INUYASHA

Story & Art by
Rumiko Takahashi

INUYASHA

Volume 18
VIZBIG Edition

Story and Art by RUMIKO TAKAHASHI

© 1997 Rumiko TAKAHASHI/Shogakukan
All rights reserved.
Original Japanese edition "INUYASHA"
published by SHOGAKUKAN Inc.

English Adaptation/Gerard Jones
Translation/Mari Morimoto
Transcription/David Smith
Touch-up Art & Lettering/Bill Schuch, Leonard Clark
VIZ Media Series Design/Yuki Ameda
VIZBIG Edition Design/Sam Elzway
Shonen Sunday Edition Editor/Annette Roman
VIZBIG Edition Editor/Annette Roman

Printed in China

Published by VIZ Media, LLC
P.O. Box 77010
San Francisco, CA 94107

10 9 8 7 6 5 4 3 2 1
First printing, February 2014

InuYasha

Volume 53
Awakening

Volume 54
The Jewel Completed

Volume 55
The Light Reborn

Volume 56
Tomorrow

Story & Art by
Rumiko Takahashi

Shonen Sunday Manga / VIZBIG Edition

CONTENTS

Cast of Characters 6

Volume 53: Awakening

Volume 54: The Jewel Completed

Volume 55: The Light Reborn

Volume 56: Tomorrow

CAST OF CHARACTERS

Kagome
A modern-day Japanese schoolgirl who is the reincarnation of Kikyo, the priestess who imprisoned Inuyasha for fifty years with her enchanted arrow. As Kikyo's reincarnation, Kagome has the power to see the Shikon Jewel shards.

Inuyasha
A half-human, half-demon hybrid, Inuyasha has doglike ears and demonic strength. He assists Kagome in her search for the shards of the Shikon Jewel, mostly because a charmed necklace allows Kagome to restrain him with a single word.

Naraku
This enigmatic demon is responsible for both Miroku's curse and for turning Kikyo and Inuyasha against each other.

Byakuya
A powerful sorcerer and master of illusions created by Naraku.

Rin
An orphaned girl devoted to Sesshomaru. He once resurrected her with Tenseiga. She brings out the best in him.

Kohaku
Naraku controlled Kohaku with a Shikon shard, then resurrected him after he was killed and used him as a puppet. Kohaku has regained his memories and is trying to redeem himself.

Miroku

An easygoing Buddhist priest of questionable morals. Miroku bears a curse passed down from his grandfather and is searching for the demon Naraku, who first inflicted the curse.

Kikyo

A village priestess who was the original protector of the Shikon Jewel. She died fifty years ago.

Sango

A proud Demon Slayer from the village where the first Shikon Jewel was born. Her clan and family lost, she fights on against the demonic Naraku along with Inuyasha.

Shippo

A young orphan fox demon. The mischievous Shippo enjoys goading Inuyasha and playing tricks with his shape-shifting abilities.

Magatsuhi

A monstrous demon who dwells inside the Shikon Jewel but can sometimes escape to wreak havoc on everyone, including Naraku.

Sesshomaru

Inuyasha's half brother by the same demon father, Sesshomaru is a pureblood demon who covets the sword left to Inuyasha by their father.

INUYASHA

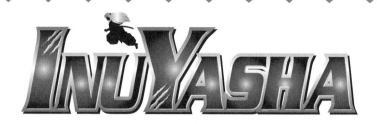

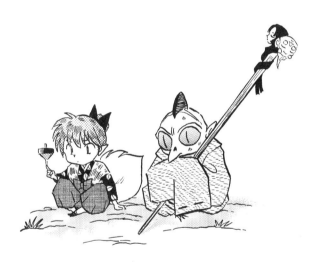

Volume 53

Awakening

SCROLL ONE
MAGATSUHI'S SHADE

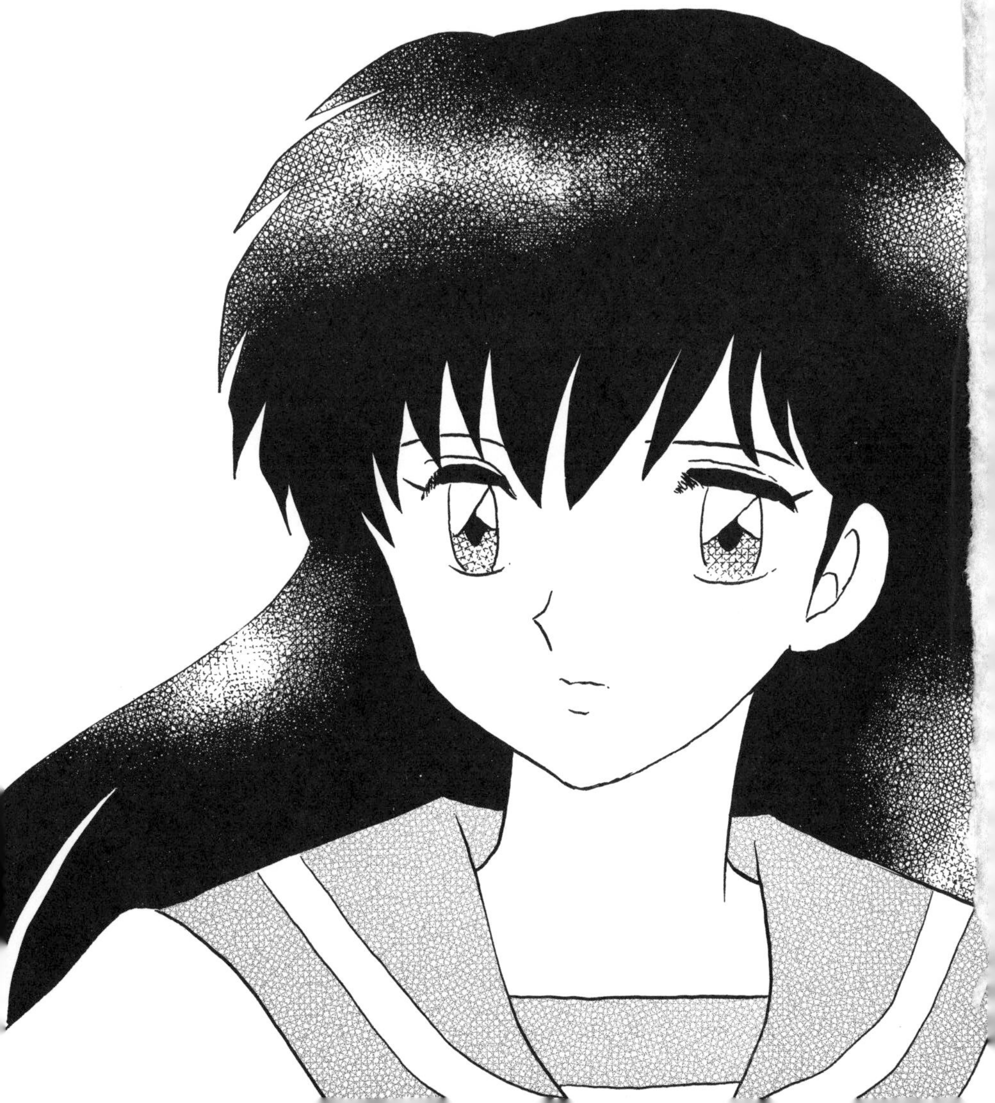

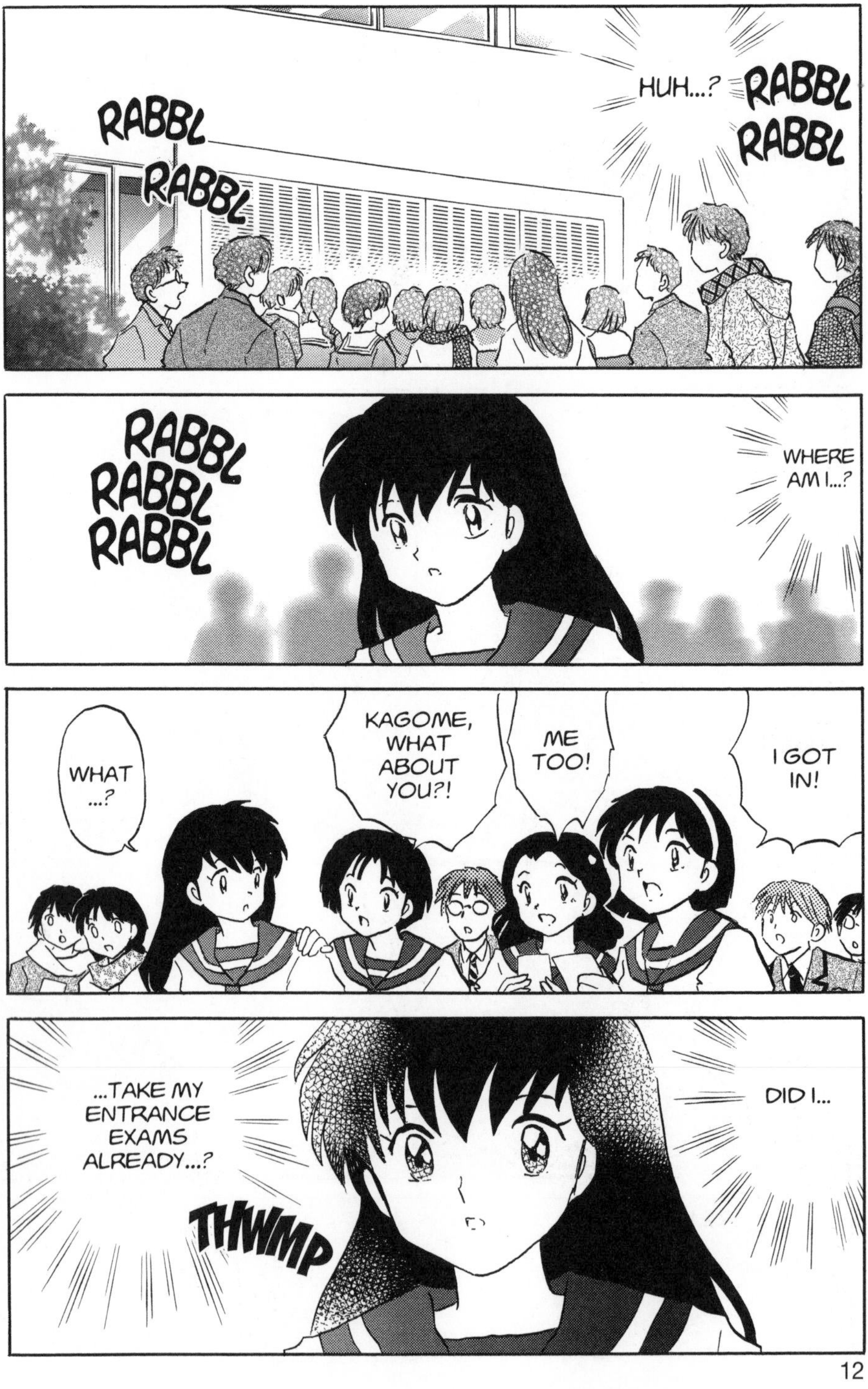
RABBL
RABBL
HUH...?
RABBL
RABBL
WHERE AM I...?
RABBL
RABBL
RABBL
I GOT IN!
ME TOO!
KAGOME, WHAT ABOUT YOU?!
WHAT ...?
DID I...
...TAKE MY ENTRANCE EXAMS ALREADY...?
THWMP

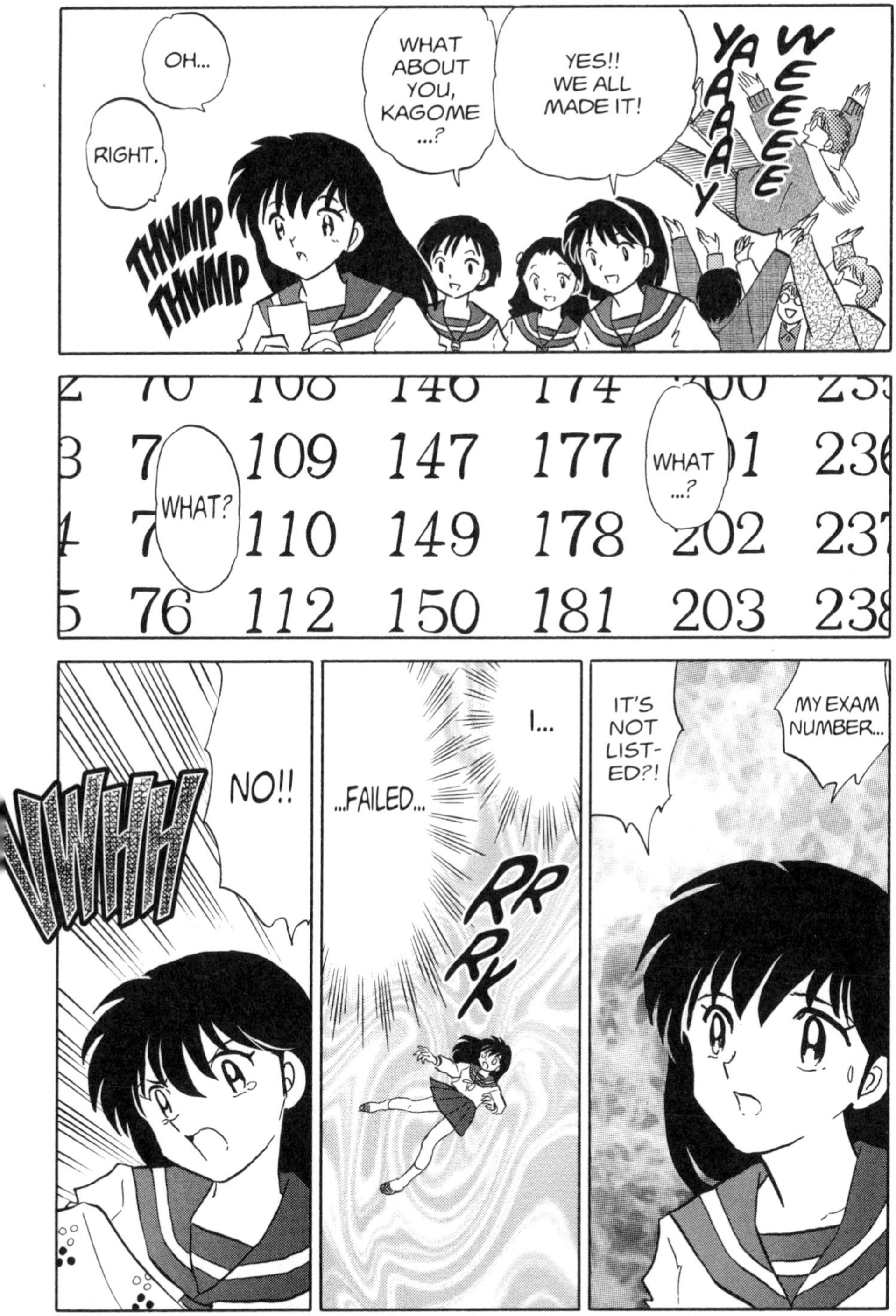
WEEEEE
YAAAAAY
YES!! WE ALL MADE IT!
WHAT ABOUT YOU, KAGOME ...?
OH...
RIGHT.
THWMP THWMP
WHAT ...?
WHAT?
MY EXAM NUMBER...
IT'S NOT LISTED?!
I...
...FAILED...
RRRK
NO!!
VWHH

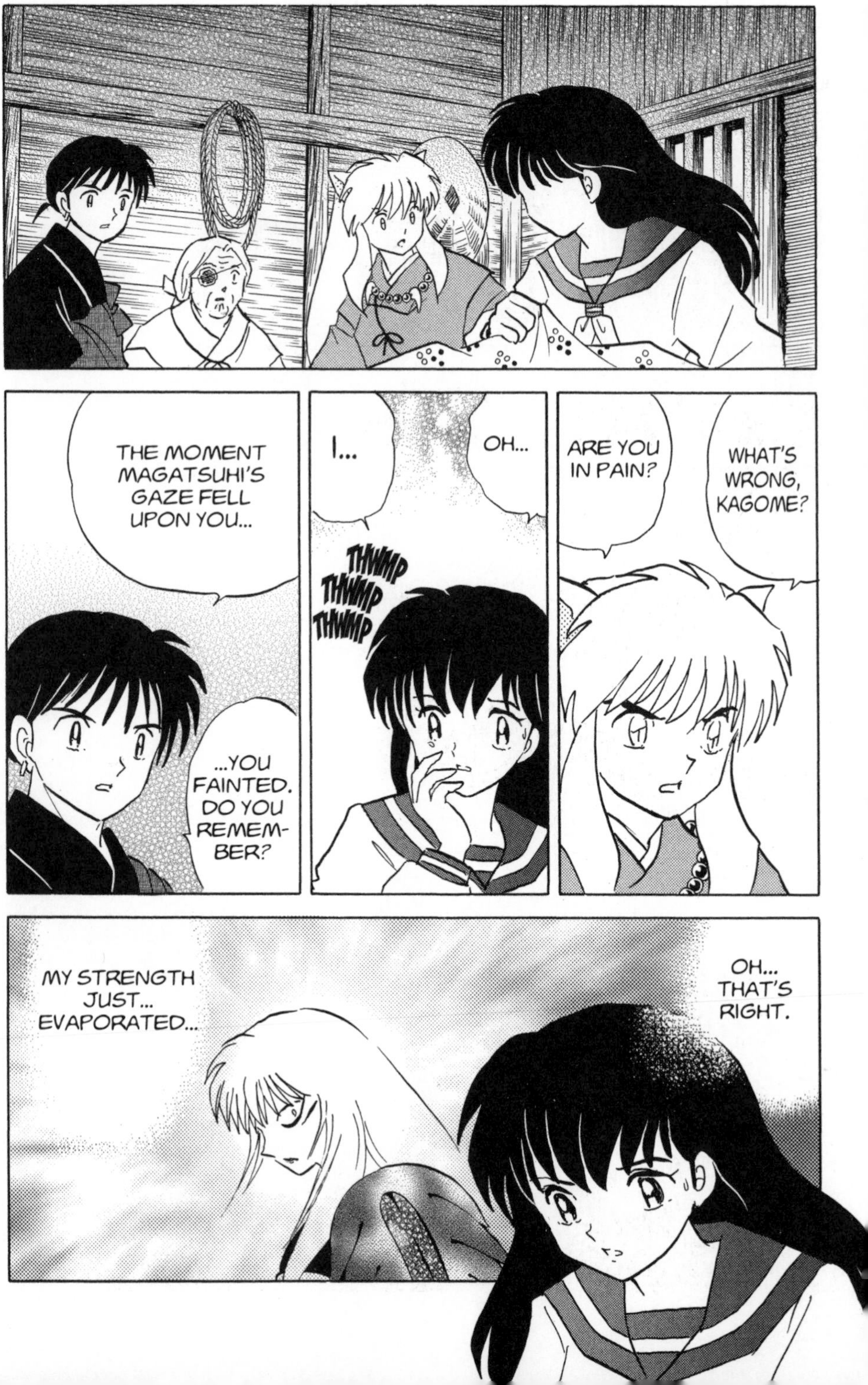
WHAT'S WRONG, KAGOME?
ARE YOU IN PAIN?
OH...
I...
THWMP THWMP THWMP
THE MOMENT MAGATSUHI'S GAZE FELL UPON YOU...
...YOU FAINTED. DO YOU REMEMBER?
OH... THAT'S RIGHT.
MY STRENGTH JUST... EVAPORATED...

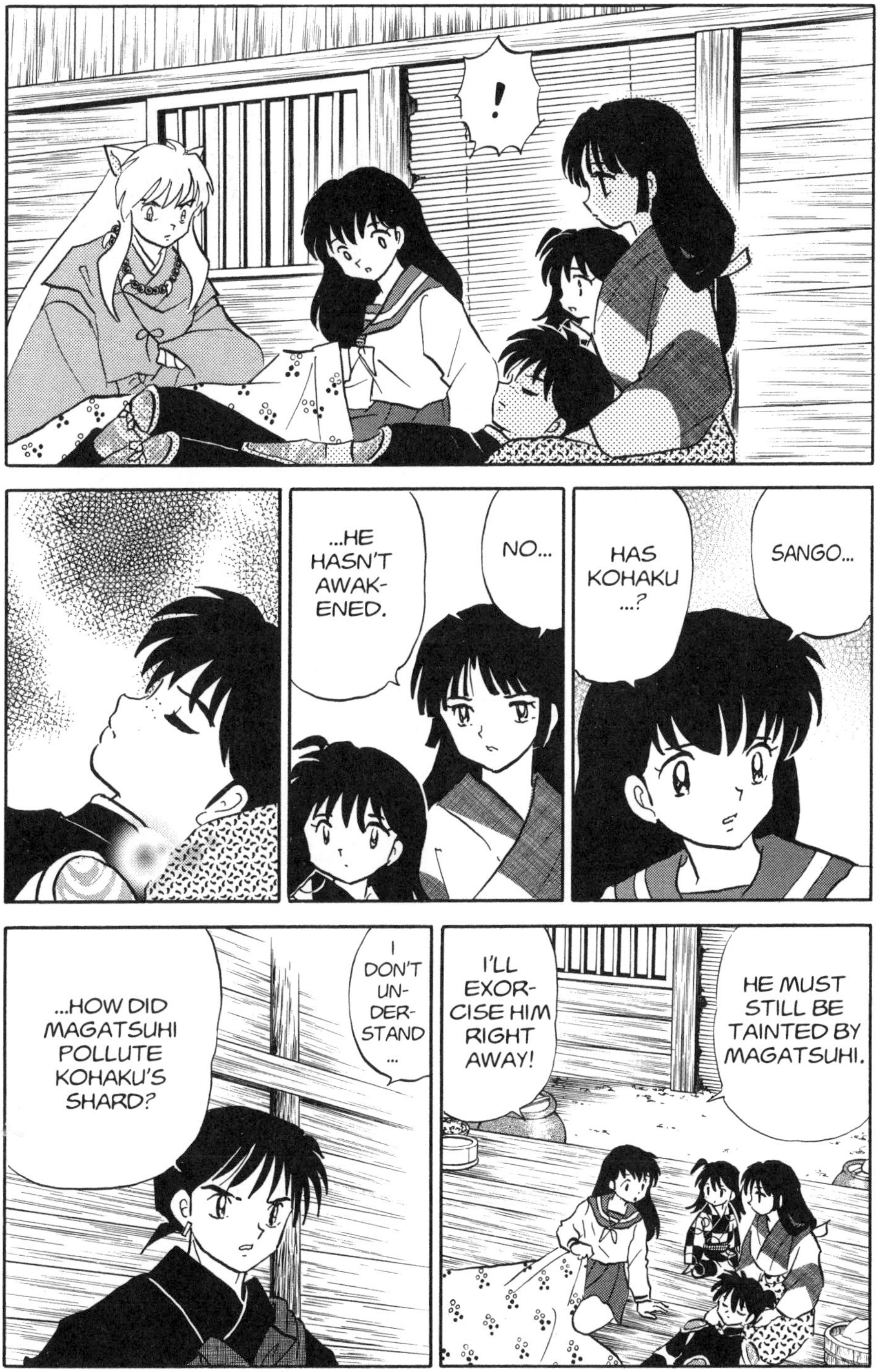
!
SANGO...
HAS KOHAKU ...?
NO...
...HE HASN'T AWAKENED.
HE MUST STILL BE TAINTED BY MAGATSUHI.
I'LL EXORCISE HIM RIGHT AWAY!
I DON'T UNDERSTAND...
...HOW DID MAGATSUHI POLLUTE KOHAKU'S SHARD?

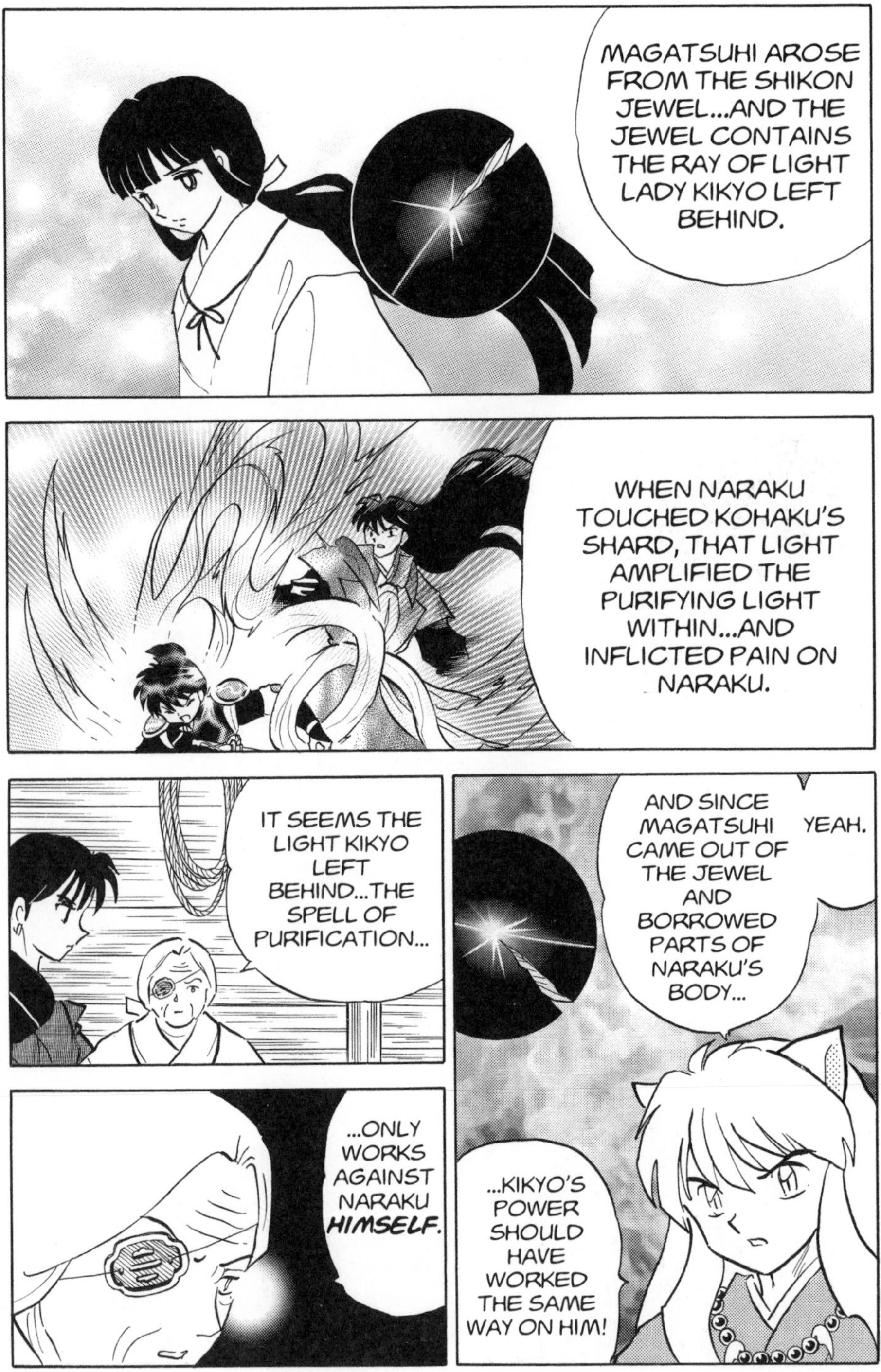
MAGATSUHI AROSE FROM THE SHIKON JEWEL...AND THE JEWEL CONTAINS THE RAY OF LIGHT LADY KIKYO LEFT BEHIND.
WHEN NARAKU TOUCHED KOHAKU'S SHARD, THAT LIGHT AMPLIFIED THE PURIFYING LIGHT WITHIN...AND INFLICTED PAIN ON NARAKU.
YEAH.
AND SINCE MAGATSUHI CAME OUT OF THE JEWEL AND BORROWED PARTS OF NARAKU'S BODY...
...KIKYO'S POWER SHOULD HAVE WORKED THE SAME WAY ON HIM!
IT SEEMS THE LIGHT KIKYO LEFT BEHIND...THE SPELL OF PURIFICATION...
...ONLY WORKS AGAINST NARAKU ***HIMSELF***.

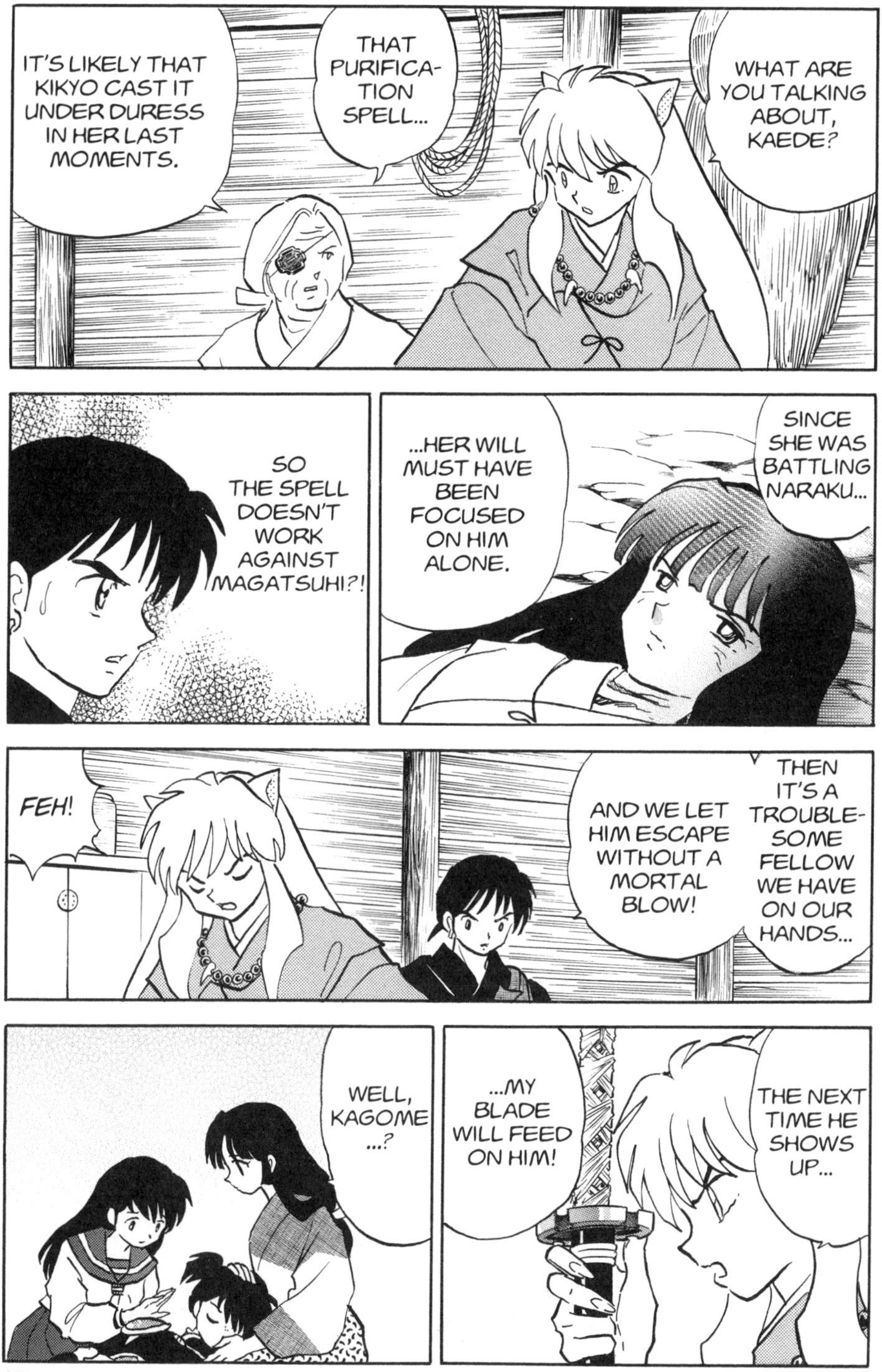

WHAT ARE YOU TALKING ABOUT, KAEDE?
THAT PURIFICATION SPELL...
IT'S LIKELY THAT KIKYO CAST IT UNDER DURESS IN HER LAST MOMENTS.
SINCE SHE WAS BATTLING NARAKU...
...HER WILL MUST HAVE BEEN FOCUSED ON HIM ALONE.
SO THE SPELL DOESN'T WORK AGAINST MAGATSUHI?!
THEN IT'S A TROUBLESOME FELLOW WE HAVE ON OUR HANDS...
AND WE LET HIM ESCAPE WITHOUT A MORTAL BLOW!
FEH!
THE NEXT TIME HE SHOWS UP...
...MY BLADE WILL FEED ON HIM!
WELL, KAGOME ...?

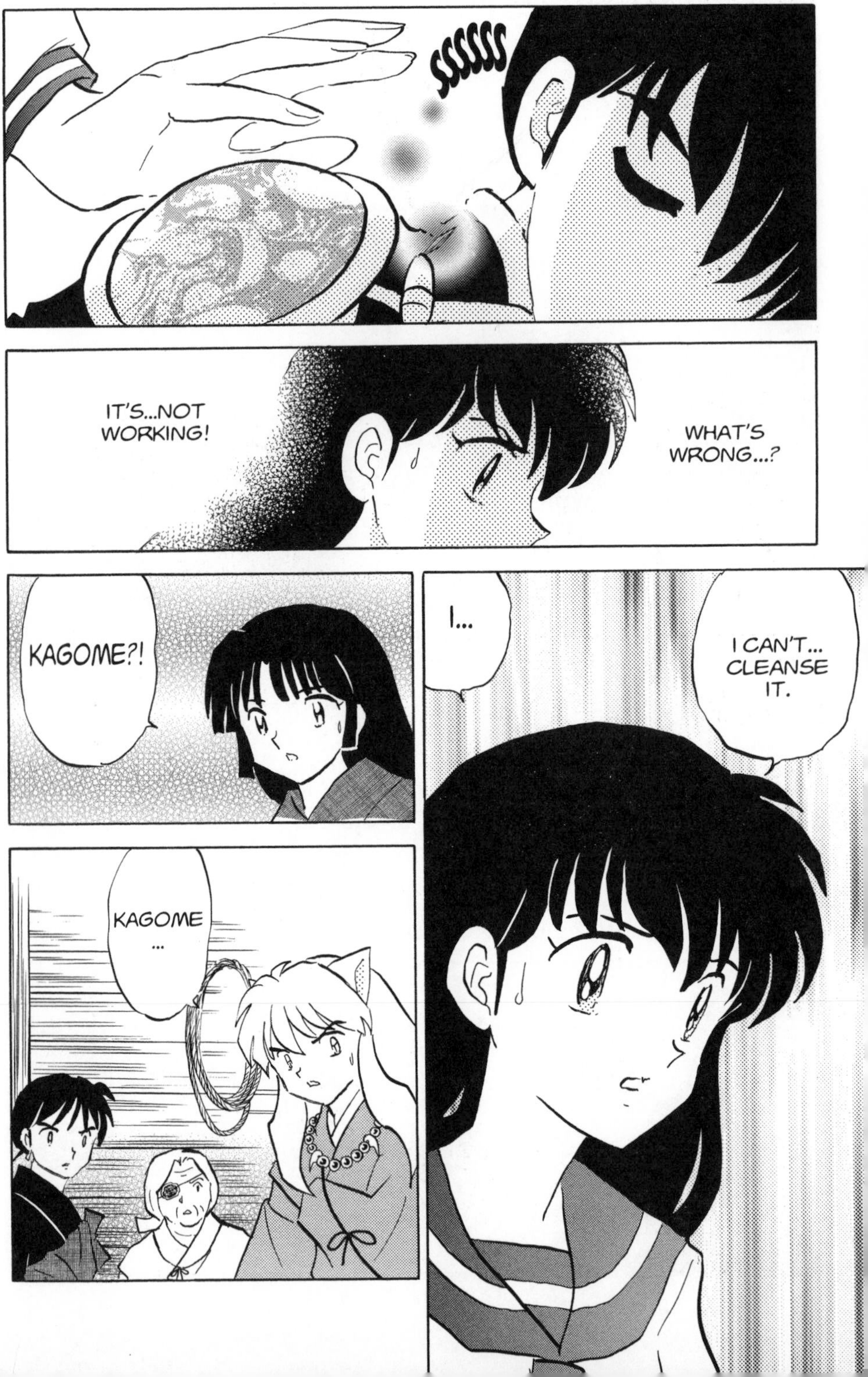
SSSSSS
WHAT'S WRONG...?
IT'S...NOT WORKING!
I...
I CAN'T... CLEANSE IT.
KAGOME?!
KAGOME ...

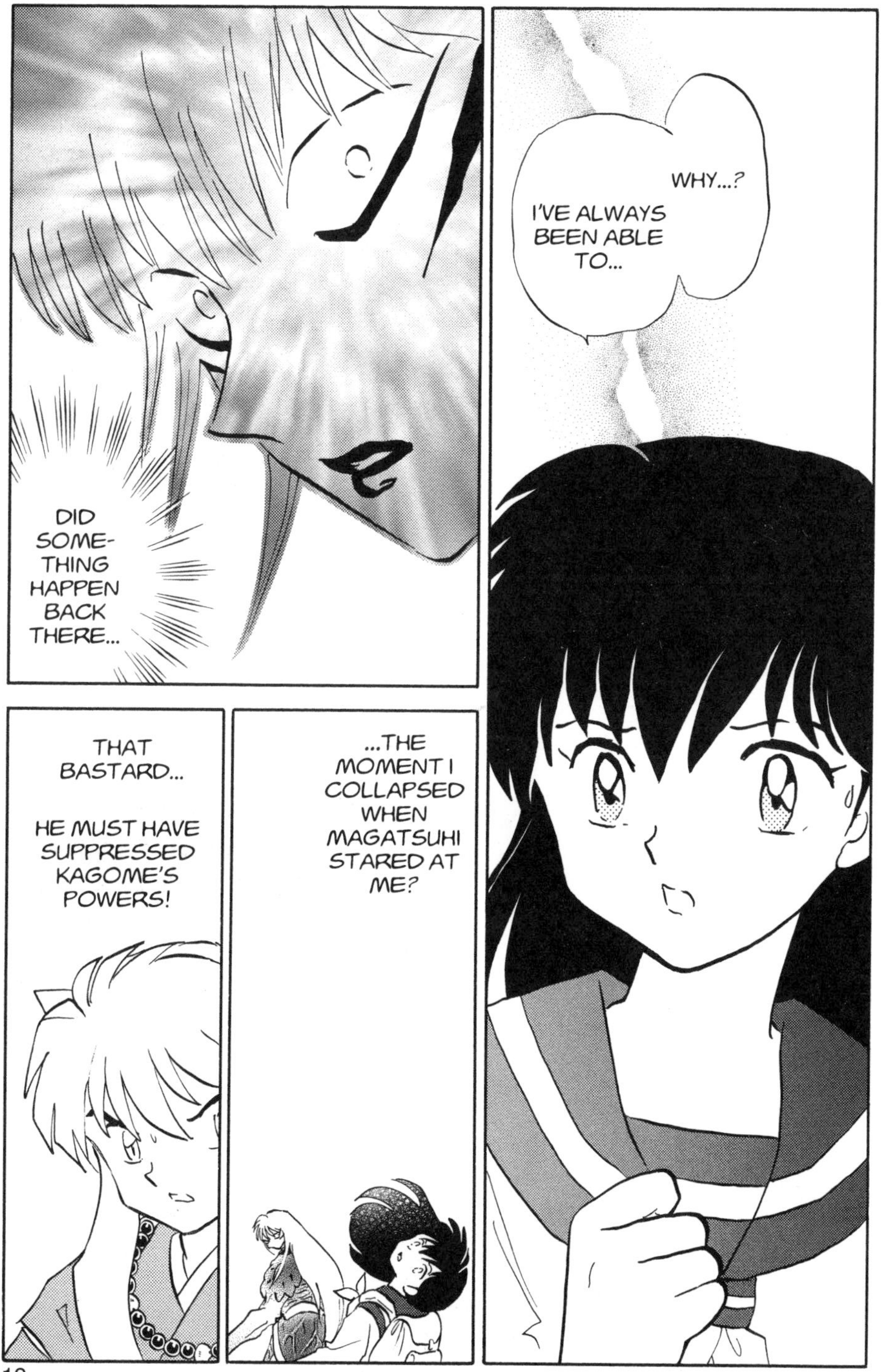
WHY...?
I'VE ALWAYS BEEN ABLE TO...
DID SOME-THING HAPPEN BACK THERE...
...THE MOMENT I COLLAPSED WHEN MAGATSUHI STARED AT ME?
THAT BASTARD...
HE MUST HAVE SUPPRESSED KAGOME'S POWERS!

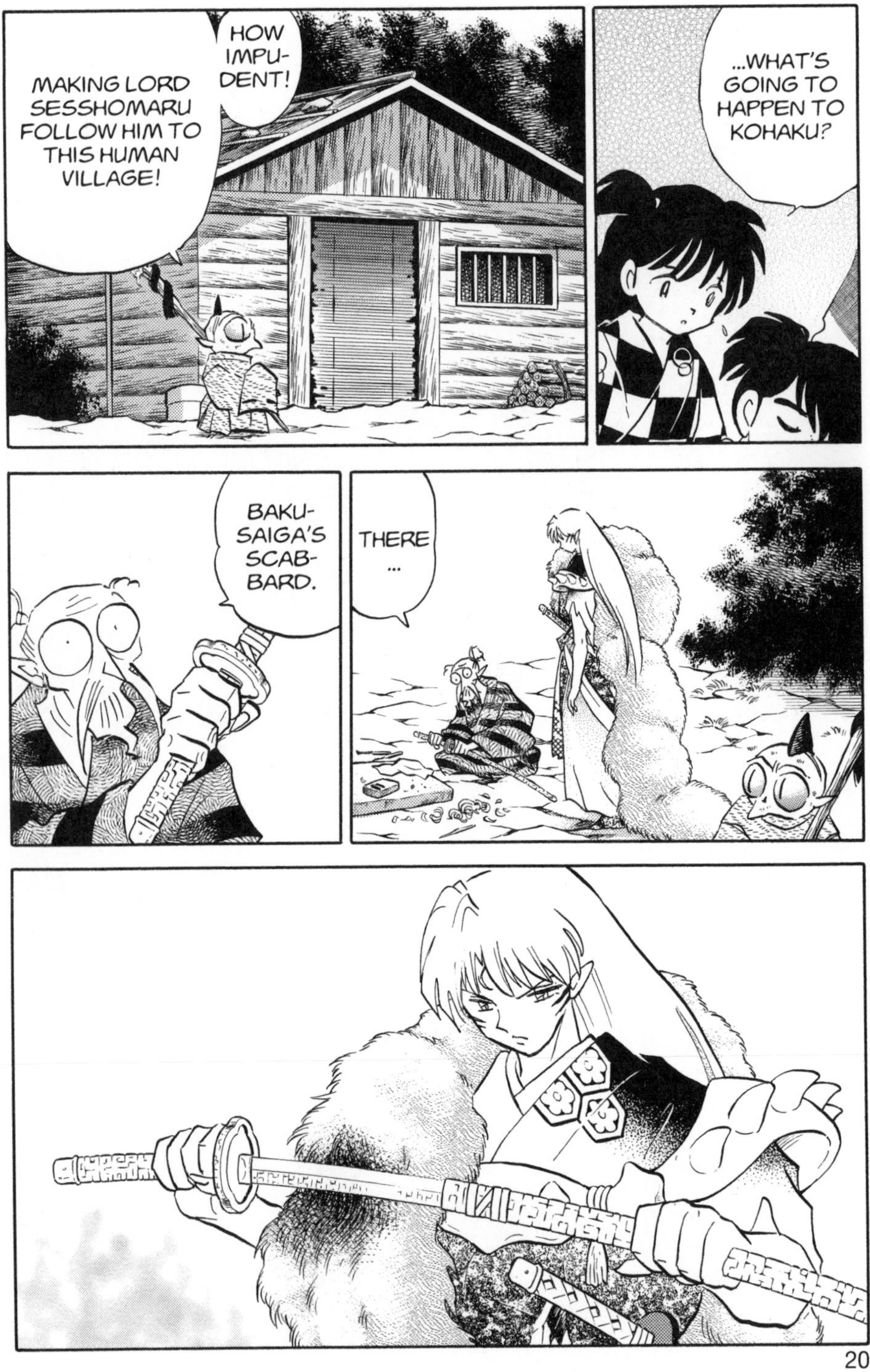

...WHAT'S GOING TO HAPPEN TO KOHAKU?
HOW IMPU-DENT!
MAKING LORD SESSHOMARU FOLLOW HIM TO THIS HUMAN VILLAGE!
THERE ...
BAKU-SAIGA'S SCAB-BARD.

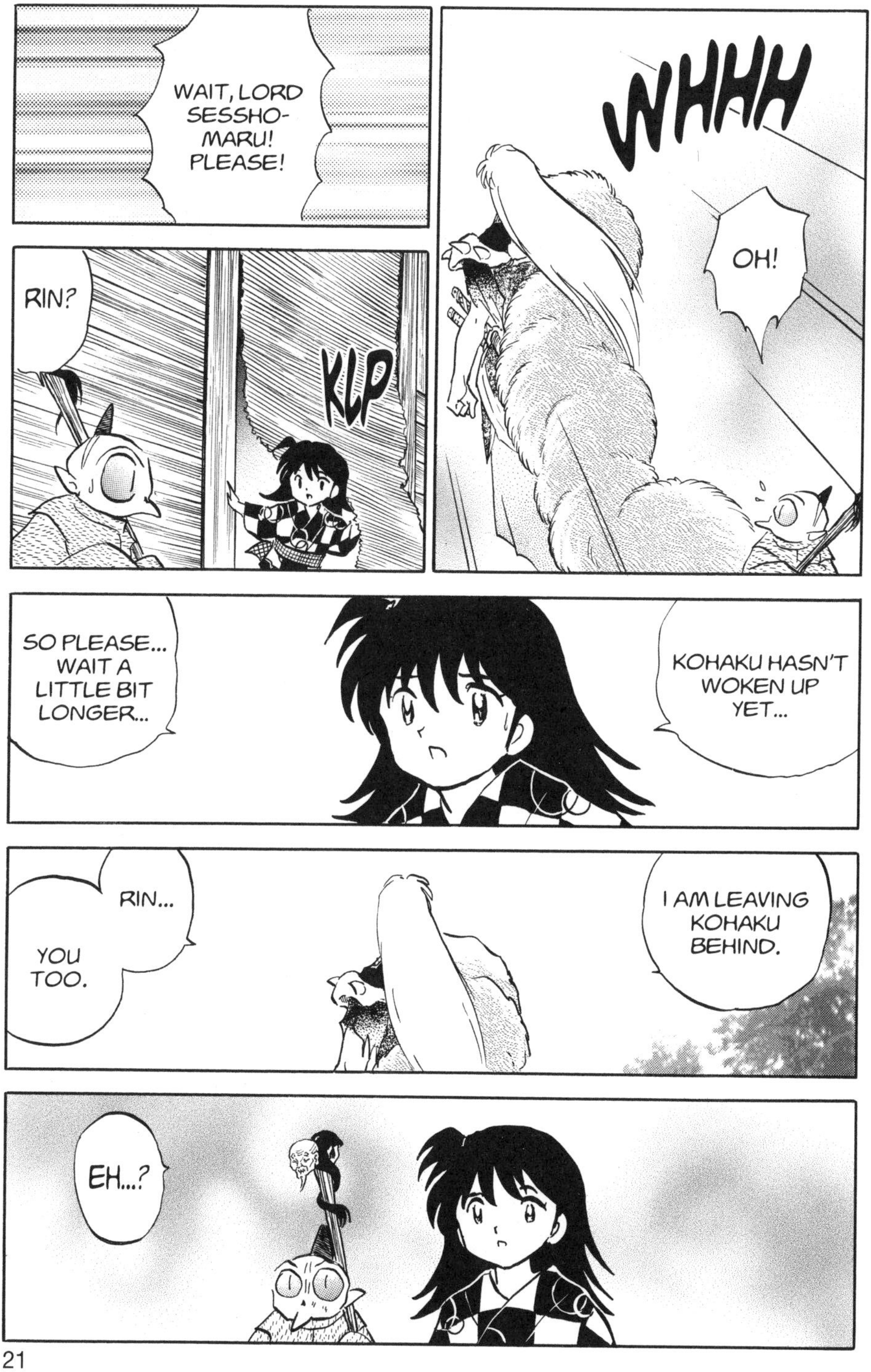
WHHH
OH!
WAIT, LORD SESSHO-MARU! PLEASE!
RIN?
KLP
KOHAKU HASN'T WOKEN UP YET...
SO PLEASE... WAIT A LITTLE BIT LONGER...
I AM LEAVING KOHAKU BEHIND.
RIN...
YOU TOO.
EH...?

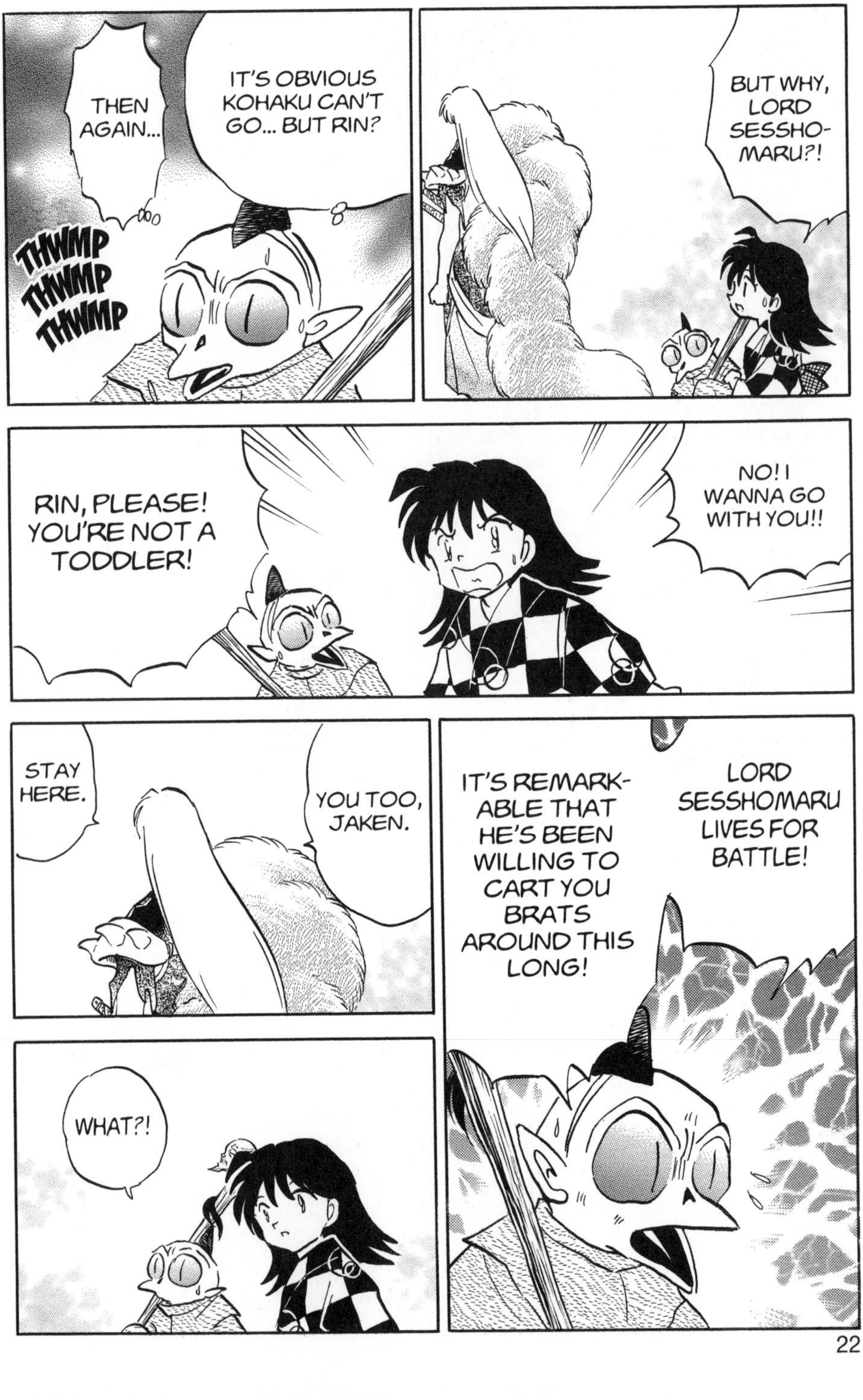
BUT WHY, LORD SESSHOMARU?!
IT'S OBVIOUS KOHAKU CAN'T GO... BUT RIN?
THEN AGAIN...
THWMP THWMP THWMP
NO! I WANNA GO WITH YOU!!
RIN, PLEASE! YOU'RE NOT A TODDLER!
LORD SESSHOMARU LIVES FOR BATTLE!
IT'S REMARKABLE THAT HE'S BEEN WILLING TO CART YOU BRATS AROUND THIS LONG!
STAY HERE.
YOU TOO, JAKEN.
WHAT?!

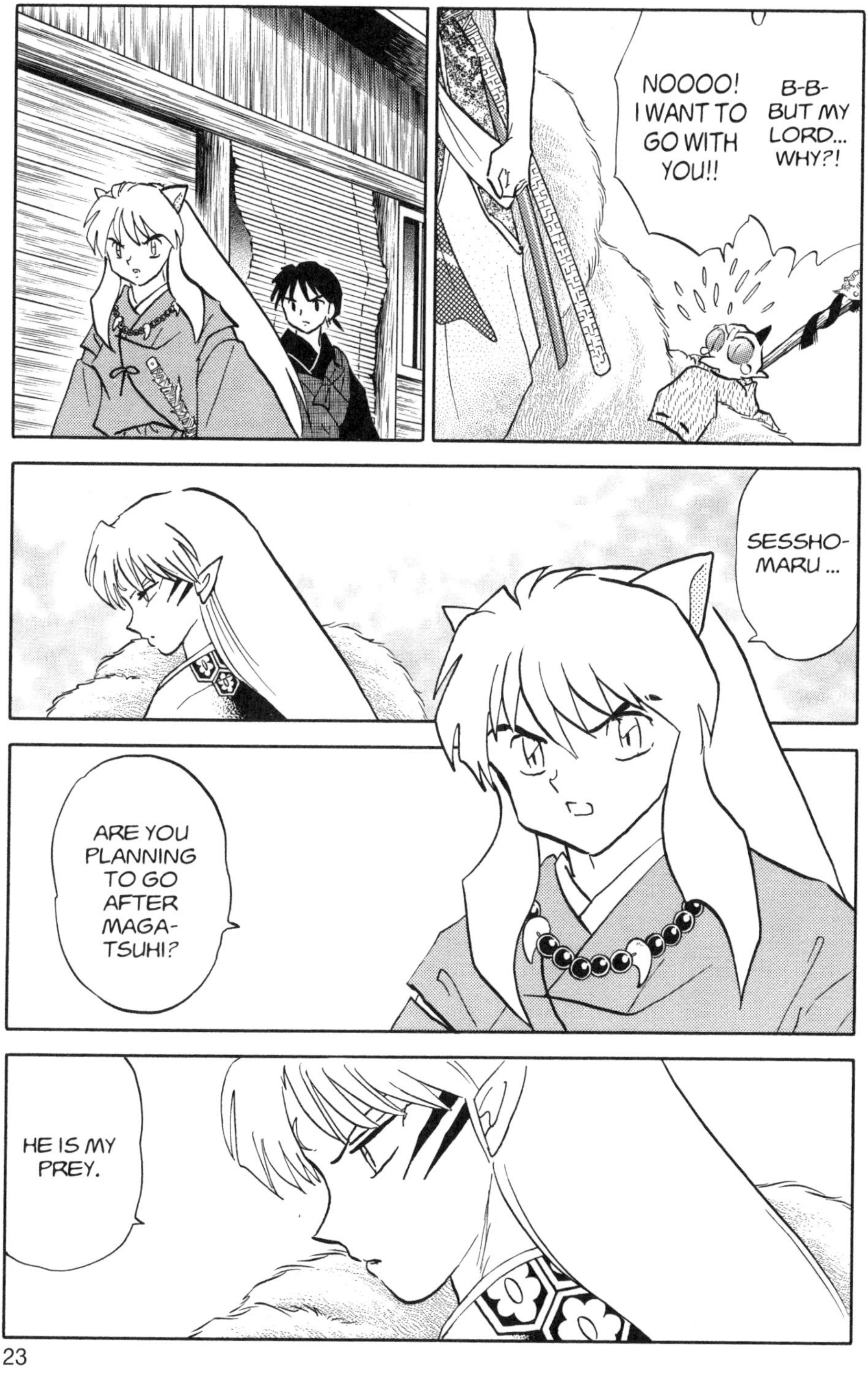
B-B- BUT MY LORD... WHY?!
NOOOO! I WANT TO GO WITH YOU!!
SESSHO-MARU ...
ARE YOU PLANNING TO GO AFTER MAGA-TSUHI?
HE IS MY PREY.

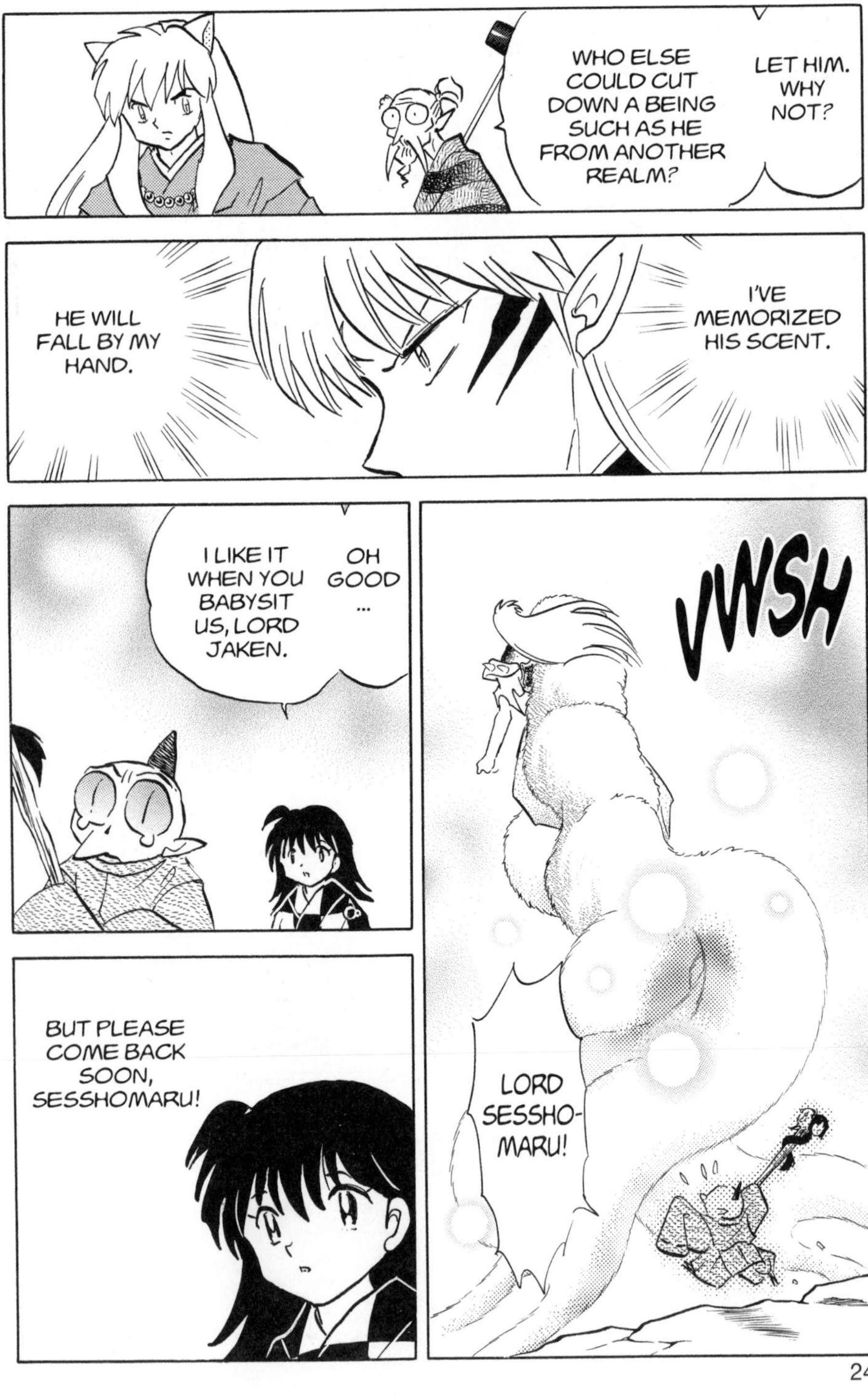
LET HIM. WHY NOT?
WHO ELSE COULD CUT DOWN A BEING SUCH AS HE FROM ANOTHER REALM?
I'VE MEMORIZED HIS SCENT.
HE WILL FALL BY MY HAND.
VWSH
LORD SESSHO-MARU!
OH GOOD ...
I LIKE IT WHEN YOU BABYSIT US, LORD JAKEN.
BUT PLEASE COME BACK SOON, SESSHOMARU!

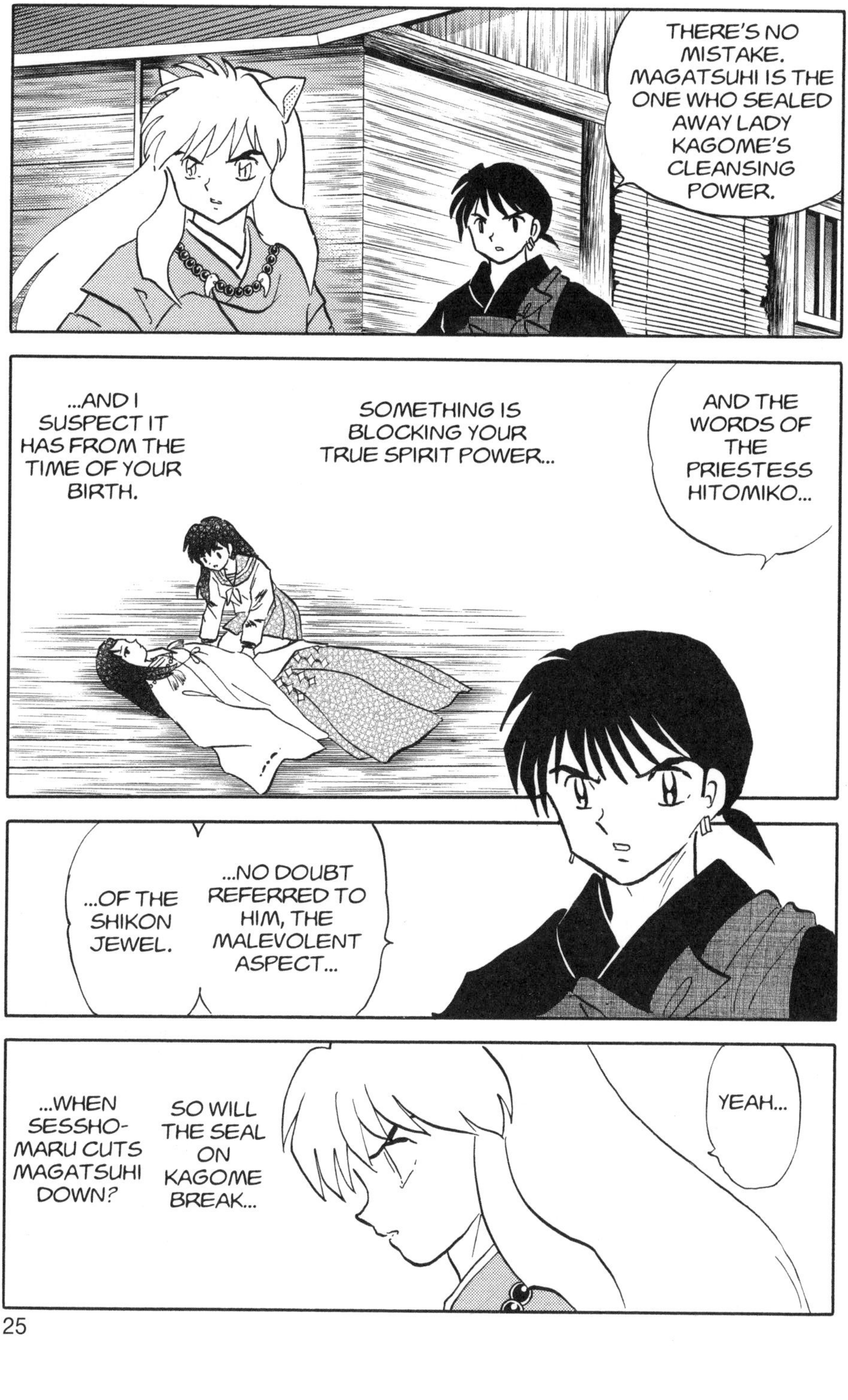
THERE'S NO MISTAKE. MAGATSUHI IS THE ONE WHO SEALED AWAY LADY KAGOME'S CLEANSING POWER.
AND THE WORDS OF THE PRIESTESS HITOMIKO...
SOMETHING IS BLOCKING YOUR TRUE SPIRIT POWER...
...AND I SUSPECT IT HAS FROM THE TIME OF YOUR BIRTH.
...NO DOUBT REFERRED TO HIM, THE MALEVOLENT ASPECT...
...OF THE SHIKON JEWEL.
YEAH...
SO WILL THE SEAL ON KAGOME BREAK...
...WHEN SESSHOMARU CUTS MAGATSUHI DOWN?

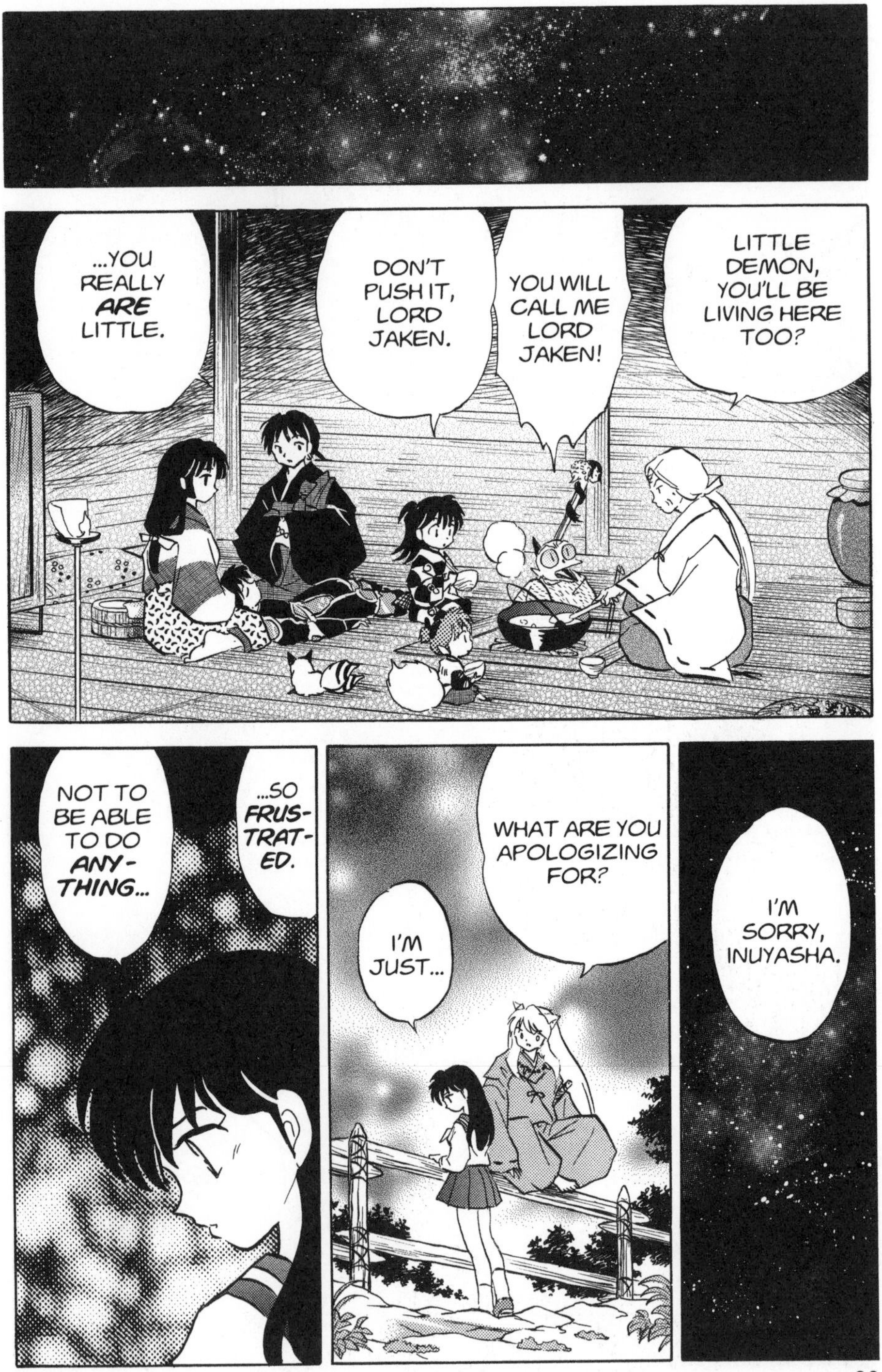
LITTLE DEMON, YOU'LL BE LIVING HERE TOO?
YOU WILL CALL ME LORD JAKEN!
DON'T PUSH IT, LORD JAKEN.
...YOU REALLY **ARE** LITTLE.
I'M SORRY, INUYASHA.
WHAT ARE YOU APOLOGIZING FOR?
I'M JUST...
...SO **FRUSTRATED.**
NOT TO BE ABLE TO DO **ANYTHING...**

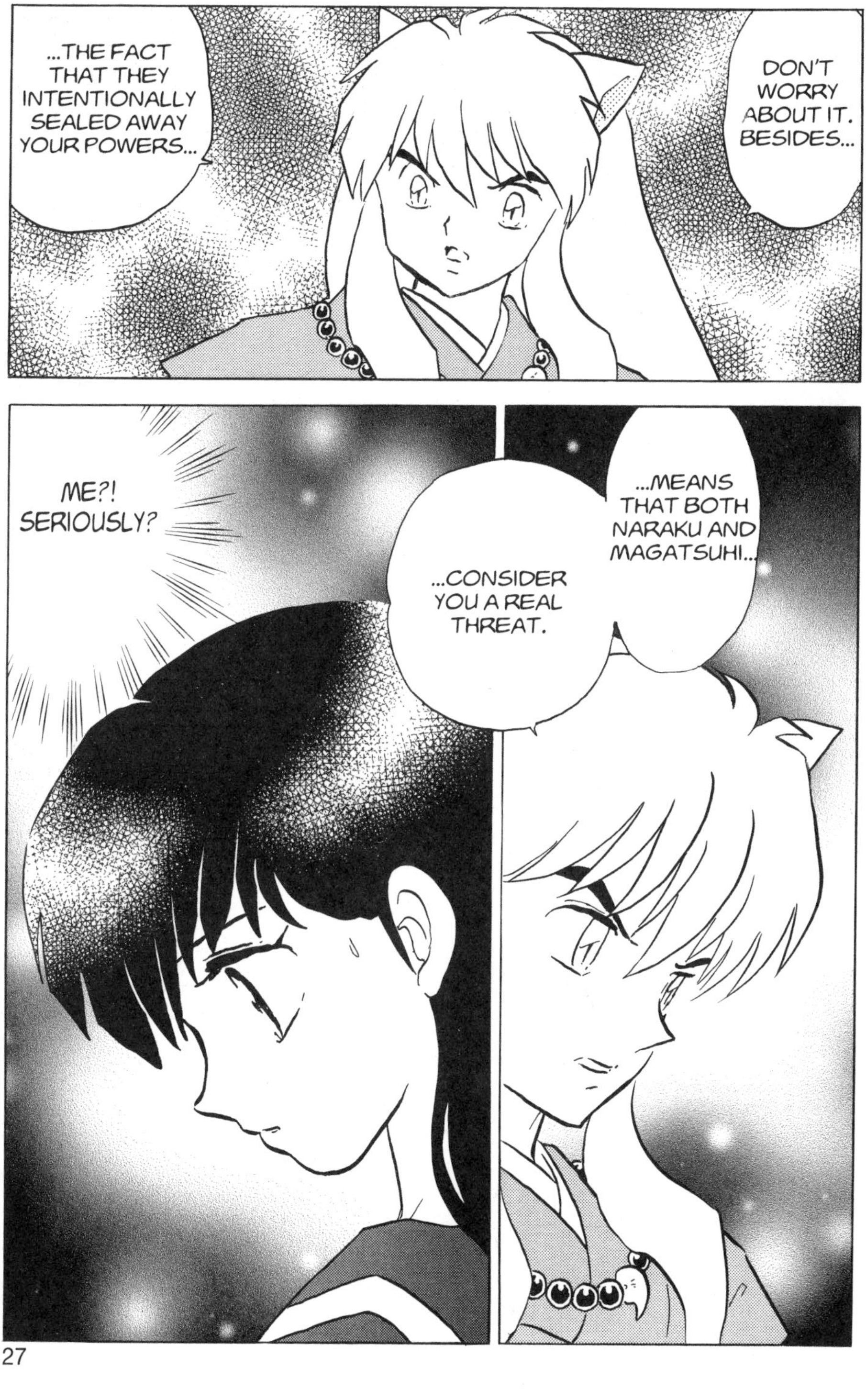
DON'T WORRY ABOUT IT. BESIDES...
...THE FACT THAT THEY INTENTIONALLY SEALED AWAY YOUR POWERS...
...MEANS THAT BOTH NARAKU AND MAGATSUHI...
...CONSIDER YOU A REAL THREAT.
ME?! SERIOUSLY?

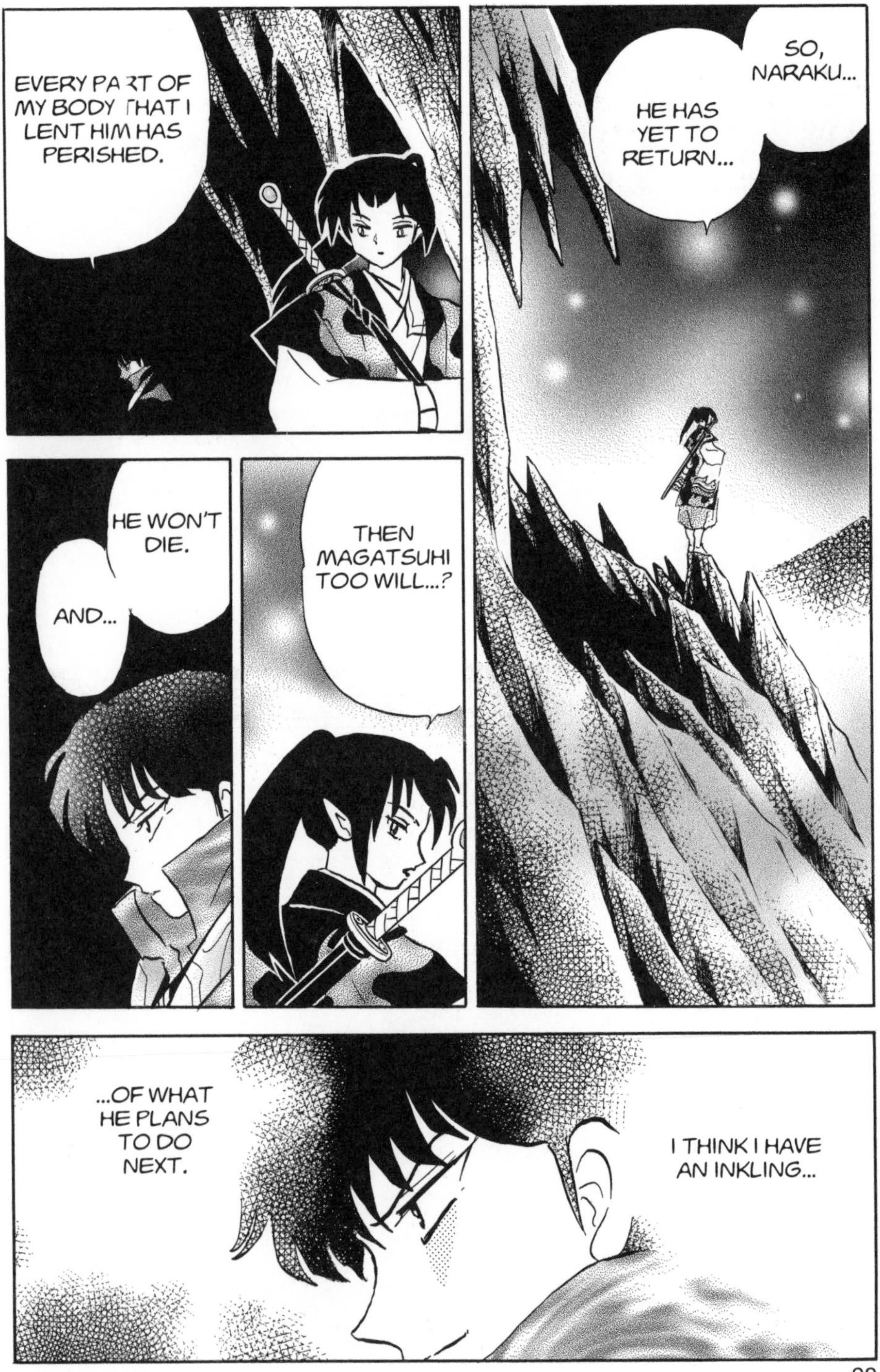
SO, NARAKU...
HE HAS YET TO RETURN...
EVERY PART OF MY BODY THAT I LENT HIM HAS PERISHED.
THEN MAGATSUHI TOO WILL...?
HE WON'T DIE.
AND...
I THINK I HAVE AN INKLING...
...OF WHAT HE PLANS TO DO NEXT.

SCROLL TWO
THE DAY OF DAYS

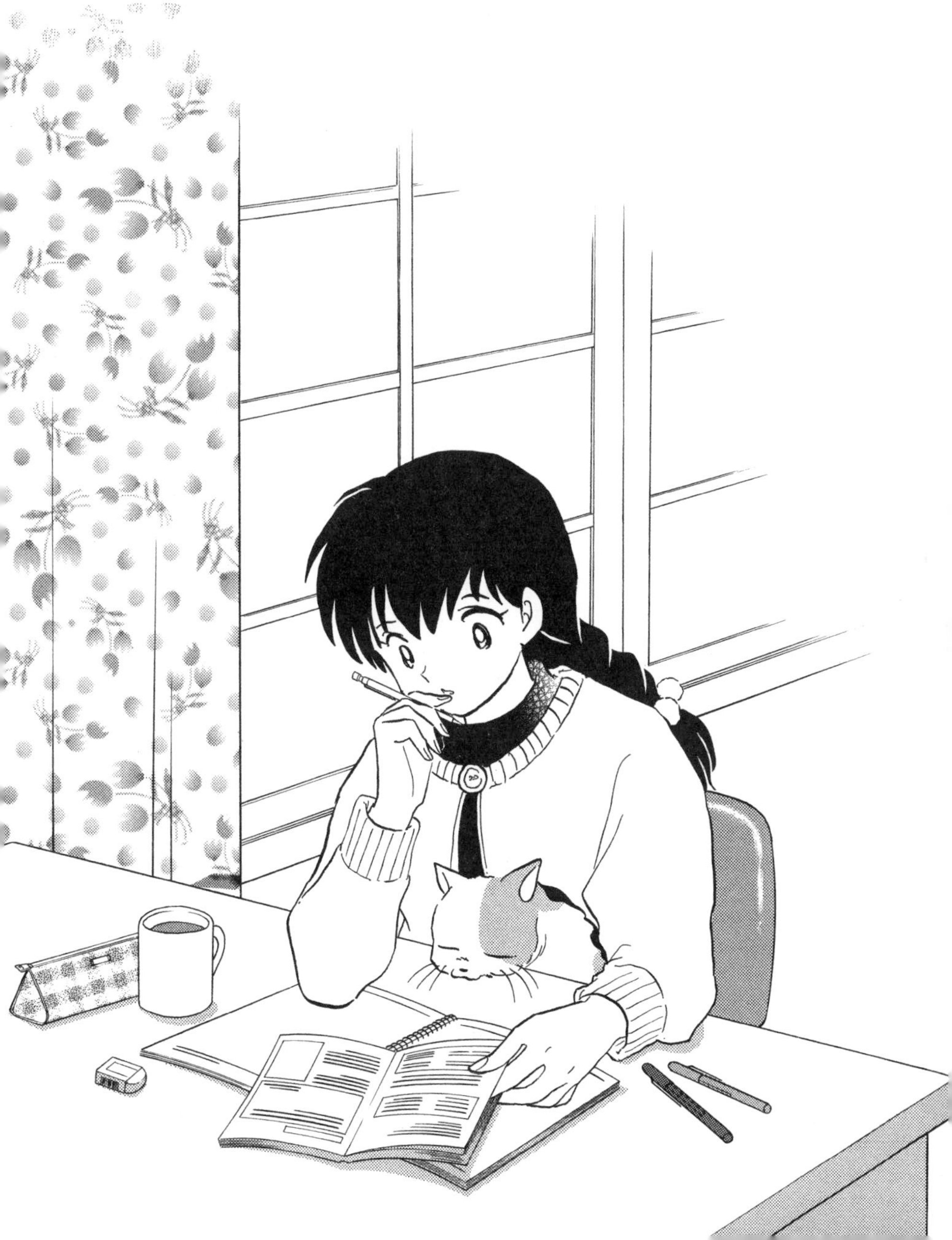

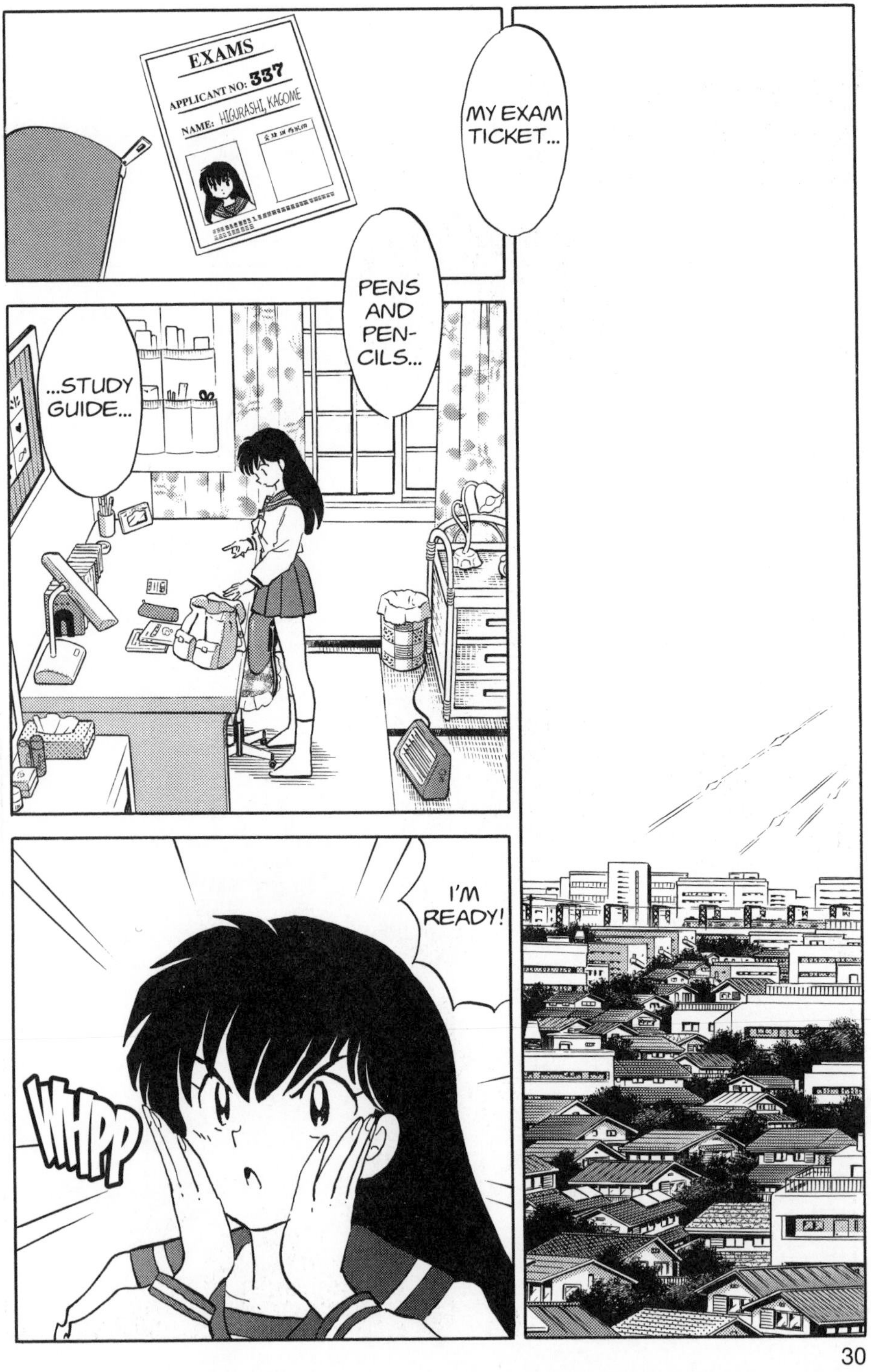
MY EXAM TICKET...
EXAMS
APPLICANT NO: 337
NAME: HIGURASHI, KAGOME
PENS AND PEN-CILS...
...STUDY GUIDE...
I'M READY!
WHPP

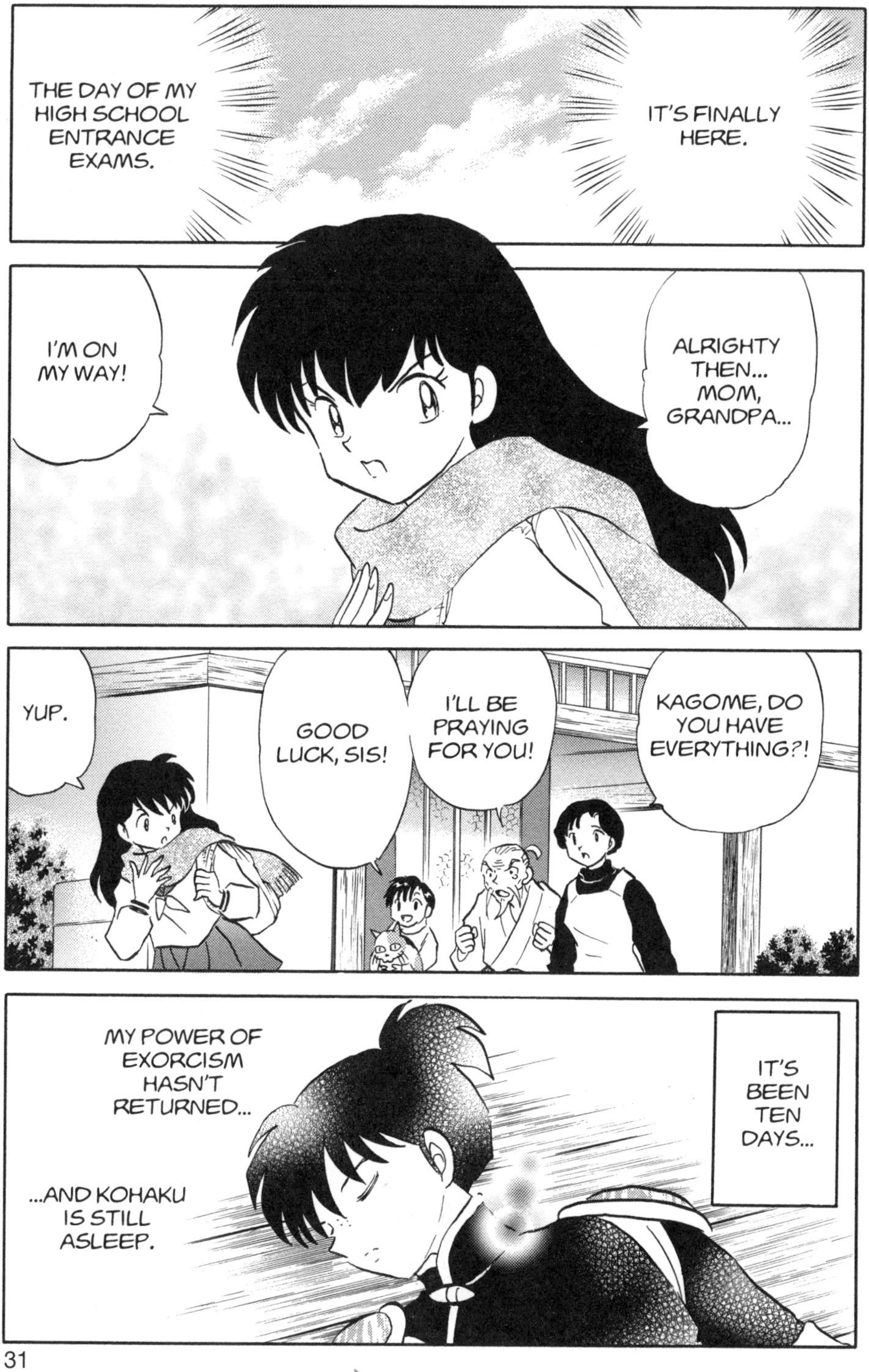
IT'S FINALLY HERE.
THE DAY OF MY HIGH SCHOOL ENTRANCE EXAMS.
ALRIGHTY THEN... MOM, GRANDPA...
I'M ON MY WAY!
KAGOME, DO YOU HAVE EVERYTHING?!
I'LL BE PRAYING FOR YOU!
GOOD LUCK, SIS!
YUP.
IT'S BEEN TEN DAYS...
MY POWER OF EXORCISM HASN'T RETURNED...
...AND KOHAKU IS STILL ASLEEP.

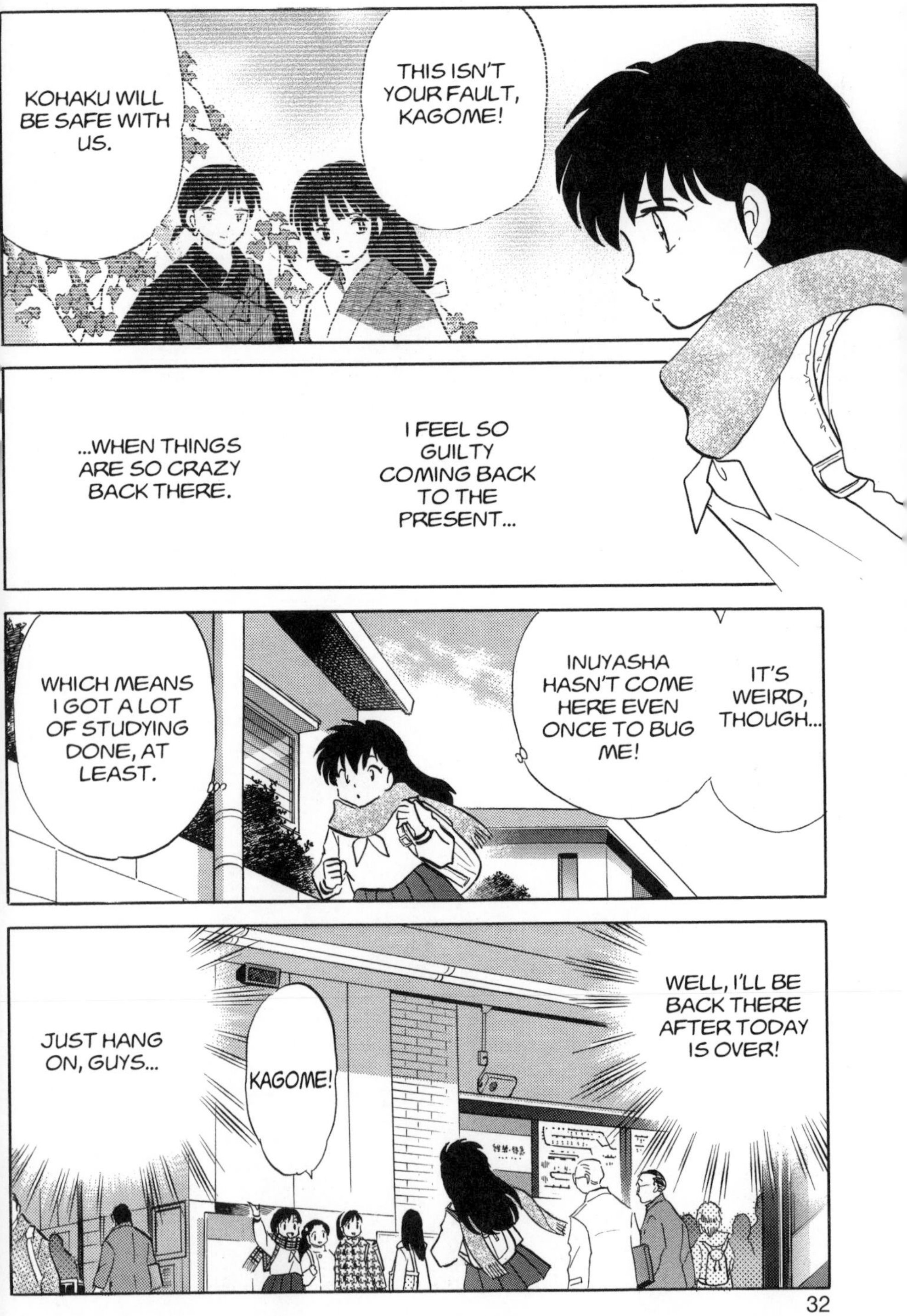
THIS ISN'T YOUR FAULT, KAGOME!
KOHAKU WILL BE SAFE WITH US.
I FEEL SO GUILTY COMING BACK TO THE PRESENT...
...WHEN THINGS ARE SO CRAZY BACK THERE.
IT'S WEIRD, THOUGH...
INUYASHA HASN'T COME HERE EVEN ONCE TO BUG ME!
WHICH MEANS I GOT A LOT OF STUDYING DONE, AT LEAST.
WELL, I'LL BE BACK THERE AFTER TODAY IS OVER!
KAGOME!
JUST HANG ON, GUYS...

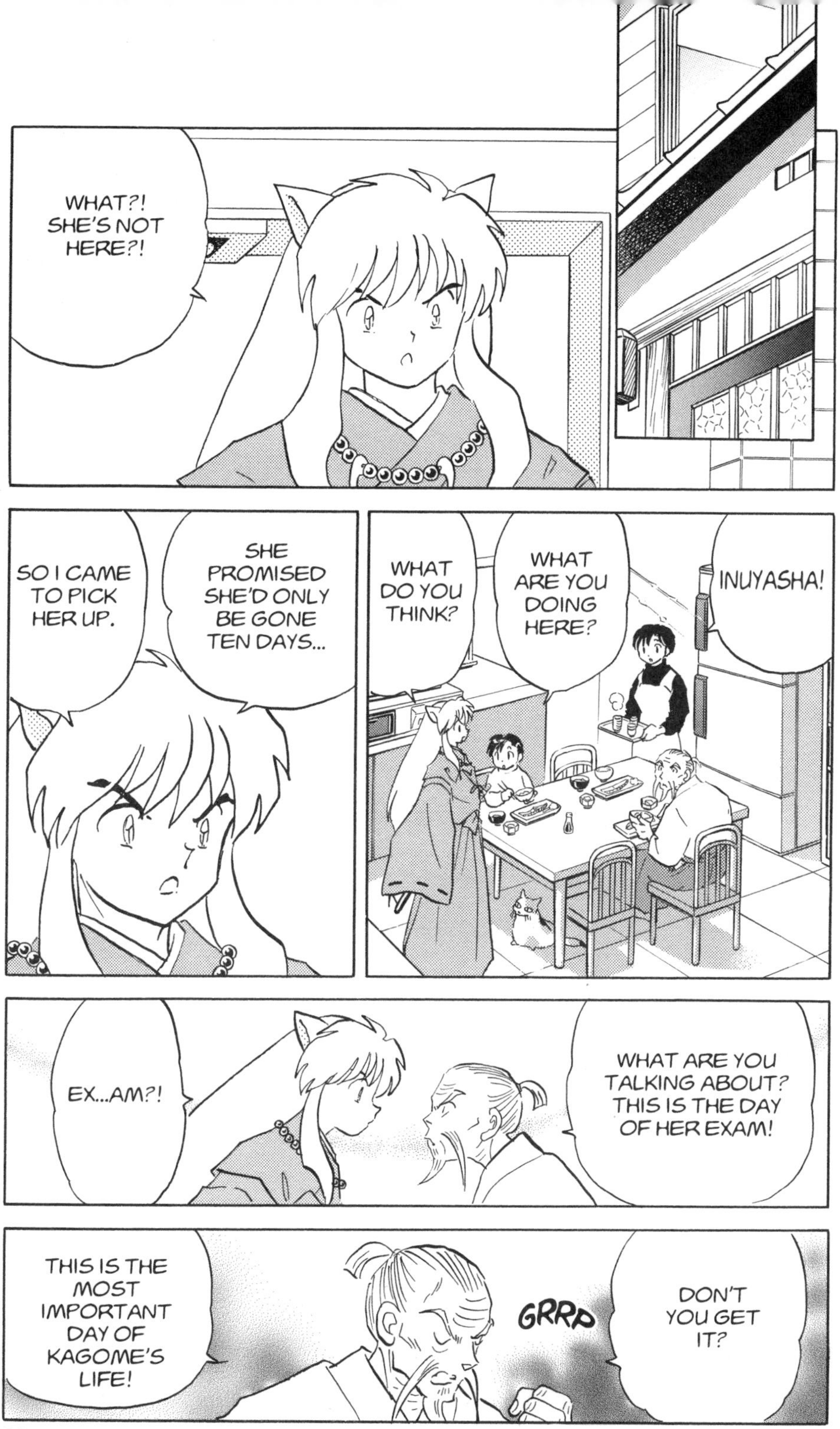
WHAT?! SHE'S NOT HERE?!
INUYASHA!
WHAT ARE YOU DOING HERE?
WHAT DO YOU THINK?
SHE PROMISED SHE'D ONLY BE GONE TEN DAYS...
SO I CAME TO PICK HER UP.
WHAT ARE YOU TALKING ABOUT? THIS IS THE DAY OF HER EXAM!
EX...AM?!
DON'T YOU GET IT?
GRRP
THIS IS THE MOST IMPORTANT DAY OF KAGOME'S LIFE!

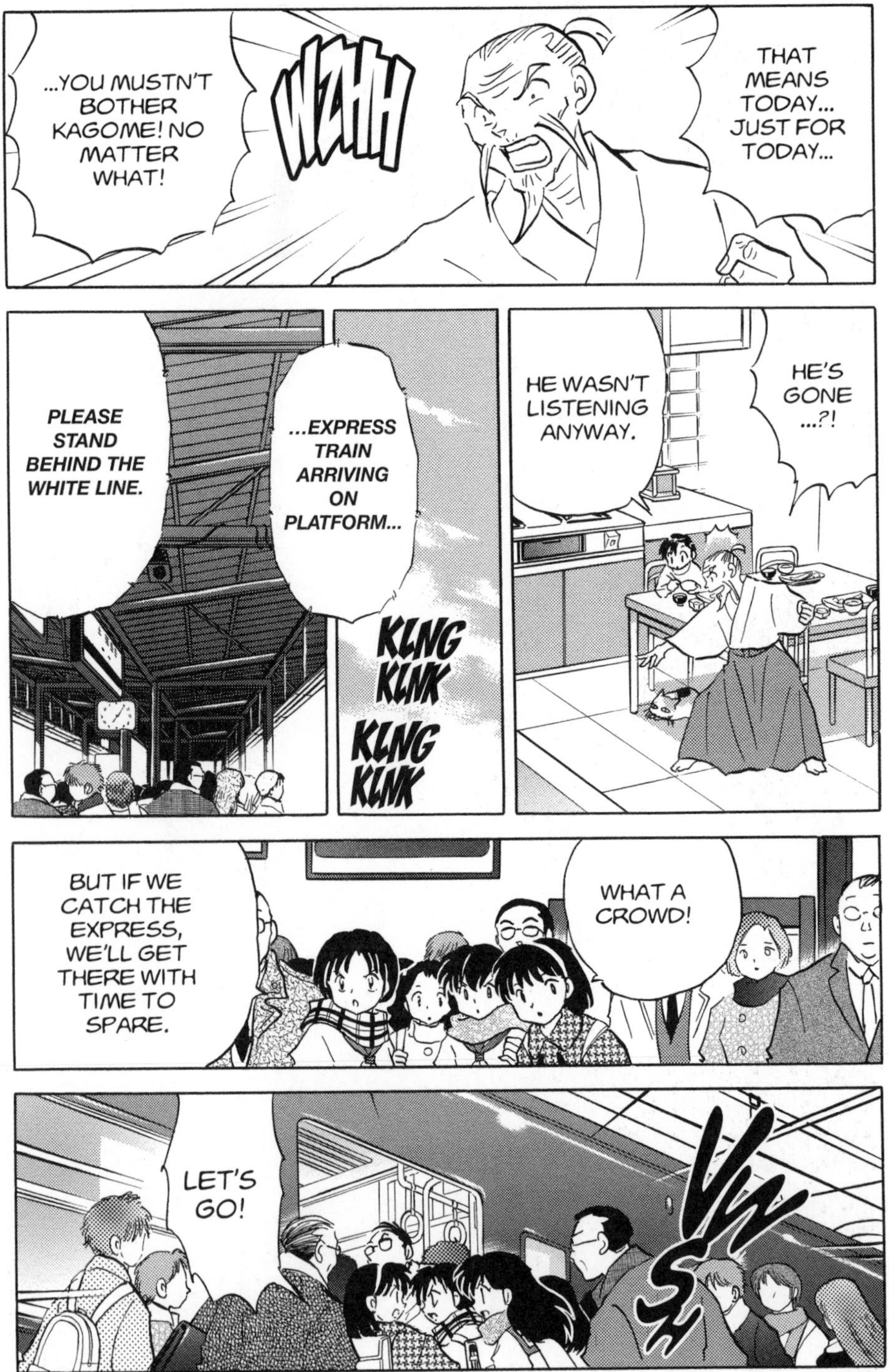
THAT MEANS TODAY... JUST FOR TODAY...
WZHH
...YOU MUSTN'T BOTHER KAGOME! NO MATTER WHAT!
HE'S GONE ...?!
HE WASN'T LISTENING ANYWAY.
...EXPRESS TRAIN ARRIVING ON PLATFORM...
KLNG KLNK
KLNG KLNK
PLEASE STAND BEHIND THE WHITE LINE.
WHAT A CROWD!
BUT IF WE CATCH THE EXPRESS, WE'LL GET THERE WITH TIME TO SPARE.
VWSH
LET'S GO!

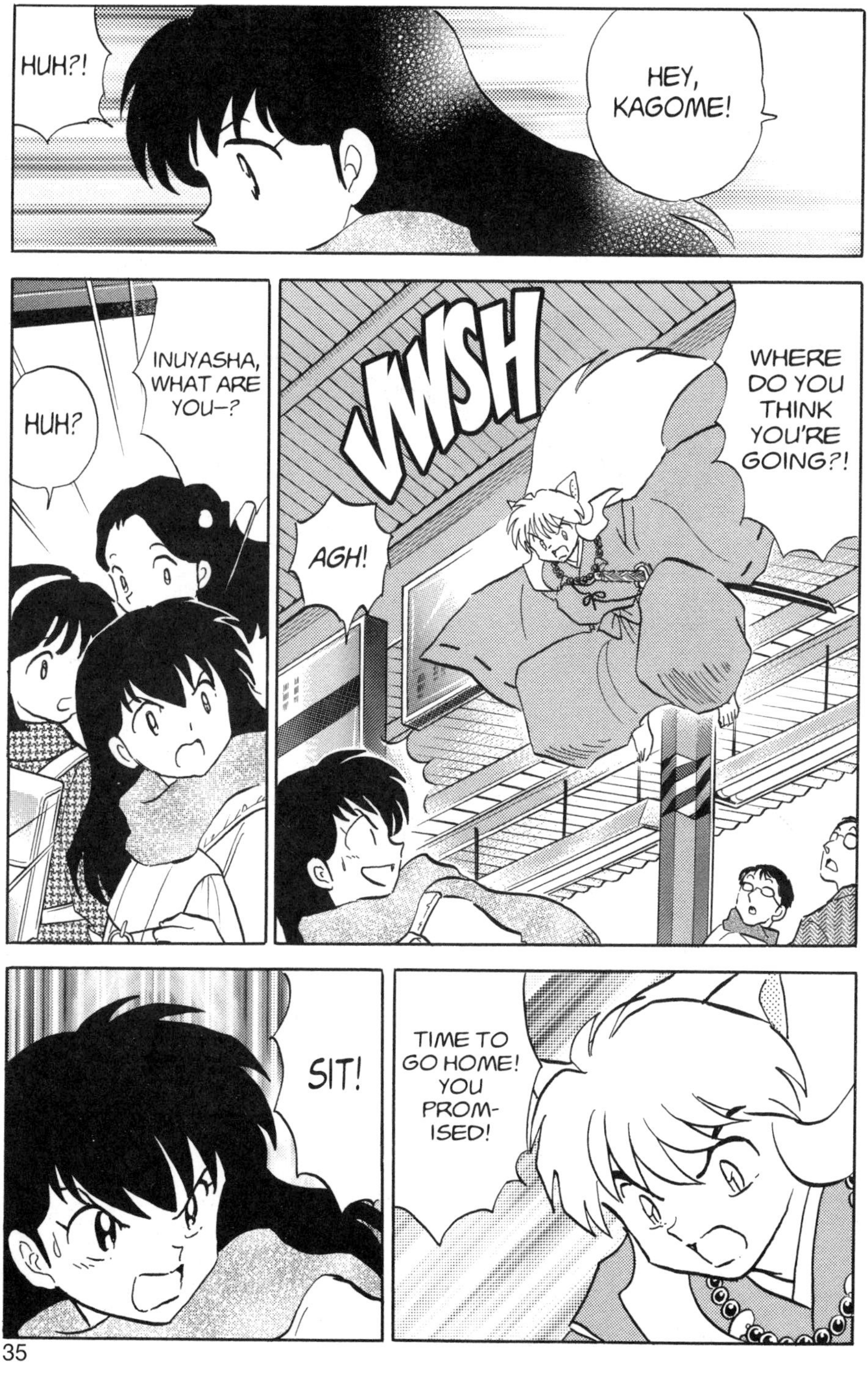
HEY, KAGOME!
HUH?!
WHERE DO YOU THINK YOU'RE GOING?!
VWSH
AGH!
INUYASHA, WHAT ARE YOU—?
HUH?
TIME TO GO HOME! YOU PROMISED!
SIT!

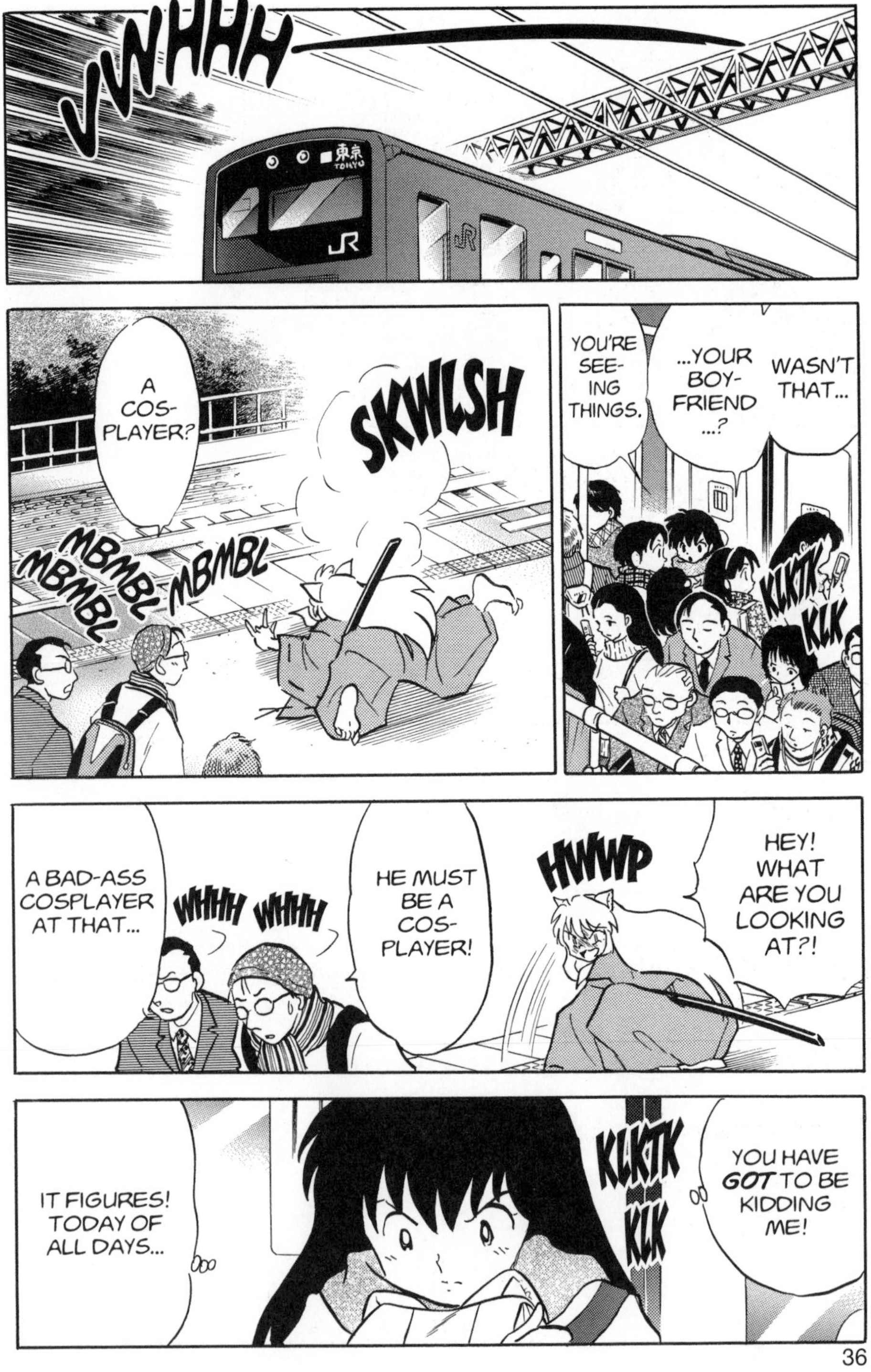
VWHHH
WASN'T THAT...
...YOUR BOY-FRIEND ...?
YOU'RE SEE-ING THINGS.
KLKTK KLK
SKWLSH
A COS-PLAYER?
MBMBL MBMBL
MBMBL
HEY! WHAT ARE YOU LOOKING AT?!
HWWP
HE MUST BE A COS-PLAYER!
WHHH WHHH
A BAD-ASS COSPLAYER AT THAT...
YOU HAVE *GOT* TO BE KIDDING ME!
KLKTK KLK
IT FIGURES! TODAY OF ALL DAYS...

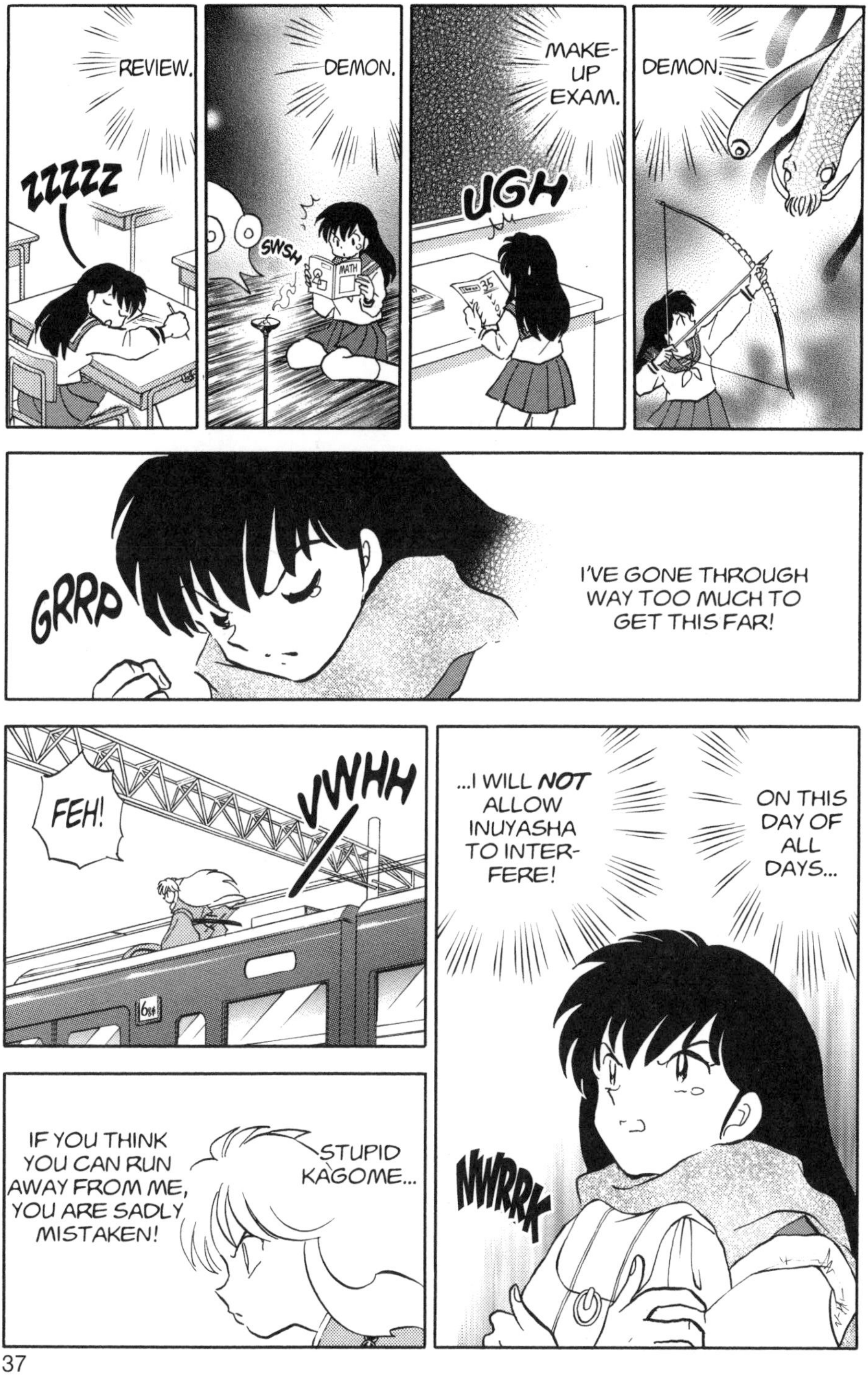
DEMON.
MAKE-UP EXAM.
UGH
DEMON.
SWSH
MATH
REVIEW.
ZZZZZ
I'VE GONE THROUGH WAY TOO MUCH TO GET THIS FAR!
GRRP
ON THIS DAY OF ALL DAYS...
...I WILL *NOT* ALLOW INUYASHA TO INTER-FERE!
NWRRK
VWHH
FEH!
STUPID KAGOME...
IF YOU THINK YOU CAN RUN AWAY FROM ME, YOU ARE SADLY MISTAKEN!

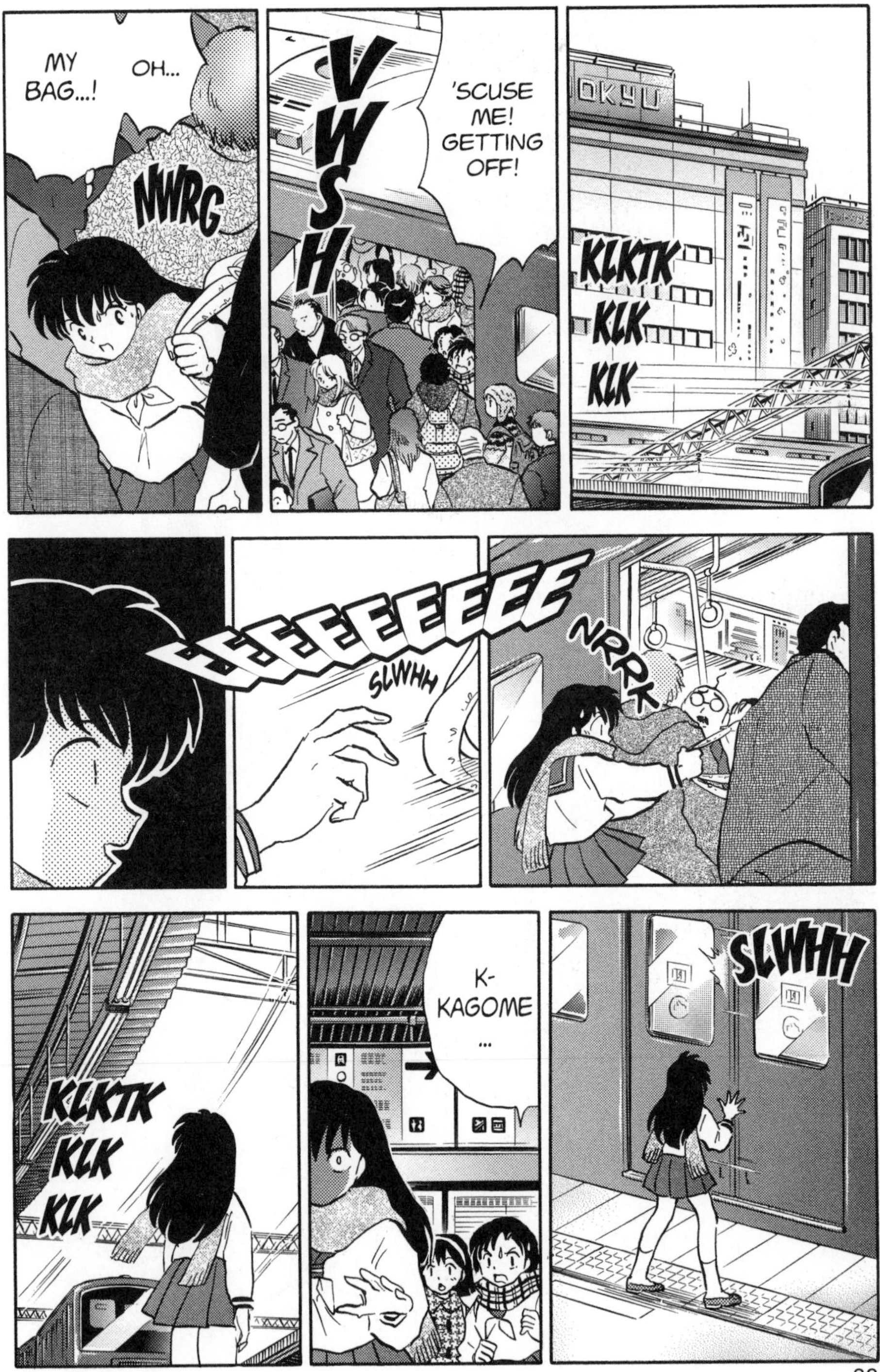
KLKTK
KLK
KLK
'SCUSE ME! GETTING OFF!
VWSH
OH...
MY BAG...!
NWRG
NRRK
SLWHH
EEEEEEEEE
SLWHH
K-KAGOME ...
KLKTK
KLK
KLK

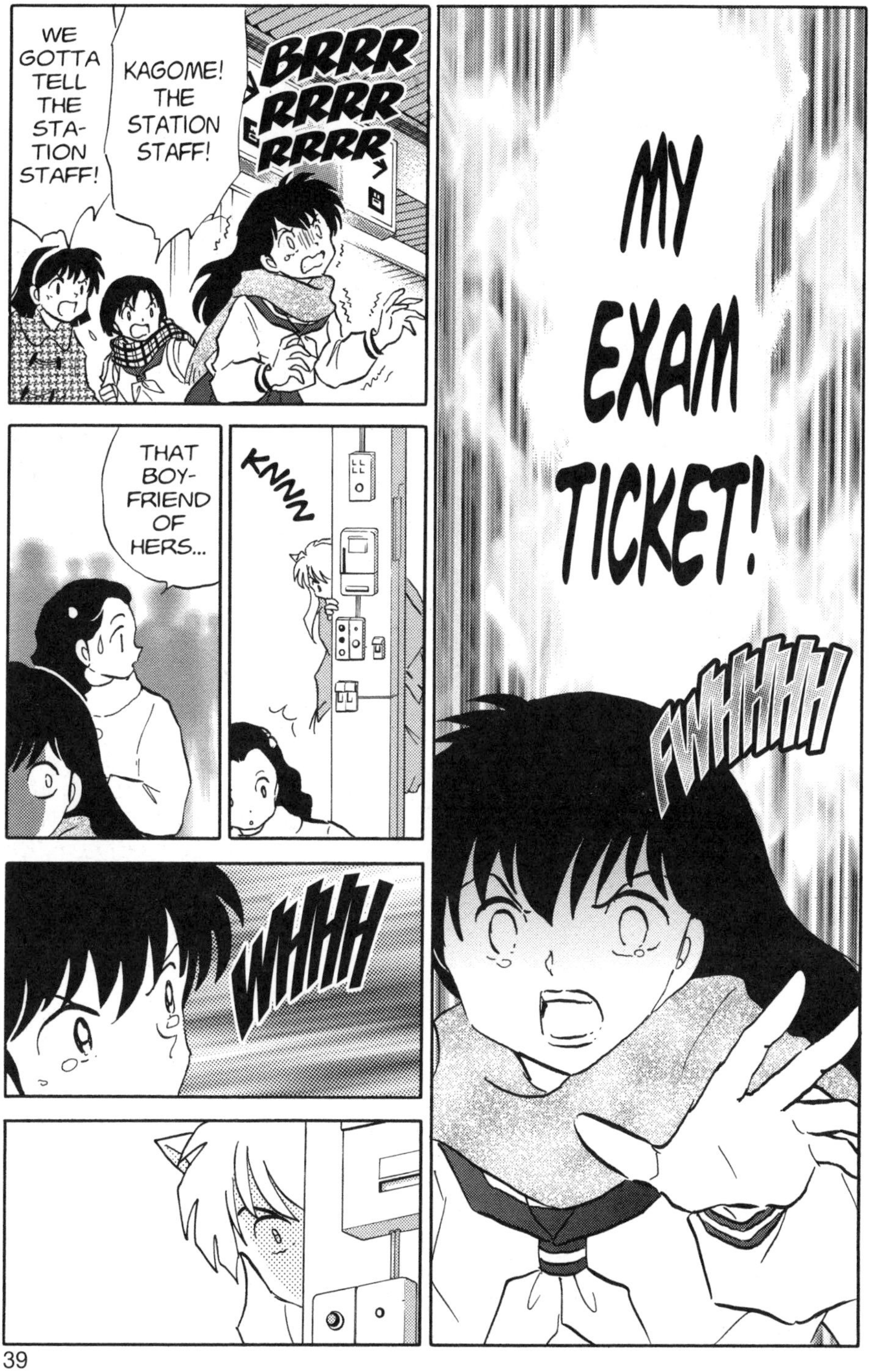
MY EXAM TICKET!
FWHHHHH
BRRRRRRRRRRRR
KAGOME! THE STATION STAFF!
WE GOTTA TELL THE STA-TION STAFF!
KNNN
THAT BOY-FRIEND OF HERS...
WHHHH

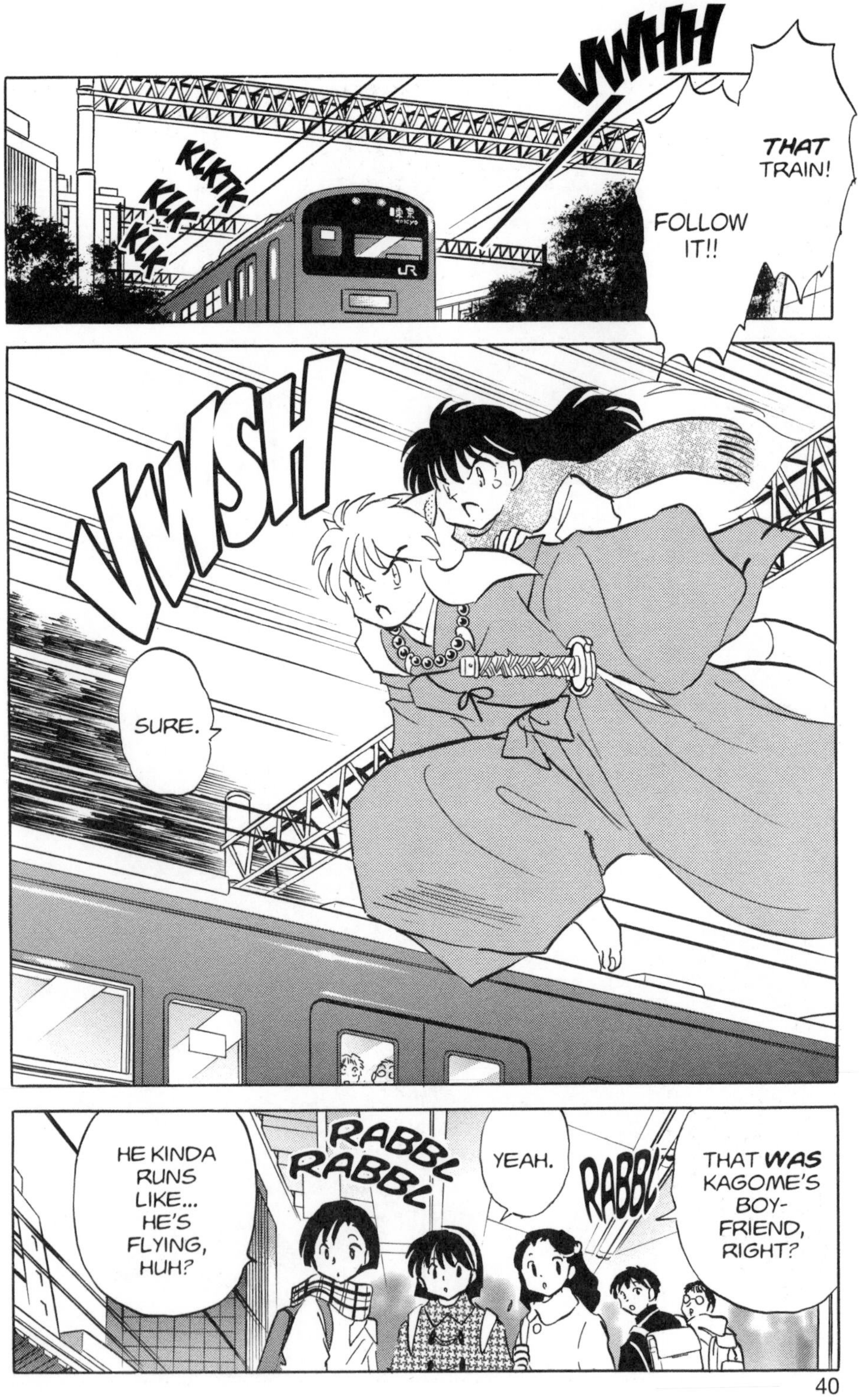
THAT TRAIN!
FOLLOW IT!!
VWHH
KLKTK
KLK
KLK
VWSH
SURE.
THAT WAS KAGOME'S BOY-FRIEND, RIGHT?
RABBL
YEAH.
RABBL
RABBL
HE KINDA RUNS LIKE... HE'S FLYING, HUH?

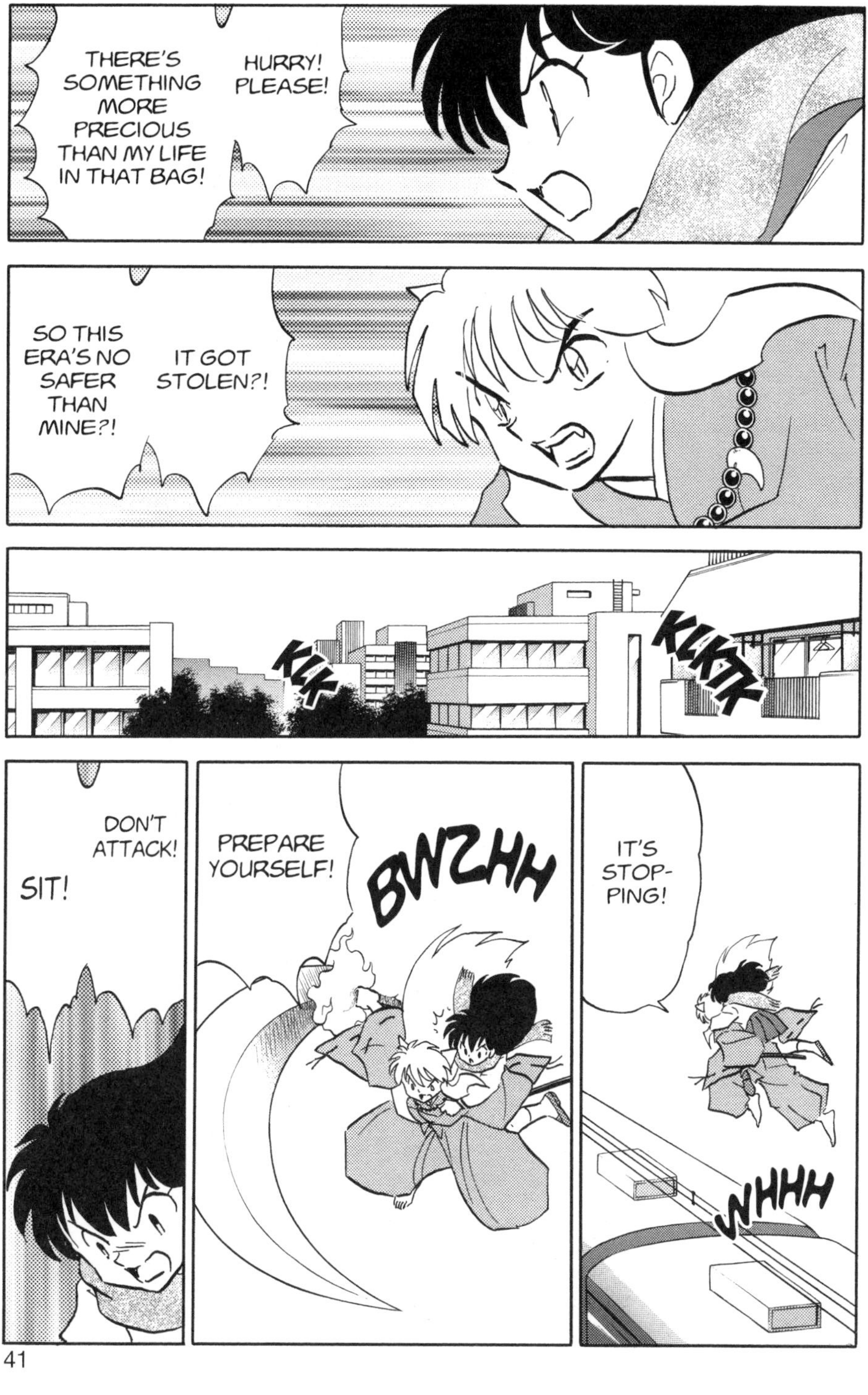
HURRY! PLEASE!
THERE'S SOMETHING MORE PRECIOUS THAN MY LIFE IN THAT BAG!
IT GOT STOLEN?!
SO THIS ERA'S NO SAFER THAN MINE?!
KLKTK
KLK
IT'S STOP-PING!
WHHH
BWZHH
PREPARE YOURSELF!
DON'T ATTACK!
SIT!

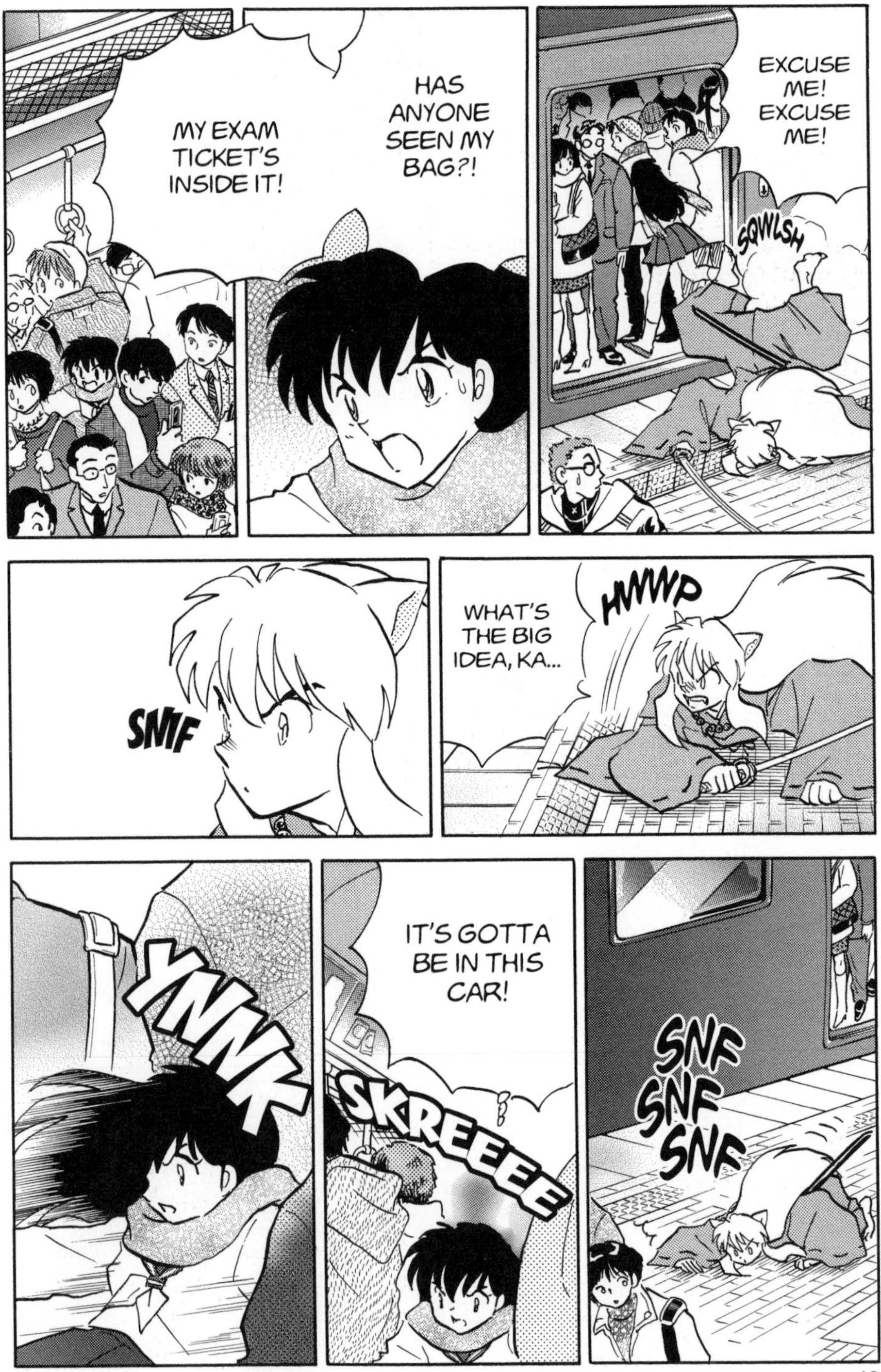
EXCUSE ME! EXCUSE ME!
SQWLSH
HAS ANYONE SEEN MY BAG?!
MY EXAM TICKET'S INSIDE IT!
WHAT'S THE BIG IDEA, KA...
HWWP
SNIF
SNF SNF SNF
IT'S GOTTA BE IN THIS CAR!
SKREEEEE
YNNK

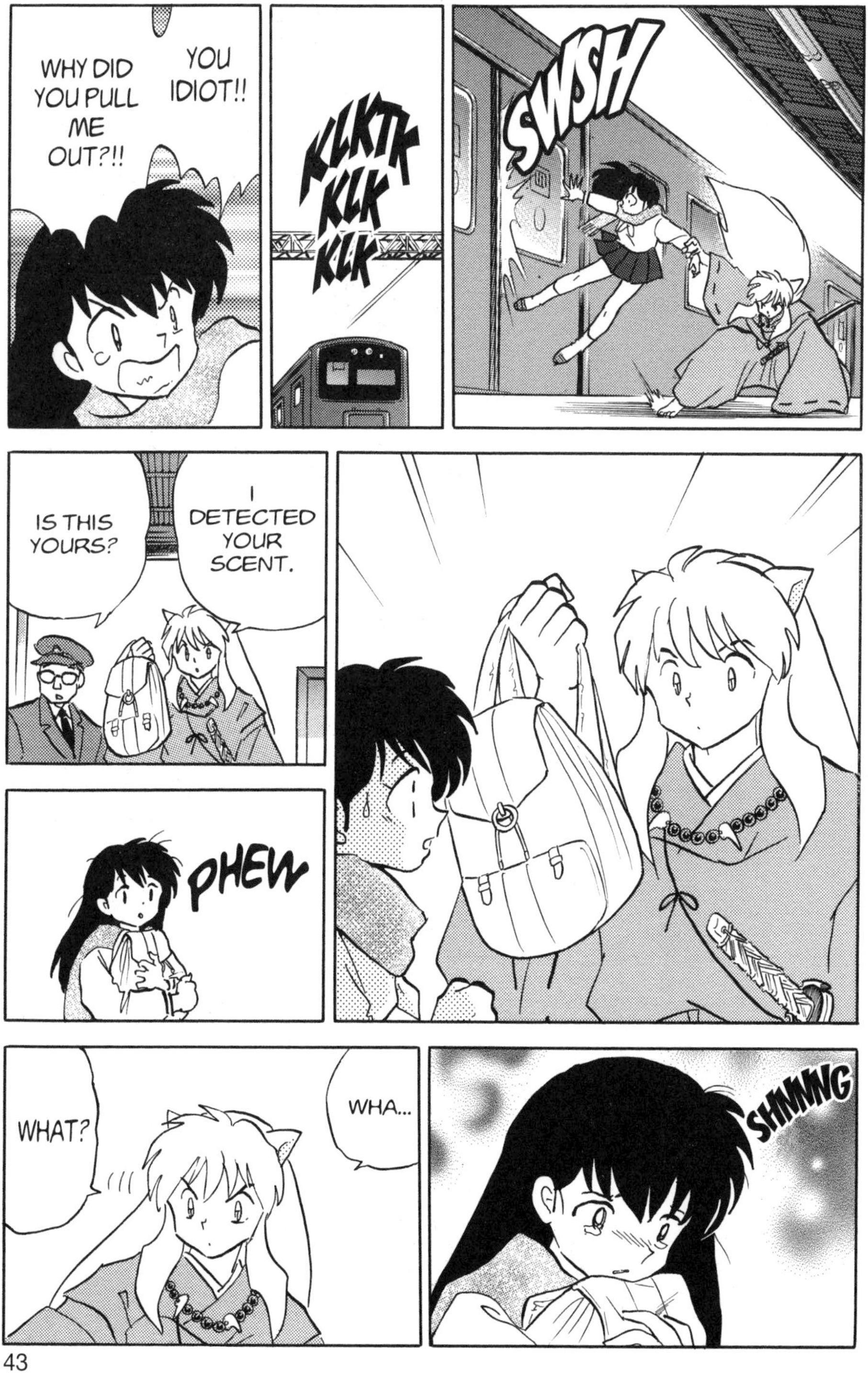
SWISH
KLKTIK KLK KLK
YOU IDIOT!!
WHY DID YOU PULL ME OUT?!!
I DETECTED YOUR SCENT.
IS THIS YOURS?
PHEW
SHNNNG
WHA...
WHAT?

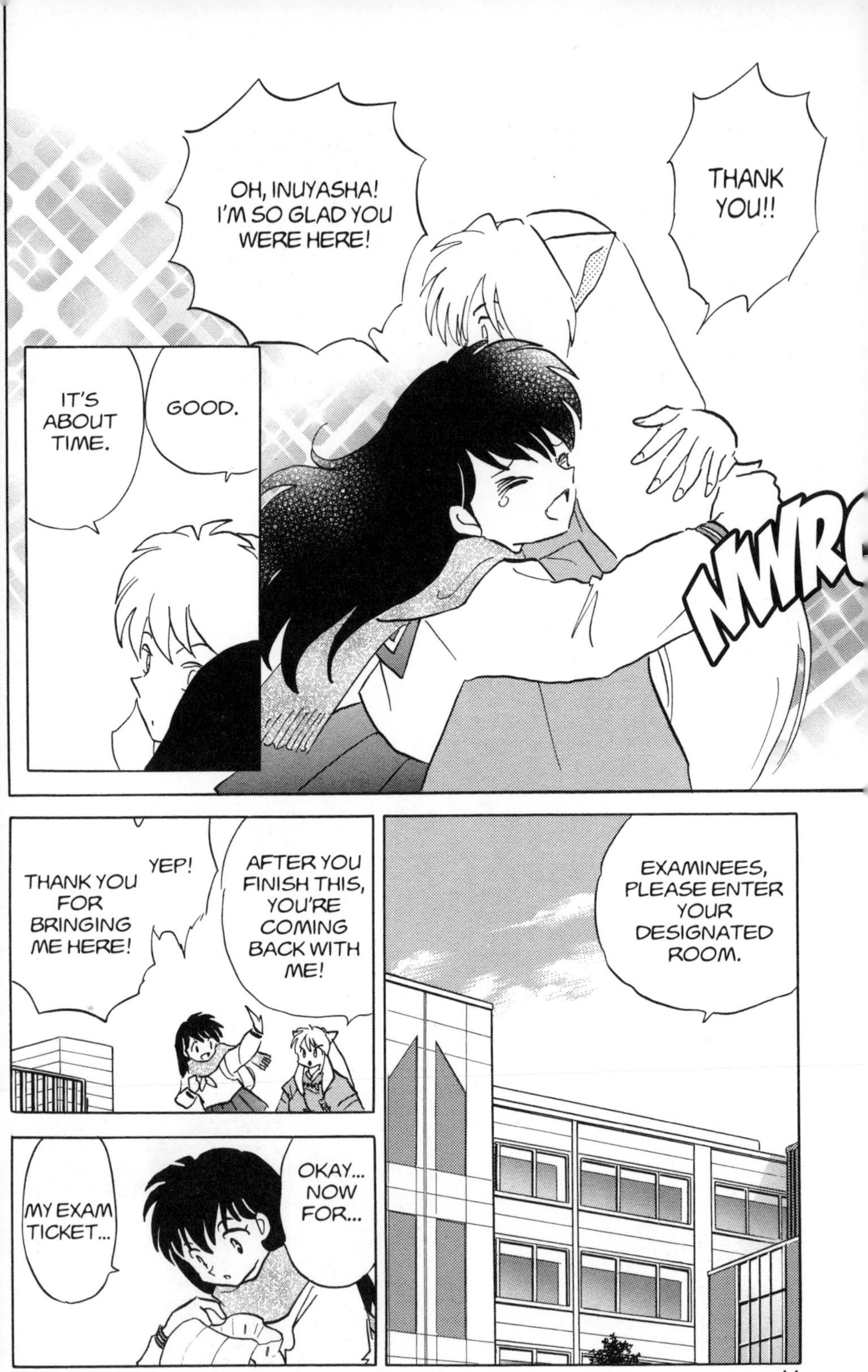
THANK YOU!!
OH, INUYASHA! I'M SO GLAD YOU WERE HERE!
NWR
GOOD.
IT'S ABOUT TIME.
EXAMINEES, PLEASE ENTER YOUR DESIGNATED ROOM.
AFTER YOU FINISH THIS, YOU'RE COMING BACK WITH ME!
YEP!
THANK YOU FOR BRINGING ME HERE!
OKAY... NOW FOR...
MY EXAM TICKET...

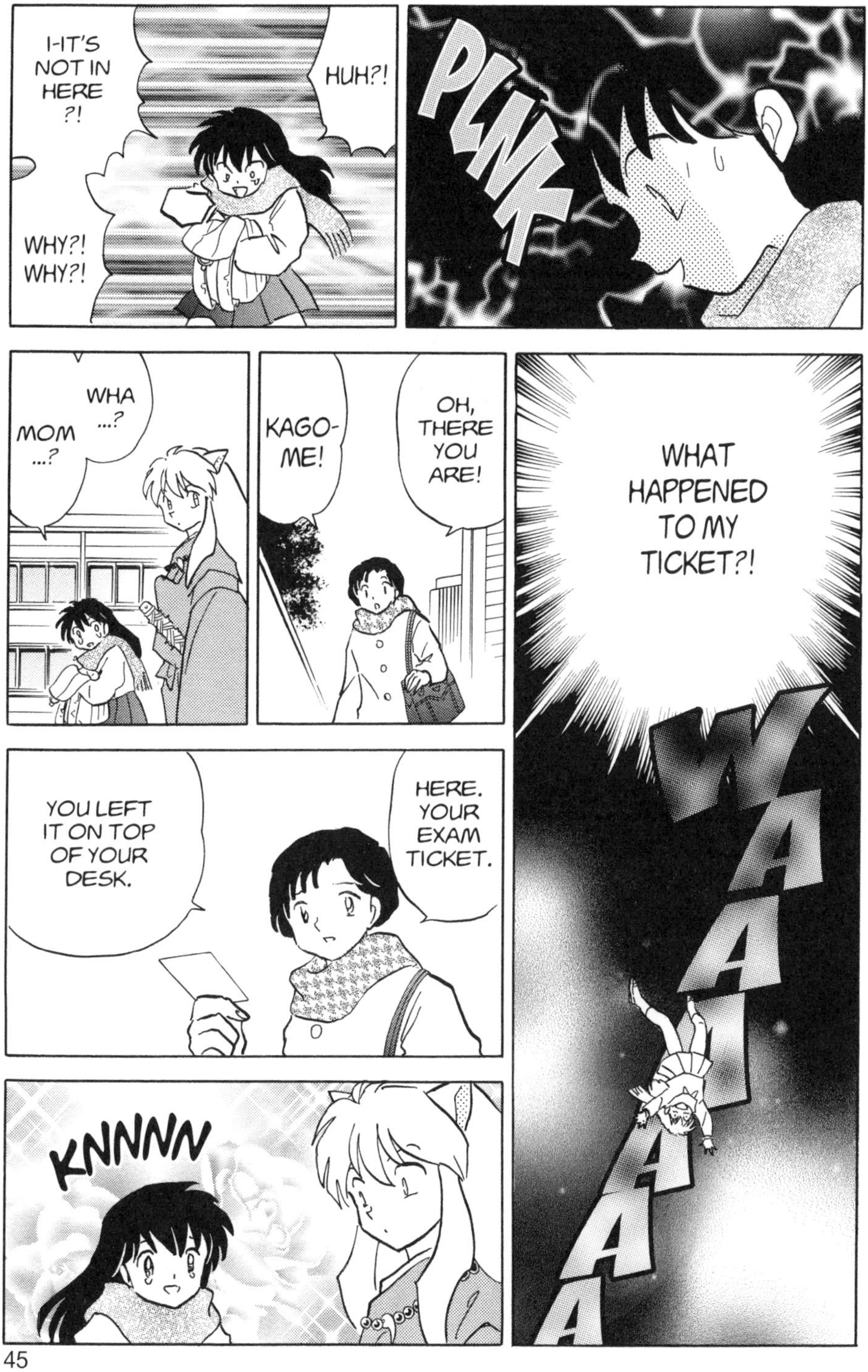
PLINK
HUH?!
I-IT'S NOT IN HERE ?!
WHY?! WHY?!
WHAT HAPPENED TO MY TICKET?!
WAAAAAAA
OH, THERE YOU ARE!
KAGO-ME!
WHA ...?
MOM ...?
HERE. YOUR EXAM TICKET.
YOU LEFT IT ON TOP OF YOUR DESK.
KNNNN

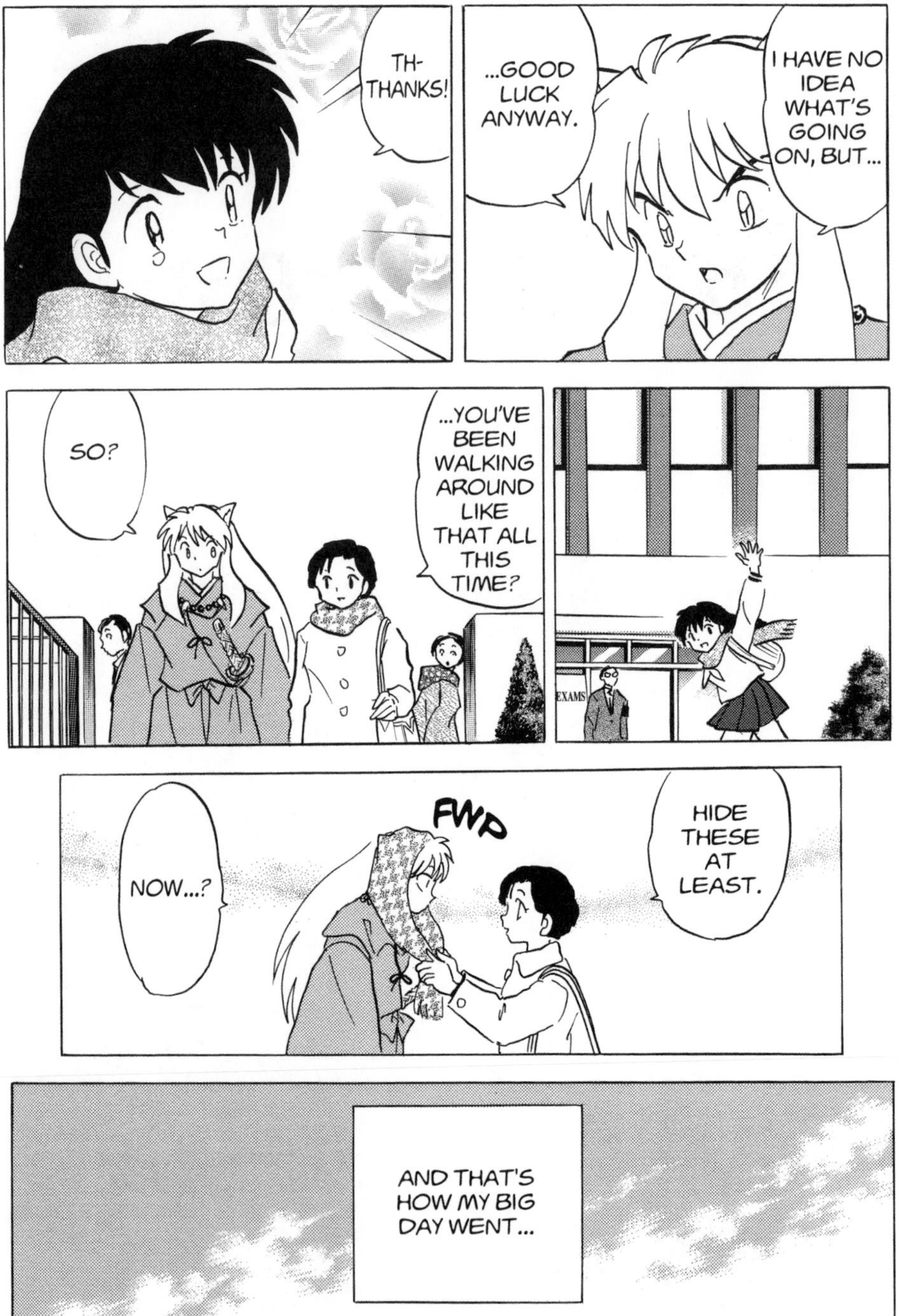
I HAVE NO IDEA WHAT'S GOING ON, BUT...
...GOOD LUCK ANYWAY.
TH- THANKS!
EXAMS
...YOU'VE BEEN WALKING AROUND LIKE THAT ALL THIS TIME?
SO?
HIDE THESE AT LEAST.
FWP
NOW...?
AND THAT'S HOW MY BIG DAY WENT...

SCROLL THREE
THE SHADOW

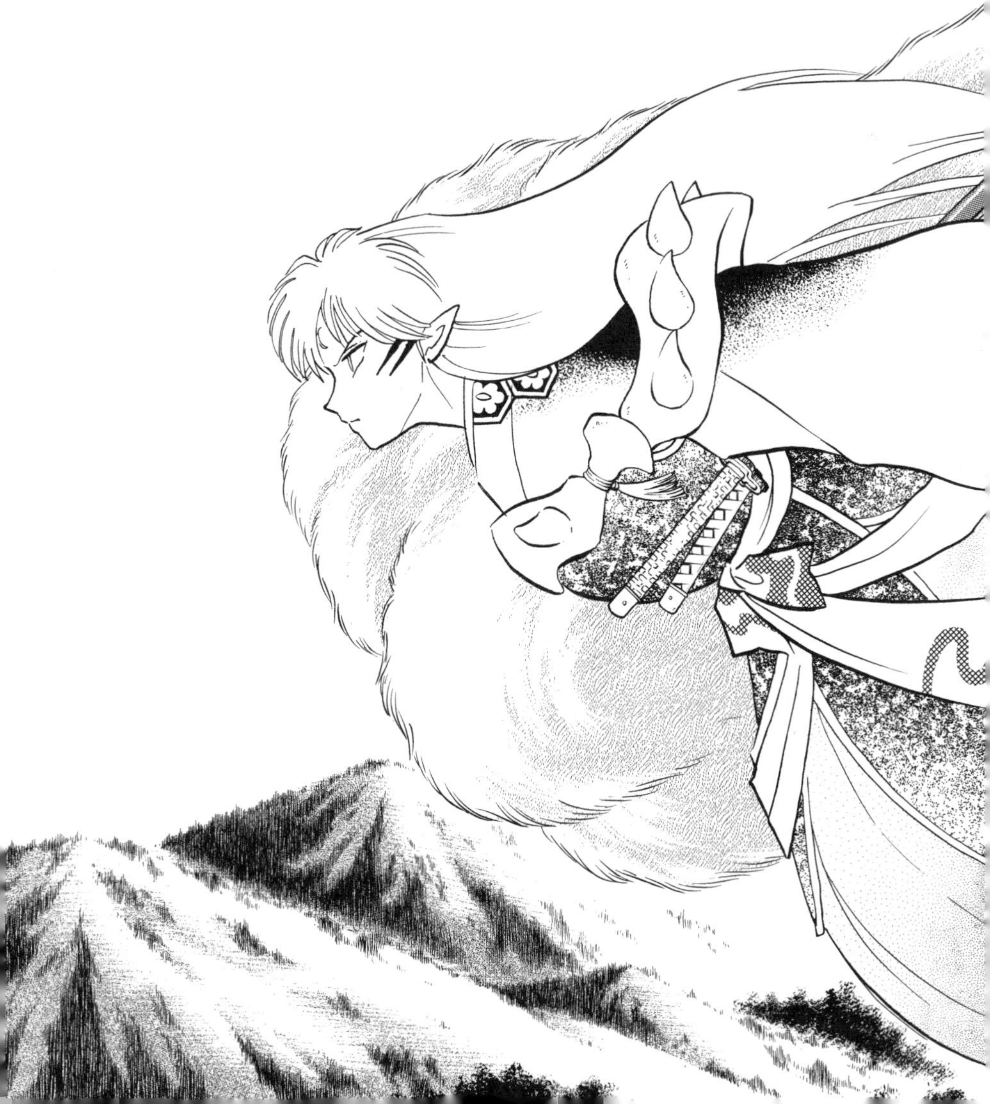

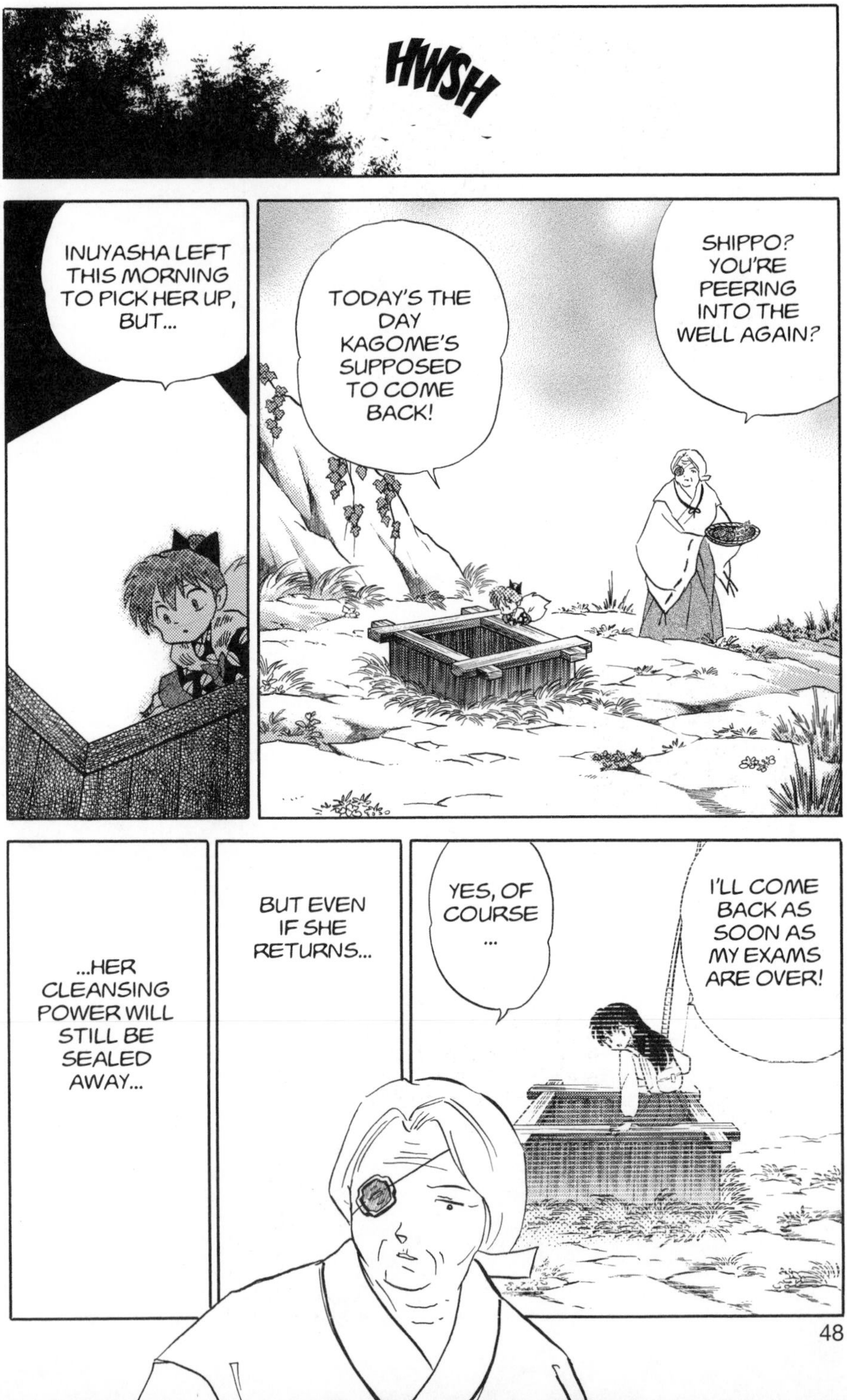
HWSH
SHIPPO? YOU'RE PEERING INTO THE WELL AGAIN?
TODAY'S THE DAY KAGOME'S SUPPOSED TO COME BACK!
INUYASHA LEFT THIS MORNING TO PICK HER UP, BUT...
I'LL COME BACK AS SOON AS MY EXAMS ARE OVER!
YES, OF COURSE...
BUT EVEN IF SHE RETURNS...
...HER CLEANSING POWER WILL STILL BE SEALED AWAY...

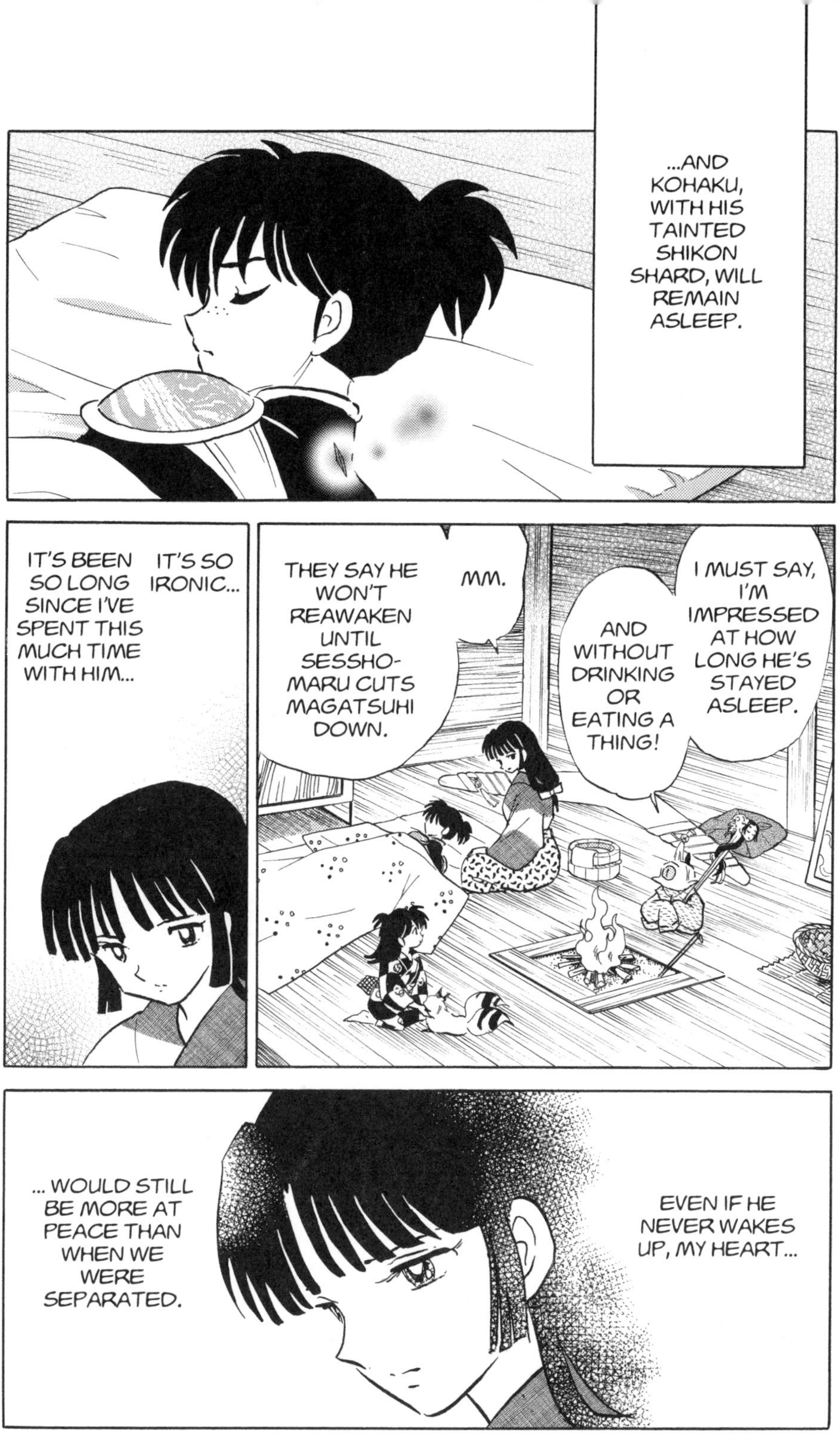
...AND KOHAKU, WITH HIS TAINTED SHIKON SHARD, WILL REMAIN ASLEEP.
I MUST SAY, I'M IMPRESSED AT HOW LONG HE'S STAYED ASLEEP.
AND WITHOUT DRINKING OR EATING A THING!
MM.
THEY SAY HE WON'T REAWAKEN UNTIL SESSHO-MARU CUTS MAGATSUHI DOWN.
IT'S SO IRONIC...
IT'S BEEN SO LONG SINCE I'VE SPENT THIS MUCH TIME WITH HIM...
EVEN IF HE NEVER WAKES UP, MY HEART...
...WOULD STILL BE MORE AT PEACE THAN WHEN WE WERE SEPARATED.

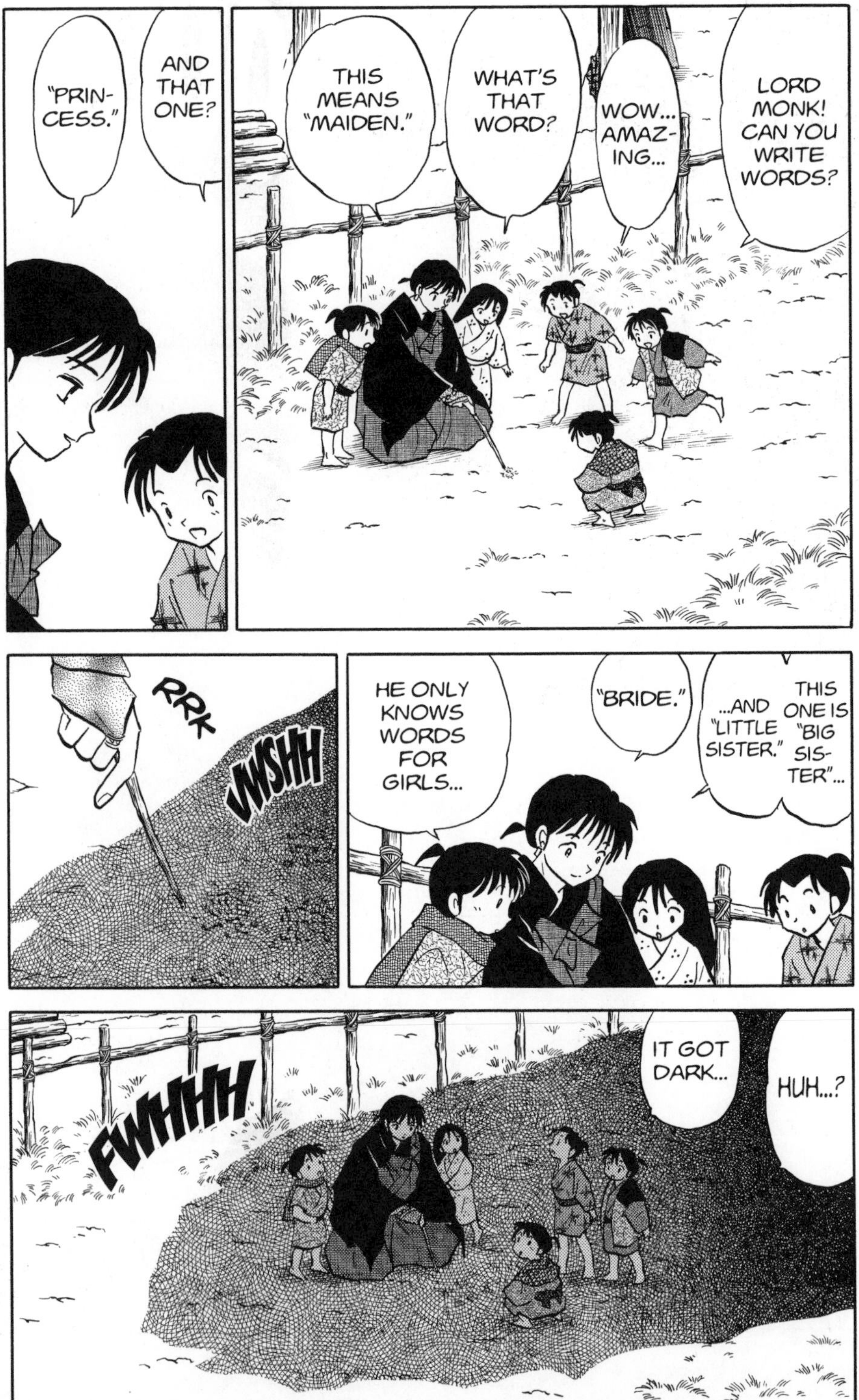

LORD MONK! CAN YOU WRITE WORDS?
WOW... AMAZ-ING...
WHAT'S THAT WORD?
THIS MEANS "MAIDEN."
AND THAT ONE?
"PRIN-CESS."
THIS ONE IS "BIG SIS-TER"...
...AND "LITTLE SISTER."
"BRIDE."
HE ONLY KNOWS WORDS FOR GIRLS...
RRK
VWSHH
HUH...?
IT GOT DARK...
FWHHHH

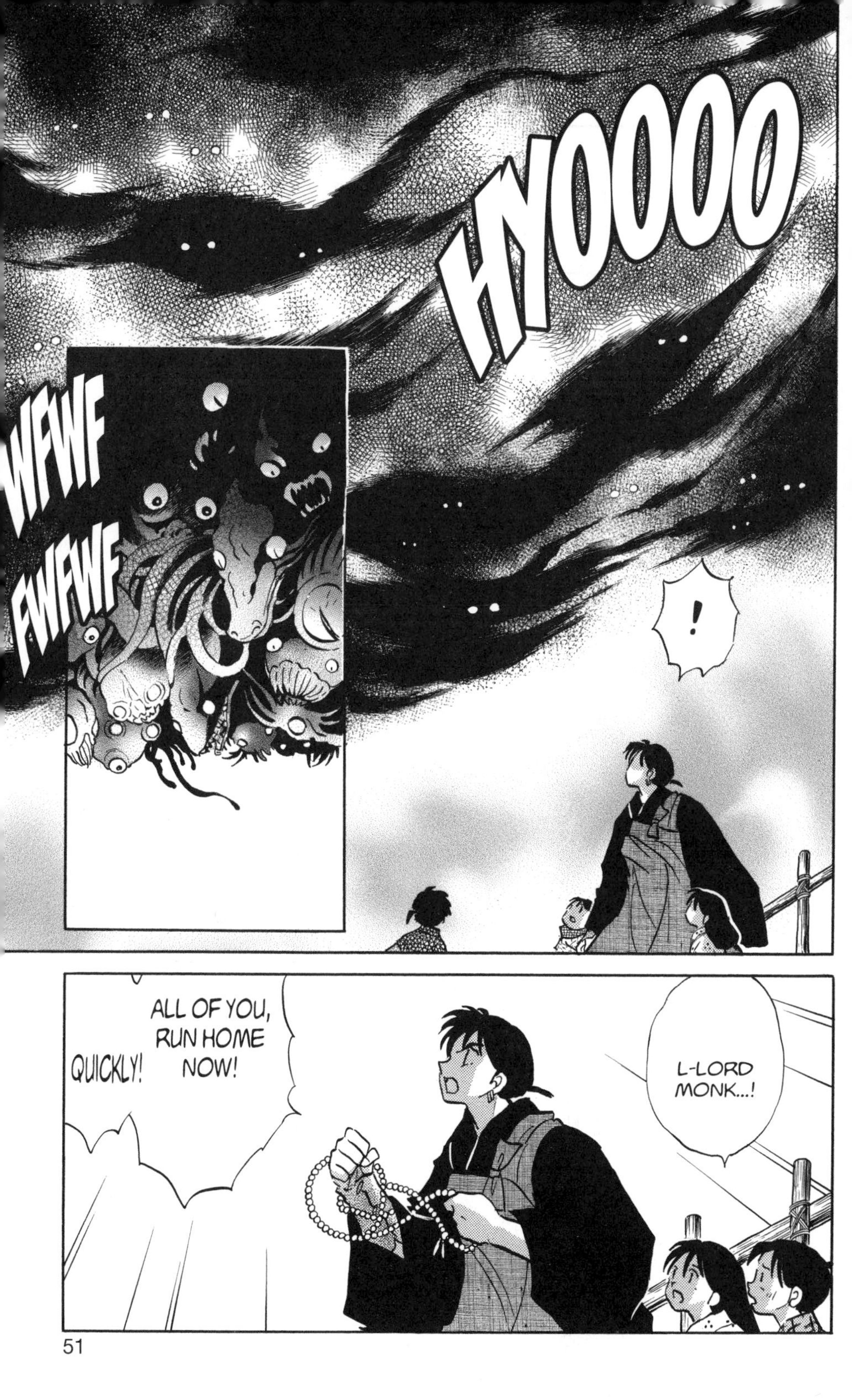
HYOOOO
!
WFWF
FWFWF
L-LORD MONK...!
ALL OF YOU, RUN HOME NOW!
QUICKLY!

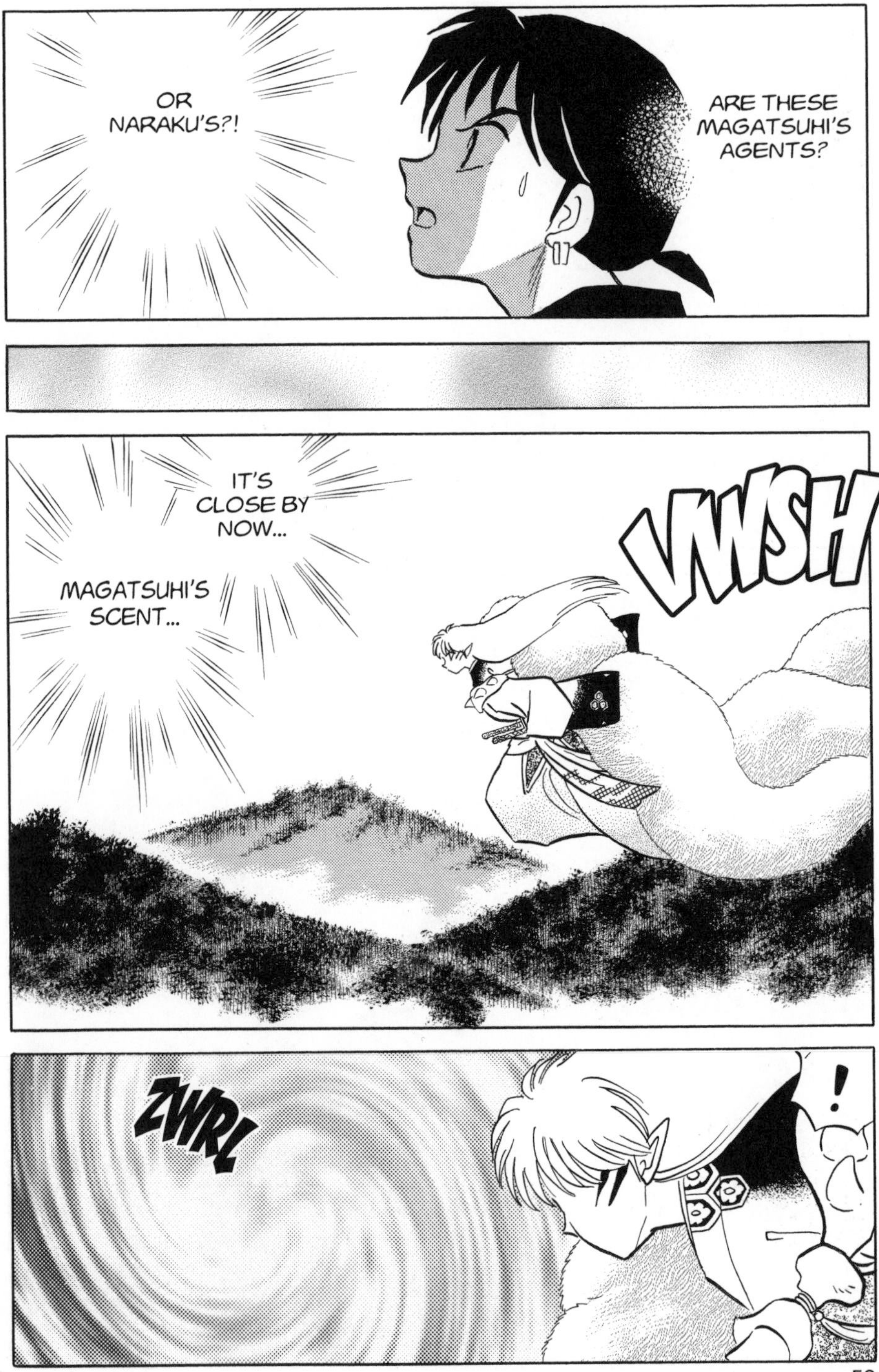
ARE THESE MAGATSUHI'S AGENTS?
OR NARAKU'S?!
VWSH
IT'S CLOSE BY NOW...
MAGATSUHI'S SCENT...
!
ZWRL

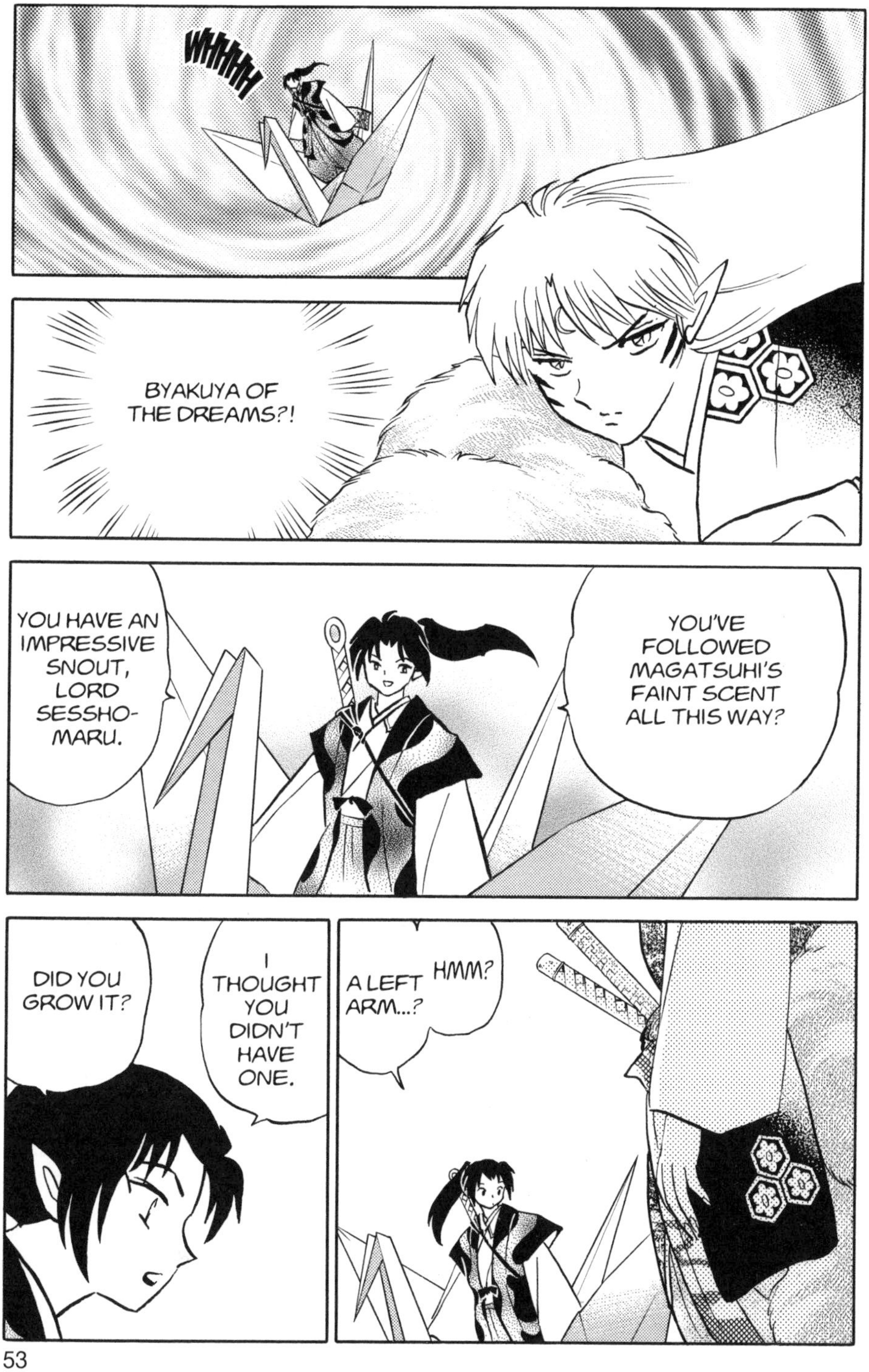
WHHHH
BYAKUYA OF THE DREAMS?!
YOU'VE FOLLOWED MAGATSUHI'S FAINT SCENT ALL THIS WAY?
YOU HAVE AN IMPRESSIVE SNOUT, LORD SESSHO-MARU.
HMM?
A LEFT ARM...?
I THOUGHT YOU DIDN'T HAVE ONE.
DID YOU GROW IT?

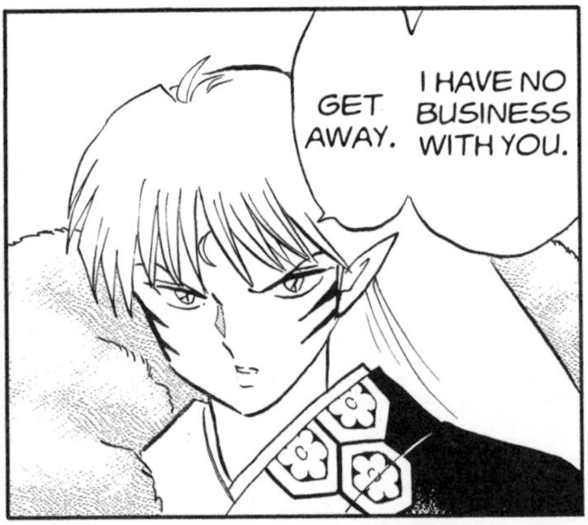
I HAVE NO BUSINESS WITH YOU.
GET AWAY.

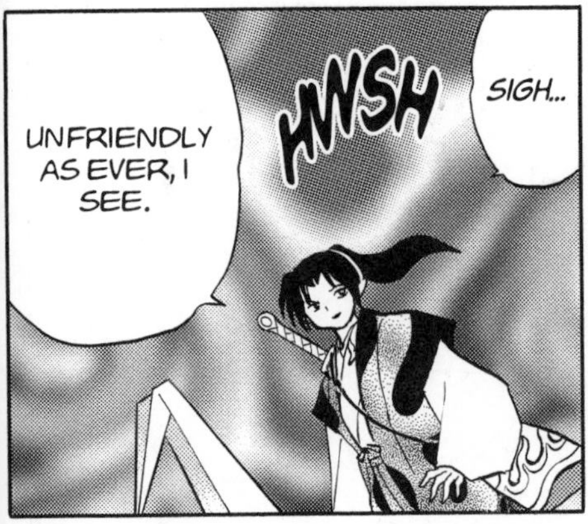
SIGH...
HWSH
UNFRIENDLY AS EVER, I SEE.

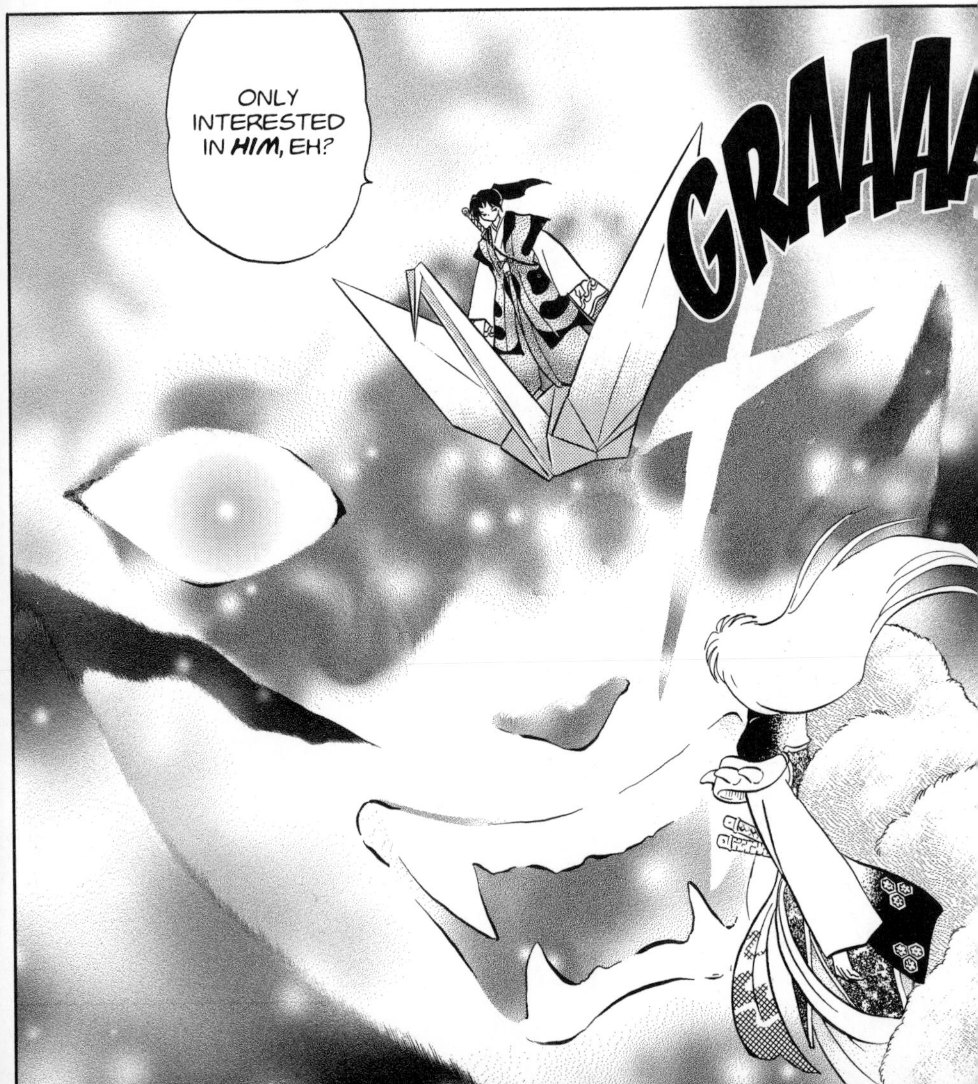
GRAAAA
ONLY INTERESTED IN ***HIM***, EH?

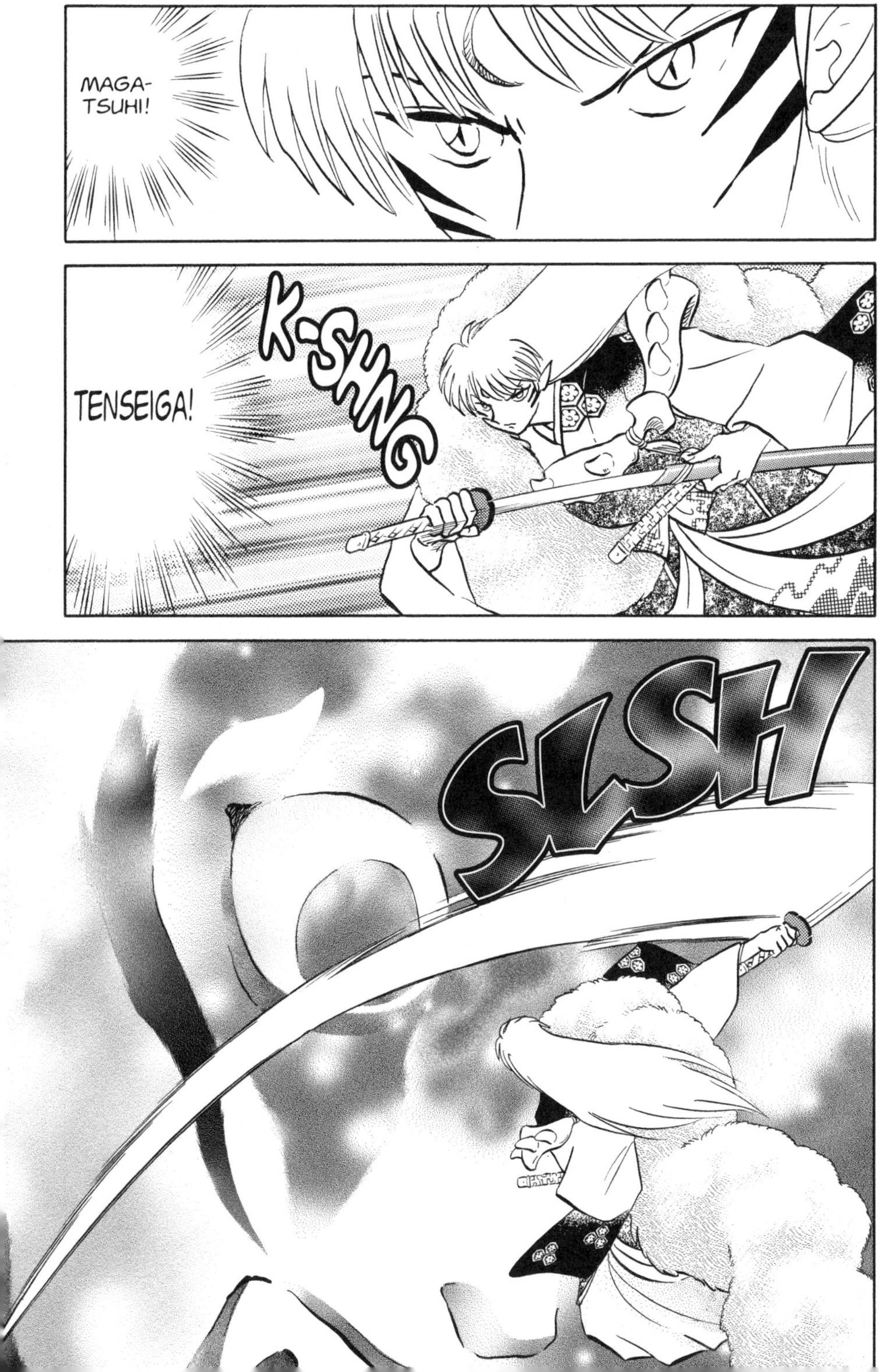
MAGA-
TSUHI!
TENSEIGA!
K-SHING
SLSH

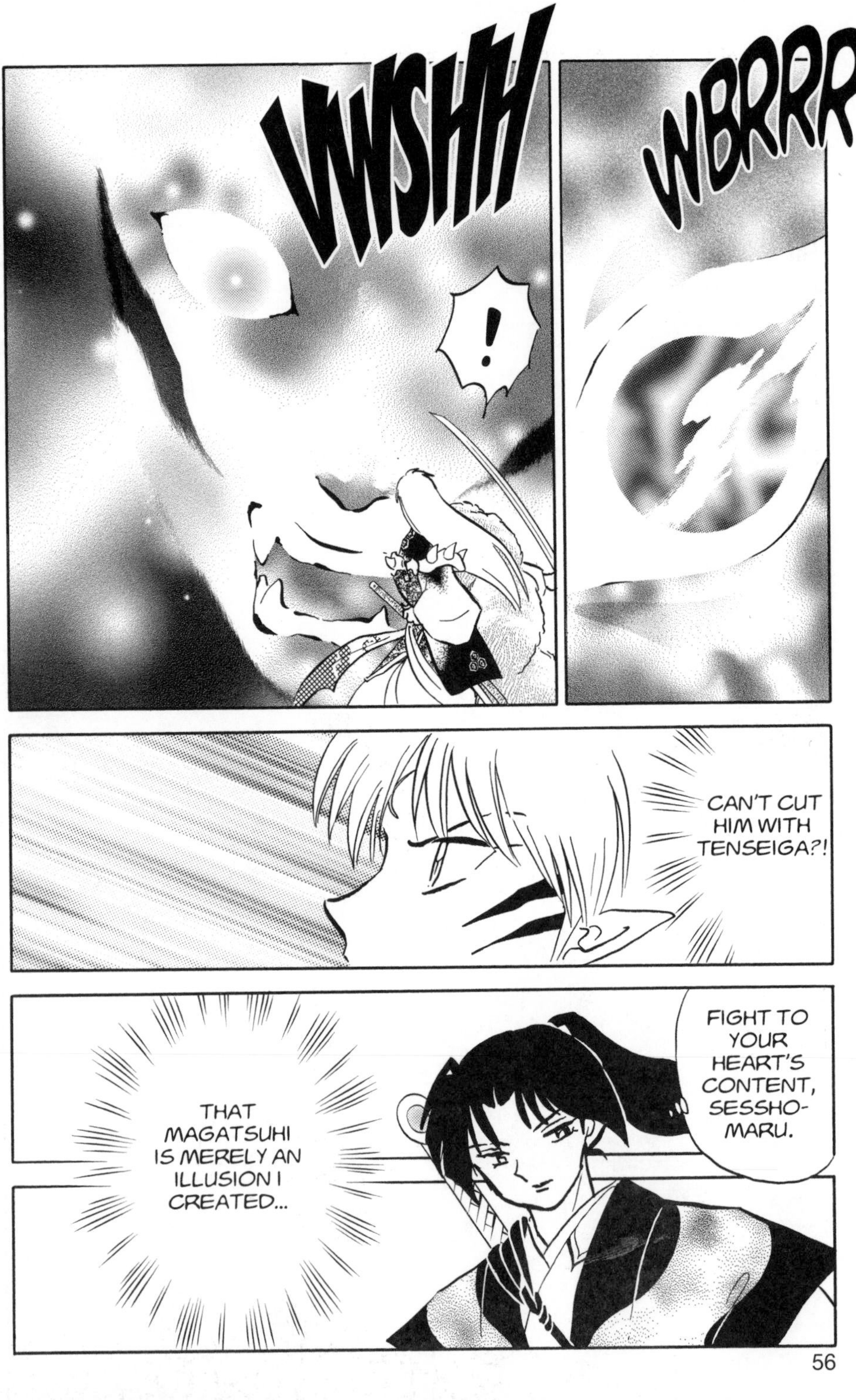
WBRRR
VWSHH
!
CAN'T CUT HIM WITH TENSEIGA?!
FIGHT TO YOUR HEART'S CONTENT, SESSHO-MARU.
THAT MAGATSUHI IS MERELY AN ILLUSION I CREATED...

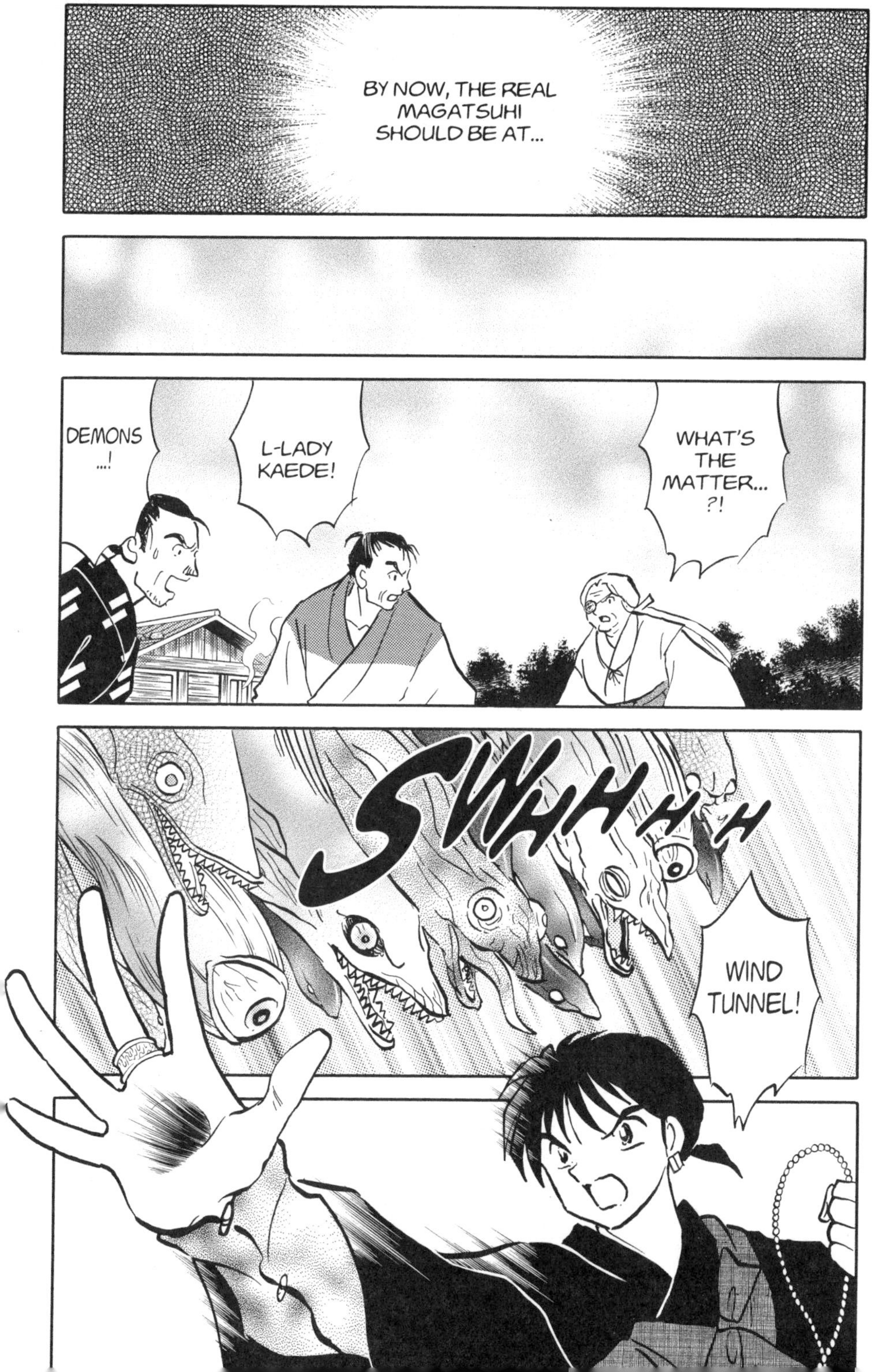
BY NOW, THE REAL MAGATSUHI SHOULD BE AT...
WHAT'S THE MATTER...?!
L-LADY KAEDE!
DEMONS...!
SWHHHH
WIND TUNNEL!

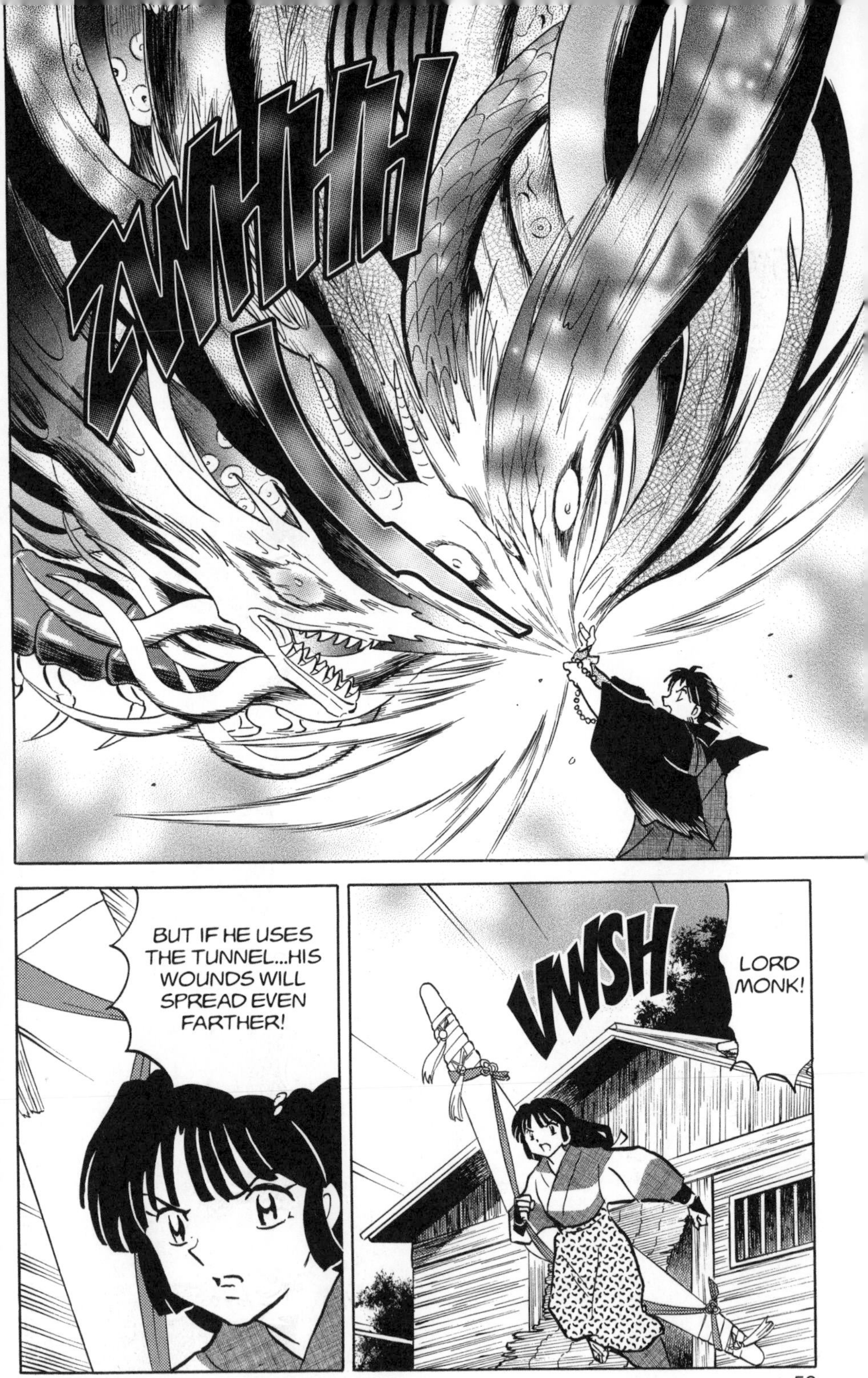
ZWHHHH
VWSH
LORD MONK!
BUT IF HE USES THE TUNNEL...HIS WOUNDS WILL SPREAD EVEN FARTHER!

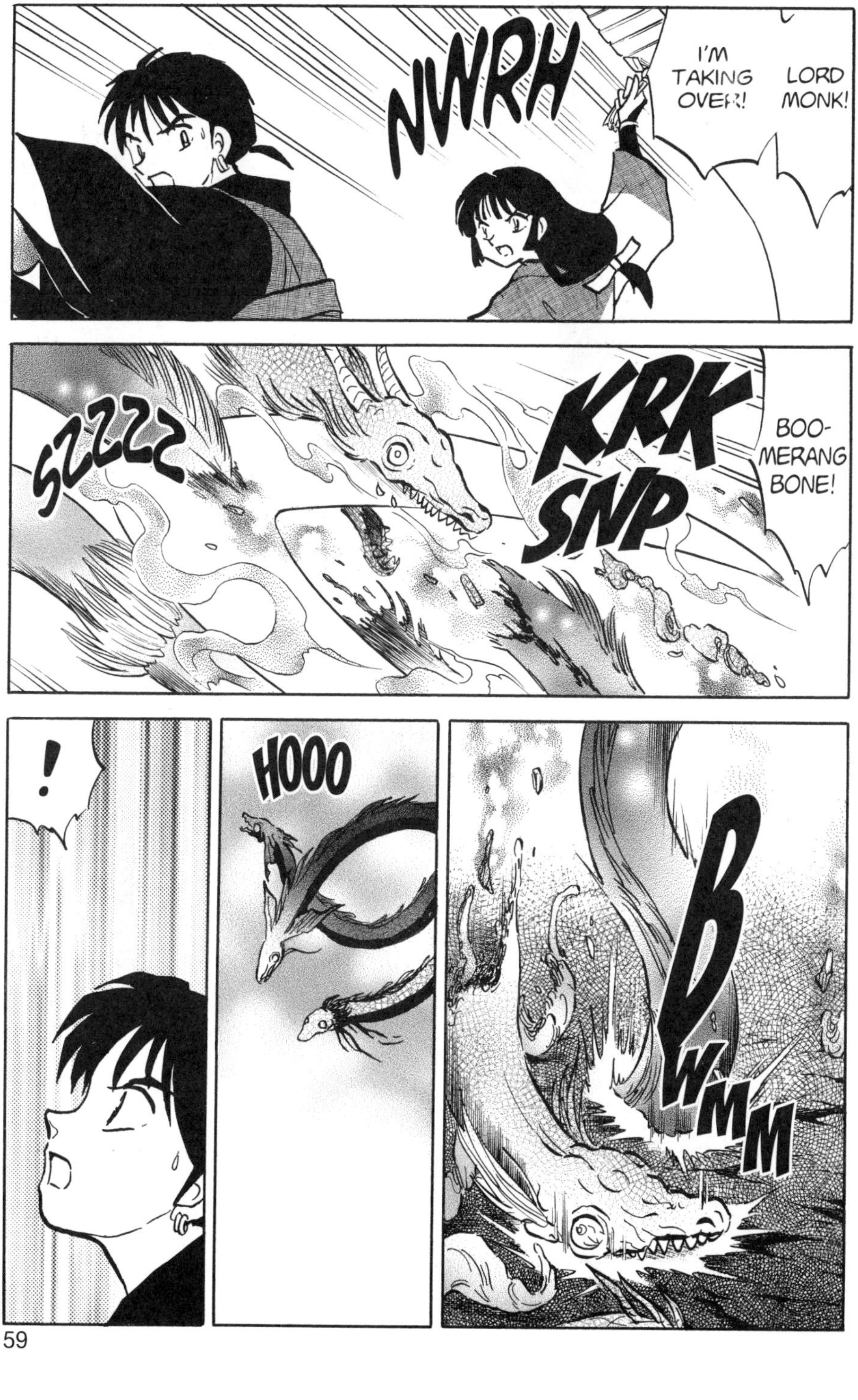
LORD MONK!
I'M TAKING OVER!
NWRH
BOO-MERANG BONE!
KRK SNP
SZZZZ
BWMM
HOOO
!

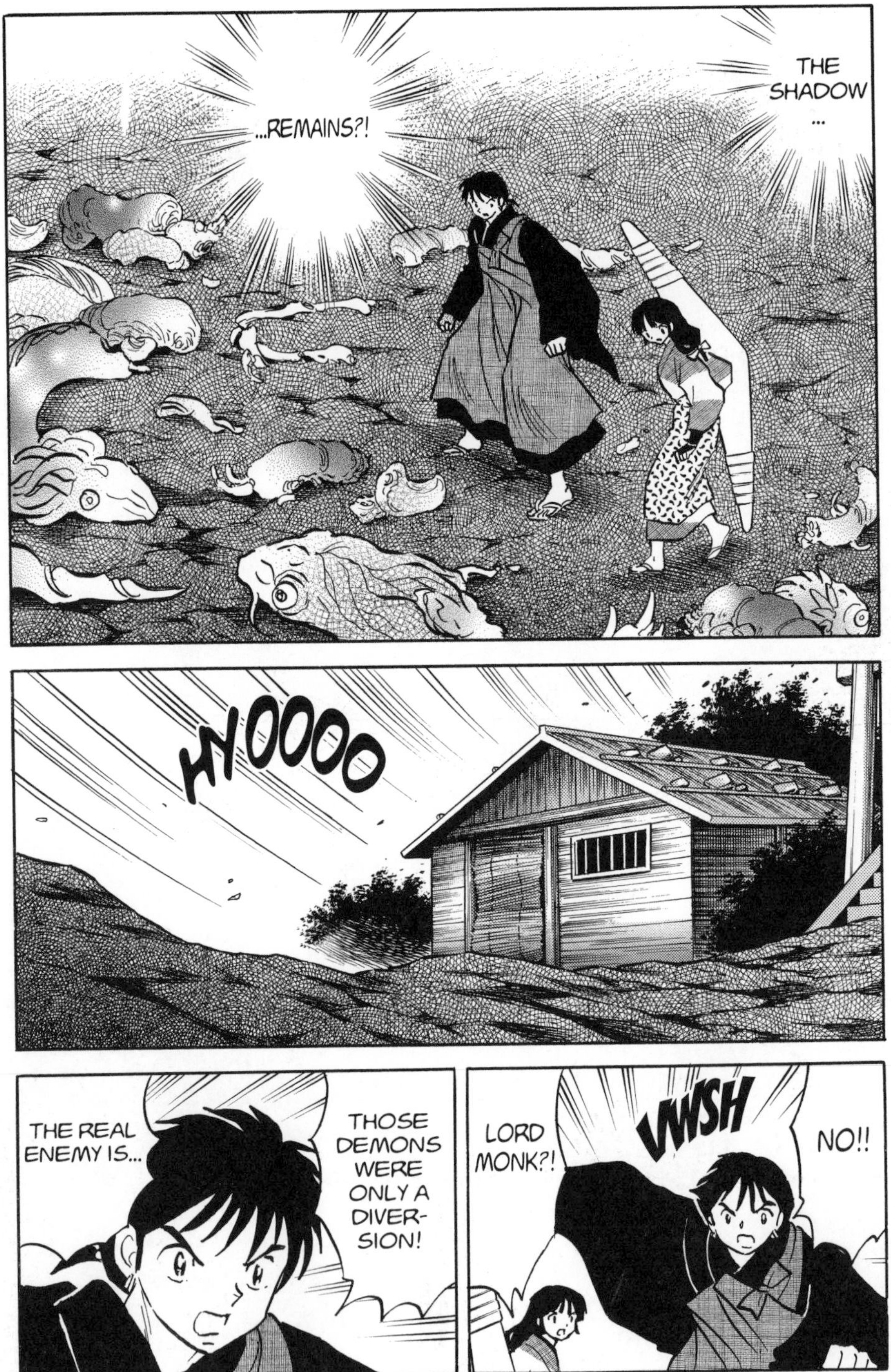
THE SHADOW ...
...REMAINS?!
HYOOOO
NO!!
VWSH
LORD MONK?!
THOSE DEMONS WERE ONLY A DIVER-SION!
THE REAL ENEMY IS...

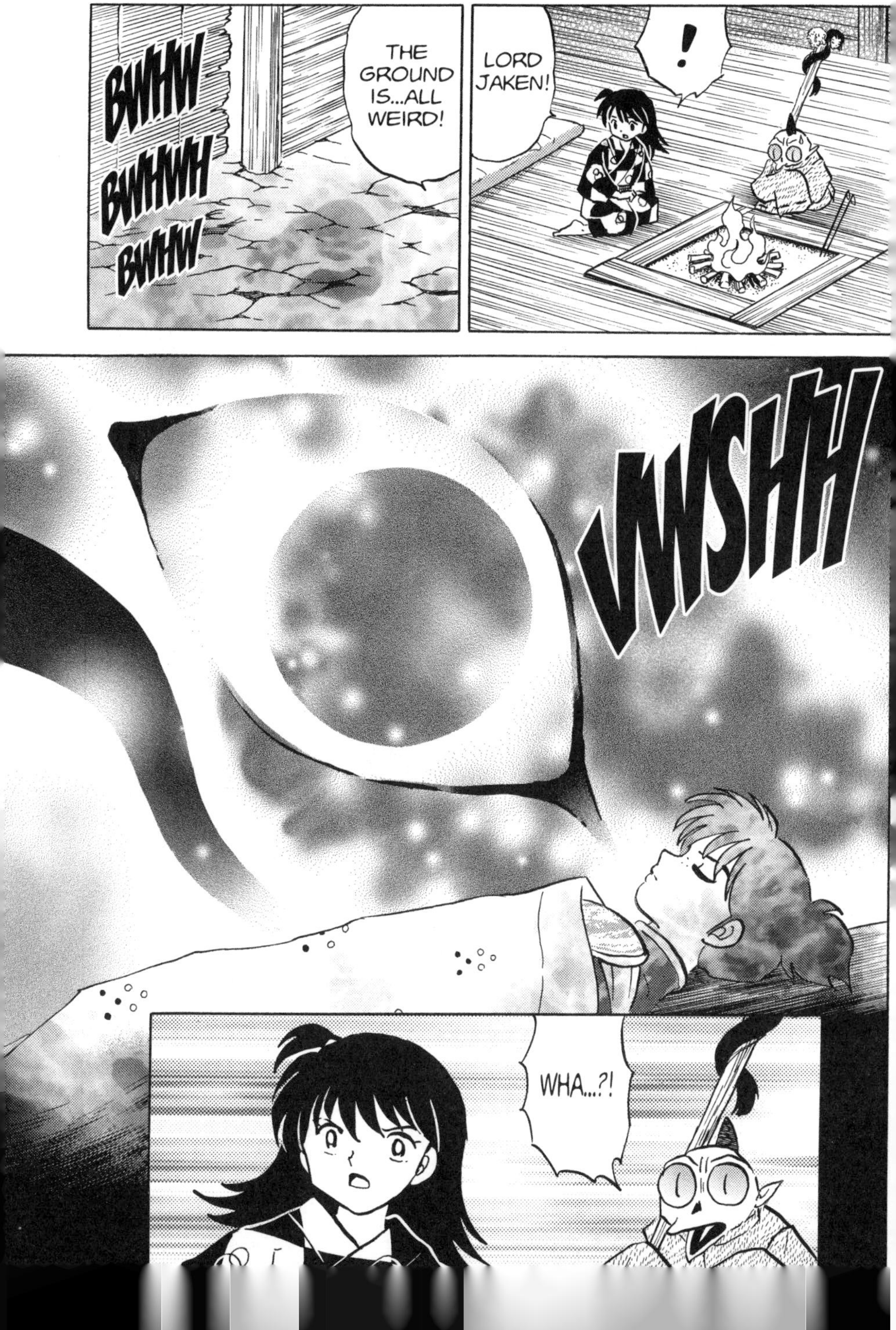
!
LORD JAKEN!
THE GROUND IS...ALL WEIRD!
BWHW BWHWH BWHW
VWSHH
WHA...?!

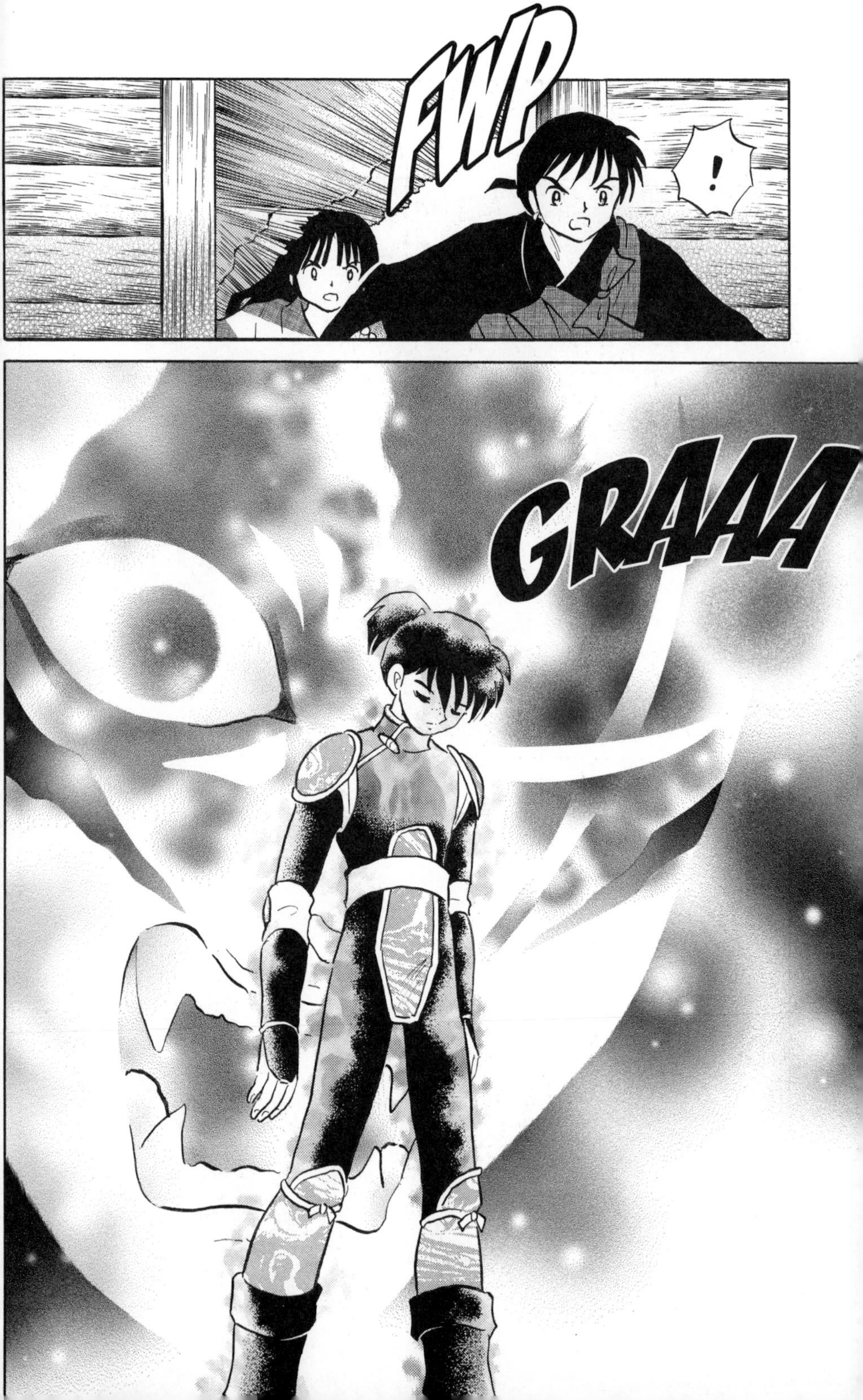
FWP
!
GRAAA

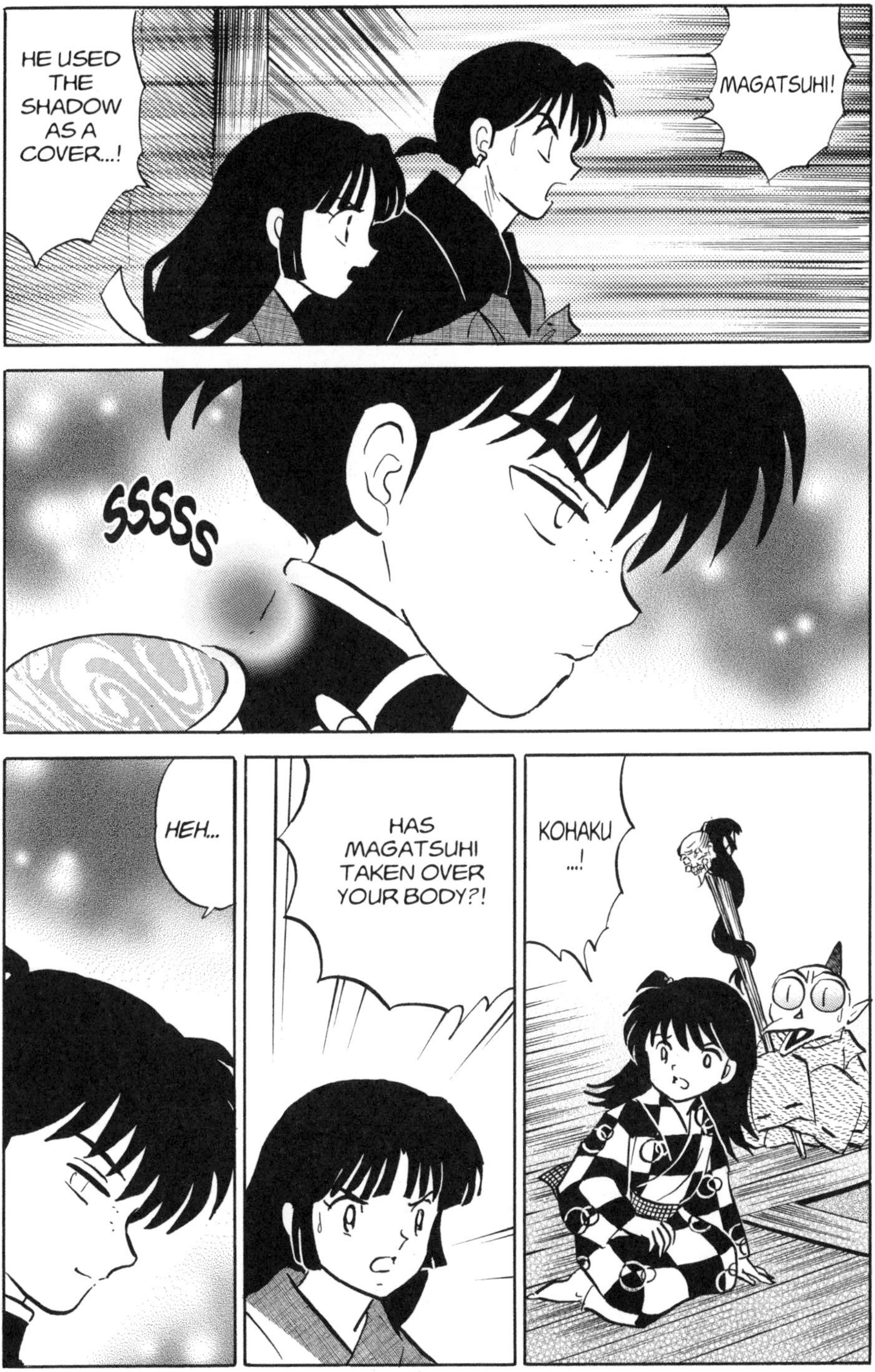
MAGATSUHI!
HE USED THE SHADOW AS A COVER...!
SSSSS
KOHAKU ...!
HAS MAGATSUHI TAKEN OVER YOUR BODY?!
HEH...

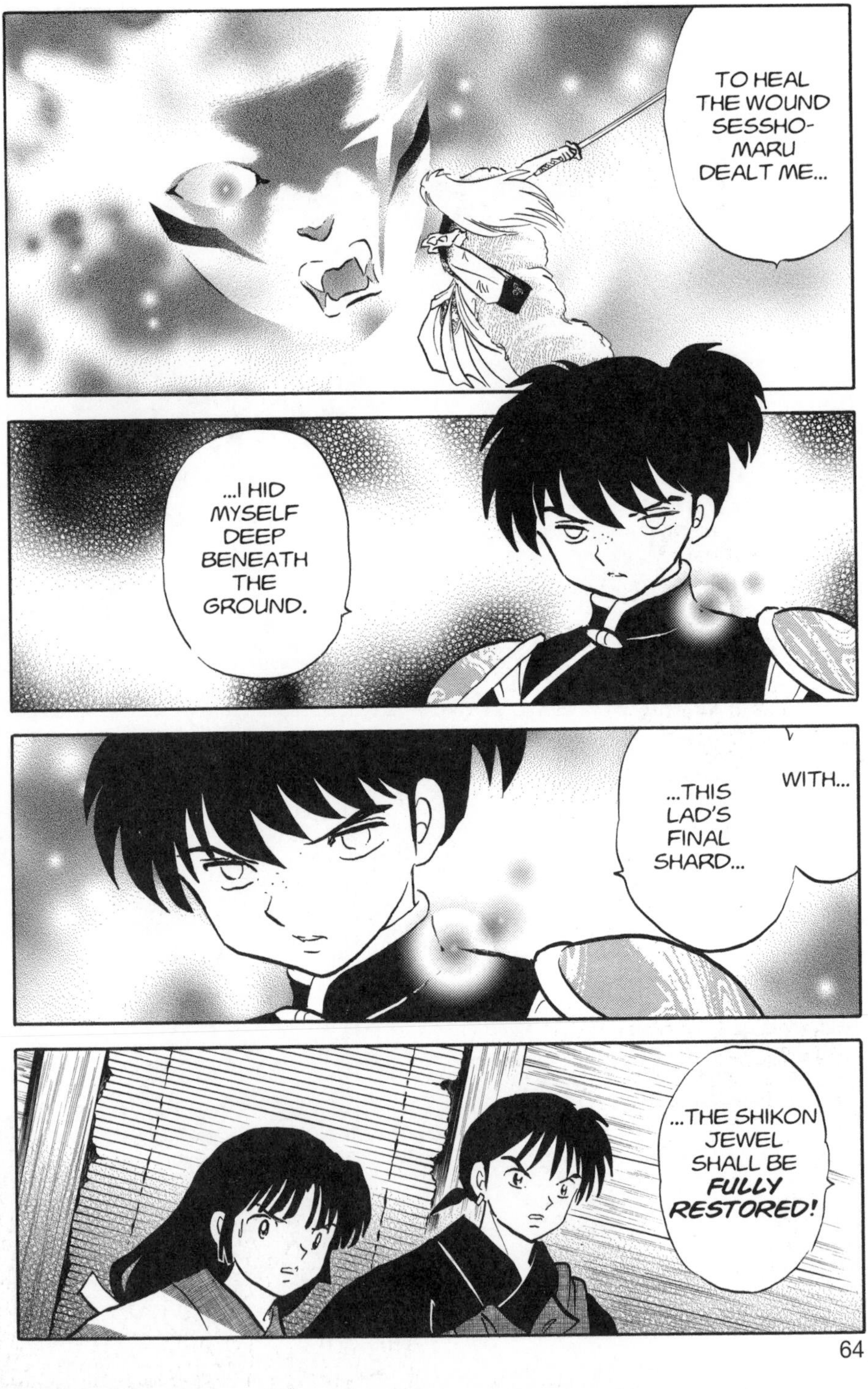
TO HEAL THE WOUND SESSHO-MARU DEALT ME...
...I HID MYSELF DEEP BENEATH THE GROUND.
WITH...
...THIS LAD'S FINAL SHARD...
...THE SHIKON JEWEL SHALL BE **FULLY RESTORED!**

SCROLL FOUR
POSSESSED

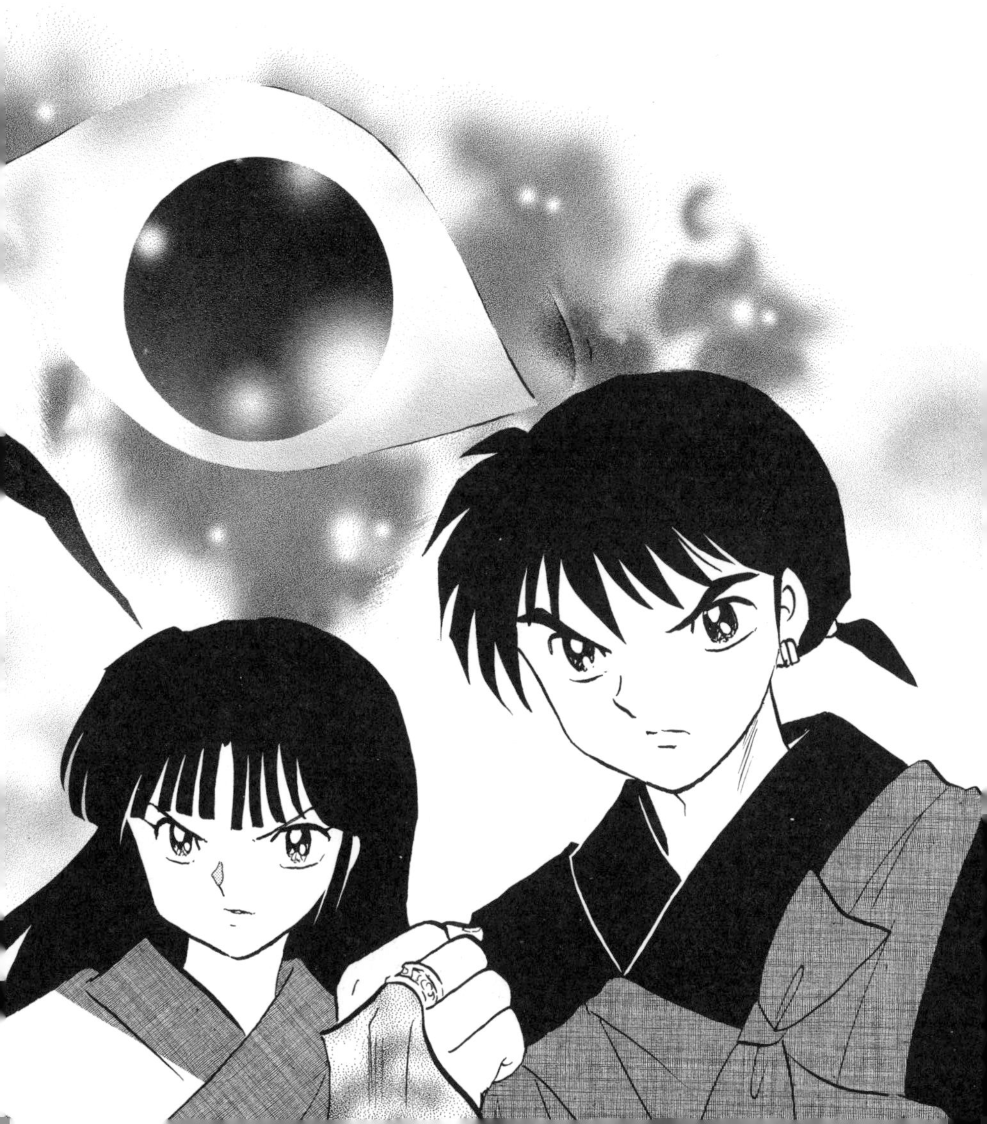

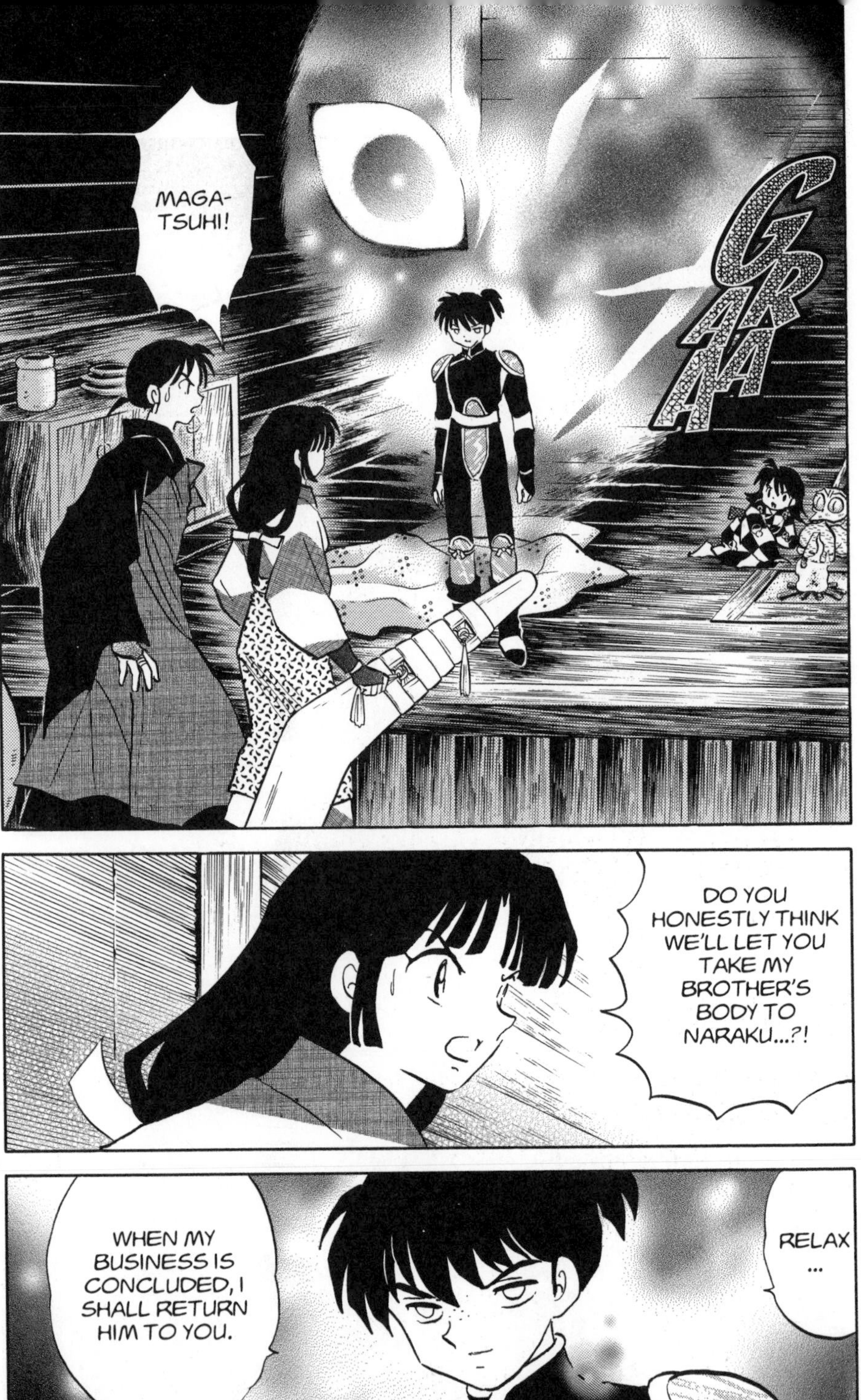

MAGA-TSUHI!
GRAAA
DO YOU HONESTLY THINK WE'LL LET YOU TAKE MY BROTHER'S BODY TO NARAKU...?!
RELAX ...
WHEN MY BUSINESS IS CONCLUDED, I SHALL RETURN HIM TO YOU.

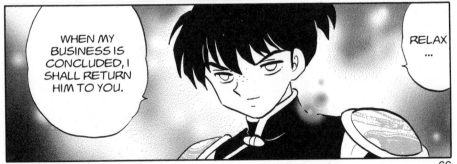

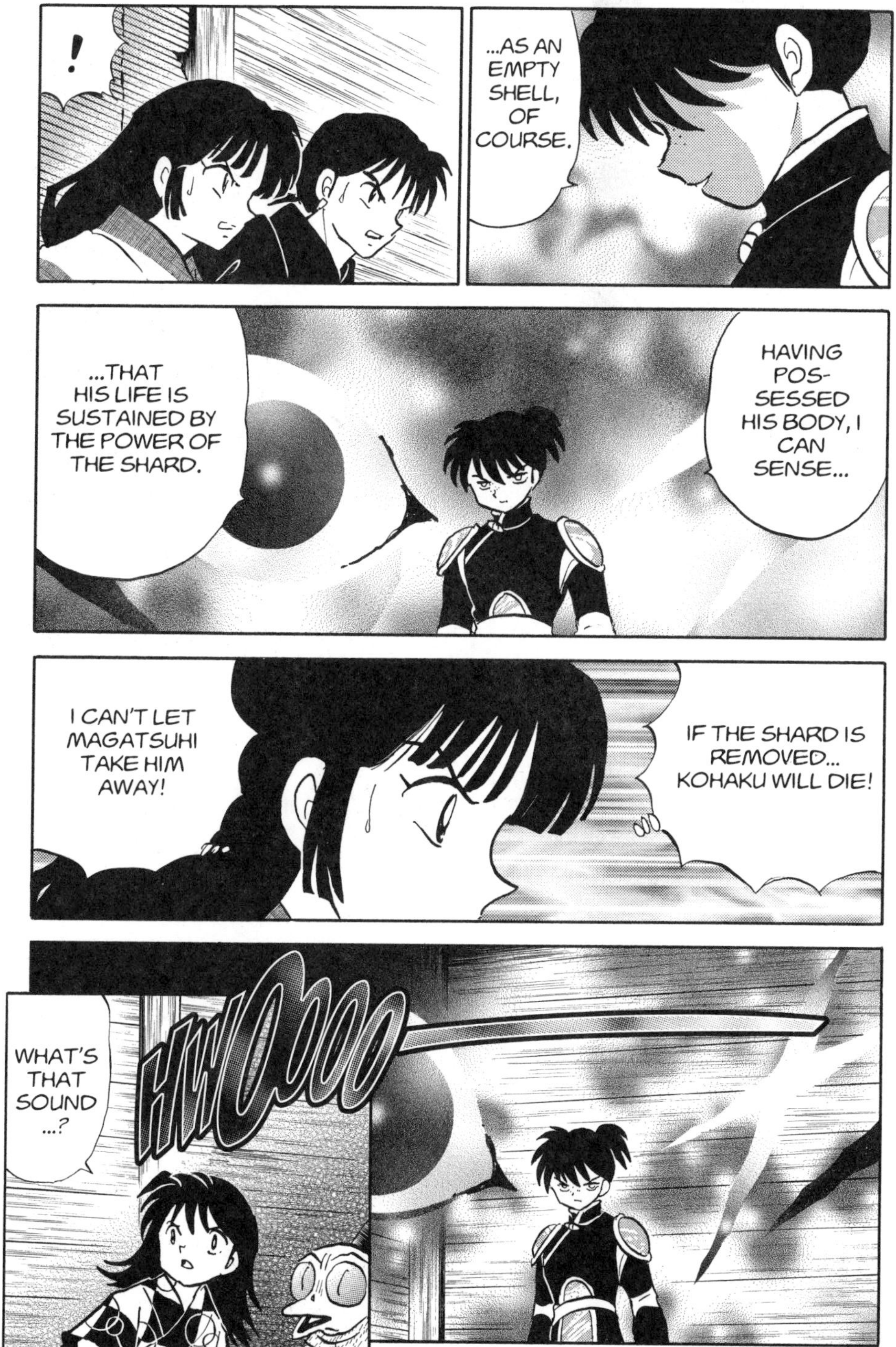
...AS AN EMPTY SHELL, OF COURSE.
!
HAVING POS-SESSED HIS BODY, I CAN SENSE...
...THAT HIS LIFE IS SUSTAINED BY THE POWER OF THE SHARD.
IF THE SHARD IS REMOVED... KOHAKU WILL DIE!
I CAN'T LET MAGATSUHI TAKE HIM AWAY!
HWOOOO
WHAT'S THAT SOUND ...?

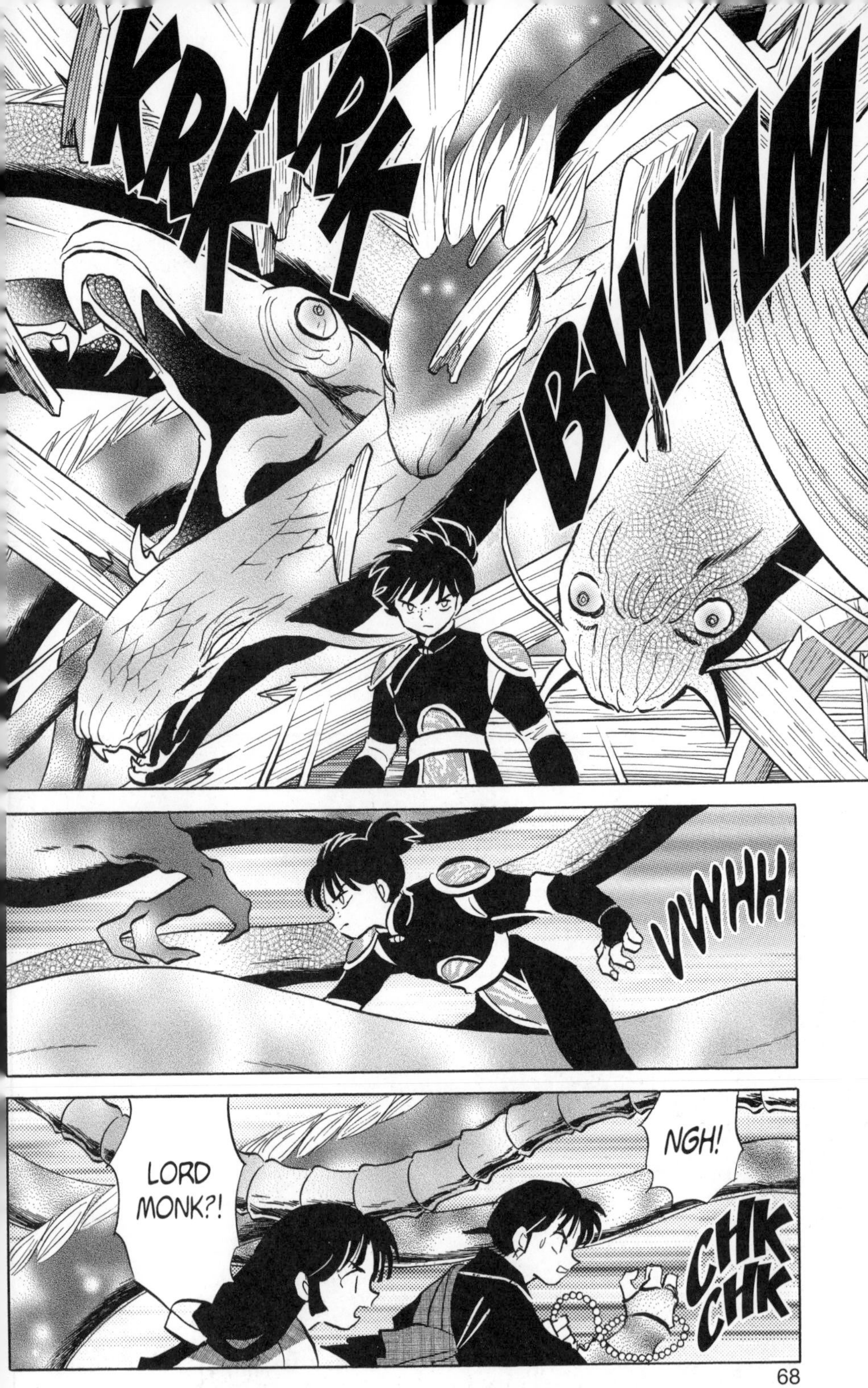

BWNM
KRAK KRAK
VWHH
NGH!
LORD MONK?!
CHK CHK

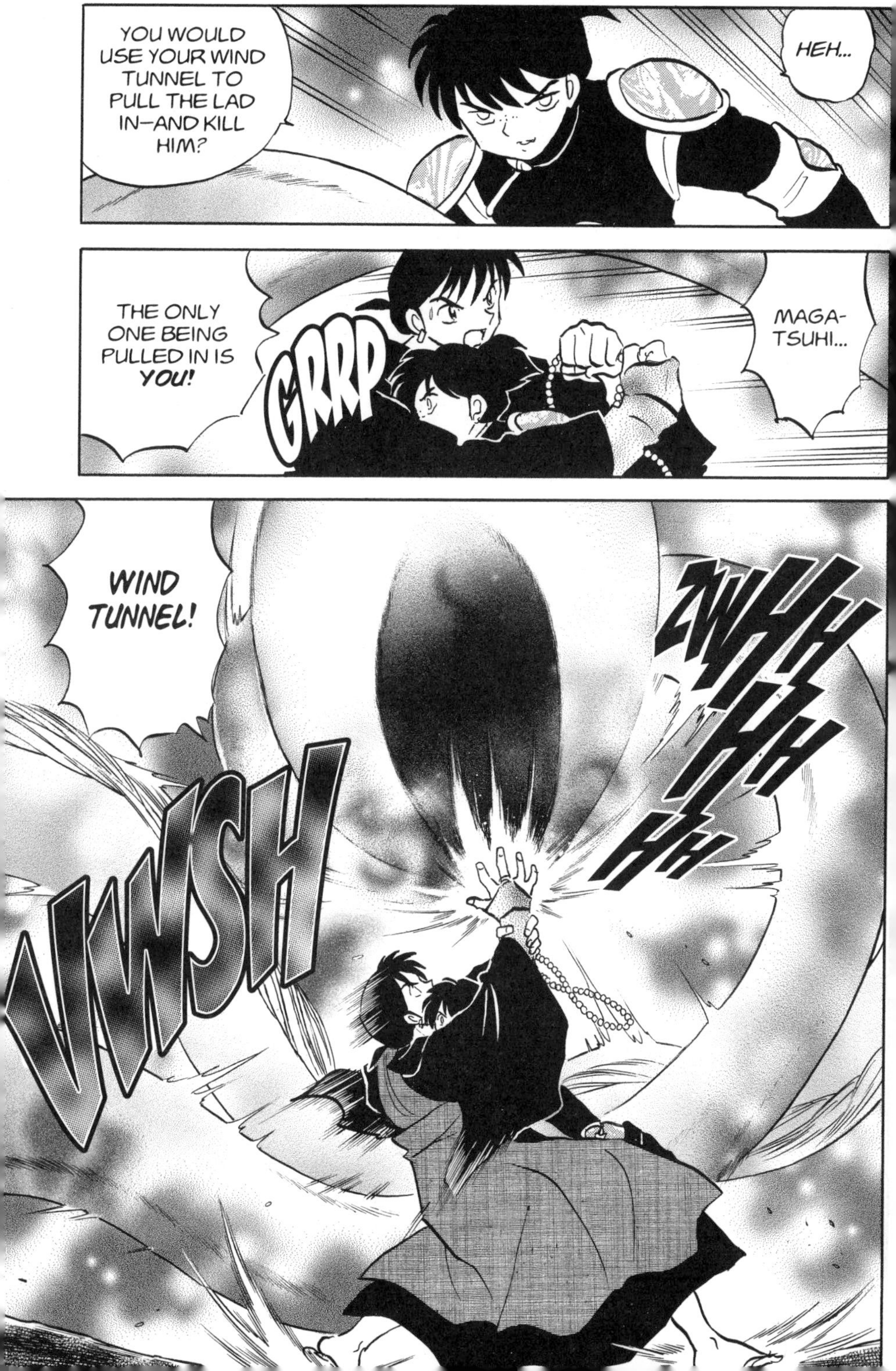
HEH...
YOU WOULD USE YOUR WIND TUNNEL TO PULL THE LAD IN—AND KILL HIM?
MAGA-TSUHI...
GRRP
THE ONLY ONE BEING PULLED IN IS *YOU!*
ZWHHHH
WIND TUNNEL!
VWSH

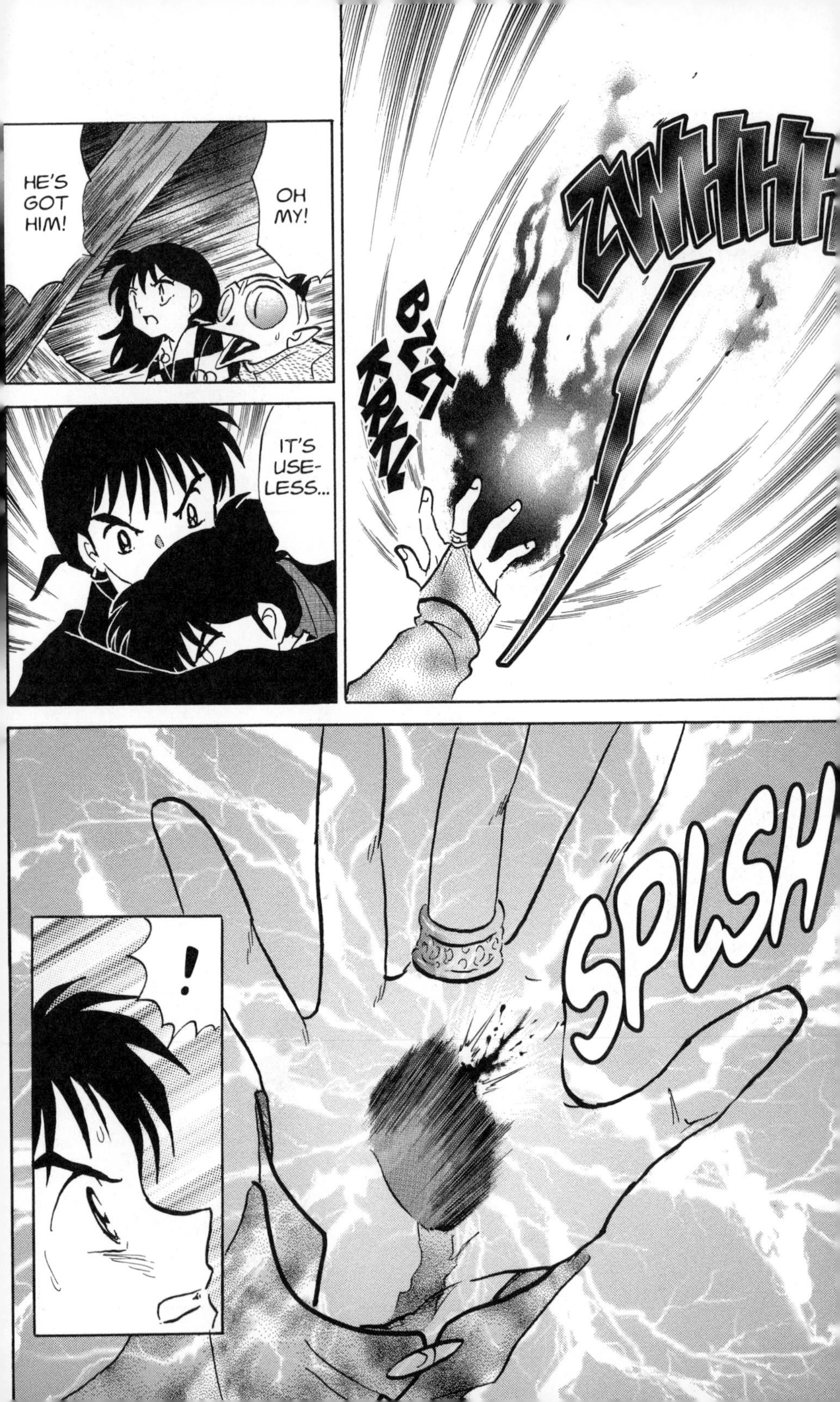
ZWHHH
BZZT KRKL
OH MY!
HE'S GOT HIM!
IT'S USELESS...
SPLSH
!

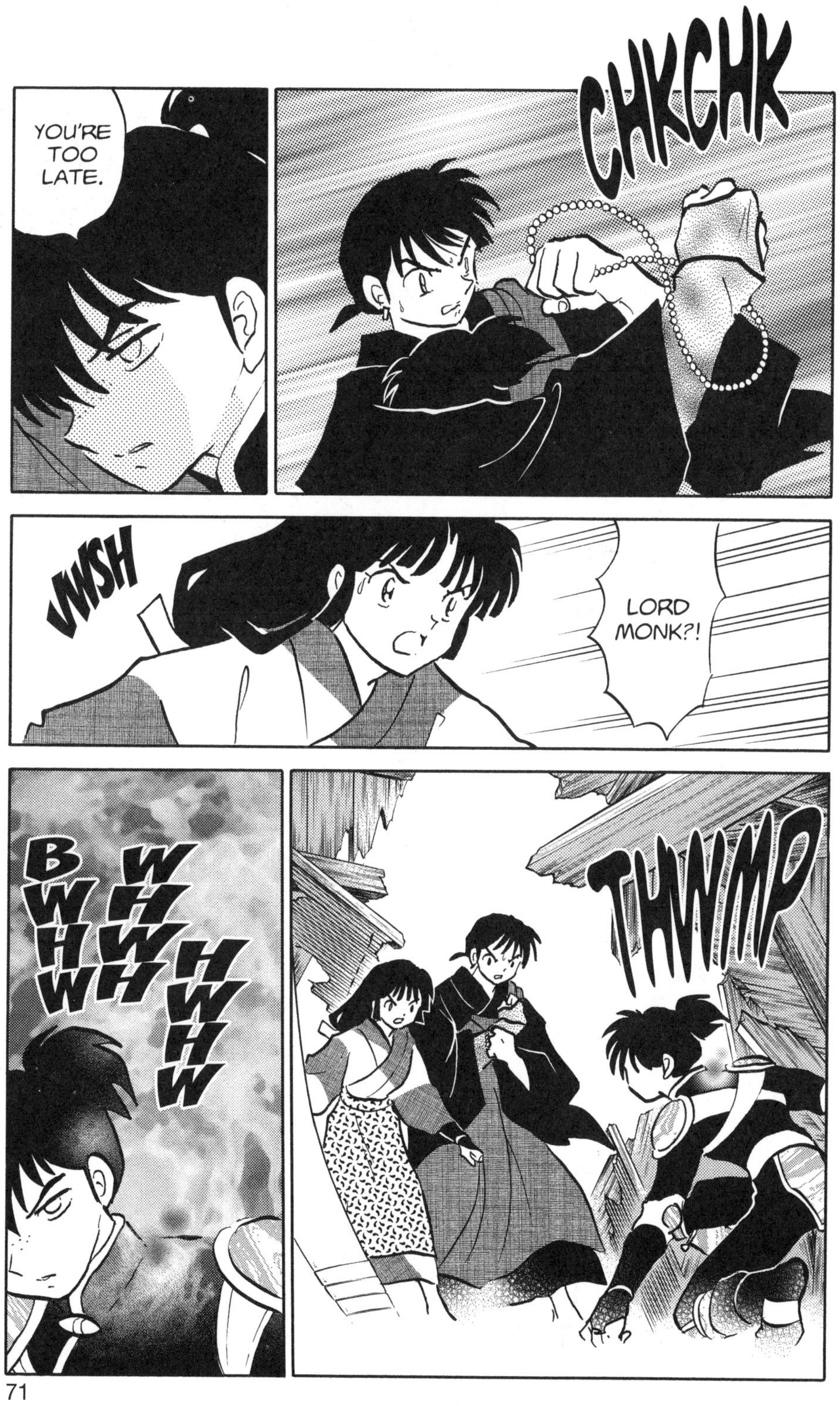
CHKCHK
YOU'RE TOO LATE.
LORD MONK?!
VWSH
THWMP
BWHW
WHWH
HWHW

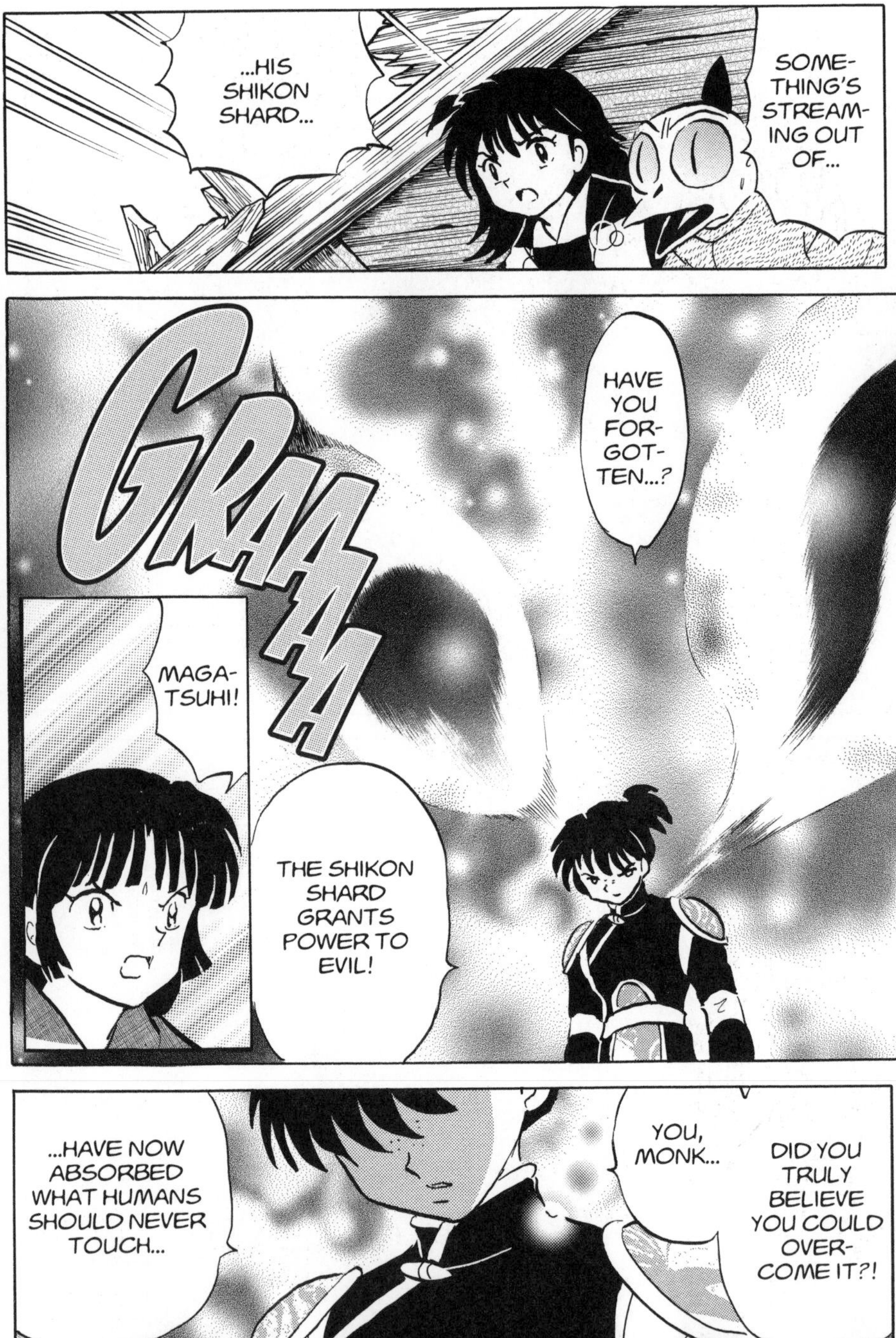
SOMETHING'S STREAMING OUT OF...
...HIS SHIKON SHARD...
HAVE YOU FORGOTTEN...?
GRAAAAA
MAGATSUHI!
THE SHIKON SHARD GRANTS POWER TO EVIL!
YOU, MONK...
...HAVE NOW ABSORBED WHAT HUMANS SHOULD NEVER TOUCH...
DID YOU TRULY BELIEVE YOU COULD OVERCOME IT?!

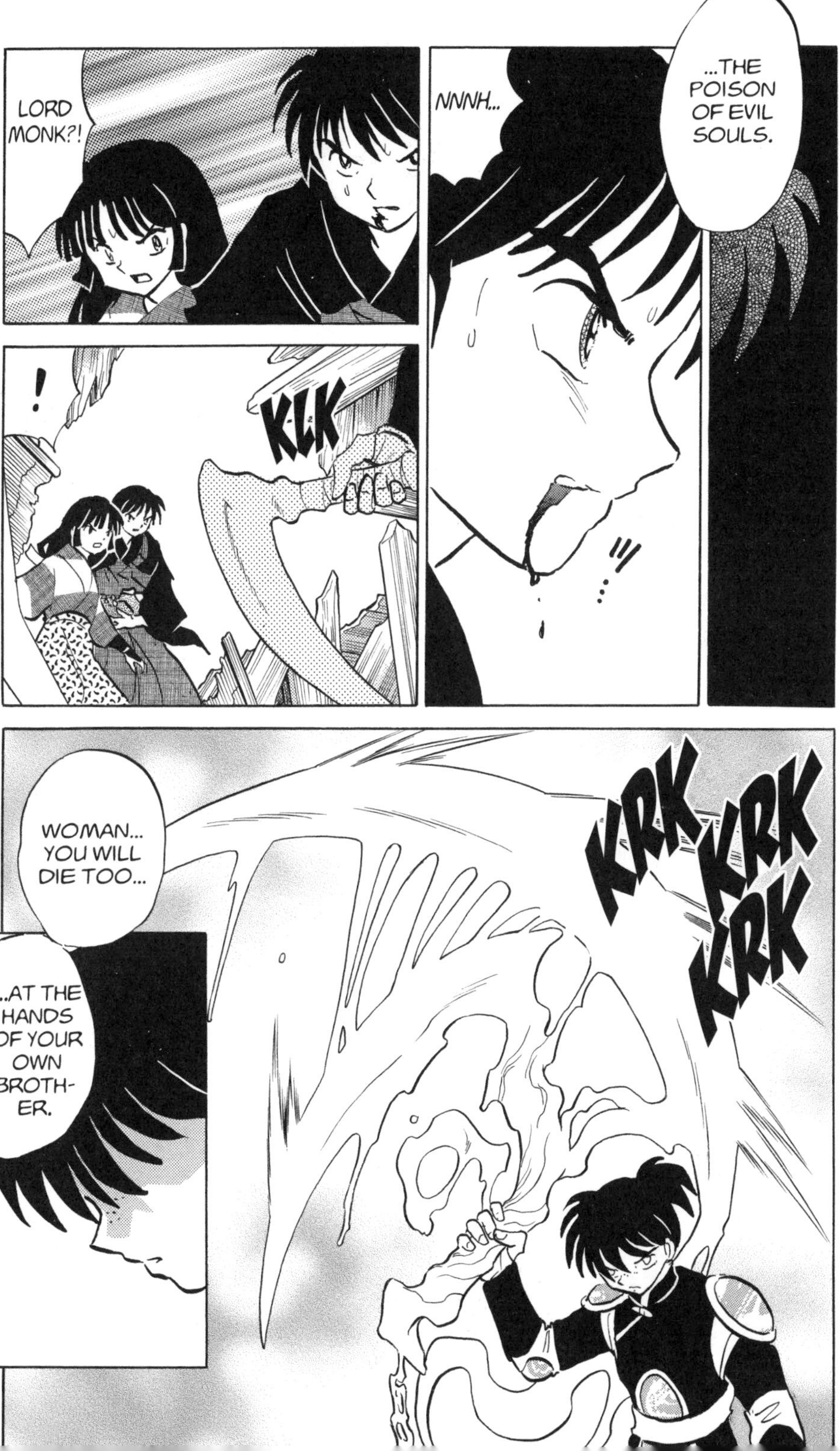
...THE POISON OF EVIL SOULS.
NNNH...
LORD MONK?!
!
KLK
KRK KRK KRK
WOMAN... YOU WILL DIE TOO...
...AT THE HANDS OF YOUR OWN BROTHER.

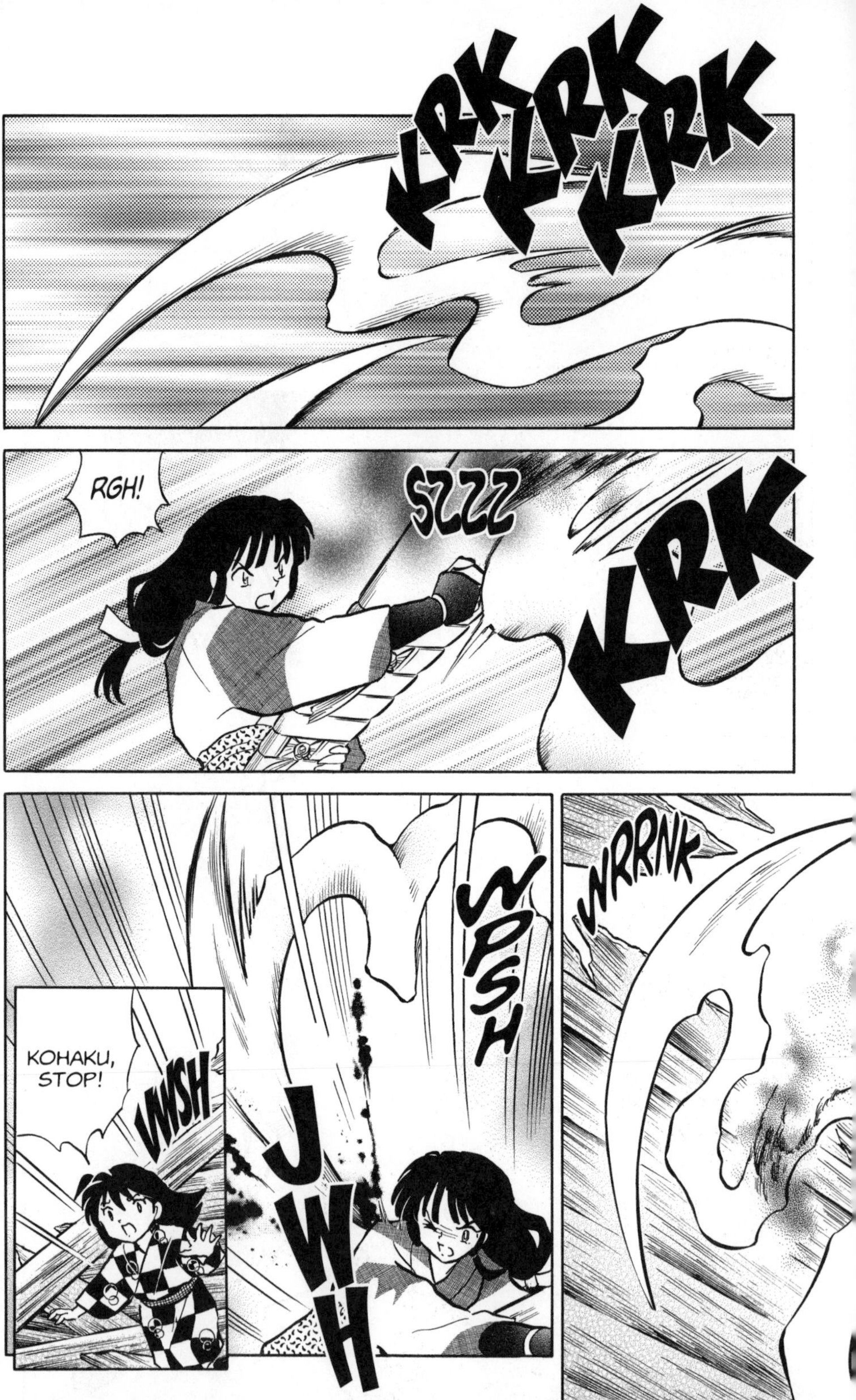
KRK
KRK
KRK
KRK
SZZZ
RGH!
WRRNK
WPSH
JWH
KOHAKU, STOP!
VWSH

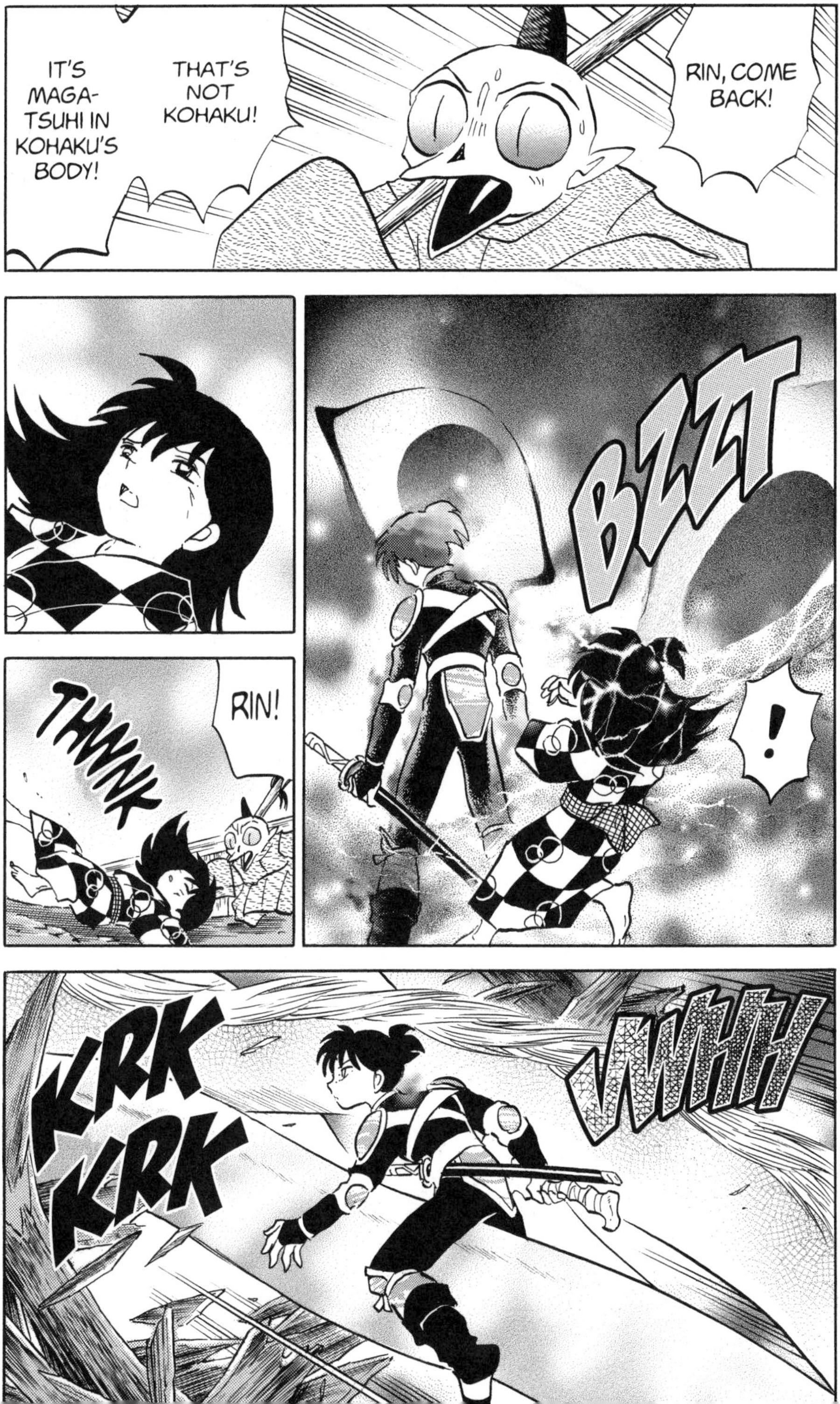
RIN, COME BACK!
THAT'S NOT KOHAKU!
IT'S MAGA-TSUHI IN KOHAKU'S BODY!
BZZT
!
RIN!
THWNK
WHHH
KRK KRK

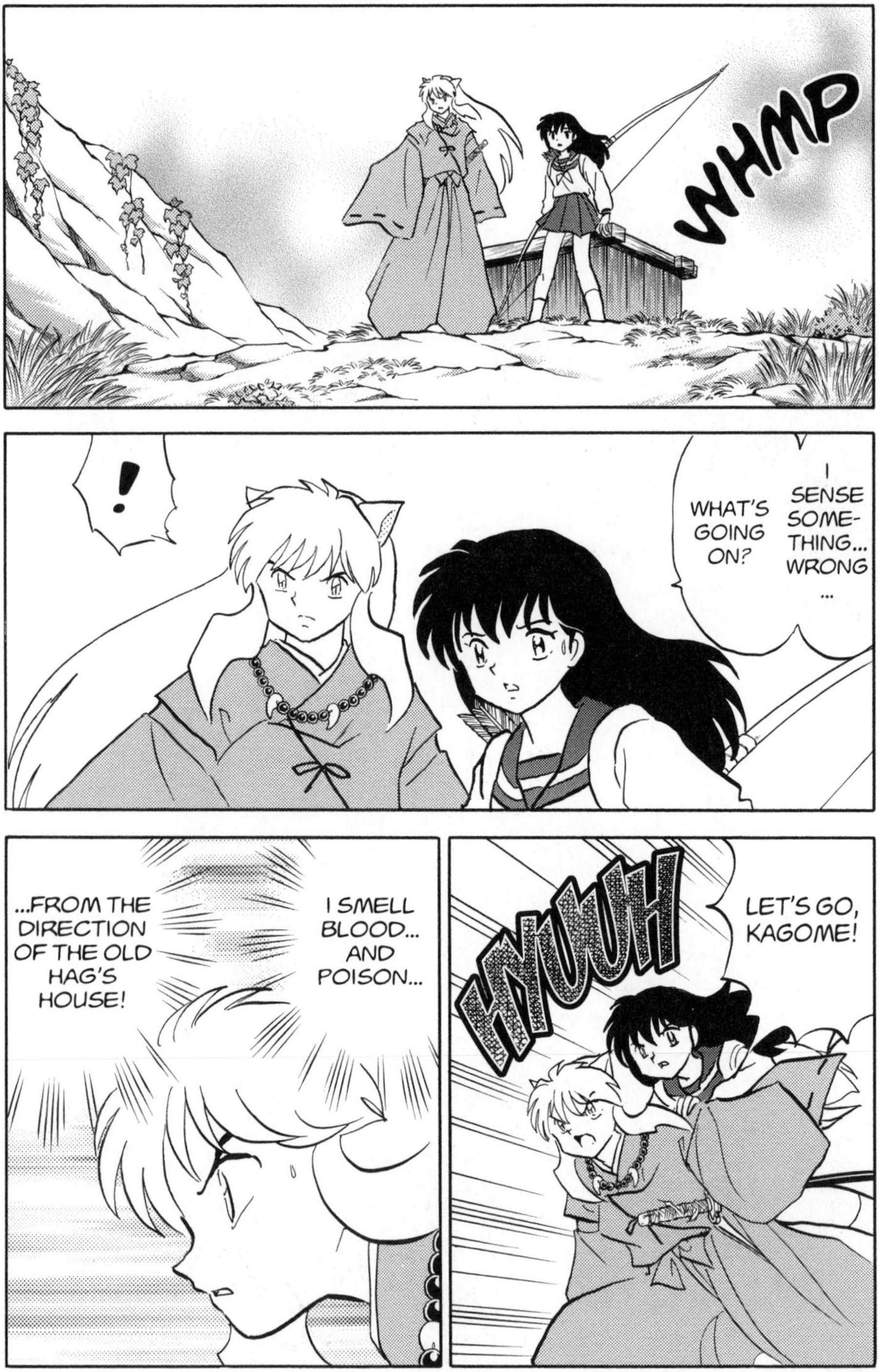
WHMP
I SENSE SOME-THING... WRONG ...
WHAT'S GOING ON?
!
HYUUH
LET'S GO, KAGOME!
I SMELL BLOOD... AND POISON...
...FROM THE DIRECTION OF THE OLD HAG'S HOUSE!

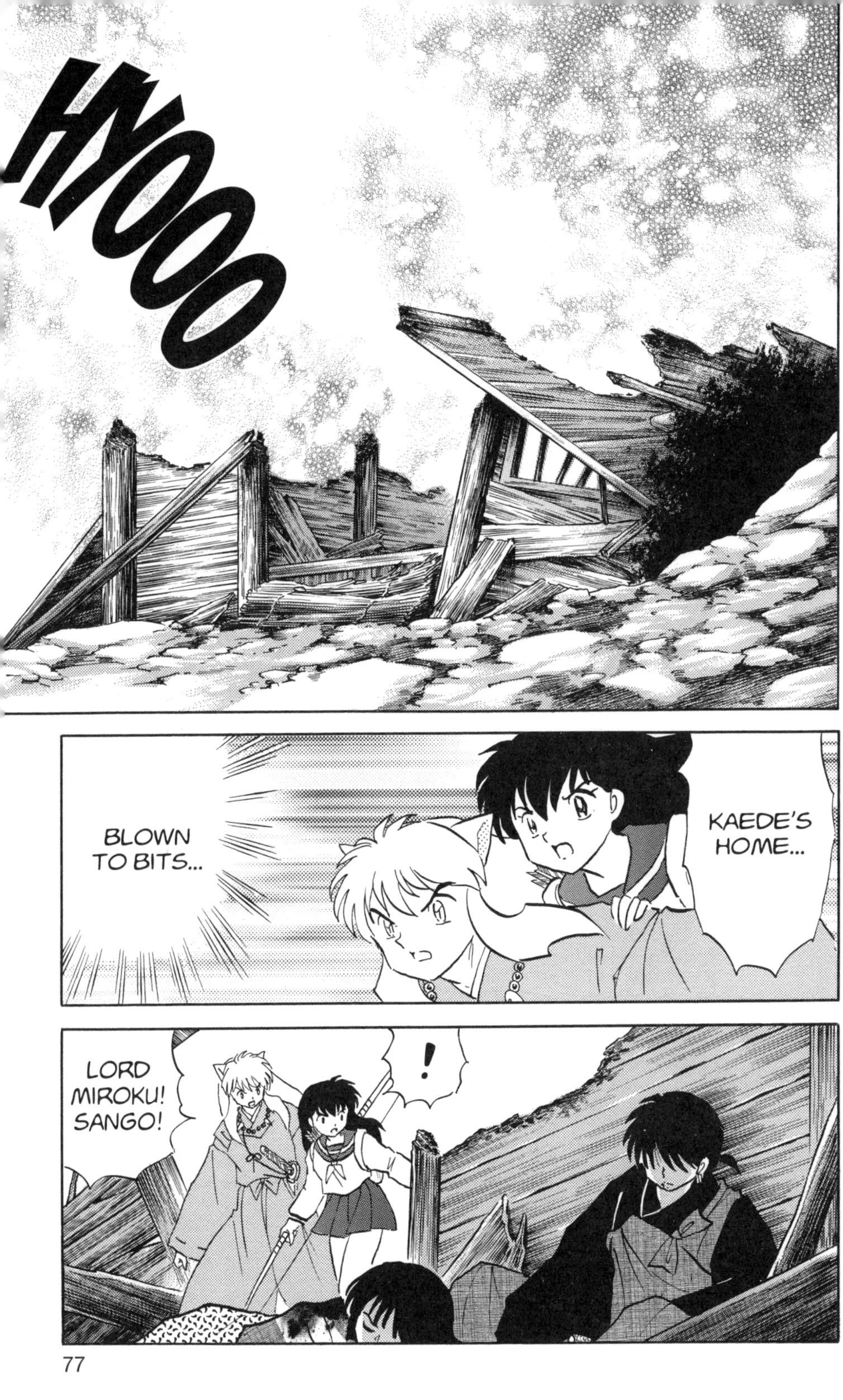
HYOOO
KAEDE'S HOME...
BLOWN TO BITS...
!
LORD MIROKU! SANGO!

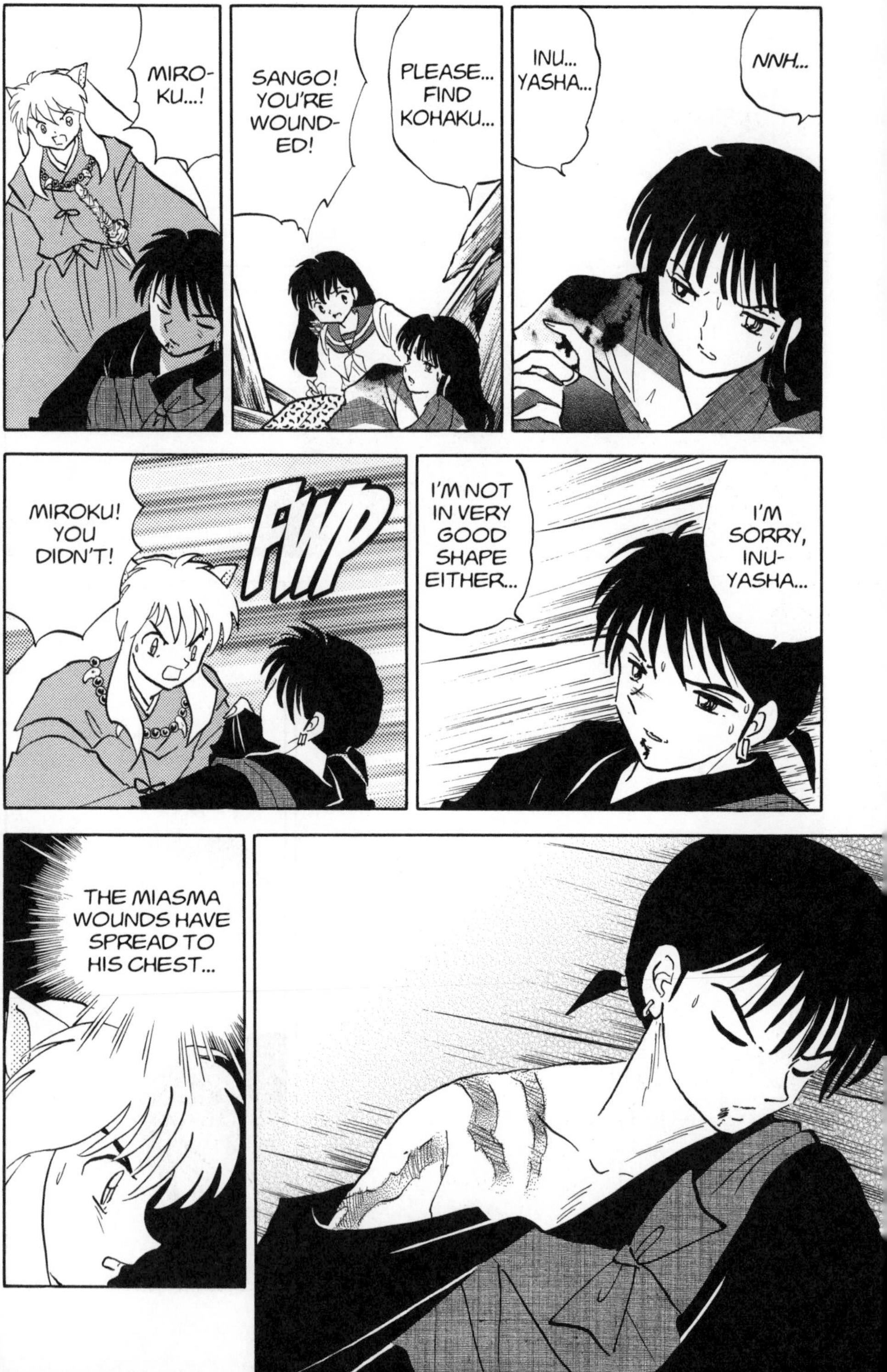
NNH...
INU... YASHA...
PLEASE... FIND KOHAKU...
SANGO! YOU'RE WOUND-ED!
MIRO-KU...!
I'M SORRY, INU-YASHA...
I'M NOT IN VERY GOOD SHAPE EITHER...
FWP
MIROKU! YOU DIDN'T!
THE MIASMA WOUNDS HAVE SPREAD TO HIS CHEST...

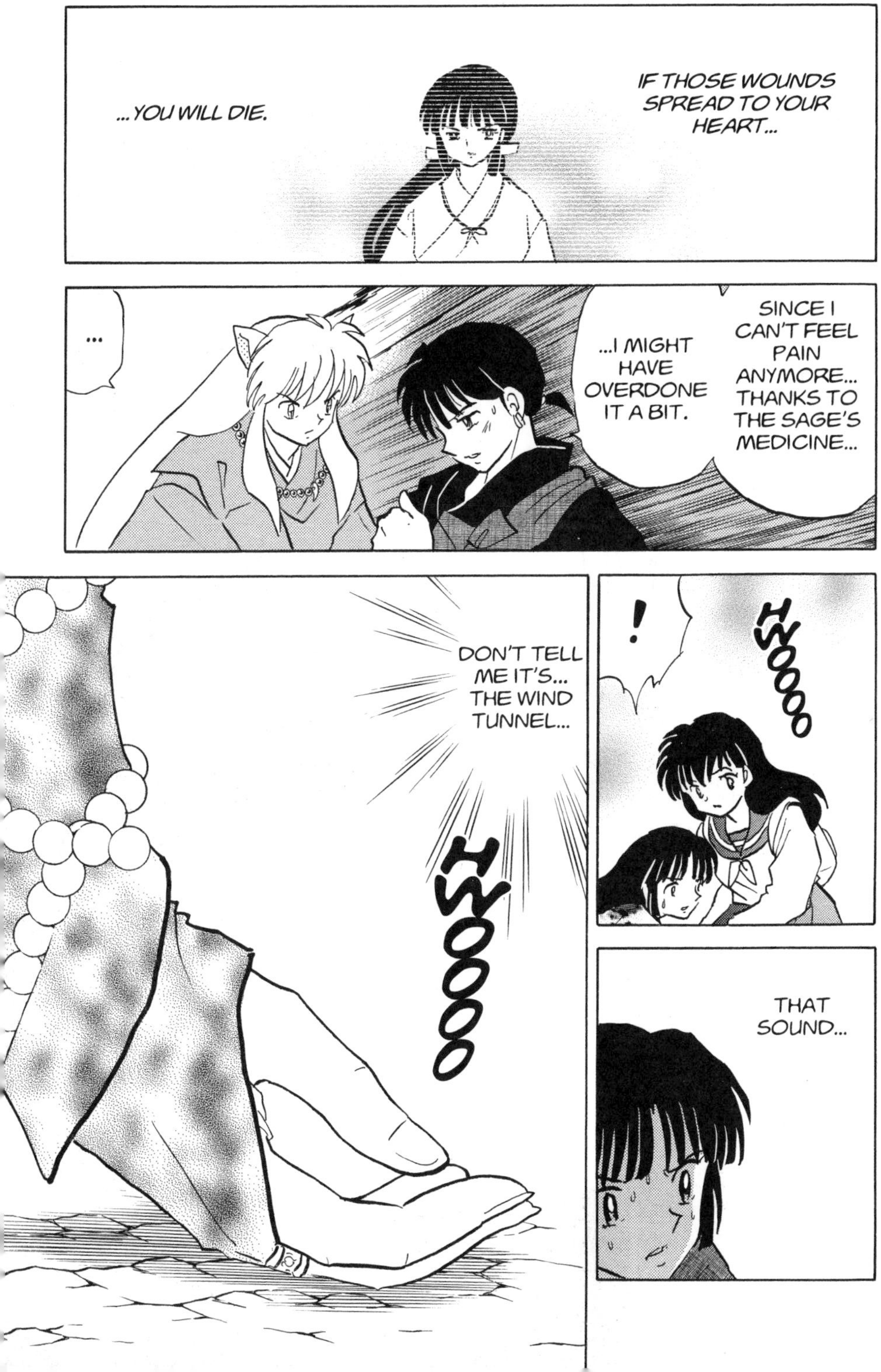
IF THOSE WOUNDS SPREAD TO YOUR HEART...
...YOU WILL DIE.
SINCE I CAN'T FEEL PAIN ANYMORE... THANKS TO THE SAGE'S MEDICINE...
...I MIGHT HAVE OVERDONE IT A BIT.
...
HWOOOO
!
THAT SOUND...
DON'T TELL ME IT'S... THE WIND TUNNEL...
HWOOOOO

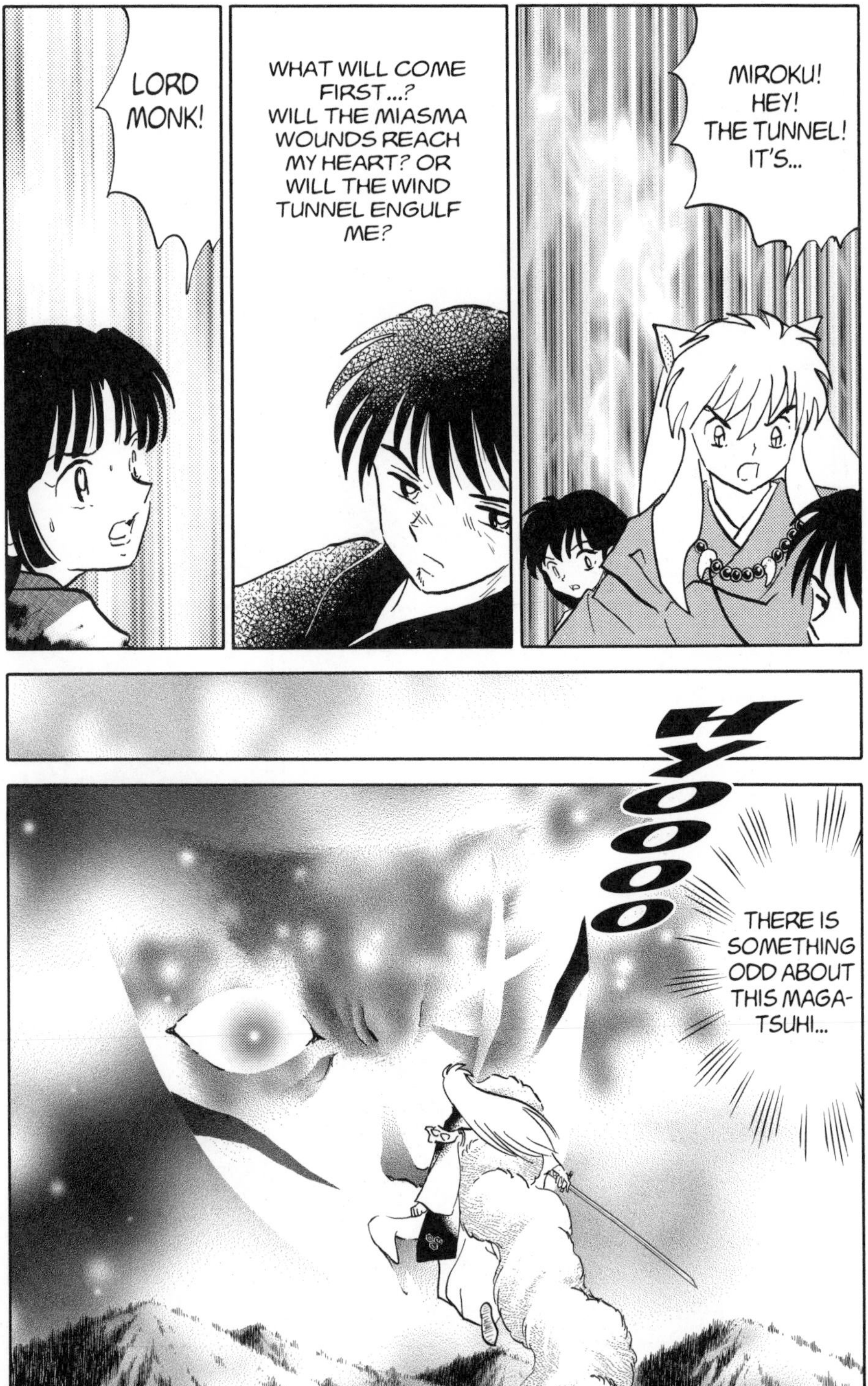
MIROKU! HEY! THE TUNNEL! IT'S...
WHAT WILL COME FIRST...? WILL THE MIASMA WOUNDS REACH MY HEART? OR WILL THE WIND TUNNEL ENGULF ME?
LORD MONK!
HYOOOOO
THERE IS SOMETHING ODD ABOUT THIS MAGA-TSUHI...

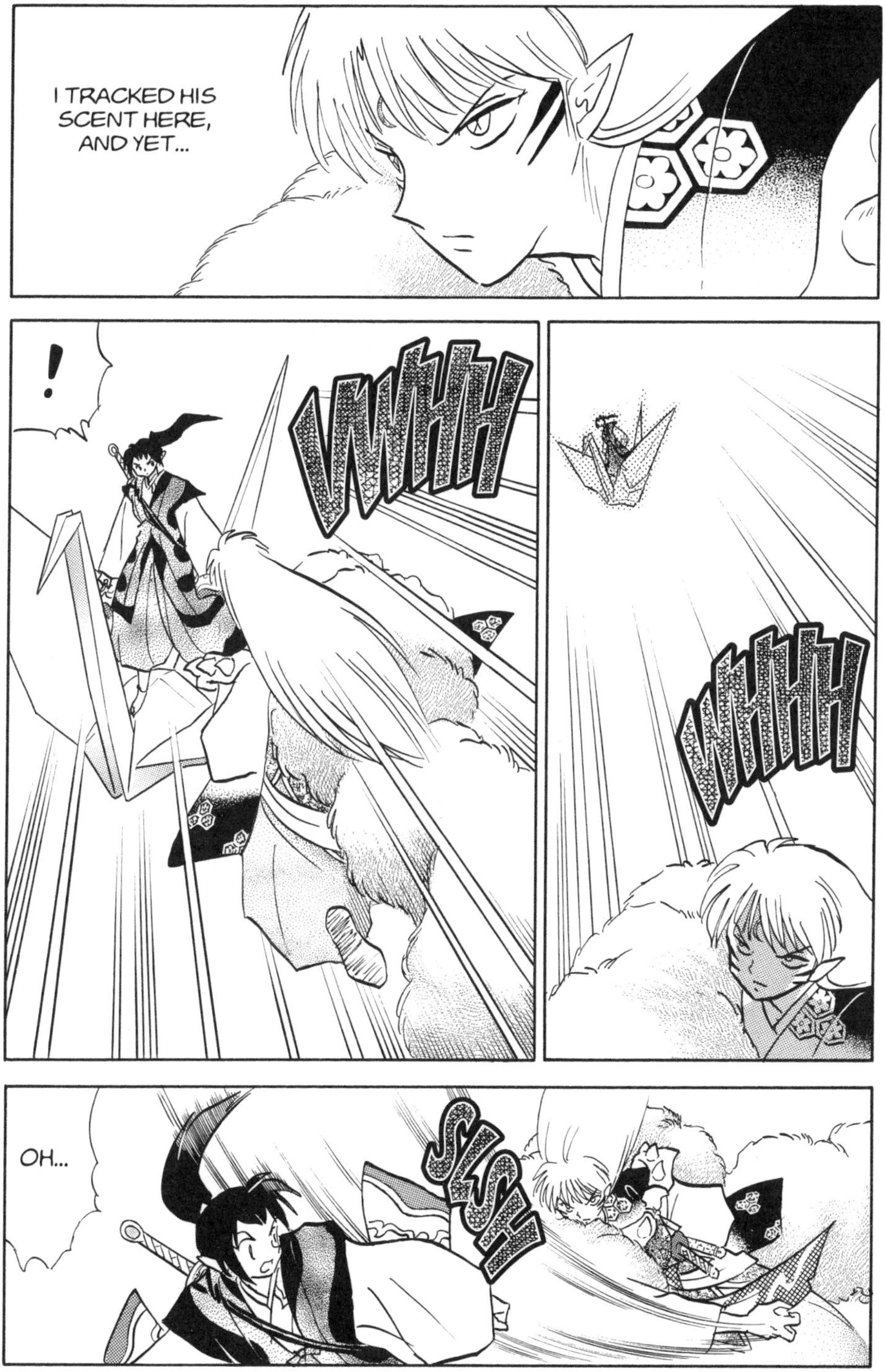

I TRACKED HIS SCENT HERE, AND YET...
WHHH
VWHH
!
SLSH
OH...

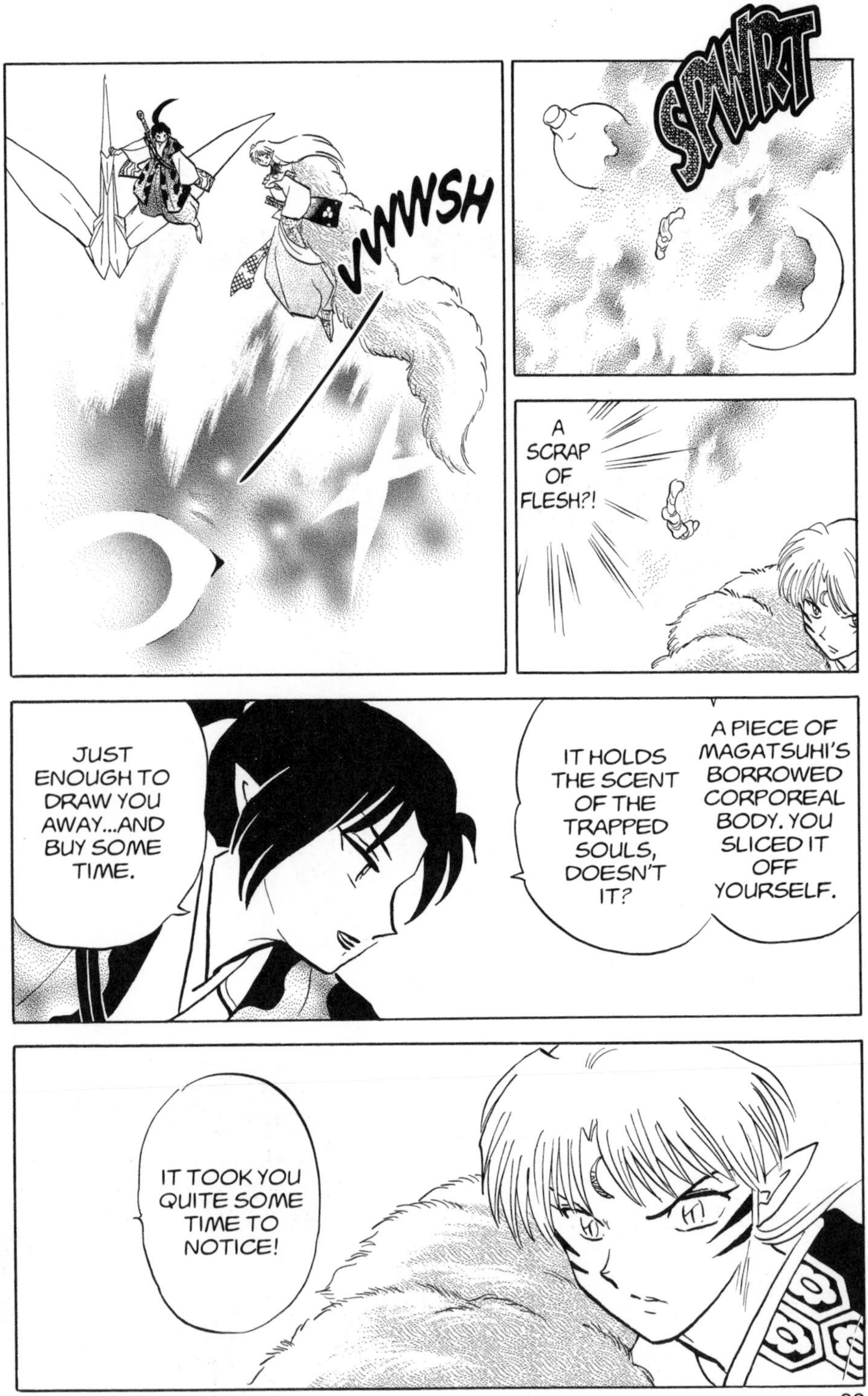
SPWRT
A SCRAP OF FLESH?!
VWWNSH
A PIECE OF MAGATSUHI'S BORROWED CORPOREAL BODY. YOU SLICED IT OFF YOURSELF.
IT HOLDS THE SCENT OF THE TRAPPED SOULS, DOESN'T IT?
JUST ENOUGH TO DRAW YOU AWAY...AND BUY SOME TIME.
IT TOOK YOU QUITE SOME TIME TO NOTICE!

SCROLL FIVE
SANGO'S WISH

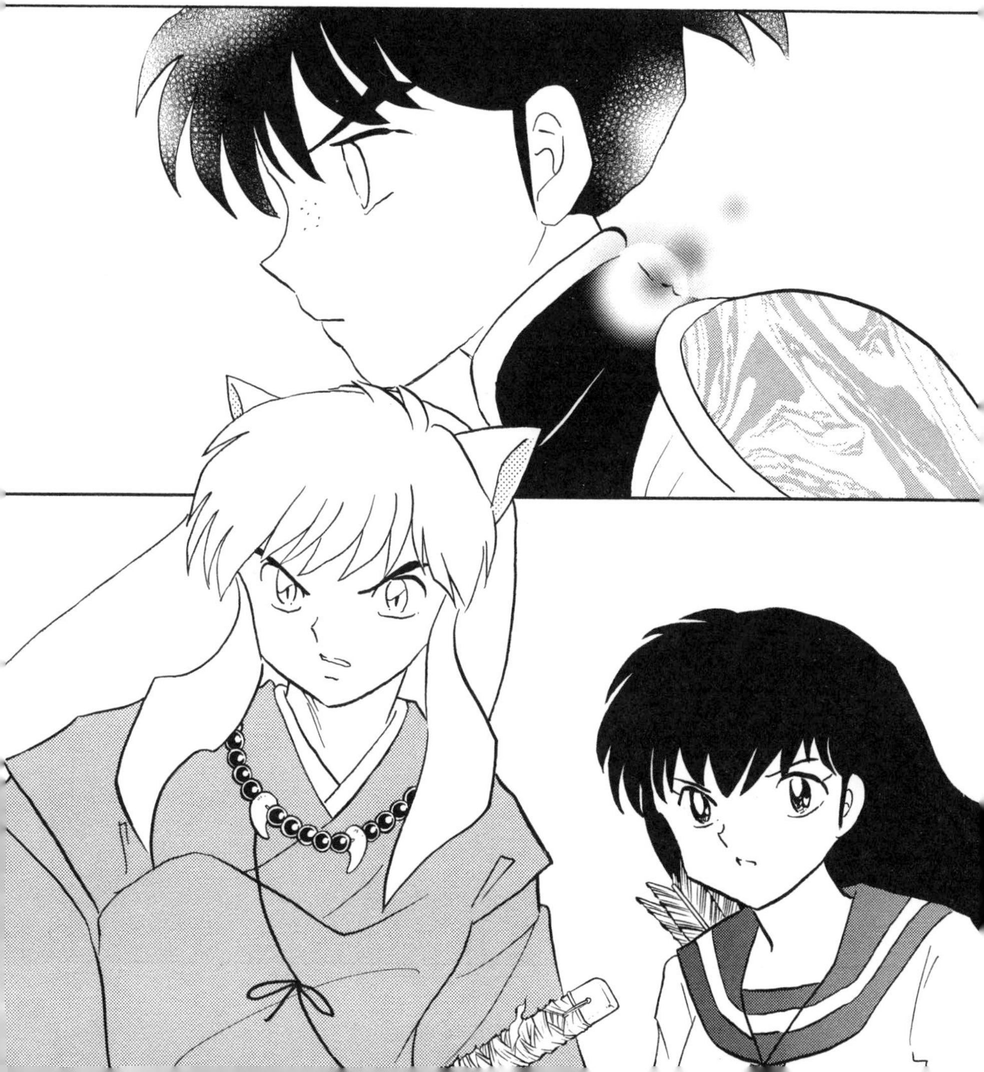

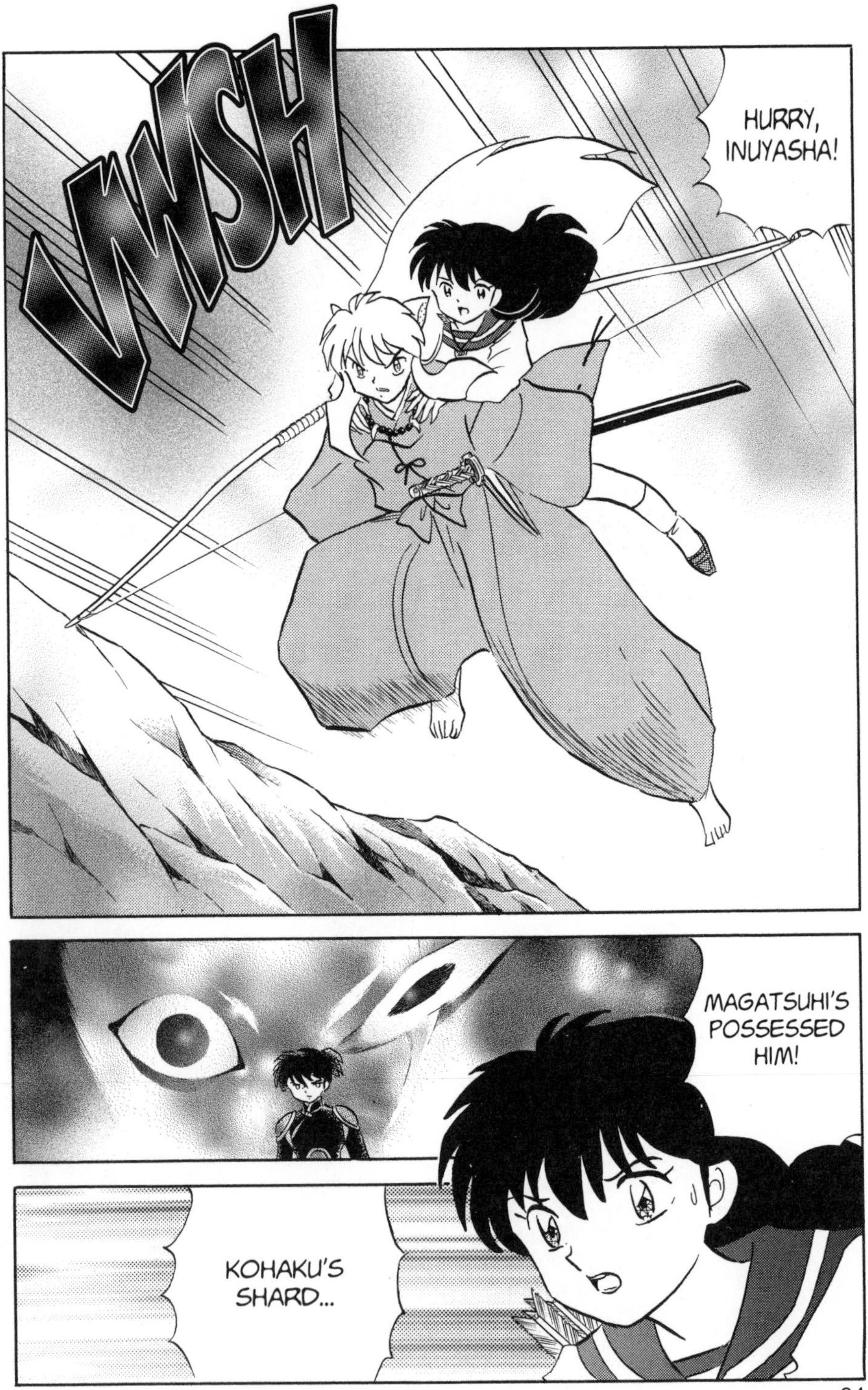
VWISH
HURRY, INUYASHA!
MAGATSUHI'S POSSESSED HIM!
KOHAKU'S SHARD...

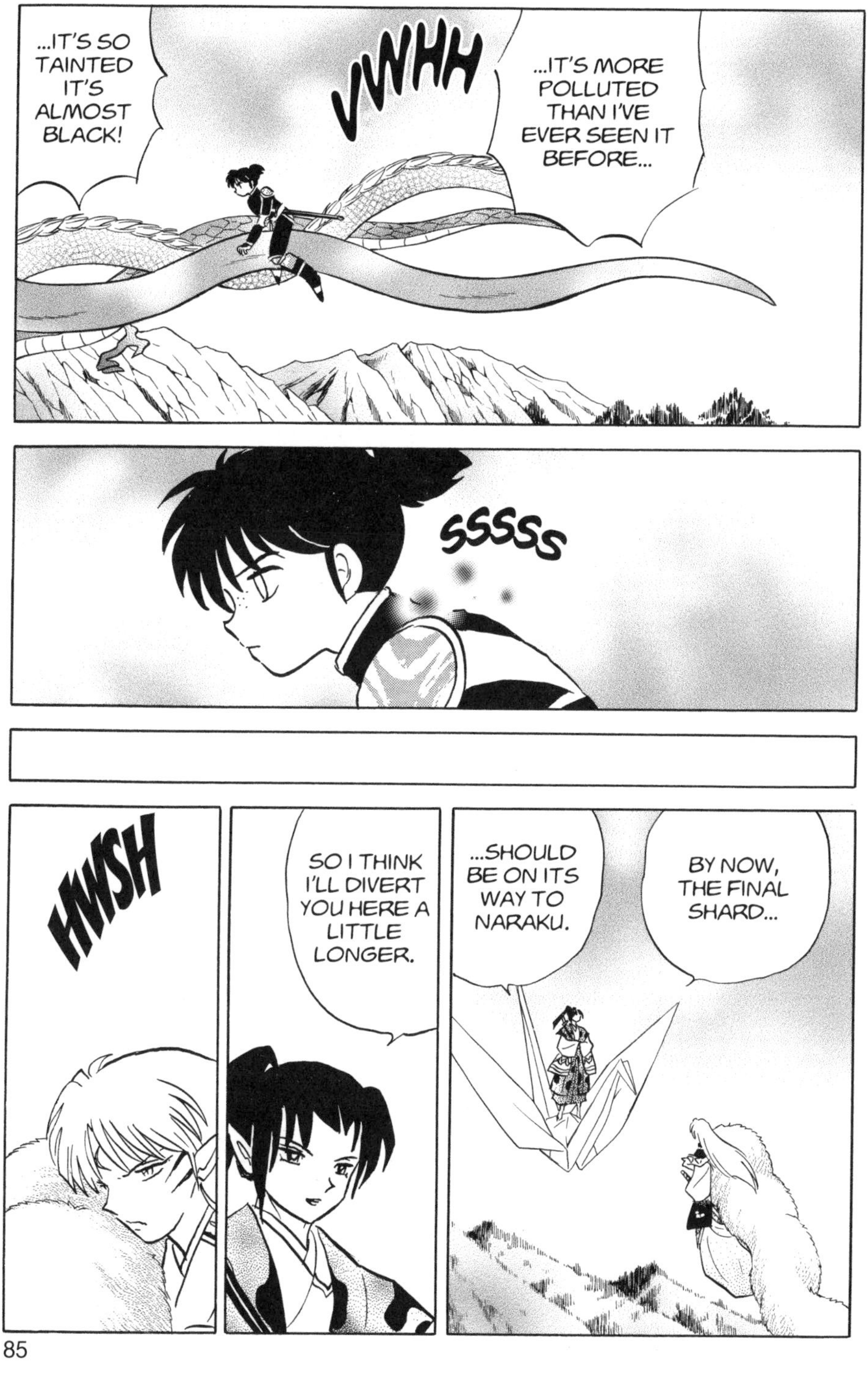
...IT'S MORE POLLUTED THAN I'VE EVER SEEN IT BEFORE...
VWHH
...IT'S SO TAINTED IT'S ALMOST BLACK!
SSSSS
BY NOW, THE FINAL SHARD...
...SHOULD BE ON ITS WAY TO NARAKU.
SO I THINK I'LL DIVERT YOU HERE A LITTLE LONGER.
HWSH

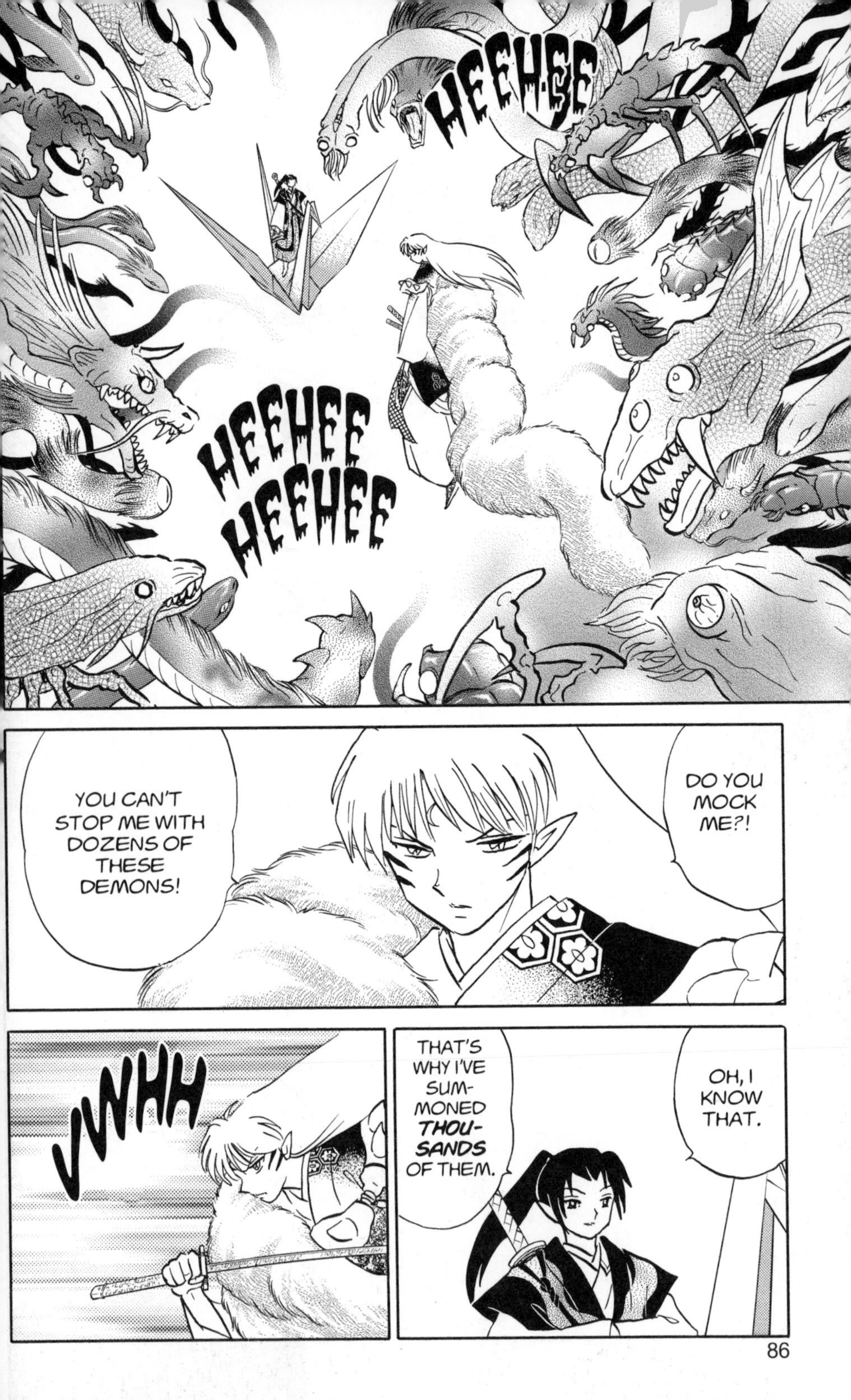
HEEHEE
HEEHEE HEEHEE
DO YOU MOCK ME?!
YOU CAN'T STOP ME WITH DOZENS OF THESE DEMONS!
OH, I KNOW THAT.
THAT'S WHY I'VE SUMMONED ***THOUSANDS*** OF THEM.
VWHH

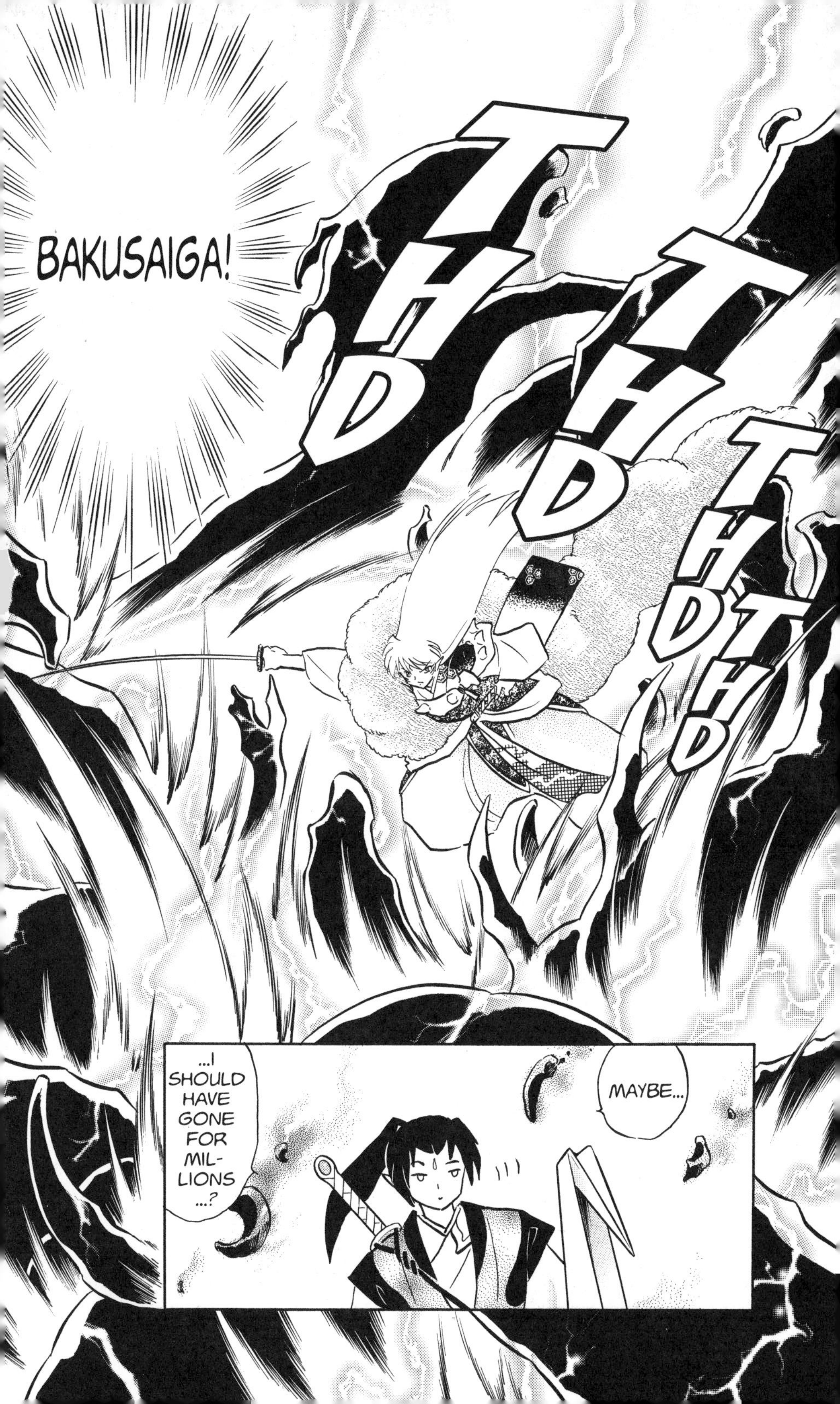
BAKUSAIGA!
THD
THD
THD
THD
MAYBE...
...I SHOULD HAVE GONE FOR MIL-LIONS ...?

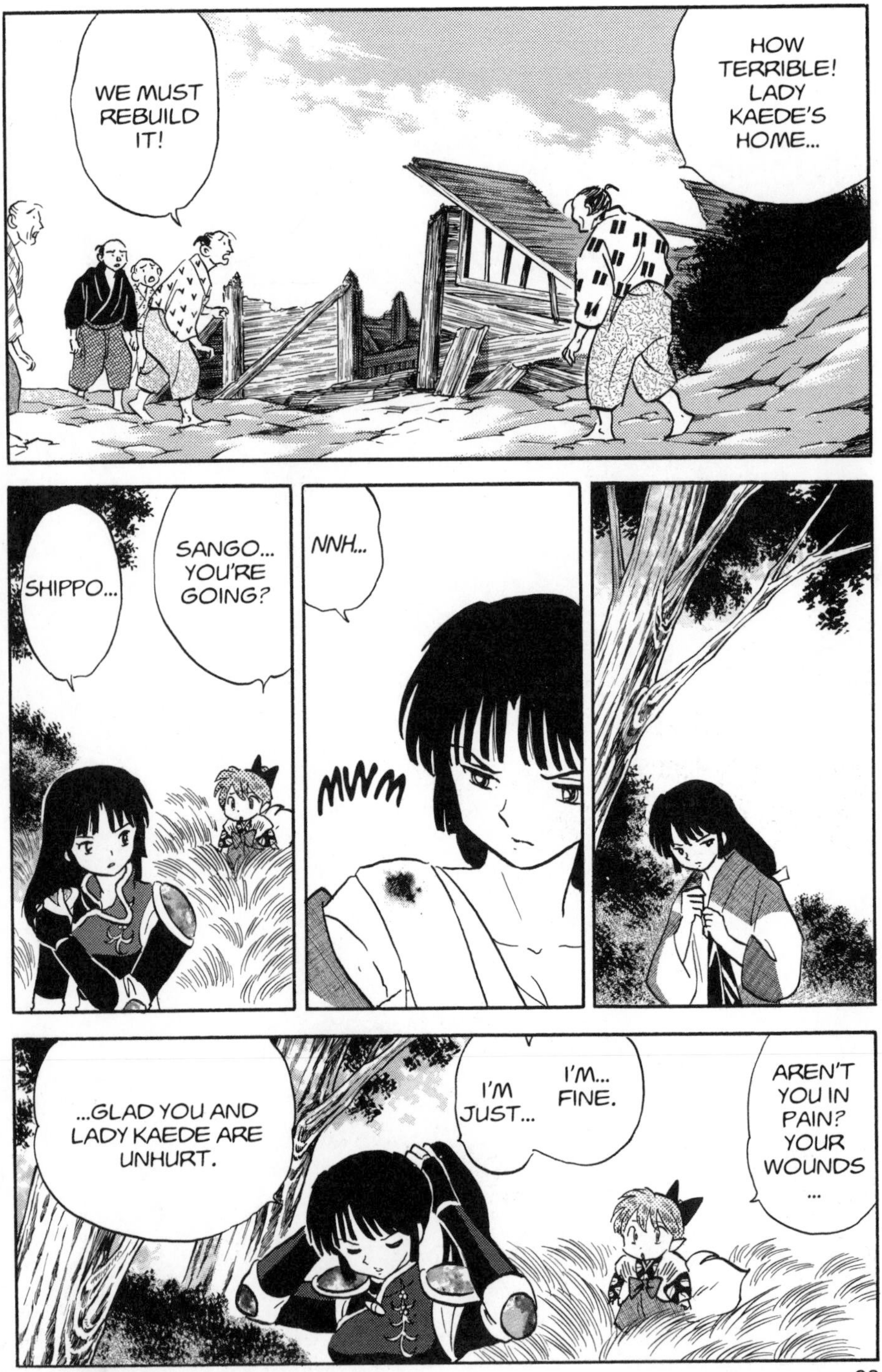
HOW TERRIBLE! LADY KAEDE'S HOME...
WE MUST REBUILD IT!
NNH...
MWM
SANGO... YOU'RE GOING?
SHIPPO...
AREN'T YOU IN PAIN? YOUR WOUNDS ...
I'M... FINE.
I'M JUST...
...GLAD YOU AND LADY KAEDE ARE UNHURT.

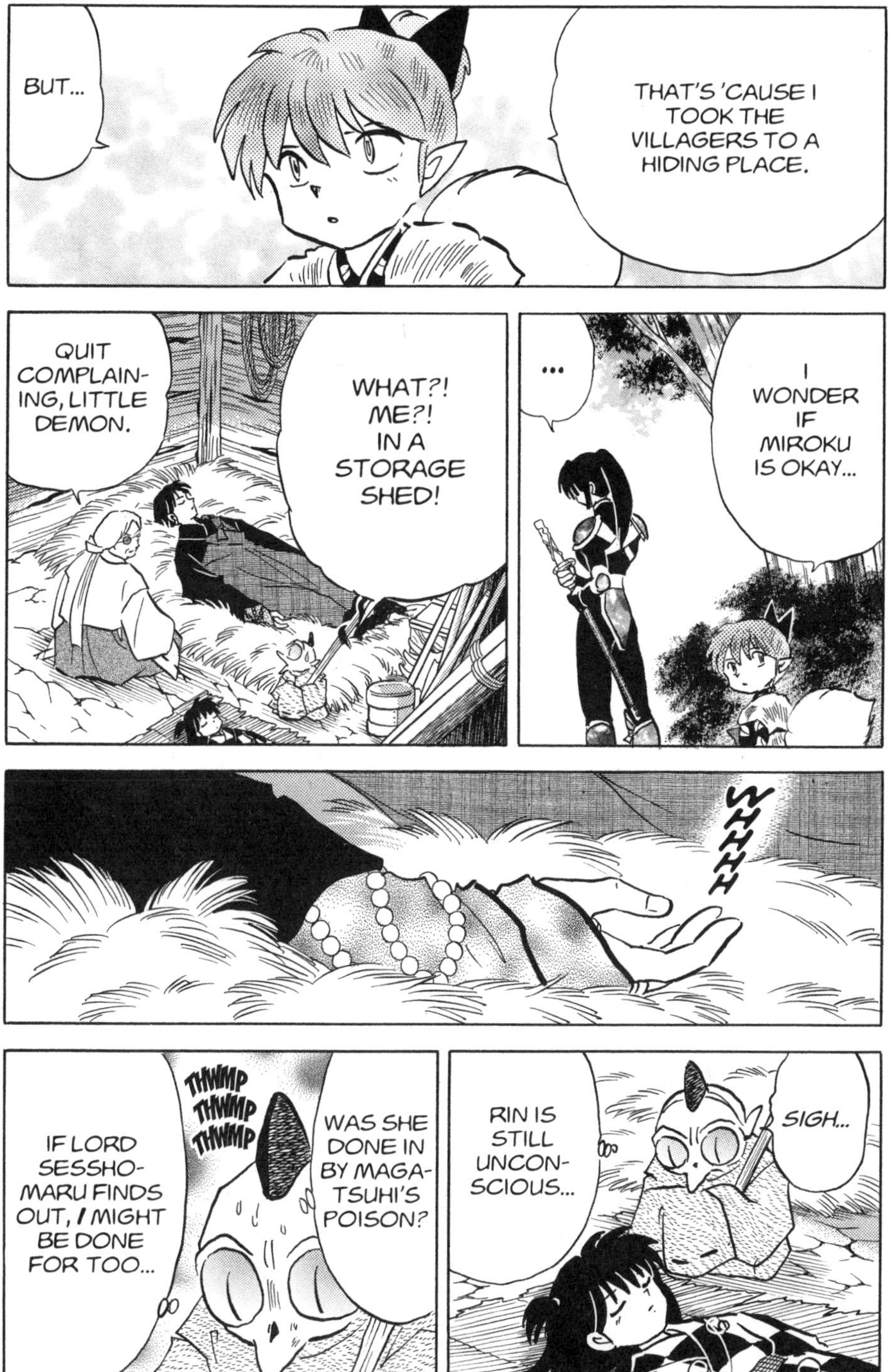
THAT'S 'CAUSE I TOOK THE VILLAGERS TO A HIDING PLACE.
BUT...
I WONDER IF MIROKU IS OKAY...
...
WHAT?! ME?! IN A STORAGE SHED!
QUIT COMPLAINING, LITTLE DEMON.
WHHHHH
SIGH...
RIN IS STILL UNCONSCIOUS...
WAS SHE DONE IN BY MAGATSUHI'S POISON?
THWMP THWMP THWMP
IF LORD SESSHOMARU FINDS OUT, *I* MIGHT BE DONE FOR TOO...

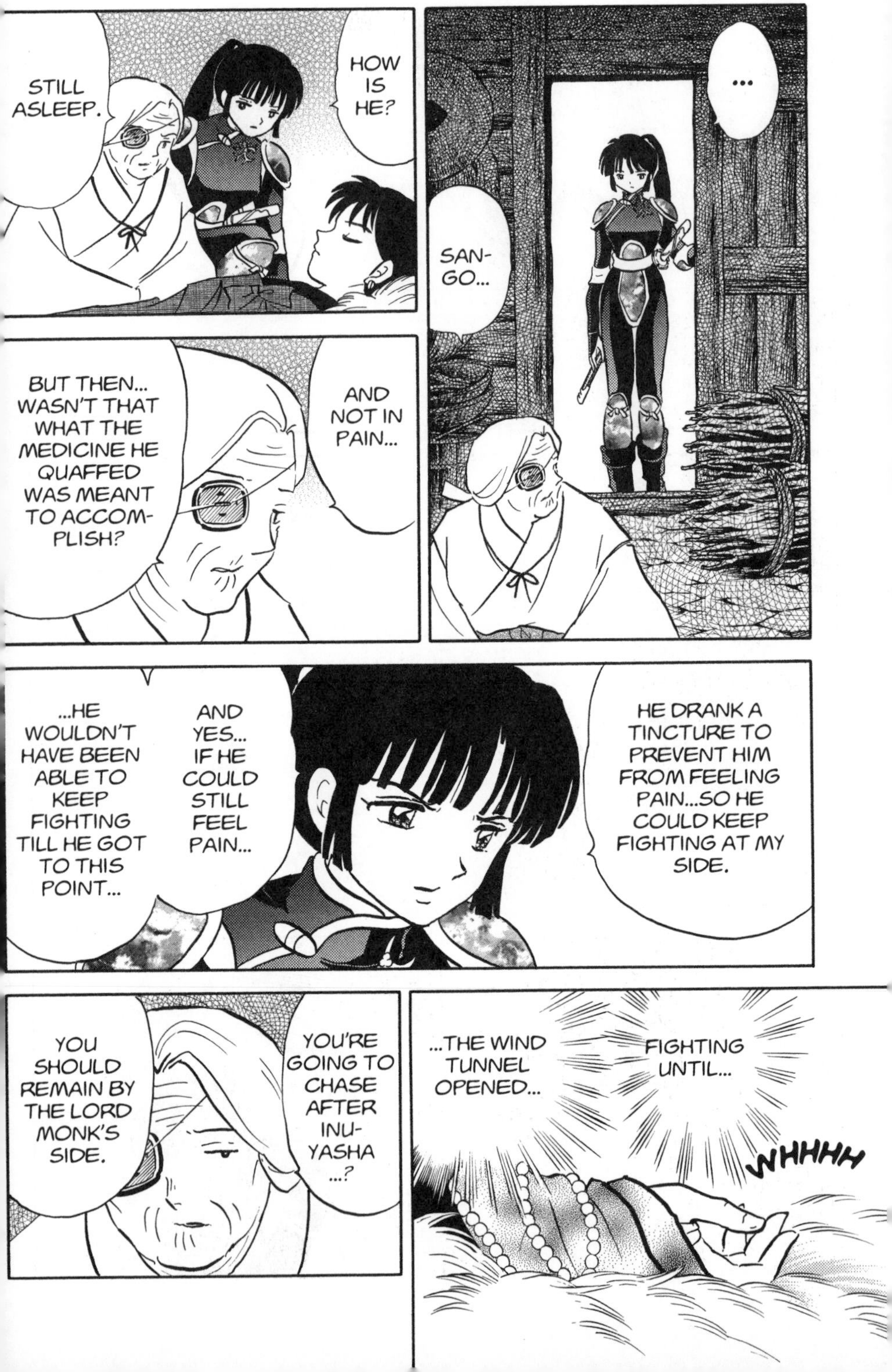
...
SAN-GO...
HOW IS HE?
STILL ASLEEP.
AND NOT IN PAIN...
BUT THEN... WASN'T THAT WHAT THE MEDICINE HE QUAFFED WAS MEANT TO ACCOMPLISH?
HE DRANK A TINCTURE TO PREVENT HIM FROM FEELING PAIN...SO HE COULD KEEP FIGHTING AT MY SIDE.
AND YES... IF HE COULD STILL FEEL PAIN...
...HE WOULDN'T HAVE BEEN ABLE TO KEEP FIGHTING TILL HE GOT TO THIS POINT...
FIGHTING UNTIL...
...THE WIND TUNNEL OPENED...
WHHHH
YOU'RE GOING TO CHASE AFTER INU-YASHA ...?
YOU SHOULD REMAIN BY THE LORD MONK'S SIDE.

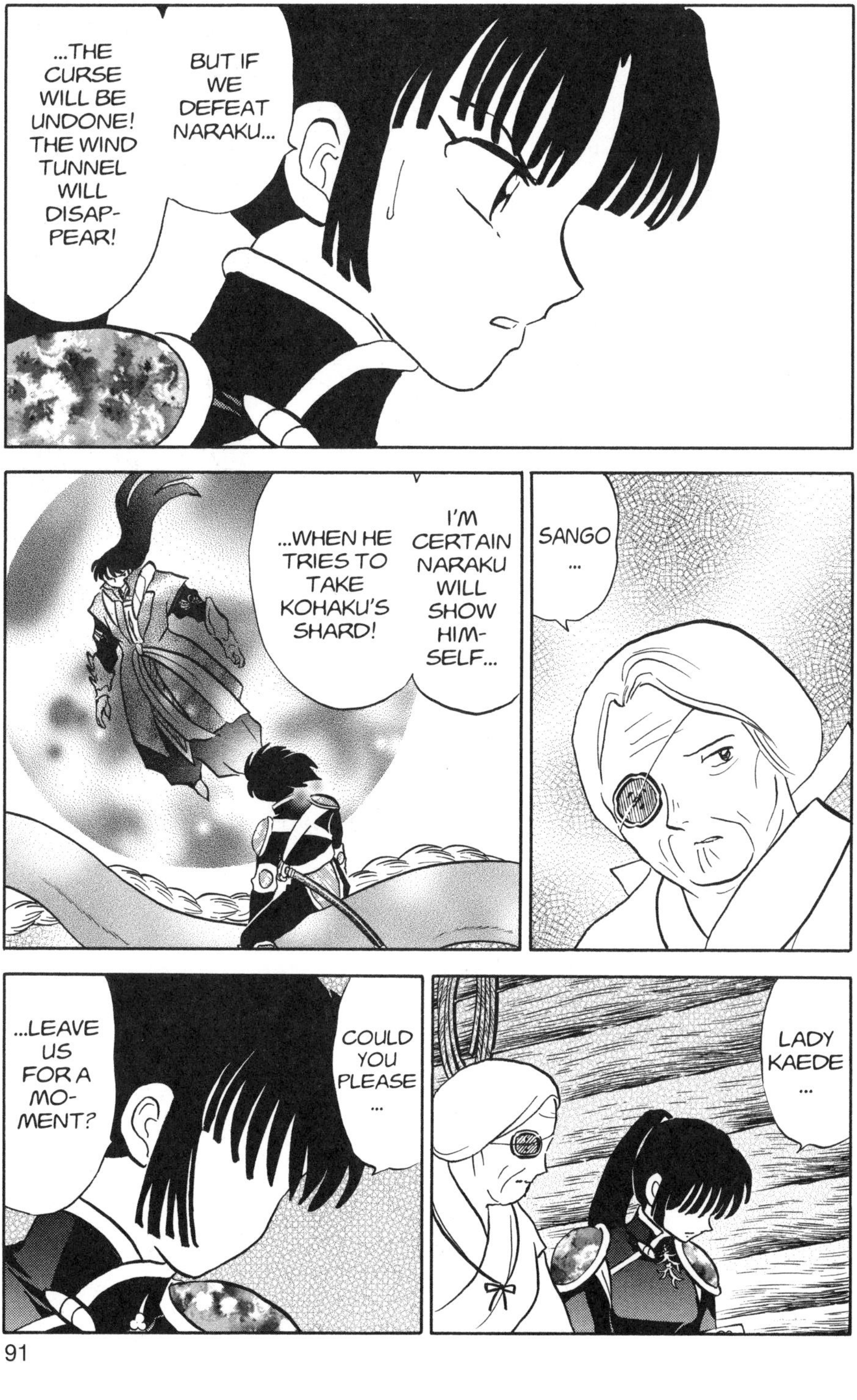
BUT IF WE DEFEAT NARAKU...
...THE CURSE WILL BE UNDONE! THE WIND TUNNEL WILL DISAPPEAR!
SANGO ...
I'M CERTAIN NARAKU WILL SHOW HIMSELF...
...WHEN HE TRIES TO TAKE KOHAKU'S SHARD!
LADY KAEDE ...
COULD YOU PLEASE ...
...LEAVE US FOR A MOMENT?

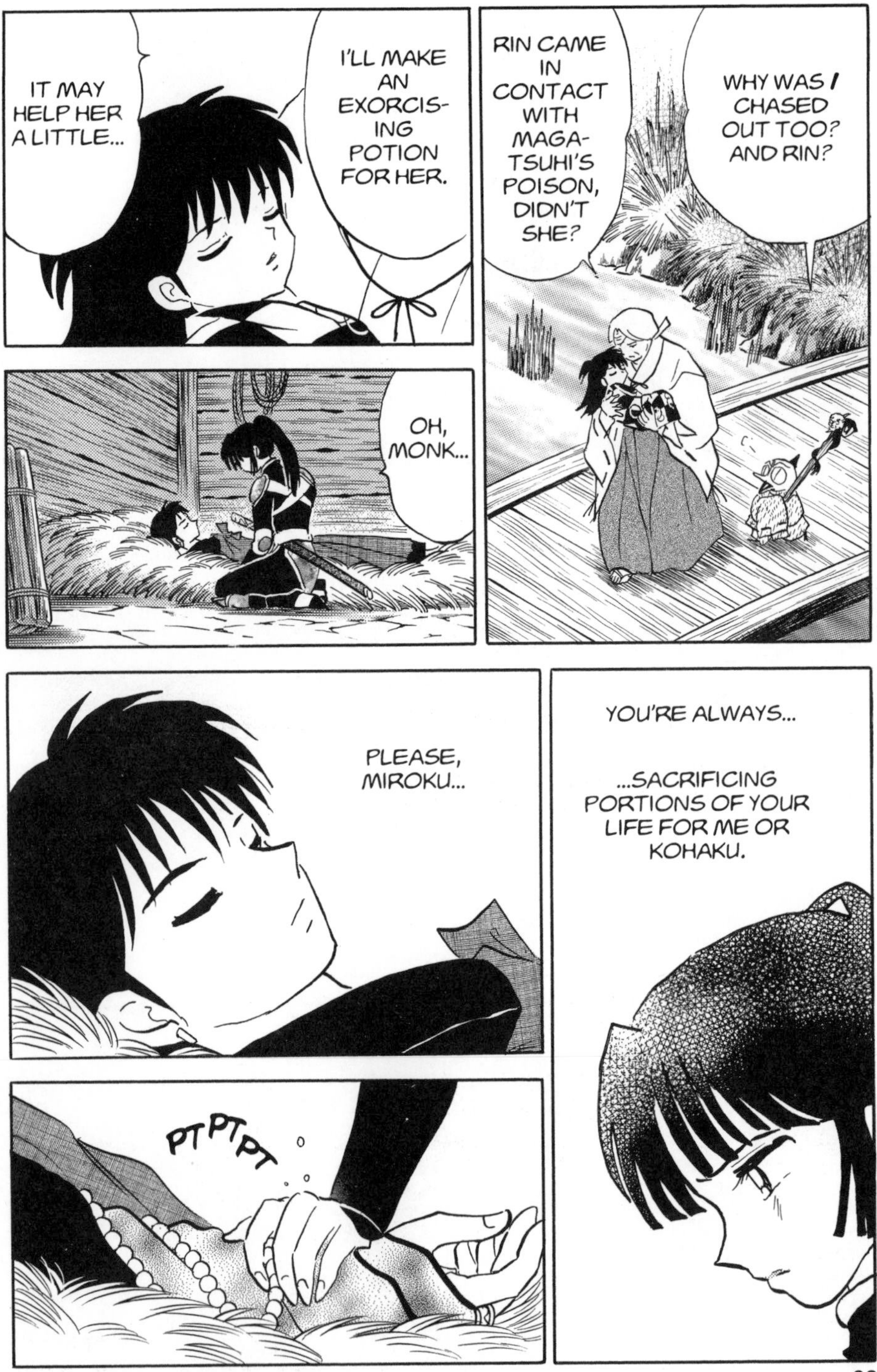
WHY WAS I CHASED OUT TOO? AND RIN?
RIN CAME IN CONTACT WITH MAGA-TSUHI'S POISON, DIDN'T SHE?
I'LL MAKE AN EXORCISING POTION FOR HER.
IT MAY HELP HER A LITTLE...
OH, MONK...
YOU'RE ALWAYS...
...SACRIFICING PORTIONS OF YOUR LIFE FOR ME OR KOHAKU.
PLEASE, MIROKU...
PT PT PT

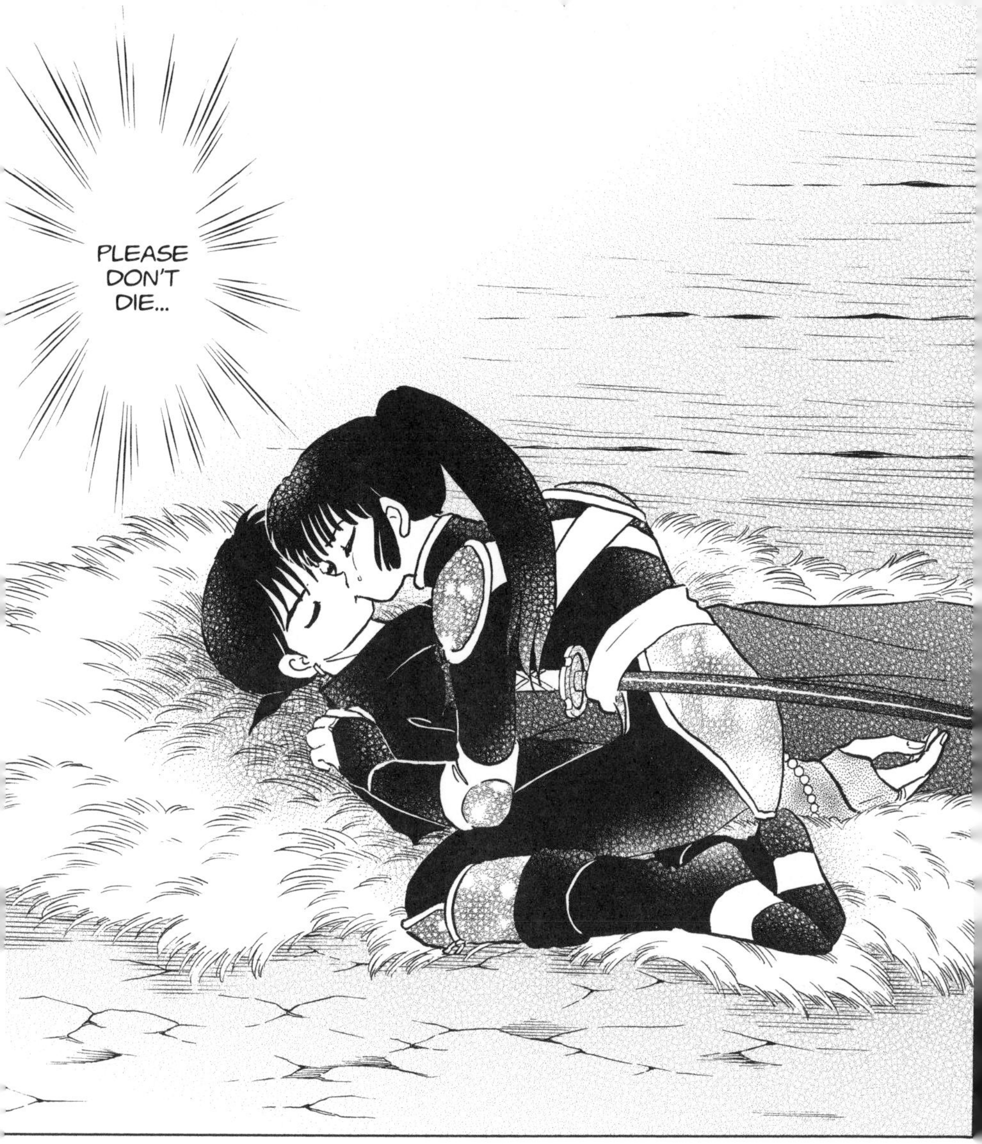
PLEASE DON'T DIE...
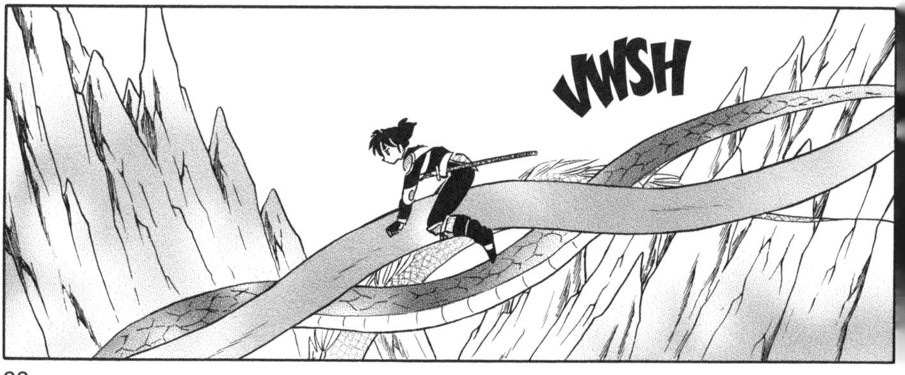
VWSH

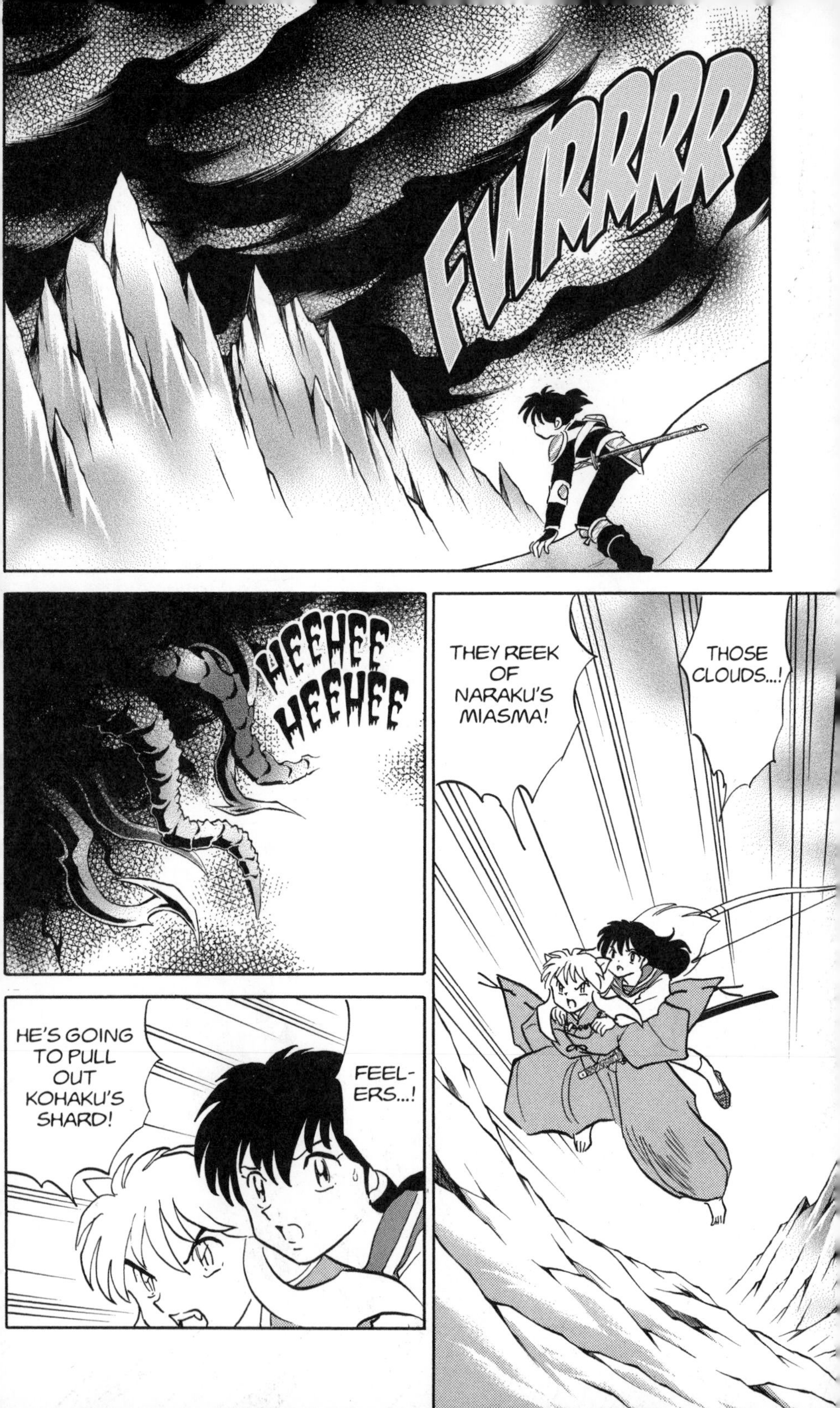
FWRRRR
THOSE CLOUDS...!
THEY REEK OF NARAKU'S MIASMA!
HEEHEE HEEHEE
FEEL-ERS...!
HE'S GOING TO PULL OUT KOHAKU'S SHARD!

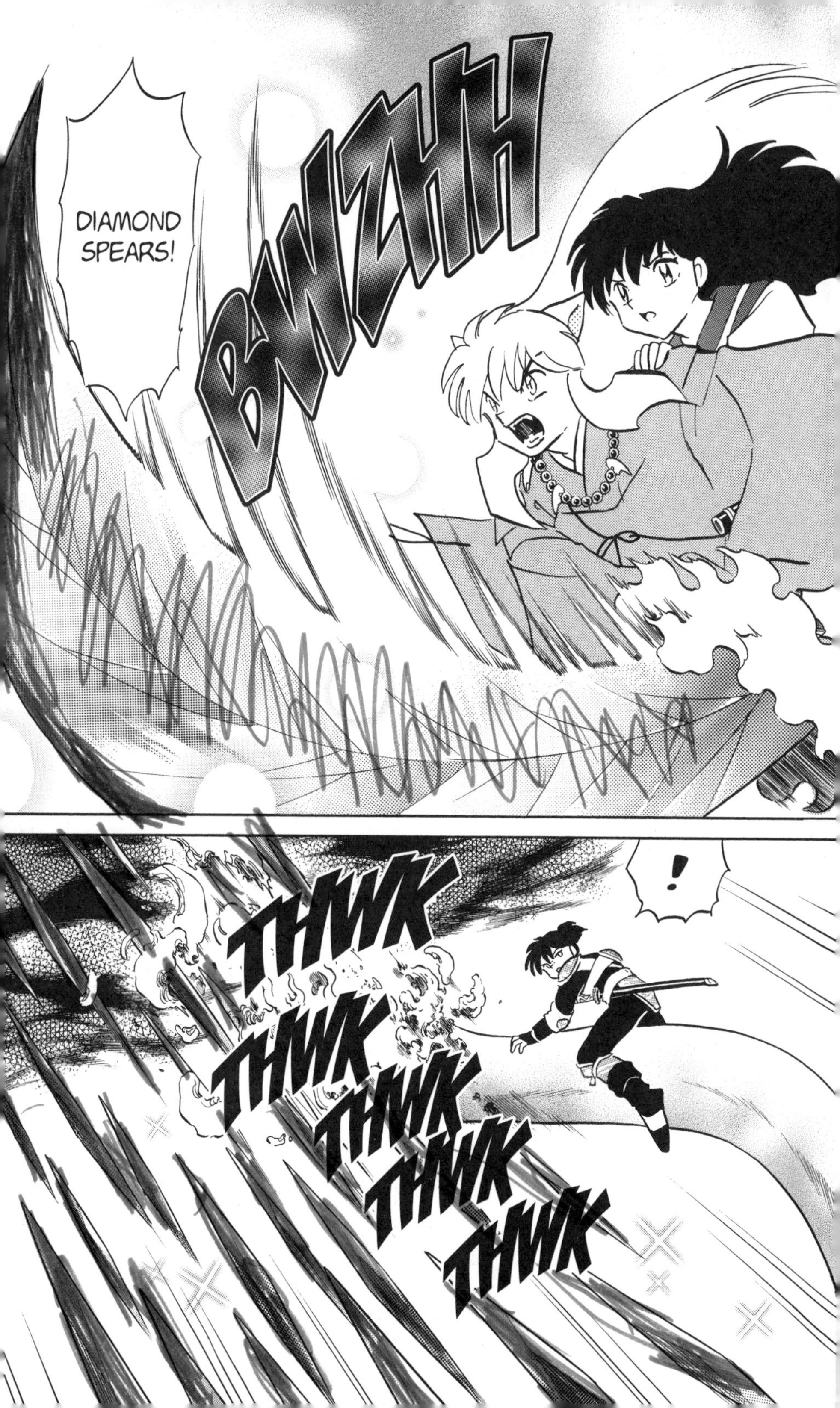
BWZHHH
DIAMOND SPEARS!
!
THWK THWK THWK THWK THWK

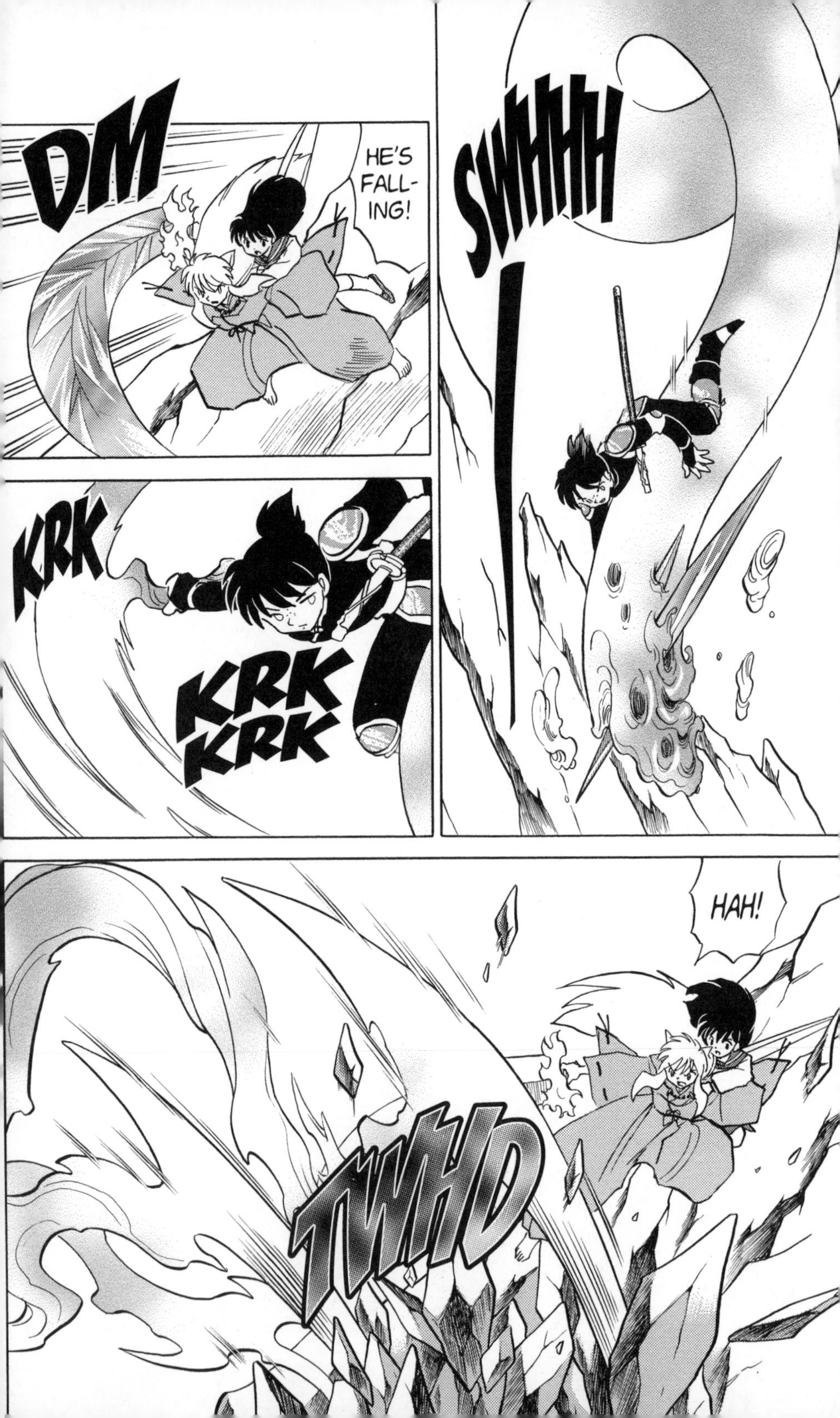
SWHHHH
HE'S FALL-ING!
DM
KRK
KRK KRK
HAH!
TWHD

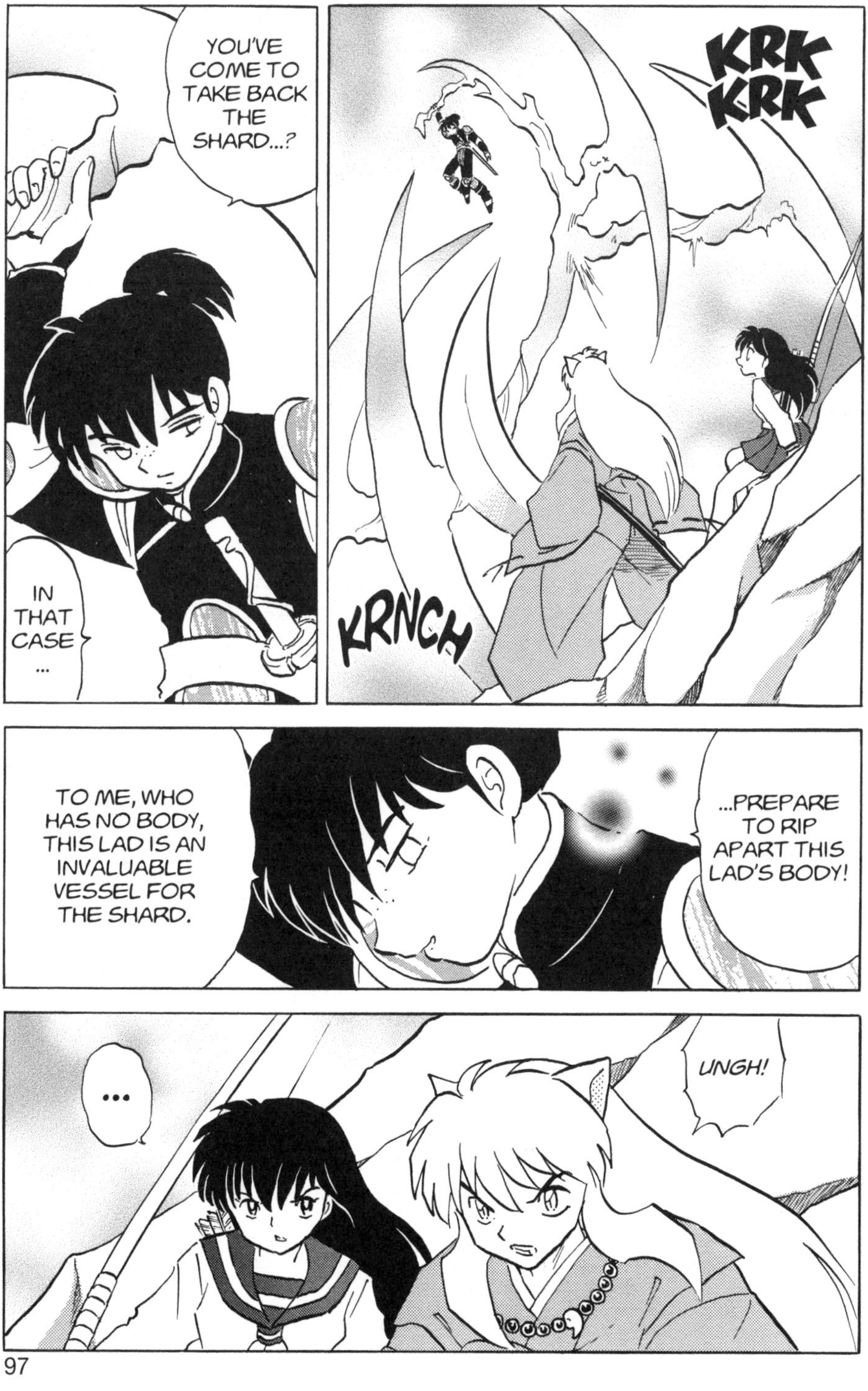
KRK KRK
KRNCH
YOU'VE COME TO TAKE BACK THE SHARD...?
IN THAT CASE ...
...PREPARE TO RIP APART THIS LAD'S BODY!
TO ME, WHO HAS NO BODY, THIS LAD IS AN INVALUABLE VESSEL FOR THE SHARD.
UNGH!
...

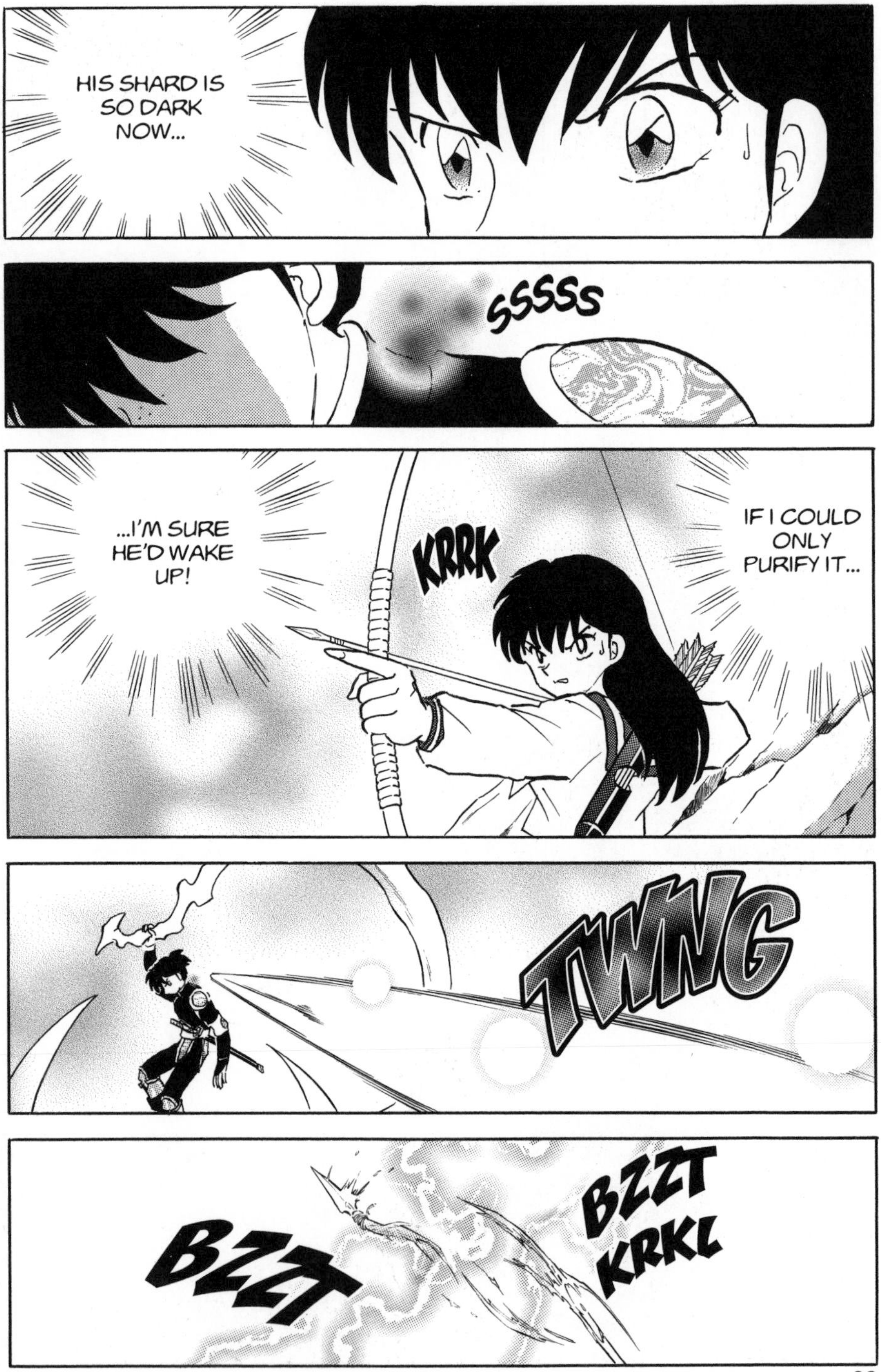
HIS SHARD IS SO DARK NOW...
SSSSS
IF I COULD ONLY PURIFY IT...
KRRK
...I'M SURE HE'D WAKE UP!
TWNG
BZZT
KRKL
BZZT

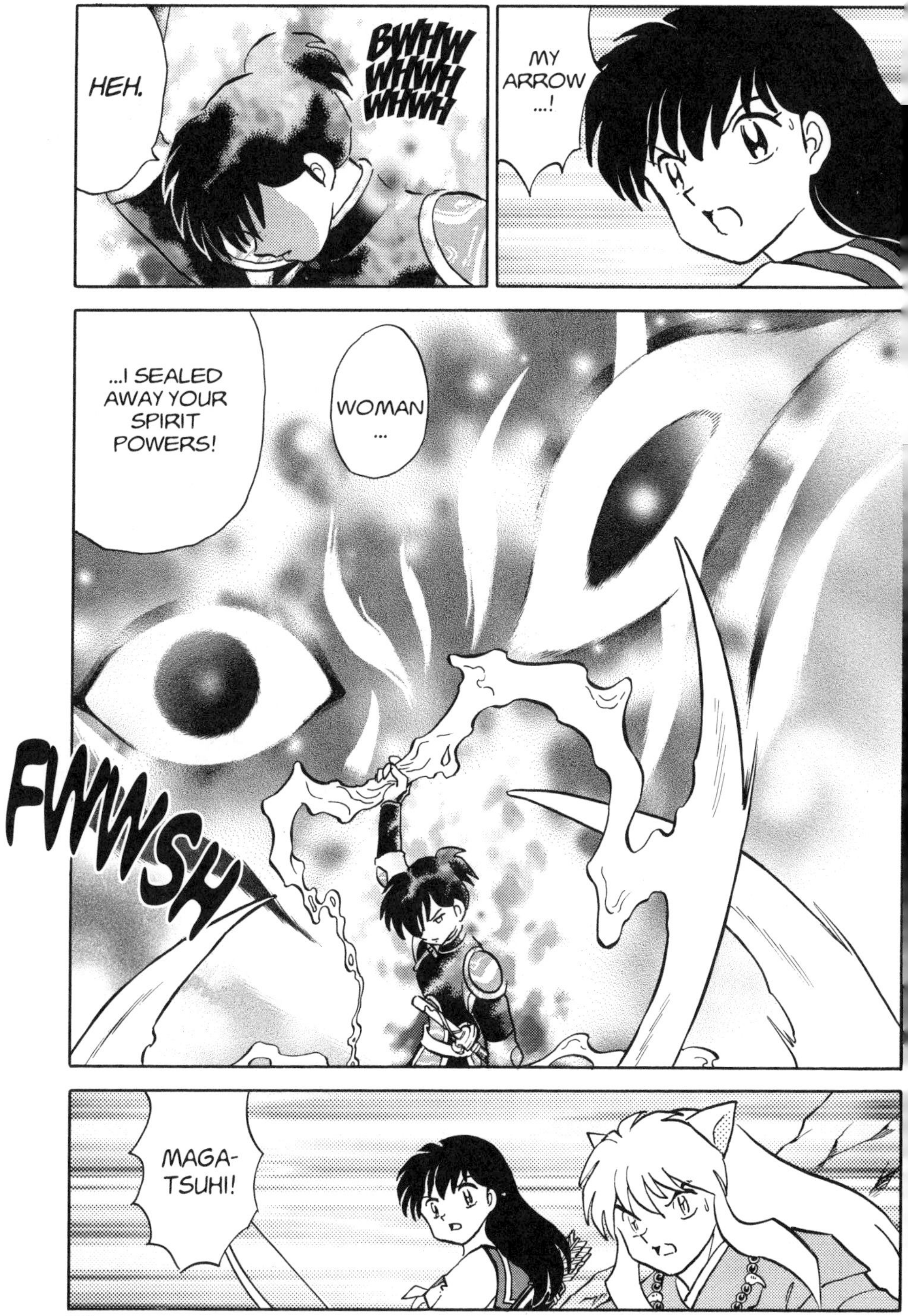
MY ARROW ...!
HEH.
BWHW WHWH WHWH
WOMAN ...
...I SEALED AWAY YOUR SPIRIT POWERS!
FWWSH
MAGA-TSUHI!

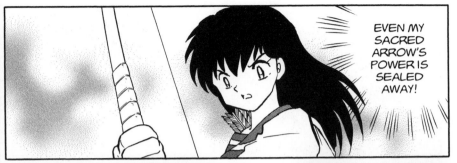

EVEN MY SACRED ARROW'S POWER IS SEALED AWAY!

SOON NOW...THE SHIKON JEWEL SHALL BE RESTORED!

SWH

KRK KRK KRK

NOT ON MY WATCH!

VWSH

SCROLL SIX
AWAKENING

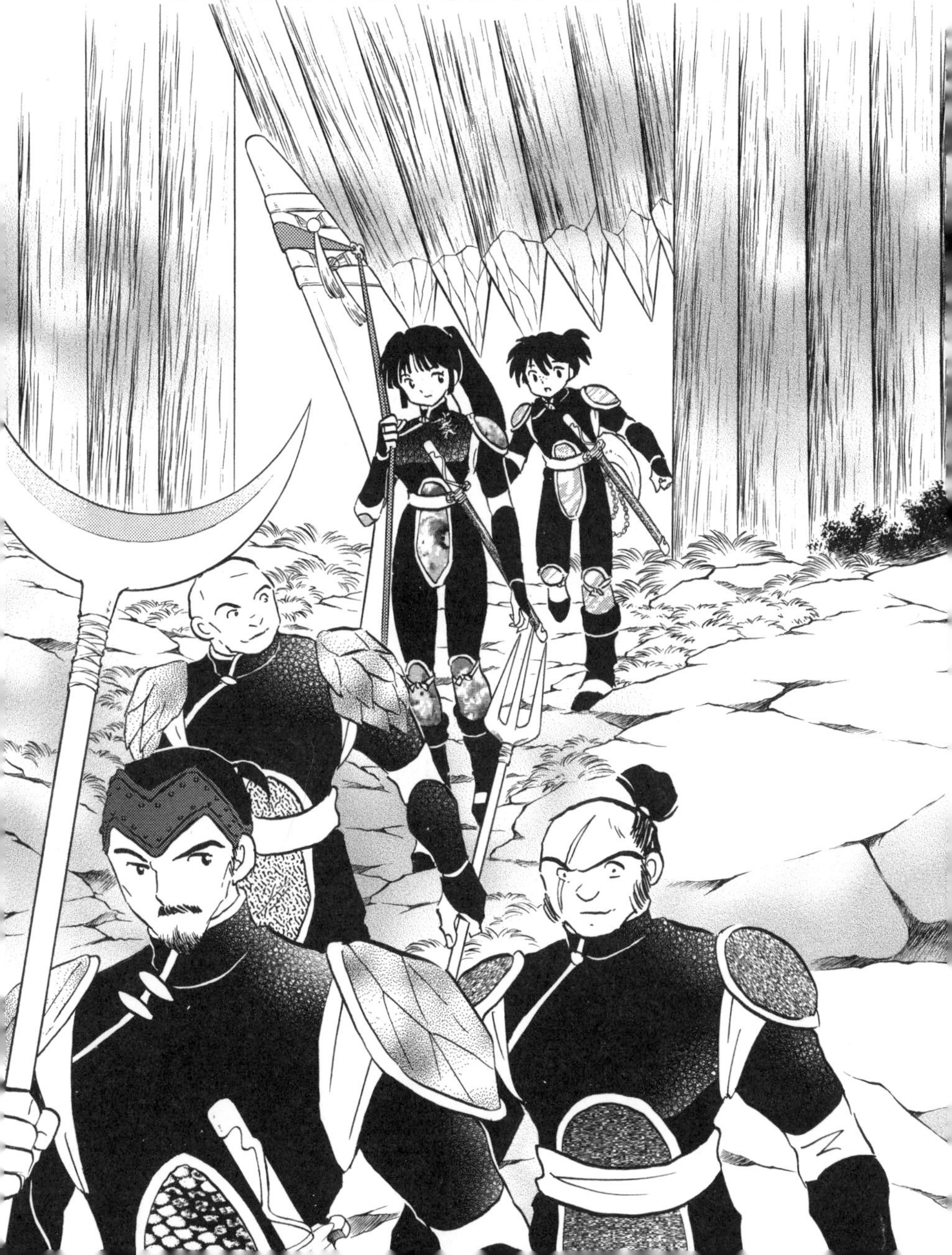

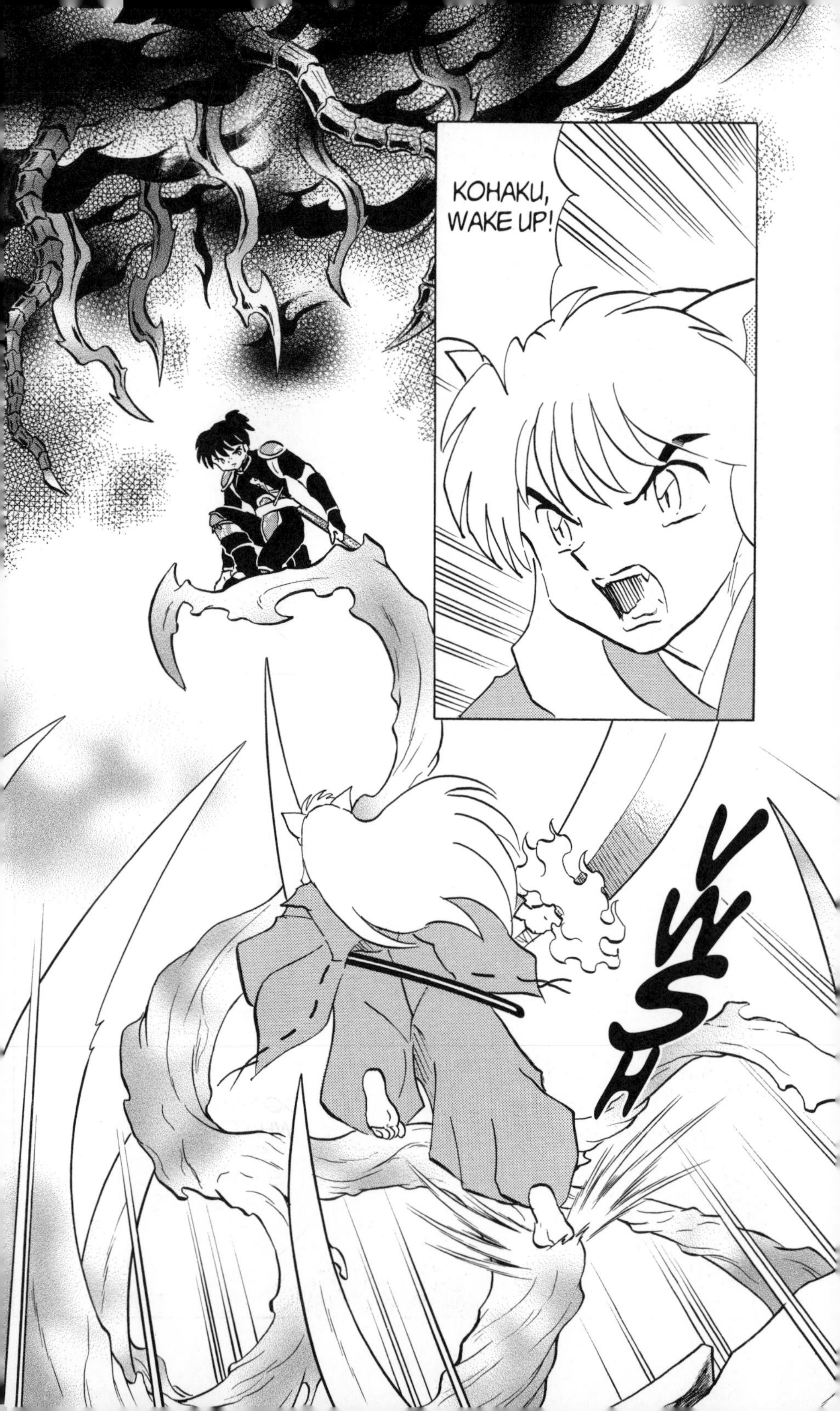
KOHAKU, WAKE UP!
VWSH

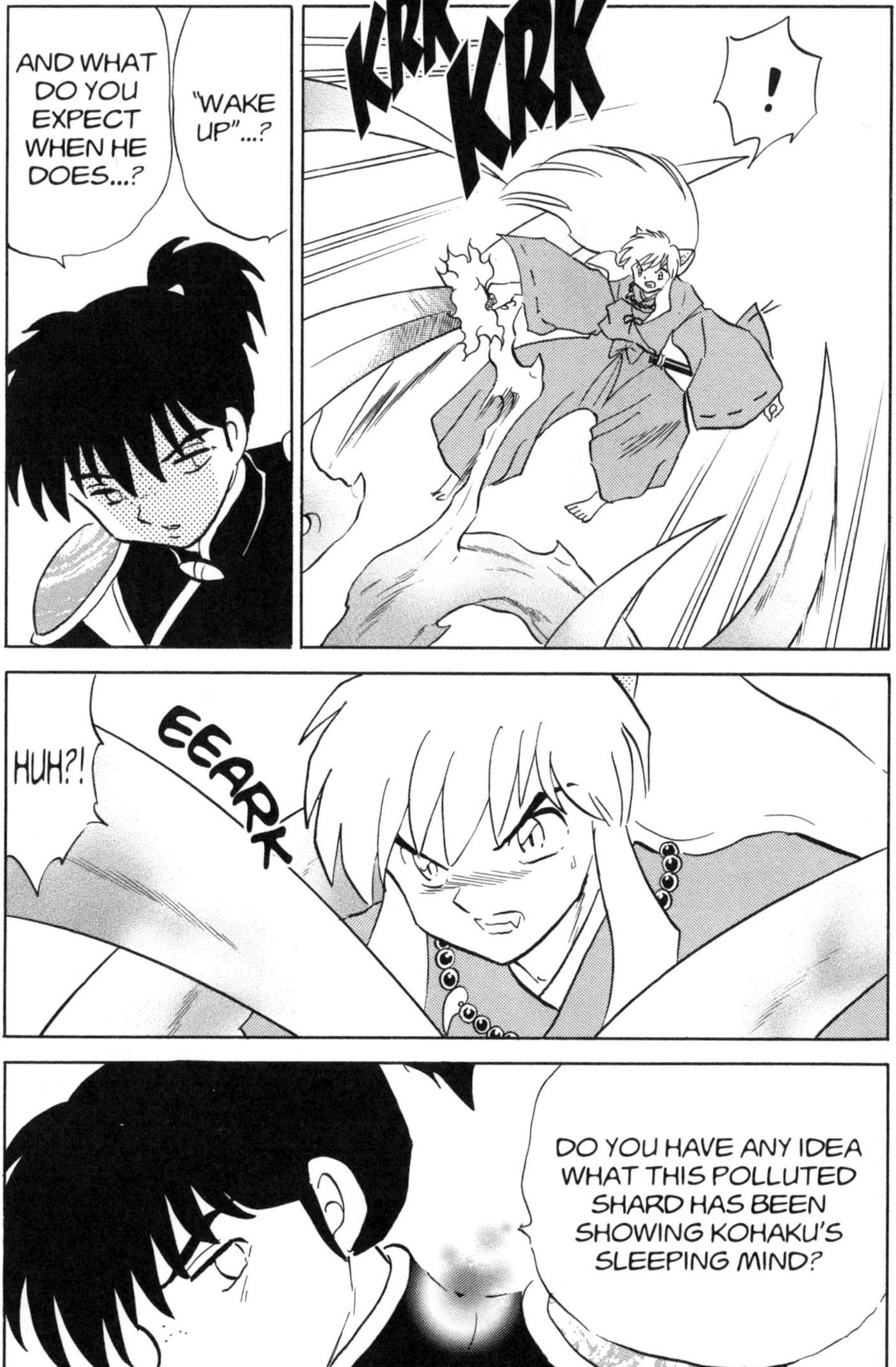
KRK KRK
!
"WAKE UP"...?
AND WHAT DO YOU EXPECT WHEN HE DOES...?
EEARK
HUH?!
DO YOU HAVE ANY IDEA WHAT THIS POLLUTED SHARD HAS BEEN SHOWING KOHAKU'S SLEEPING MIND?

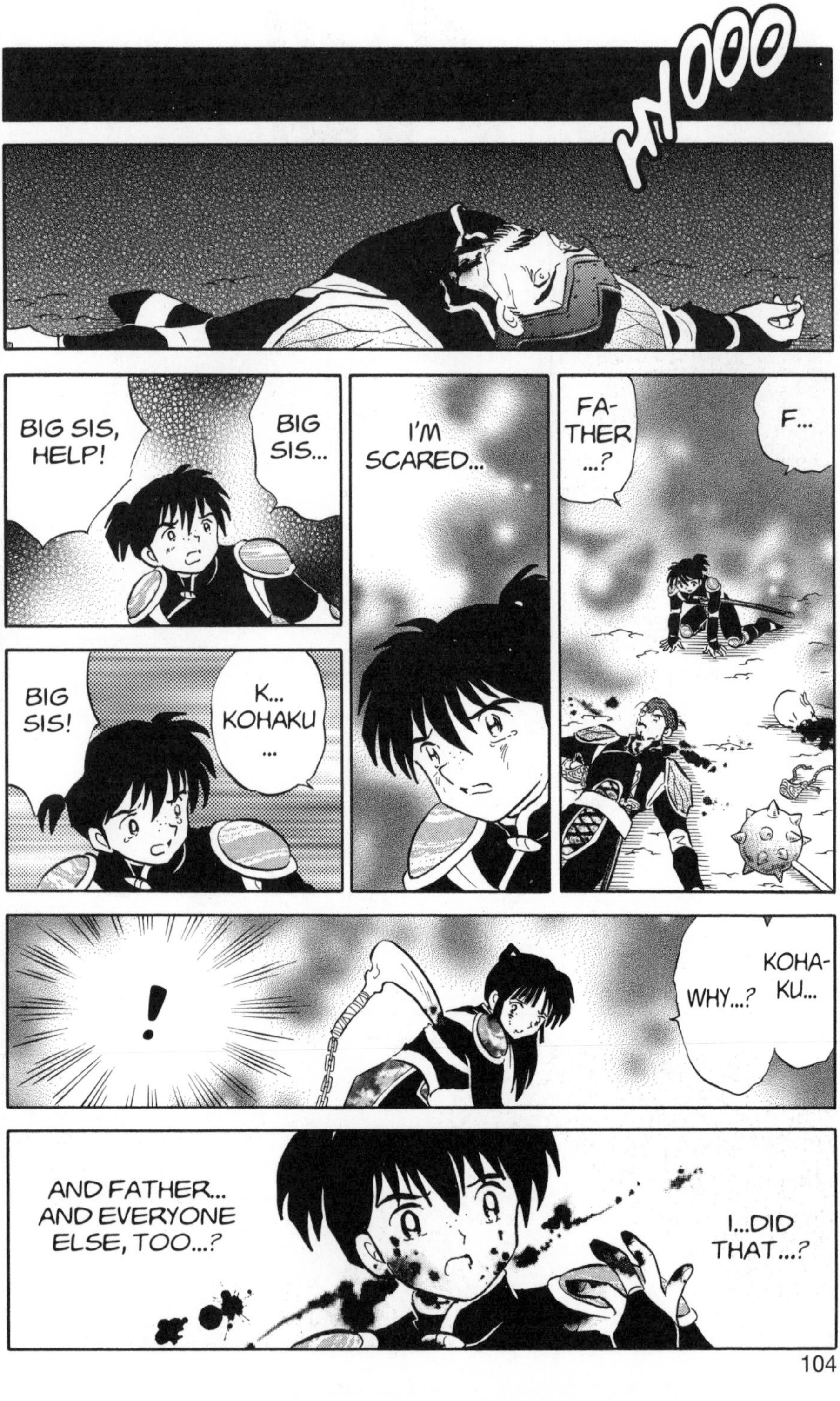
HYOOO
F...
FA-THER...?
I'M SCARED...
BIG SIS...
BIG SIS, HELP!
K... KOHAKU...
BIG SIS!
KOHA-KU...
WHY...?
!
I...DID THAT...?
AND FATHER... AND EVERYONE ELSE, TOO...?

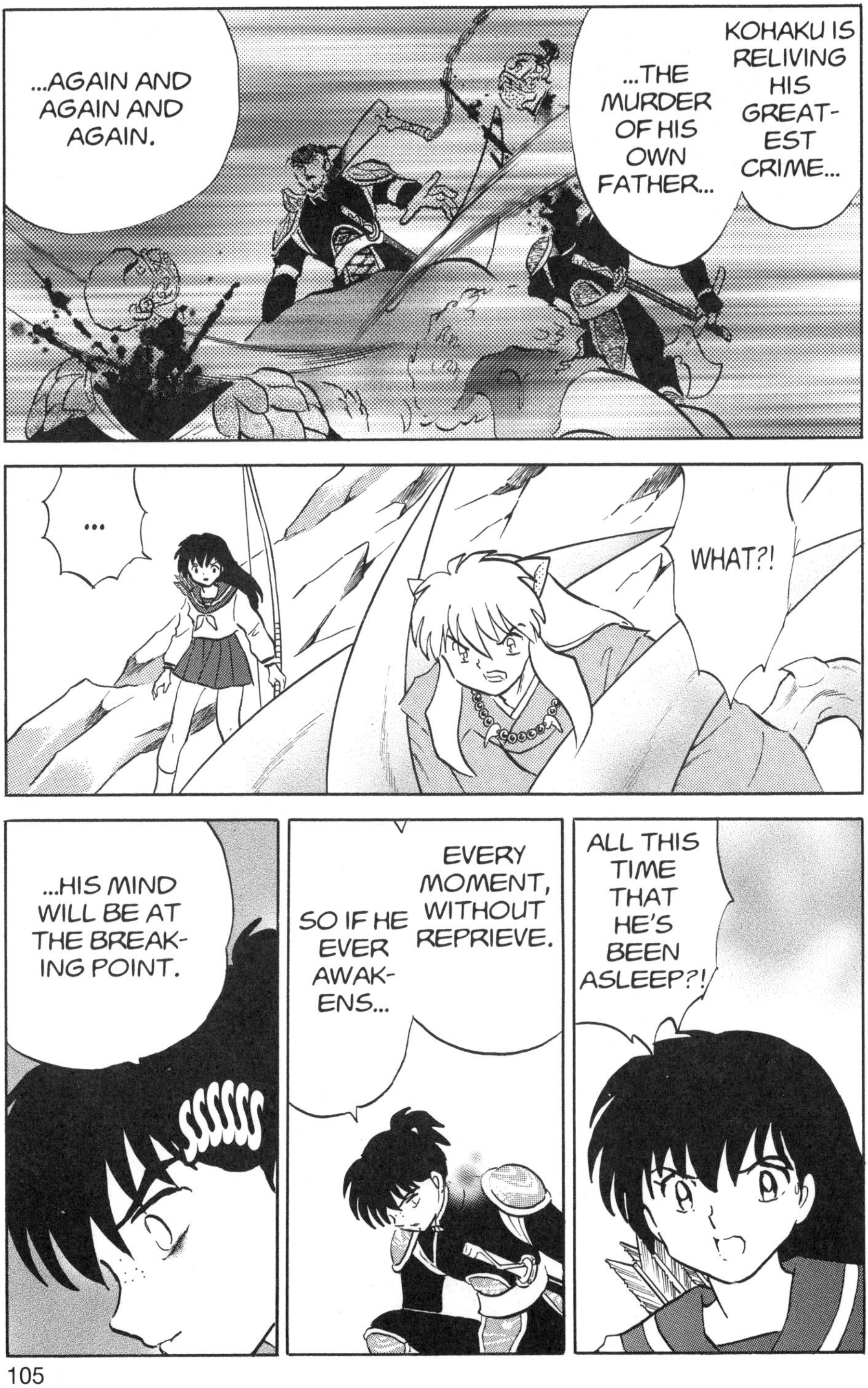
KOHAKU IS RELIVING HIS GREATEST CRIME...
...THE MURDER OF HIS OWN FATHER...
...AGAIN AND AGAIN AND AGAIN.
WHAT?!
...
ALL THIS TIME THAT HE'S BEEN ASLEEP?!
EVERY MOMENT, WITHOUT REPRIEVE.
SO IF HE EVER AWAKENS...
...HIS MIND WILL BE AT THE BREAKING POINT.
SSSSSS

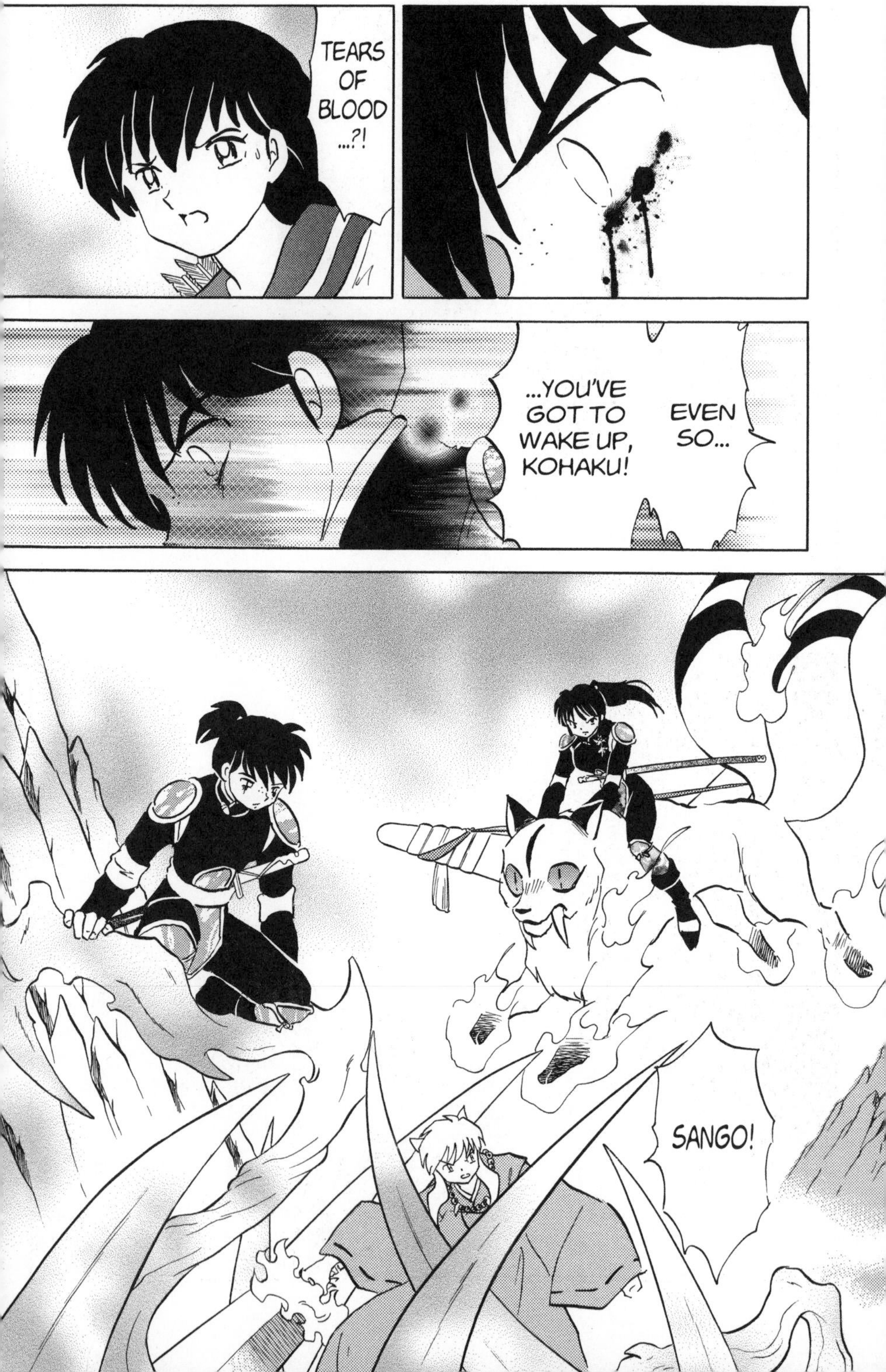
TEARS OF BLOOD ...?!
EVEN SO...
...YOU'VE GOT TO WAKE UP, KOHAKU!
SANGO!

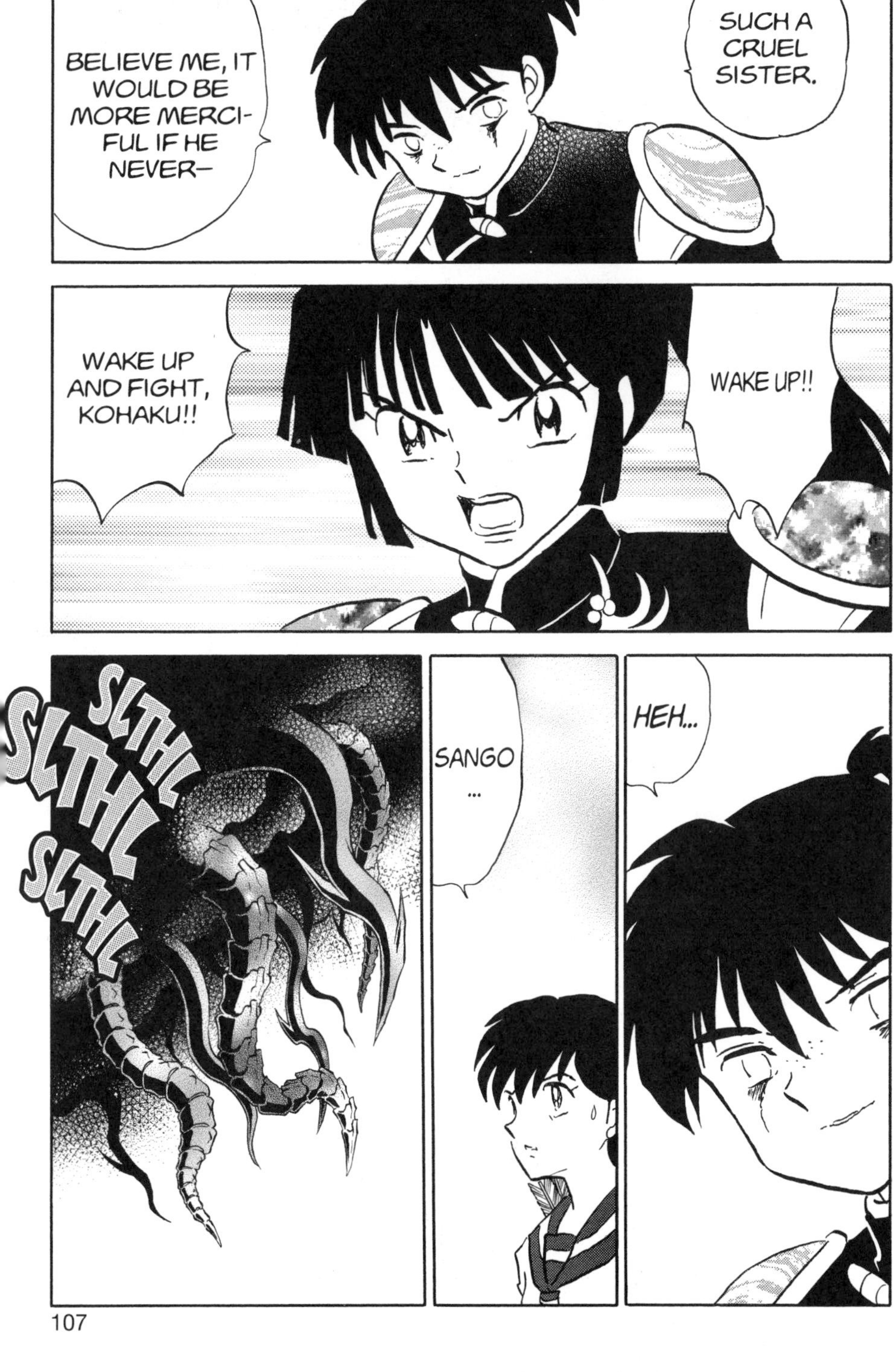
SUCH A CRUEL SISTER.
BELIEVE ME, IT WOULD BE MORE MERCI- FUL IF HE NEVER–
WAKE UP!!
WAKE UP AND FIGHT, KOHAKU!!
HEH...
SANGO ...
SLTHL
SLTHL
SLTHL

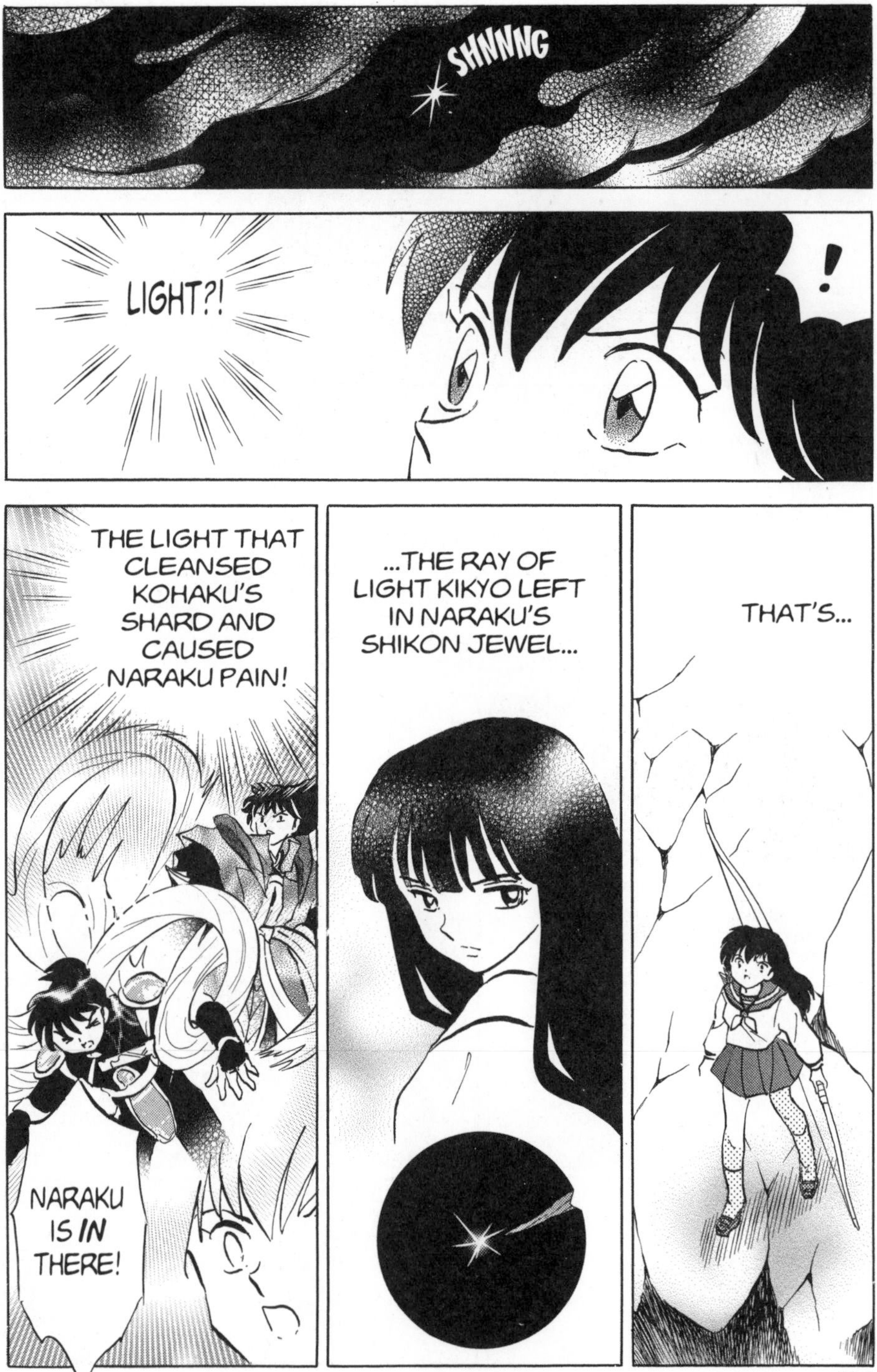
SHNNNG
!
LIGHT?!
THAT'S...
...THE RAY OF LIGHT KIKYO LEFT IN NARAKU'S SHIKON JEWEL...
THE LIGHT THAT CLEANSED KOHAKU'S SHARD AND CAUSED NARAKU PAIN!
NARAKU IS *IN* THERE!

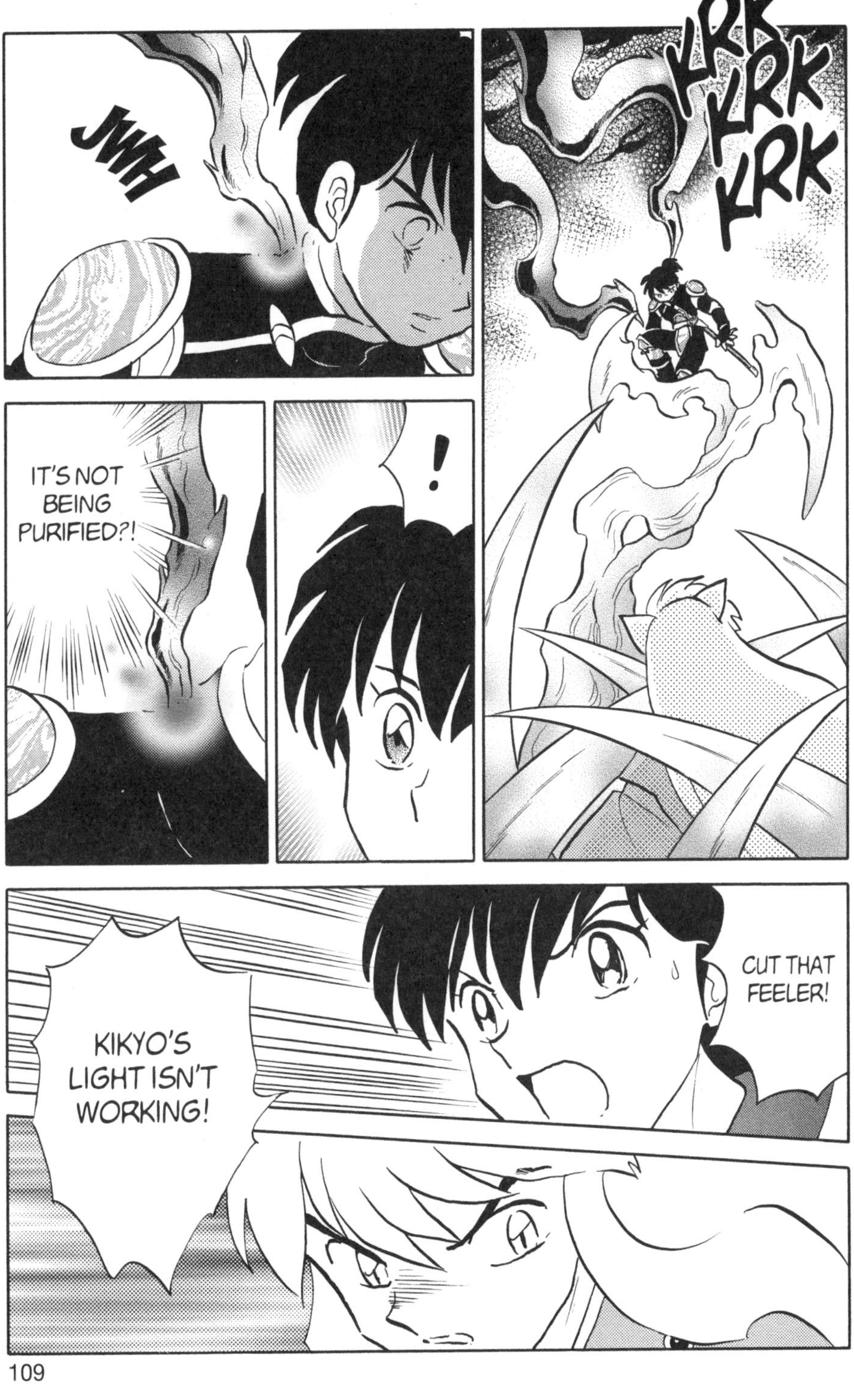
KRK
KRK
KRK
JWH
!
IT'S NOT BEING PURIFIED?!
CUT THAT FEELER!
KIKYO'S LIGHT ISN'T WORKING!

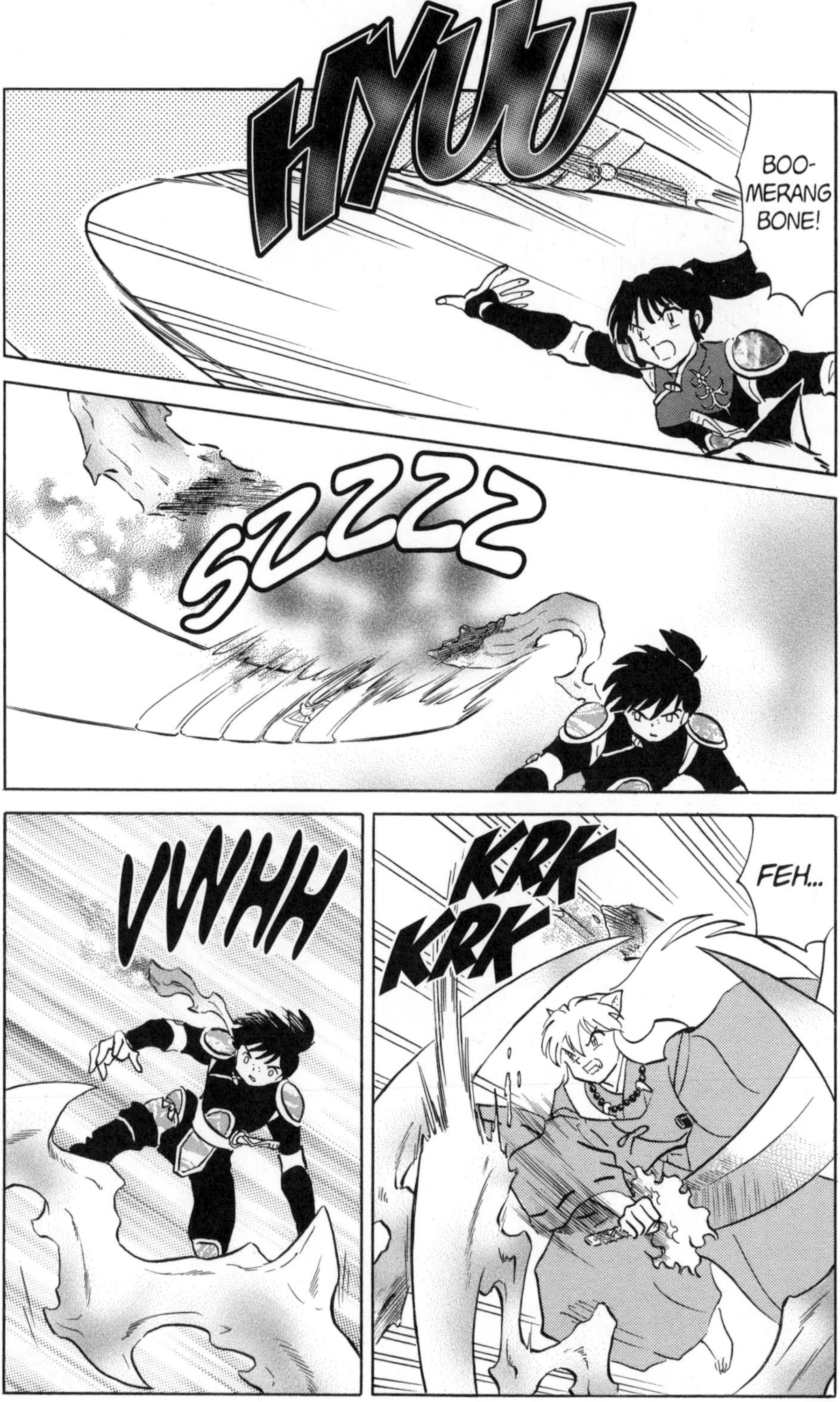
HYUU
BOO-
MERANG
BONE!
SZZZZ
FEH...
KRK
KRK
VWHH

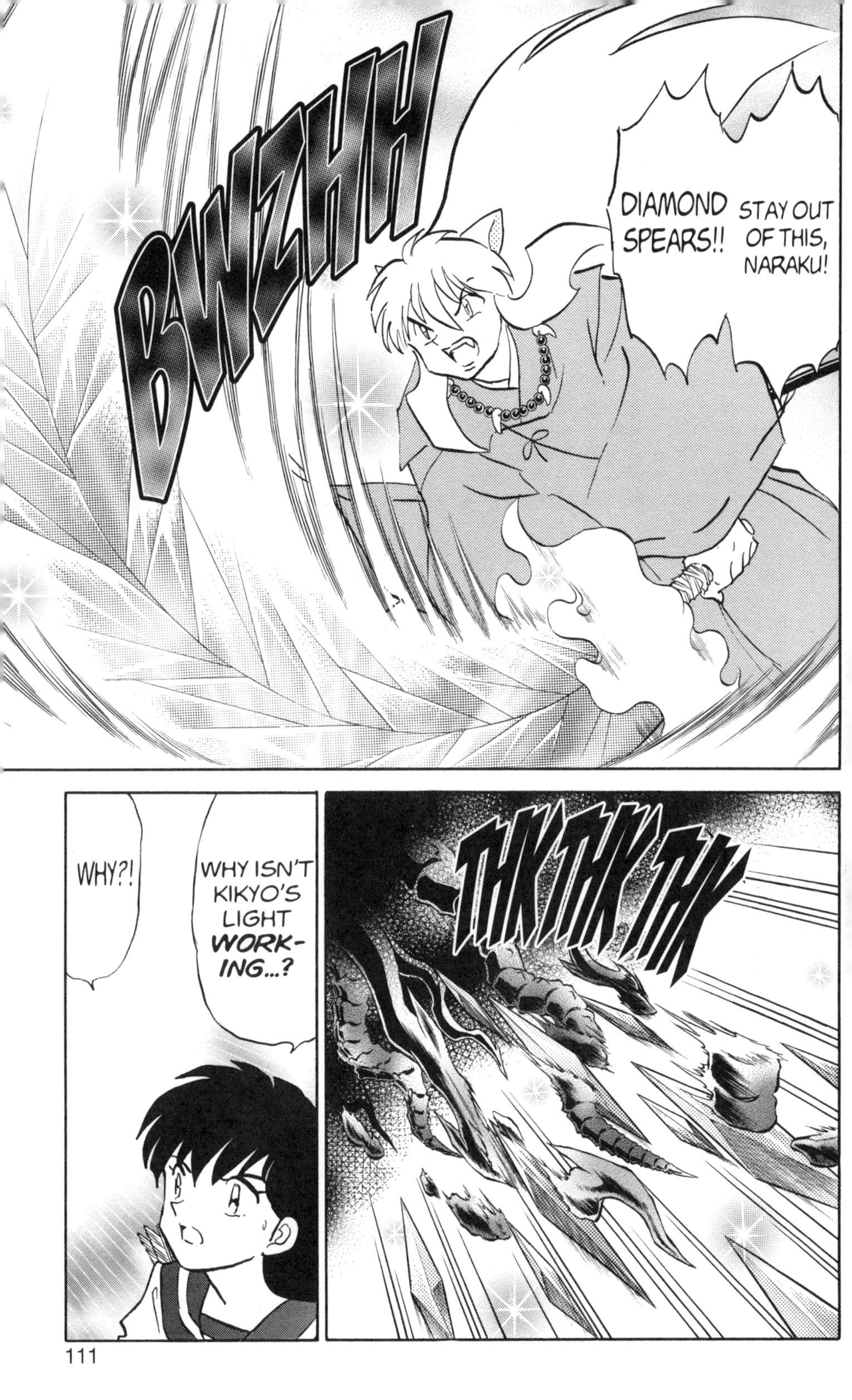
STAY OUT OF THIS, NARAKU!
DIAMOND SPEARS!!
BWZHH
THK THK THK
WHY ISN'T KIKYO'S LIGHT ***WORKING***...?
WHY?!

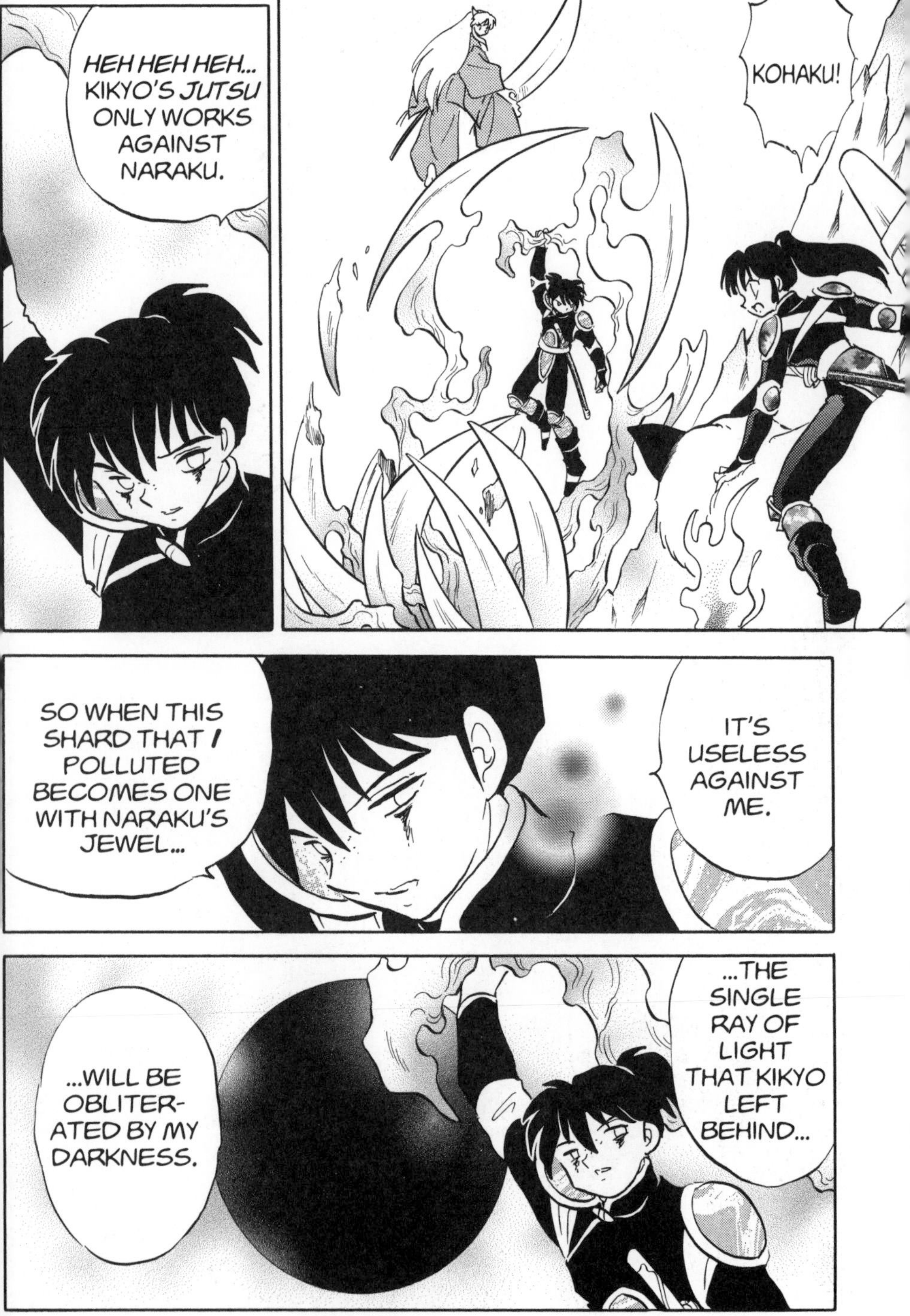
KOHAKU!
HEH HEH HEH... KIKYO'S JUTSU ONLY WORKS AGAINST NARAKU.
IT'S USELESS AGAINST ME.
SO WHEN THIS SHARD THAT I POLLUTED BECOMES ONE WITH NARAKU'S JEWEL...
...THE SINGLE RAY OF LIGHT THAT KIKYO LEFT BEHIND...
...WILL BE OBLITERATED BY MY DARKNESS.

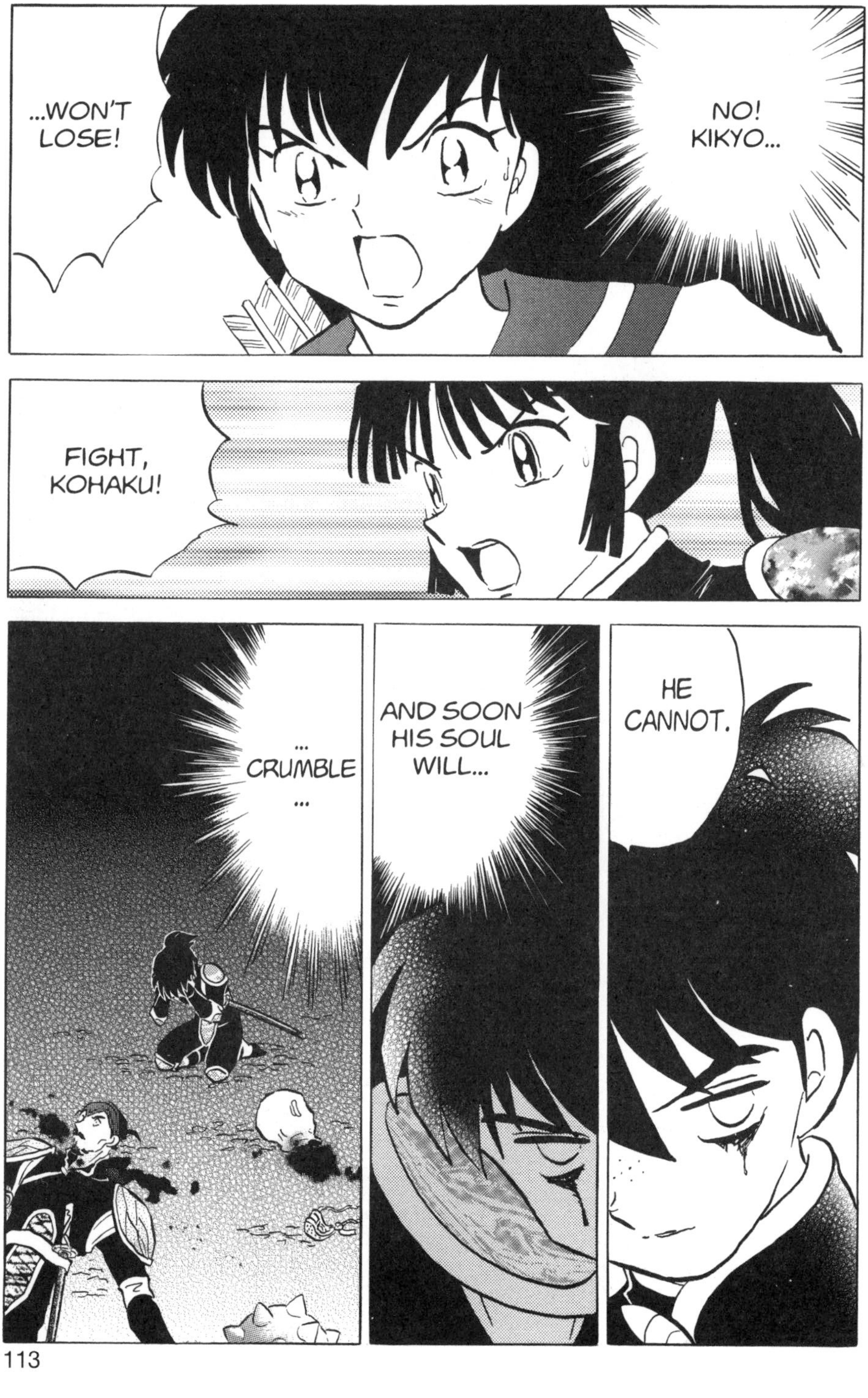
NO! KIKYO...
...WON'T LOSE!
FIGHT, KOHAKU!
HE CANNOT.
AND SOON HIS SOUL WILL...
... CRUMBLE ...

BIG SIS...

I'M AFRAID...

SANGO ...HELP ME...

FA- THER ...?

KNNNN

WBWHW

LIGHT ...!

114

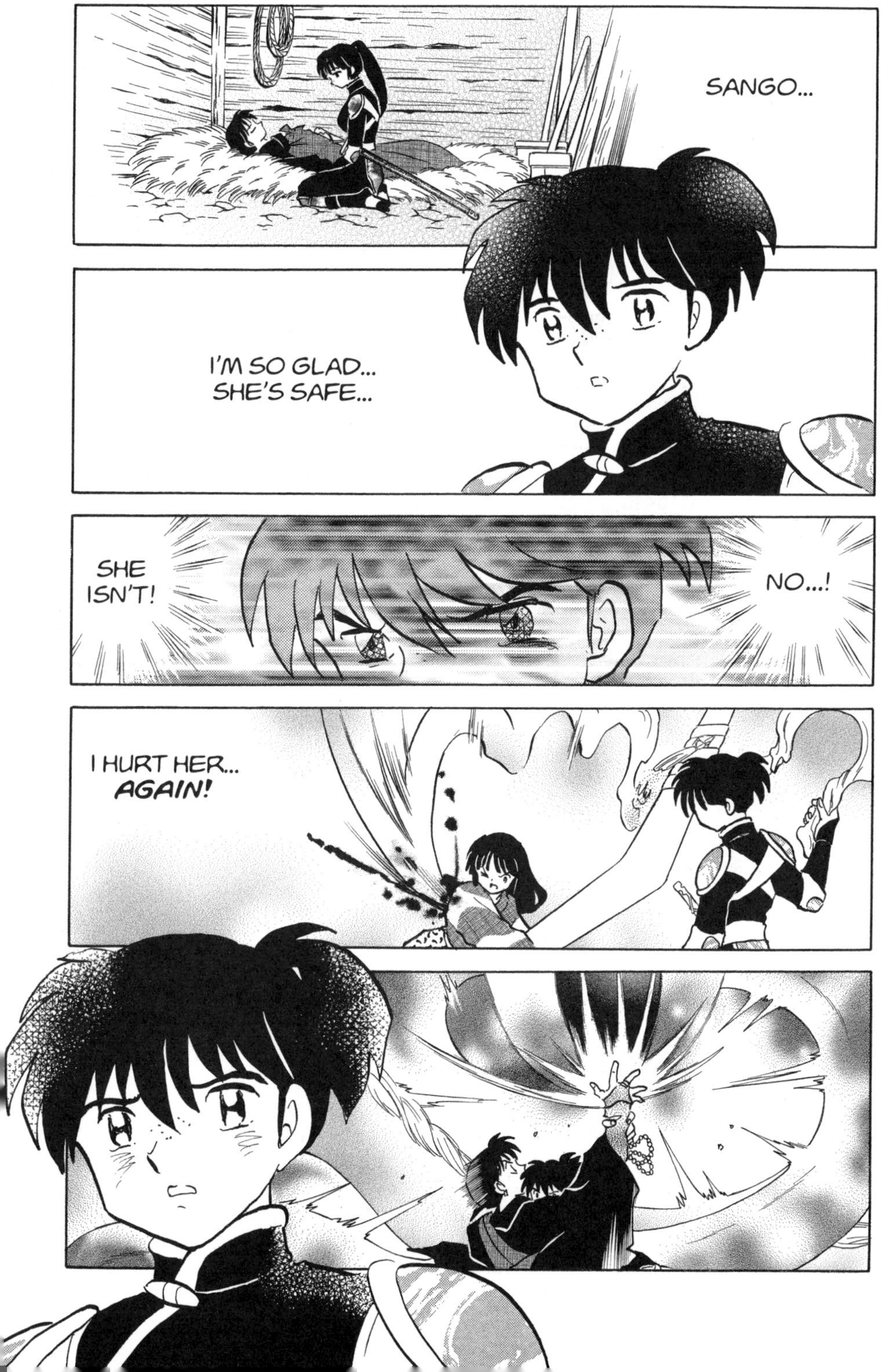
SANGO...
I'M SO GLAD... SHE'S SAFE...
NO...!
SHE ISN'T!
I HURT HER... ***AGAIN!***

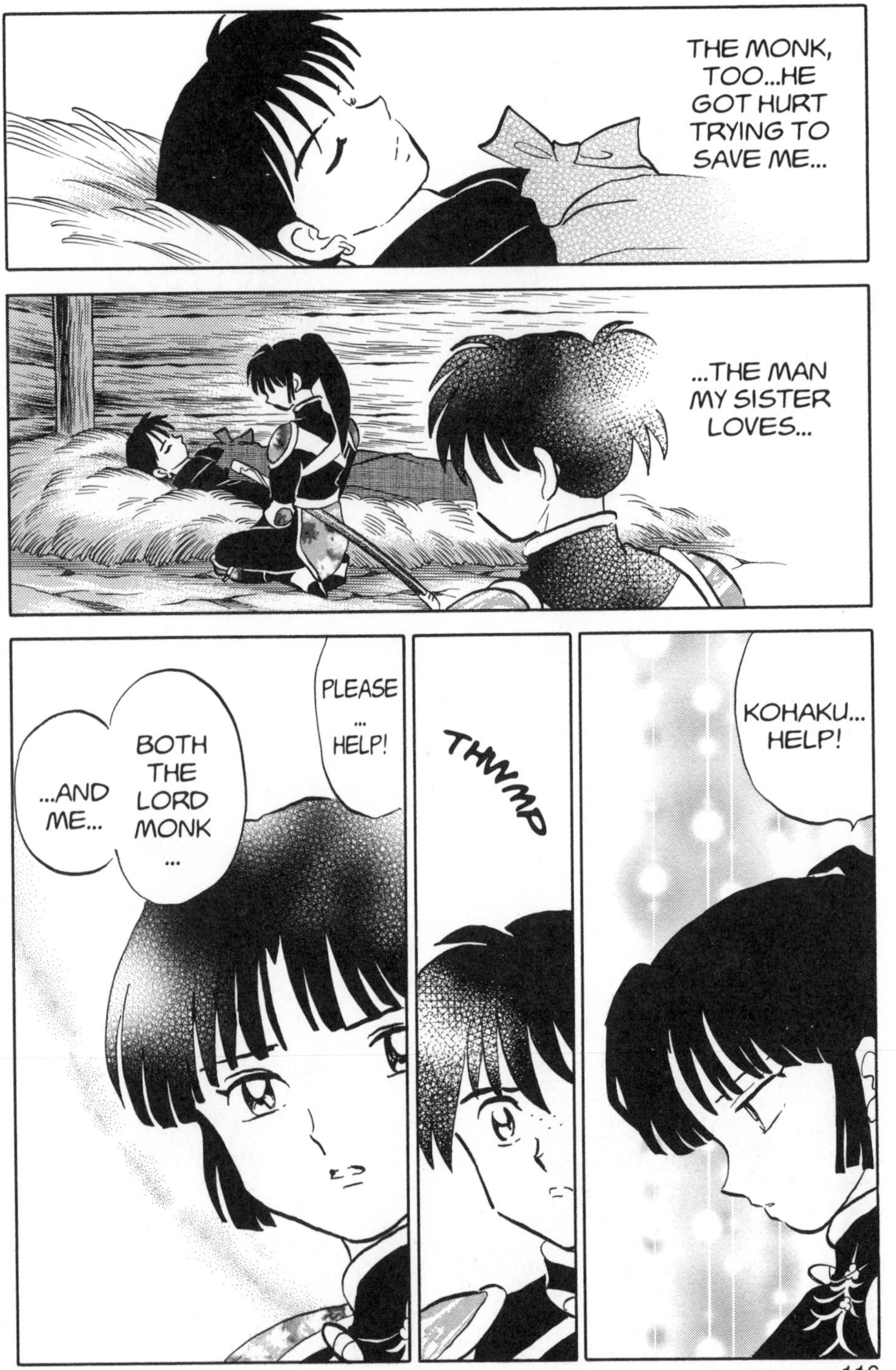

THE MONK, TOO...HE GOT HURT TRYING TO SAVE ME...
...THE MAN MY SISTER LOVES...
KOHAKU... HELP!
THWMP
PLEASE ... HELP!
BOTH THE LORD MONK ...
...AND ME...

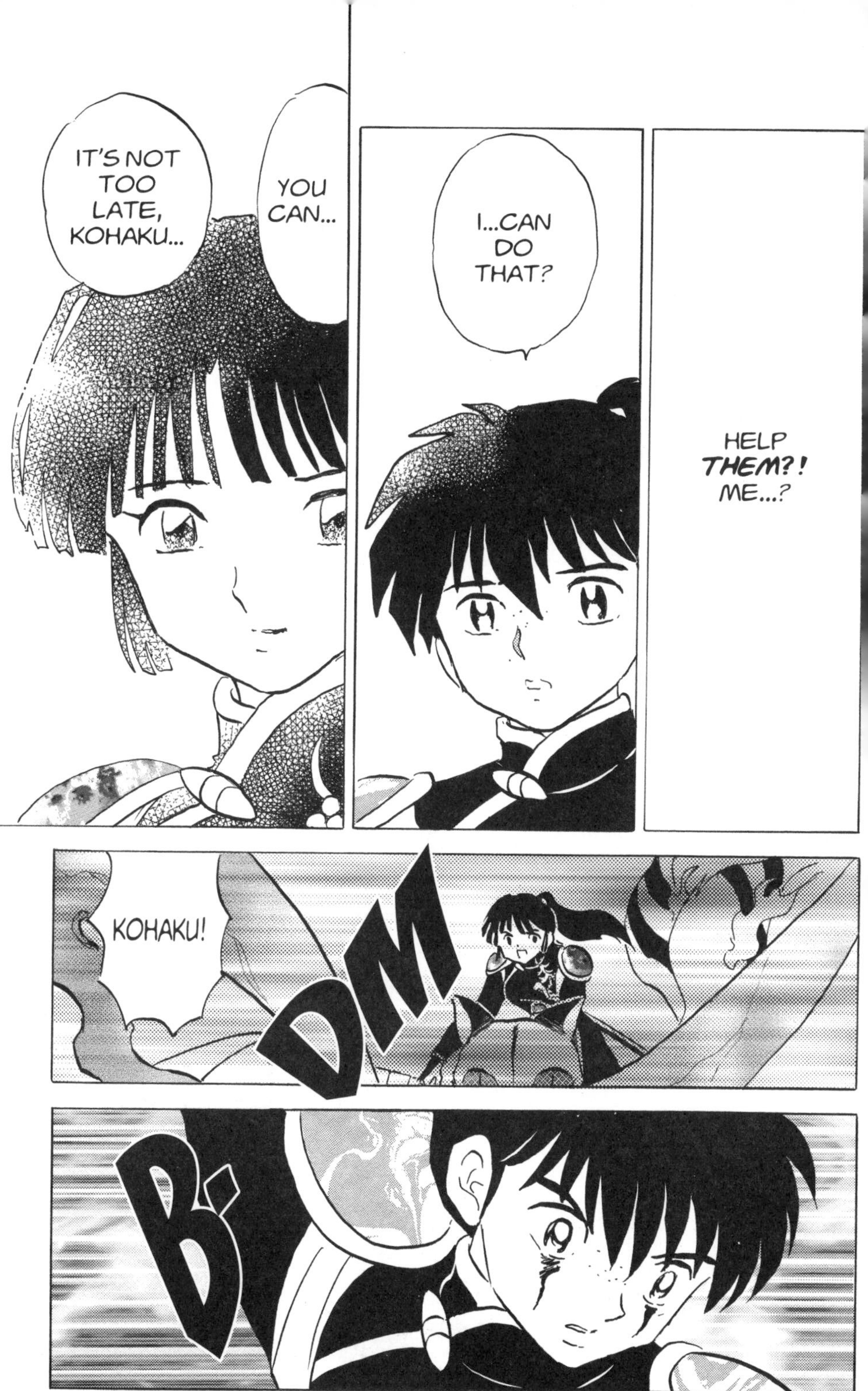
HELP *THEM?!* ME...?
I...CAN DO THAT?
YOU CAN...
IT'S NOT TOO LATE, KOHAKU...
DM
KOHAKU!
B'

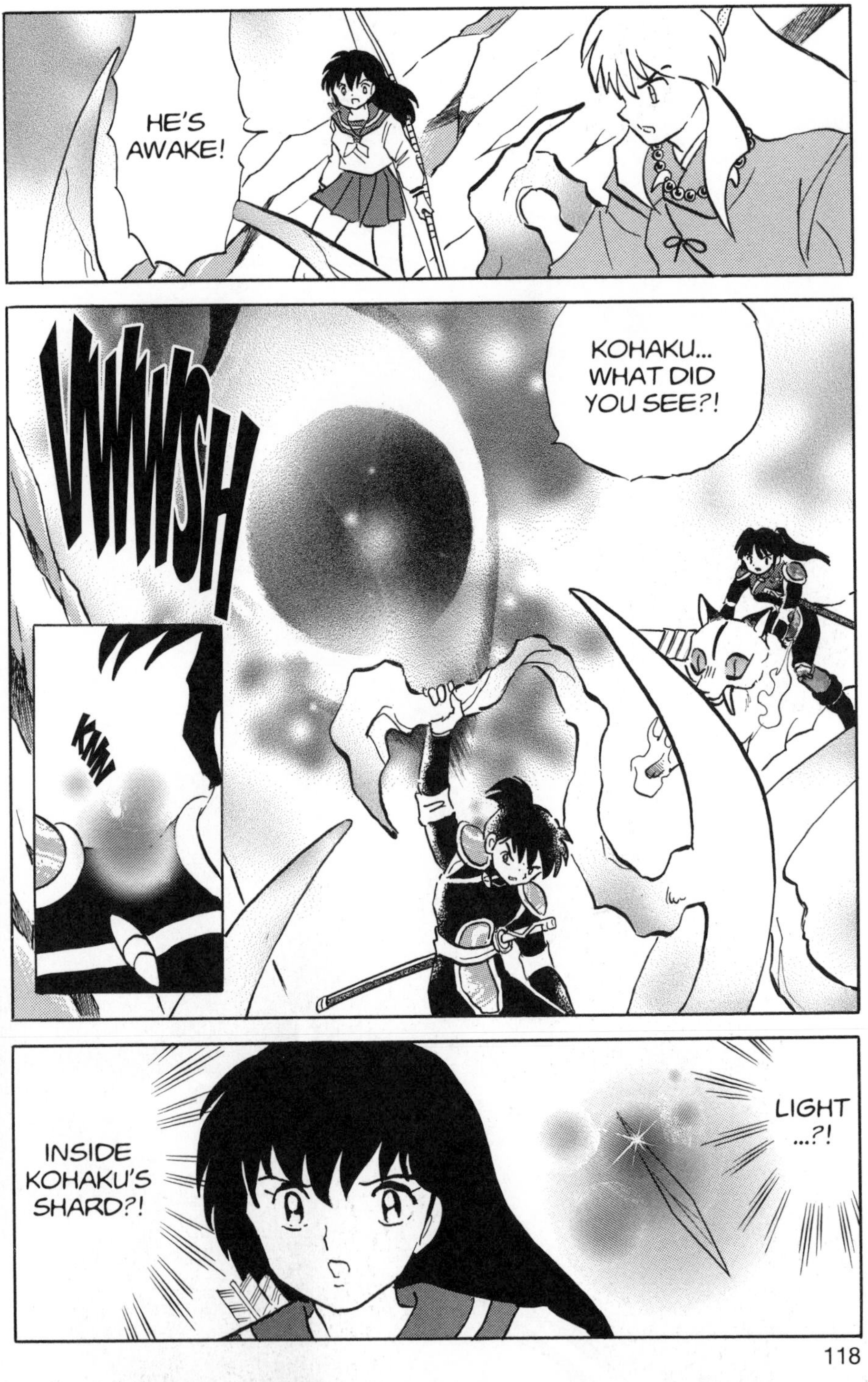
HE'S AWAKE!
KOHAKU... WHAT DID YOU SEE?!
VWWISH
KNN
LIGHT ...?!
INSIDE KOHAKU'S SHARD?!

SCROLL SEVEN
RELEASE

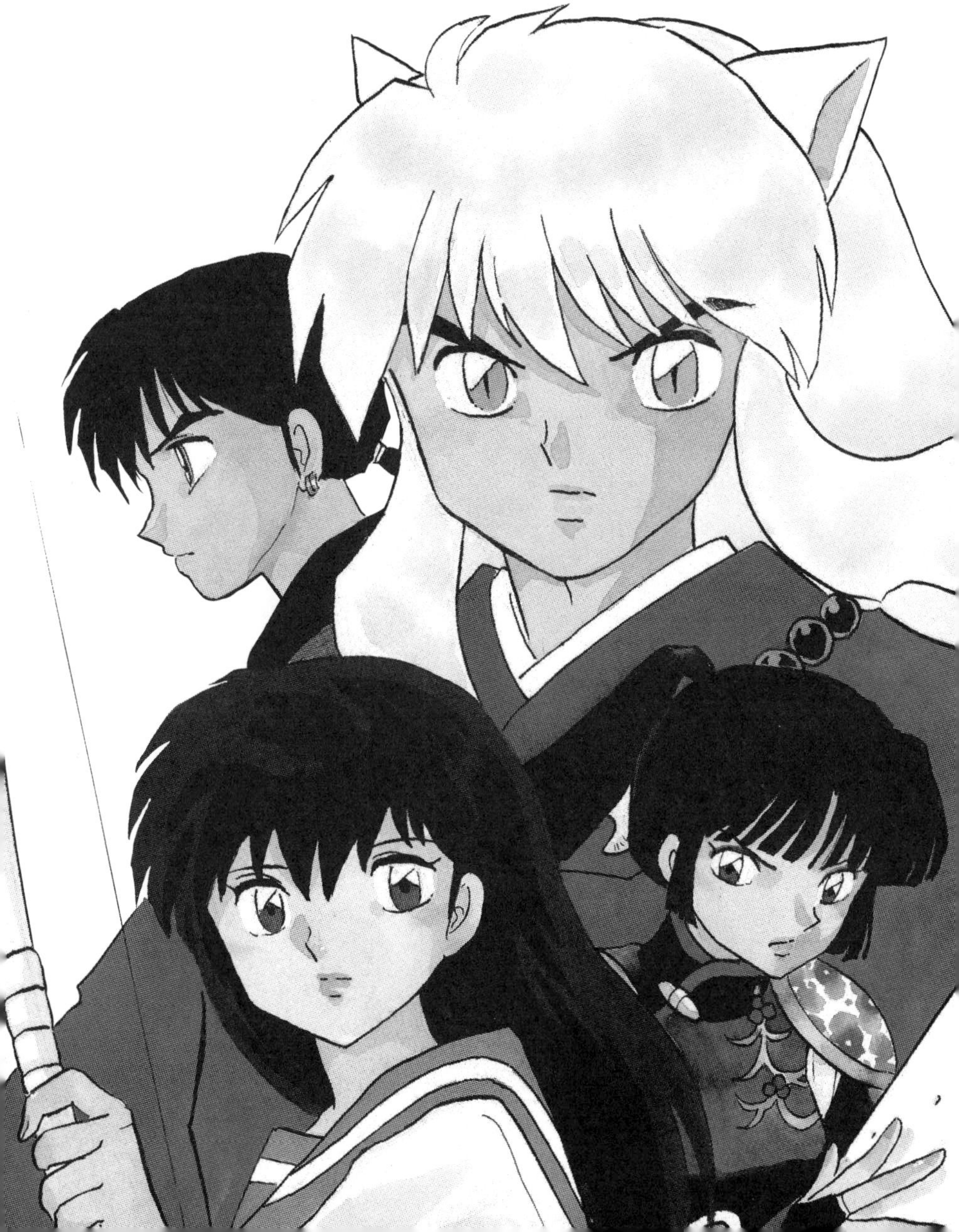

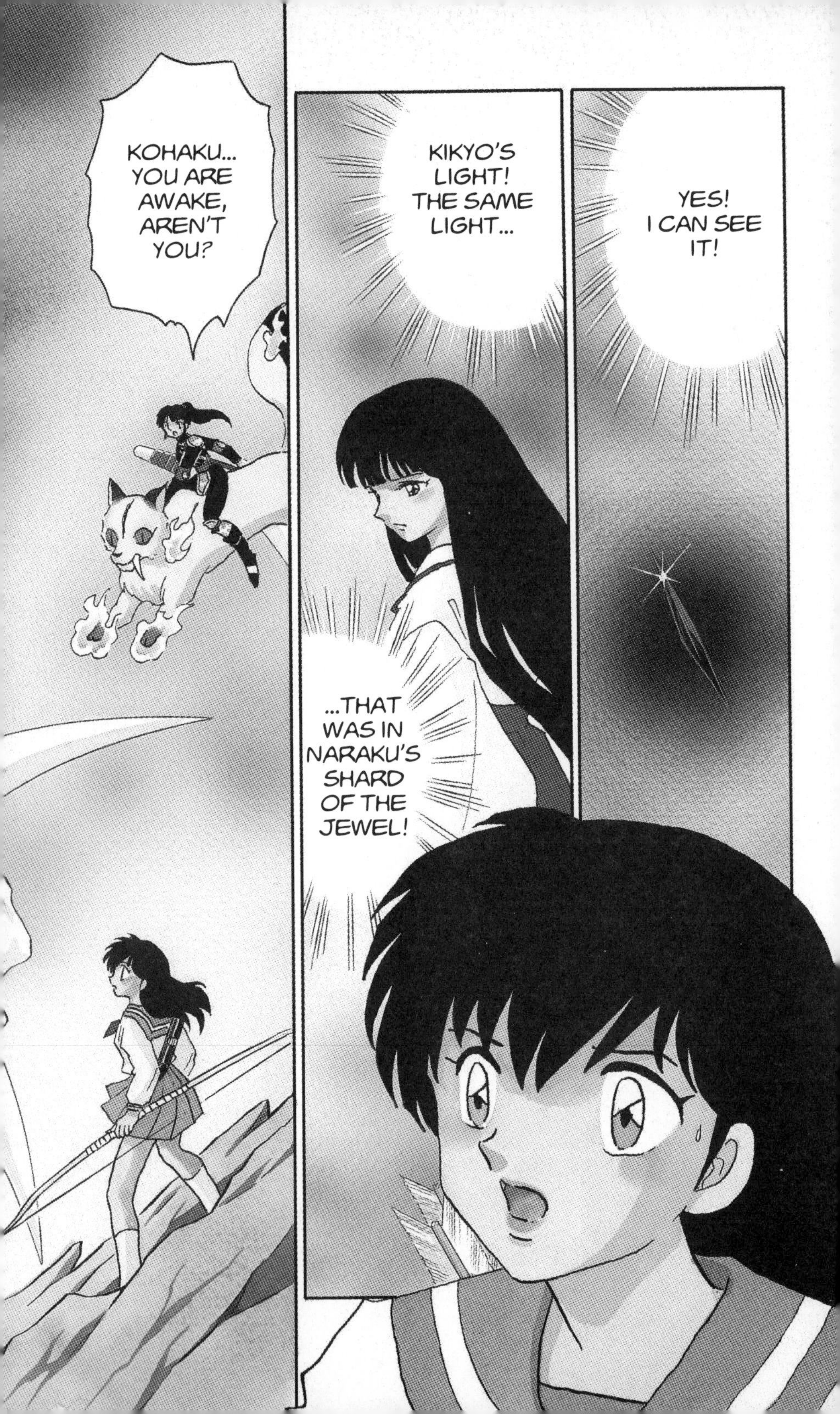

YES! I CAN SEE IT!
KIKYO'S LIGHT! THE SAME LIGHT...
...THAT WAS IN NARAKU'S SHARD OF THE JEWEL!
KOHAKU... YOU ARE AWAKE, AREN'T YOU?

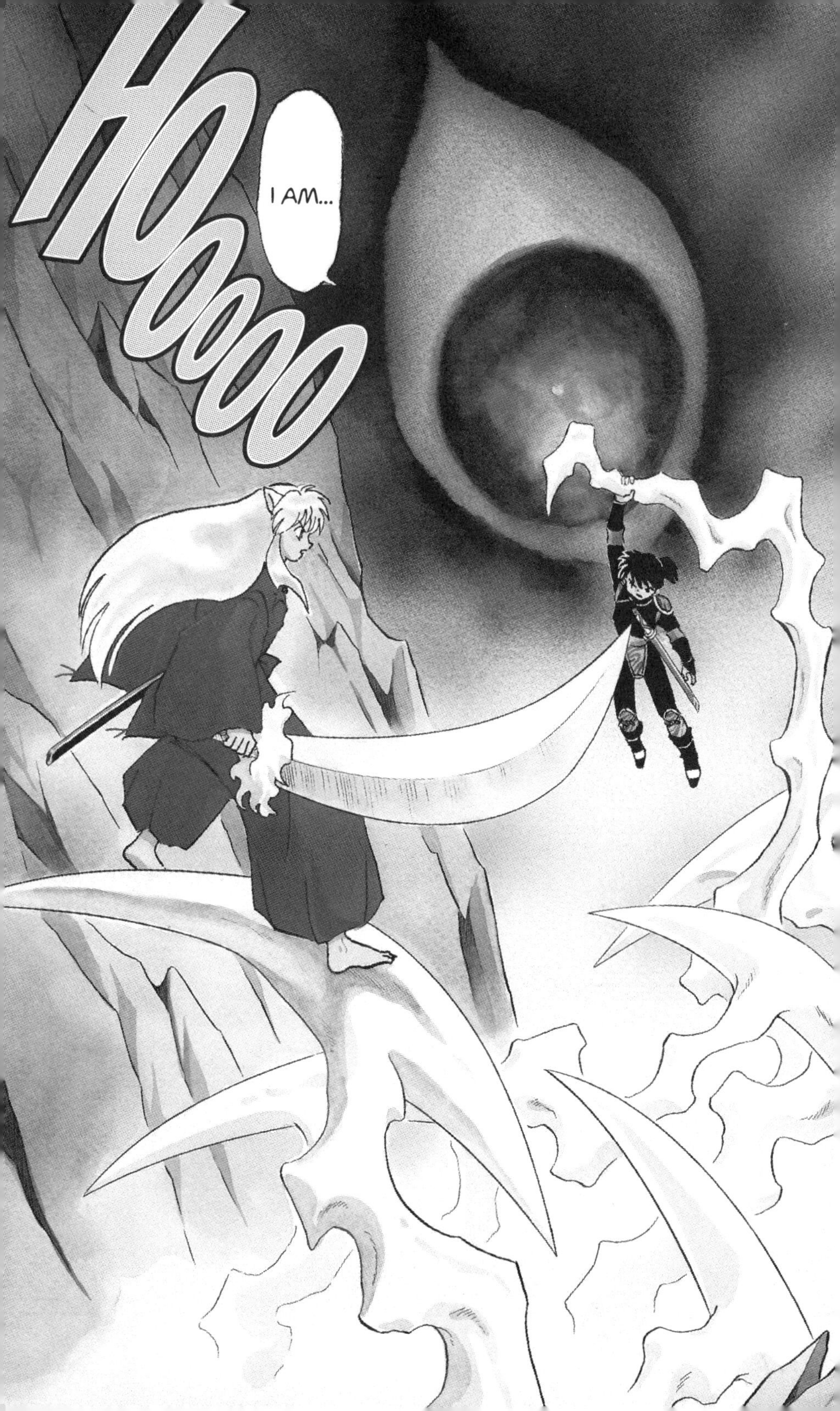
HOOOOO
I AM...

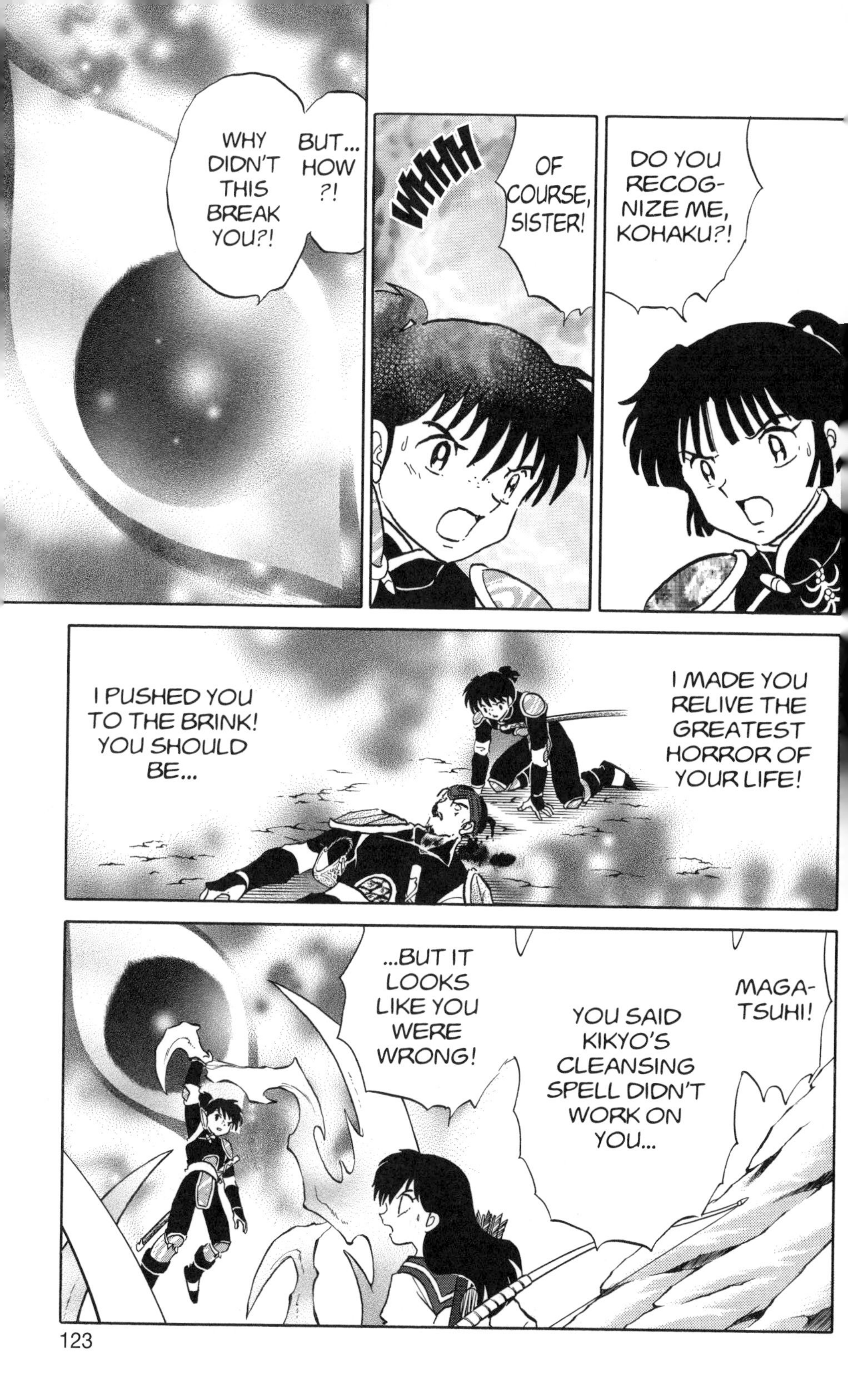
DO YOU RECOGNIZE ME, KOHAKU?!
WHHH
OF COURSE, SISTER!
BUT... HOW?!
WHY DIDN'T THIS BREAK YOU?!
I MADE YOU RELIVE THE GREATEST HORROR OF YOUR LIFE!
I PUSHED YOU TO THE BRINK! YOU SHOULD BE...
MAGATSUHI!
YOU SAID KIKYO'S CLEANSING SPELL DIDN'T WORK ON YOU...
...BUT IT LOOKS LIKE YOU WERE WRONG!

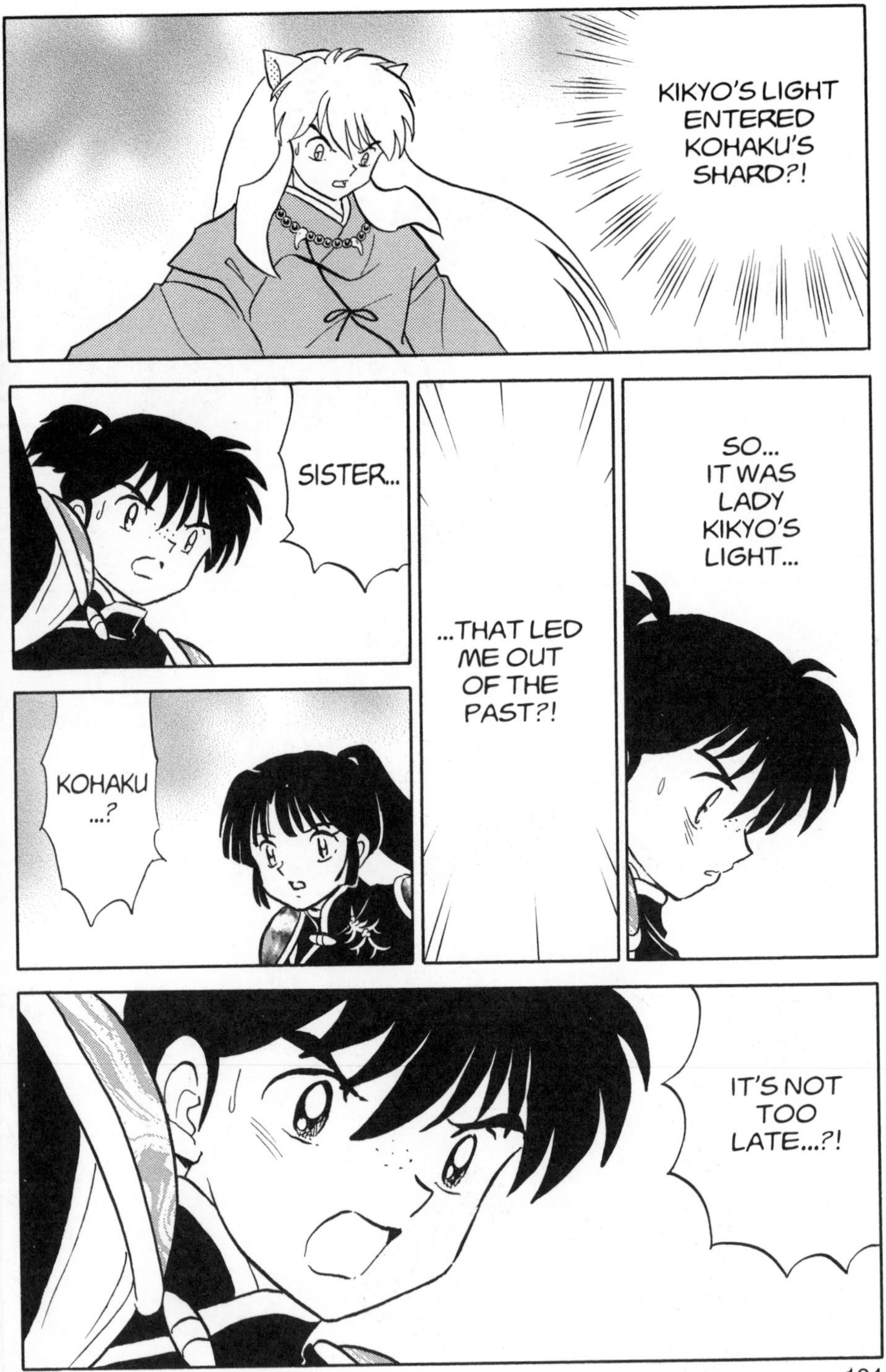

KIKYO'S LIGHT ENTERED KOHAKU'S SHARD?!
SO... IT WAS LADY KIKYO'S LIGHT...
...THAT LED ME OUT OF THE PAST?!
SISTER...
KOHAKU ...?
IT'S NOT TOO LATE...?!

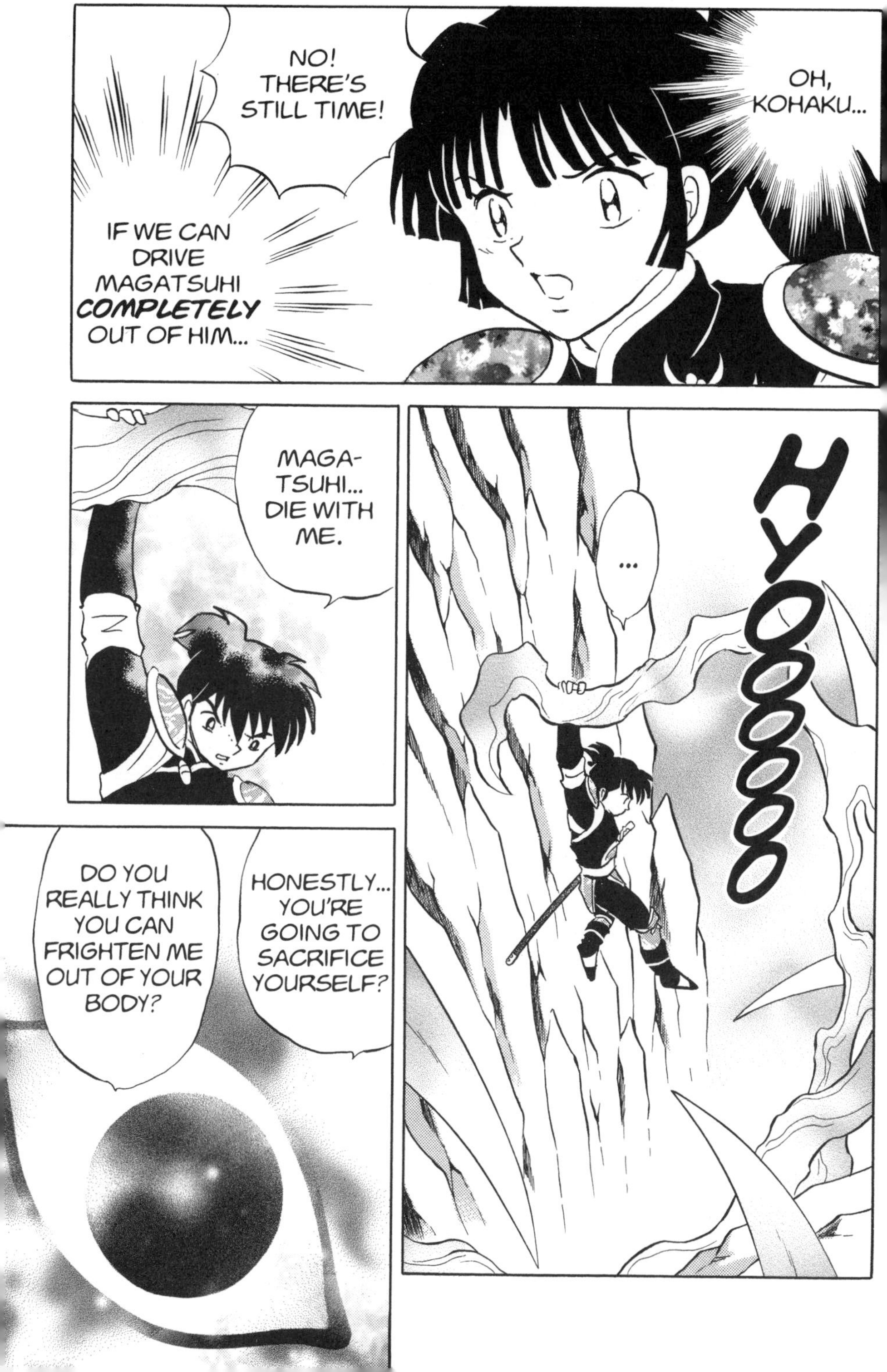
OH, KOHAKU...
NO! THERE'S STILL TIME!
IF WE CAN DRIVE MAGATSUHI **COMPLETELY** OUT OF HIM...
HYOOOOOO
...
MAGA-TSUHI... DIE WITH ME.
HONESTLY... YOU'RE GOING TO SACRIFICE YOURSELF?
DO YOU REALLY THINK YOU CAN FRIGHTEN ME OUT OF YOUR BODY?

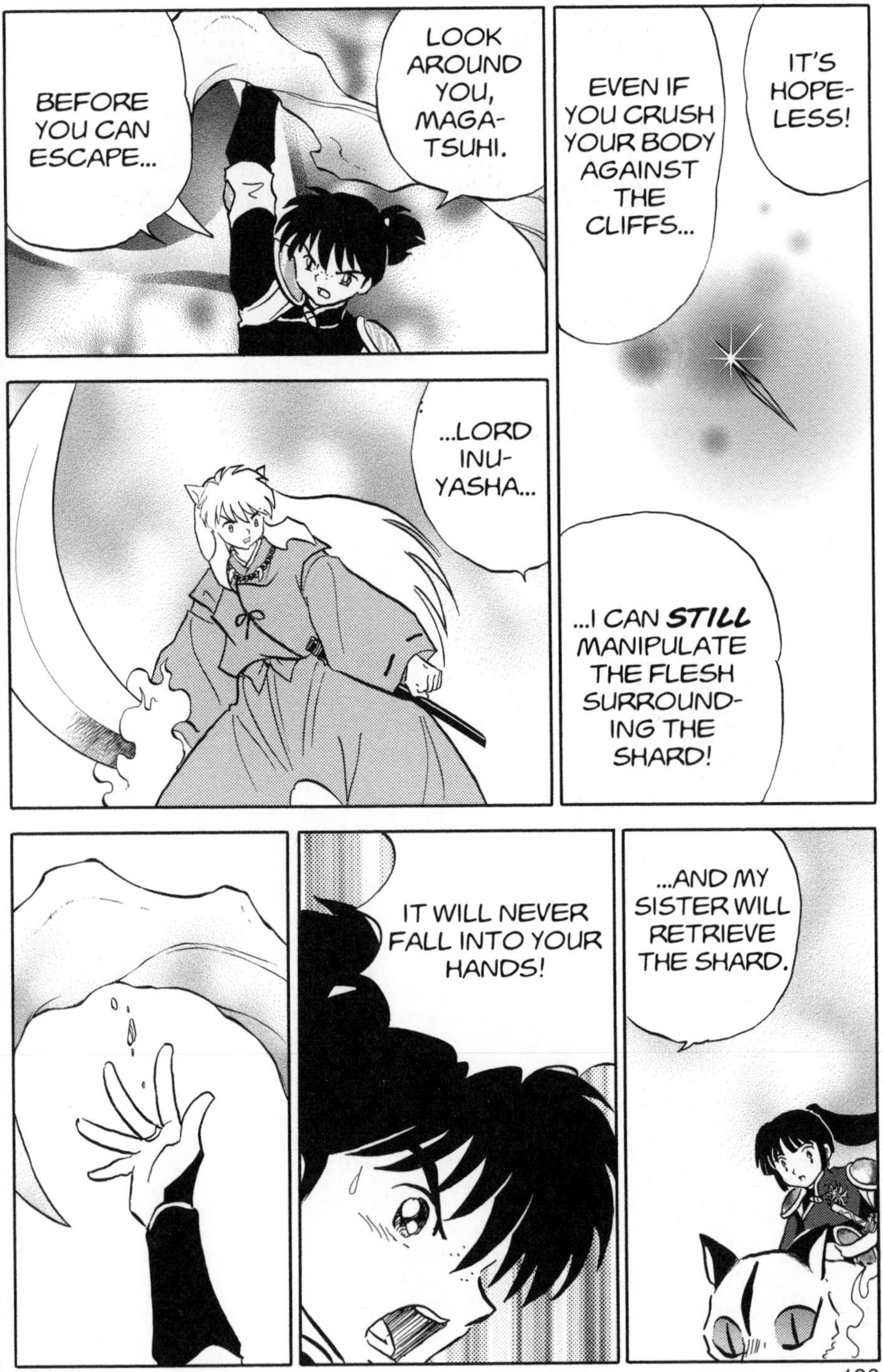
IT'S HOPE-LESS!
EVEN IF YOU CRUSH YOUR BODY AGAINST THE CLIFFS...
...I CAN **STILL** MANIPULATE THE FLESH SURROUND-ING THE SHARD!
LOOK AROUND YOU, MAGA-TSUHI.
BEFORE YOU CAN ESCAPE...
...LORD INU-YASHA...
...AND MY SISTER WILL RETRIEVE THE SHARD.
IT WILL NEVER FALL INTO YOUR HANDS!

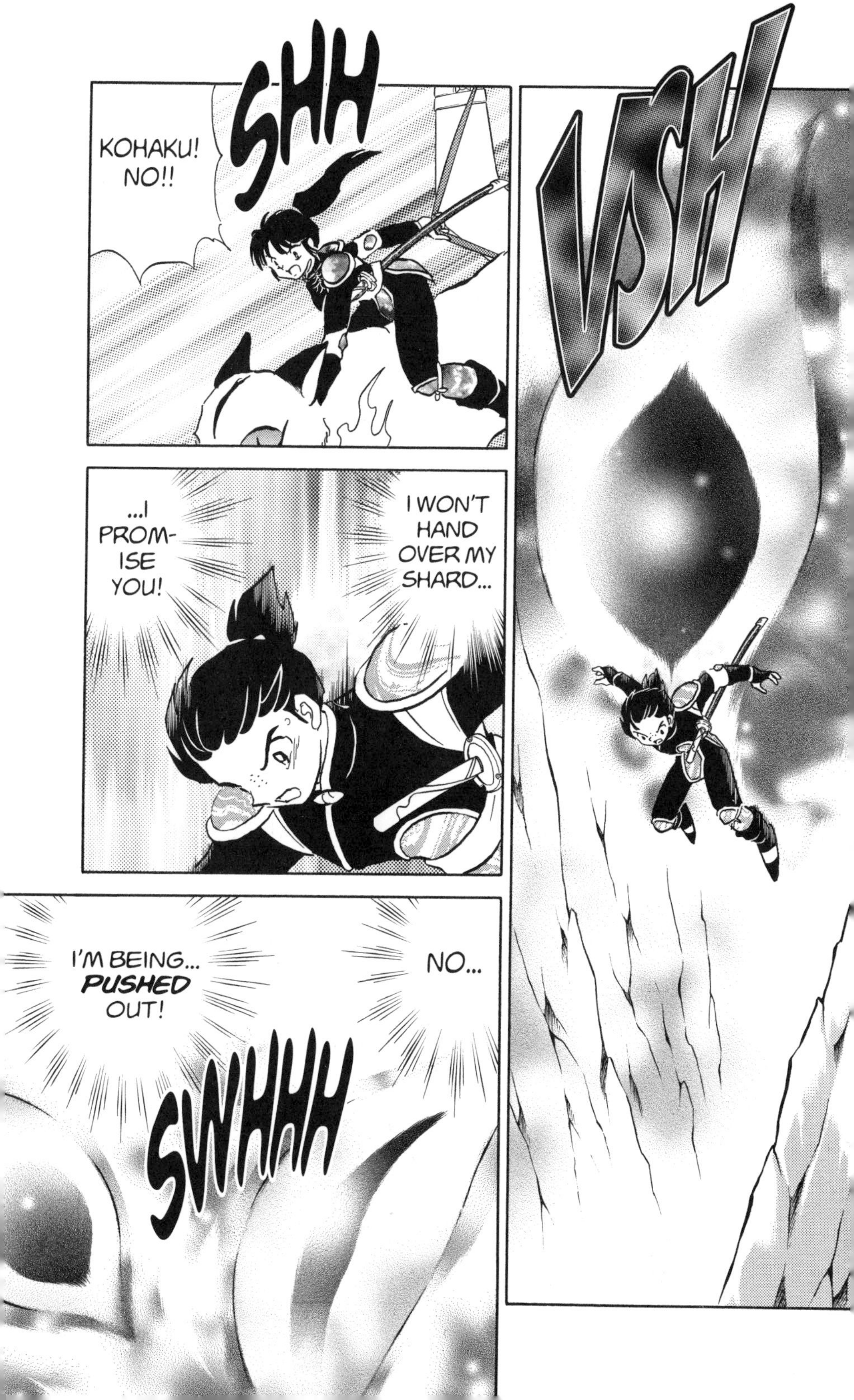
VSH
SHH
KOHAKU! NO!!
I WON'T HAND OVER MY SHARD...
...I PROM-ISE YOU!
NO...
I'M BEING... **PUSHED** OUT!
SWHHH

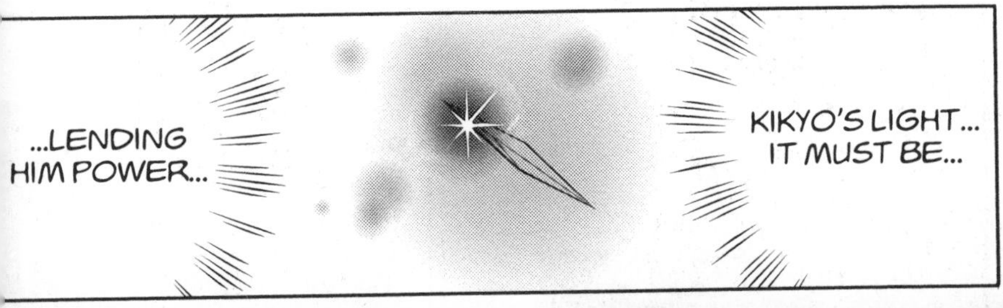
KIKYO'S LIGHT... IT MUST BE...
...LENDING HIM POWER...
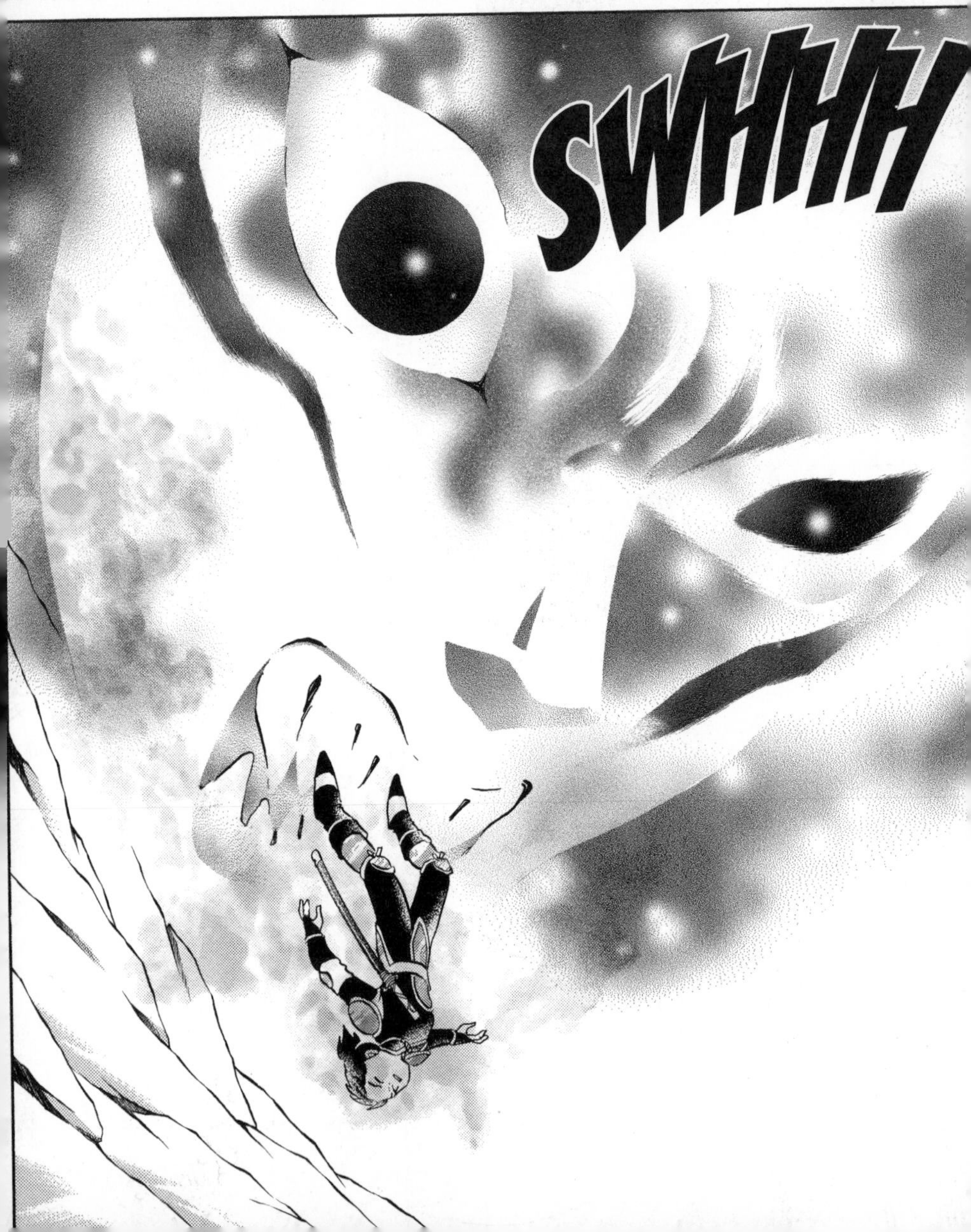
SWHHHH

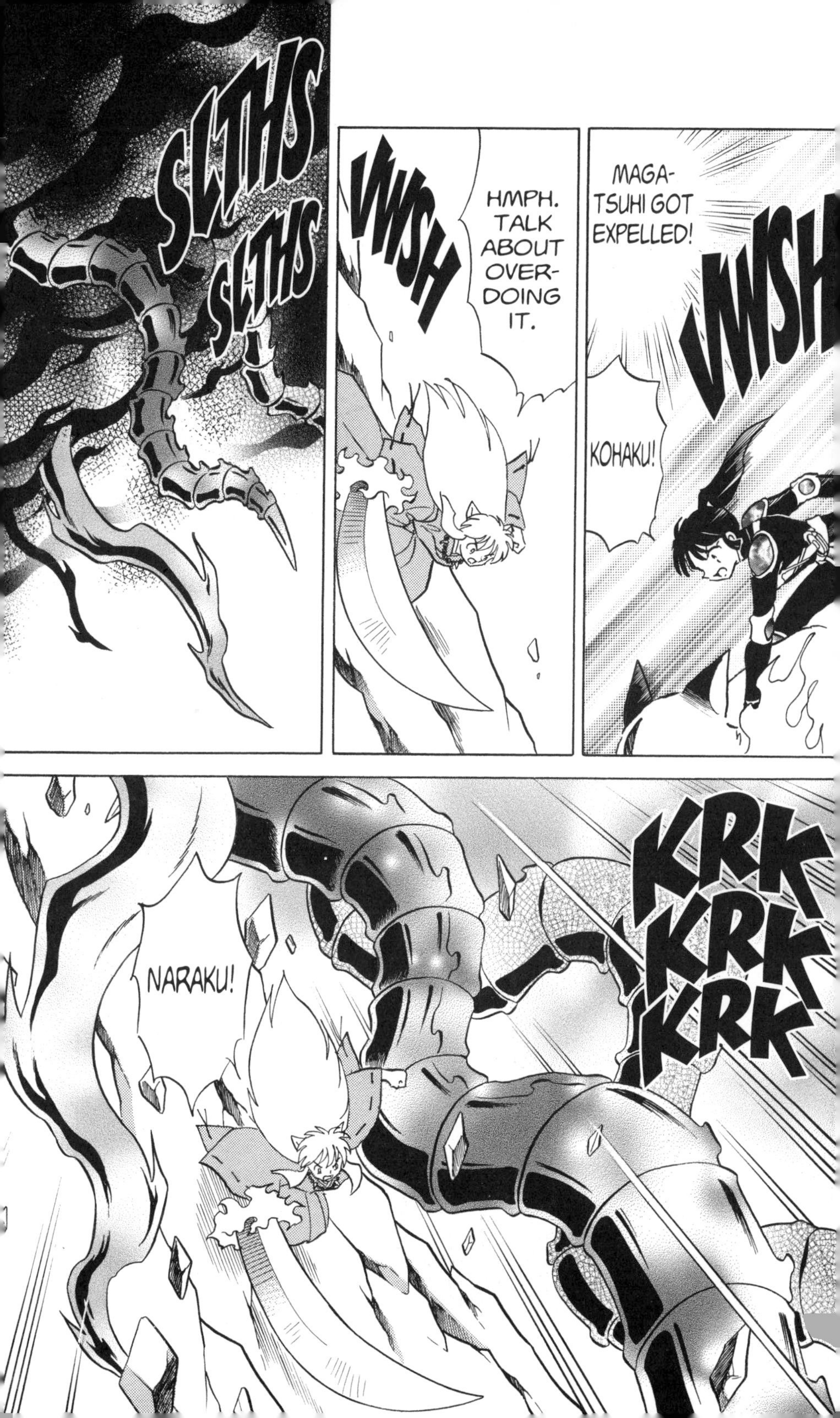

MAGA-TSUHI GOT EXPELLED!
VWISH
KOHAKU!
HMPH. TALK ABOUT OVER-DOING IT.
VWISH
SLITHS SLITHS
KRK KRK KRK
NARAKU!

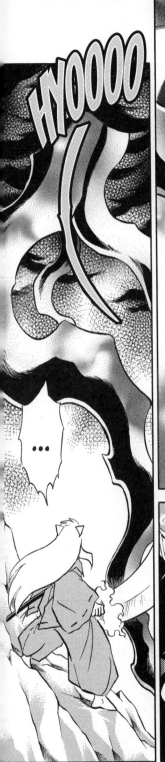

HYOOOO

...

HEH
HEH
HEH...

NRRG

KRK
KRK

SISTER...CUT
THE FEELER!
PLEASE!

KOHA-
KU!

VWSH

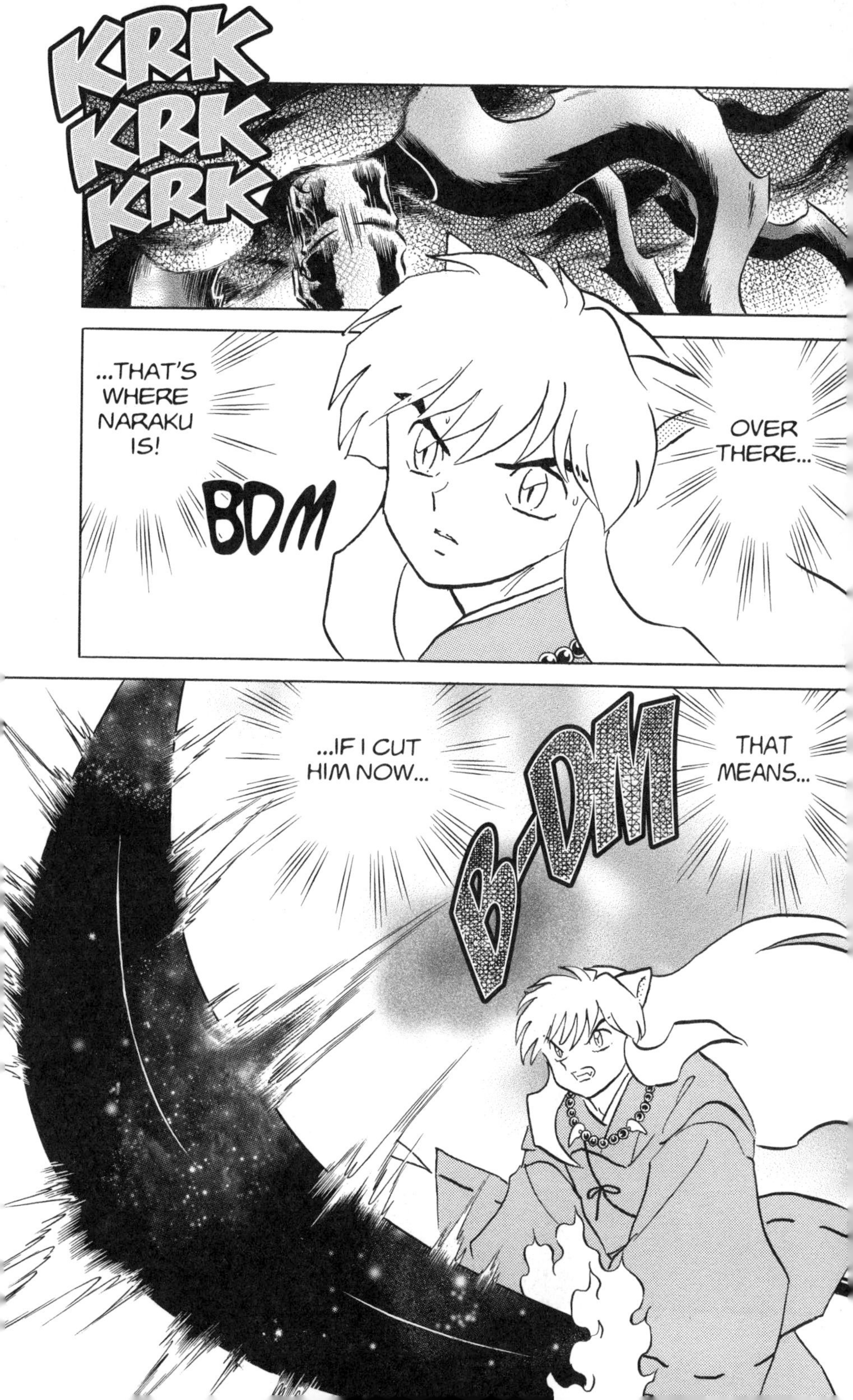
KRK KRK KRK
OVER THERE...
...THAT'S WHERE NARAKU IS!
BDM
THAT MEANS...
...IF I CUT HIM NOW...
B-DM

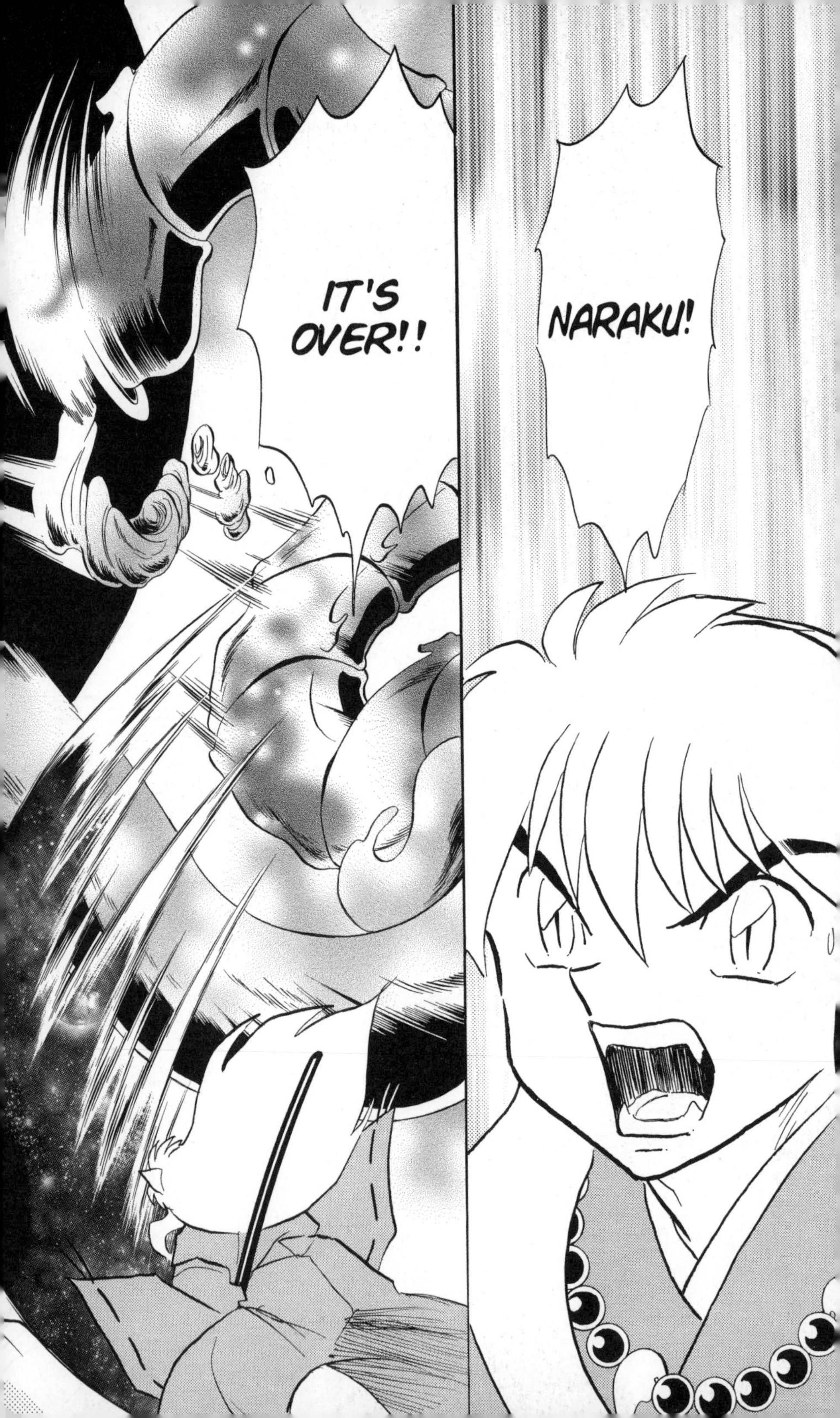
NARAKU!
IT'S OVER!!

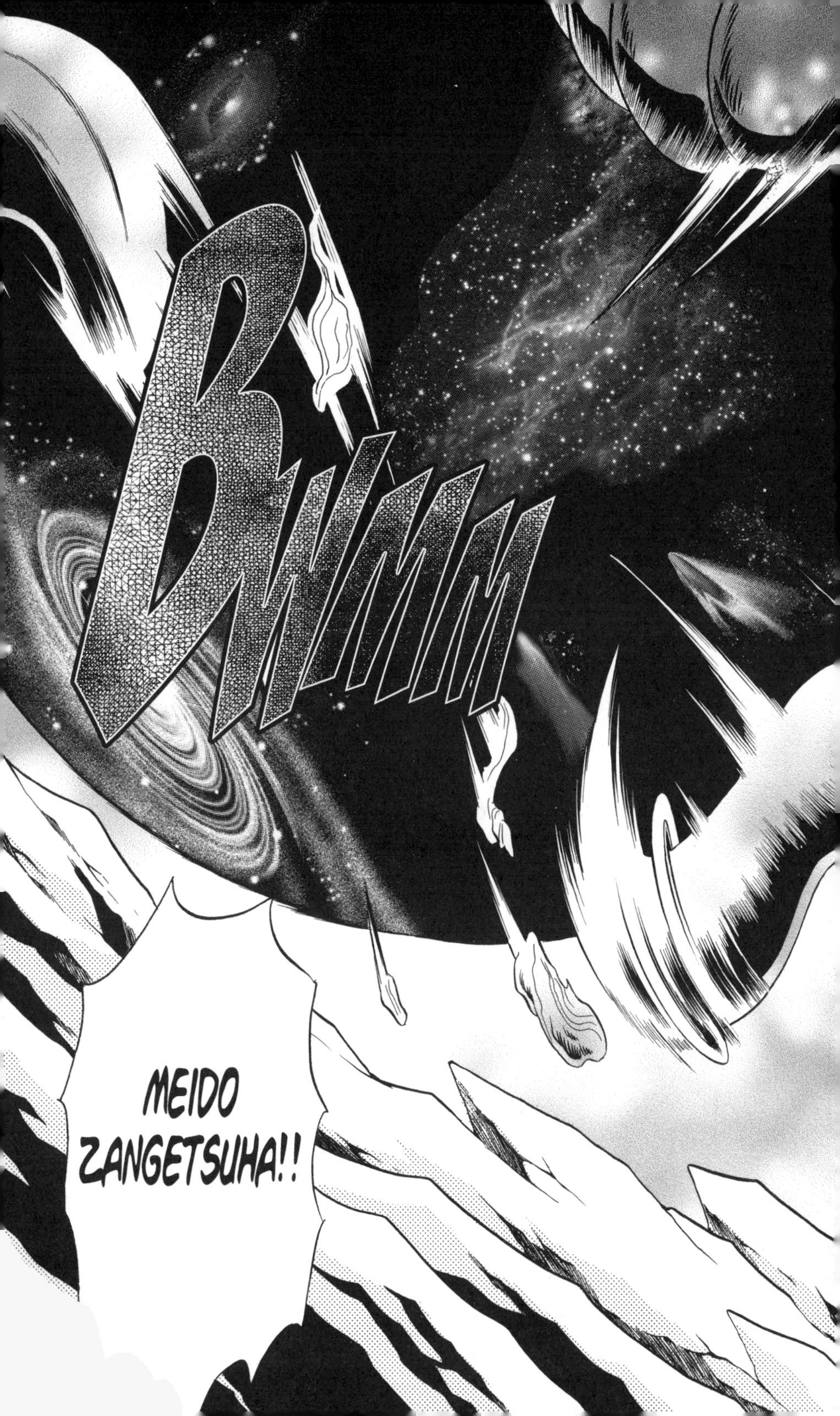
BWMMM
MEIDO ZANGETSUHA!!

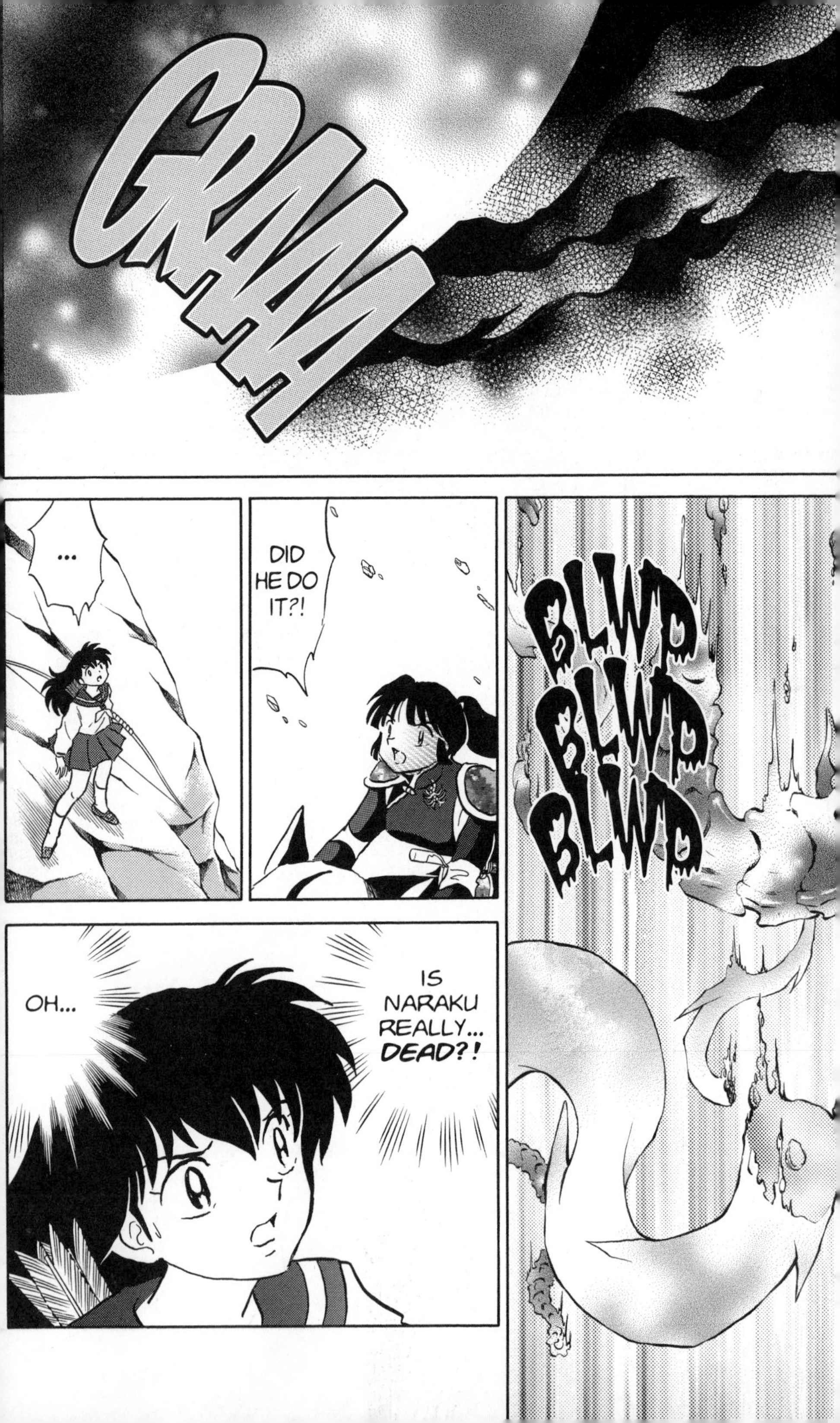
GRAAA
BLWP BLWP BLWP
DID HE DO IT?!
...
IS NARAKU REALLY... *DEAD?!*
OH...

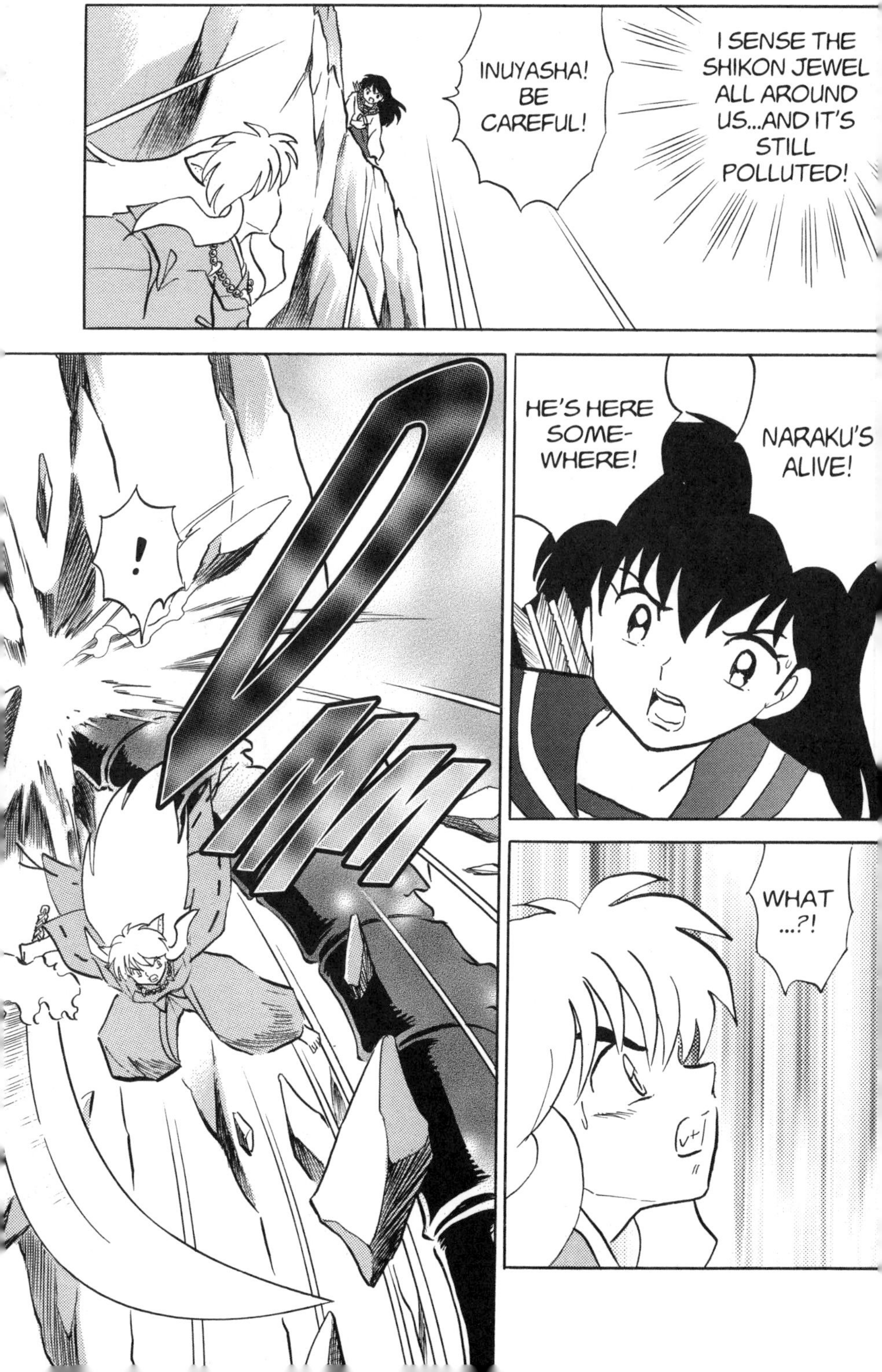
I SENSE THE SHIKON JEWEL ALL AROUND US...AND IT'S STILL POLLUTED!
INUYASHA! BE CAREFUL!
NARAKU'S ALIVE!
HE'S HERE SOME-WHERE!
WHAT ...?!
!

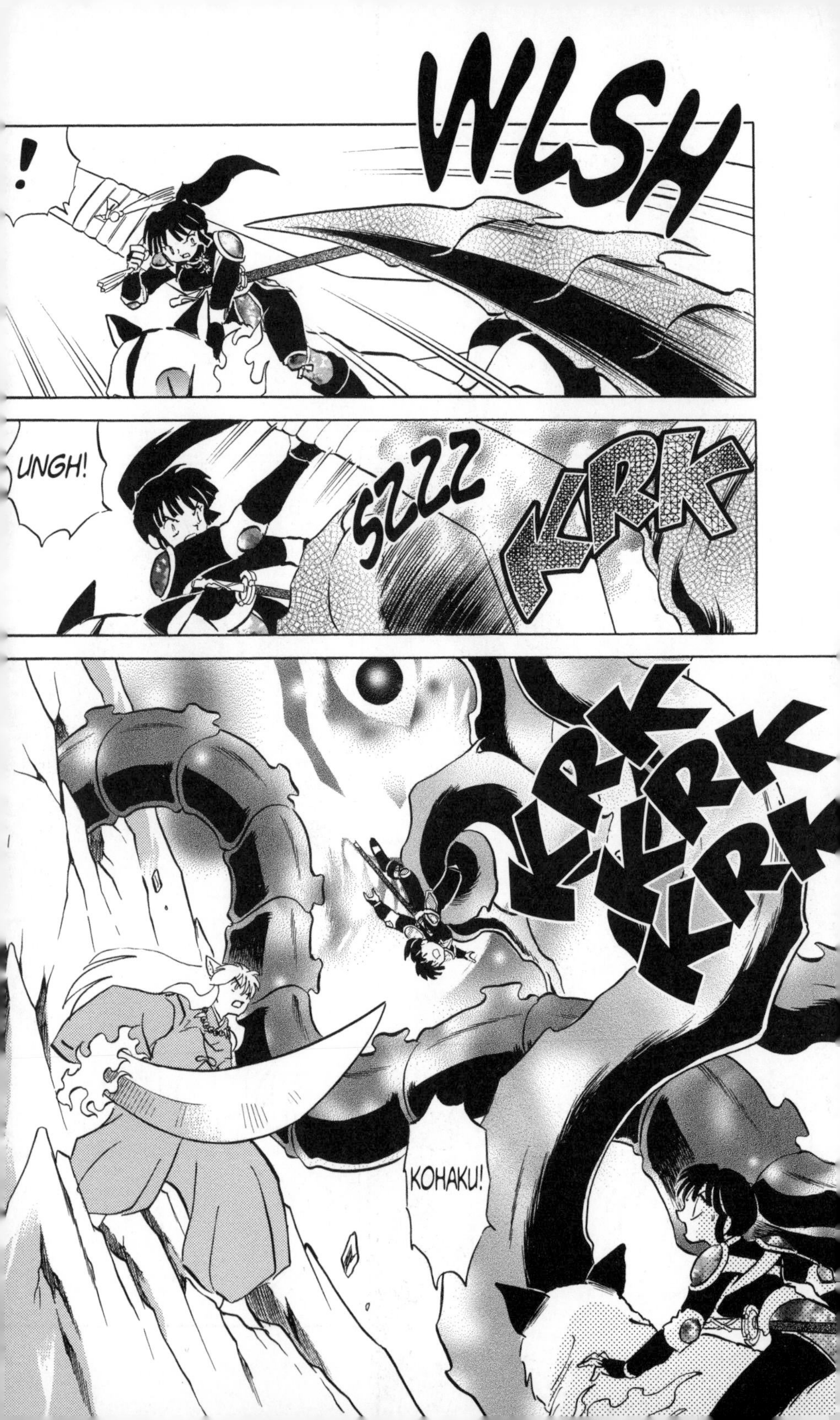
WLSH
!
SZZZ
KRK
UNGH!
KRK KRK KRK KRK
KOHAKU!

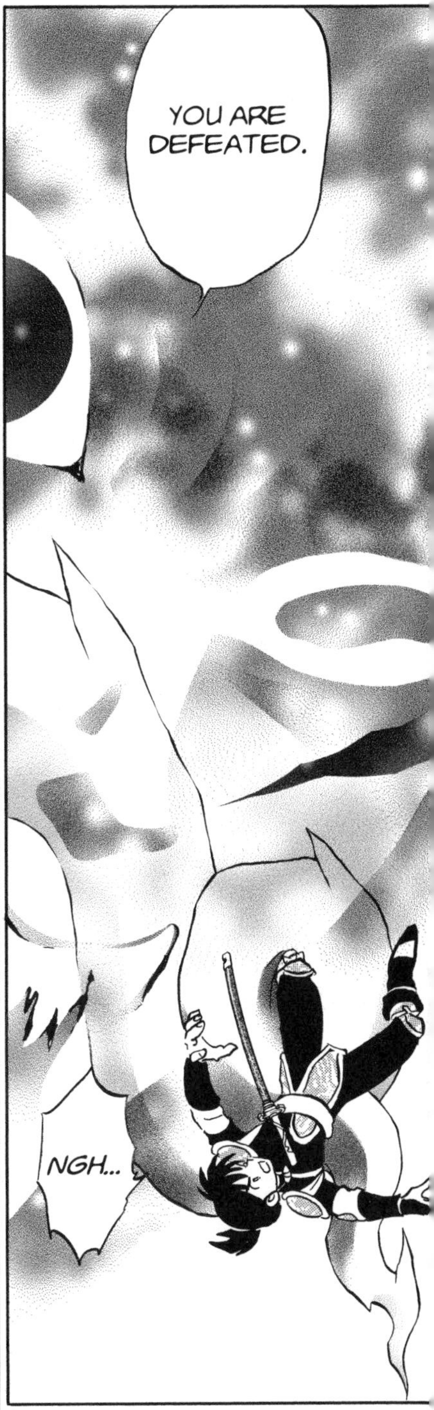
YOU ARE DEFEATED.
NGH...

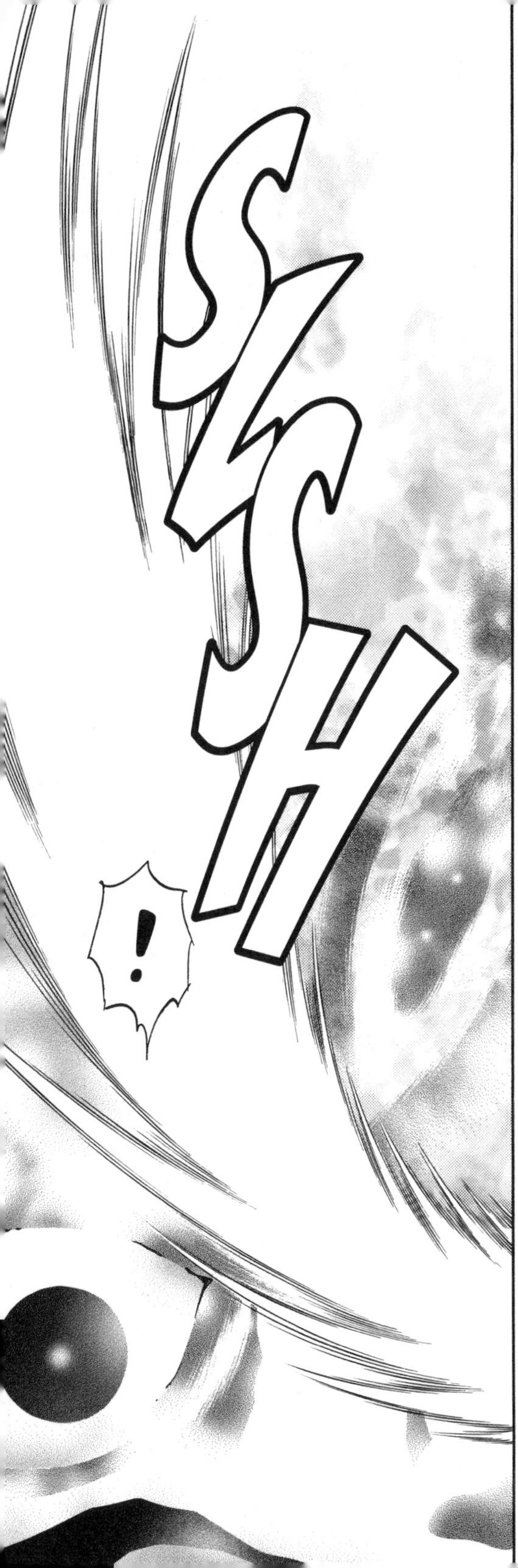
SSSH
!

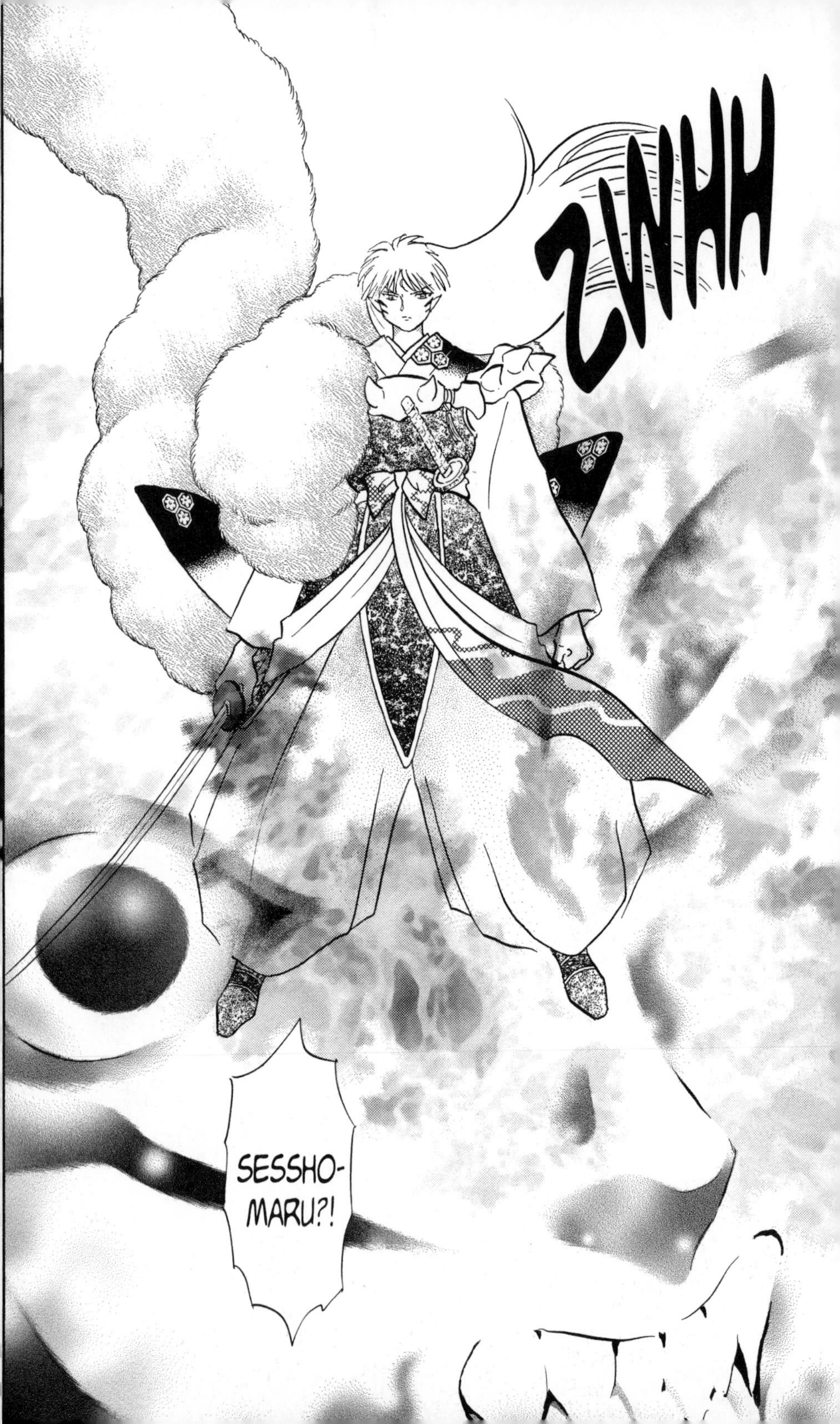
ZWHH
SESSHO-MARU?!

SCROLL EIGHT
THE LOST POWERS

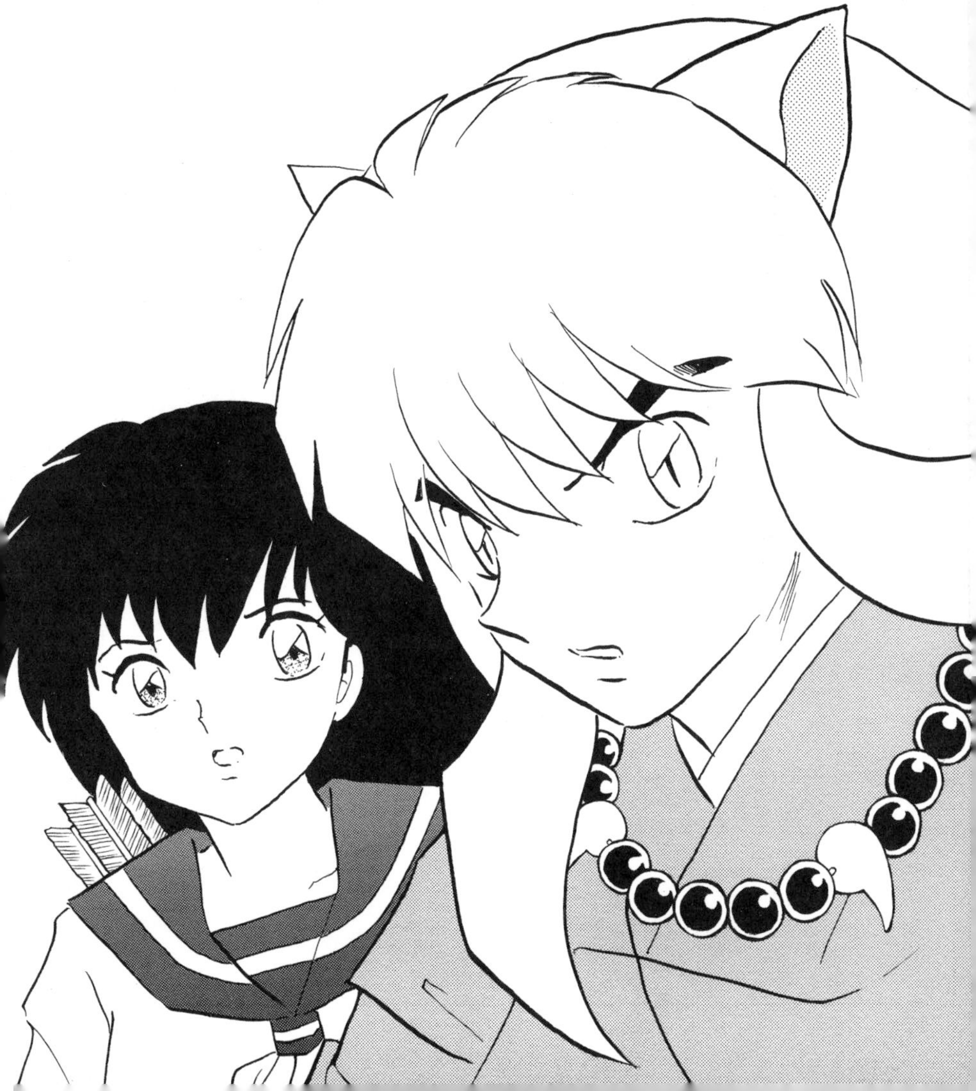

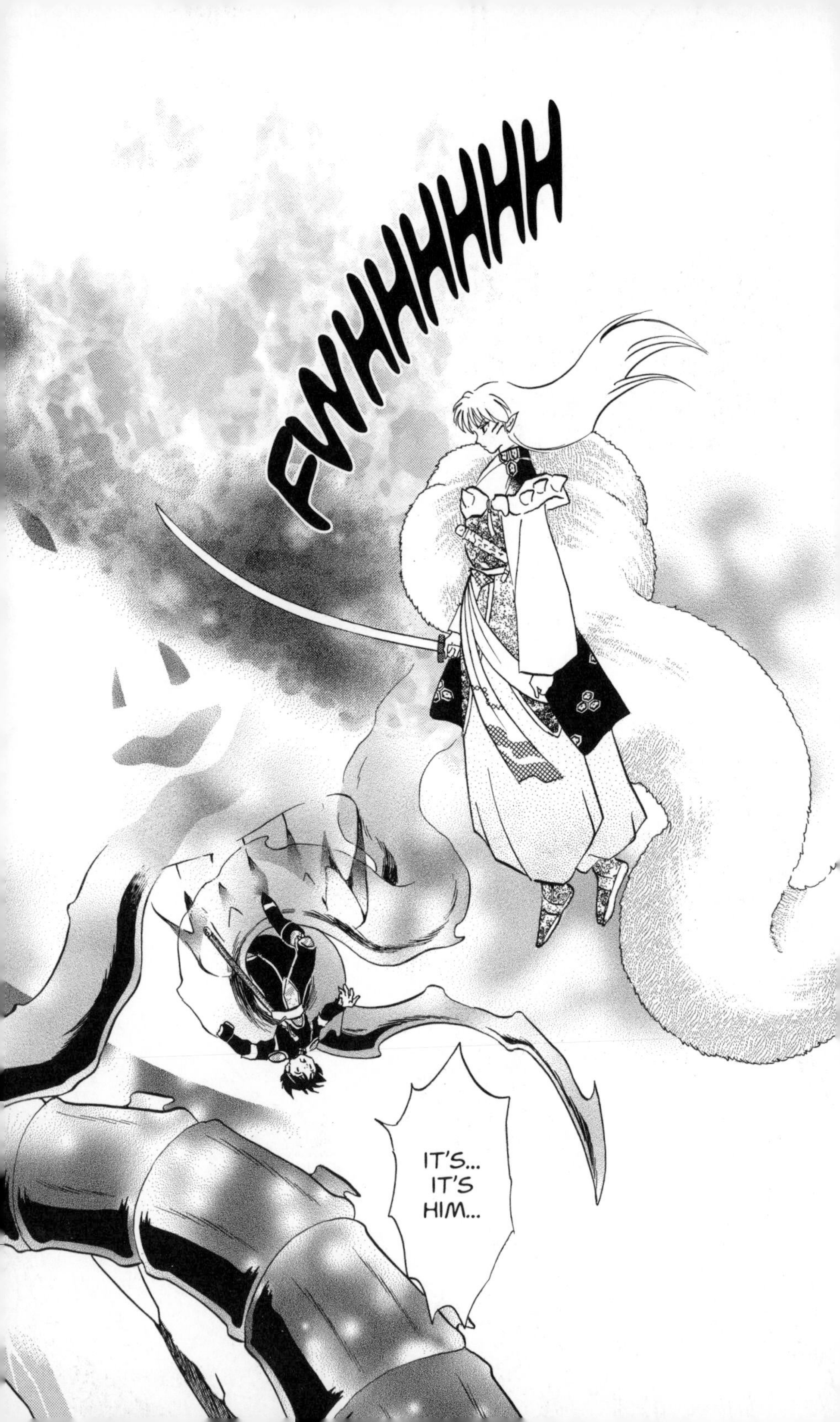
FWHHHHHH
IT'S... IT'S HIM...

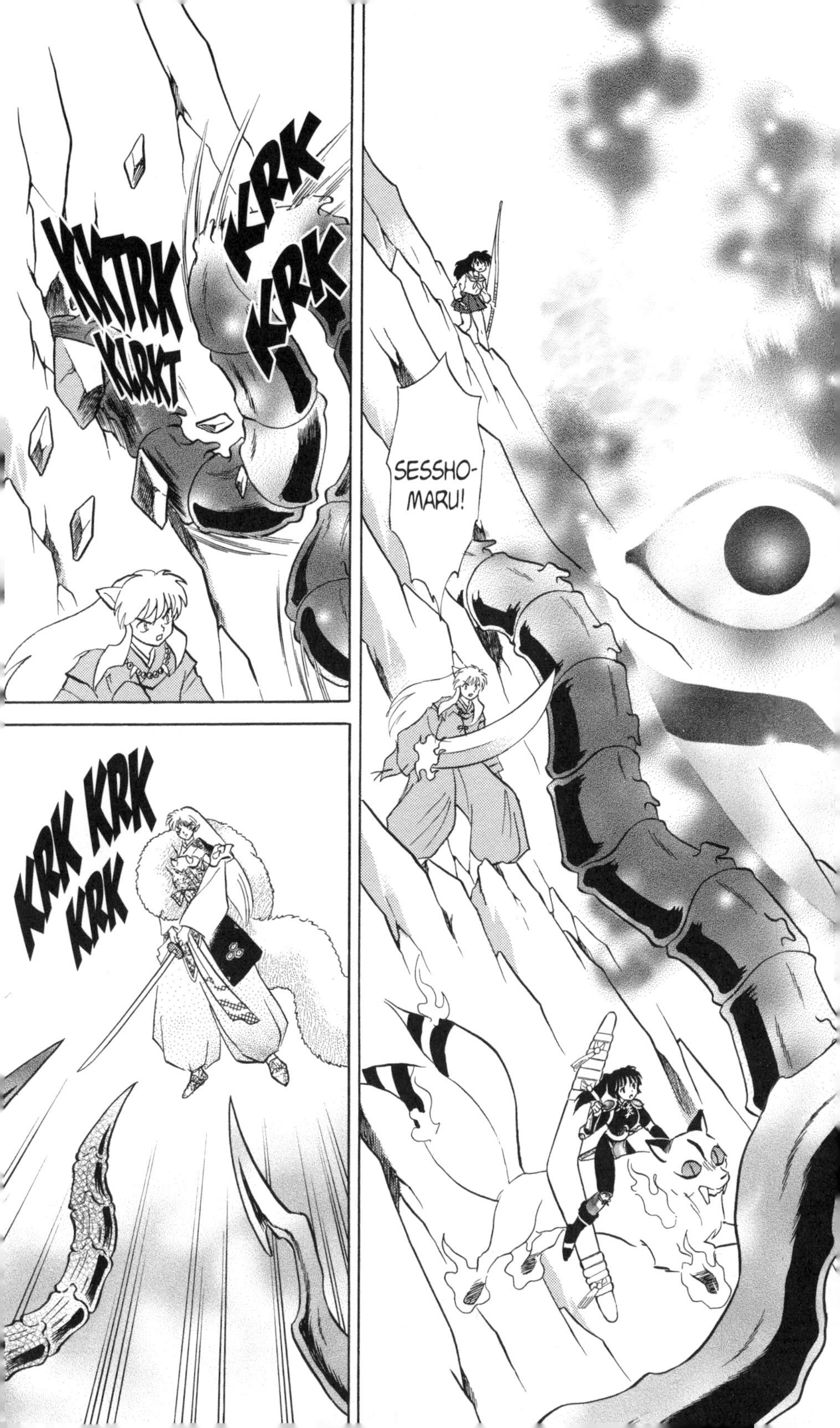
SESSHO-MARU!
KRK KRK
KKTRK KLRKT
KRK KRK KRK

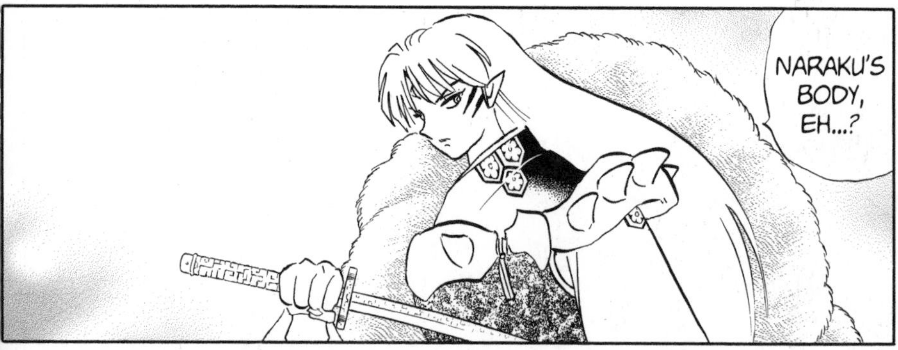
NARAKU'S BODY, EH...?

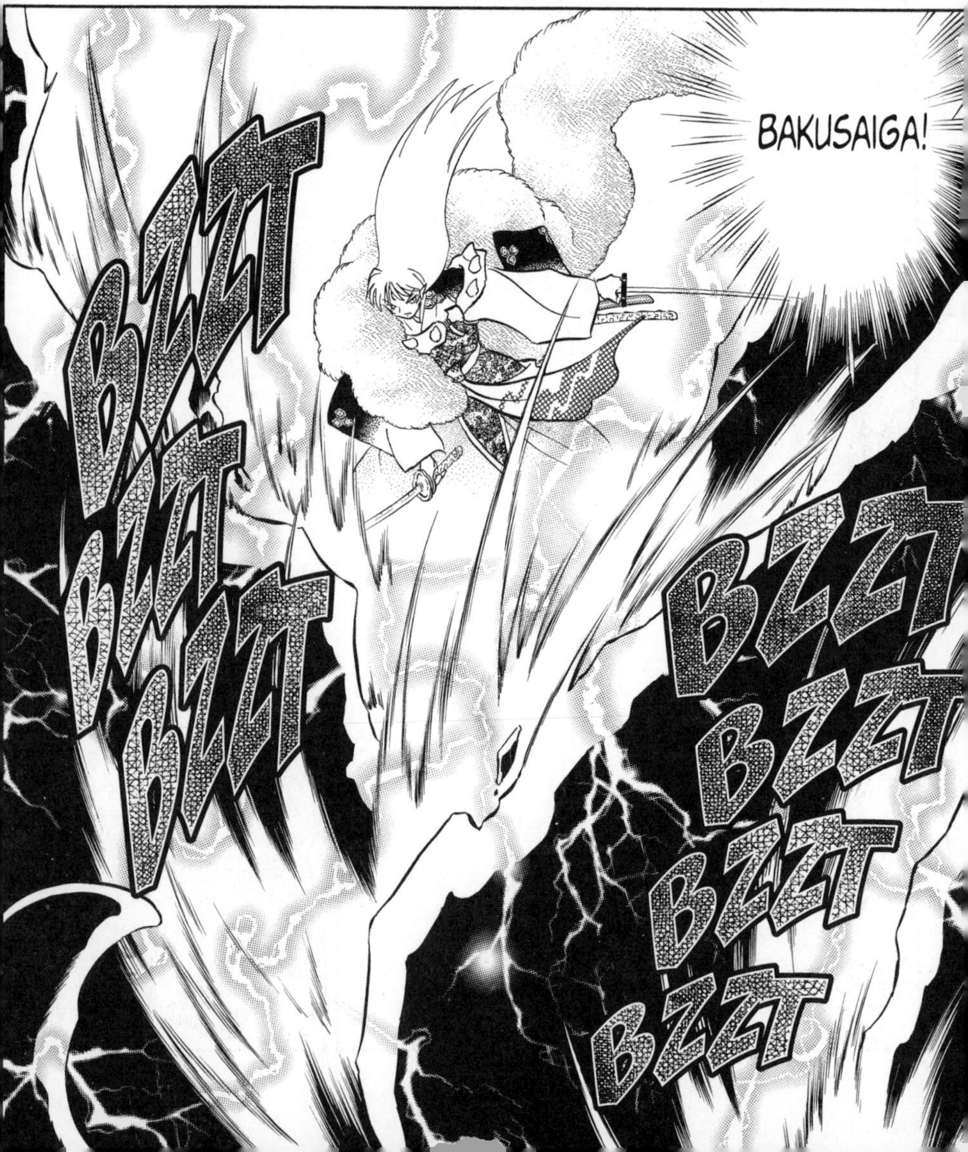
BAKUSAIGA!
BZZT BZZT BZZT BZZT
BZZT BZZT BZZT

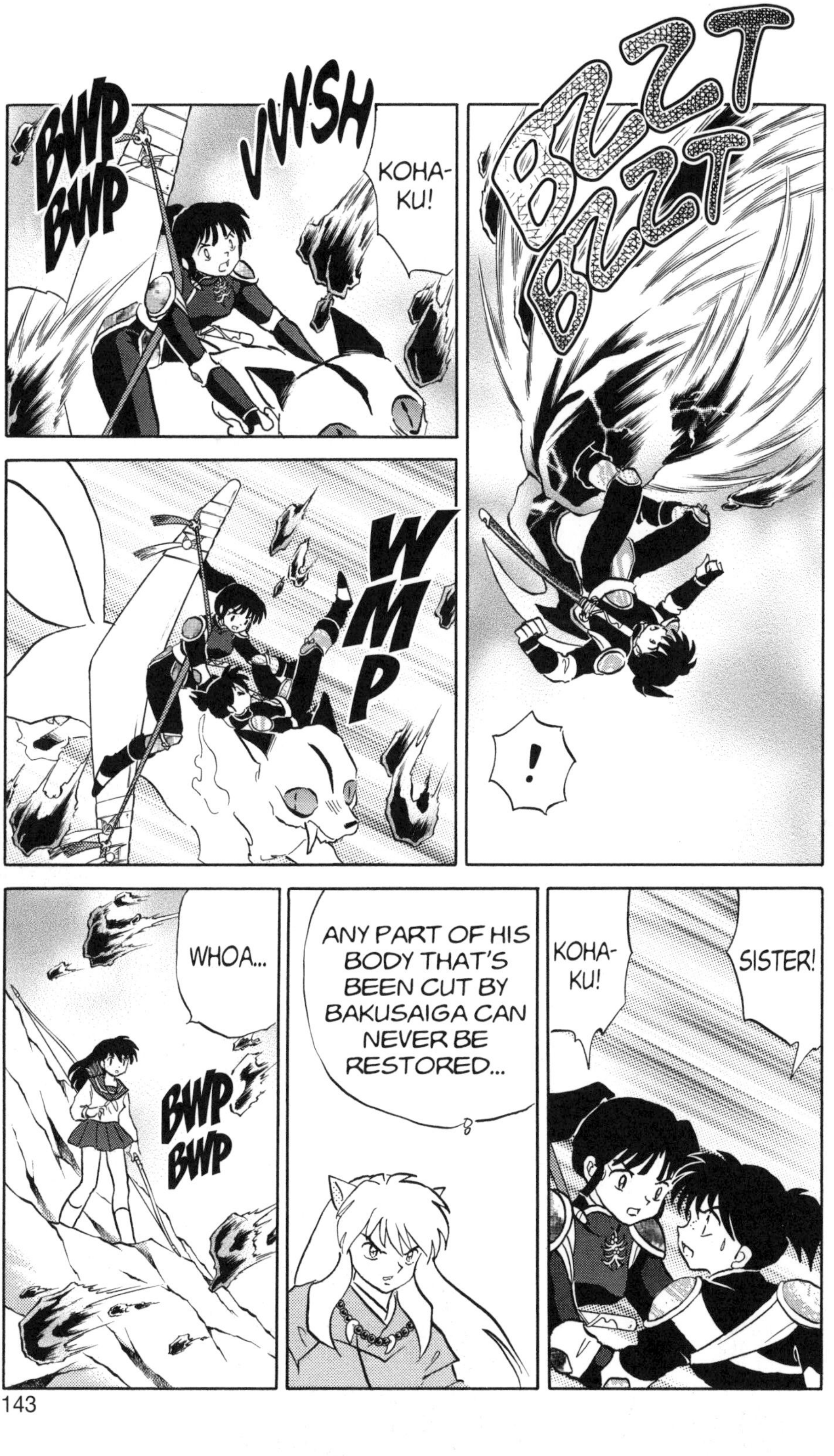
BZZT BZZT
!
VWSH
KOHA-KU!
BWP BWP
WMP
SISTER!
KOHA-KU!
ANY PART OF HIS BODY THAT'S BEEN CUT BY BAKUSAIGA CAN NEVER BE RESTORED...
WHOA...
BWP BWP

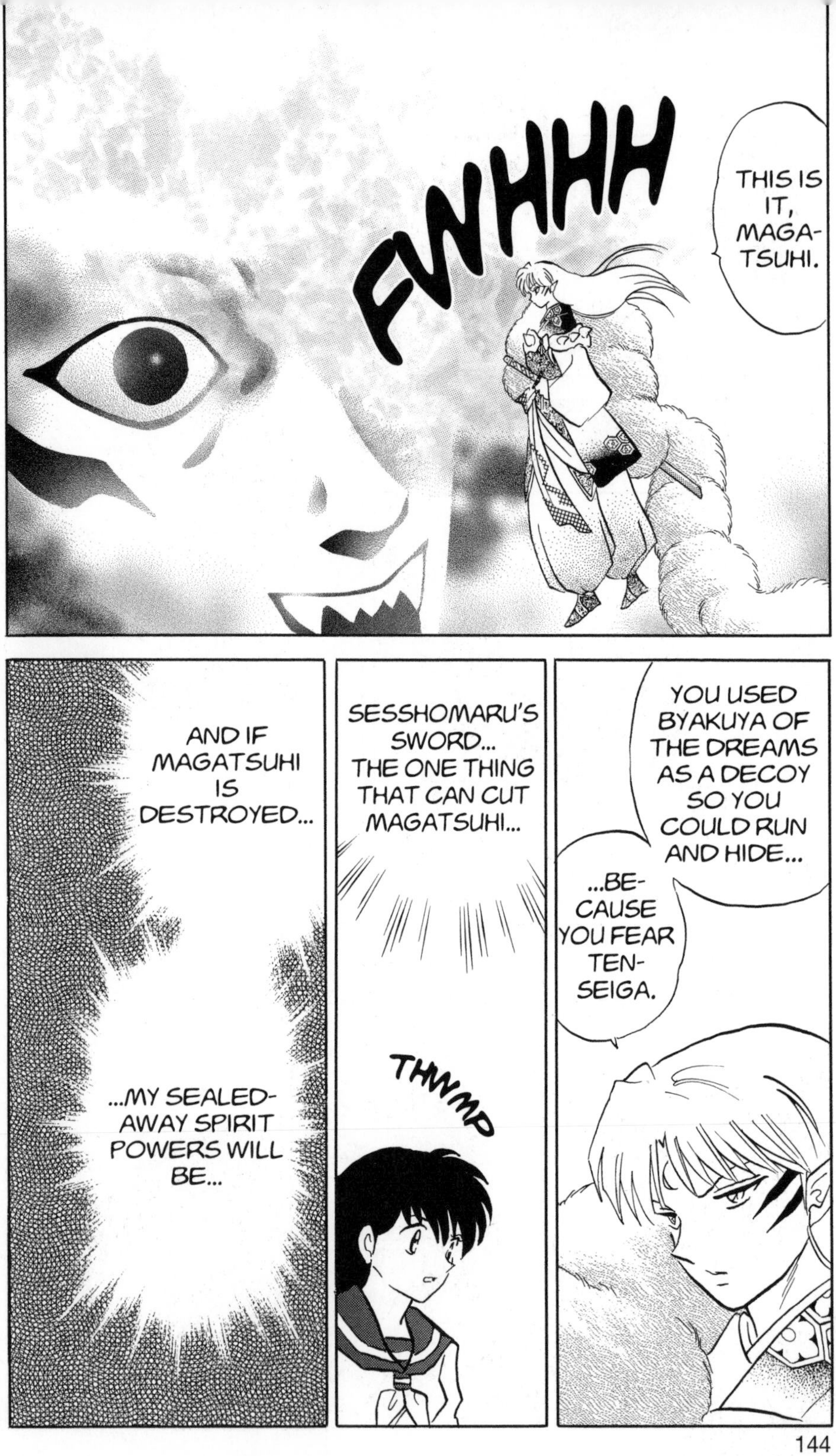
THIS IS IT, MAGA-TSUHI.
FWHHH
YOU USED BYAKUYA OF THE DREAMS AS A DECOY SO YOU COULD RUN AND HIDE...
...BE-CAUSE YOU FEAR TEN-SEIGA.
SESSHOMARU'S SWORD... THE ONE THING THAT CAN CUT MAGATSUHI...
THWMP
AND IF MAGATSUHI IS DESTROYED...
...MY SEALED-AWAY SPIRIT POWERS WILL BE...

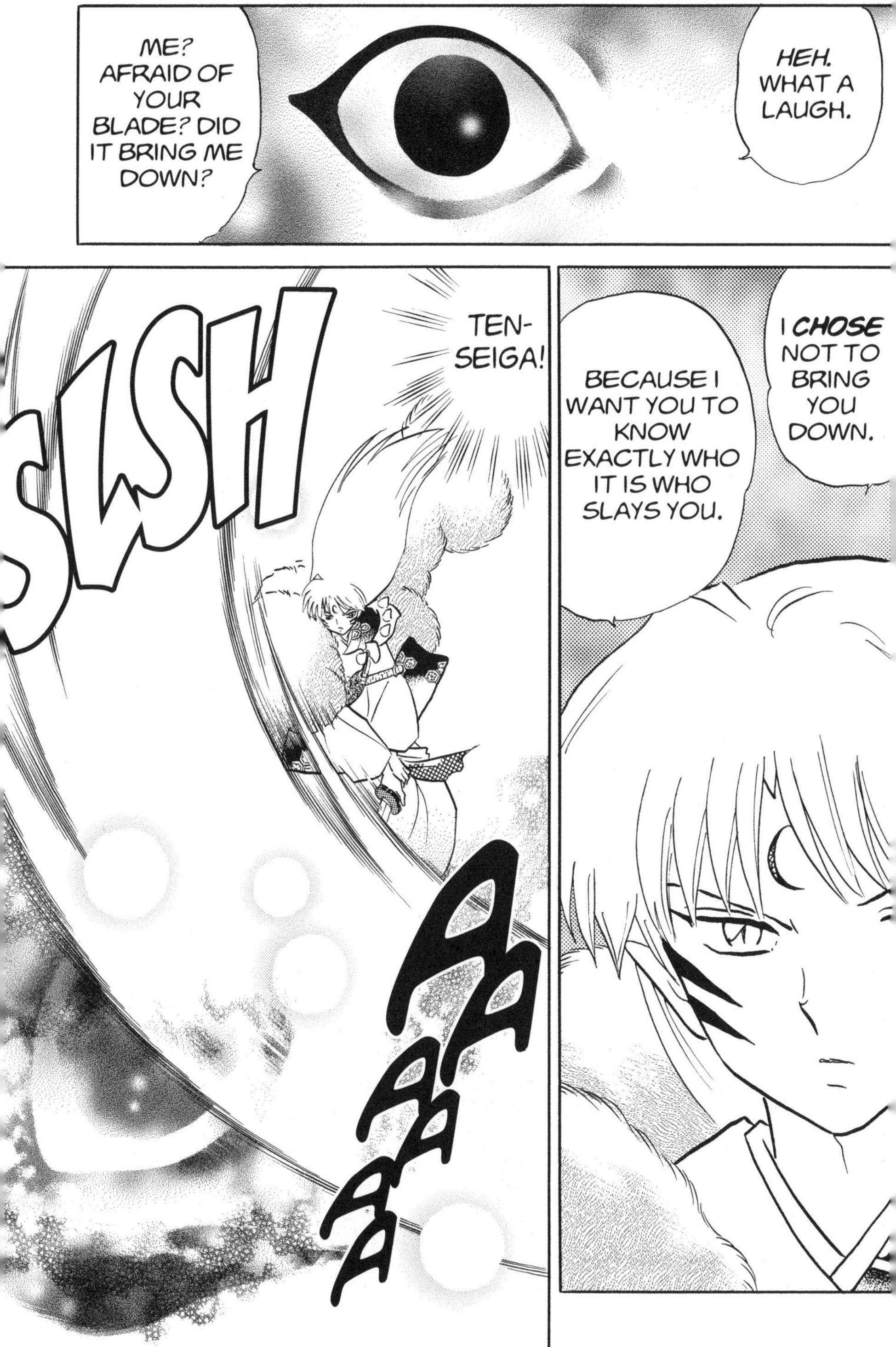
HEH. WHAT A LAUGH.
ME? AFRAID OF YOUR BLADE? DID IT BRING ME DOWN?
I *CHOSE* NOT TO BRING YOU DOWN.
BECAUSE I WANT YOU TO KNOW EXACTLY WHO IT IS WHO SLAYS YOU.
TEN-SEIGA!
SLSH
AAAAAA

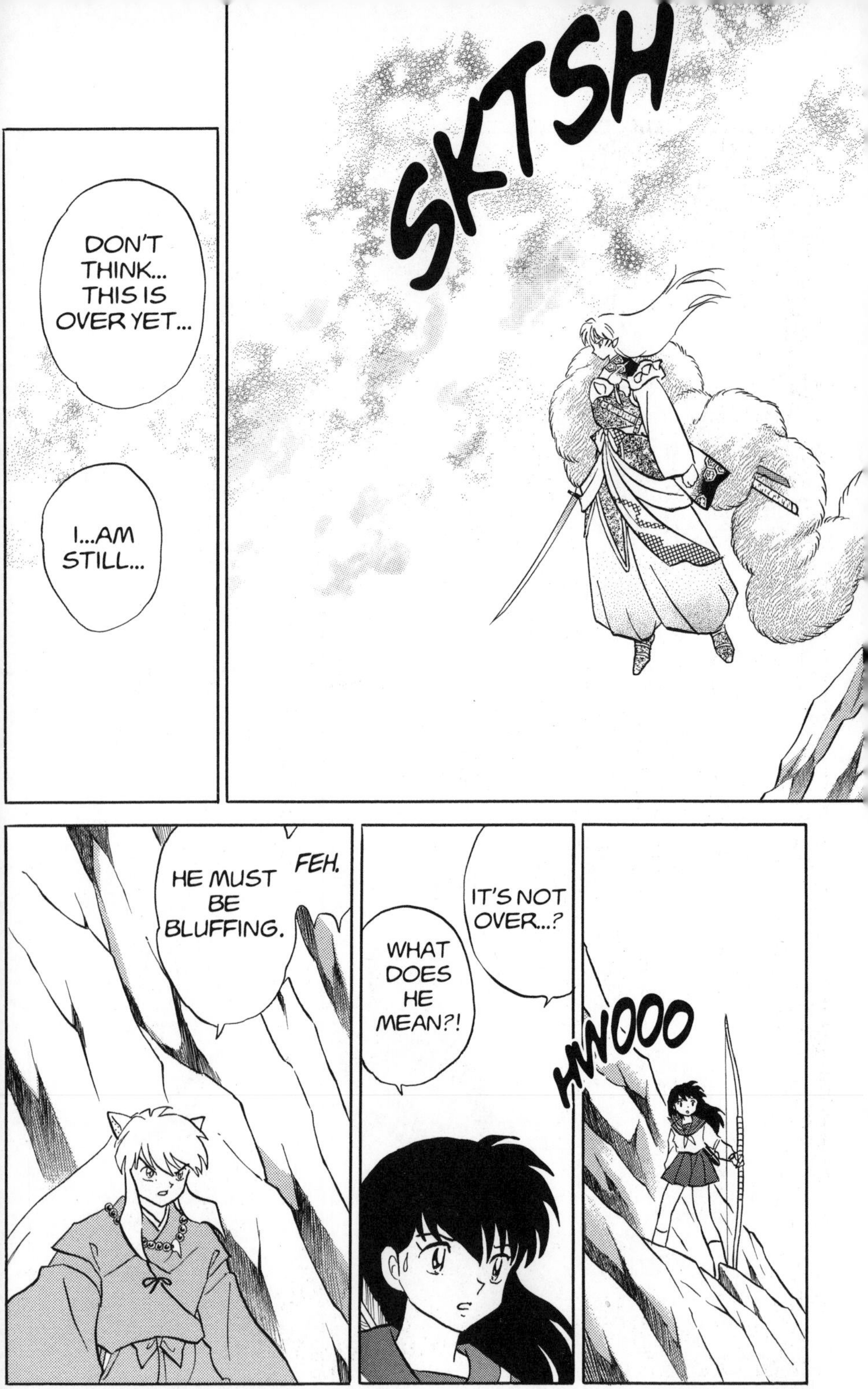
SKTSH
DON'T THINK... THIS IS OVER YET...
I...AM STILL...
HWOOO
IT'S NOT OVER...?
WHAT DOES HE MEAN?!
FEH.
HE MUST BE BLUFFING.

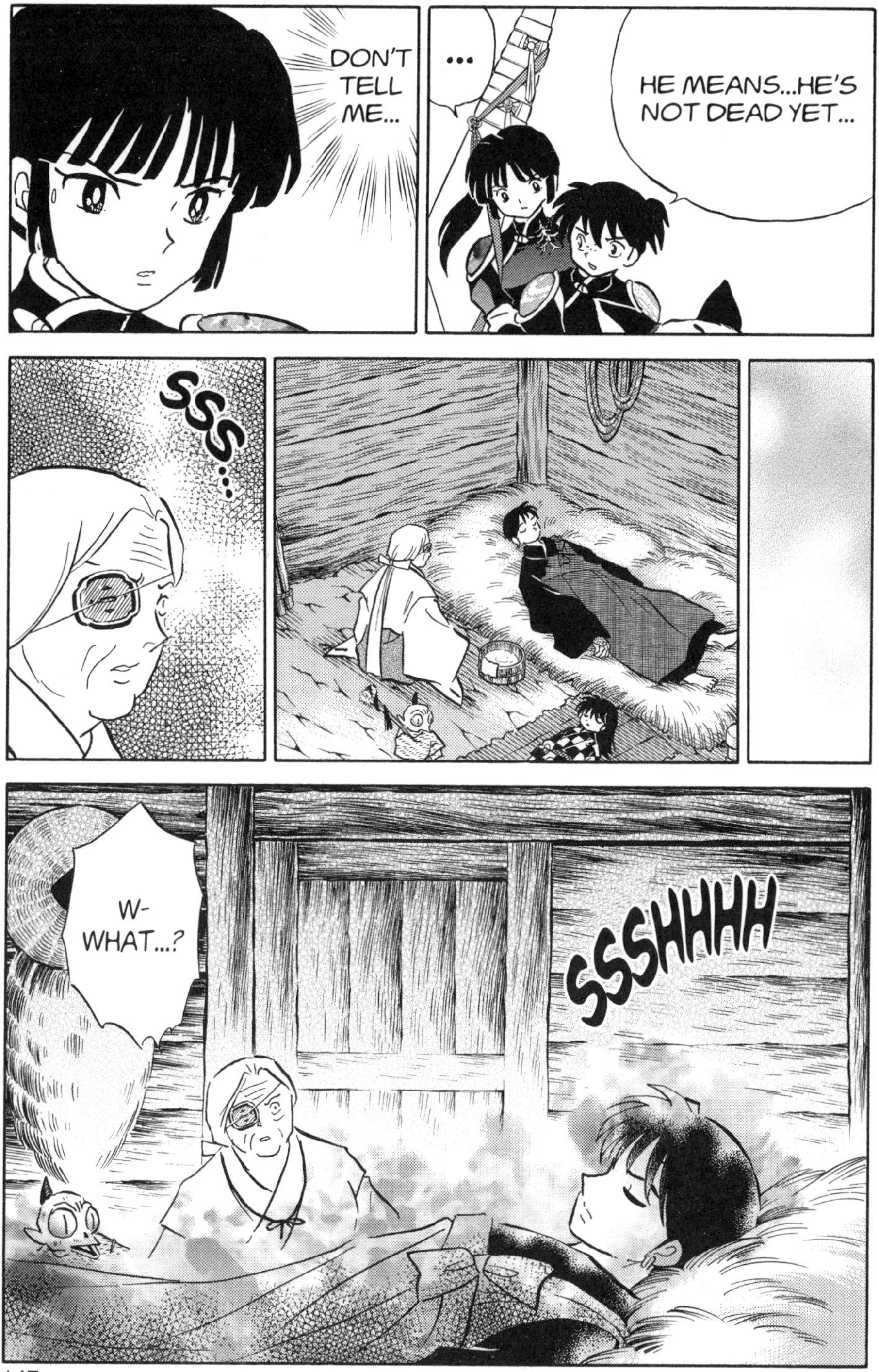
HE MEANS...HE'S NOT DEAD YET...
...
DON'T TELL ME...
SSS...
SSSHHHH
W-WHAT...?

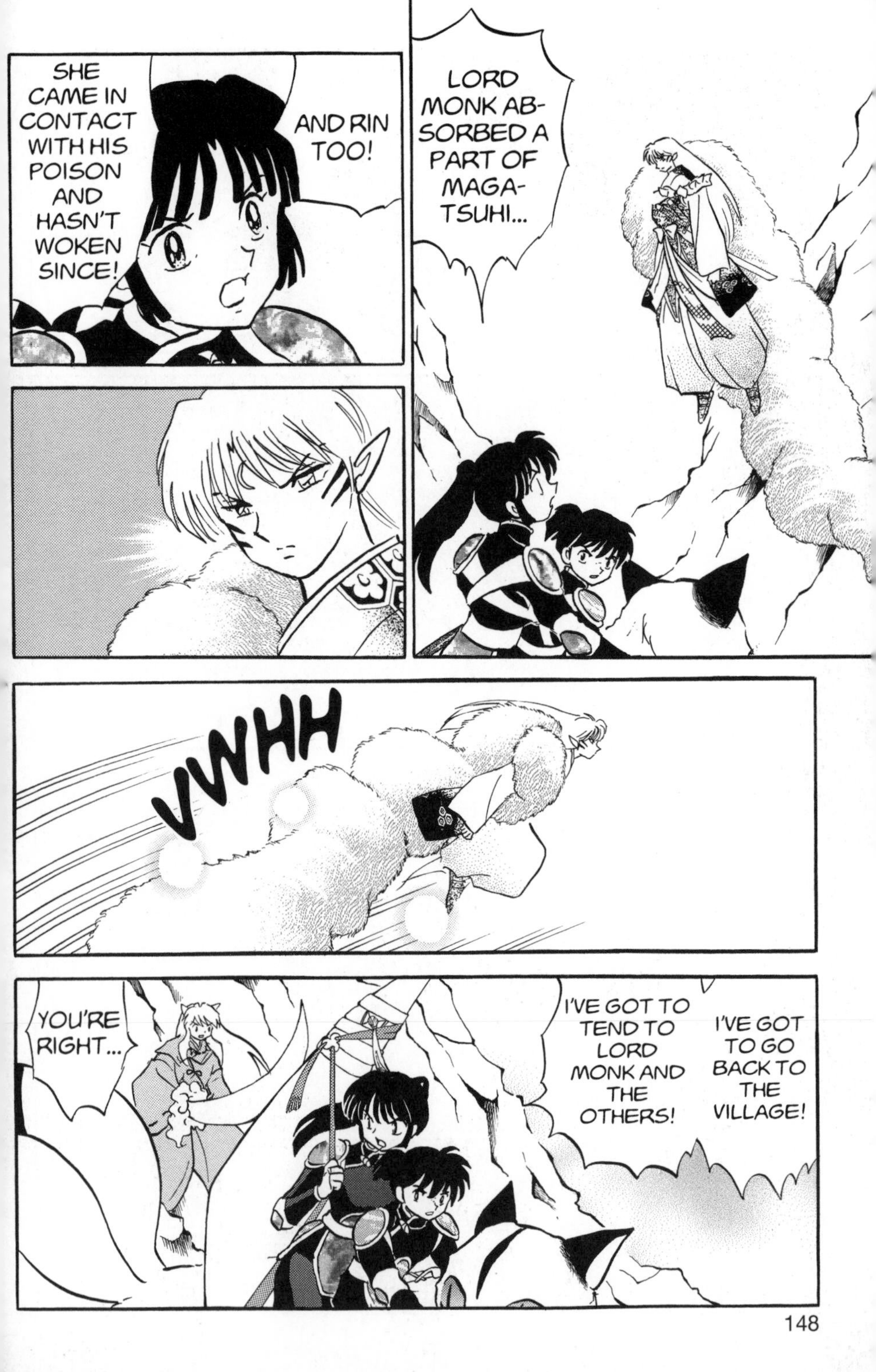
LORD MONK ABSORBED A PART OF MAGATSUHI...
SHE CAME IN CONTACT WITH HIS POISON AND HASN'T WOKEN SINCE!
AND RIN TOO!
VWHH
I'VE GOT TO GO BACK TO THE VILLAGE!
I'VE GOT TO TEND TO LORD MONK AND THE OTHERS!
YOU'RE RIGHT...

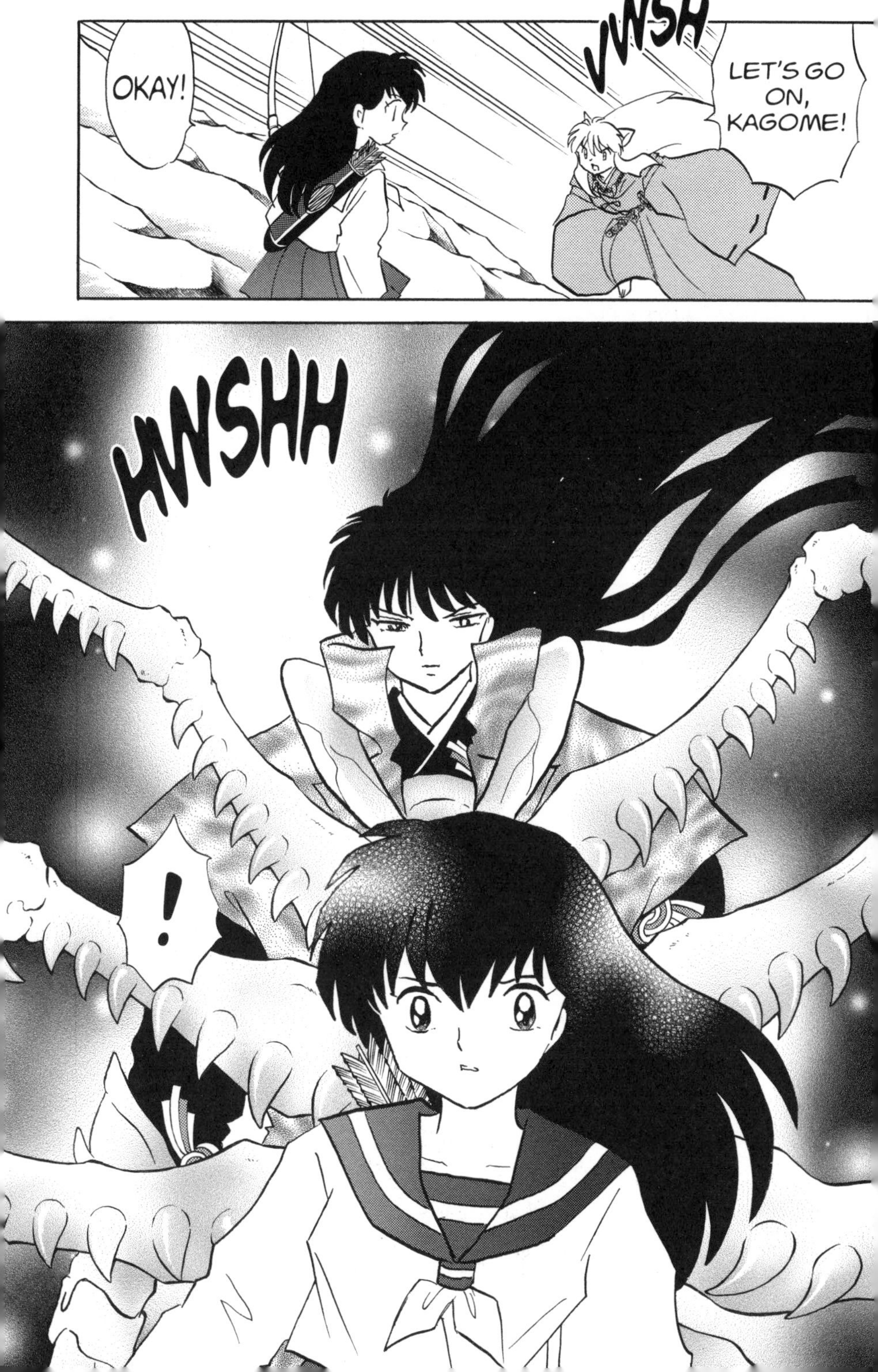
LET'S GO ON, KAGOME!
VWSH
OKAY!
HWSHH
!

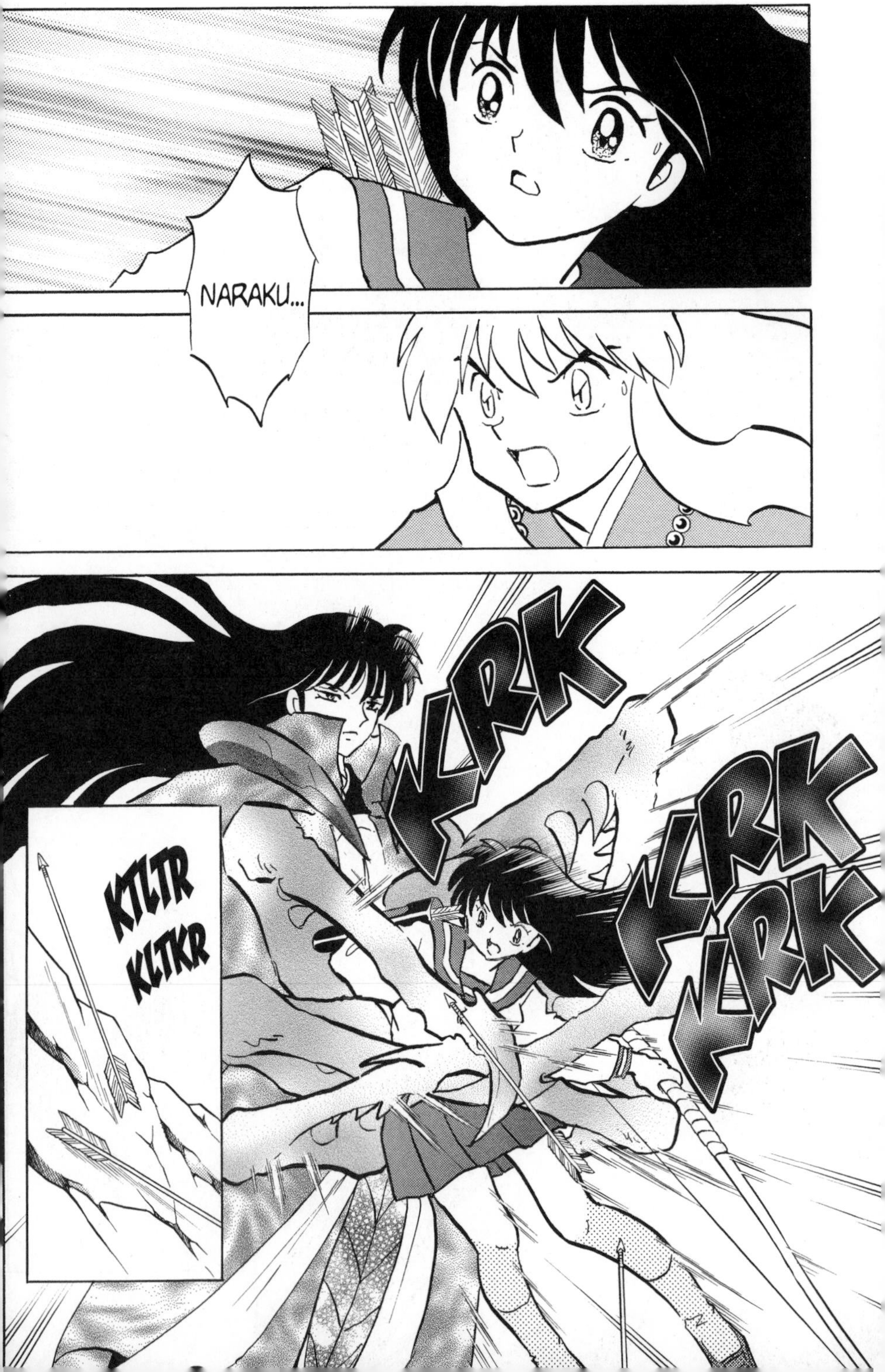
NARAKU...
KRK
KRK
KRK
KTLTR
KLTKR

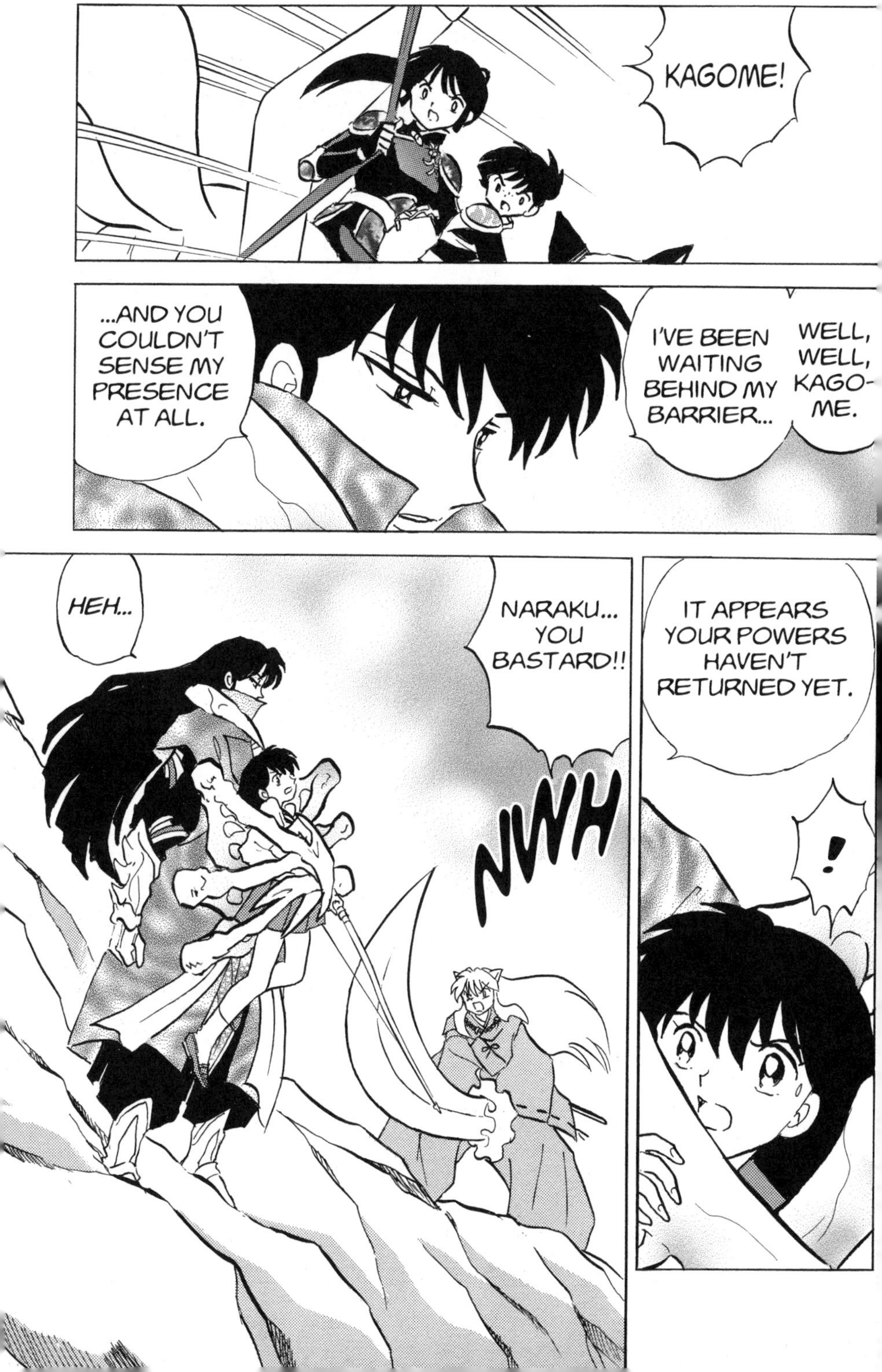
KAGOME!
WELL, WELL, KAGO-ME.
I'VE BEEN WAITING BEHIND MY BARRIER...
...AND YOU COULDN'T SENSE MY PRESENCE AT ALL.
IT APPEARS YOUR POWERS HAVEN'T RETURNED YET.
!
NARAKU... YOU BASTARD!!
HEH...
NWH

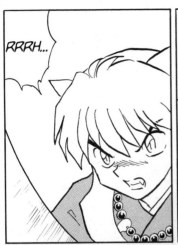

WHAT'S THE MATTER, INU-YASHA?
STAB ME TO YOUR HEART'S CON-TENT.
NWRRK
RRRH...
DON'T WORRY. I WON'T KILL HER.
NOT UNTIL I'VE TAKEN KOHAKU'S SHARD AT LEAST.
SHKSHK
!
KRK KRK KRK

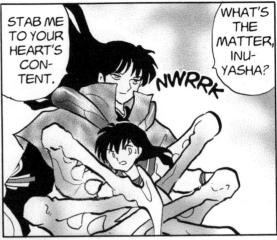

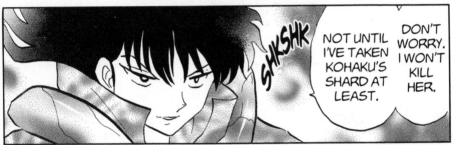

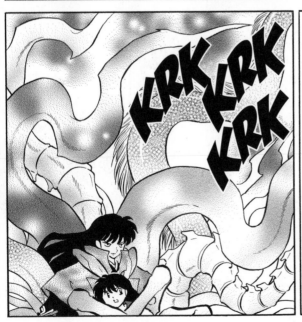

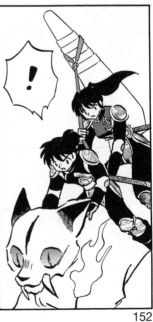

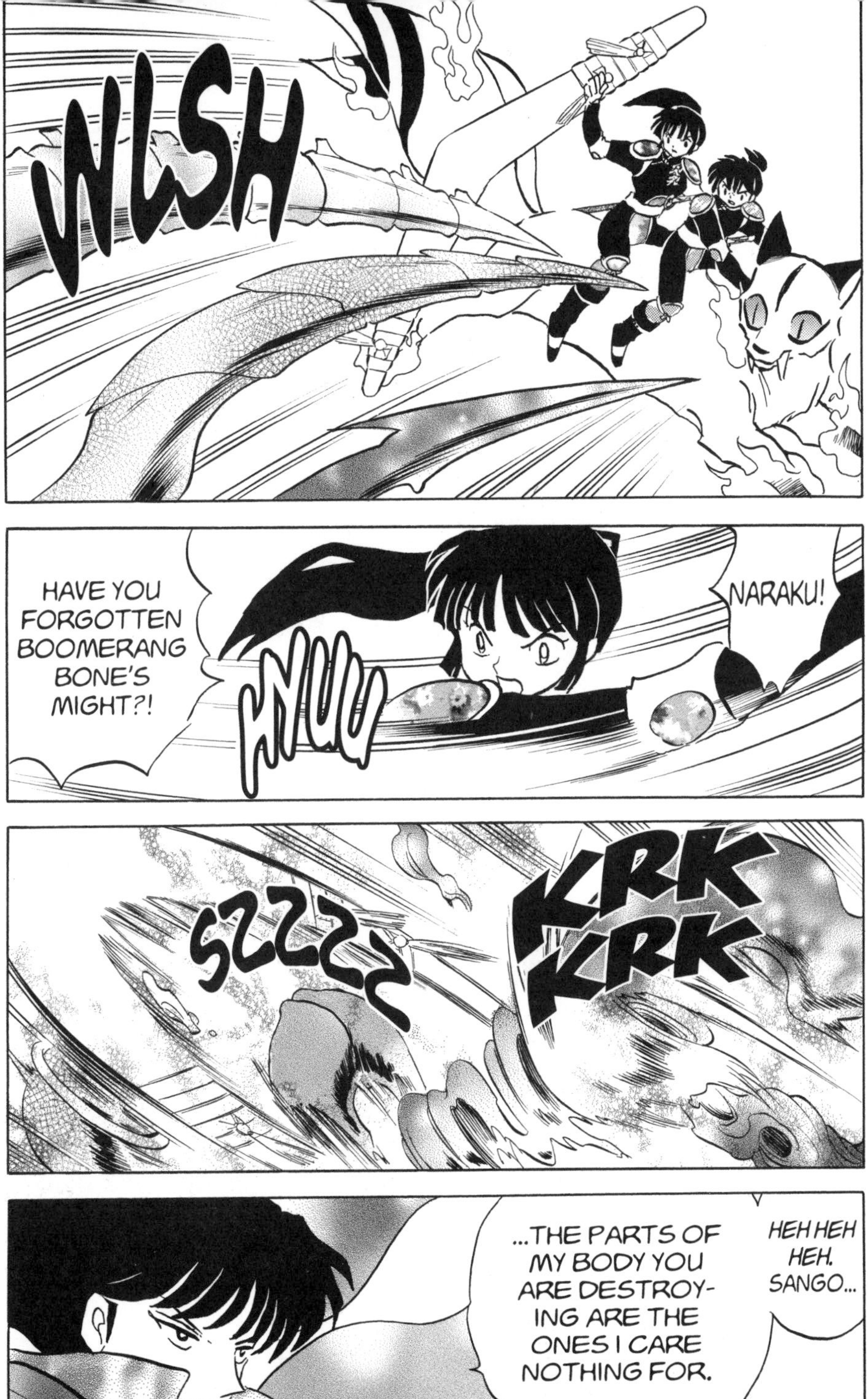
WLSH
NARAKU!
HAVE YOU FORGOTTEN BOOMERANG BONE'S MIGHT?!
HNUU
KRK KRK
SZZZZ
HEH HEH HEH. SANGO...
...THE PARTS OF MY BODY YOU ARE DESTROY-ING ARE THE ONES I CARE NOTHING FOR.

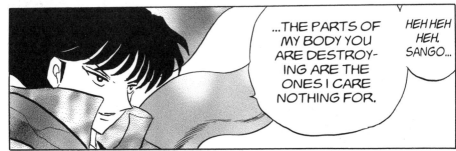

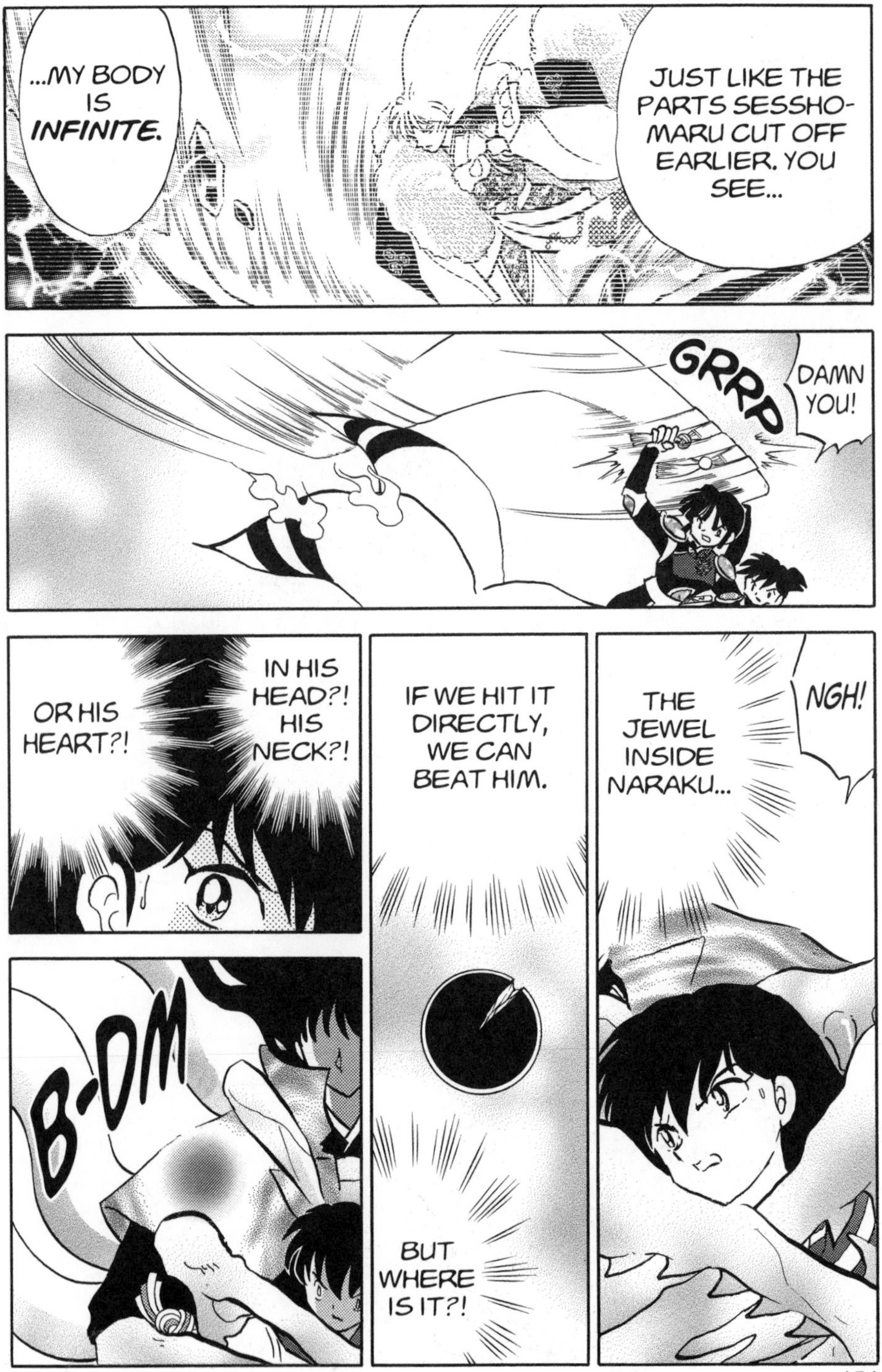
JUST LIKE THE PARTS SESSHO-MARU CUT OFF EARLIER. YOU SEE...
...MY BODY IS INFINITE.
DAMN YOU!
GRRP
NGH!
THE JEWEL INSIDE NARAKU...
IF WE HIT IT DIRECTLY, WE CAN BEAT HIM.
BUT WHERE IS IT?!
IN HIS HEAD?! HIS NECK?!
OR HIS HEART?!
B-DM

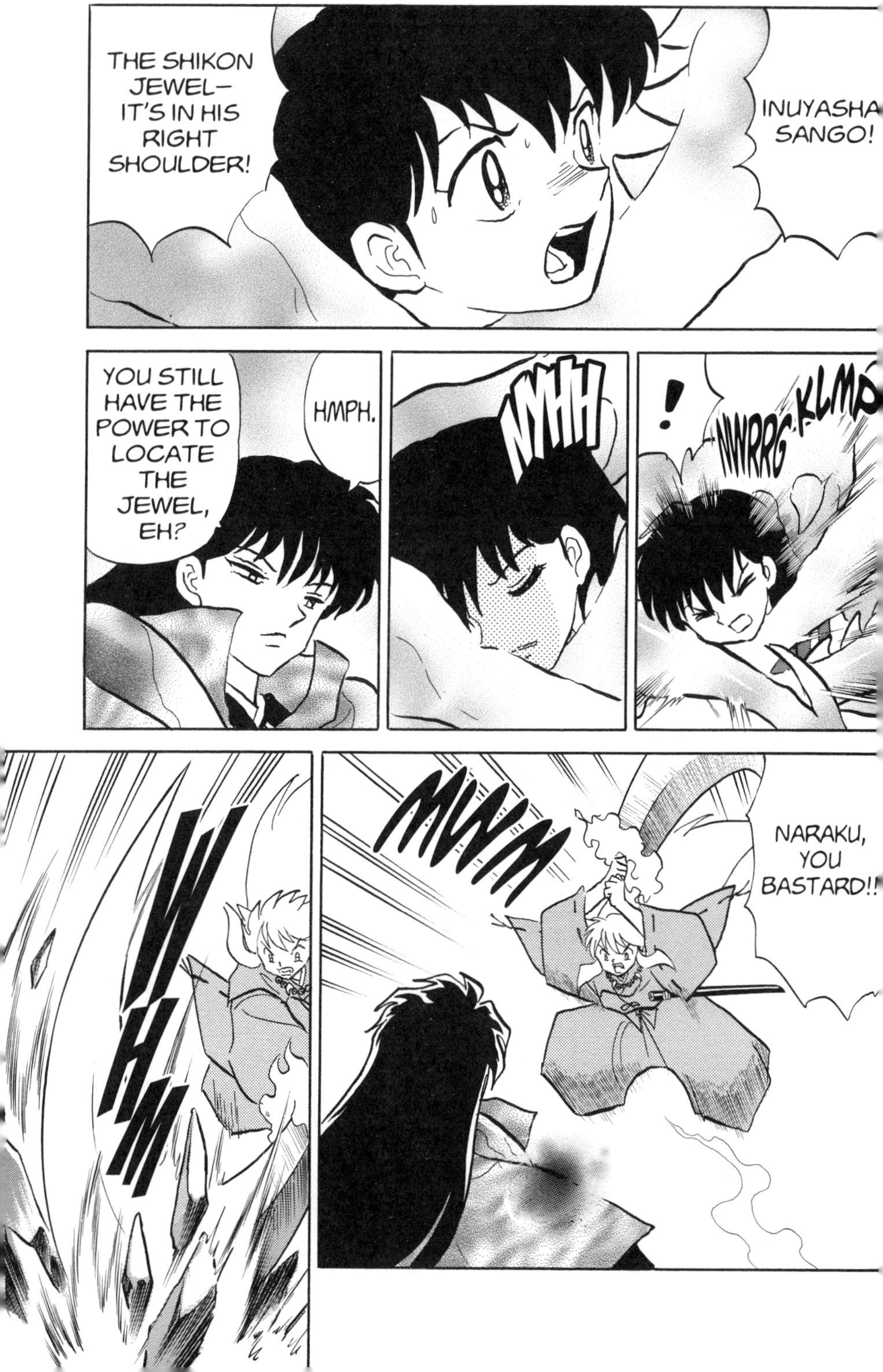
INUYASHA SANGO!
THE SHIKON JEWEL— IT'S IN HIS RIGHT SHOULDER!
!
NWRRG
KLMP
NYHH
HMPH.
YOU STILL HAVE THE POWER TO LOCATE THE JEWEL, EH?
MWM
NARAKU, YOU BASTARD!!
WHHM

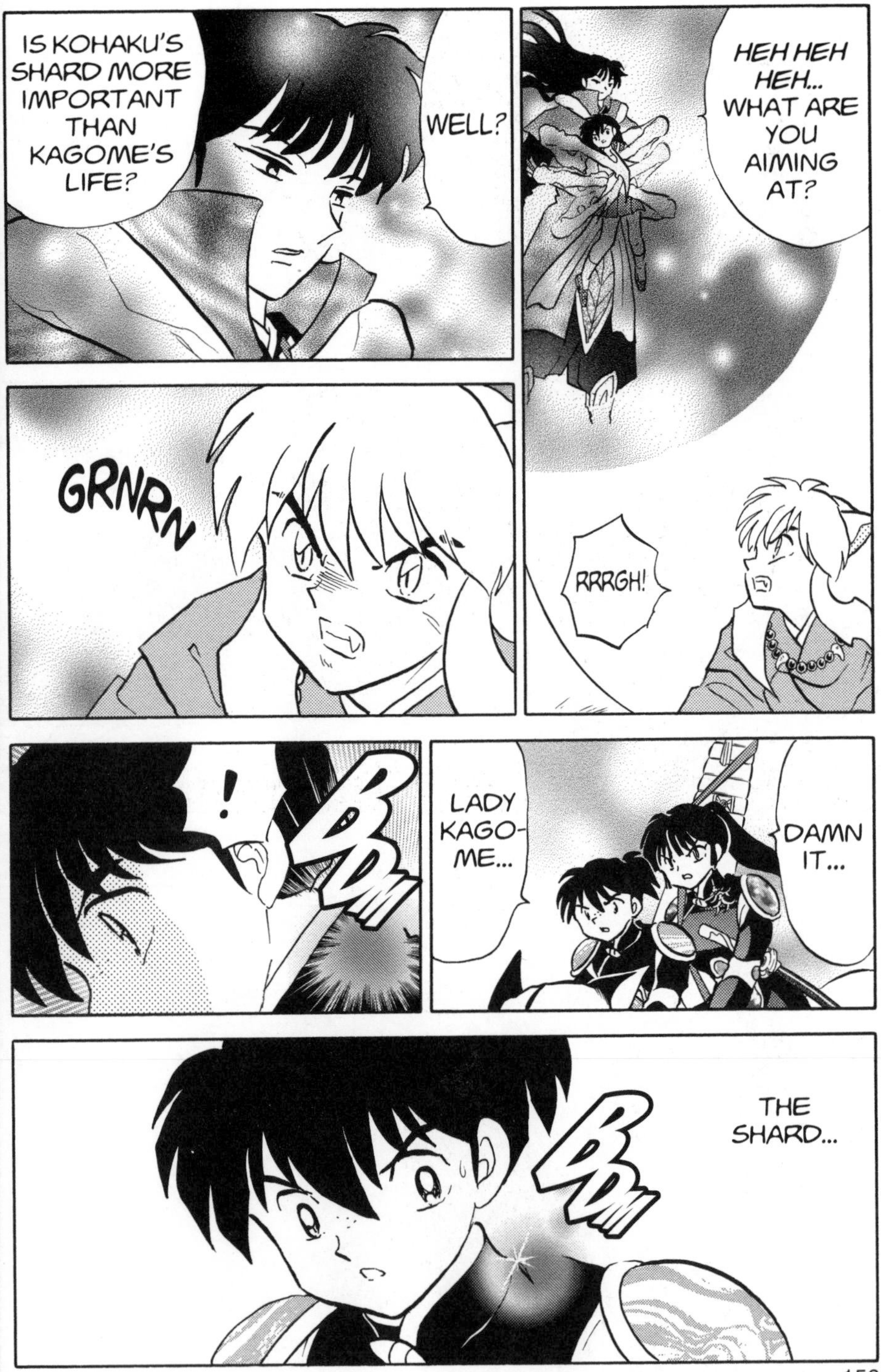
HEH HEH HEH... WHAT ARE YOU AIMING AT?
RRRGH!
IS KOHAKU'S SHARD MORE IMPORTANT THAN KAGOME'S LIFE?
WELL?
GRNRN
DAMN IT...
LADY KAGO-ME...
!
BDM
THE SHARD...
BDM

SCROLL NINE
A LIFE ONCE LOST

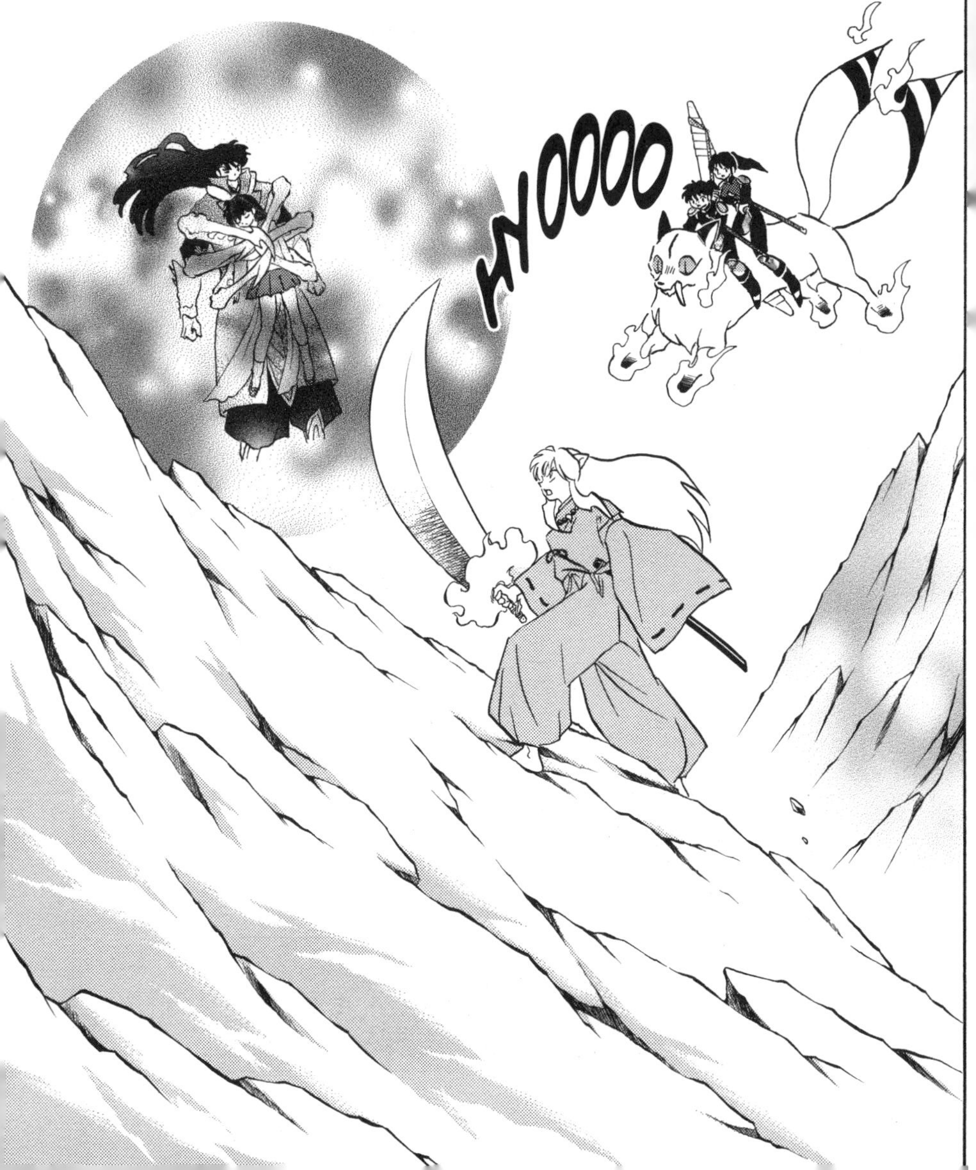
HYOOOO

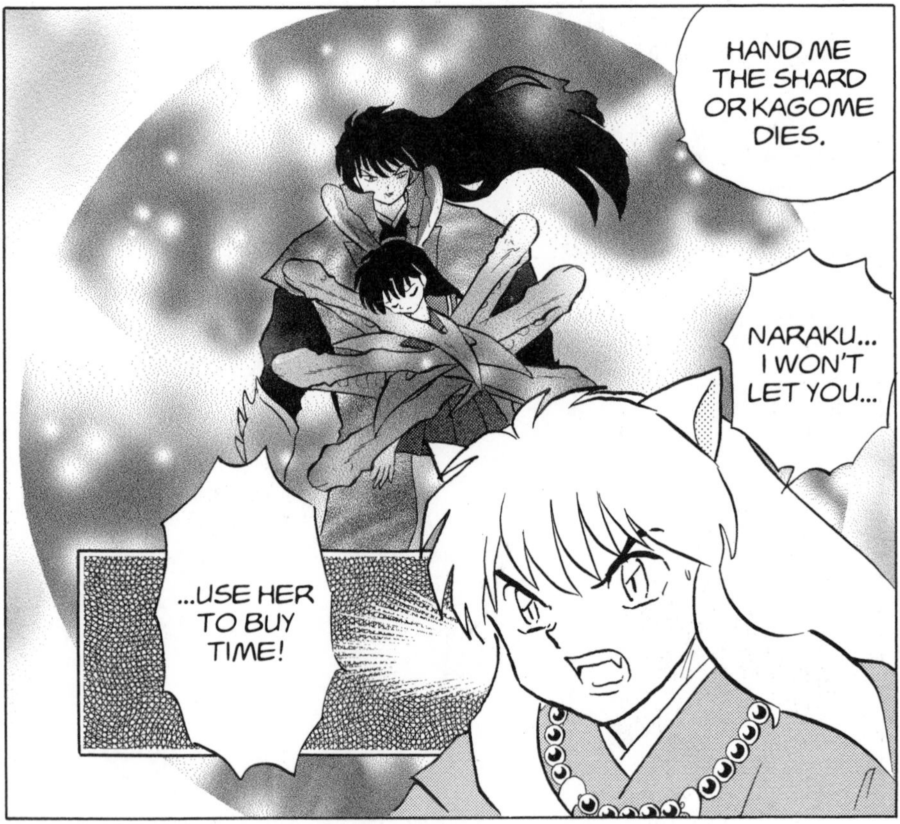
HAND ME THE SHARD OR KAGOME DIES.
NARAKU... I WON'T LET YOU...
...USE HER TO BUY TIME!

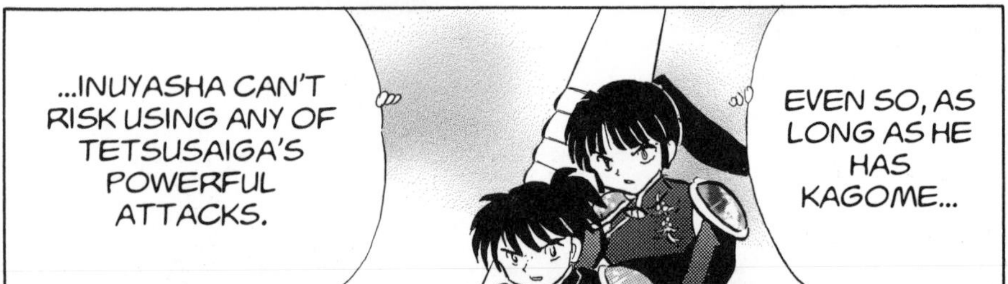
EVEN SO, AS LONG AS HE HAS KAGOME...
...INUYASHA CAN'T RISK USING ANY OF TETSUSAIGA'S POWERFUL ATTACKS.

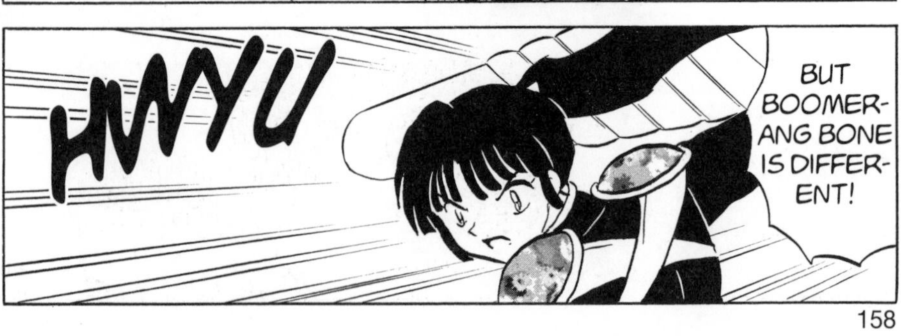
BUT BOOMERANG BONE IS DIFFERENT!
HWYU

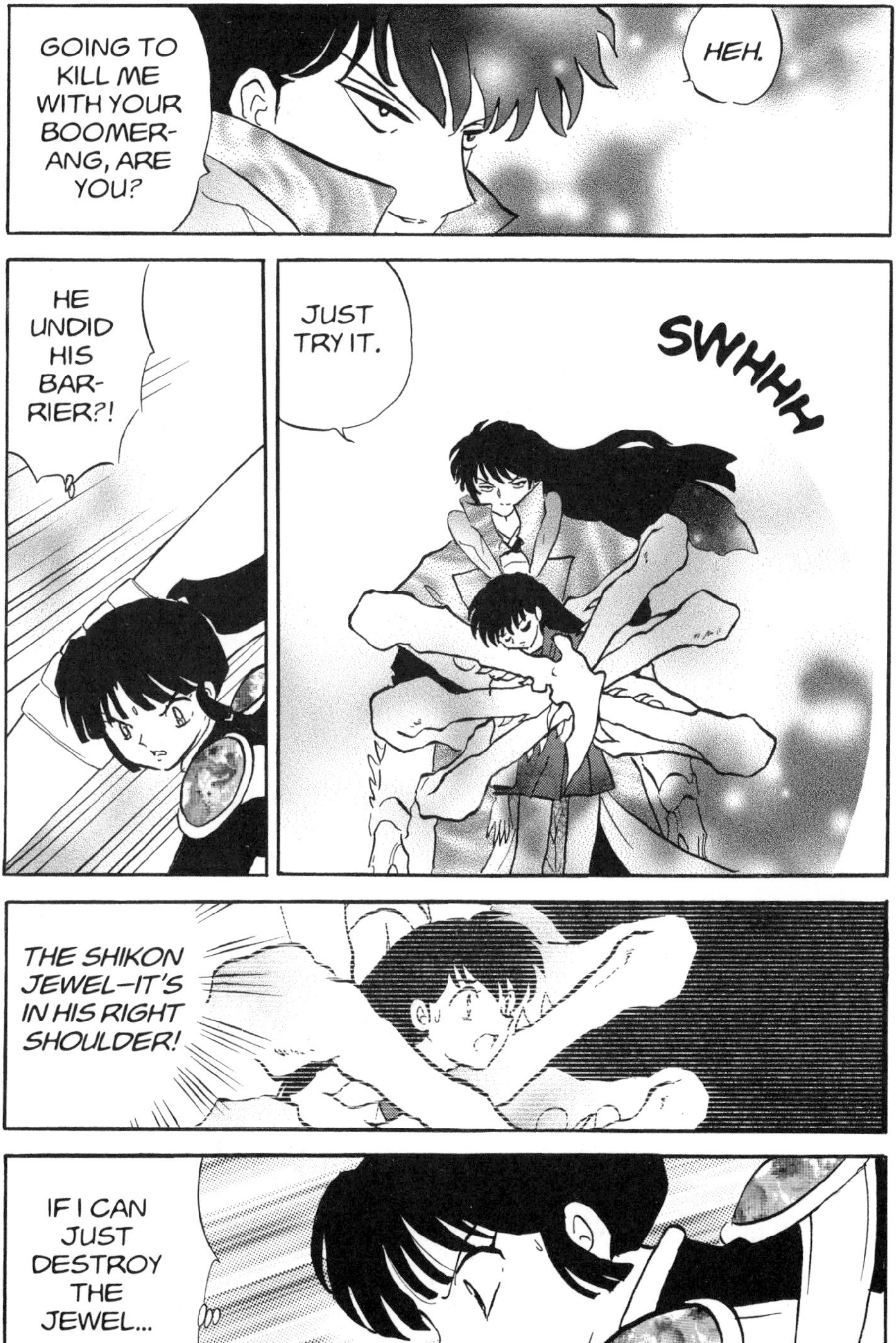
HEH.
GOING TO KILL ME WITH YOUR BOOMER-ANG, ARE YOU?
JUST TRY IT.
SWHHH
HE UNDID HIS BAR-RIER?!
THE SHIKON JEWEL—IT'S IN HIS RIGHT SHOULDER!
IF I CAN JUST DESTROY THE JEWEL...

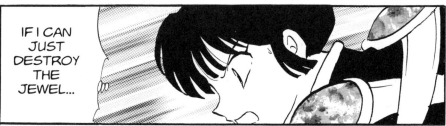

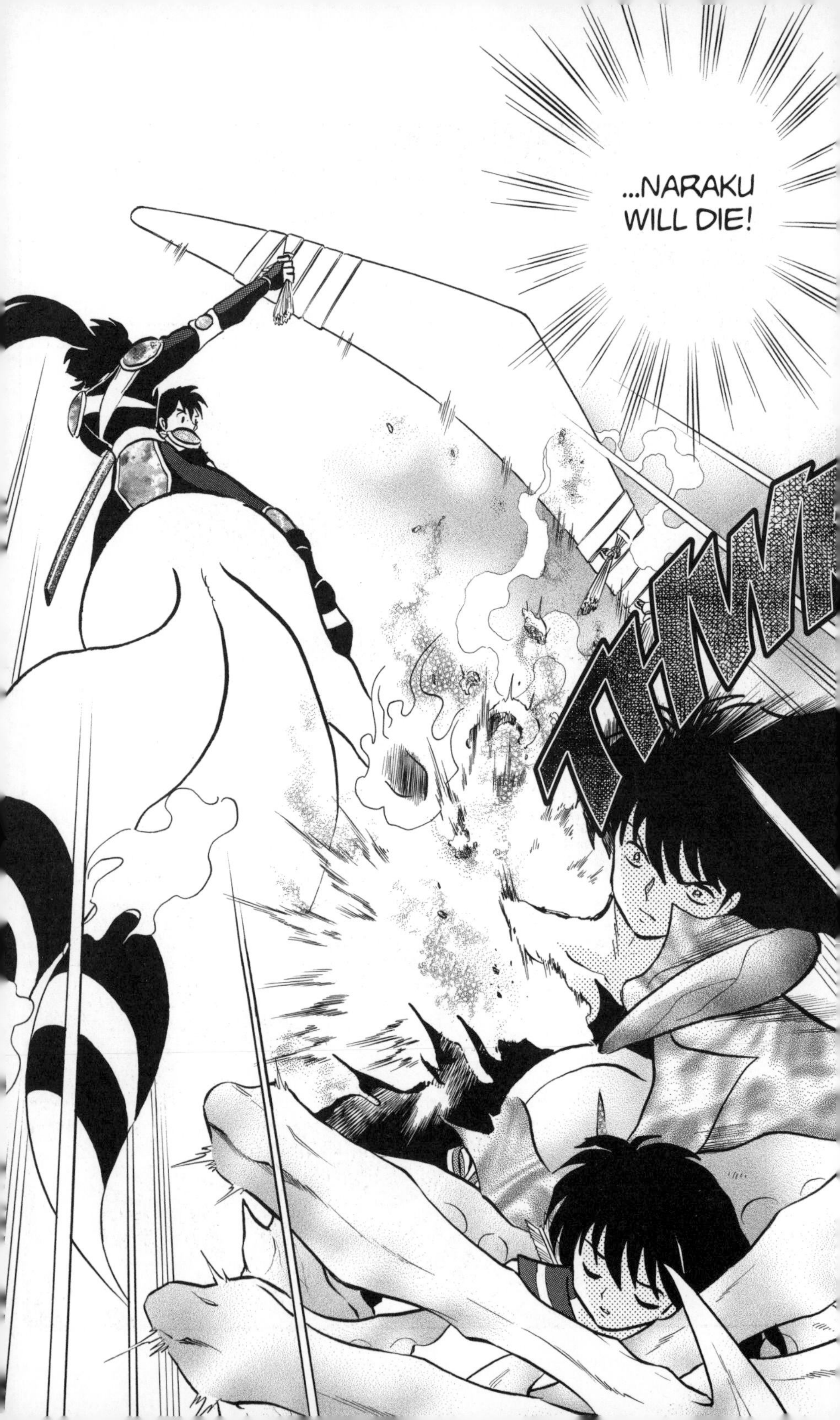
...NARAKU
WILL DIE!
THWN

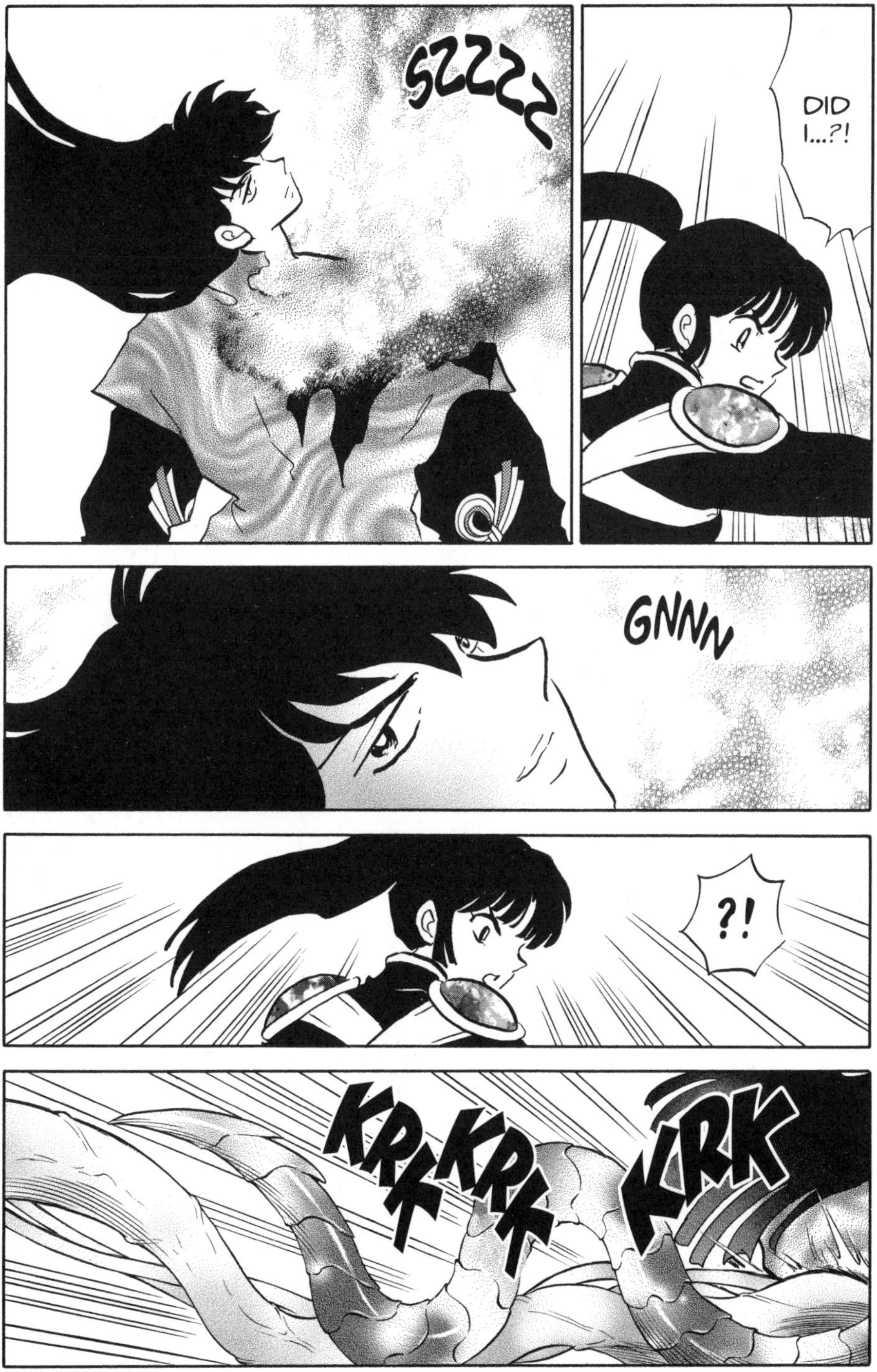
DID I...?!
SZZZZ
GNNN
?!
KRK
KRK
KRK

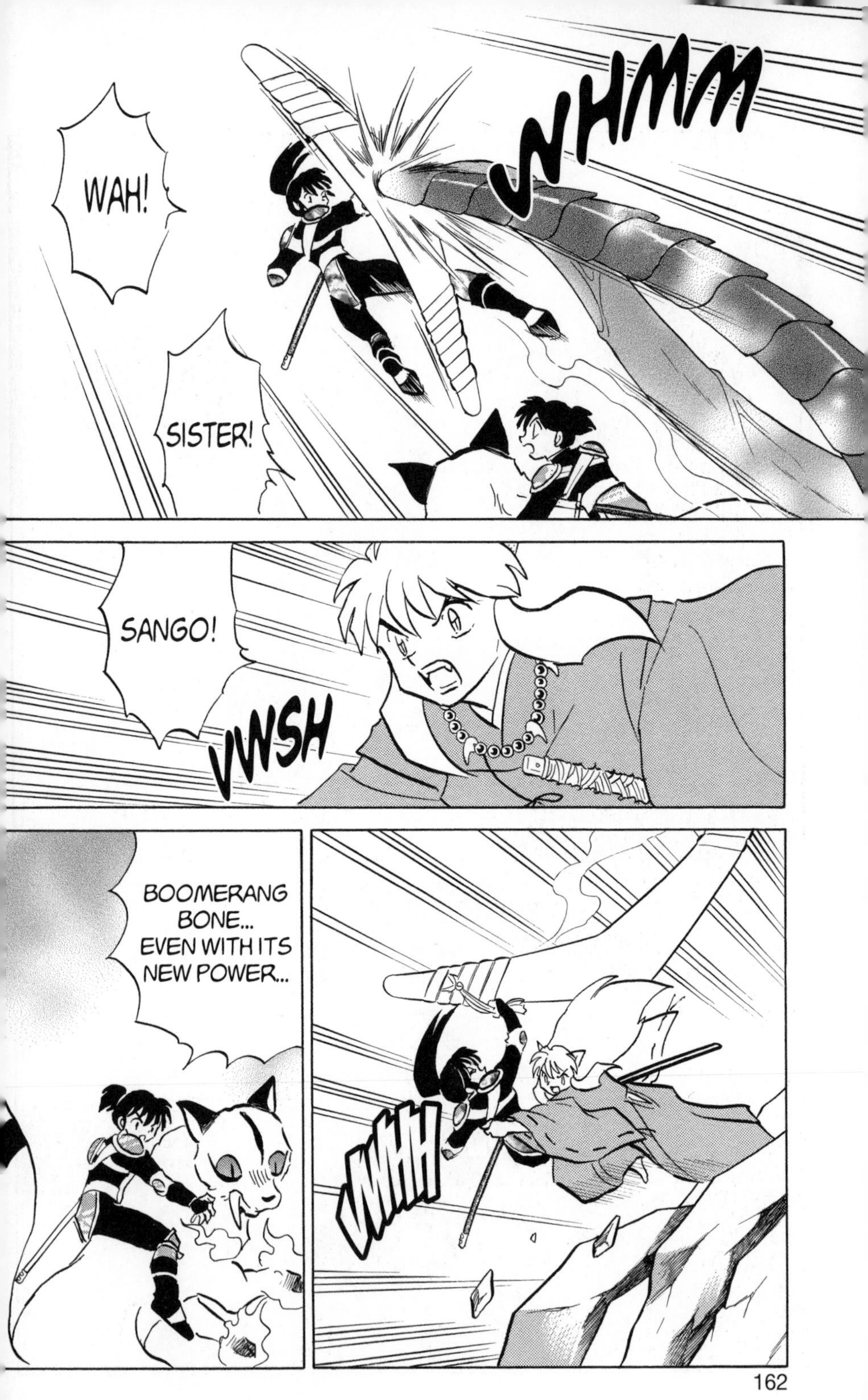
WHMM
WAH!
SISTER!
SANGO!
VWSH
VWHH
BOOMERANG BONE... EVEN WITH ITS NEW POWER...

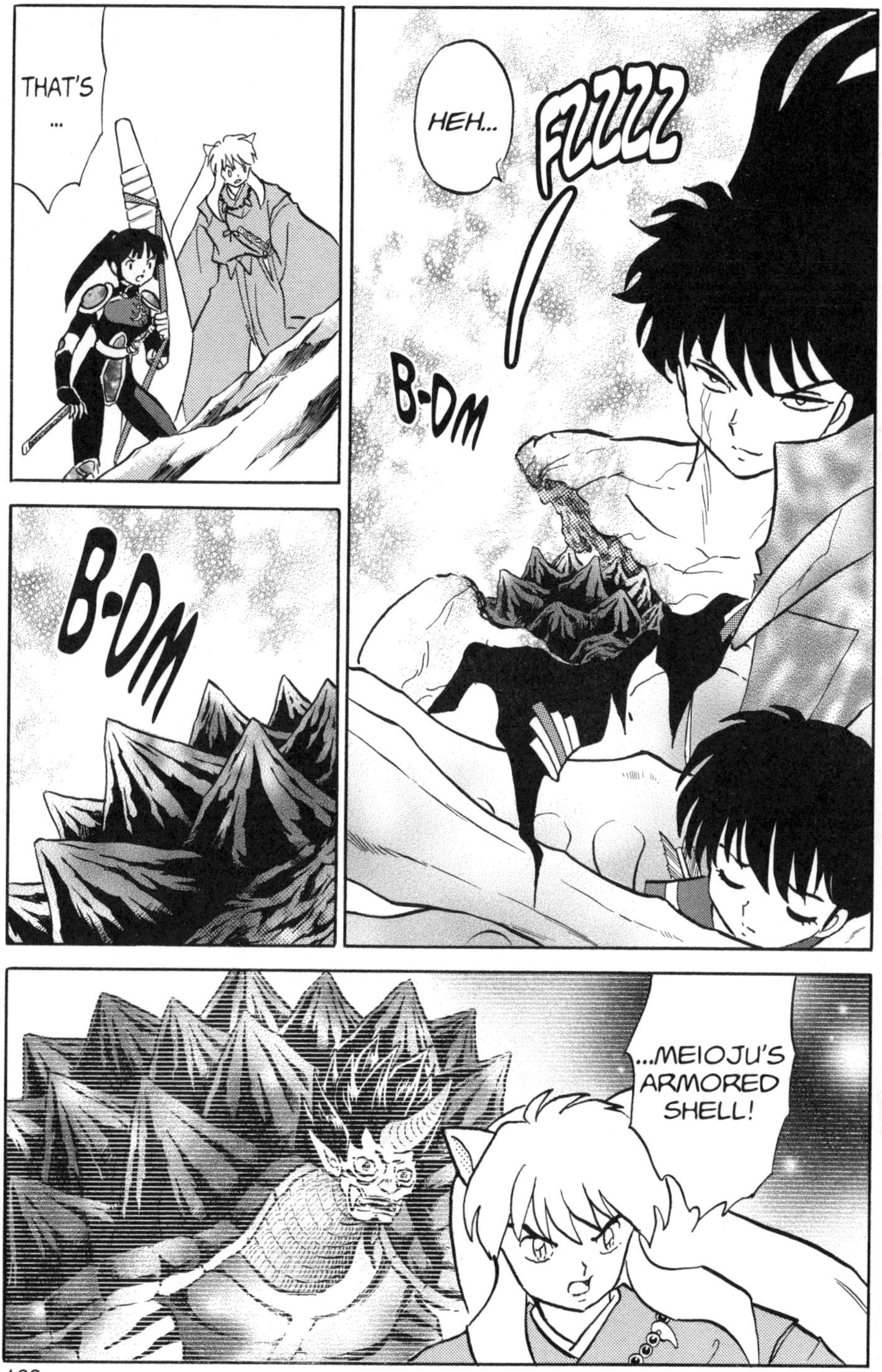
HEH...
FZZZZ
B-DM
THAT'S ...
B-DM
...MEIOJU'S ARMORED SHELL!

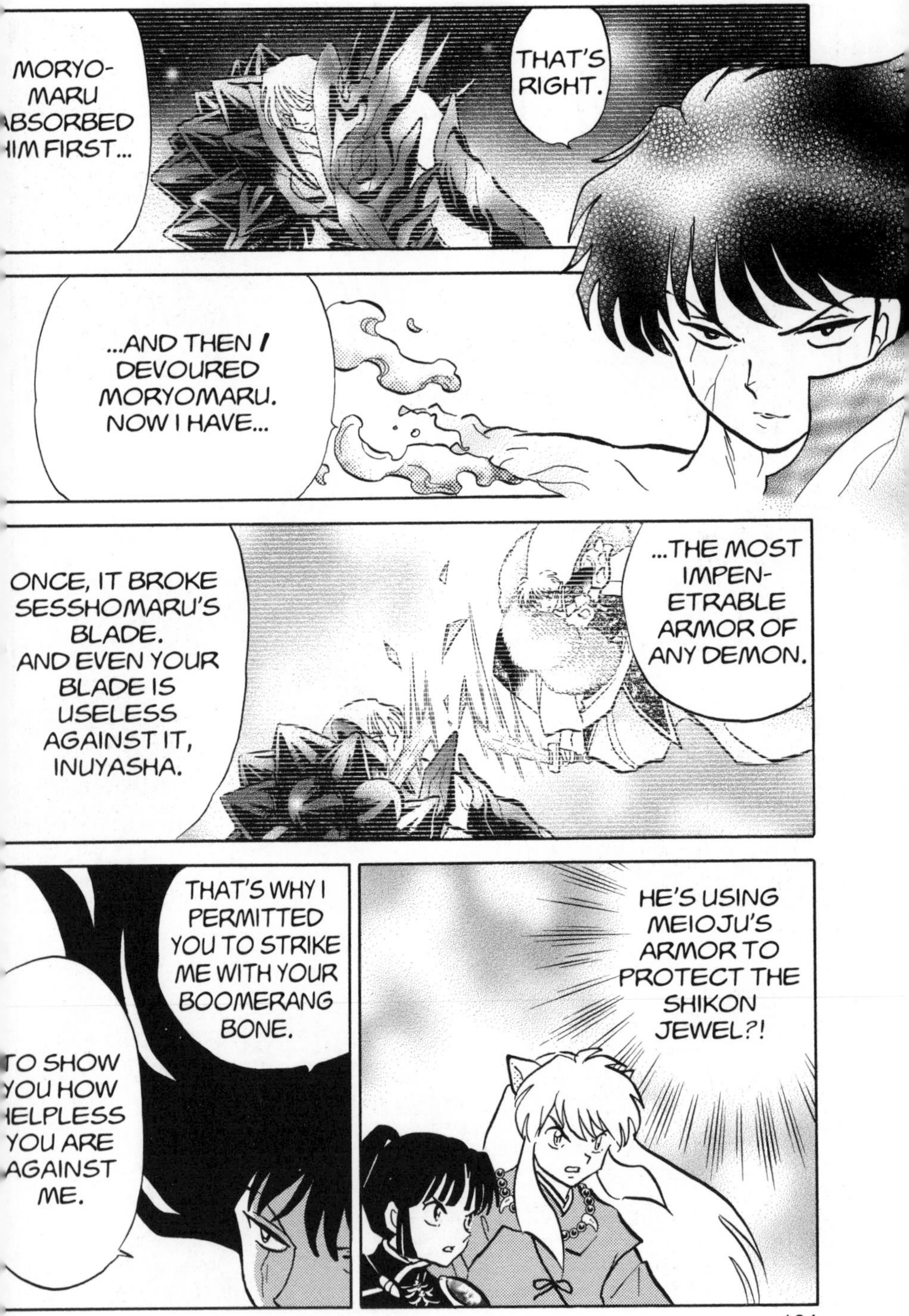
THAT'S RIGHT.
MORYO-MARU ABSORBED HIM FIRST...
...AND THEN I DEVOURED MORYOMARU. NOW I HAVE...
...THE MOST IMPEN-ETRABLE ARMOR OF ANY DEMON.
ONCE, IT BROKE SESSHOMARU'S BLADE. AND EVEN YOUR BLADE IS USELESS AGAINST IT, INUYASHA.
HE'S USING MEIOJU'S ARMOR TO PROTECT THE SHIKON JEWEL?!
THAT'S WHY I PERMITTED YOU TO STRIKE ME WITH YOUR BOOMERANG BONE.
TO SHOW YOU HOW HELPLESS YOU ARE AGAINST ME.

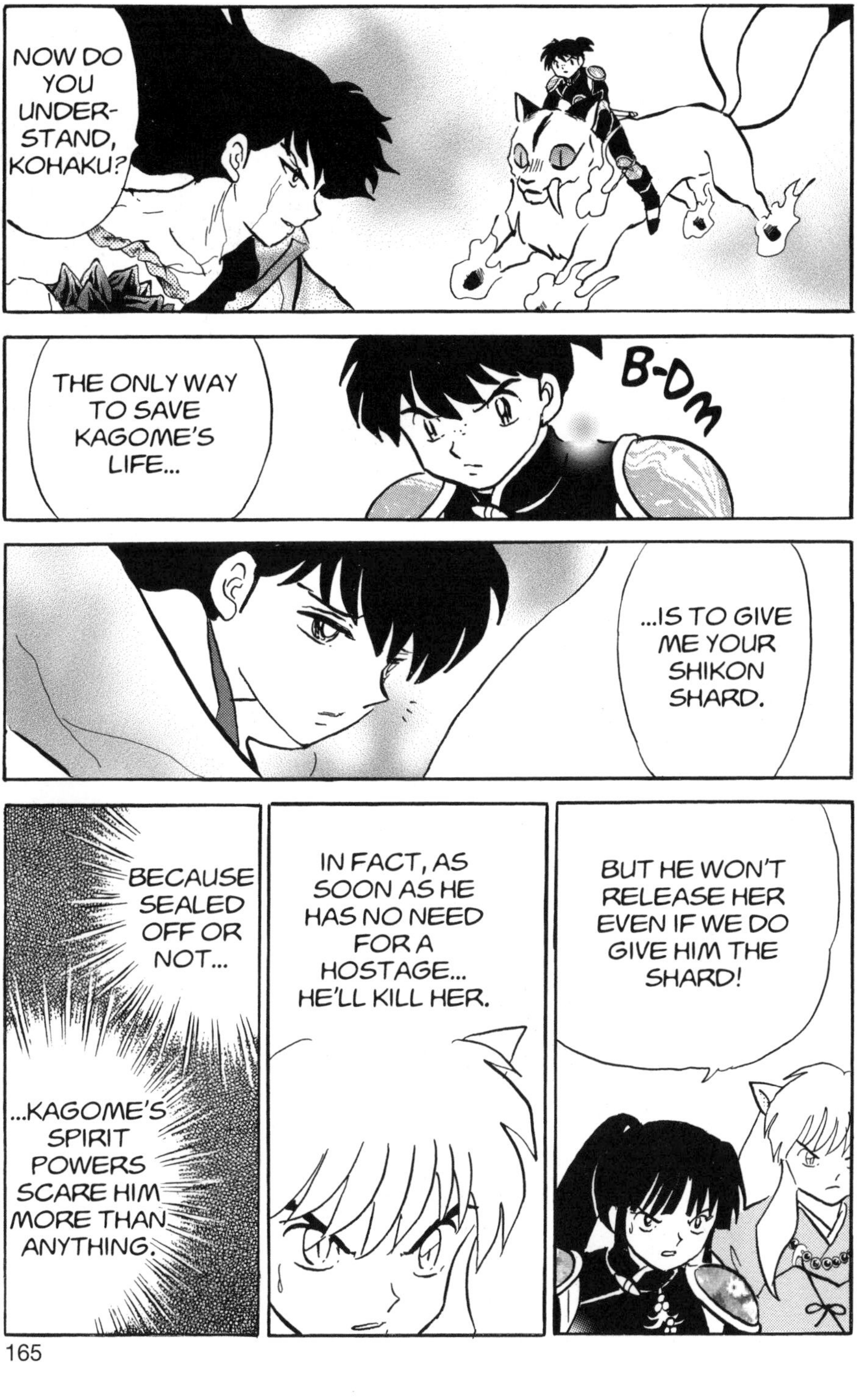
NOW DO YOU UNDER-STAND, KOHAKU?
B-DM
THE ONLY WAY TO SAVE KAGOME'S LIFE...
...IS TO GIVE ME YOUR SHIKON SHARD.
BUT HE WON'T RELEASE HER EVEN IF WE DO GIVE HIM THE SHARD!
IN FACT, AS SOON AS HE HAS NO NEED FOR A HOSTAGE... HE'LL KILL HER.
BECAUSE SEALED OFF OR NOT...
...KAGOME'S SPIRIT POWERS SCARE HIM MORE THAN ANYTHING.

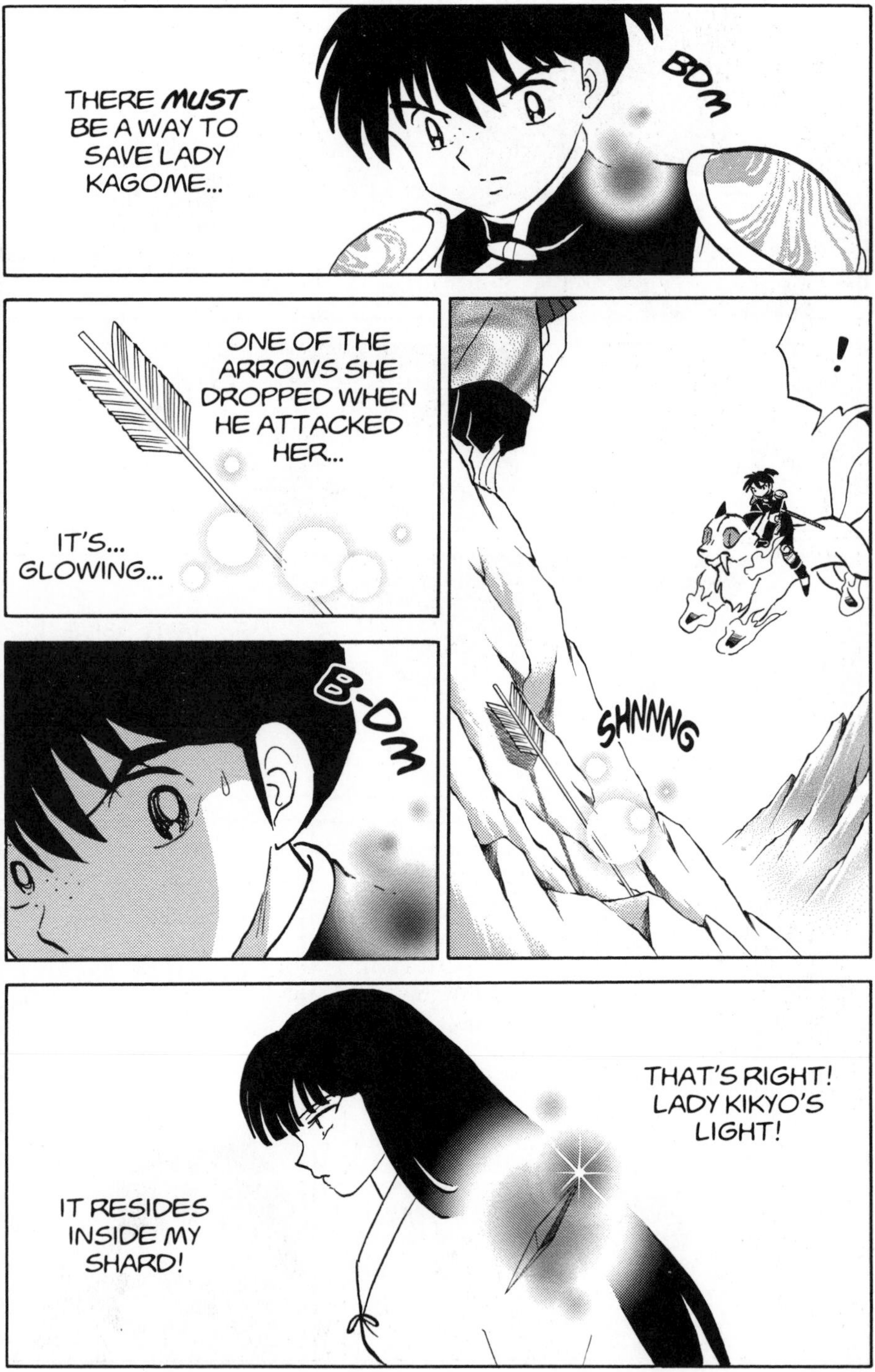
BDM
THERE MUST BE A WAY TO SAVE LADY KAGOME...
!
SHNNNG
ONE OF THE ARROWS SHE DROPPED WHEN HE ATTACKED HER...
IT'S... GLOWING...
B-DM
THAT'S RIGHT! LADY KIKYO'S LIGHT!
IT RESIDES INSIDE MY SHARD!

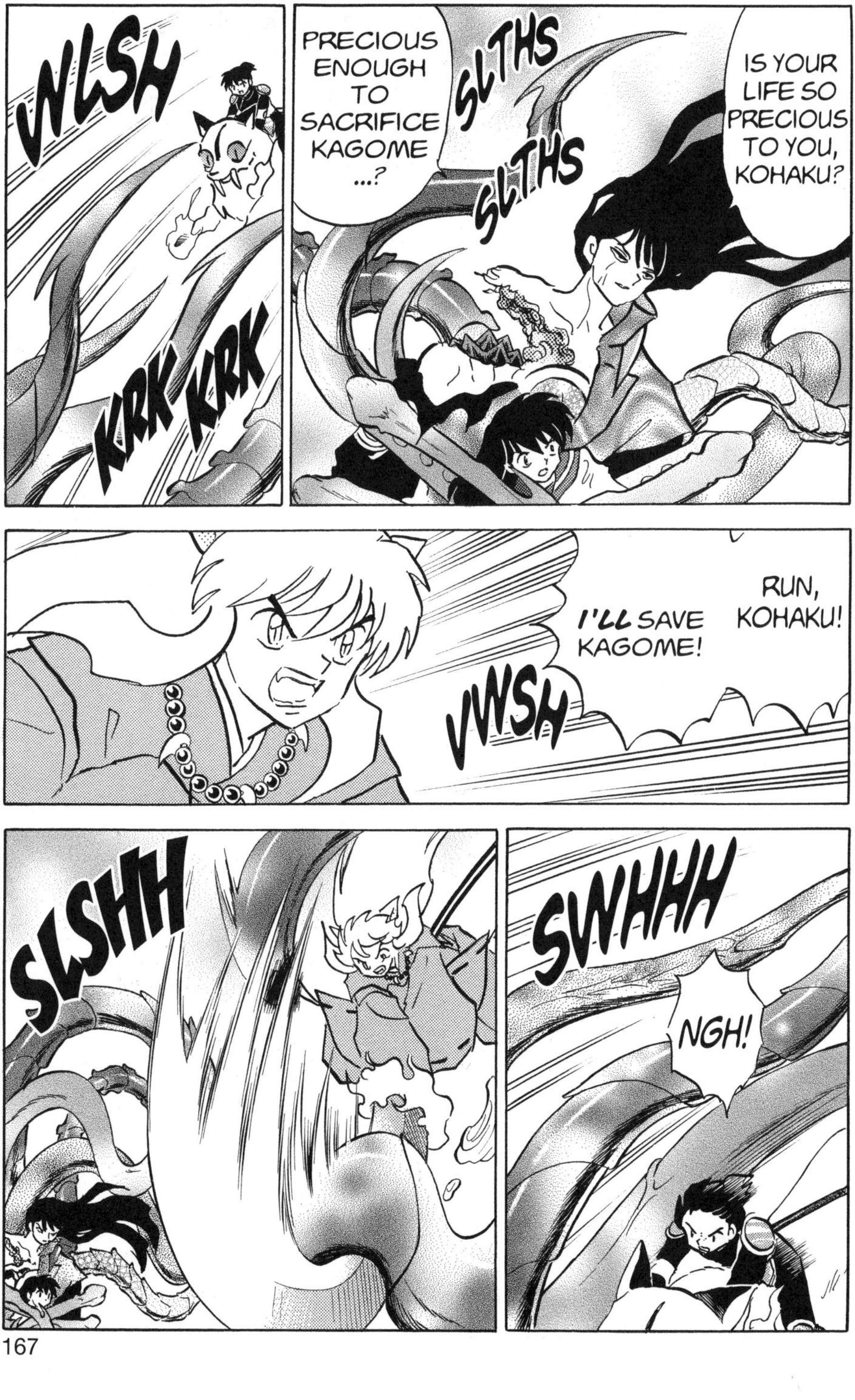
IS YOUR LIFE SO PRECIOUS TO YOU, KOHAKU?
PRECIOUS ENOUGH TO SACRIFICE KAGOME ...?
SLTHS
SLTHS
WLSH
KRK
KRK
RUN, KOHAKU!
I'LL SAVE KAGOME!
VWSH
SWHHH
NGH!
SLSHH

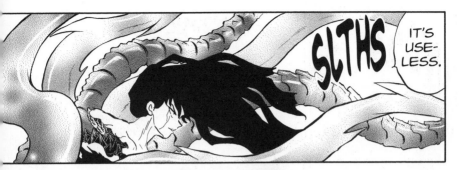

SLTHS

IT'S USE-LESS.

SLSHH

DAMN YOU!

ZNNHH

!

KAGO-ME!

INU-YASHA!!

I-I'M GETTING SUCKED IN!

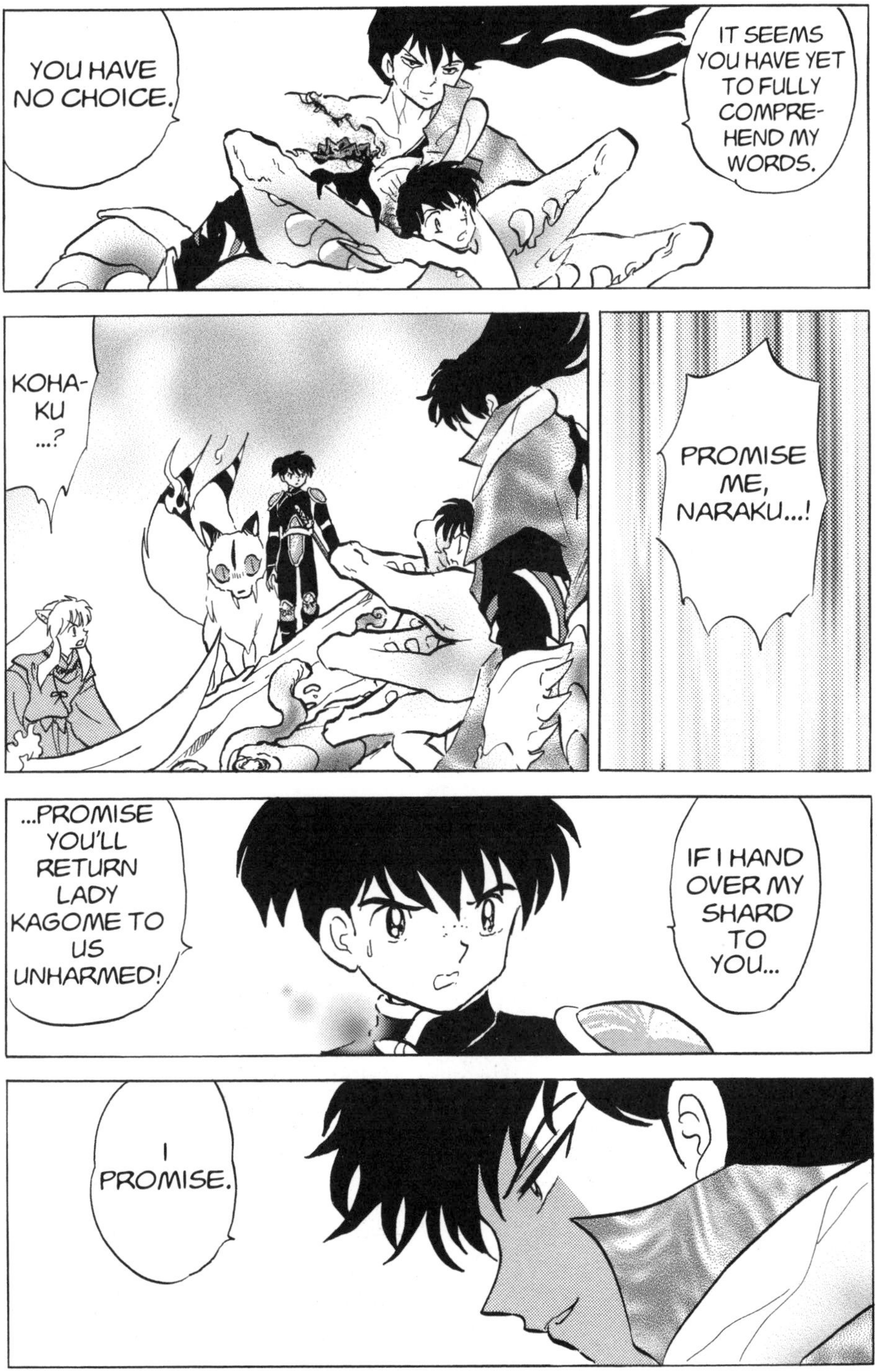
IT SEEMS YOU HAVE YET TO FULLY COMPRE-HEND MY WORDS.
YOU HAVE NO CHOICE.
PROMISE ME, NARAKU...!
KOHA-KU ...?
IF I HAND OVER MY SHARD TO YOU...
...PROMISE YOU'LL RETURN LADY KAGOME TO US UNHARMED!
I PROMISE.

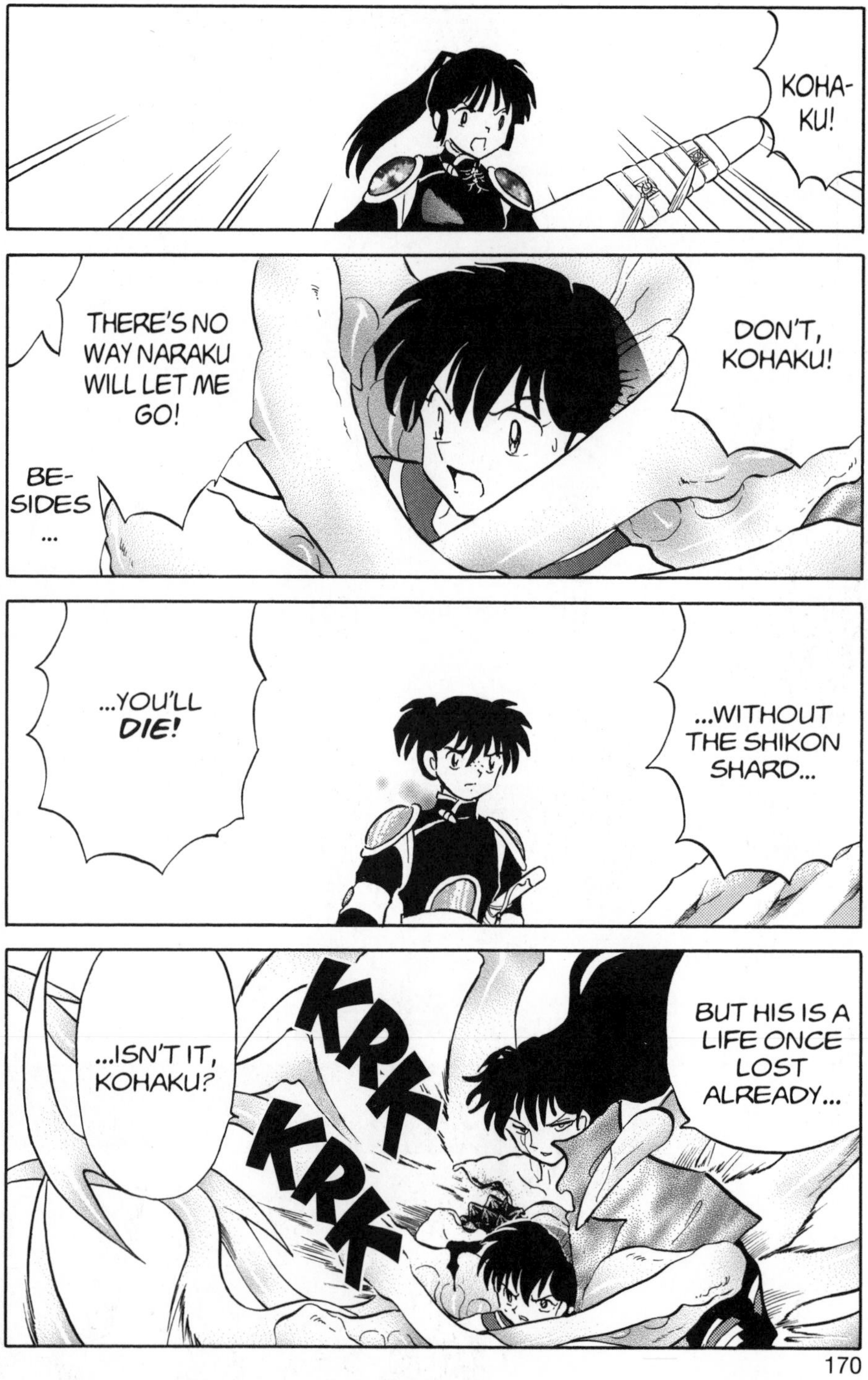
KOHA-KU!
DON'T, KOHAKU!
THERE'S NO WAY NARAKU WILL LET ME GO!
BE-SIDES ...
...WITHOUT THE SHIKON SHARD...
...YOU'LL **DIE!**
BUT HIS IS A LIFE ONCE LOST ALREADY...
KRK KRK
...ISN'T IT, KOHAKU?

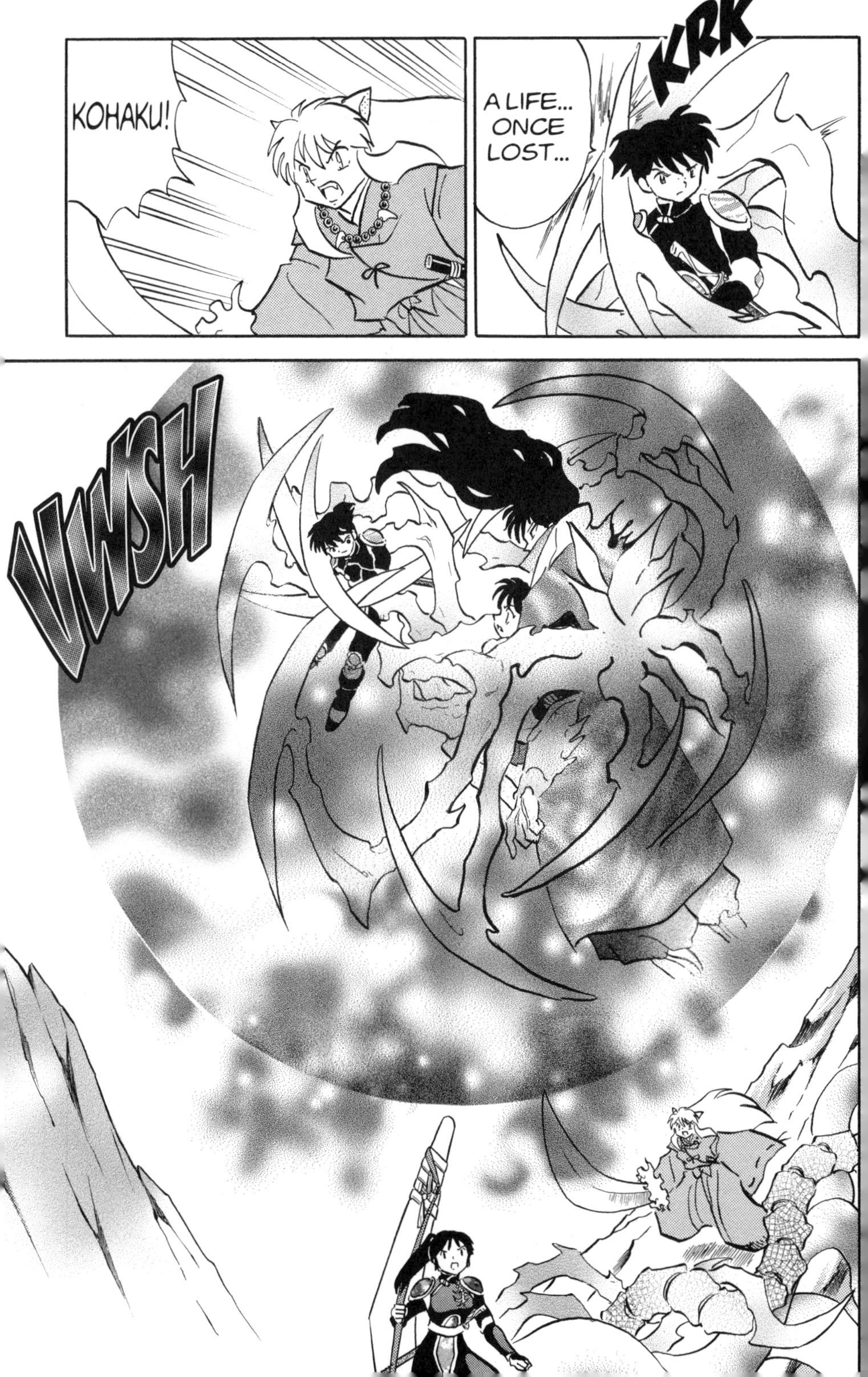
KRK
A LIFE... ONCE LOST...
KOHAKU!
VWSH

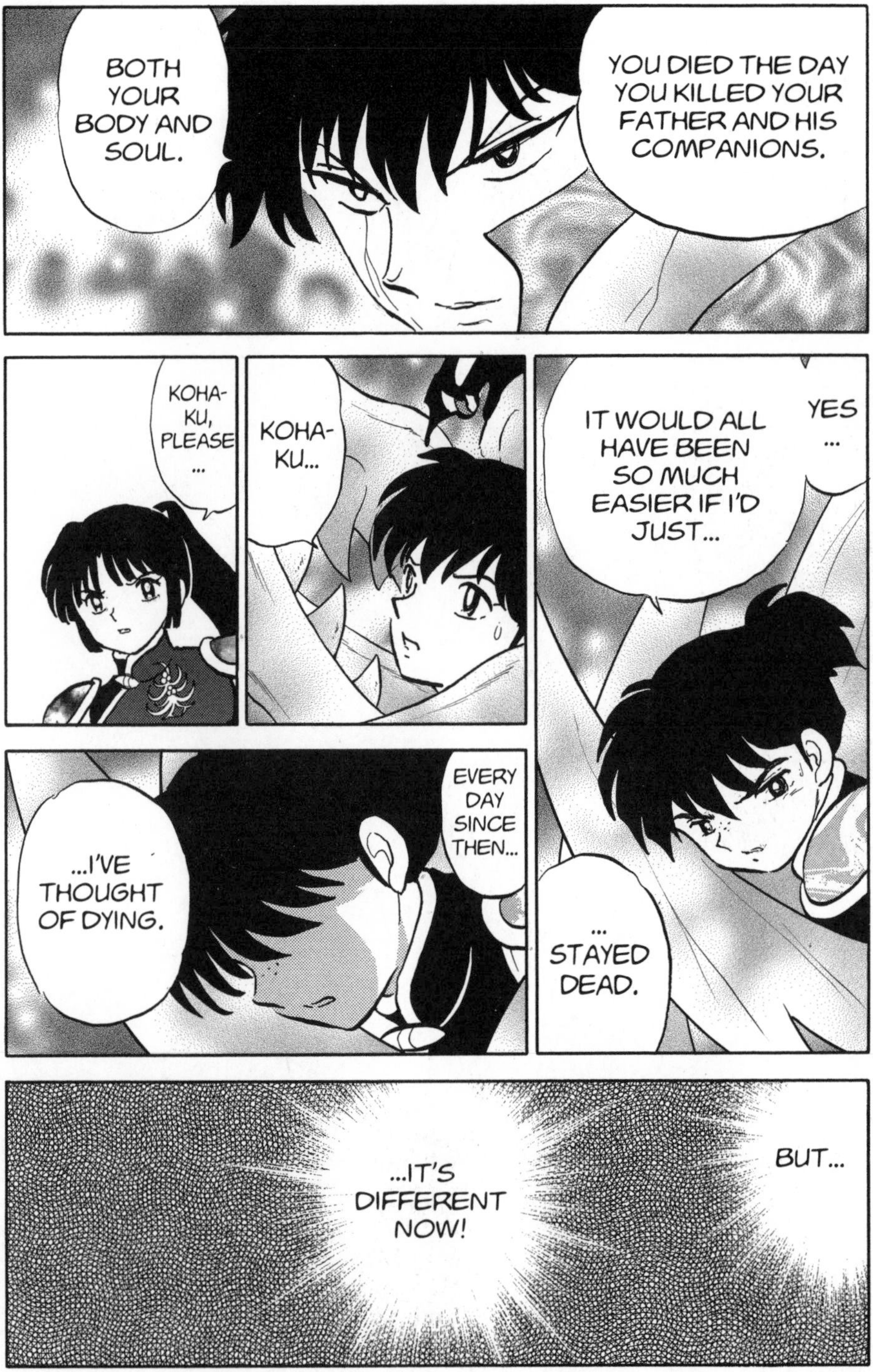
YOU DIED THE DAY YOU KILLED YOUR FATHER AND HIS COMPANIONS.
BOTH YOUR BODY AND SOUL.
YES ...
IT WOULD ALL HAVE BEEN SO MUCH EASIER IF I'D JUST...
... STAYED DEAD.
KOHA-KU...
KOHA-KU, PLEASE ...
EVERY DAY SINCE THEN...
...I'VE THOUGHT OF DYING.
BUT...
...IT'S DIFFERENT NOW!

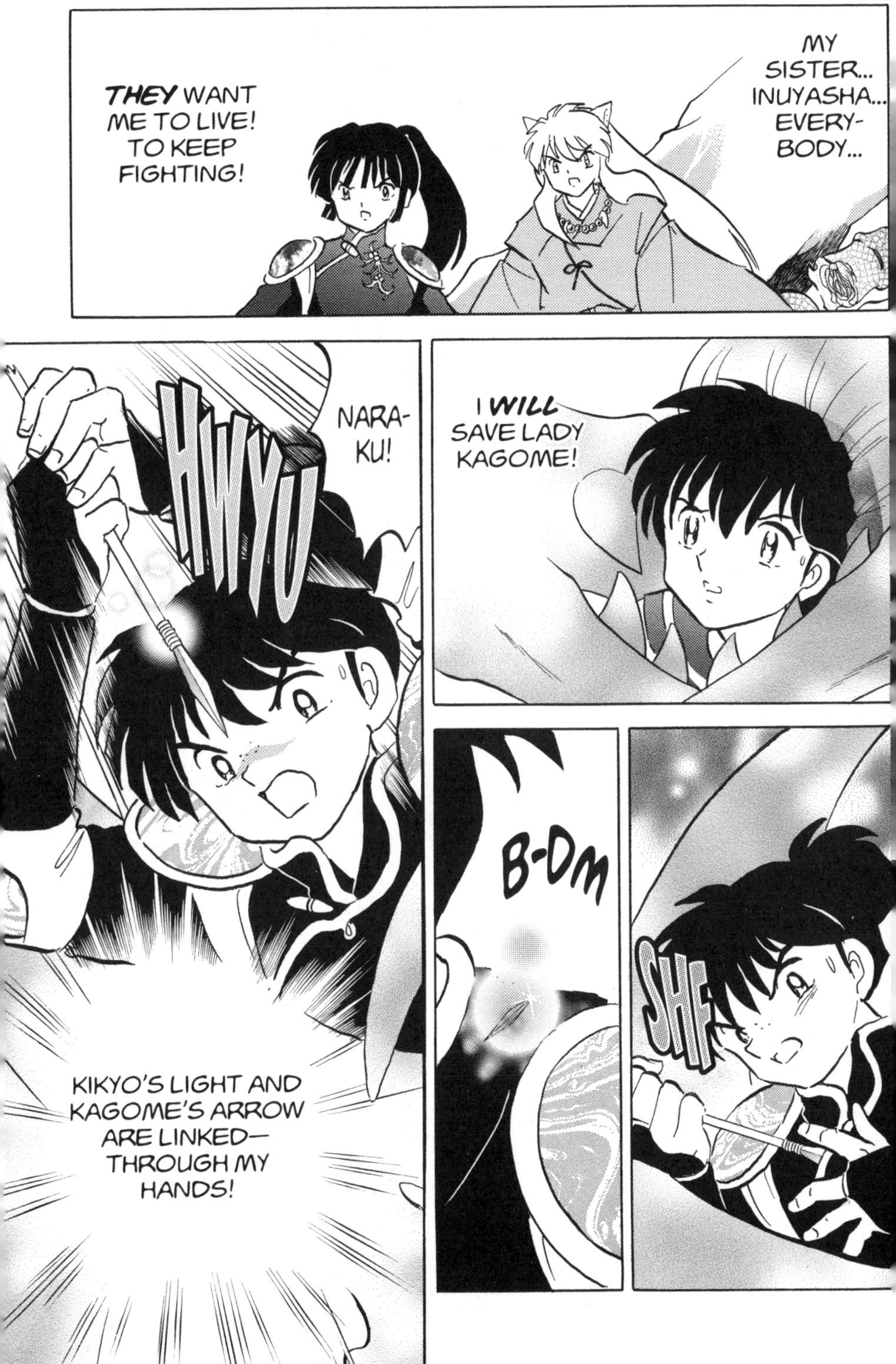
MY SISTER... INUYASHA... EVERY-BODY...
THEY WANT ME TO LIVE! TO KEEP FIGHTING!
I WILL SAVE LADY KAGOME!
SHF
B-DM
NARA-KU!
HWYU
KIKYO'S LIGHT AND KAGOME'S ARROW ARE LINKED— THROUGH MY HANDS!

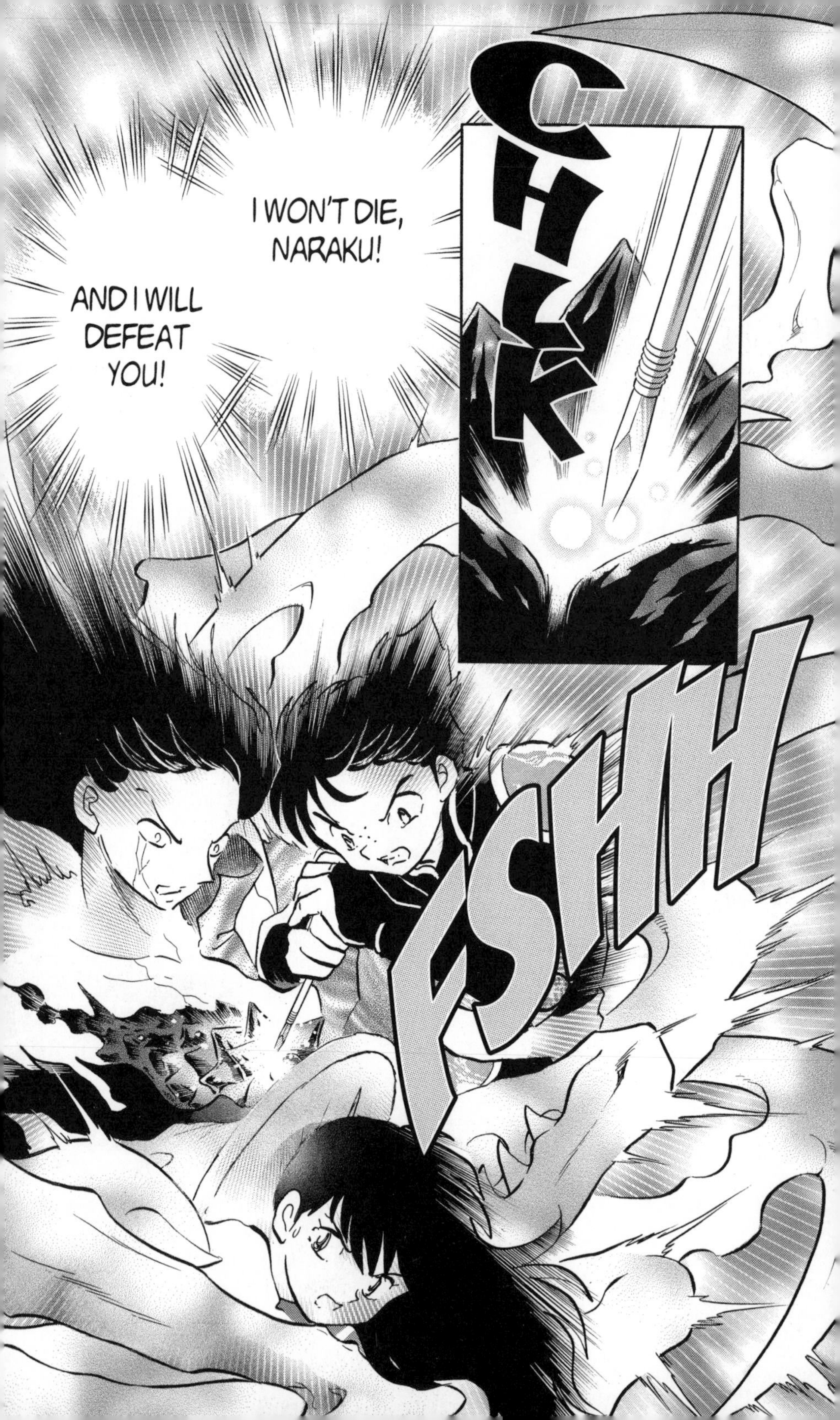

CHUK
I WON'T DIE, NARAKU!
AND I WILL DEFEAT YOU!
FSHH

SCROLL TEN
FROM HERE ON OUT

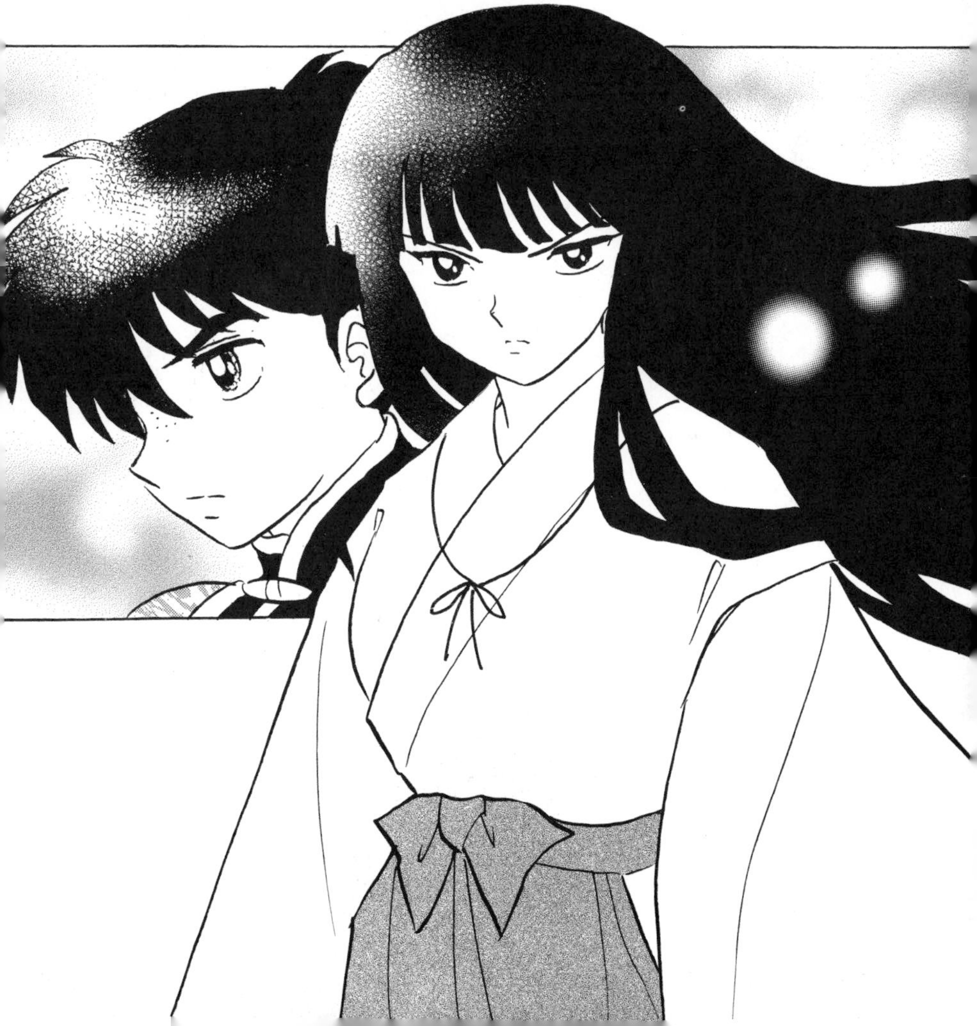

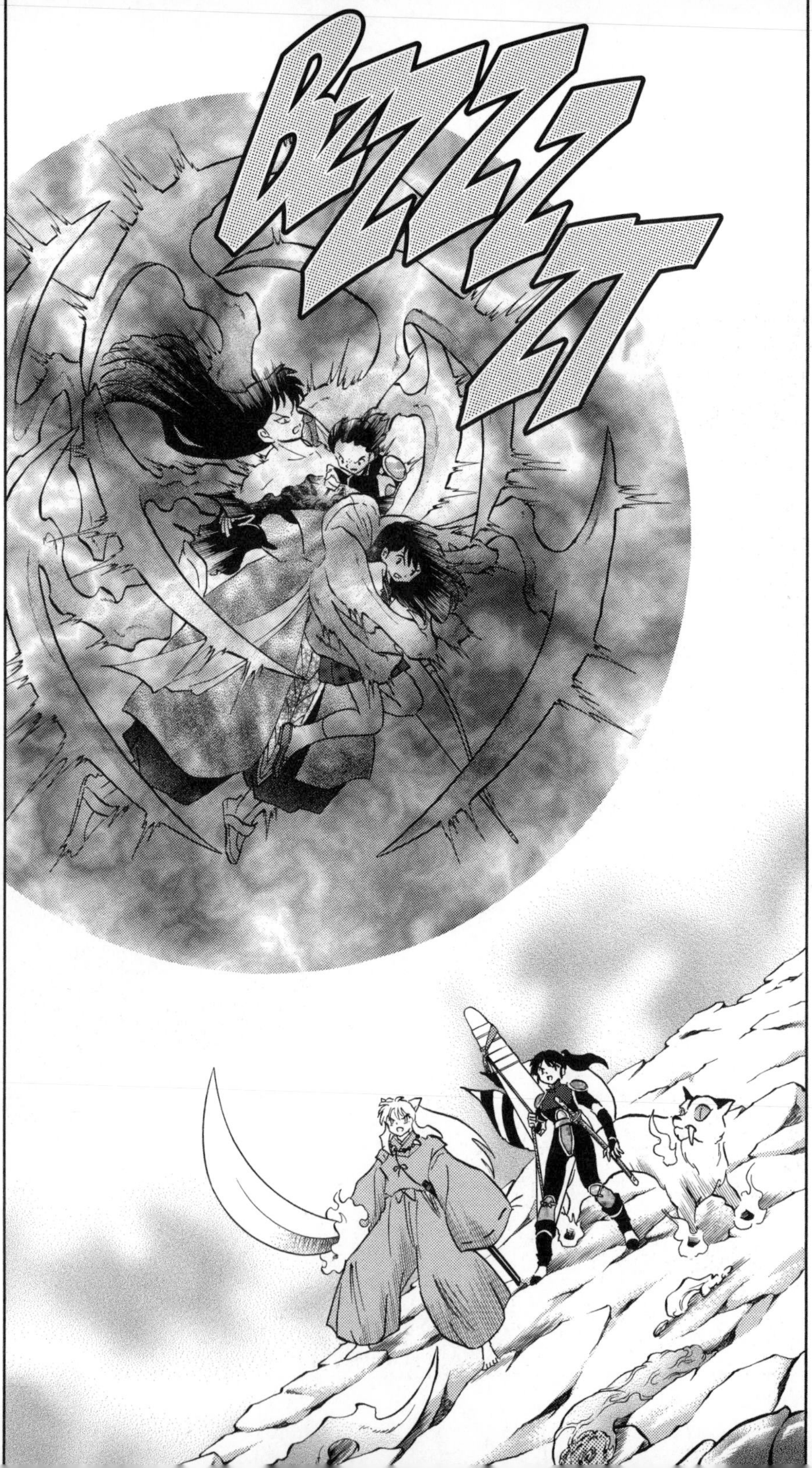
BZZZT

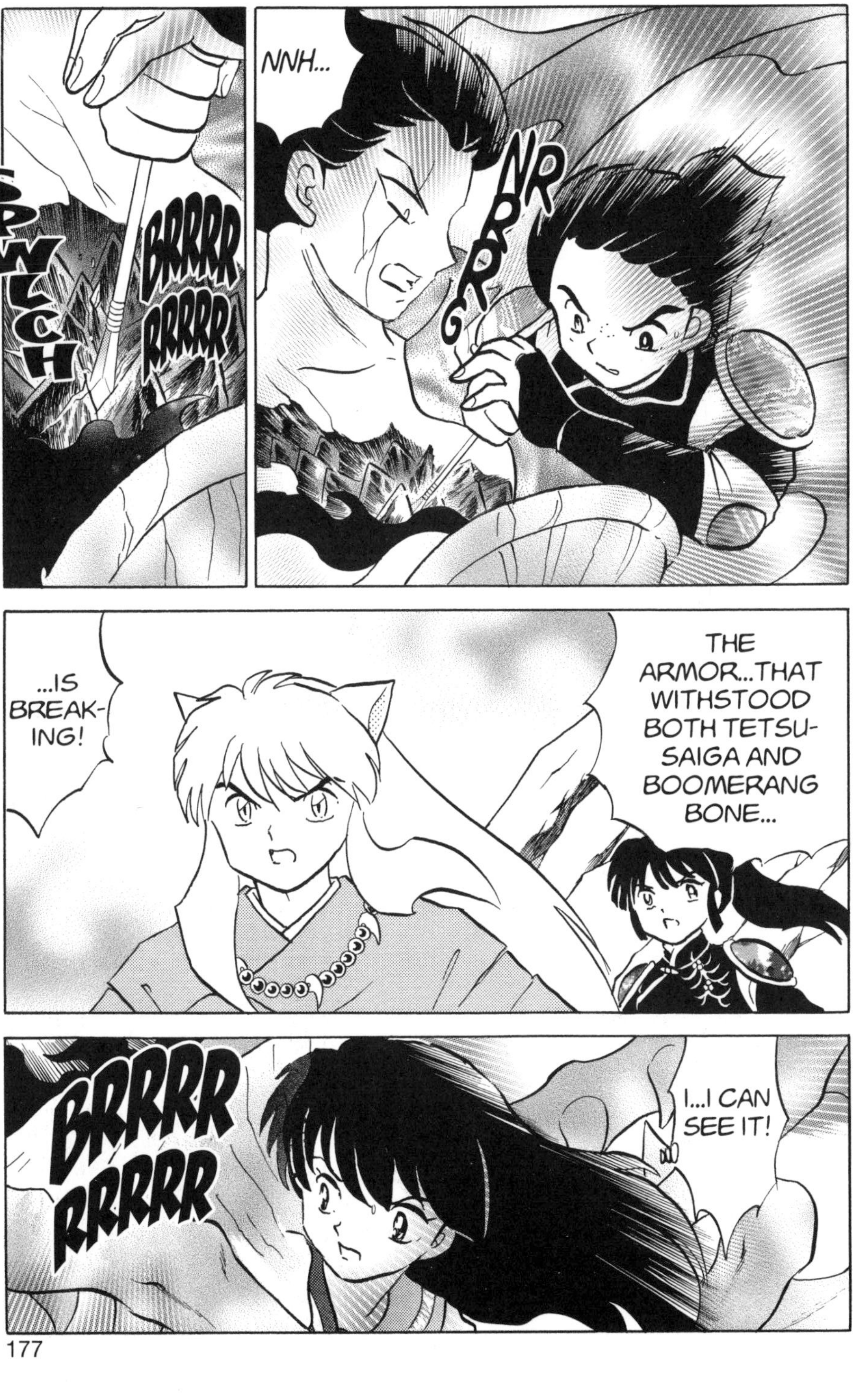
NNH...
NRRRG
SPWLCH
BRRRR
RRRRR
THE ARMOR...THAT WITHSTOOD BOTH TETSU-SAIGA AND BOOMERANG BONE...
...IS BREAK-ING!
I...I CAN SEE IT!
BRRRR
RRRRR

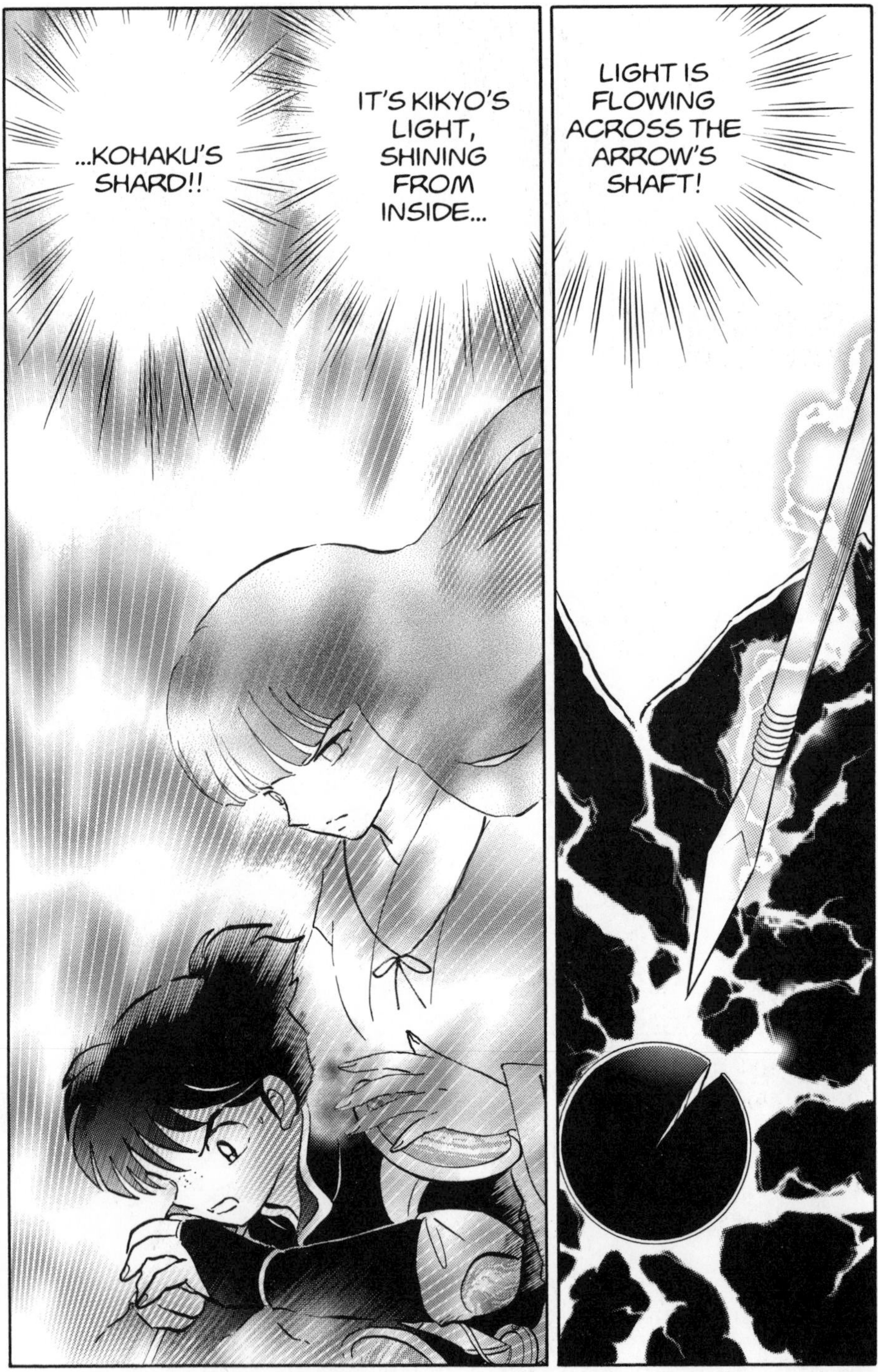
LIGHT IS FLOWING ACROSS THE ARROW'S SHAFT!
IT'S KIKYO'S LIGHT, SHINING FROM INSIDE...
...KOHAKU'S SHARD!!

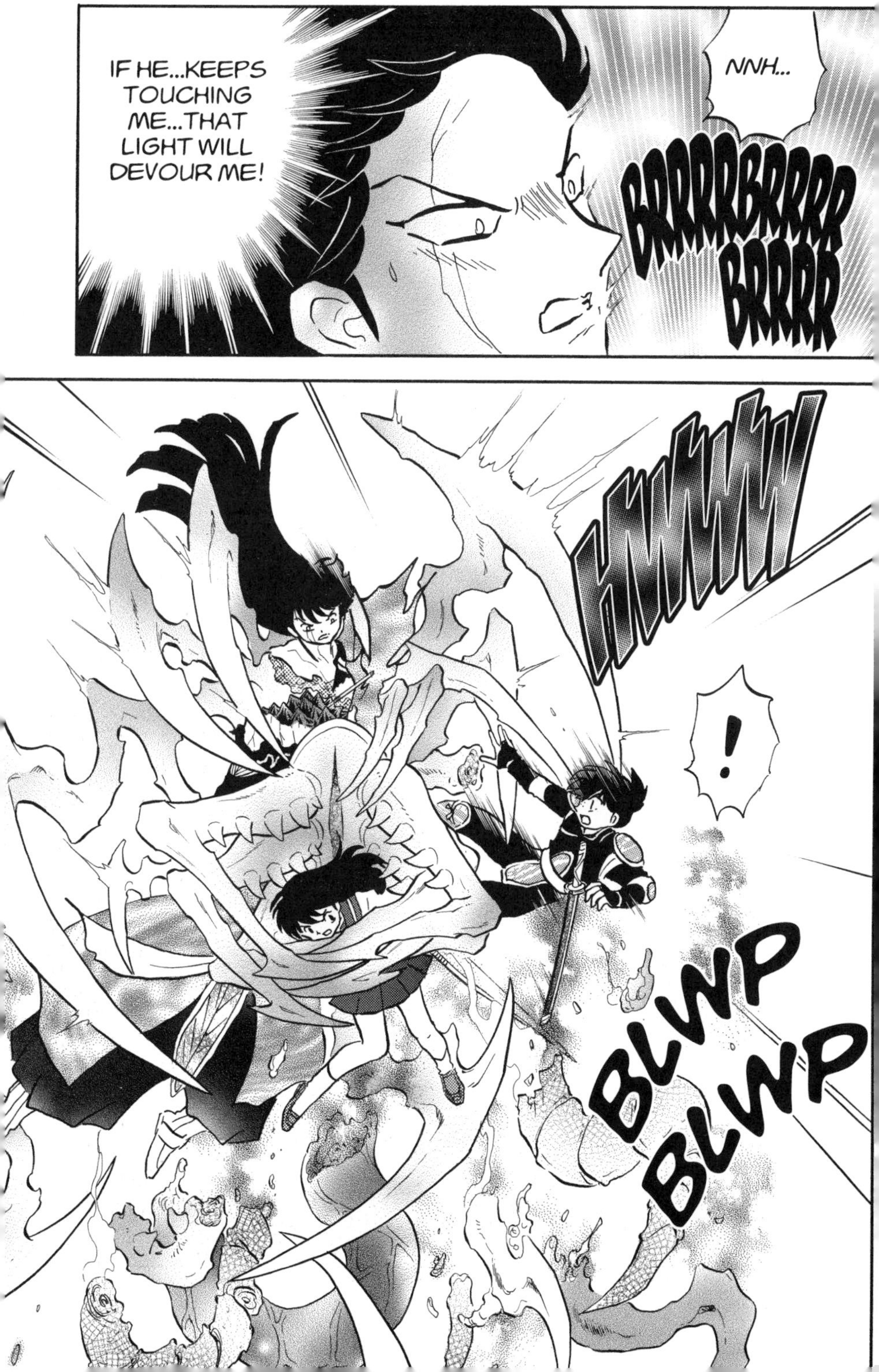
NNH...
BRRRRBRRRR
BRRRR
IF HE...KEEPS TOUCHING ME...THAT LIGHT WILL DEVOUR ME!
!
BLWP
BLWP

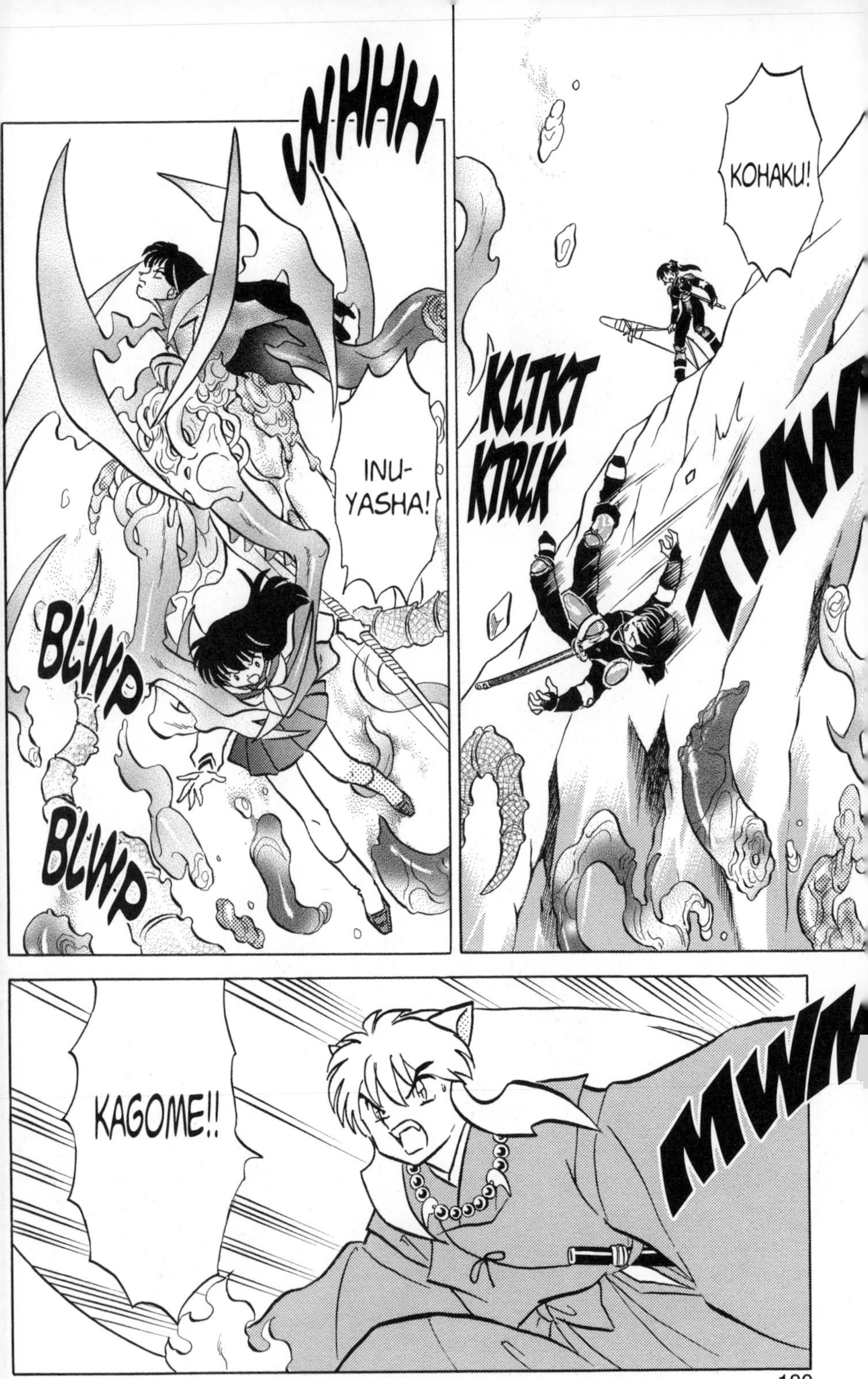
KOHAKU!
KLTKT KTRLK
THW
WHHH
INU-YASHA!
BLWP
BLWP
KAGOME!!
MWM

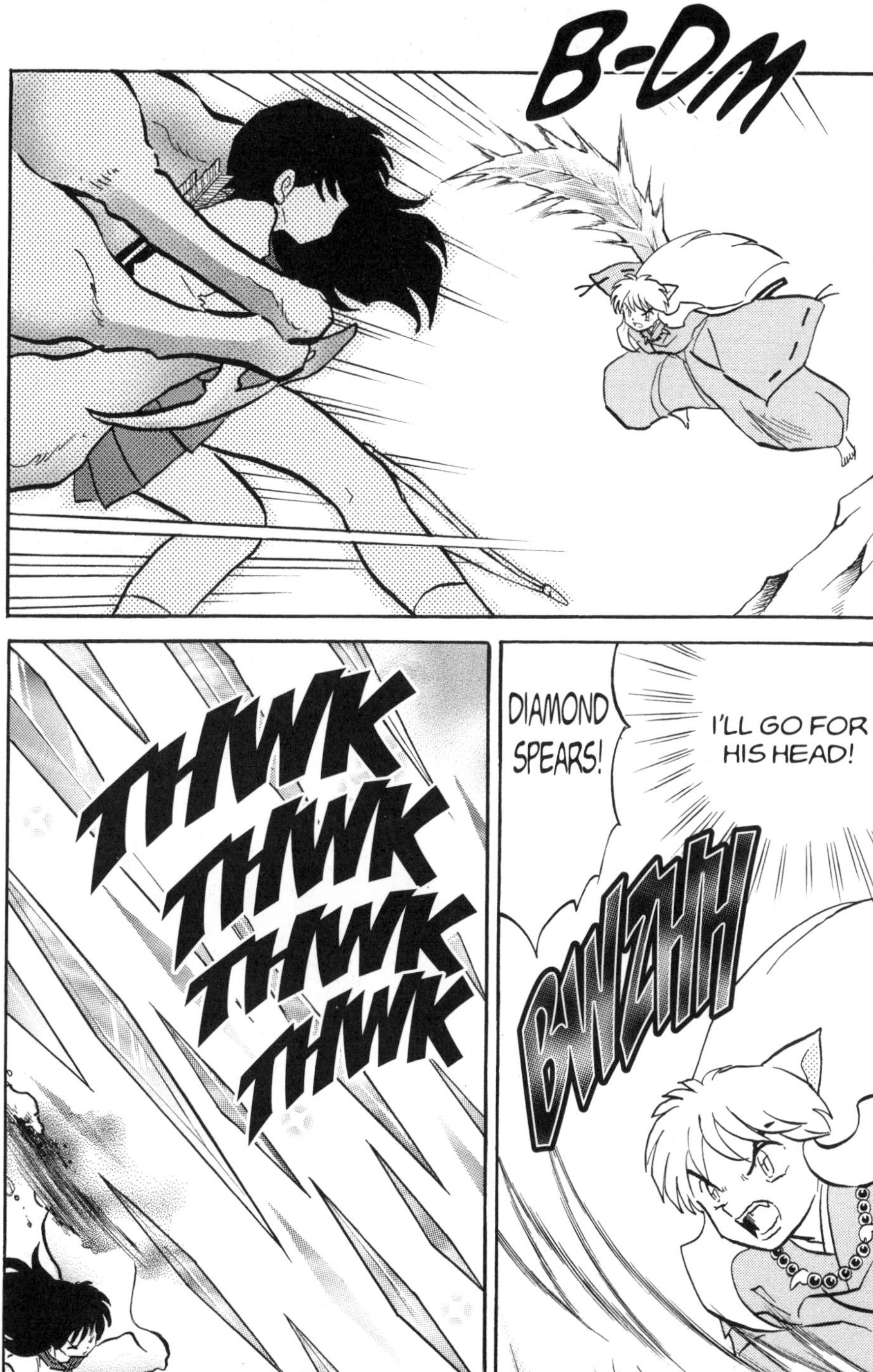
B-DM
I'LL GO FOR HIS HEAD!
DIAMOND SPEARS!
BWZHH
THWK
THWK
THWK
THWK

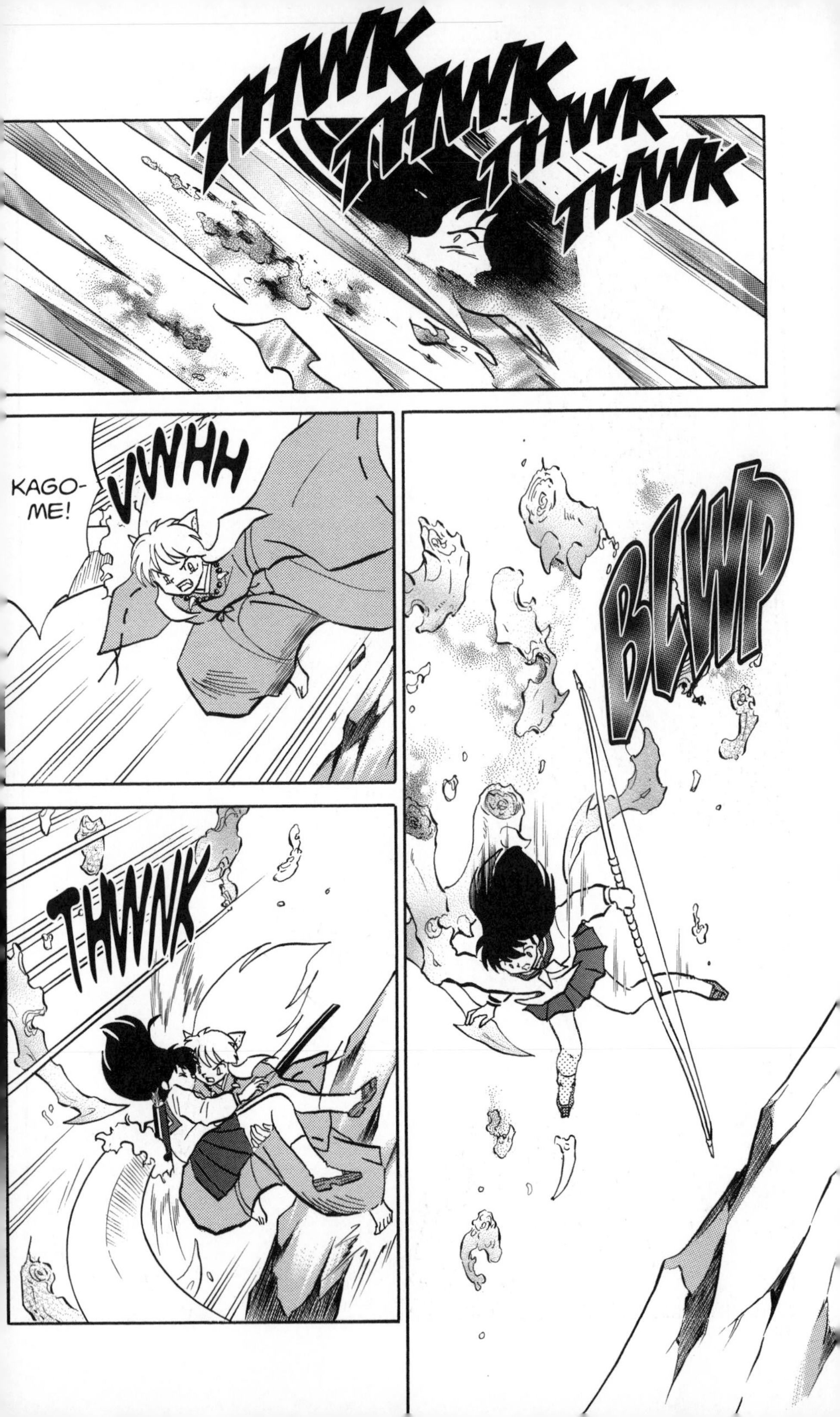
THWK
THWK
THWK
THWK
BLWP
VWHH
KAGO-ME!
THWNK

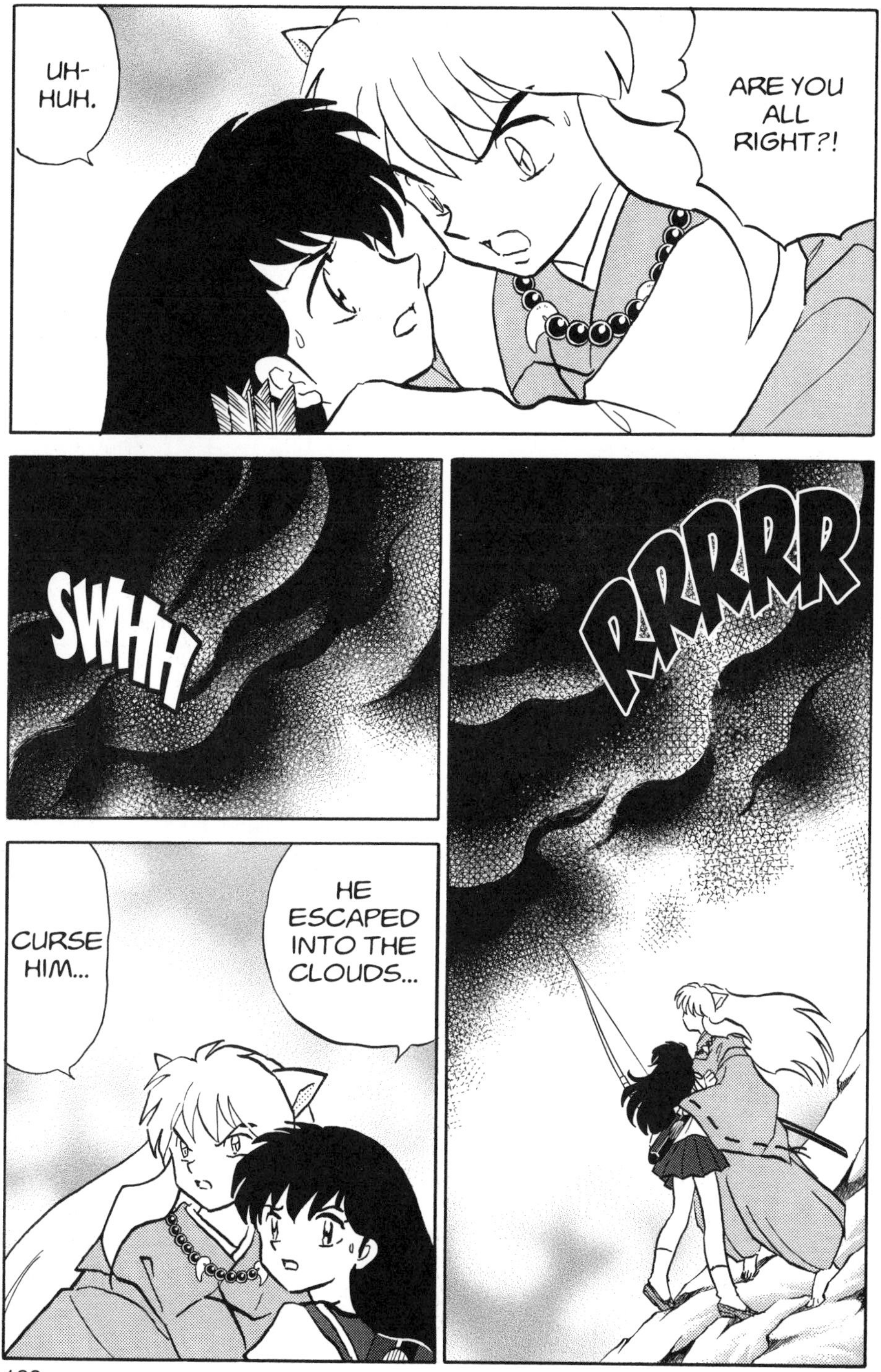
ARE YOU ALL RIGHT?!
UH-HUH.
RRRRR
SWHH
HE ESCAPED INTO THE CLOUDS...
CURSE HIM...

KOHAKU!

KO-
HAKU!

YOU DID
WELL.

THANK
GOD...

KO-
HAKU
...

BIG
SISTER
...

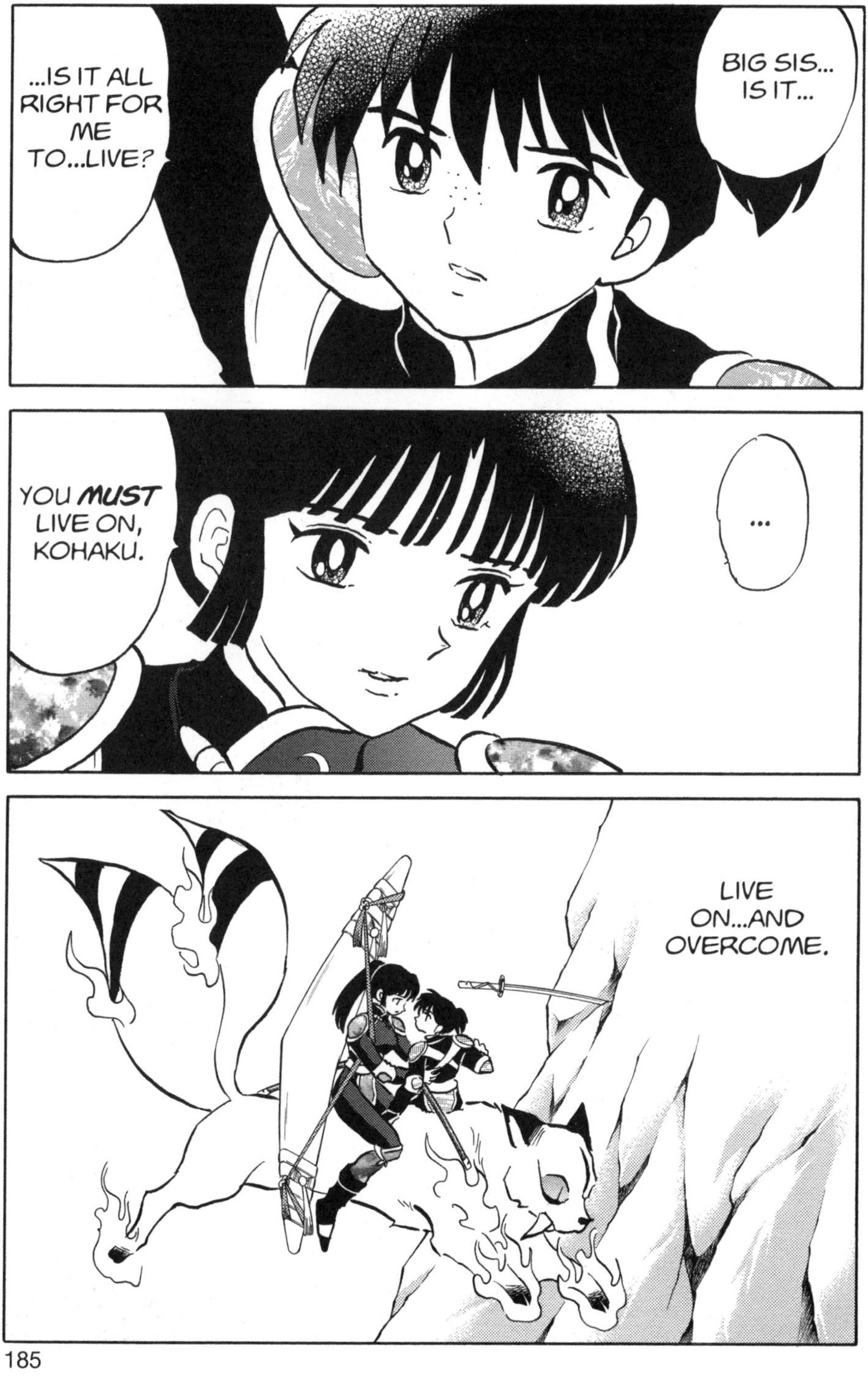
BIG SIS... IS IT...
...IS IT ALL RIGHT FOR ME TO...LIVE?
...
YOU **MUST** LIVE ON, KOHAKU.
LIVE ON...AND OVERCOME.

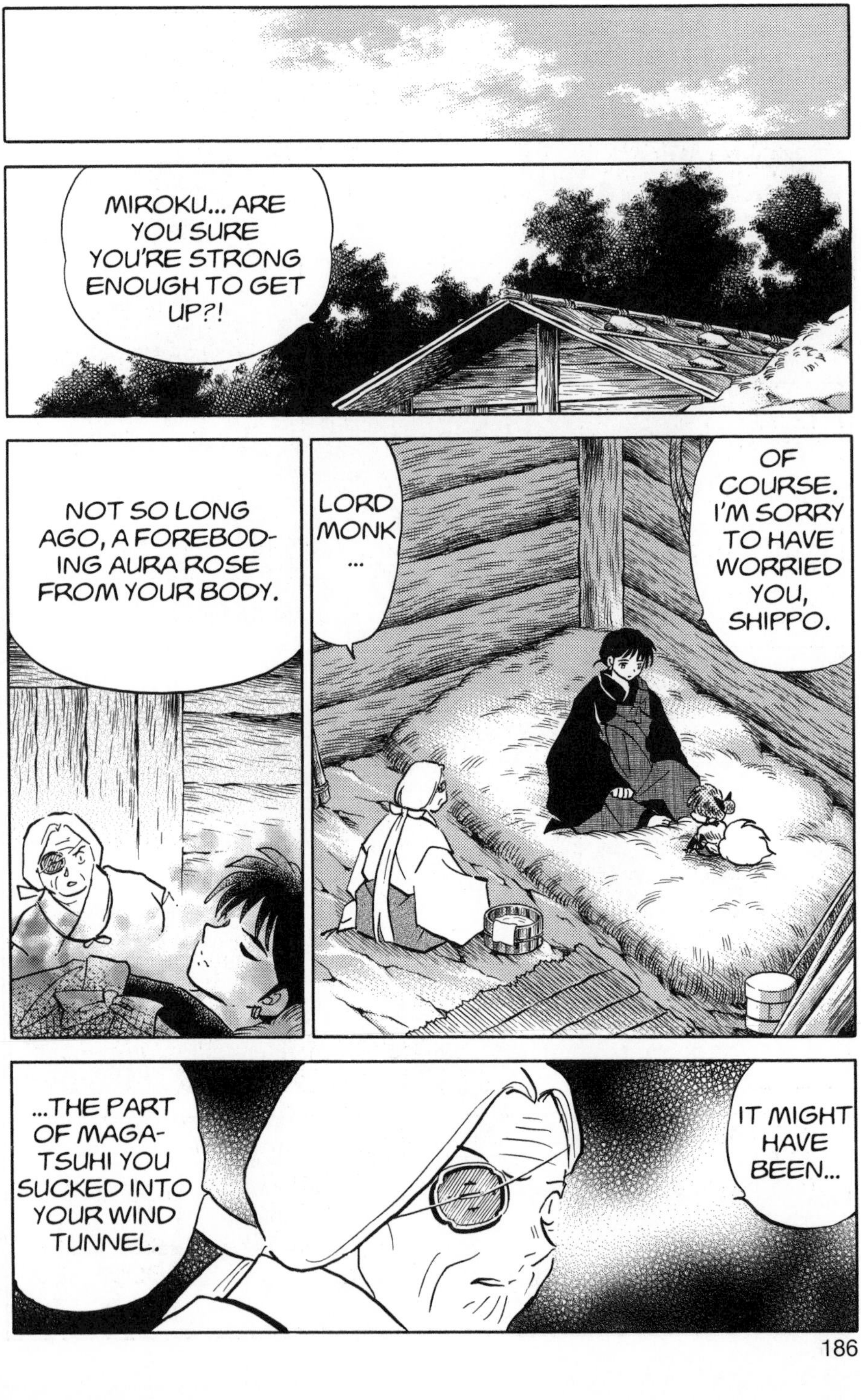
MIROKU... ARE YOU SURE YOU'RE STRONG ENOUGH TO GET UP?!
OF COURSE. I'M SORRY TO HAVE WORRIED YOU, SHIPPO.
LORD MONK ...
NOT SO LONG AGO, A FOREBODING AURA ROSE FROM YOUR BODY.
IT MIGHT HAVE BEEN...
...THE PART OF MAGATSUHI YOU SUCKED INTO YOUR WIND TUNNEL.

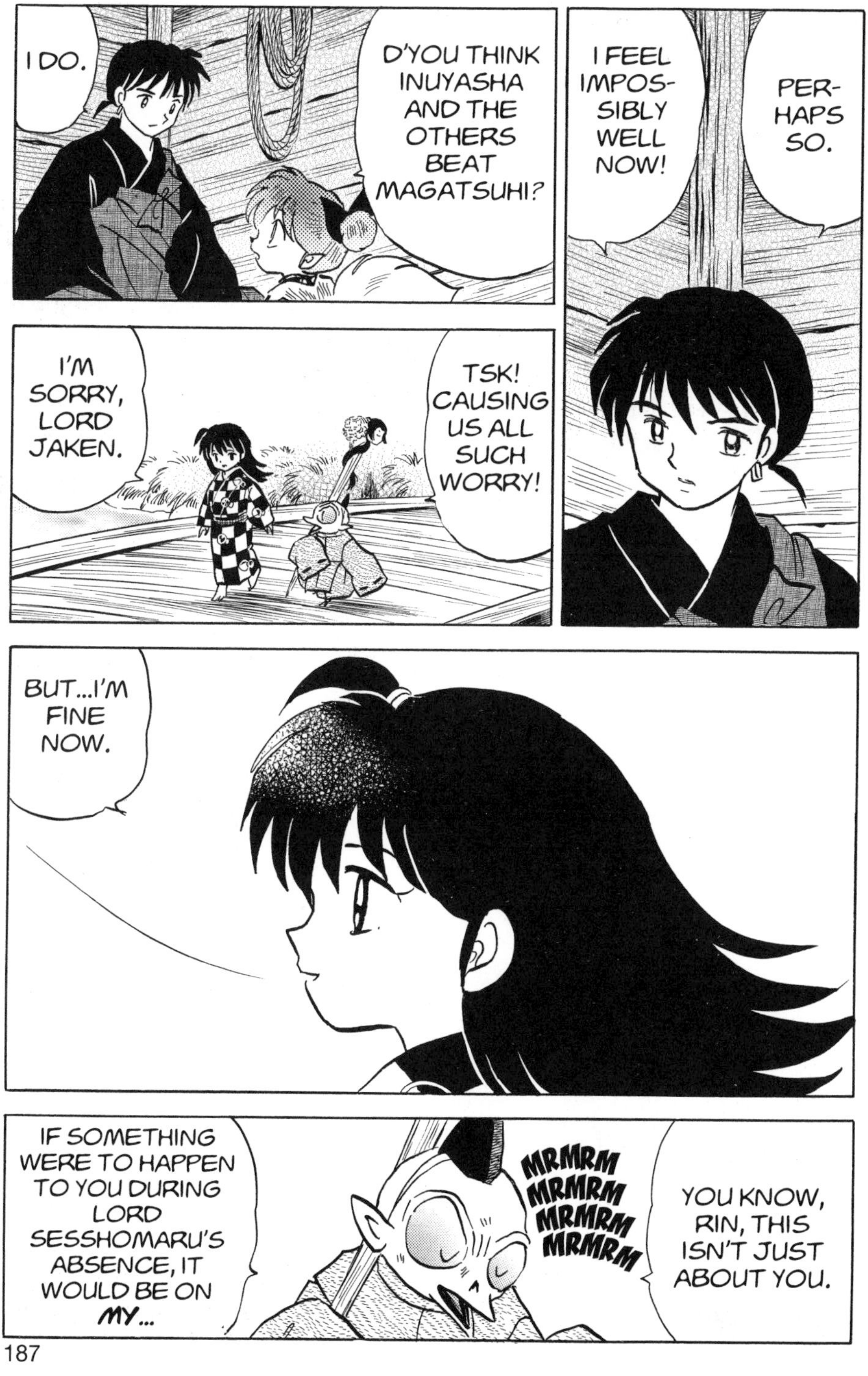
PER-HAPS SO.
I FEEL IMPOS-SIBLY WELL NOW!
D'YOU THINK INUYASHA AND THE OTHERS BEAT MAGATSUHI?
I DO.
TSK! CAUSING US ALL SUCH WORRY!
I'M SORRY, LORD JAKEN.
BUT...I'M FINE NOW.
YOU KNOW, RIN, THIS ISN'T JUST ABOUT YOU.
MRMRM MRMRM MRMRM MRMRM
IF SOMETHING WERE TO HAPPEN TO YOU DURING LORD SESSHOMARU'S ABSENCE, IT WOULD BE ON ***MY***...

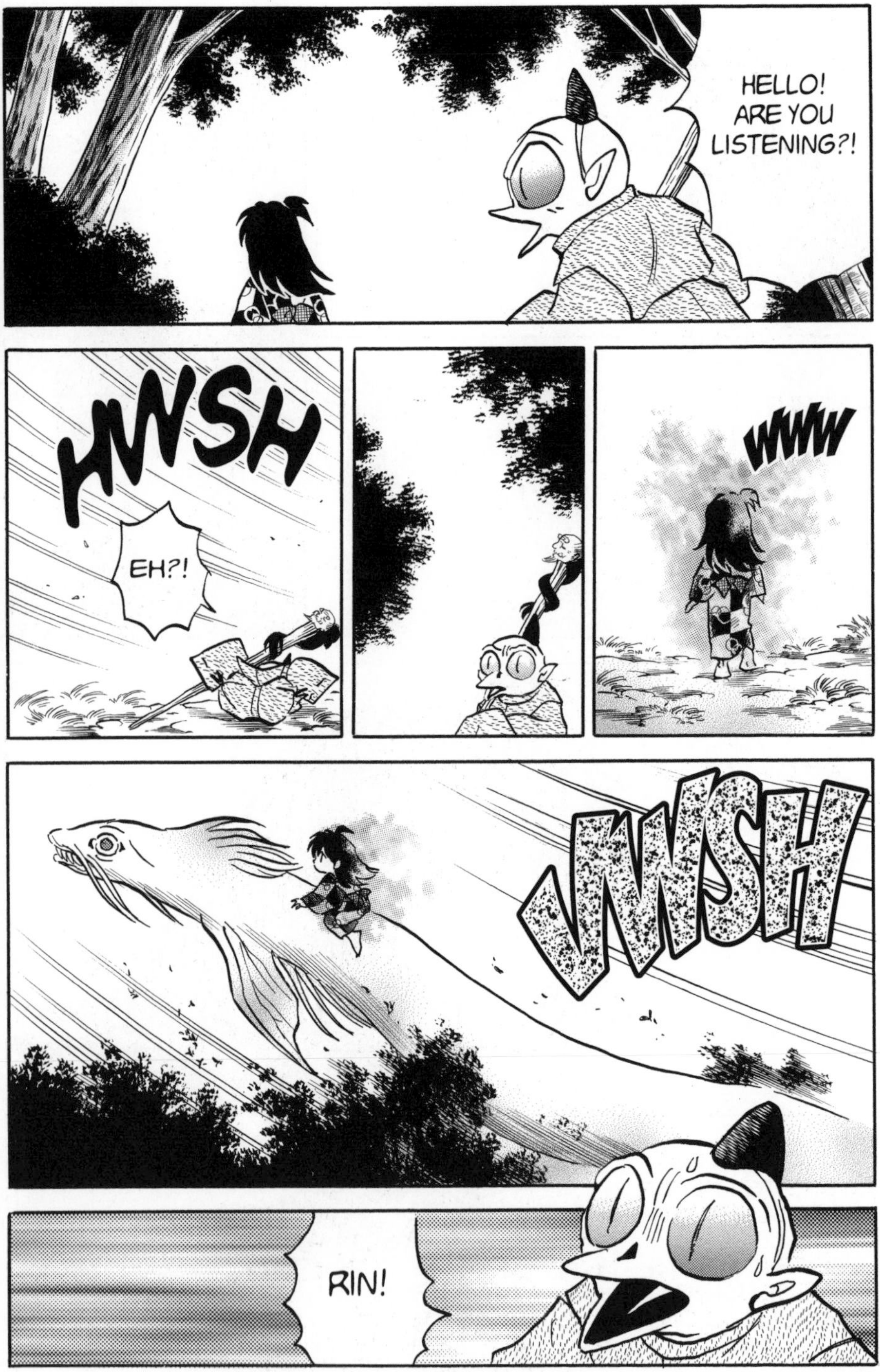
HELLO! ARE YOU LISTENING?!
WWW
HWSH
EH?!
WHSH
RIN!

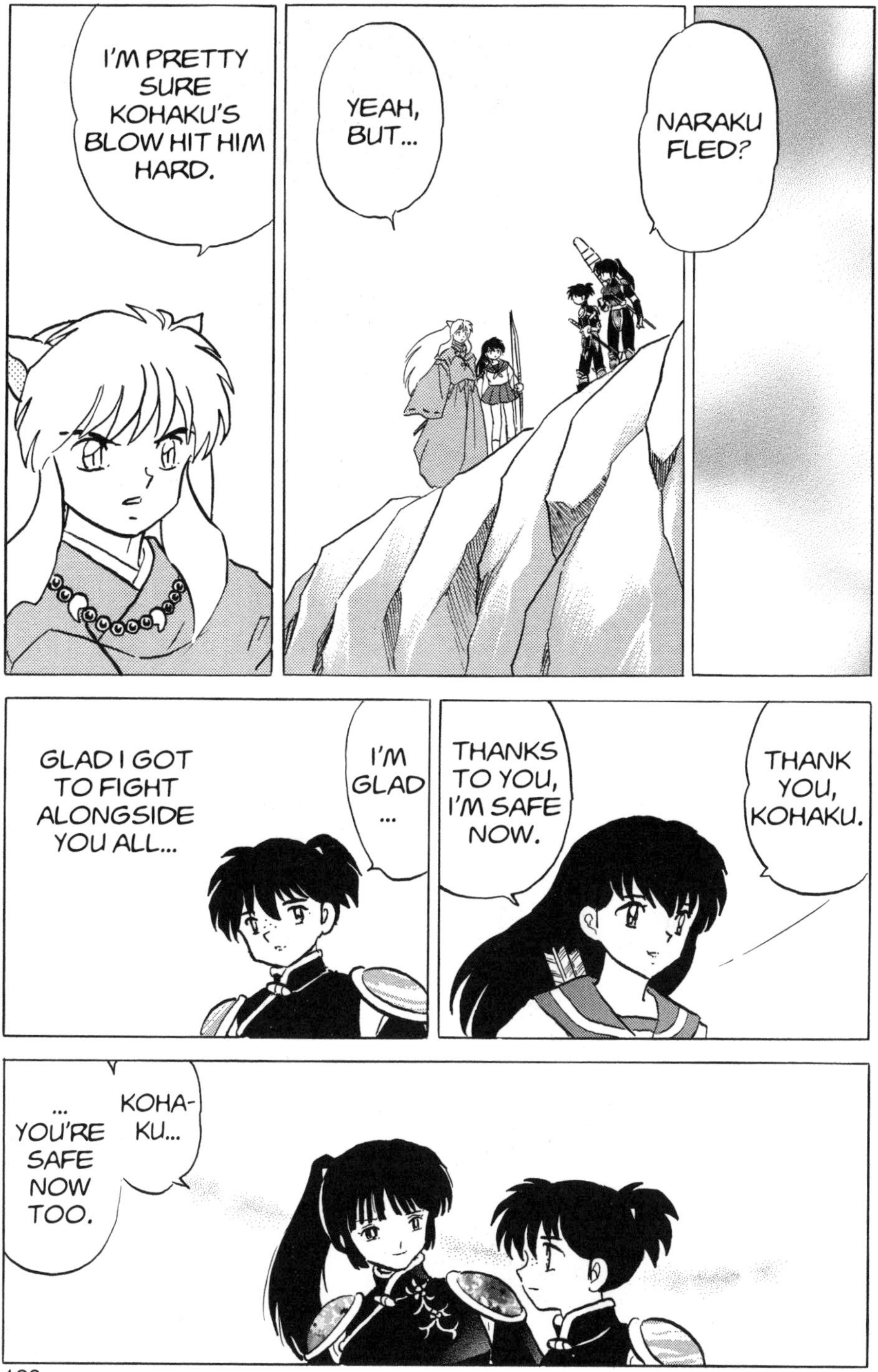
NARAKU FLED?
YEAH, BUT...
I'M PRETTY SURE KOHAKU'S BLOW HIT HIM HARD.
THANK YOU, KOHAKU.
THANKS TO YOU, I'M SAFE NOW.
I'M GLAD ...
GLAD I GOT TO FIGHT ALONGSIDE YOU ALL...
KOHA-KU...
... YOU'RE SAFE NOW TOO.

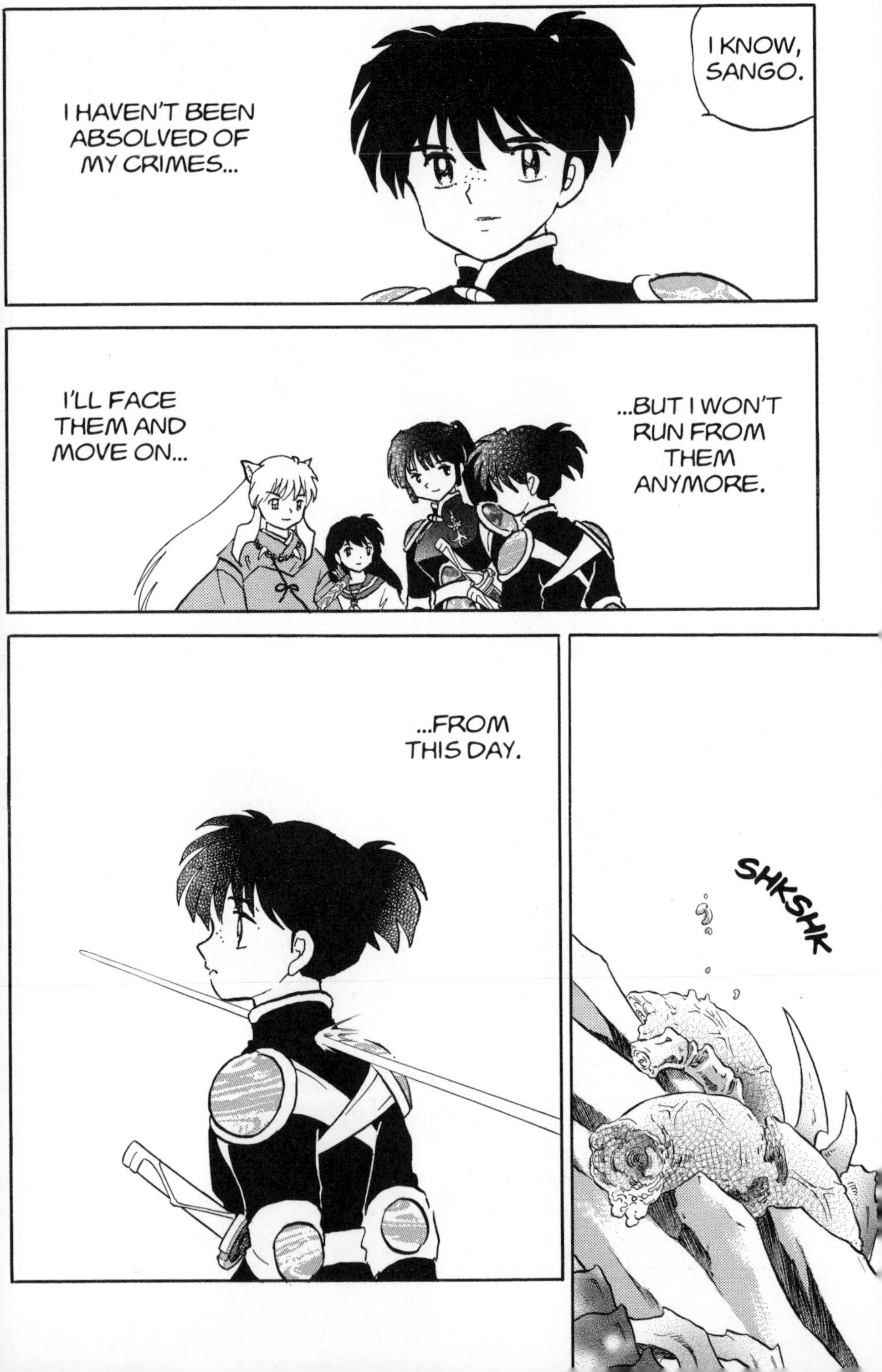
I KNOW, SANGO.
I HAVEN'T BEEN ABSOLVED OF MY CRIMES...
...BUT I WON'T RUN FROM THEM ANYMORE.
I'LL FACE THEM AND MOVE ON...
SHKSHK
...FROM THIS DAY.

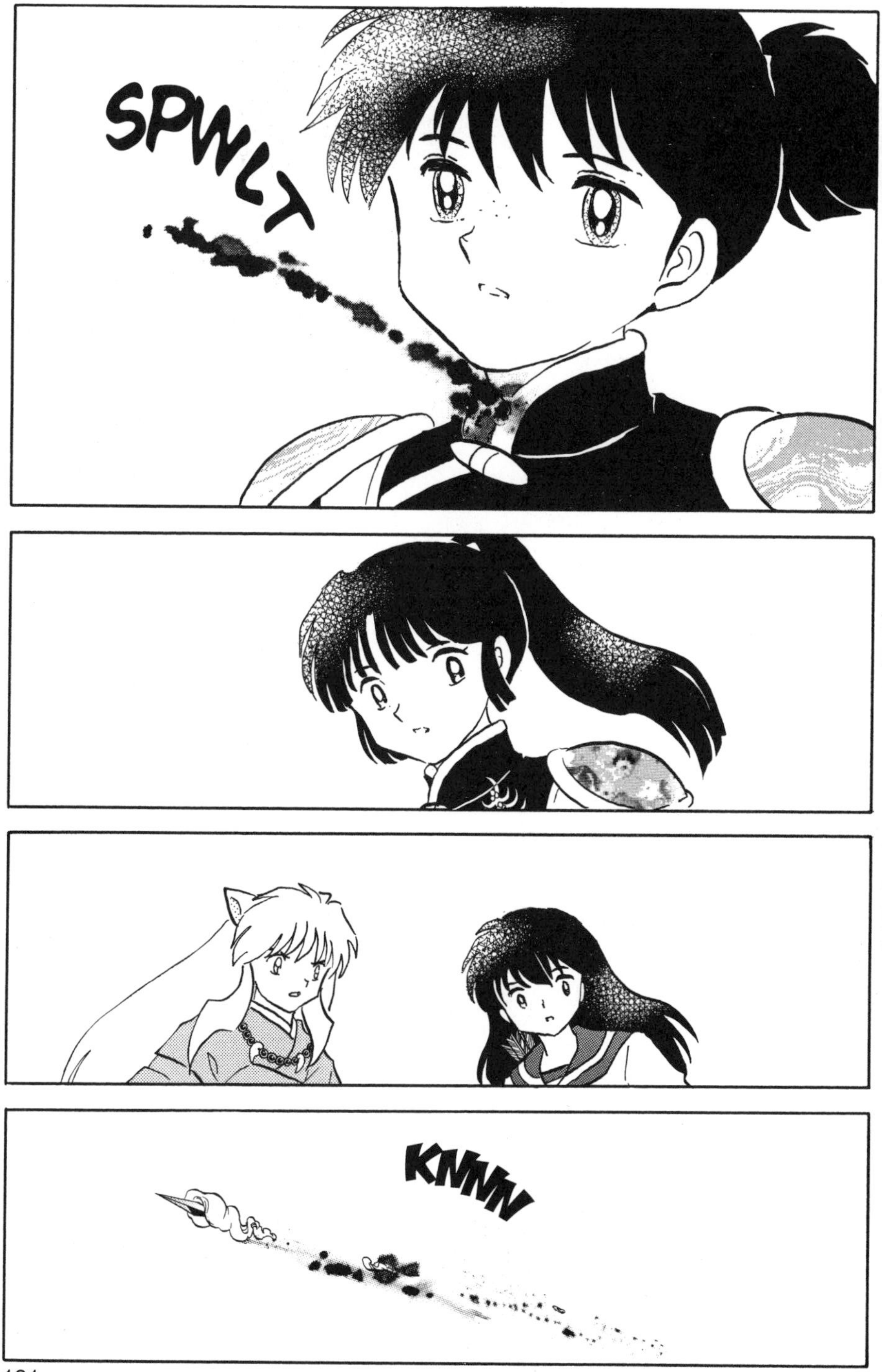
SPWLT
KNNN

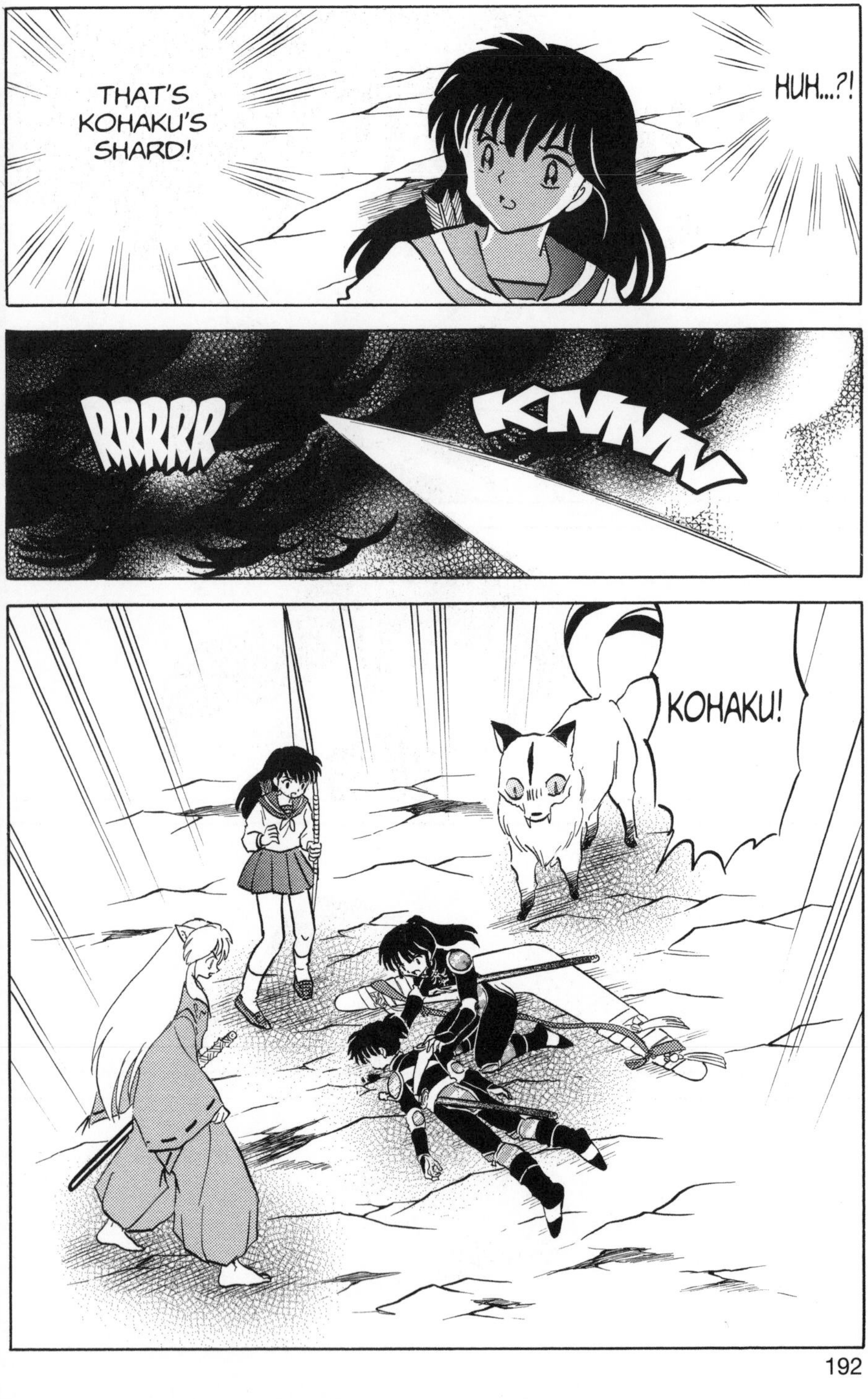
HUH...?!
THAT'S KOHAKU'S SHARD!
KNNN
RRRRR
KOHAKU!

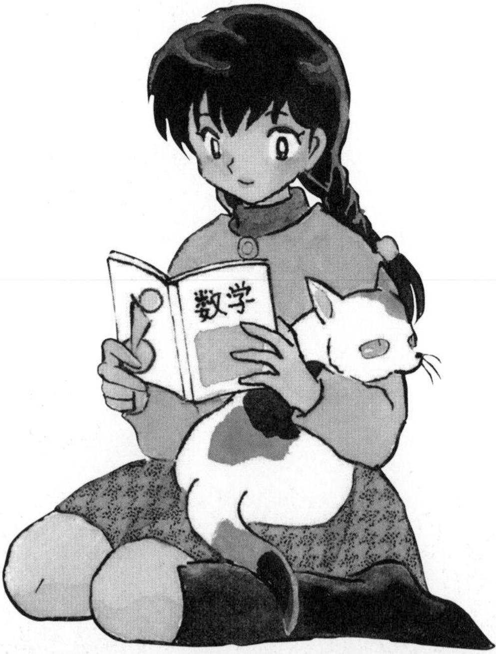
数学

Volume 54
The Jewel Completed

SCROLL ONE
THE JEWEL COMPLETED

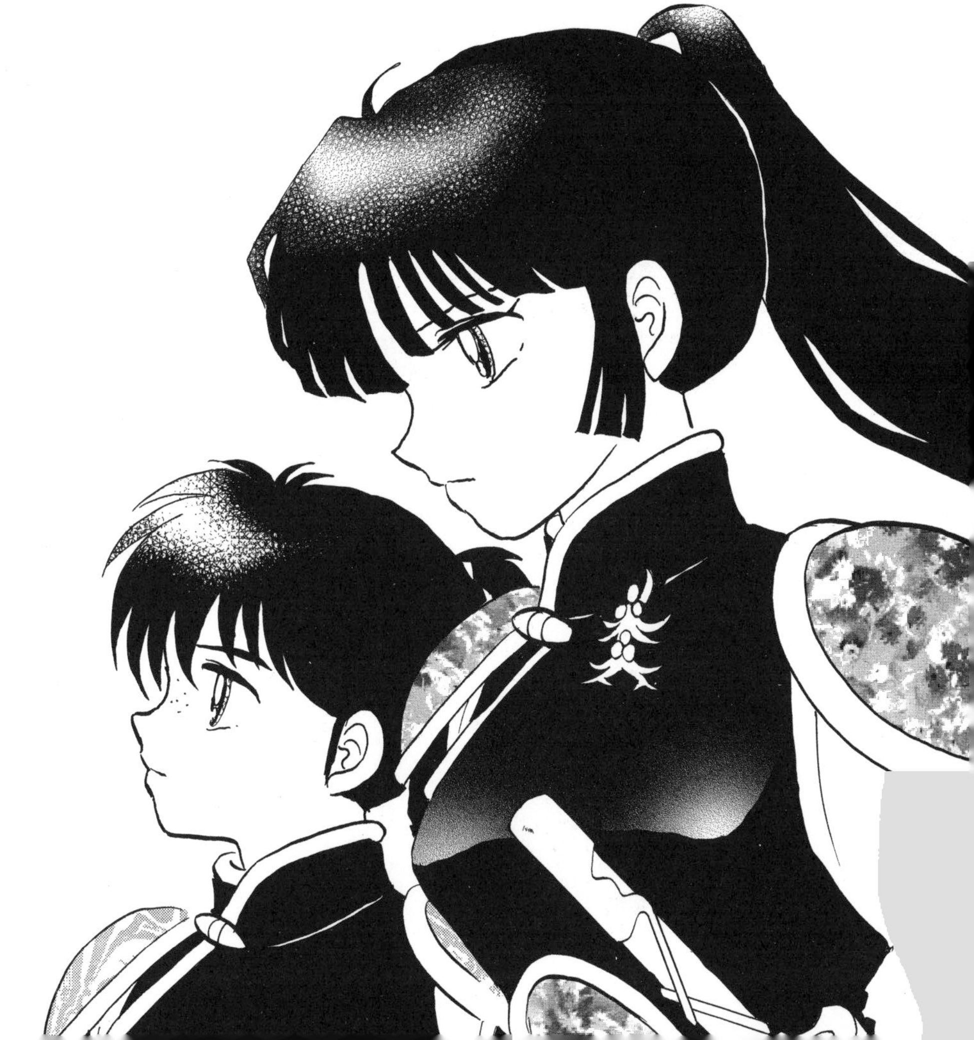

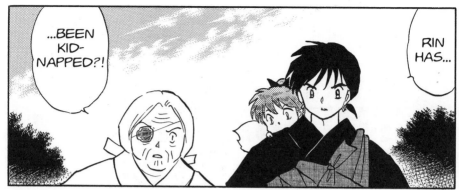

RIN HAS...
...BEEN KID-NAPPED?!
IT'S YOUR FAULT, MONK! THAT EVIL AURA THAT SEEPED OUT OF YOUR BODY...
IT SWAL-LOWED THE GIRL UP AND—
EVIL AURA ...?
MAGA-TSUHI...
MAGATSUHI? **HE** TOOK HER?!

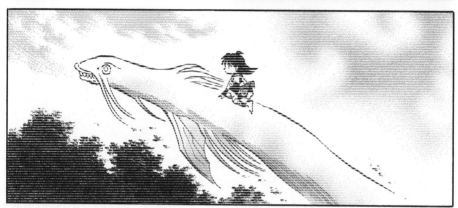

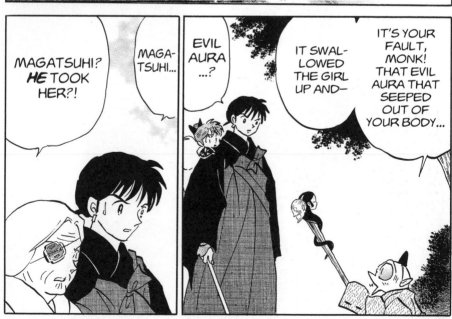

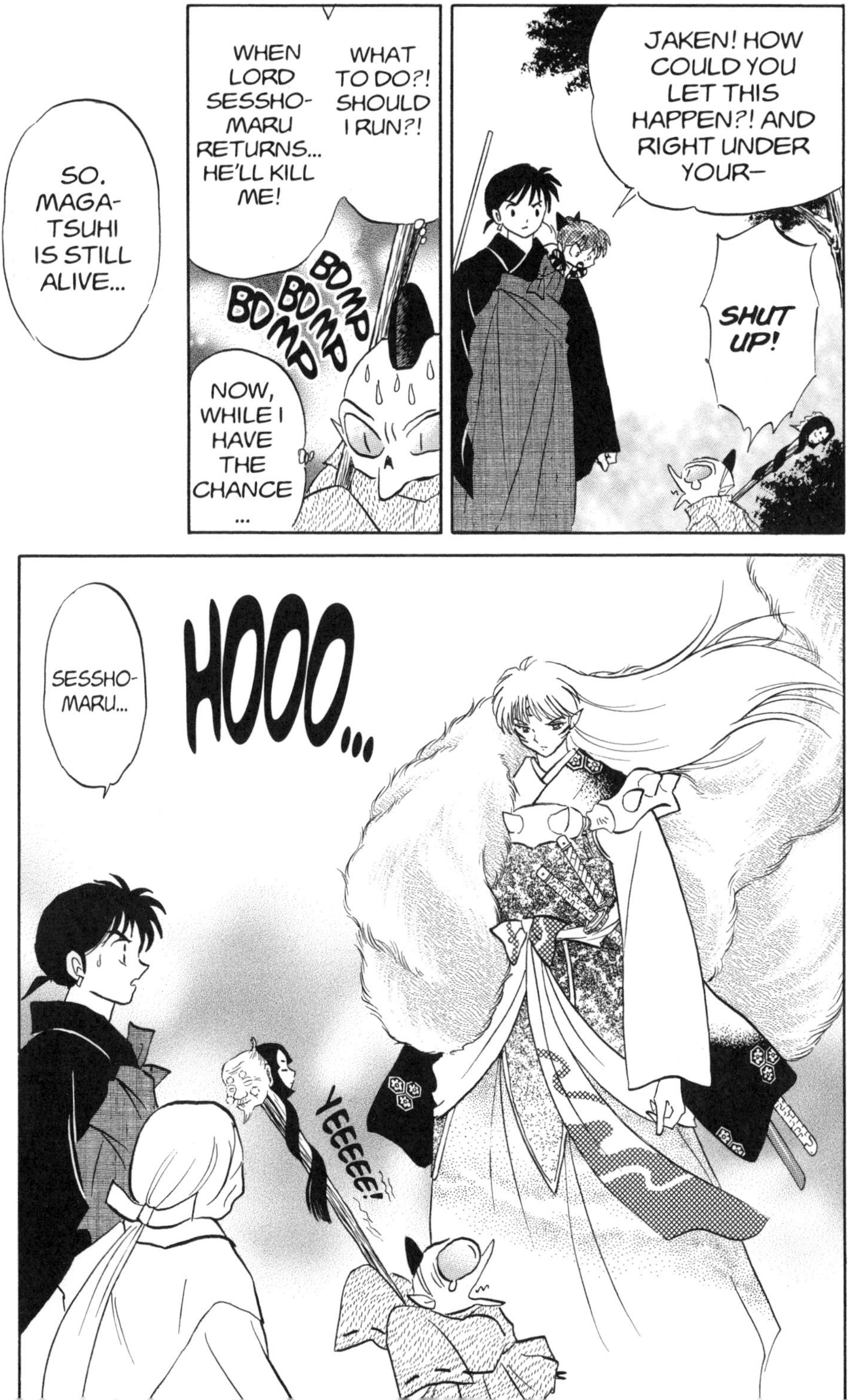
JAKEN! HOW COULD YOU LET THIS HAPPEN?! AND RIGHT UNDER YOUR—
SHUT UP!
WHAT TO DO?! SHOULD I RUN?!
WHEN LORD SESSHO-MARU RETURNS... HE'LL KILL ME!
BDMP BDMP BDMP
NOW, WHILE I HAVE THE CHANCE ...
SO. MAGA-TSUHI IS STILL ALIVE...
HOOO...
SESSHO-MARU...
YEEEEE!

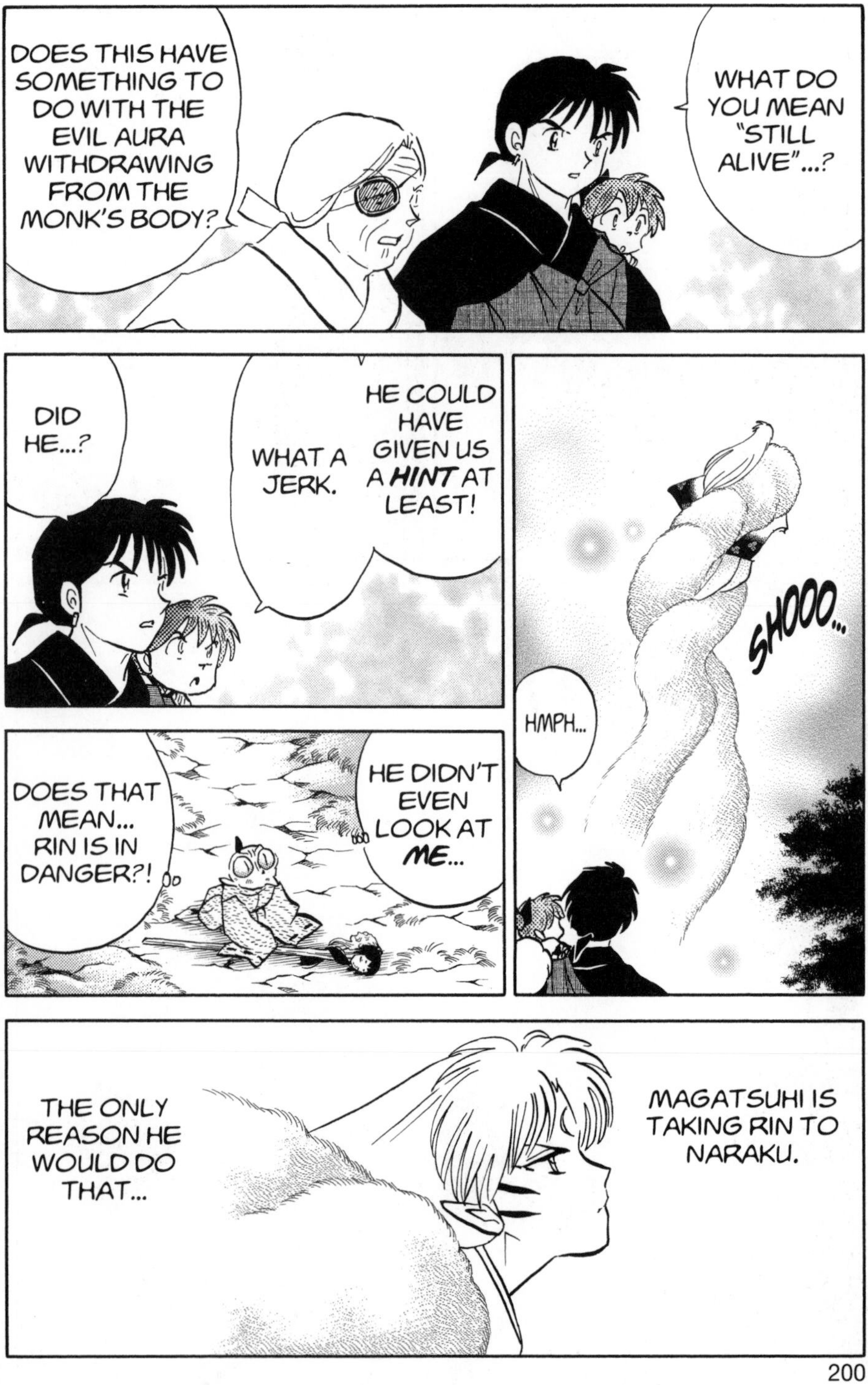
WHAT DO YOU MEAN "STILL ALIVE"...?
DOES THIS HAVE SOMETHING TO DO WITH THE EVIL AURA WITHDRAWING FROM THE MONK'S BODY?
SHOOO...
HMPH...
HE COULD HAVE GIVEN US A **HINT** AT LEAST!
WHAT A JERK.
DID HE...?
HE DIDN'T EVEN LOOK AT **ME**...
DOES THAT MEAN... RIN IS IN DANGER?!
MAGATSUHI IS TAKING RIN TO NARAKU.
THE ONLY REASON HE WOULD DO THAT...

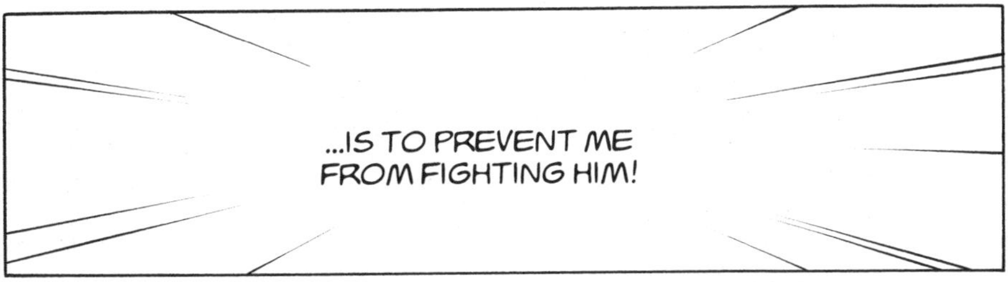
...IS TO PREVENT ME FROM FIGHTING HIM!

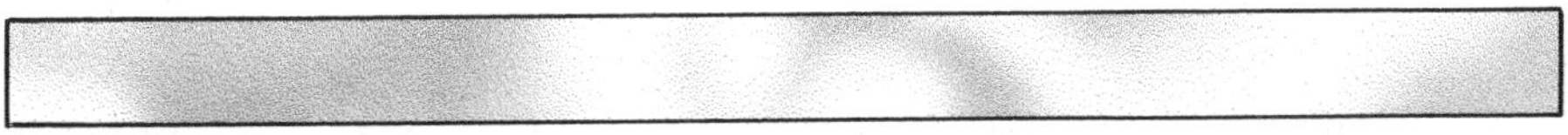

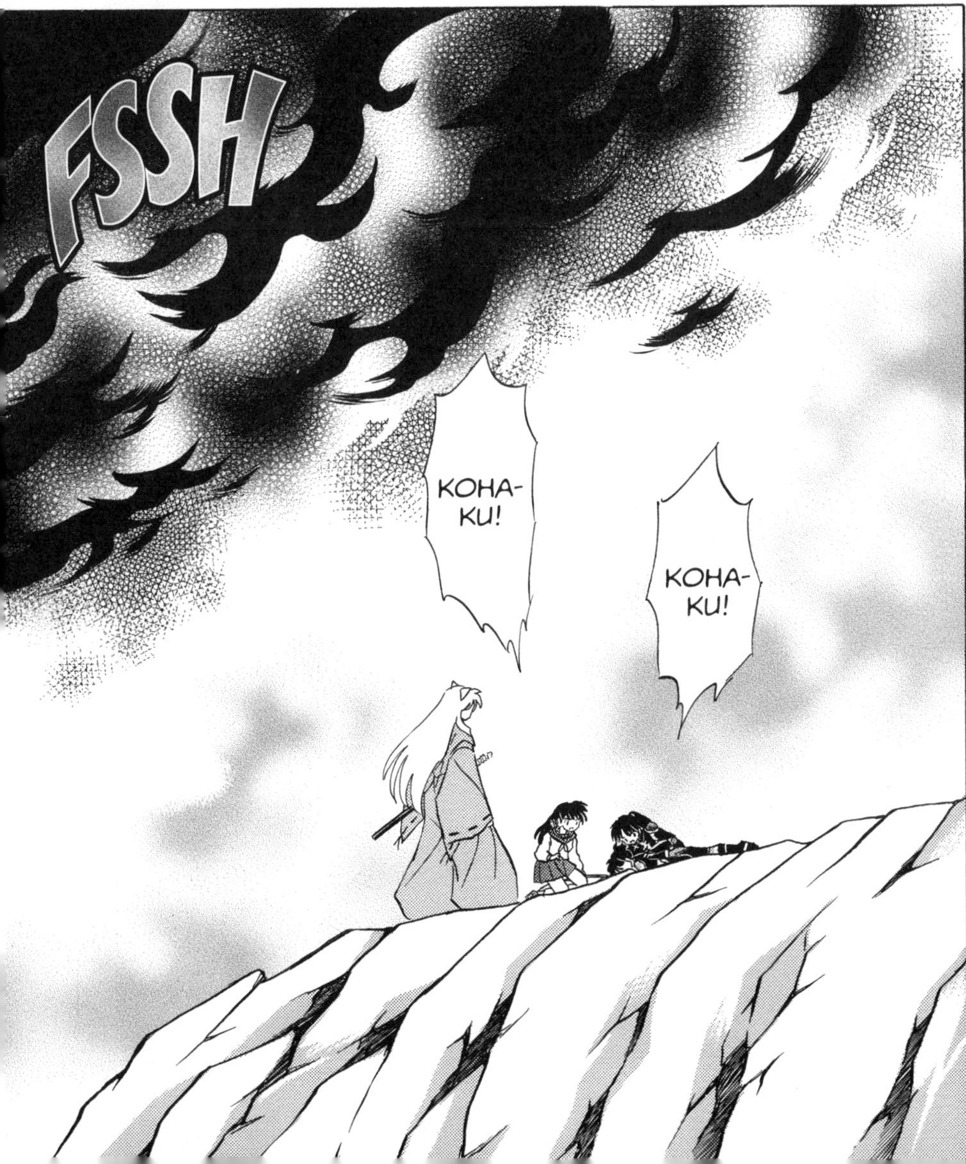
FSSH
KOHA-KU!
KOHA-KU!

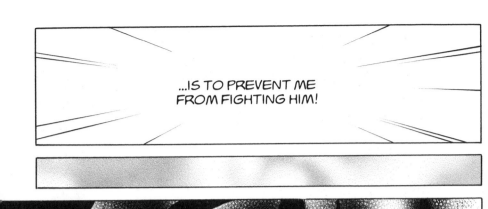

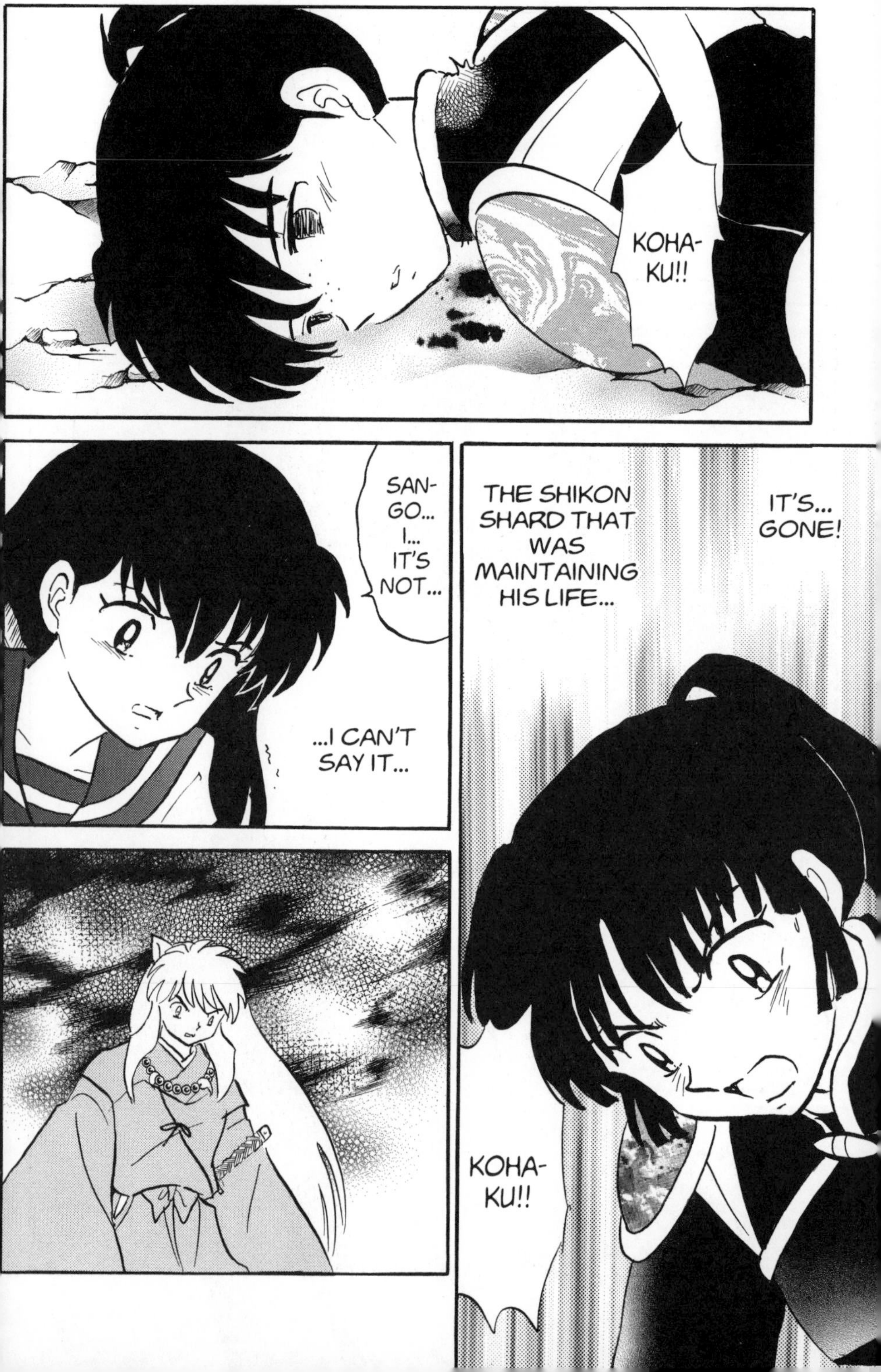
KOHA-KU!!
IT'S... GONE!
THE SHIKON SHARD THAT WAS MAINTAINING HIS LIFE...
KOHA-KU!!
SAN-GO... I... IT'S NOT...
...I CAN'T SAY IT...

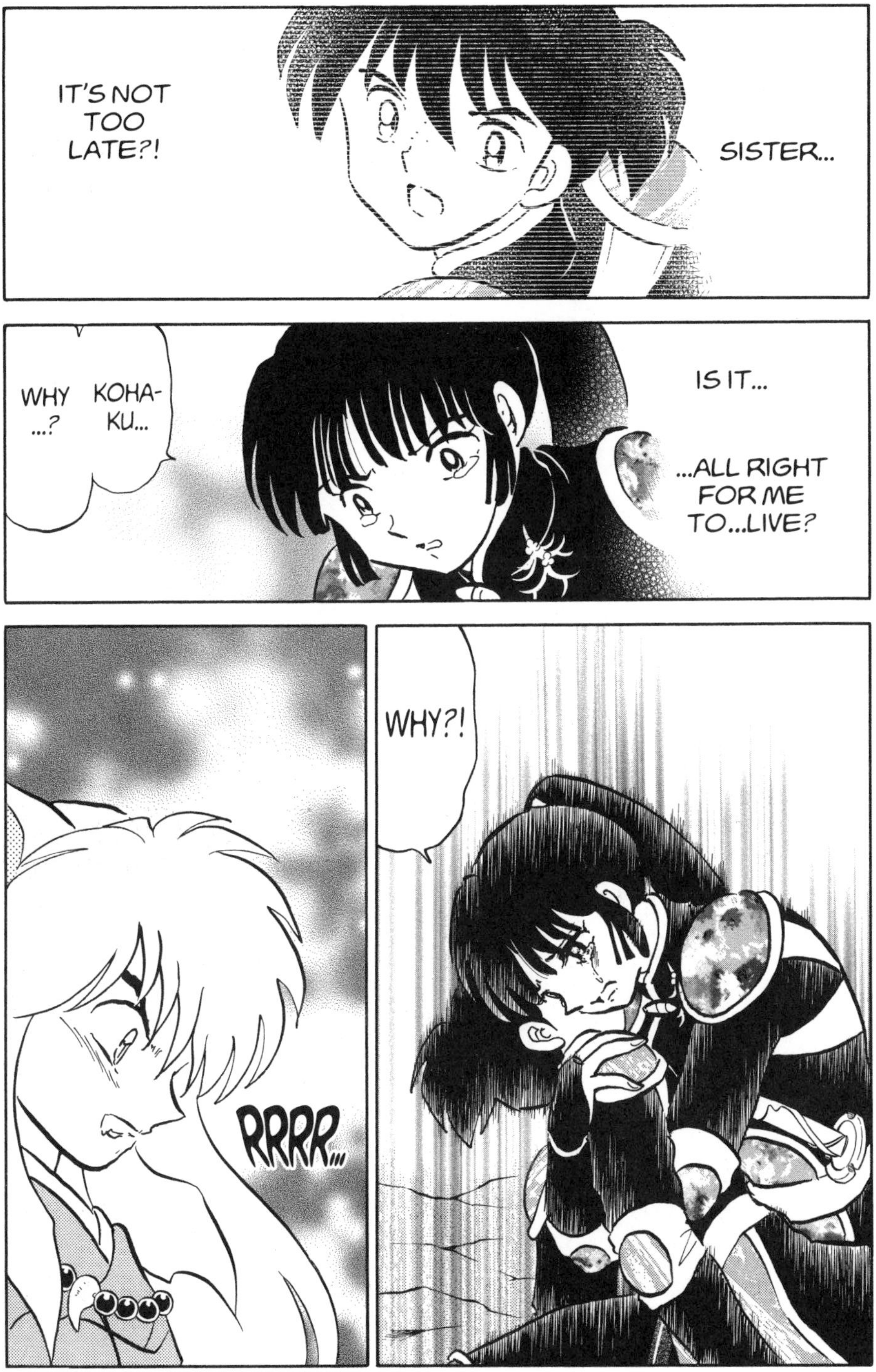
SISTER...
IT'S NOT TOO LATE?!
IS IT...
...ALL RIGHT FOR ME TO...LIVE?
WHY ...? KOHA-KU...
WHY?!
RRRR...

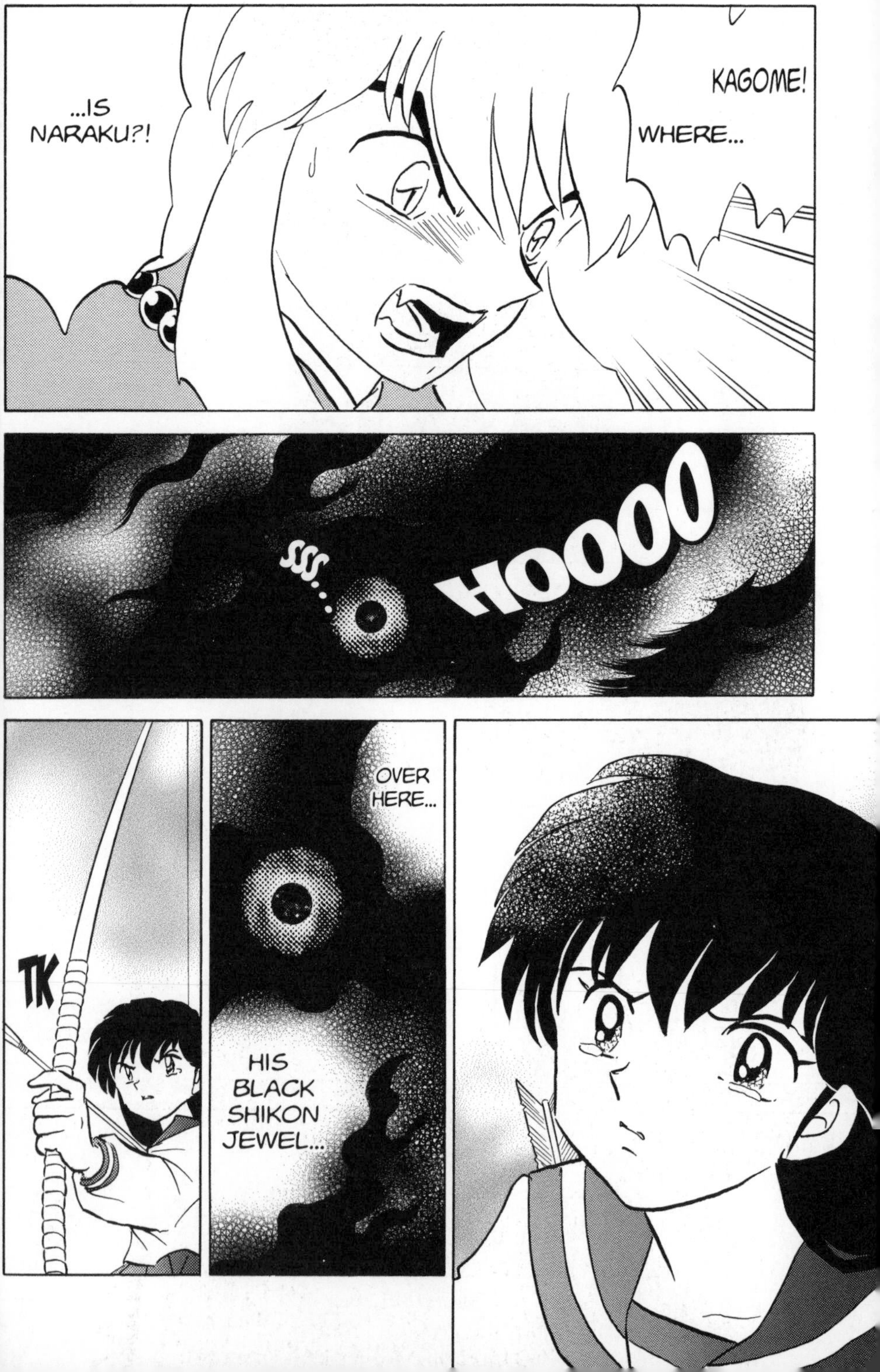
KAGOME!
WHERE...
...IS NARAKU?!
HOOOO
SSS...
OVER HERE...
HIS BLACK SHIKON JEWEL...
TK

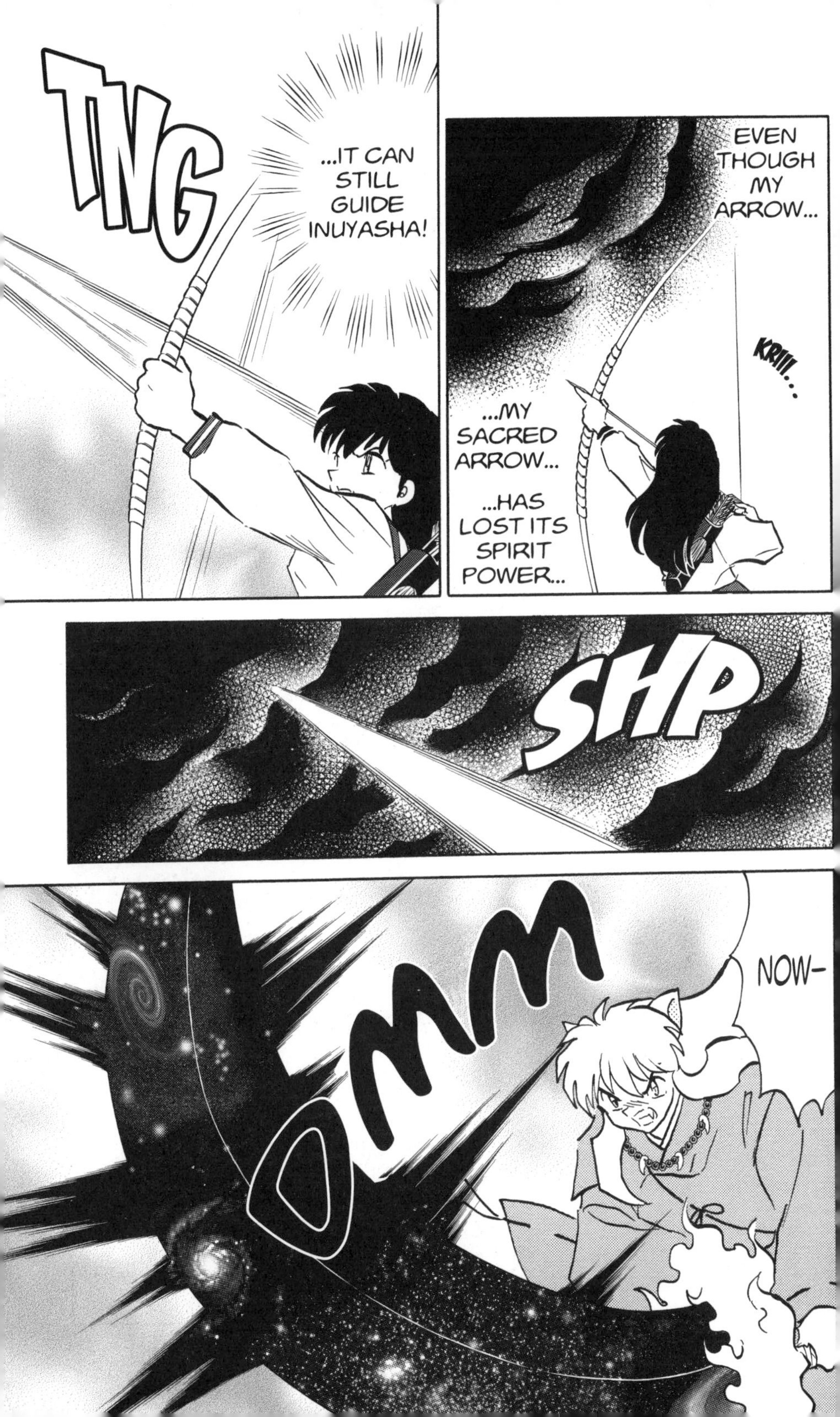
EVEN THOUGH MY ARROW...
KRIII...
...MY SACRED ARROW...
...HAS LOST ITS SPIRIT POWER...
...IT CAN STILL GUIDE INUYASHA!
TNG
SHP
NOW-
OMM

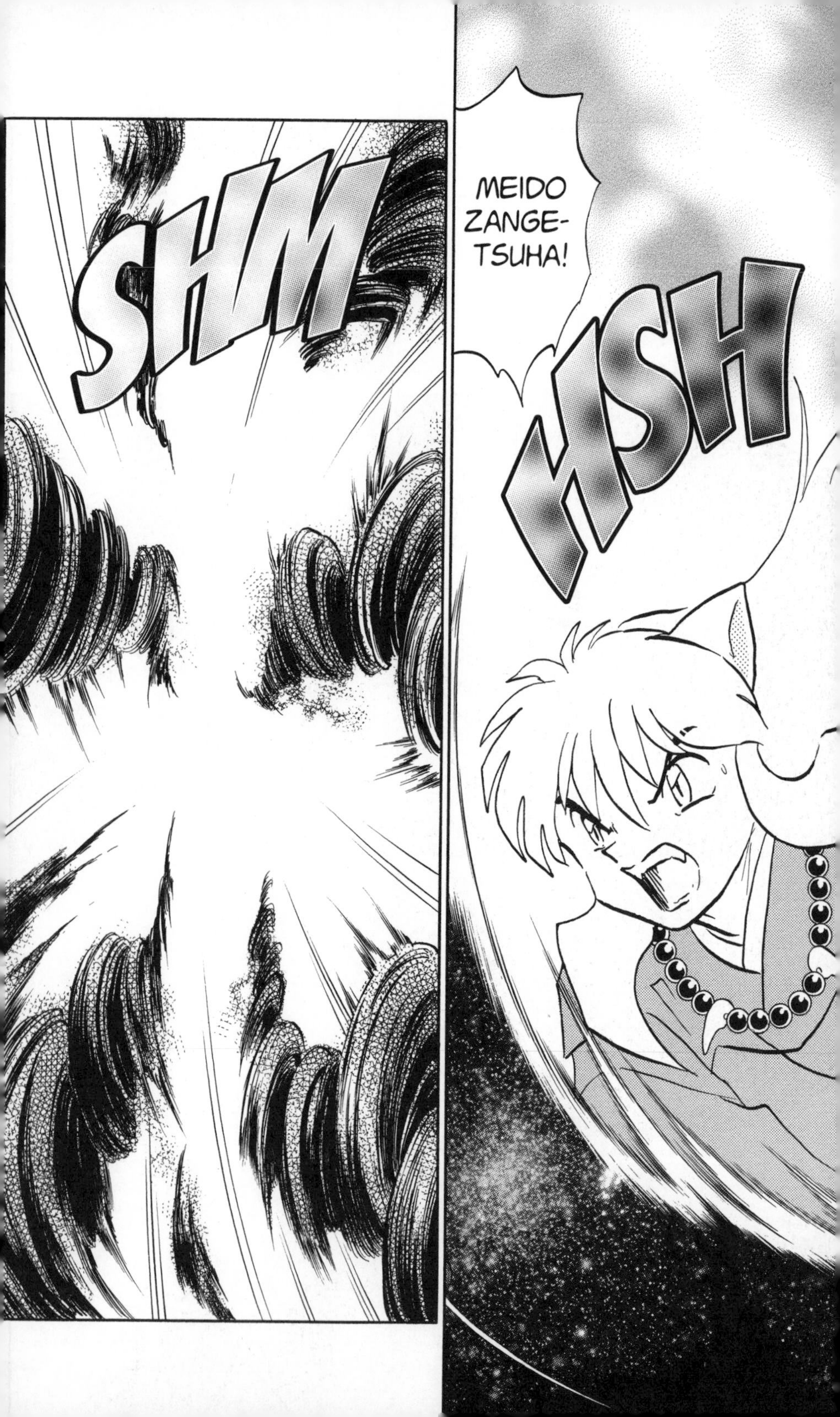
MEIDO ZANGE-TSUHA!
HSH
SHM

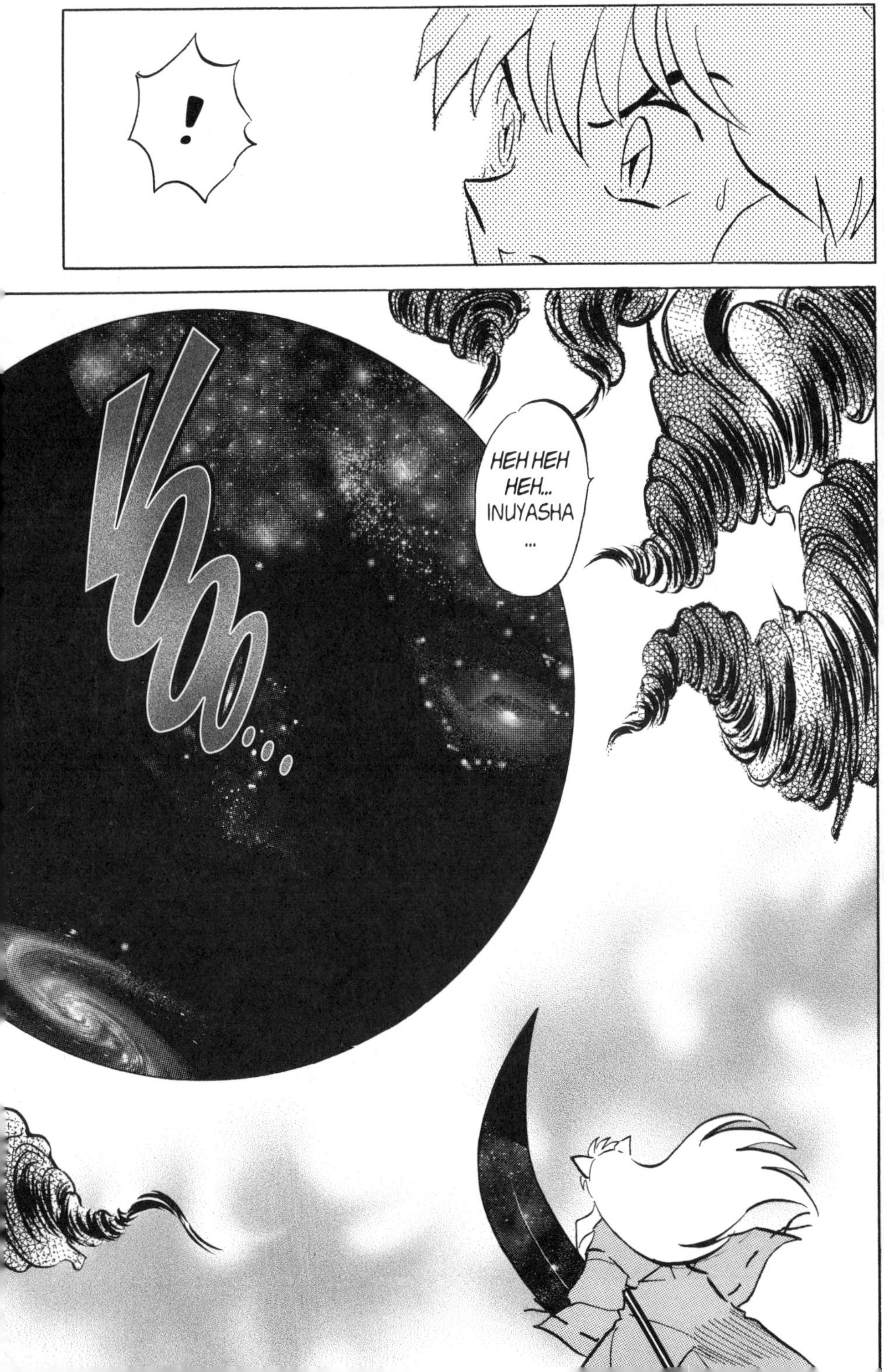
!
HEH HEH HEH... INUYASHA ...
VOOO...

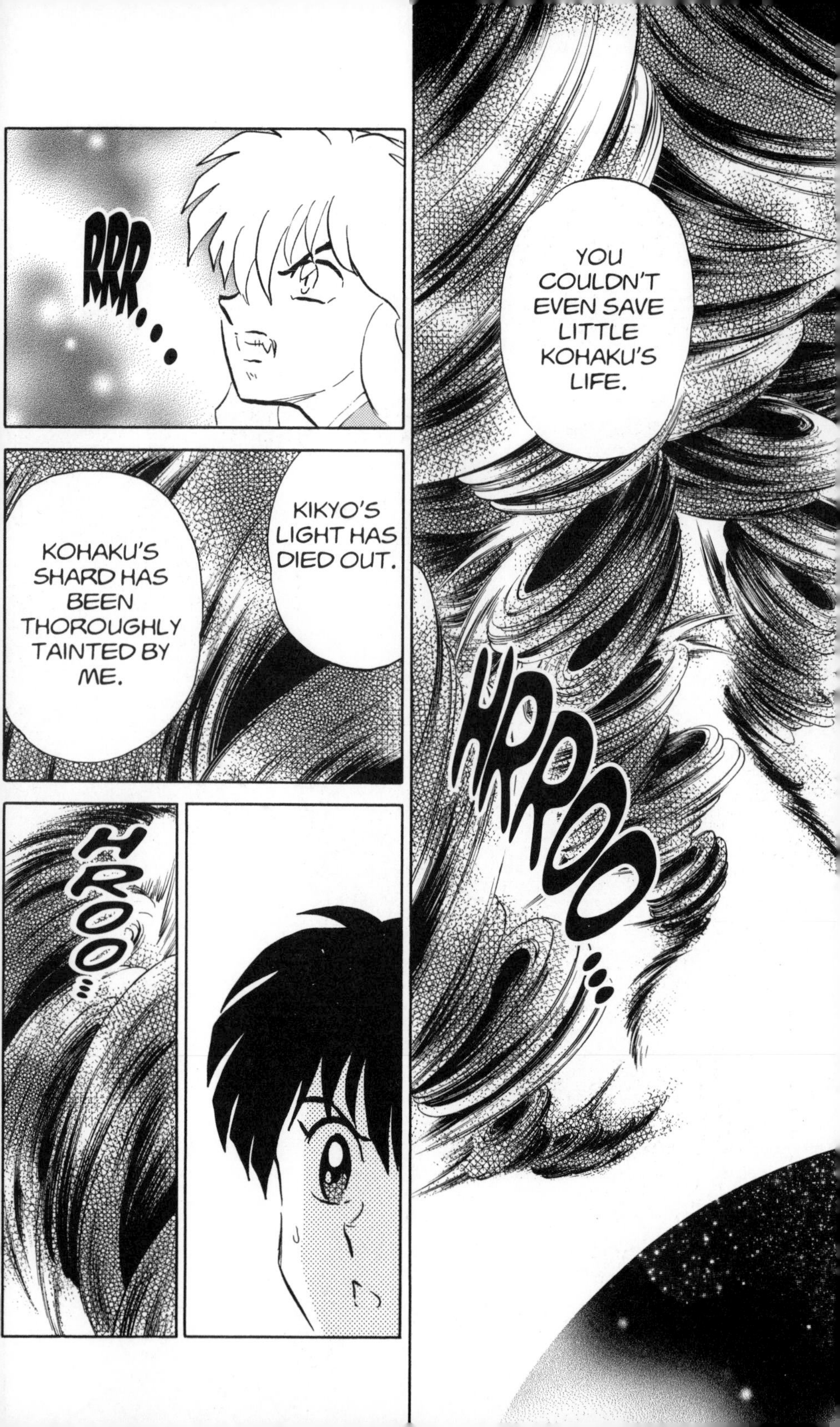
YOU COULDN'T EVEN SAVE LITTLE KOHAKU'S LIFE.
HRROO...
RRR...
KIKYO'S LIGHT HAS DIED OUT.
KOHAKU'S SHARD HAS BEEN THOROUGHLY TAINTED BY ME.
HROO...

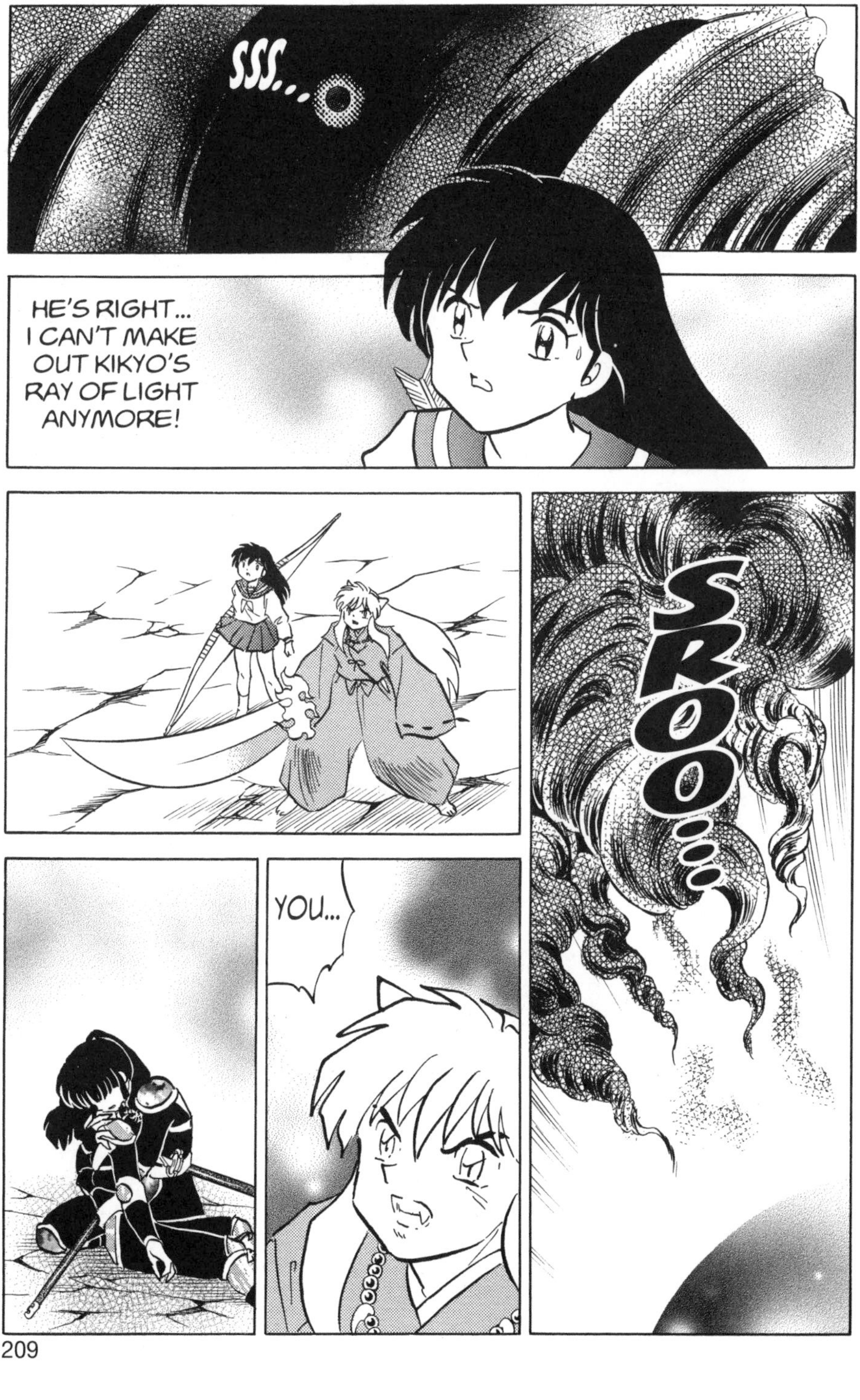
SSS...
HE'S RIGHT... I CAN'T MAKE OUT KIKYO'S RAY OF LIGHT ANYMORE!
SROO....
YOU...

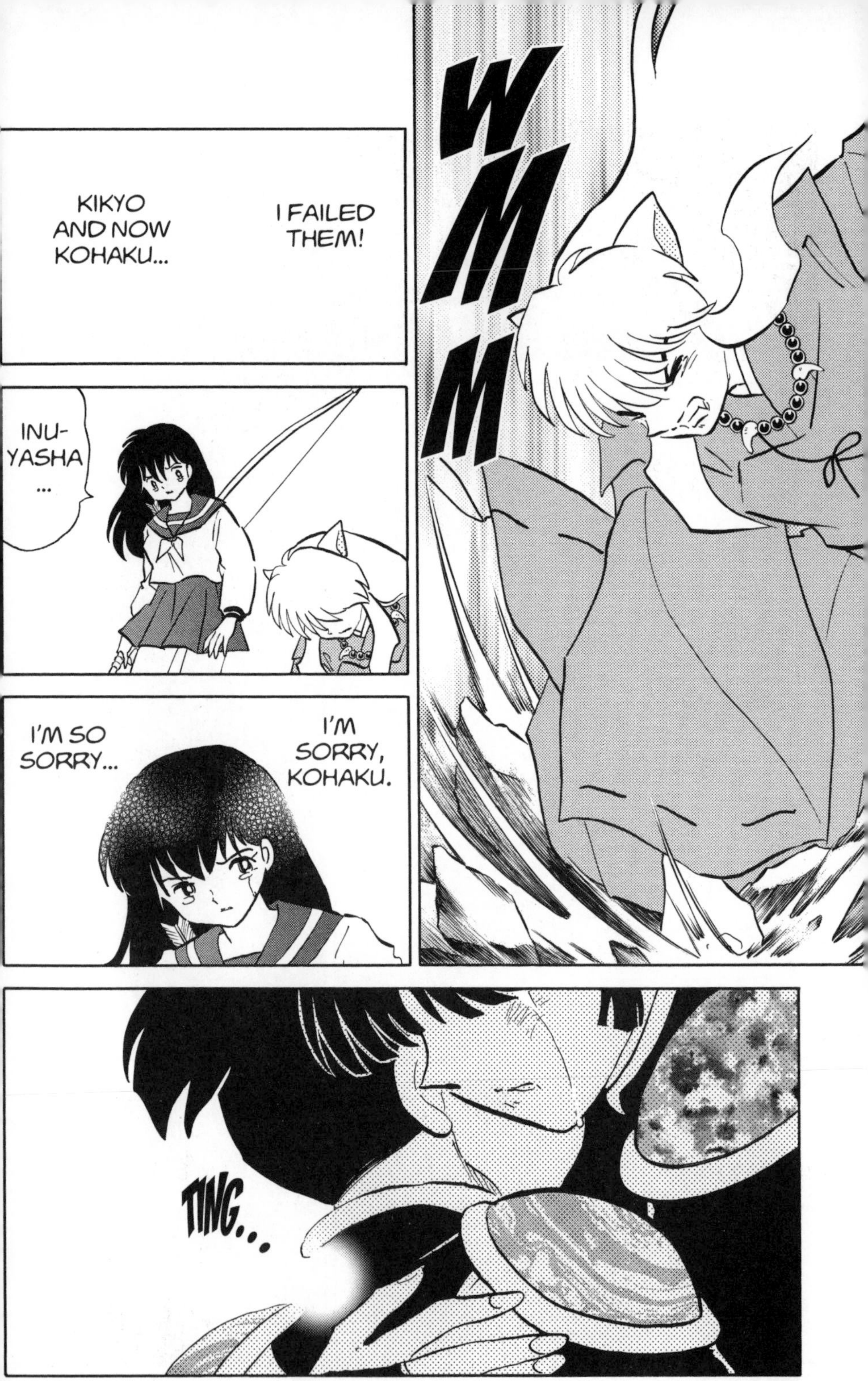
WMMM
I FAILED THEM!
KIKYO AND NOW KOHAKU...
INU-YASHA ...
I'M SORRY, KOHAKU.
I'M SO SORRY...
TING...

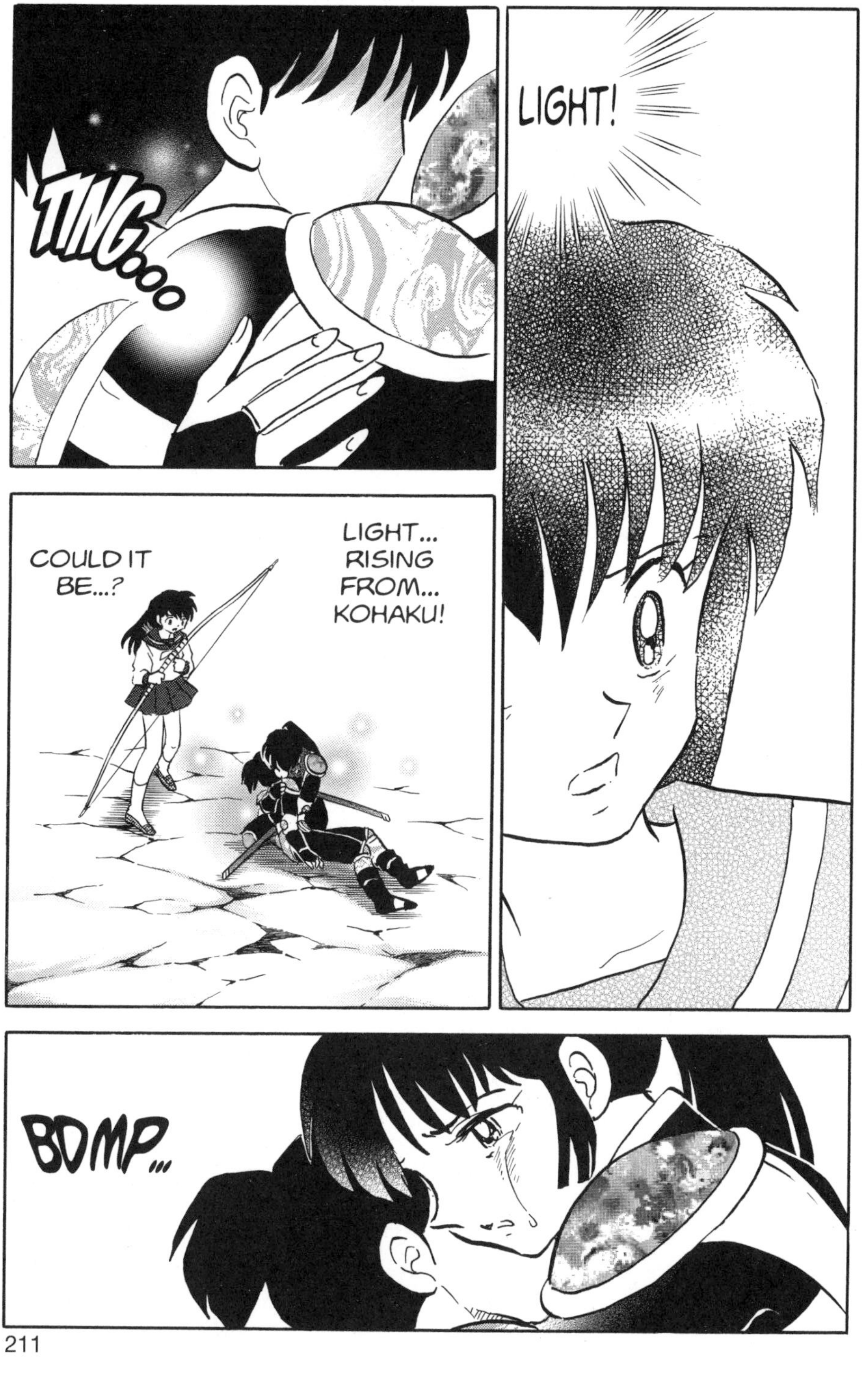
LIGHT!
TING...
LIGHT... RISING FROM... KOHAKU!
COULD IT BE...?
BDMP...

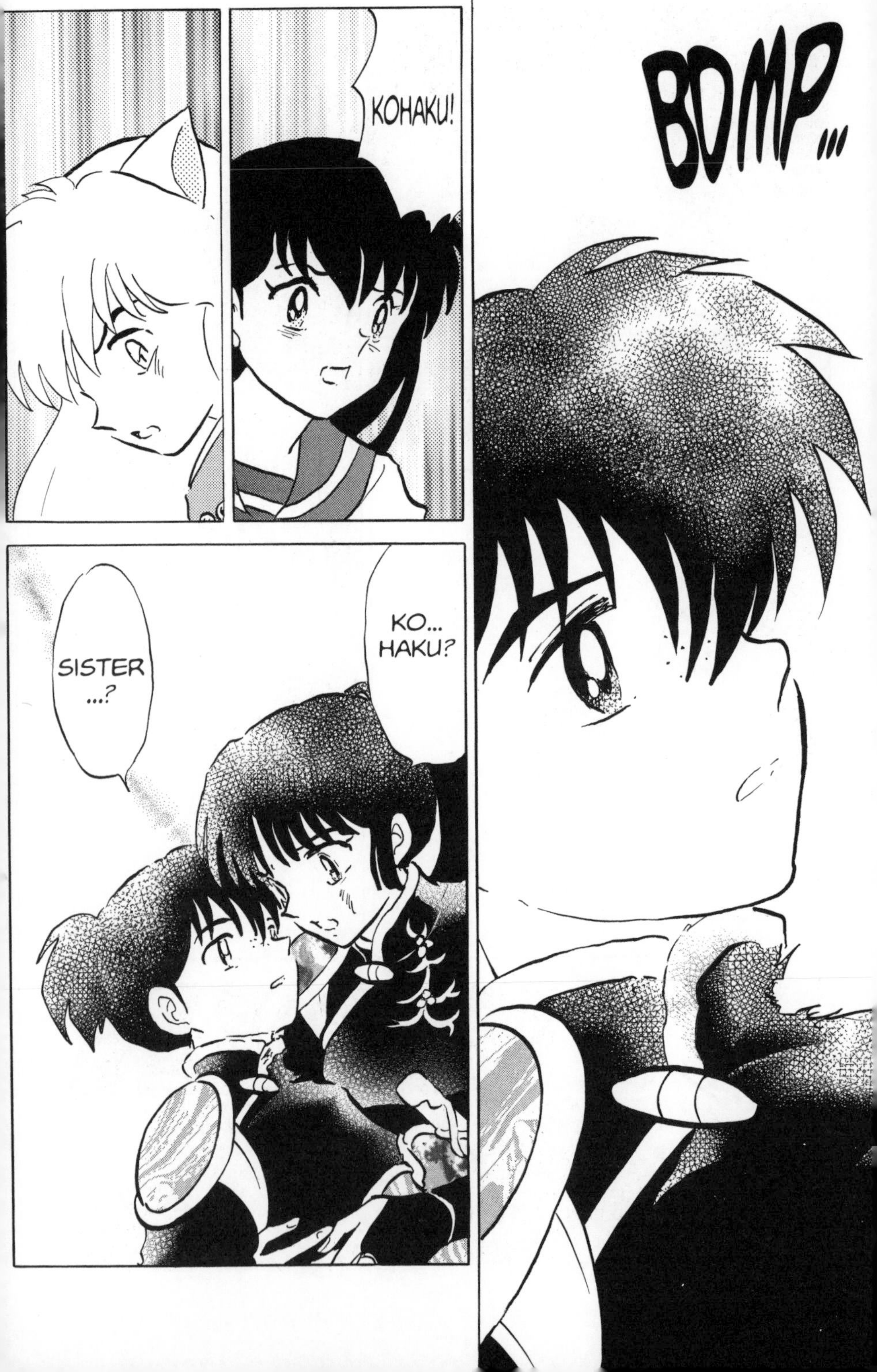
BOMP...
KOHAKU!
KO... HAKU?
SISTER ...?

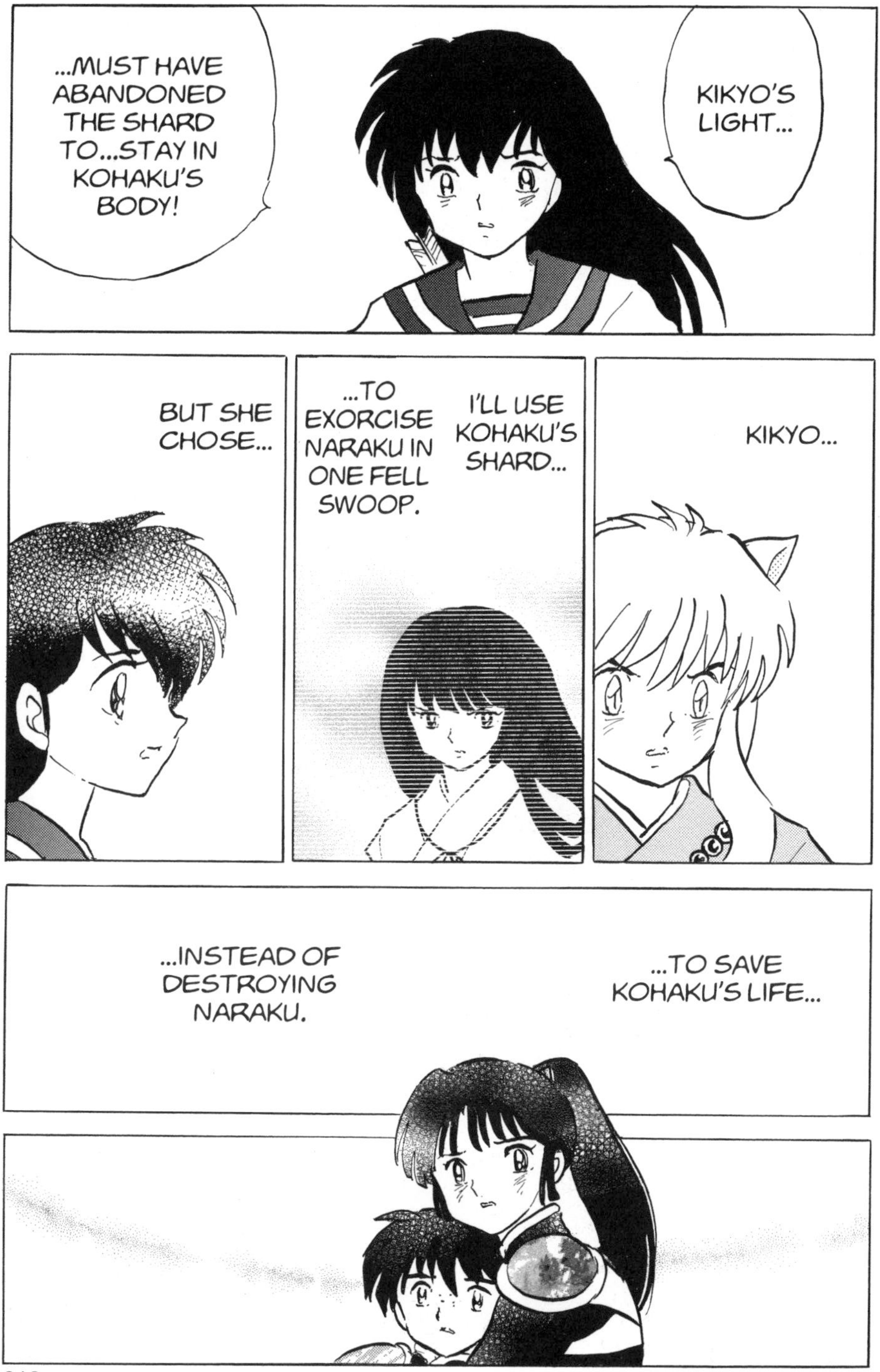
KIKYO'S LIGHT...
...MUST HAVE ABANDONED THE SHARD TO...STAY IN KOHAKU'S BODY!
KIKYO...
I'LL USE KOHAKU'S SHARD...
...TO EXORCISE NARAKU IN ONE FELL SWOOP.
BUT SHE CHOSE...
...TO SAVE KOHAKU'S LIFE...
...INSTEAD OF DESTROYING NARAKU.

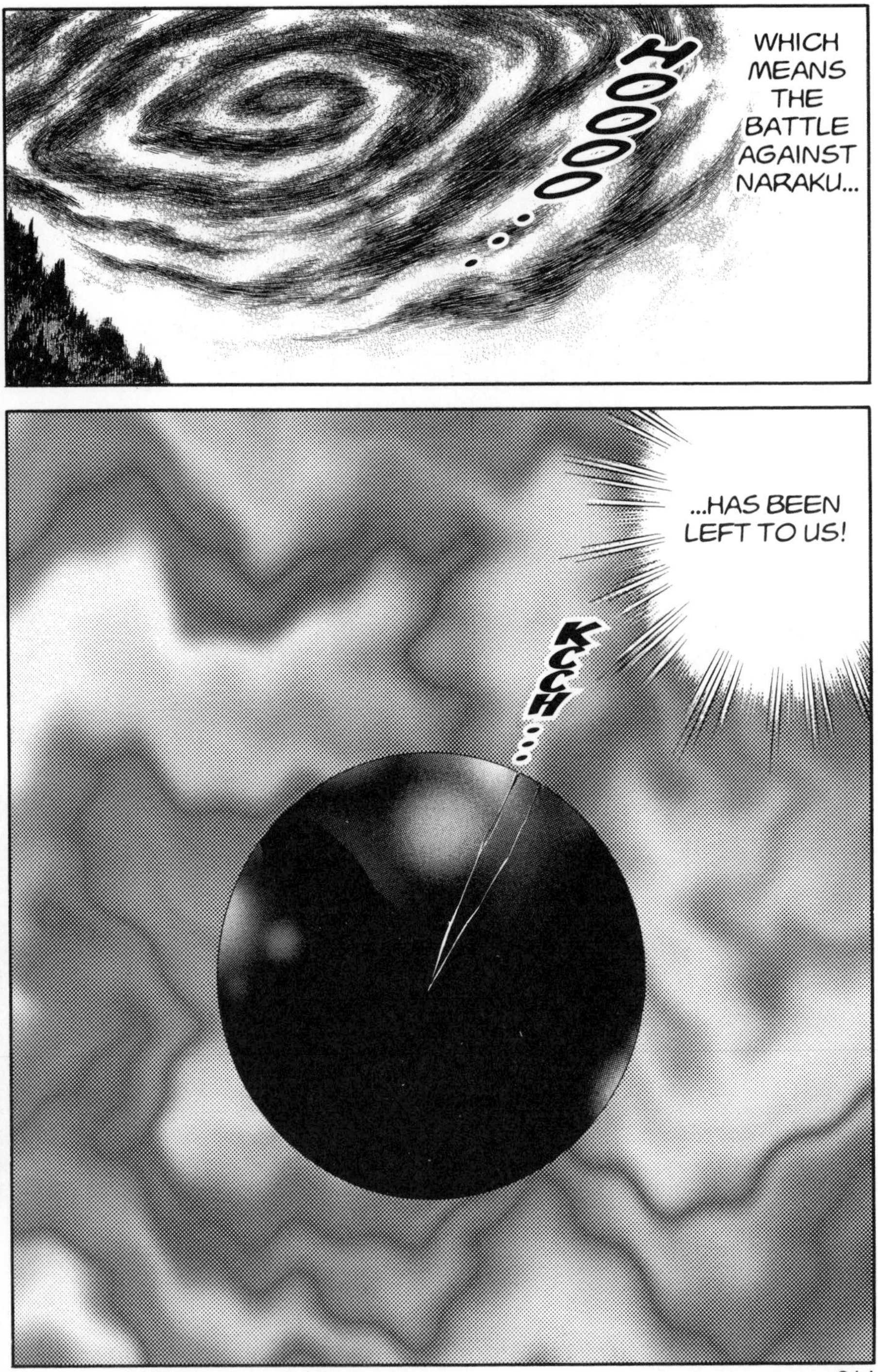
WHICH MEANS THE BATTLE AGAINST NARAKU...
HOOOOO......
...HAS BEEN LEFT TO US!
KCCH...

SCROLL TWO
GRADUATION

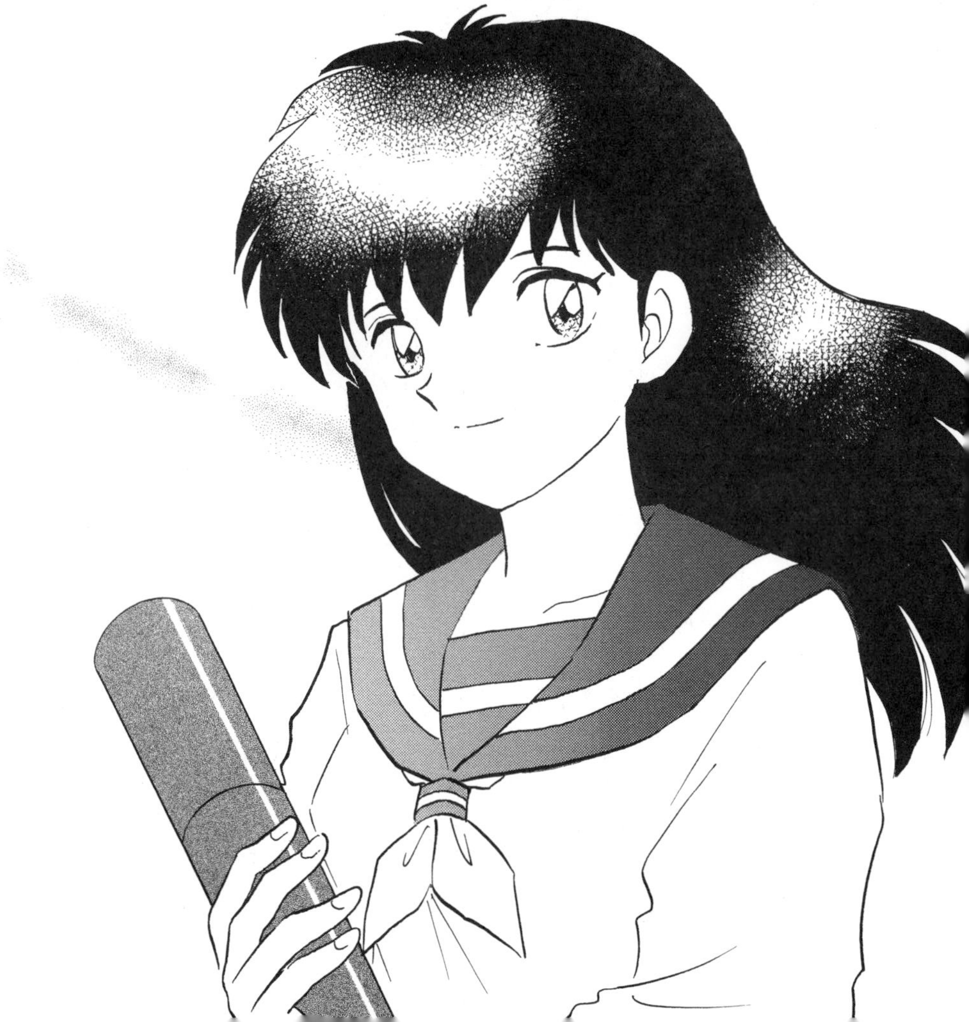

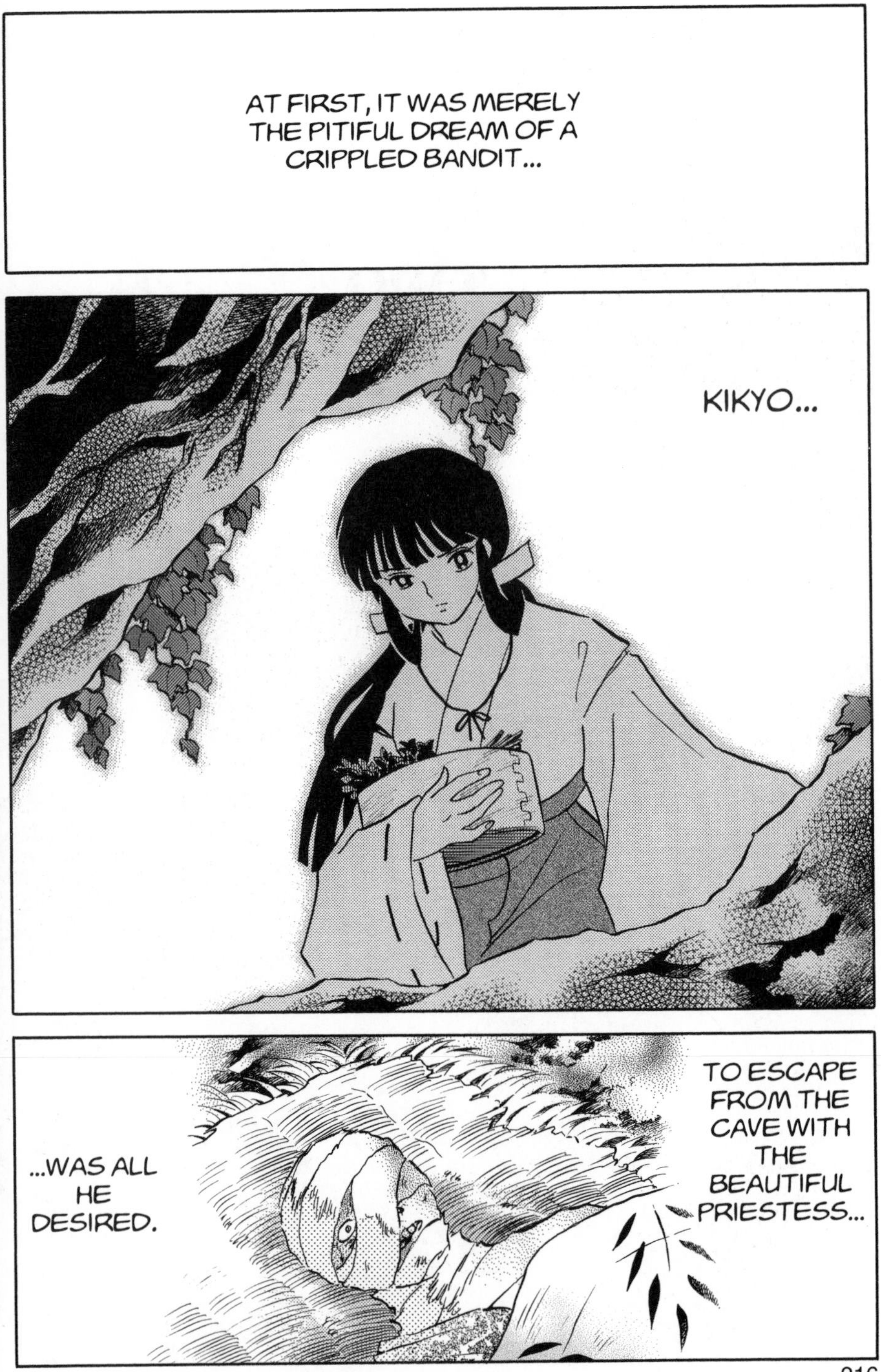
AT FIRST, IT WAS MERELY THE PITIFUL DREAM OF A CRIPPLED BANDIT...
KIKYO...
TO ESCAPE FROM THE CAVE WITH THE BEAUTIFUL PRIESTESS...
...WAS ALL HE DESIRED.

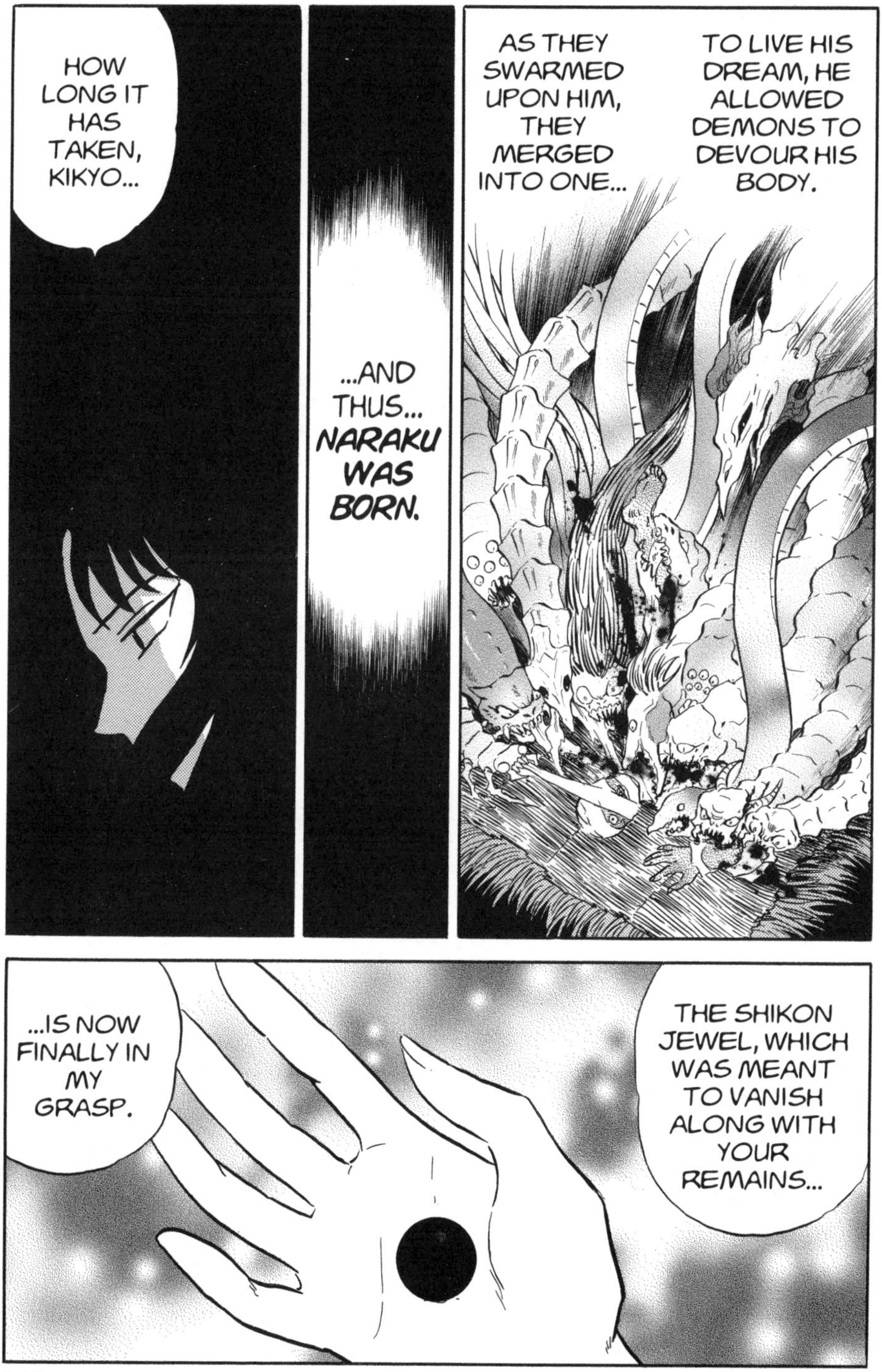
TO LIVE HIS DREAM, HE ALLOWED DEMONS TO DEVOUR HIS BODY.
AS THEY SWARMED UPON HIM, THEY MERGED INTO ONE...
...AND THUS... NARAKU WAS BORN.
HOW LONG IT HAS TAKEN, KIKYO...
THE SHIKON JEWEL, WHICH WAS MEANT TO VANISH ALONG WITH YOUR REMAINS...
...IS NOW FINALLY IN MY GRASP.

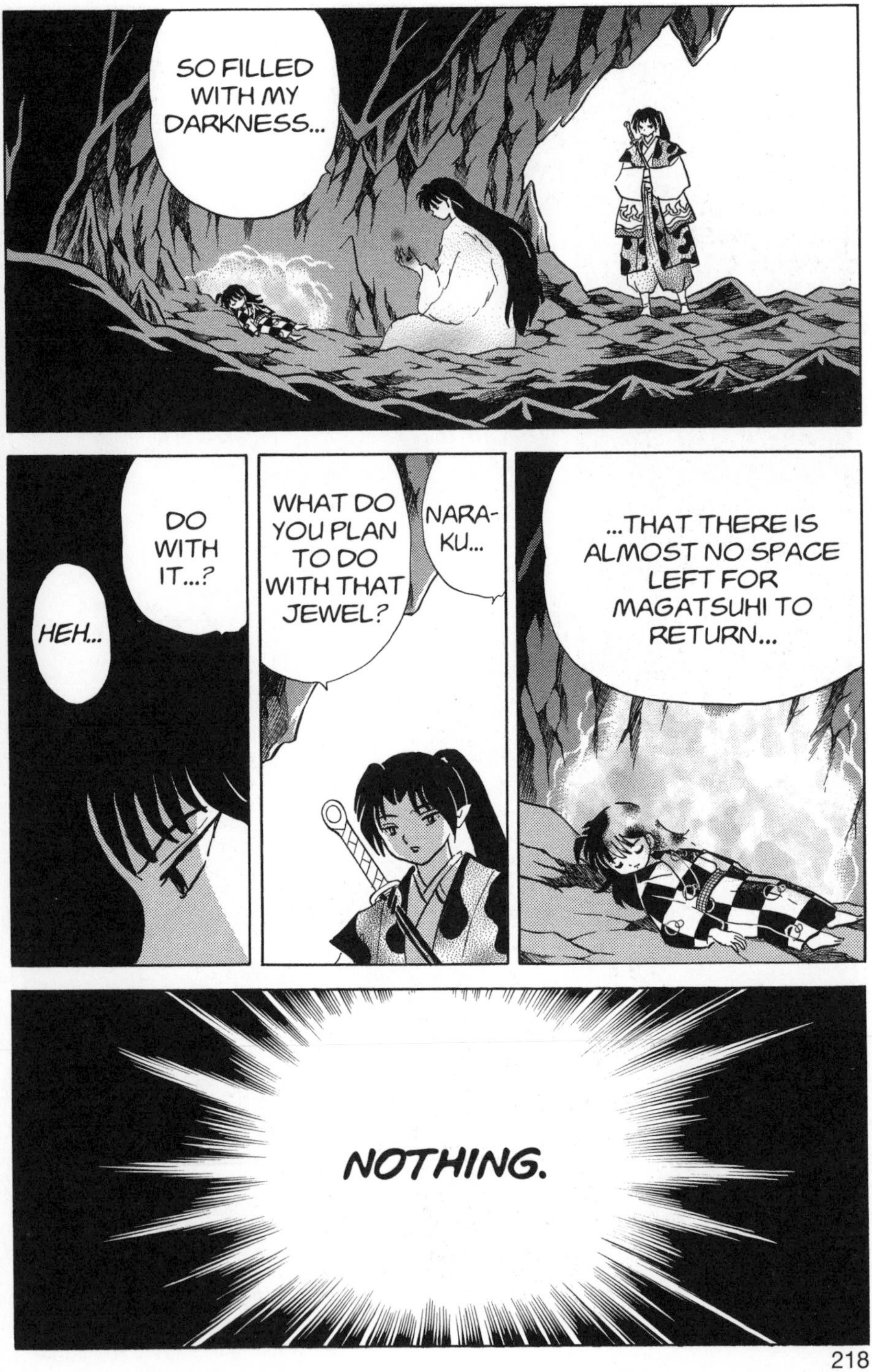
SO FILLED WITH MY DARKNESS...
...THAT THERE IS ALMOST NO SPACE LEFT FOR MAGATSUHI TO RETURN...
NARA-KU...
WHAT DO YOU PLAN TO DO WITH THAT JEWEL?
DO WITH IT...?
HEH...
NOTHING.

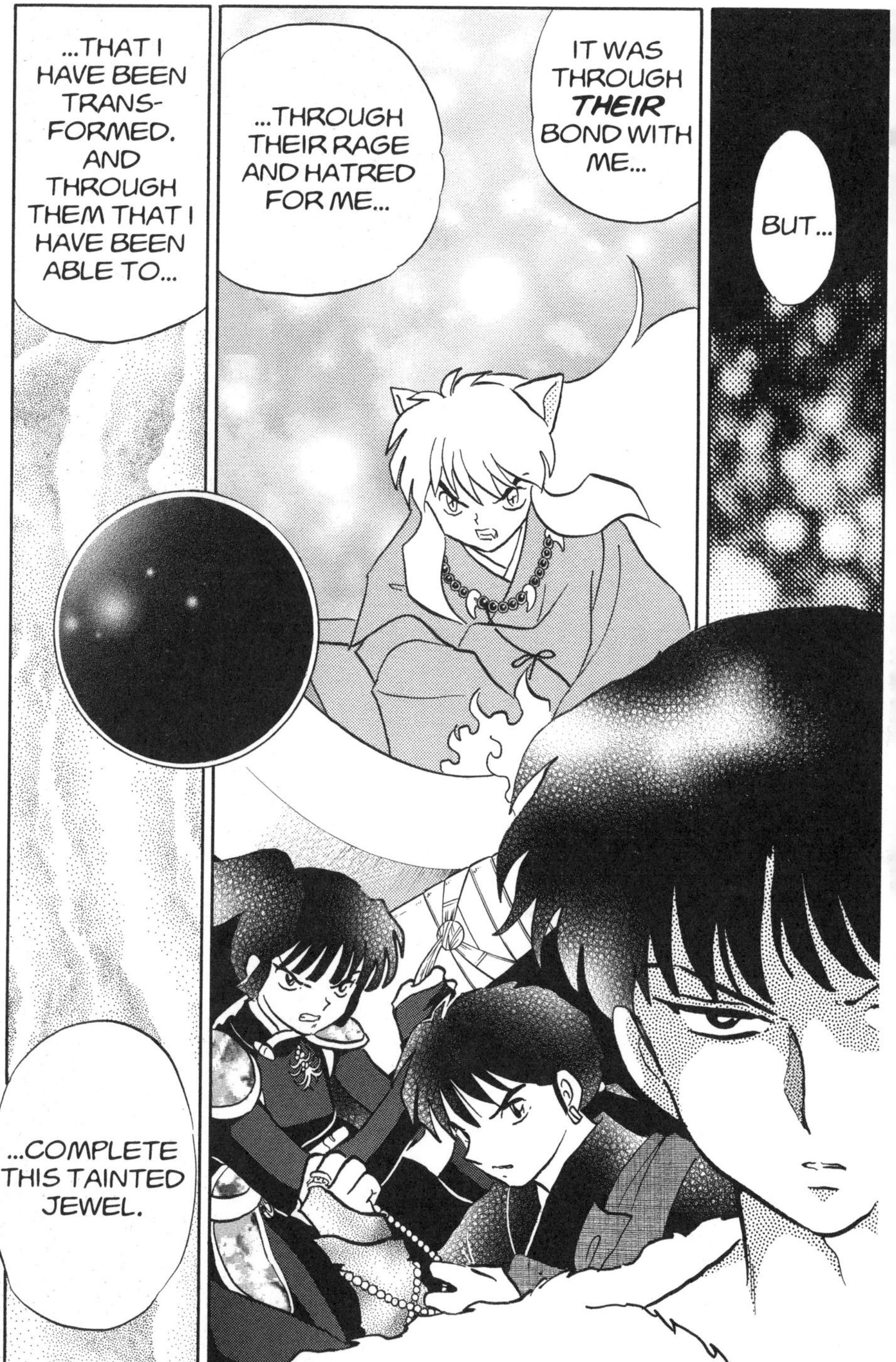
BUT...
IT WAS THROUGH THEIR BOND WITH ME...
...THROUGH THEIR RAGE AND HATRED FOR ME...
...THAT I HAVE BEEN TRANS-FORMED. AND THROUGH THEM THAT I HAVE BEEN ABLE TO...
...COMPLETE THIS TAINTED JEWEL.

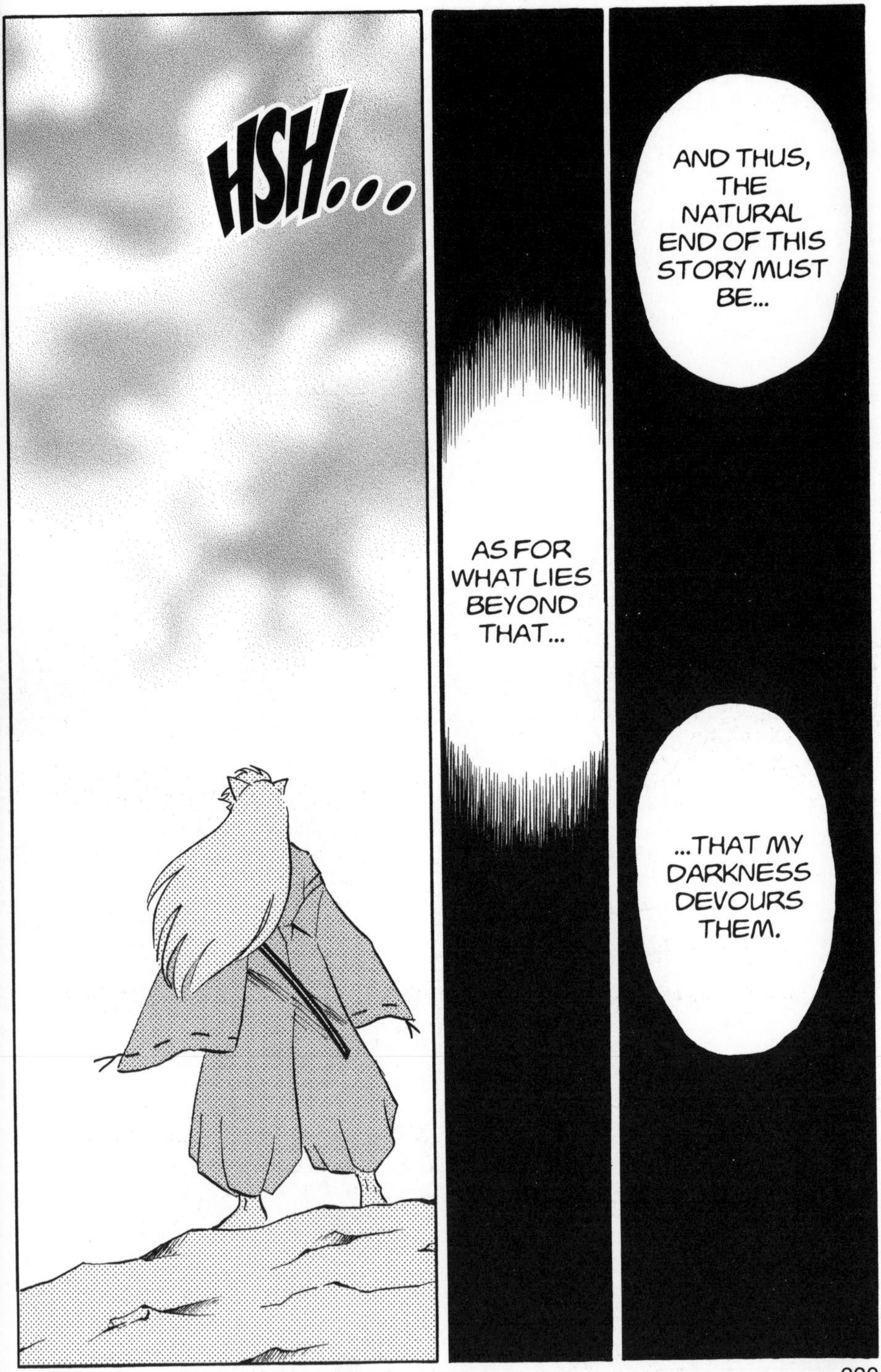
AND THUS, THE NATURAL END OF THIS STORY MUST BE...
...THAT MY DARKNESS DEVOURS THEM.
AS FOR WHAT LIES BEYOND THAT...
HSH...

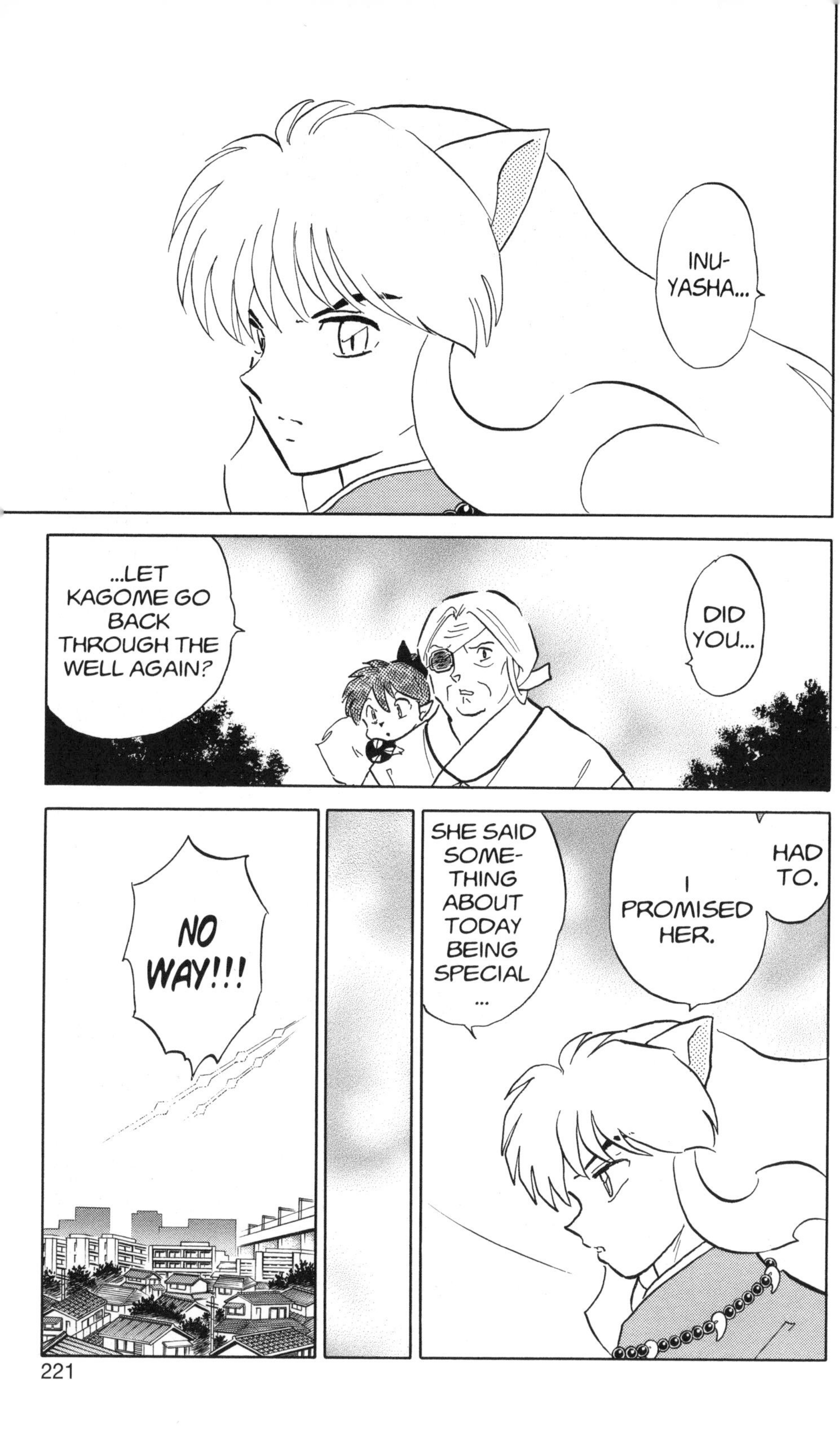
INU-YASHA...
DID YOU...
...LET KAGOME GO BACK THROUGH THE WELL AGAIN?
HAD TO.
I PROMISED HER.
SHE SAID SOME-THING ABOUT TODAY BEING SPECIAL...
NO WAY!!!

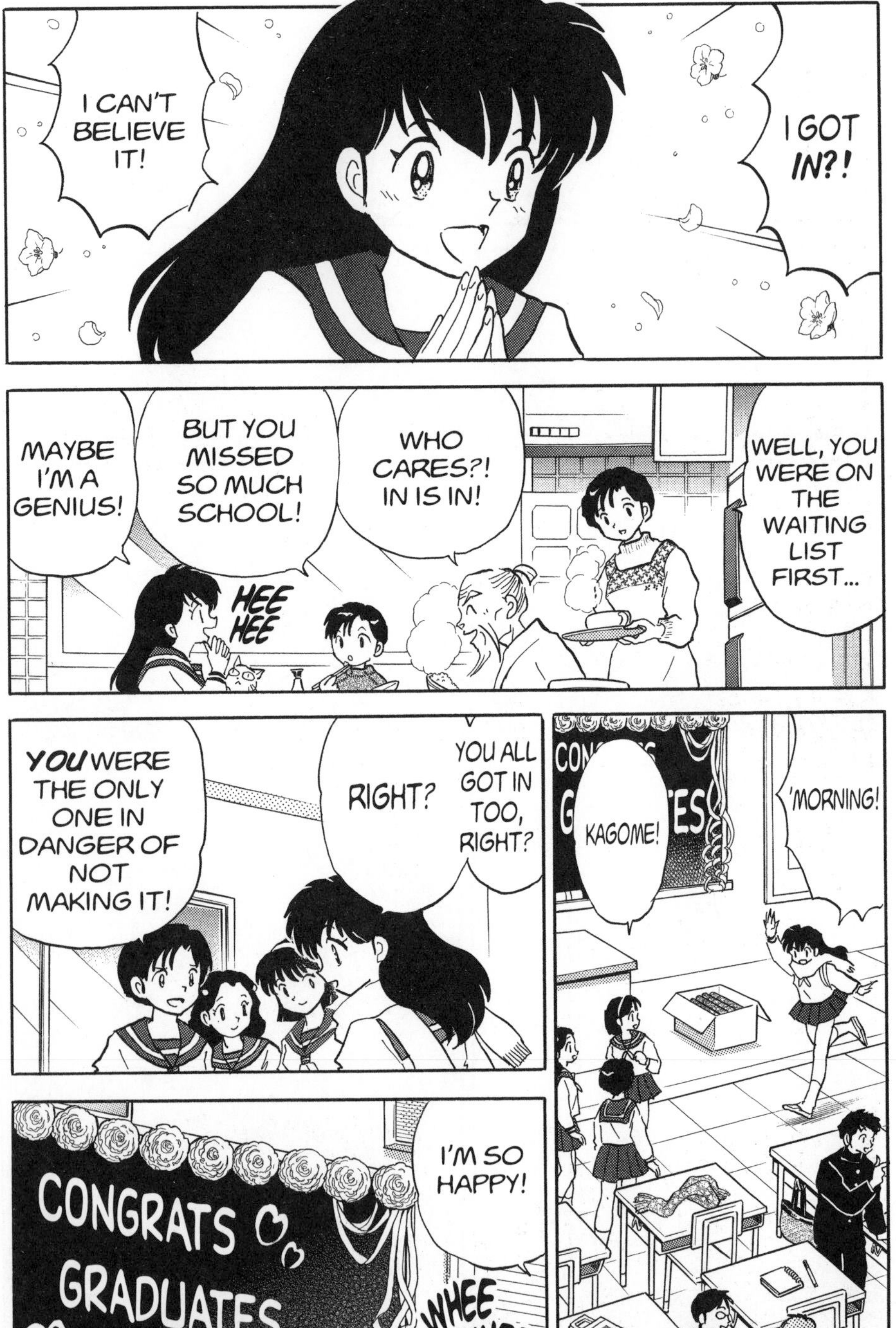
I GOT IN?!
I CAN'T BELIEVE IT!
WELL, YOU WERE ON THE WAITING LIST FIRST...
WHO CARES?! IN IS IN!
BUT YOU MISSED SO MUCH SCHOOL!
HEE HEE
MAYBE I'M A GENIUS!
'MORNING!
KAGOME!
YOU ALL GOT IN TOO, RIGHT?
RIGHT?
YOU WERE THE ONLY ONE IN DANGER OF NOT MAKING IT!
I'M SO HAPPY!
WHEE WHEE
CONGRATS GRADUATES

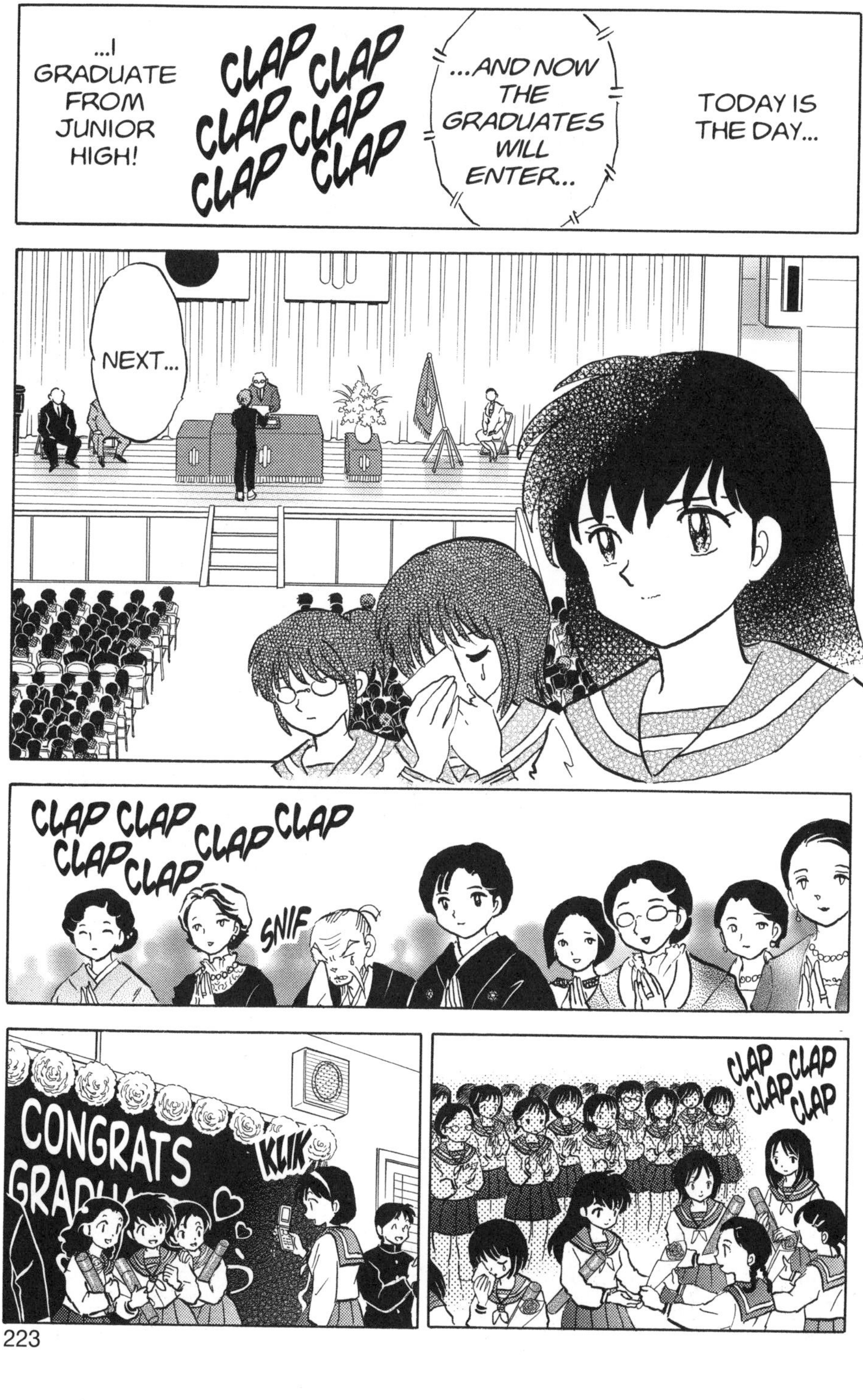
TODAY IS THE DAY...
...AND NOW THE GRADUATES WILL ENTER...
CLAP CLAP CLAP CLAP CLAP CLAP
...I GRADUATE FROM JUNIOR HIGH!
NEXT...
CLAP CLAP CLAP CLAP CLAP CLAP
SNIF
CLAP CLAP CLAP CLAP
KLIK
CONGRATS

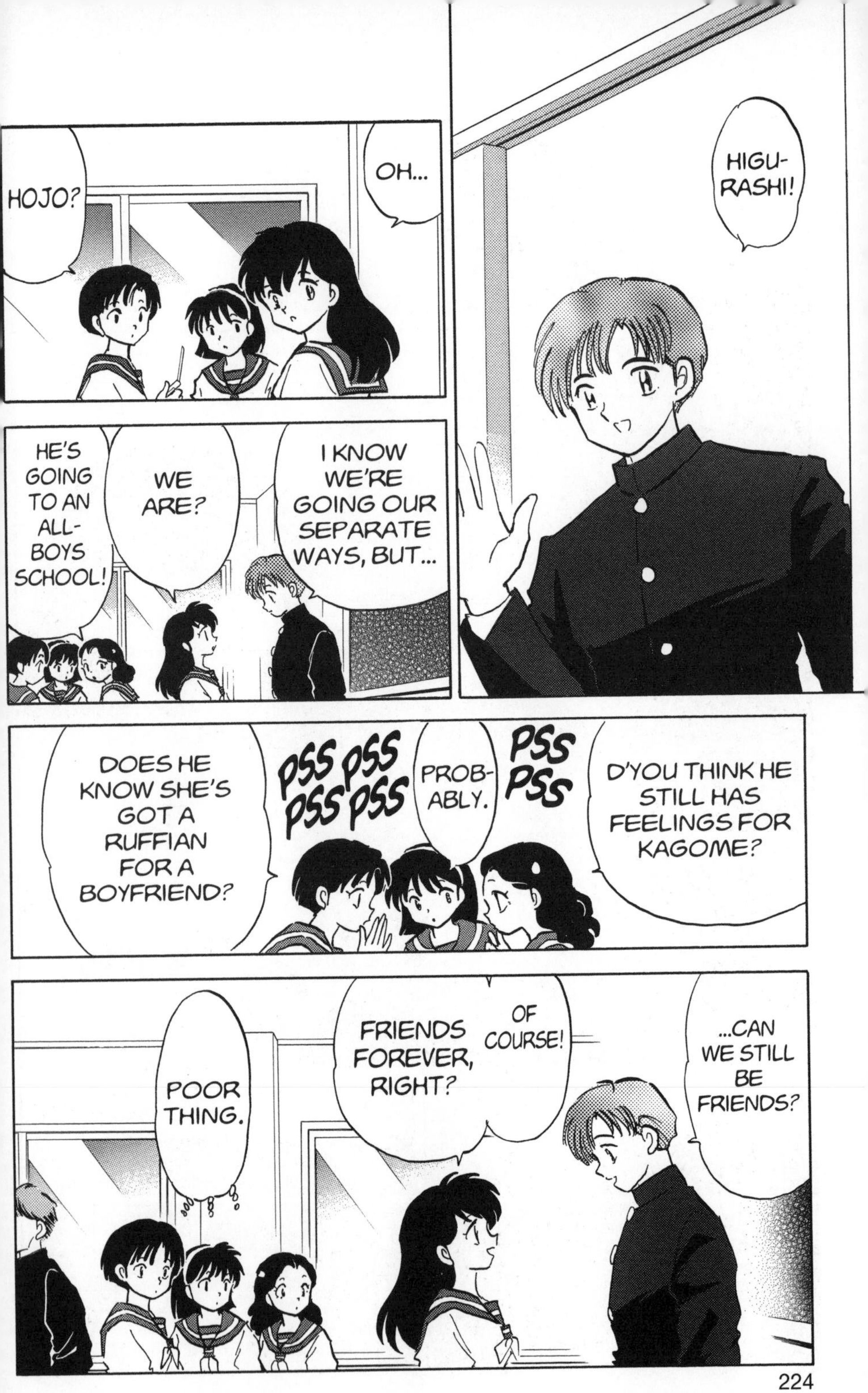
HIGU-RASHI!
OH...
HOJO?
I KNOW WE'RE GOING OUR SEPARATE WAYS, BUT...
WE ARE?
HE'S GOING TO AN ALL-BOYS SCHOOL!
D'YOU THINK HE STILL HAS FEELINGS FOR KAGOME?
PSS PSS
PROB-ABLY.
PSS PSS PSS PSS
DOES HE KNOW SHE'S GOT A RUFFIAN FOR A BOYFRIEND?
...CAN WE STILL BE FRIENDS?
OF COURSE!
FRIENDS FOREVER, RIGHT?
POOR THING.

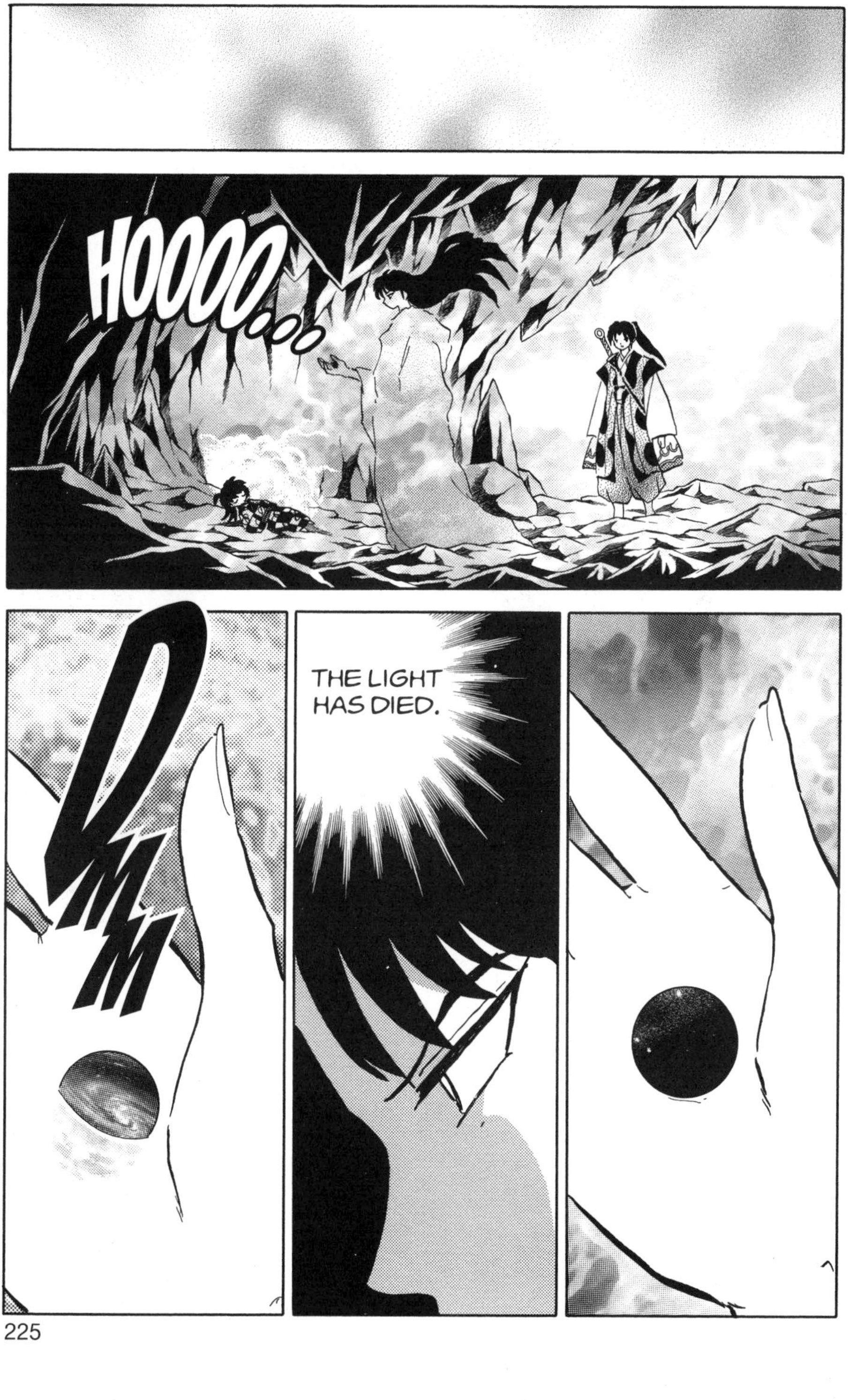
HOOOO...
THE LIGHT HAS DIED.
DMM

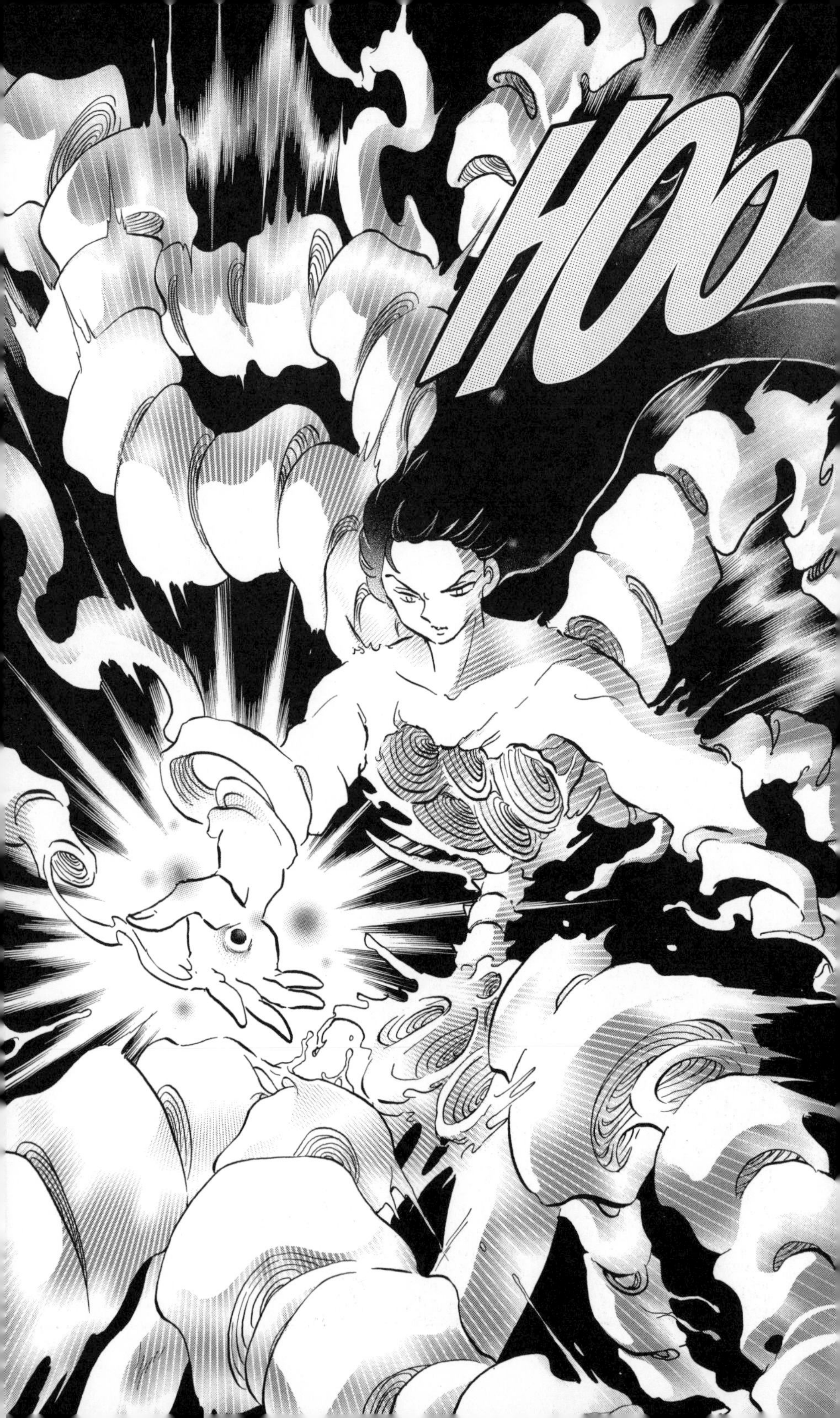
HOO

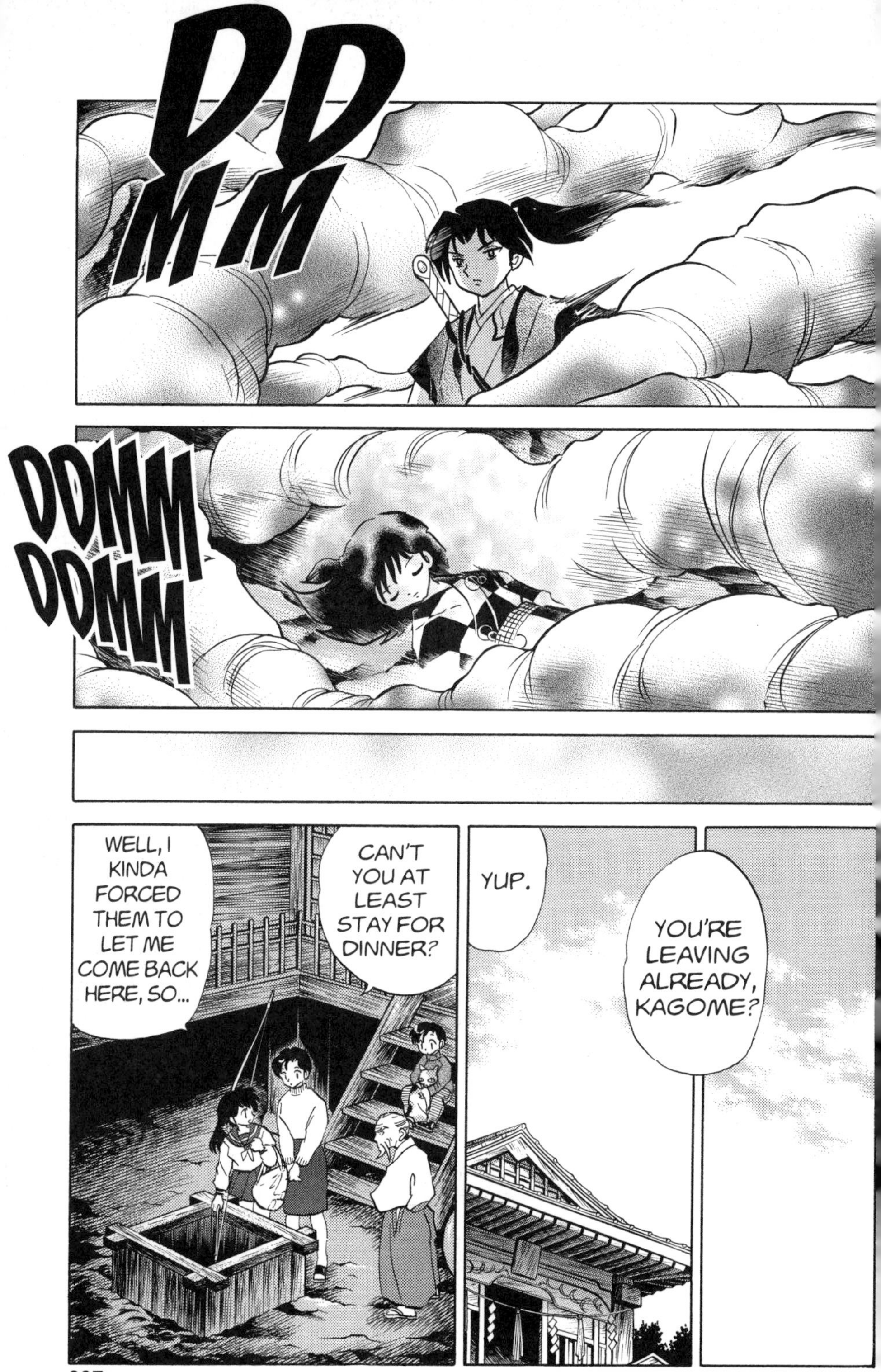
DDMM
DDMM DDMM
YOU'RE LEAVING ALREADY, KAGOME?
YUP.
CAN'T YOU AT LEAST STAY FOR DINNER?
WELL, I KINDA FORCED THEM TO LET ME COME BACK HERE, SO...

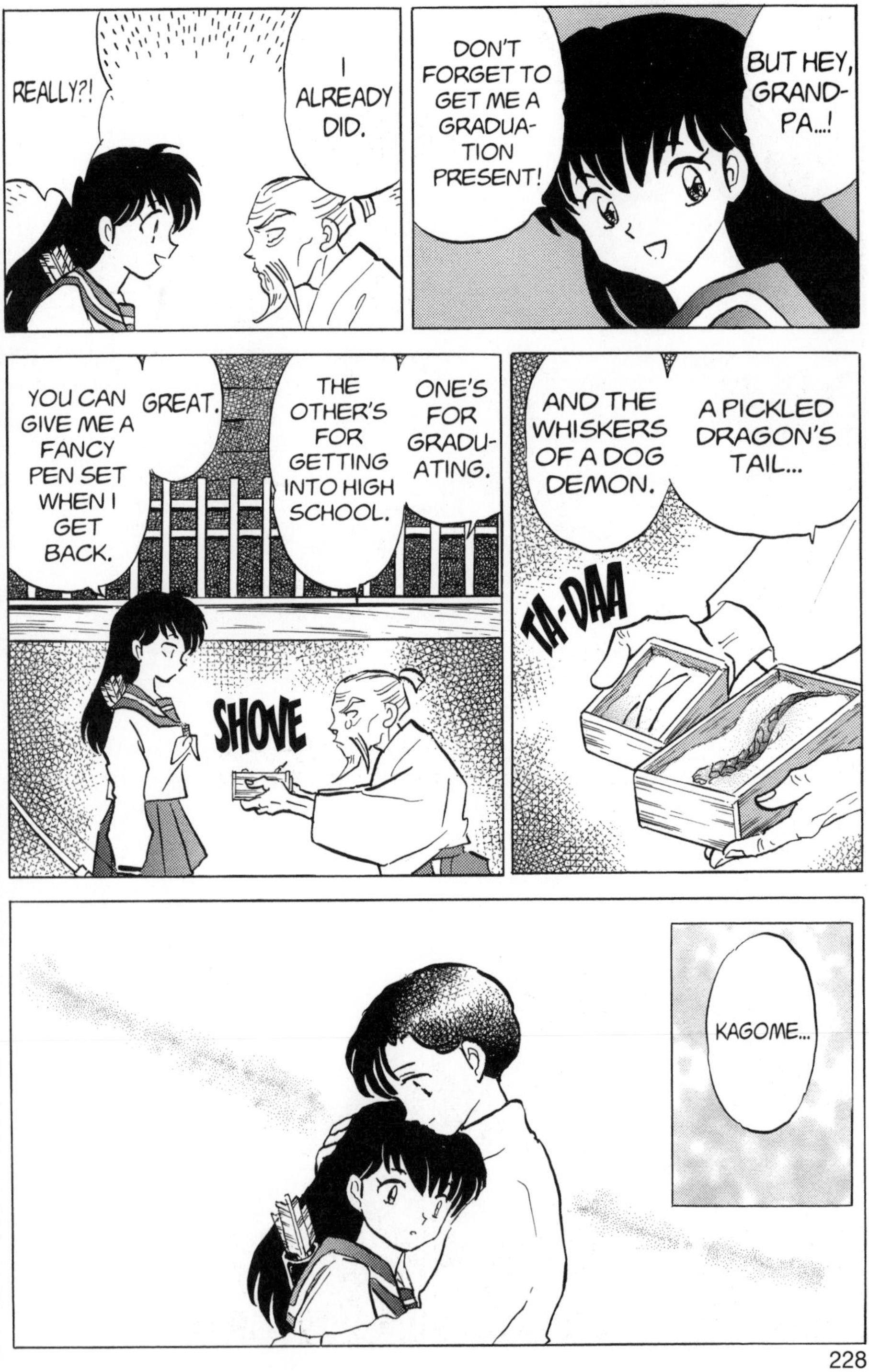
BUT HEY, GRAND-PA...!
DON'T FORGET TO GET ME A GRADUA-TION PRESENT!
I ALREADY DID.
REALLY?!
A PICKLED DRAGON'S TAIL...
AND THE WHISKERS OF A DOG DEMON.
TA-DAA
ONE'S FOR GRADU-ATING.
THE OTHER'S FOR GETTING INTO HIGH SCHOOL.
GREAT.
YOU CAN GIVE ME A FANCY PEN SET WHEN I GET BACK.
SHOVE
KAGOME...

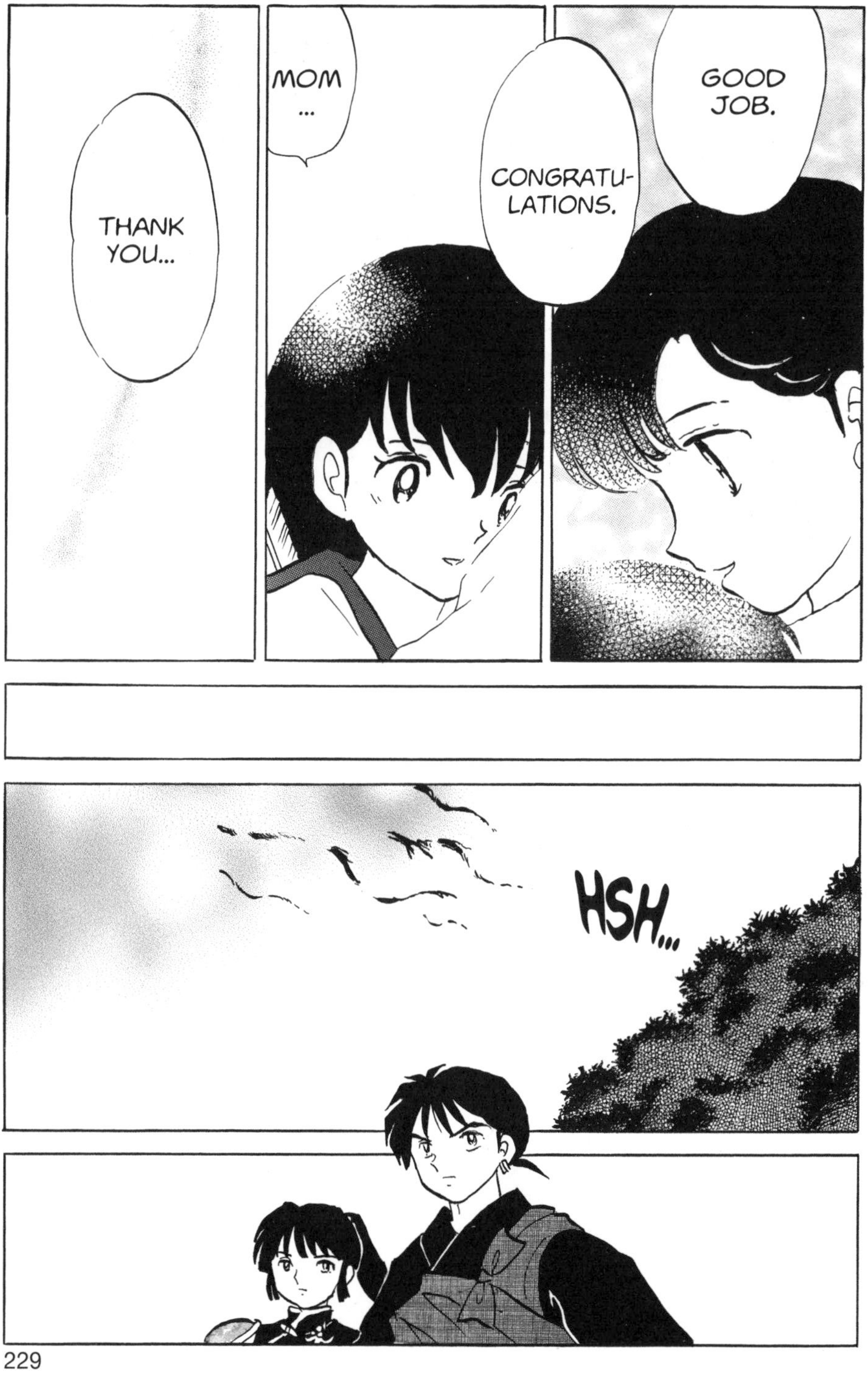
GOOD JOB.
CONGRATU-LATIONS.
MOM ...
THANK YOU...
HSH...

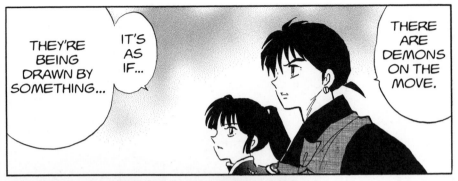

THERE ARE DEMONS ON THE MOVE.
IT'S AS IF...
THEY'RE BEING DRAWN BY SOMETHING...
HOOOOO
AN EVIL AURA IS SPREADING ACROSS THE SKY.
...
LORD INUYASHA... DID NARAKU USE...
...THE JEW-EL?
YEAH. HE DID.

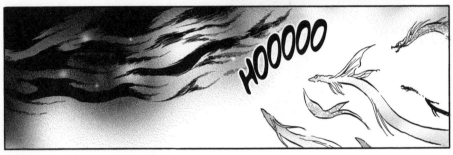

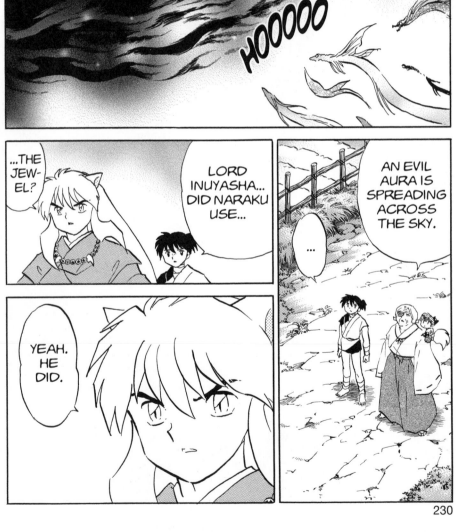

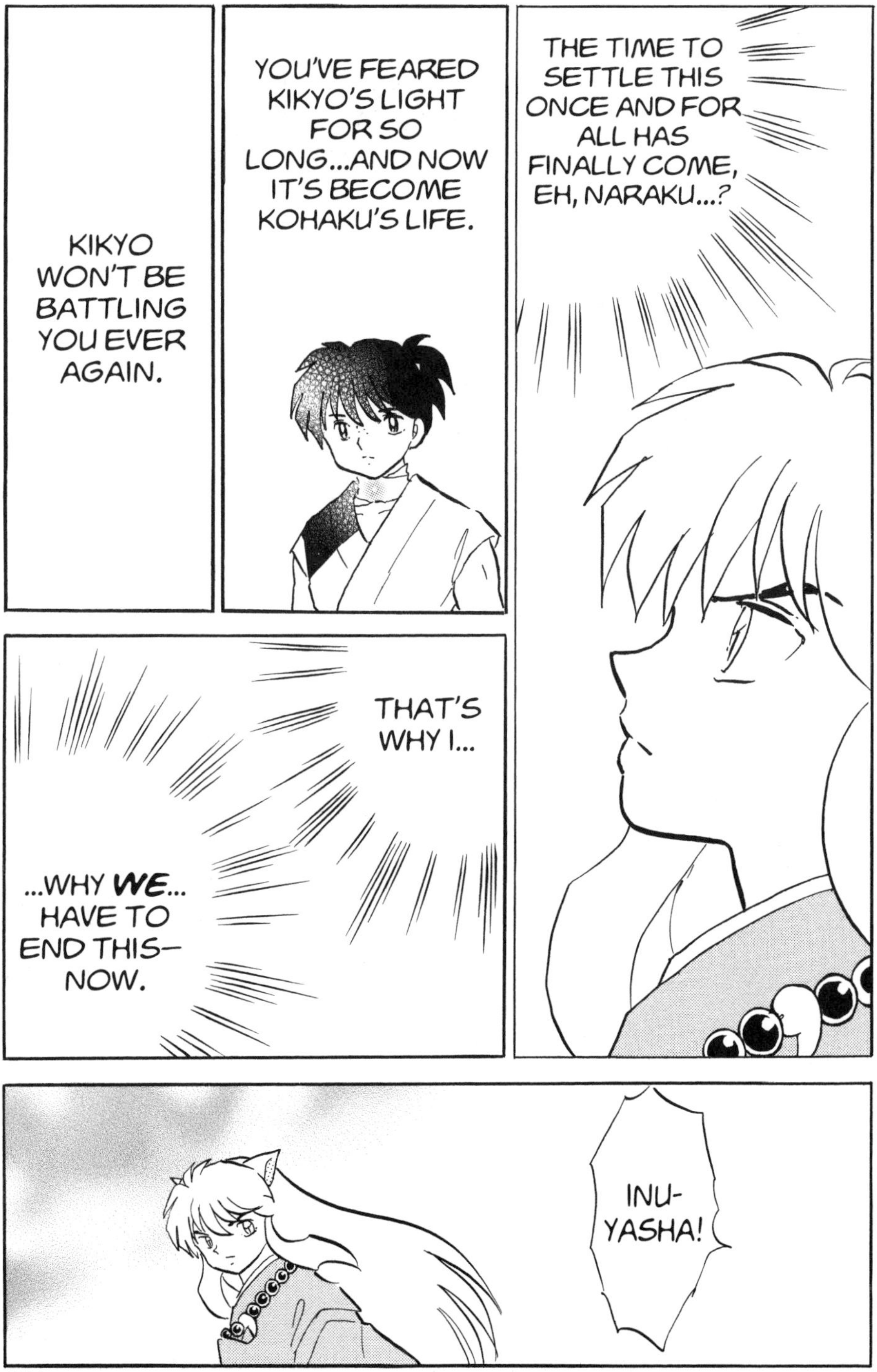
THE TIME TO SETTLE THIS ONCE AND FOR ALL HAS FINALLY COME, EH, NARAKU...?
YOU'VE FEARED KIKYO'S LIGHT FOR SO LONG...AND NOW IT'S BECOME KOHAKU'S LIFE.
KIKYO WON'T BE BATTLING YOU EVER AGAIN.
THAT'S WHY I...
...WHY **WE**... HAVE TO END THIS— NOW.
INU-YASHA!

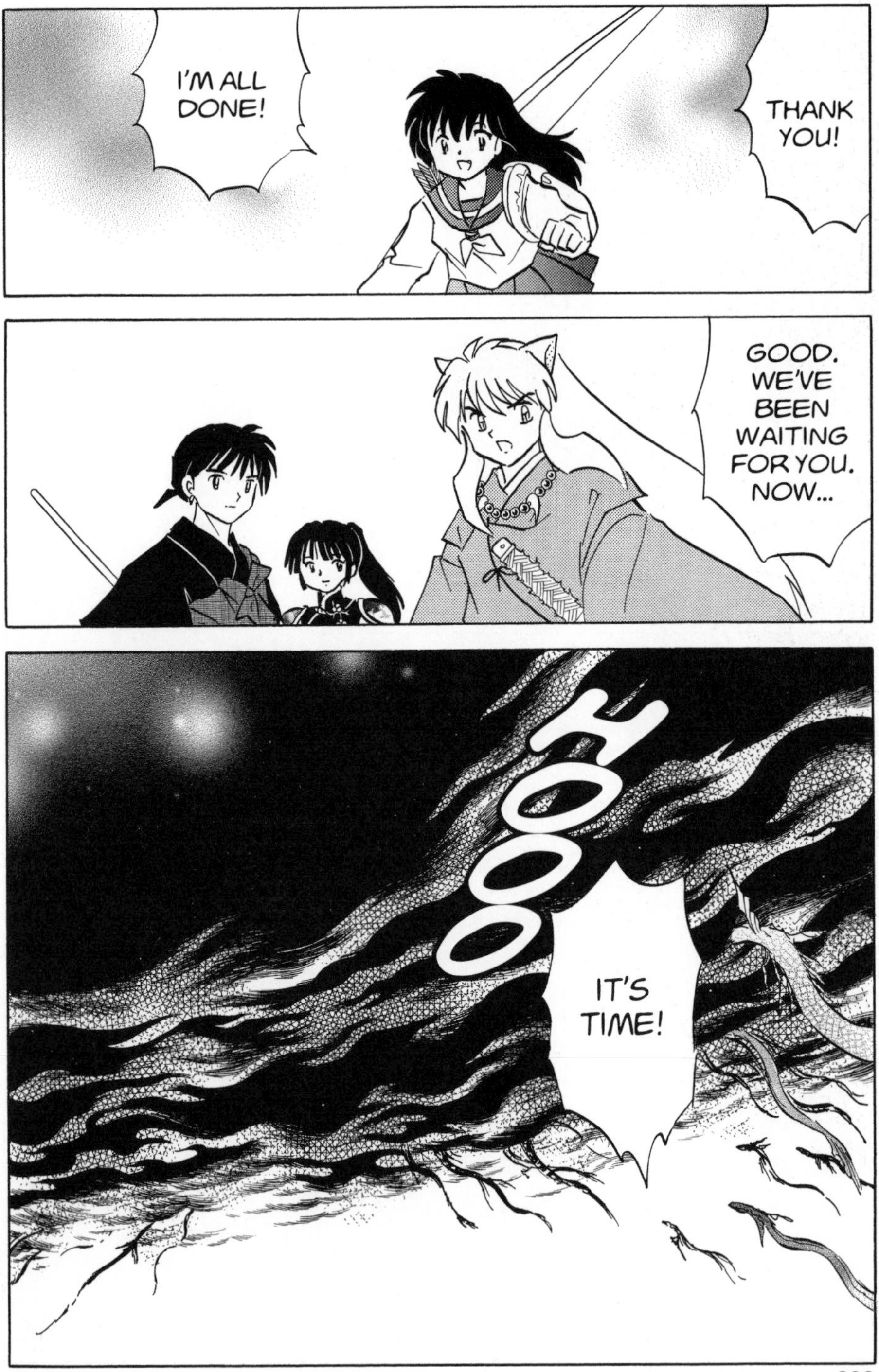
THANK YOU!
I'M ALL DONE!
GOOD. WE'VE BEEN WAITING FOR YOU. NOW...
HOOOO
IT'S TIME!

SCROLL THREE
CLOUD OF EVIL

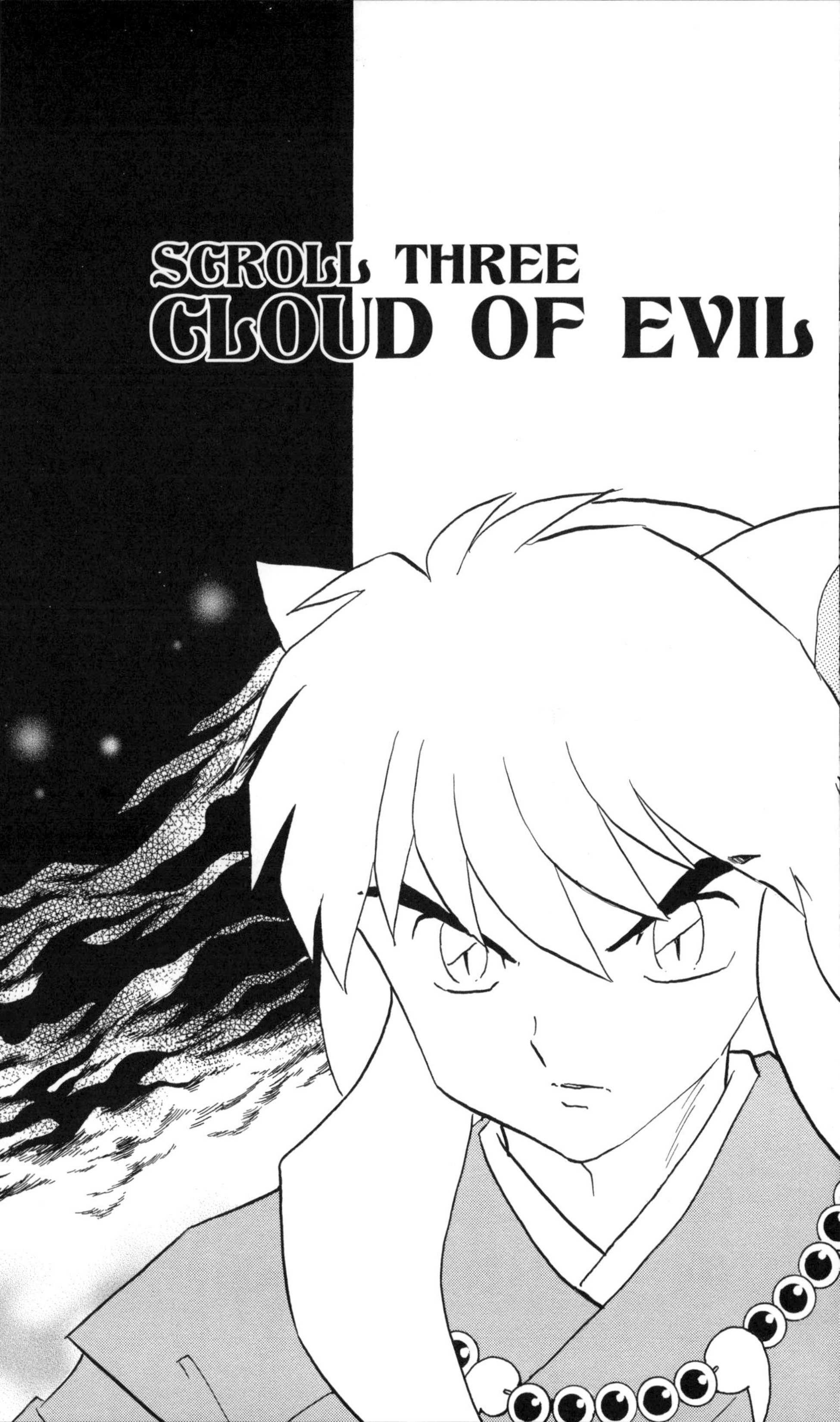

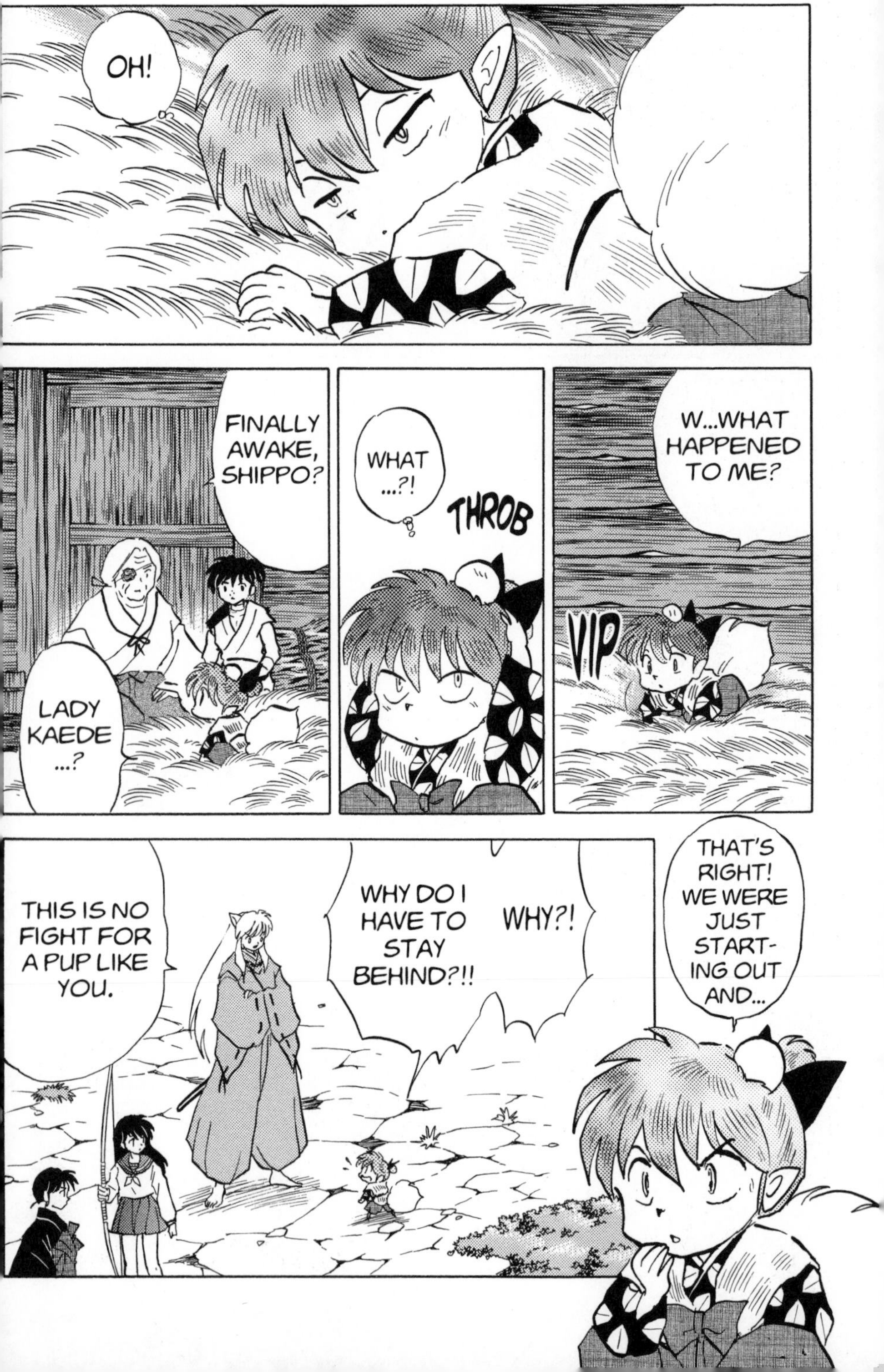
OH!
W...WHAT HAPPENED TO ME?
VIP
WHAT ...?!
THROB
FINALLY AWAKE, SHIPPO?
LADY KAEDE ...?
THAT'S RIGHT! WE WERE JUST START-ING OUT AND...
WHY?!
WHY DO I HAVE TO STAY BEHIND?!!
THIS IS NO FIGHT FOR A PUP LIKE YOU.

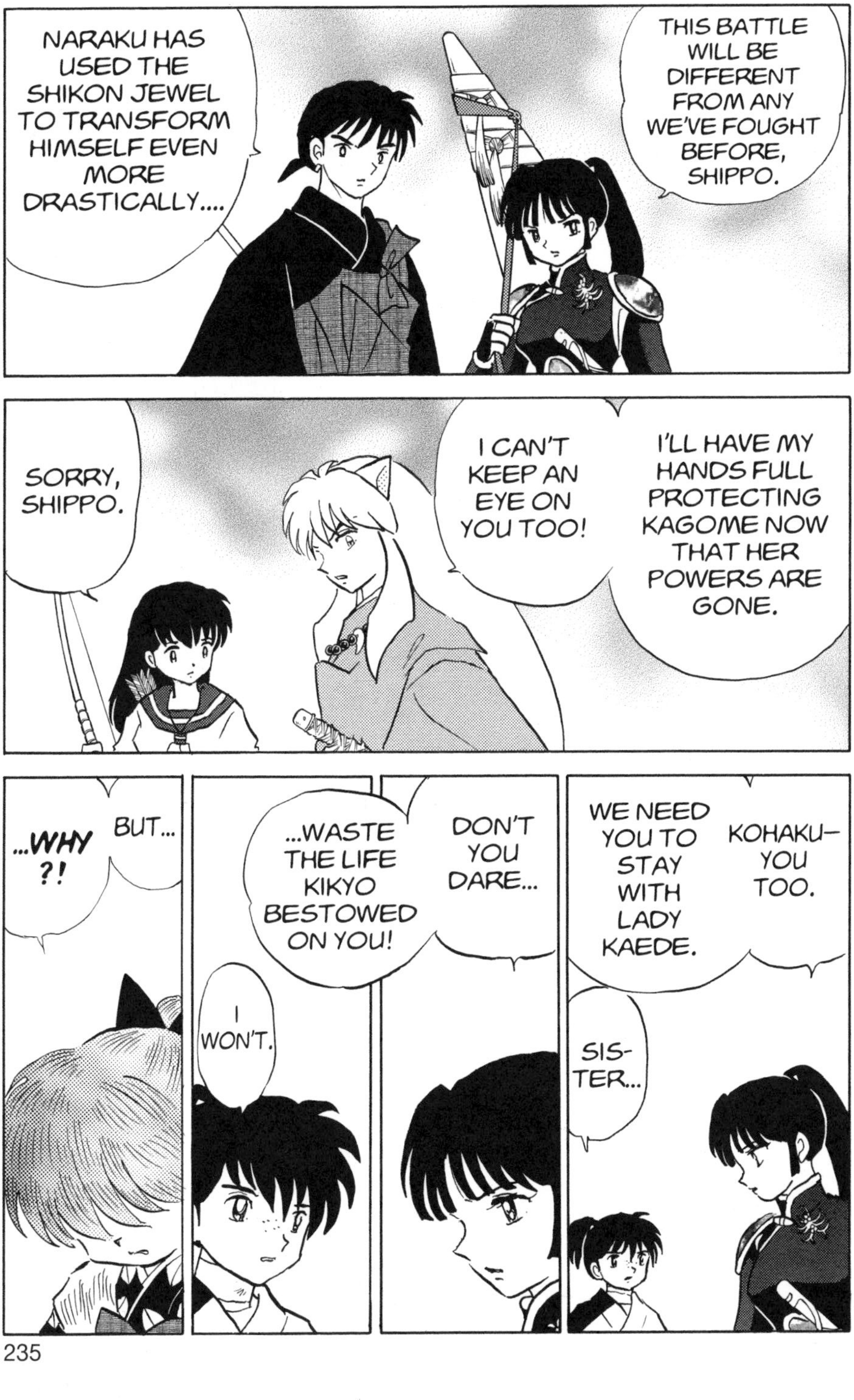
THIS BATTLE WILL BE DIFFERENT FROM ANY WE'VE FOUGHT BEFORE, SHIPPO.
NARAKU HAS USED THE SHIKON JEWEL TO TRANSFORM HIMSELF EVEN MORE DRASTICALLY....
I'LL HAVE MY HANDS FULL PROTECTING KAGOME NOW THAT HER POWERS ARE GONE.
I CAN'T KEEP AN EYE ON YOU TOO!
SORRY, SHIPPO.
KOHAKU— YOU TOO.
WE NEED YOU TO STAY WITH LADY KAEDE.
SIS- TER...
DON'T YOU DARE...
...WASTE THE LIFE KIKYO BESTOWED ON YOU!
I WON'T.
BUT...
...WHY ?!

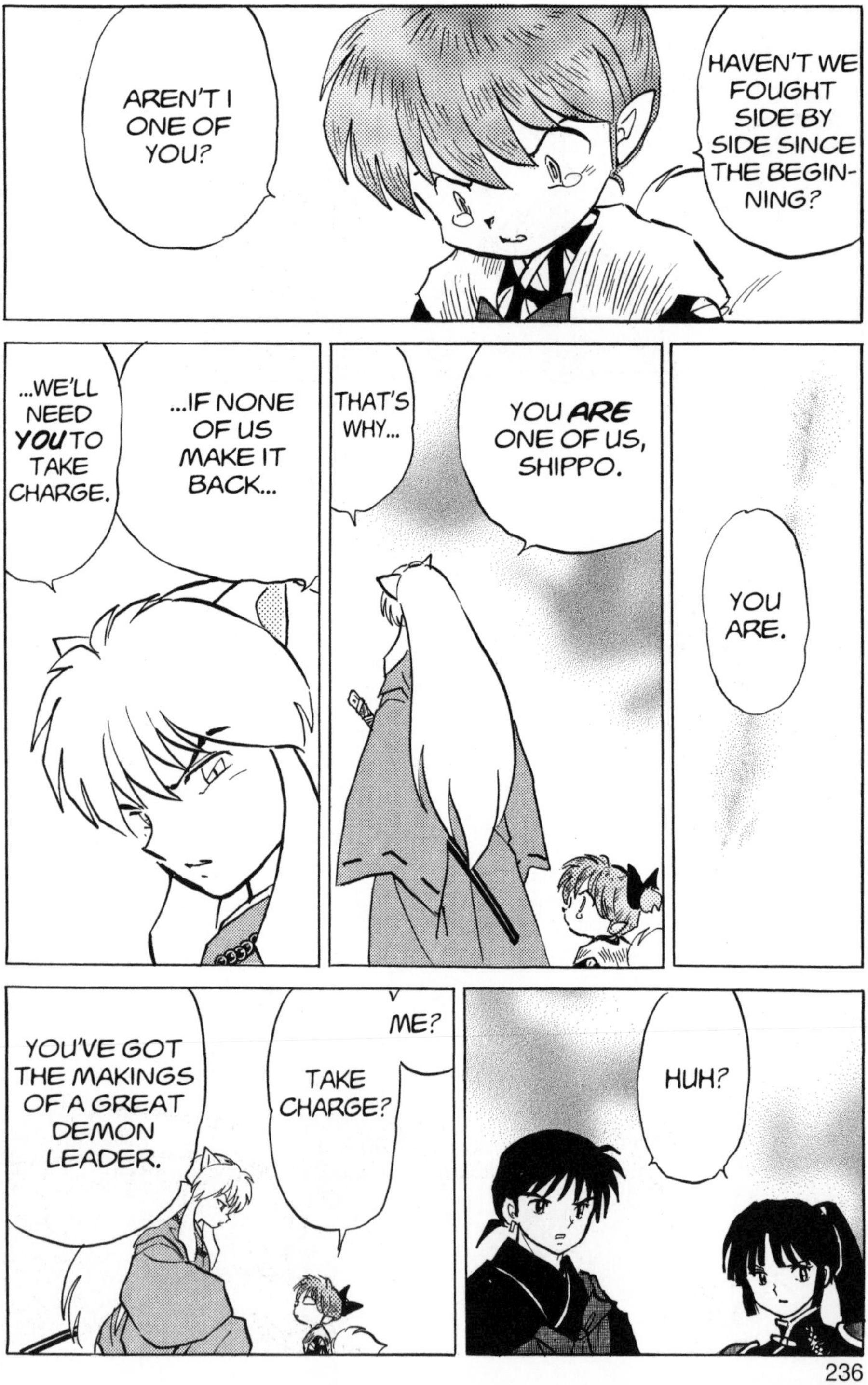
HAVEN'T WE FOUGHT SIDE BY SIDE SINCE THE BEGINNING?
AREN'T I ONE OF YOU?
YOU ARE.
YOU **ARE** ONE OF US, SHIPPO.
THAT'S WHY...
...IF NONE OF US MAKE IT BACK...
...WE'LL NEED **YOU** TO TAKE CHARGE.
HUH?
TAKE CHARGE?
ME?
YOU'VE GOT THE MAKINGS OF A GREAT DEMON LEADER.

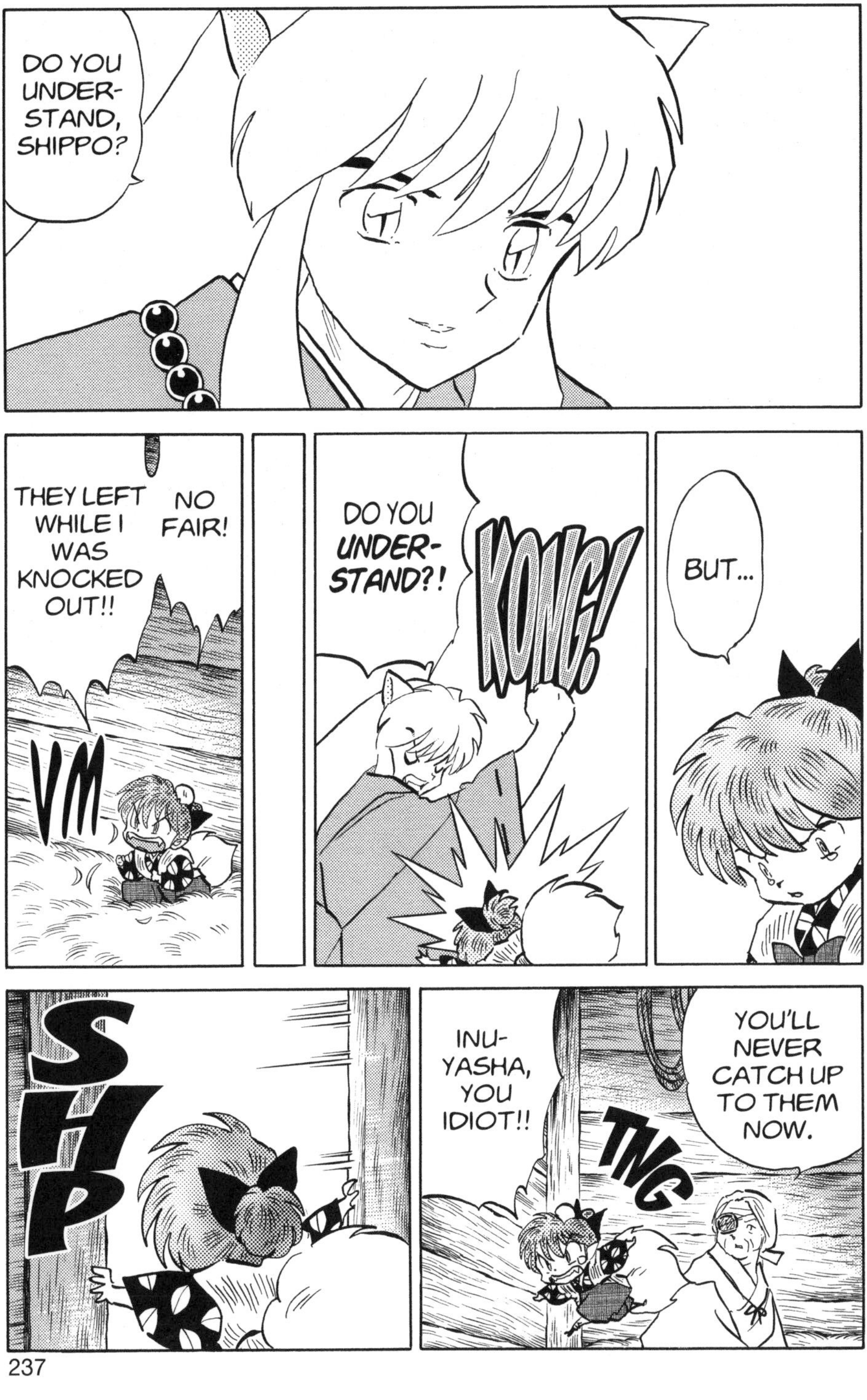
DO YOU UNDER-STAND, SHIPPO?
BUT...
DO YOU UNDER-STAND?!
KONG!
NO FAIR!
THEY LEFT WHILE I WAS KNOCKED OUT!!
VM
YOU'LL NEVER CATCH UP TO THEM NOW.
INU-YASHA, YOU IDIOT!!
TNG
SHP

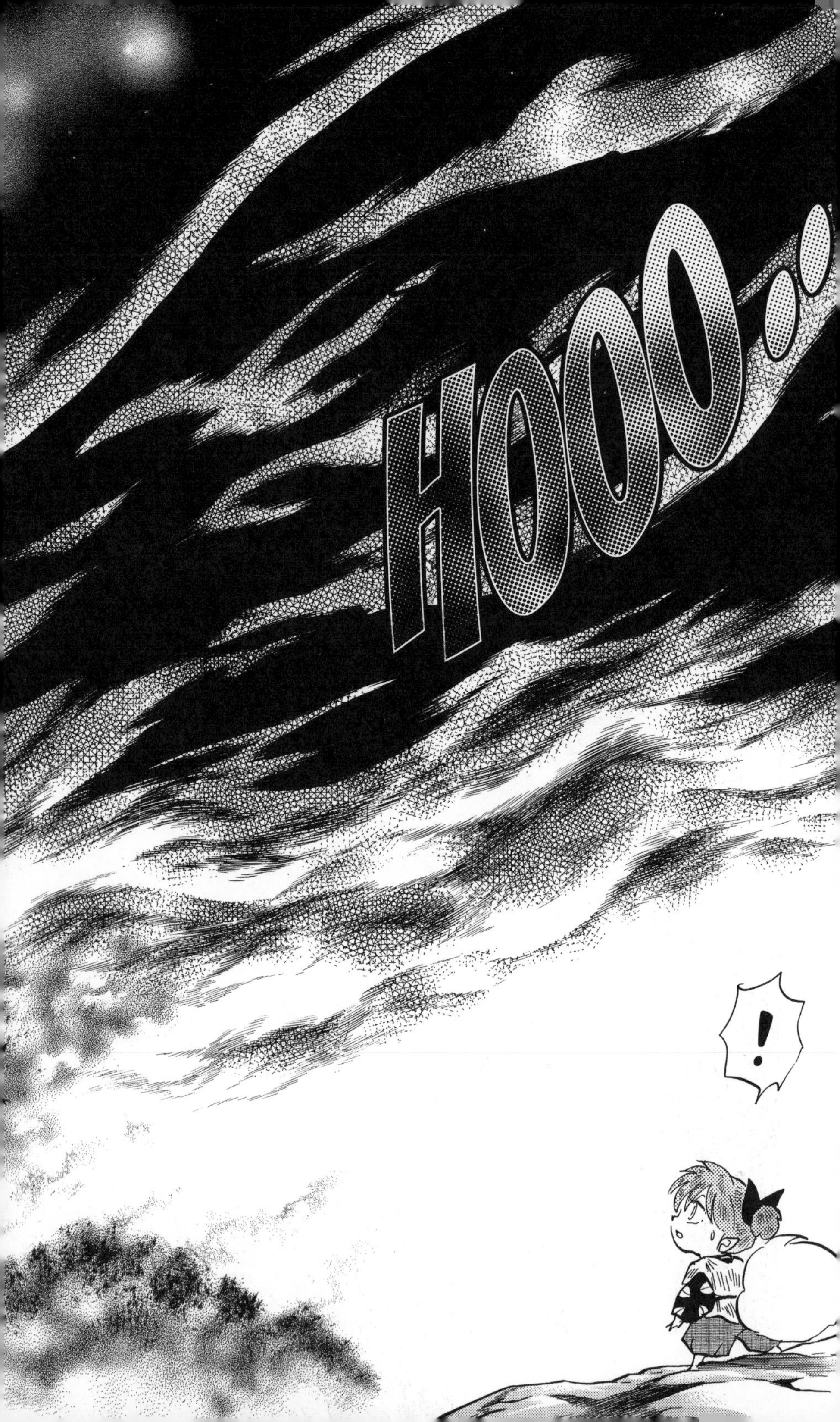
HOOO...
!

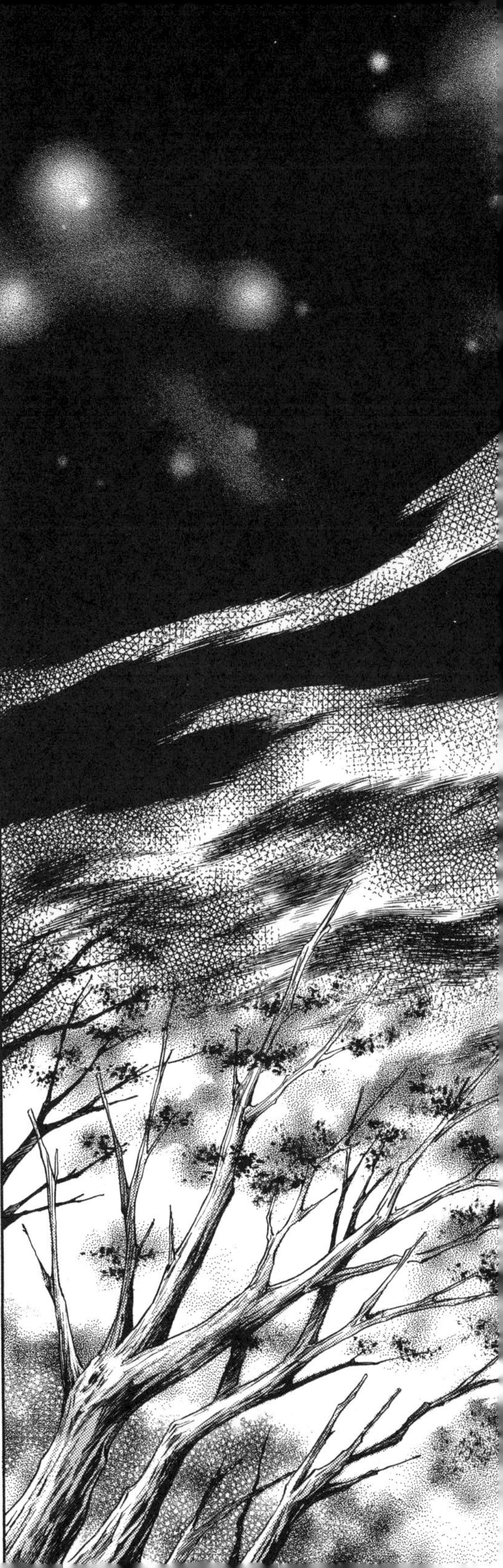

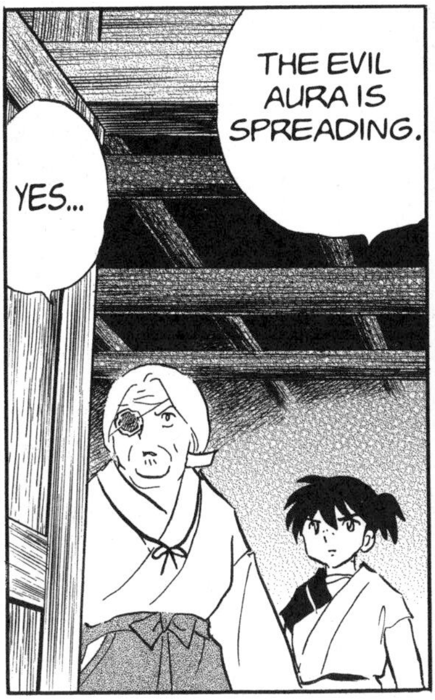
THE EVIL AURA IS SPREADING.
YES...

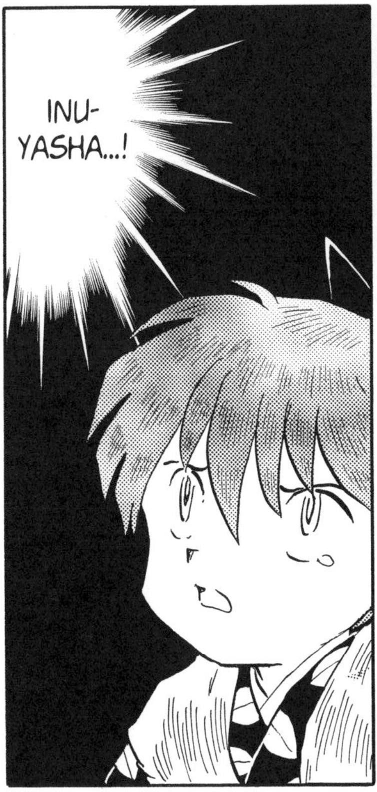
INU-YASHA...!

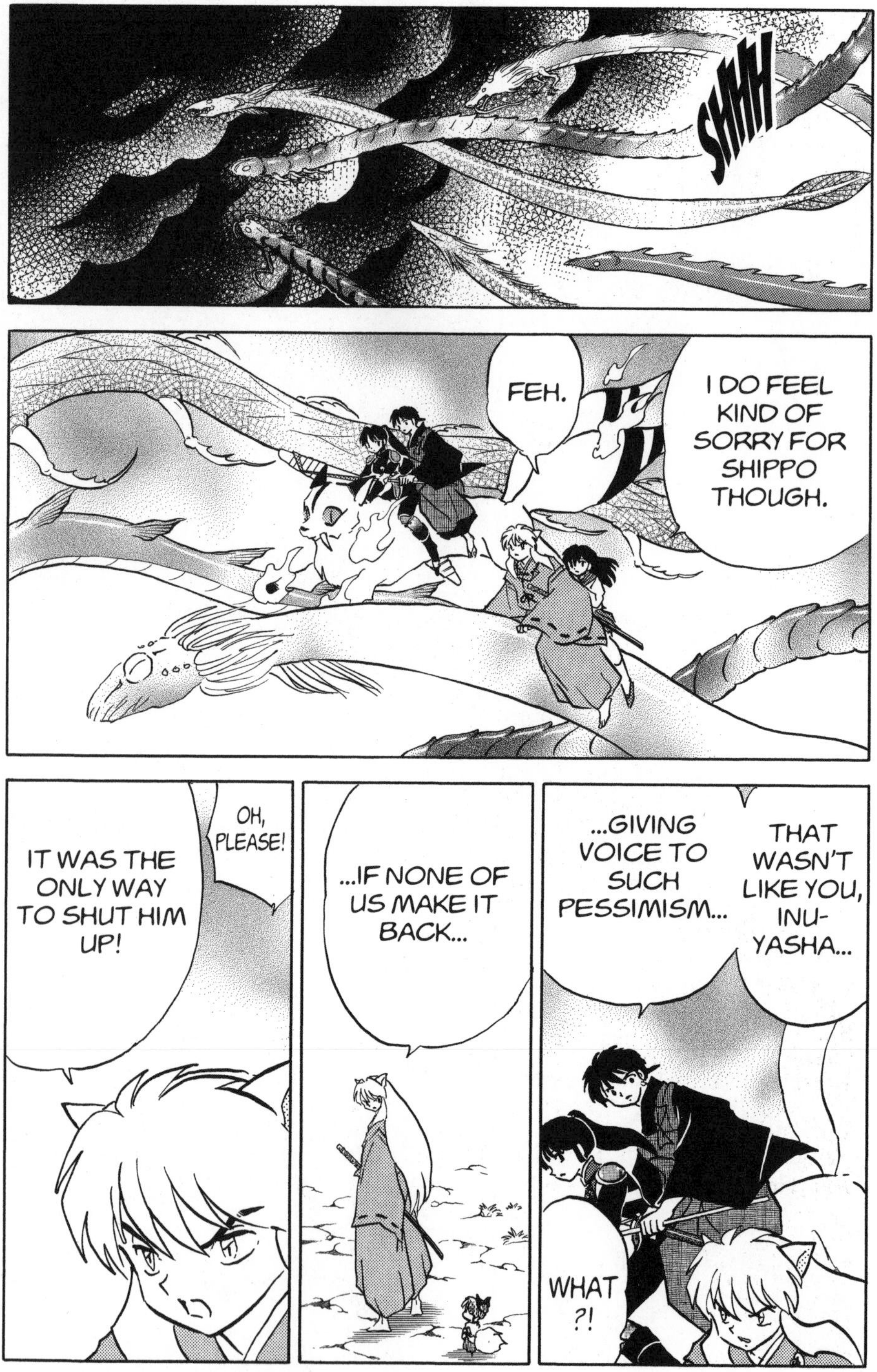
SHHHH
I DO FEEL KIND OF SORRY FOR SHIPPO THOUGH.
FEH.
THAT WASN'T LIKE YOU, INU-YASHA...
...GIVING VOICE TO SUCH PESSIMISM...
WHAT?!
...IF NONE OF US MAKE IT BACK...
OH, PLEASE!
IT WAS THE ONLY WAY TO SHUT HIM UP!

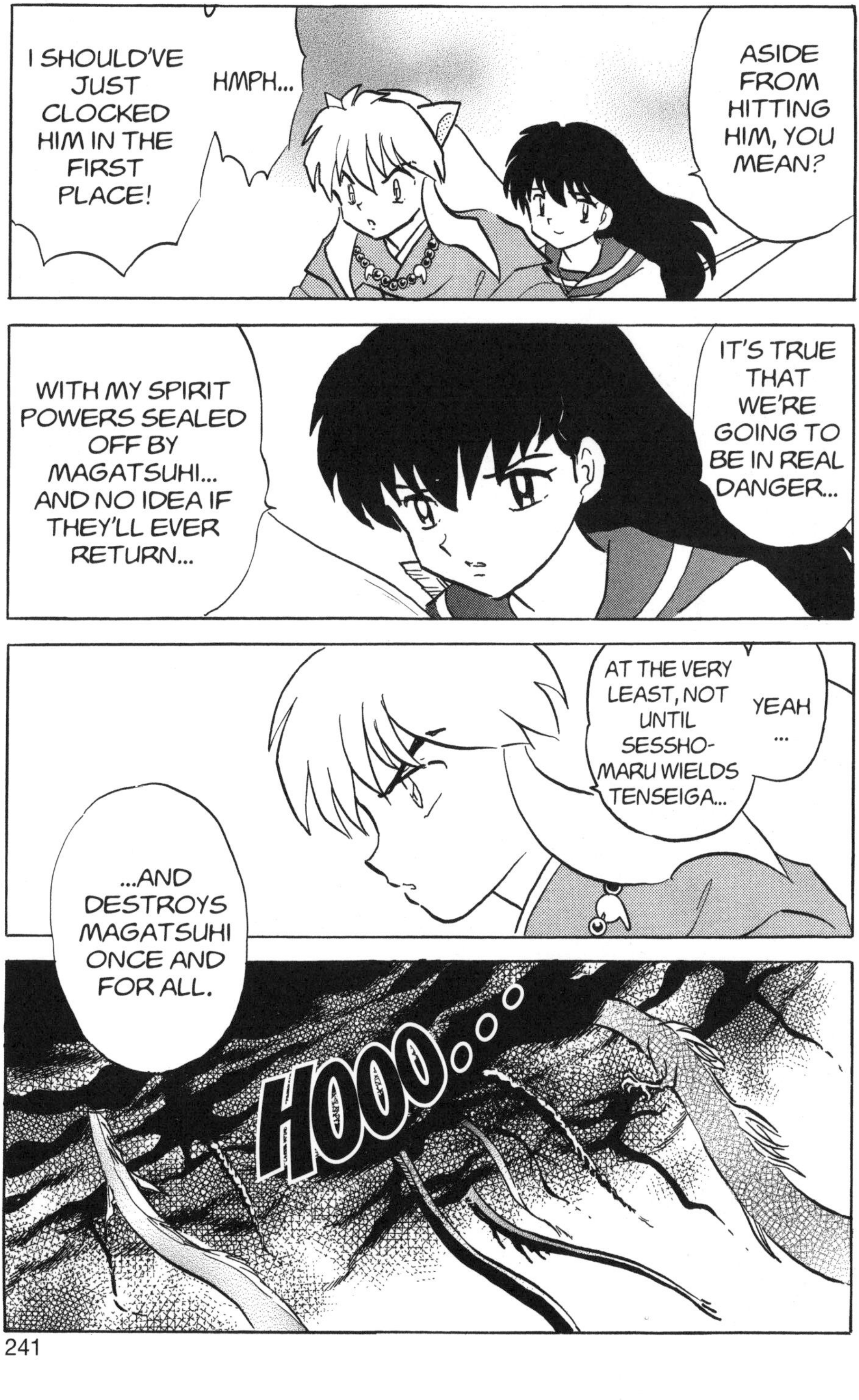
ASIDE FROM HITTING HIM, YOU MEAN?
HMPH...
I SHOULD'VE JUST CLOCKED HIM IN THE FIRST PLACE!
IT'S TRUE THAT WE'RE GOING TO BE IN REAL DANGER...
WITH MY SPIRIT POWERS SEALED OFF BY MAGATSUHI... AND NO IDEA IF THEY'LL EVER RETURN...
YEAH ...
AT THE VERY LEAST, NOT UNTIL SESSHO-MARU WIELDS TENSEIGA...
...AND DESTROYS MAGATSUHI ONCE AND FOR ALL.
HOOO...

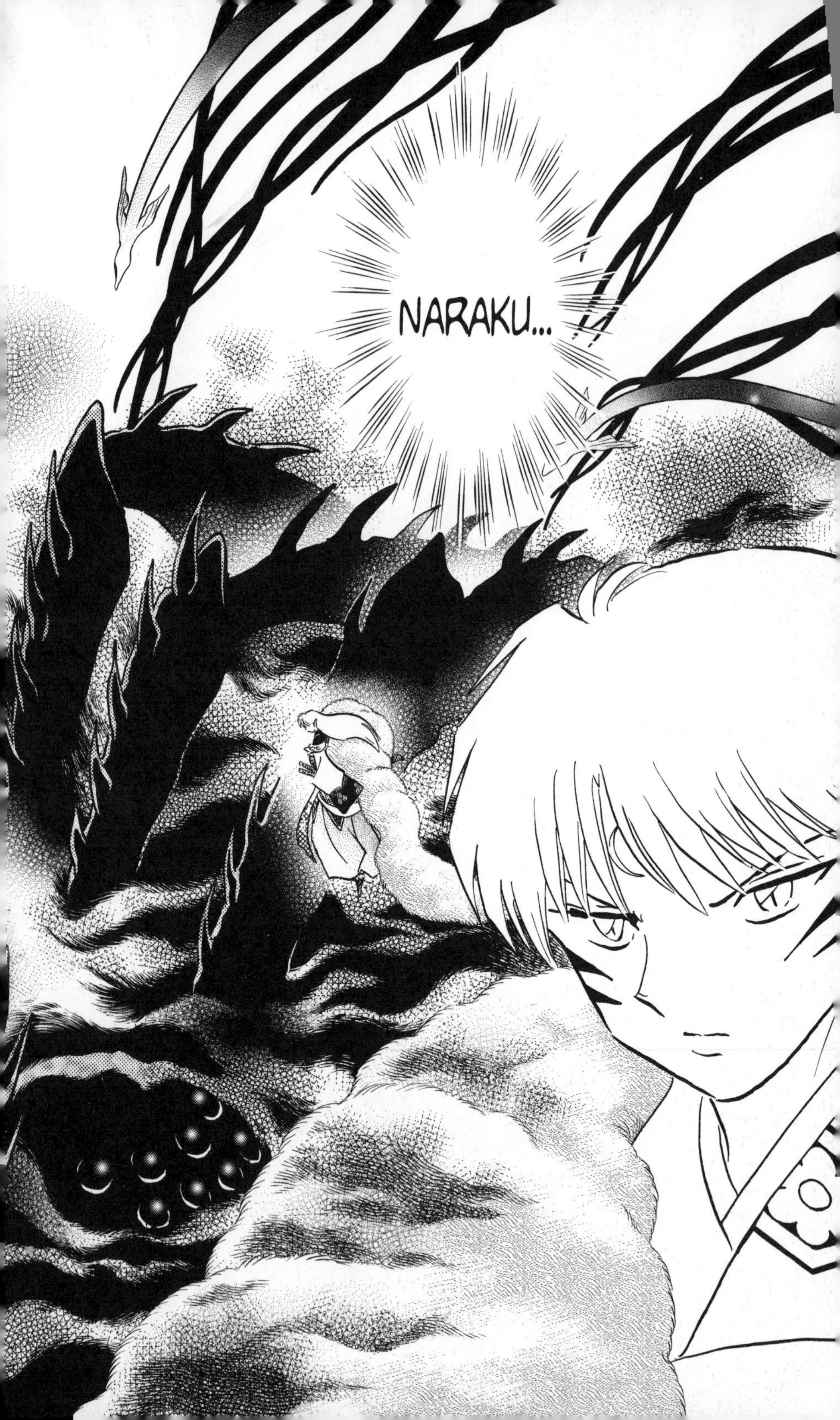
NARAKU...

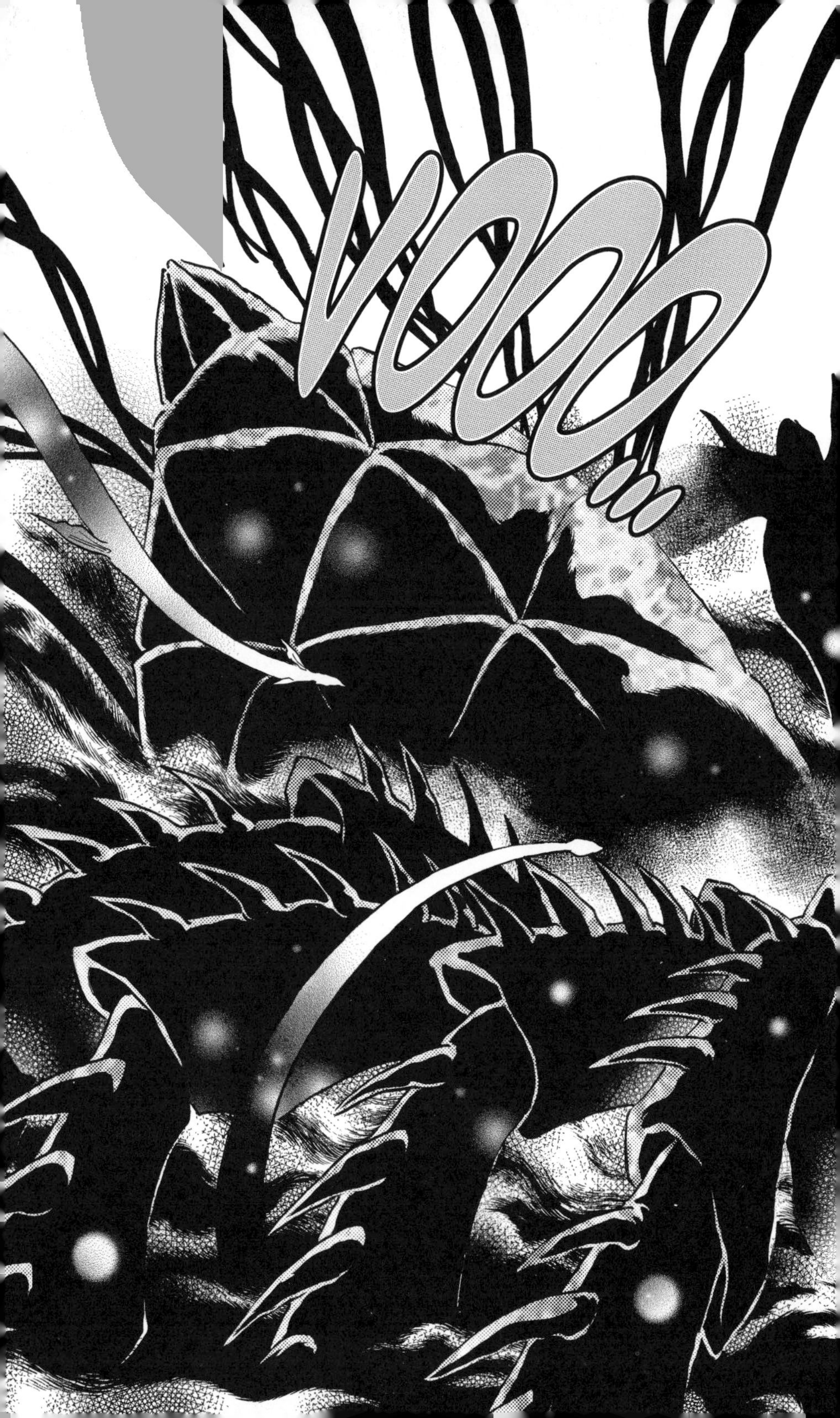
VOOOO...

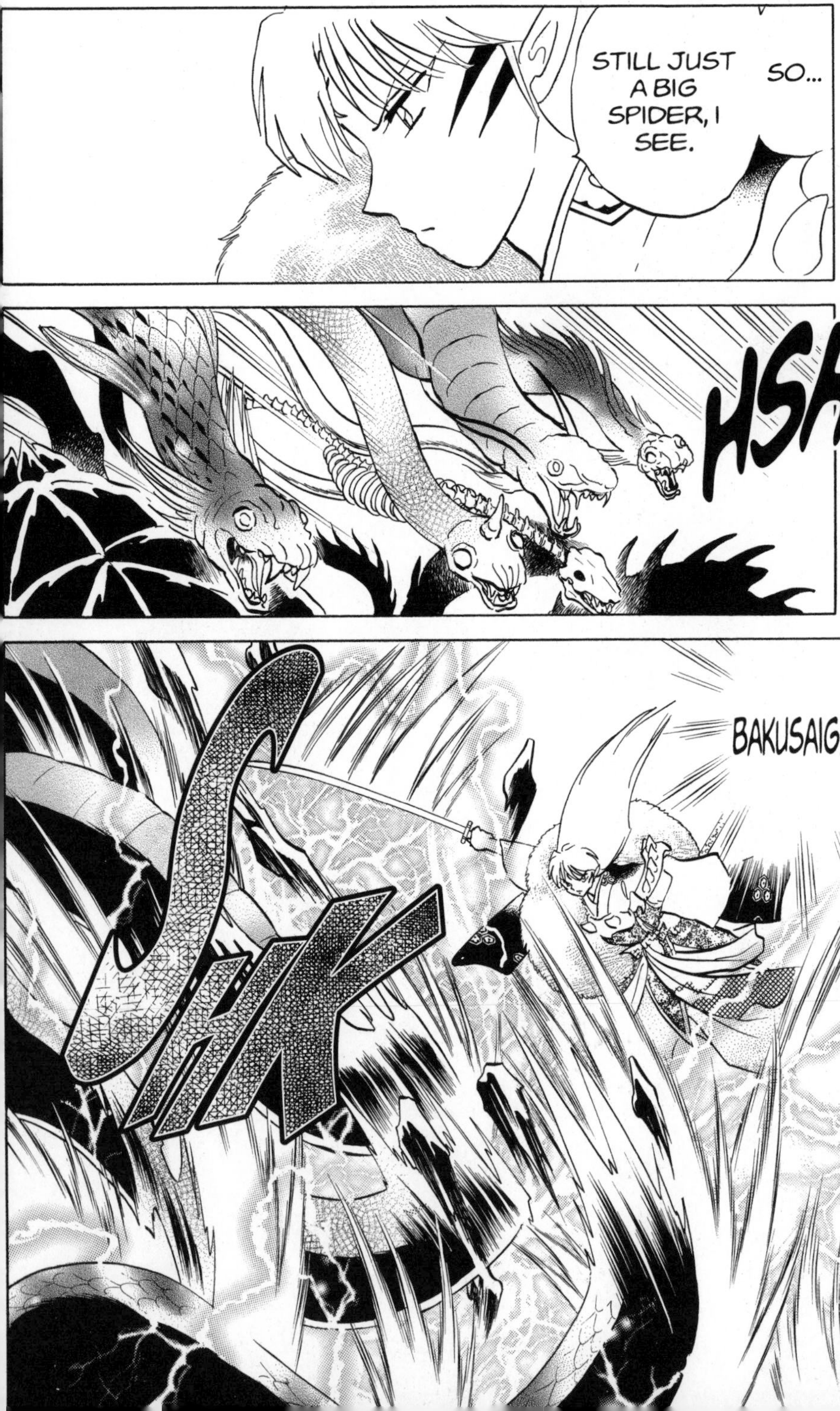
SO...
STILL JUST A BIG SPIDER, I SEE.
HSH
BAKUSAIGA!
SHK

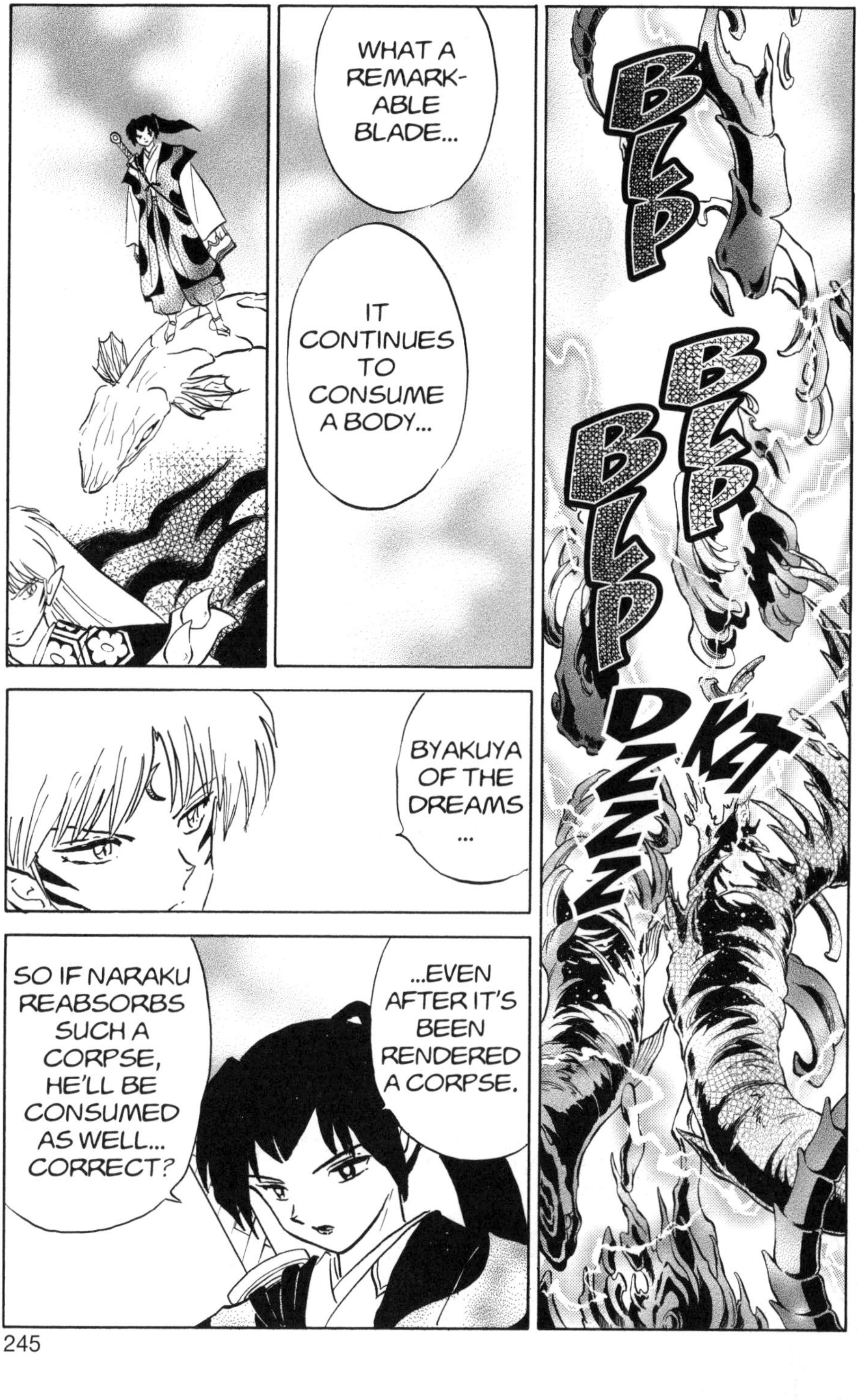
BLP
BLP
BLP
DZZZ
DKT
WHAT A REMARK-ABLE BLADE...
IT CONTINUES TO CONSUME A BODY...
BYAKUYA OF THE DREAMS...
...EVEN AFTER IT'S BEEN RENDERED A CORPSE.
SO IF NARAKU REABSORBS SUCH A CORPSE, HE'LL BE CONSUMED AS WELL... CORRECT?

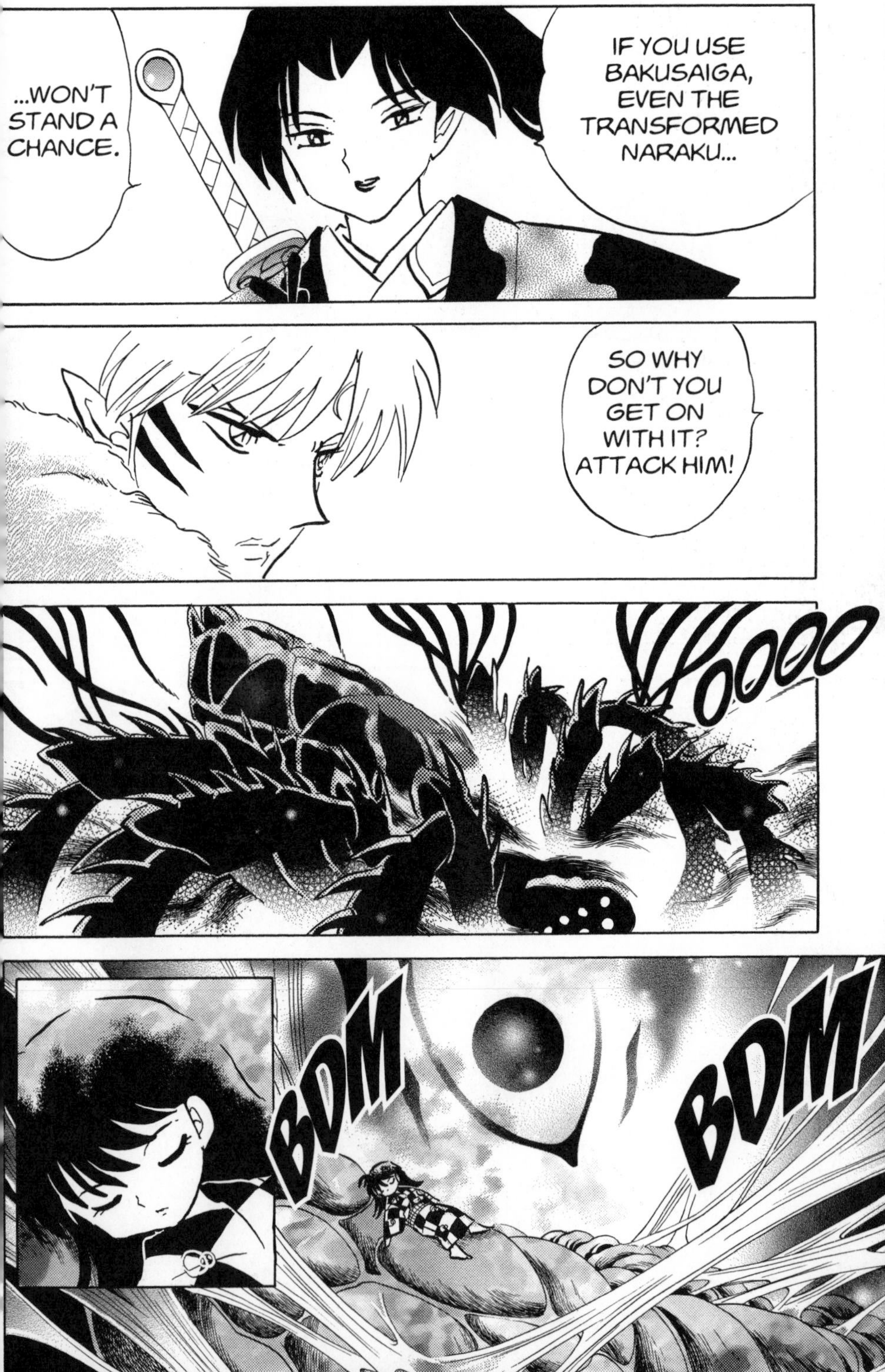
IF YOU USE BAKUSAIGA, EVEN THE TRANSFORMED NARAKU...
...WON'T STAND A CHANCE.
SO WHY DON'T YOU GET ON WITH IT? ATTACK HIM!
OOOO
BDM
BDM

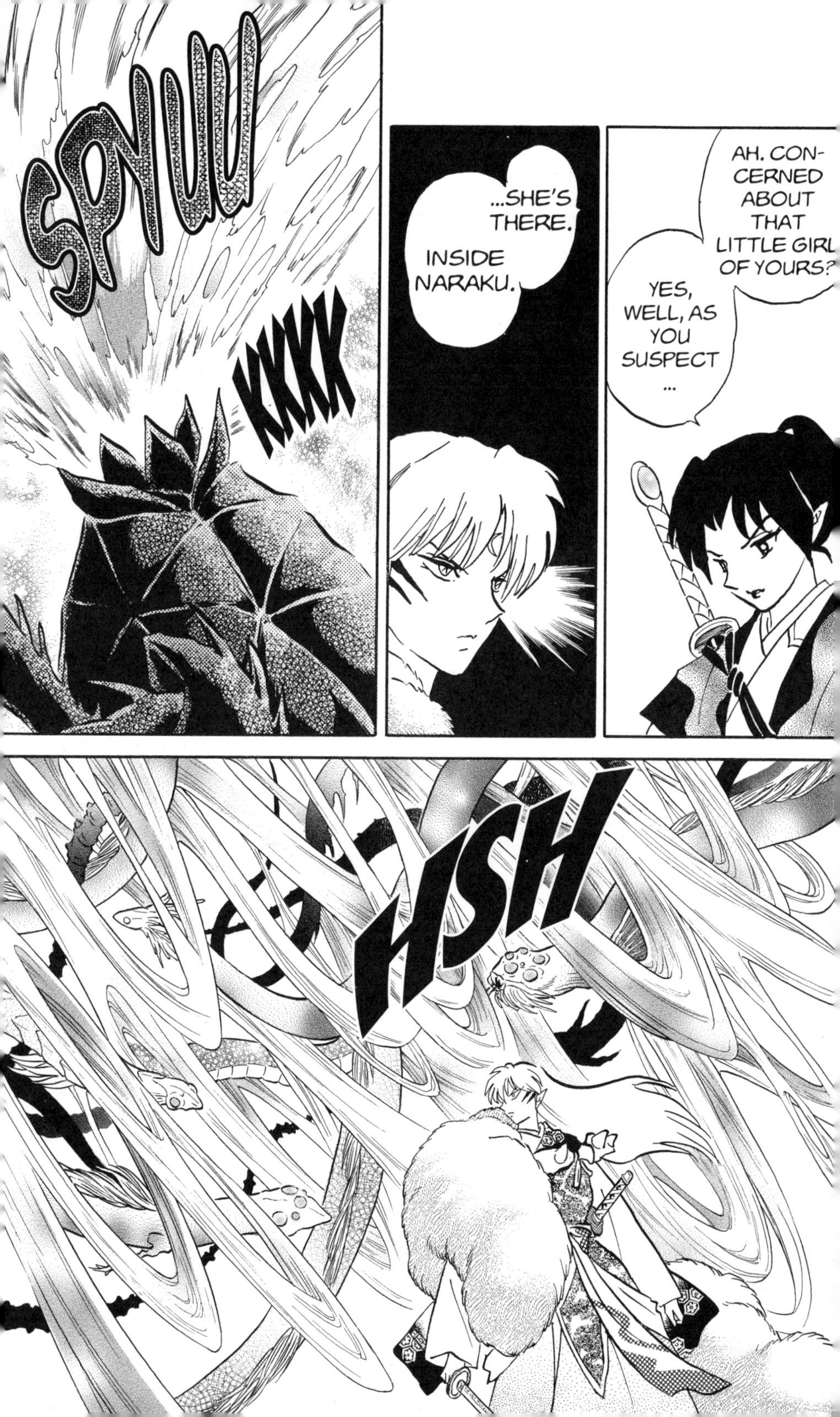

AH. CON-CERNED ABOUT THAT LITTLE GIRL OF YOURS?
YES, WELL, AS YOU SUSPECT ...
...SHE'S THERE.
INSIDE NARAKU.
SPYUU
KKKK
HSH

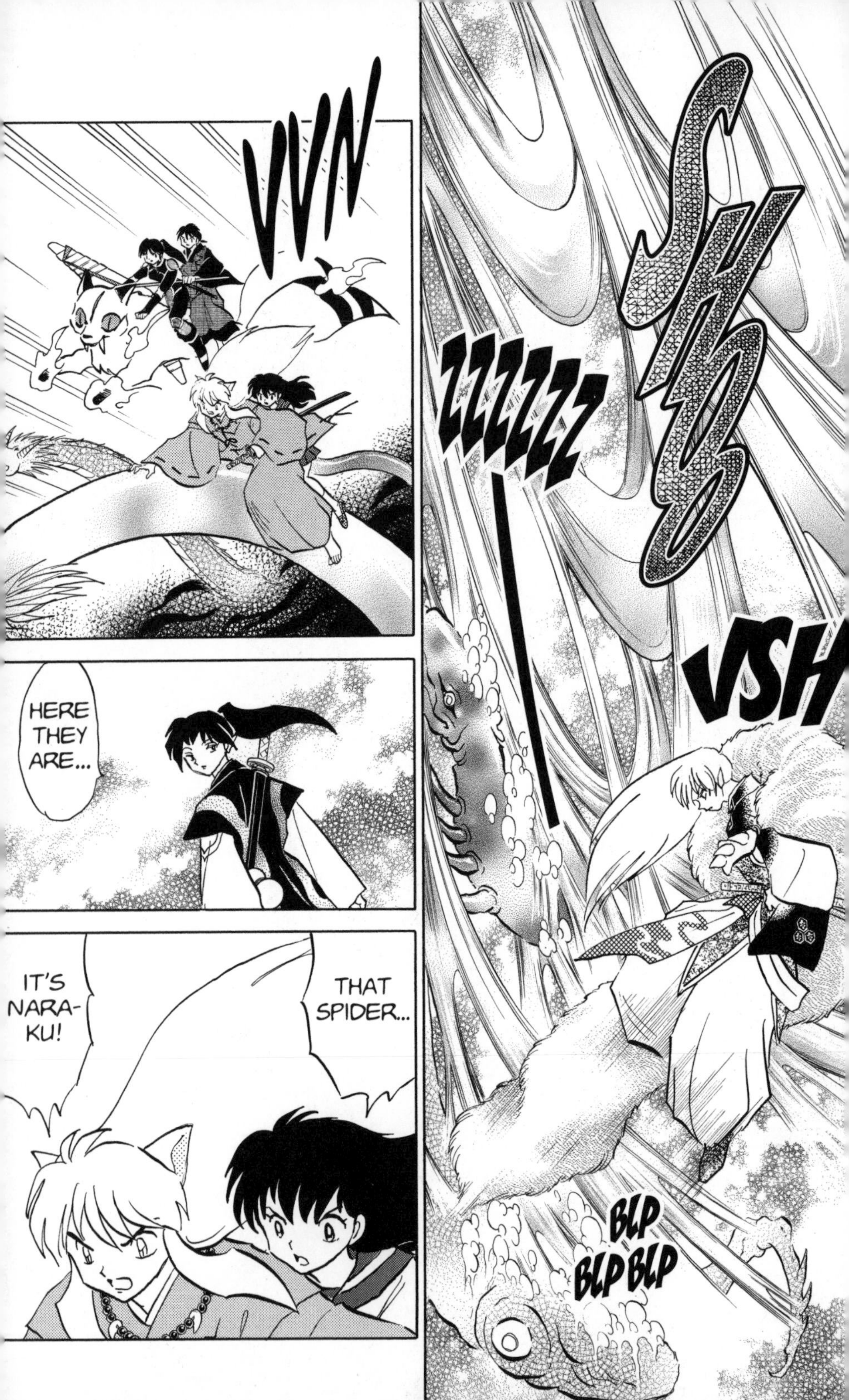
SHS
ZZZZZZZ
VSH
BLP
BLP BLP
VVN
HERE THEY ARE...
THAT SPIDER...
IT'S NARA-KU!

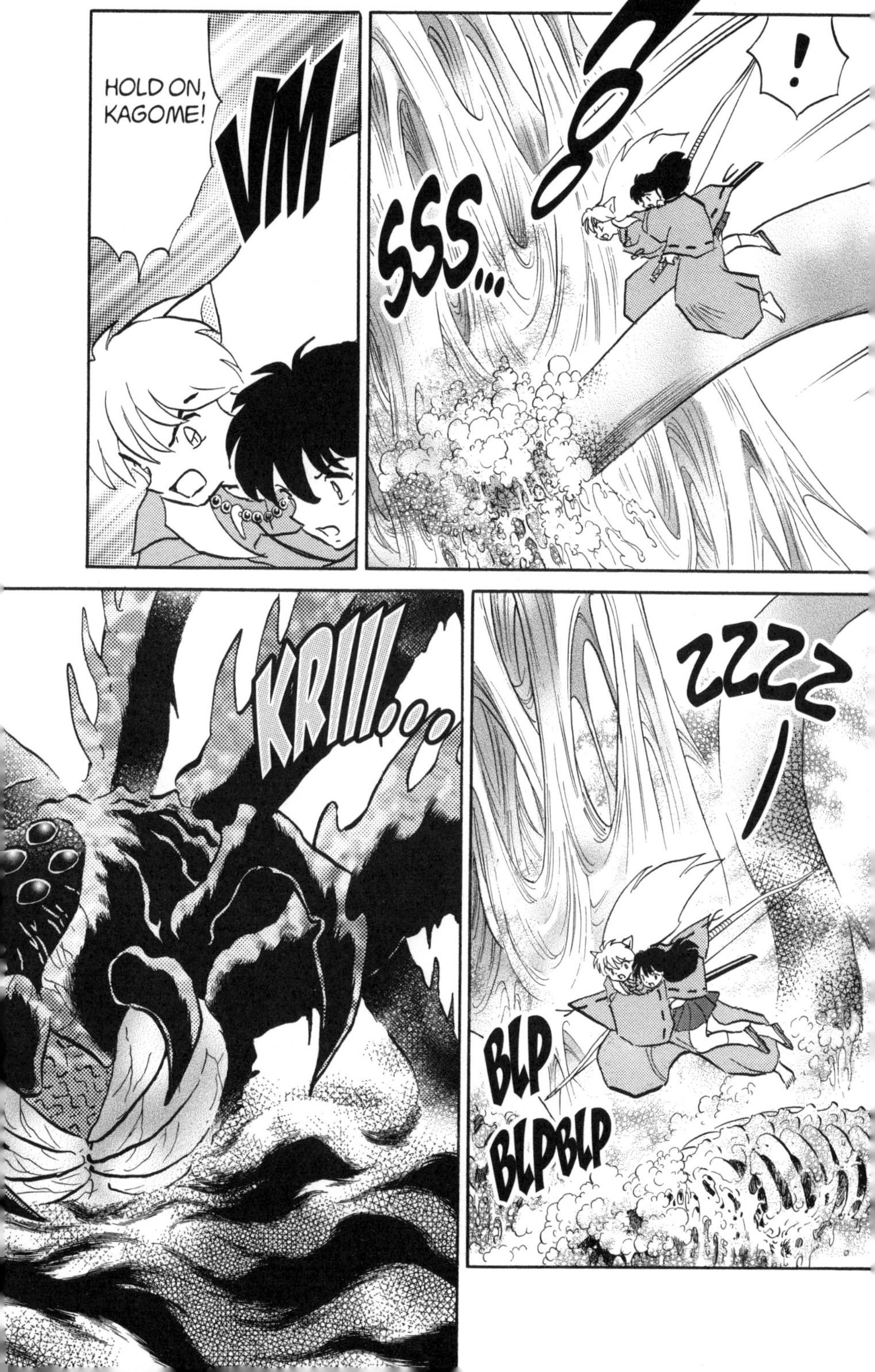
HOO
!
SSS...
HOLD ON, KAGOME!
VM
ZZZZ
BLP
BLPBLP
KRIII...

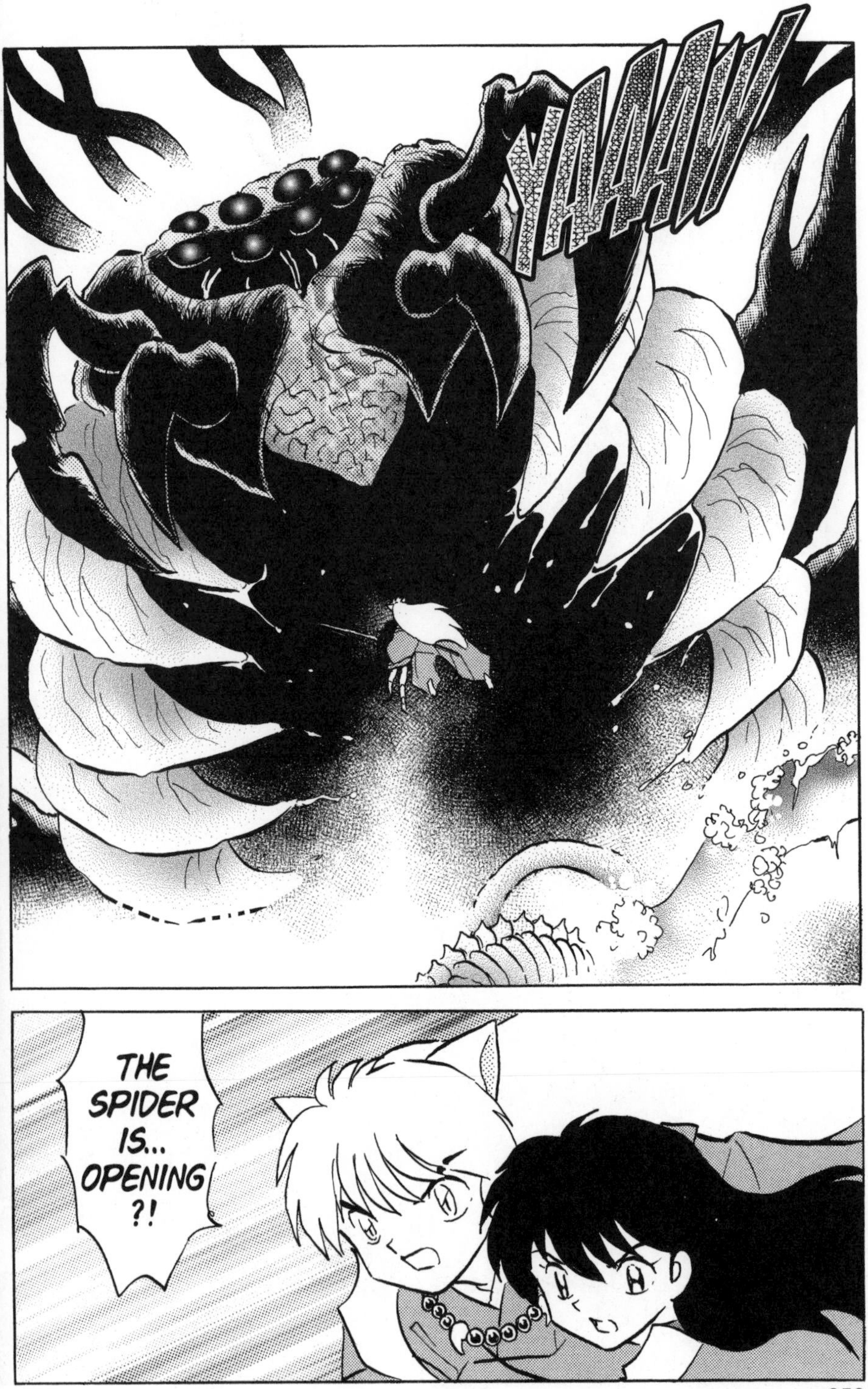
YAAAAW
THE SPIDER IS... OPENING ?!

SCROLL FOUR
INSIDE NARAKU

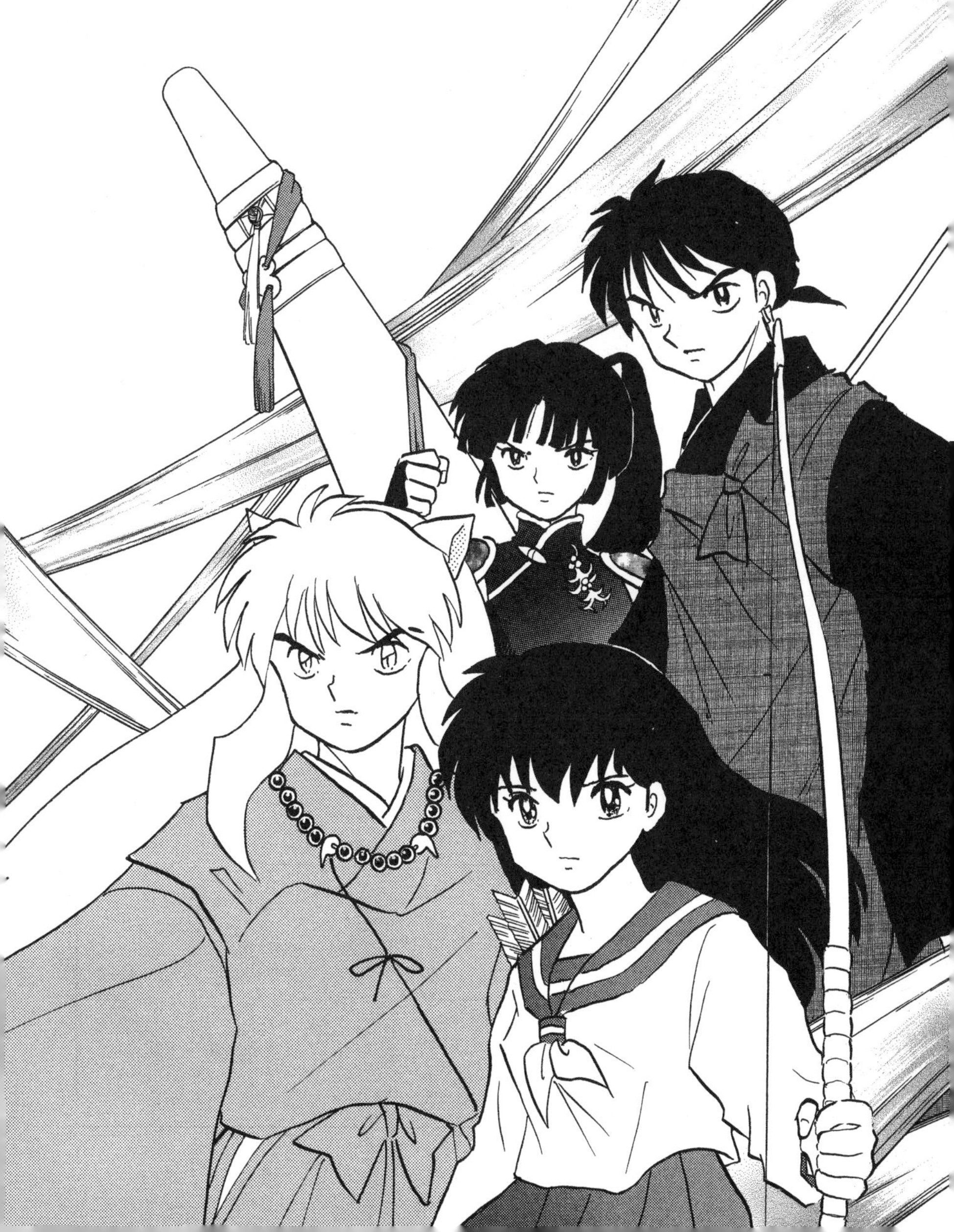

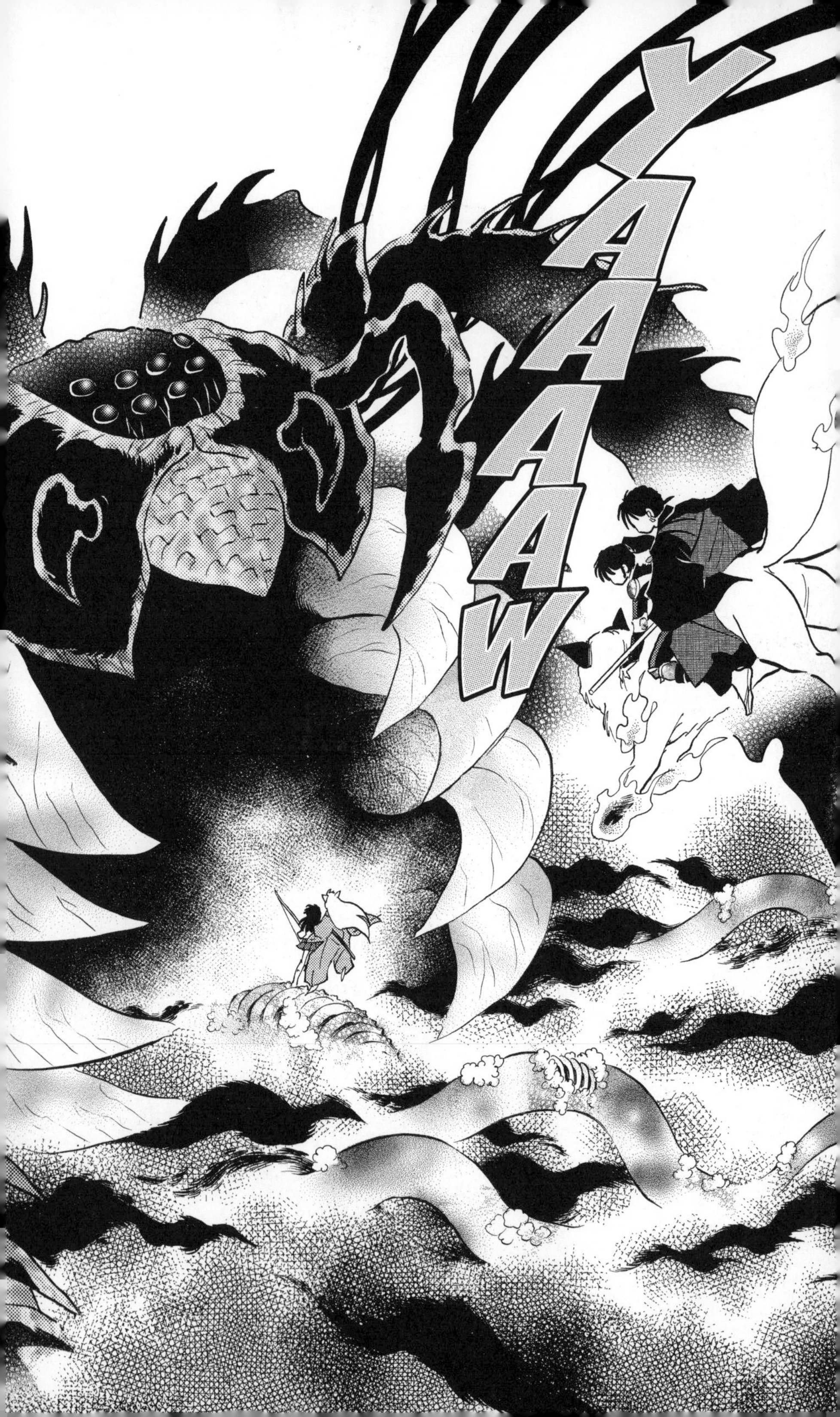
YAAAAW

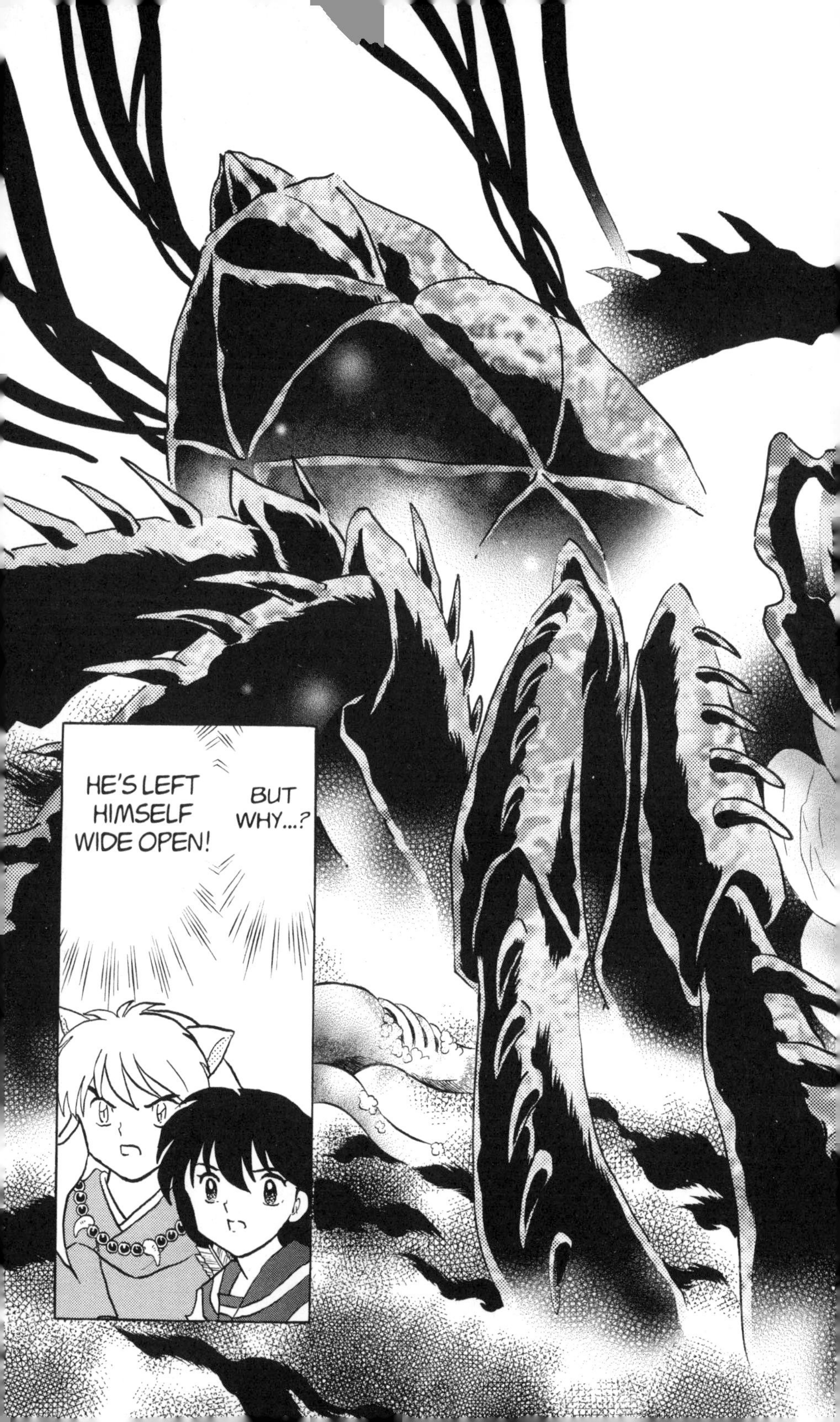
BUT WHY...?
HE'S LEFT HIMSELF WIDE OPEN!

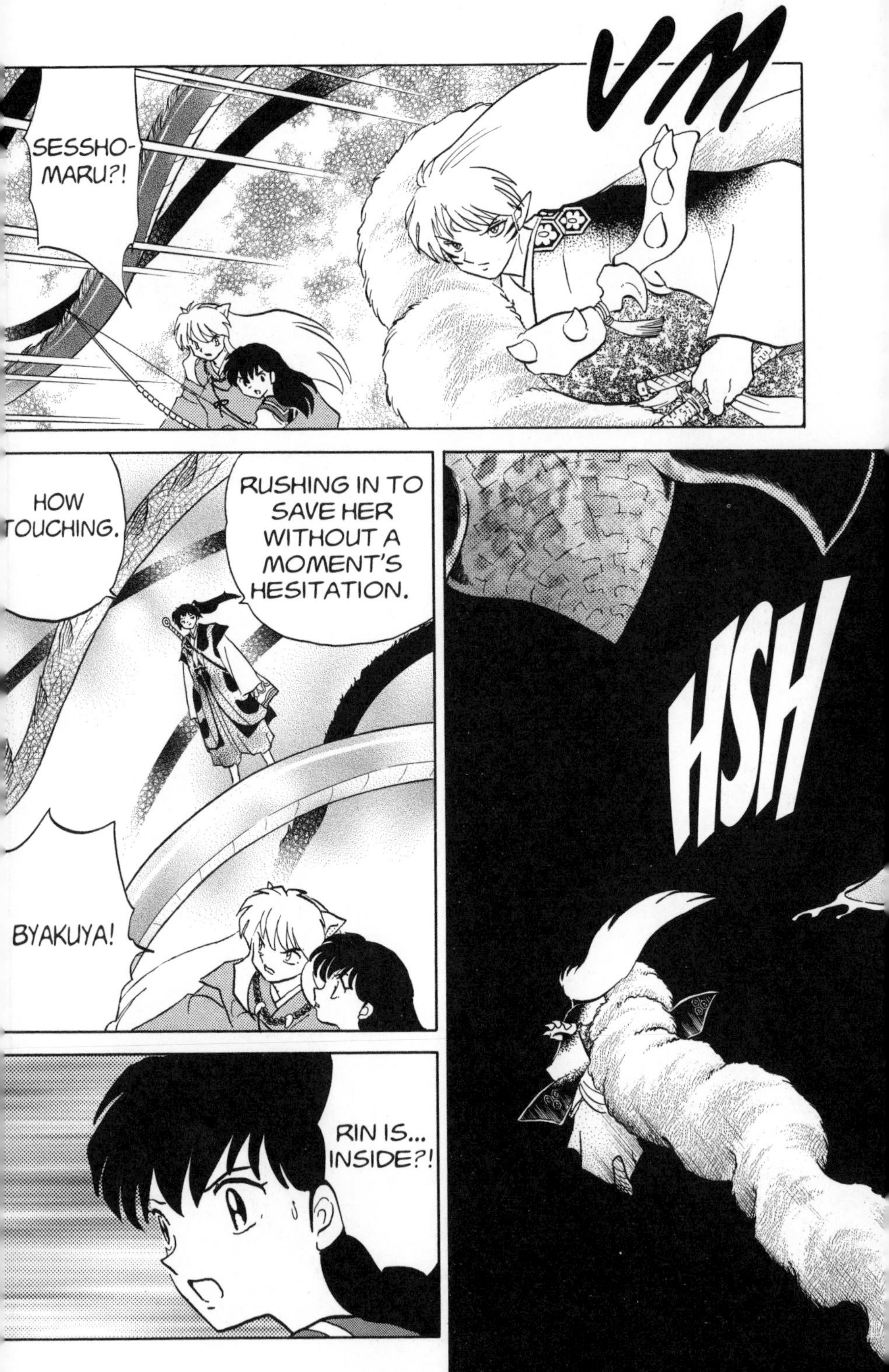
VM
SESSHO-MARU?!
HSH
RUSHING IN TO SAVE HER WITHOUT A MOMENT'S HESITATION.
HOW TOUCHING.
BYAKUYA!
RIN IS... INSIDE?!

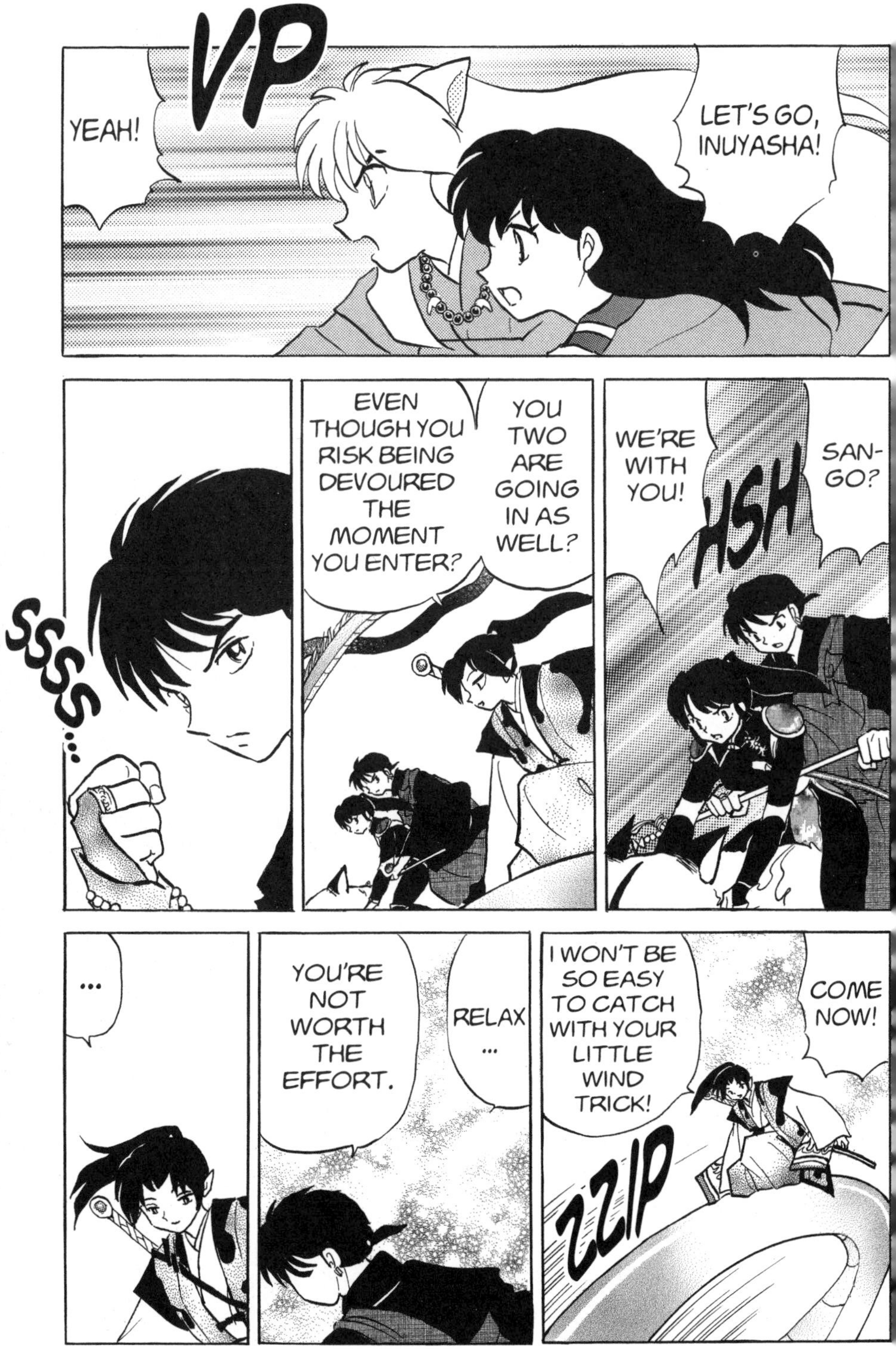
LET'S GO, INUYASHA!
VP
YEAH!
SAN-GO?
HSH
WE'RE WITH YOU!
YOU TWO ARE GOING IN AS WELL?
EVEN THOUGH YOU RISK BEING DEVOURED THE MOMENT YOU ENTER?
SSSS...
COME NOW!
I WON'T BE SO EASY TO CATCH WITH YOUR LITTLE WIND TRICK!
ZZIP
RELAX...
YOU'RE NOT WORTH THE EFFORT.
...

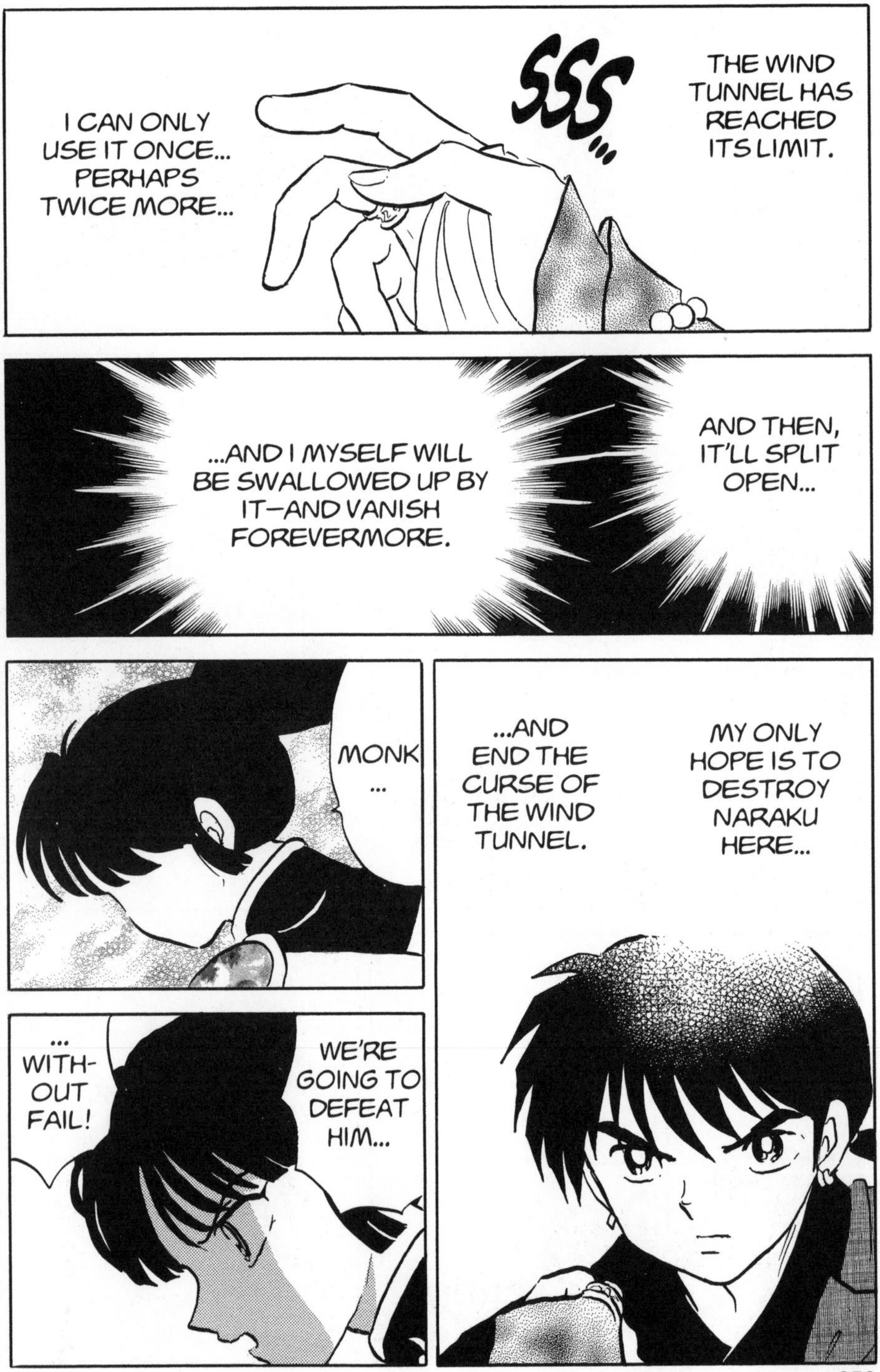
THE WIND TUNNEL HAS REACHED ITS LIMIT.
SSS...
I CAN ONLY USE IT ONCE... PERHAPS TWICE MORE...
AND THEN, IT'LL SPLIT OPEN...
...AND I MYSELF WILL BE SWALLOWED UP BY IT—AND VANISH FOREVERMORE.
MY ONLY HOPE IS TO DESTROY NARAKU HERE...
...AND END THE CURSE OF THE WIND TUNNEL.
MONK ...
WE'RE GOING TO DEFEAT HIM...
... WITH-OUT FAIL!

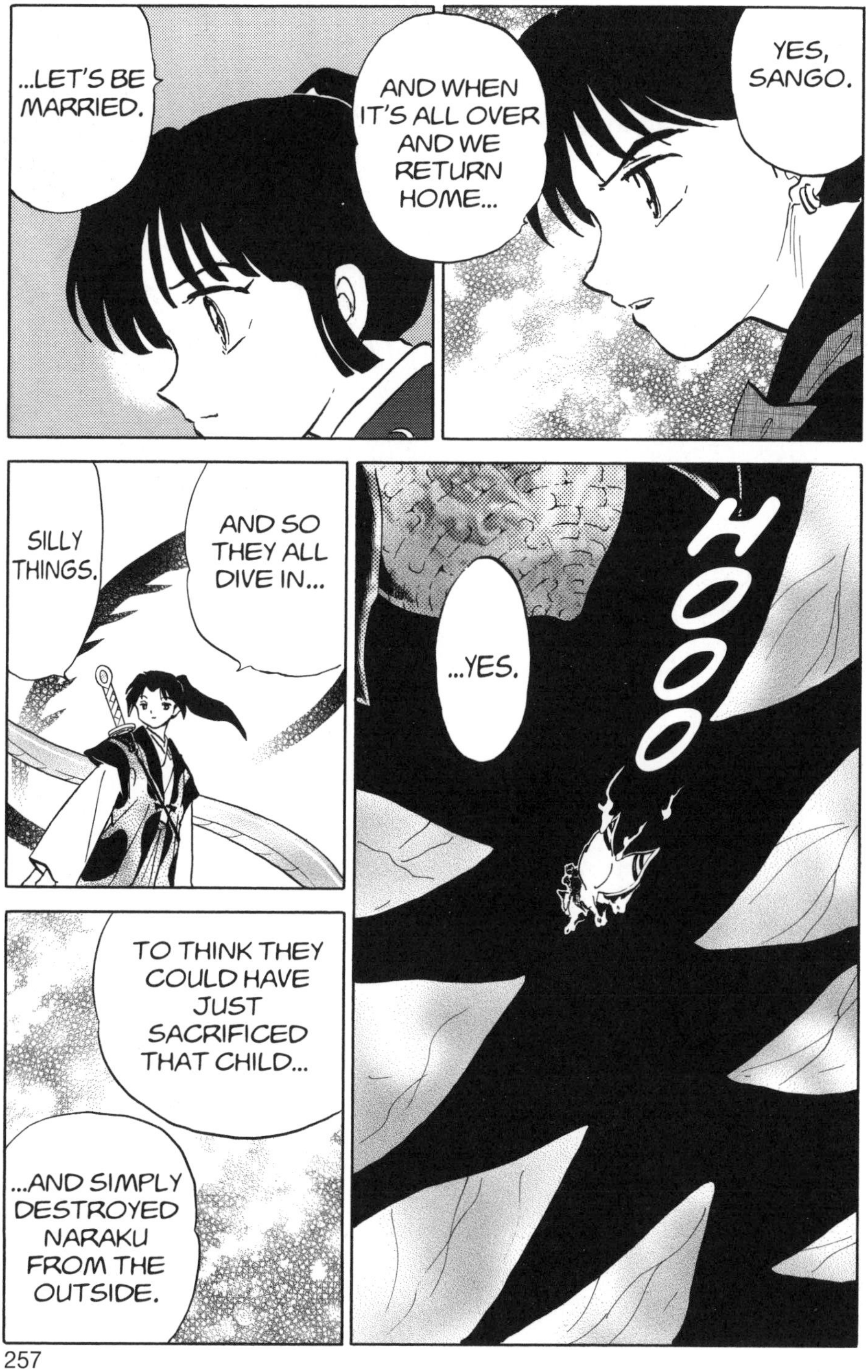
YES, SANGO.
AND WHEN IT'S ALL OVER AND WE RETURN HOME...
...LET'S BE MARRIED.
HOOOO
...YES.
AND SO THEY ALL DIVE IN...
SILLY THINGS.
TO THINK THEY COULD HAVE JUST SACRIFICED THAT CHILD...
...AND SIMPLY DESTROYED NARAKU FROM THE OUTSIDE.

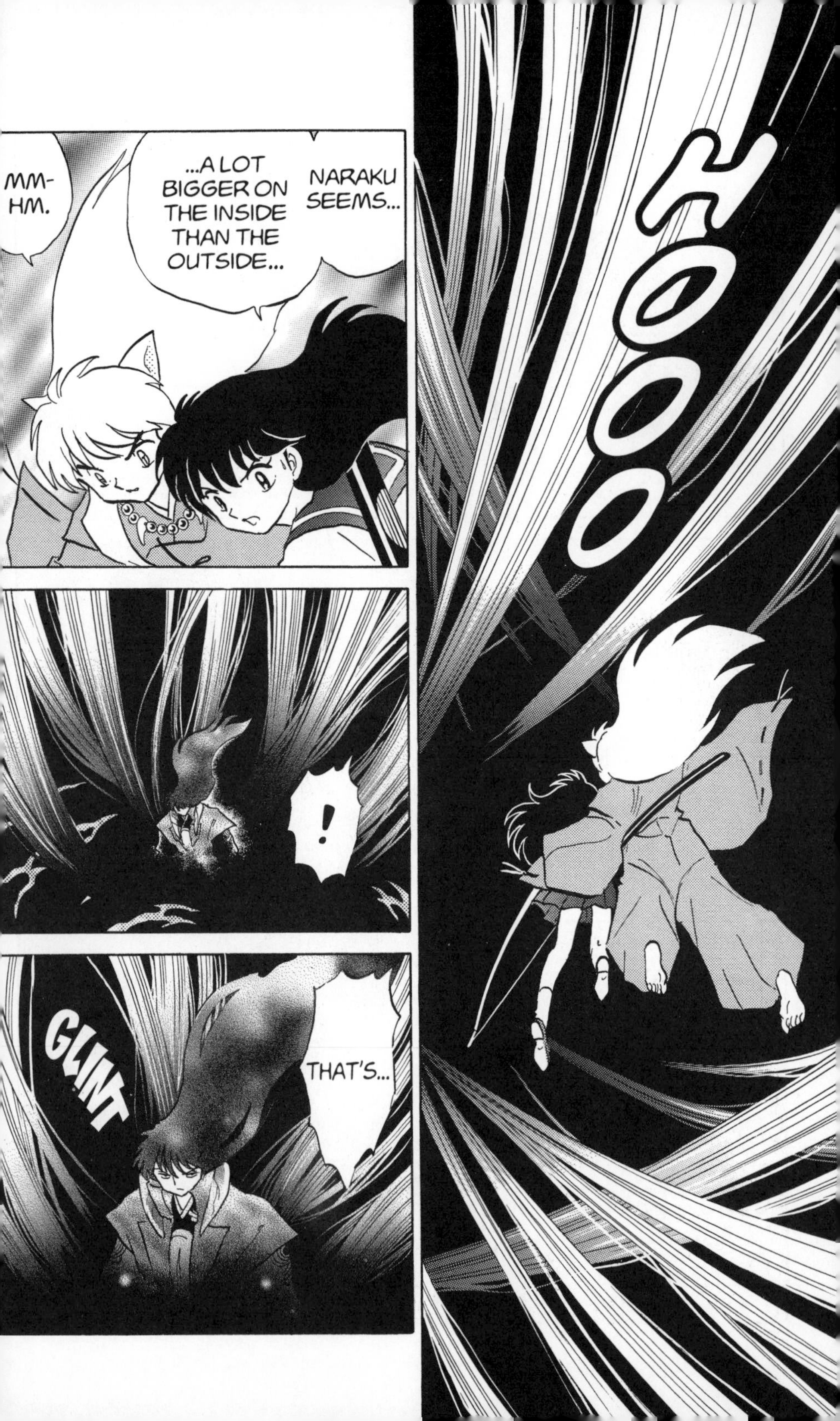
HOOOO
NARAKU SEEMS...
...A LOT BIGGER ON THE INSIDE THAN THE OUTSIDE...
MM-HM.
!
THAT'S...
GLINT

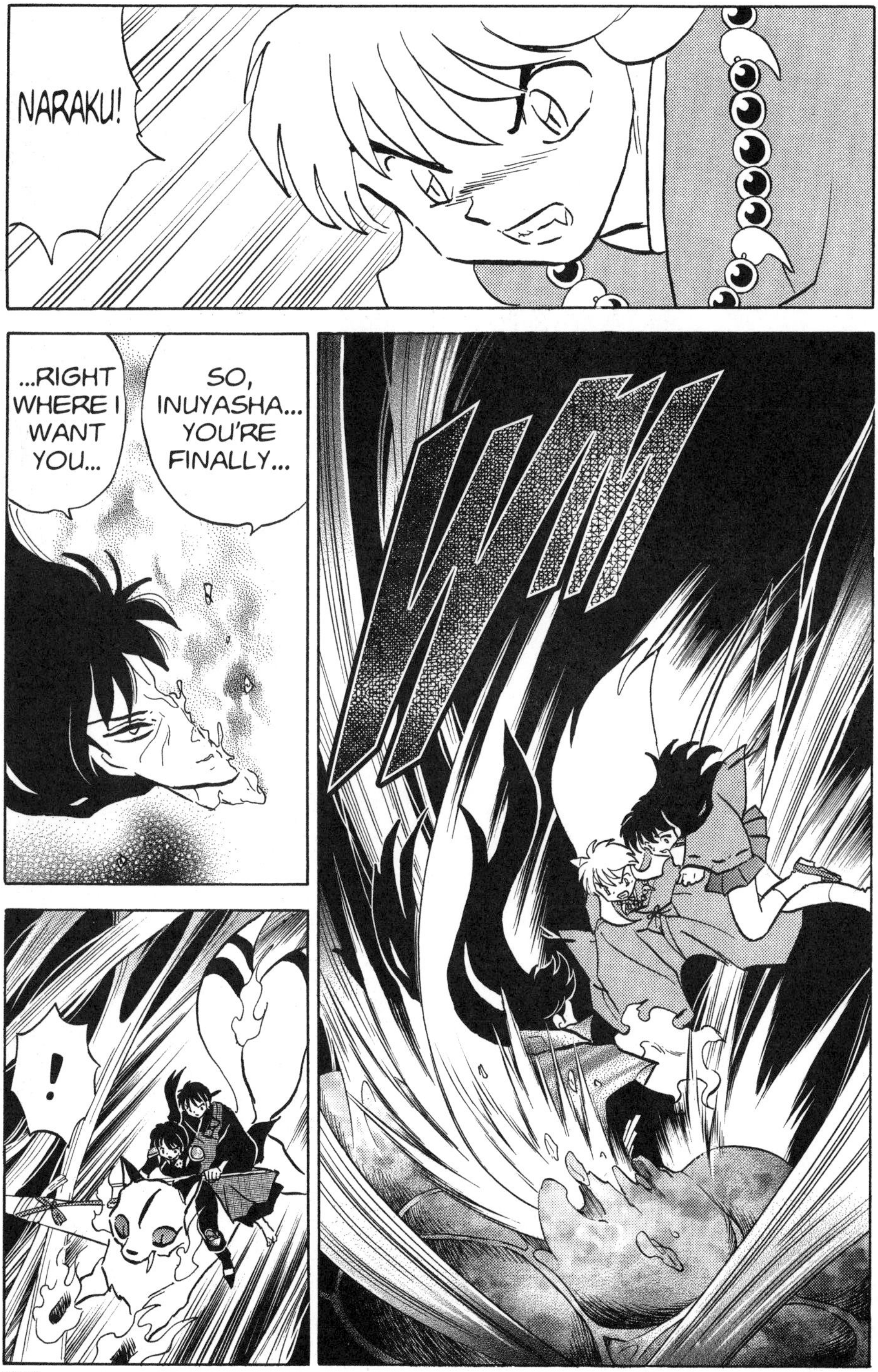
NARAKU!
SO, INUYASHA... YOU'RE FINALLY...
...RIGHT WHERE I WANT YOU...
!

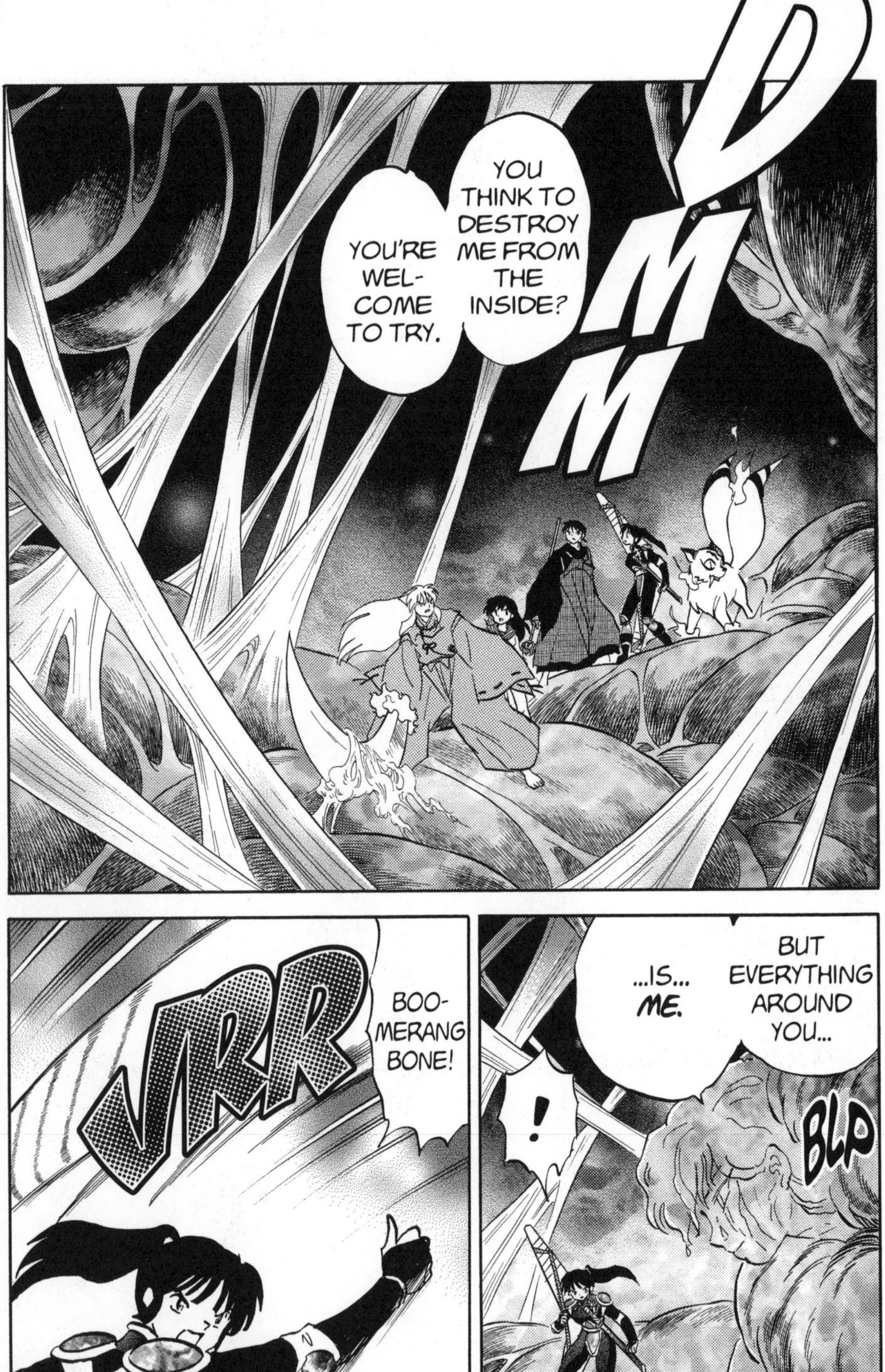
DMMM
YOU THINK TO DESTROY ME FROM THE INSIDE?
YOU'RE WEL-COME TO TRY.
BUT EVERYTHING AROUND YOU...
...IS... **ME.**
!
BLP
BOO-MERANG BONE!
VRR

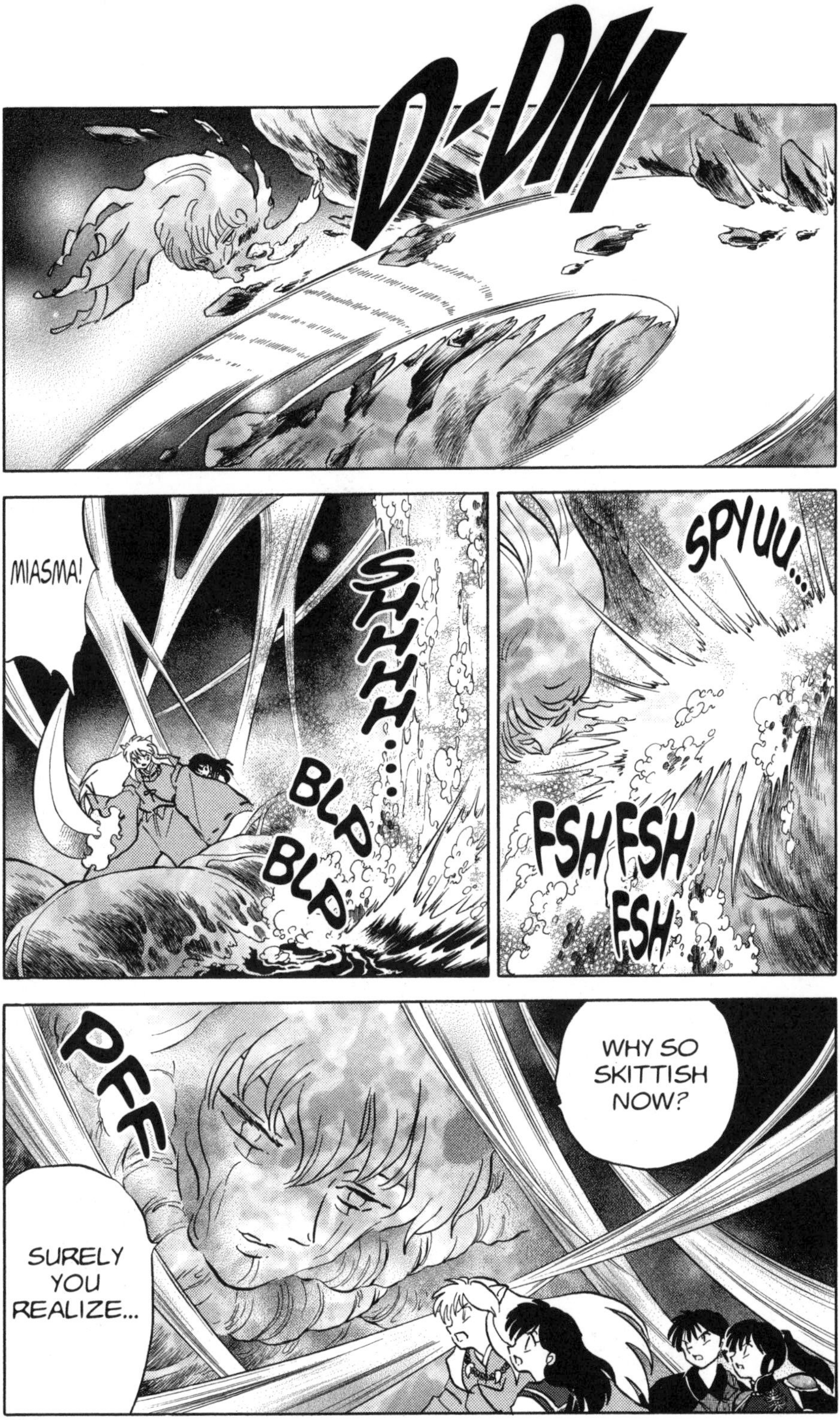
D-DM
SPYUU...
FSH FSH
FSH
MIASMA!
SHHHH...
BLP BLP
WHY SO SKITTISH NOW?
PFF
SURELY YOU REALIZE...

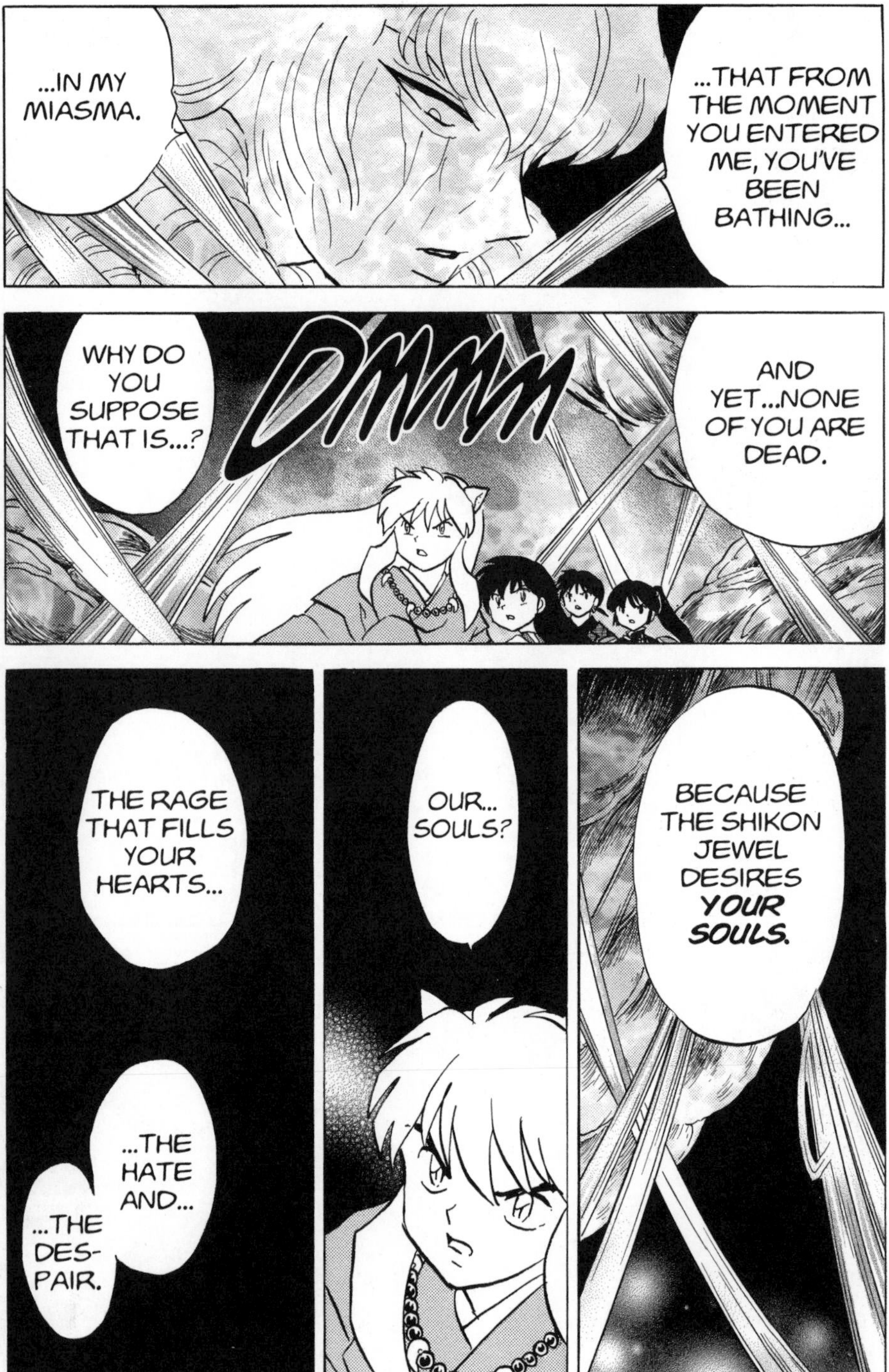
...THAT FROM THE MOMENT YOU ENTERED ME, YOU'VE BEEN BATHING...
...IN MY MIASMA.
AND YET...NONE OF YOU ARE DEAD.
DMMM
WHY DO YOU SUPPOSE THAT IS...?
BECAUSE THE SHIKON JEWEL DESIRES ***YOUR SOULS.***
OUR... SOULS?
THE RAGE THAT FILLS YOUR HEARTS...
...THE HATE AND...
...THE DES-PAIR.

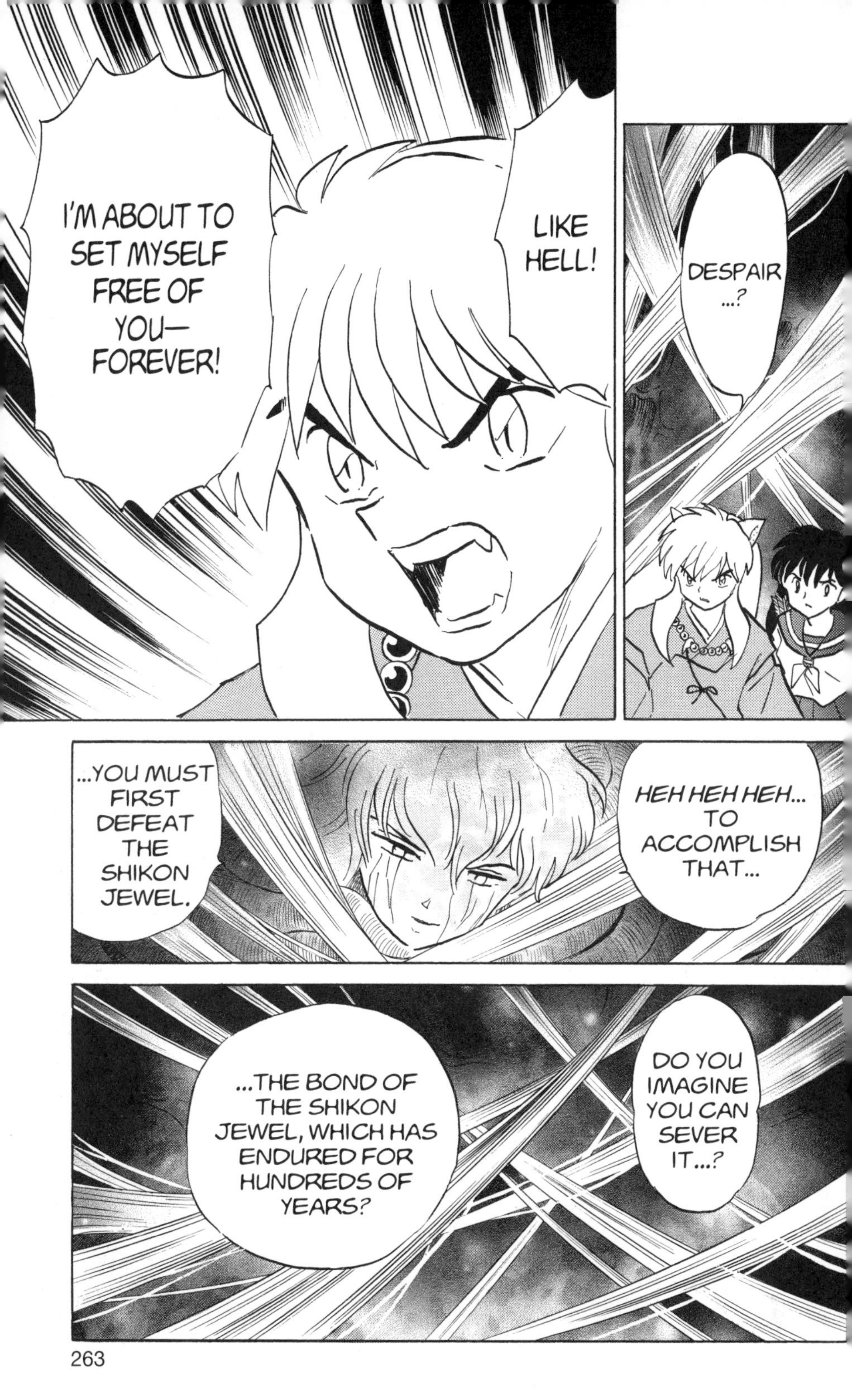
DESPAIR ...?
LIKE HELL!
I'M ABOUT TO SET MYSELF FREE OF YOU— FOREVER!
HEH HEH HEH... TO ACCOMPLISH THAT...
...YOU MUST FIRST DEFEAT THE SHIKON JEWEL.
DO YOU IMAGINE YOU CAN SEVER IT...?
...THE BOND OF THE SHIKON JEWEL, WHICH HAS ENDURED FOR HUNDREDS OF YEARS?

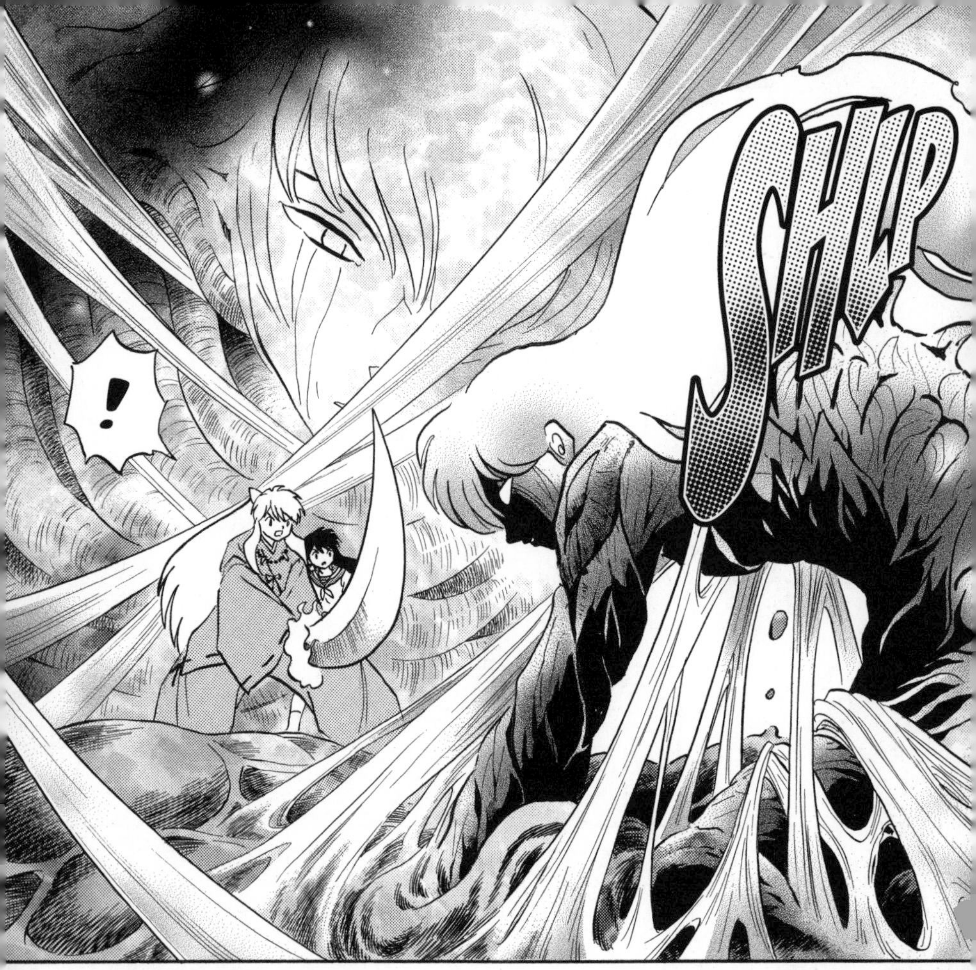
SHLP
!
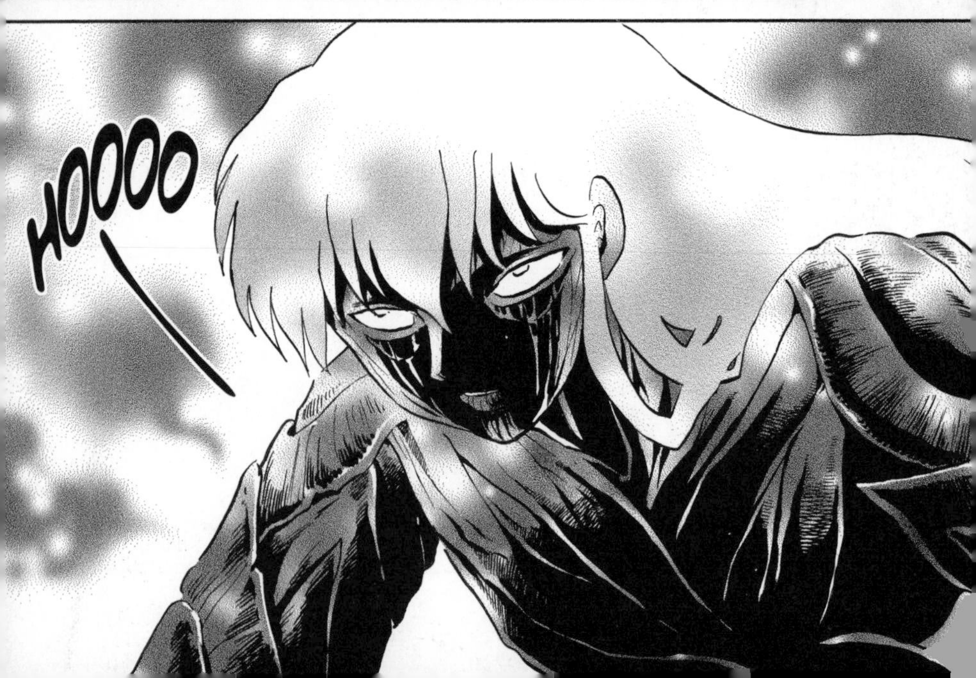
HOOOO

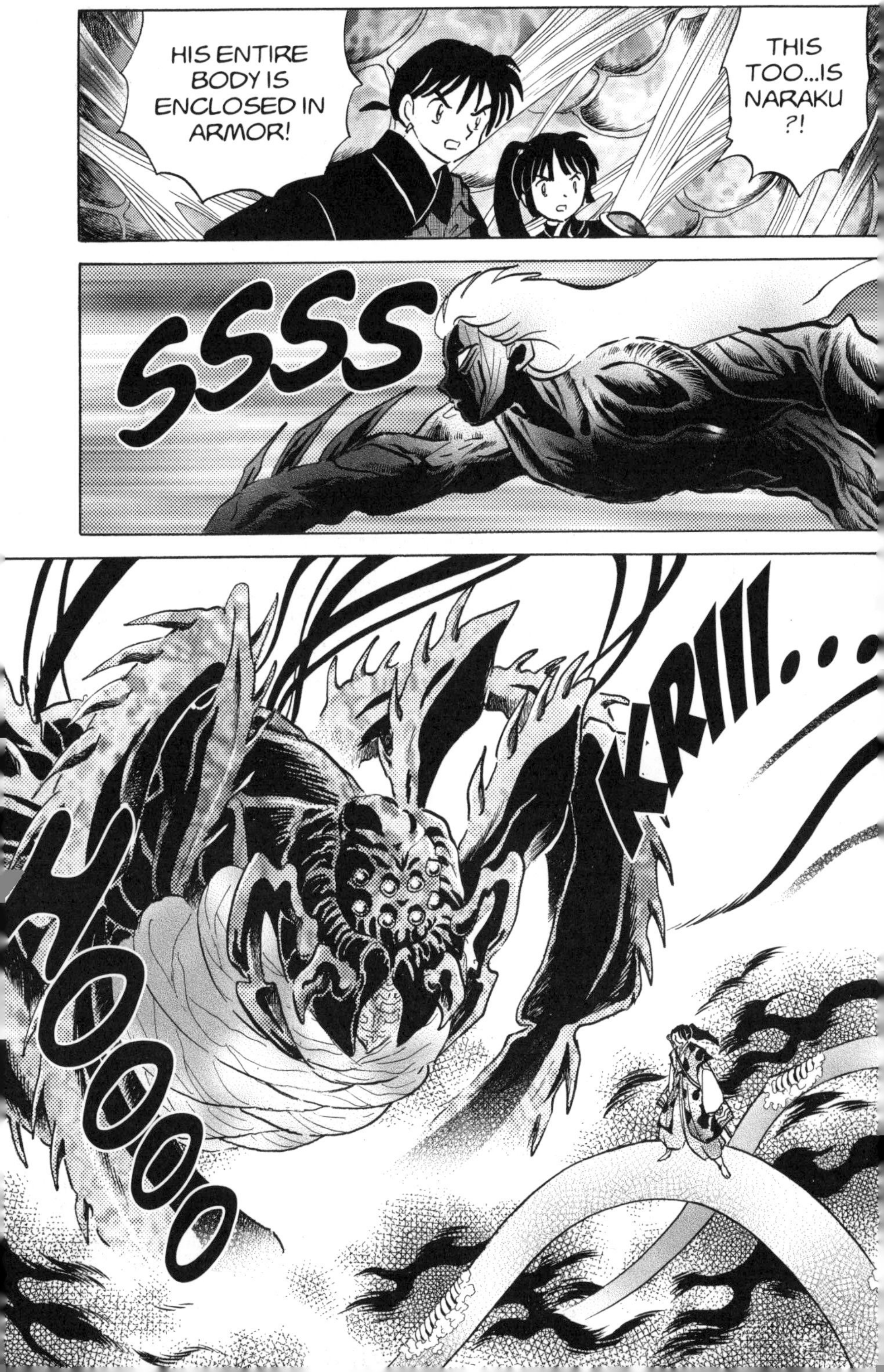
THIS TOO...IS NARAKU ?!
HIS ENTIRE BODY IS ENCLOSED IN ARMOR!
SSSS
KRIII...
HOOOOOO

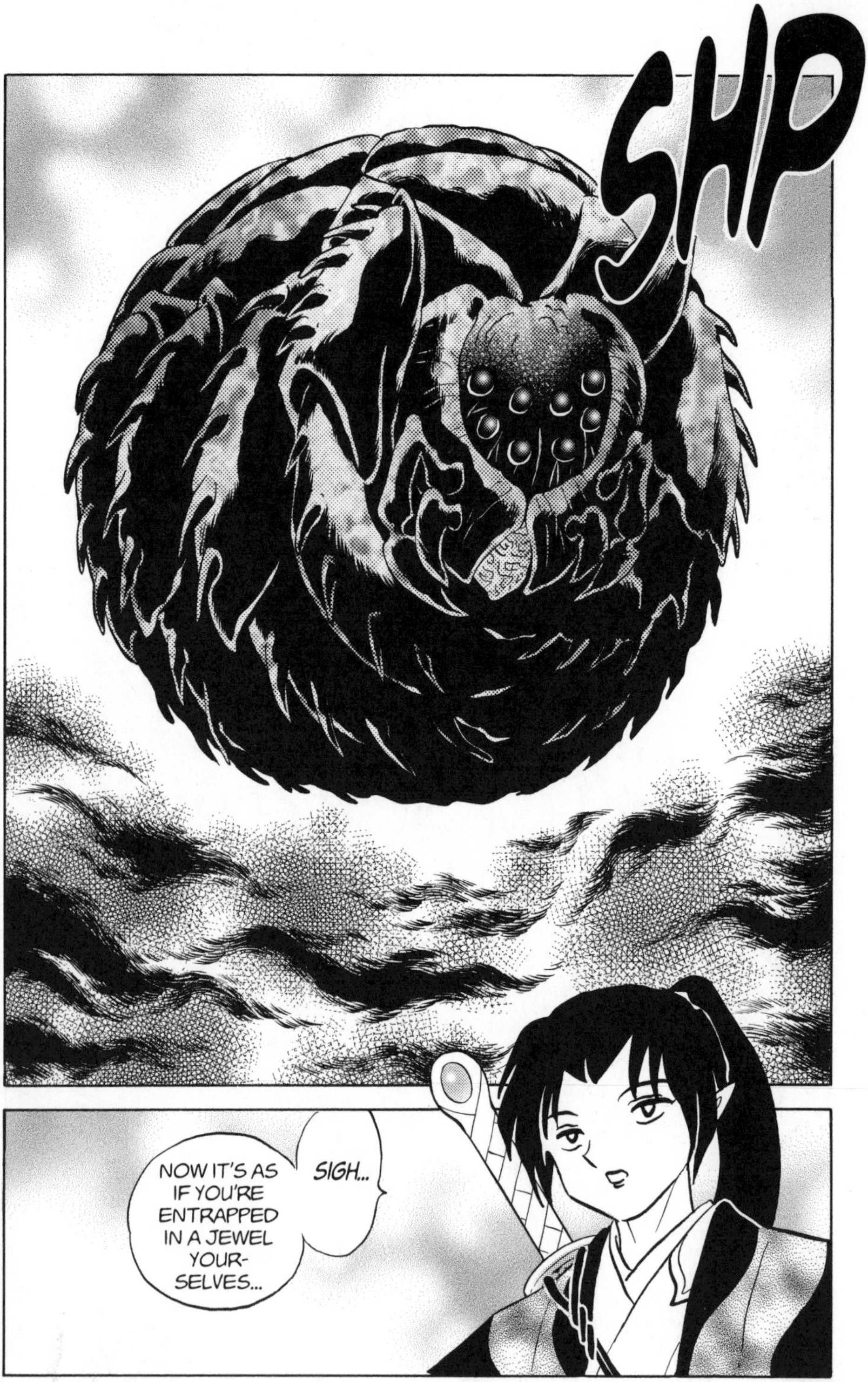
SHP
SIGH...
NOW IT'S AS IF YOU'RE ENTRAPPED IN A JEWEL YOUR-SELVES...

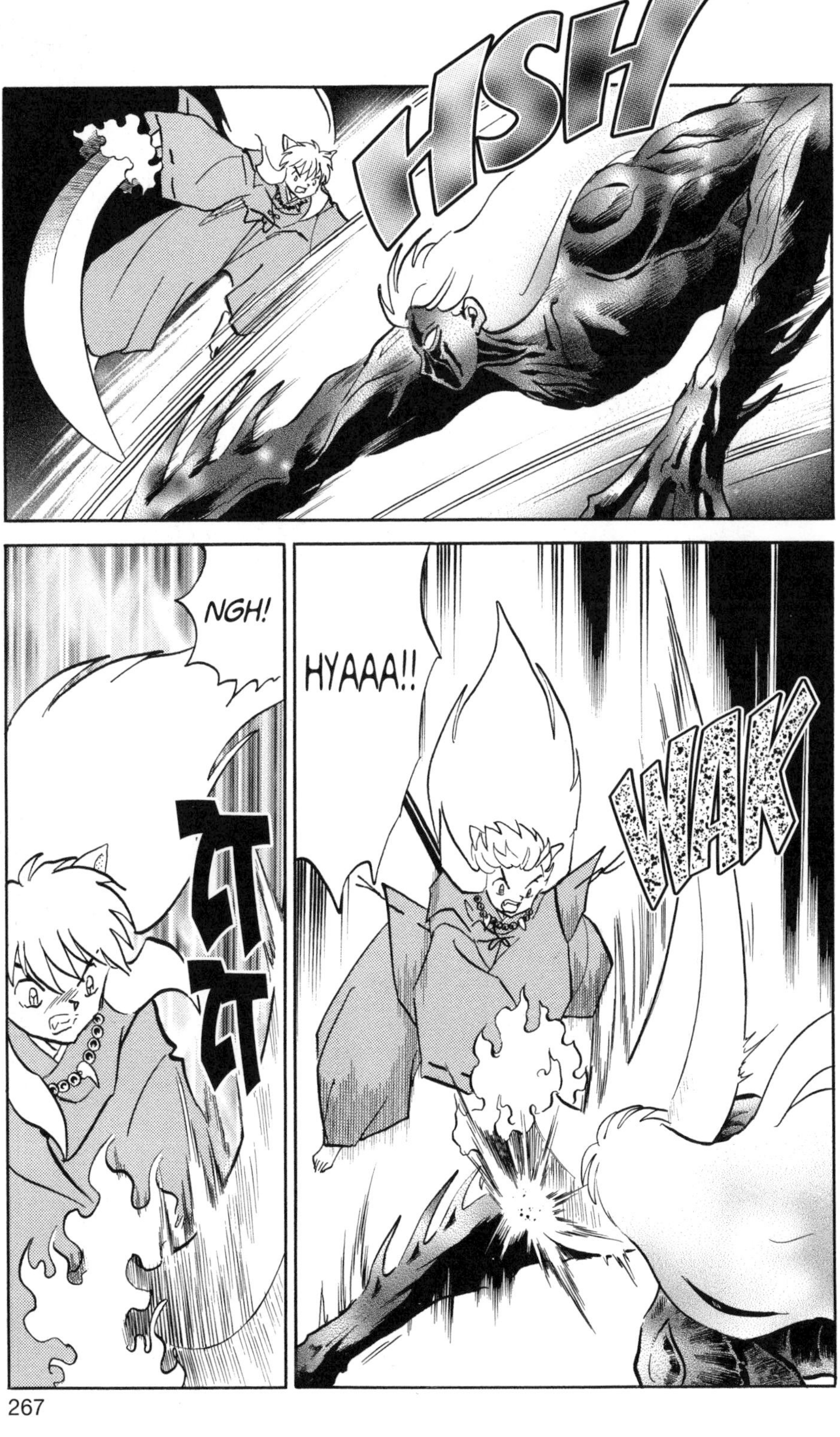
HISH
HYAAA!!
WAK
NGH!

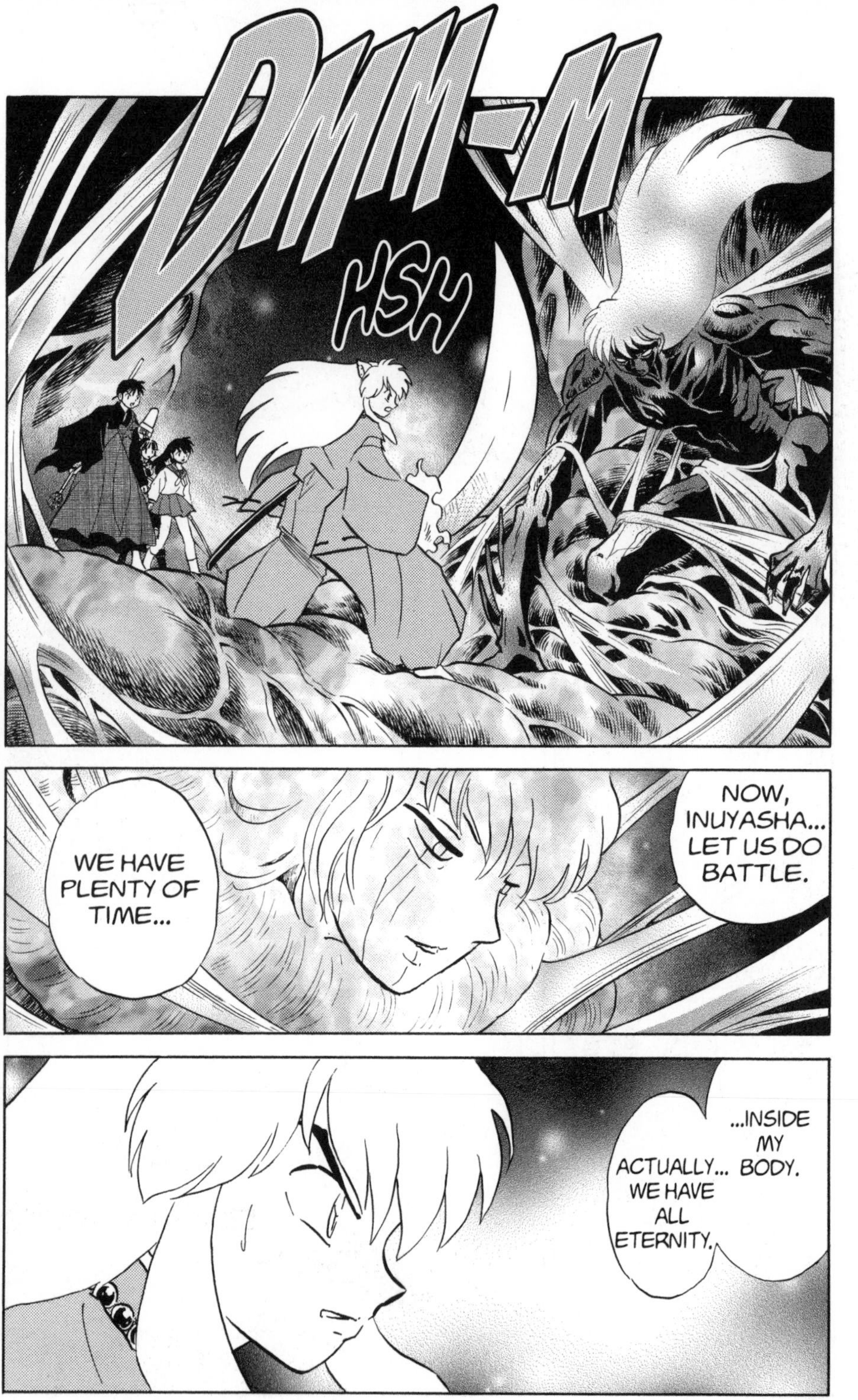
DMM-M
HSH
NOW, INUYASHA... LET US DO BATTLE.
WE HAVE PLENTY OF TIME...
ACTUALLY... WE HAVE ALL ETERNITY.
...INSIDE MY BODY.

SCROLL FIVE
A HINT OF THE JEWEL

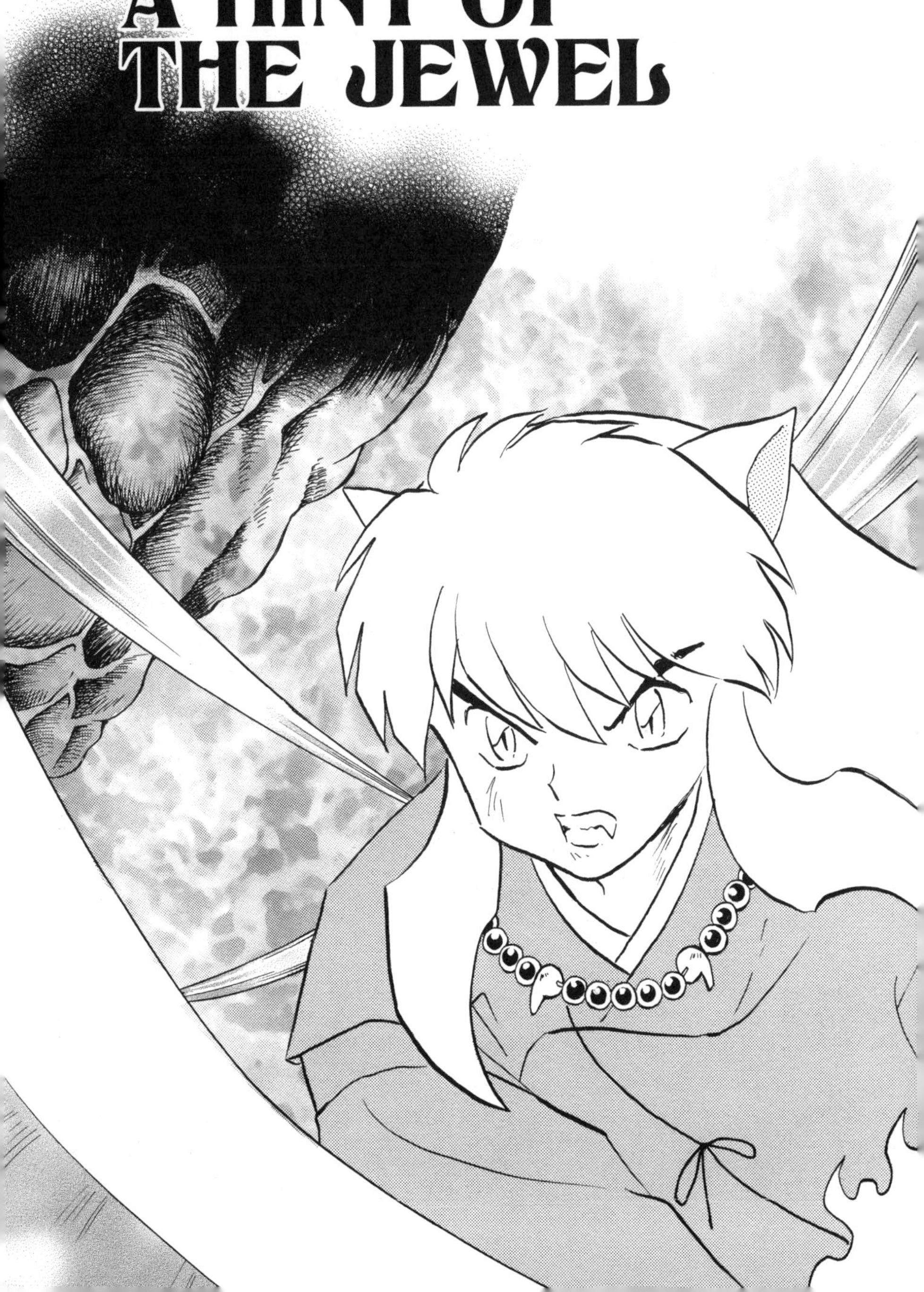

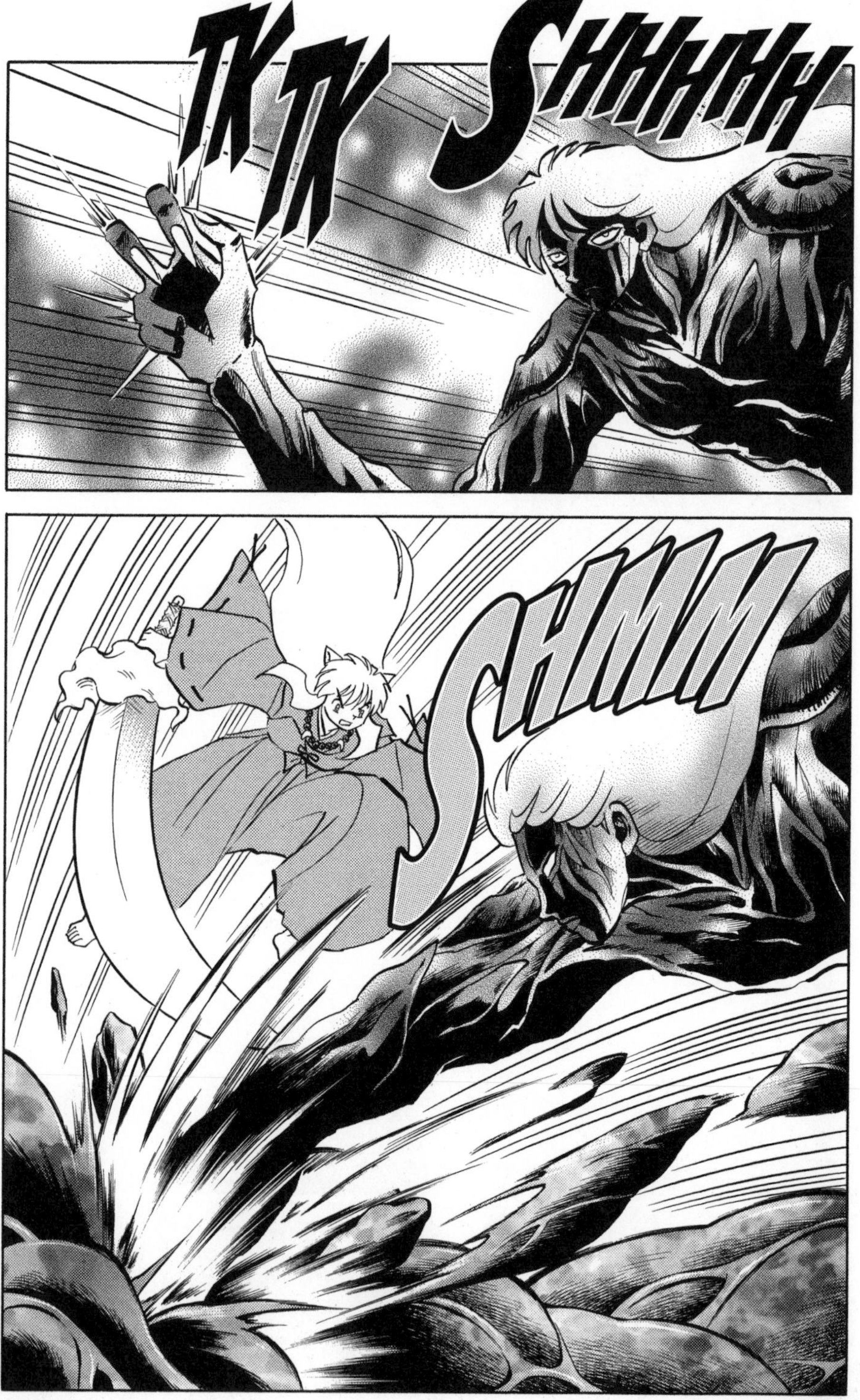
TK TK
SHHHH
SHMM

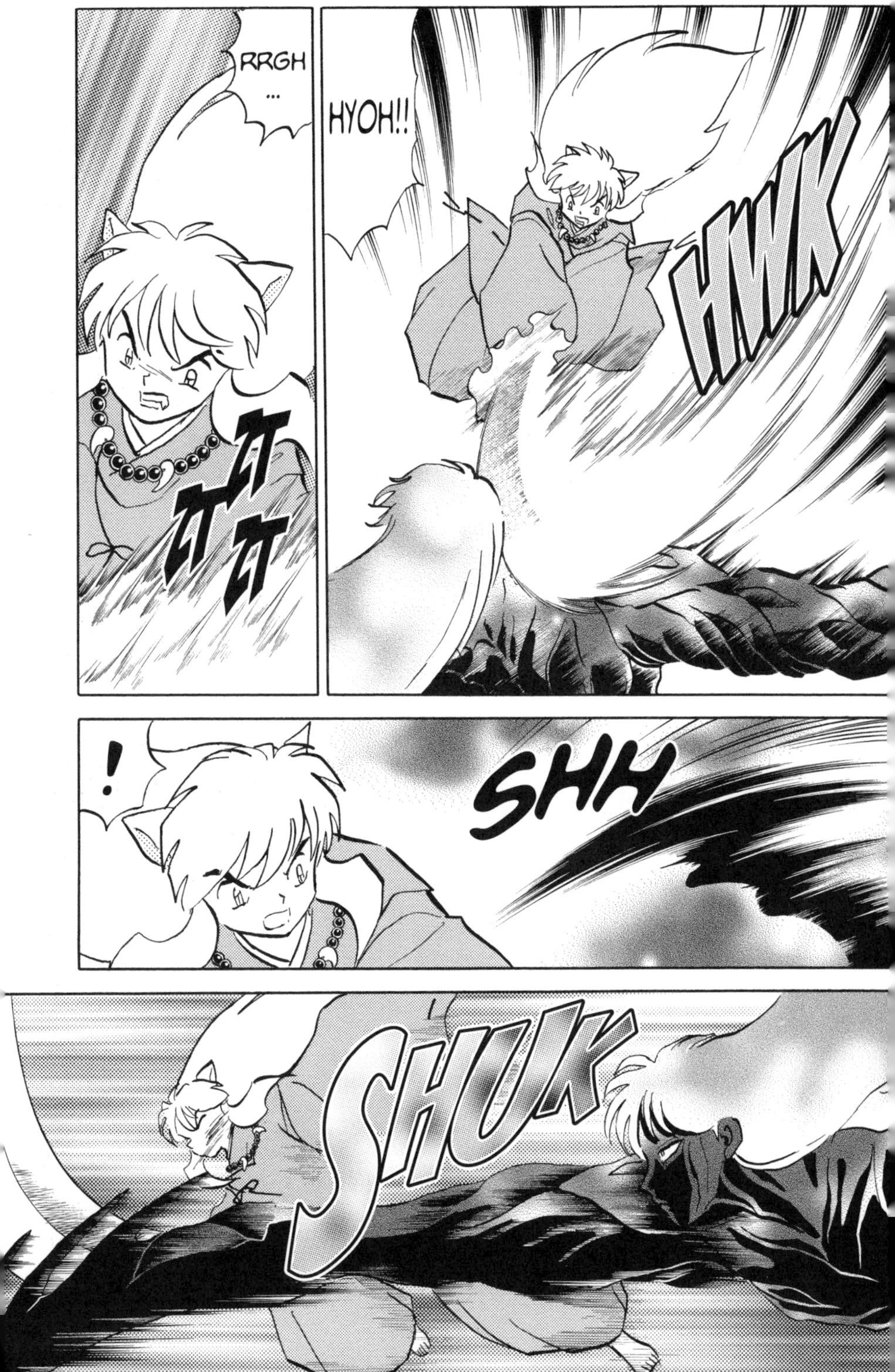
HYOH!!
HWWK
RRGH ...
SHH
!
SHUK

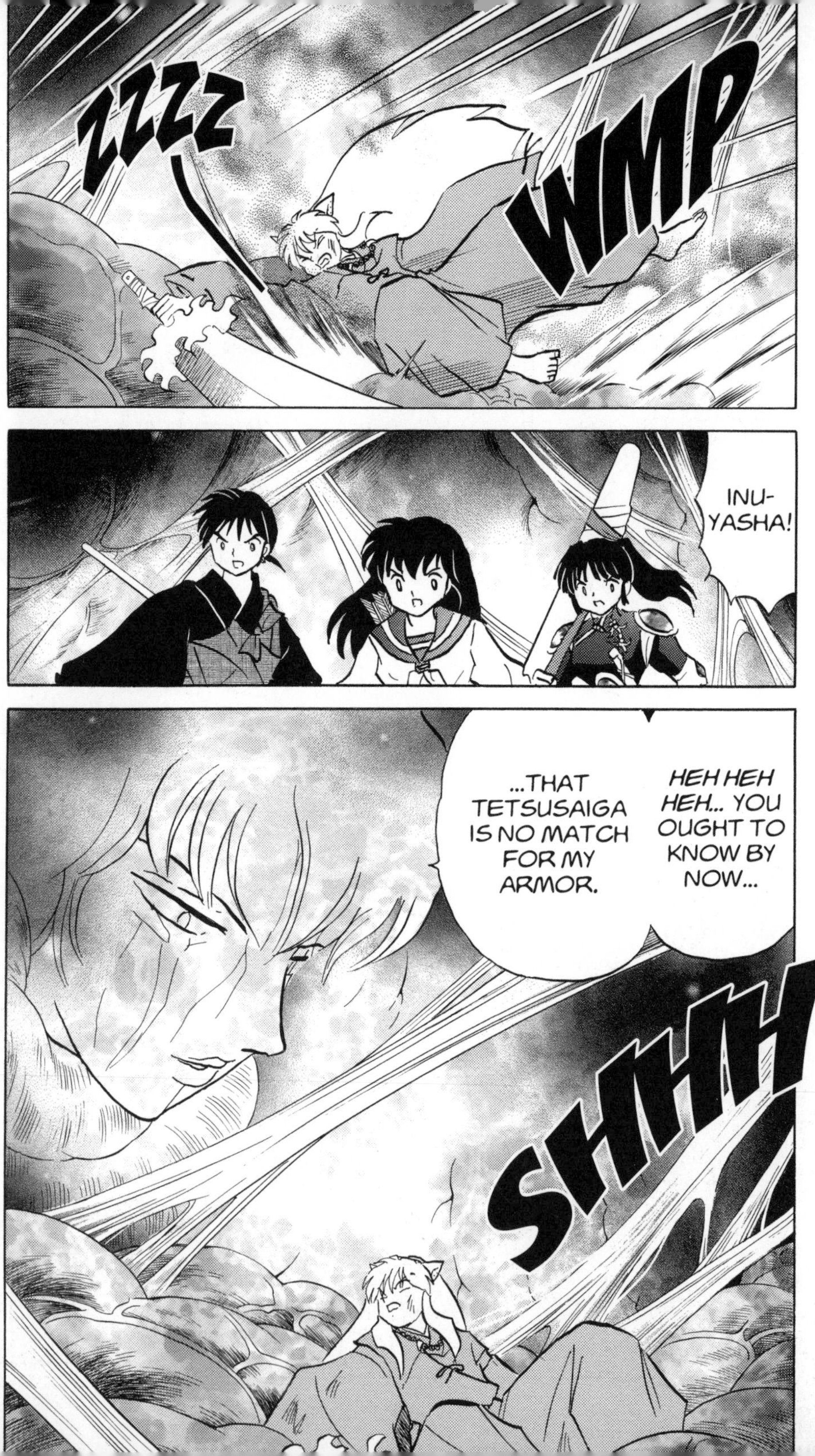
WMP
ZZZZ
INU-YASHA!
HEH HEH HEH... YOU OUGHT TO KNOW BY NOW...
...THAT TETSUSAIGA IS NO MATCH FOR MY ARMOR.
SHHH

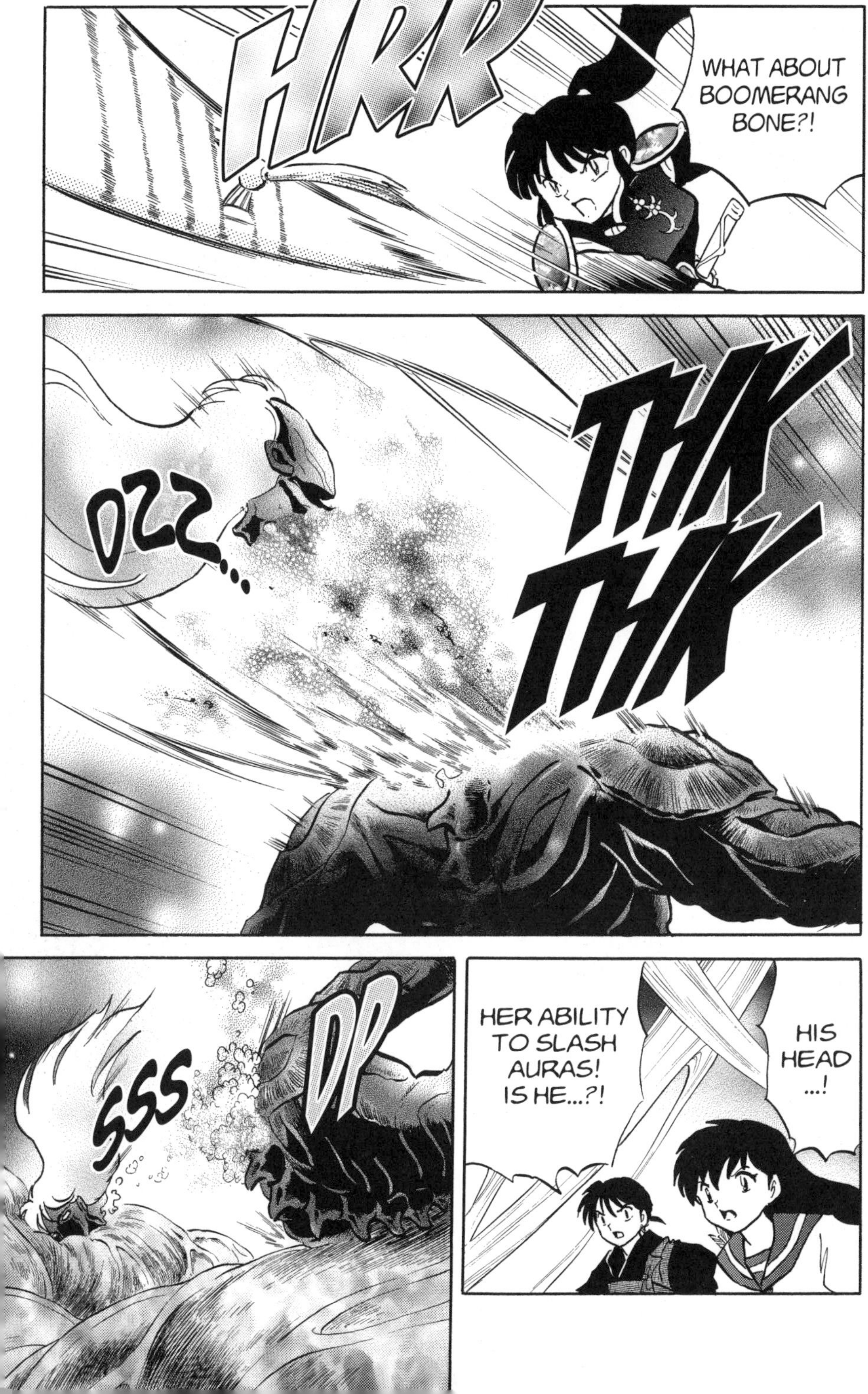
WHAT ABOUT BOOMERANG BONE?!
HRR
THK THK
DZZ...
HIS HEAD ...!
HER ABILITY TO SLASH AURAS! IS HE...?!
DP
SSS

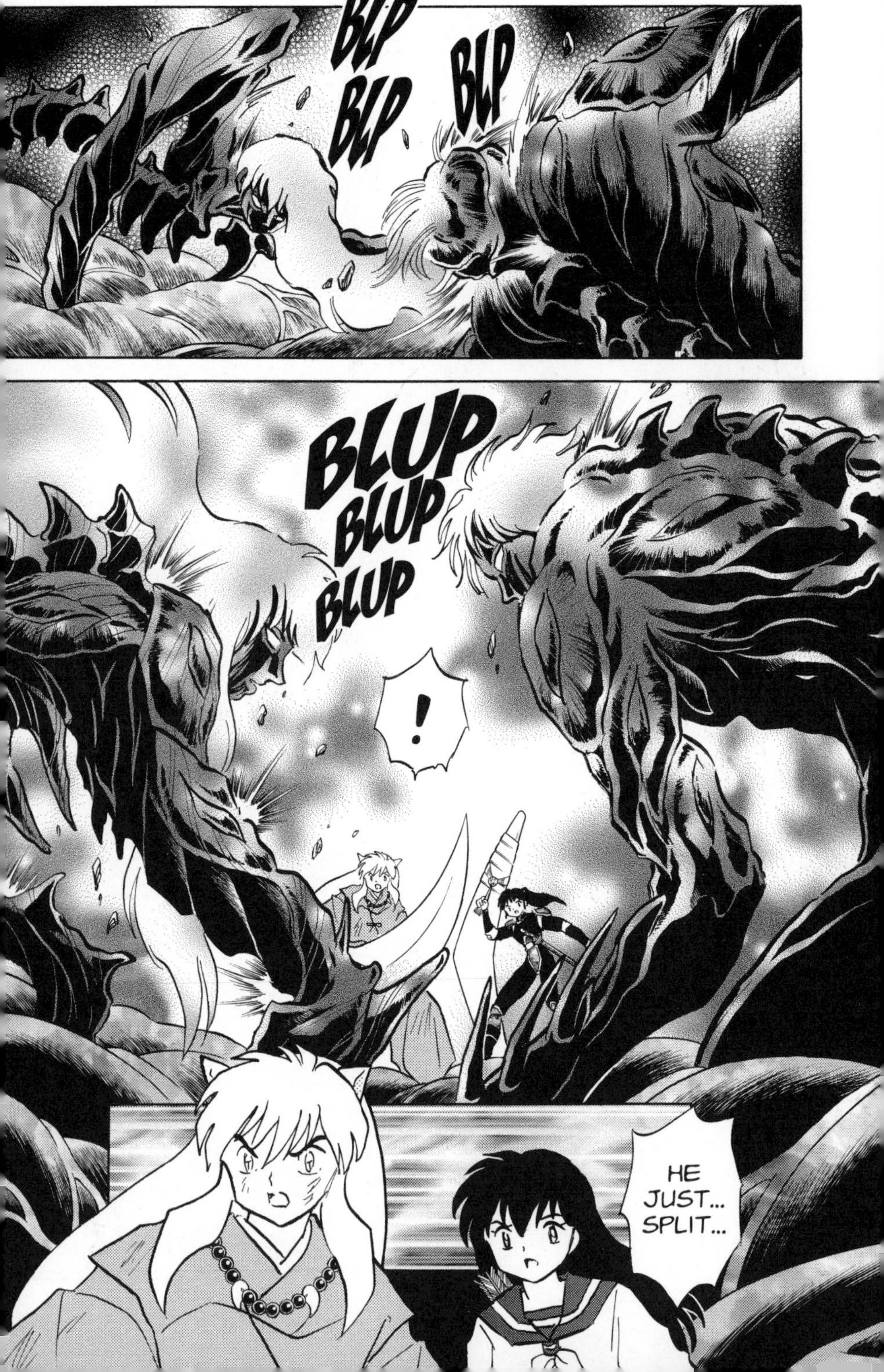
BLP
BLP
BLP
BLUP
BLUP
BLUP
!
HE JUST... SPLIT...

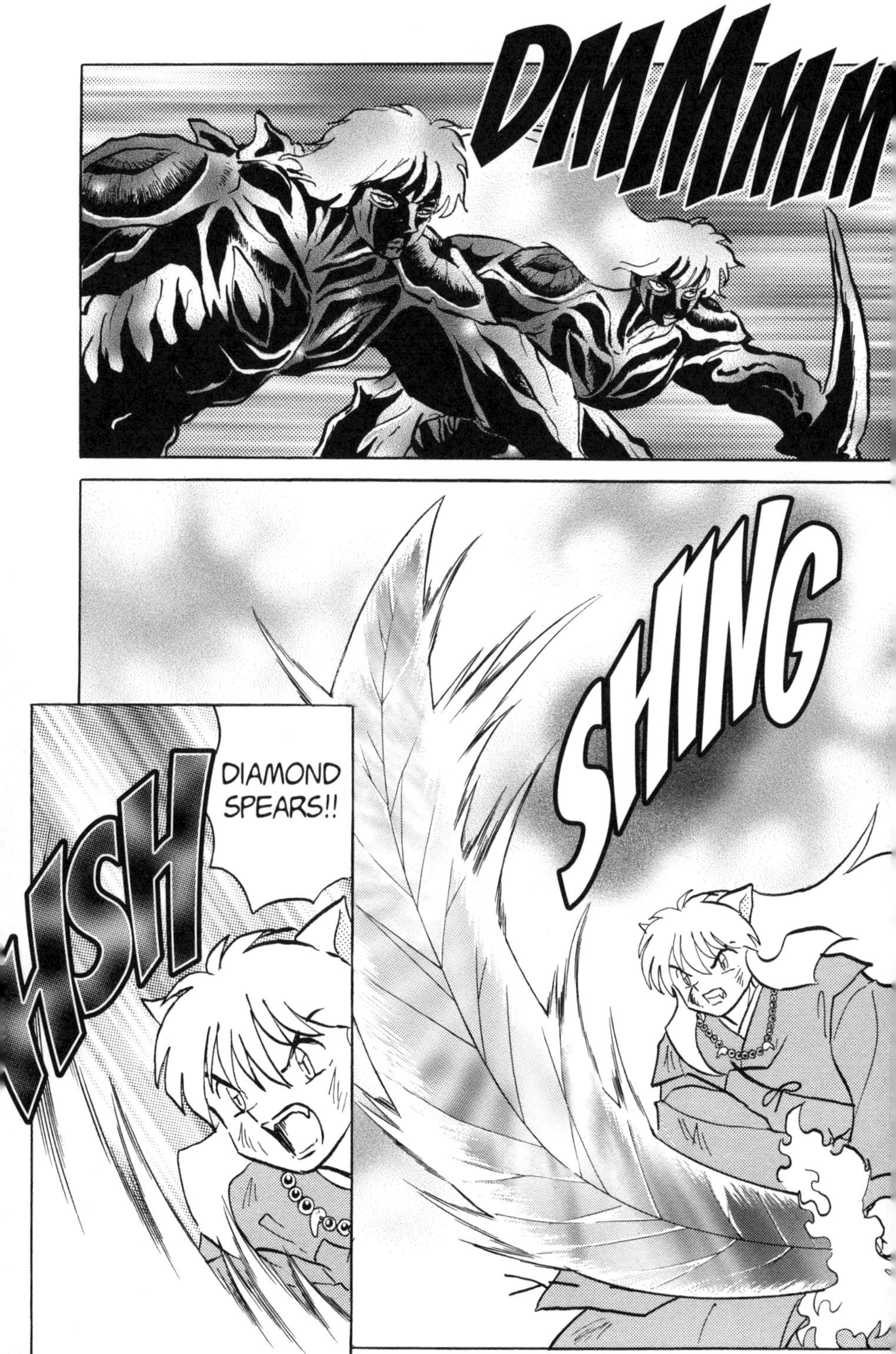
DMMMM
SHING
DIAMOND SPEARS!!
HSH

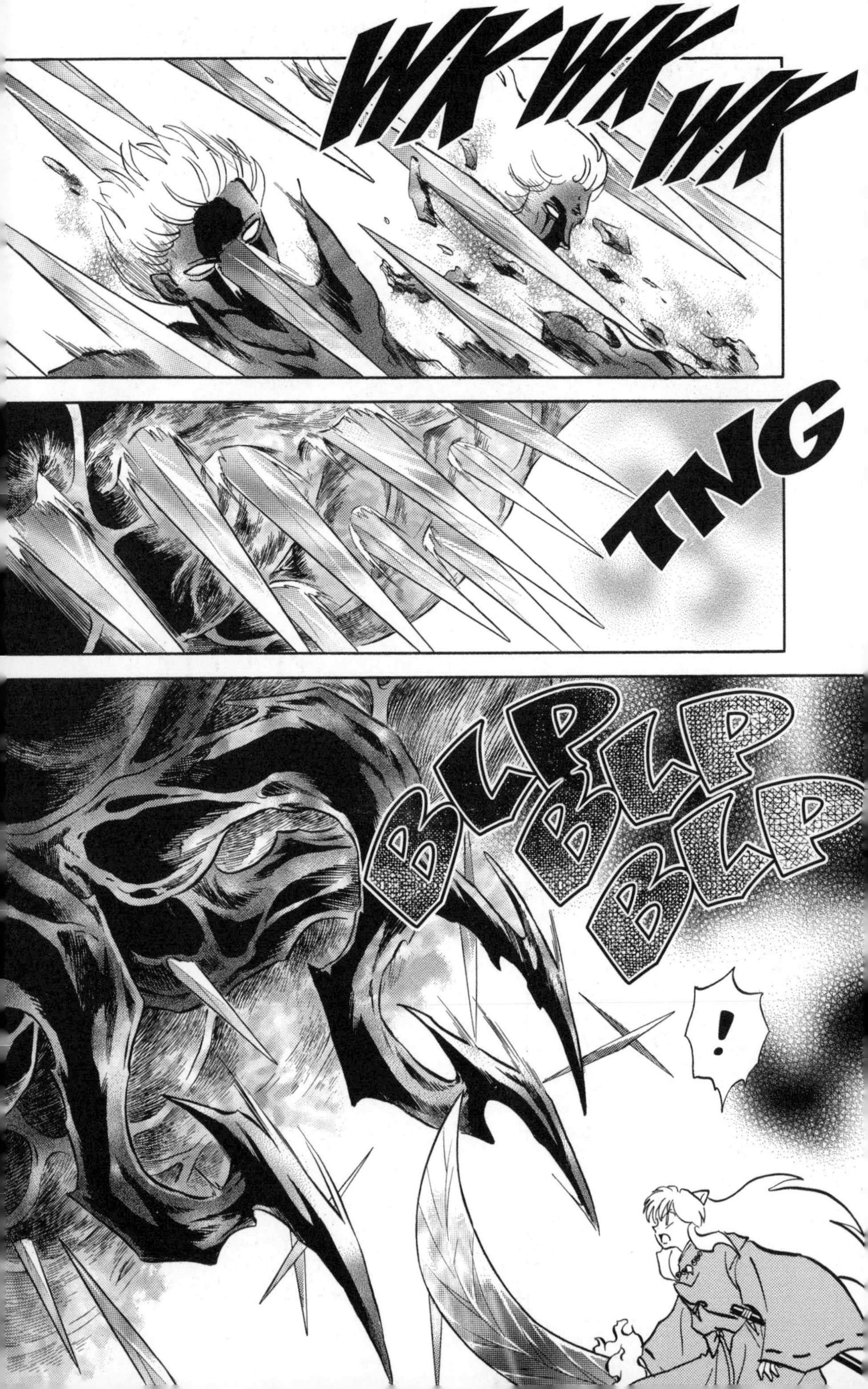
WK WK WK
TNG
BLP BLP BLP
!

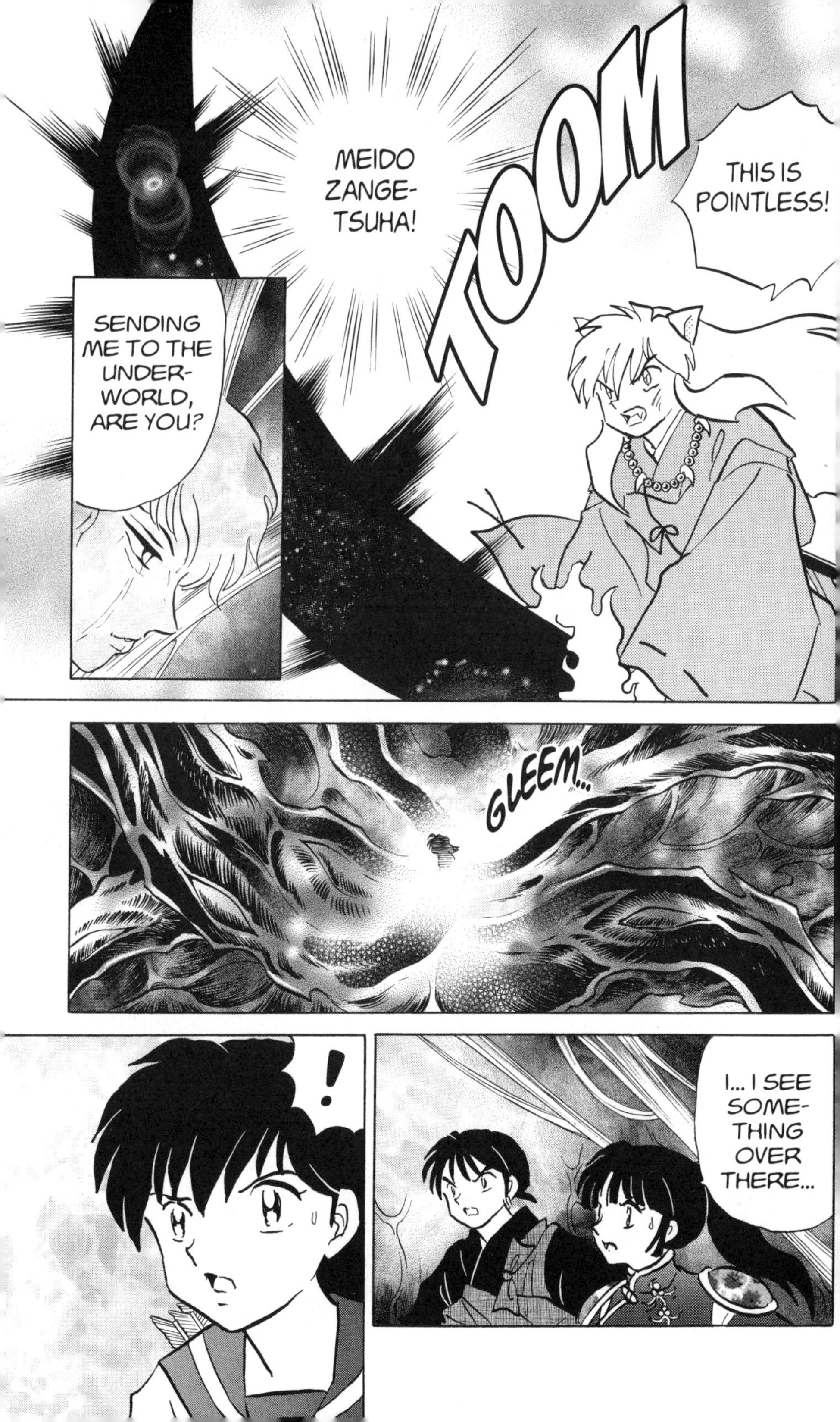
THIS IS POINTLESS!
TOOM
MEIDO ZANGE-TSUHA!
SENDING ME TO THE UNDER-WORLD, ARE YOU?
GLEEM...
I... I SEE SOME-THING OVER THERE...
!

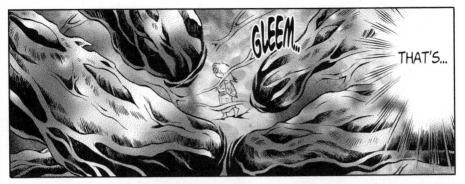

THAT'S...
GLEEM...
RIN!
SO...THE CHILD HAS AWAKENED.
IT'S JUST ANOTHER ONE OF YOUR ILLUSIONS!
PER-HAPS...

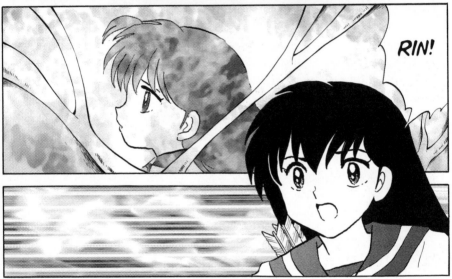

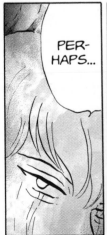

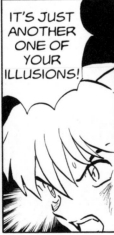

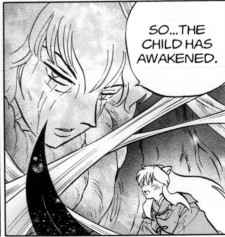

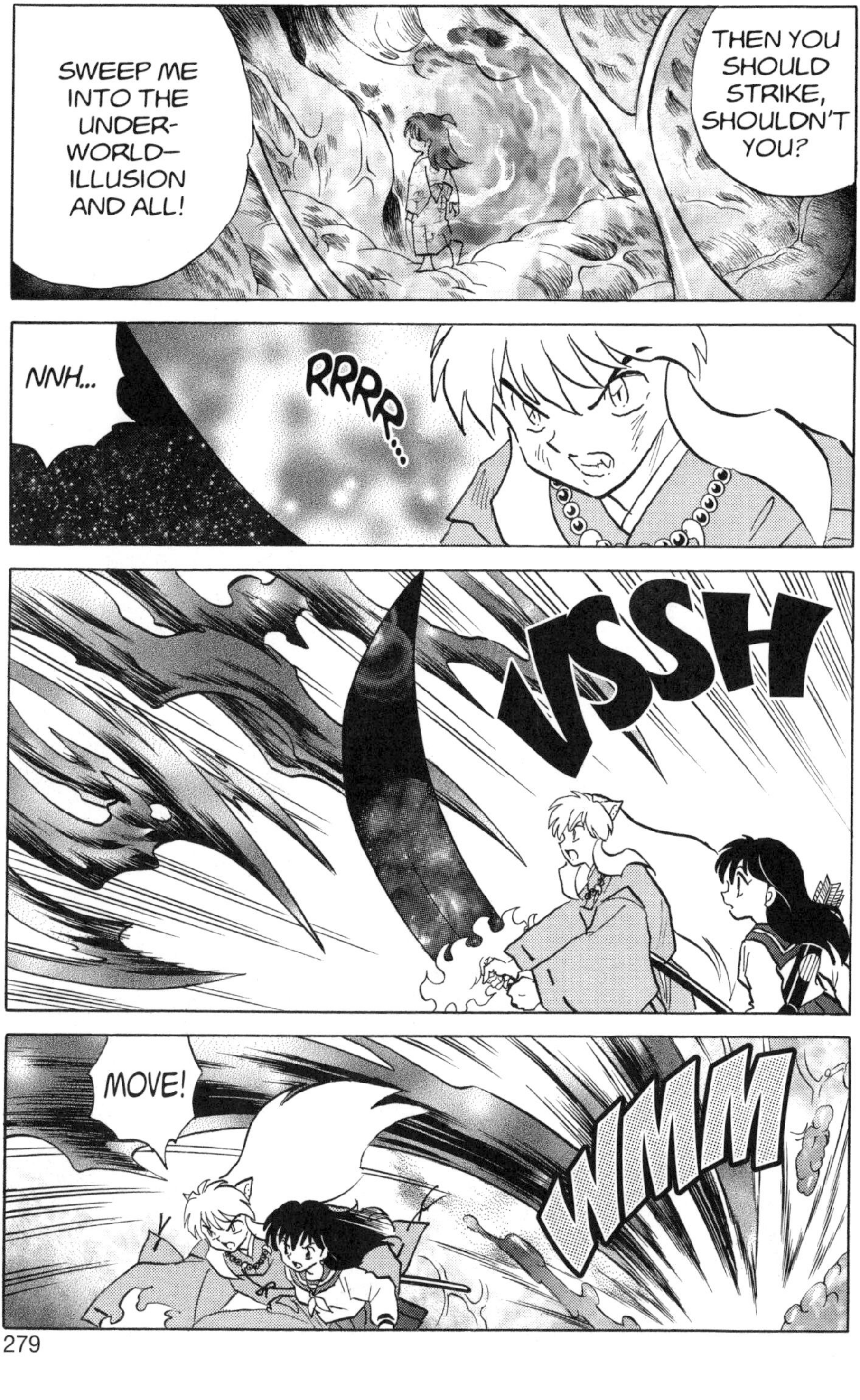
THEN YOU SHOULD STRIKE, SHOULDN'T YOU?
SWEEP ME INTO THE UNDER-WORLD—ILLUSION AND ALL!
RRRR...
NNH...
VSSH
WMMM
MOVE!

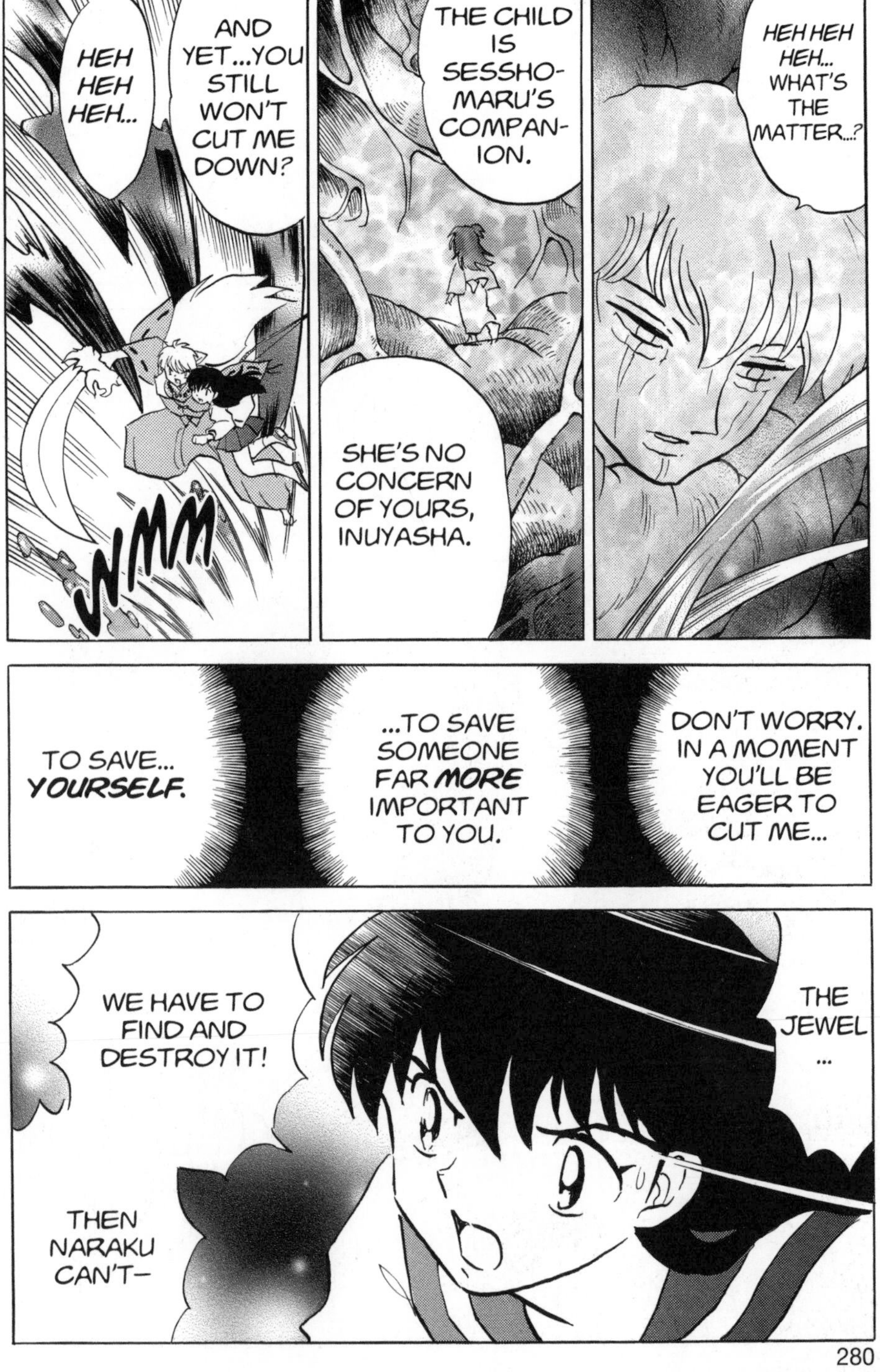
HEH HEH HEH... WHAT'S THE MATTER...?
THE CHILD IS SESSHOMARU'S COMPANION.
SHE'S NO CONCERN OF YOURS, INUYASHA.
AND YET...YOU STILL WON'T CUT ME DOWN?
HEH HEH HEH...
WMM
DON'T WORRY. IN A MOMENT YOU'LL BE EAGER TO CUT ME...
...TO SAVE SOMEONE FAR **MORE** IMPORTANT TO YOU.
TO SAVE... ***YOURSELF***.
THE JEWEL ...
WE HAVE TO FIND AND DESTROY IT!
THEN NARAKU CAN'T—

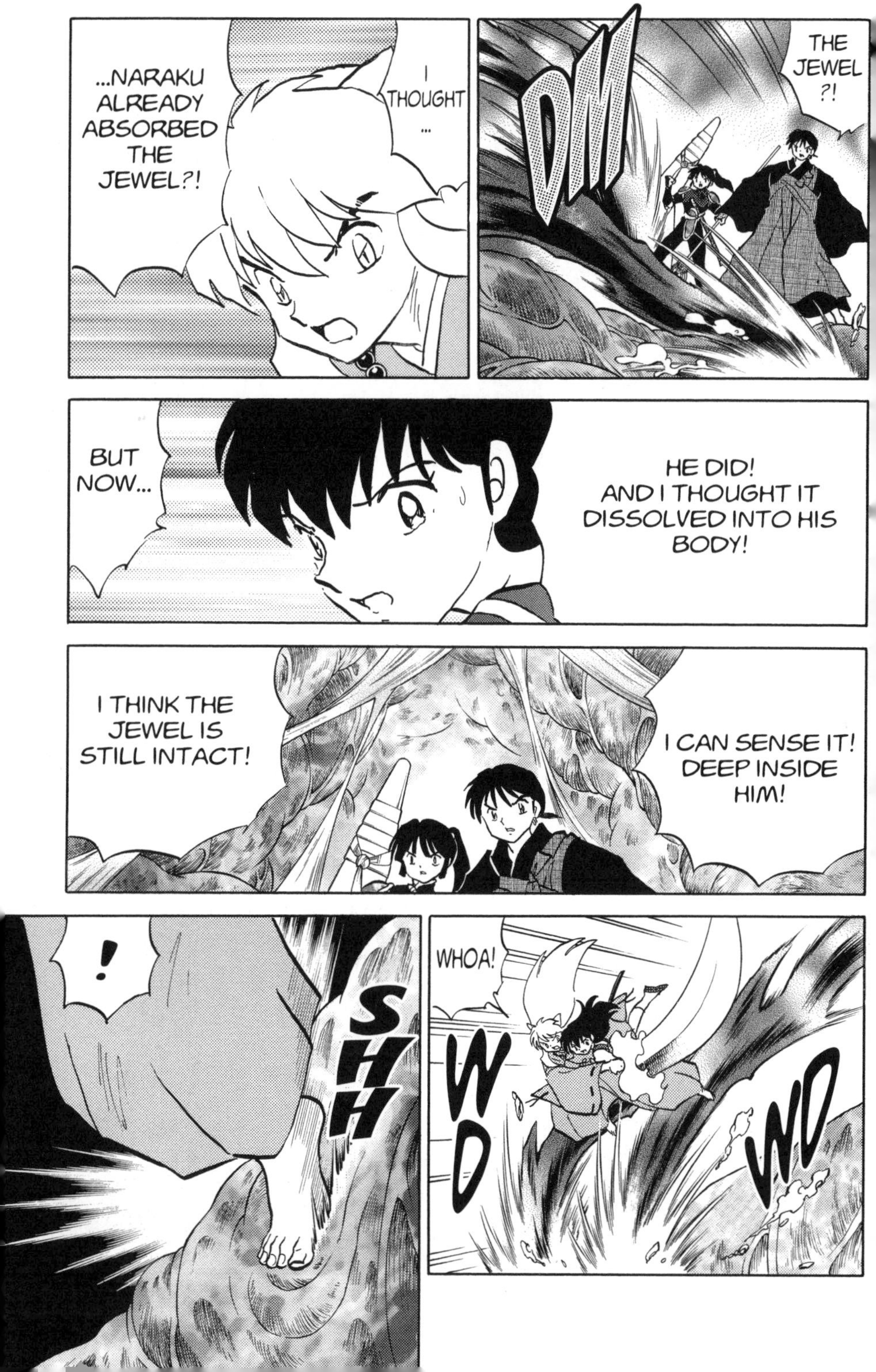
DM
THE JEWEL ?!
I THOUGHT ...
...NARAKU ALREADY ABSORBED THE JEWEL?!
HE DID! AND I THOUGHT IT DISSOLVED INTO HIS BODY!
BUT NOW...
I CAN SENSE IT! DEEP INSIDE HIM!
I THINK THE JEWEL IS STILL INTACT!
WHOA!
WD
WD
SHH
!

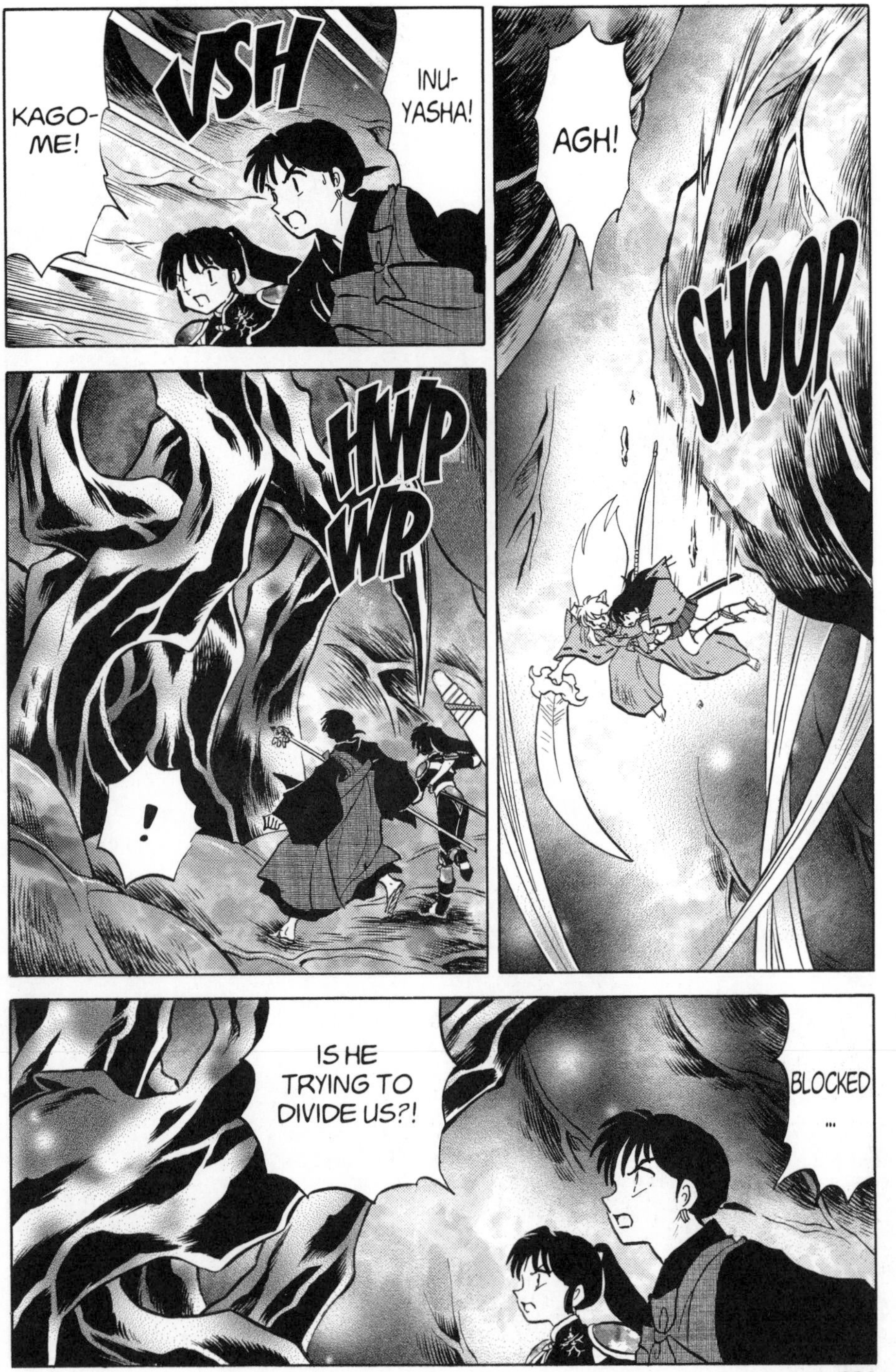
AGH!
SHOOP
INU-YASHA!
VSH
KAGO-ME!
HWP WP
!
BLOCKED...
IS HE TRYING TO DIVIDE US?!

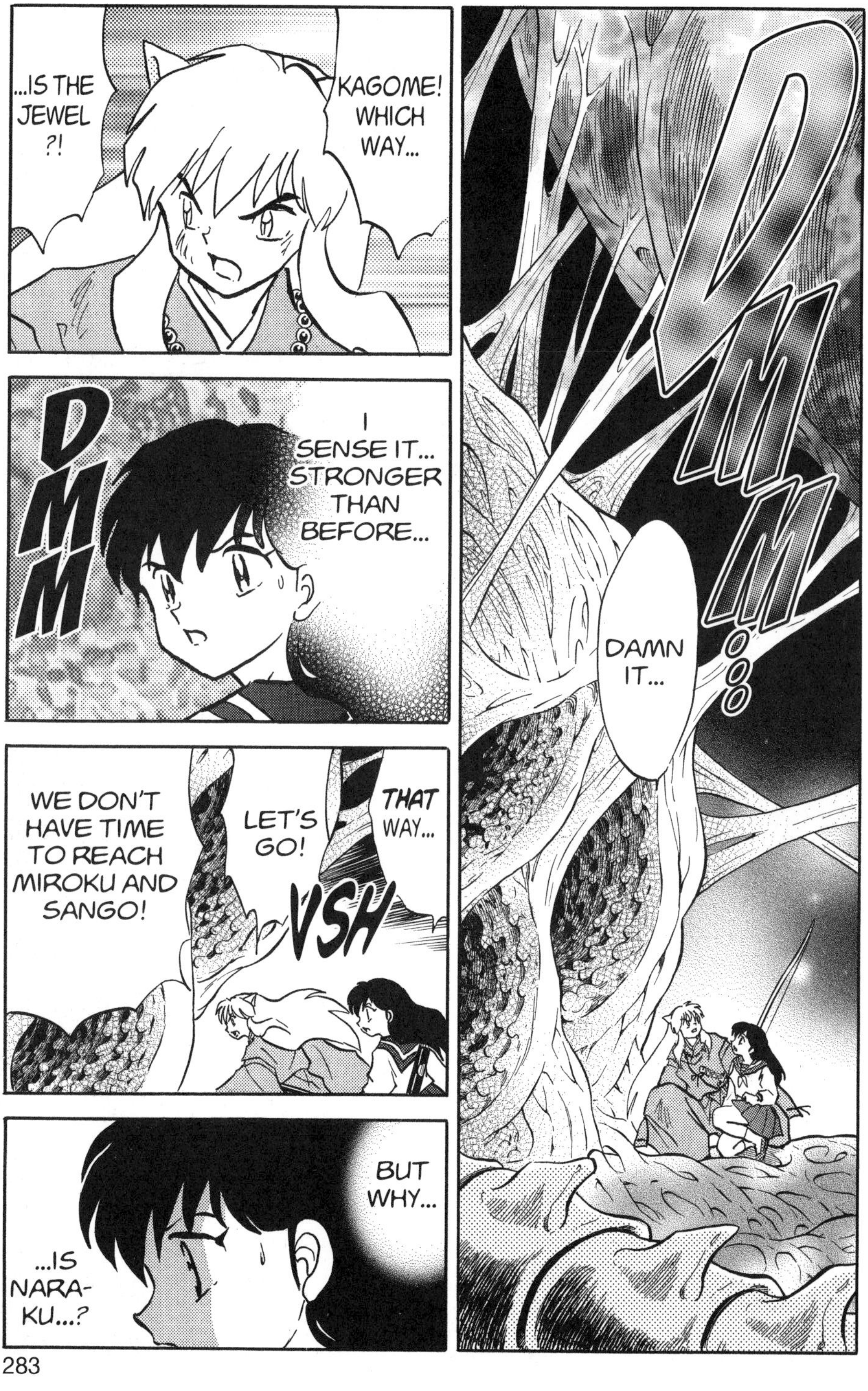
DMMMM...
DAMN IT...
KAGOME! WHICH WAY...
...IS THE JEWEL ?!
I SENSE IT... STRONGER THAN BEFORE...
DMMM
THAT WAY...
LET'S GO!
VSH
WE DON'T HAVE TIME TO REACH MIROKU AND SANGO!
BUT WHY...
...IS NARA-KU...?

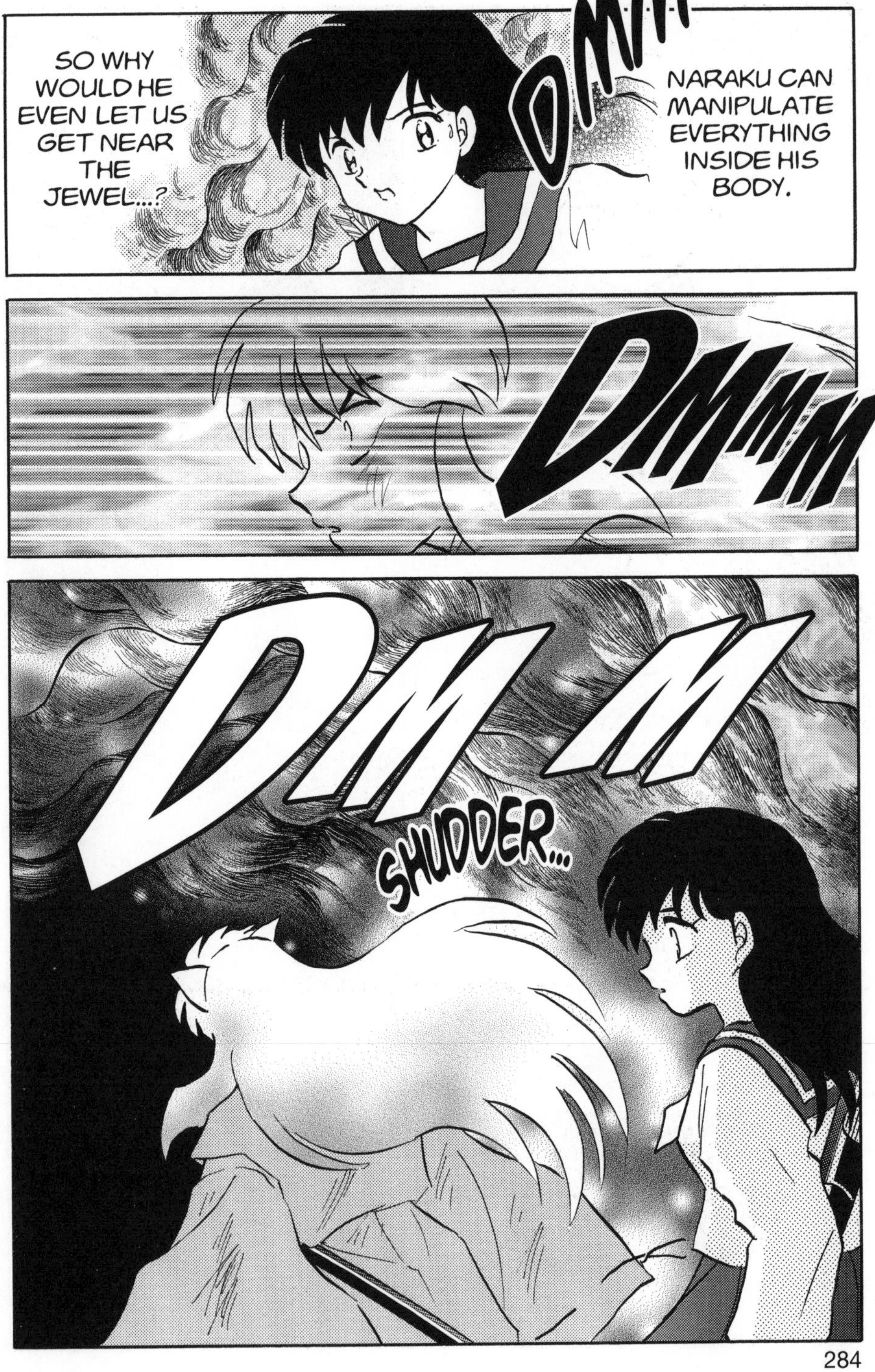
DMMM
NARAKU CAN MANIPULATE EVERYTHING INSIDE HIS BODY.
SO WHY WOULD HE EVEN LET US GET NEAR THE JEWEL...?
DMMMM
DMM
SHUDDER...

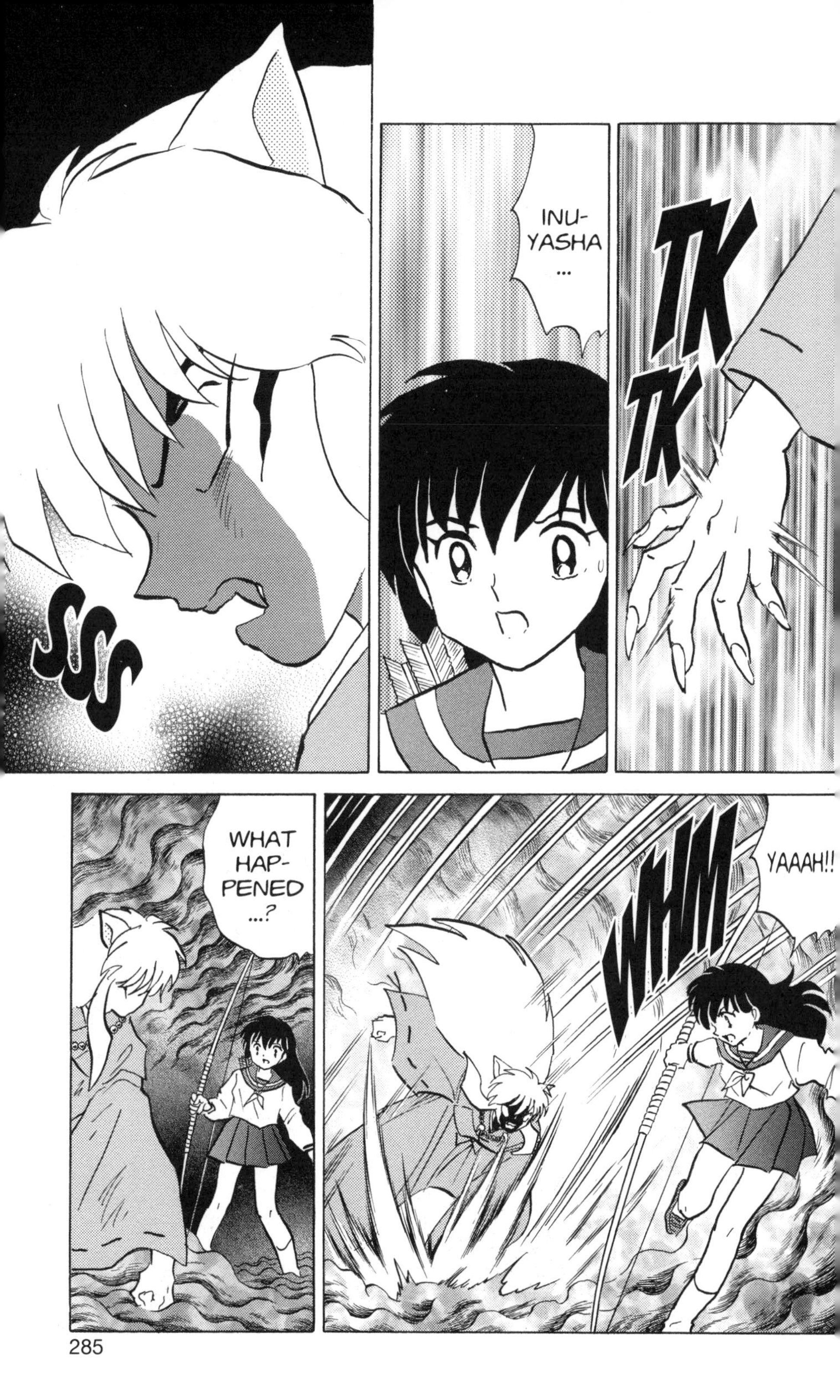
TK TK
INU-YASHA ...
SSS
YAAAH!!
WHM
WHAT HAP-PENED ...?

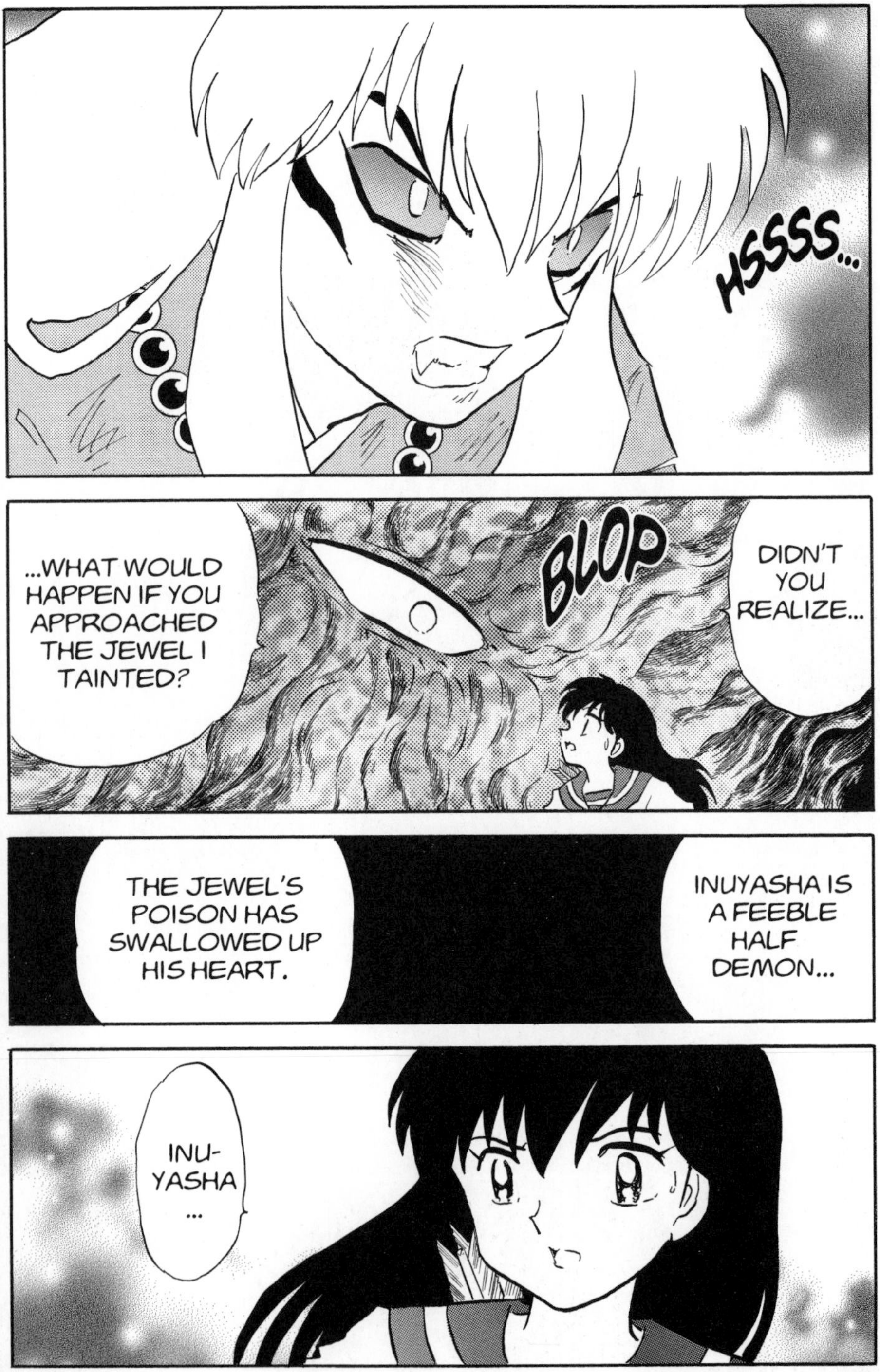
HSSSS...
DIDN'T YOU REALIZE...
BLOP
...WHAT WOULD HAPPEN IF YOU APPROACHED THE JEWEL I TAINTED?
INUYASHA IS A FEEBLE HALF DEMON...
THE JEWEL'S POISON HAS SWALLOWED UP HIS HEART.
INU-YASHA ...

SCROLL SIX
THE MIASMA ARROW

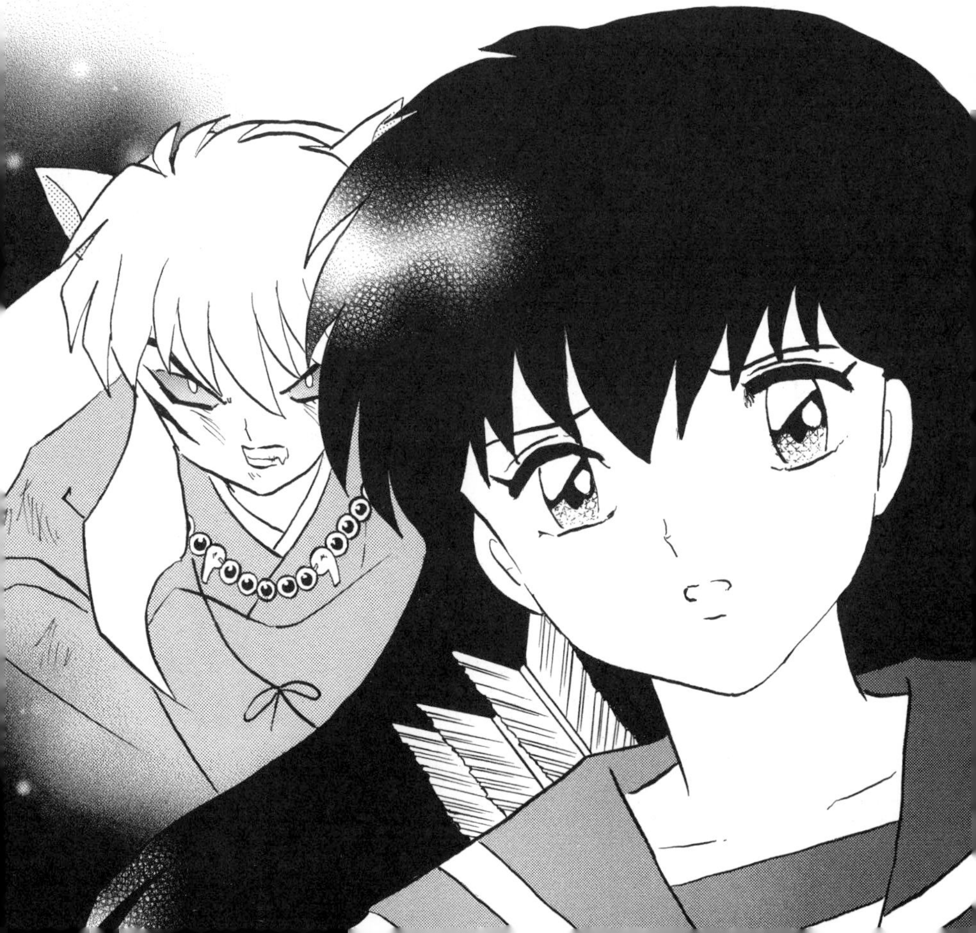

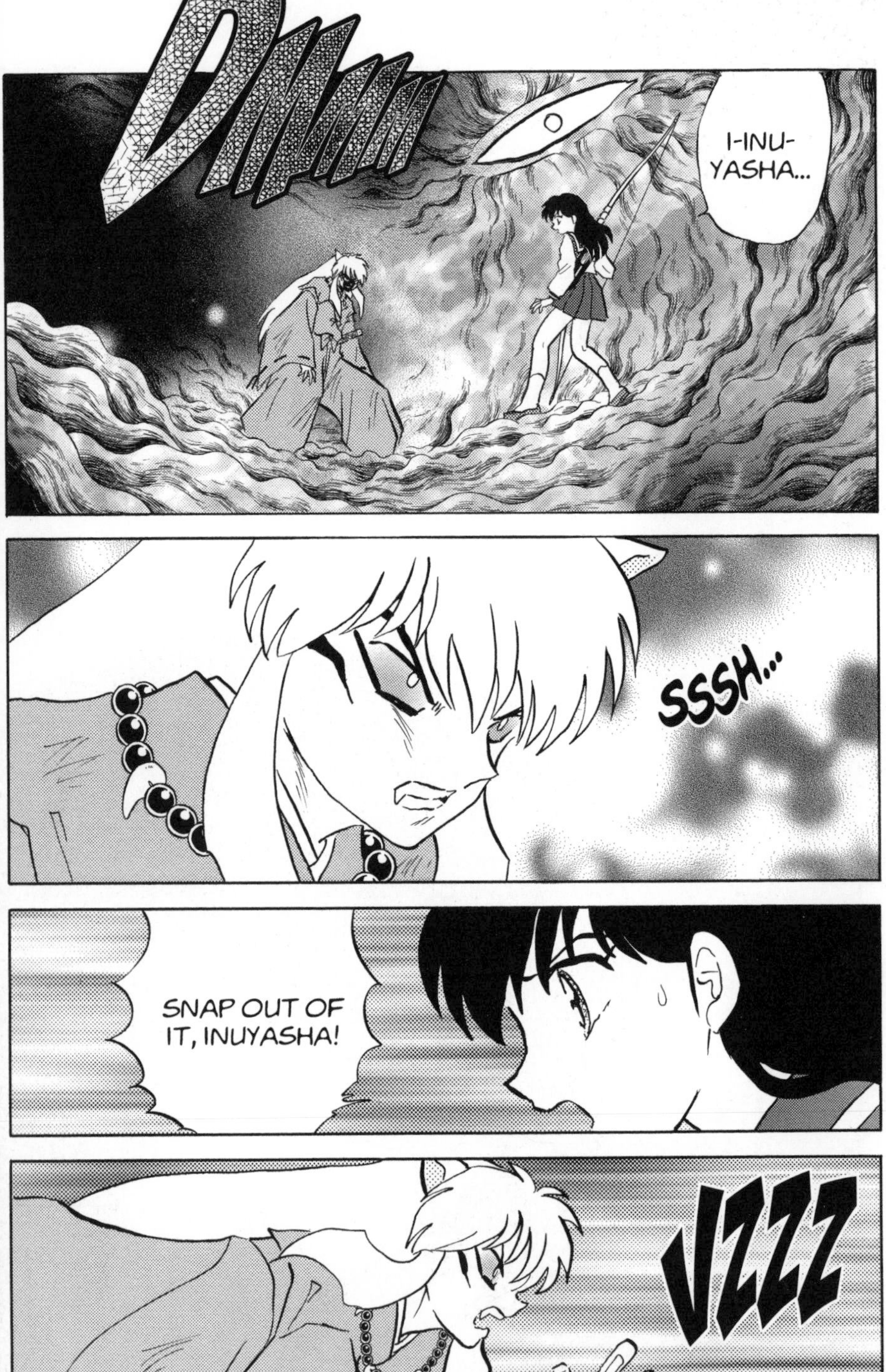

DMMM
I-INU-YASHA...
SSSH...
SNAP OUT OF IT, INUYASHA!
VZZZ

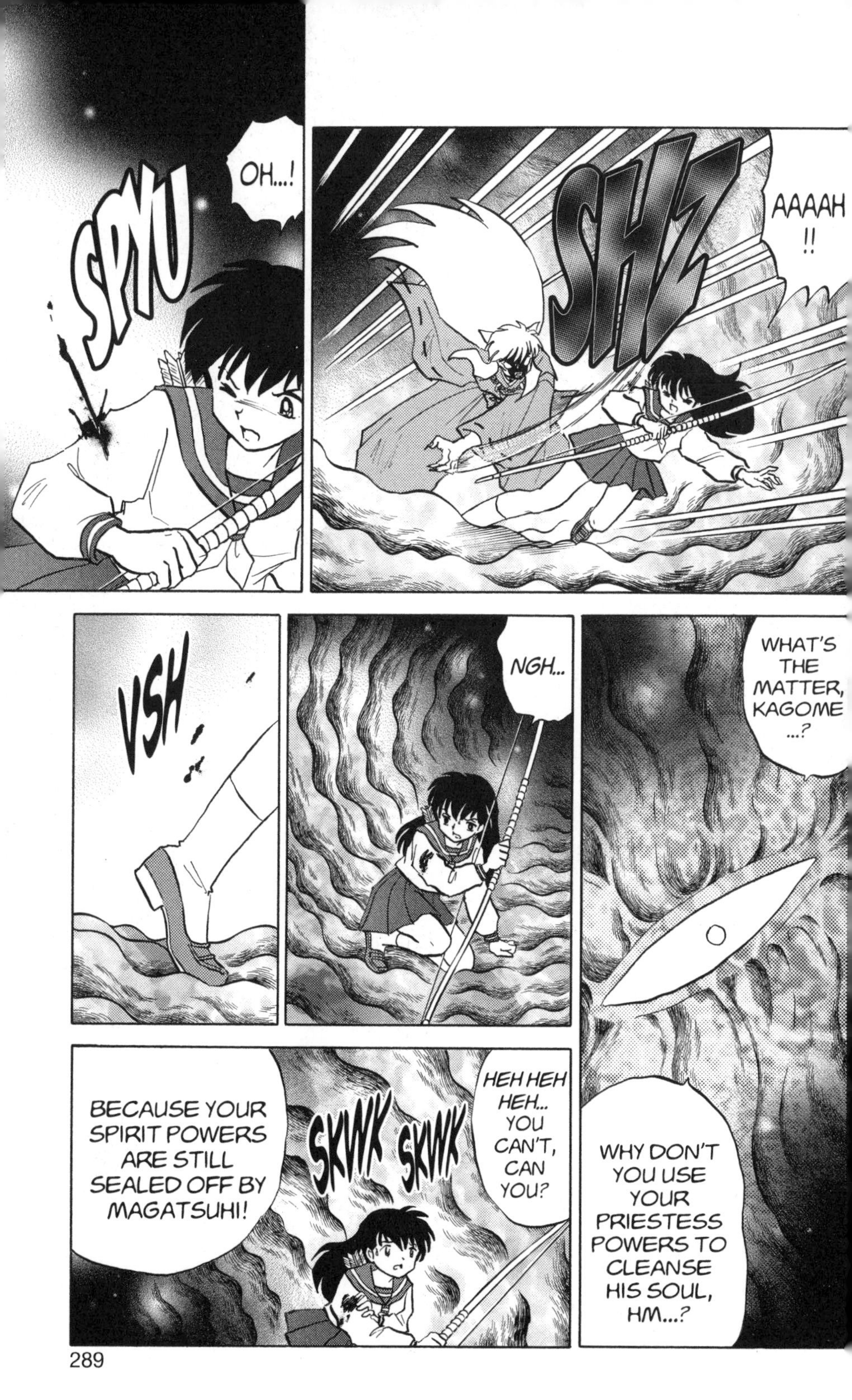
SHZ
AAAAH !!
OH...!
SPYU
WHAT'S THE MATTER, KAGOME ...?
WHY DON'T YOU USE YOUR PRIESTESS POWERS TO CLEANSE HIS SOUL, HM...?
NGH...
VSH
HEH HEH HEH... YOU CAN'T, CAN YOU?
SKWK SKWK
BECAUSE YOUR SPIRIT POWERS ARE STILL SEALED OFF BY MAGATSUHI!

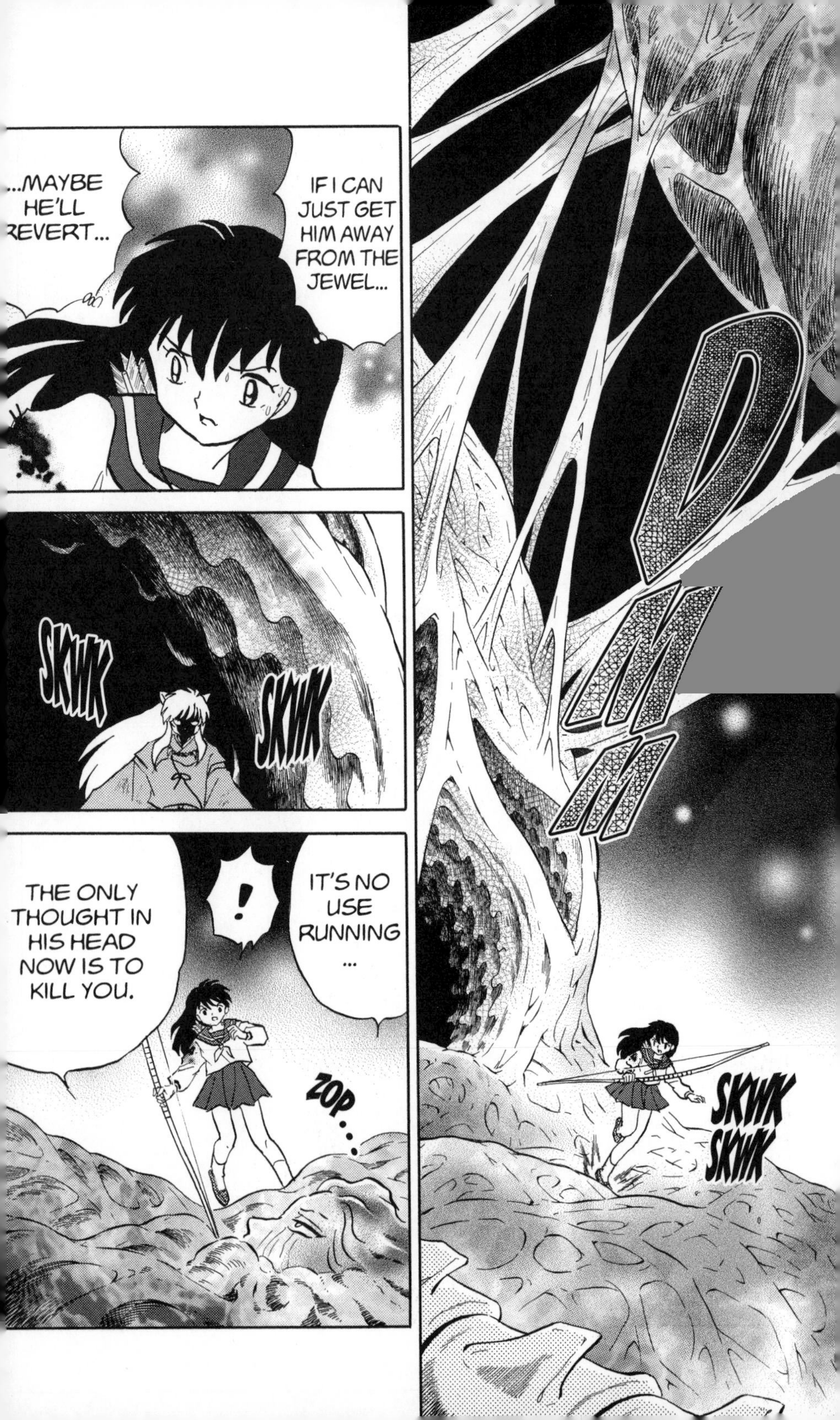
DOMMM
SKWK SKWK
IF I CAN JUST GET HIM AWAY FROM THE JEWEL...
...MAYBE HE'LL REVERT...
SKWK
SKWK
IT'S NO USE RUNNING ...
!
THE ONLY THOUGHT IN HIS HEAD NOW IS TO KILL YOU.
ZOP...

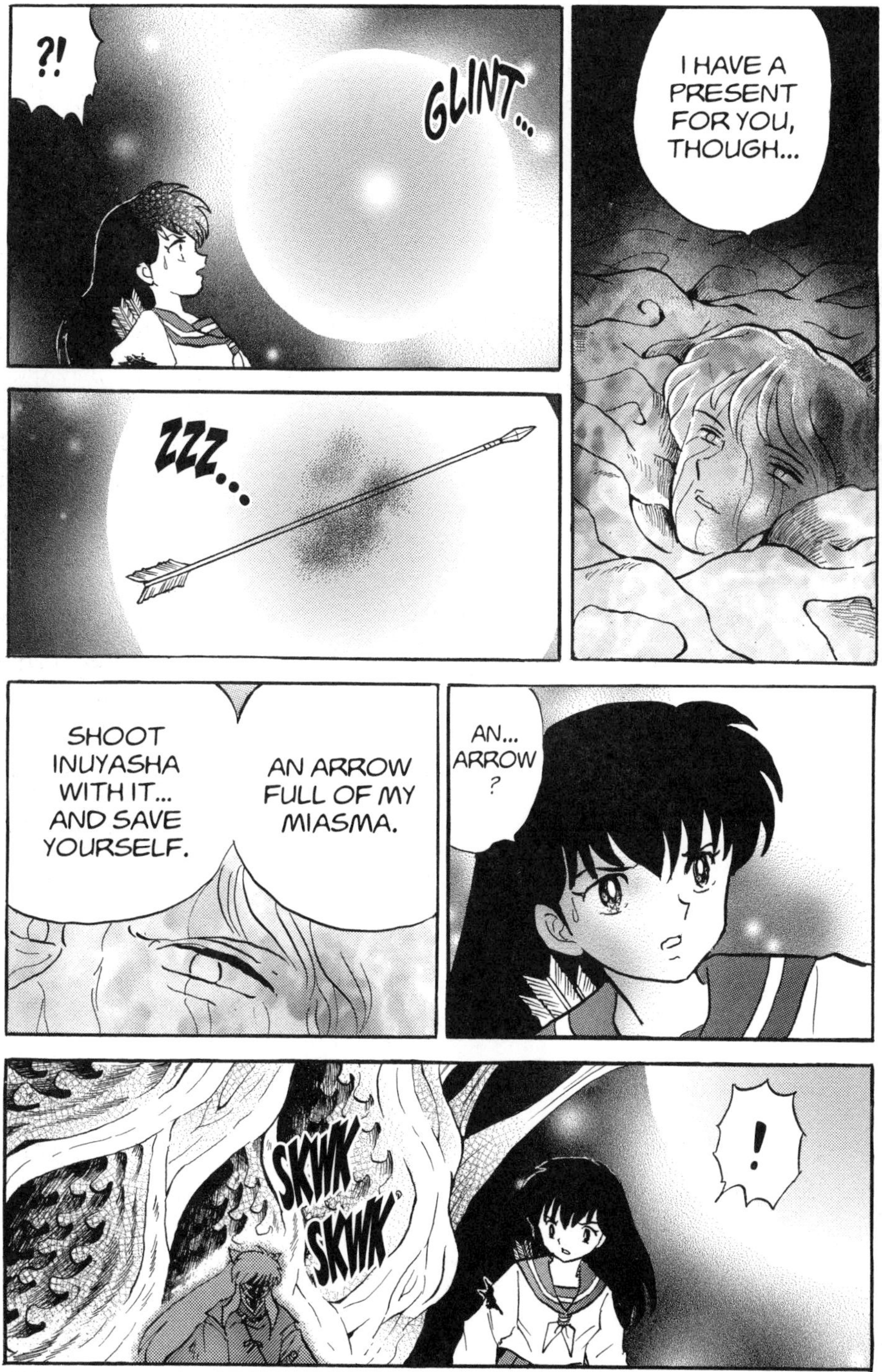

I HAVE A PRESENT FOR YOU, THOUGH...
?!
GLINT...
ZZZ...
AN... ARROW?
AN ARROW FULL OF MY MIASMA.
SHOOT INUYASHA WITH IT... AND SAVE YOURSELF.
!
SKWK SKWK

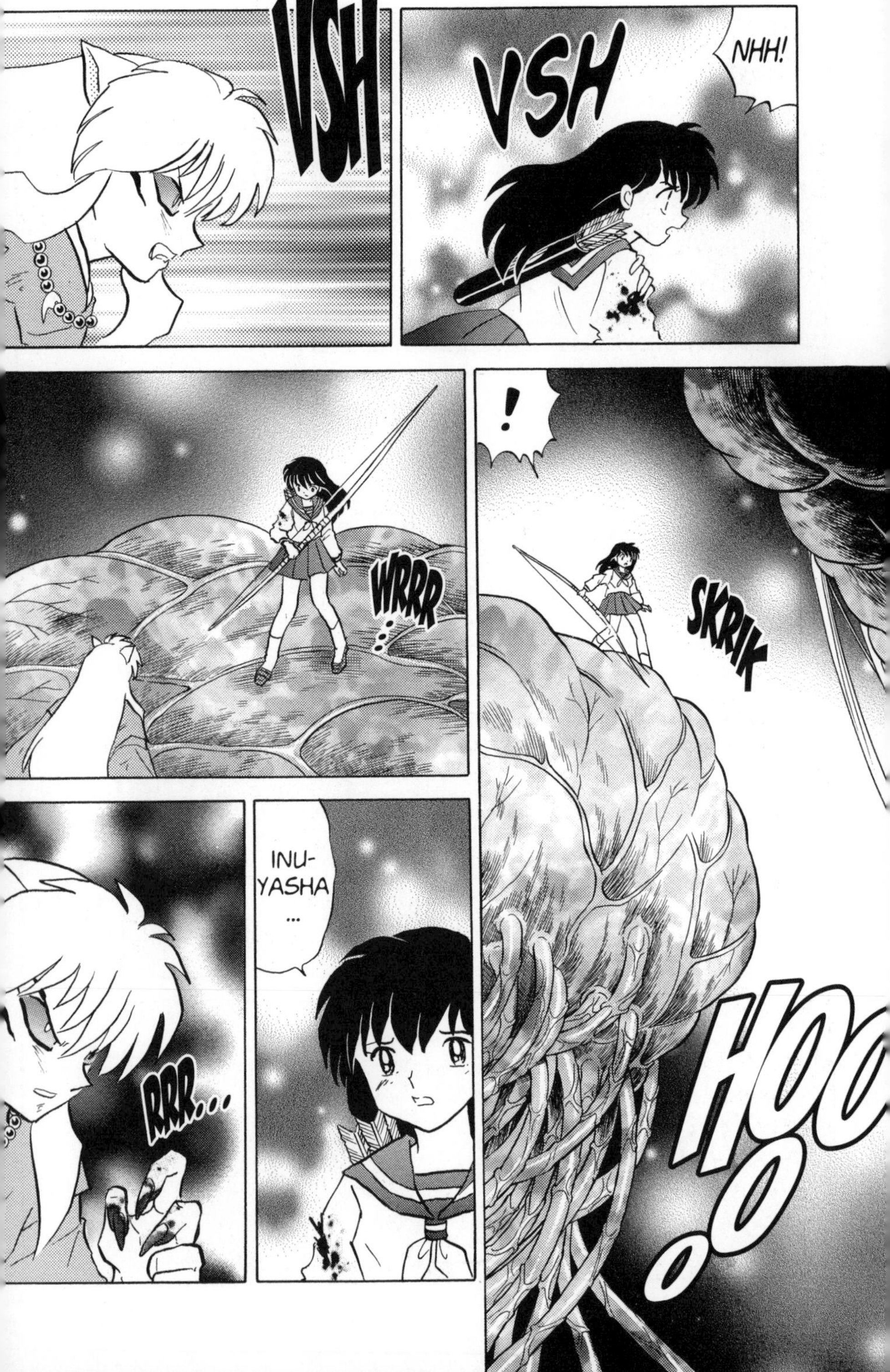
VSH
NHH!
VSH
!
SKRIK
HOOOO
WRRR...
INU-YASHA...
RRR...

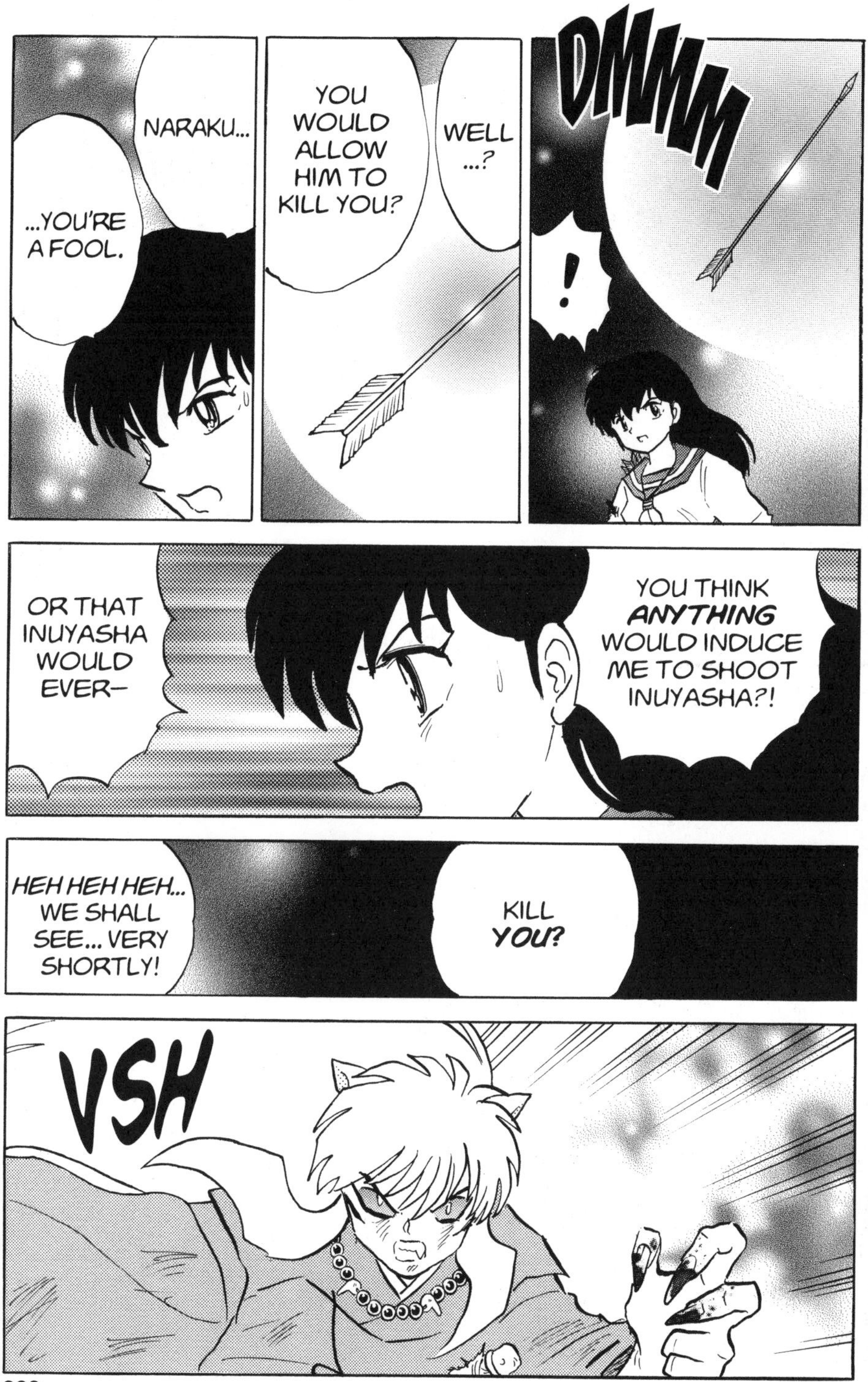
DMMM
!
WELL ...?
YOU WOULD ALLOW HIM TO KILL YOU?
NARAKU...
...YOU'RE A FOOL.
YOU THINK **ANYTHING** WOULD INDUCE ME TO SHOOT INUYASHA?!
OR THAT INUYASHA WOULD EVER–
KILL ***YOU?***
HEH HEH HEH... WE SHALL SEE... VERY SHORTLY!
VSH

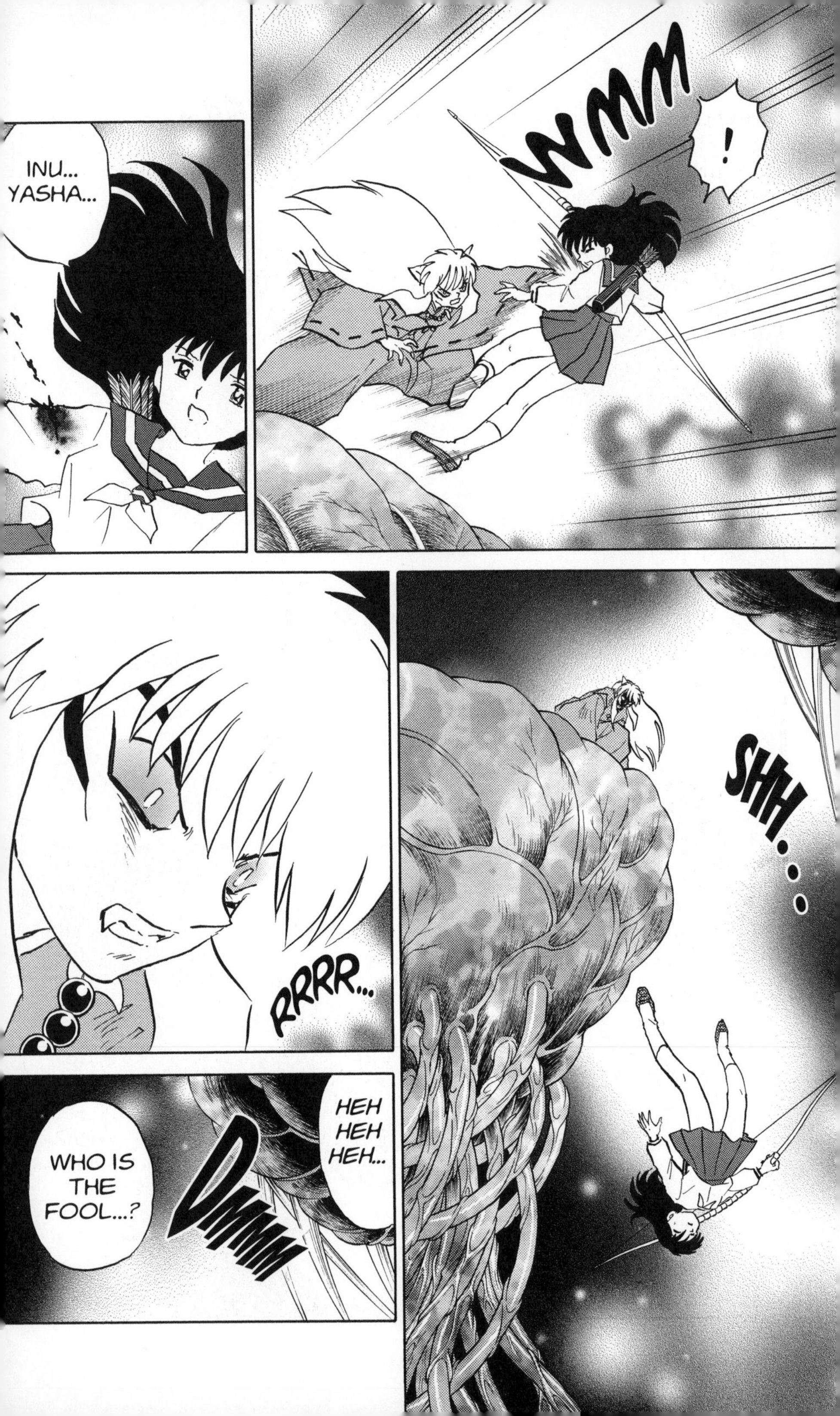
WMM
!
INU... YASHA...
SHH...
RRRR...
HEH HEH HEH...
DMMMM
WHO IS THE FOOL...?

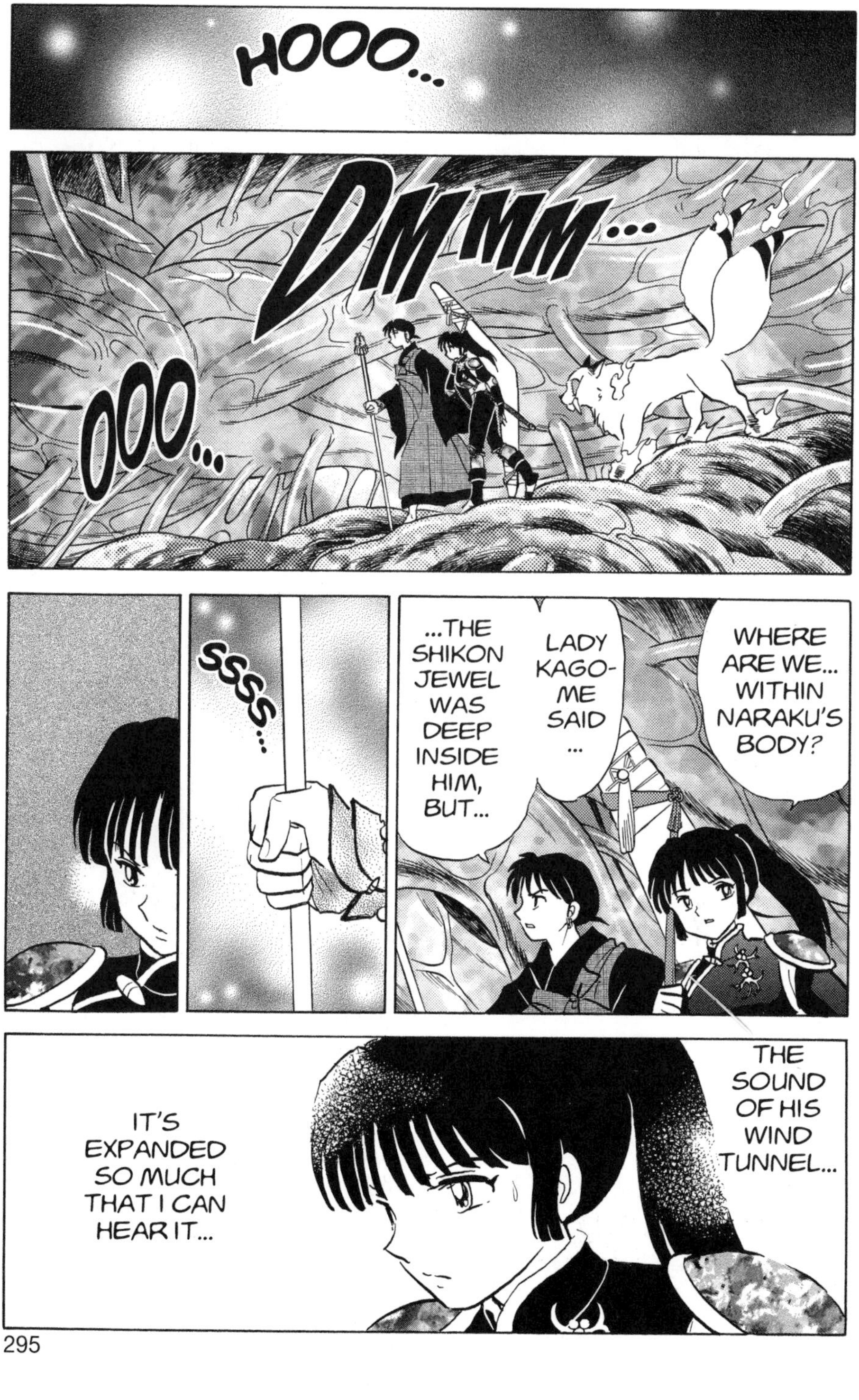
HOOO...
DMMM...
OOO...
WHERE ARE WE... WITHIN NARAKU'S BODY?
LADY KAGO-ME SAID ...
...THE SHIKON JEWEL WAS DEEP INSIDE HIM, BUT...
SSSS...
THE SOUND OF HIS WIND TUNNEL...
IT'S EXPANDED SO MUCH THAT I CAN HEAR IT...

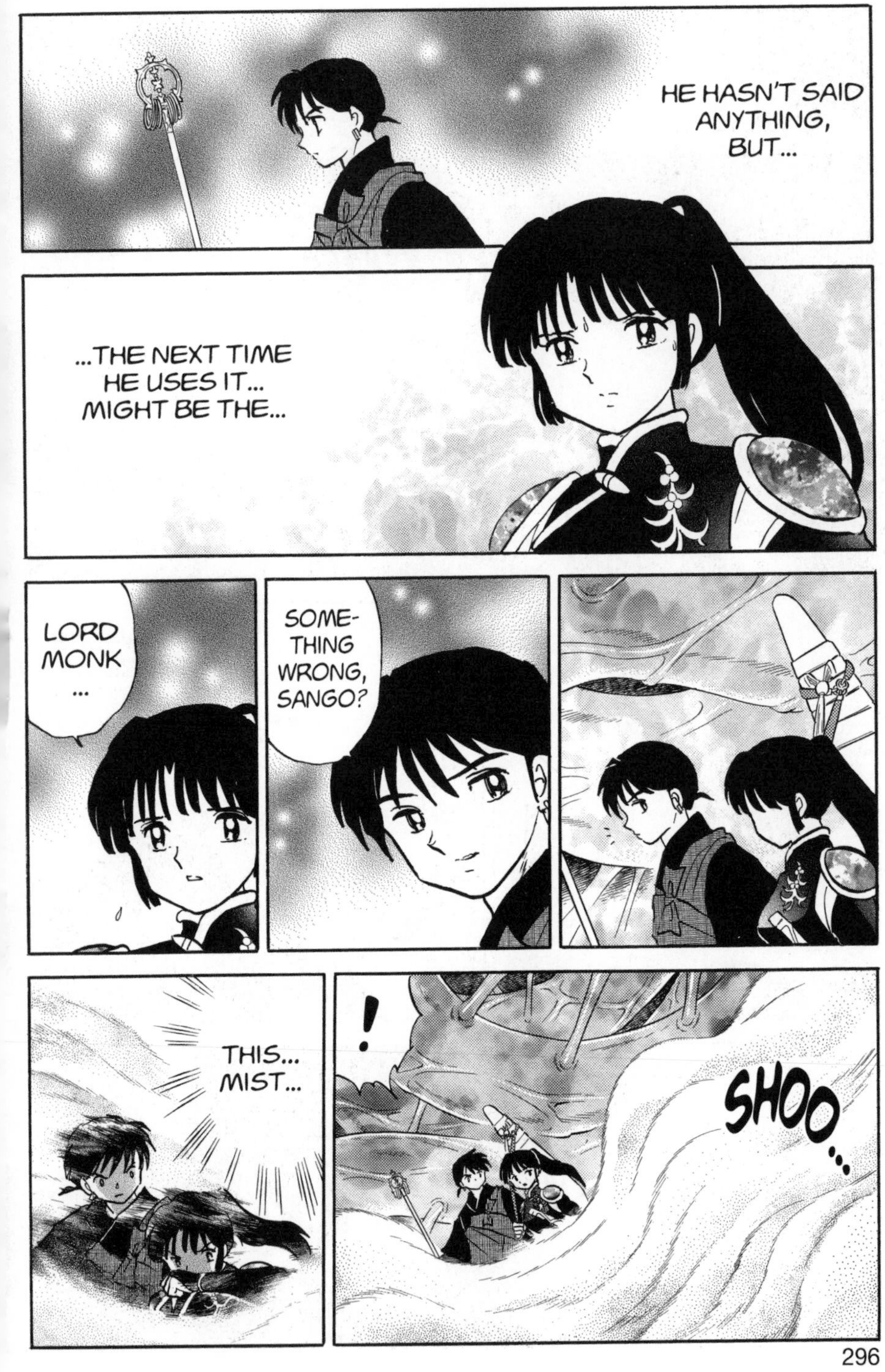
HE HASN'T SAID ANYTHING, BUT...
...THE NEXT TIME HE USES IT... MIGHT BE THE...
SOME-THING WRONG, SANGO?
LORD MONK ...
!
SHOO...
THIS... MIST...

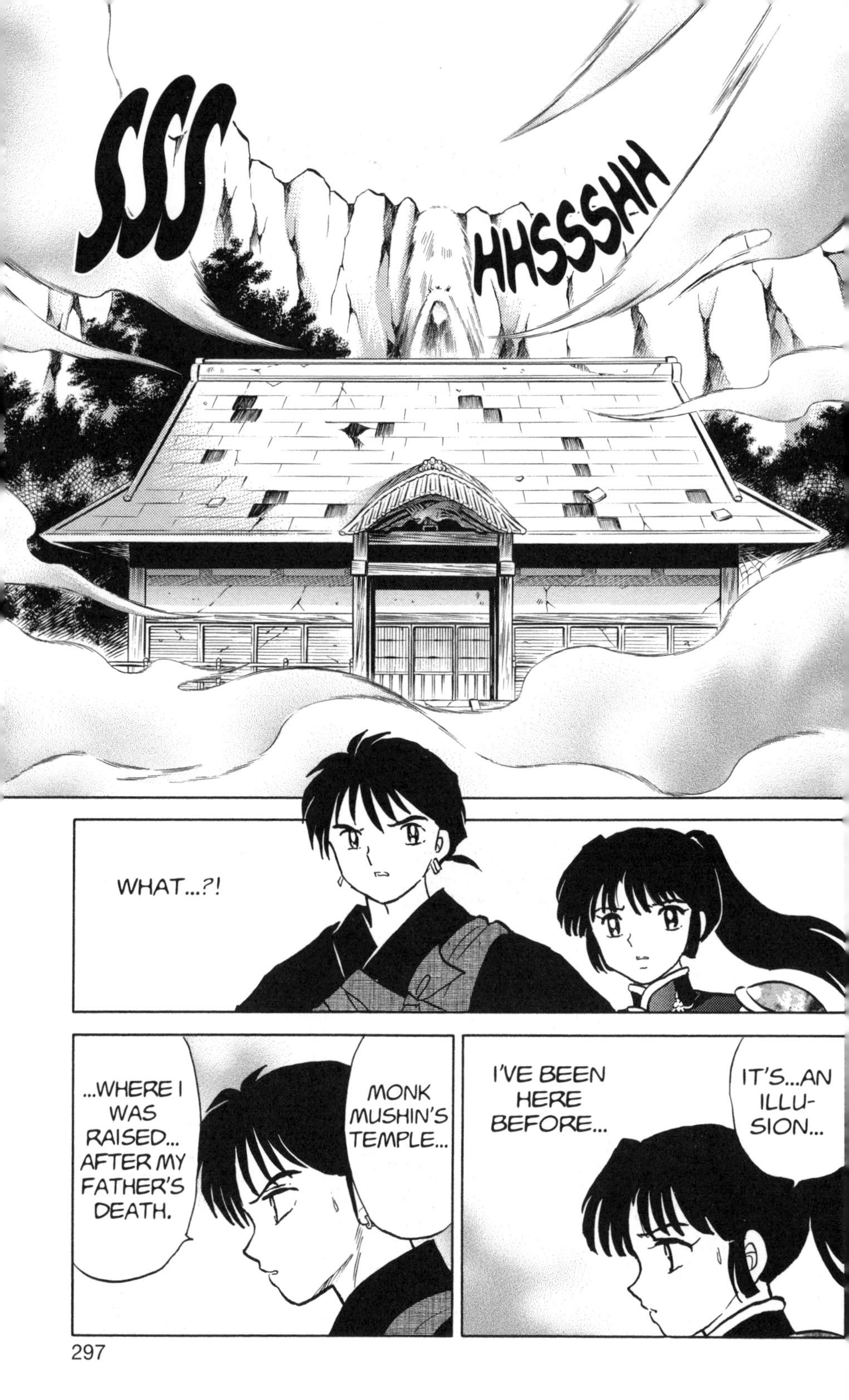
SSS
HHSSSHH
WHAT...?!
IT'S...AN ILLU-SION...
I'VE BEEN HERE BEFORE...
MONK MUSHIN'S TEMPLE...
...WHERE I WAS RAISED... AFTER MY FATHER'S DEATH.

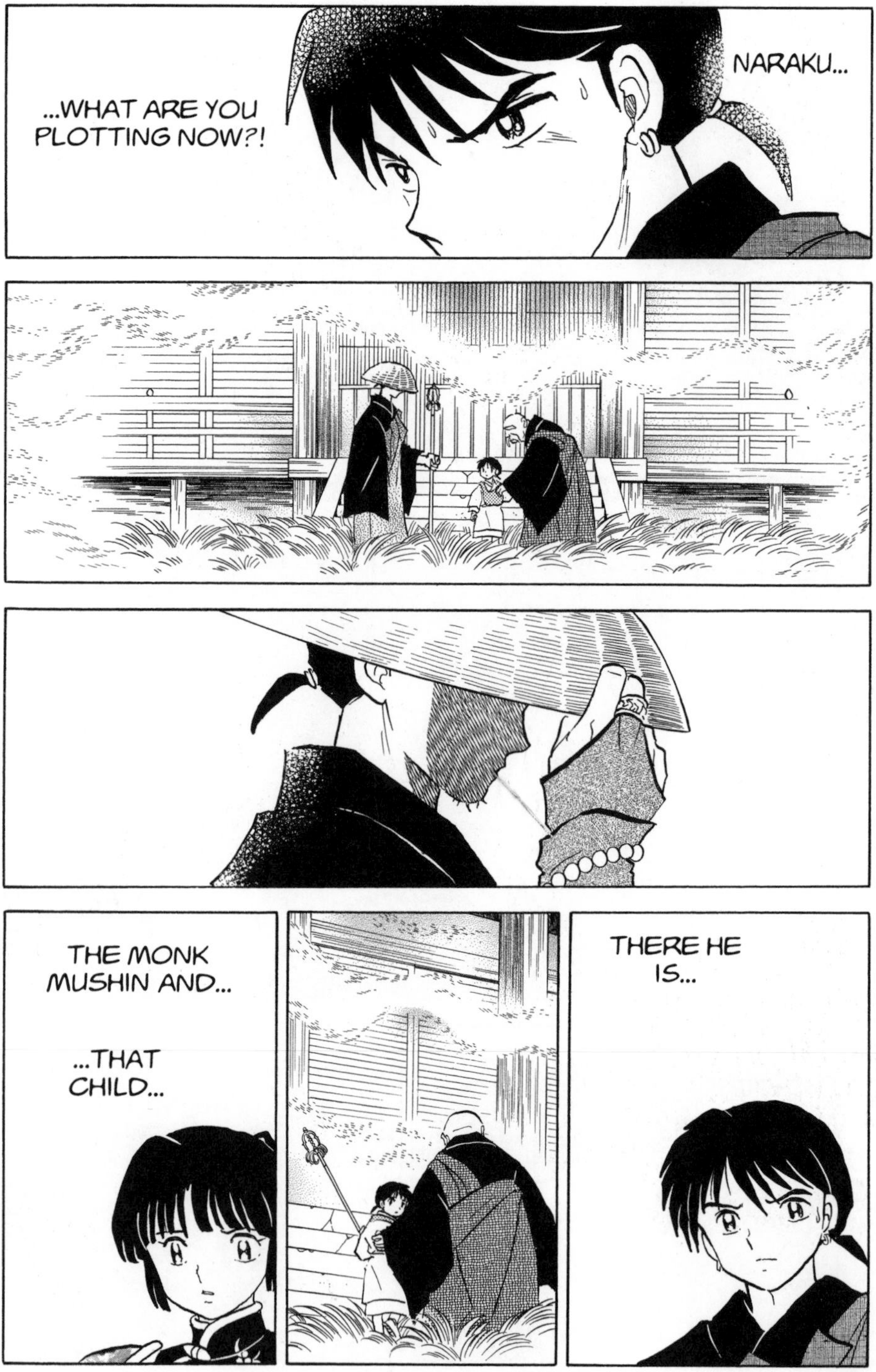
NARAKU...
...WHAT ARE YOU PLOTTING NOW?!
THERE HE IS...
THE MONK MUSHIN AND...
...THAT CHILD...

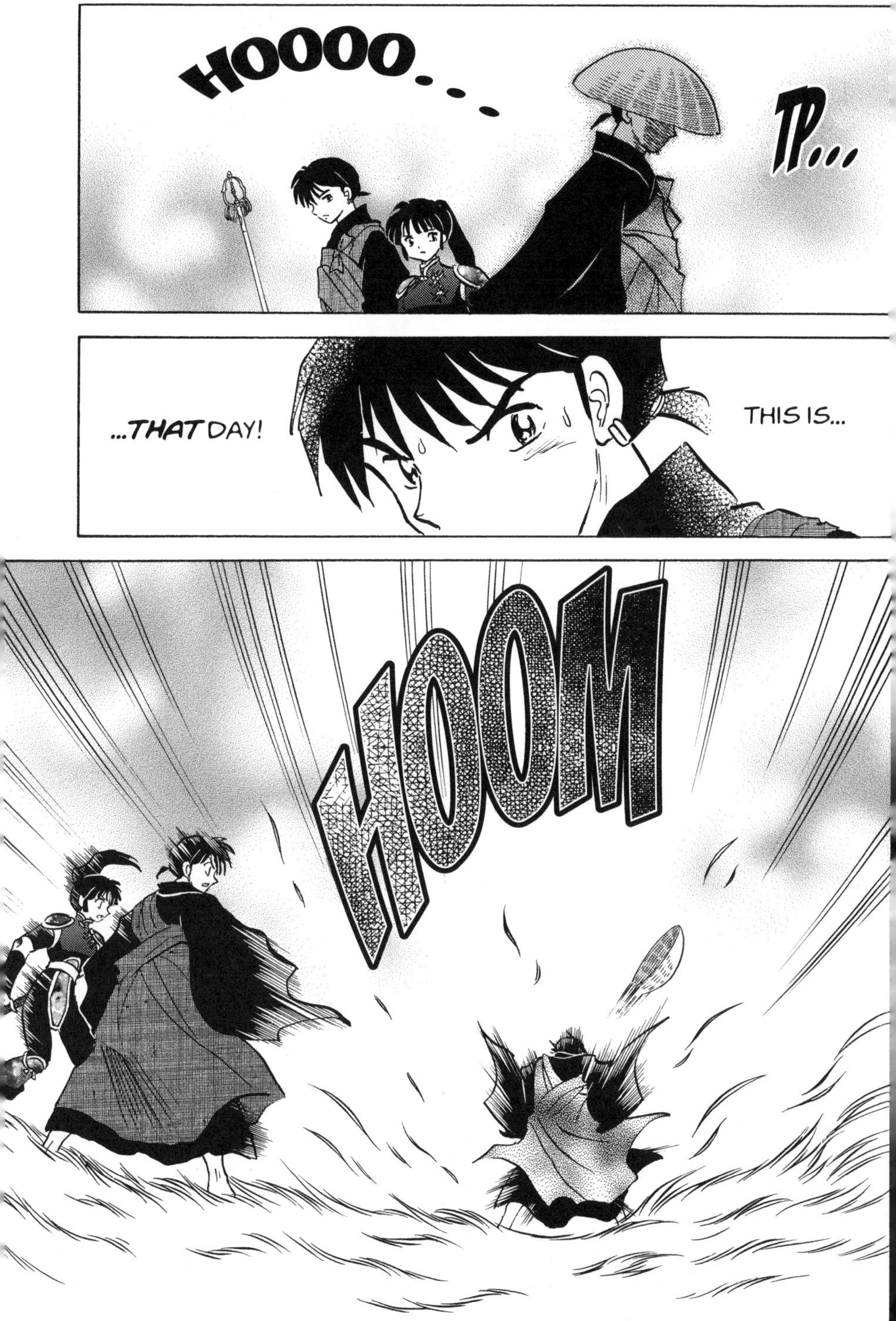
TP...
HOOOO...
THIS IS...
...THAT DAY!
HOOM

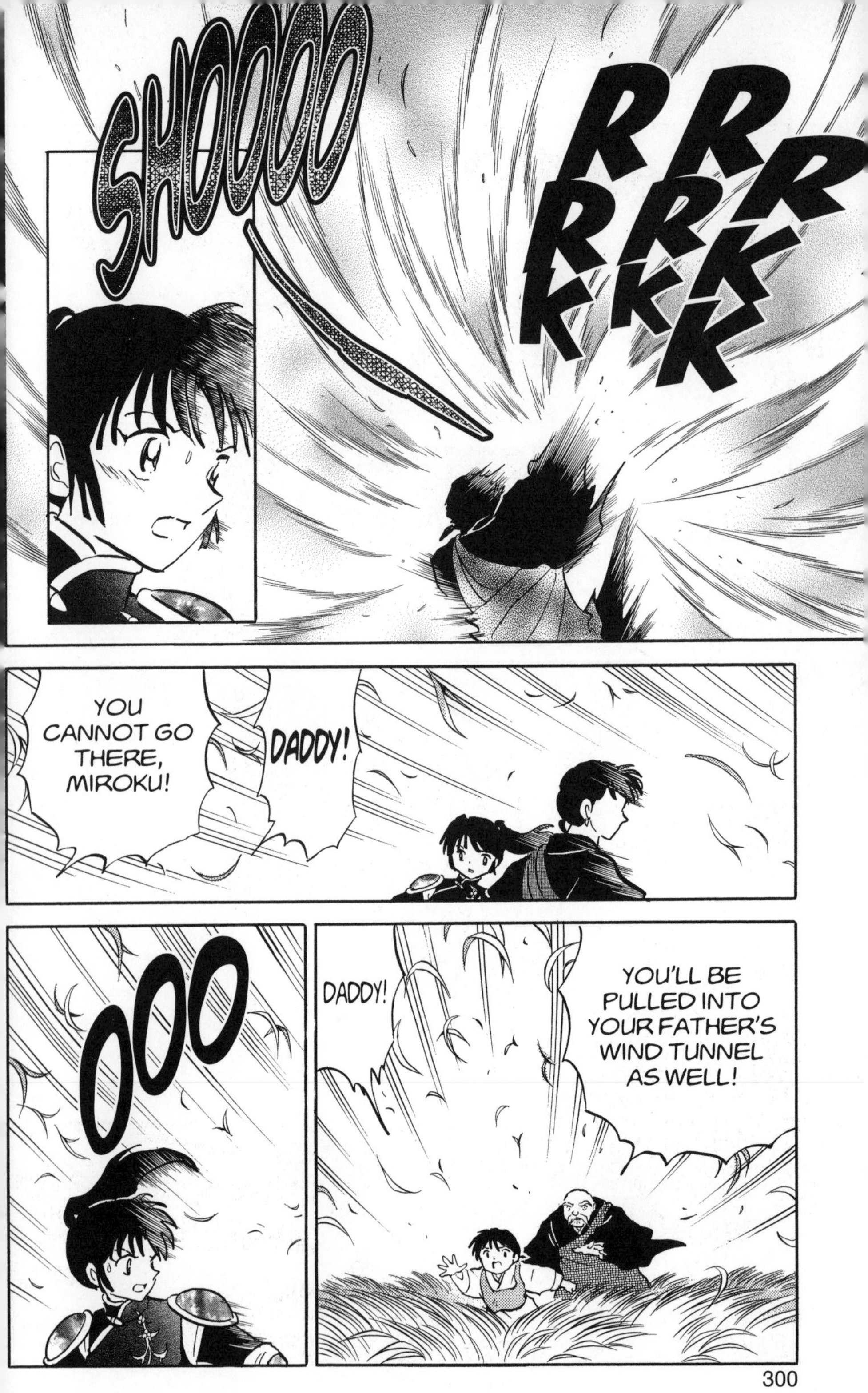
RRRRRRKKKK
SHOOOO
DADDY!
YOU CANNOT GO THERE, MIROKU!
YOU'LL BE PULLED INTO YOUR FATHER'S WIND TUNNEL AS WELL!
DADDY!
OOO

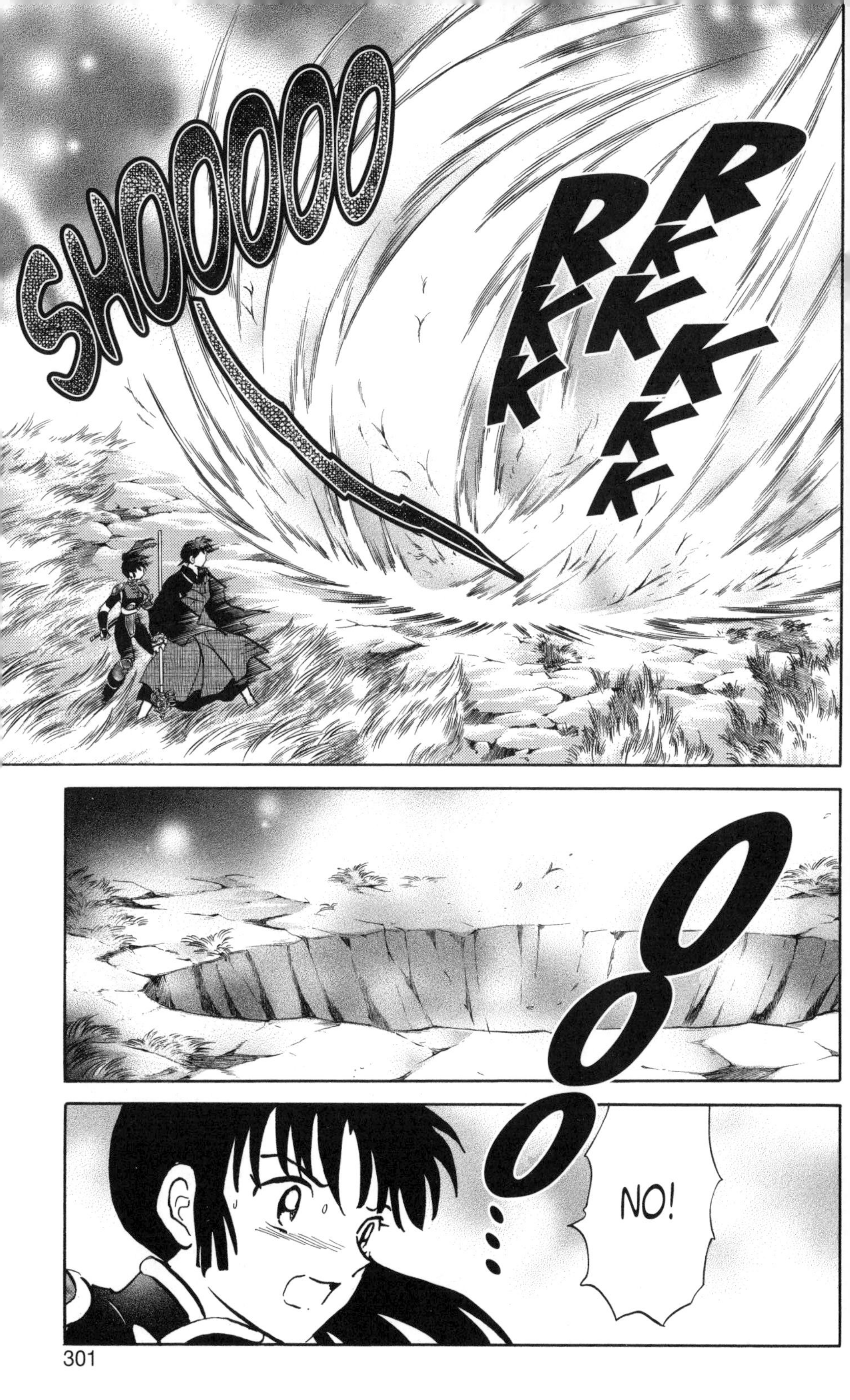
RRKKKKK
SHOOOOO
OOO...
NO!

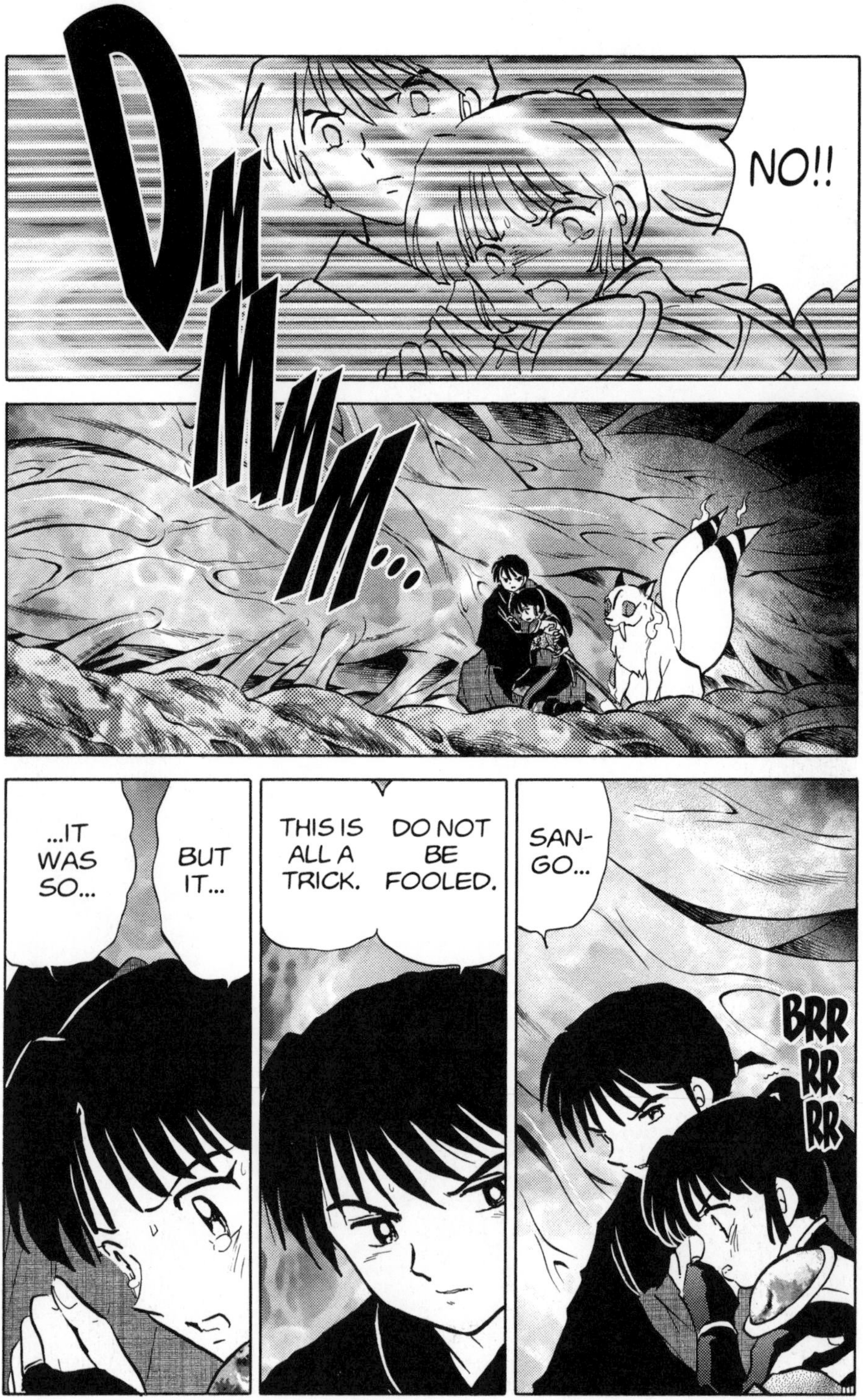
NO!!
DMMMM...
SAN-GO...
BRRRRRRR
THIS IS ALL A TRICK.
DO NOT BE FOOLED.
BUT IT...
...IT WAS SO...

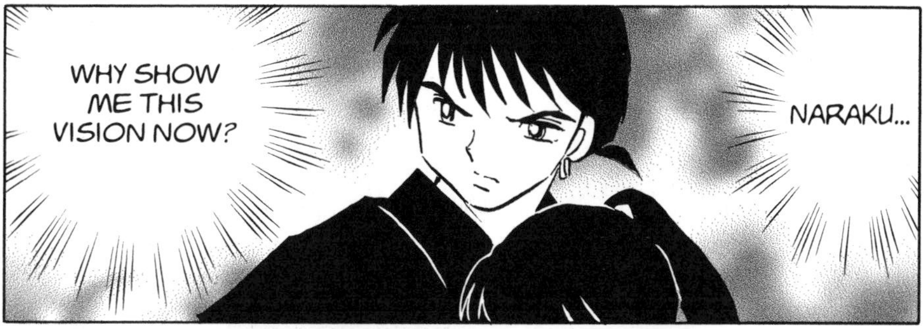
NARAKU...
WHY SHOW ME THIS VISION NOW?

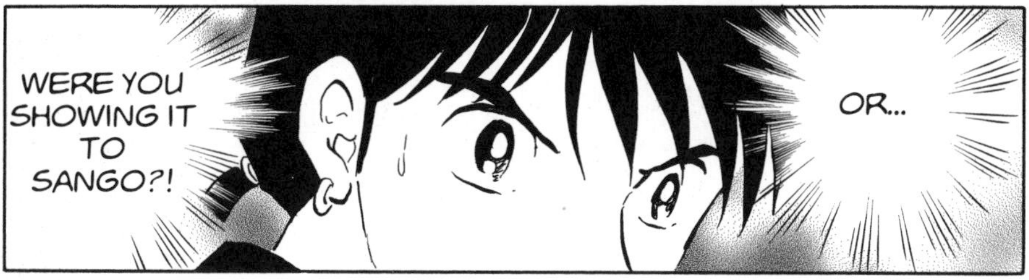
OR...
WERE YOU SHOWING IT TO SANGO?!

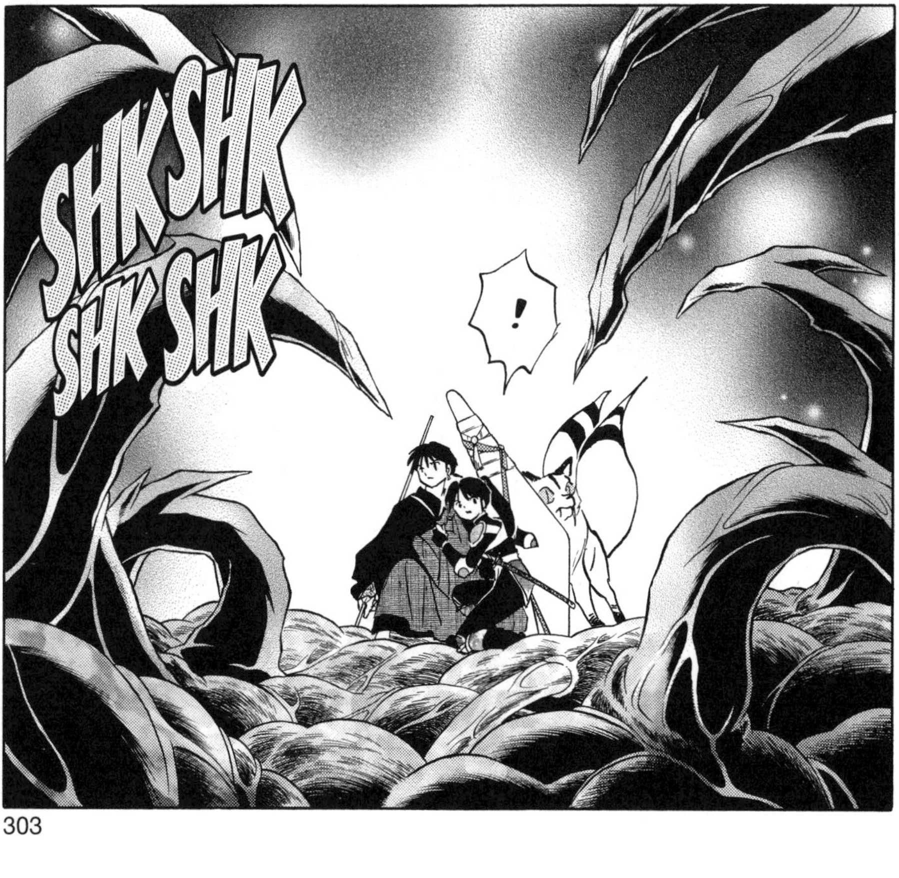
!
SHK SHK
SHK SHK

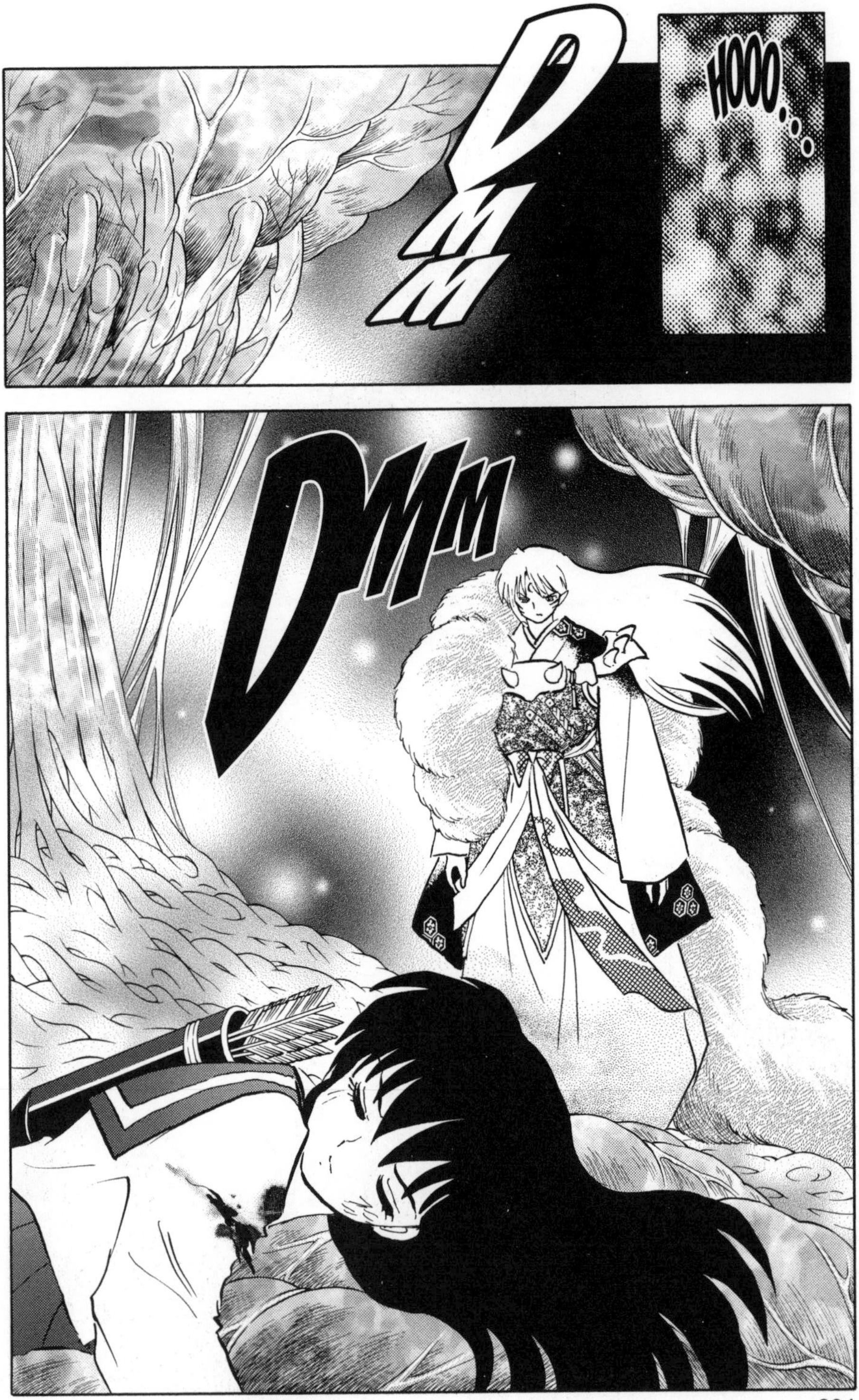
HOOO...
DMMM
DMMM

SCROLL SEVEN
NARAKU'S DARKNESS

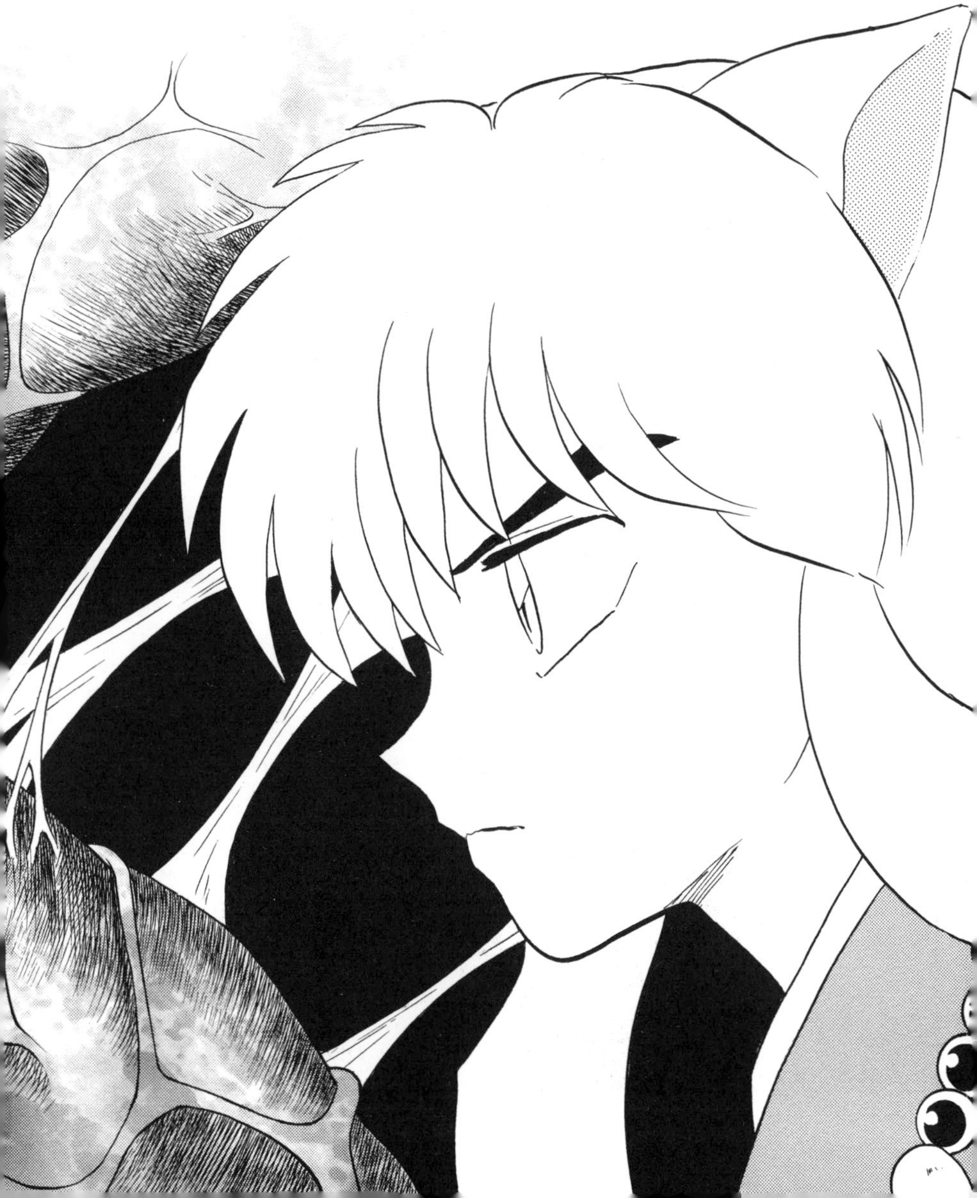

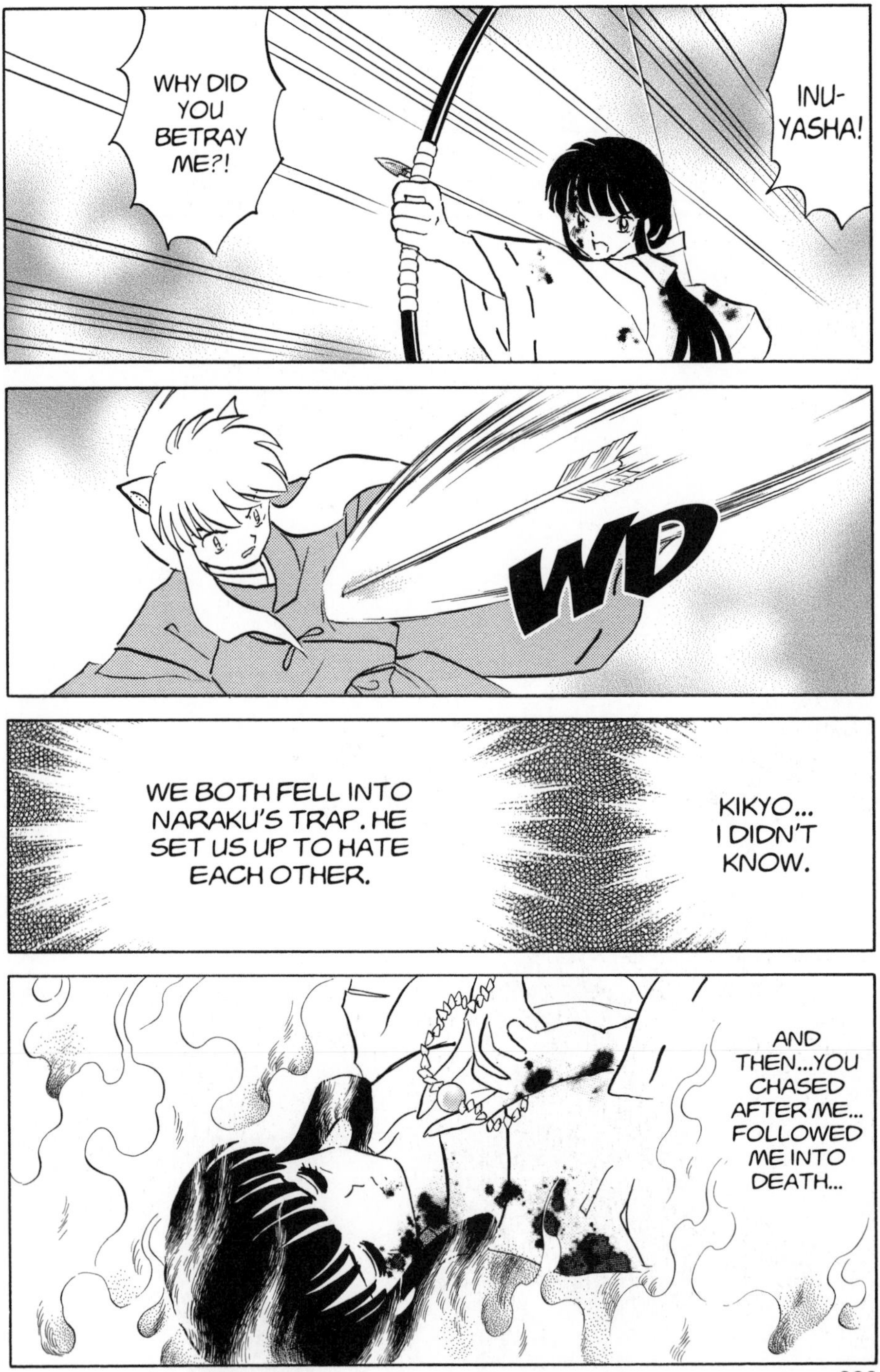
INU-YASHA!
WHY DID YOU BETRAY ME?!
WD
KIKYO... I DIDN'T KNOW.
WE BOTH FELL INTO NARAKU'S TRAP. HE SET US UP TO HATE EACH OTHER.
AND THEN...YOU CHASED AFTER ME... FOLLOWED ME INTO DEATH...

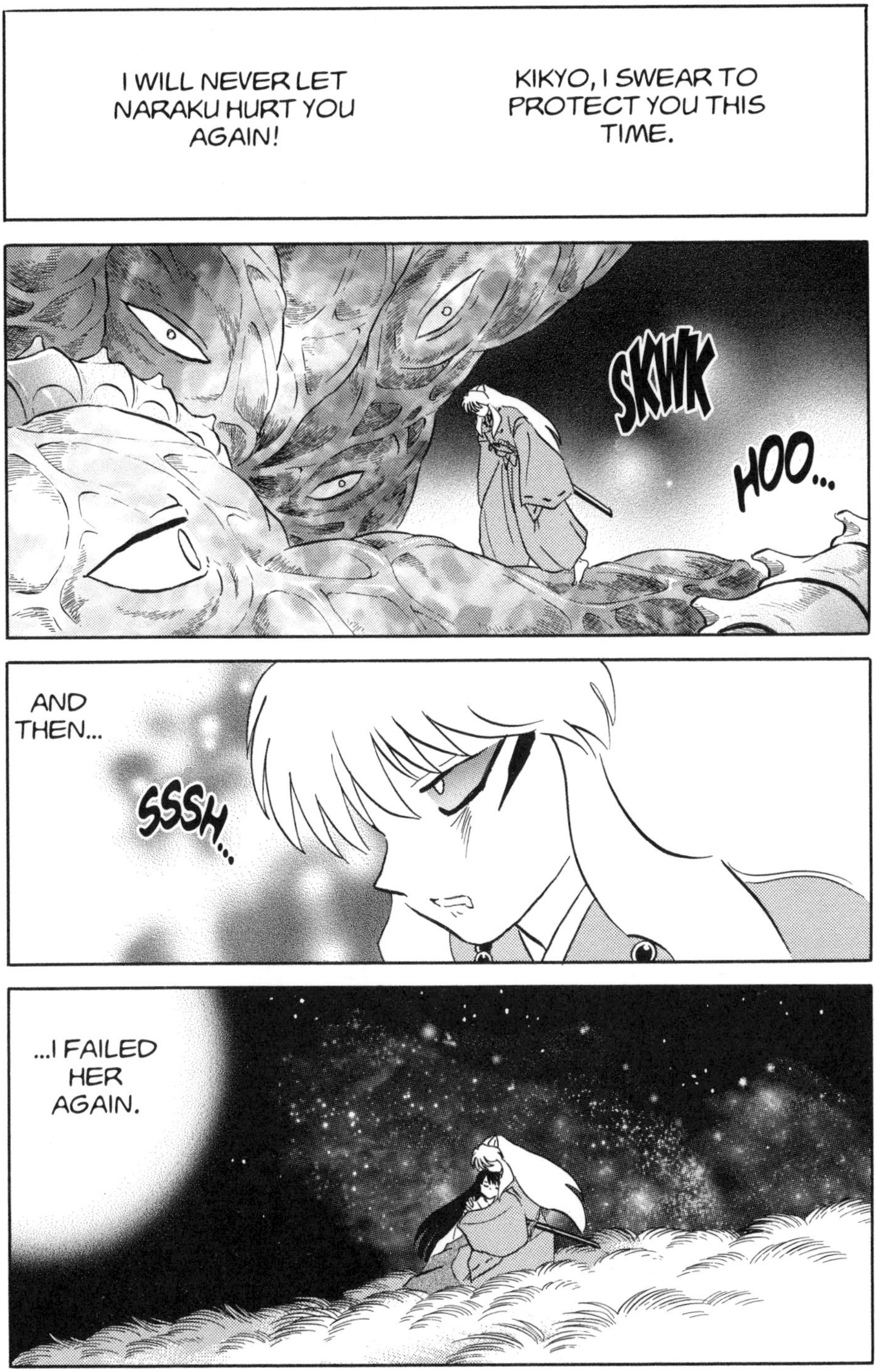
KIKYO, I SWEAR TO PROTECT YOU THIS TIME.
I WILL NEVER LET NARAKU HURT YOU AGAIN!
SKWK
HOO...
AND THEN...
SSSH...
...I FAILED HER AGAIN.

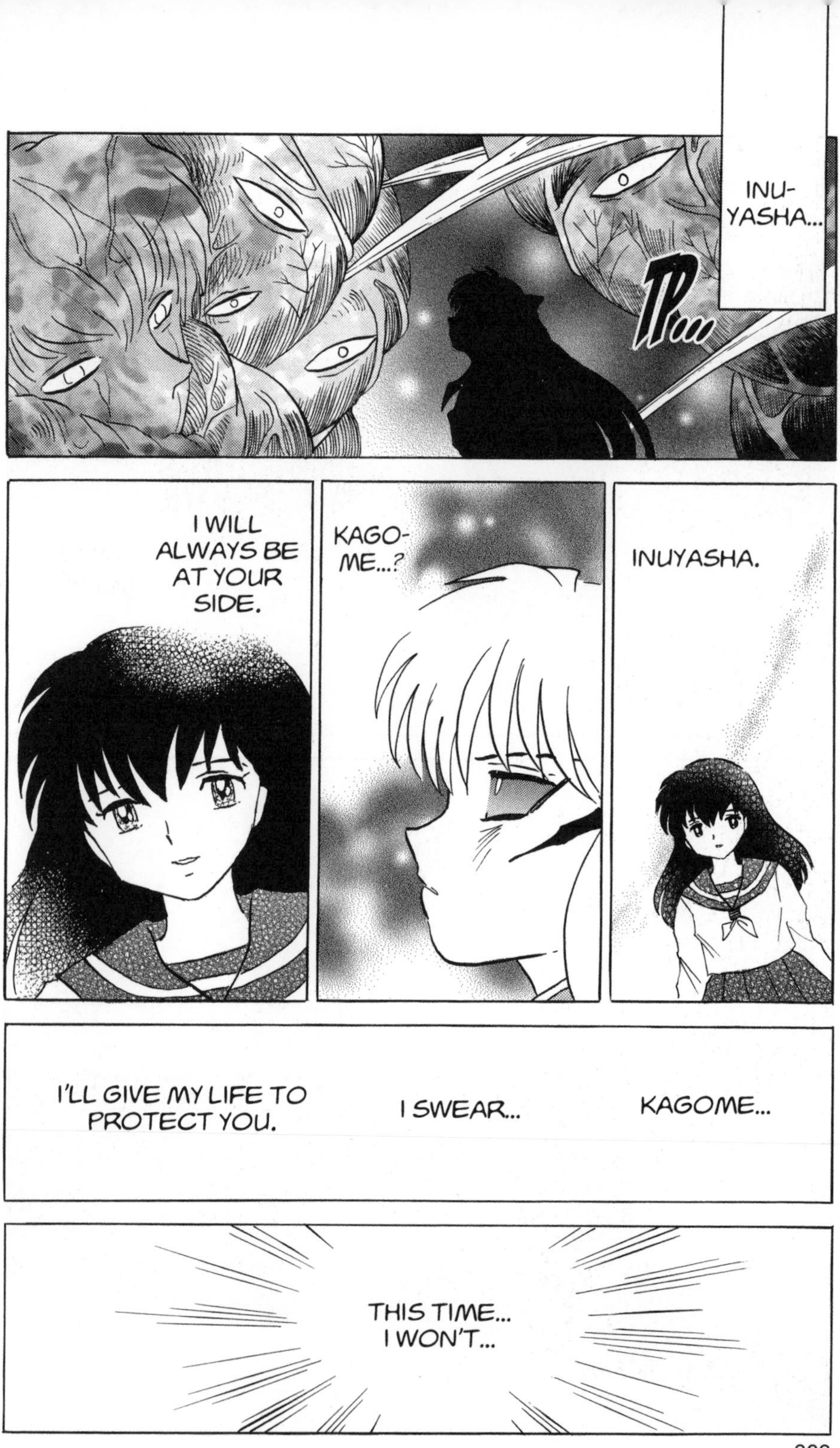
INU-YASHA...
INUYASHA.
KAGO-ME...?
I WILL ALWAYS BE AT YOUR SIDE.
KAGOME...
I SWEAR...
I'LL GIVE MY LIFE TO PROTECT YOU.
THIS TIME... I WON'T...

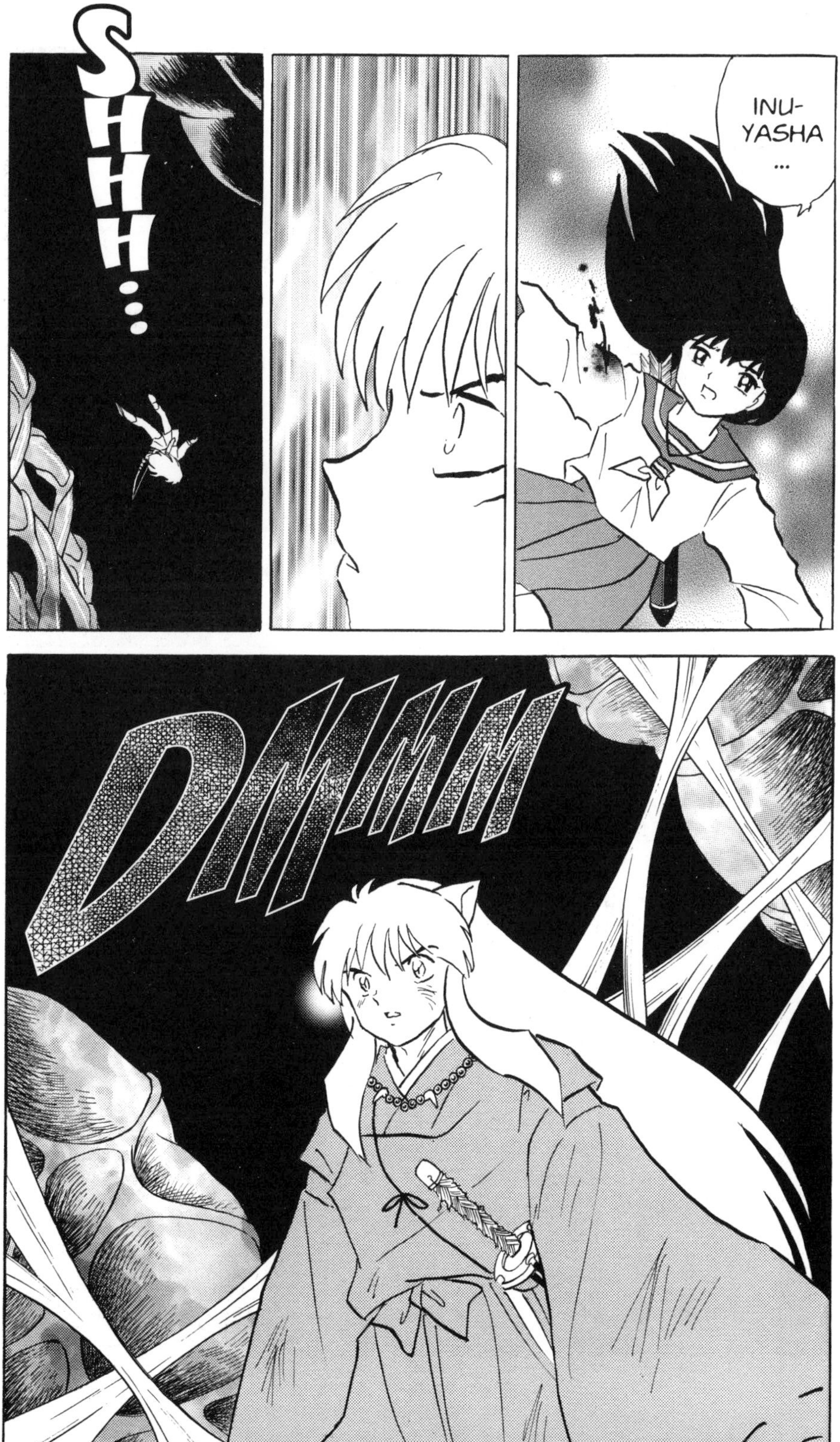
INU-YASHA ...
SHHH...
DMMM

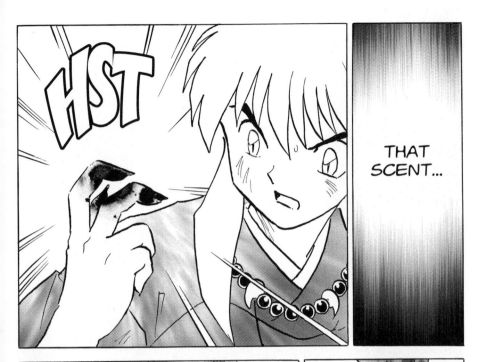

THAT SCENT...
HST
BLOOD ...
KAGO-ME'S BLOOD ...?!
DON'T YOU REMEM-BER...?
ZWP
ZWP
I SUPPOSE NOT...
...SINCE YOU'VE HARDLY BEEN YOURSELF OF LATE.

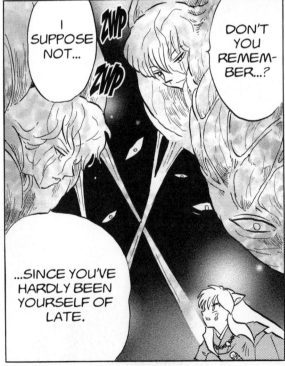

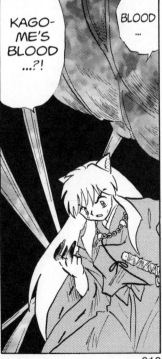

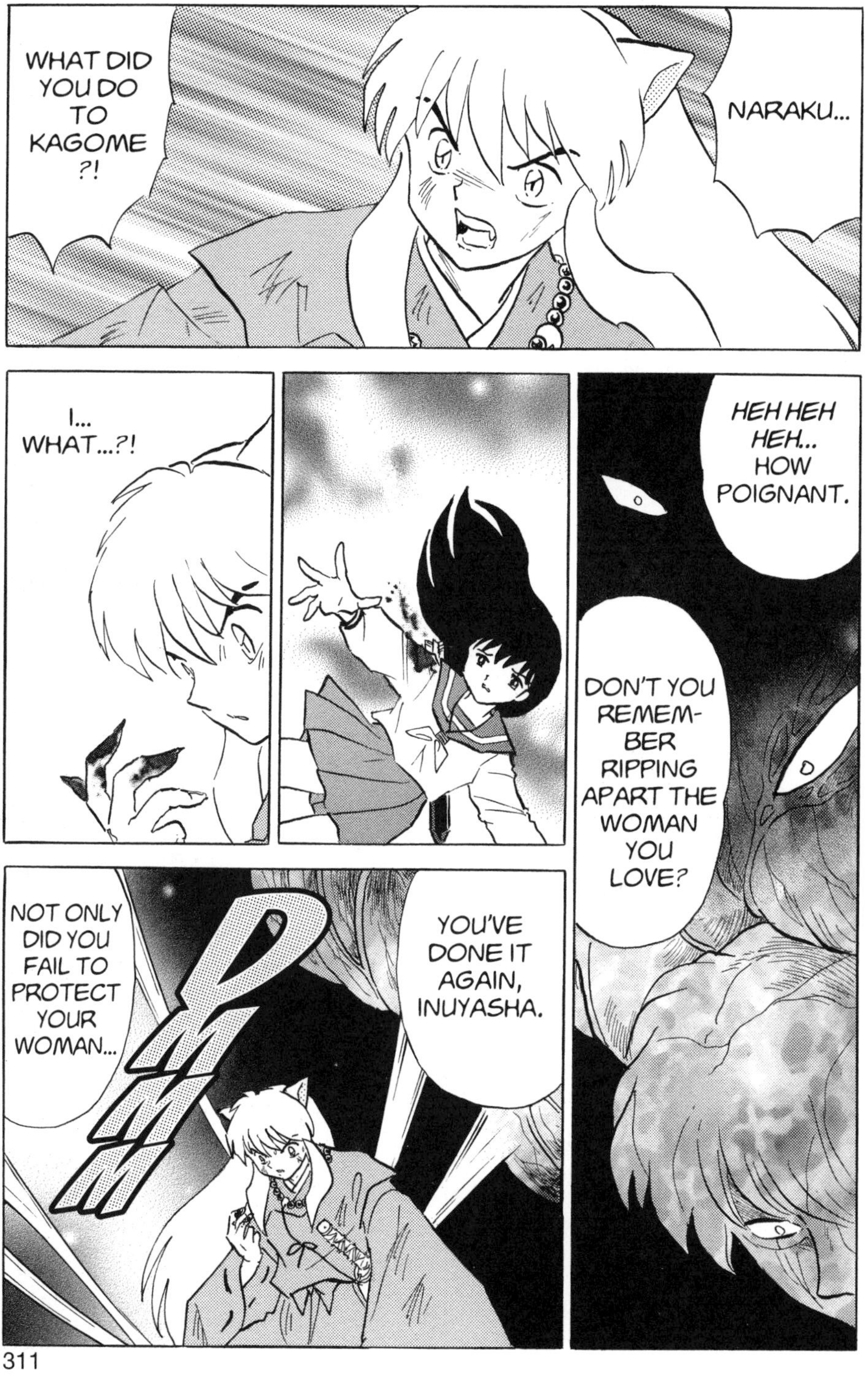
NARAKU...
WHAT DID YOU DO TO KAGOME ?!
HEH HEH HEH... HOW POIGNANT.
DON'T YOU REMEMBER RIPPING APART THE WOMAN YOU LOVE?
I... WHAT...?!
YOU'VE DONE IT AGAIN, INUYASHA.
NOT ONLY DID YOU FAIL TO PROTECT YOUR WOMAN...

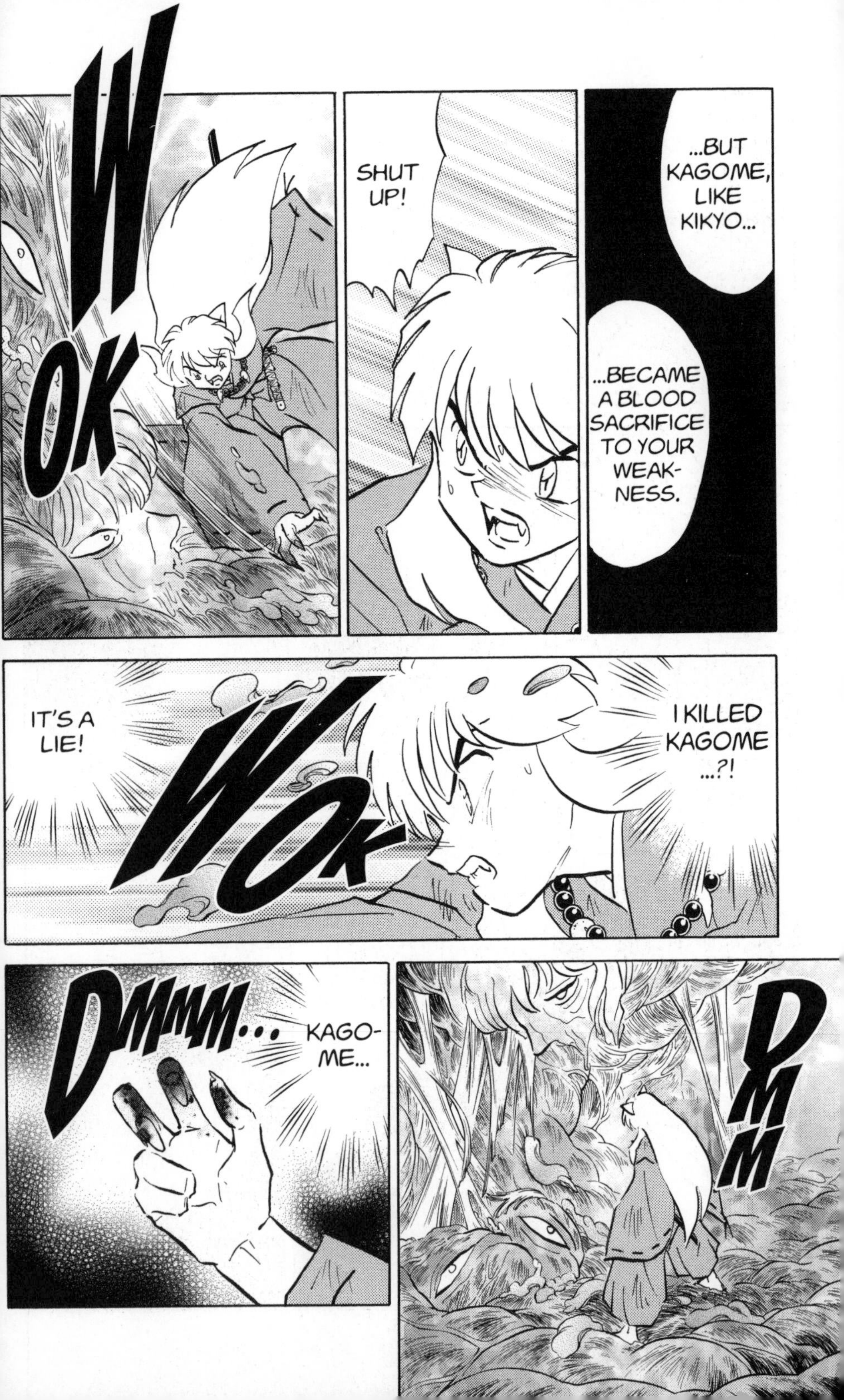

...BUT KAGOME, LIKE KIKYO...
...BECAME A BLOOD SACRIFICE TO YOUR WEAK-NESS.
SHUT UP!
WOK
I KILLED KAGOME ...?!
WOK
IT'S A LIE!
DMM
KAGO-ME...
DMMM...

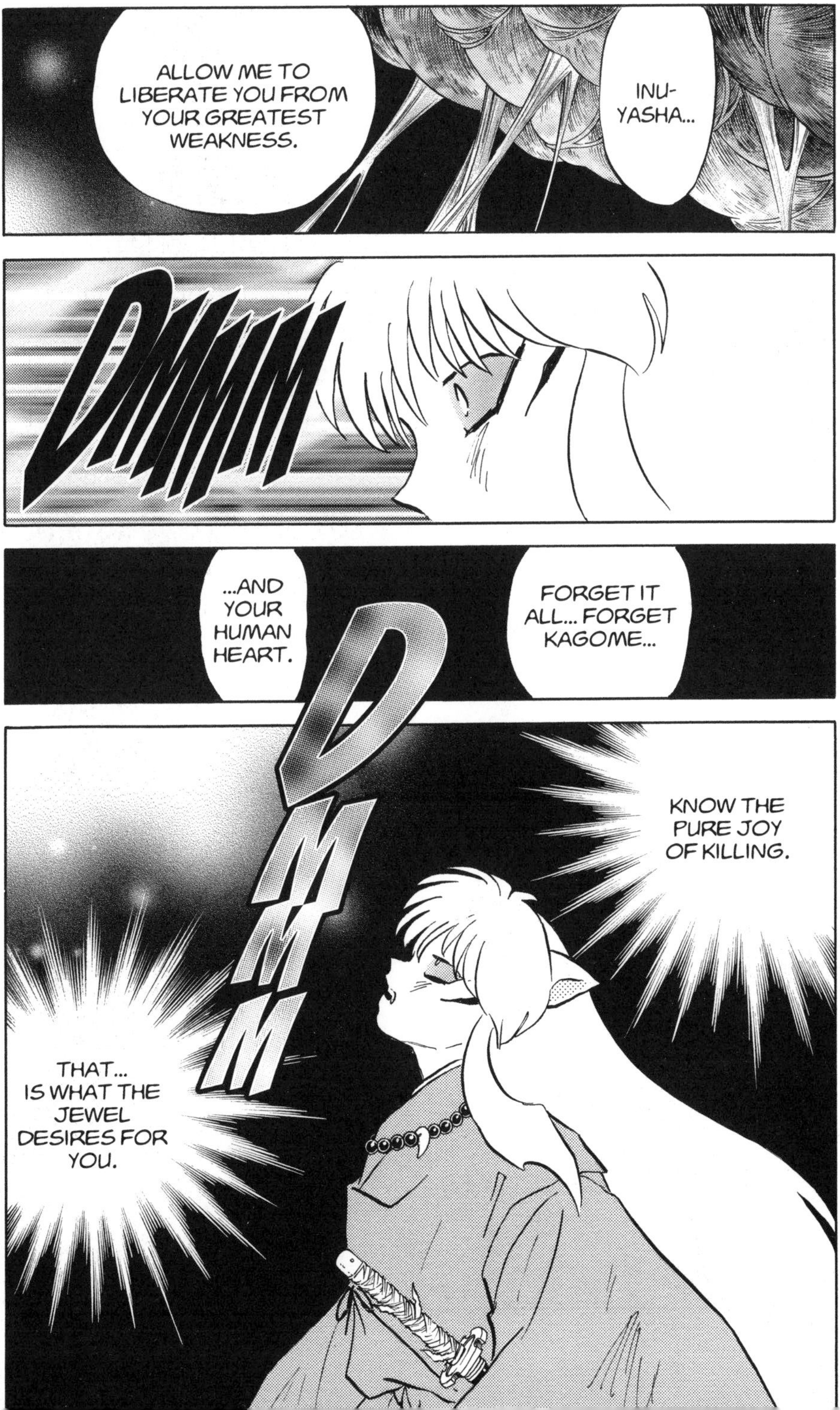
INU-YASHA...
ALLOW ME TO LIBERATE YOU FROM YOUR GREATEST WEAKNESS.
DMMM
FORGET IT ALL... FORGET KAGOME...
...AND YOUR HUMAN HEART.
KNOW THE PURE JOY OF KILLING.
DMMM
THAT... IS WHAT THE JEWEL DESIRES FOR YOU.

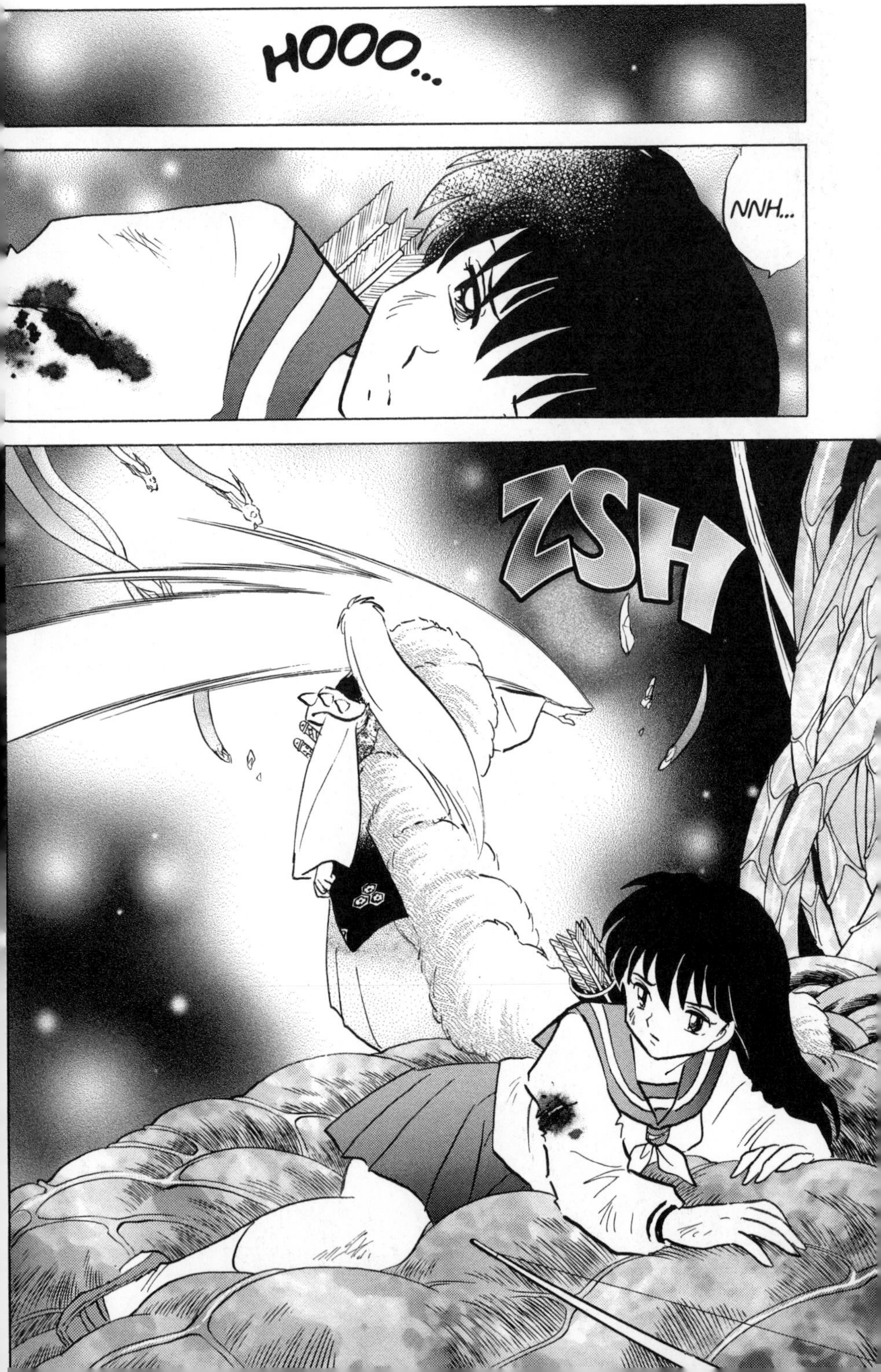
HOOO...
NNH...
ZSH

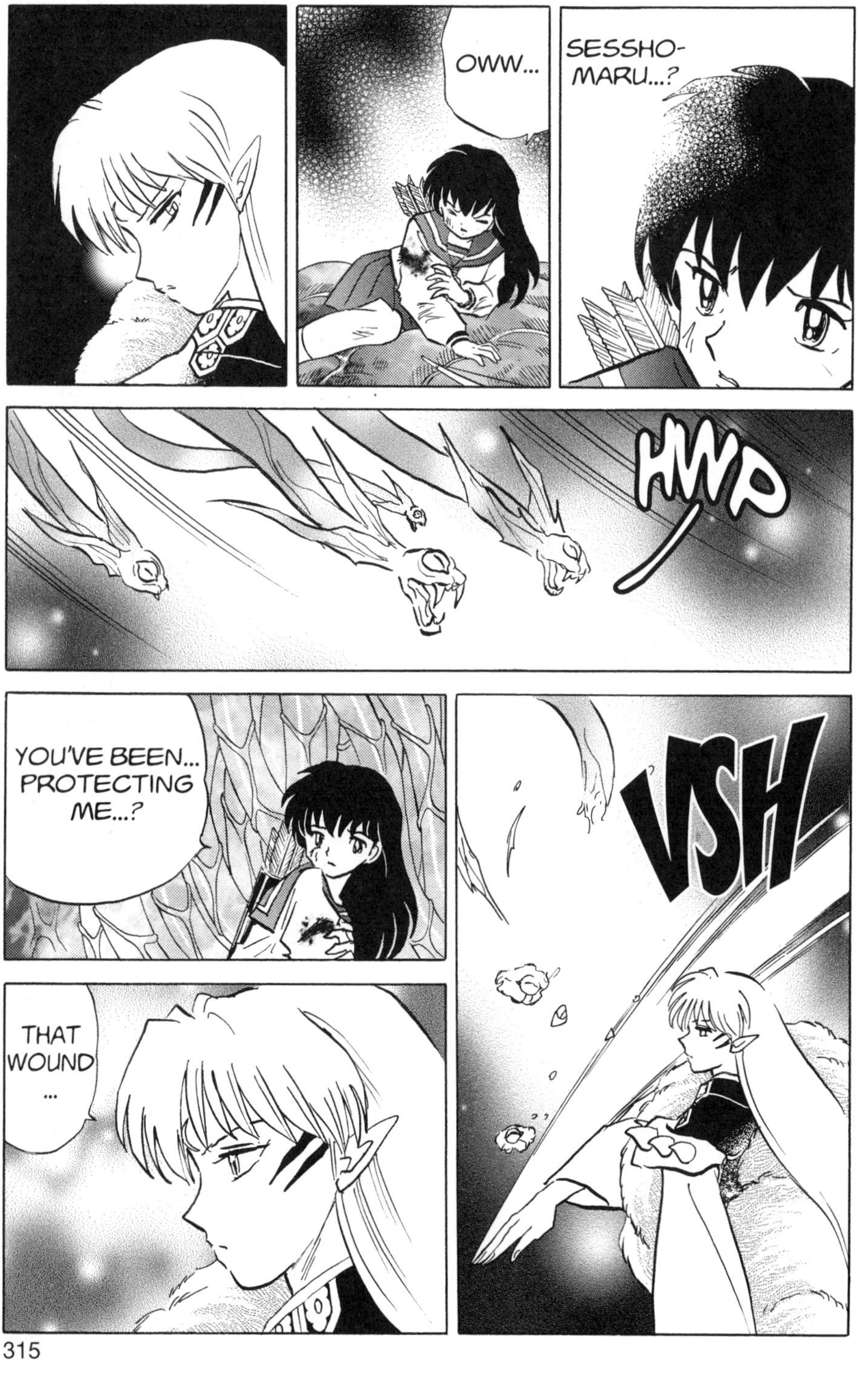
SESSHO-MARU...?
OWW...
HWP
VSH
YOU'VE BEEN... PROTECTING ME...?
THAT WOUND ...

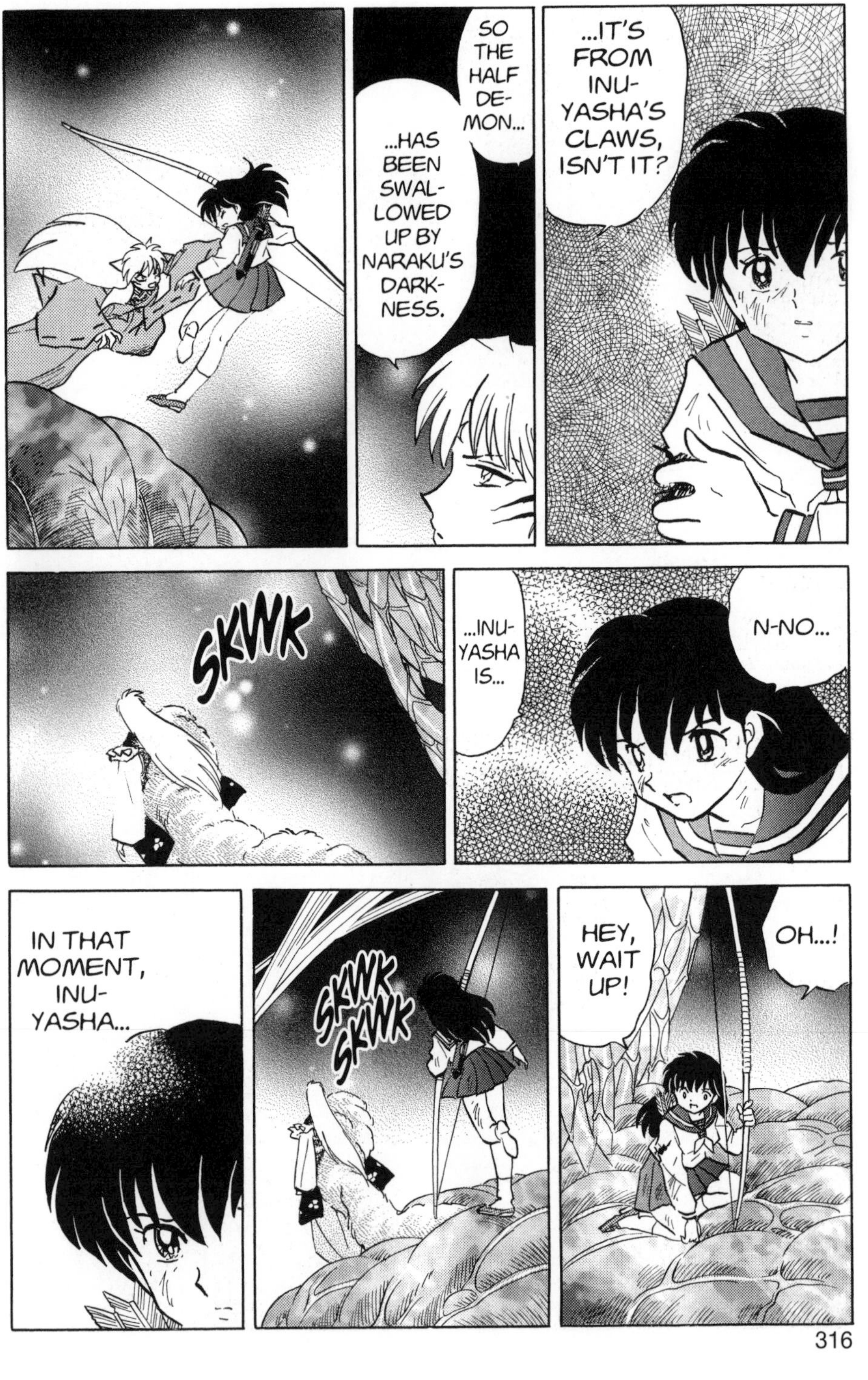
...IT'S FROM INU-YASHA'S CLAWS, ISN'T IT?
SO THE HALF DE-MON...
...HAS BEEN SWAL-LOWED UP BY NARAKU'S DARK-NESS.
N-NO...
...INU-YASHA IS...
SKWK
OH...!
HEY, WAIT UP!
SKWK SKWK
IN THAT MOMENT, INU-YASHA...

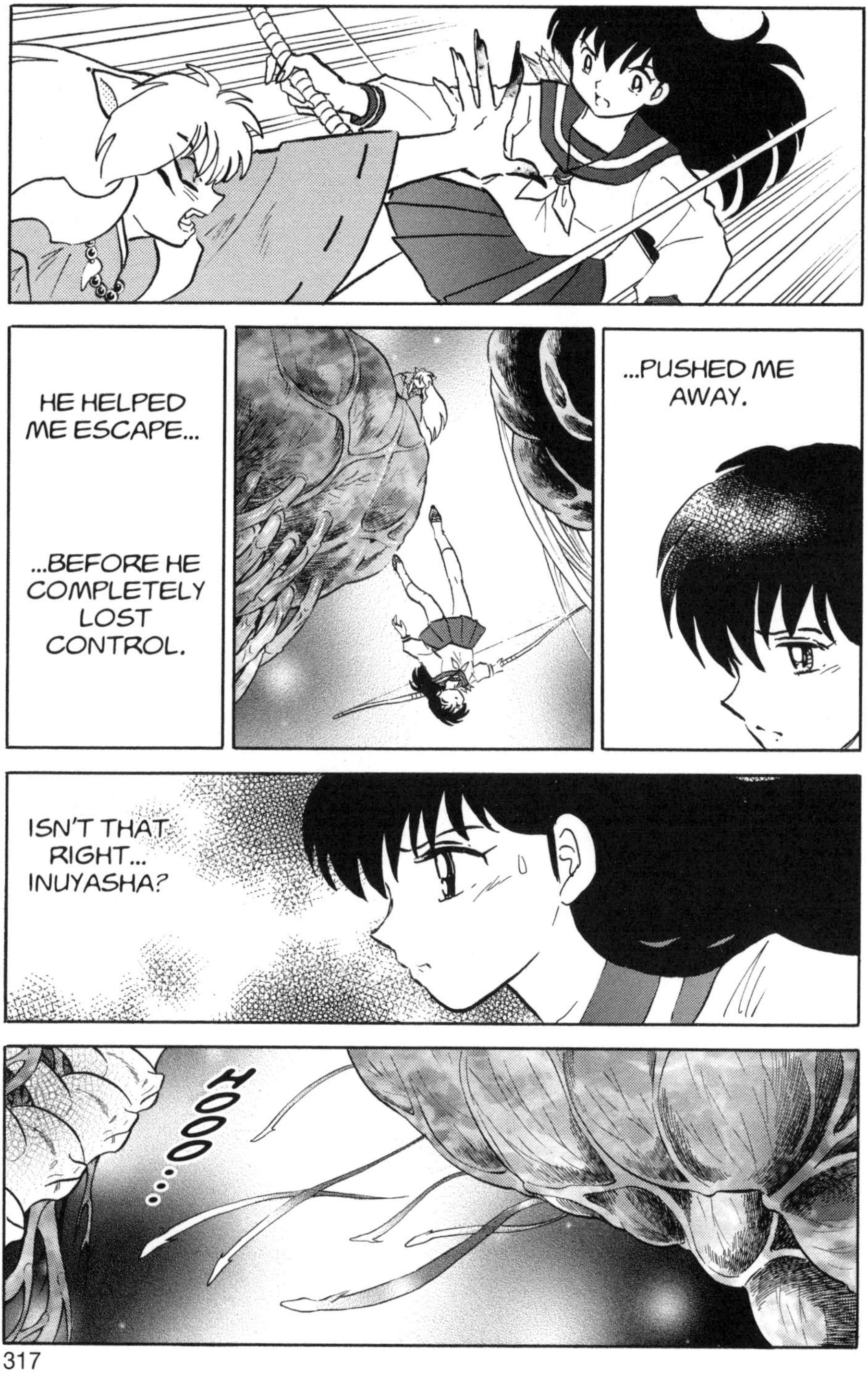
HE HELPED ME ESCAPE...
...BEFORE HE COMPLETELY LOST CONTROL.
...PUSHED ME AWAY.
ISN'T THAT RIGHT... INUYASHA?
HOOO...

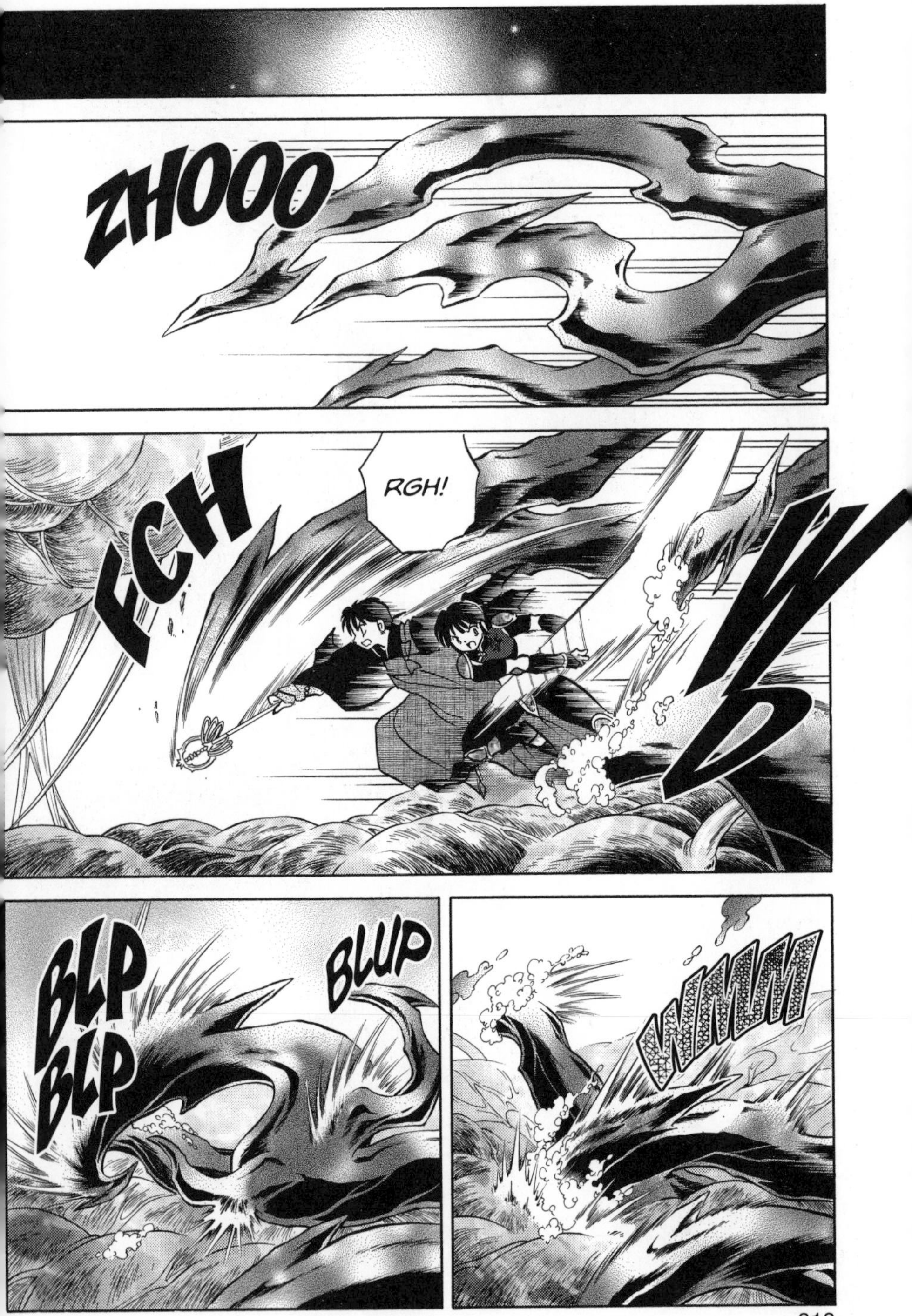
ZHOOO
RGH!
FCH
WMMM
BLUP
BLP BLP

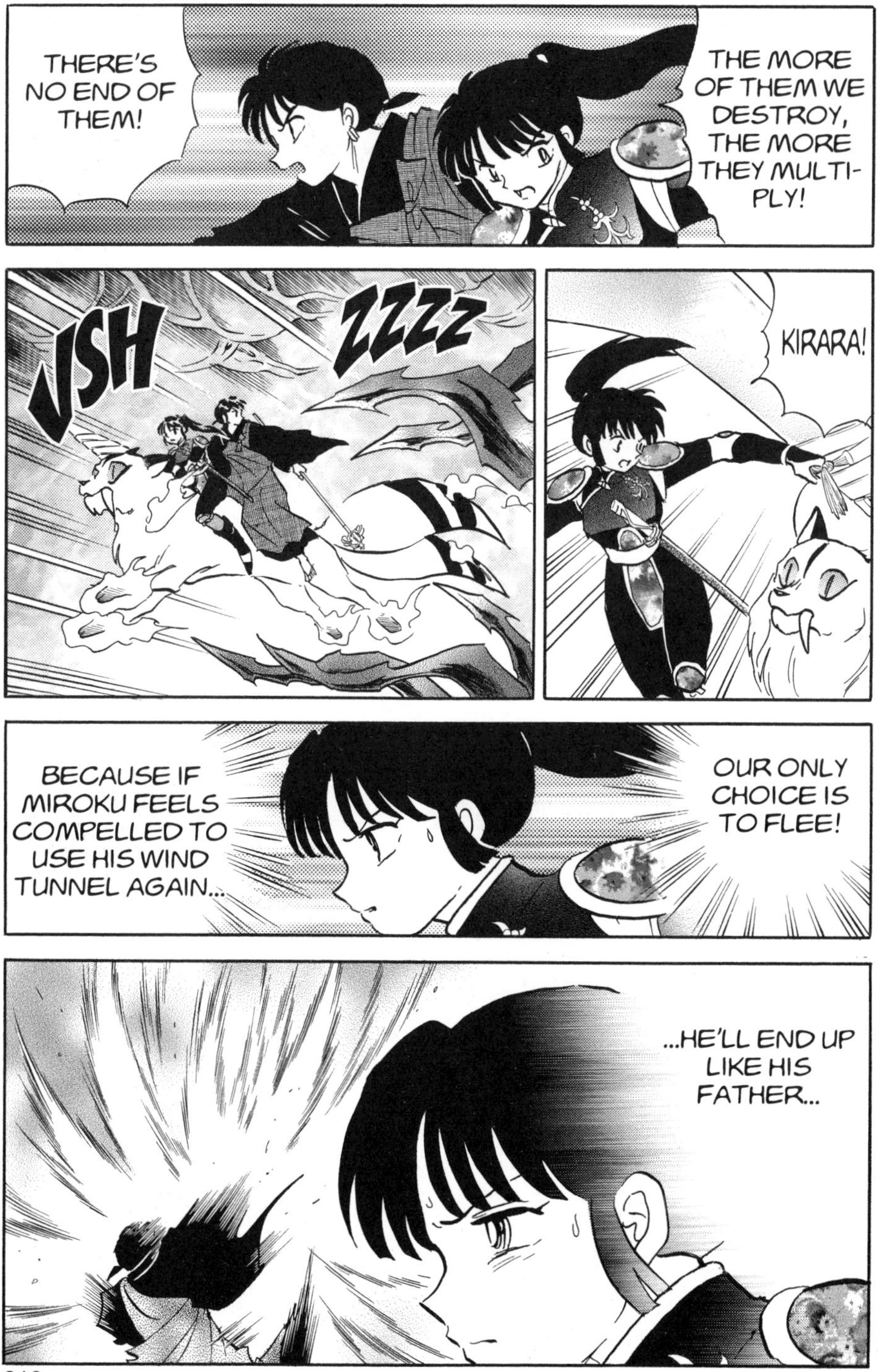
THE MORE OF THEM WE DESTROY, THE MORE THEY MULTIPLY!
THERE'S NO END OF THEM!
KIRARA!
VSH ZZZZ
OUR ONLY CHOICE IS TO FLEE!
BECAUSE IF MIROKU FEELS COMPELLED TO USE HIS WIND TUNNEL AGAIN...
...HE'LL END UP LIKE HIS FATHER...

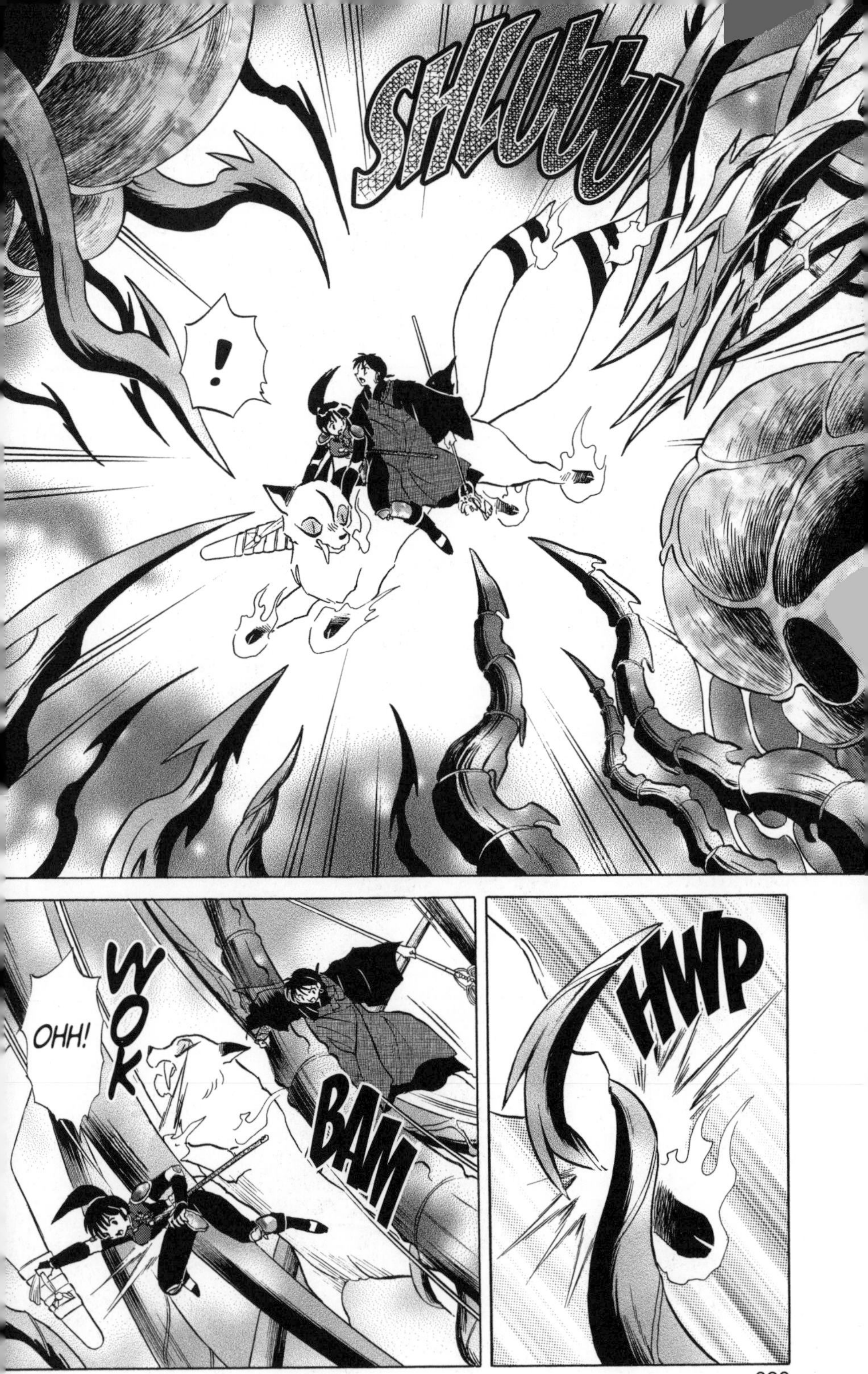
SHLUUU
!
HWP
WOK
OHH!
BAM

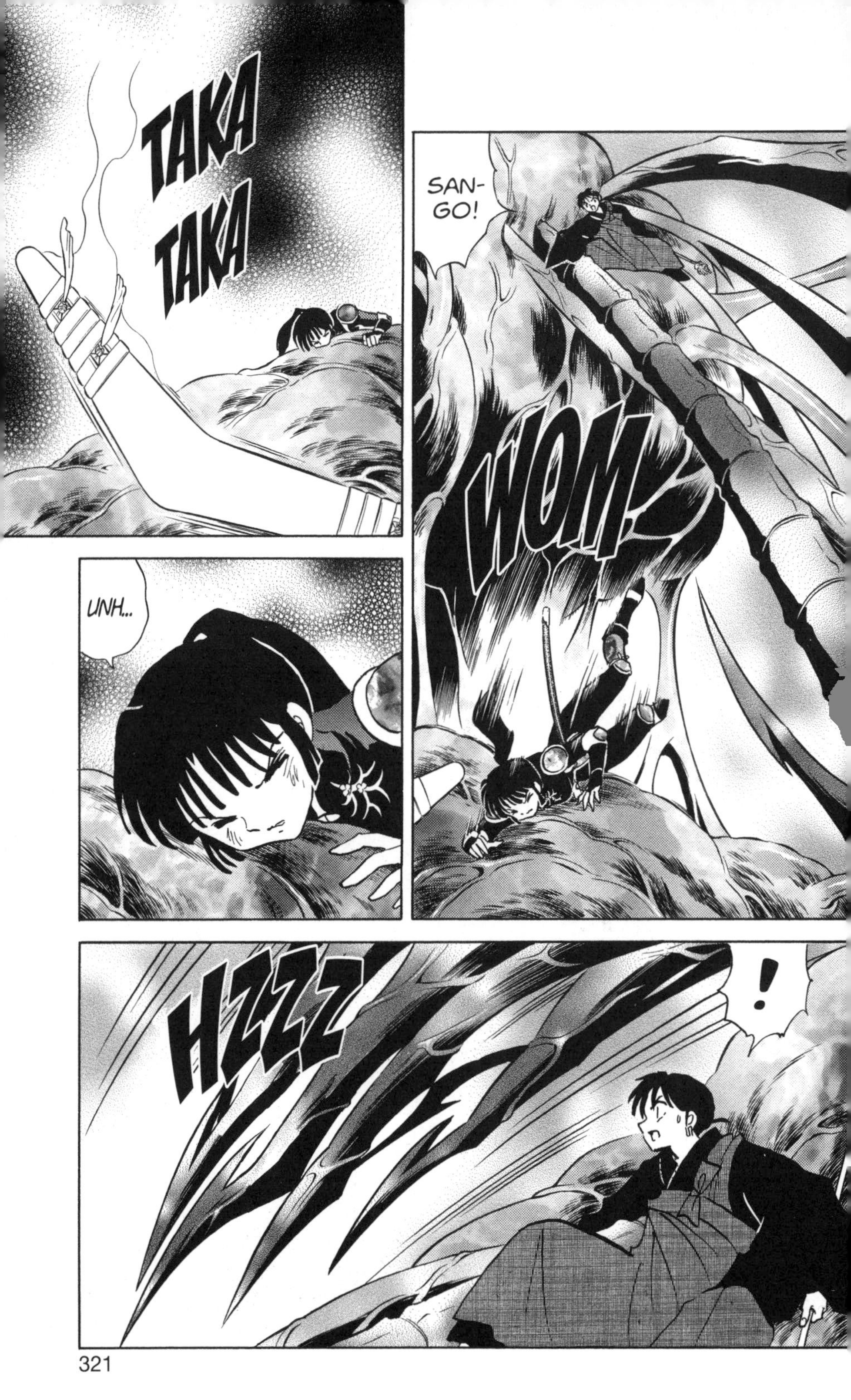
SAN-GO!
WOM
TAKA TAKA
UNH...
!
HZZZ

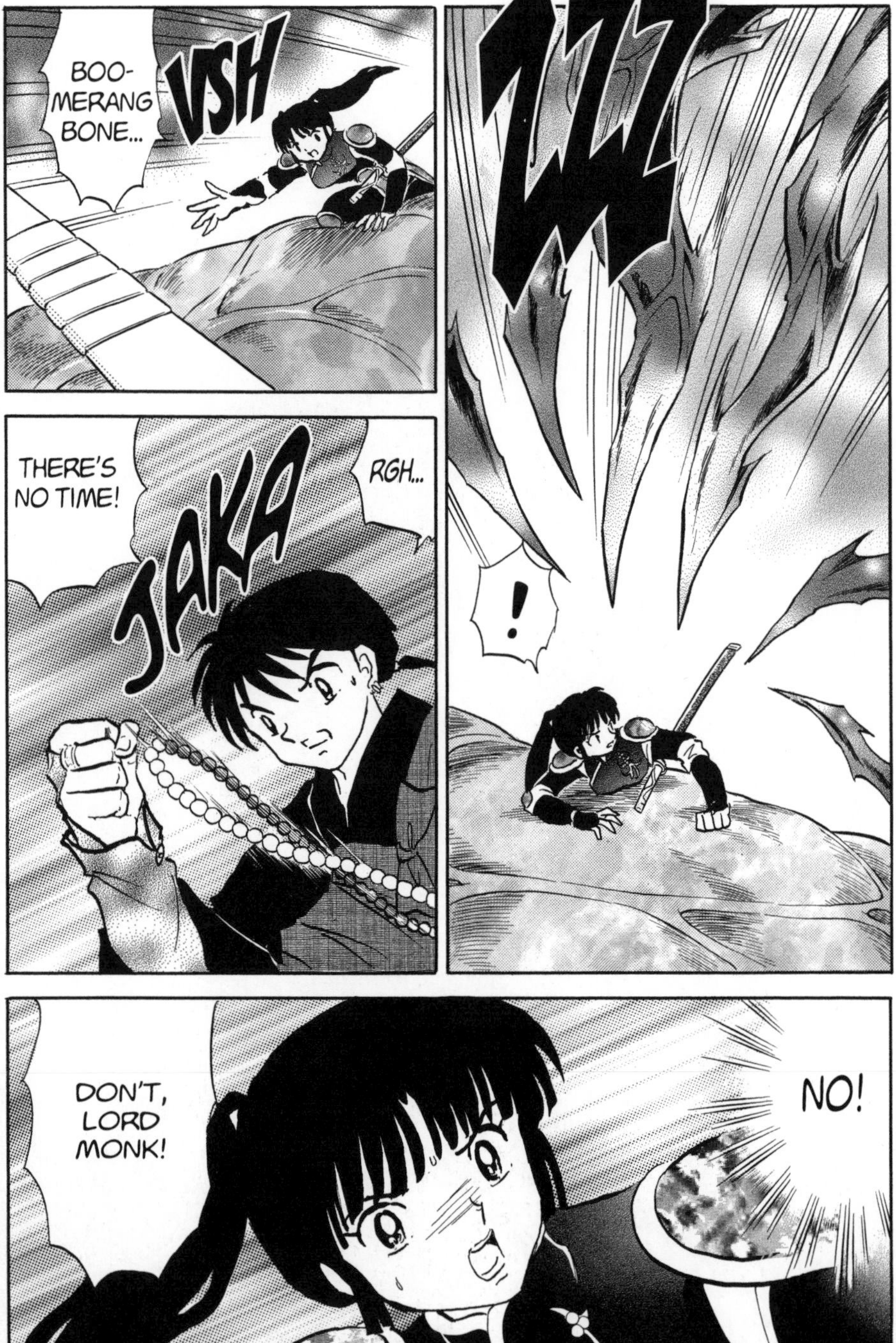
ZZZ
!
VSH
BOO-MERANG BONE...
RGH...
JAKA
THERE'S NO TIME!
NO!
DON'T, LORD MONK!

SCROLL EIGHT
THE WIND TUNNEL'S LIMIT

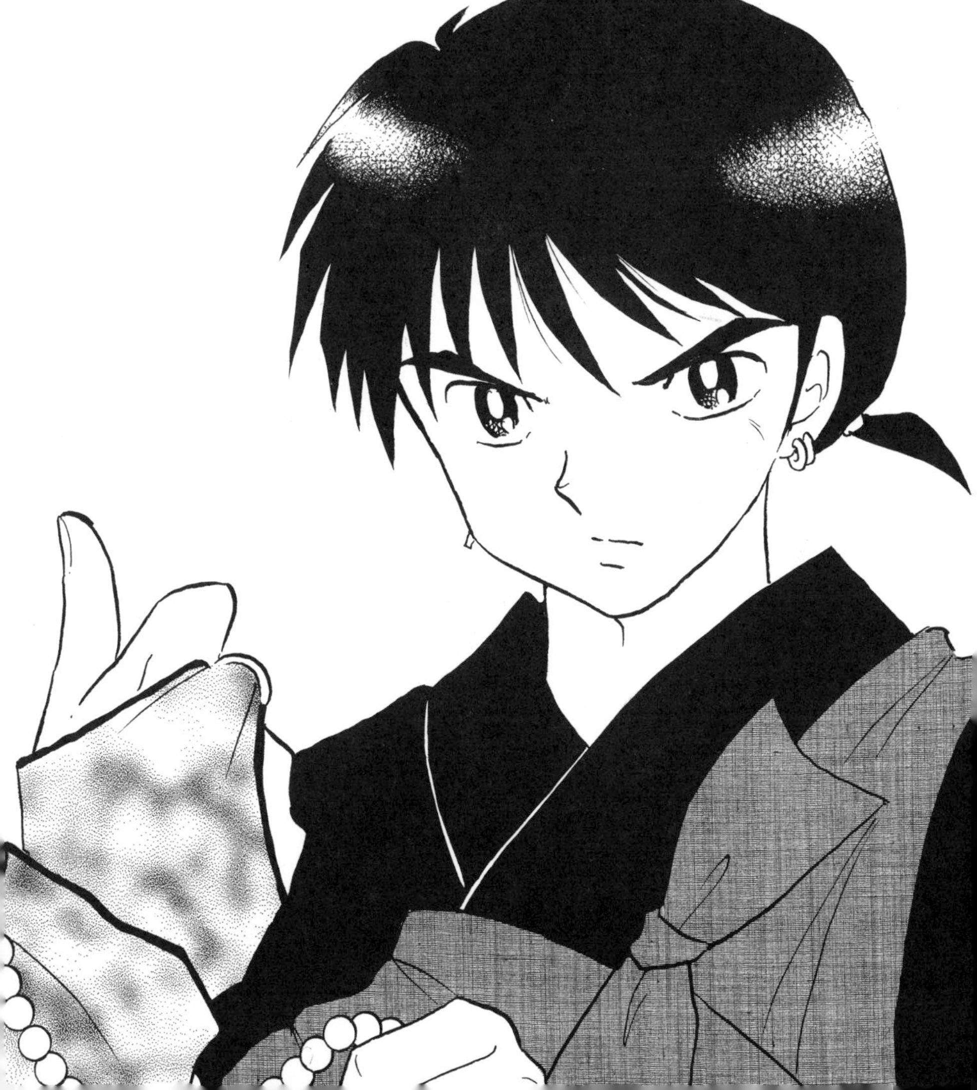

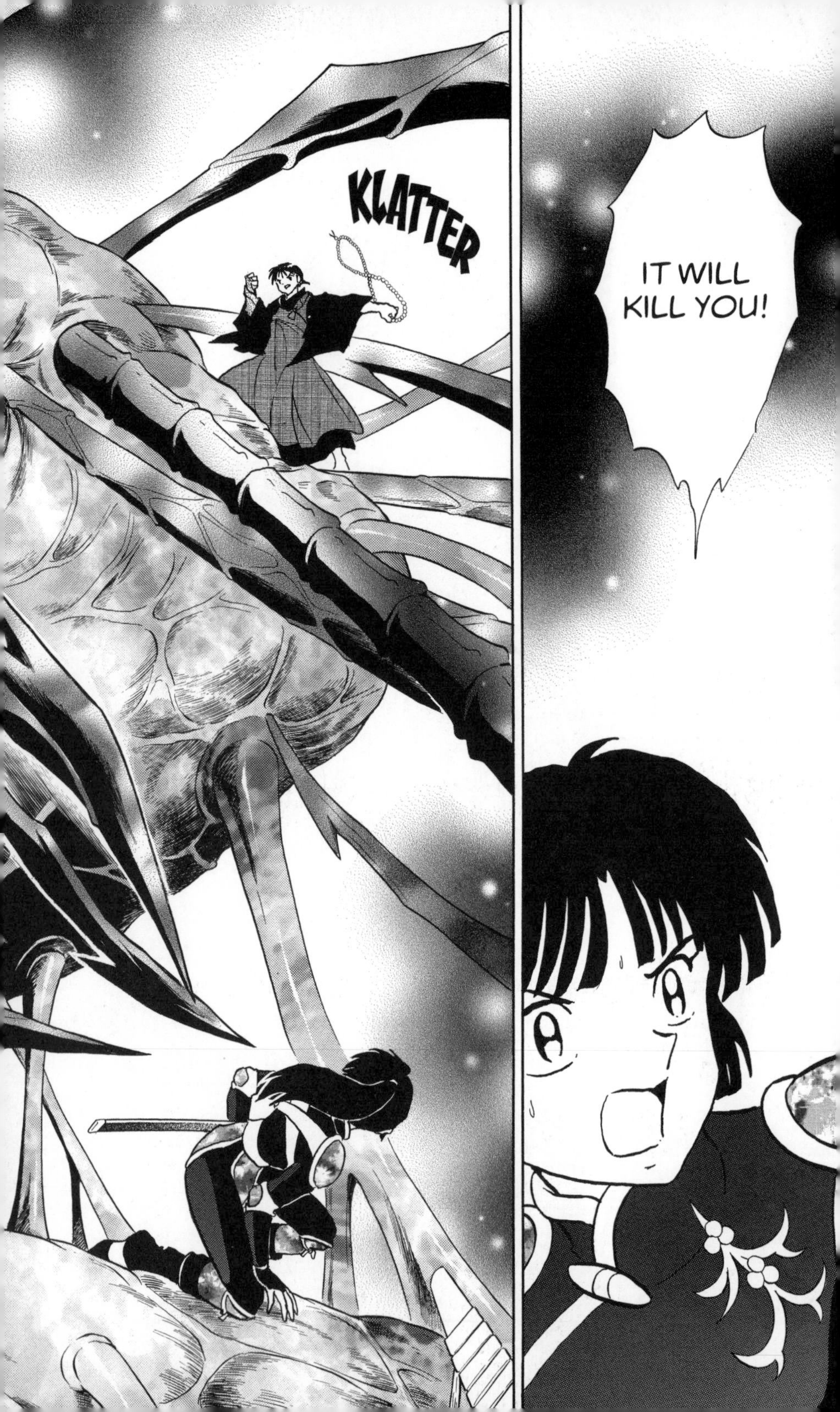
IT WILL KILL YOU!
KLATTER

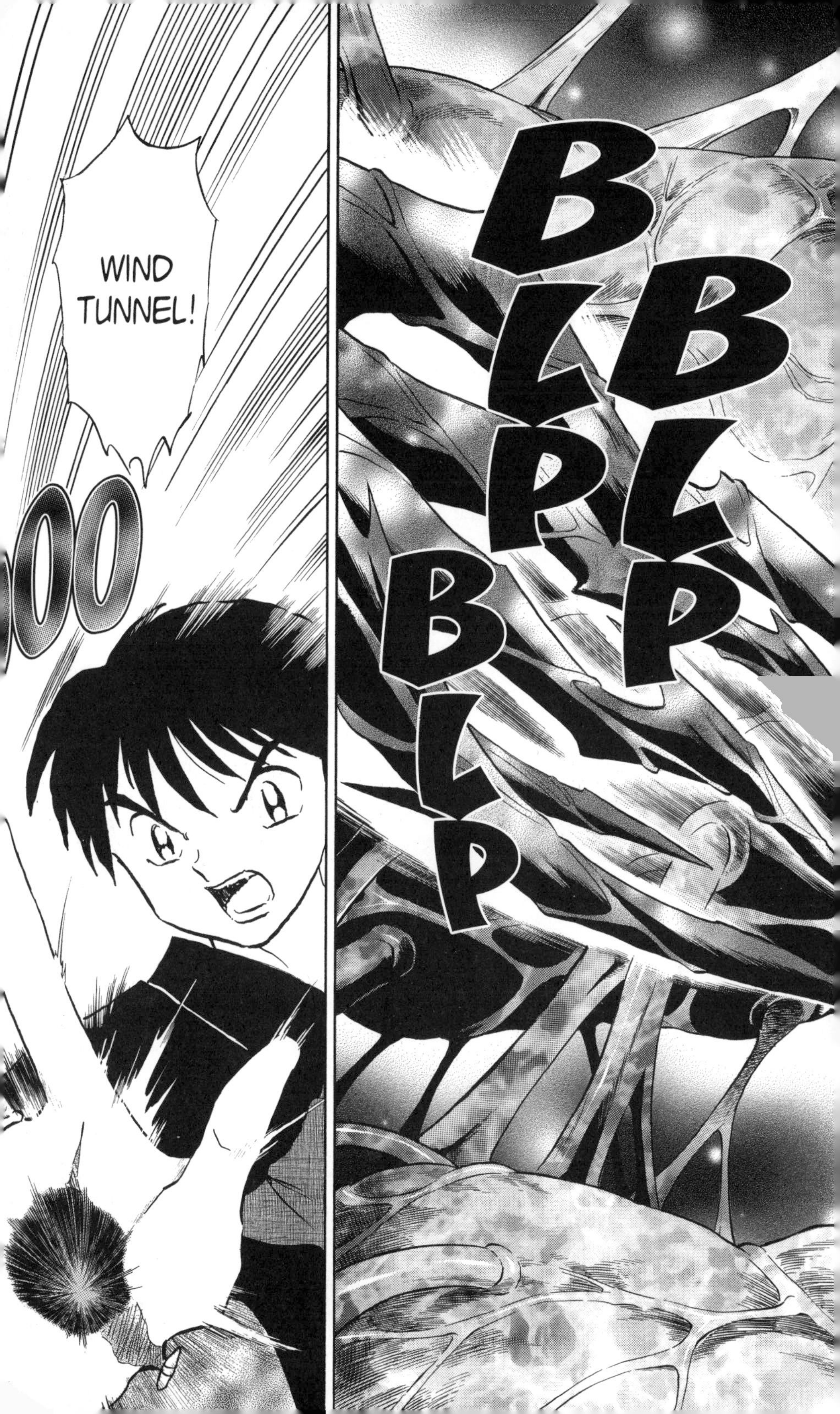
BLP
BLP
BLP
WIND TUNNEL!
OO

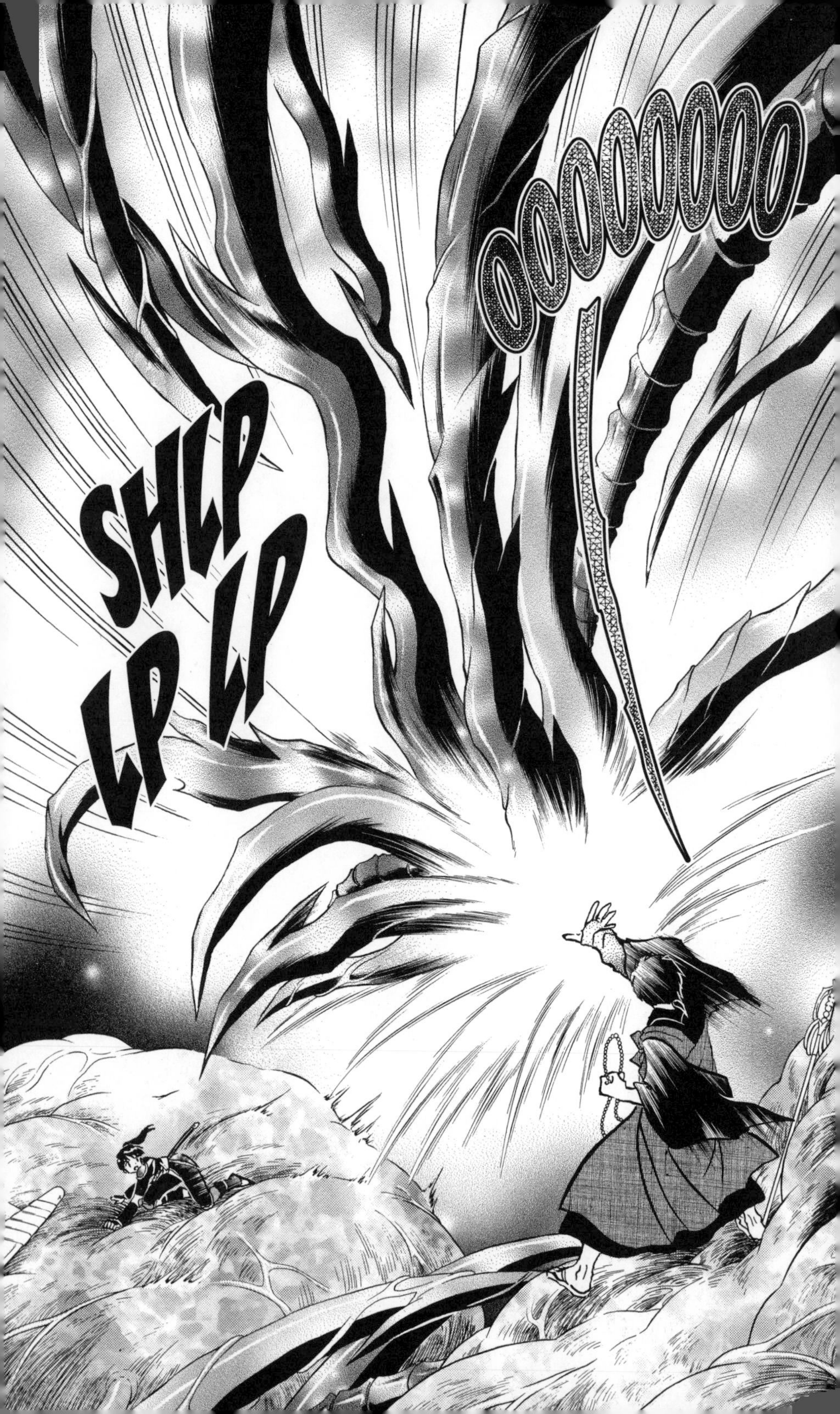

OOOOOOOOO
SHLP LP LP

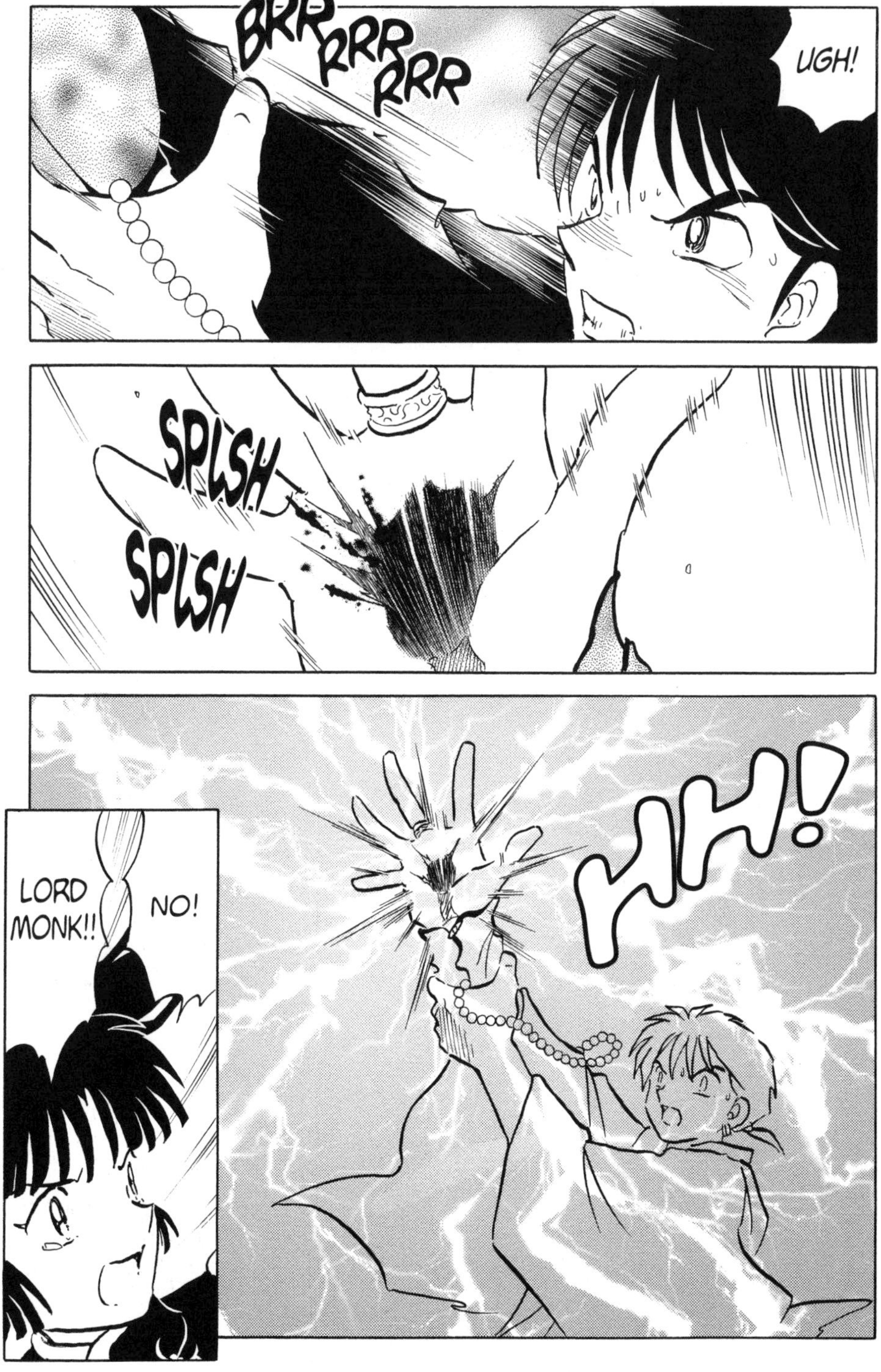
UGH!
BRR RRR RRR
SPLSH
SPLSH
HH!
NO!
LORD MONK!!

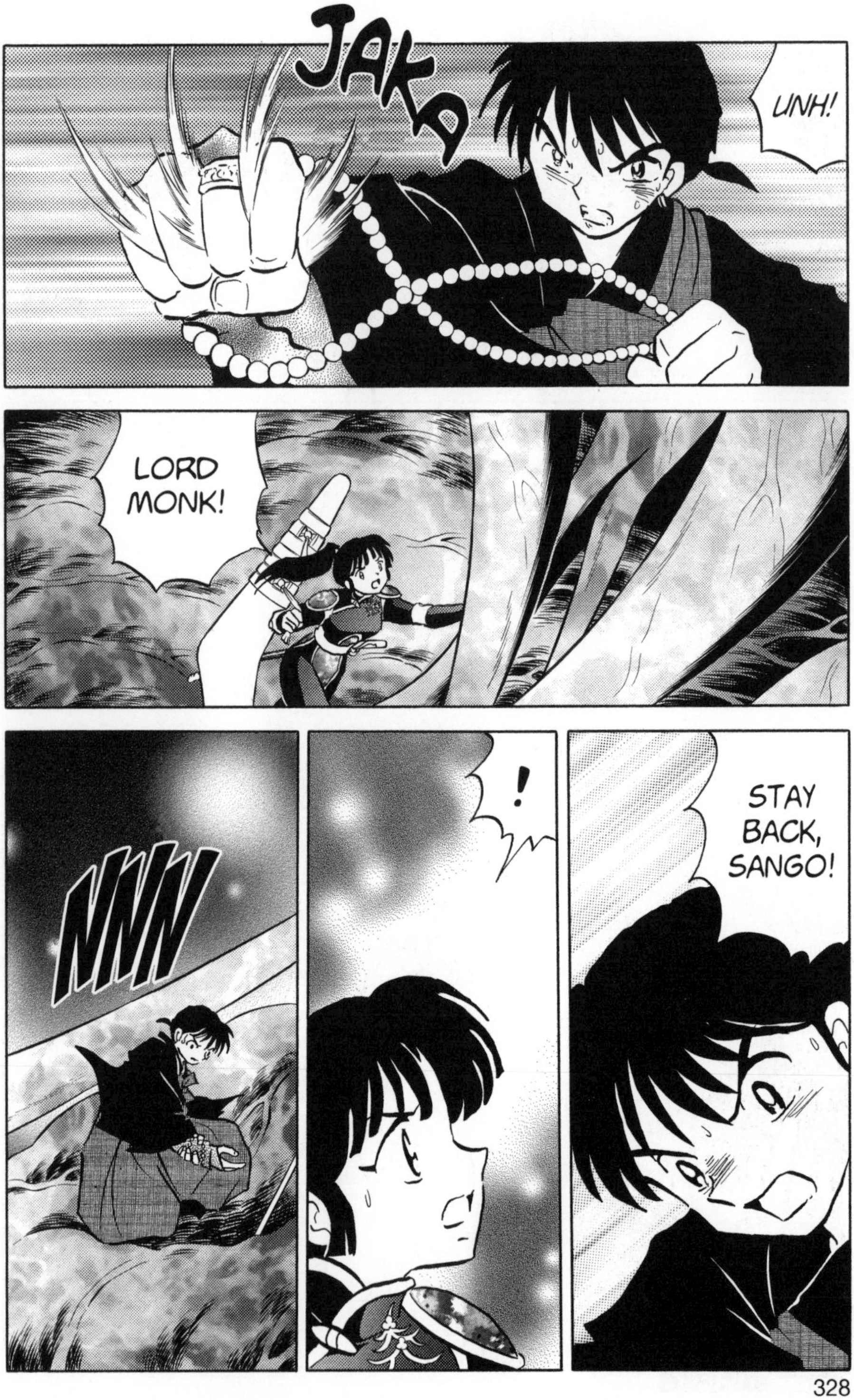
UNH!
JAKA
LORD MONK!
STAY BACK, SANGO!
!
NNN

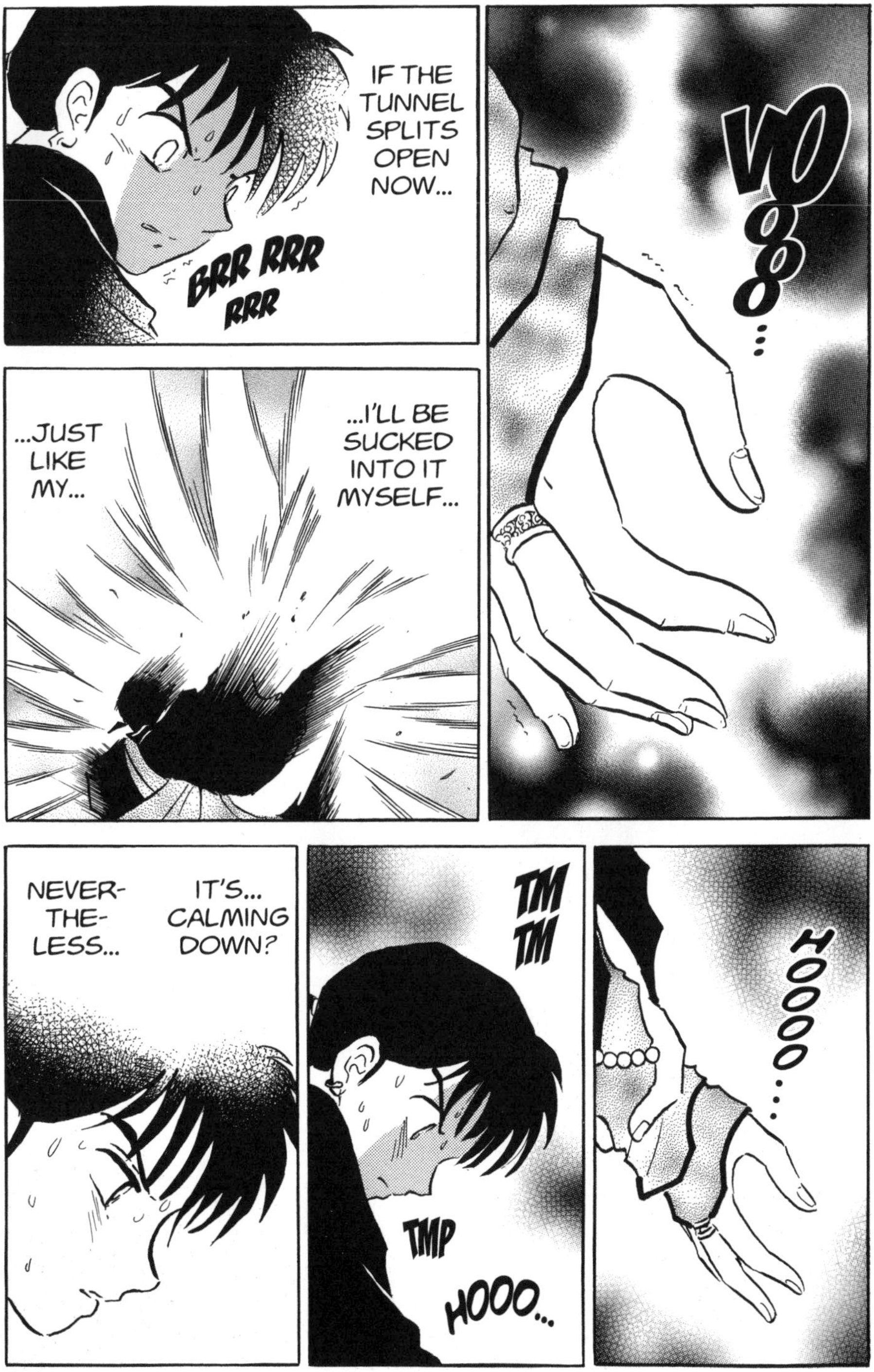
VOOOO...
IF THE TUNNEL SPLITS OPEN NOW...
BRR RRR RRR
...I'LL BE SUCKED INTO IT MYSELF...
...JUST LIKE MY...
HOOOOO...
TM TM
TMP
HOOO...
IT'S... CALMING DOWN?
NEVER-THE-LESS...

LORD MONK...

SKWK

...THE TIME...

...HAS COME!!

SANGO... HERE WE MUST PART WAYS.

WHAT...?!

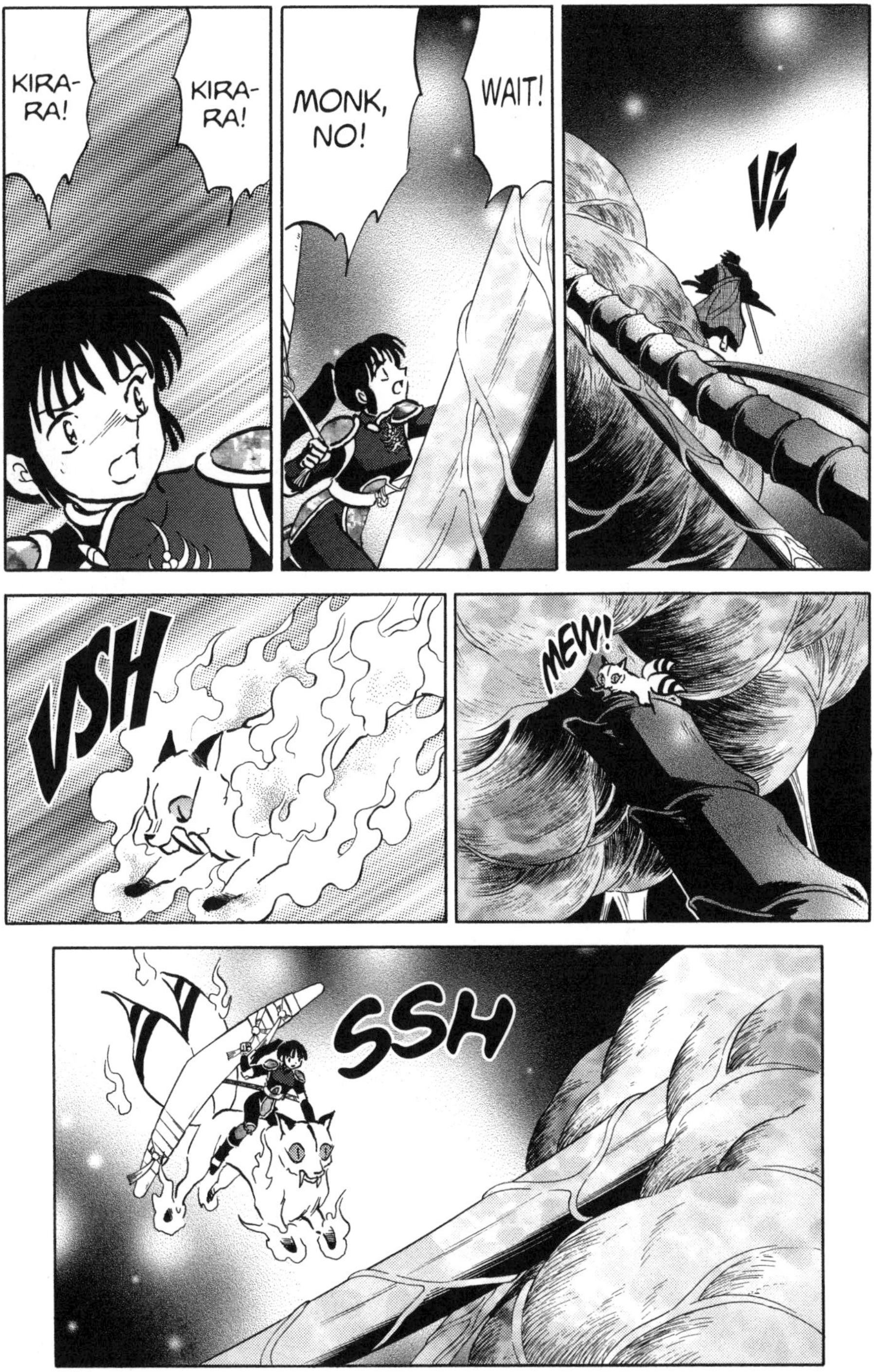
VZ
WAIT!
MONK, NO!
KIRA-RA!
KIRA-RA!
MEW!
VSH
SSH

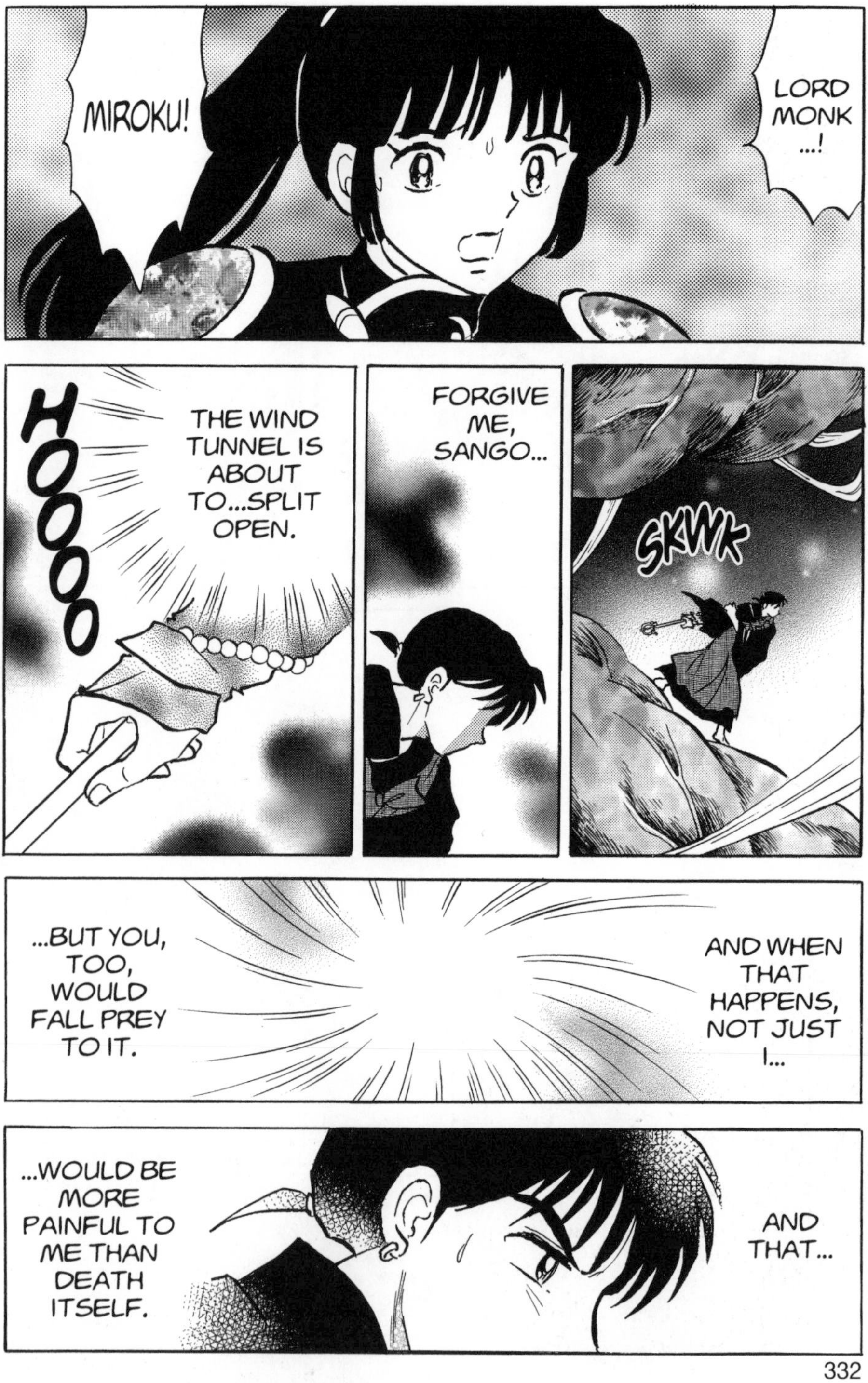
LORD MONK ...!
MIROKU!
SKWK
FORGIVE ME, SANGO...
THE WIND TUNNEL IS ABOUT TO...SPLIT OPEN.
HOOOO
AND WHEN THAT HAPPENS, NOT JUST I...
...BUT YOU, TOO, WOULD FALL PREY TO IT.
AND THAT...
...WOULD BE MORE PAINFUL TO ME THAN DEATH ITSELF.

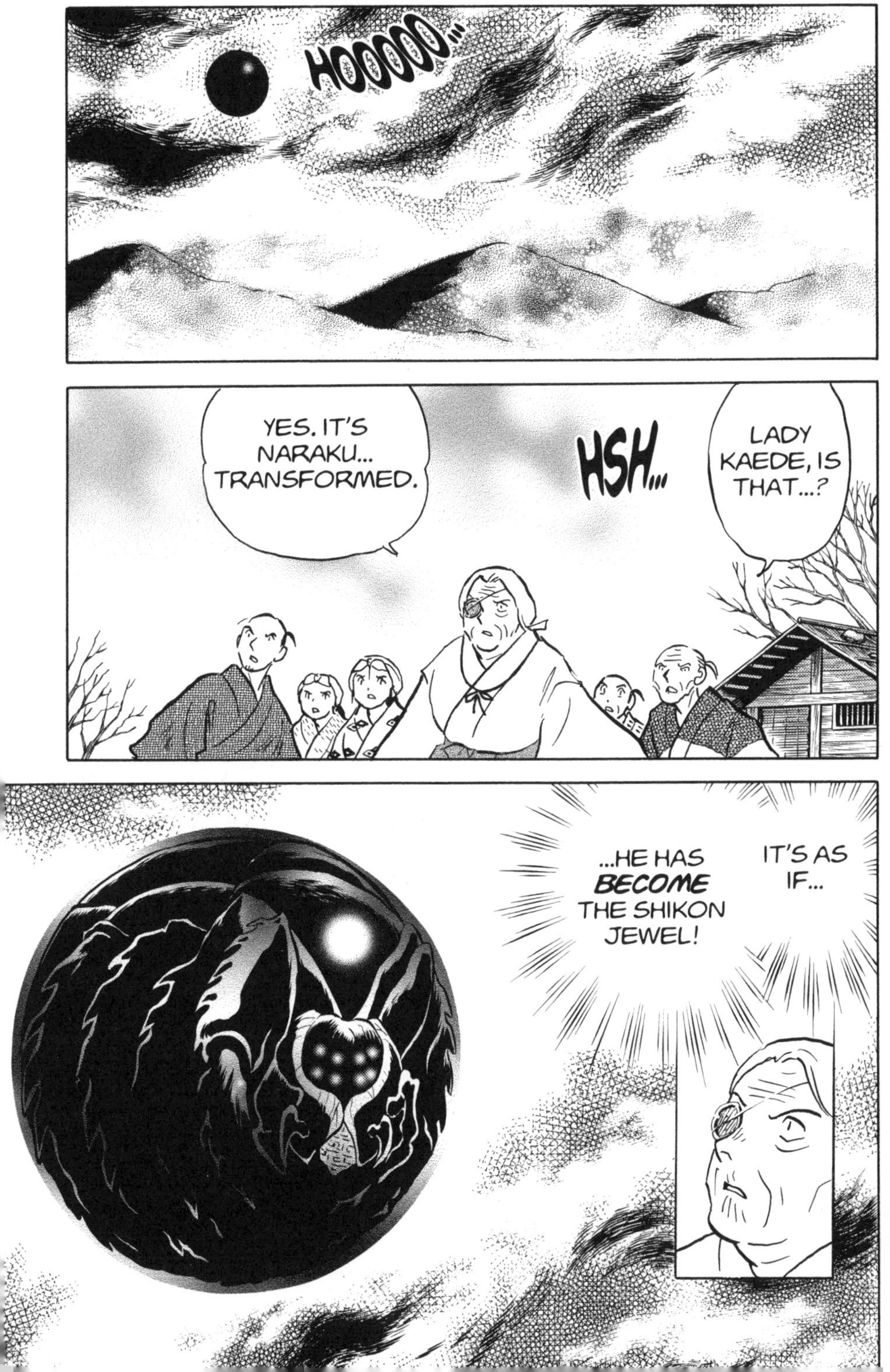
HOOOOO...
LADY KAEDE, IS THAT...?
HSH...
YES. IT'S NARAKU... TRANSFORMED.
IT'S AS IF...
...HE HAS *BECOME* THE SHIKON JEWEL!

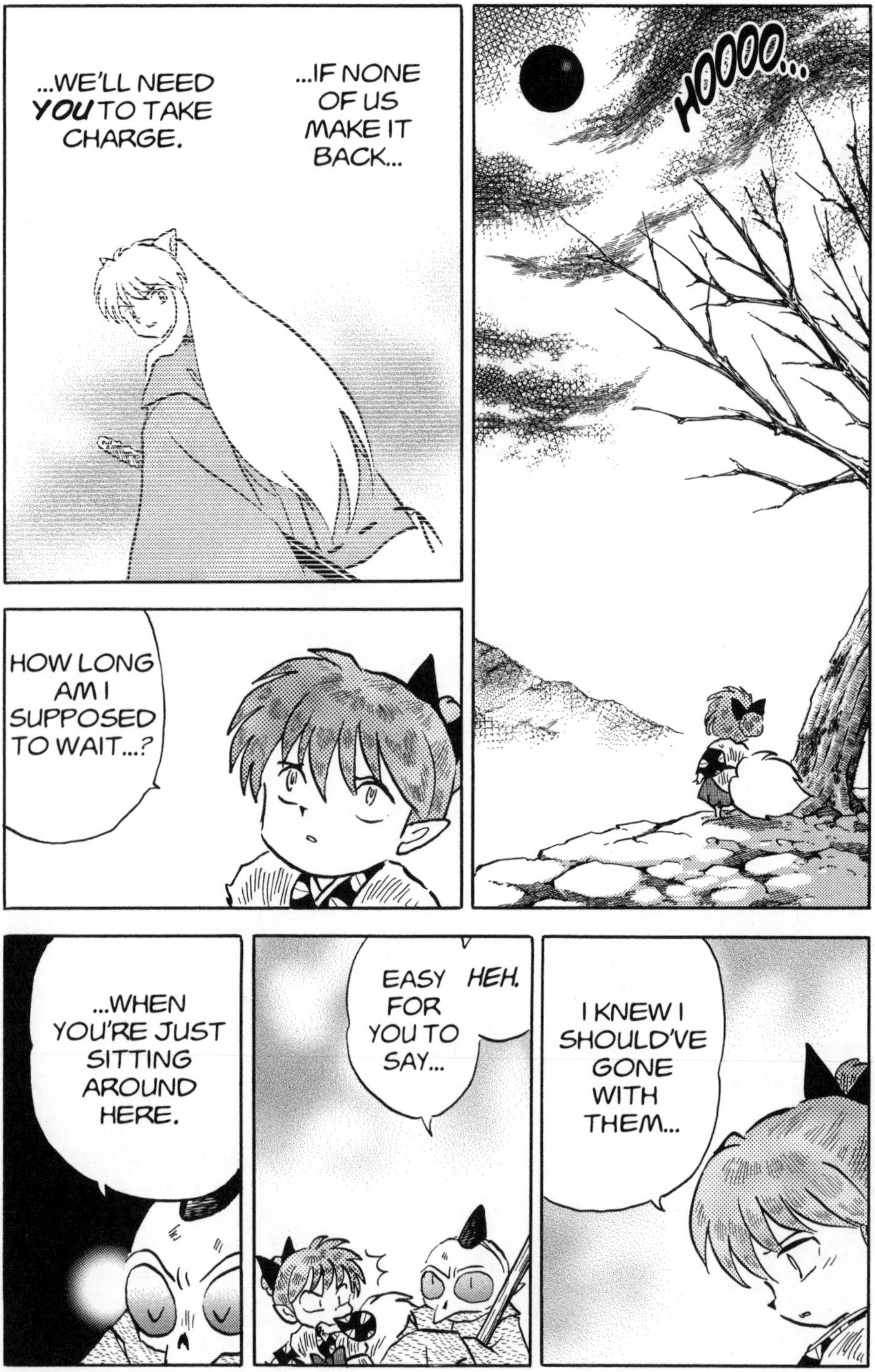
HOOOO...
...IF NONE OF US MAKE IT BACK...
...WE'LL NEED **YOU** TO TAKE CHARGE.
HOW LONG AM I SUPPOSED TO WAIT...?
I KNEW I SHOULD'VE GONE WITH THEM...
HEH.
EASY FOR YOU TO SAY...
...WHEN YOU'RE JUST SITTING AROUND HERE.

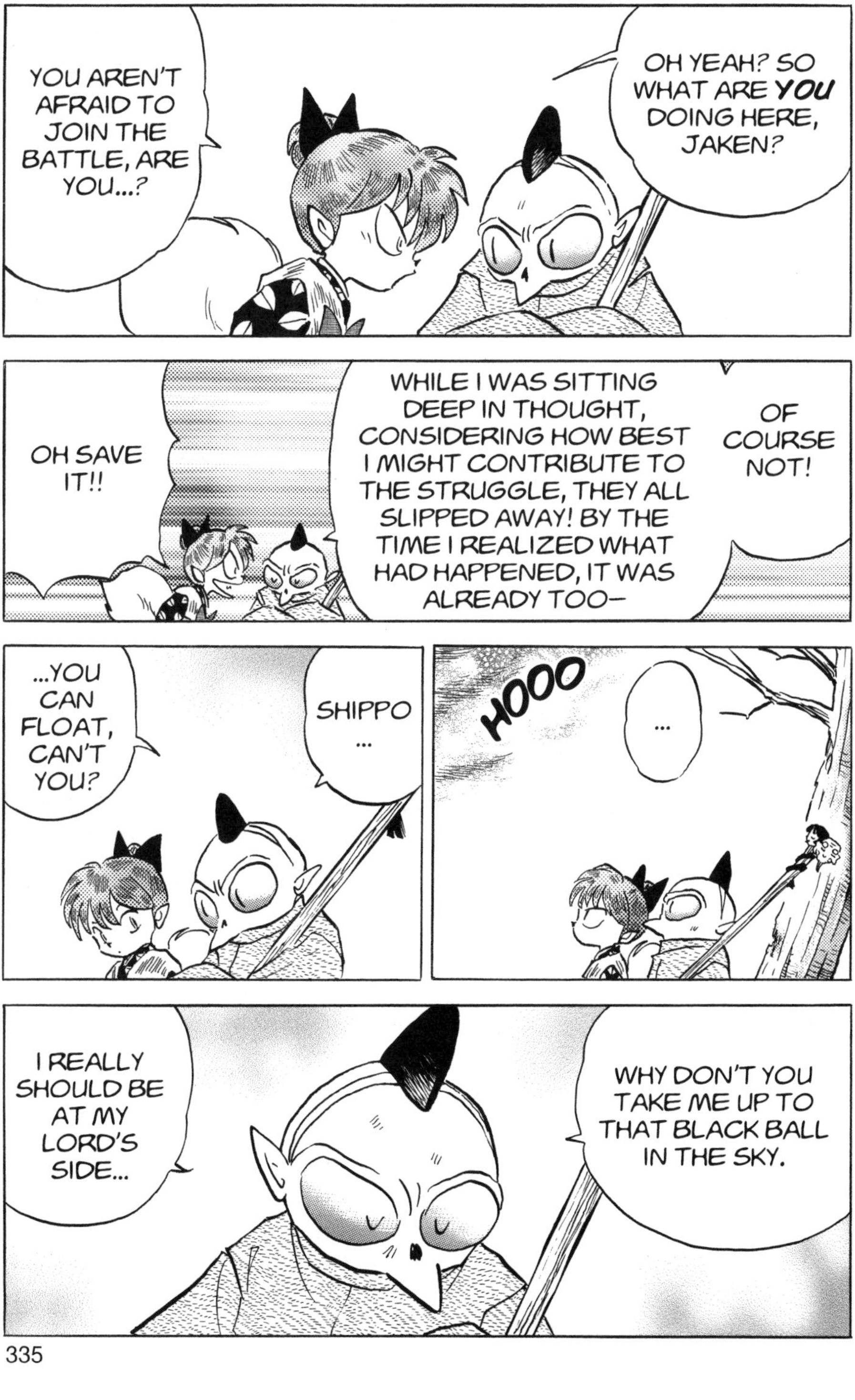
OH YEAH? SO WHAT ARE **YOU** DOING HERE, JAKEN?
YOU AREN'T AFRAID TO JOIN THE BATTLE, ARE YOU...?
OF COURSE NOT!
WHILE I WAS SITTING DEEP IN THOUGHT, CONSIDERING HOW BEST I MIGHT CONTRIBUTE TO THE STRUGGLE, THEY ALL SLIPPED AWAY! BY THE TIME I REALIZED WHAT HAD HAPPENED, IT WAS ALREADY TOO–
OH SAVE IT!!
HOOO
...
SHIPPO ...
...YOU CAN FLOAT, CAN'T YOU?
WHY DON'T YOU TAKE ME UP TO THAT BLACK BALL IN THE SKY.
I REALLY SHOULD BE AT MY LORD'S SIDE...

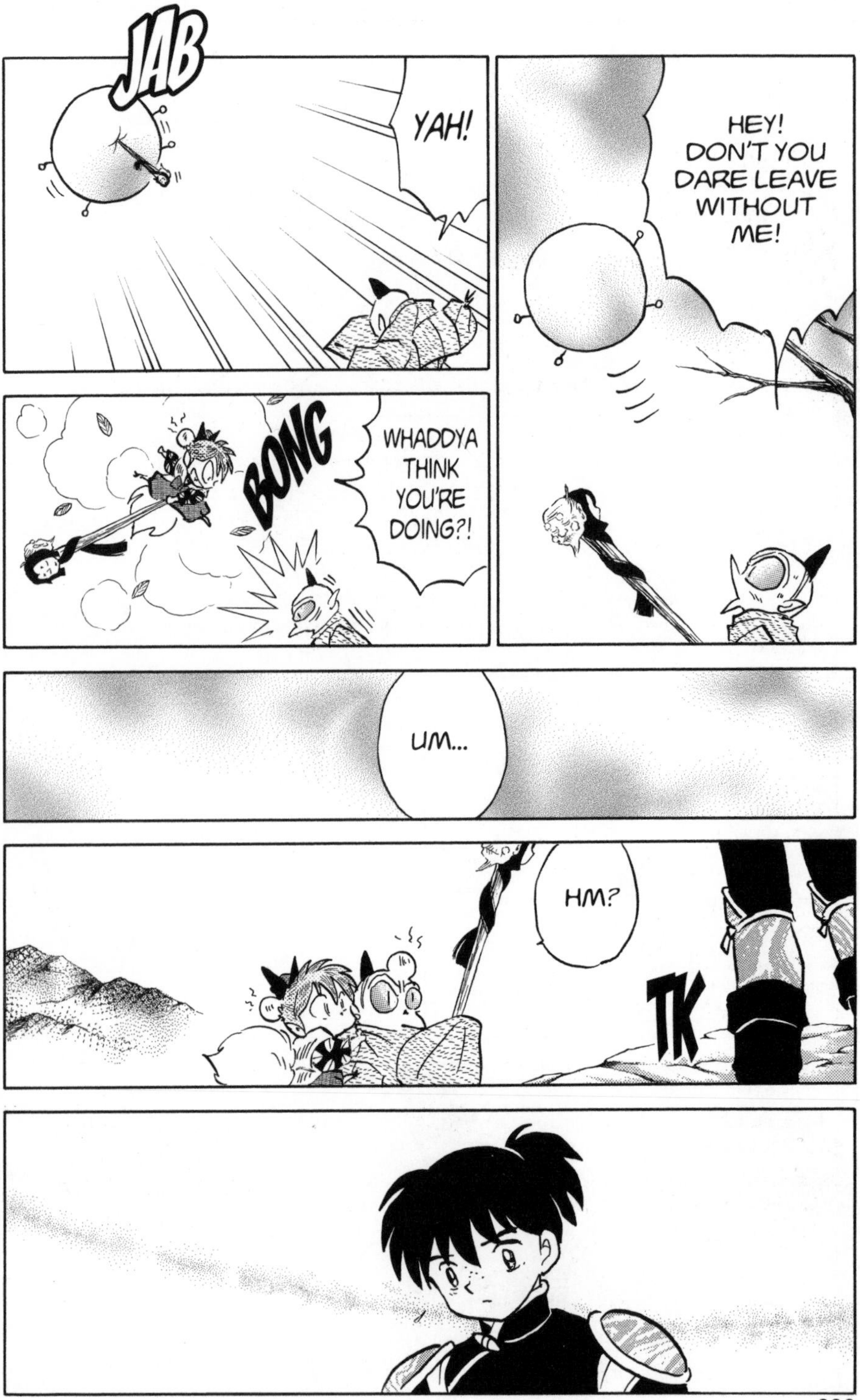
HEY! DON'T YOU DARE LEAVE WITHOUT ME!
JAB
YAH!
WHADDYA THINK YOU'RE DOING?!
BONG
UM...
HM?
TK

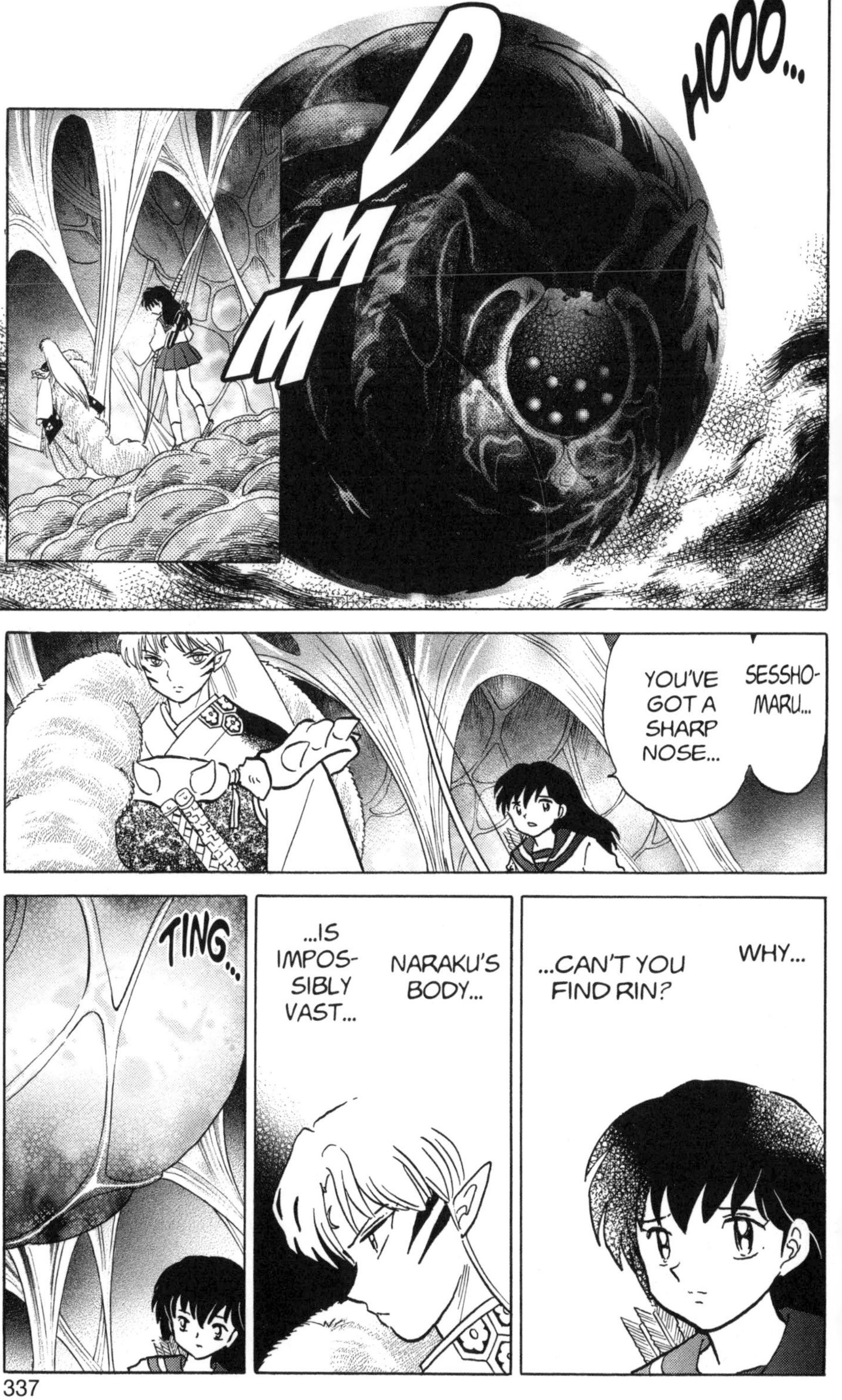
HOOO...
DOMMM
SESSHO-MARU...
YOU'VE GOT A SHARP NOSE...
WHY...
...CAN'T YOU FIND RIN?
NARAKU'S BODY...
...IS IMPOS-SIBLY VAST...
TING...

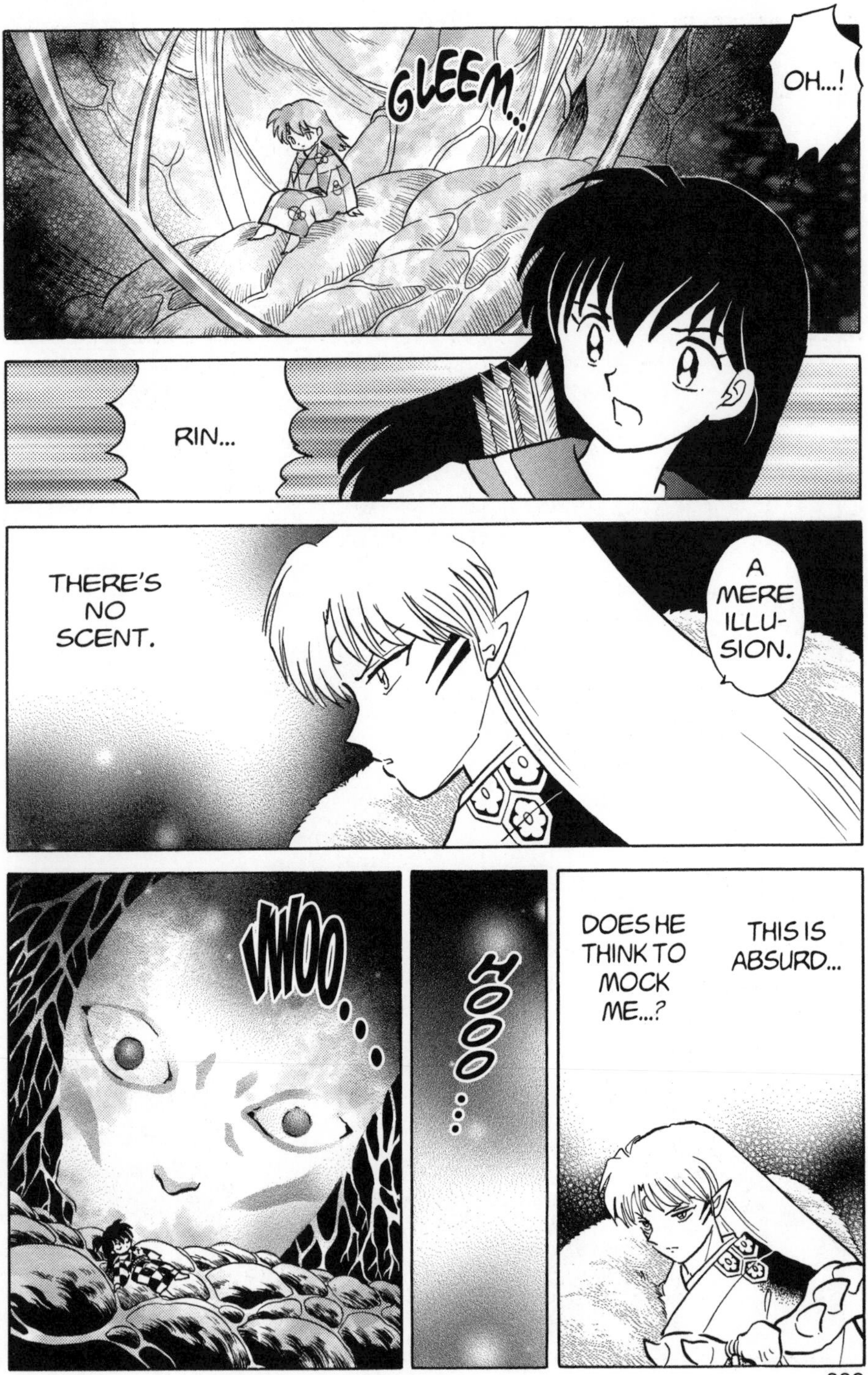
OH...!
GLEEM...
RIN...
A MERE ILLUSION.
THERE'S NO SCENT.
THIS IS ABSURD...
DOES HE THINK TO MOCK ME...?
HOOOO...
WOO....

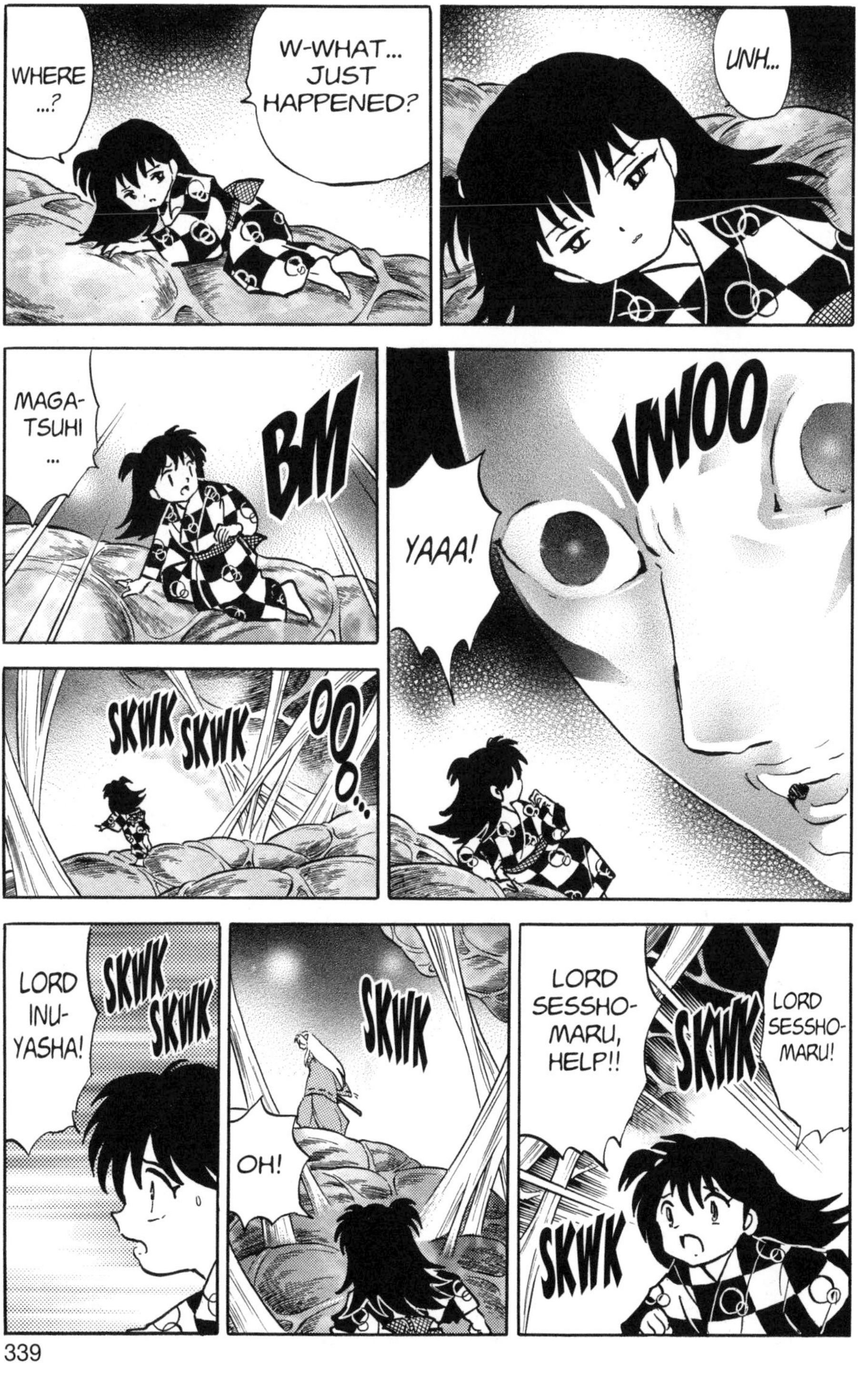
UNH...
W-WHAT... JUST HAPPENED?
WHERE ...?
VWOO
YAAA!
MAGA-TSUHI ...
BM
SKWK SKWK
OOO...
LORD SESSHO-MARU!
SKWK
LORD SESSHO-MARU, HELP!!
SKWK
SKWK
OH!
SKWK SKWK
LORD INU-YASHA!

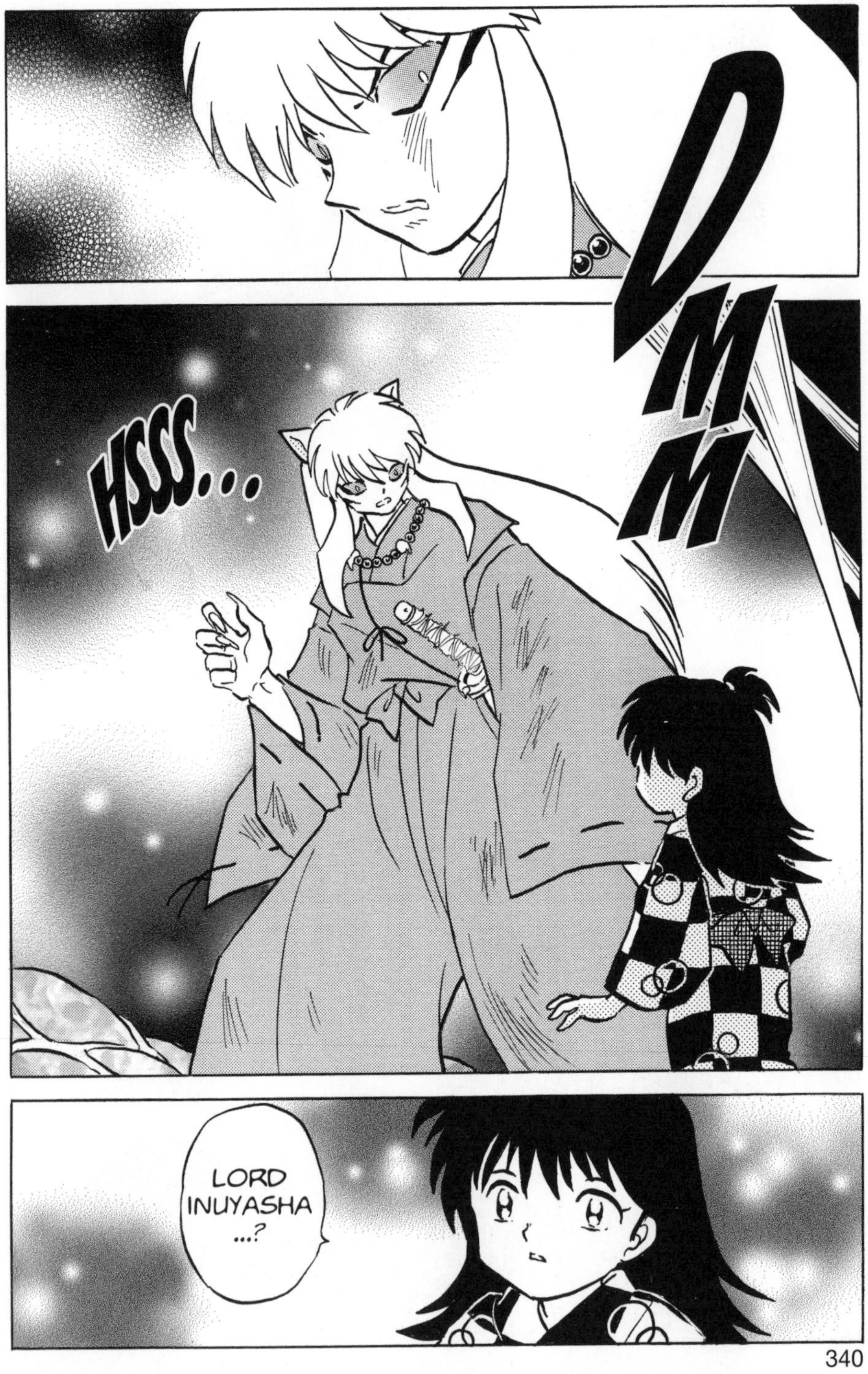
DMMM
HSSS...
LORD INUYASHA ...?

SCROLL NINE
THE LAST BIT OF REASON

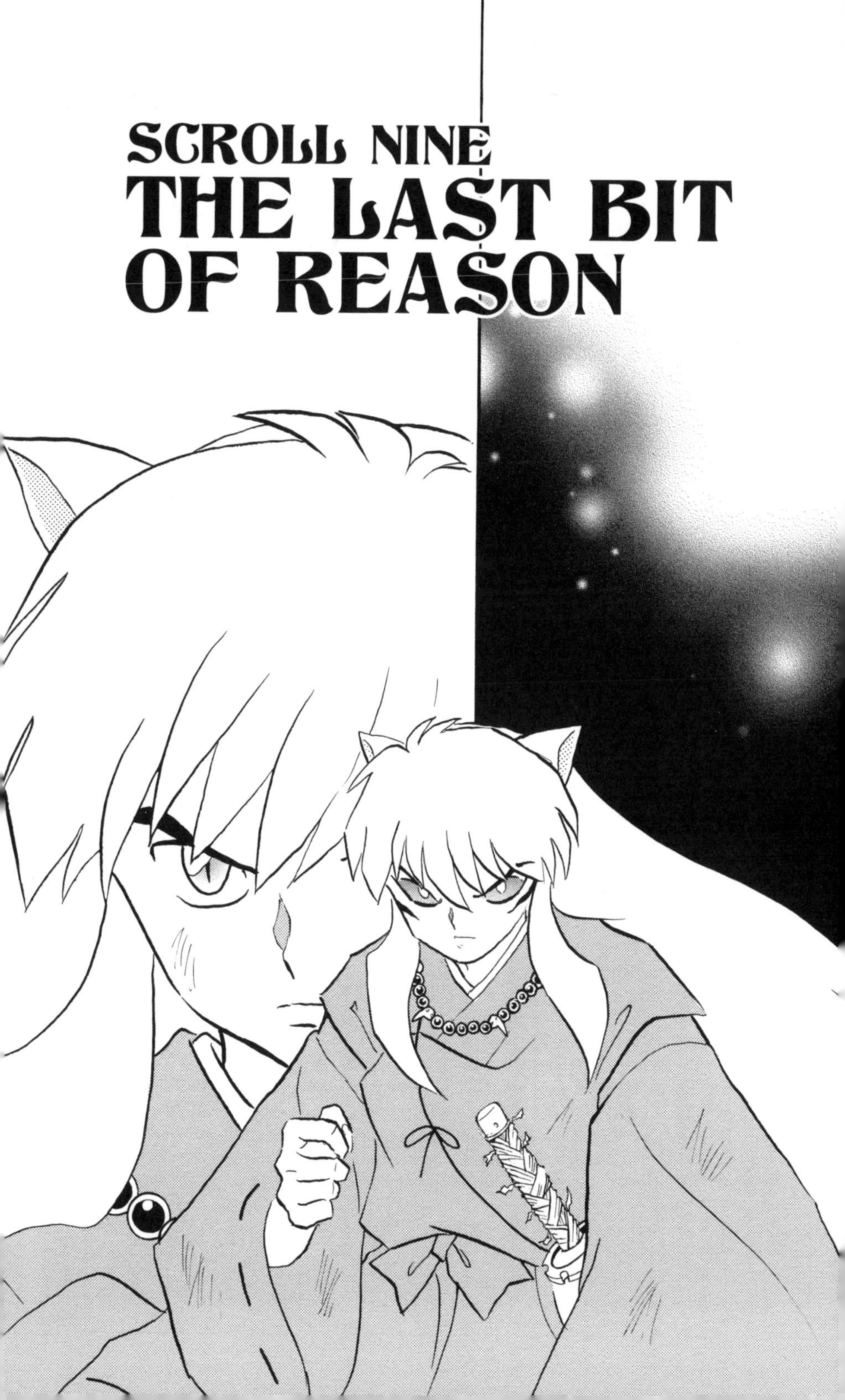

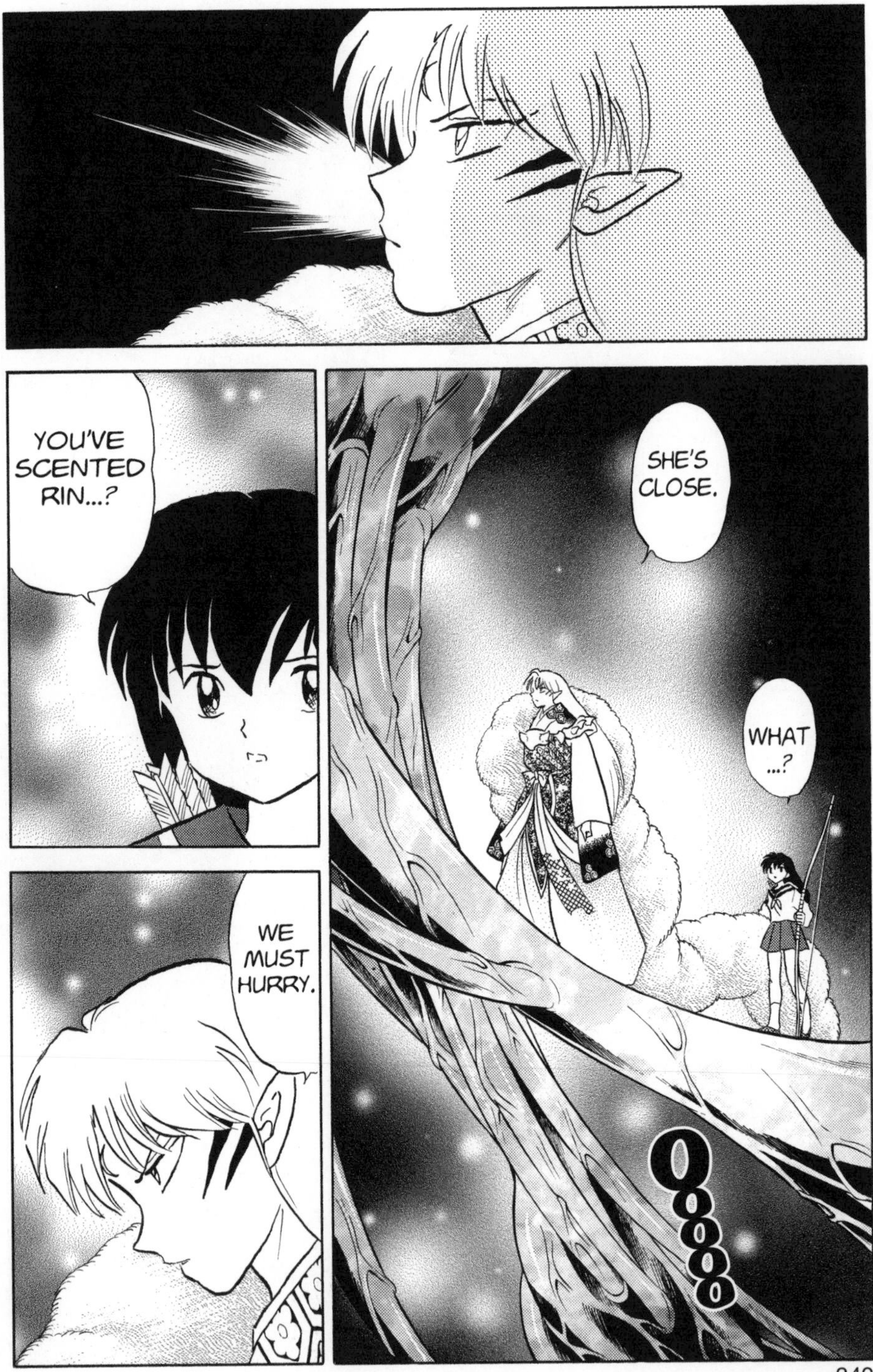
SHE'S CLOSE.
WHAT ...?
Ooooo
YOU'VE SCENTED RIN...?
WE MUST HURRY.

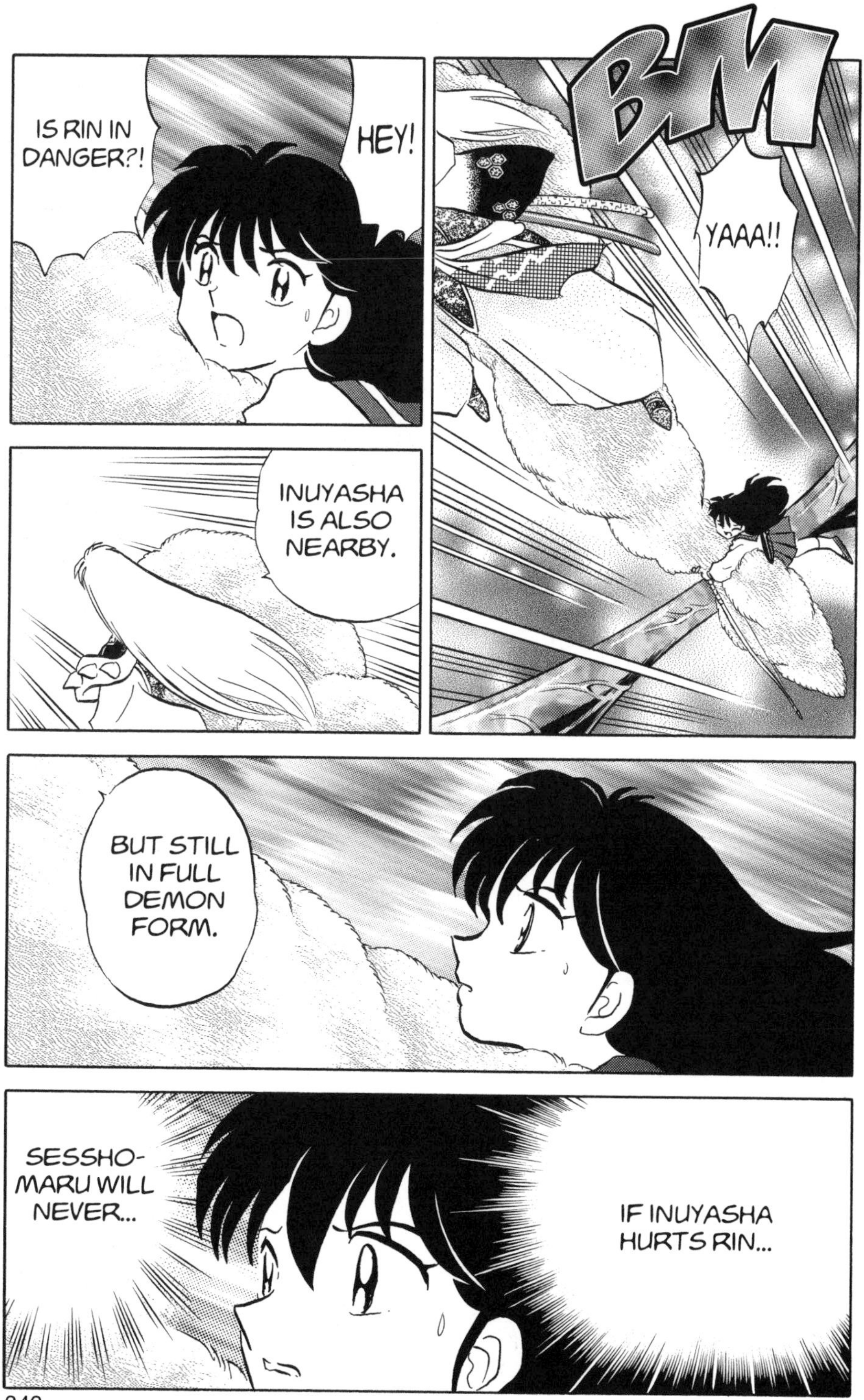
BM
YAAA!!
HEY!
IS RIN IN DANGER?!
INUYASHA IS ALSO NEARBY.
BUT STILL IN FULL DEMON FORM.
IF INUYASHA HURTS RIN...
SESSHO-MARU WILL NEVER...

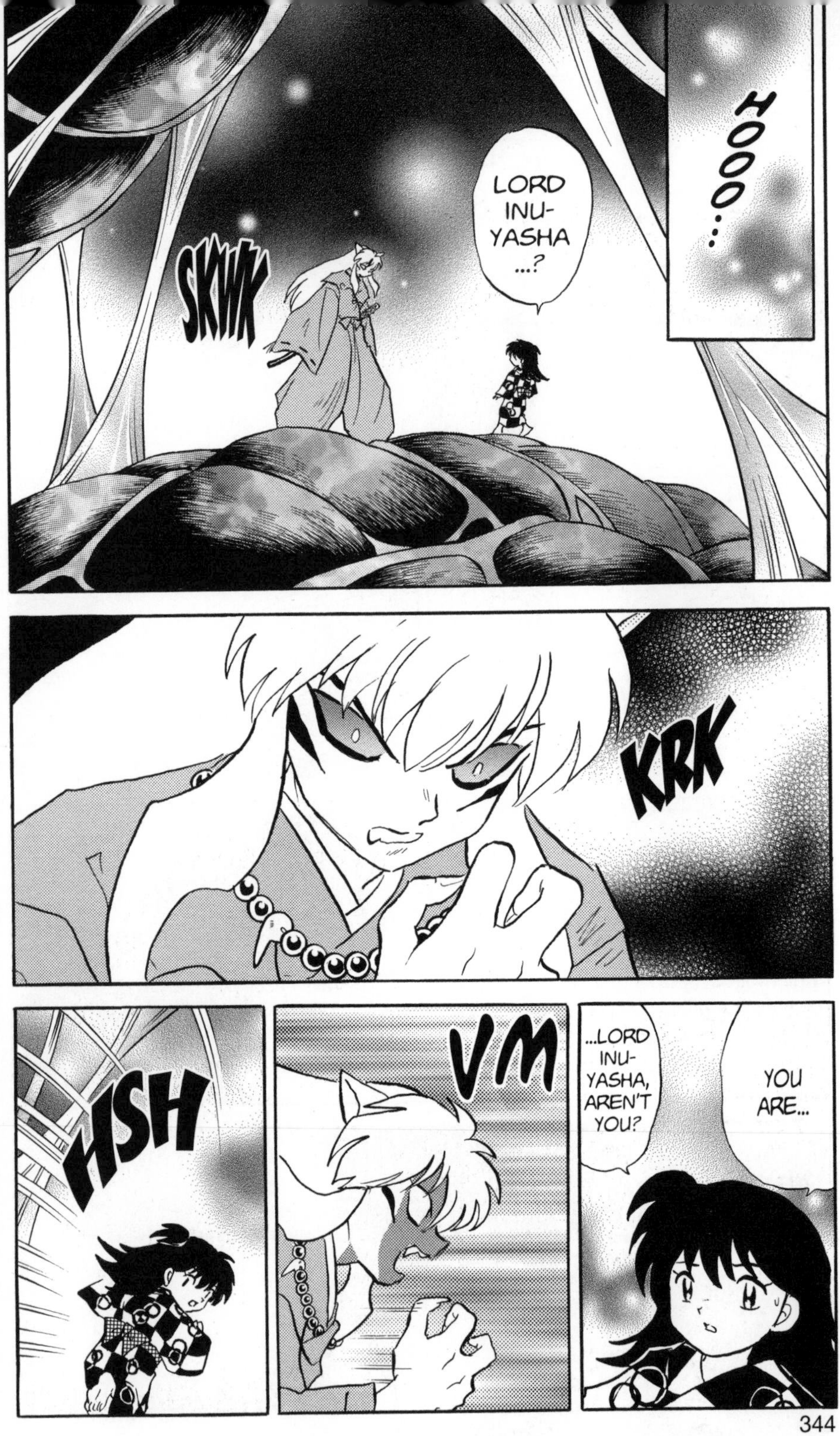
HOOOO...
LORD INU-YASHA ...?
SKWK
KRK
YOU ARE...
...LORD INU-YASHA, AREN'T YOU?
VM
HSH

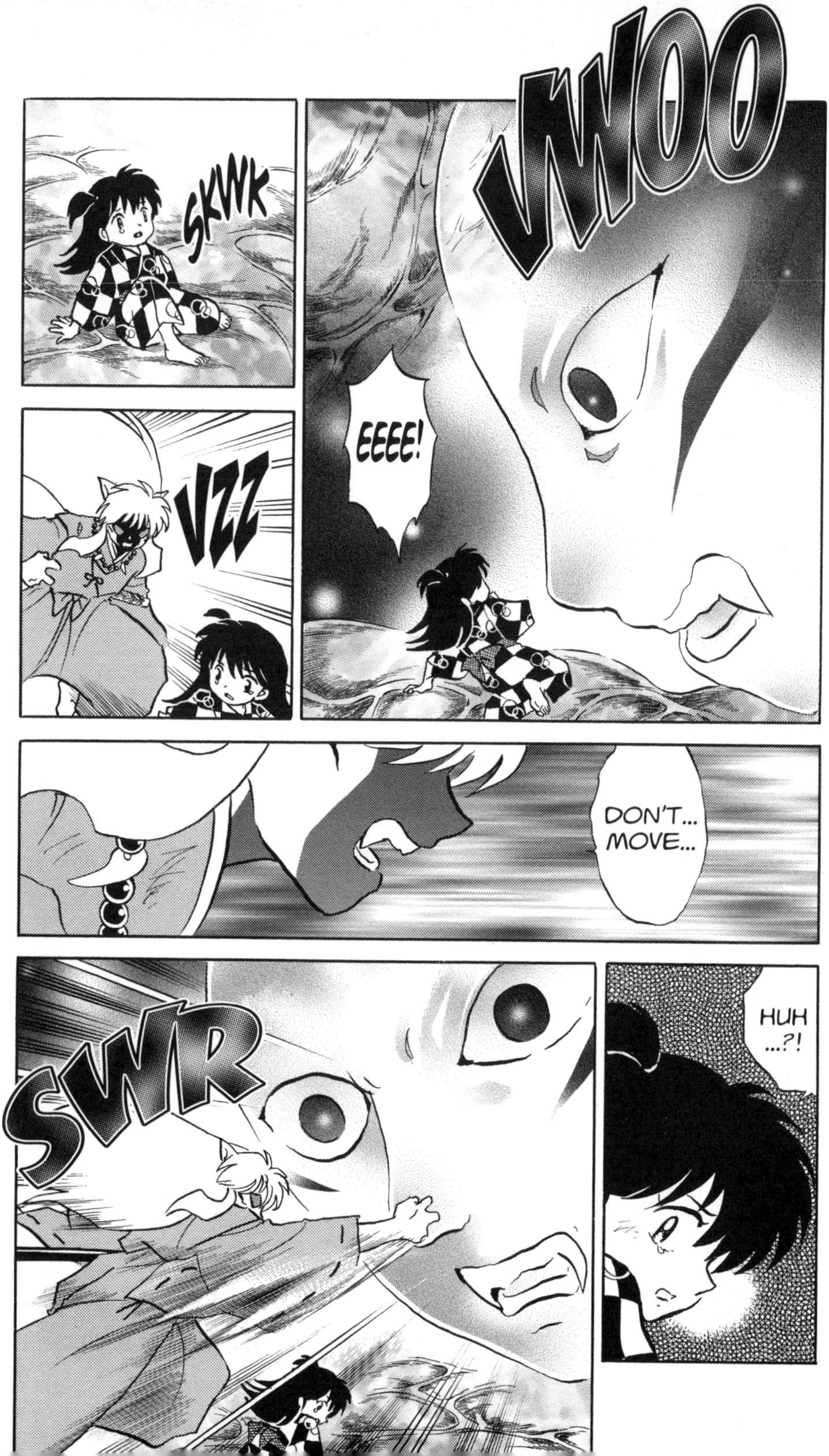
VWOO
EEEE!
SKWK
VZZ
DON'T... MOVE...
HUH ...?!
SWR

LORD INUYASHA...

WOK

HEH HEH HEH...

SKWK

WELL...

STILL A SCRAP OF HUMAN HEART IN YOU, EH?

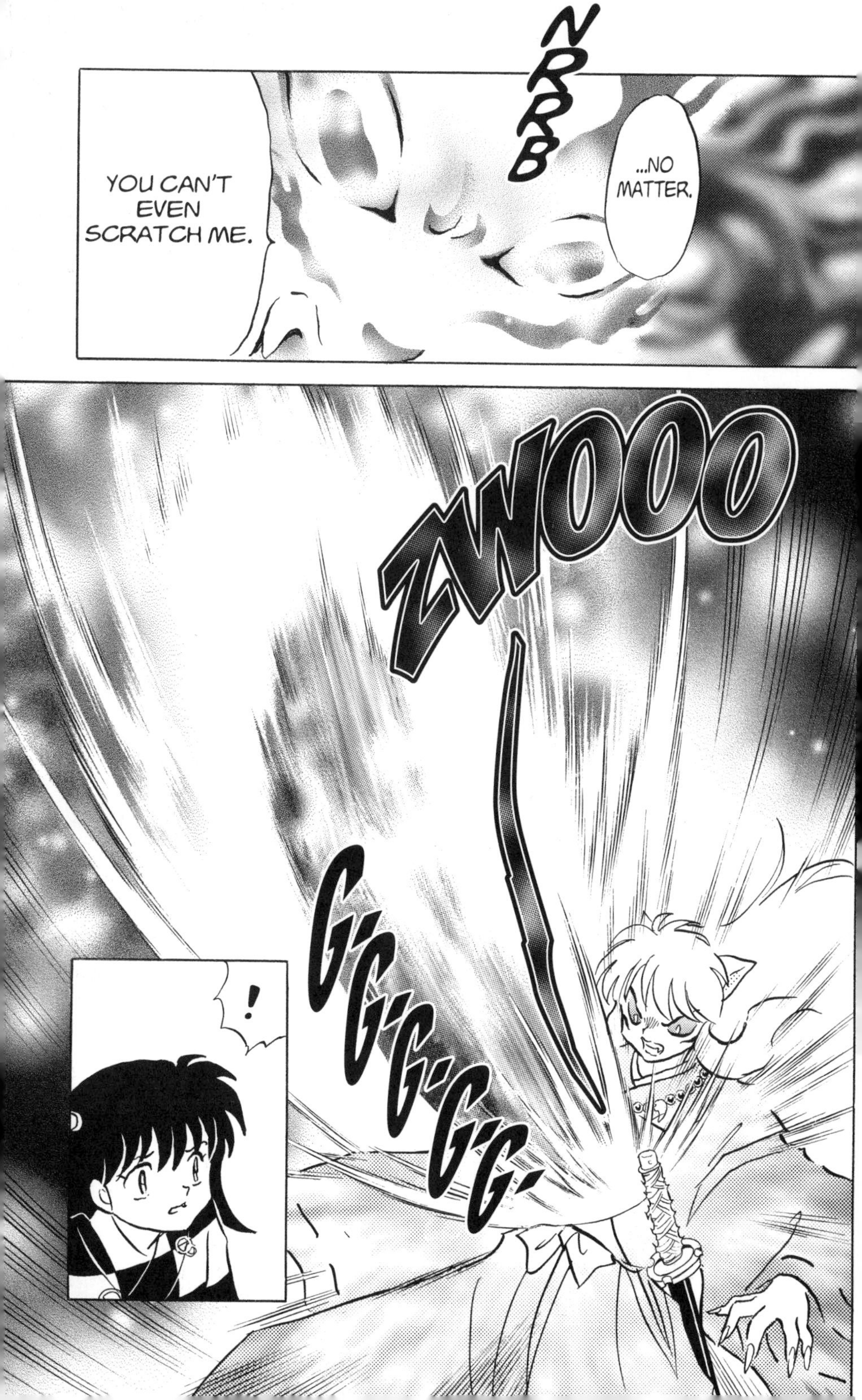
NRRB
...NO MATTER.
YOU CAN'T EVEN SCRATCH ME.
ZWOOO
G'G'G'G'G'
!

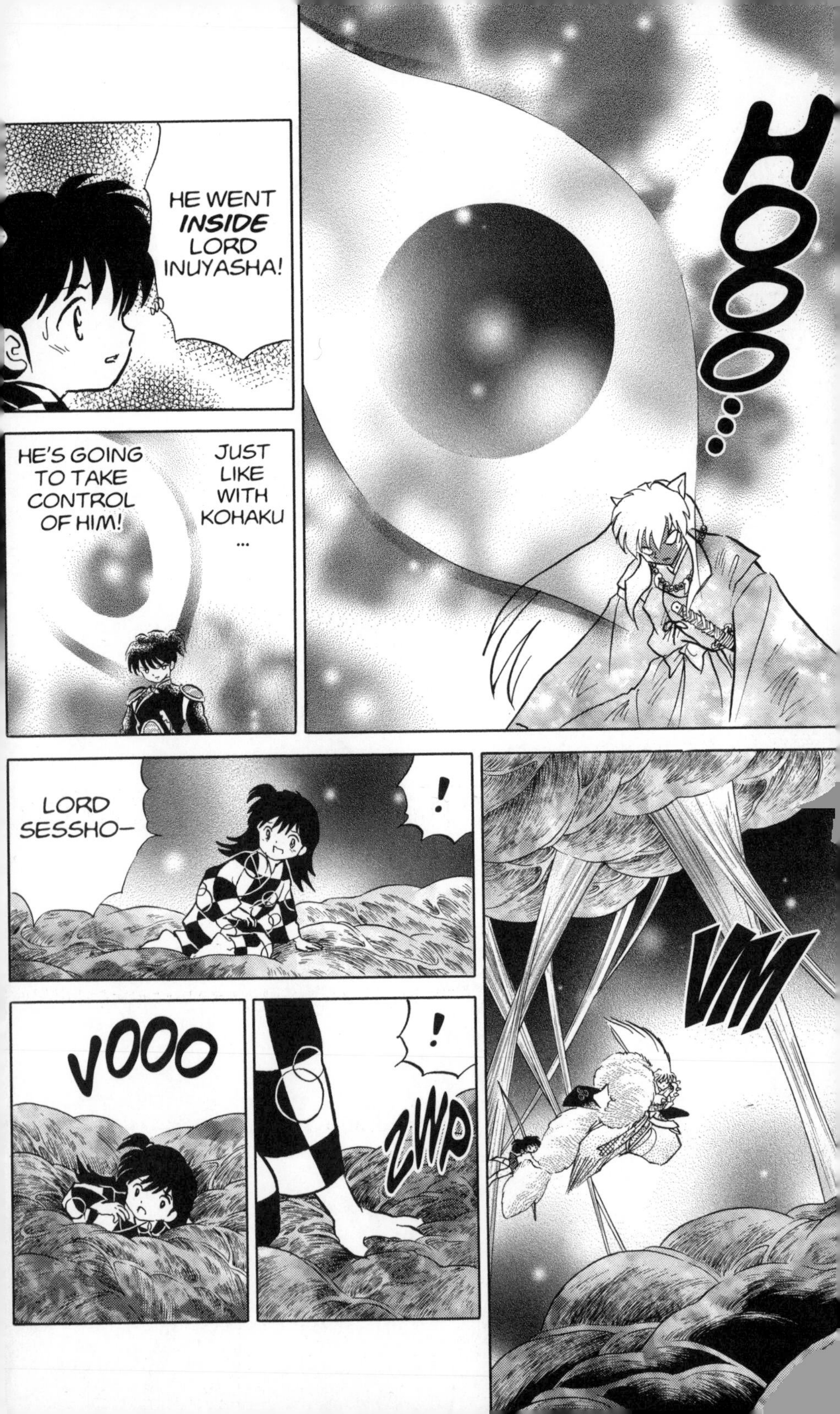
HOOOO...
HE WENT *INSIDE* LORD INUYASHA!
JUST LIKE WITH KOHAKU ...
HE'S GOING TO TAKE CONTROL OF HIM!
VM
LORD SESSHO-
!
!
ZWP
VOOO

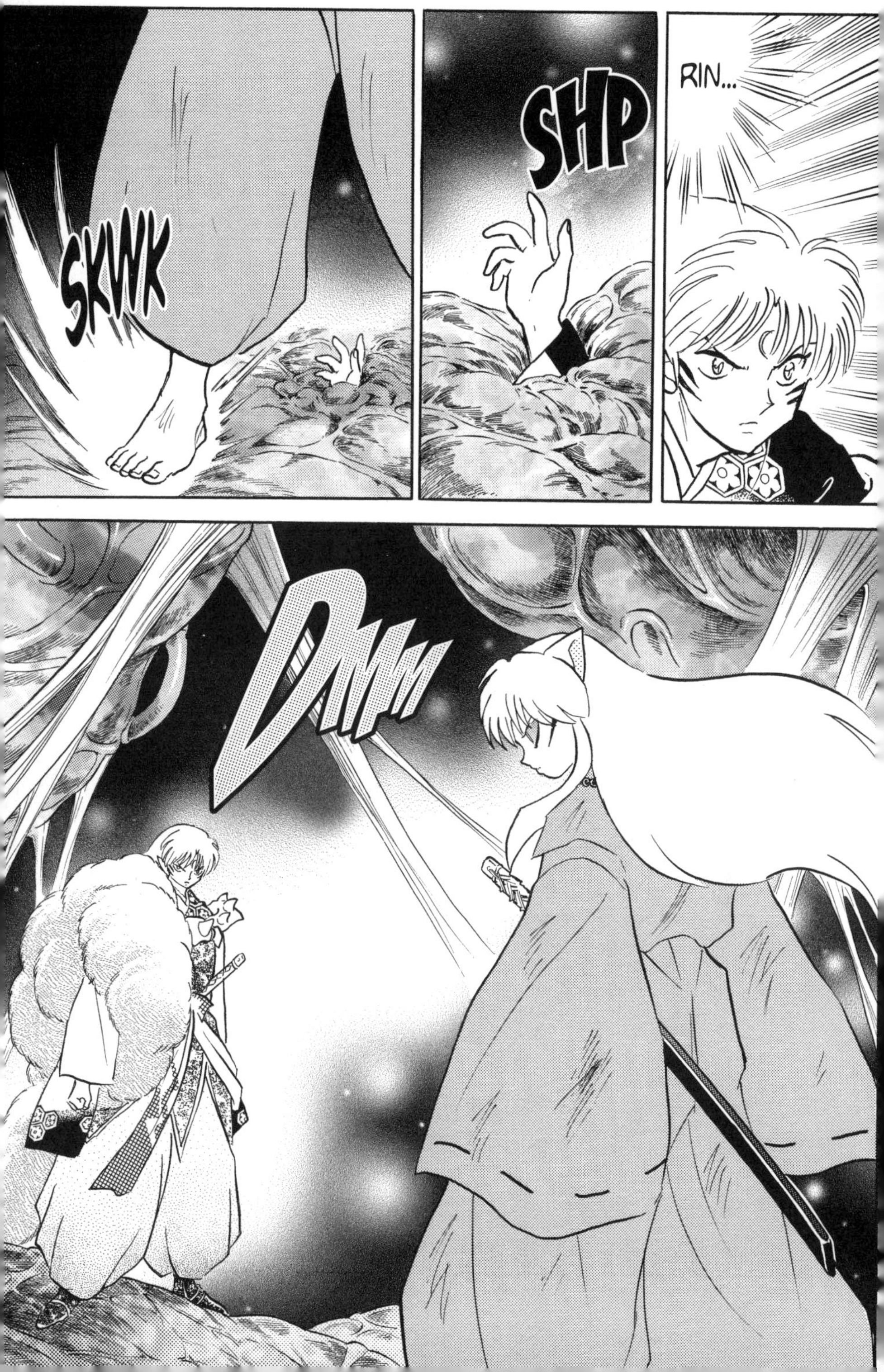
RIN...
SHP
SKWK
DMM

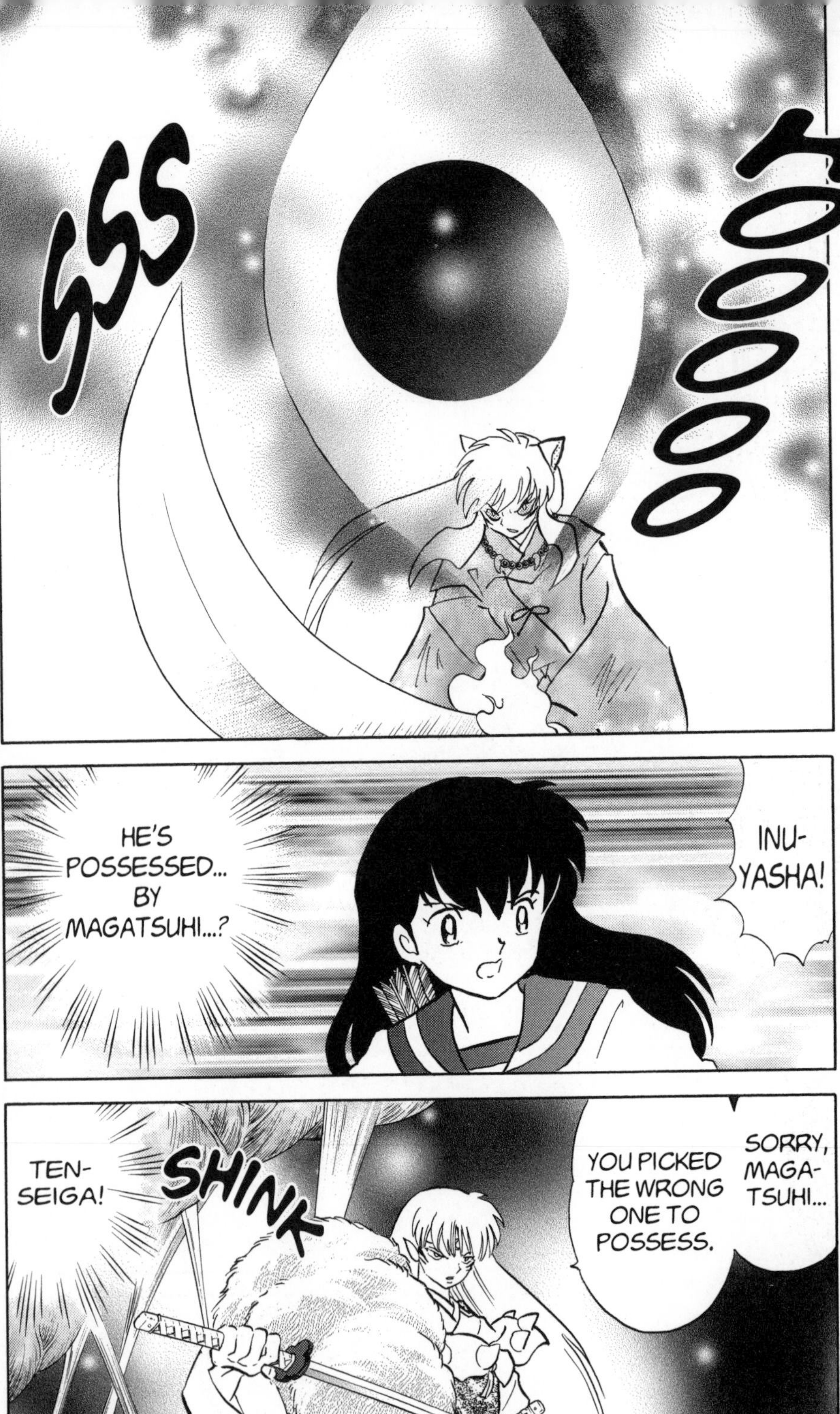
HOOOOOO
SSS
INU-YASHA!
HE'S POSSESSED... BY MAGATSUHI...?
SORRY, MAGA-TSUHI...
YOU PICKED THE WRONG ONE TO POSSESS.
SHINK
TEN-SEIGA!

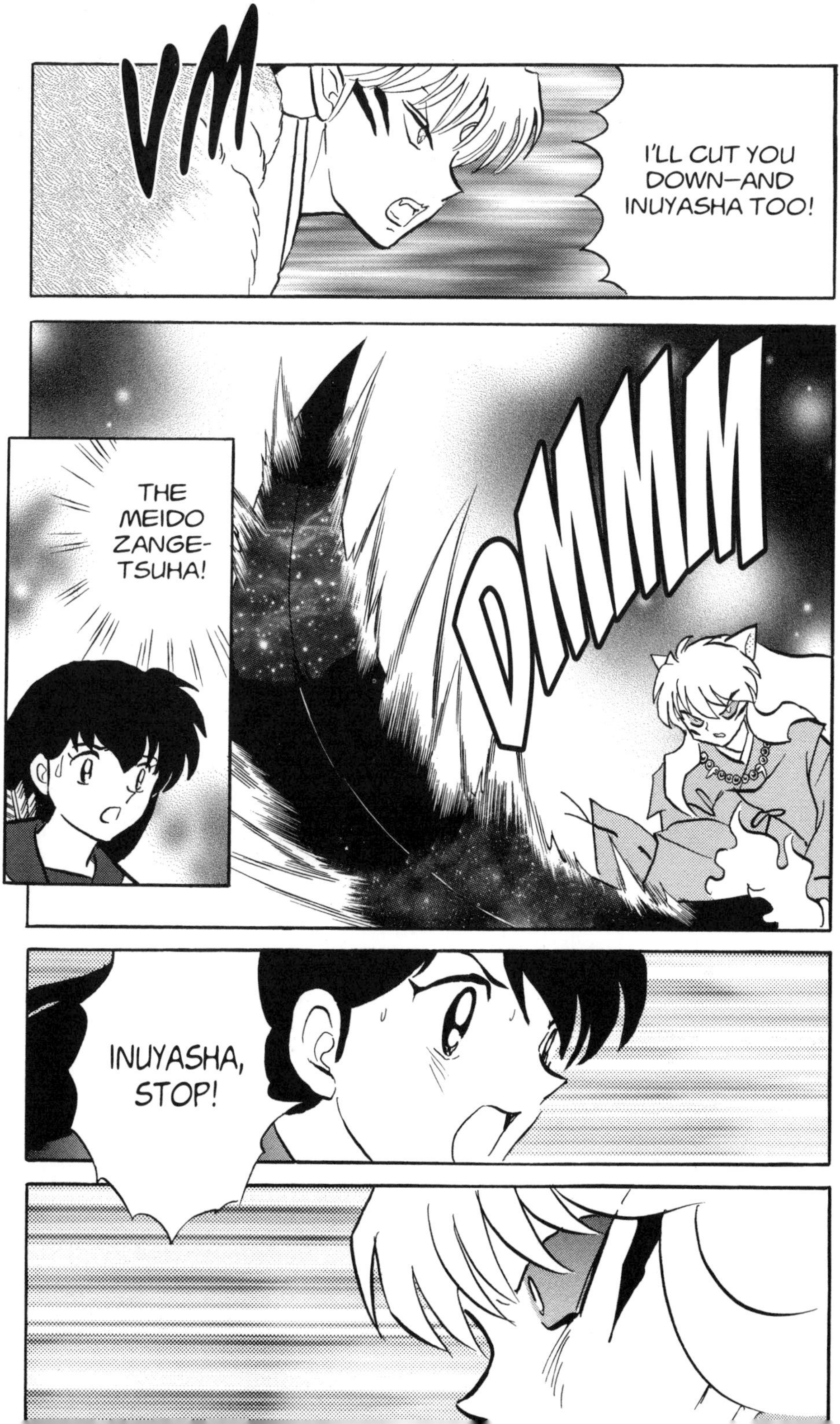
VM
I'LL CUT YOU DOWN—AND INUYASHA TOO!
DMMMM
THE MEIDO ZANGE-TSUHA!
INUYASHA, STOP!

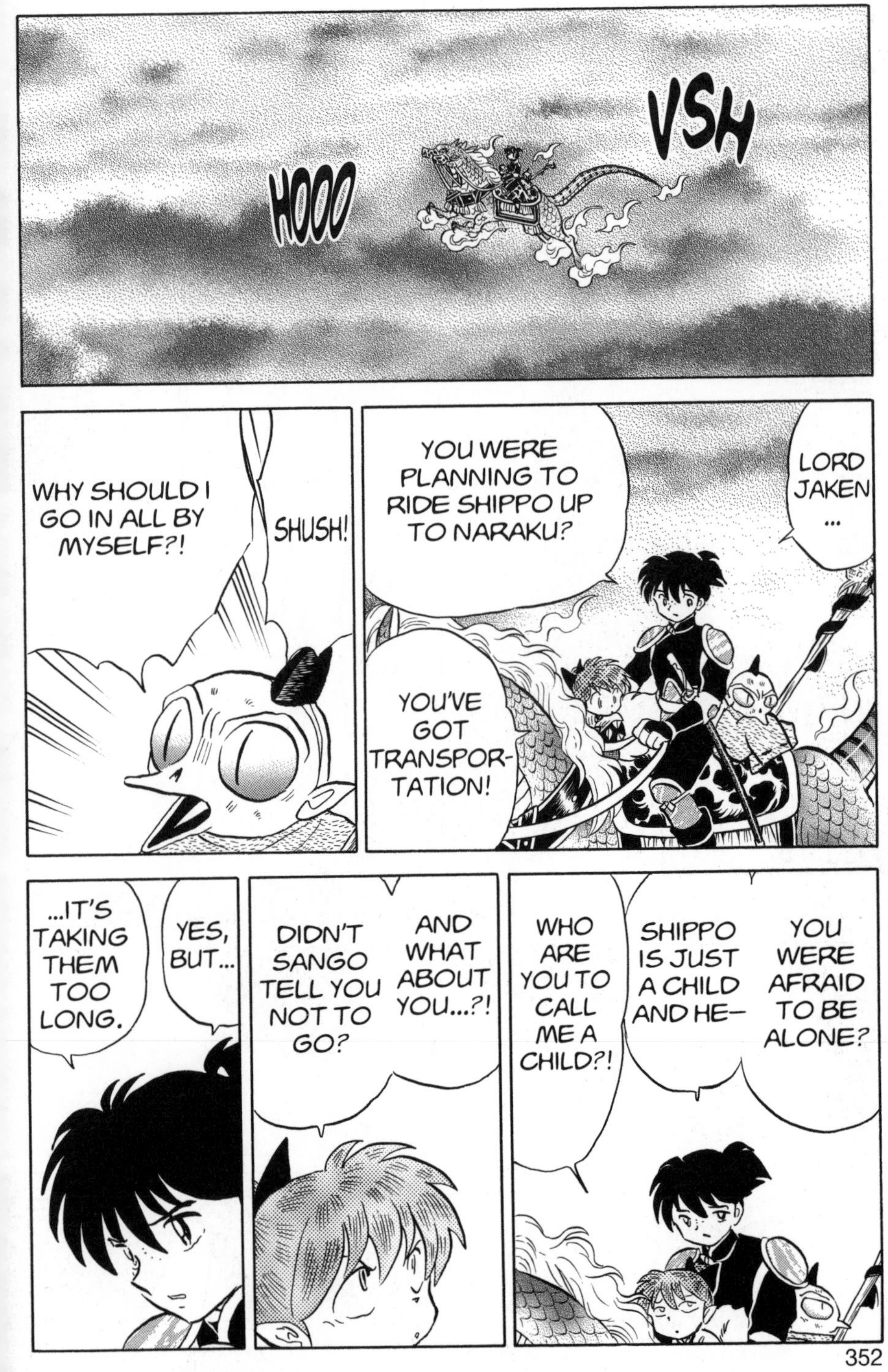
VSH
HOOO
LORD JAKEN ...
YOU WERE PLANNING TO RIDE SHIPPO UP TO NARAKU?
YOU'VE GOT TRANSPORTATION!
SHUSH!
WHY SHOULD I GO IN ALL BY MYSELF?!
YOU WERE AFRAID TO BE ALONE?
SHIPPO IS JUST A CHILD AND HE—
WHO ARE YOU TO CALL ME A CHILD?!
AND WHAT ABOUT YOU...?!
DIDN'T SANGO TELL YOU NOT TO GO?
YES, BUT...
...IT'S TAKING THEM TOO LONG.

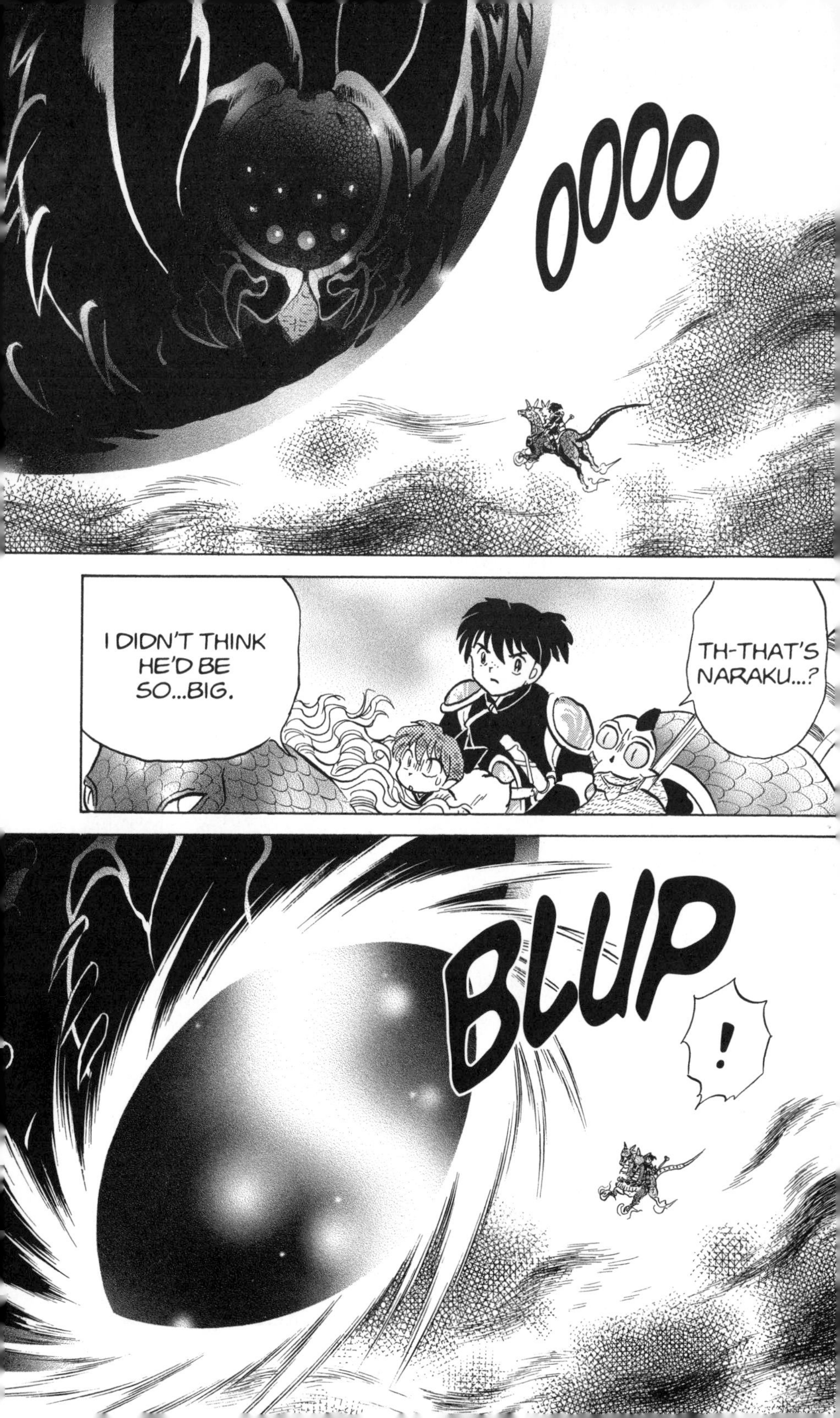
OOOO
TH-THAT'S NARAKU...?
I DIDN'T THINK HE'D BE SO...BIG.
BLUP
!

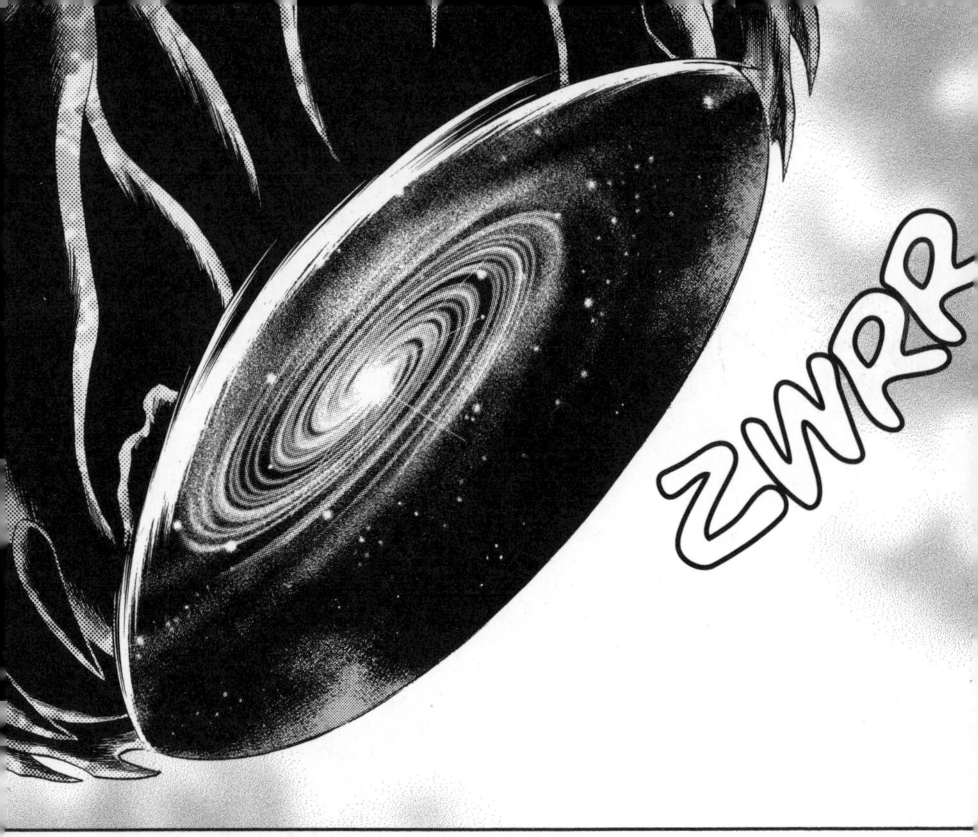
ZWRR

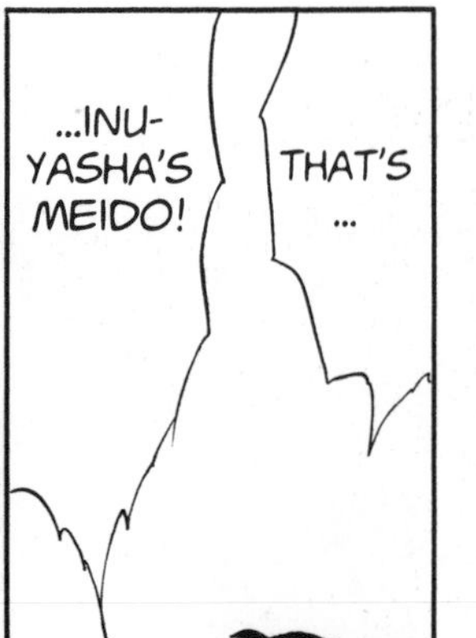
THAT'S ...
...INU-YASHA'S MEIDO!

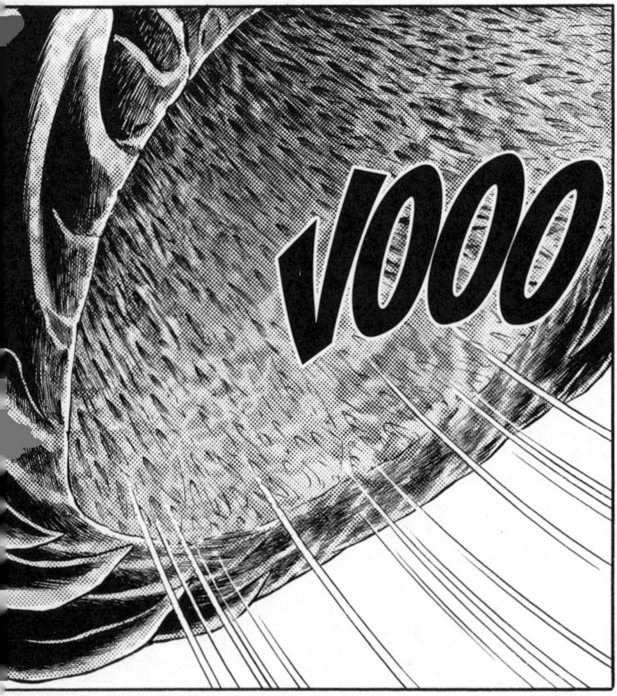
VOOO

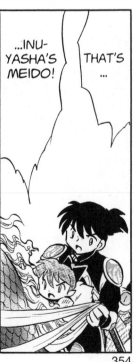

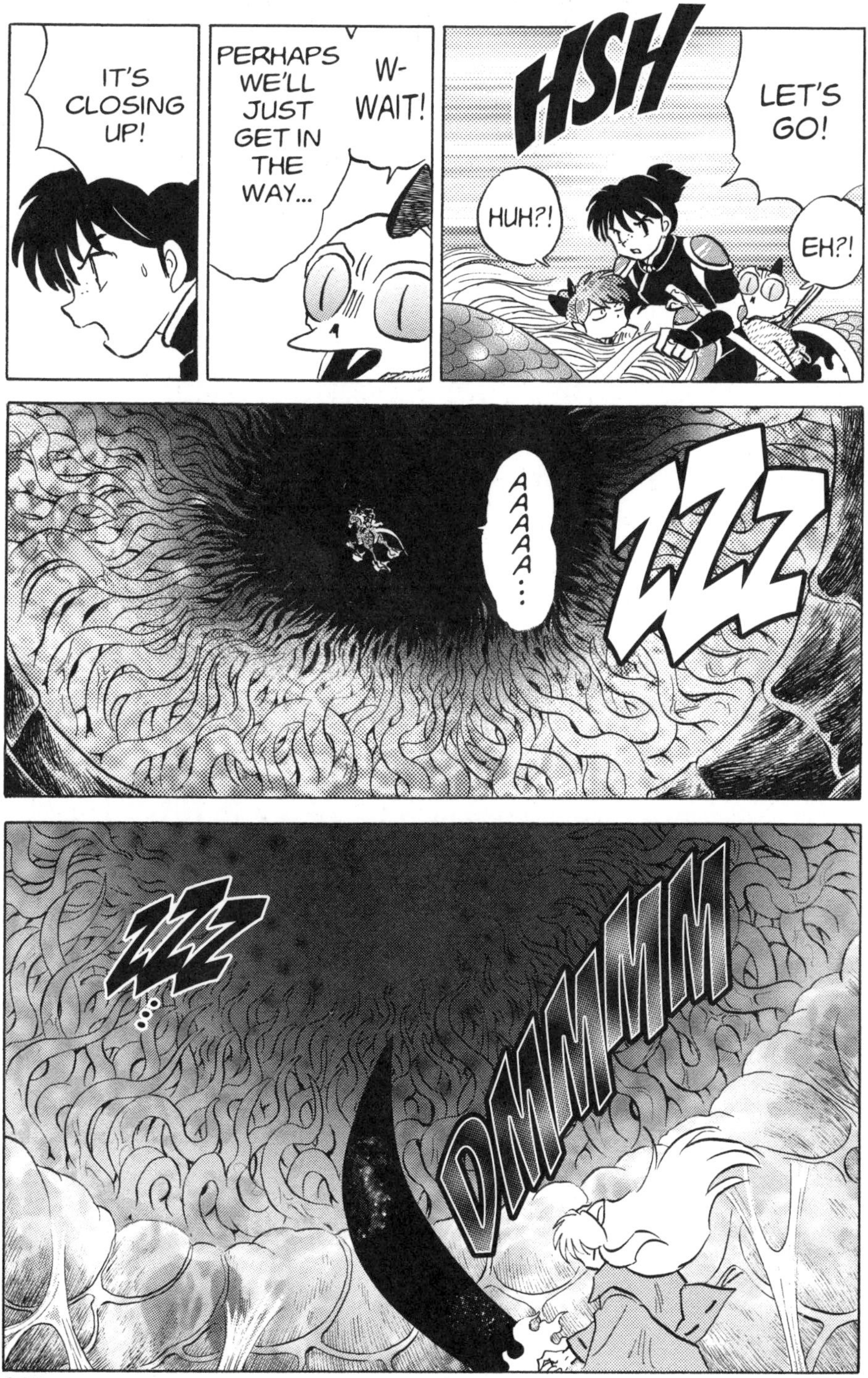
LET'S GO!
HSH
EH?!
HUH?!
W- WAIT!
PERHAPS WE'LL JUST GET IN THE WAY...
IT'S CLOSING UP!
ZZZ
AAAAA...
DMMMMM
ZZZ

...INTEN-
TIONALLY
?!

HE
MISSED
...

HOOO...

INU-
YASHA
...

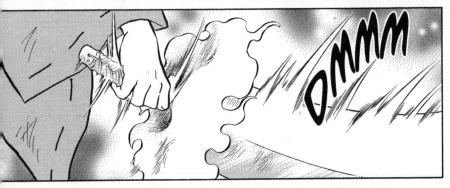

OMMM

TETSU-
SAIGA...?

356

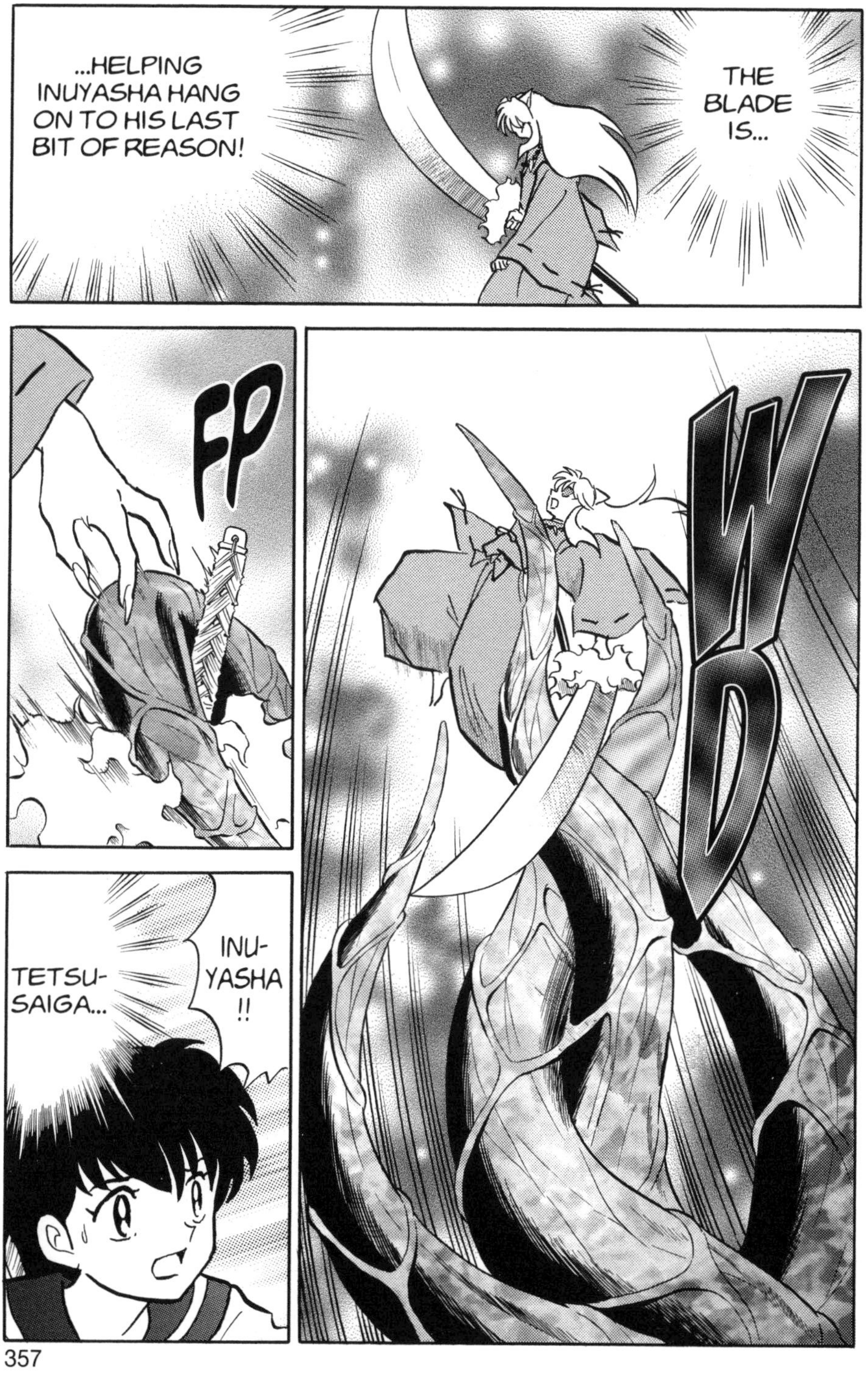
THE BLADE IS...
...HELPING INUYASHA HANG ON TO HIS LAST BIT OF REASON!
WD
FP
INU-YASHA !!
TETSU-SAIGA...

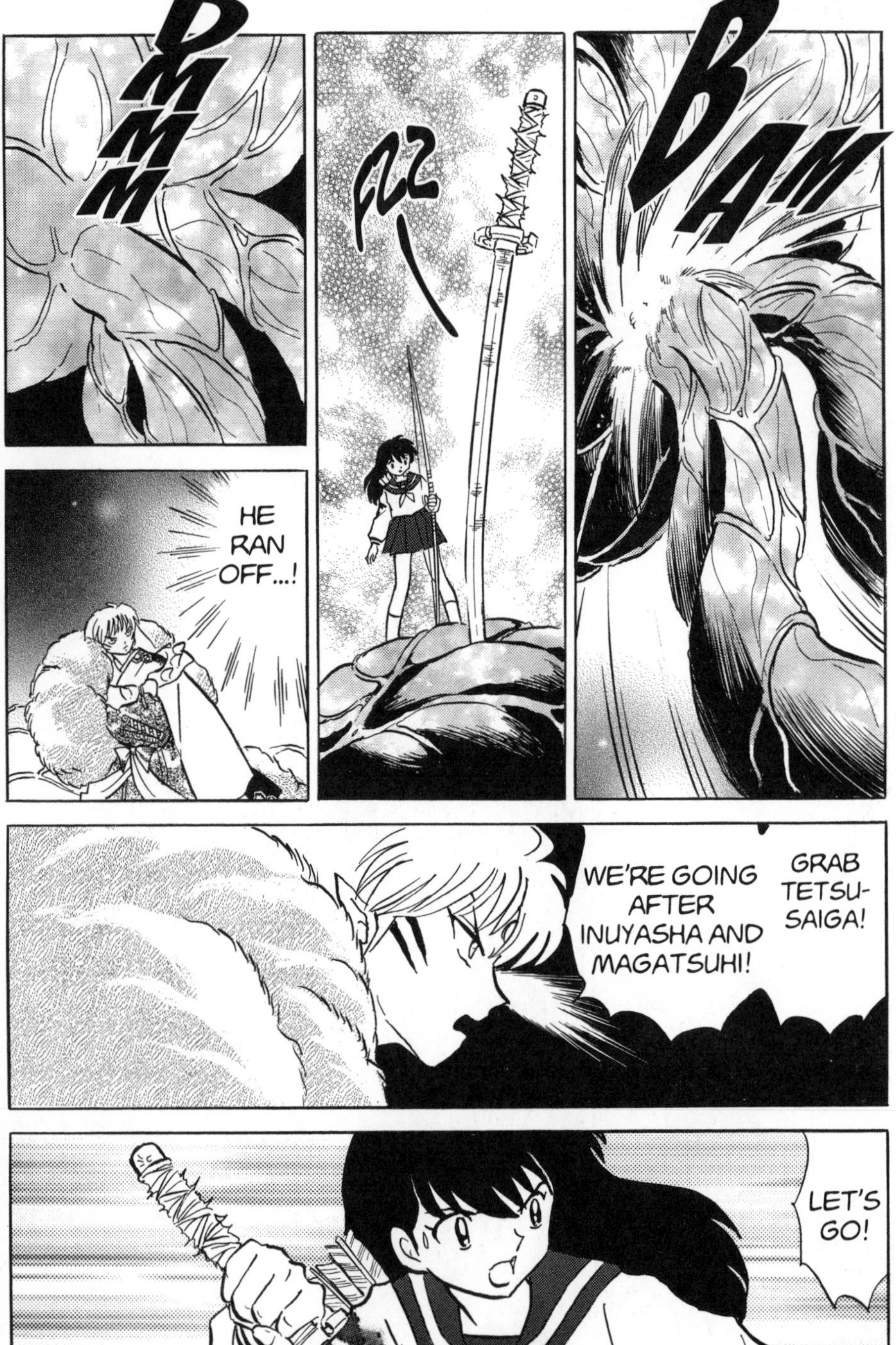
BAM
FZZ
DMMM
HE RAN OFF...!
GRAB TETSU-SAIGA!
WE'RE GOING AFTER INUYASHA AND MAGATSUHI!
LET'S GO!

SCROLL TEN
THE SCENT OF KAGOME'S BLOOD

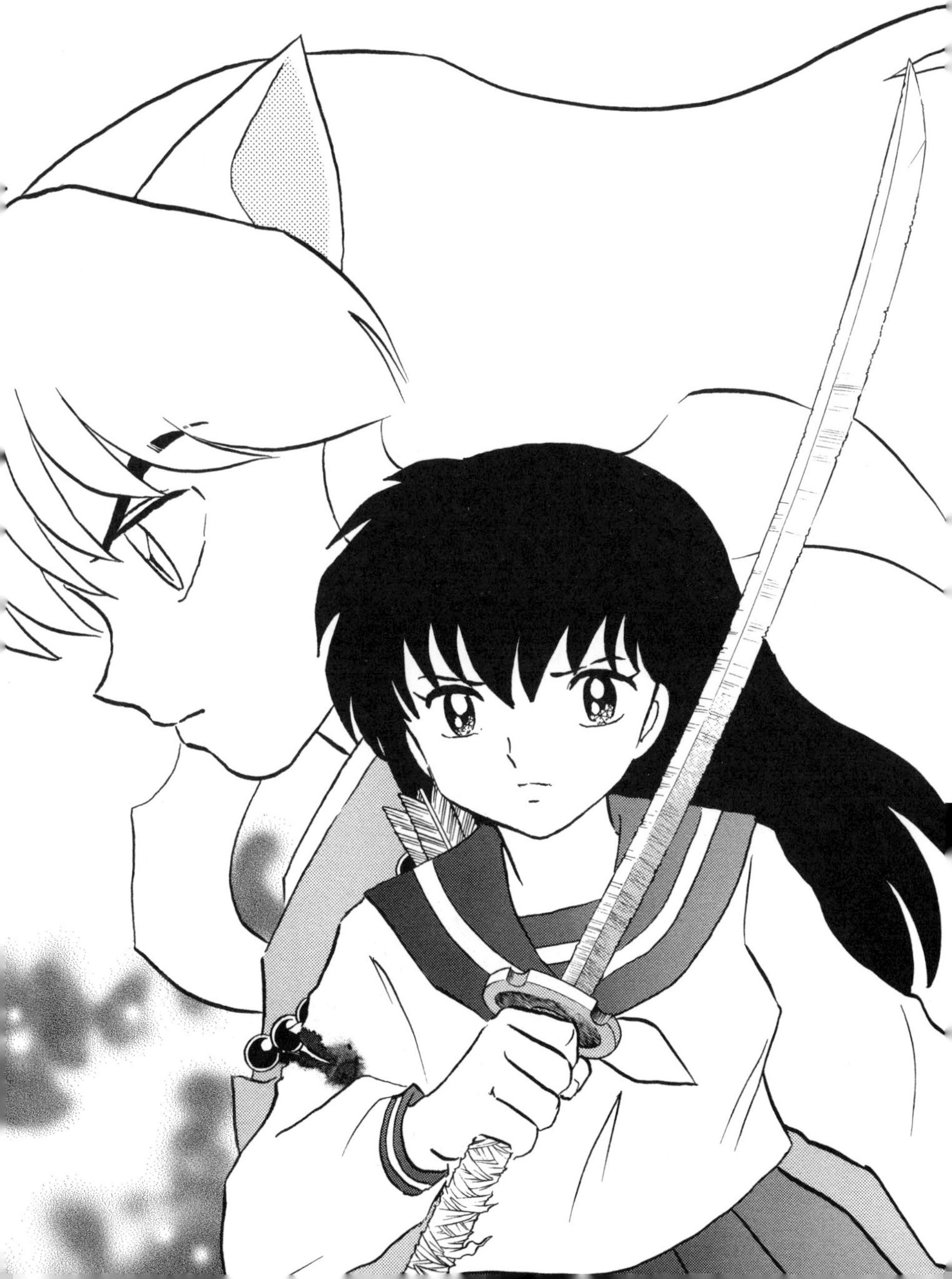

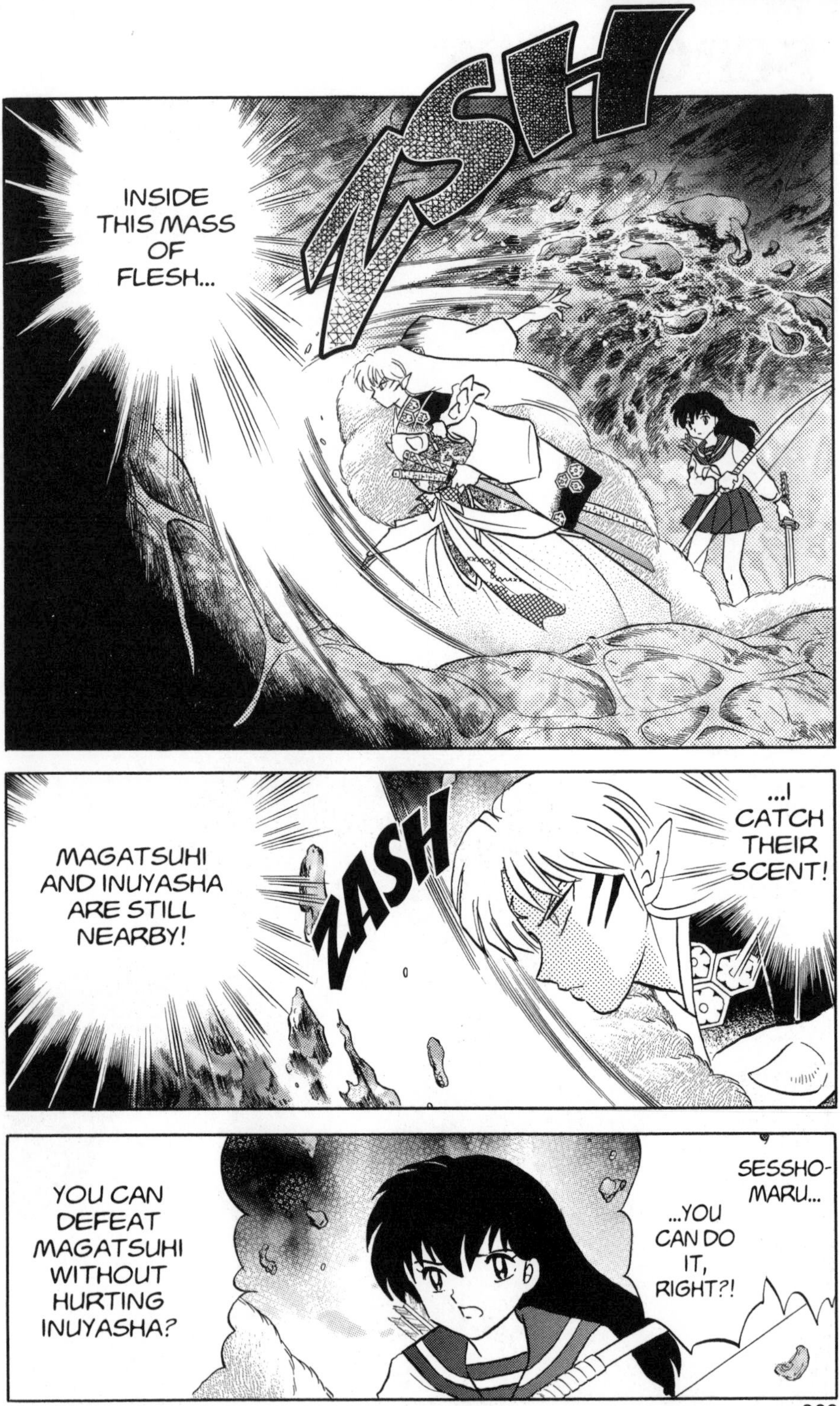
ZSH
INSIDE THIS MASS OF FLESH...
...I CATCH THEIR SCENT!
ZASH
MAGATSUHI AND INUYASHA ARE STILL NEARBY!
SESSHO-MARU...
...YOU CAN DO IT, RIGHT?!
YOU CAN DEFEAT MAGATSUHI WITHOUT HURTING INUYASHA?

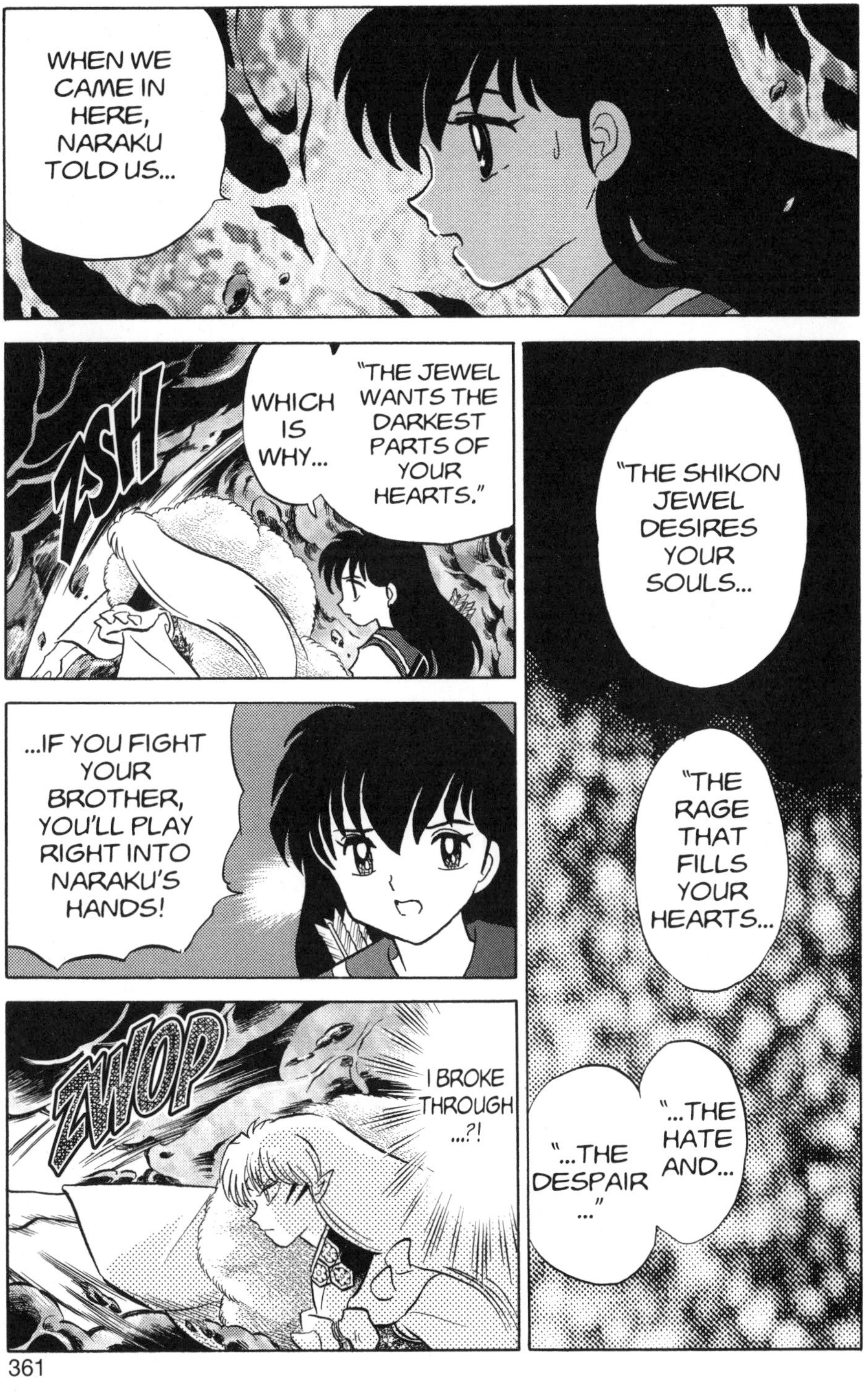
WHEN WE CAME IN HERE, NARAKU TOLD US...
"THE SHIKON JEWEL DESIRES YOUR SOULS...
"THE RAGE THAT FILLS YOUR HEARTS...
"...THE HATE AND...
"...THE DESPAIR..."
"THE JEWEL WANTS THE DARKEST PARTS OF YOUR HEARTS."
WHICH IS WHY...
ZSH
...IF YOU FIGHT YOUR BROTHER, YOU'LL PLAY RIGHT INTO NARAKU'S HANDS!
I BROKE THROUGH ...?!
ZWOP

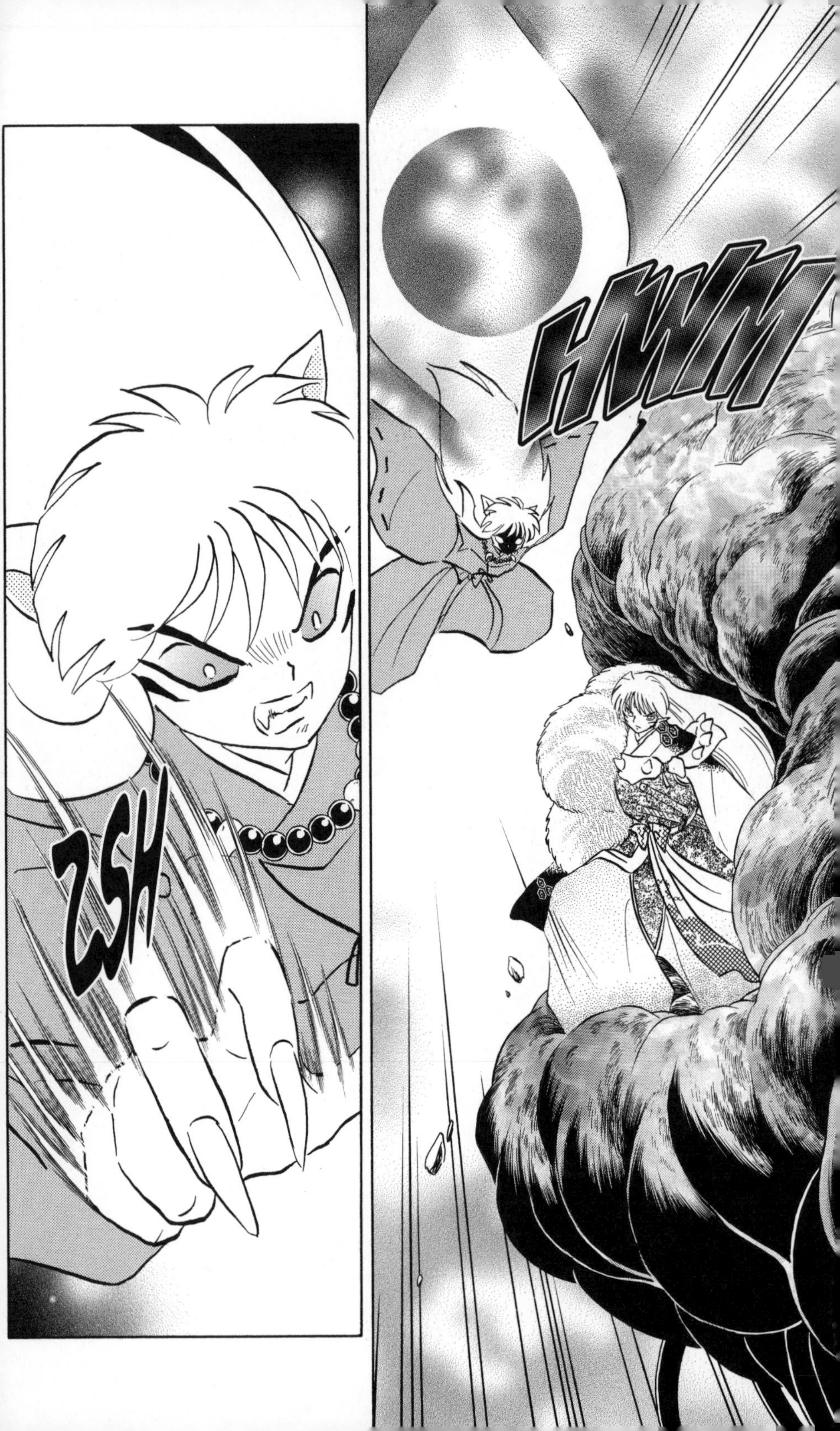
ZSH

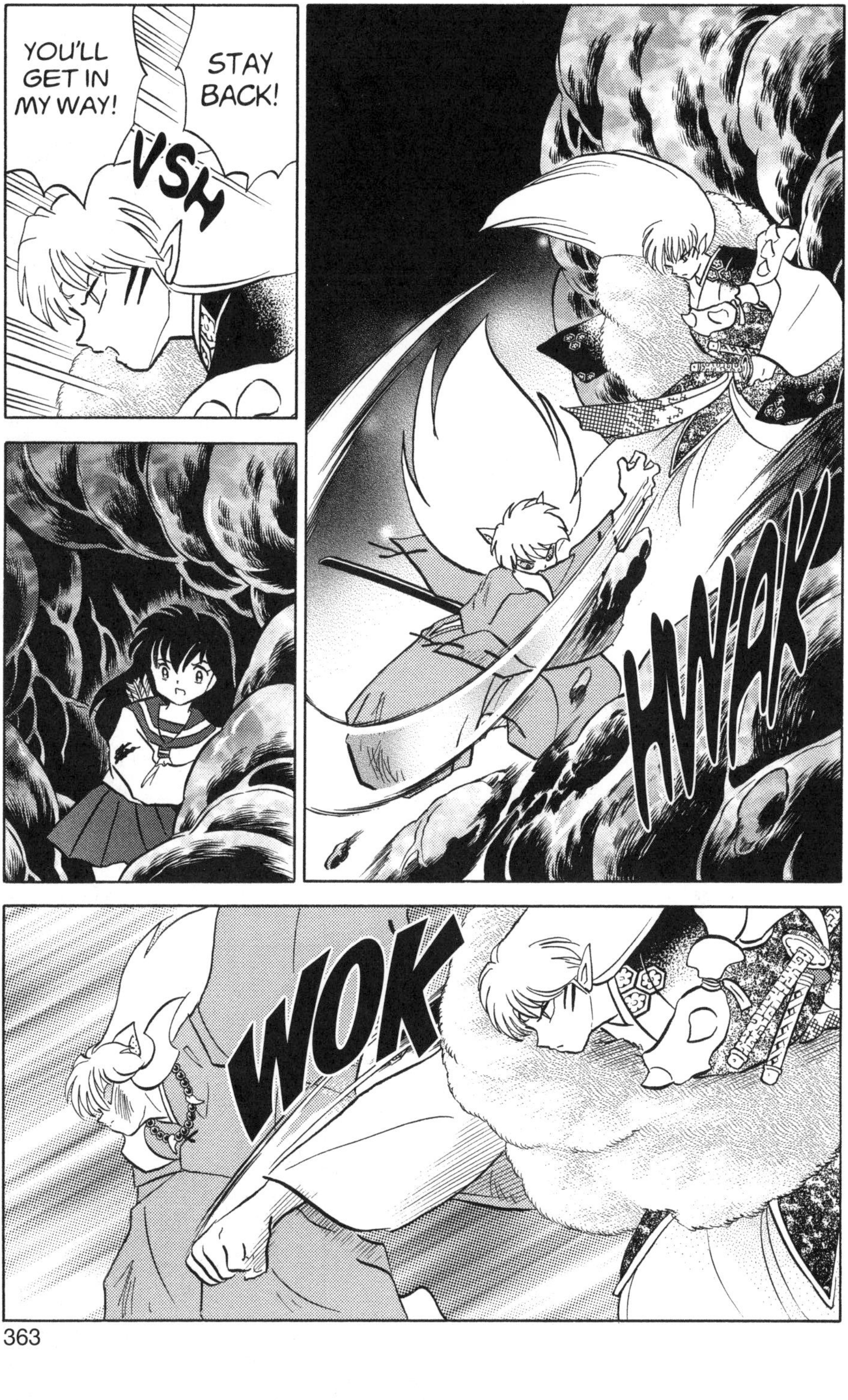
HWAK
STAY BACK!
YOU'LL GET IN MY WAY!
VSH
WOK

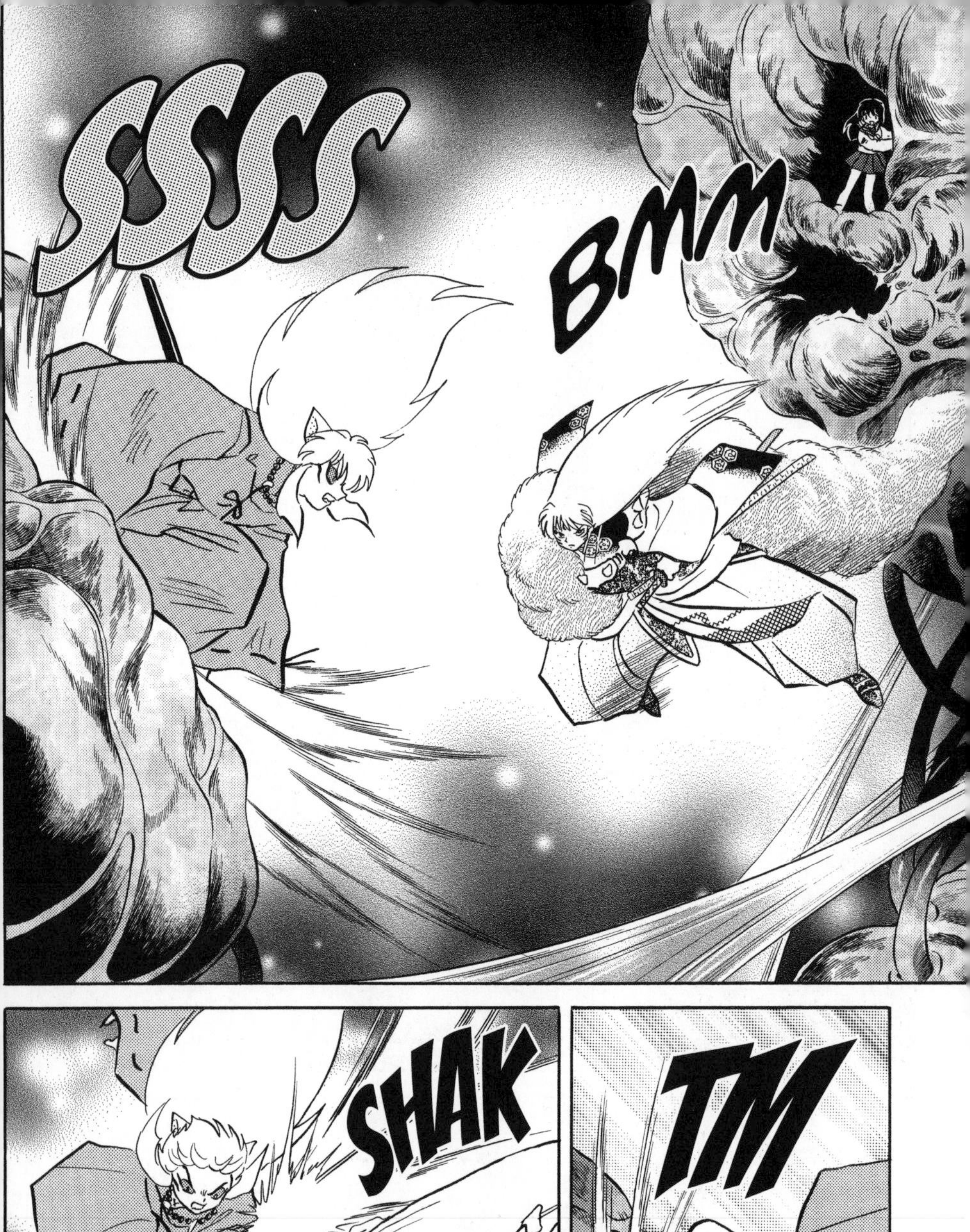
BMM
SSSS
TM
SHAK

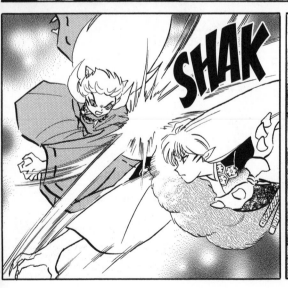

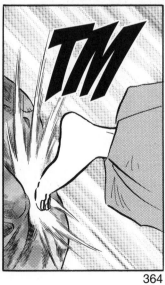

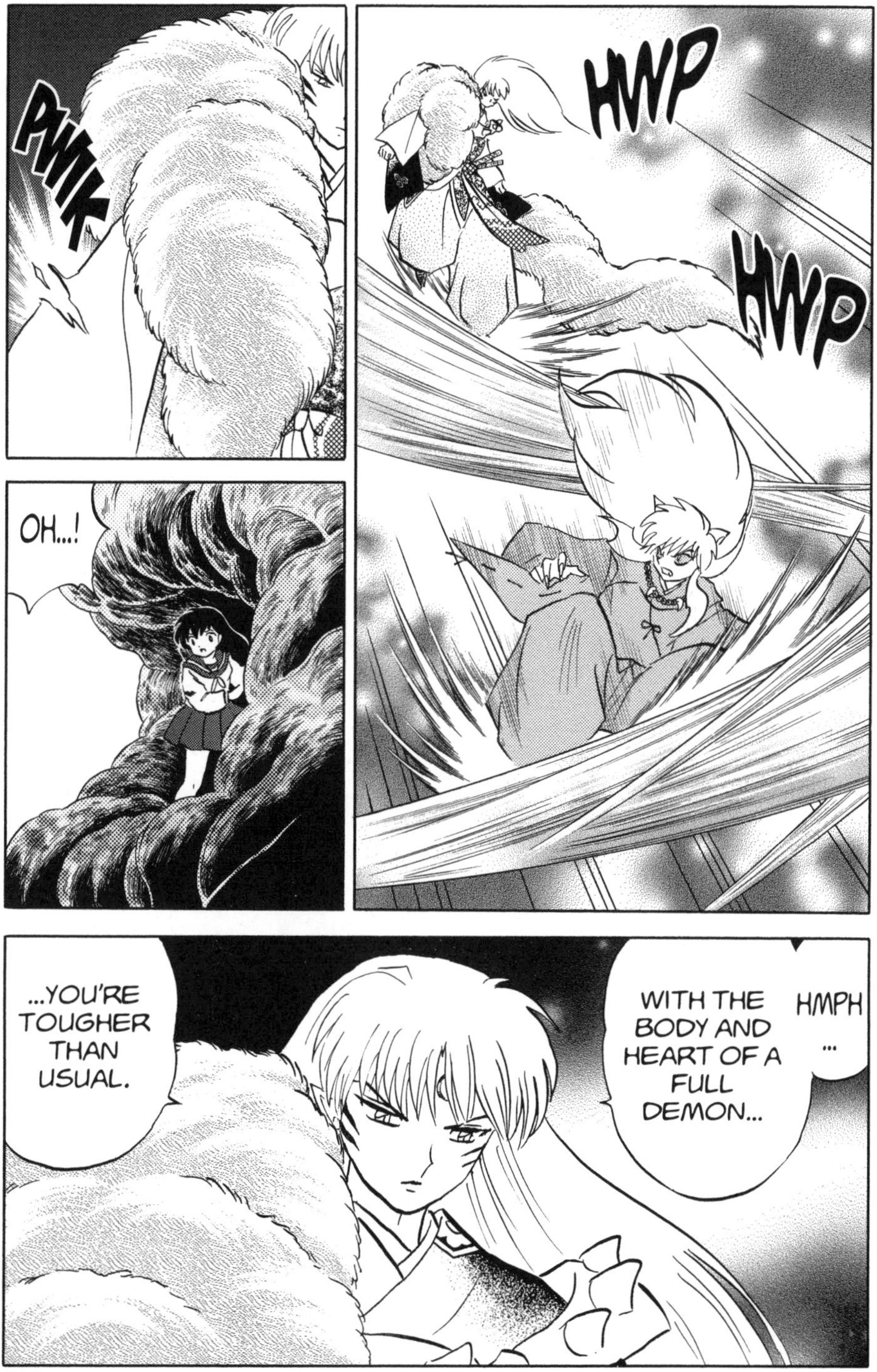
HWP
HWP
PWIK
OH...!
HMPH ...
WITH THE BODY AND HEART OF A FULL DEMON...
...YOU'RE TOUGHER THAN USUAL.

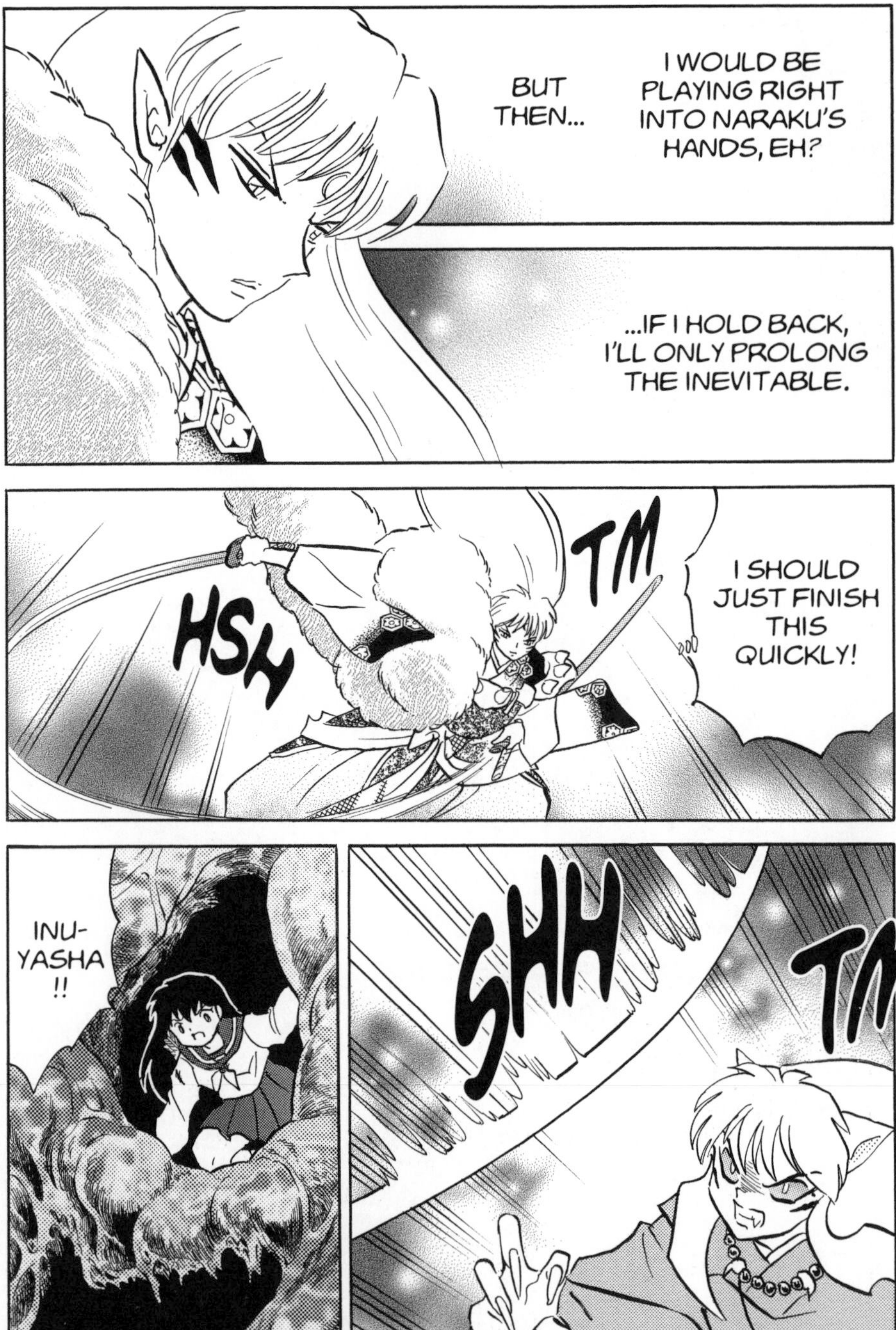
I WOULD BE PLAYING RIGHT INTO NARAKU'S HANDS, EH?
BUT THEN...
...IF I HOLD BACK, I'LL ONLY PROLONG THE INEVITABLE.
TM
I SHOULD JUST FINISH THIS QUICKLY!
HSH
TM
SHH
INU-YASHA !!

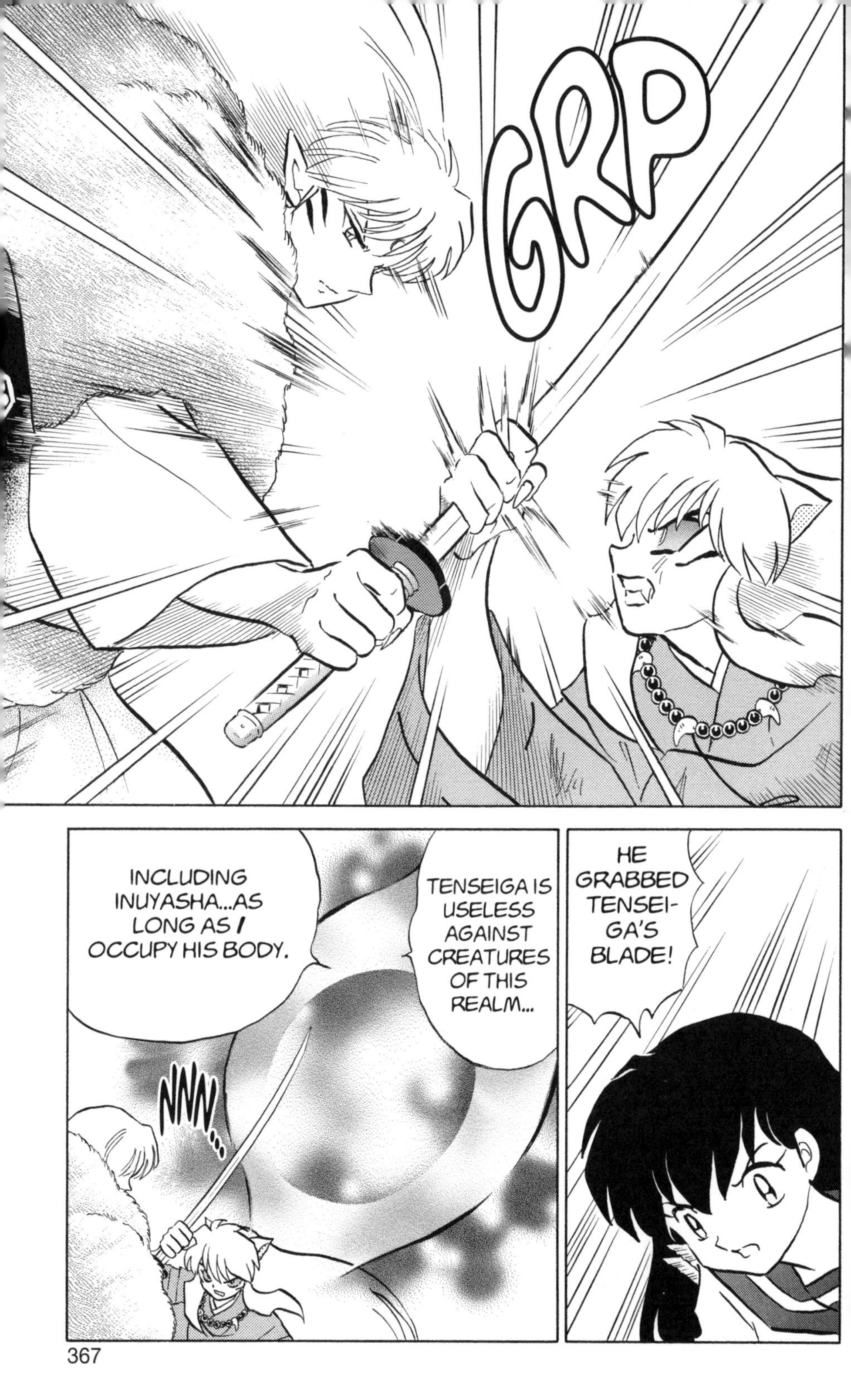
GRP
HE GRABBED TENSEI-GA'S BLADE!
TENSEIGA IS USELESS AGAINST CREATURES OF THIS REALM...
INCLUDING INUYASHA...AS LONG AS *I* OCCUPY HIS BODY.
NNN...

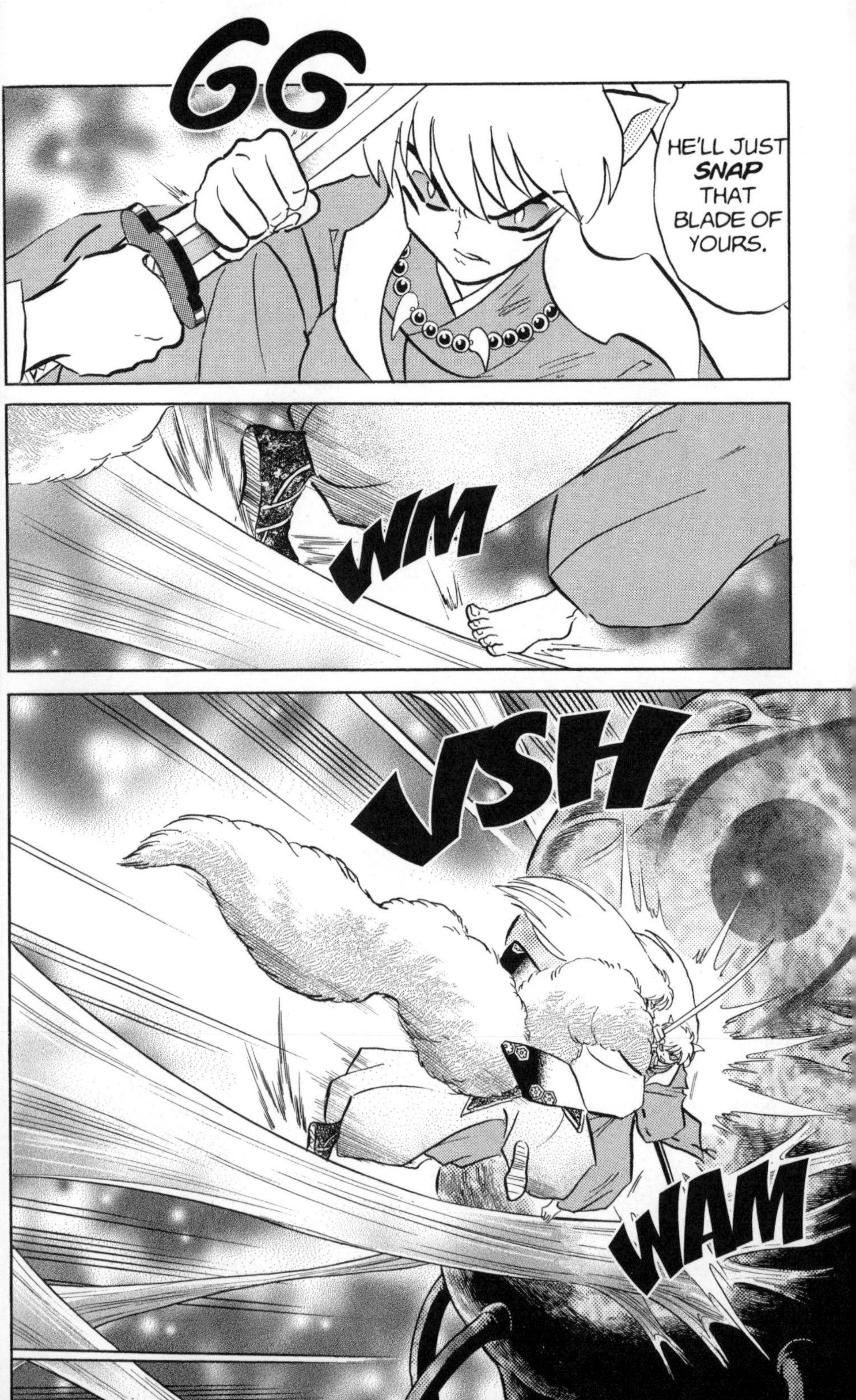
GG
HE'LL JUST **SNAP** THAT BLADE OF YOURS.
WM
VSH
WAM

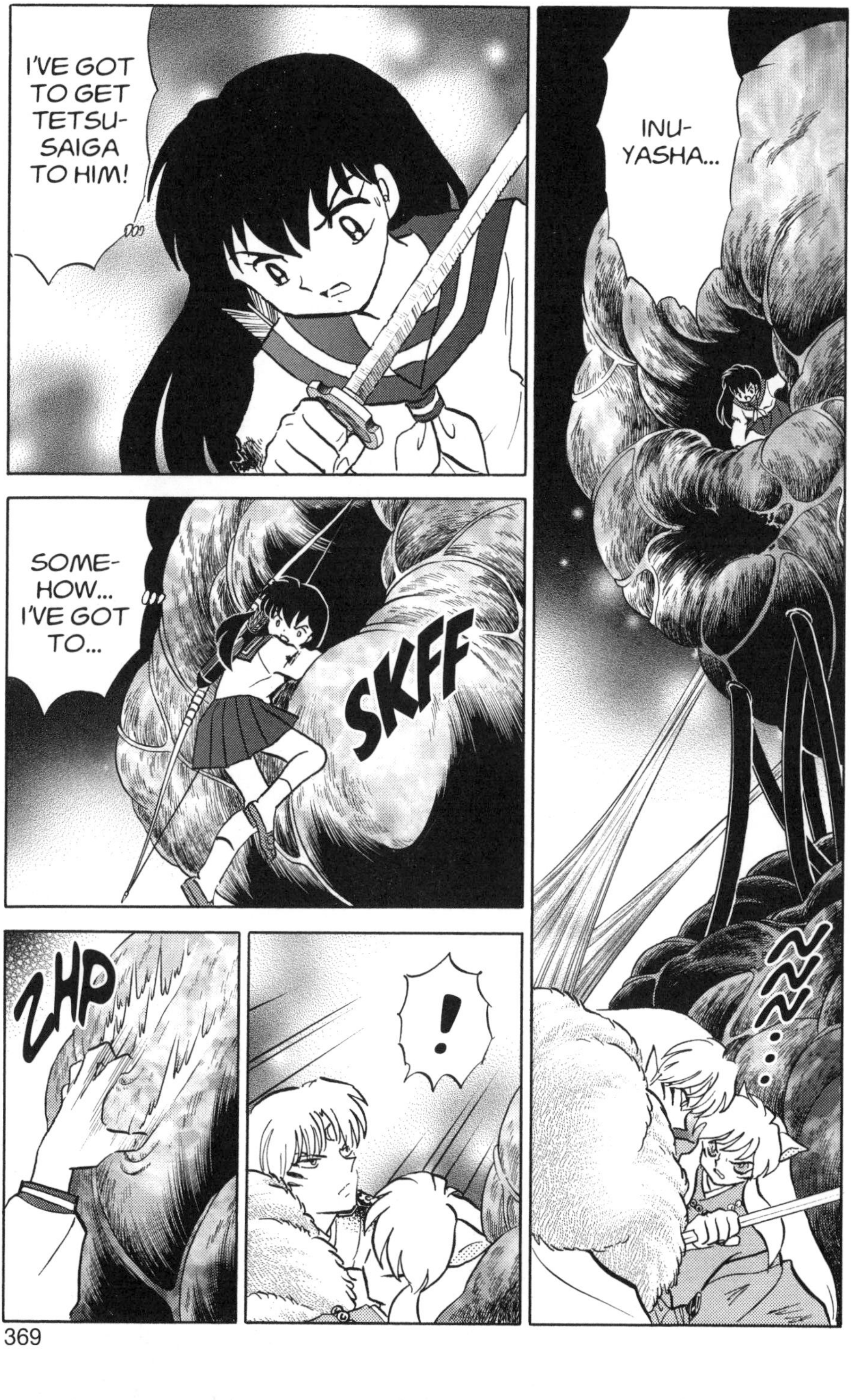
INU-YASHA...
NNN...
I'VE GOT TO GET TETSU-SAIGA TO HIM!
SOME-HOW... I'VE GOT TO...
SKFF
!
ZHP

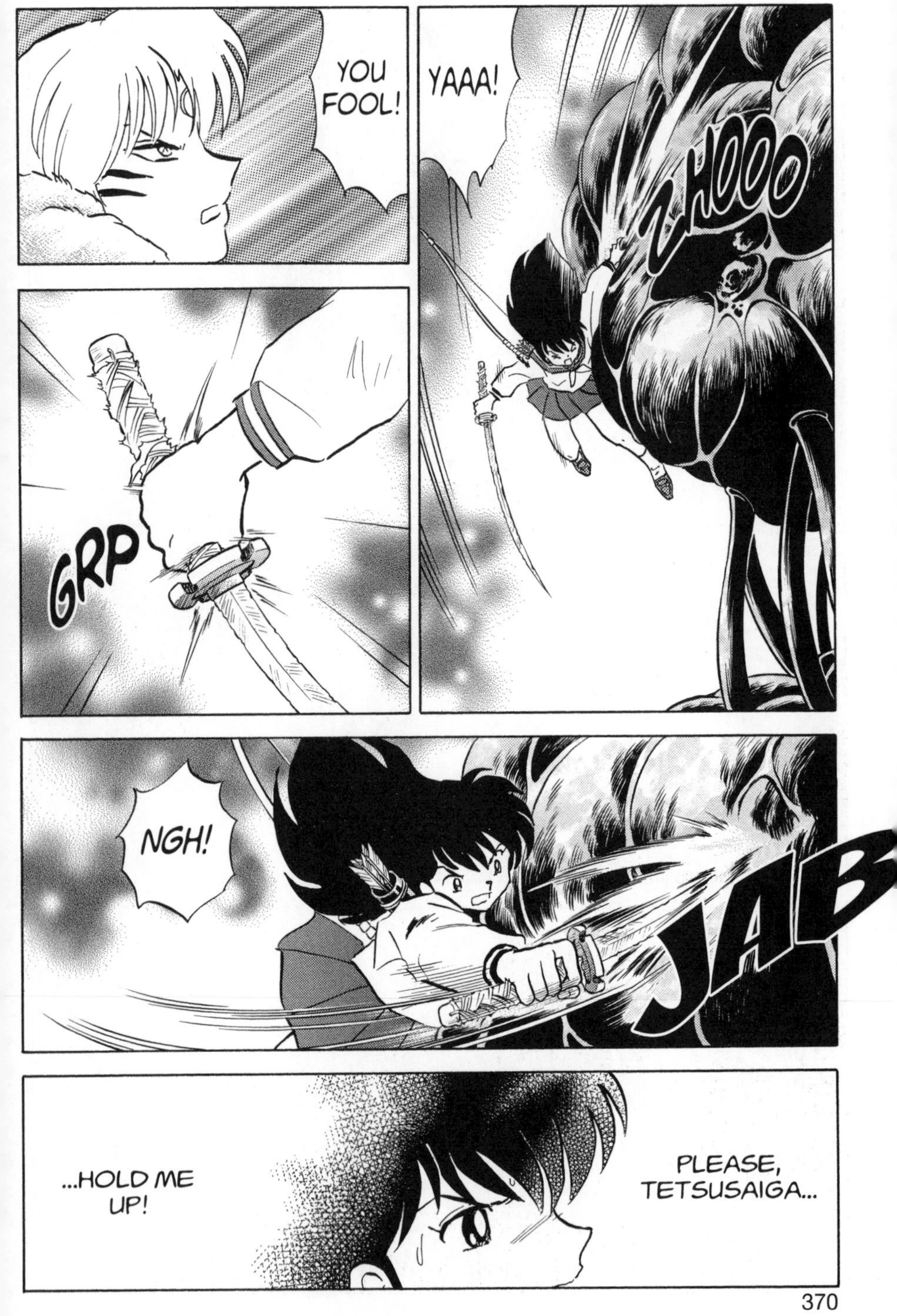
YAAA!
ZHOOO
YOU FOOL!
GRP
JAB
NGH!
PLEASE, TETSUSAIGA...
...HOLD ME UP!

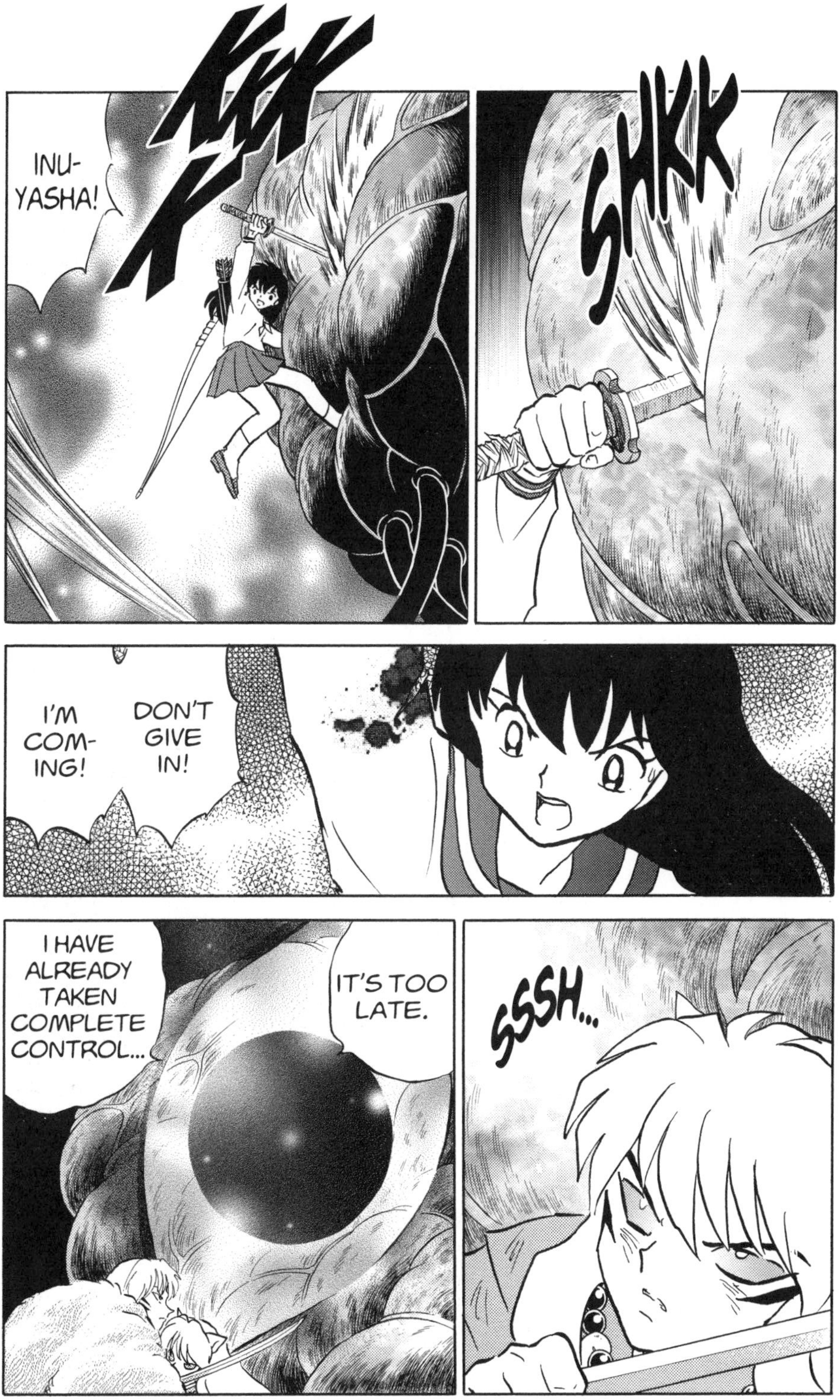
SHKK
INU-YASHA!
DON'T GIVE IN!
I'M COMING!
SSSH...
IT'S TOO LATE.
I HAVE ALREADY TAKEN COMPLETE CONTROL...

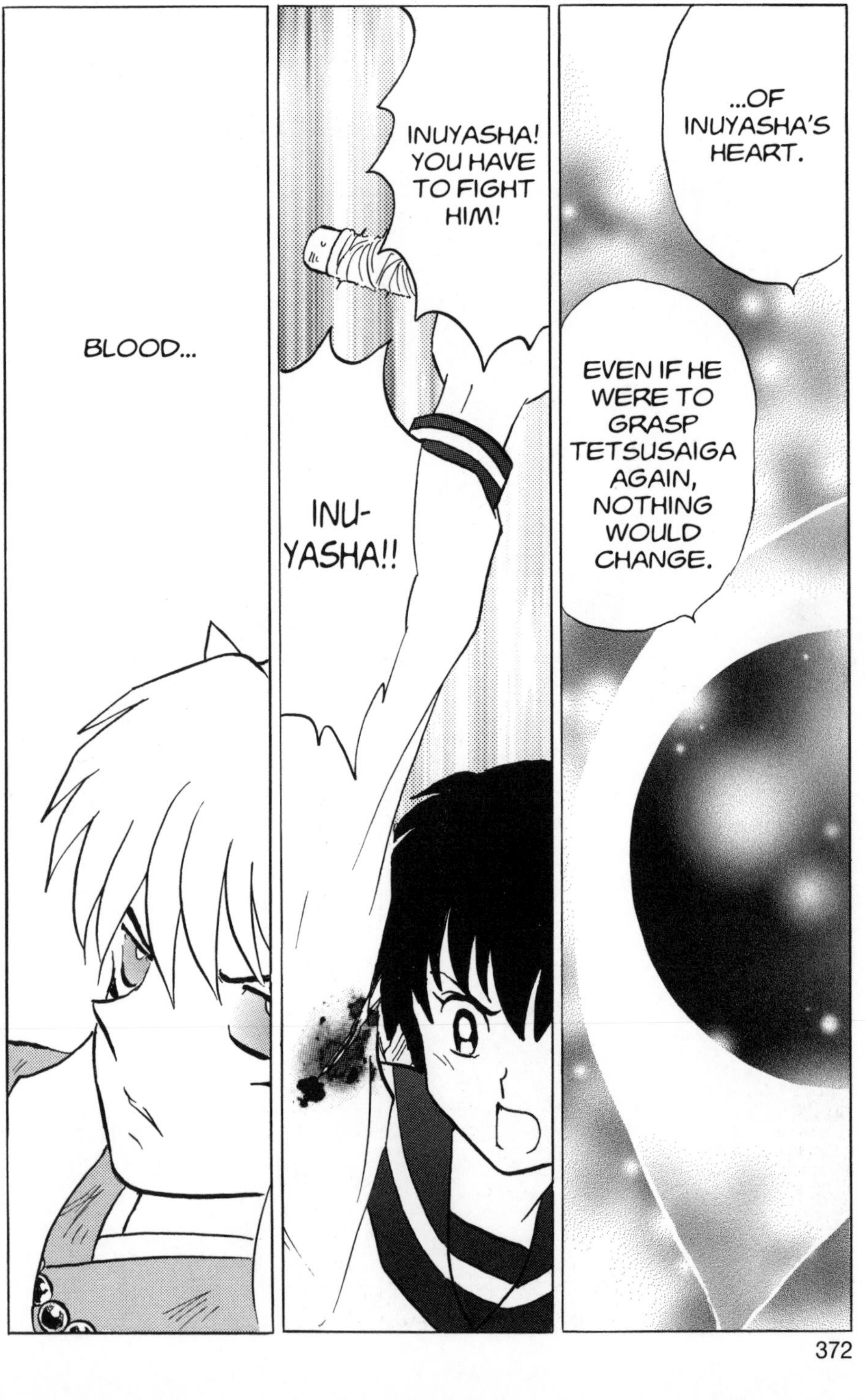
...OF INUYASHA'S HEART.
EVEN IF HE WERE TO GRASP TETSUSAIGA AGAIN, NOTHING WOULD CHANGE.
INUYASHA! YOU HAVE TO FIGHT HIM!
INU-YASHA!!
BLOOD...

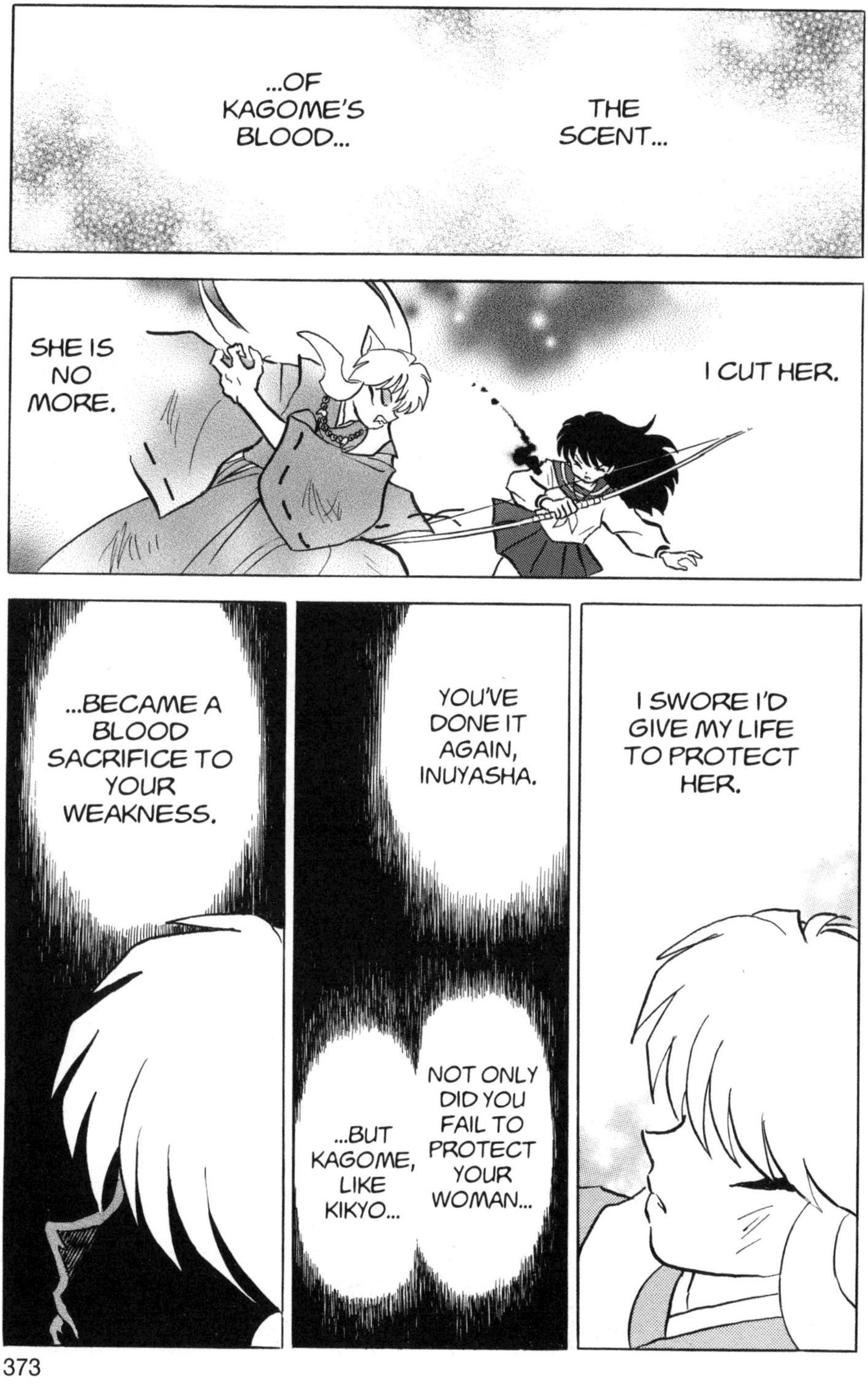
THE SCENT...
...OF KAGOME'S BLOOD...
I CUT HER.
SHE IS NO MORE.
I SWORE I'D GIVE MY LIFE TO PROTECT HER.
YOU'VE DONE IT AGAIN, INUYASHA.
NOT ONLY DID YOU FAIL TO PROTECT YOUR WOMAN...
...BUT KAGOME, LIKE KIKYO...
...BECAME A BLOOD SACRIFICE TO YOUR WEAKNESS.

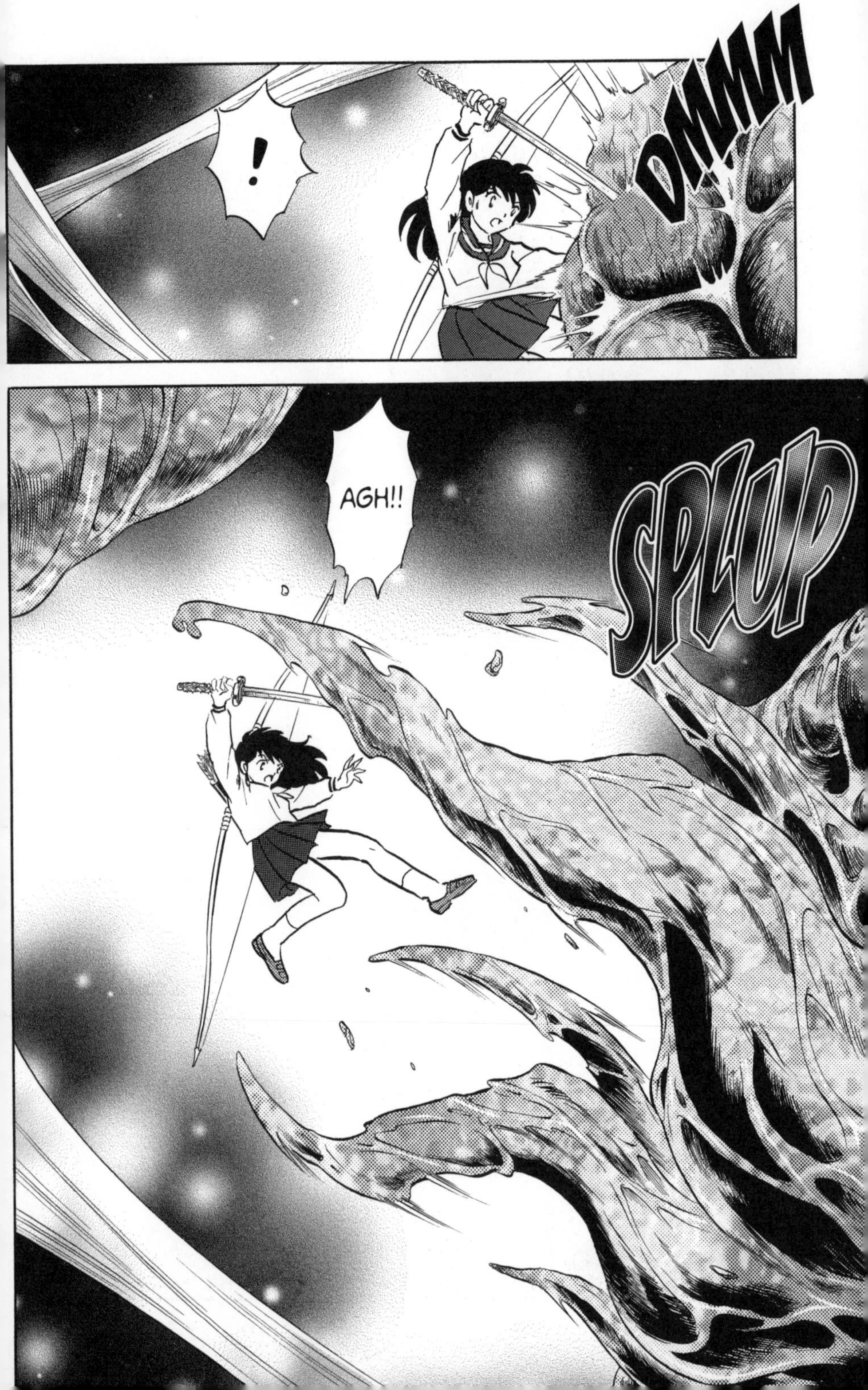
DMMM
!
SPLUP
AGH!!

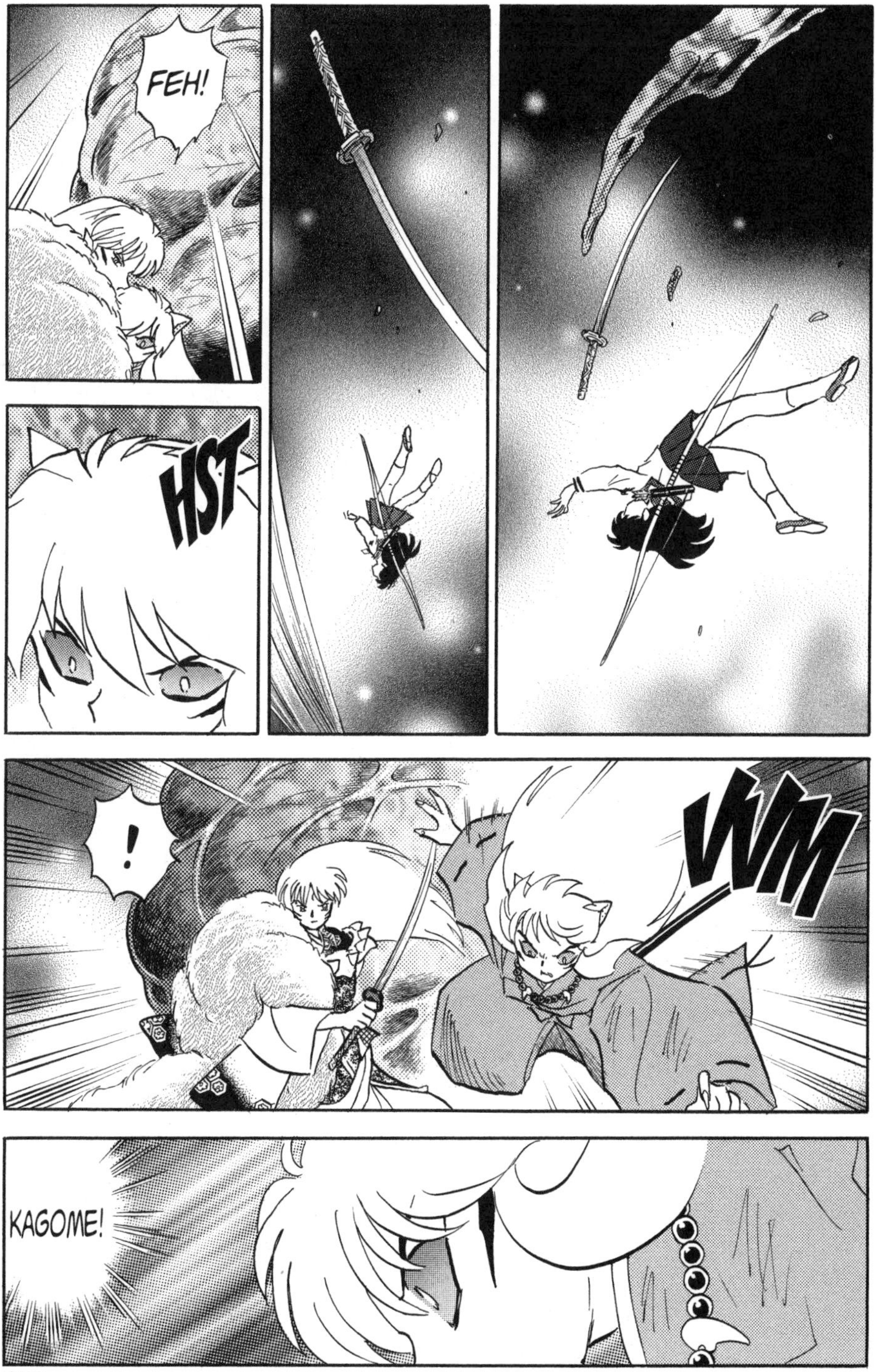
FEH!
HST
WM
!
KAGOME!

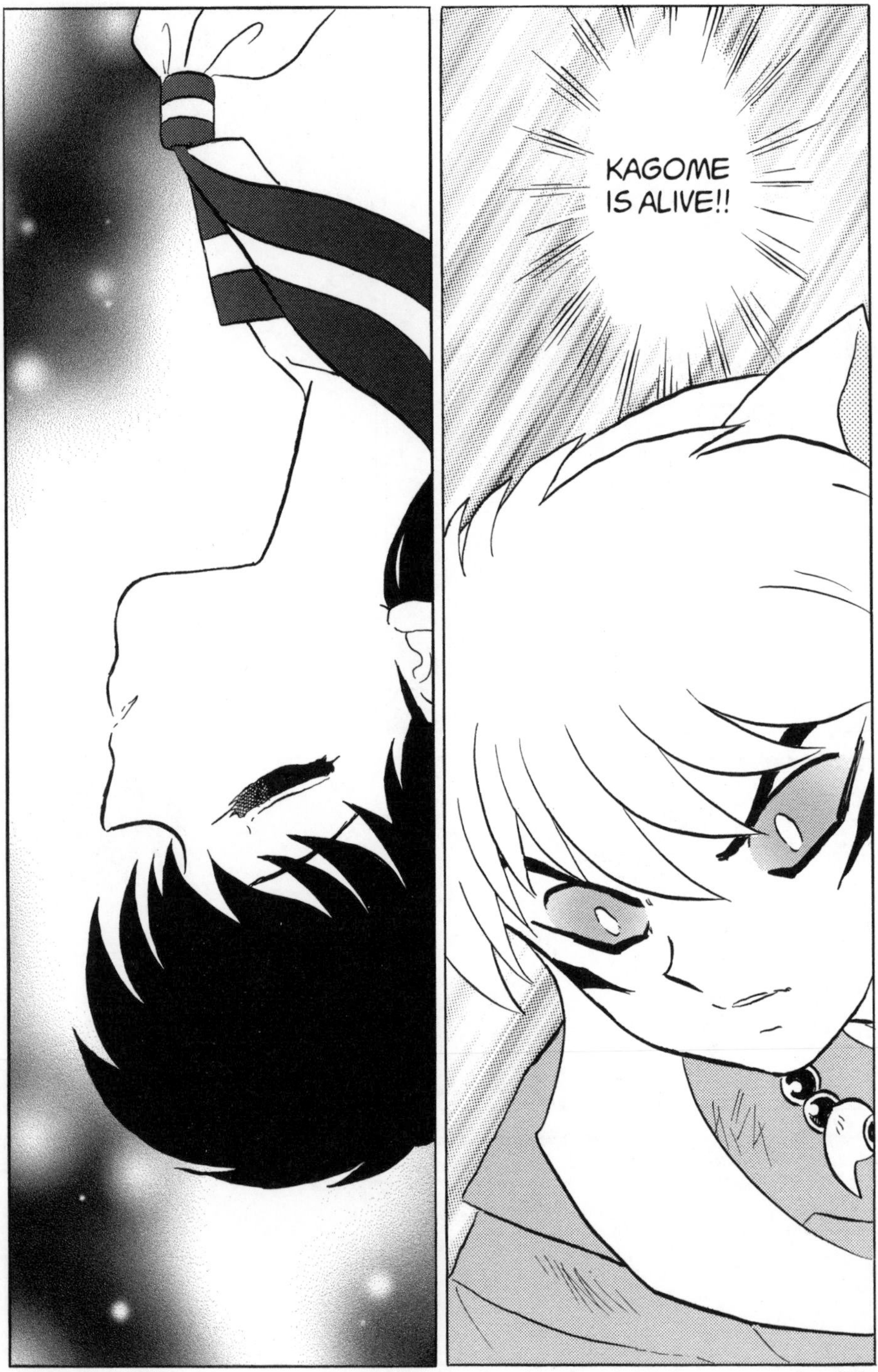
KAGOME
IS ALIVE!!

Volume 55
The Light Reborn

SCROLL ONE
ENTRAPPED

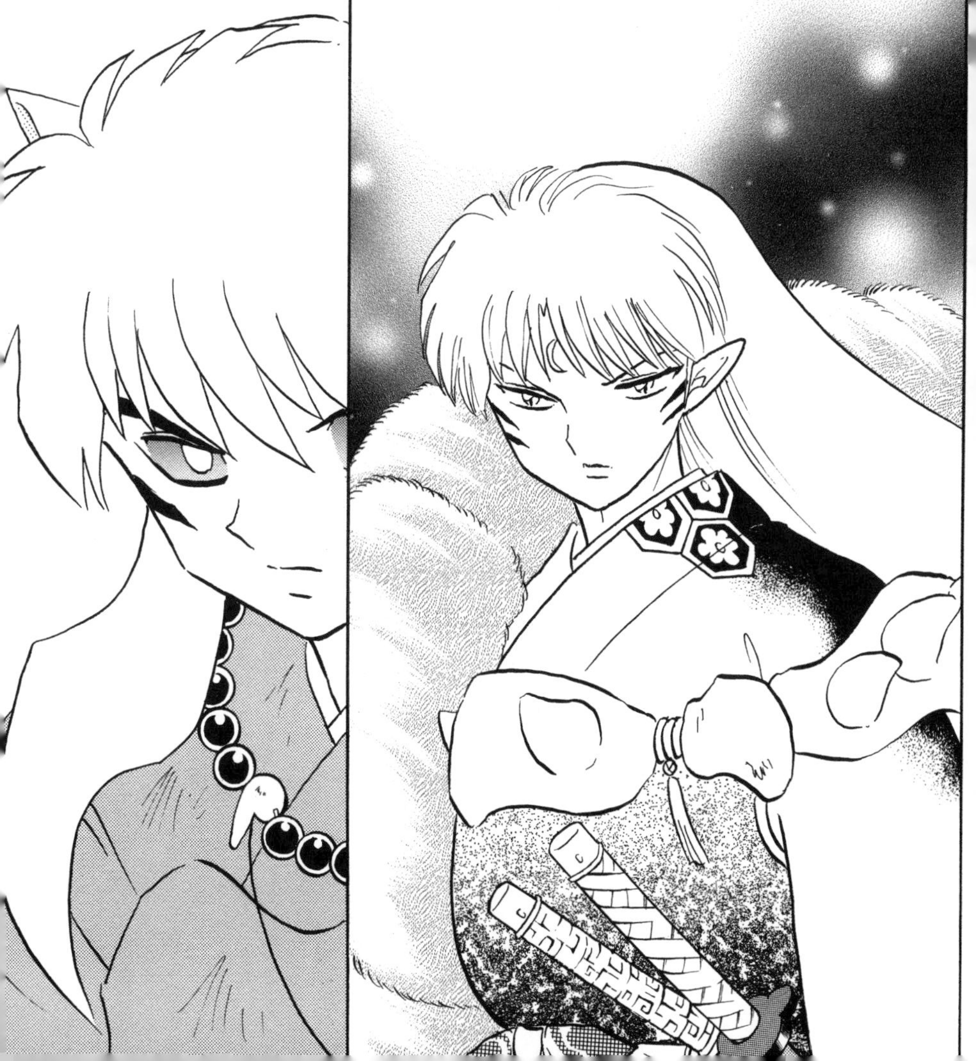

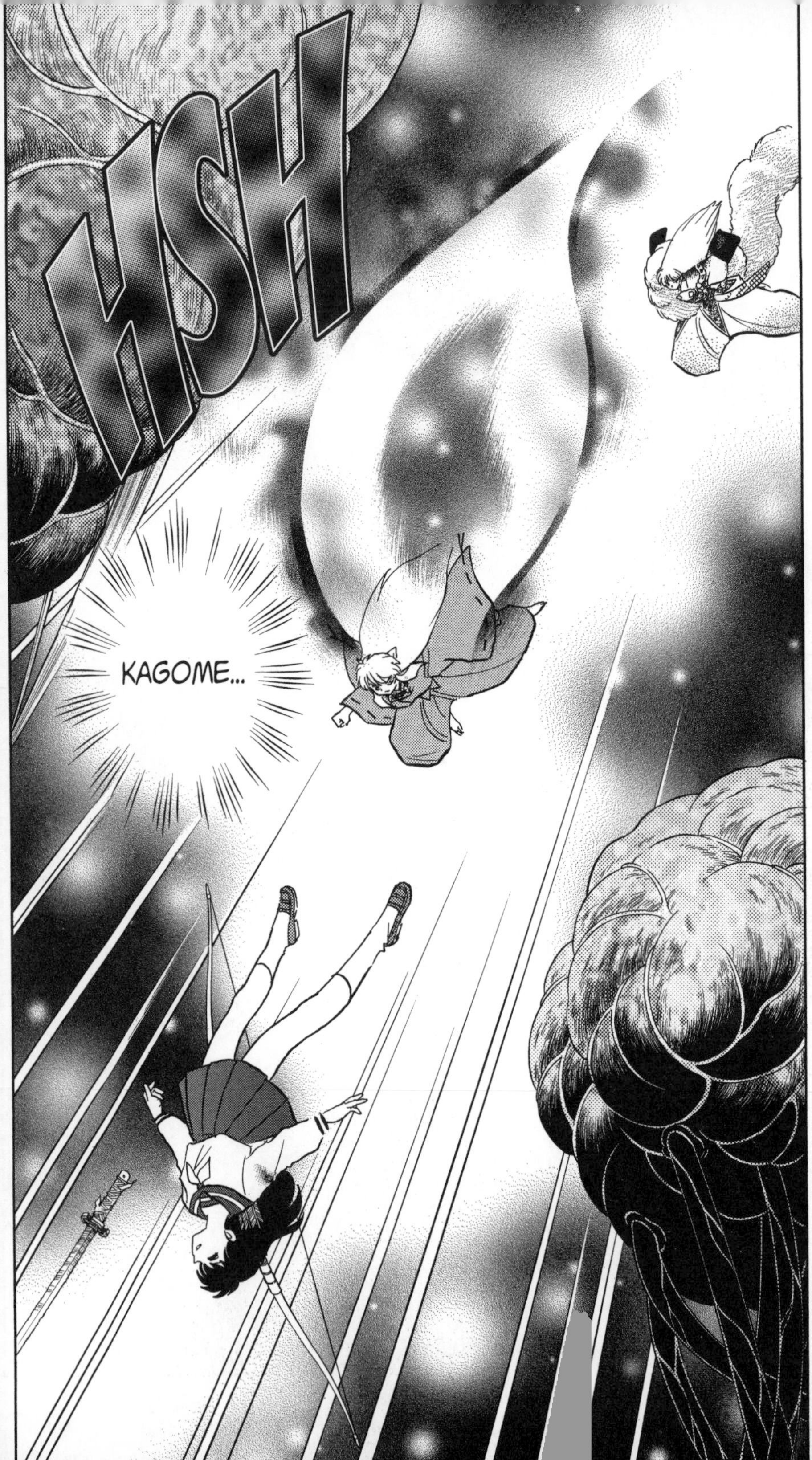
HSH
KAGOME...

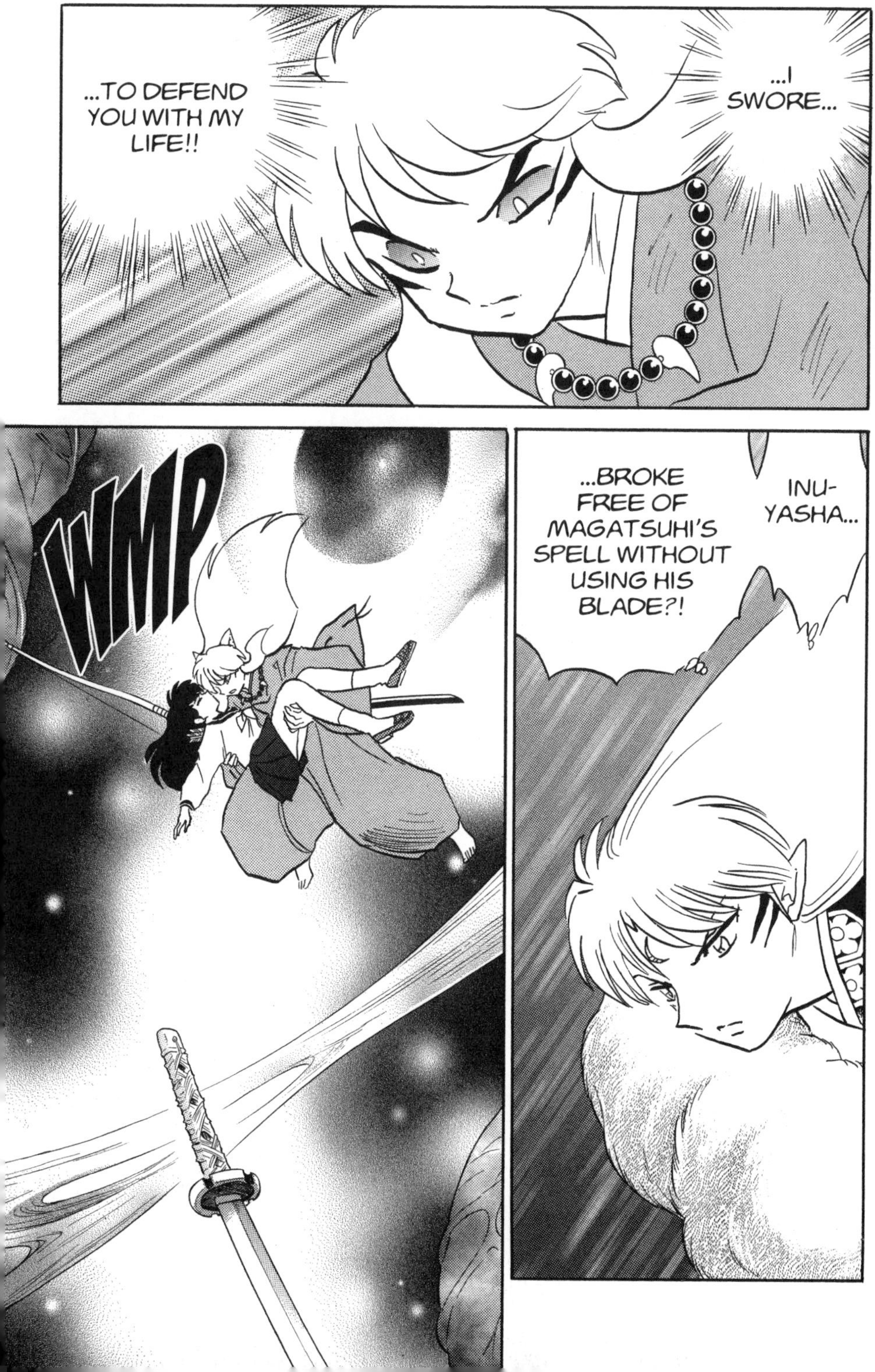
...I SWORE...
...TO DEFEND YOU WITH MY LIFE!!
INU-YASHA...
...BROKE FREE OF MAGATSUHI'S SPELL WITHOUT USING HIS BLADE?!
WMP

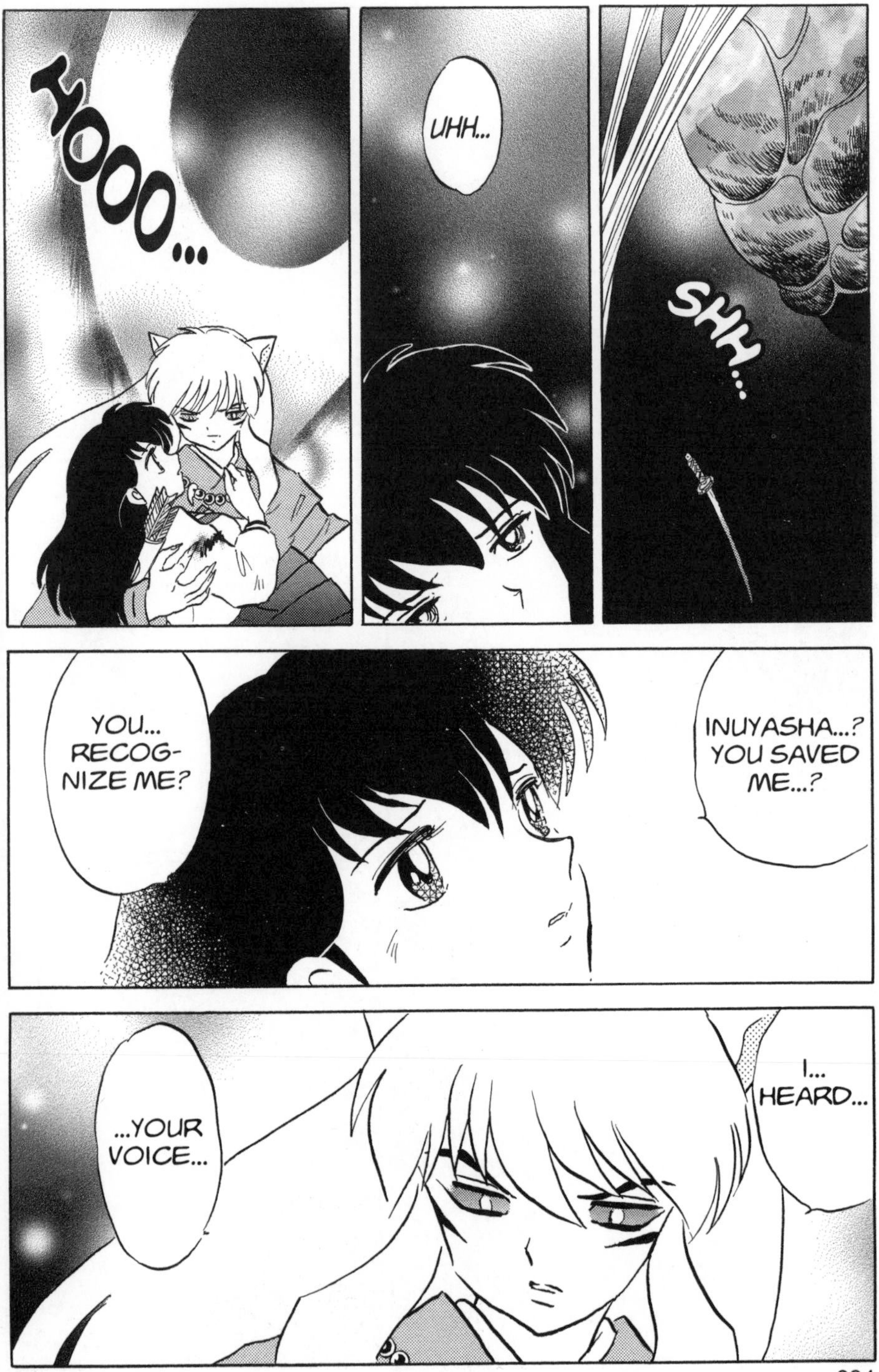
SHH...
UHH...
HOOO...
INUYASHA...? YOU SAVED ME...?
YOU... RECOG-NIZE ME?
I... HEARD...
...YOUR VOICE...

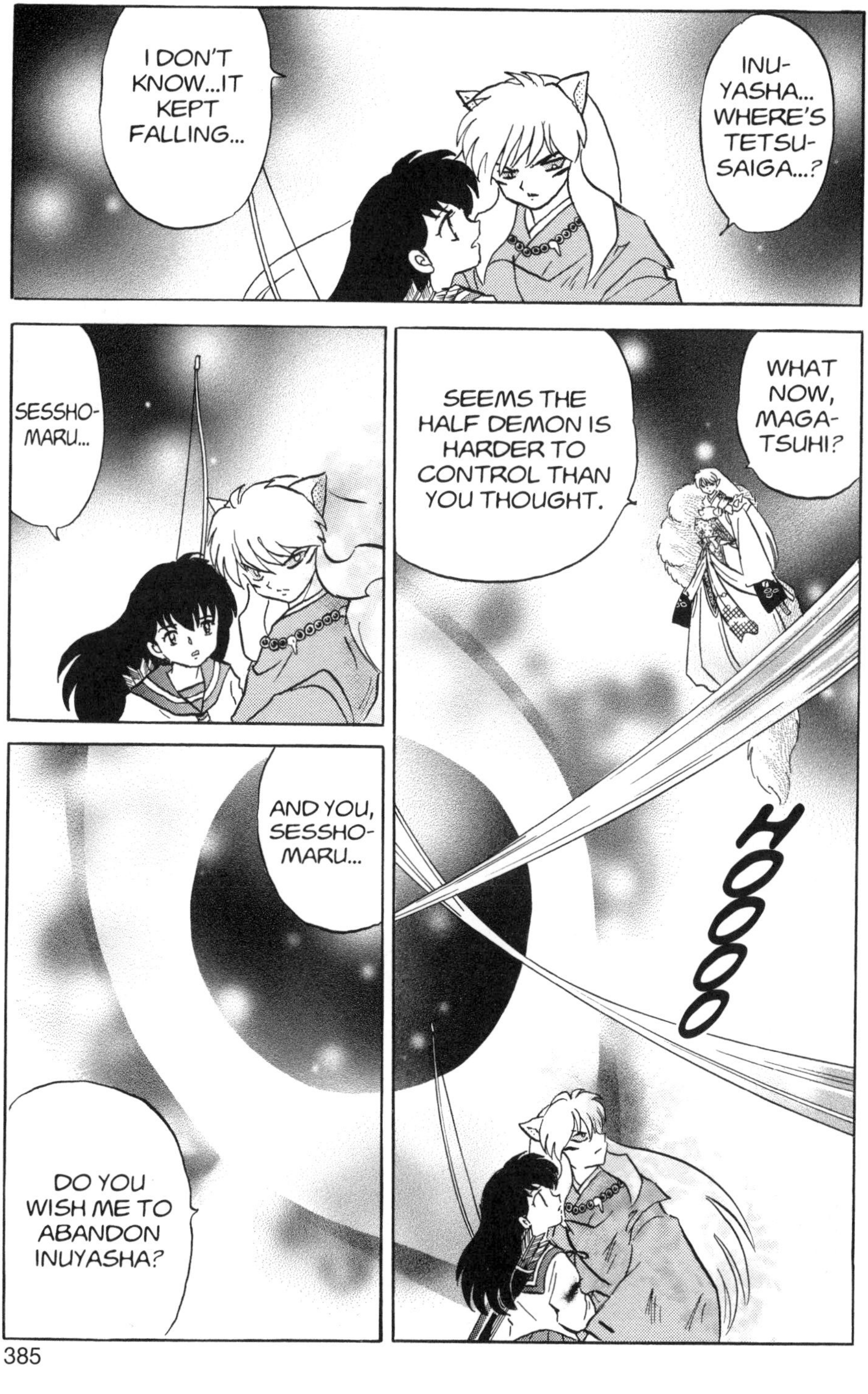
INU-YASHA... WHERE'S TETSU-SAIGA...?
I DON'T KNOW...IT KEPT FALLING...
WHAT NOW, MAGA-TSUHI?
SEEMS THE HALF DEMON IS HARDER TO CONTROL THAN YOU THOUGHT.
HOOOOO
SESSHO-MARU...
AND YOU, SESSHO-MARU...
DO YOU WISH ME TO ABANDON INUYASHA?

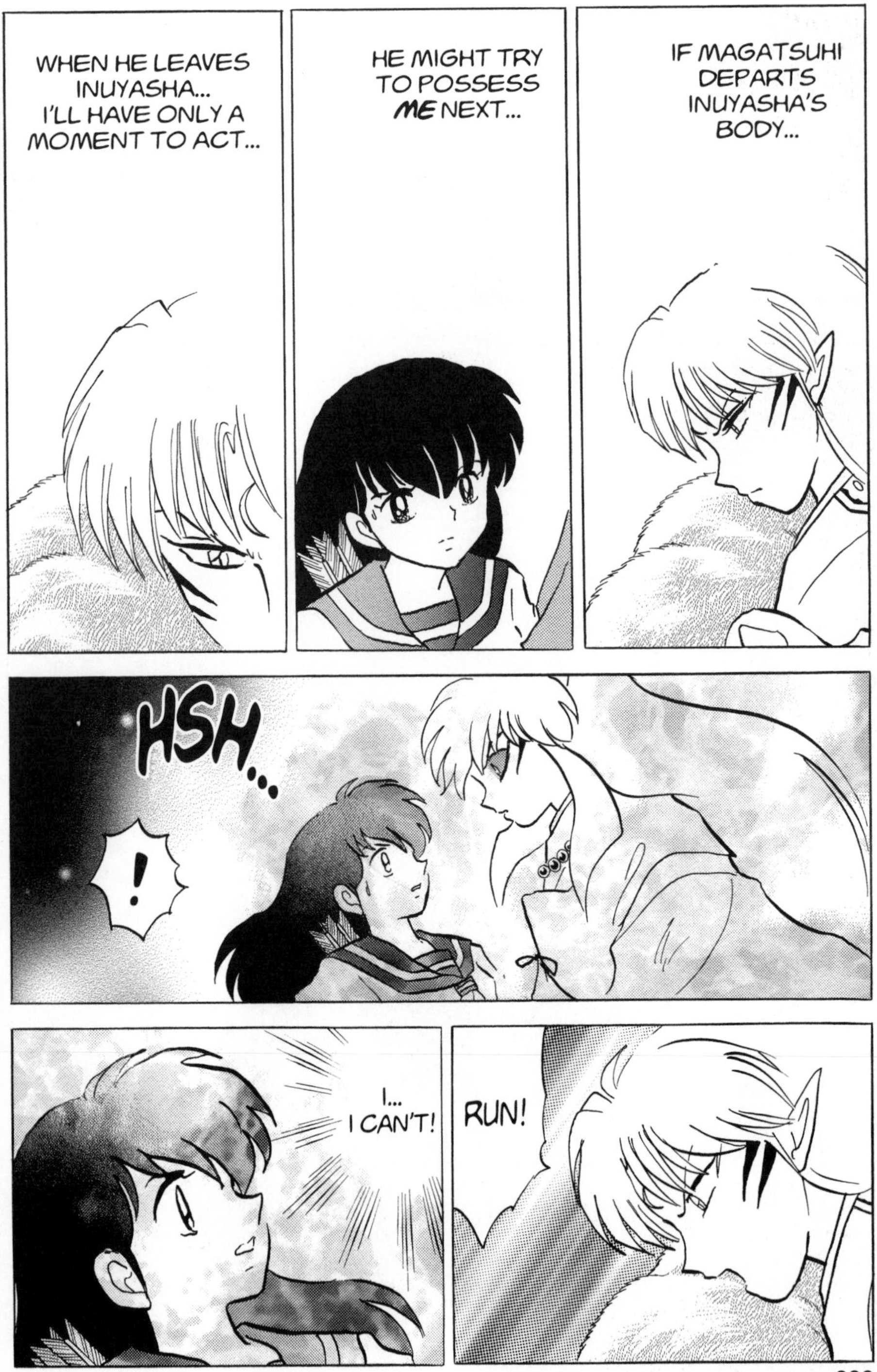
IF MAGATSUHI DEPARTS INUYASHA'S BODY...
HE MIGHT TRY TO POSSESS *ME* NEXT...
WHEN HE LEAVES INUYASHA... I'LL HAVE ONLY A MOMENT TO ACT...
HSH...
!
RUN!
I... I CAN'T!

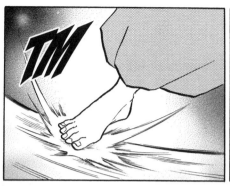

TM

HE'S GOING INTO KAGOME!

INU-YASHA...

VAH

VSH

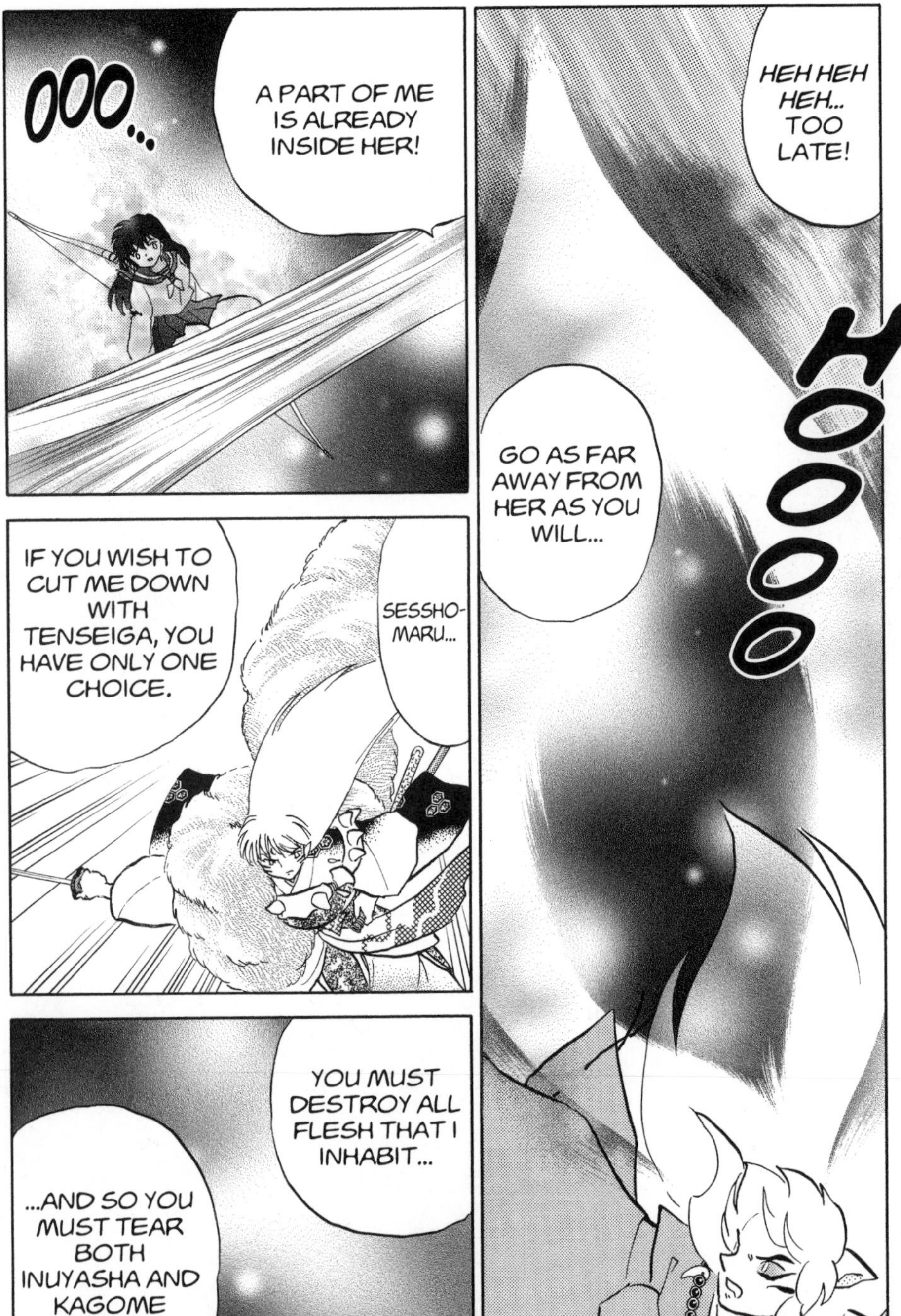
HEH HEH HEH... TOO LATE!
HOOOOO
GO AS FAR AWAY FROM HER AS YOU WILL...
A PART OF ME IS ALREADY INSIDE HER!
OOO...
SESSHO-MARU...
IF YOU WISH TO CUT ME DOWN WITH TENSEIGA, YOU HAVE ONLY ONE CHOICE.
YOU MUST DESTROY ALL FLESH THAT I INHABIT...
...AND SO YOU MUST TEAR BOTH INUYASHA AND KAGOME APART.

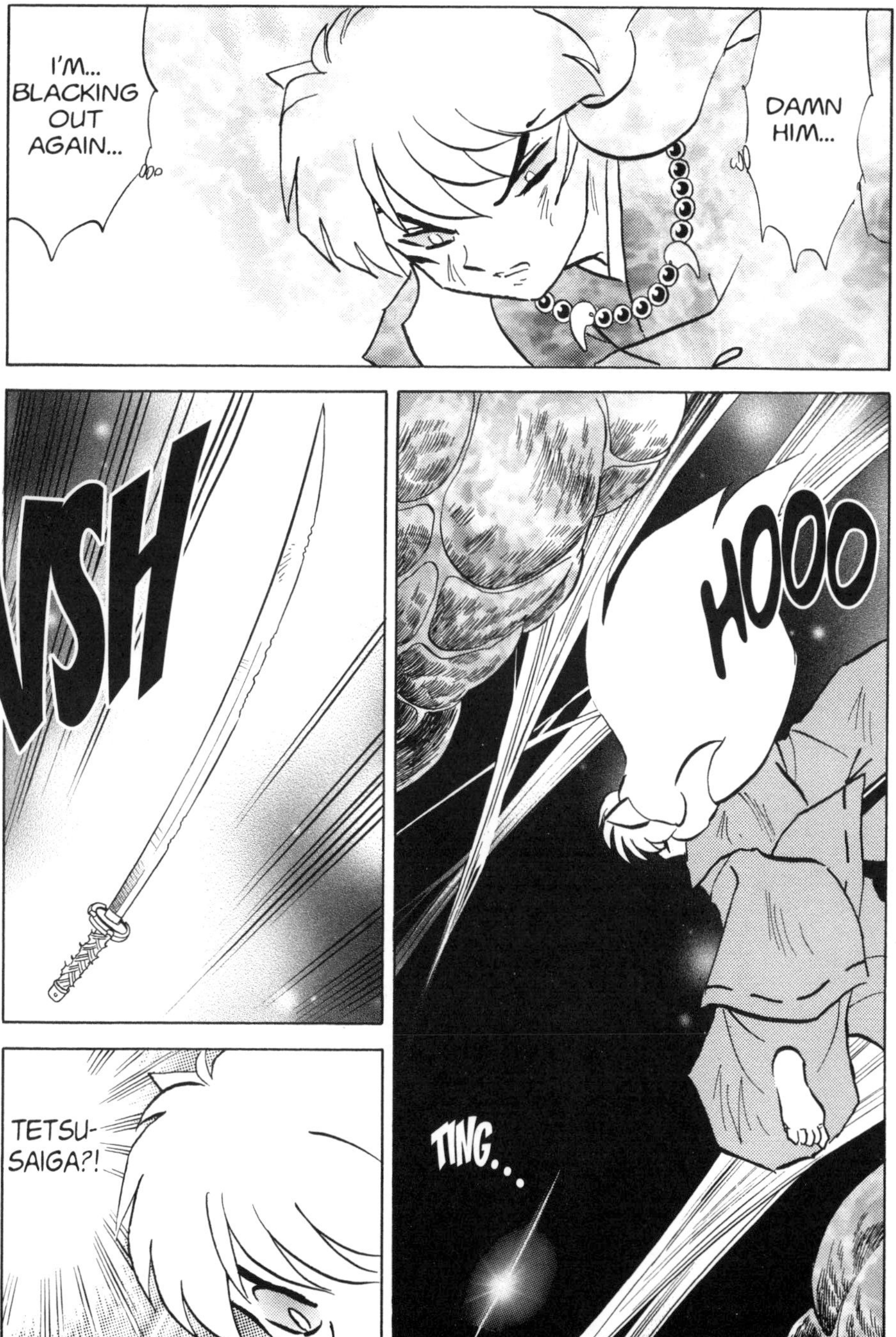
DAMN HIM...
I'M... BLACKING OUT AGAIN...
HOOO
TING...
VSH
TETSU-SAIGA?!

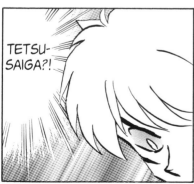

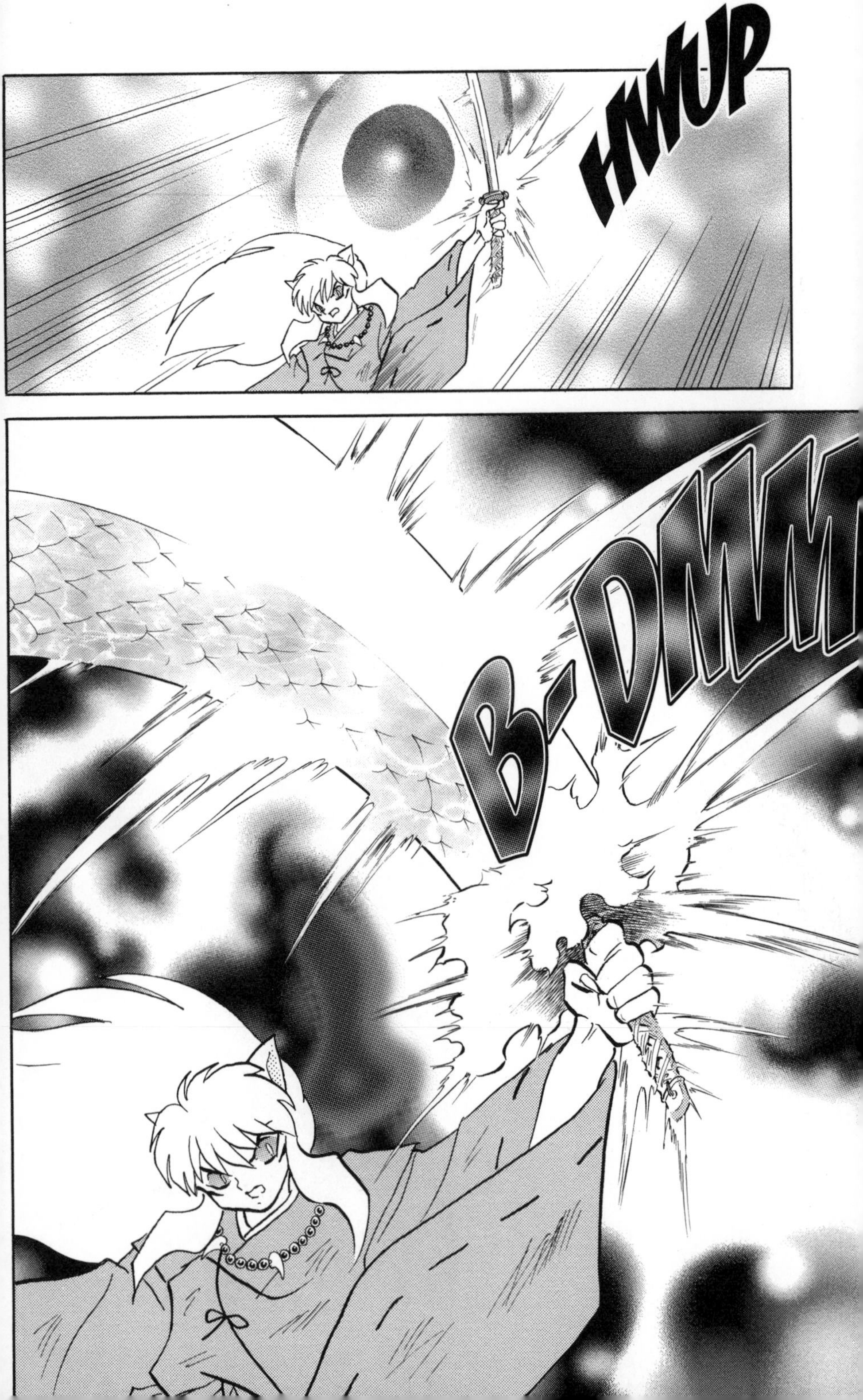
HWUP
B-DMMM

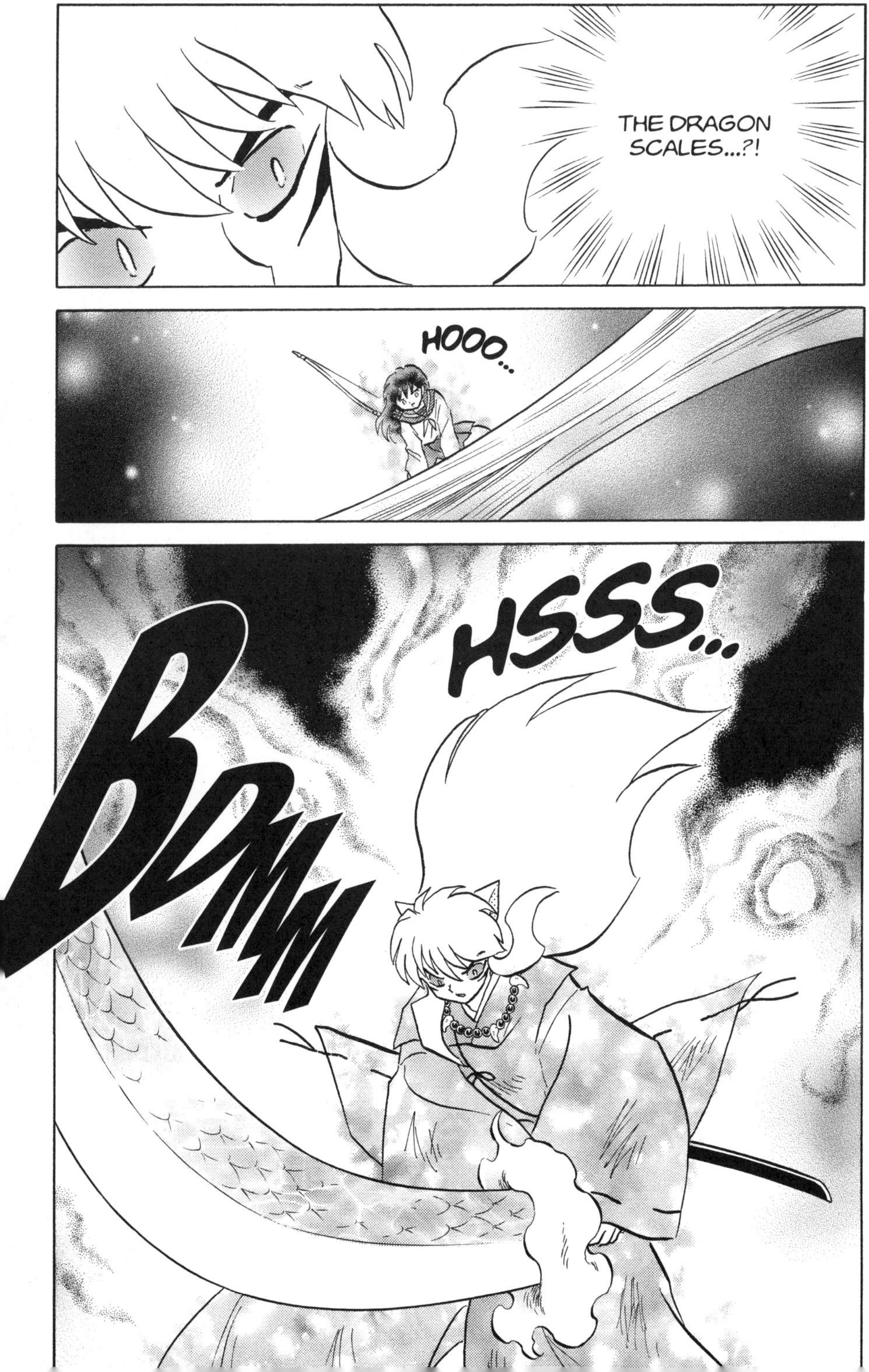
THE DRAGON SCALES...?!
HOOO...
HSSS...
BOMM

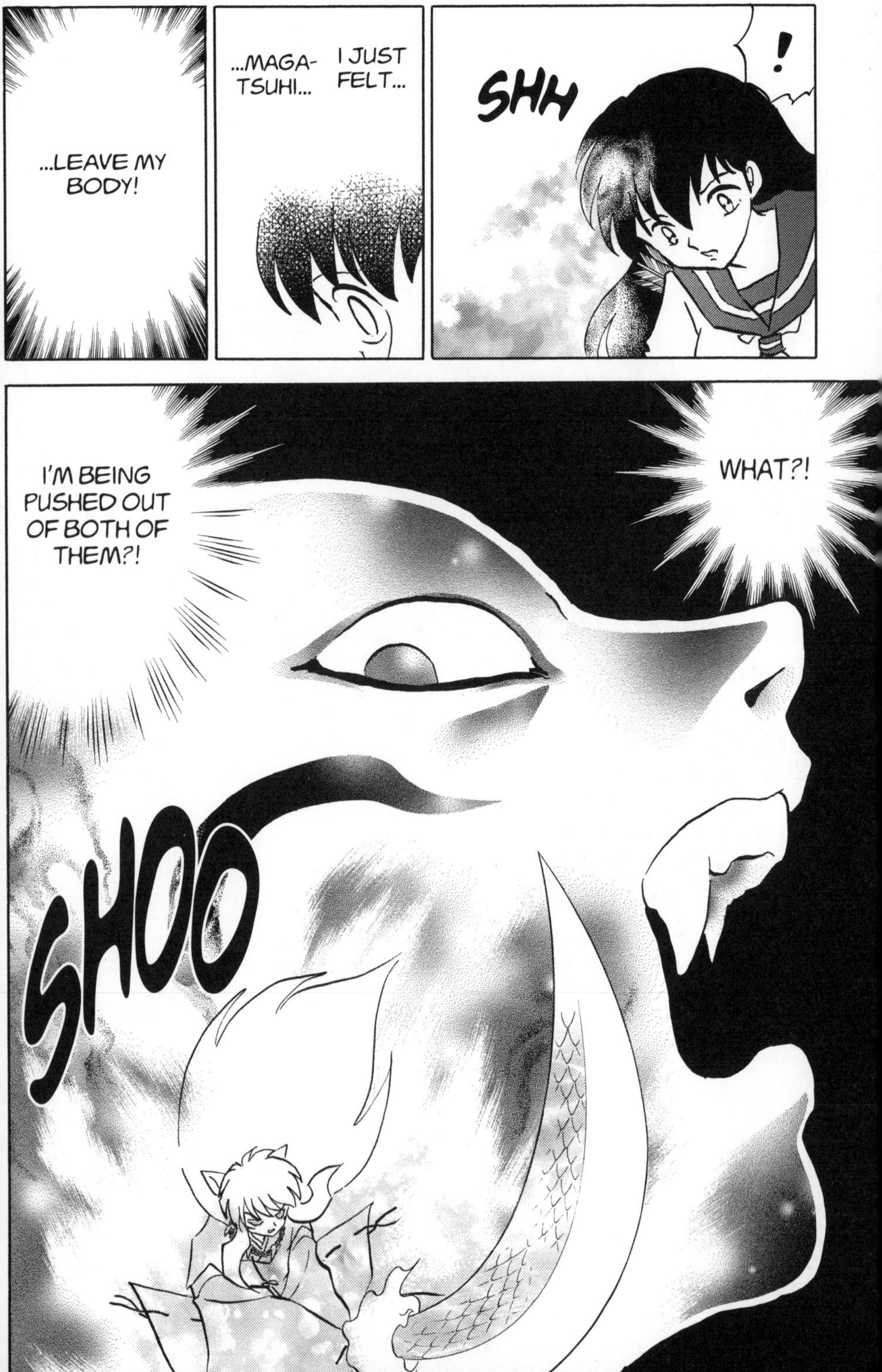
!
SHH
I JUST FELT...
...MAGA-TSUHI...
...LEAVE MY BODY!
WHAT?!
I'M BEING PUSHED OUT OF BOTH OF THEM?!
SHOO

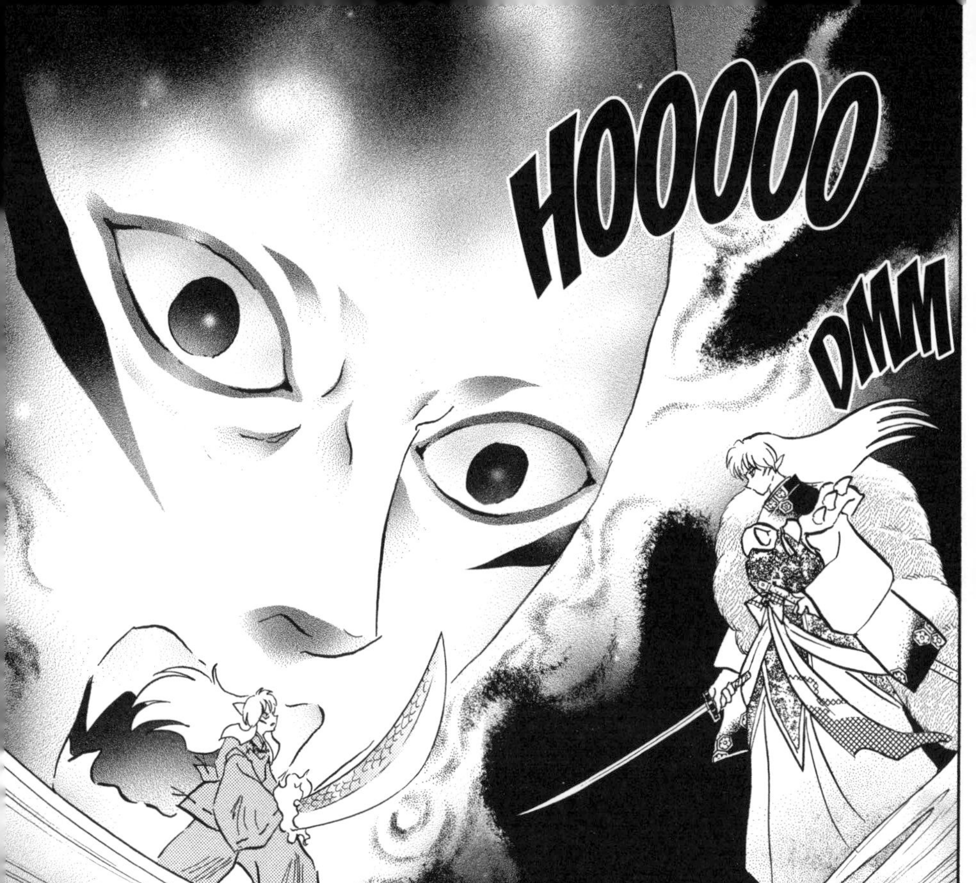
HOOOOO
DMM
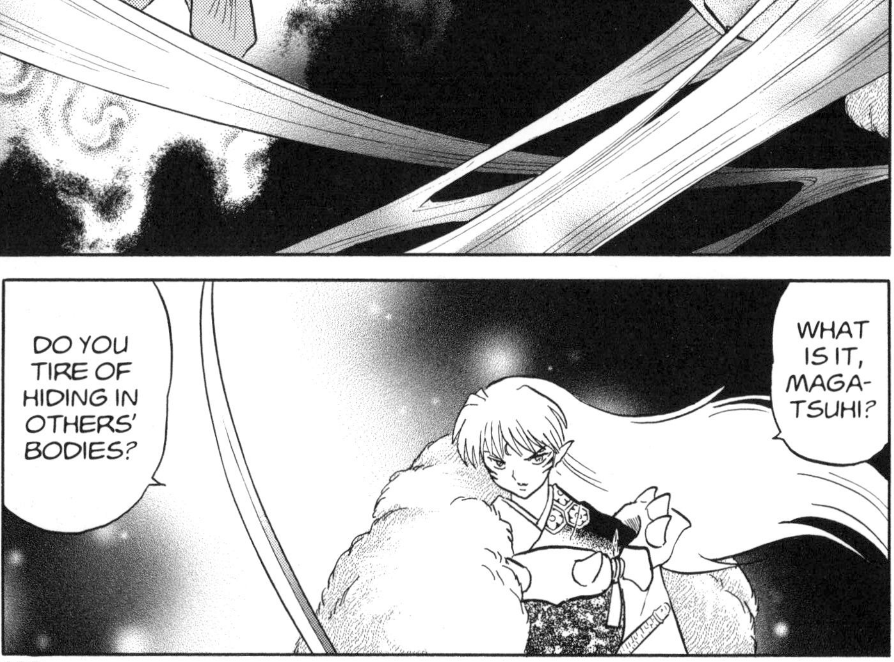
WHAT IS IT, MAGA-TSUHI?
DO YOU TIRE OF HIDING IN OTHERS' BODIES?

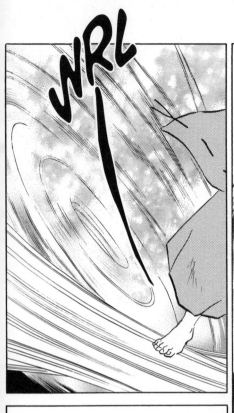

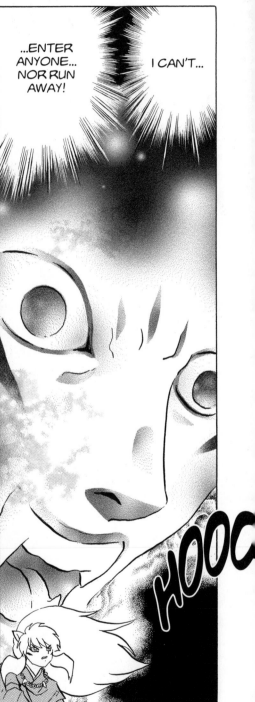

I CAN'T...
...ENTER ANYONE... NOR RUN AWAY!
HOO
WRL
I'VE GOT HIM TRAPPED...
...IN MY DEMON VORTEX!

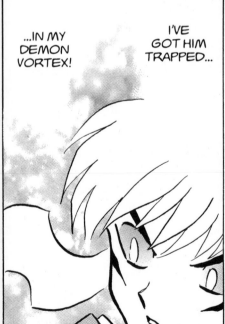

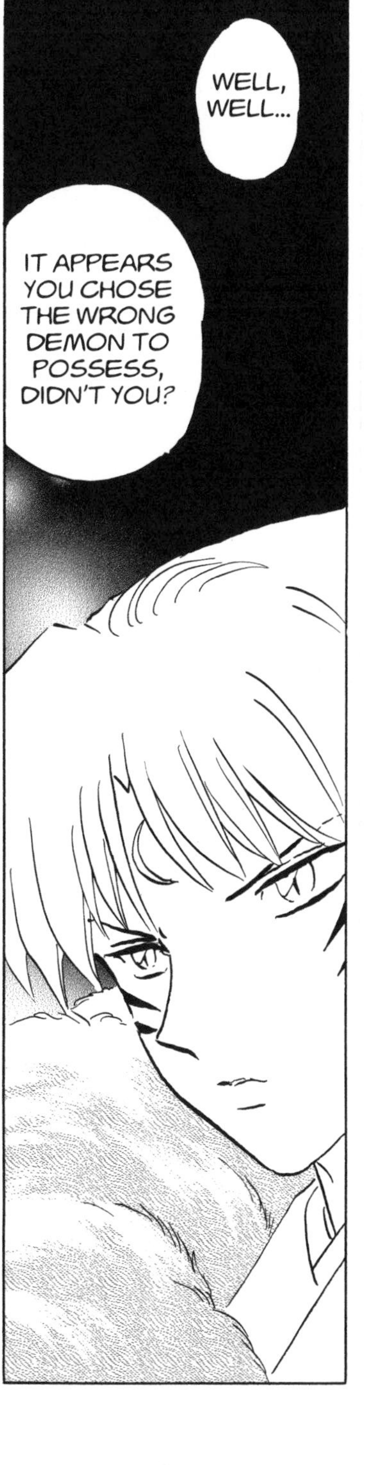
WELL, WELL...
IT APPEARS YOU CHOSE THE WRONG DEMON TO POSSESS, DIDN'T YOU?
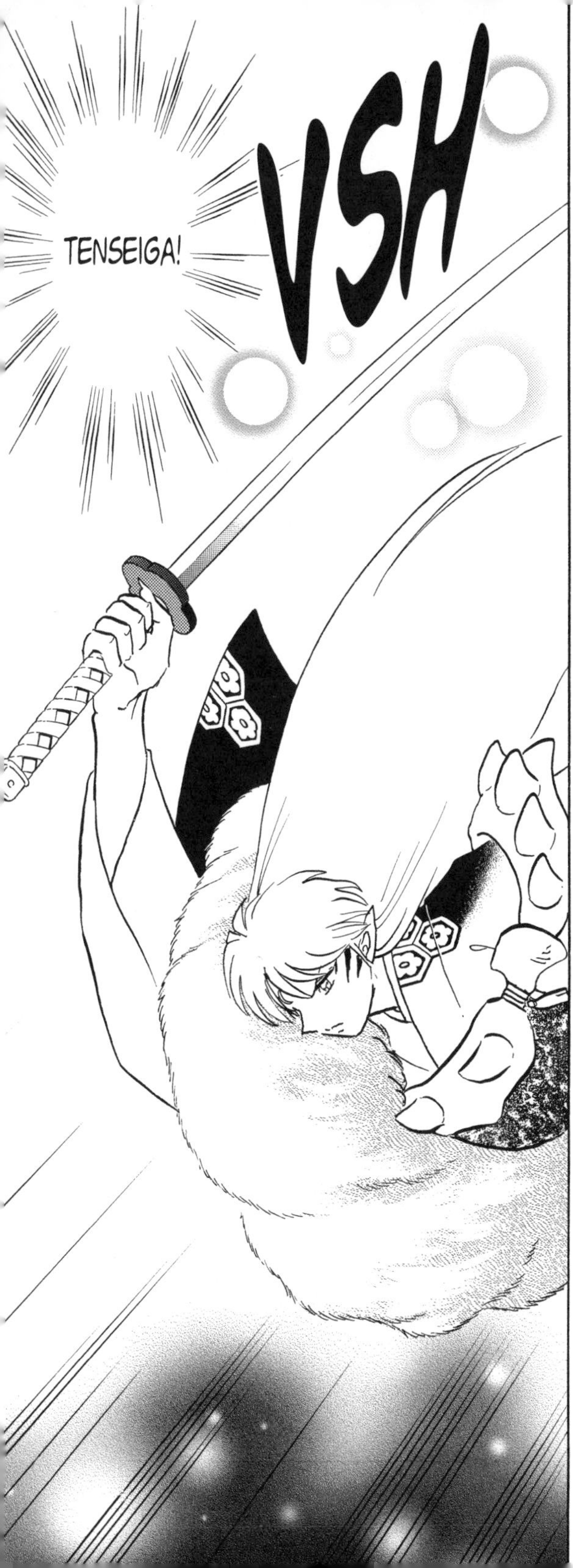
TENSEIGA!
VSH

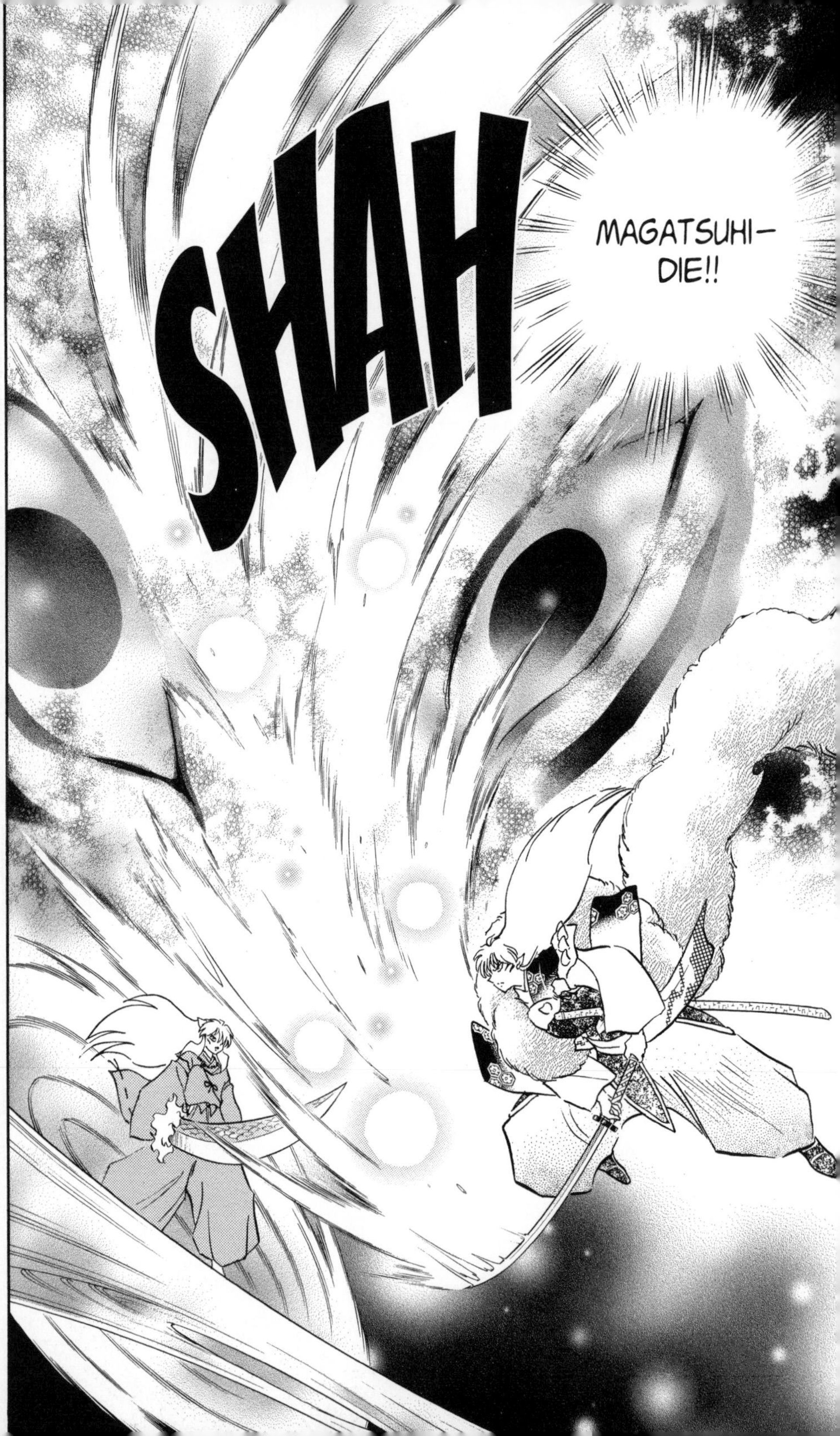
MAGATSUHI—
DIE!!
SHAH

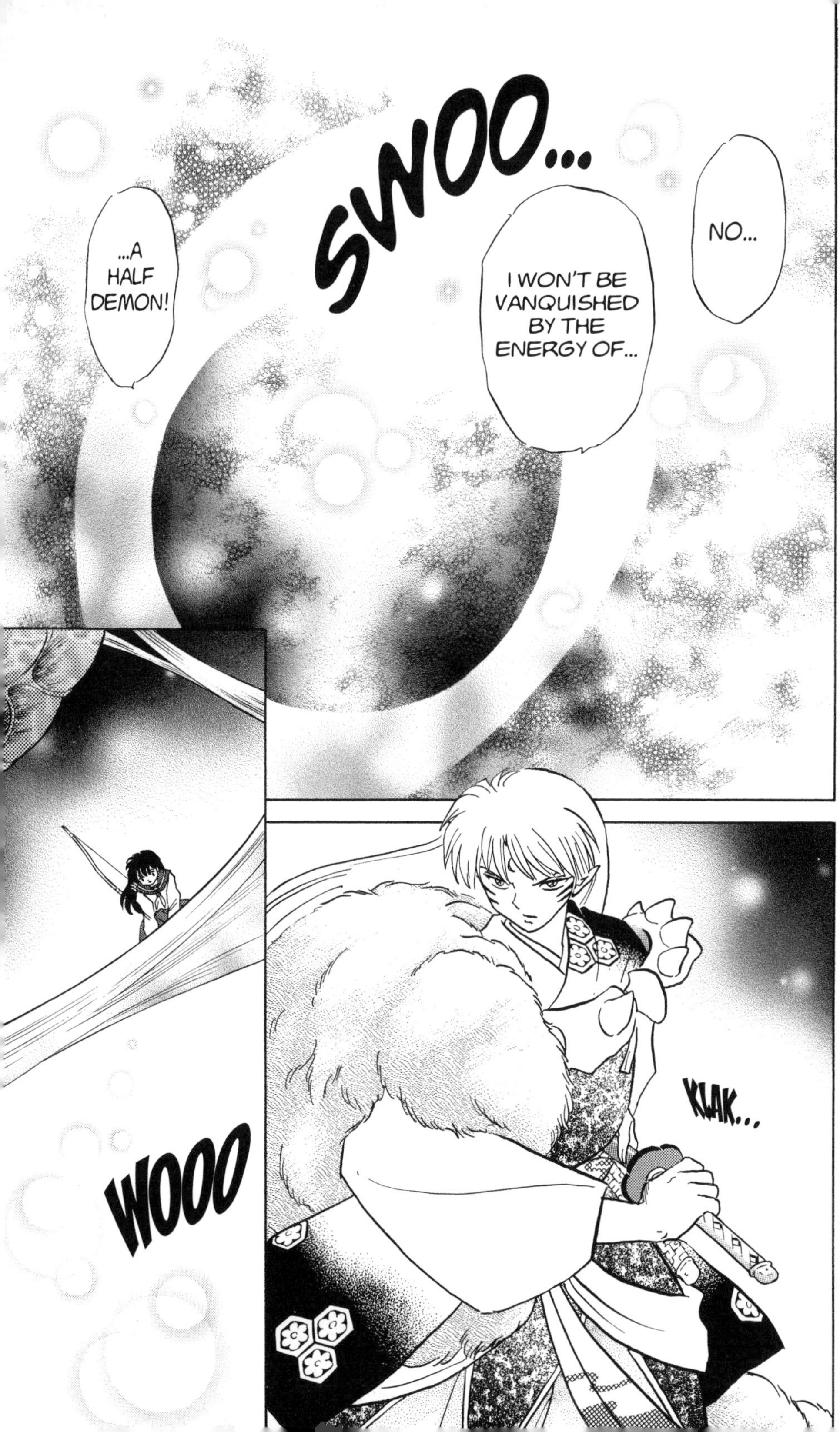
NO...
I WON'T BE VANQUISHED BY THE ENERGY OF...
SWOO...
...A HALF DEMON!
KLAK...
WOOO

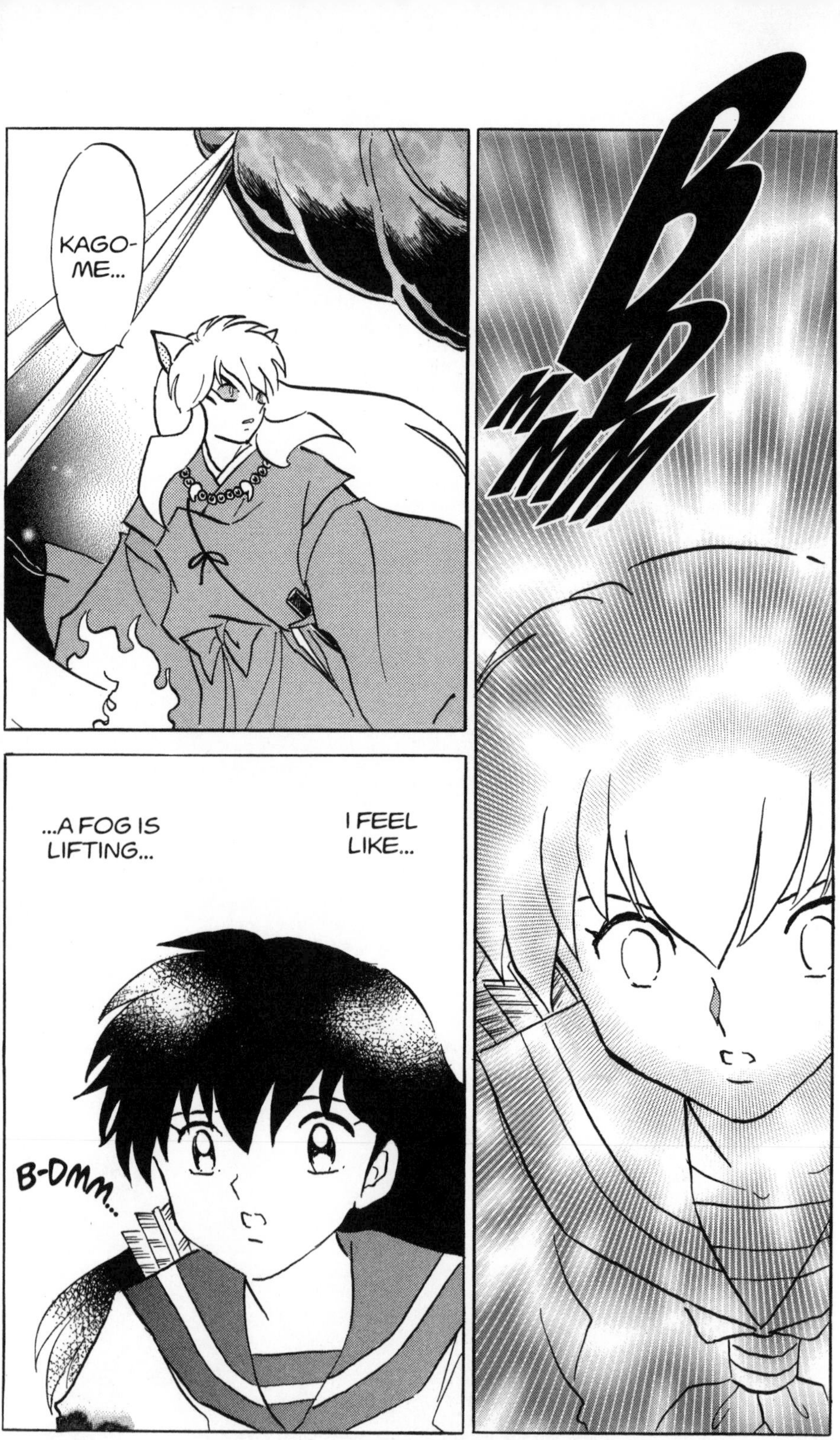
BMMM
KAGO-ME...
I FEEL LIKE...
...A FOG IS LIFTING...
B-DMM...

SCROLL TWO
THE LIGHT REBORN

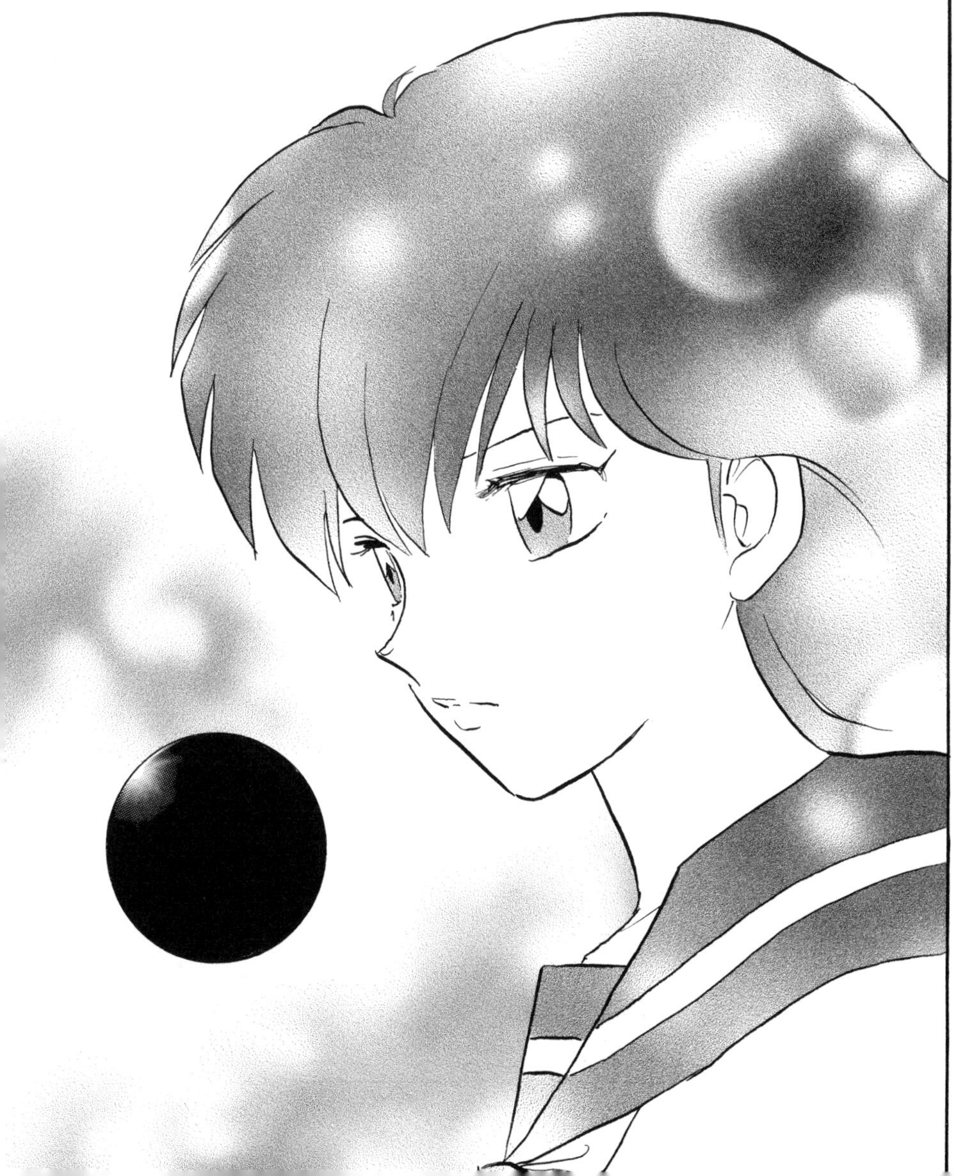

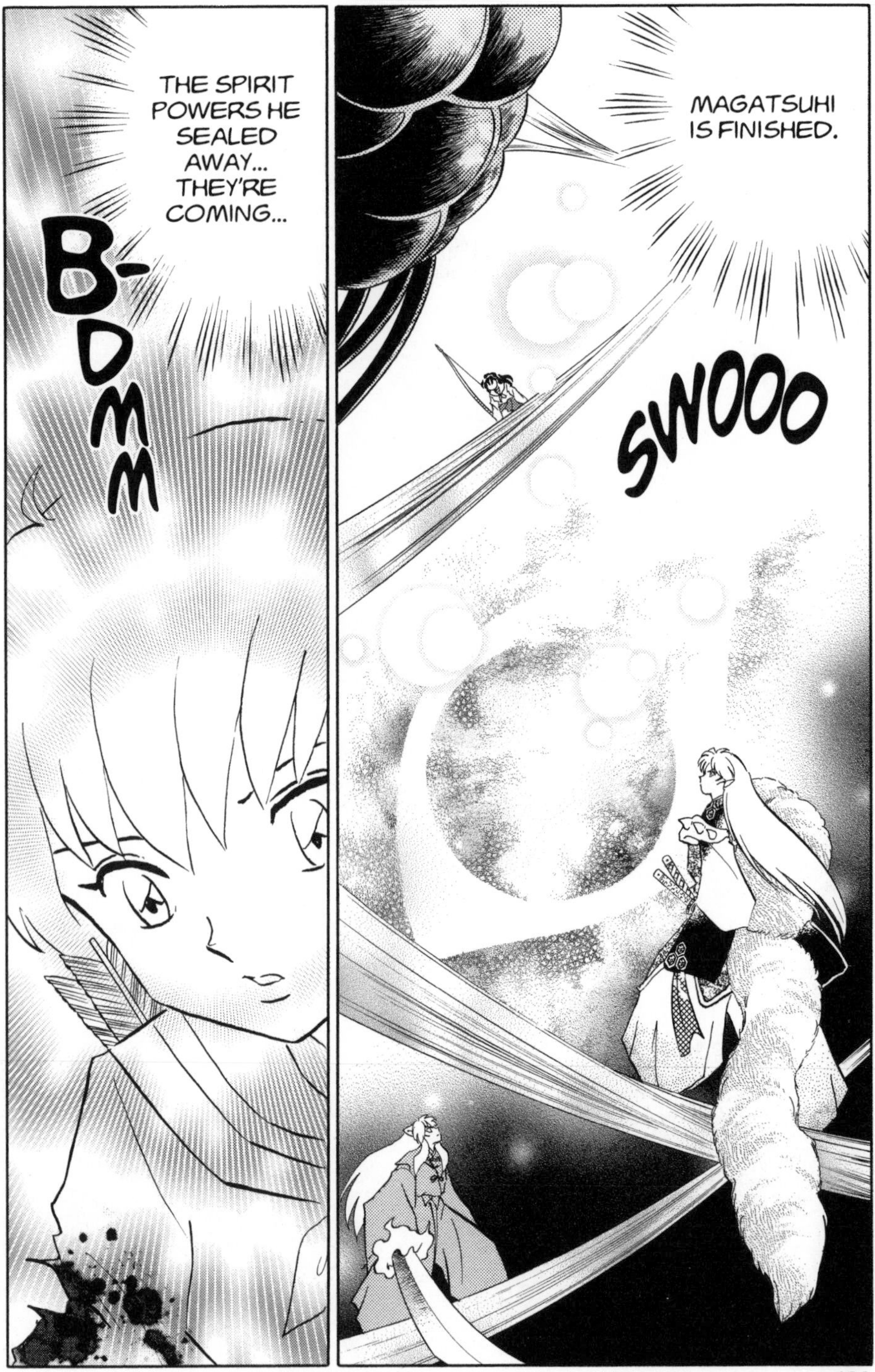
MAGATSUHI IS FINISHED.
SWOOO
THE SPIRIT POWERS HE SEALED AWAY... THEY'RE COMING...
B-DMM

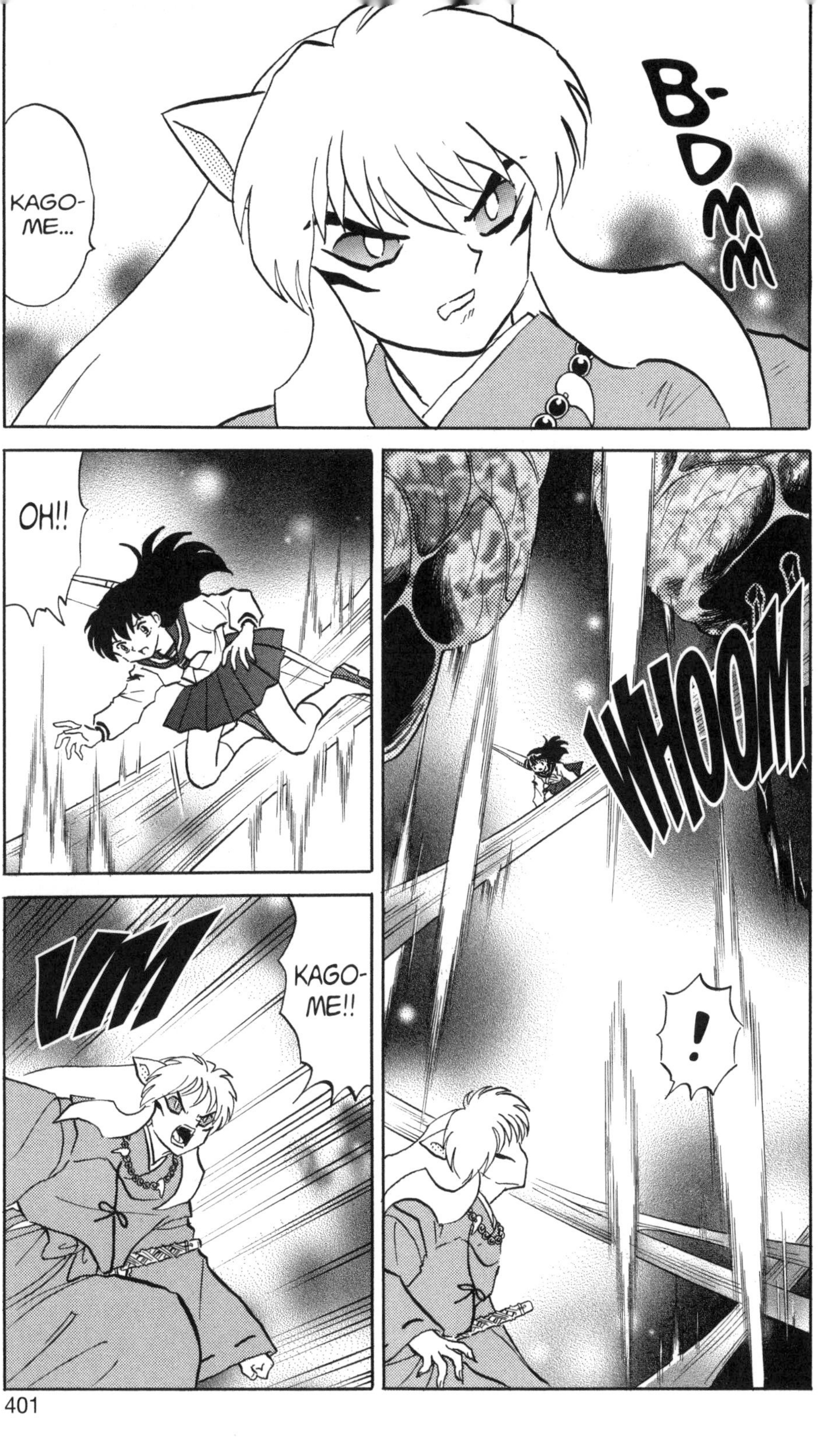
B-DMMM
KAGO-ME...
WHOOM
!
OH!!
VM
KAGO-ME!!

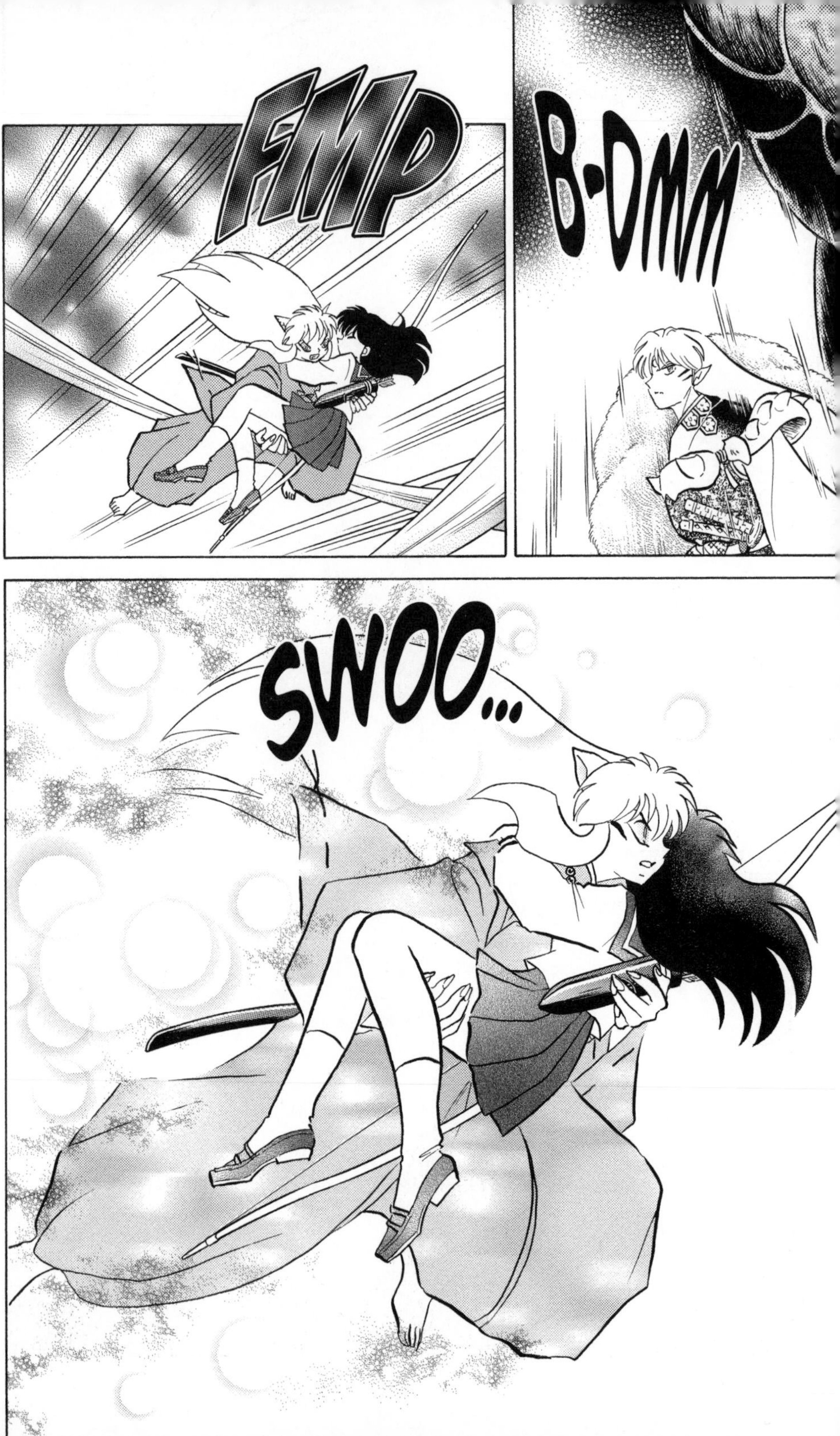
B-DMM
FMP
SWOO...

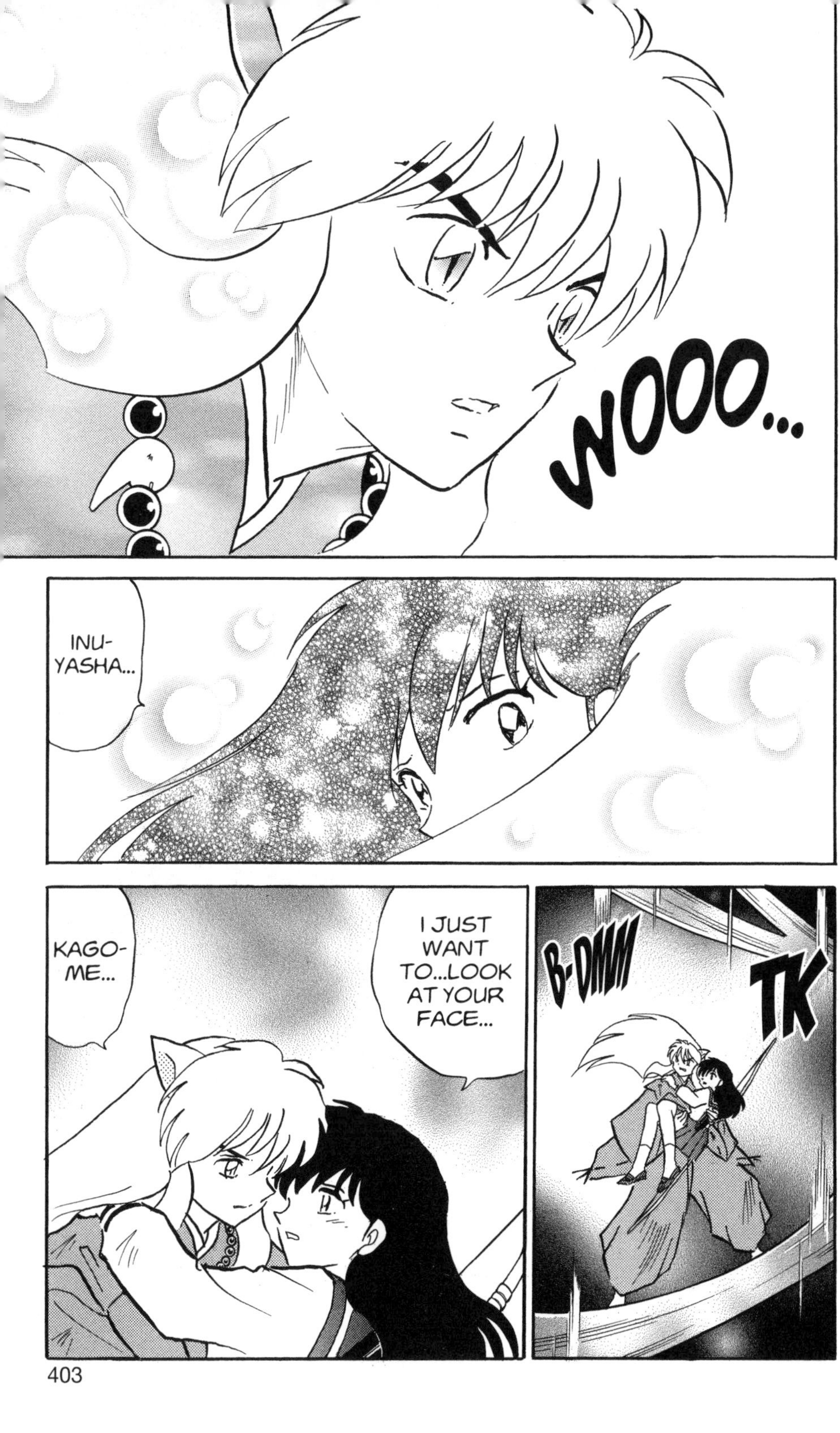
WOOO...
INU-YASHA...
B-DMM
TK
I JUST WANT TO...LOOK AT YOUR FACE...
KAGO-ME...

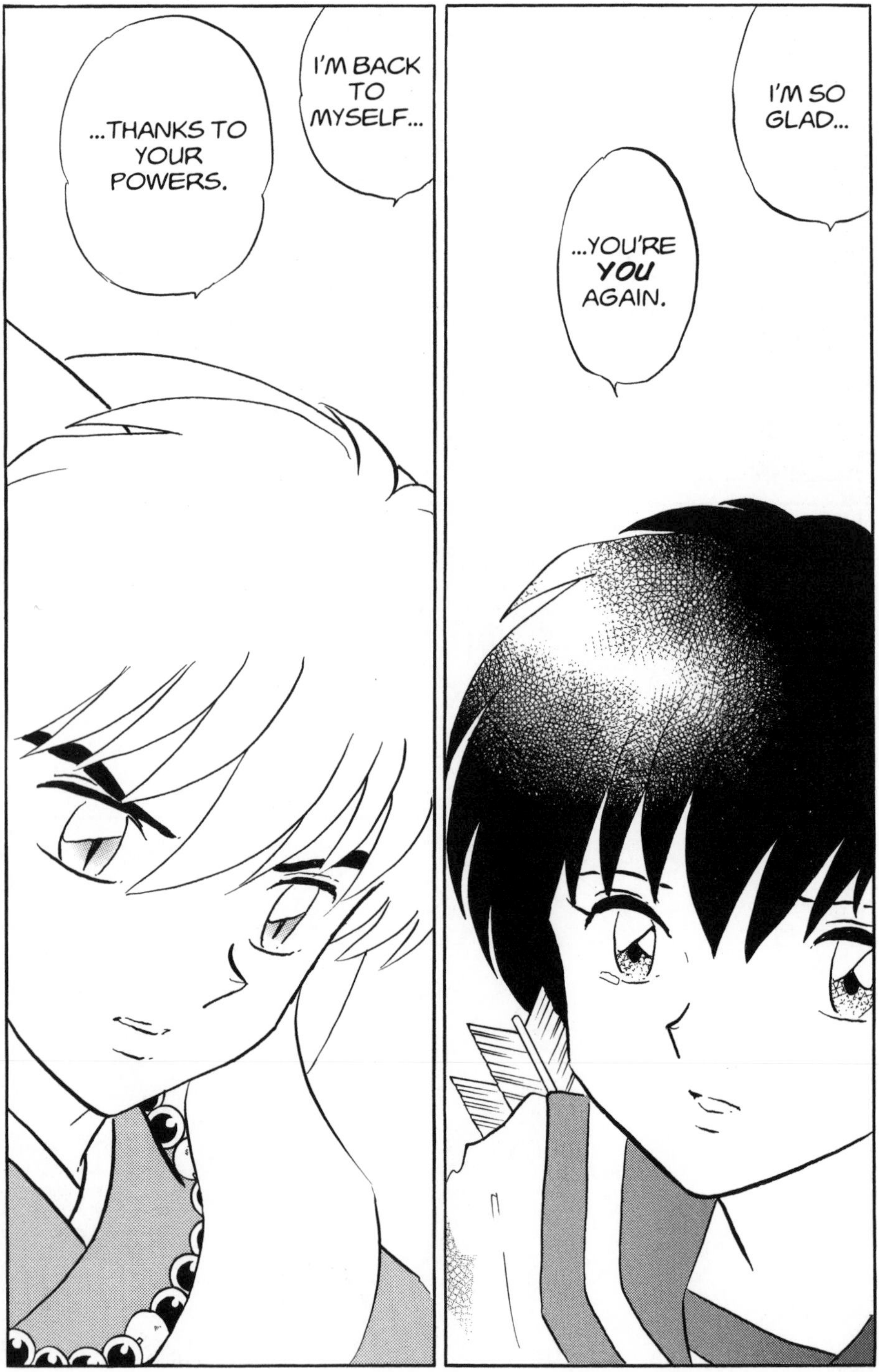
I'M SO GLAD...
...YOU'RE **YOU** AGAIN.
I'M BACK TO MYSELF...
...THANKS TO YOUR POWERS.

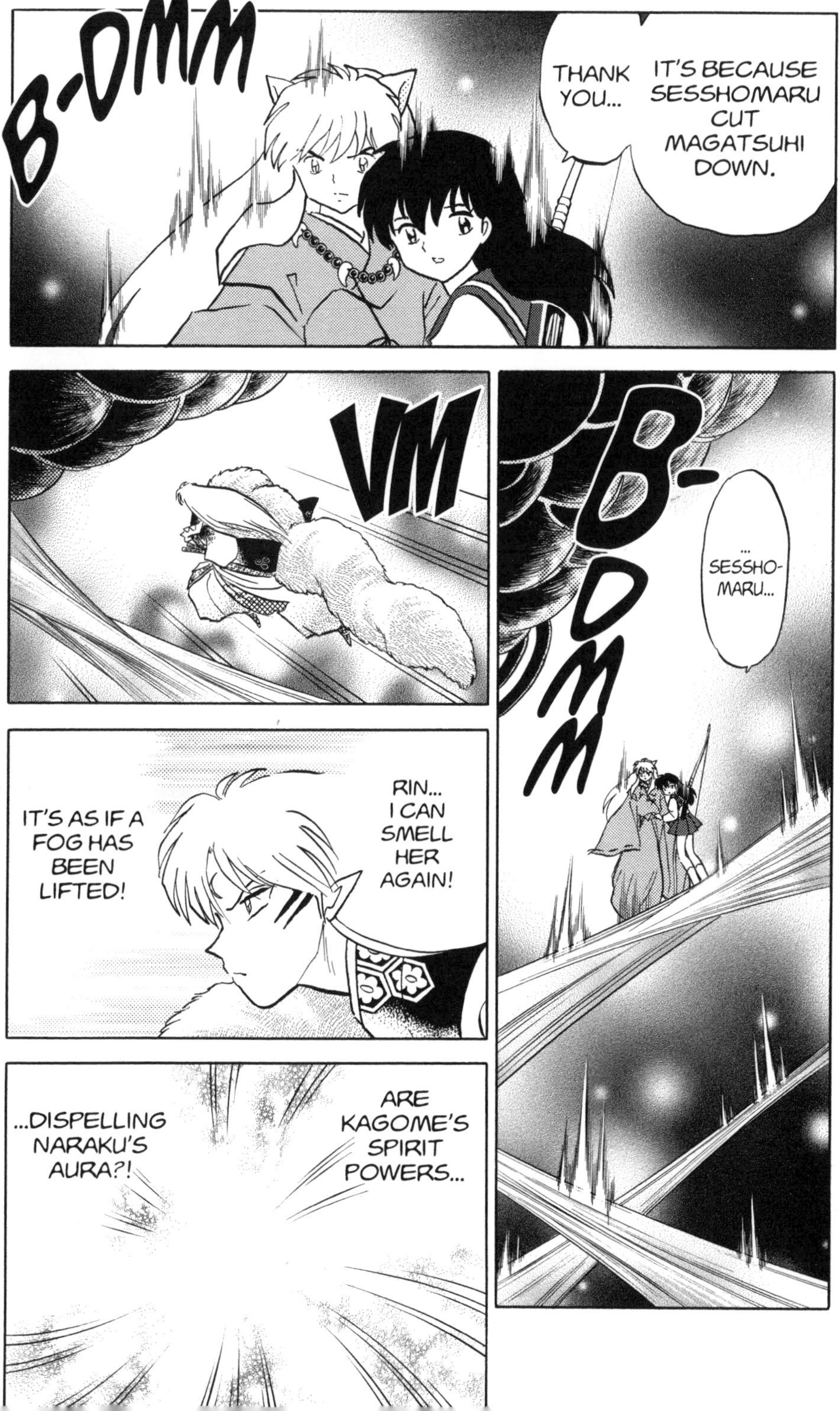
B-DMM
IT'S BECAUSE SESSHOMARU CUT MAGATSUHI DOWN.
THANK YOU...
B-DMM
...SESSHO-MARU...
VM
RIN... I CAN SMELL HER AGAIN!
IT'S AS IF A FOG HAS BEEN LIFTED!
ARE KAGOME'S SPIRIT POWERS...
...DISPELLING NARAKU'S AURA?!

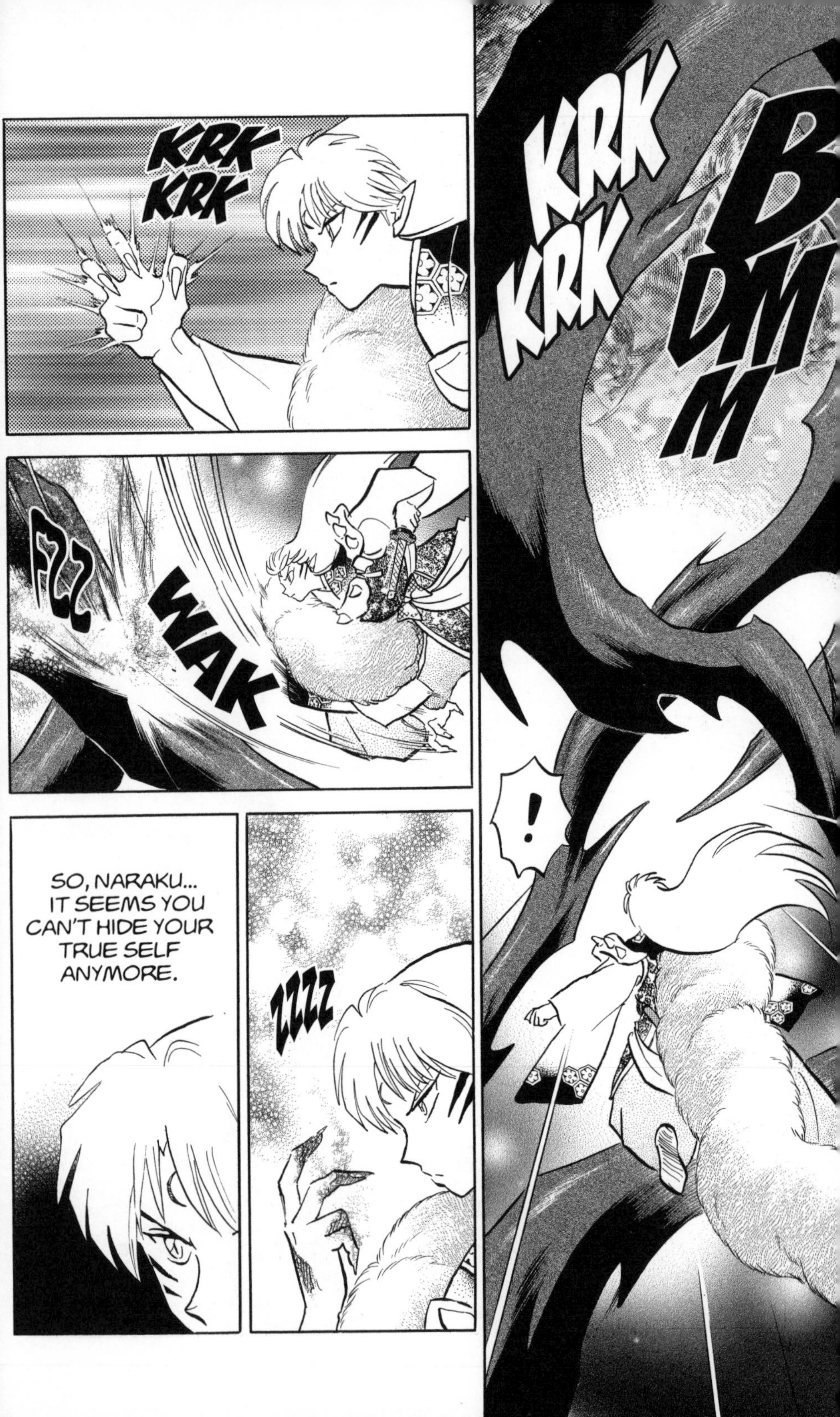
KRK
KRK
BDMM
!
KRK
KRK
WAK
FZZ
ZZZZ
SO, NARAKU... IT SEEMS YOU CAN'T HIDE YOUR TRUE SELF ANYMORE.

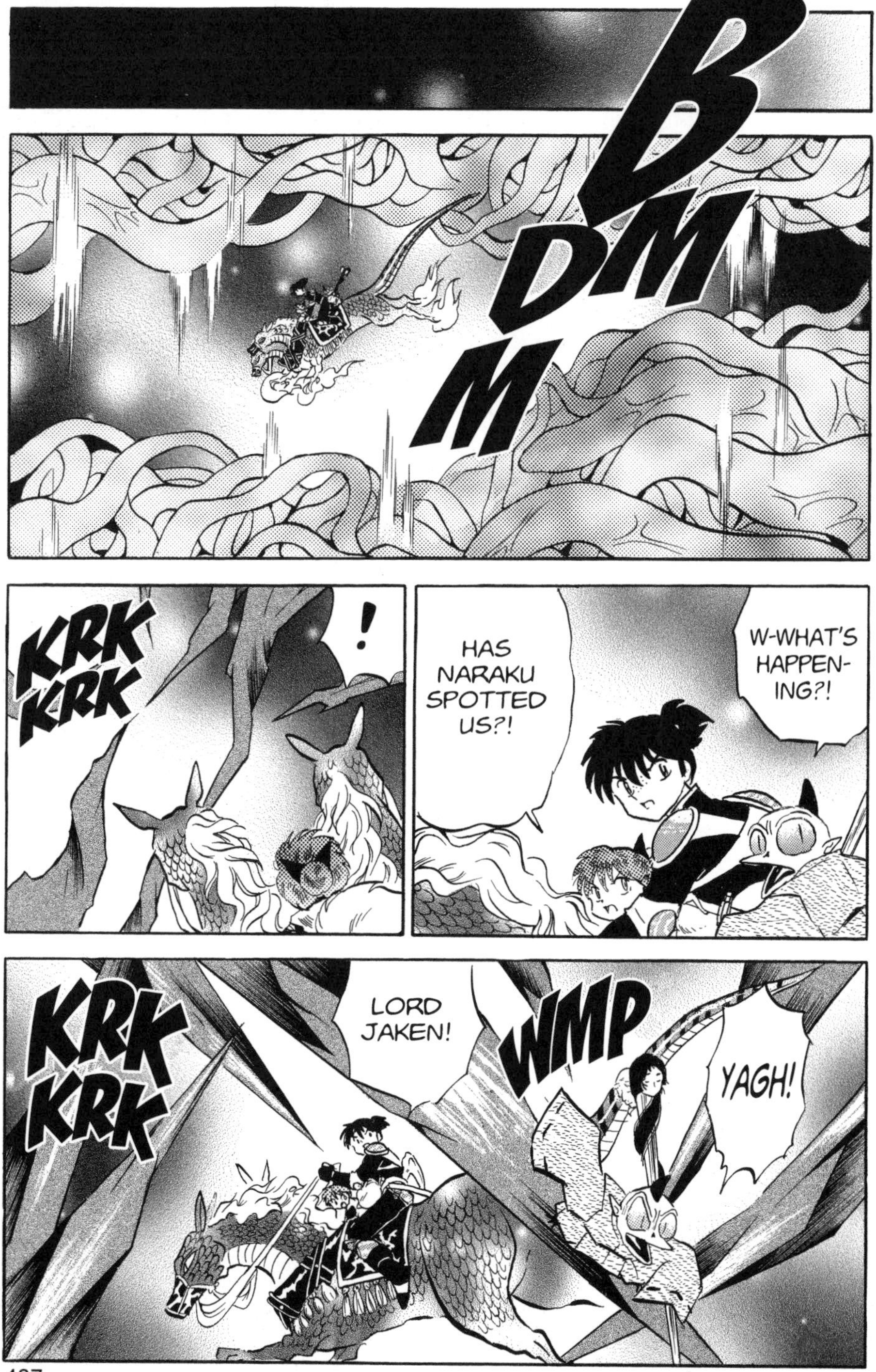
BDMM
W-WHAT'S HAPPEN-ING?!
HAS NARAKU SPOTTED US?!
!
KRK KRK
YAGH!
WMP
LORD JAKEN!
KRK KRK

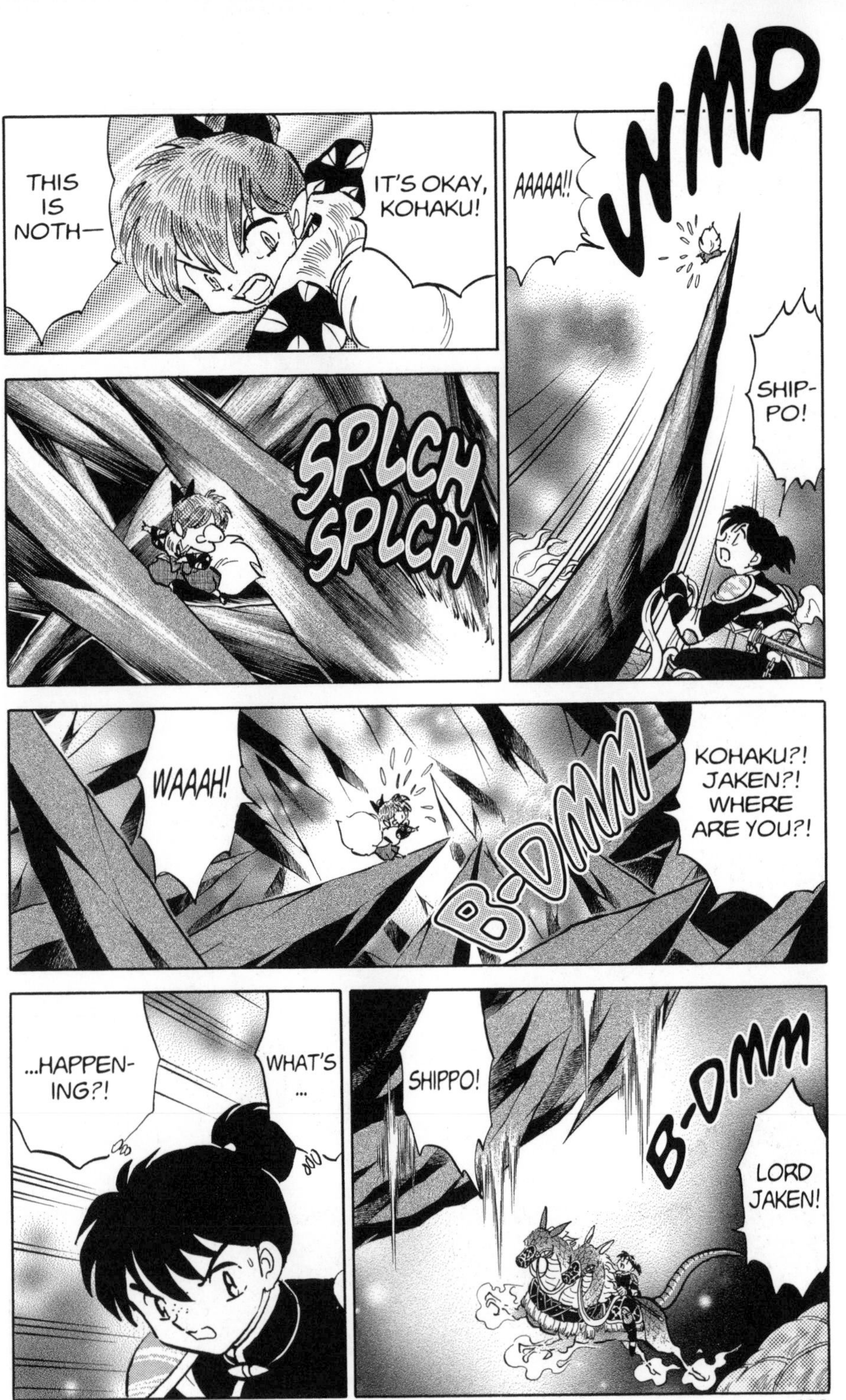
WMP
AAAAA!!
SHIP-PO!
IT'S OKAY, KOHAKU!
THIS IS NOTH—
SPLCH SPLCH
KOHAKU?! JAKEN?! WHERE ARE YOU?!
B-DMM
WAAAH!
B-DMM
LORD JAKEN!
SHIPPO!
WHAT'S ...
...HAPPEN-ING?!

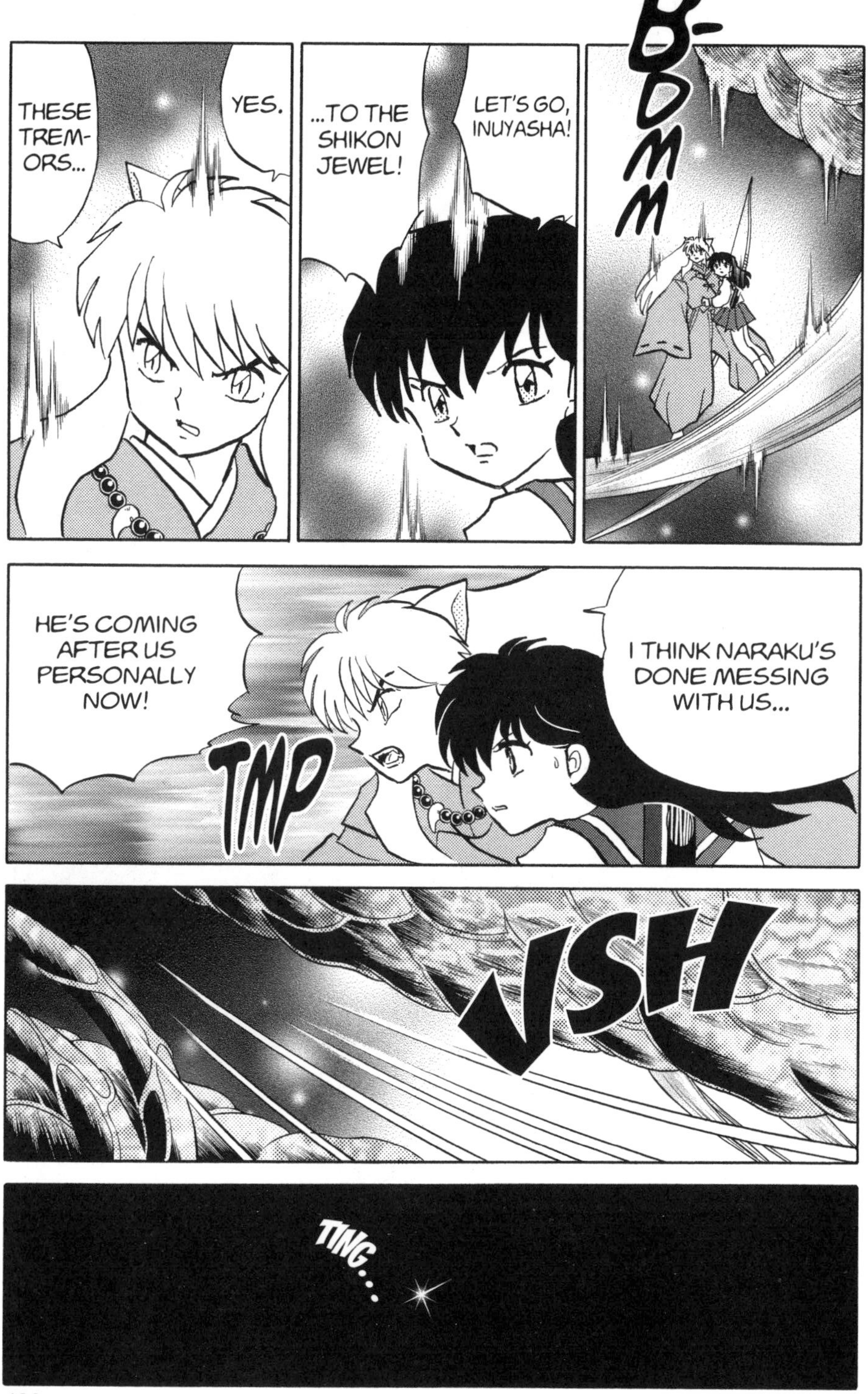
B-DOMM
LET'S GO, INUYASHA!
...TO THE SHIKON JEWEL!
YES.
THESE TREM-ORS...
I THINK NARAKU'S DONE MESSING WITH US...
TMP
HE'S COMING AFTER US PERSONALLY NOW!
VSH
TING...

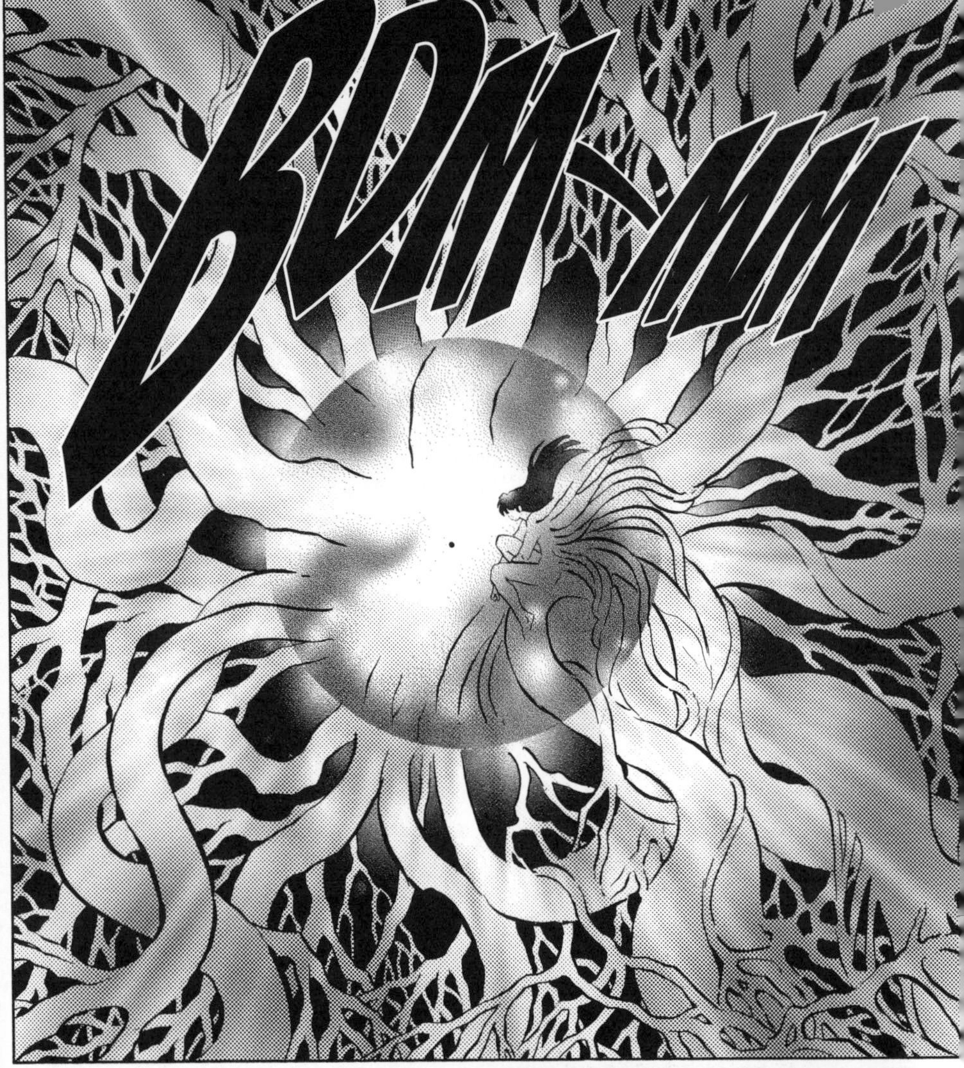
BROM-MM

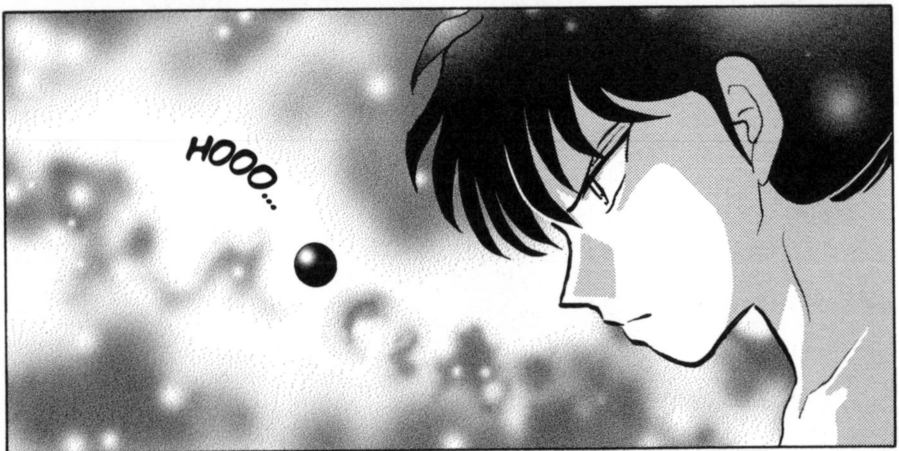
HOOO...

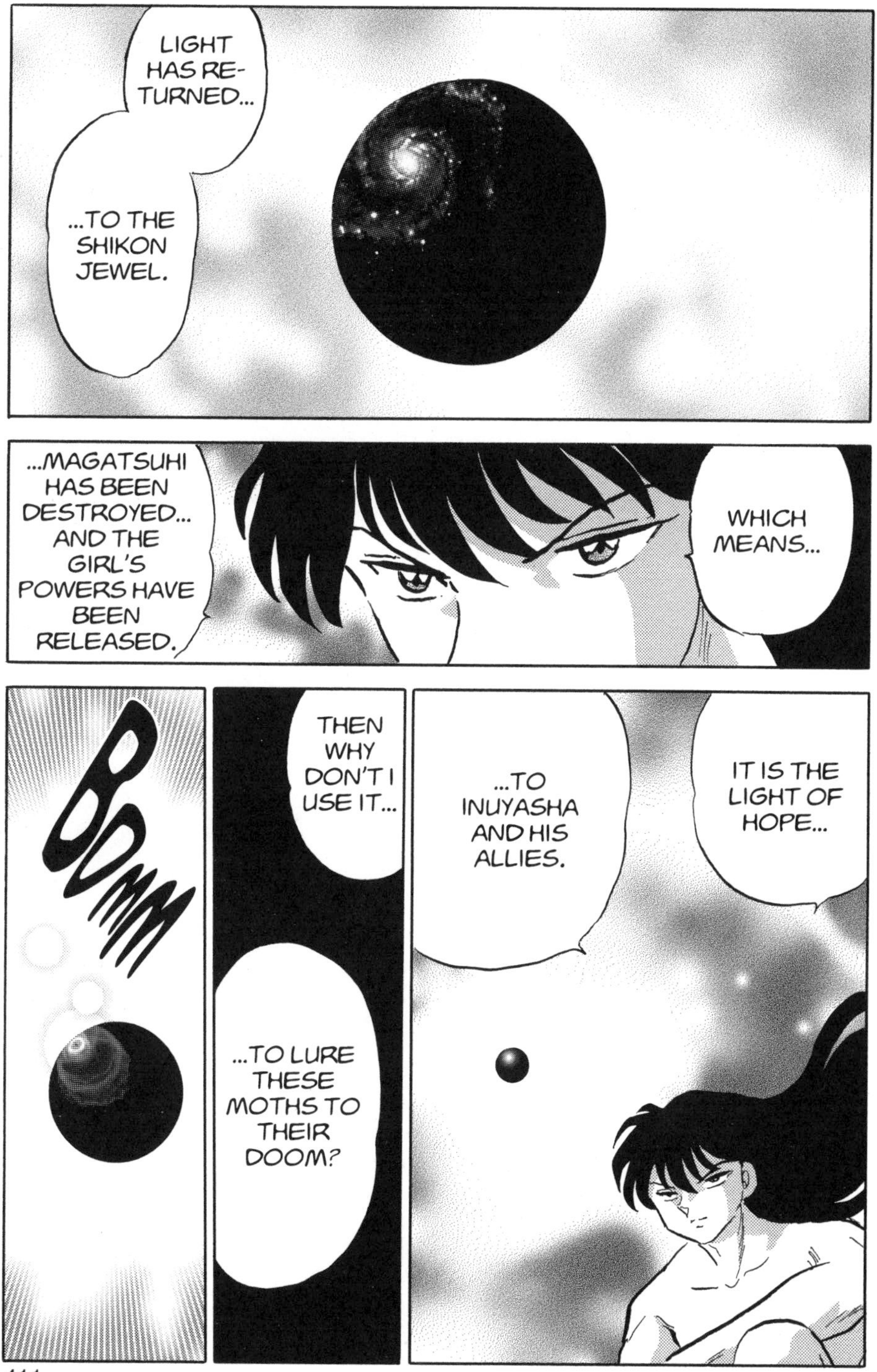
LIGHT HAS RE-TURNED...
...TO THE SHIKON JEWEL.
WHICH MEANS...
...MAGATSUHI HAS BEEN DESTROYED... AND THE GIRL'S POWERS HAVE BEEN RELEASED.
IT IS THE LIGHT OF HOPE...
...TO INUYASHA AND HIS ALLIES.
THEN WHY DON'T I USE IT...
...TO LURE THESE MOTHS TO THEIR DOOM?
BDMM

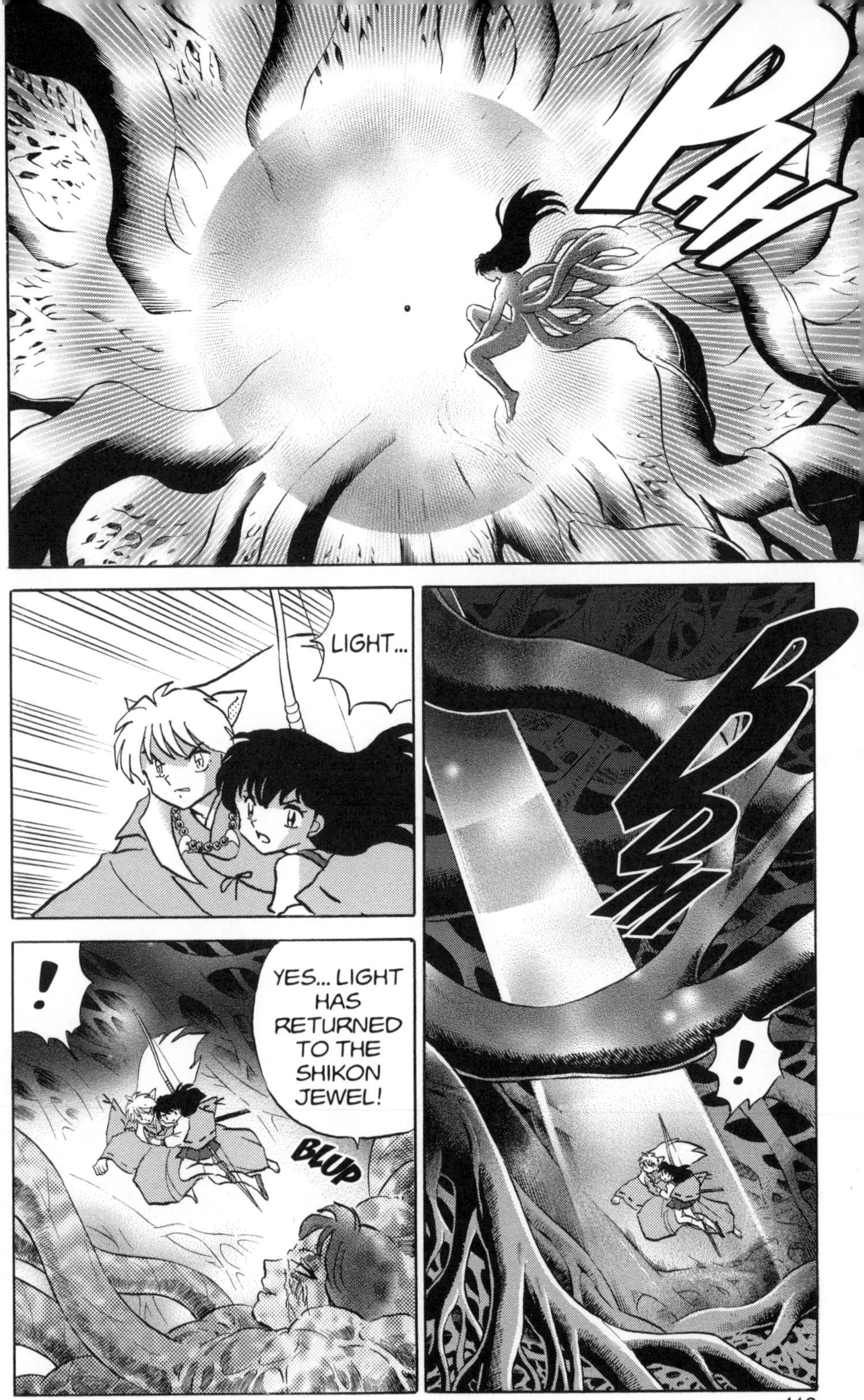
PAH
BOMM
!
LIGHT...
YES... LIGHT HAS RETURNED TO THE SHIKON JEWEL!
!
BLUP

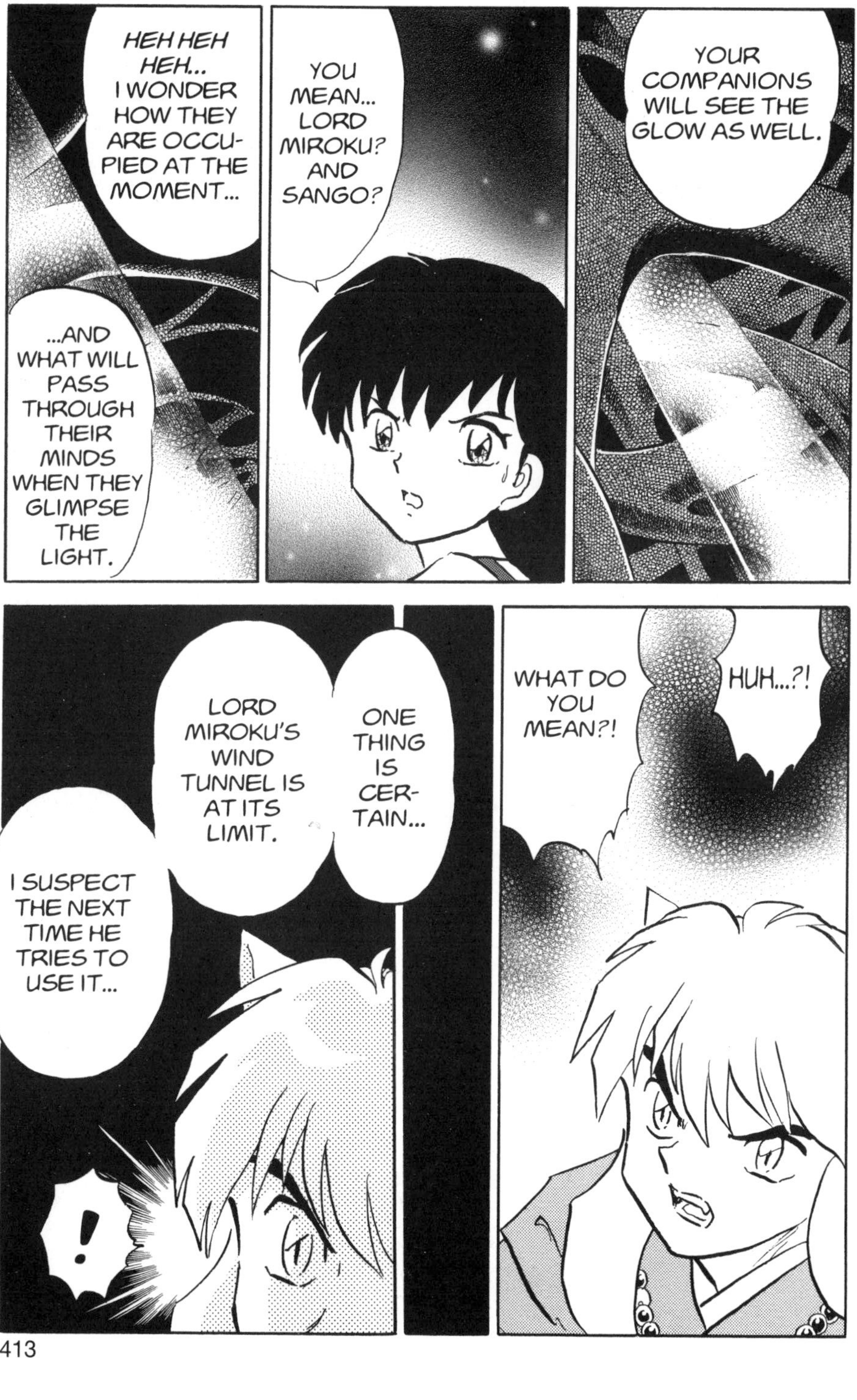
YOUR COMPANIONS WILL SEE THE GLOW AS WELL.
YOU MEAN... LORD MIROKU? AND SANGO?
HEH HEH HEH... I WONDER HOW THEY ARE OCCUPIED AT THE MOMENT...
...AND WHAT WILL PASS THROUGH THEIR MINDS WHEN THEY GLIMPSE THE LIGHT.
HUH...?!
WHAT DO YOU MEAN?!
ONE THING IS CERTAIN...
LORD MIROKU'S WIND TUNNEL IS AT ITS LIMIT.
I SUSPECT THE NEXT TIME HE TRIES TO USE IT...
!

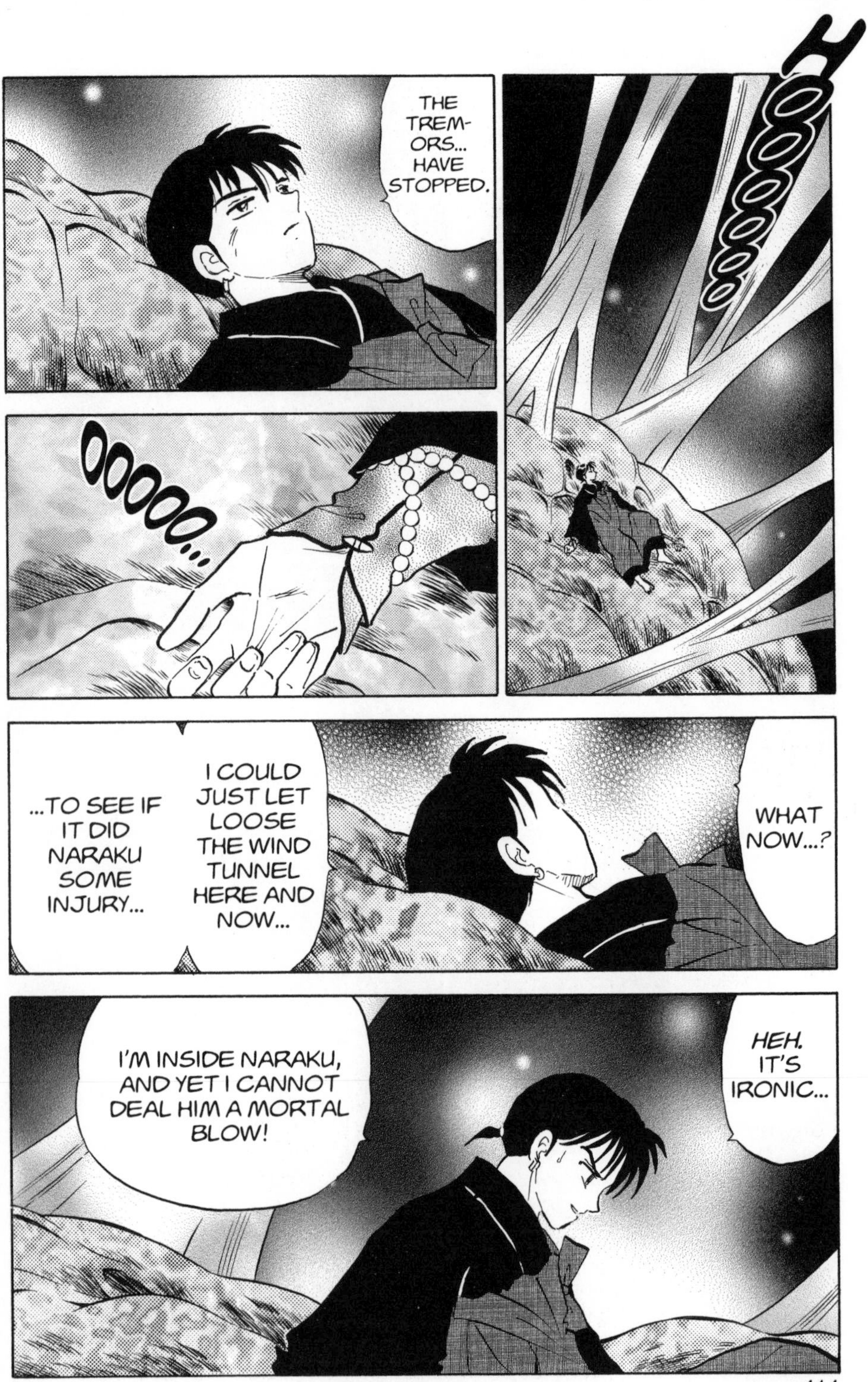
HOOOOOOOO
THE TREM-ORS... HAVE STOPPED.
OOOOO...
WHAT NOW...?
I COULD JUST LET LOOSE THE WIND TUNNEL HERE AND NOW...
...TO SEE IF IT DID NARAKU SOME INJURY...
HEH. IT'S IRONIC...
I'M INSIDE NARAKU, AND YET I CANNOT DEAL HIM A MORTAL BLOW!

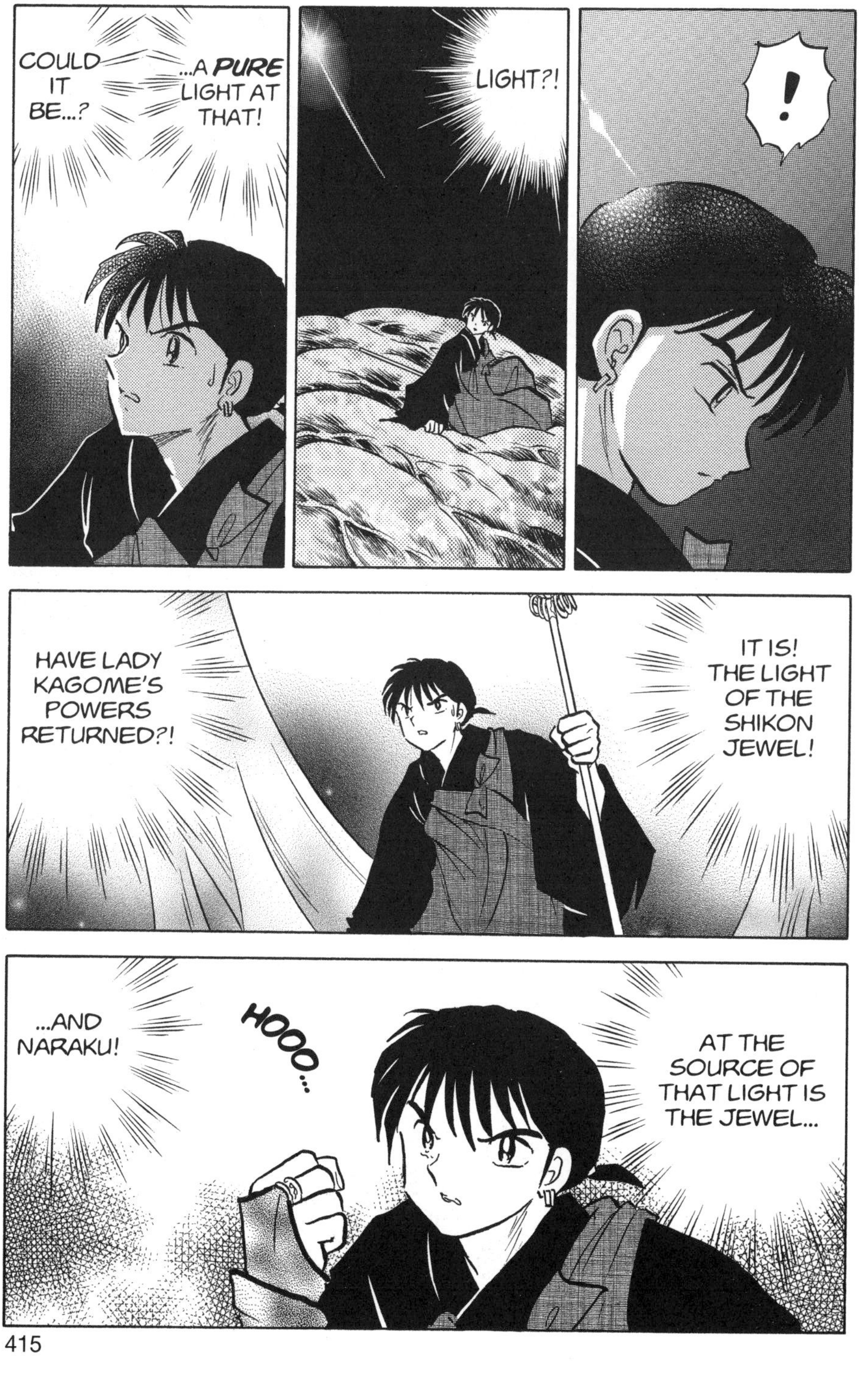
!
LIGHT?!
COULD IT BE...?
...A PURE LIGHT AT THAT!
IT IS! THE LIGHT OF THE SHIKON JEWEL!
HAVE LADY KAGOME'S POWERS RETURNED?!
AT THE SOURCE OF THAT LIGHT IS THE JEWEL...
HOOO...
...AND NARAKU!

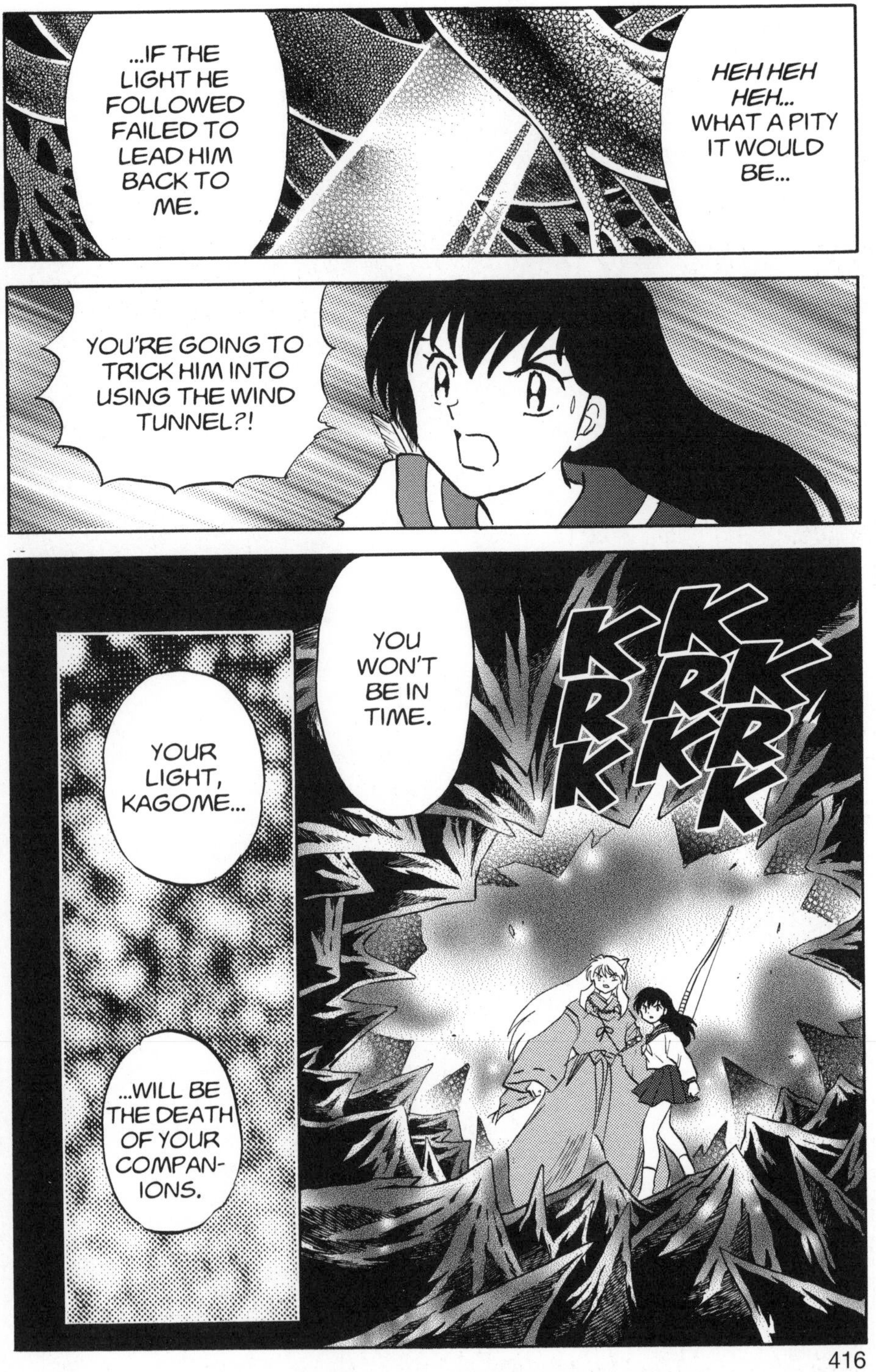
HEH HEH HEH... WHAT A PITY IT WOULD BE...
...IF THE LIGHT HE FOLLOWED FAILED TO LEAD HIM BACK TO ME.
YOU'RE GOING TO TRICK HIM INTO USING THE WIND TUNNEL?!
KRKRKKRKRK
YOU WON'T BE IN TIME.
YOUR LIGHT, KAGOME...
...WILL BE THE DEATH OF YOUR COMPANIONS.

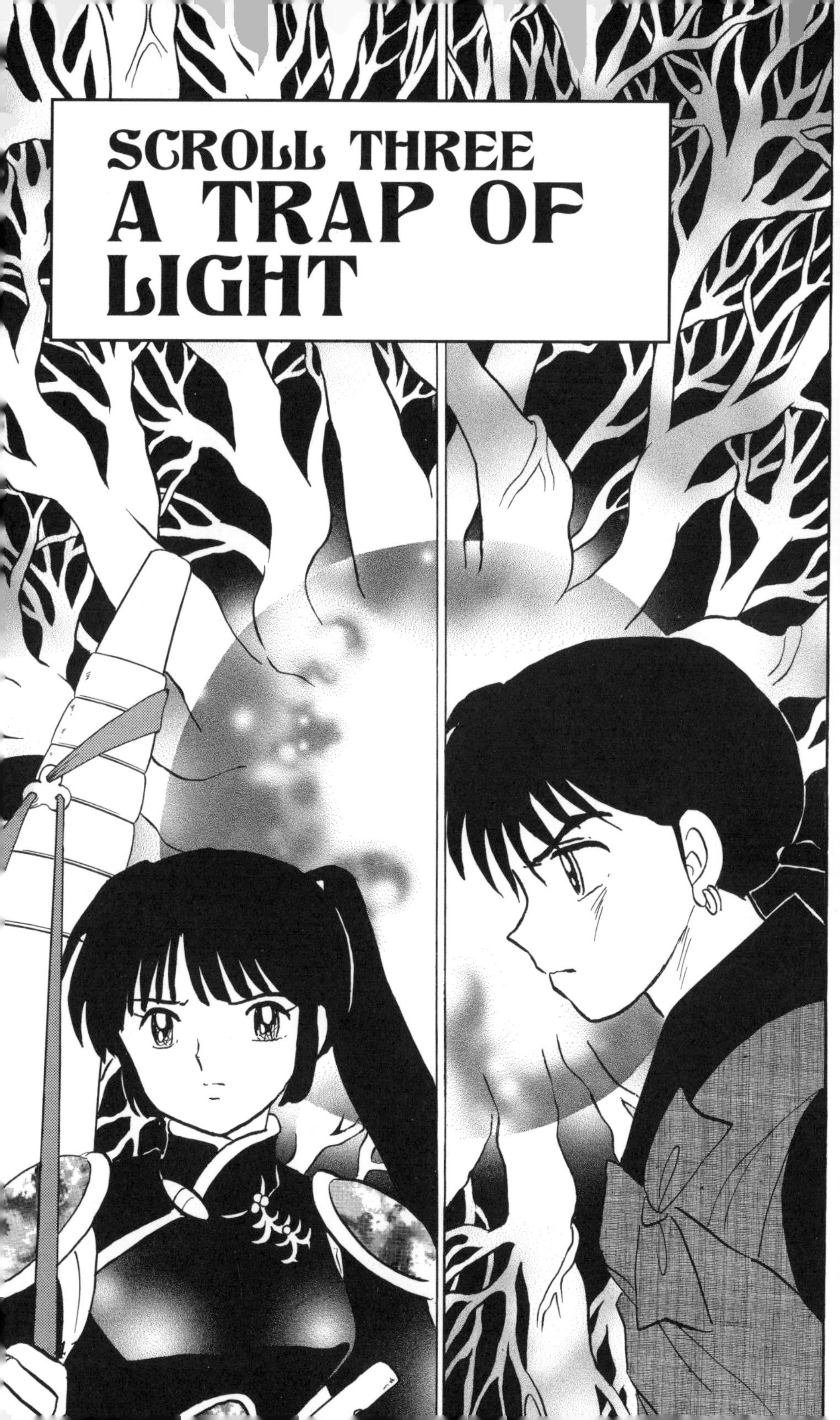
SCROLL THREE
A TRAP OF LIGHT

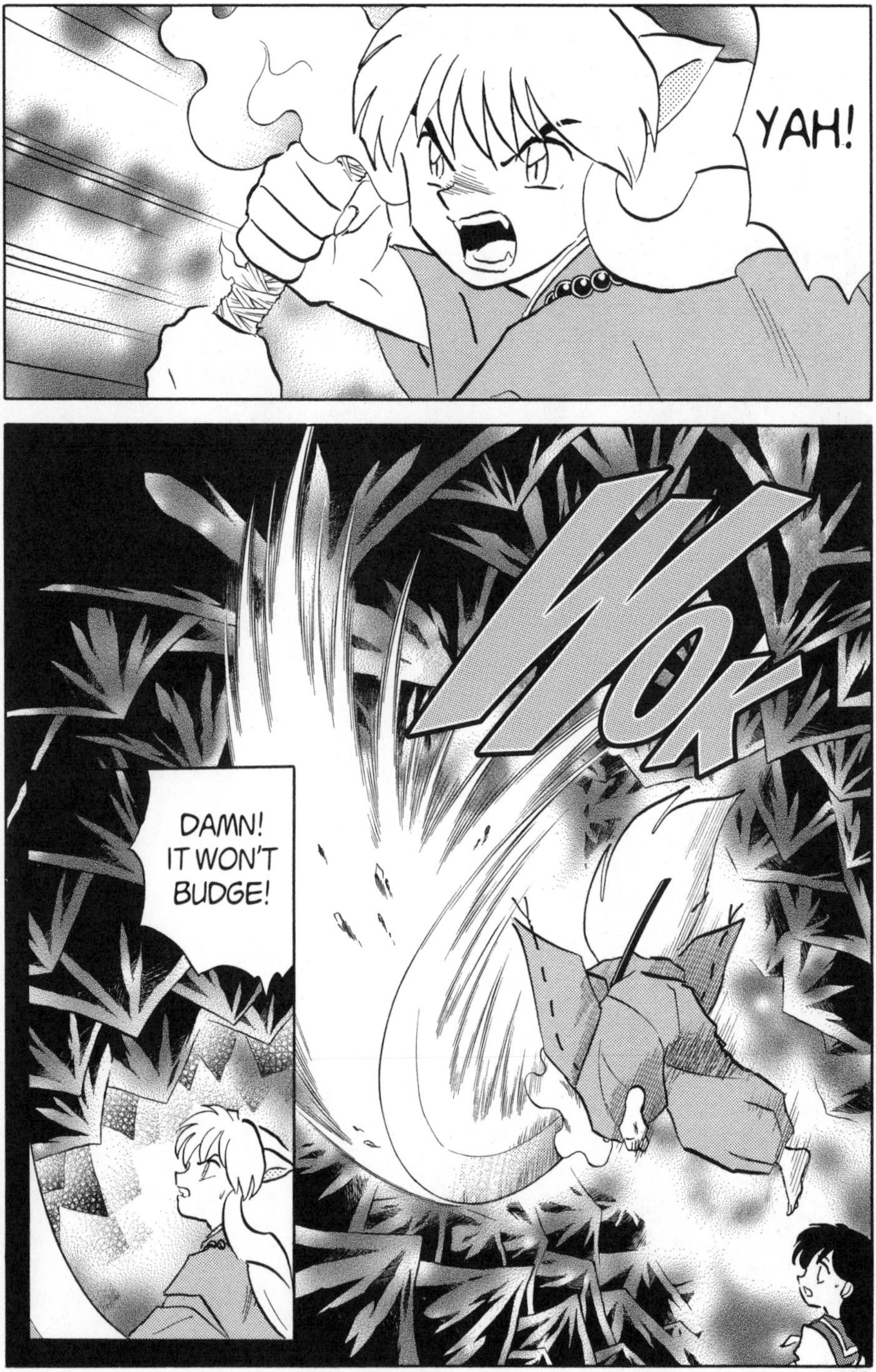
YAH!
WOK
DAMN! IT WON'T BUDGE!

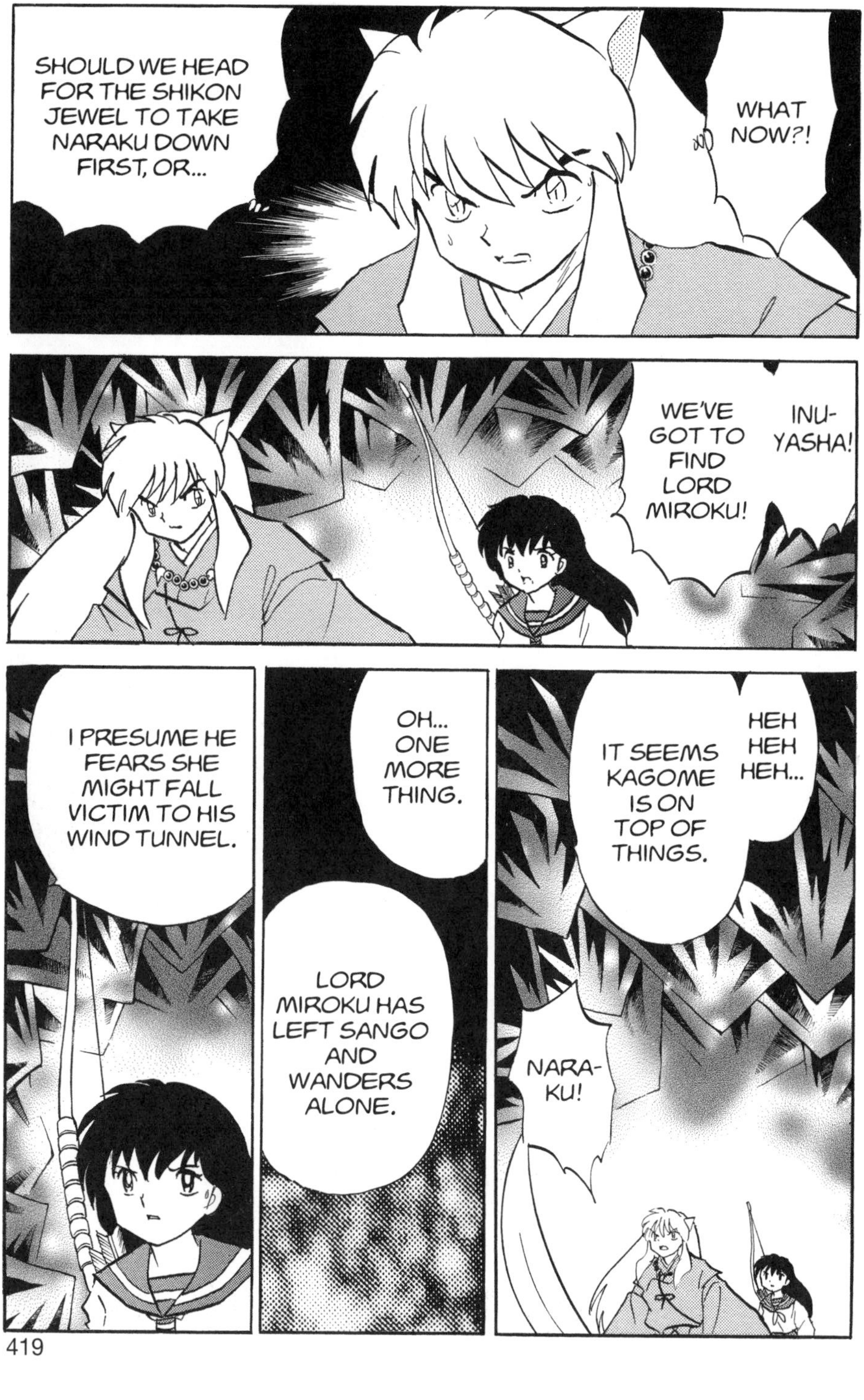

WHAT NOW?!
SHOULD WE HEAD FOR THE SHIKON JEWEL TO TAKE NARAKU DOWN FIRST, OR...
INU-YASHA!
WE'VE GOT TO FIND LORD MIROKU!
HEH HEH HEH...
IT SEEMS KAGOME IS ON TOP OF THINGS.
NARA-KU!
OH... ONE MORE THING.
LORD MIROKU HAS LEFT SANGO AND WANDERS ALONE.
I PRESUME HE FEARS SHE MIGHT FALL VICTIM TO HIS WIND TUNNEL.

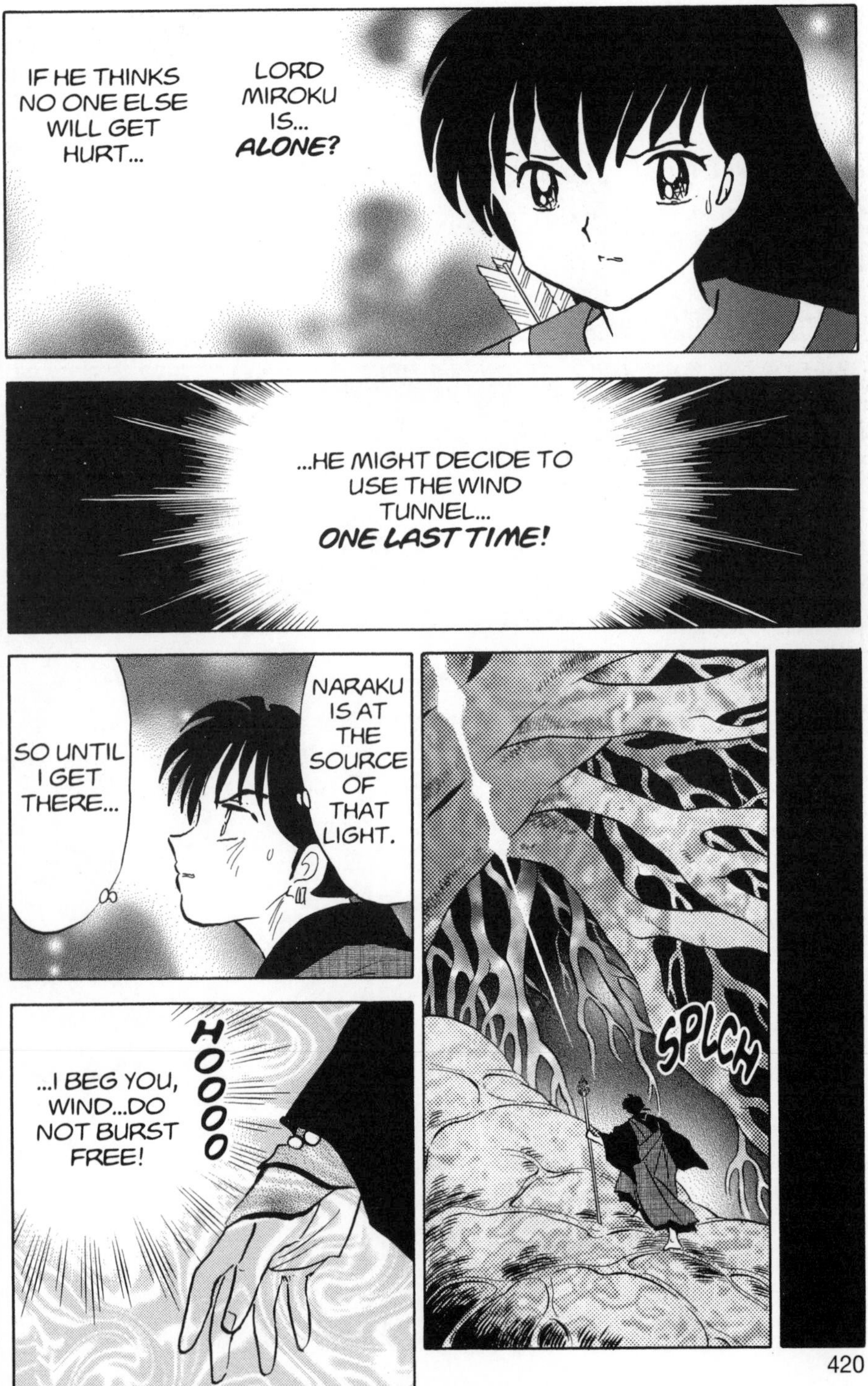
LORD MIROKU IS... ALONE?
IF HE THINKS NO ONE ELSE WILL GET HURT...
...HE MIGHT DECIDE TO USE THE WIND TUNNEL... ONE LAST TIME!
SPLCH
NARAKU IS AT THE SOURCE OF THAT LIGHT.
SO UNTIL I GET THERE...
HOOOOO
...I BEG YOU, WIND...DO NOT BURST FREE!

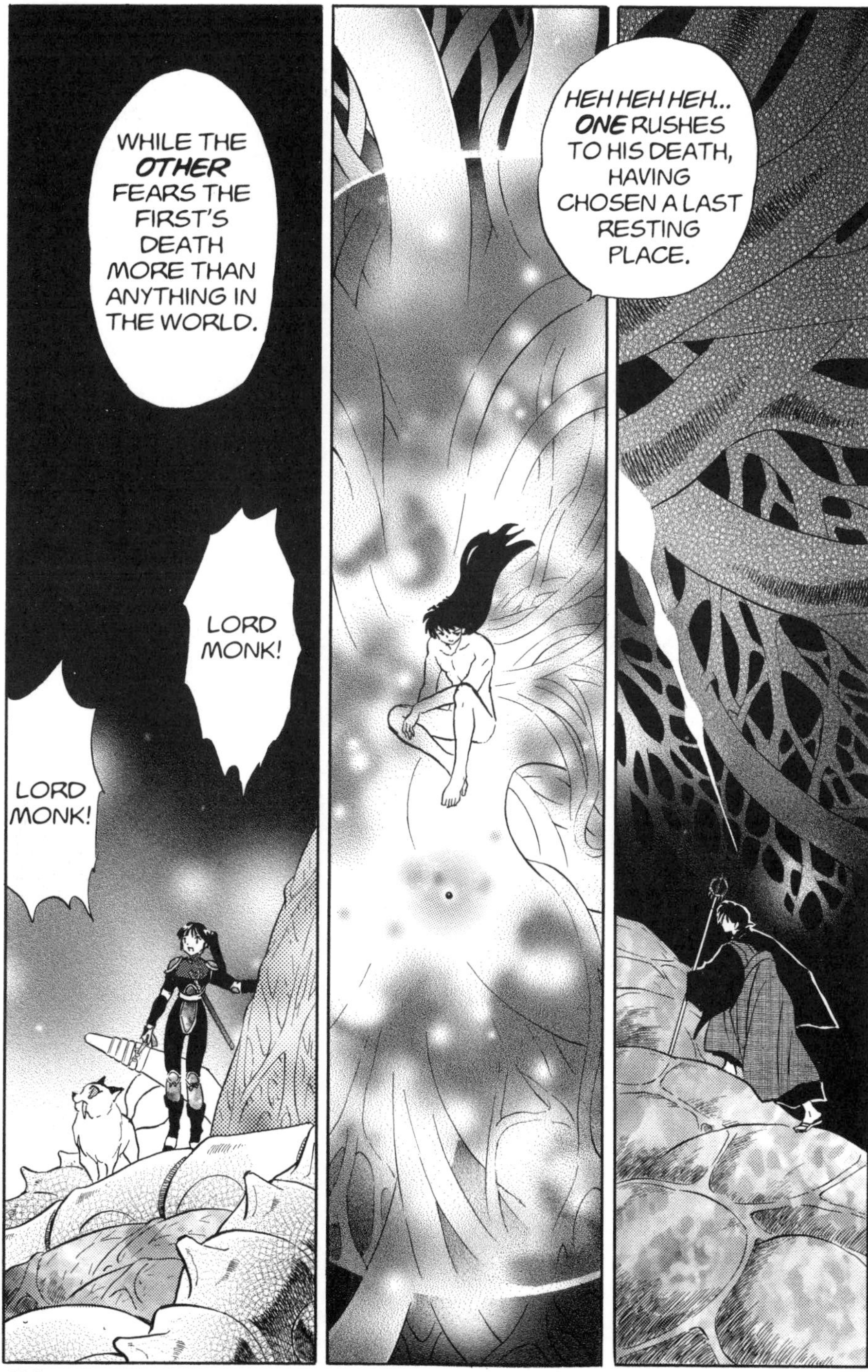
HEH HEH HEH... ONE RUSHES TO HIS DEATH, HAVING CHOSEN A LAST RESTING PLACE.
WHILE THE OTHER FEARS THE FIRST'S DEATH MORE THAN ANYTHING IN THE WORLD.
LORD MONK!
LORD MONK!

HOOO...

SANGO... HERE, WE MUST PART WAYS.

LORD MONK...

FMP

ARE YOU PLANNING TO DIE ALONE?

BUT... WHY?

...I DIE TOO!

IF YOU DIE, LORD MONK...

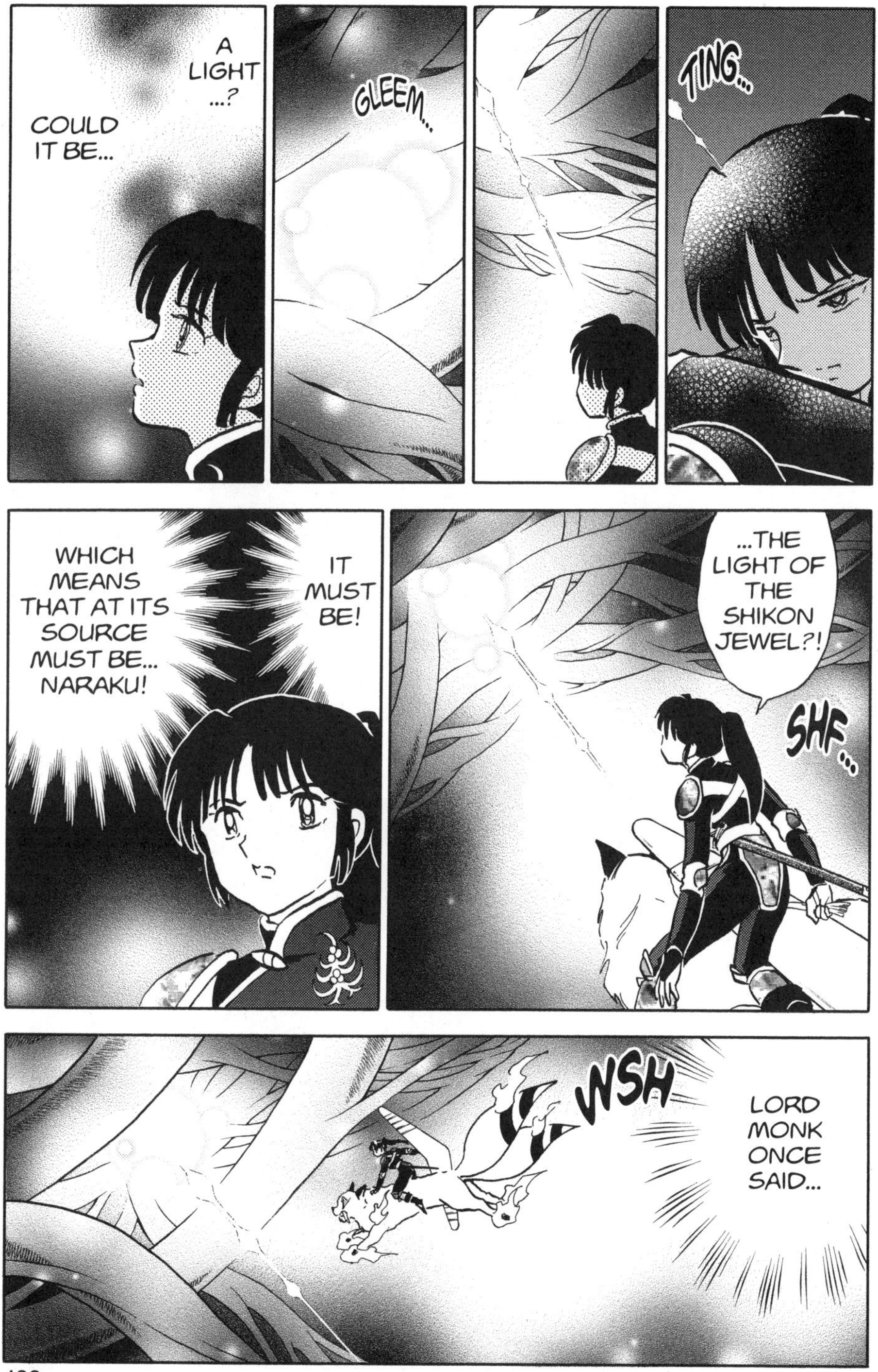
TING...
GLEEM...
A LIGHT ...?
COULD IT BE...
...THE LIGHT OF THE SHIKON JEWEL?!
SHF...
IT MUST BE!
WHICH MEANS THAT AT ITS SOURCE MUST BE... NARAKU!
LORD MONK ONCE SAID...
WSH

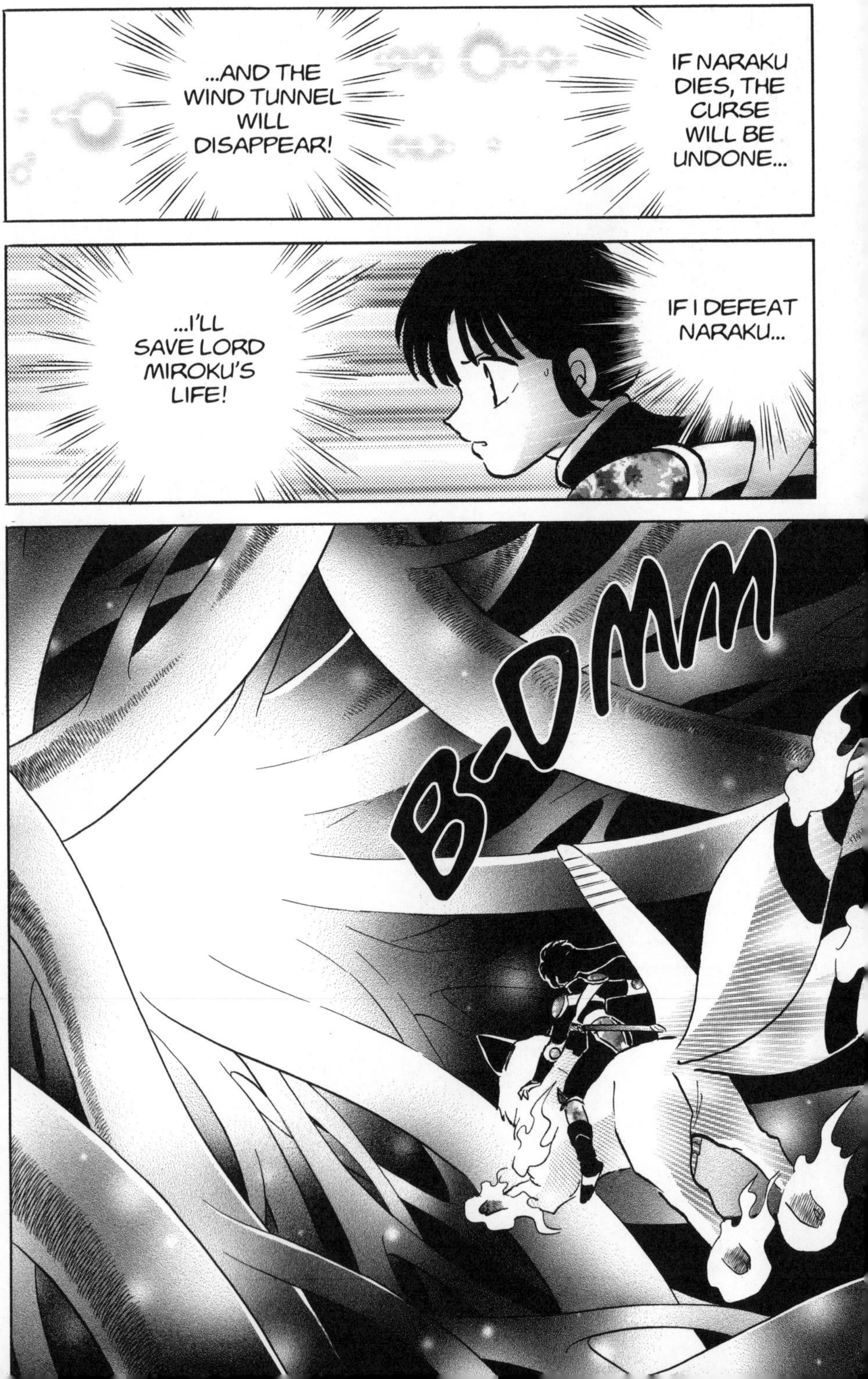
IF NARAKU DIES, THE CURSE WILL BE UNDONE...
...AND THE WIND TUNNEL WILL DISAPPEAR!
IF I DEFEAT NARAKU...
...I'LL SAVE LORD MIROKU'S LIFE!
B-DMM

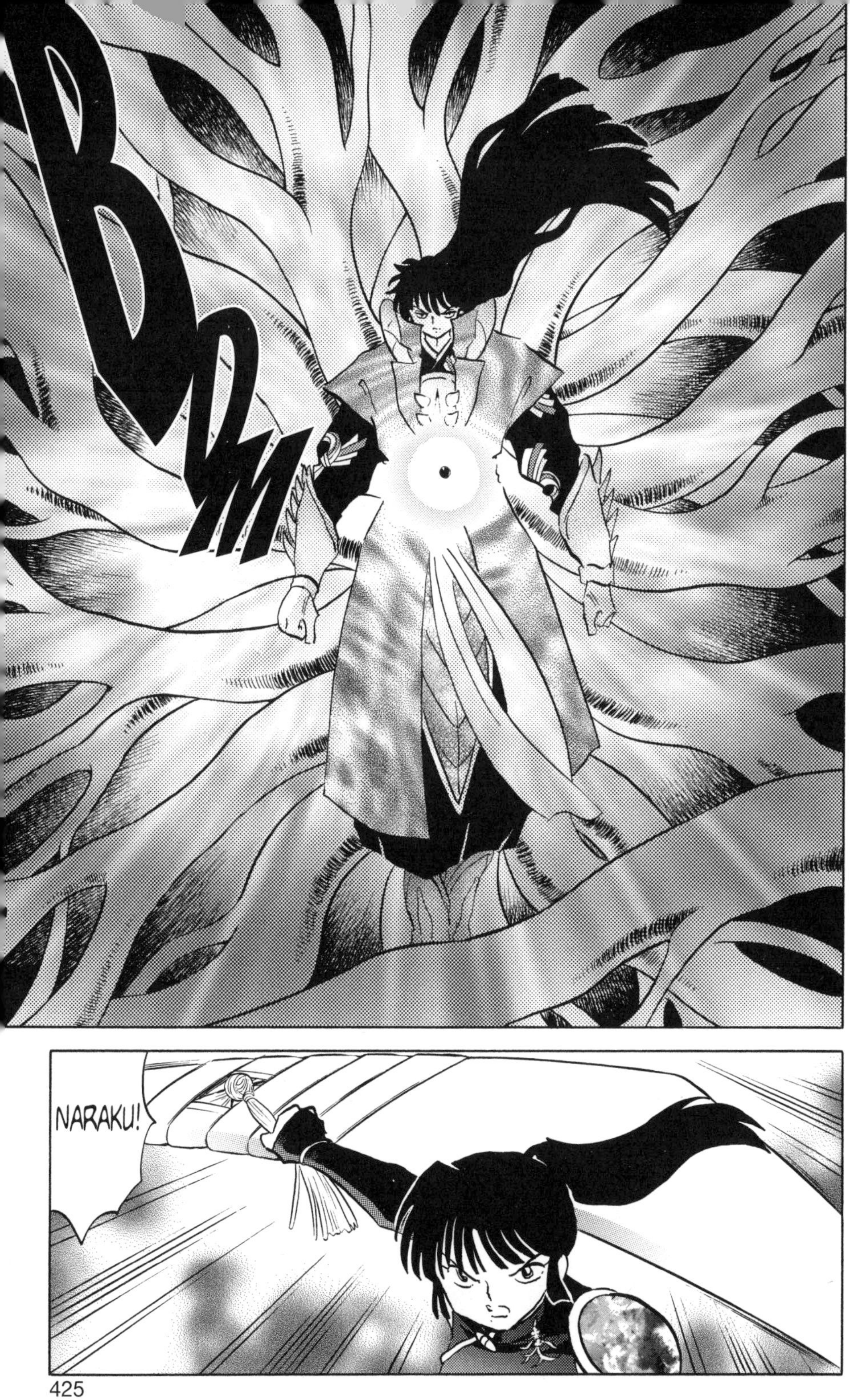
BOOM
NARAKU!

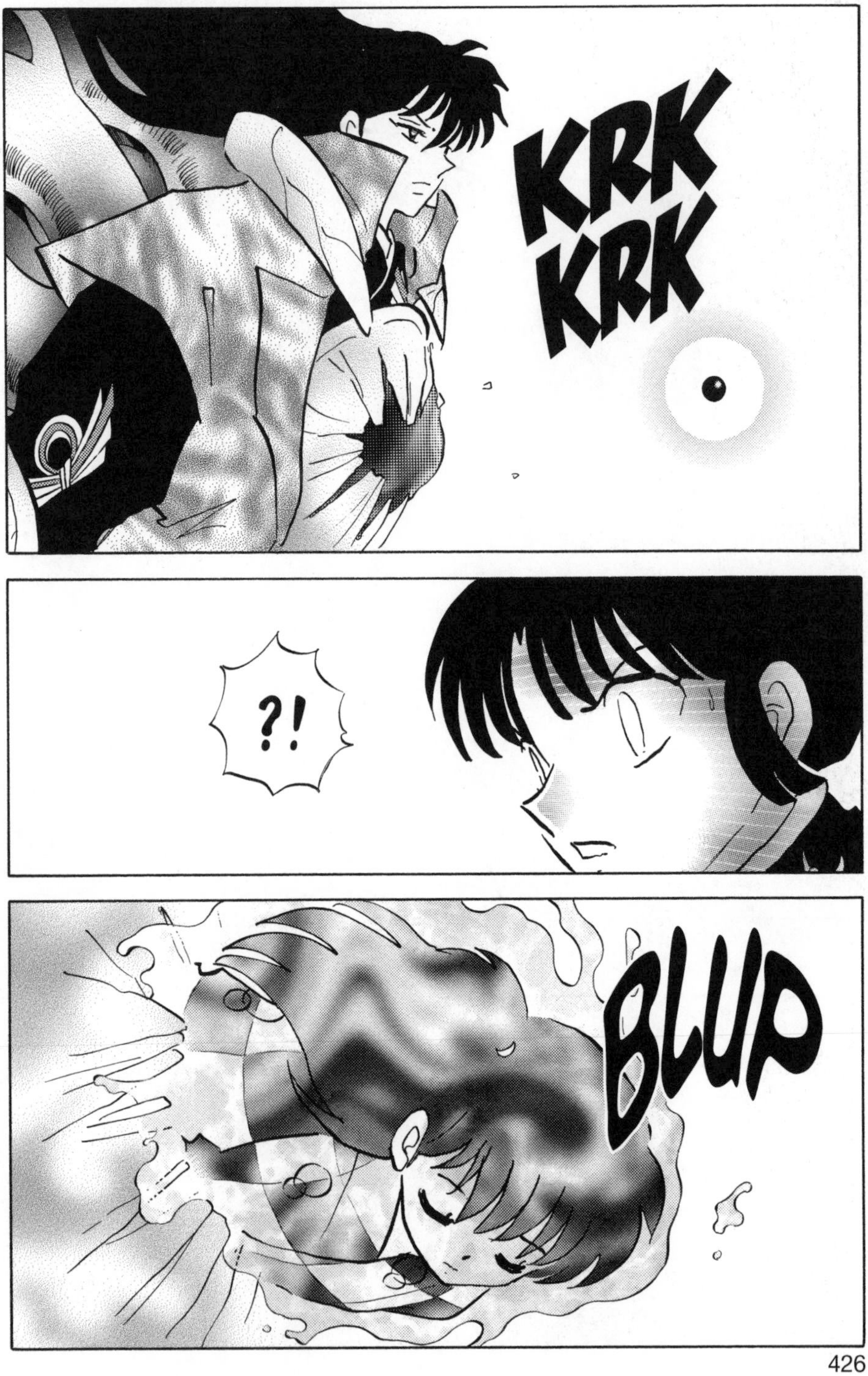
KRK KRK
?!
BLUP

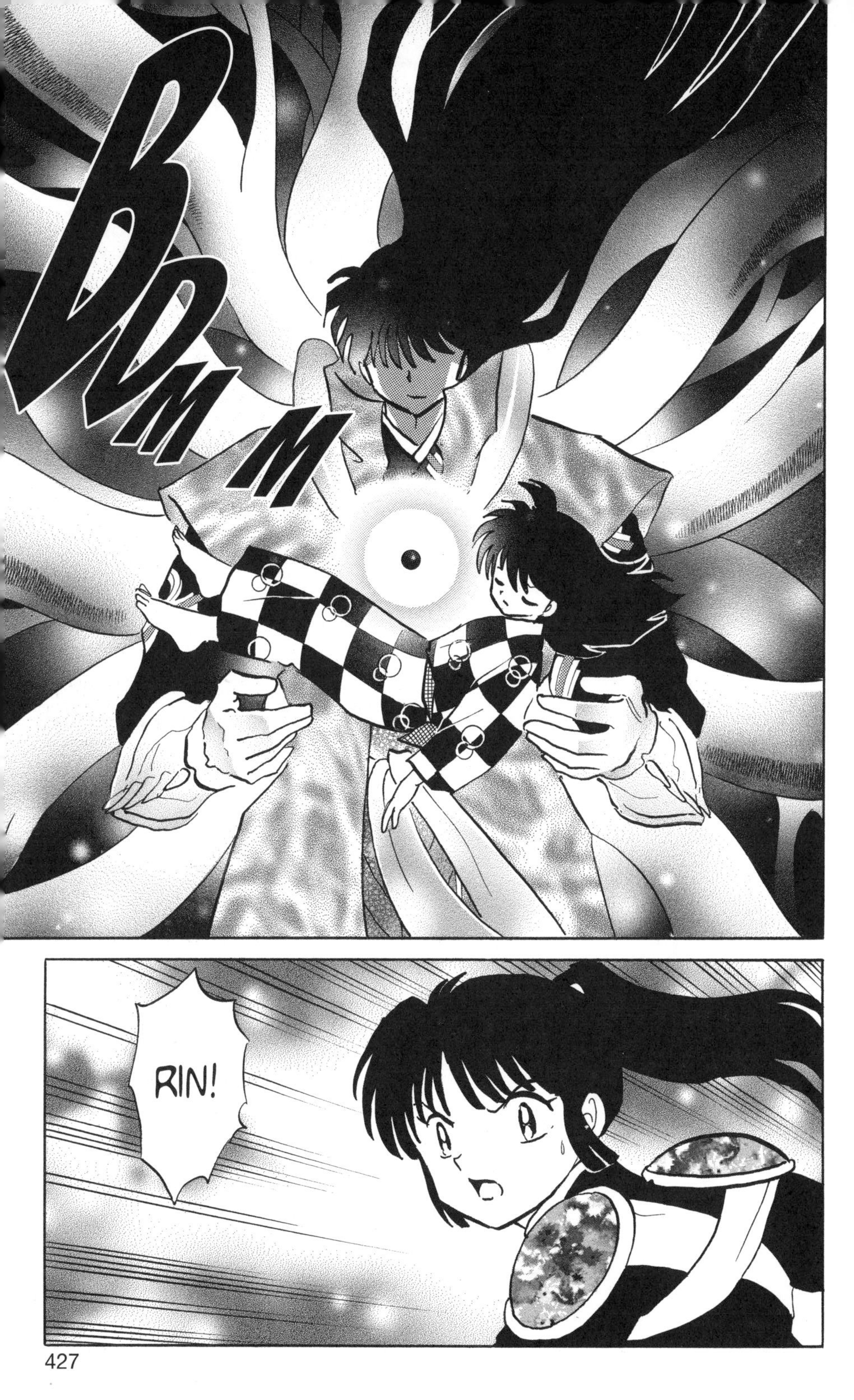
BOMMM
RIN!

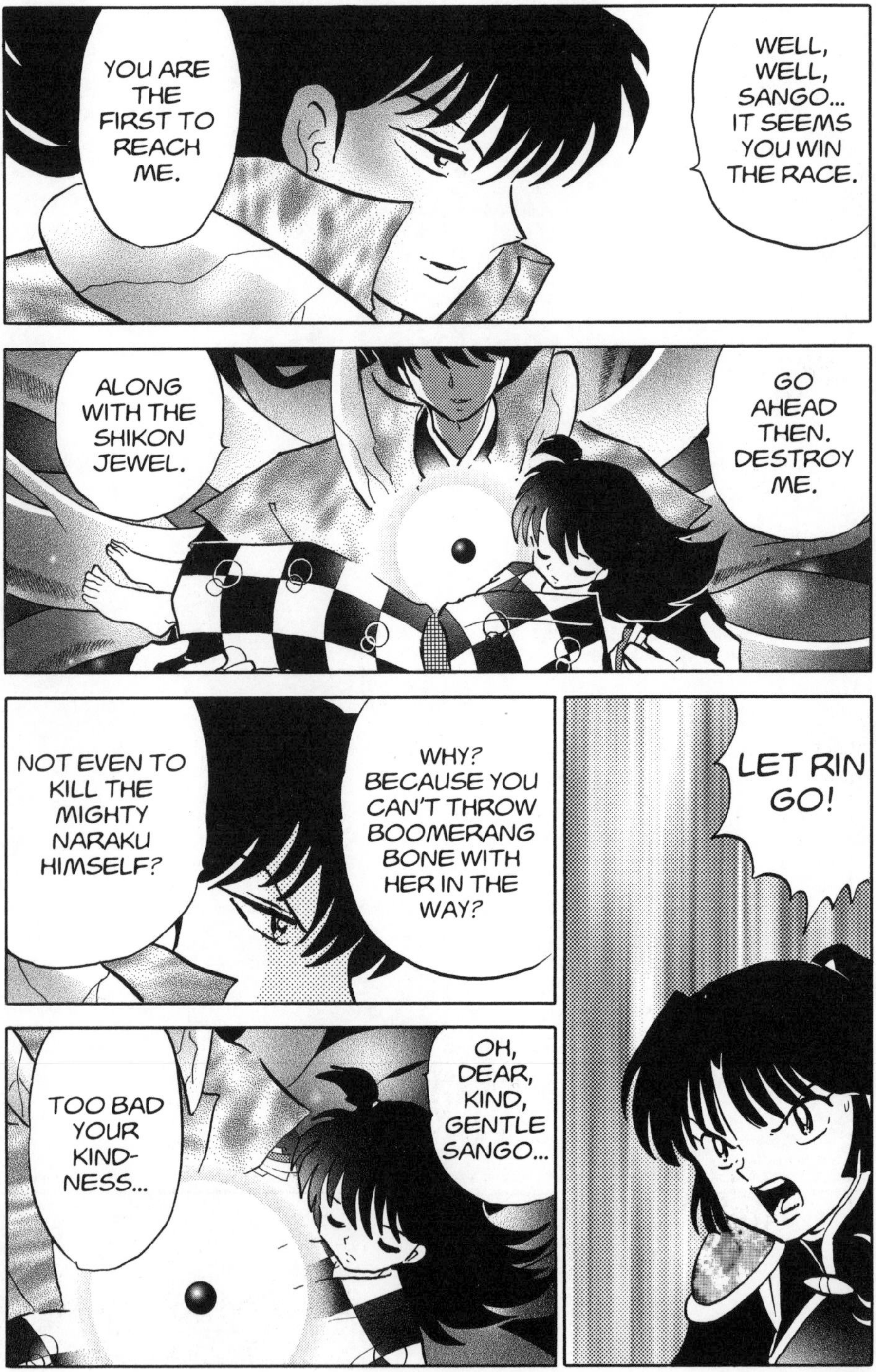
WELL, WELL, SANGO... IT SEEMS YOU WIN THE RACE.
YOU ARE THE FIRST TO REACH ME.
GO AHEAD THEN. DESTROY ME.
ALONG WITH THE SHIKON JEWEL.
LET RIN GO!
WHY? BECAUSE YOU CAN'T THROW BOOMERANG BONE WITH HER IN THE WAY?
NOT EVEN TO KILL THE MIGHTY NARAKU HIMSELF?
OH, DEAR, KIND, GENTLE SANGO...
TOO BAD YOUR KIND-NESS...

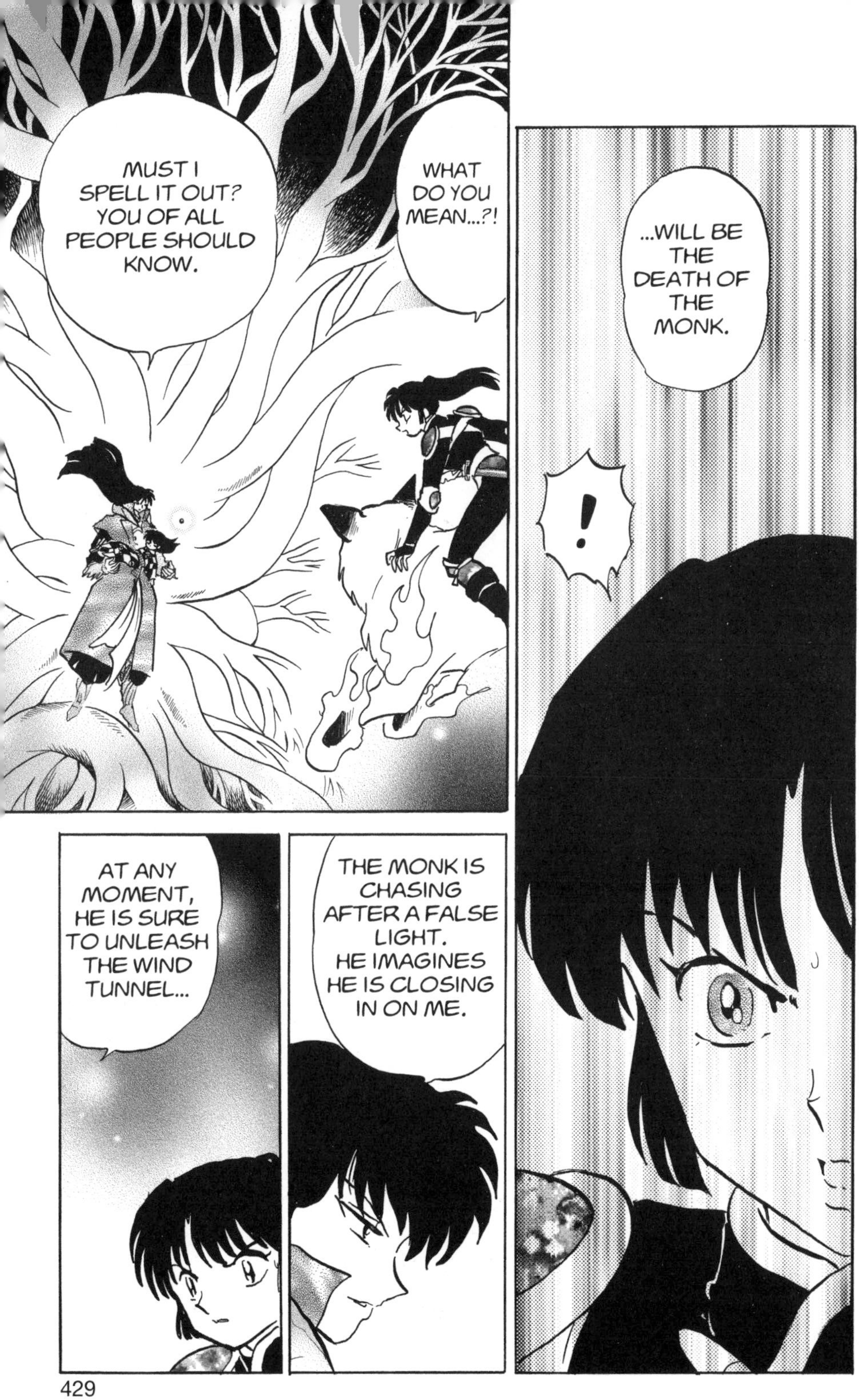
MUST I SPELL IT OUT? YOU OF ALL PEOPLE SHOULD KNOW.
WHAT DO YOU MEAN...?!
AT ANY MOMENT, HE IS SURE TO UNLEASH THE WIND TUNNEL...
THE MONK IS CHASING AFTER A FALSE LIGHT. HE IMAGINES HE IS CLOSING IN ON ME.
...WILL BE THE DEATH OF THE MONK.
!

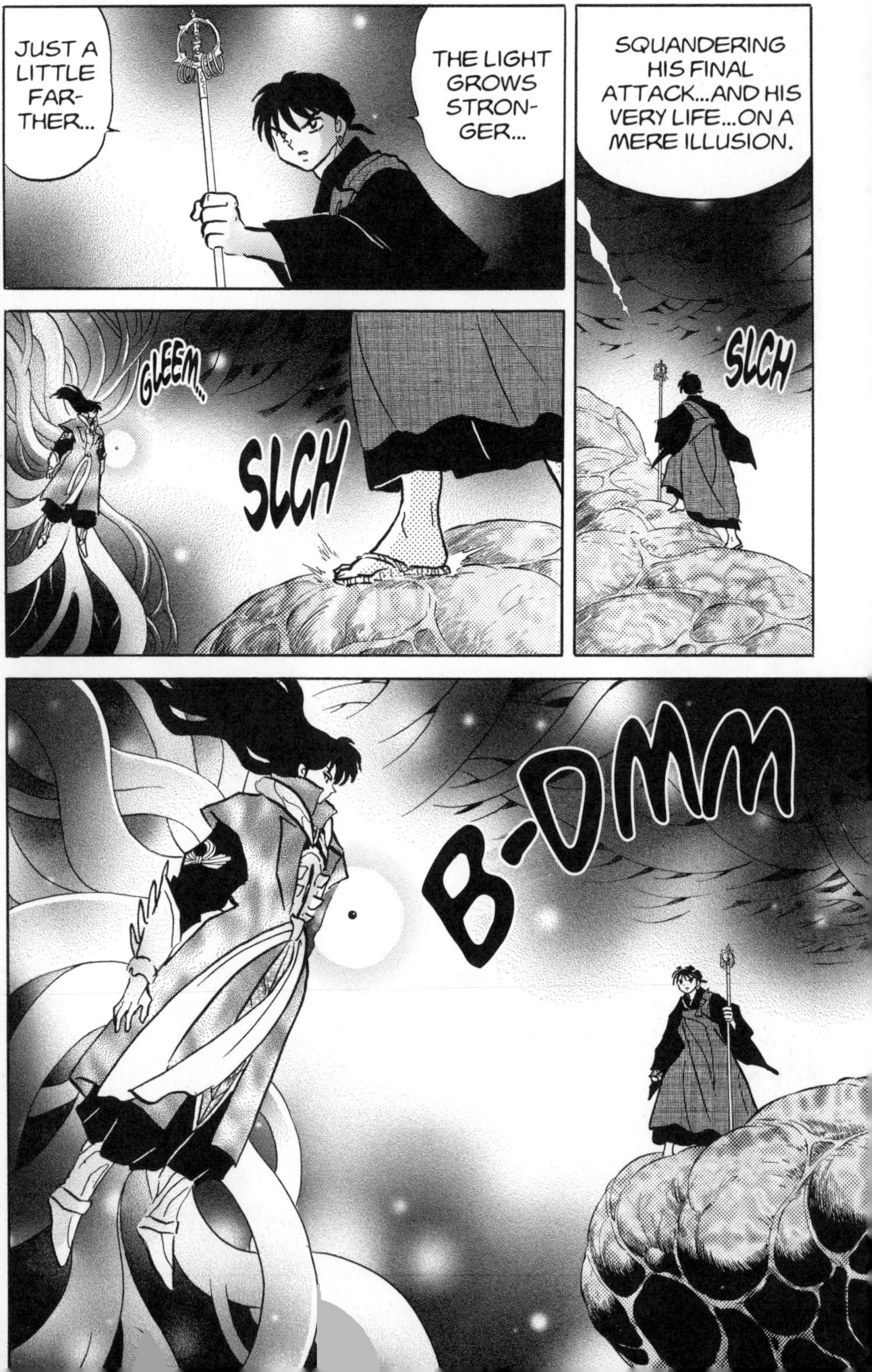
SQUANDERING HIS FINAL ATTACK...AND HIS VERY LIFE...ON A MERE ILLUSION.
SLCH
THE LIGHT GROWS STRON-GER...
JUST A LITTLE FAR-THER...
SLCH
GLEEM...
B-DMM

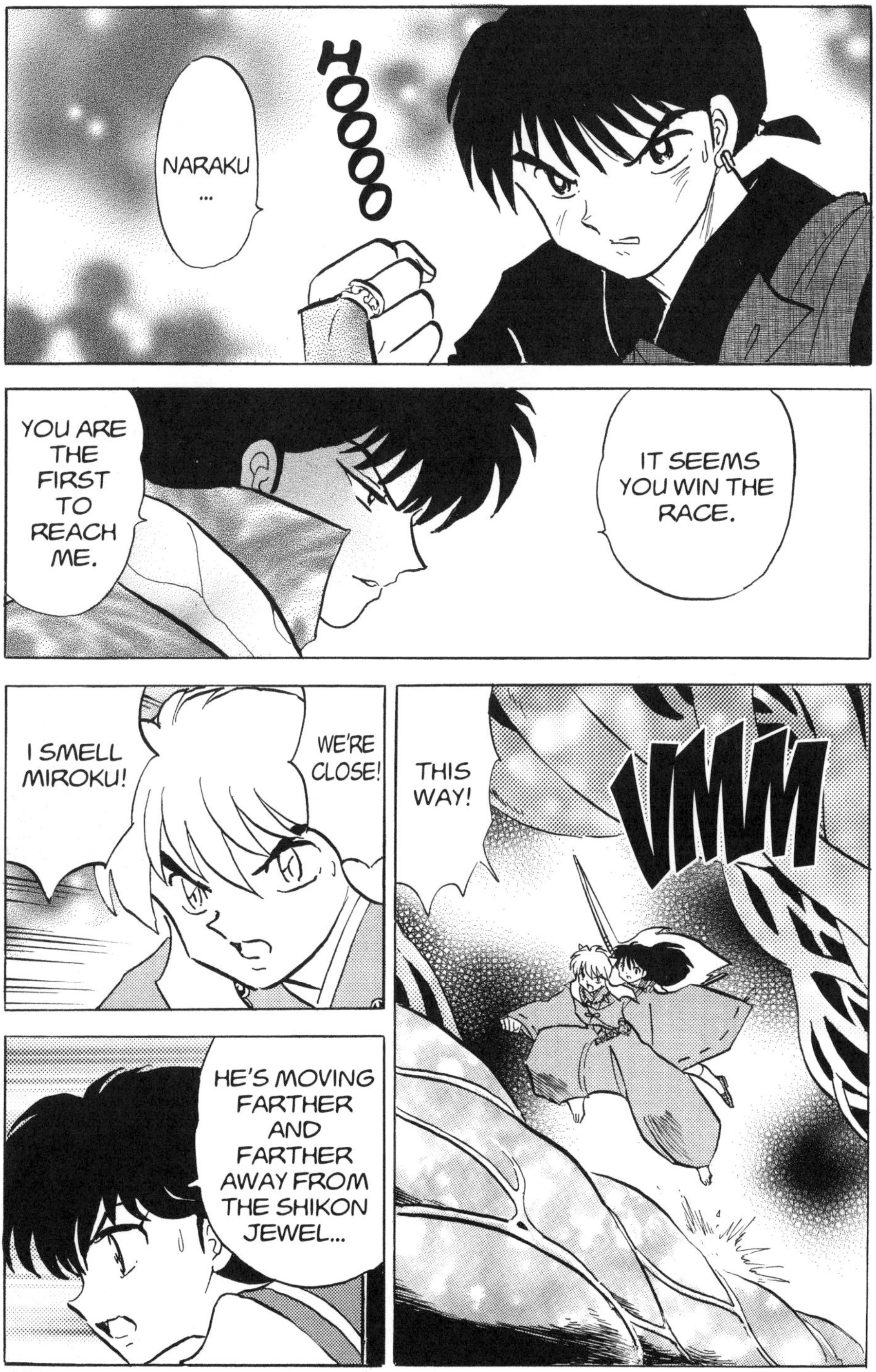
HOOOO
NARAKU ...
IT SEEMS YOU WIN THE RACE.
YOU ARE THE FIRST TO REACH ME.
VMMM
THIS WAY!
WE'RE CLOSE!
I SMELL MIROKU!
HE'S MOVING FARTHER AND FARTHER AWAY FROM THE SHIKON JEWEL...

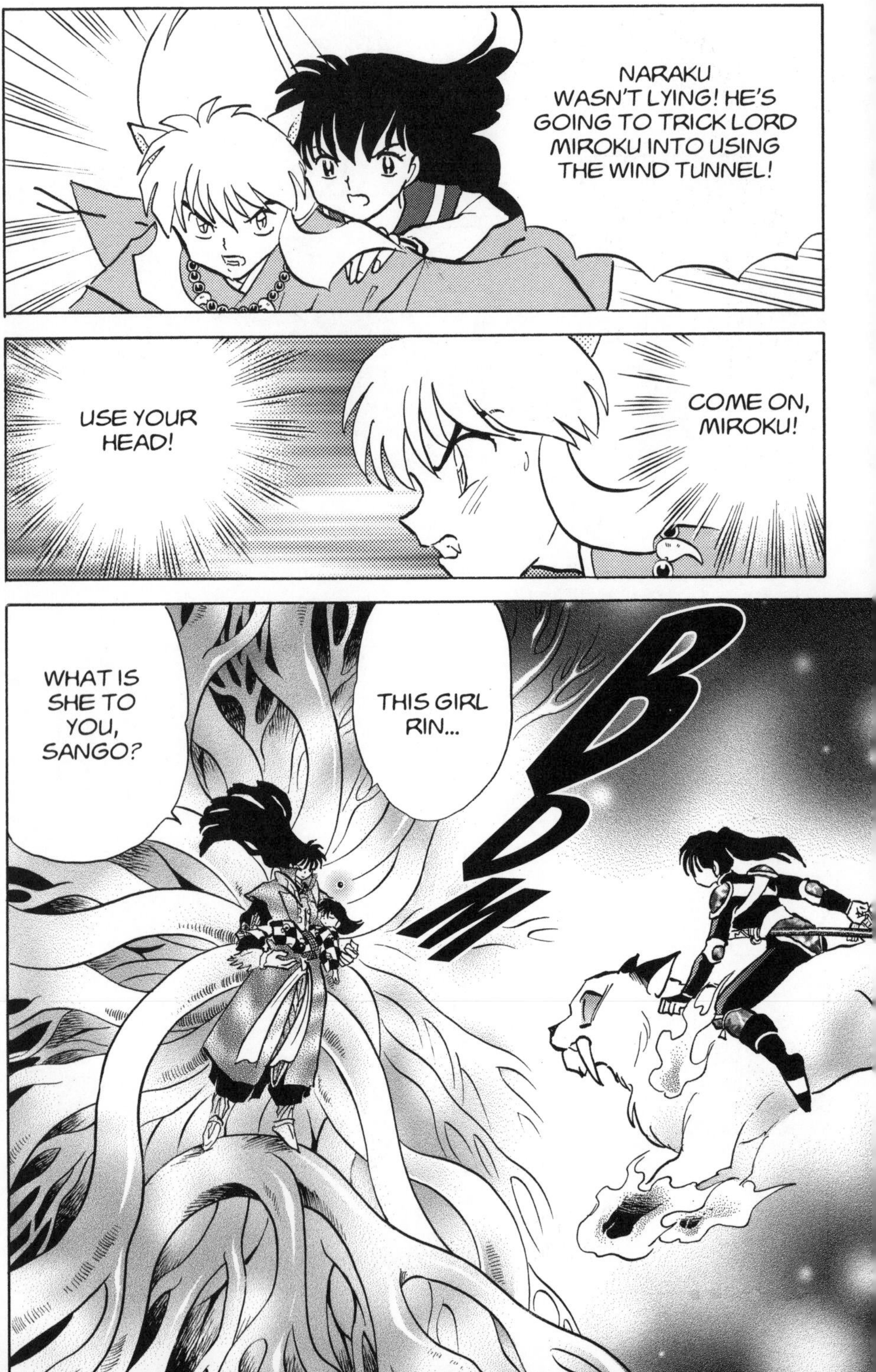
NARAKU WASN'T LYING! HE'S GOING TO TRICK LORD MIROKU INTO USING THE WIND TUNNEL!
COME ON, MIROKU!
USE YOUR HEAD!
BDM
THIS GIRL RIN...
WHAT IS SHE TO YOU, SANGO?

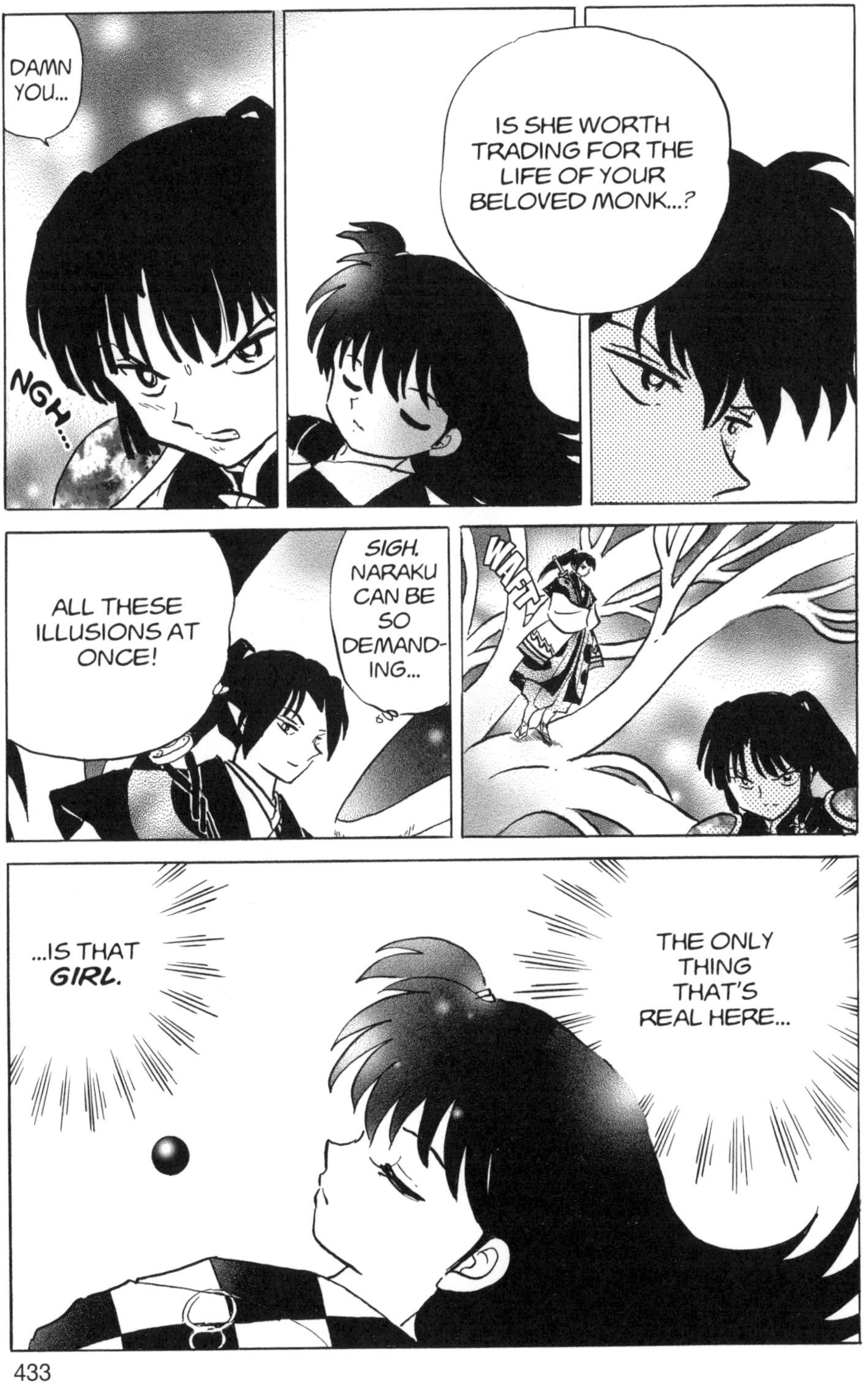
IS SHE WORTH TRADING FOR THE LIFE OF YOUR BELOVED MONK...?
DAMN YOU...
NGH...
WAFT
SIGH. NARAKU CAN BE SO DEMAND-ING...
ALL THESE ILLUSIONS AT ONCE!
THE ONLY THING THAT'S REAL HERE...
...IS THAT **GIRL**.

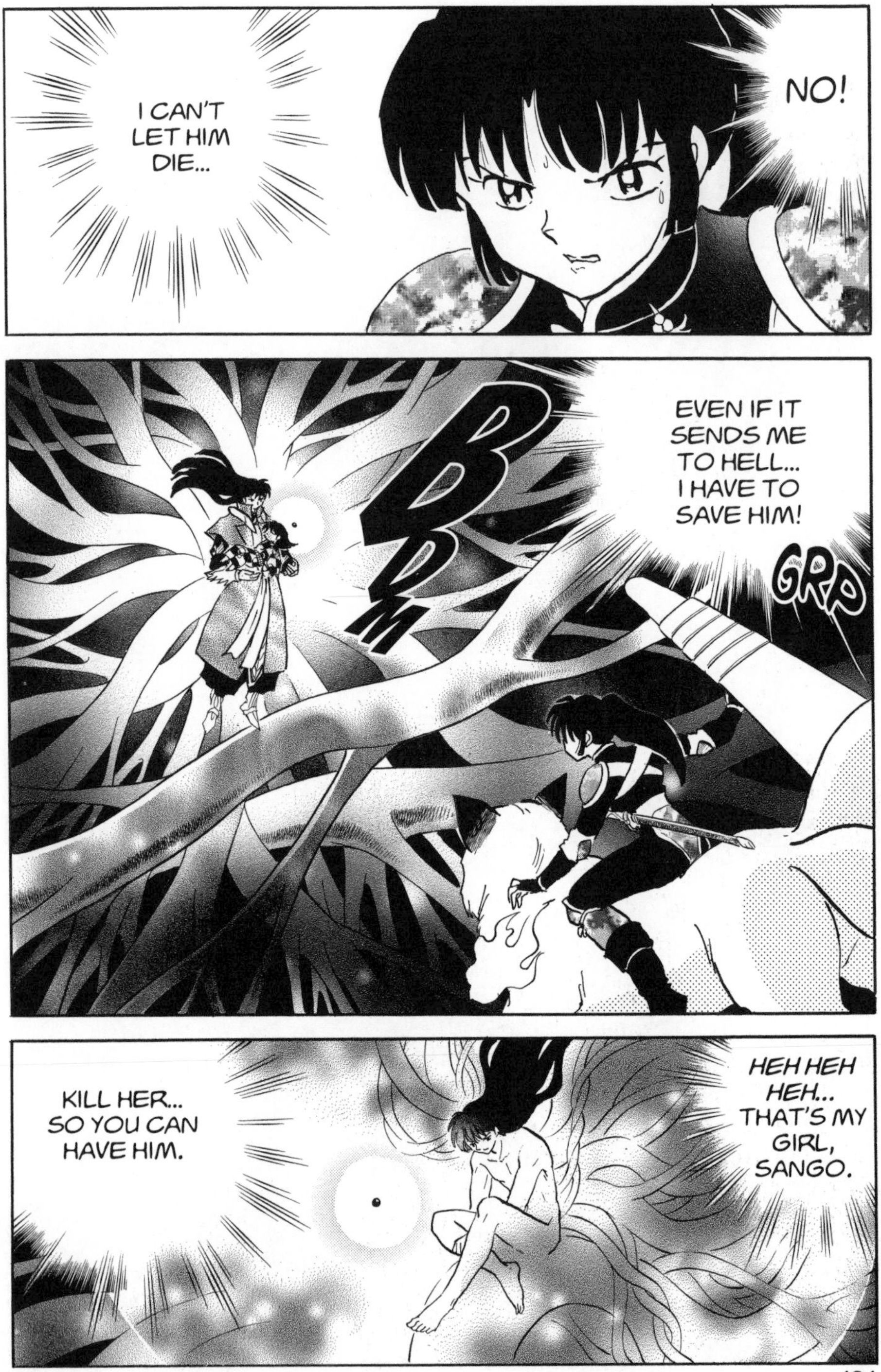
NO!
I CAN'T LET HIM DIE...
EVEN IF IT SENDS ME TO HELL... I HAVE TO SAVE HIM!
GRP
BDM
HEH HEH HEH... THAT'S MY GIRL, SANGO.
KILL HER... SO YOU CAN HAVE HIM.

SCROLL FOUR
LIGHT DEVOURED

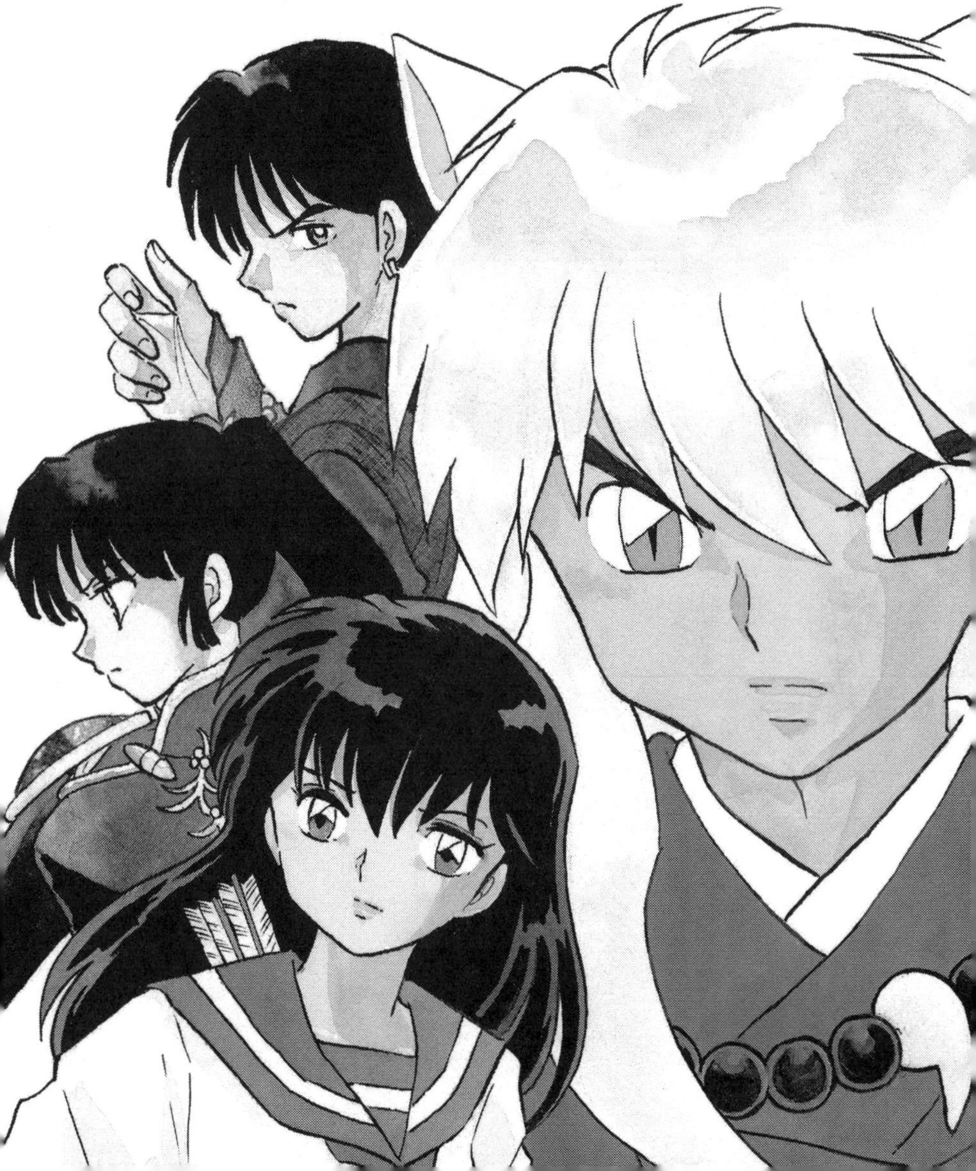

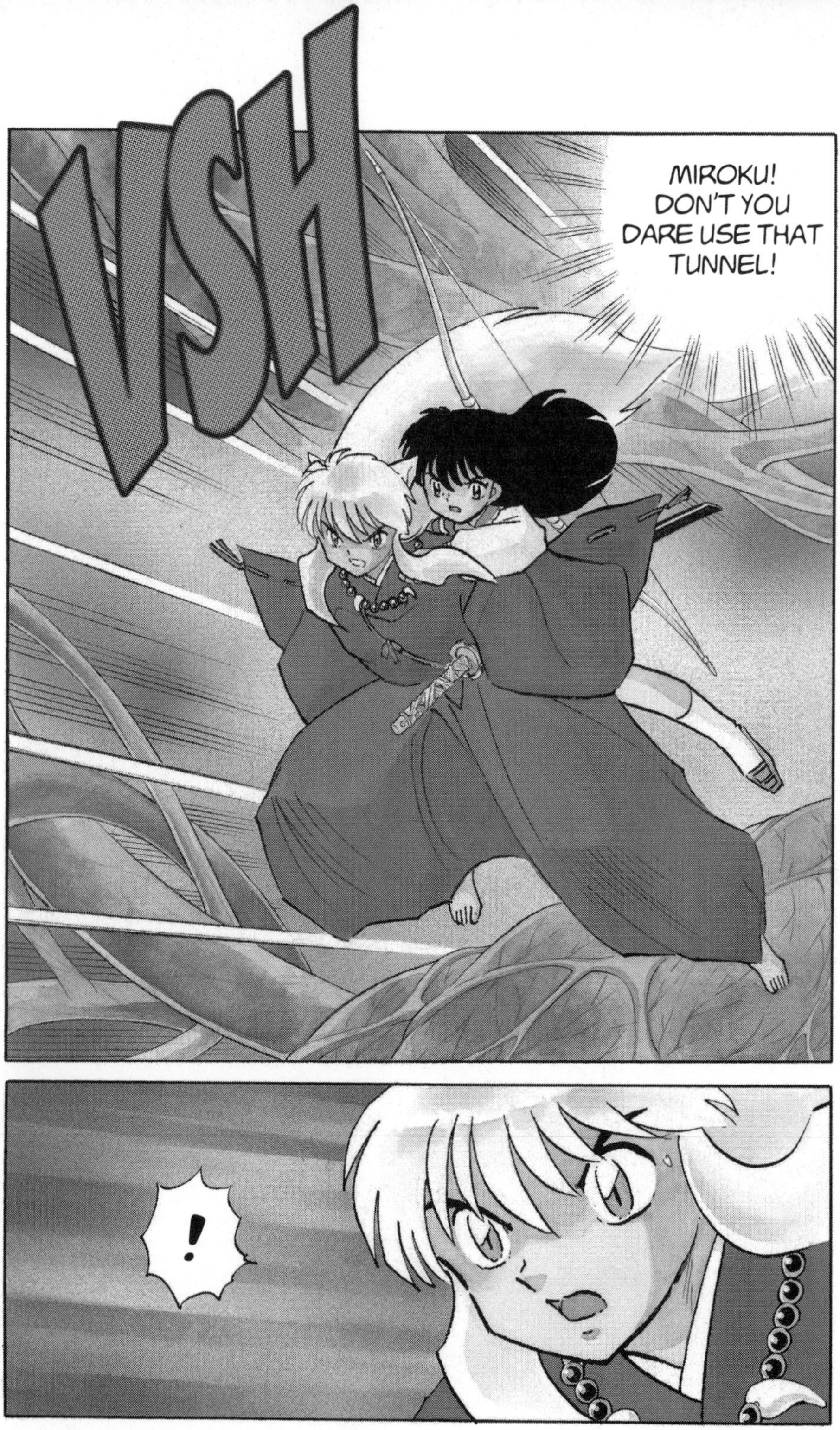
VSH
MIROKU! DON'T YOU DARE USE THAT TUNNEL!
!

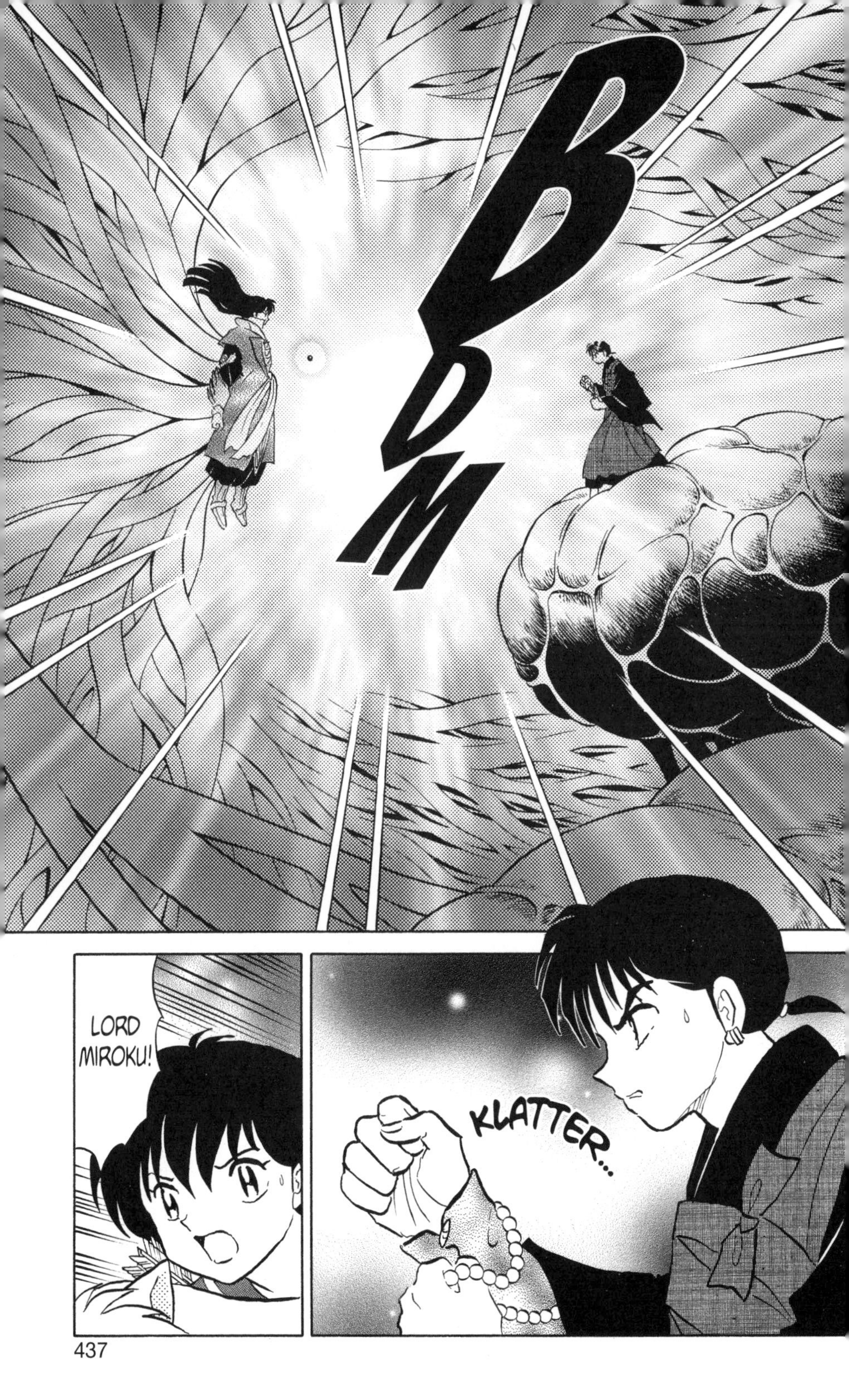
BDM
KLATTER...
LORD MIROKU!

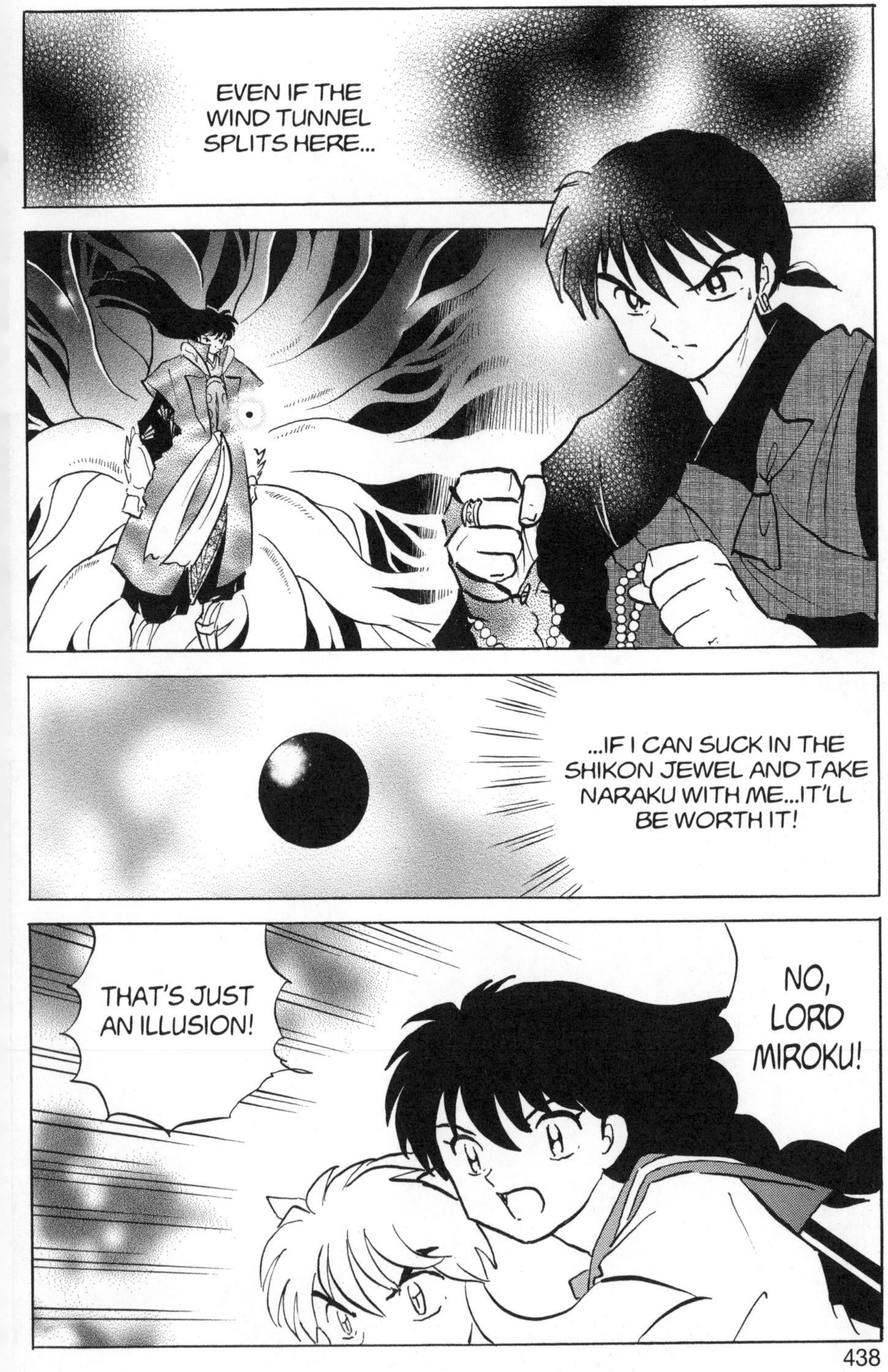
EVEN IF THE WIND TUNNEL SPLITS HERE...
...IF I CAN SUCK IN THE SHIKON JEWEL AND TAKE NARAKU WITH ME...IT'LL BE WORTH IT!
NO, LORD MIROKU!
THAT'S JUST AN ILLUSION!

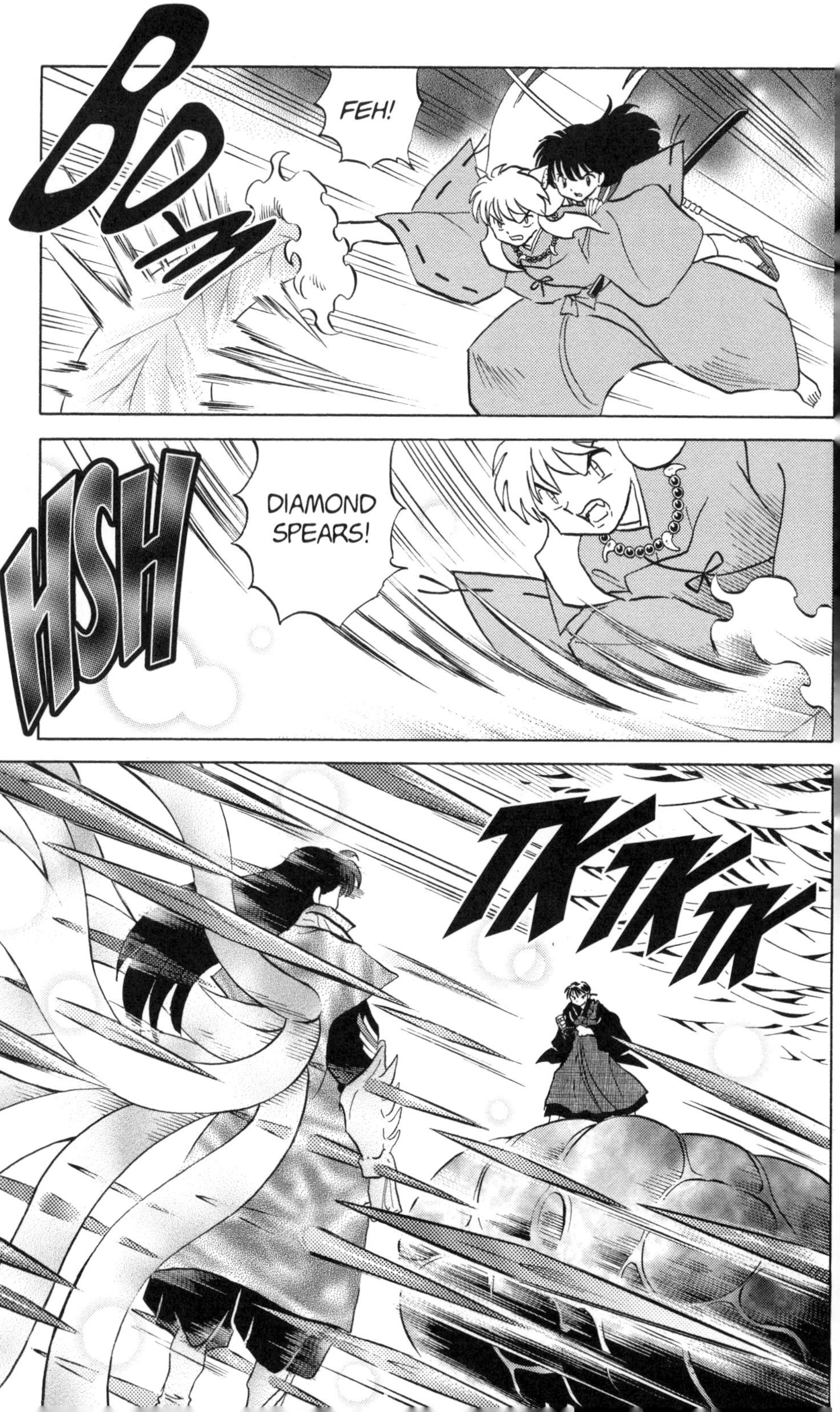
FEH!
BOOM
DIAMOND SPEARS!
HSH
TKTKTK

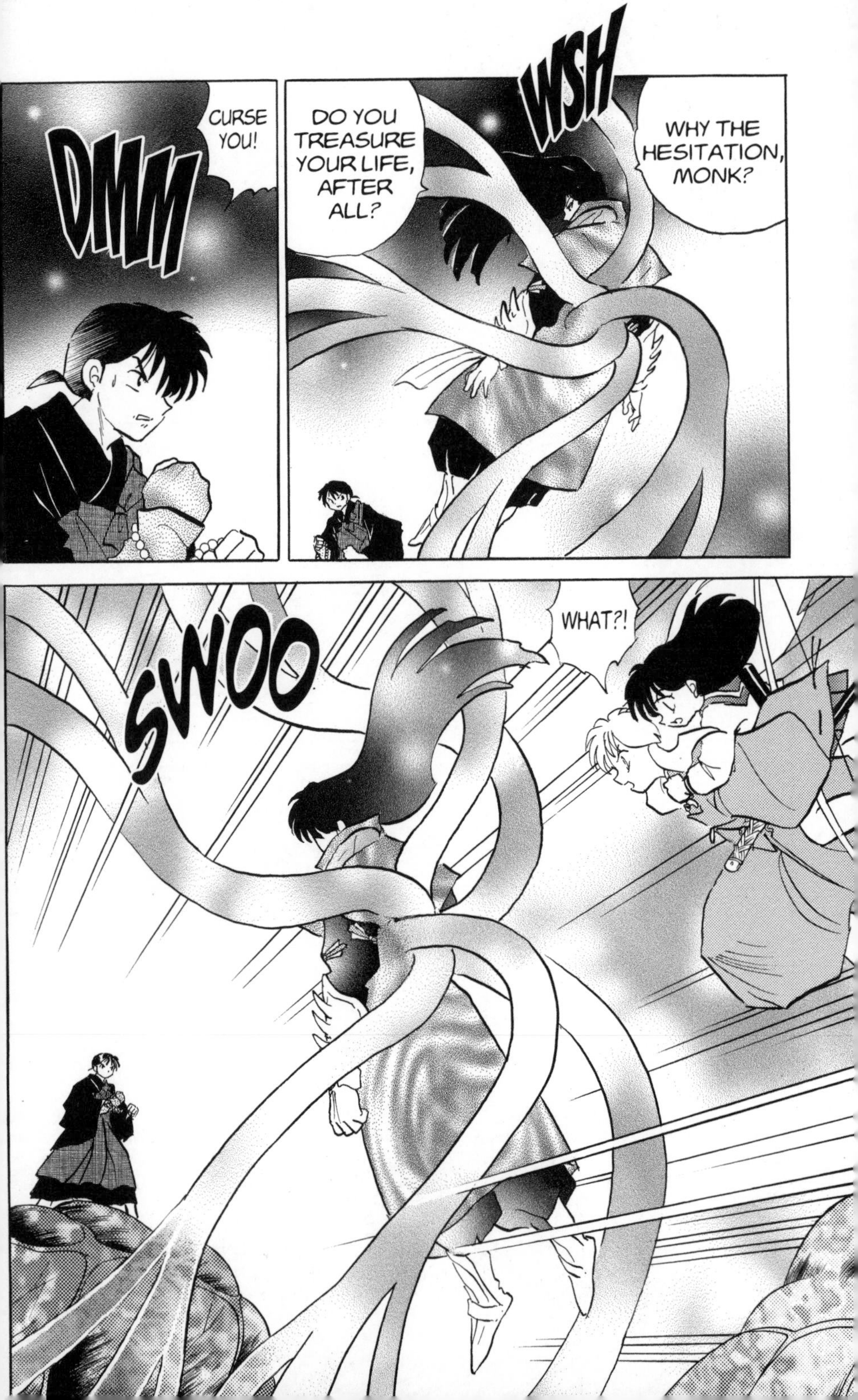
WHY THE HESITATION, MONK?
WSH
DO YOU TREASURE YOUR LIFE, AFTER ALL?
CURSE YOU!
DMM
WHAT?!
SWOO

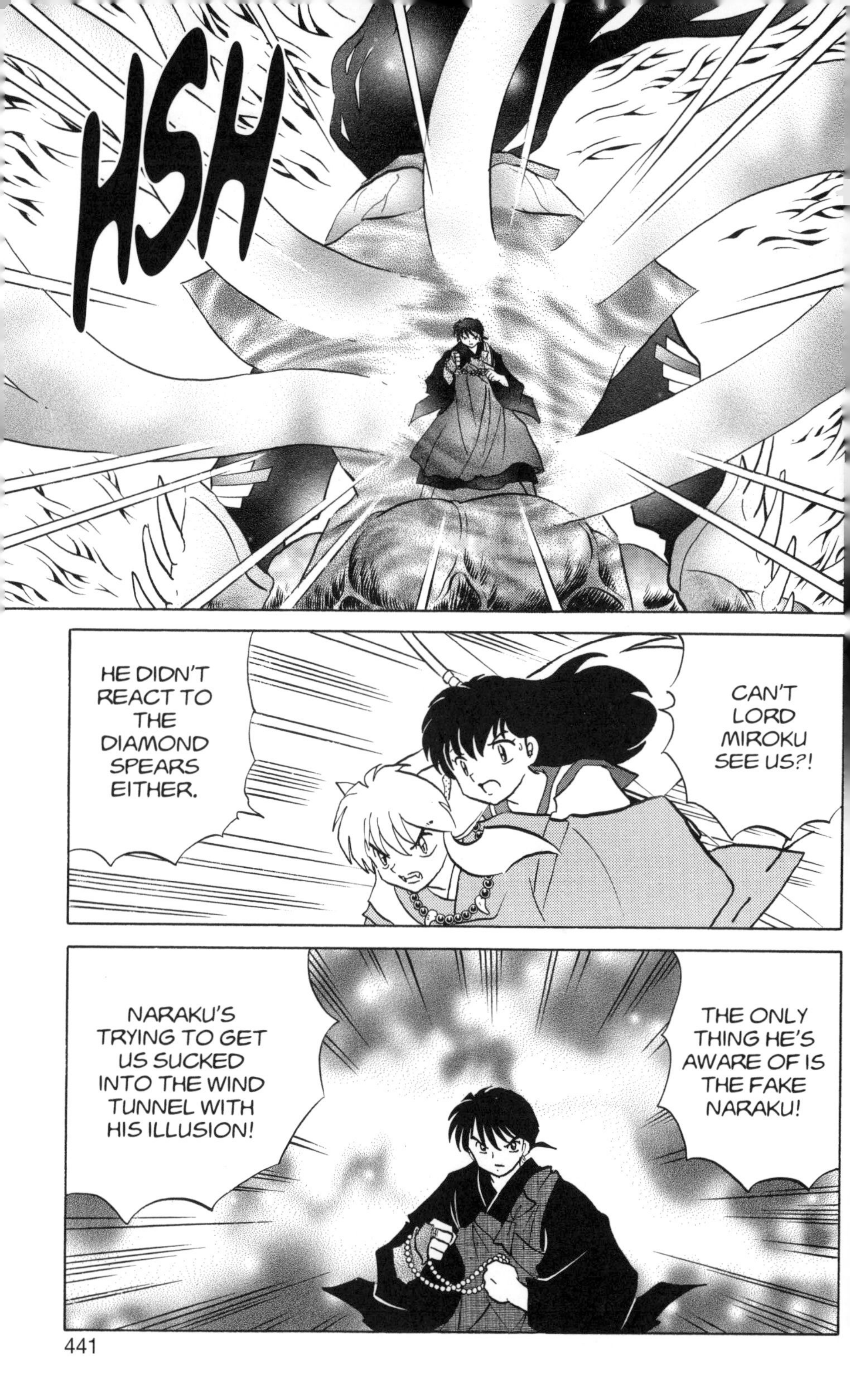
HSH
CAN'T LORD MIROKU SEE US?!
HE DIDN'T REACT TO THE DIAMOND SPEARS EITHER.
THE ONLY THING HE'S AWARE OF IS THE FAKE NARAKU!
NARAKU'S TRYING TO GET US SUCKED INTO THE WIND TUNNEL WITH HIS ILLUSION!

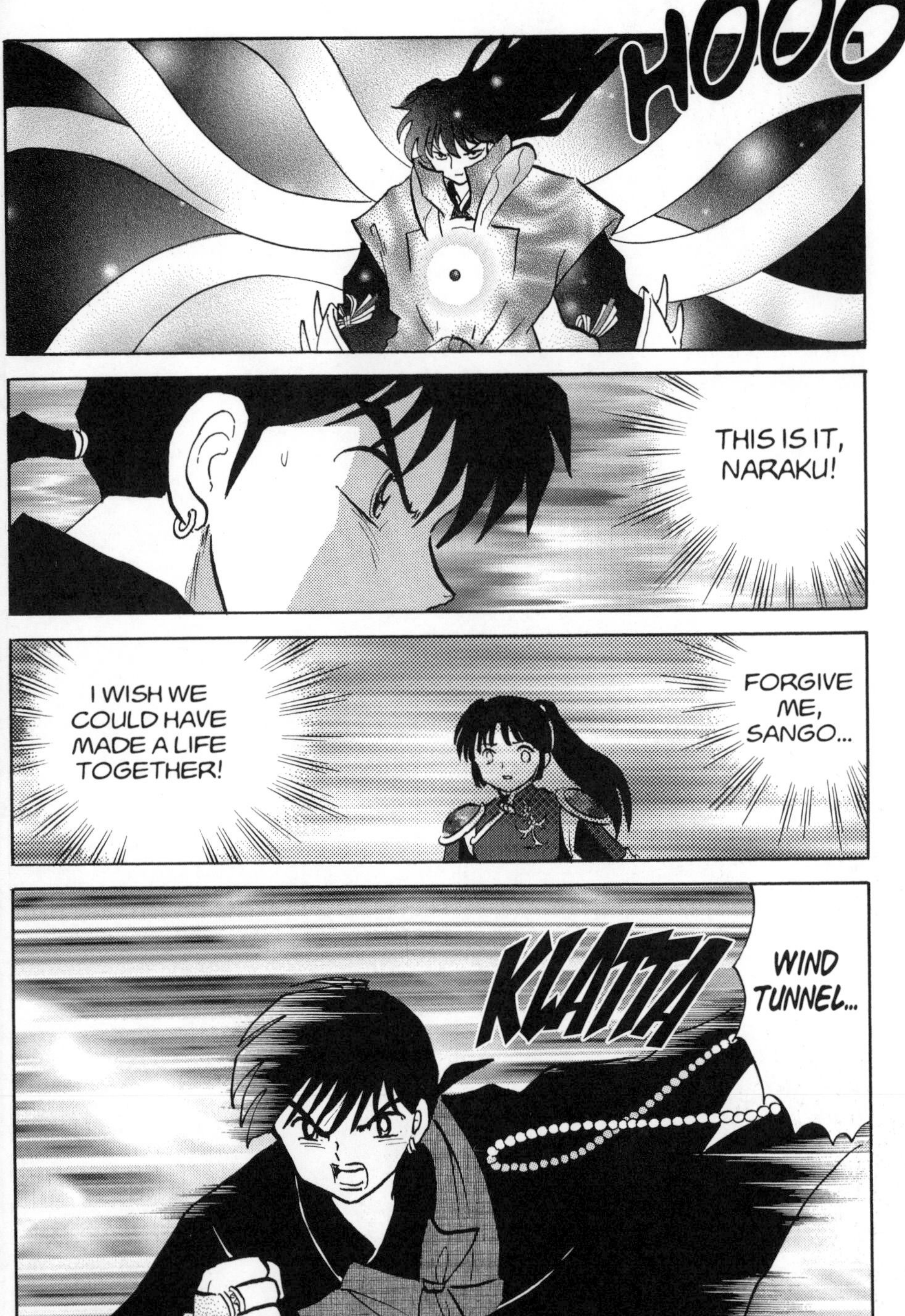
HOOO
THIS IS IT, NARAKU!
FORGIVE ME, SANGO...
I WISH WE COULD HAVE MADE A LIFE TOGETHER!
WIND TUNNEL...
KWATTA

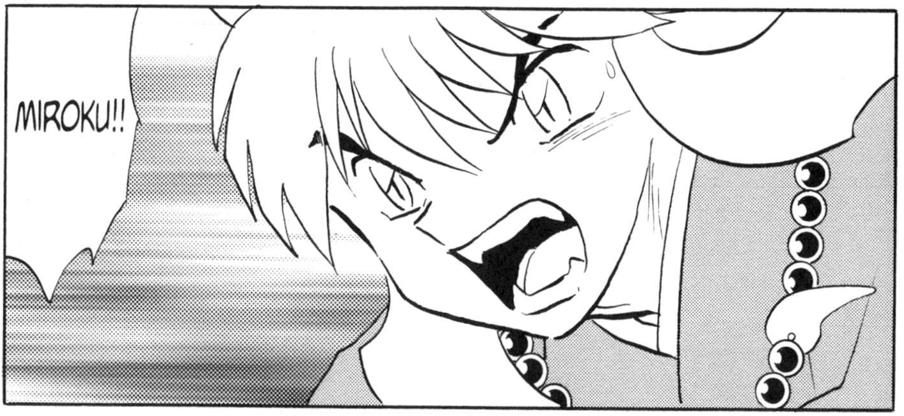
MIROKU!!

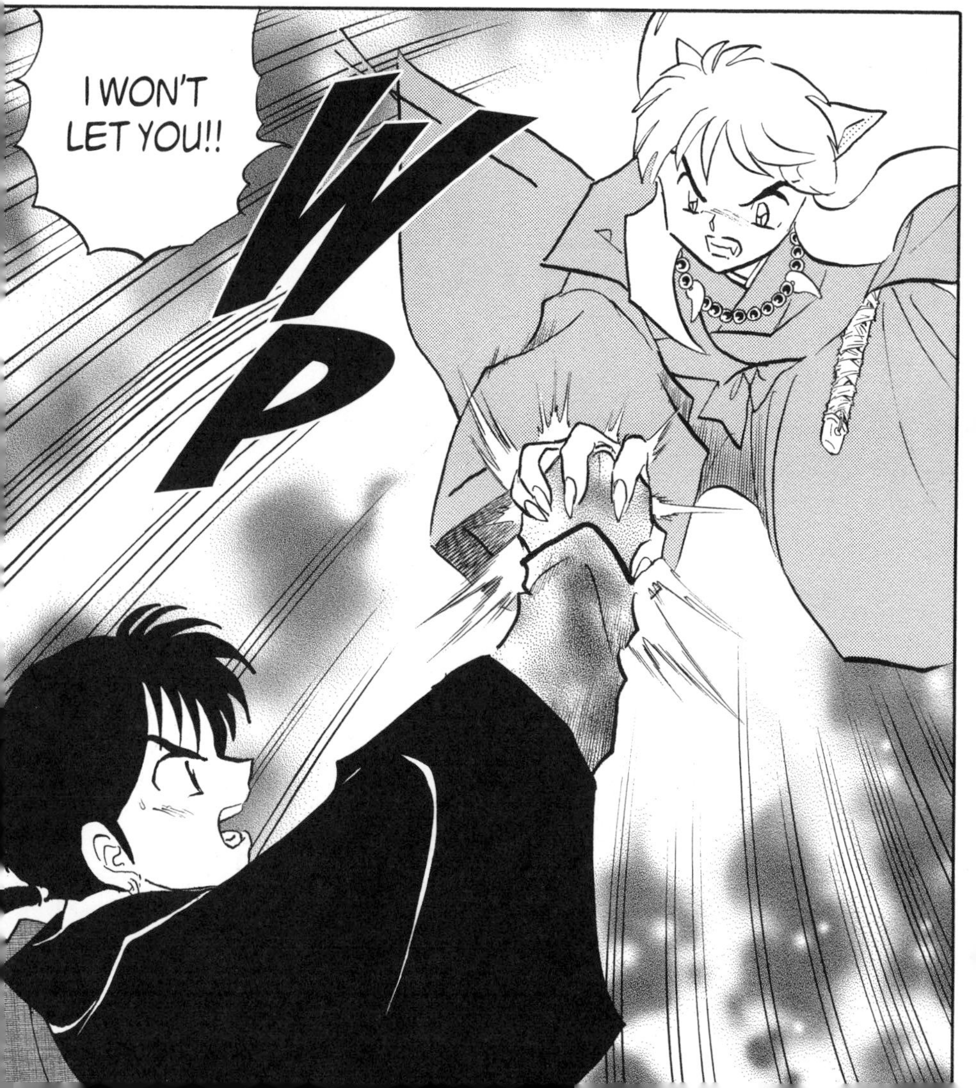
I WON'T LET YOU!!
WP

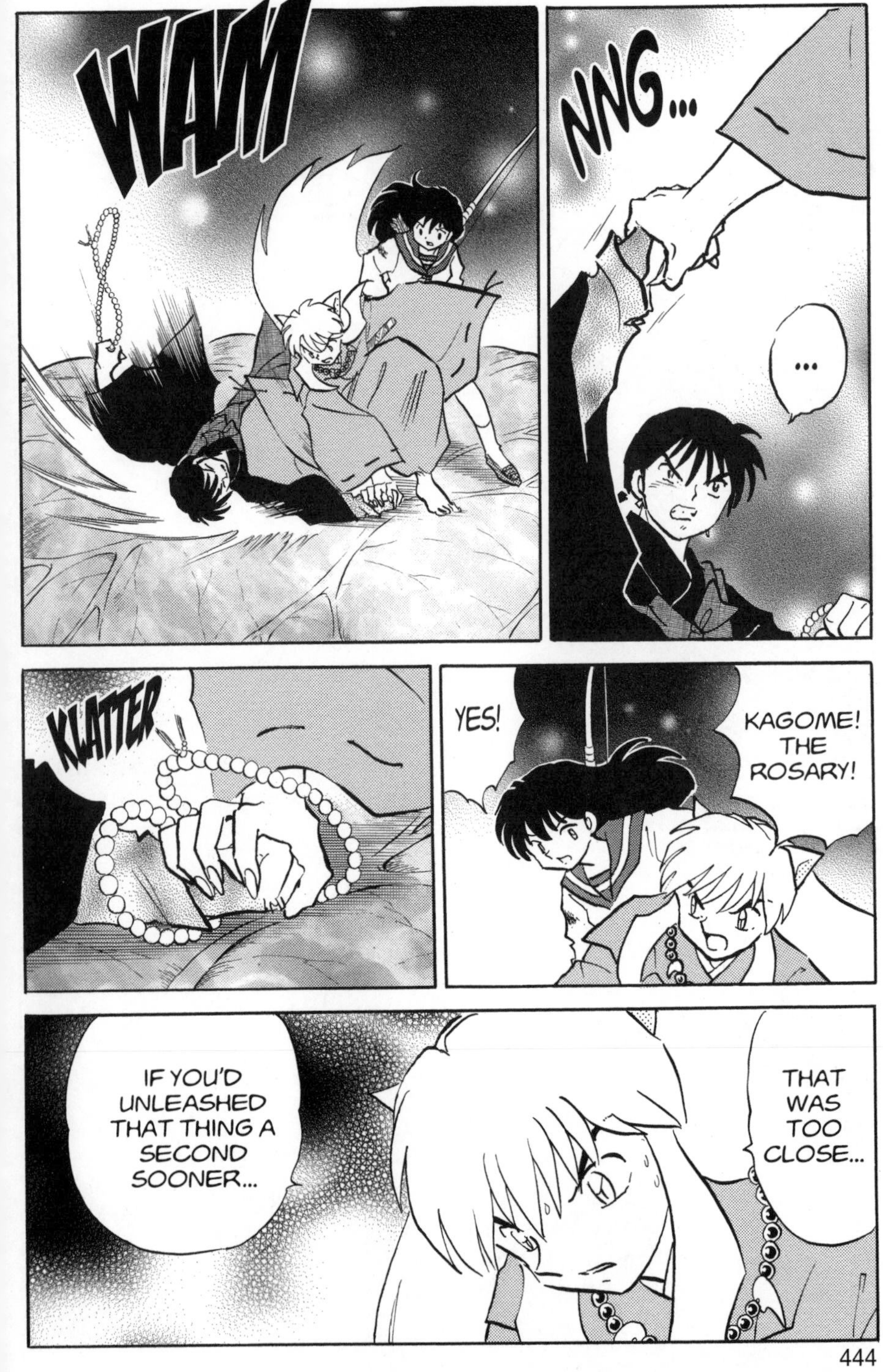
NNG...
...
WAM
KAGOME! THE ROSARY!
YES!
KLATTER
THAT WAS TOO CLOSE...
IF YOU'D UNLEASHED THAT THING A SECOND SOONER...

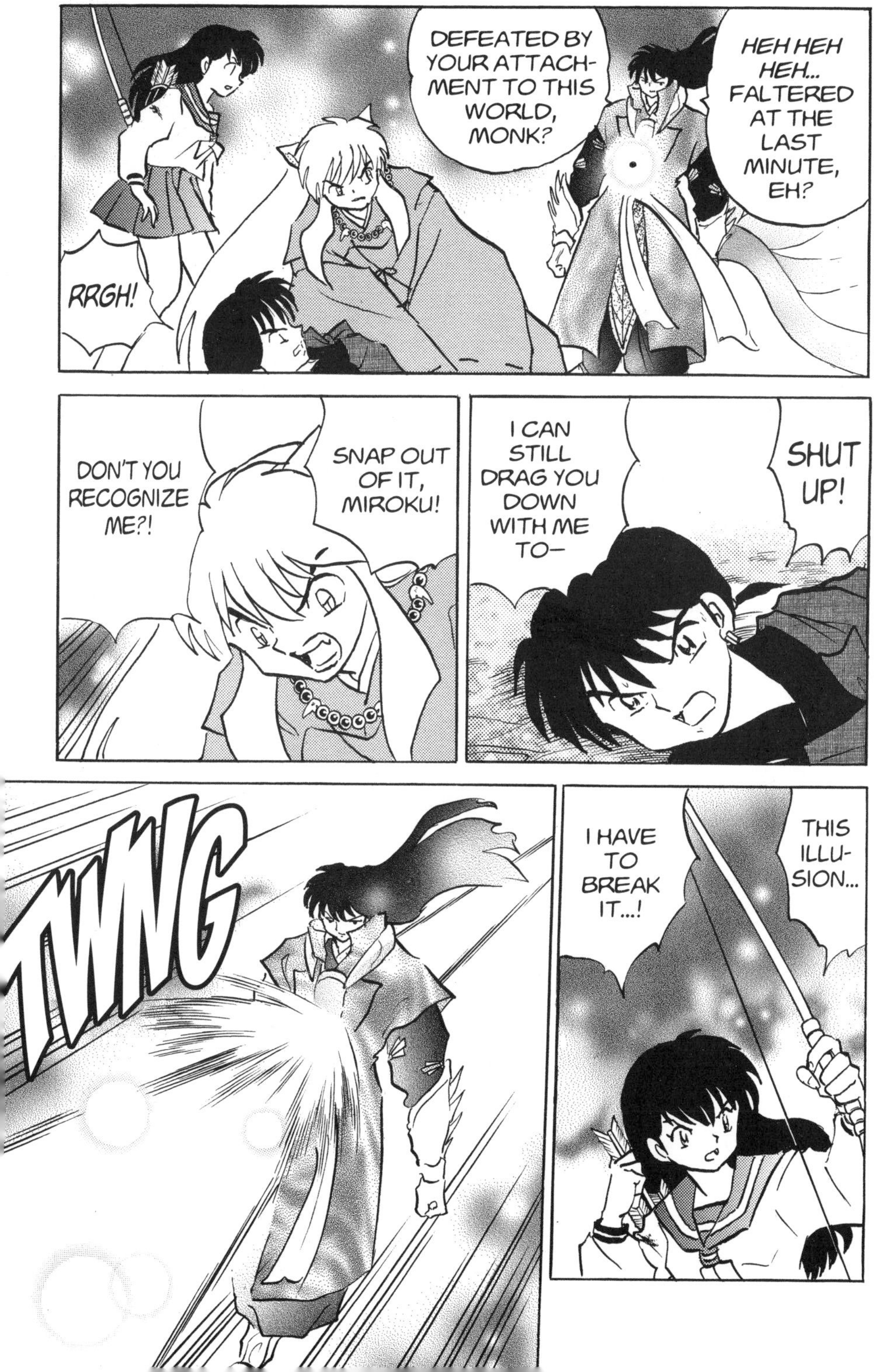
HEH HEH HEH... FALTERED AT THE LAST MINUTE, EH?
DEFEATED BY YOUR ATTACHMENT TO THIS WORLD, MONK?
RRGH!
SHUT UP!
I CAN STILL DRAG YOU DOWN WITH ME TO—
SNAP OUT OF IT, MIROKU!
DON'T YOU RECOGNIZE ME?!
THIS ILLUSION...
I HAVE TO BREAK IT...!
TWNG

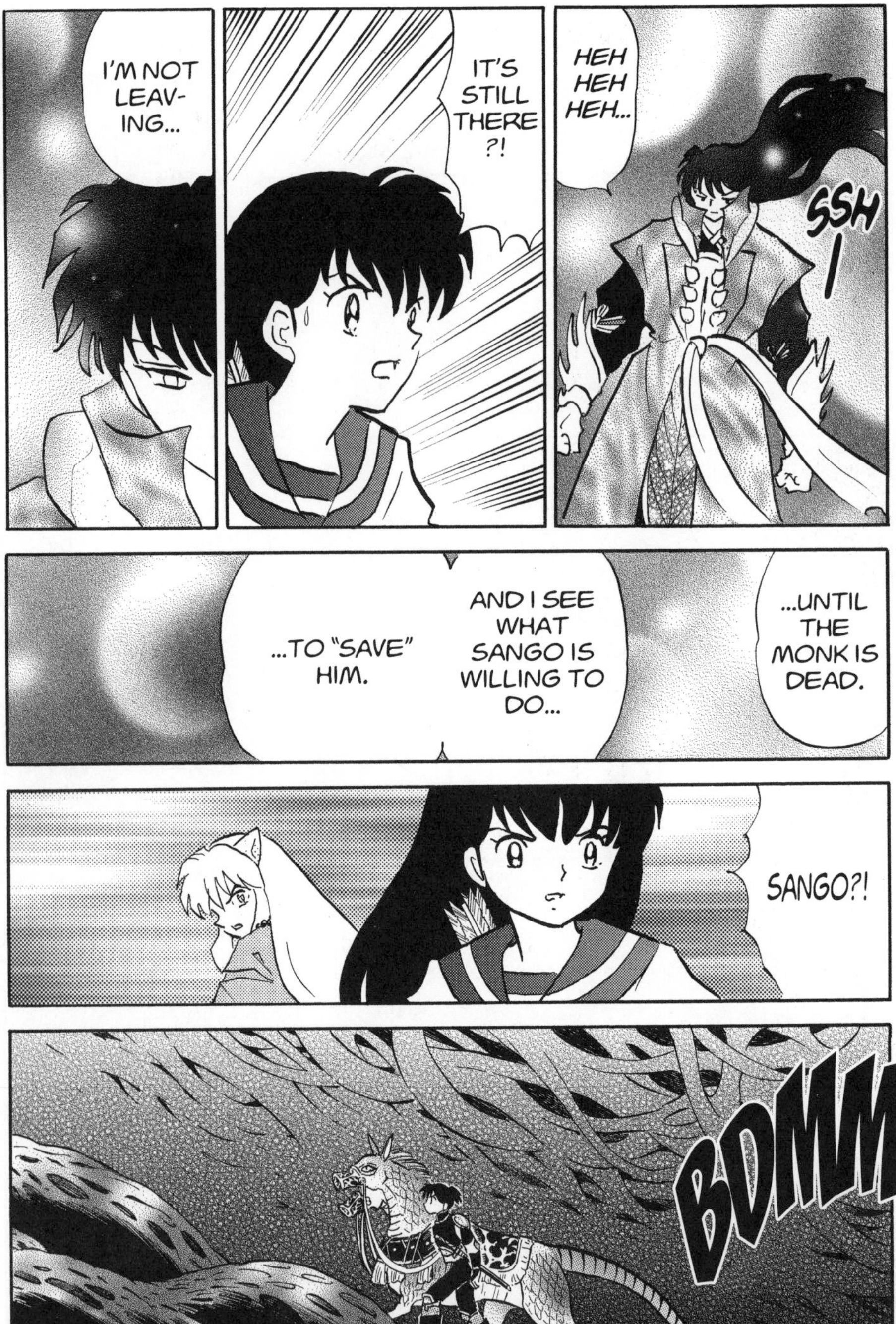
HEH HEH HEH...
SSHI
IT'S STILL THERE?!
I'M NOT LEAVING...
...UNTIL THE MONK IS DEAD.
AND I SEE WHAT SANGO IS WILLING TO DO...
...TO "SAVE" HIM.
SANGO?!
BOMM

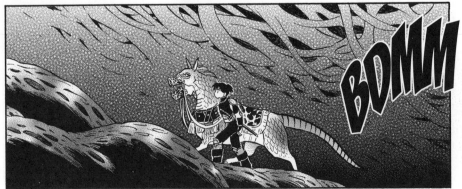

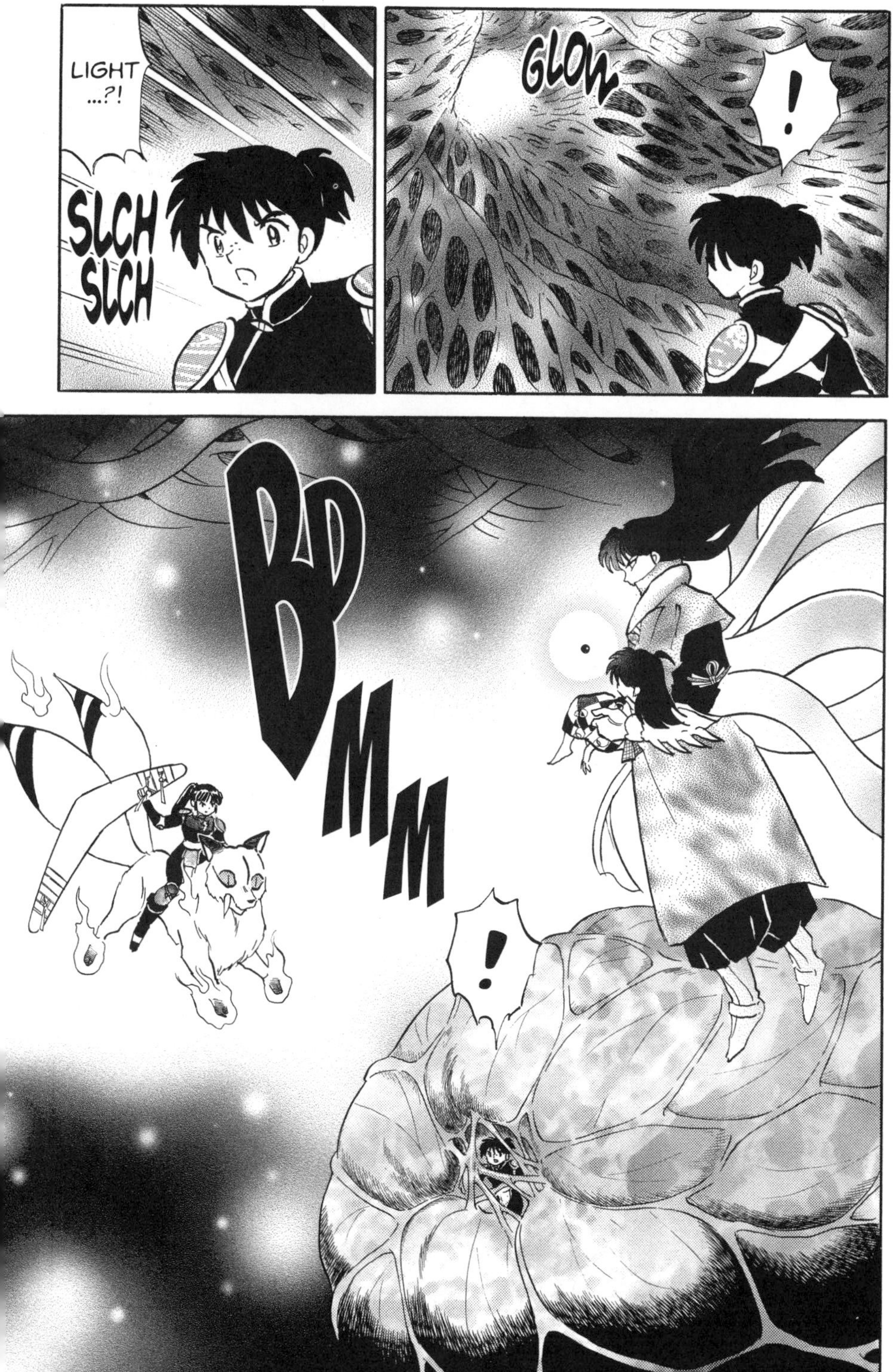
GLOW
!
LIGHT ...?!
SLCH SLCH
BDMMM
!

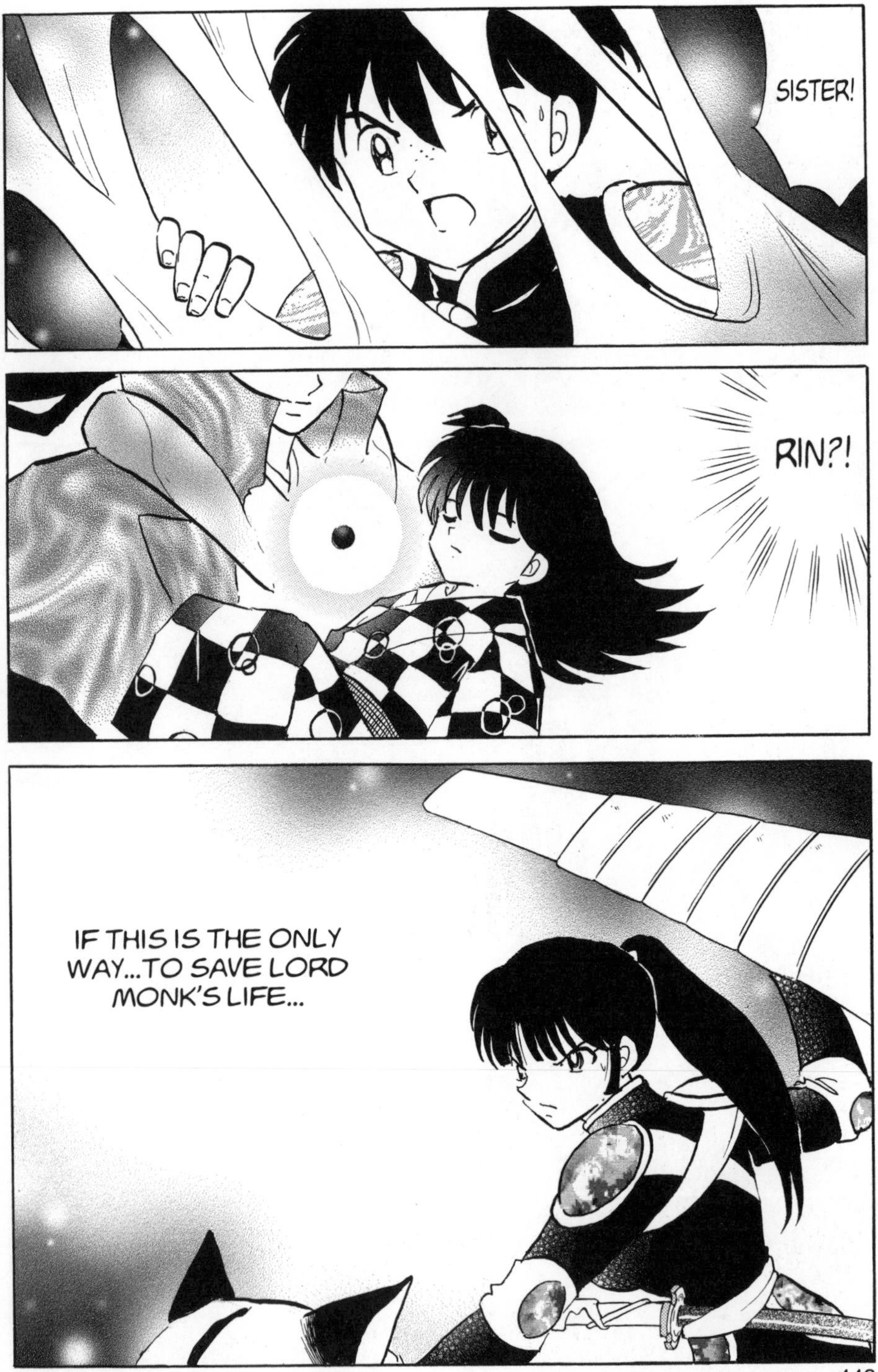

SISTER!
RIN?!
IF THIS IS THE ONLY WAY...TO SAVE LORD MONK'S LIFE...

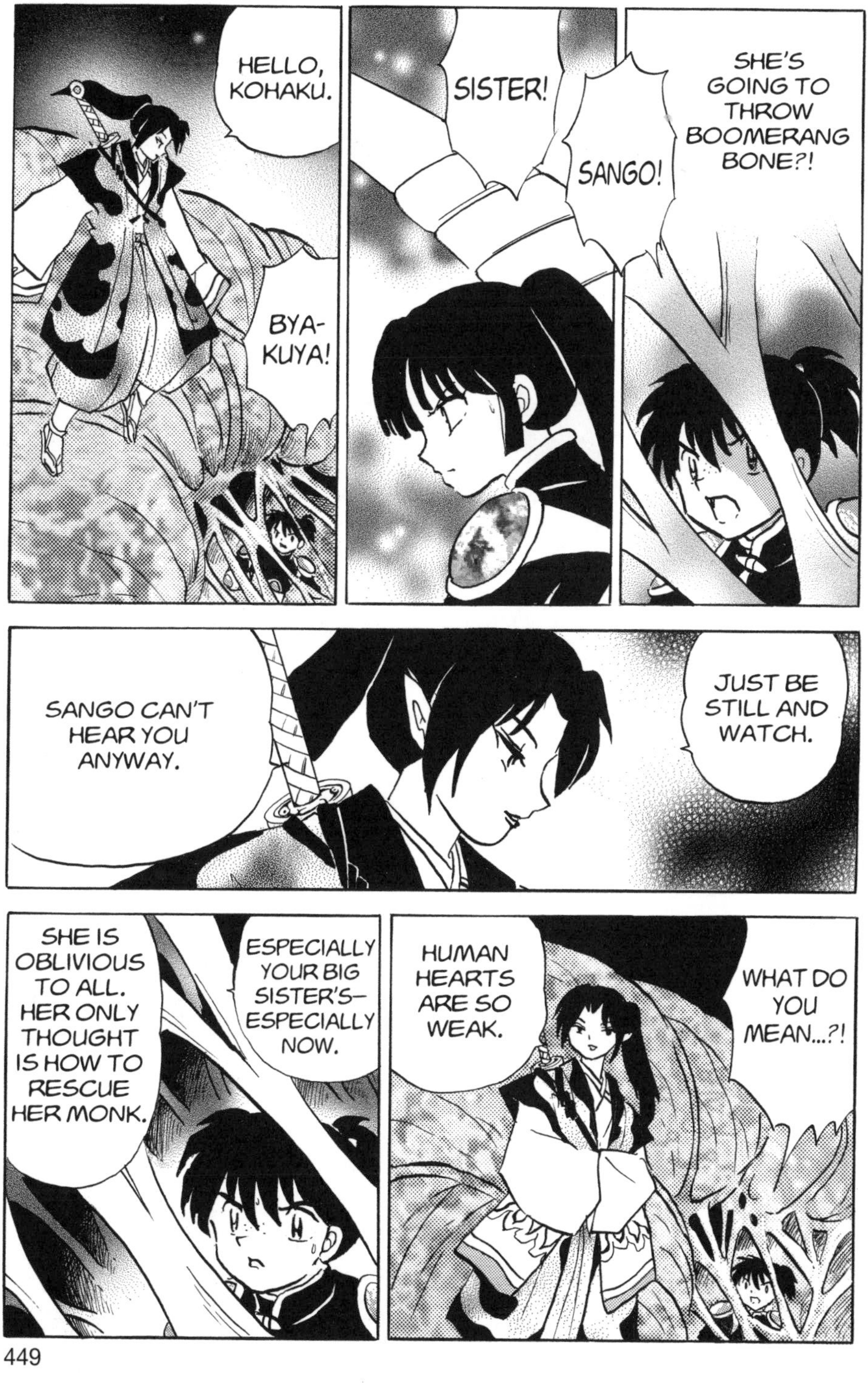
SHE'S GOING TO THROW BOOMERANG BONE?!
SANGO!
SISTER!
HELLO, KOHAKU.
BYA-KUYA!
JUST BE STILL AND WATCH.
SANGO CAN'T HEAR YOU ANYWAY.
WHAT DO YOU MEAN...?!
HUMAN HEARTS ARE SO WEAK.
ESPECIALLY YOUR BIG SISTER'S— ESPECIALLY NOW.
SHE IS OBLIVIOUS TO ALL. HER ONLY THOUGHT IS HOW TO RESCUE HER MONK.

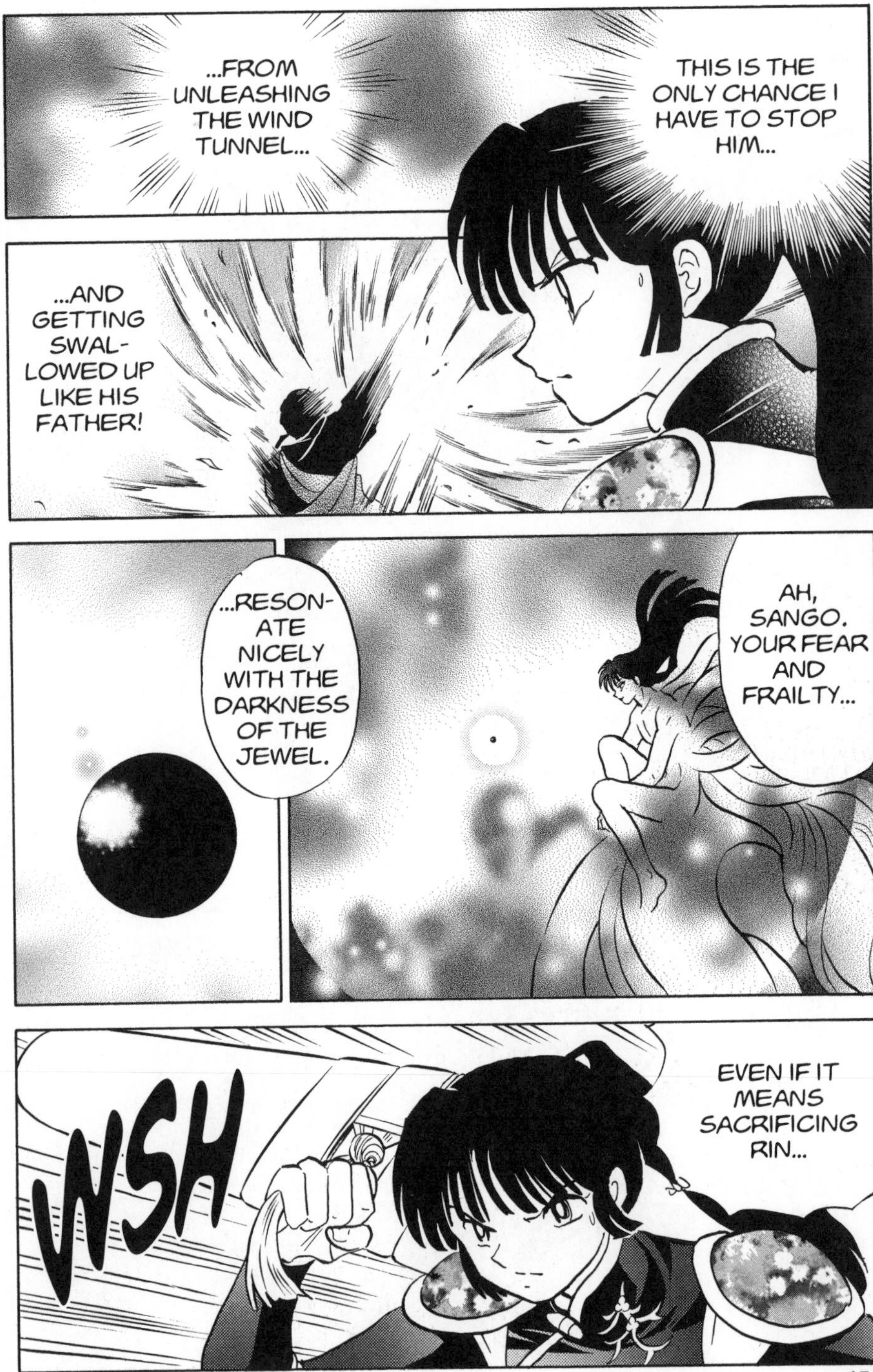
THIS IS THE ONLY CHANCE I HAVE TO STOP HIM...
...FROM UNLEASHING THE WIND TUNNEL...
...AND GETTING SWAL-LOWED UP LIKE HIS FATHER!
AH, SANGO. YOUR FEAR AND FRAILTY...
...RESON-ATE NICELY WITH THE DARKNESS OF THE JEWEL.
EVEN IF IT MEANS SACRIFICING RIN...
WSH

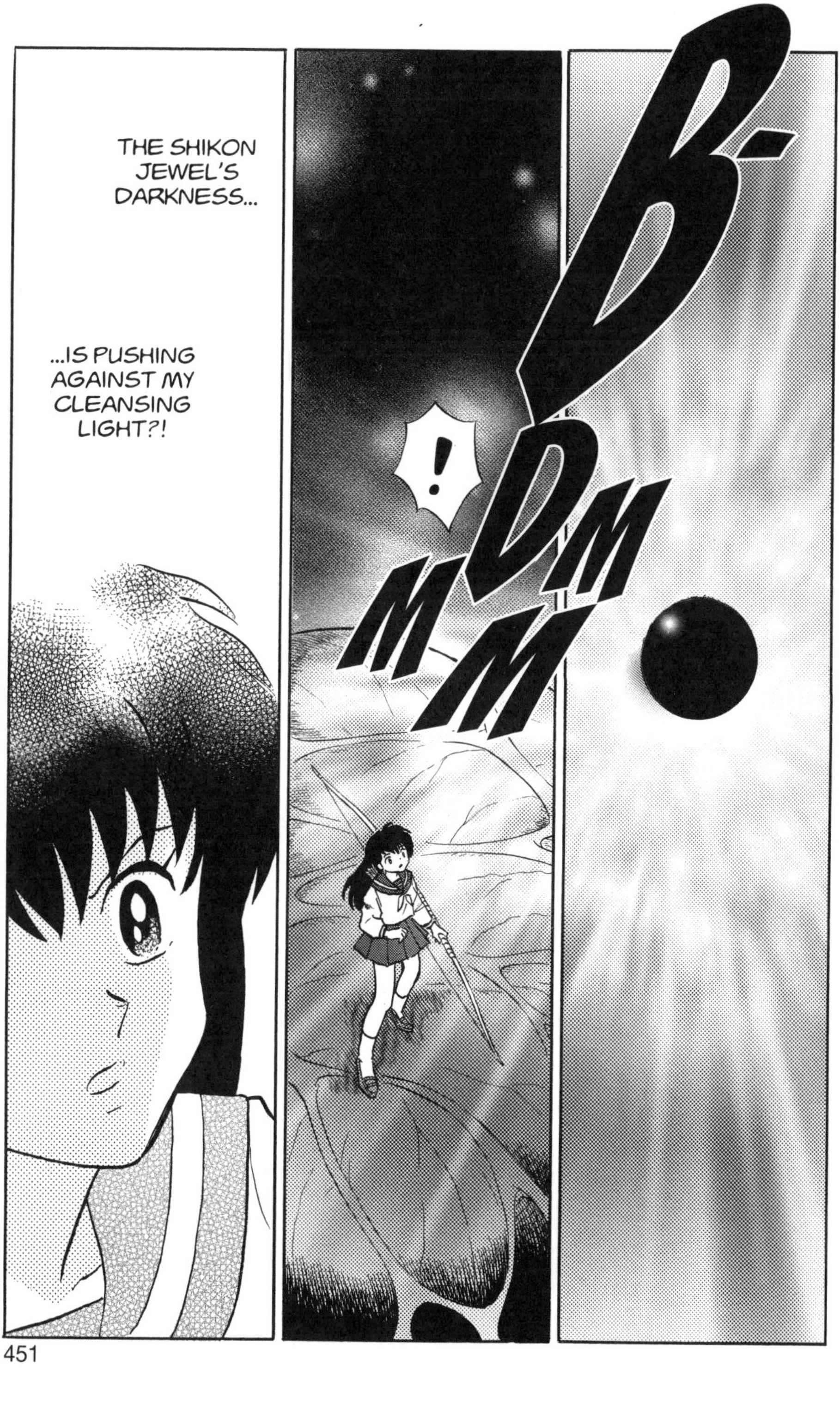
B-DMMM
!
THE SHIKON JEWEL'S DARKNESS...
...IS PUSHING AGAINST MY CLEANSING LIGHT?!

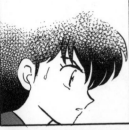

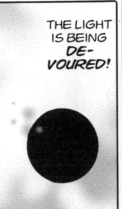

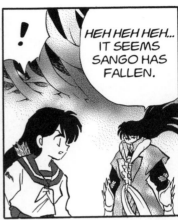

!
HEH HEH HEH... IT SEEMS SANGO HAS FALLEN.
THE LIGHT IS BEING DE-VOURED!
I HAVE TO STOP IT...
...BEFORE NARAKU REGAINS HIS POWER!
MY TARGET NOW IS...
B-DOMM
...WATCH FOR IT...
HOOOO...
KAGO-ME...?!
GLEEM...

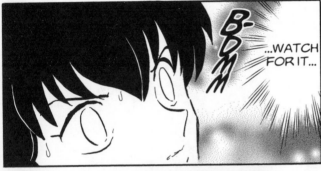

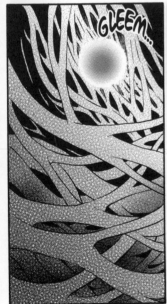

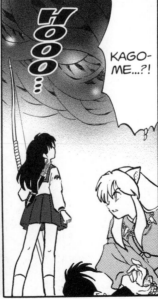

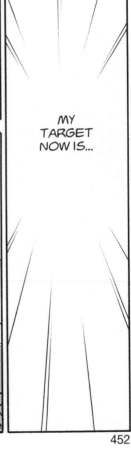

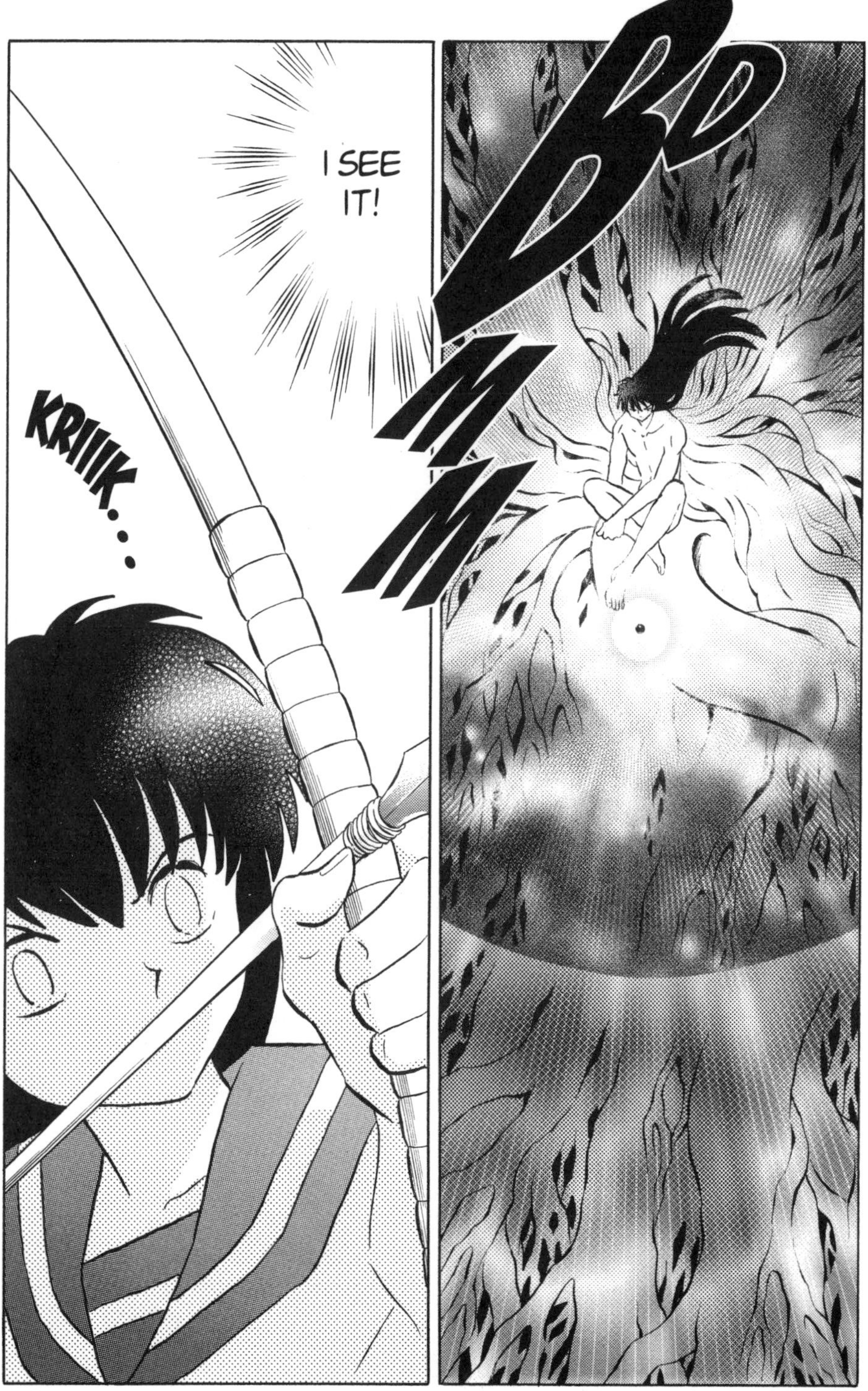
BDMMM
I SEE IT!
KRIIIK...

TWING
ONE CHANCE !!
HRR
FORGIVE ME, RIN!
SANGO!

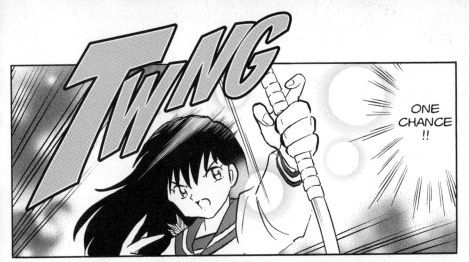

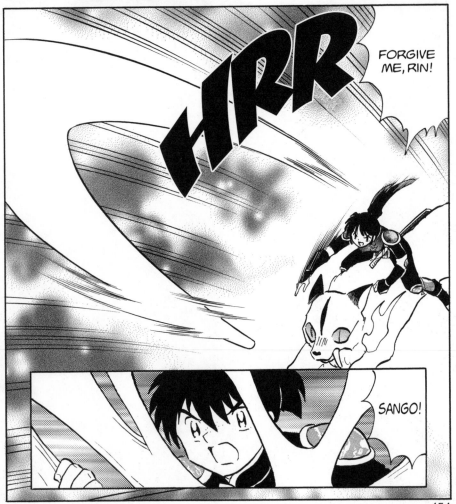

SCROLL FIVE
THE VANISHING ARROW

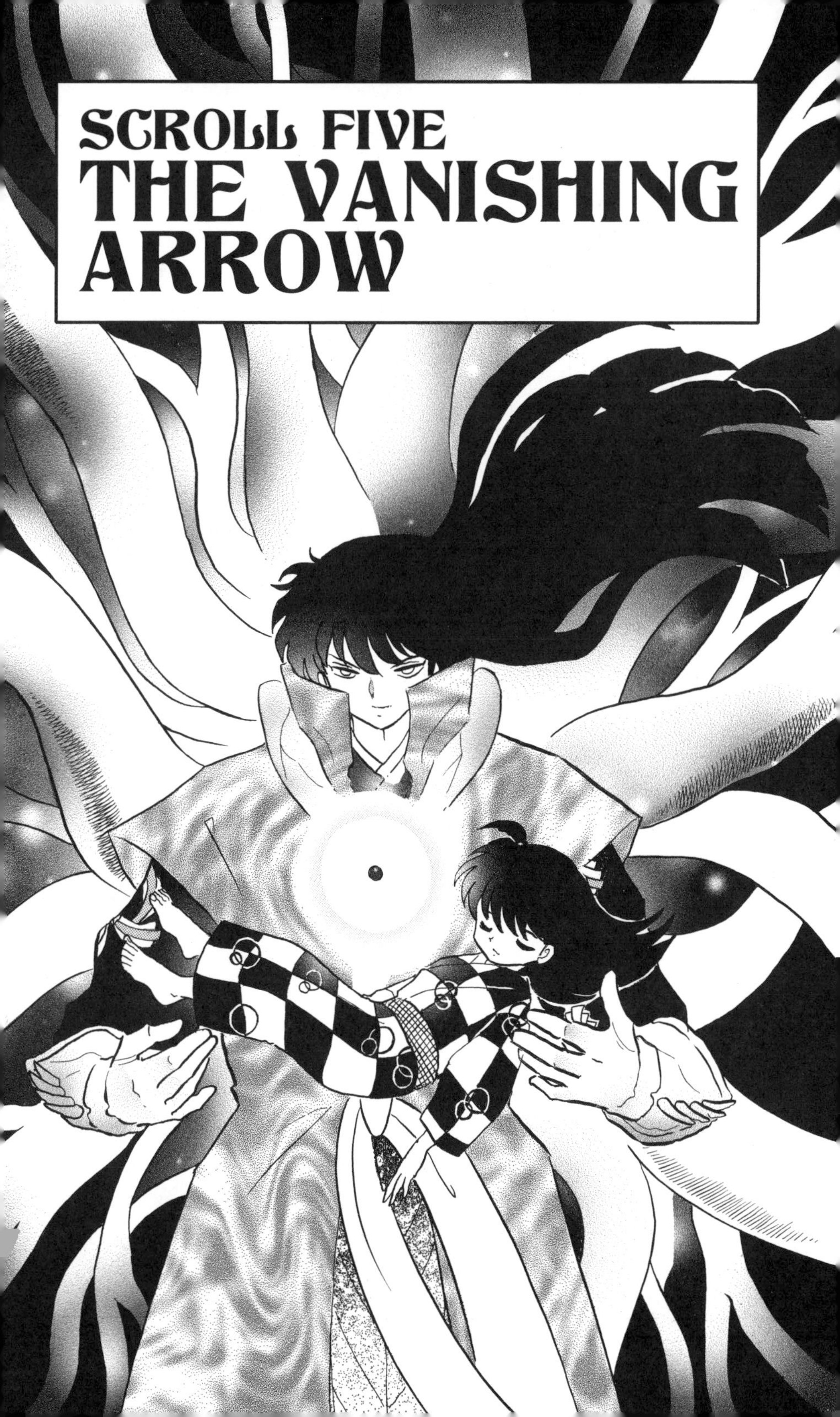

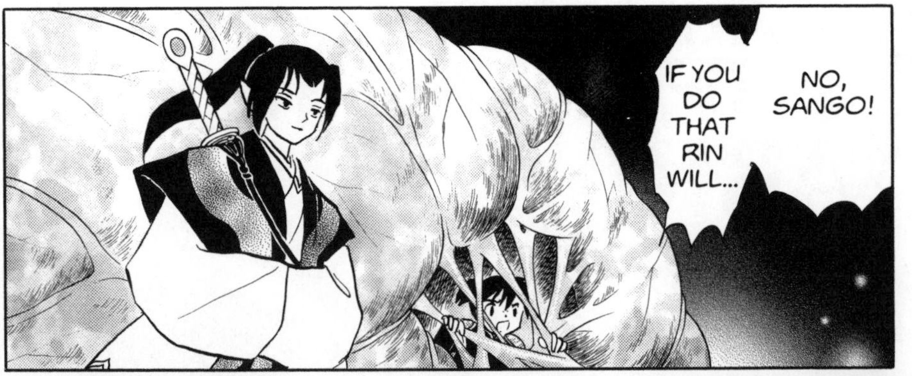
NO, SANGO!
IF YOU DO THAT RIN WILL...

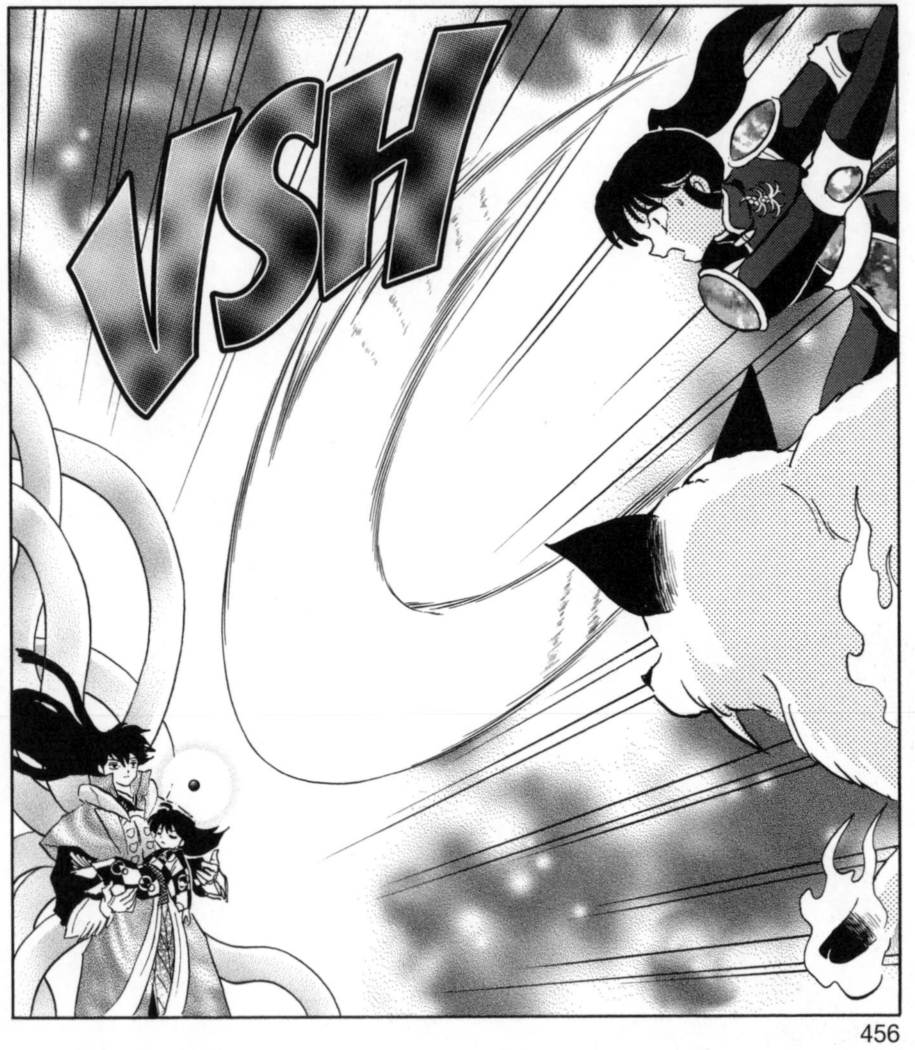
VSH

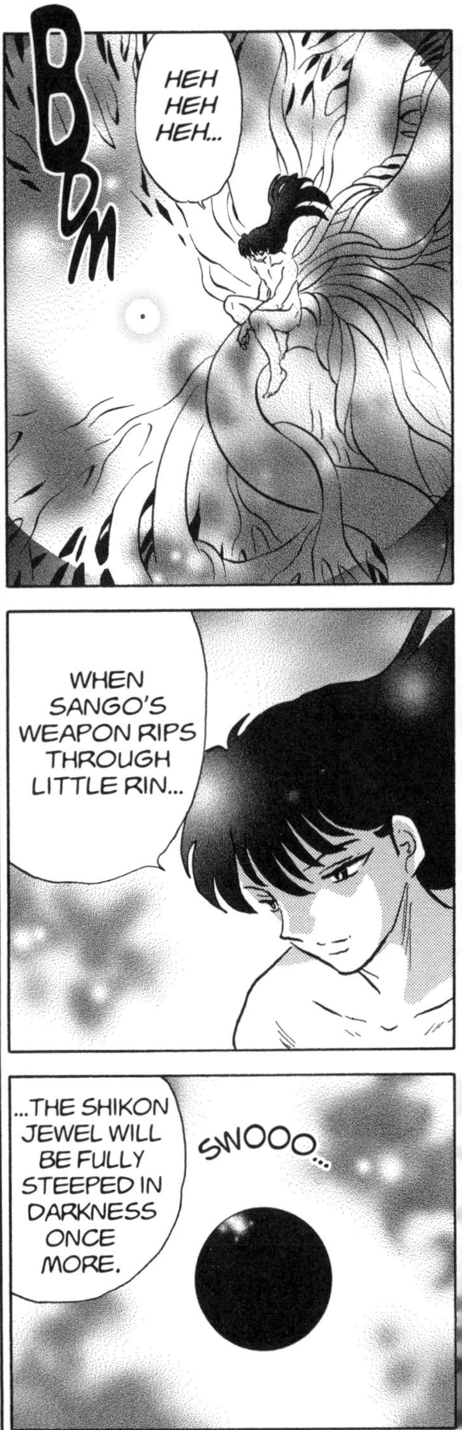
BDM
HEH HEH HEH...
WHEN SANGO'S WEAPON RIPS THROUGH LITTLE RIN...
...THE SHIKON JEWEL WILL BE FULLY STEEPED IN DARKNESS ONCE MORE.
SWOOO...
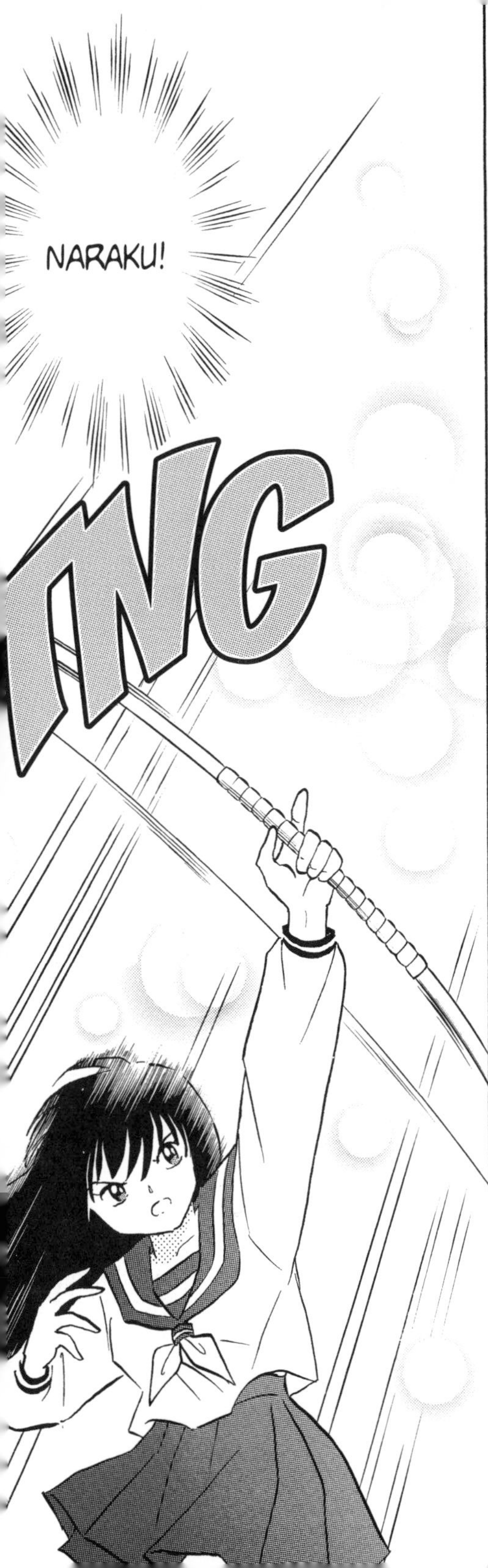
NARAKU!
TNG

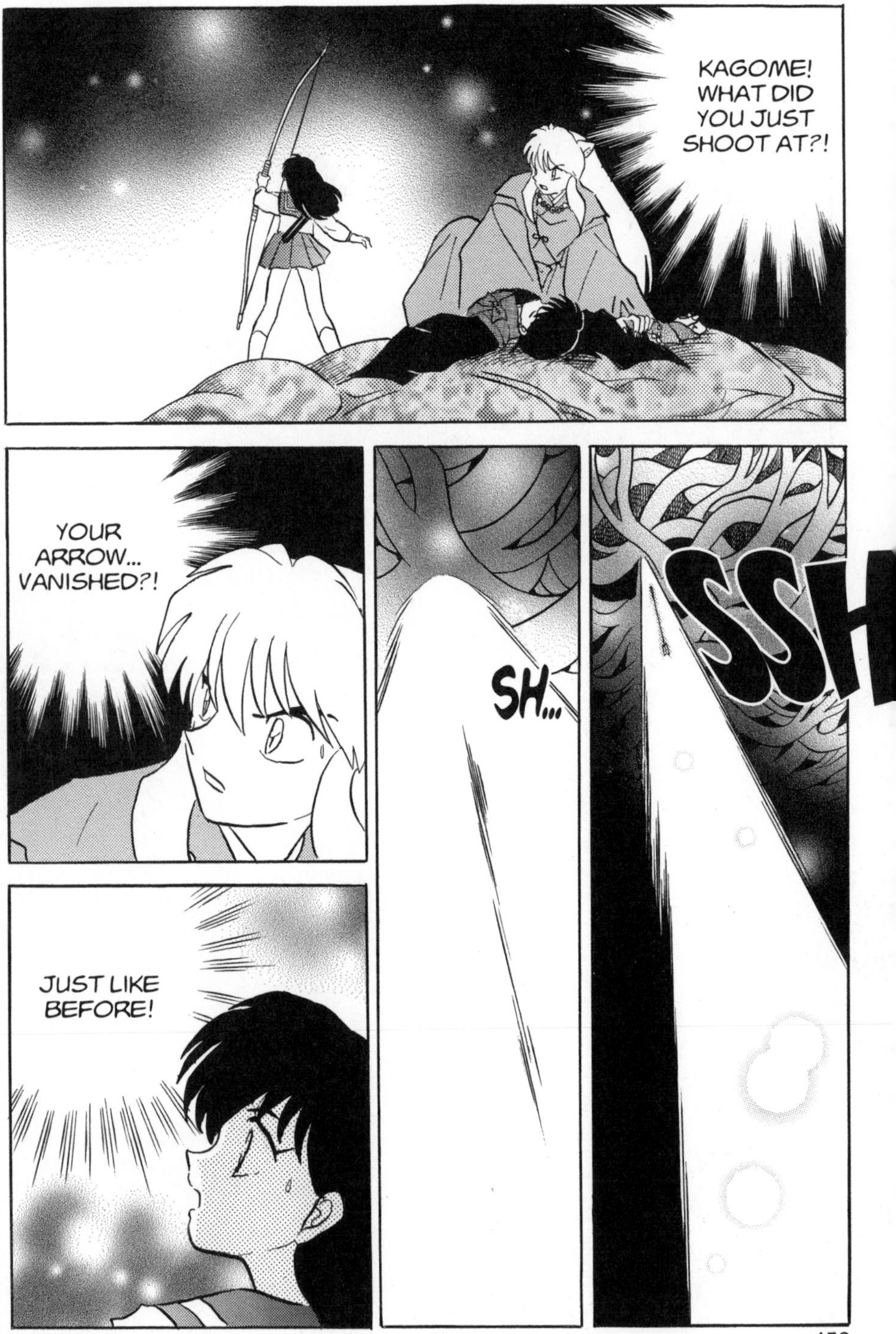
KAGOME! WHAT DID YOU JUST SHOOT AT?!
SSH
SH...
YOUR ARROW... VANISHED?!
JUST LIKE BEFORE!

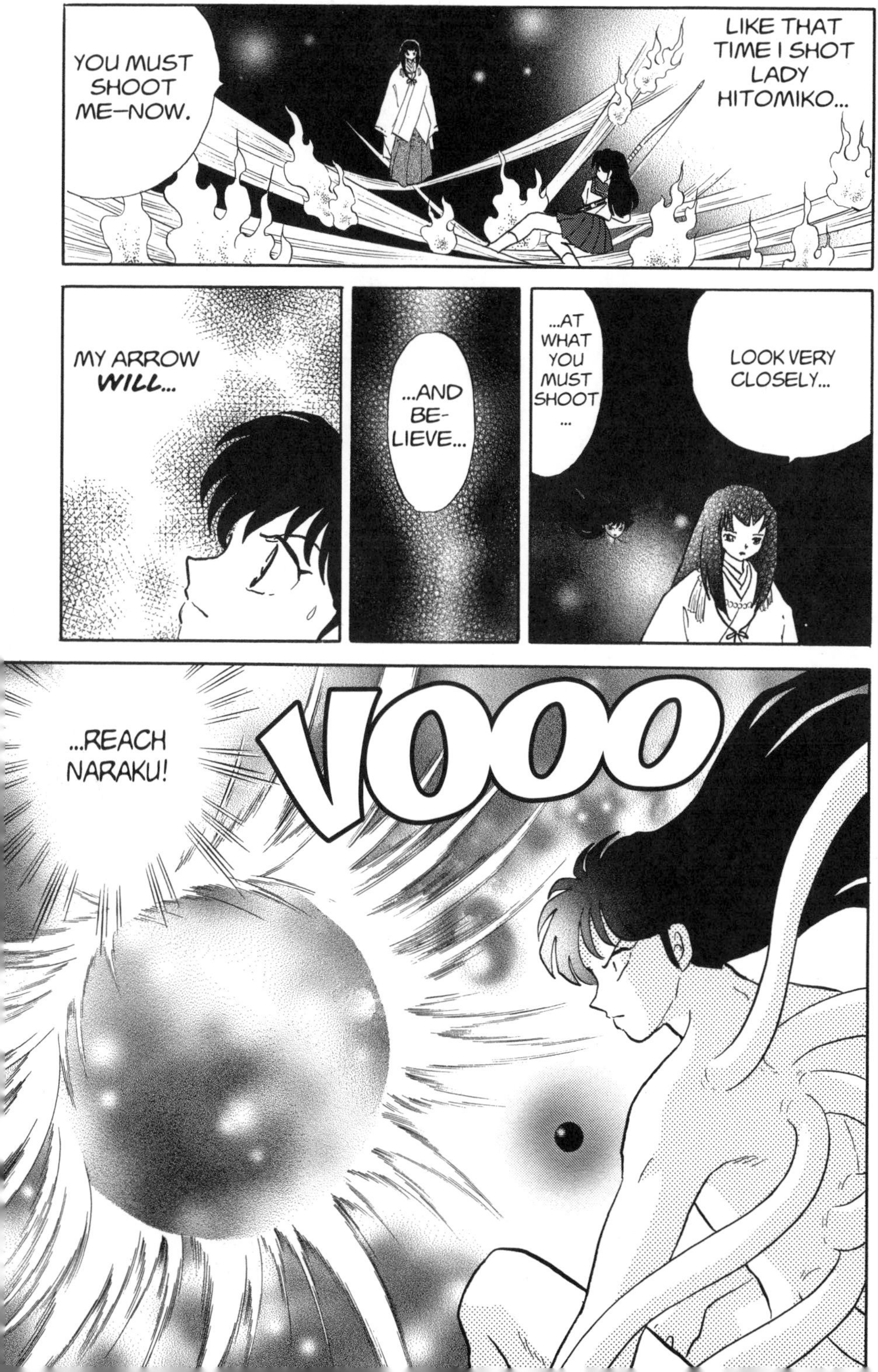
LIKE THAT TIME I SHOT LADY HITOMIKO...
YOU MUST SHOOT ME—NOW.
LOOK VERY CLOSELY...
...AT WHAT YOU MUST SHOOT ...
...AND BE-LIEVE...
MY ARROW **WILL**...
VOOO
...REACH NARAKU!

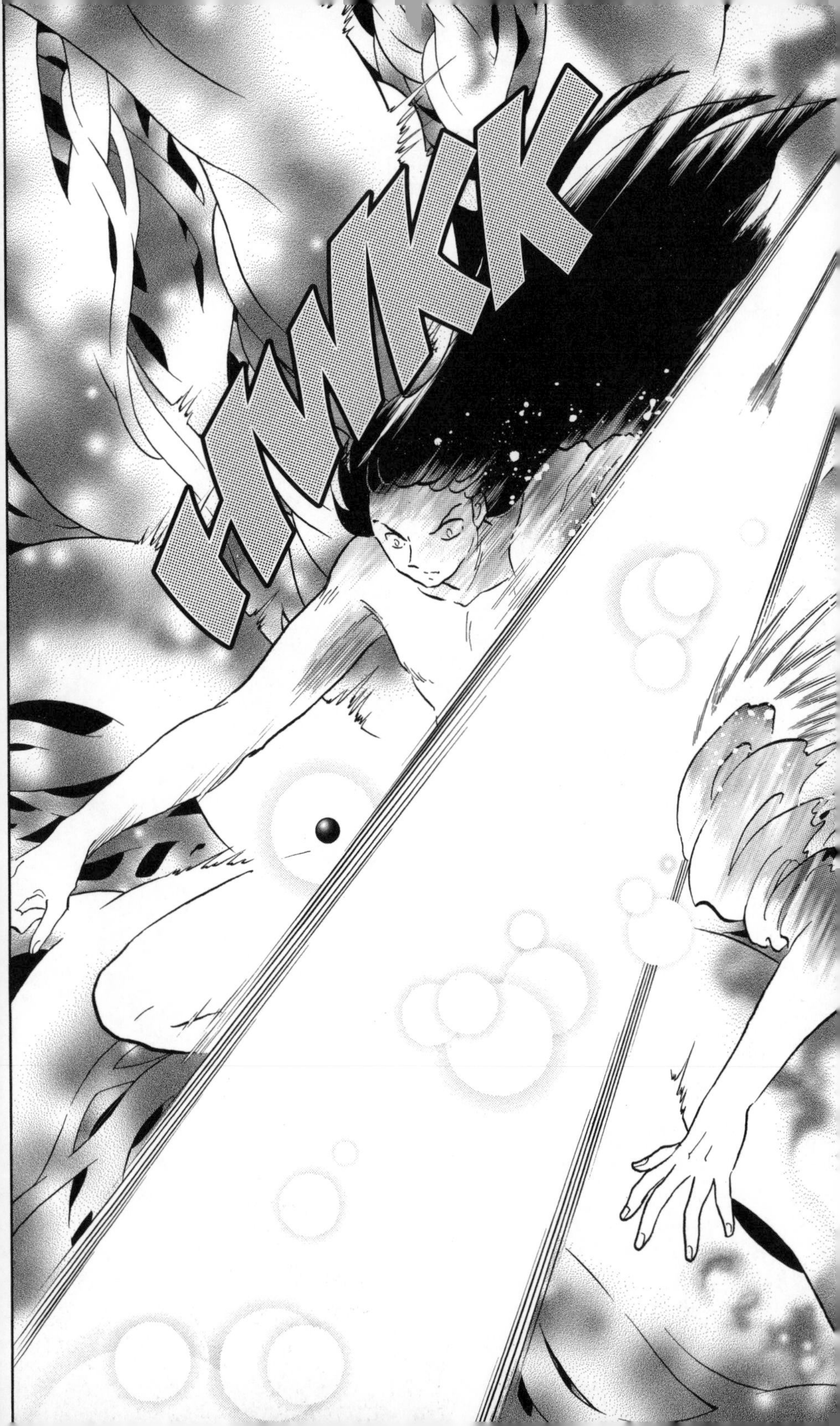

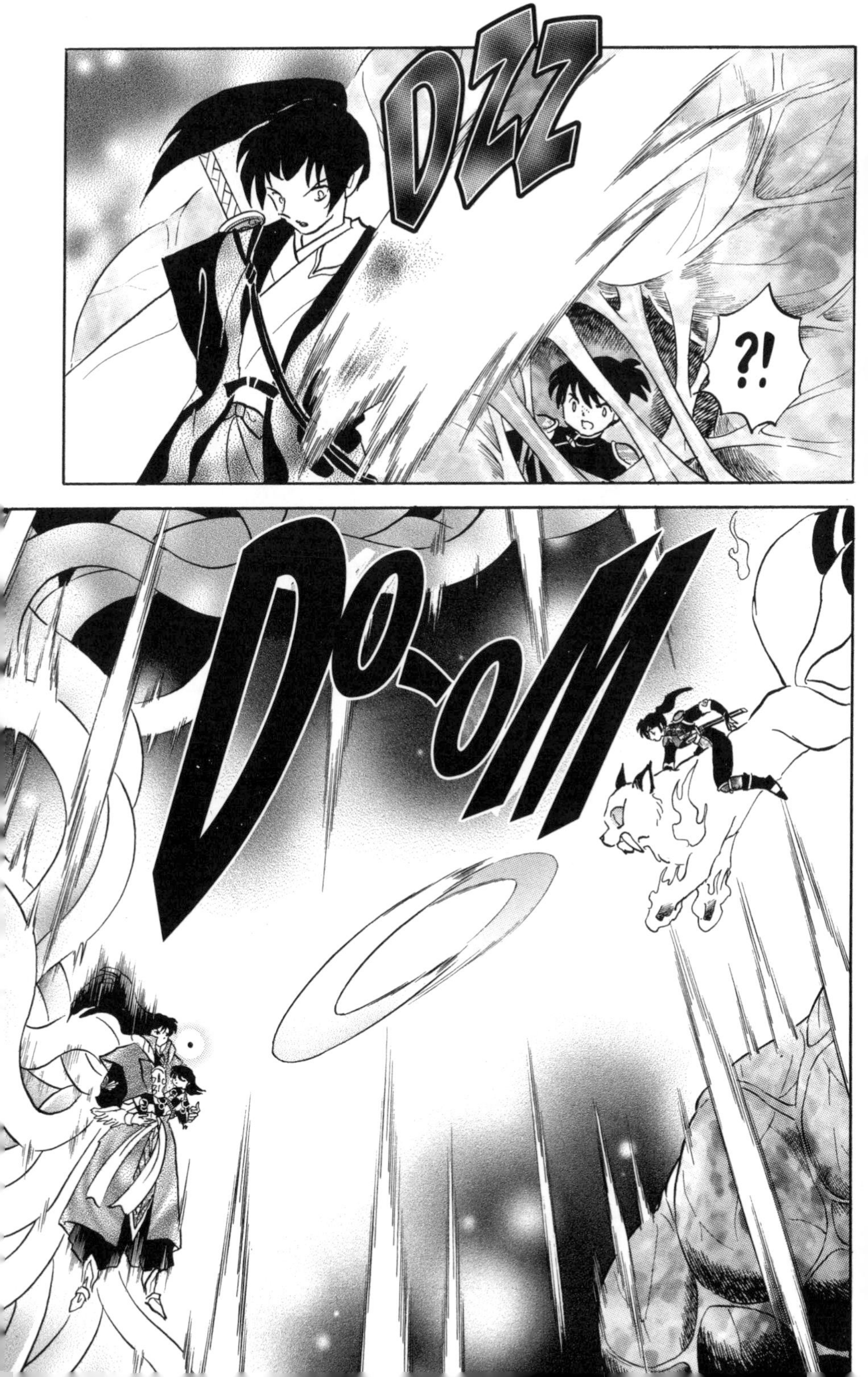
DZZ
?!
DO-OM

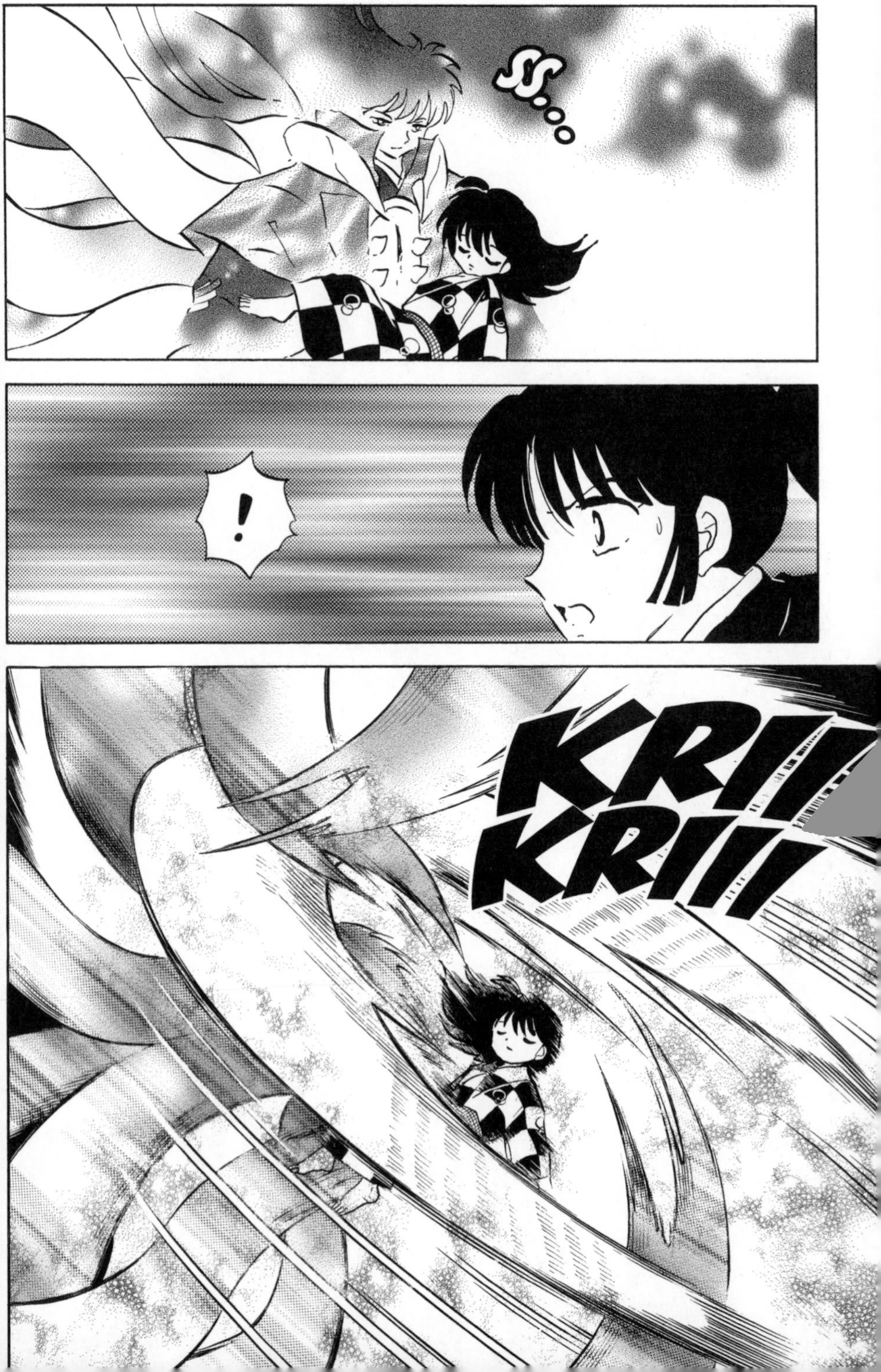
SS...
!
KRII
KRIII

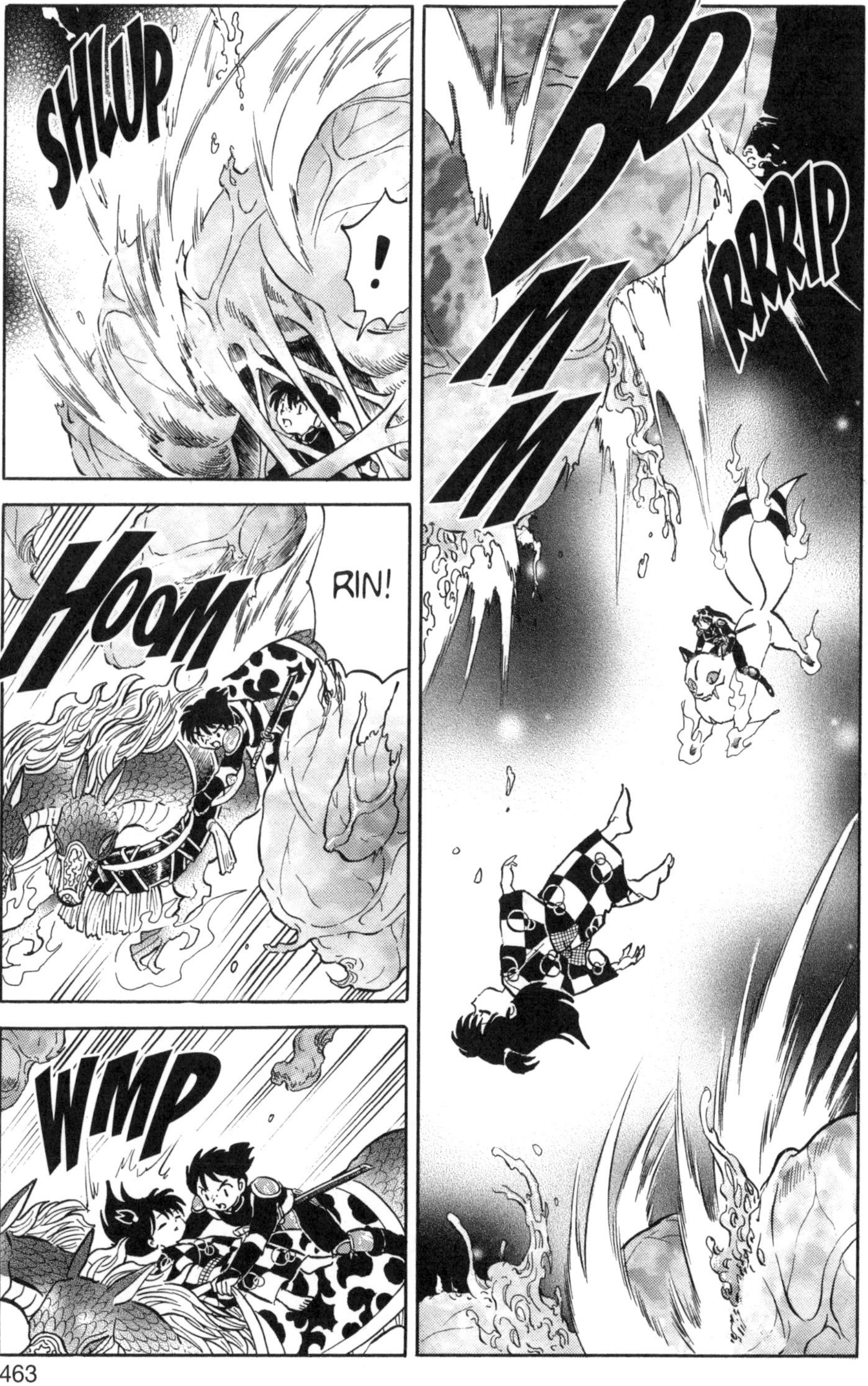
BDMMM
RRRIP
SHLUP
!
HOOM
RIN!
WMP

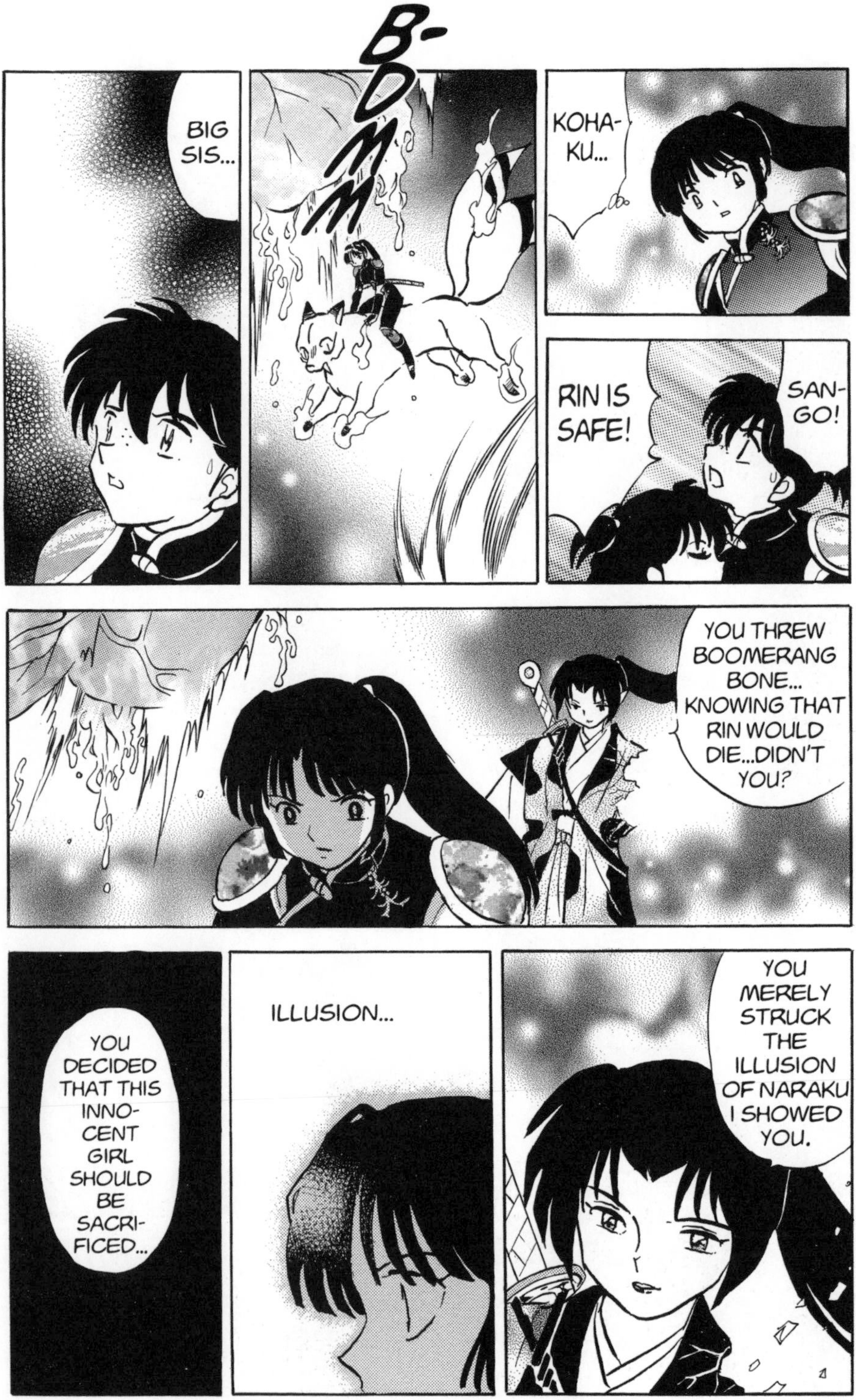
KOHA-KU...
SAN-GO!
RIN IS SAFE!
B-DOMM
BIG SIS...
YOU THREW BOOMERANG BONE... KNOWING THAT RIN WOULD DIE...DIDN'T YOU?
YOU MERELY STRUCK THE ILLUSION OF NARAKU I SHOWED YOU.
ILLUSION...
YOU DECIDED THAT THIS INNO-CENT GIRL SHOULD BE SACRI-FICED...

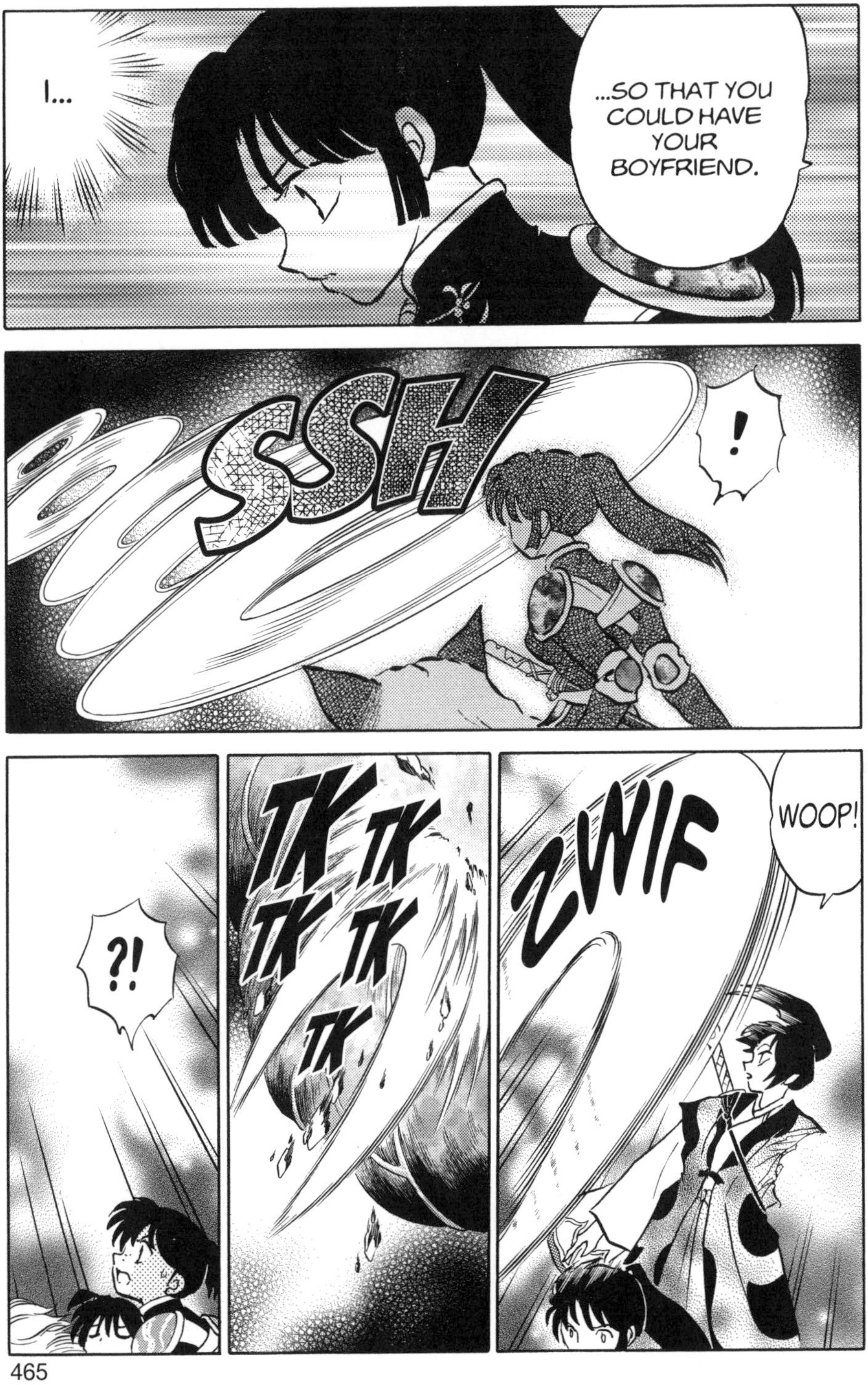

...SO THAT YOU COULD HAVE YOUR BOYFRIEND.
I...
!
SSH
WOOP!
ZWIF
TK TK TK TK TK TK
?!

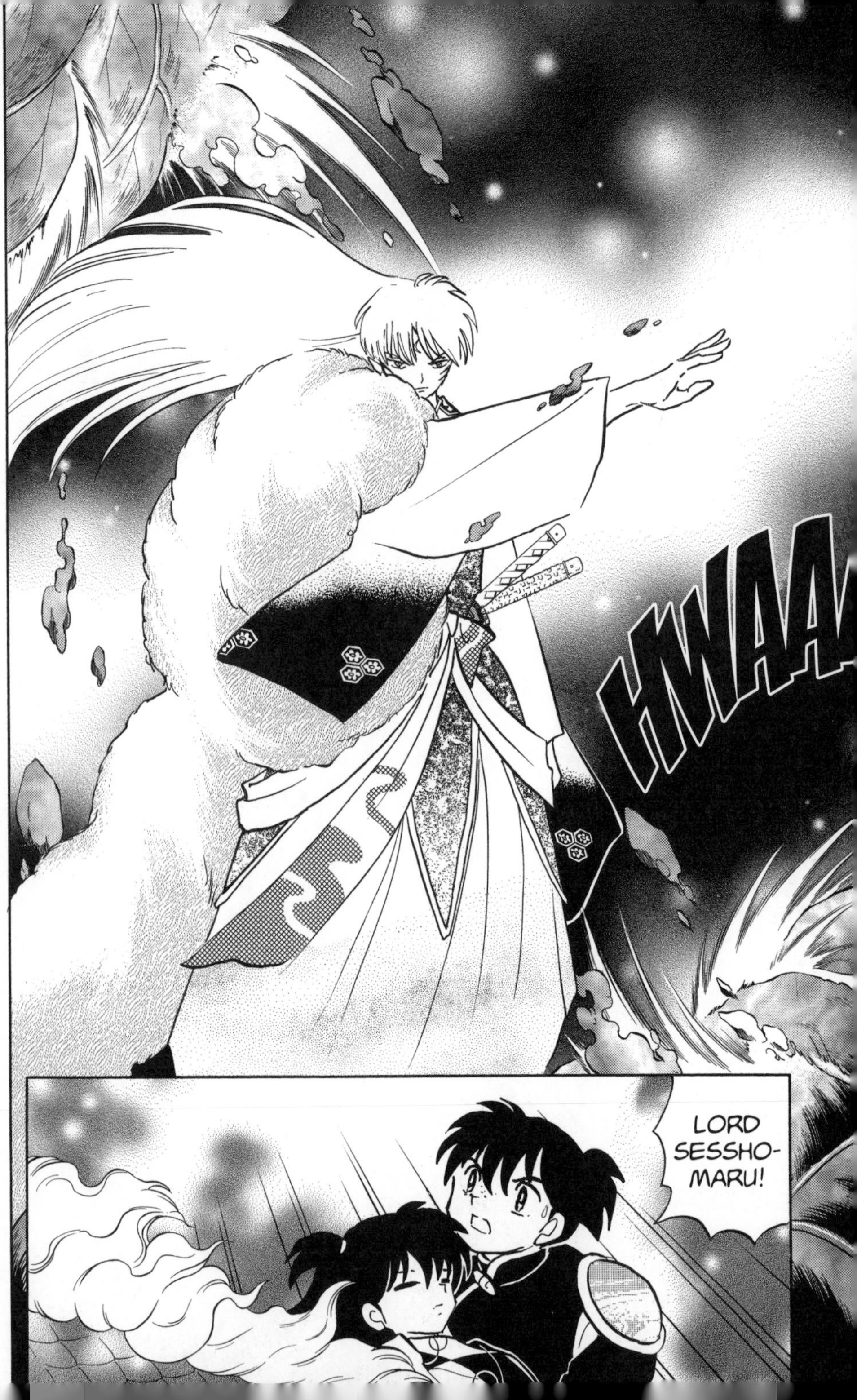
HWAA
LORD SESSHO-MARU!

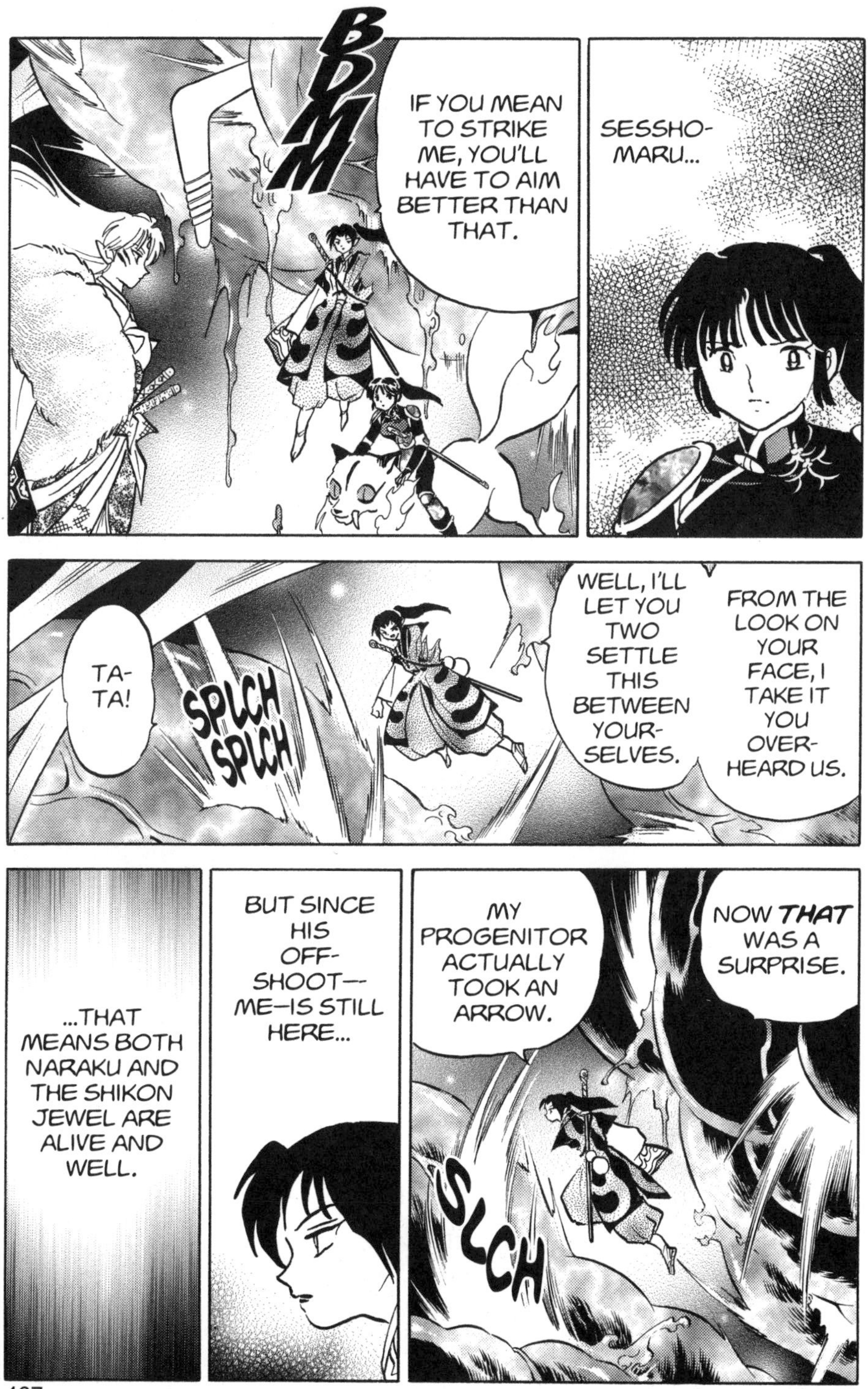
SESSHO-MARU...
IF YOU MEAN TO STRIKE ME, YOU'LL HAVE TO AIM BETTER THAN THAT.
BDM
FROM THE LOOK ON YOUR FACE, I TAKE IT YOU OVER-HEARD US.
WELL, I'LL LET YOU TWO SETTLE THIS BETWEEN YOUR-SELVES.
SPLCH SPLCH
TA-TA!
NOW *THAT* WAS A SURPRISE.
MY PROGENITOR ACTUALLY TOOK AN ARROW.
SLCH
BUT SINCE HIS OFF-SHOOT—ME—IS STILL HERE...
...THAT MEANS BOTH NARAKU AND THE SHIKON JEWEL ARE ALIVE AND WELL.

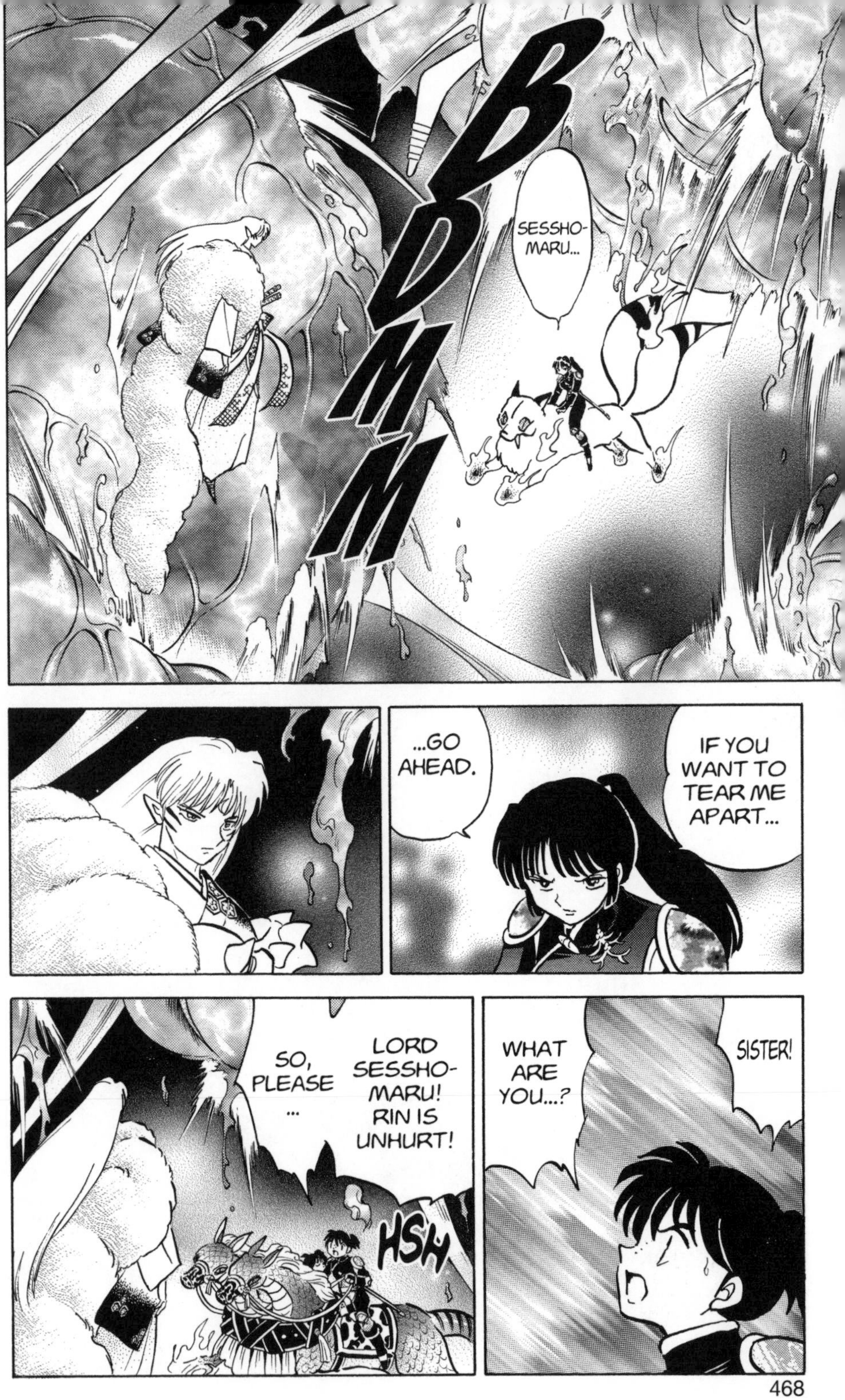
SESSHO-MARU...
BDMMM
IF YOU WANT TO TEAR ME APART...
...GO AHEAD.
SISTER!
WHAT ARE YOU...?
LORD SESSHO-MARU! RIN IS UNHURT!
SO, PLEASE ...
HSH

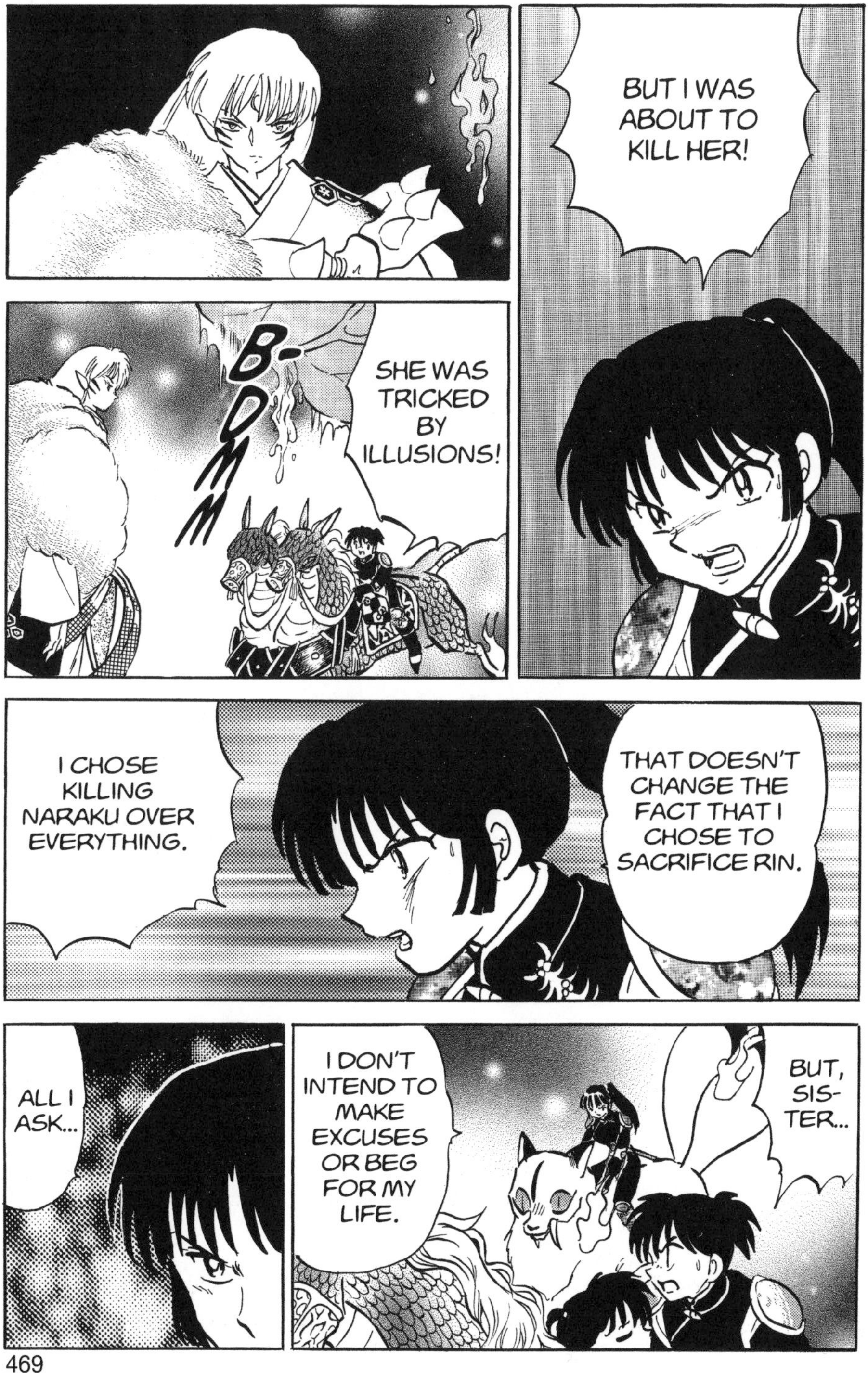
BUT I WAS ABOUT TO KILL HER!
SHE WAS TRICKED BY ILLUSIONS!
B-DOMM
THAT DOESN'T CHANGE THE FACT THAT I CHOSE TO SACRIFICE RIN.
I CHOSE KILLING NARAKU OVER EVERYTHING.
BUT, SIS-TER...
I DON'T INTEND TO MAKE EXCUSES OR BEG FOR MY LIFE.
ALL I ASK...

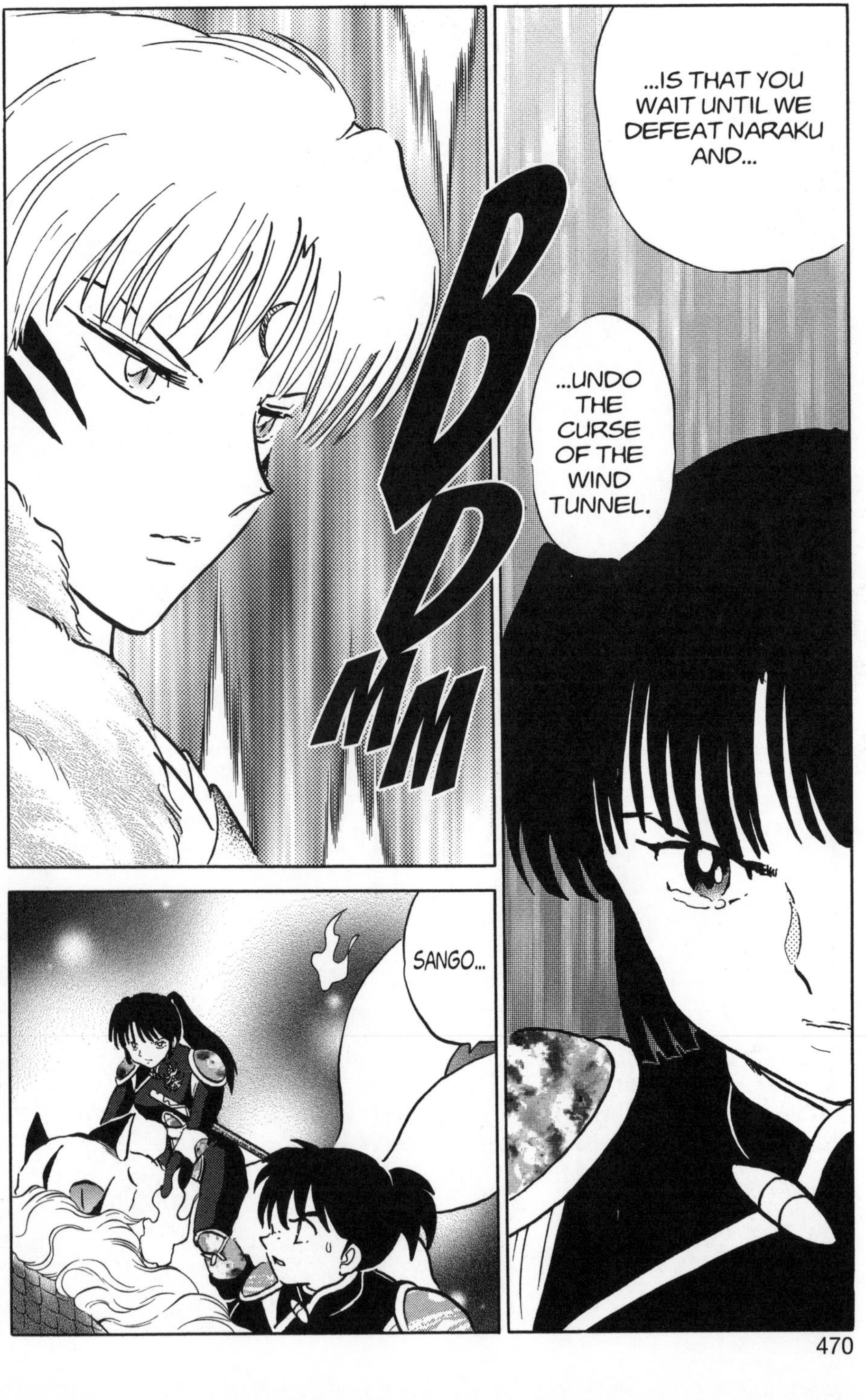
...IS THAT YOU WAIT UNTIL WE DEFEAT NARAKU AND...
...UNDO THE CURSE OF THE WIND TUNNEL.
BDMM
SANGO...

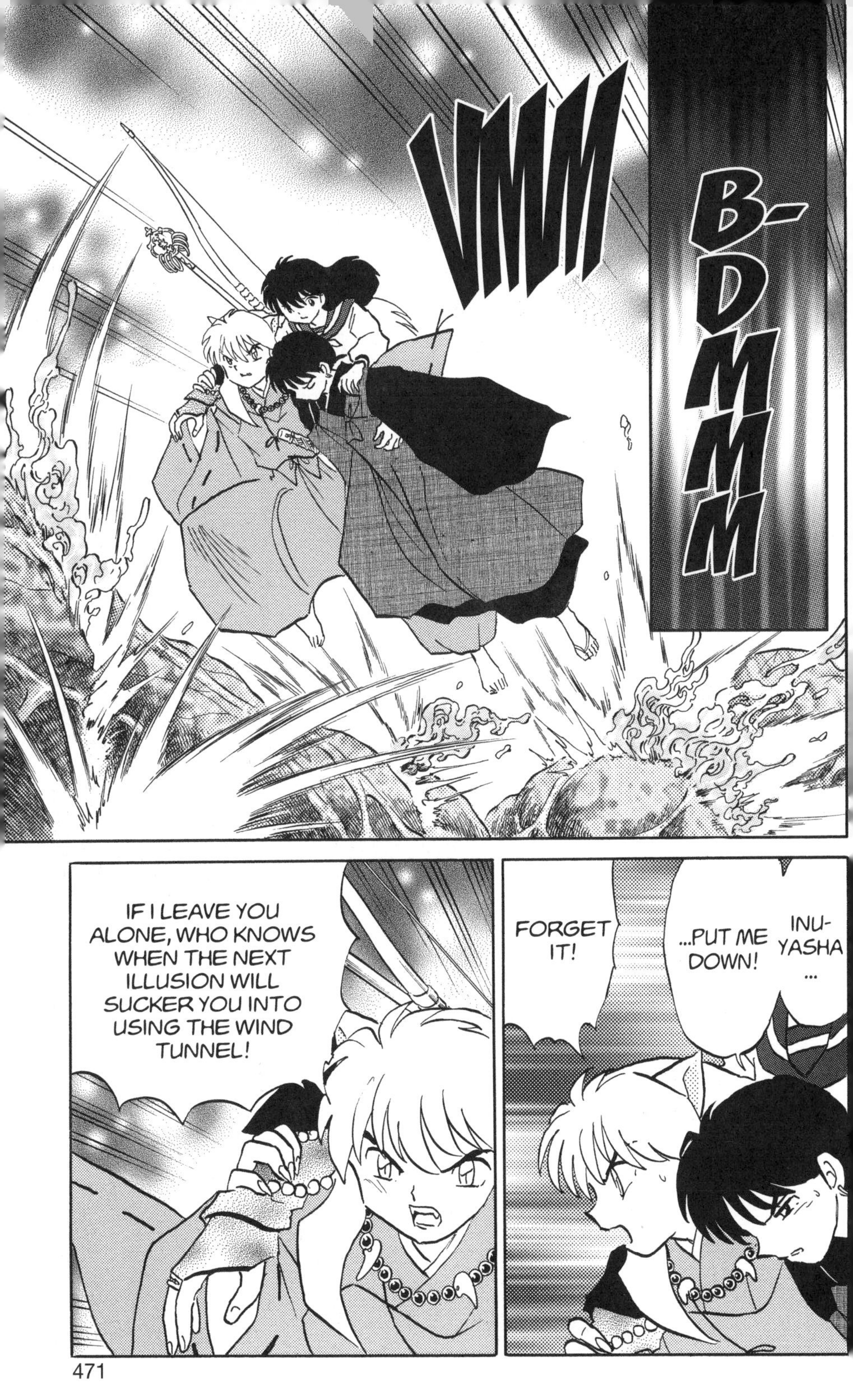
VMM
B-DMMM
INU-YASHA...
...PUT ME DOWN!
FORGET IT!
IF I LEAVE YOU ALONE, WHO KNOWS WHEN THE NEXT ILLUSION WILL SUCKER YOU INTO USING THE WIND TUNNEL!

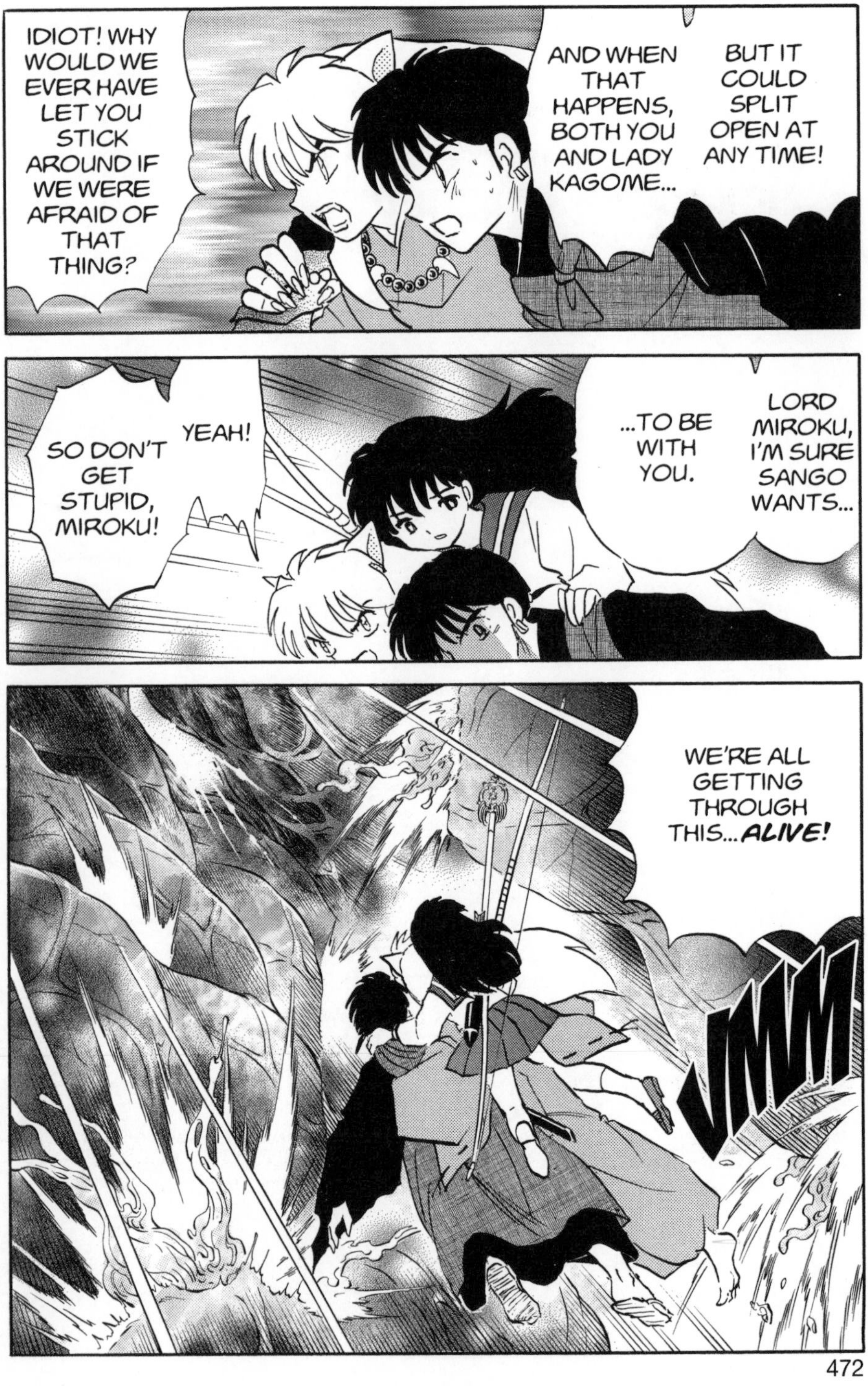
BUT IT COULD SPLIT OPEN AT ANY TIME!
AND WHEN THAT HAPPENS, BOTH YOU AND LADY KAGOME...
IDIOT! WHY WOULD WE EVER HAVE LET YOU STICK AROUND IF WE WERE AFRAID OF THAT THING?
LORD MIROKU, I'M SURE SANGO WANTS...
...TO BE WITH YOU.
YEAH!
SO DON'T GET STUPID, MIROKU!
WE'RE ALL GETTING THROUGH THIS...*ALIVE!*

SCROLL SIX
THE CENTER

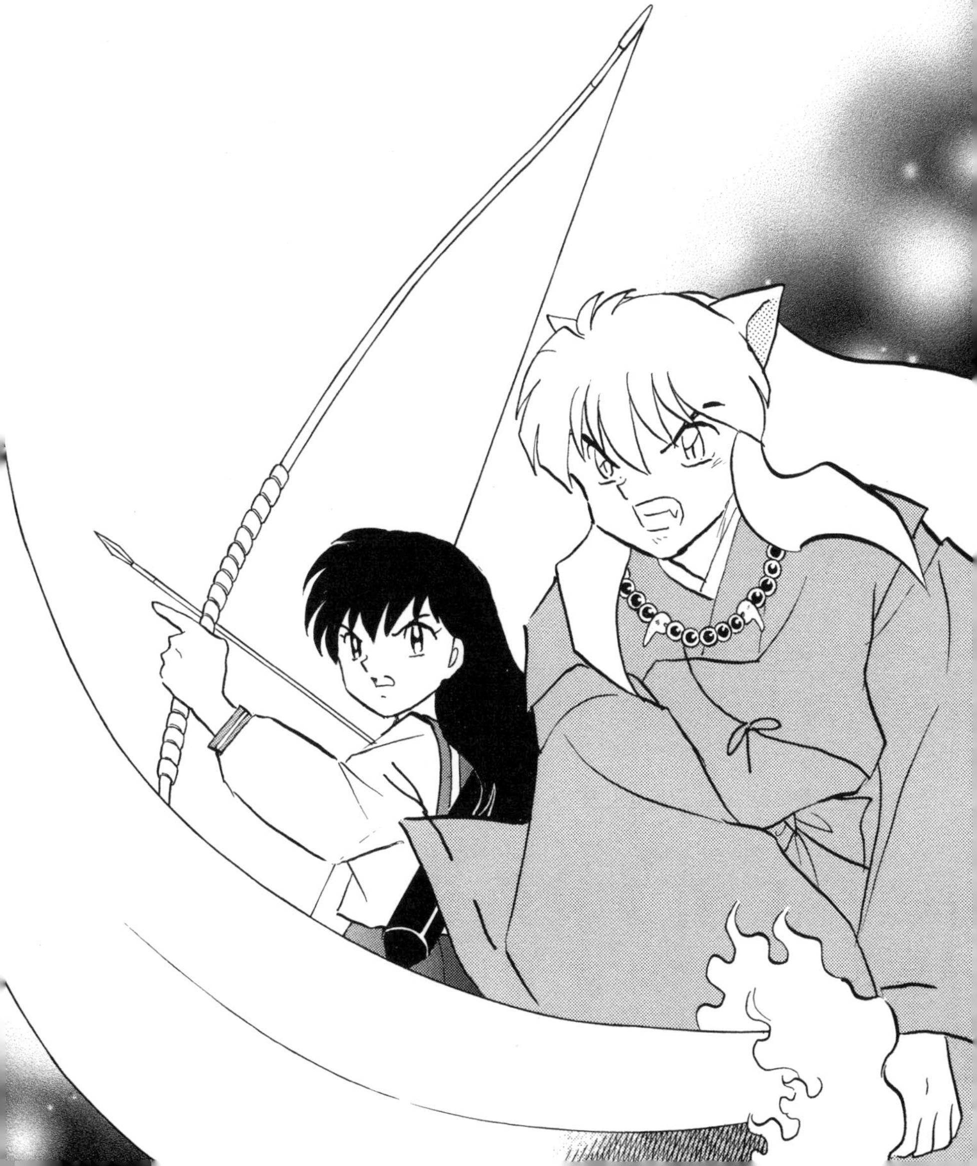

DOOM
PL-PLUP
PLUP
PLUP
PLUPP
PLUPP
SWOO

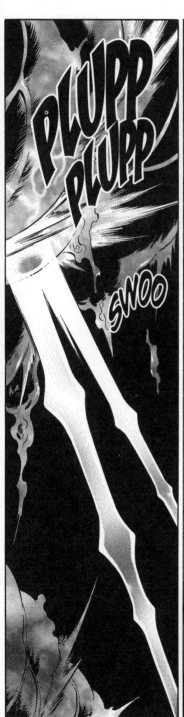

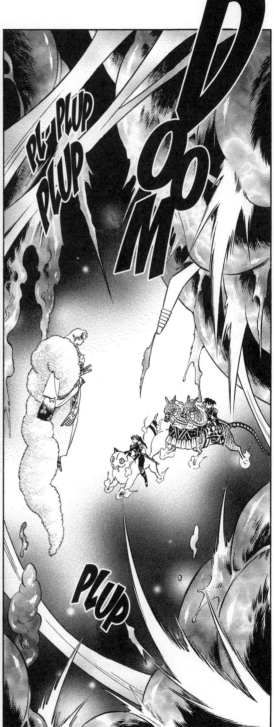

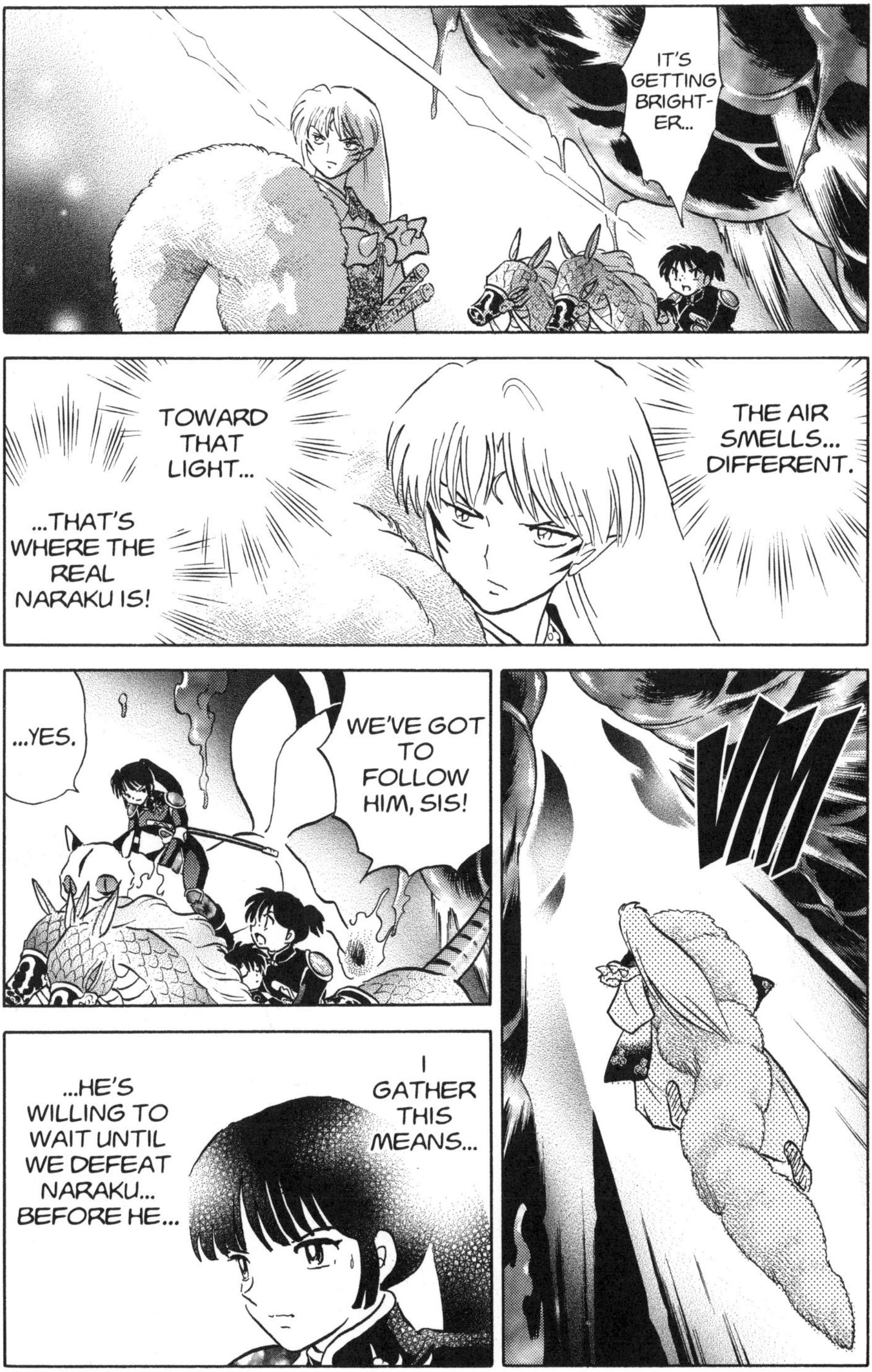
IT'S GETTING BRIGHT-ER...
THE AIR SMELLS... DIFFERENT.
TOWARD THAT LIGHT...
...THAT'S WHERE THE REAL NARAKU IS!
VM
WE'VE GOT TO FOLLOW HIM, SIS!
...YES.
I GATHER THIS MEANS...
...HE'S WILLING TO WAIT UNTIL WE DEFEAT NARAKU... BEFORE HE...

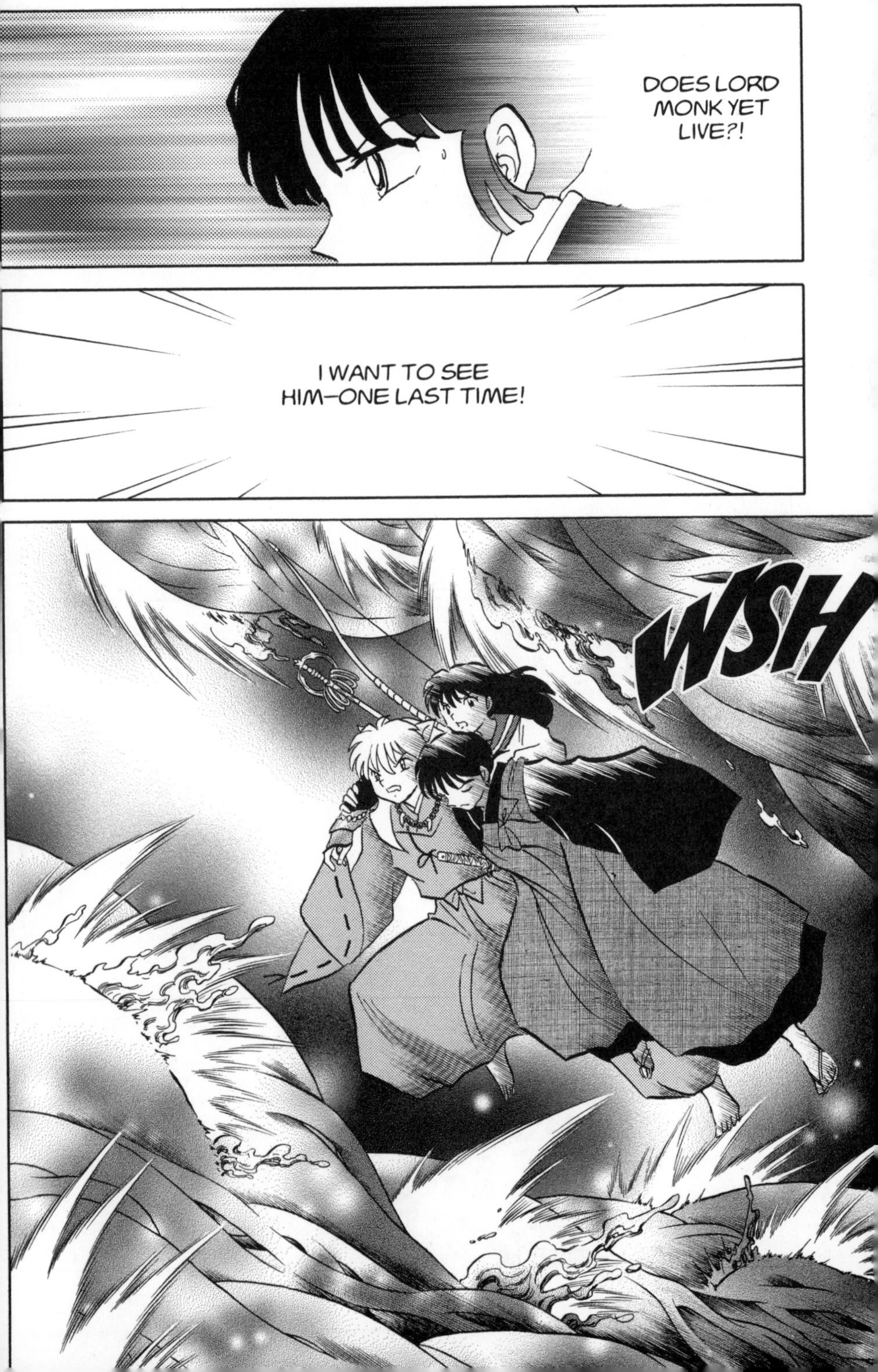
DOES LORD MONK YET LIVE?!
I WANT TO SEE HIM—ONE LAST TIME!
WSH

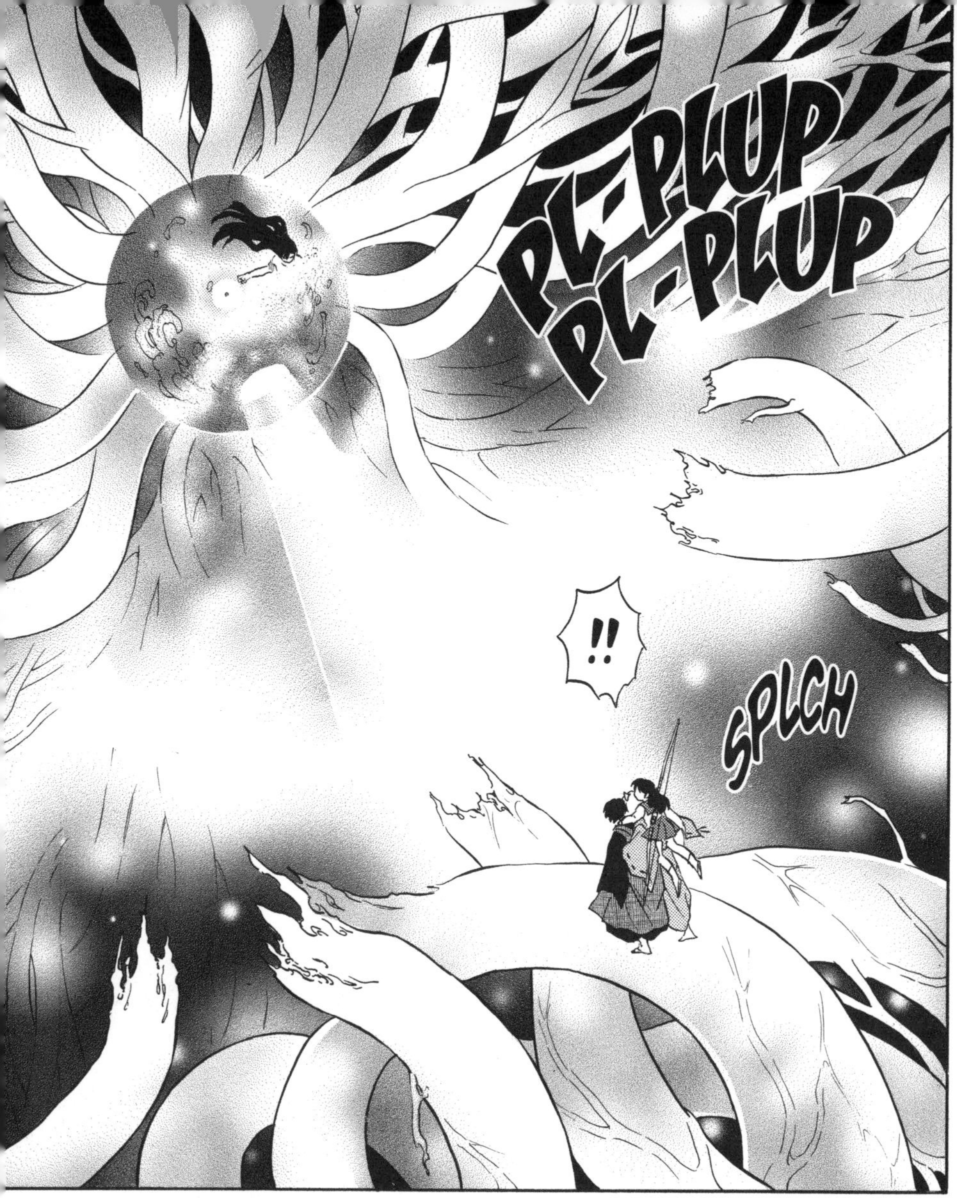
PL-PLUP PL-PLUP
!!
SPLCH
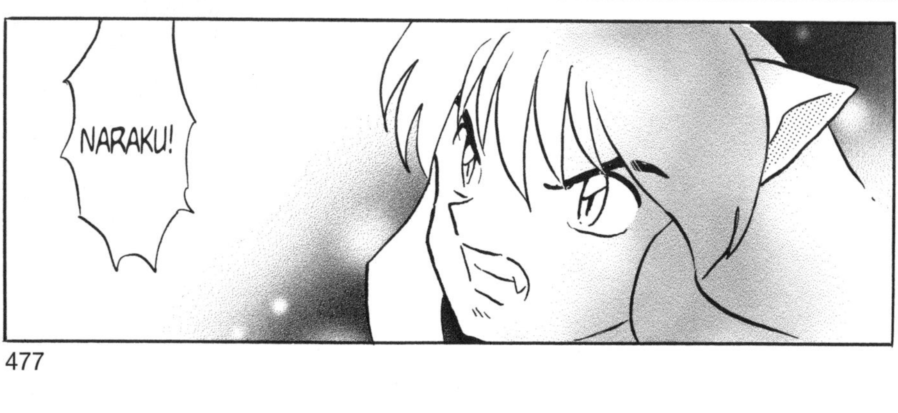
NARAKU!

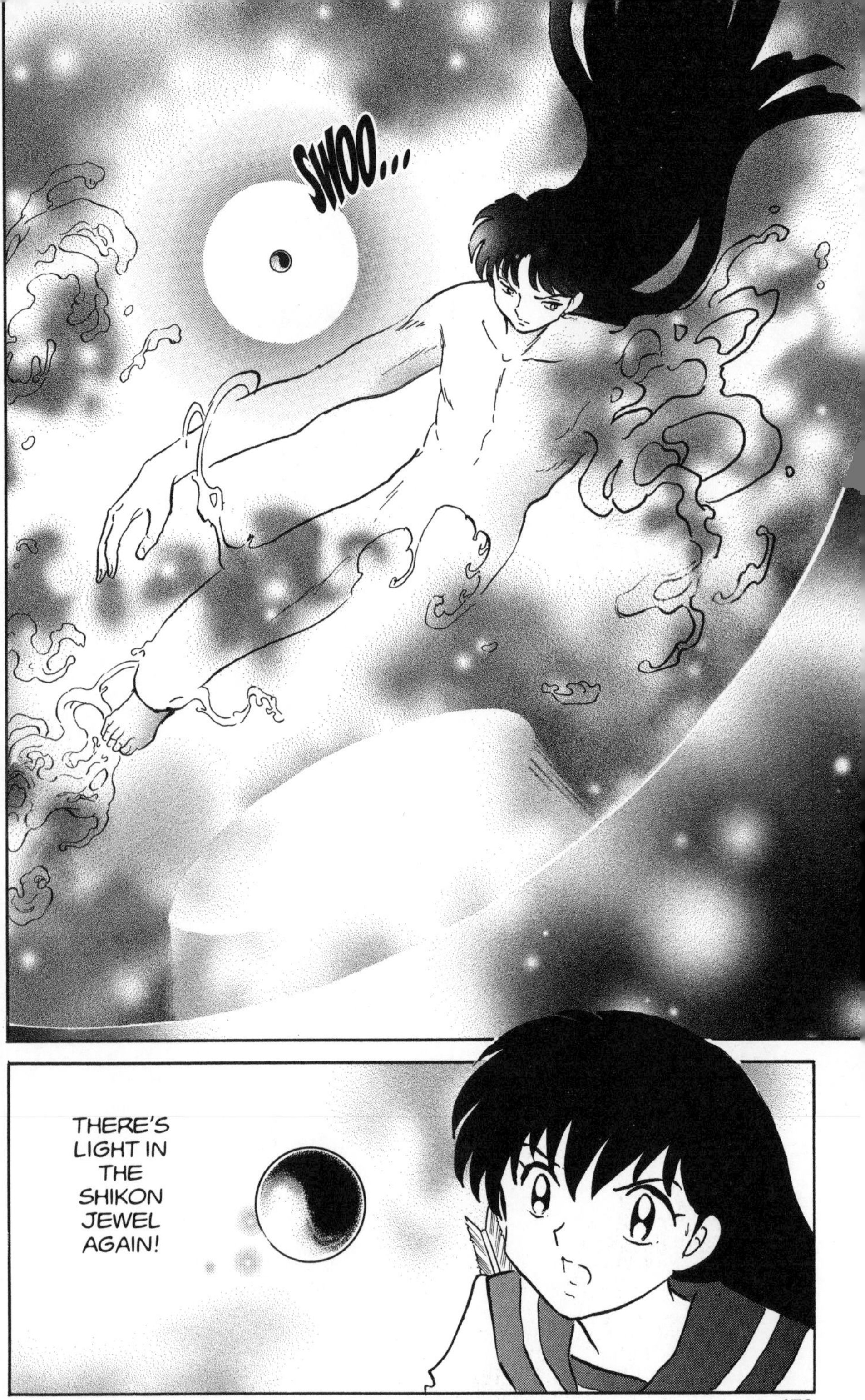
SWOO...
THERE'S LIGHT IN THE SHIKON JEWEL AGAIN!

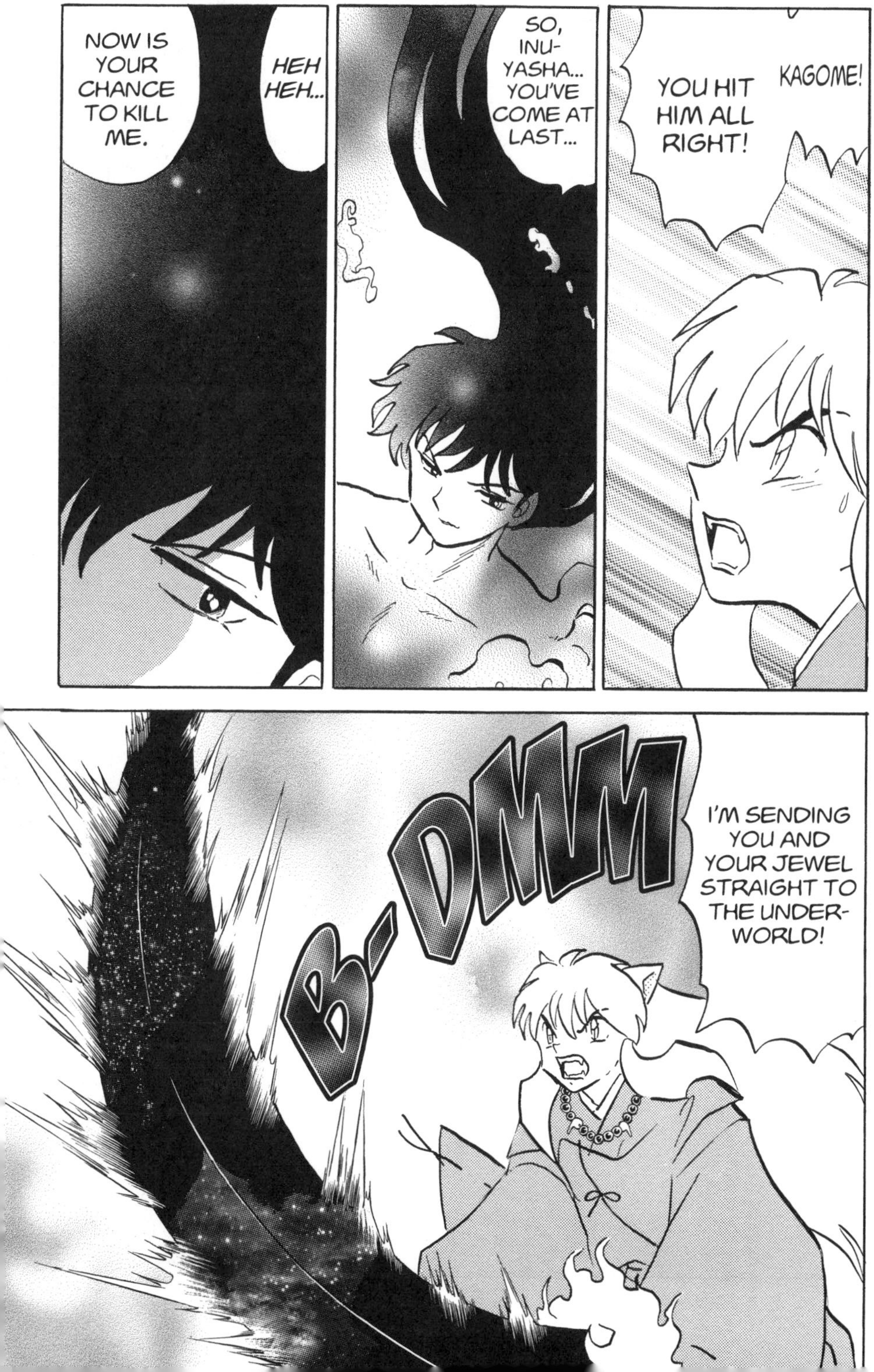
KAGOME!
YOU HIT HIM ALL RIGHT!
SO, INU-YASHA... YOU'VE COME AT LAST...
HEH HEH...
NOW IS YOUR CHANCE TO KILL ME.
I'M SENDING YOU AND YOUR JEWEL STRAIGHT TO THE UNDER-WORLD!
B-DMMM

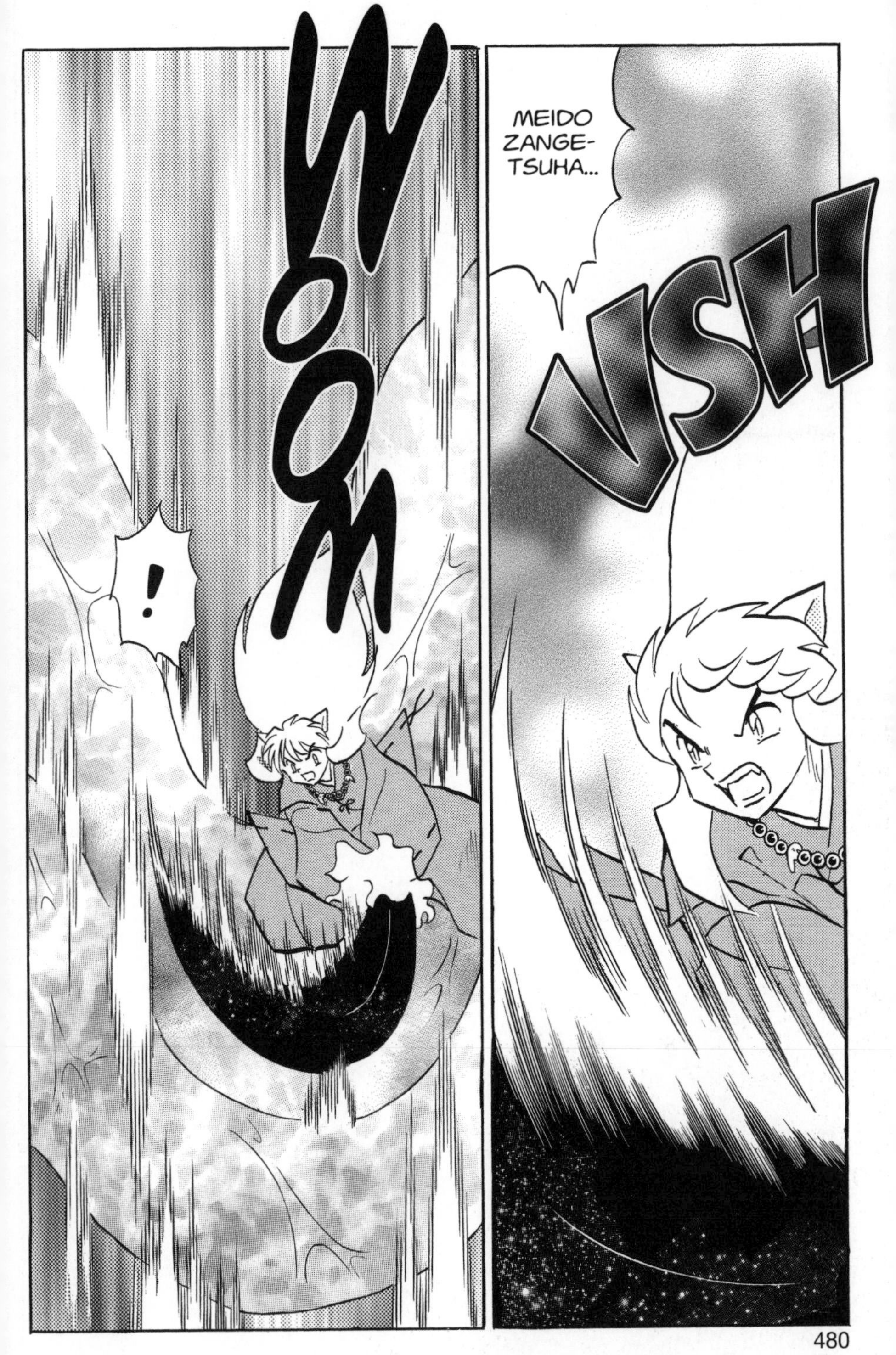
MEIDO ZANGE-TSUHA...
VSH
WOOM
!

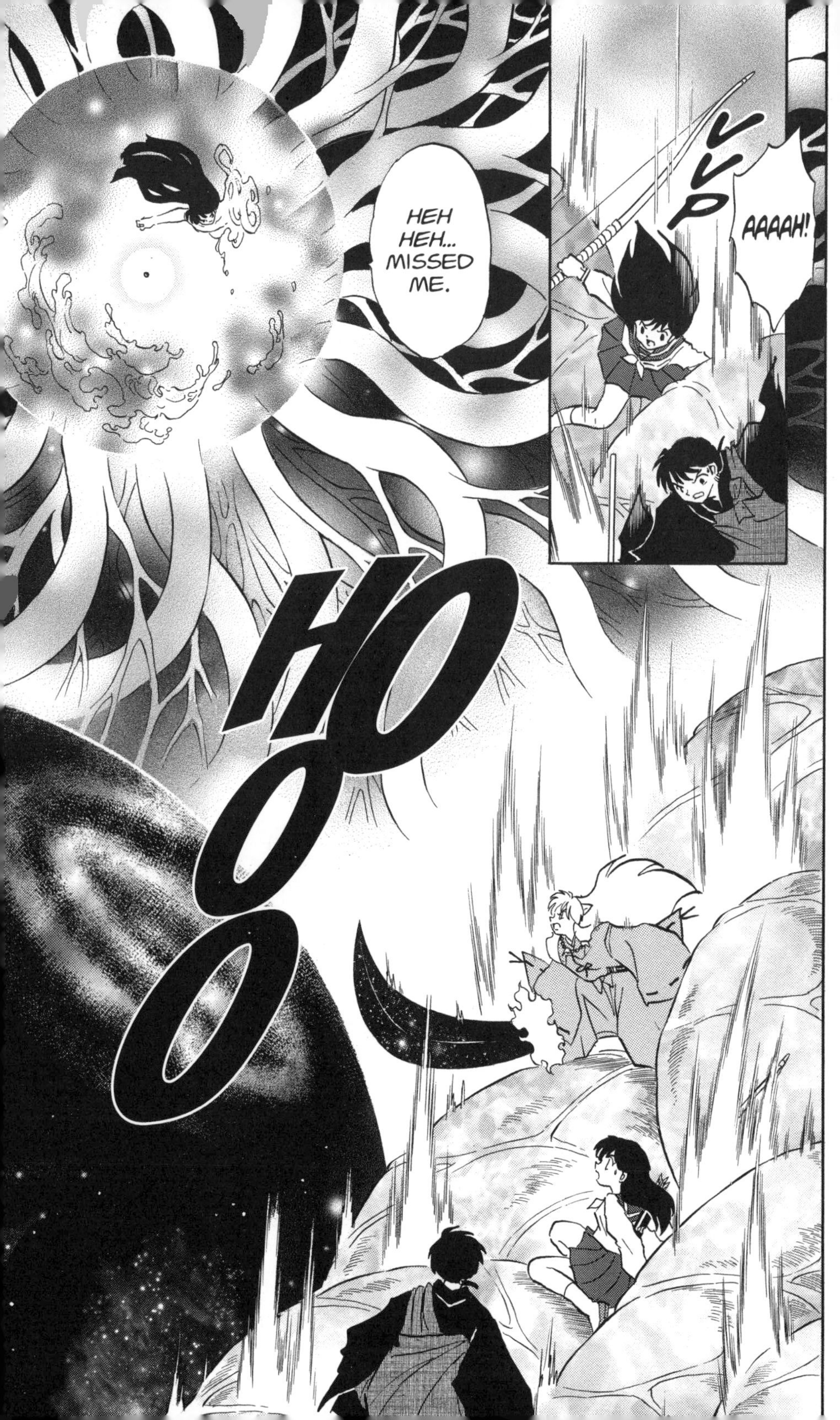
VVVP
AAAAH!
HEH HEH... MISSED ME.
HOOO

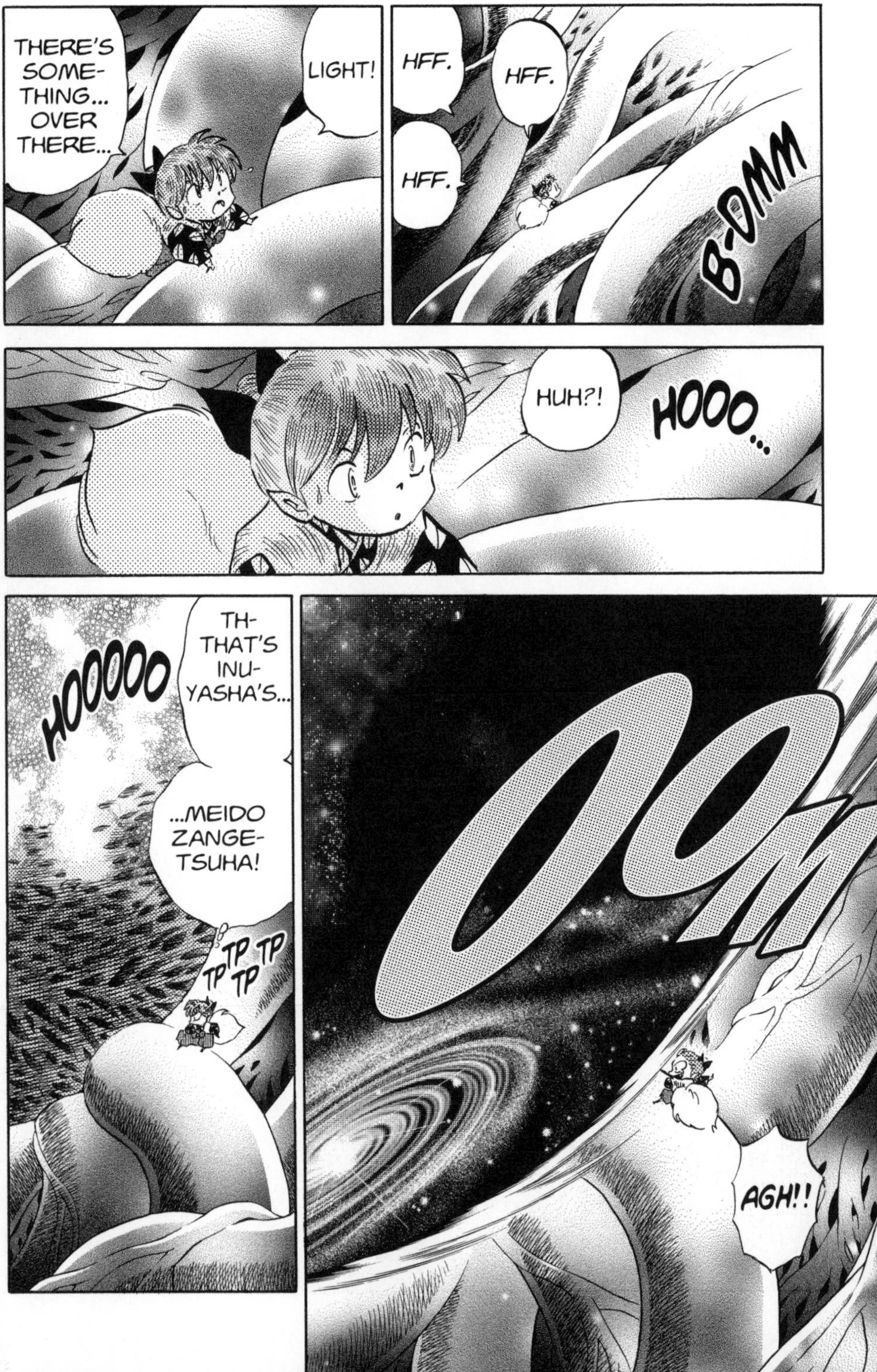
HFF.
HFF.
HFF.
B-DMM
LIGHT!
THERE'S SOME-THING... OVER THERE...
HOOO...
HUH?!
OOM
AGH!!
TH-THAT'S INU-YASHA'S...
...MEIDO ZANGE-TSUHA!
HOOOOO
TP TP TP TP

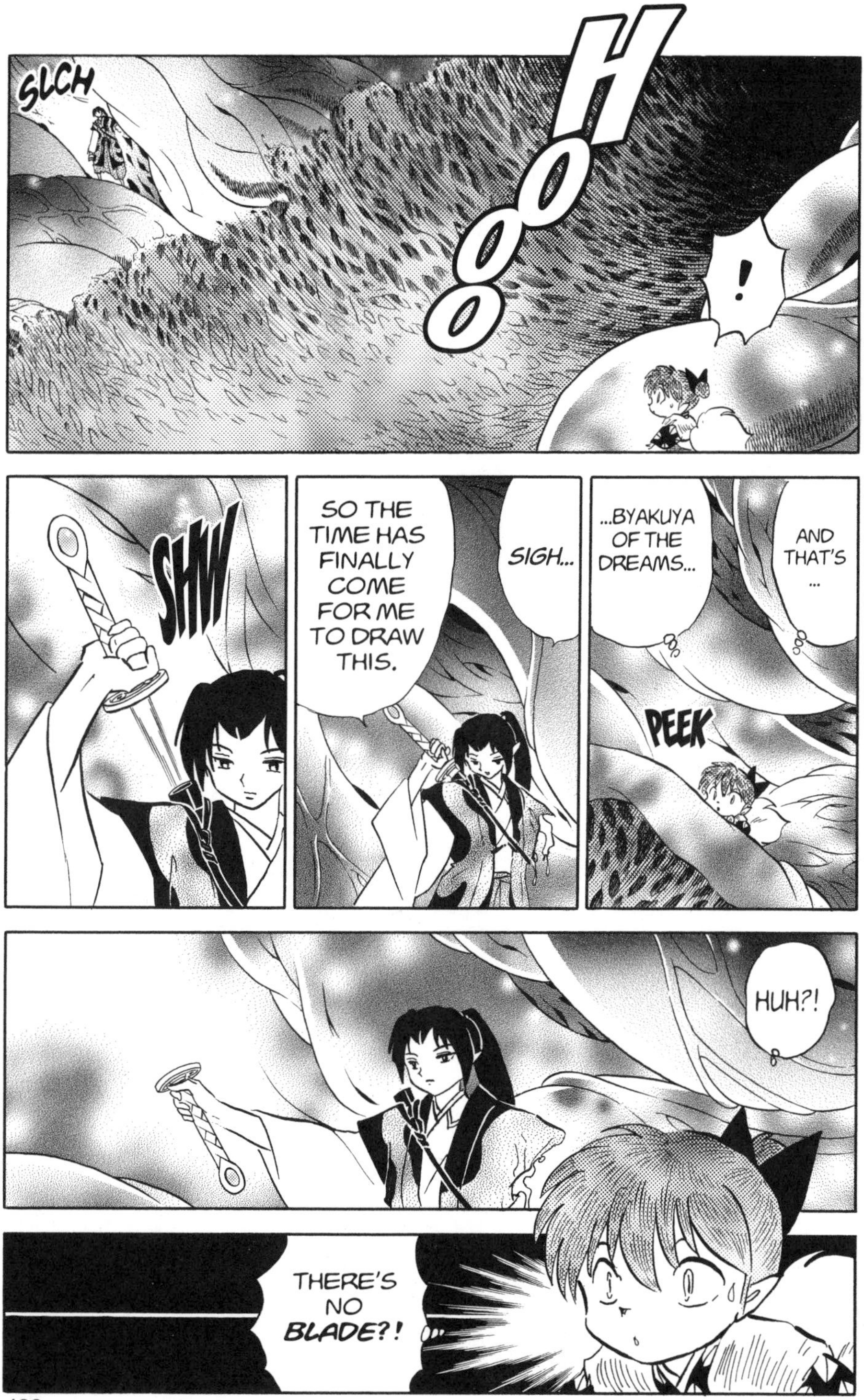
HOOOOO
!
SLCH
AND THAT'S ...
...BYAKUYA OF THE DREAMS...
PEEK
SIGH...
SO THE TIME HAS FINALLY COME FOR ME TO DRAW THIS.
SHW
HUH?!
THERE'S NO *BLADE?!*

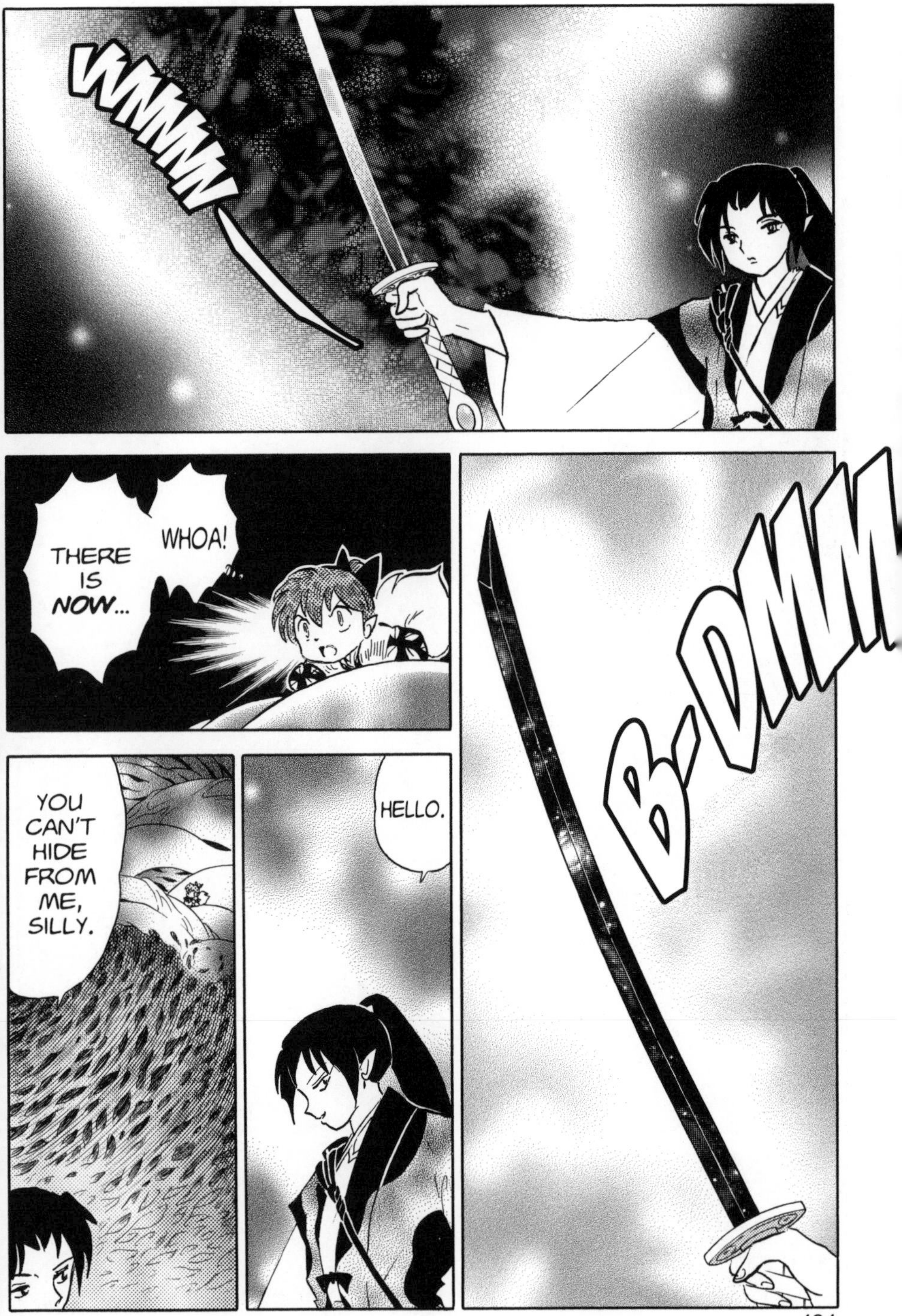
VWMMMM
B-DMM
WHOA!
THERE IS NOW...
HELLO.
YOU CAN'T HIDE FROM ME, SILLY.

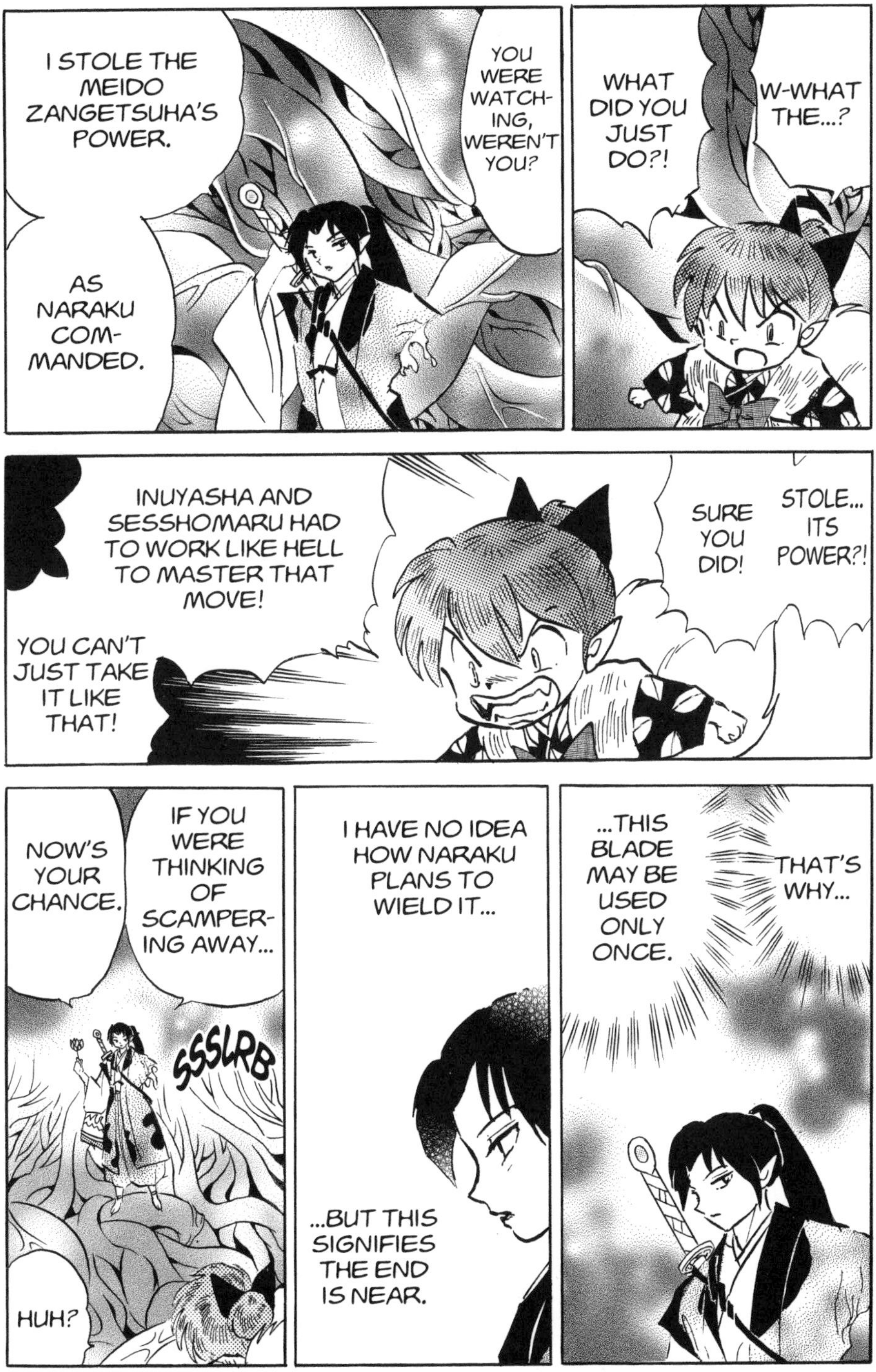
W-WHAT THE...?
WHAT DID YOU JUST DO?!
YOU WERE WATCHING, WEREN'T YOU?
I STOLE THE MEIDO ZANGETSUHA'S POWER.
AS NARAKU COMMANDED.
STOLE... ITS POWER?!
SURE YOU DID!
INUYASHA AND SESSHOMARU HAD TO WORK LIKE HELL TO MASTER THAT MOVE!
YOU CAN'T JUST TAKE IT LIKE THAT!
THAT'S WHY...
...THIS BLADE MAY BE USED ONLY ONCE.
I HAVE NO IDEA HOW NARAKU PLANS TO WIELD IT...
...BUT THIS SIGNIFIES THE END IS NEAR.
IF YOU WERE THINKING OF SCAMPERING AWAY...
NOW'S YOUR CHANCE.
SSSLRB
HUH?

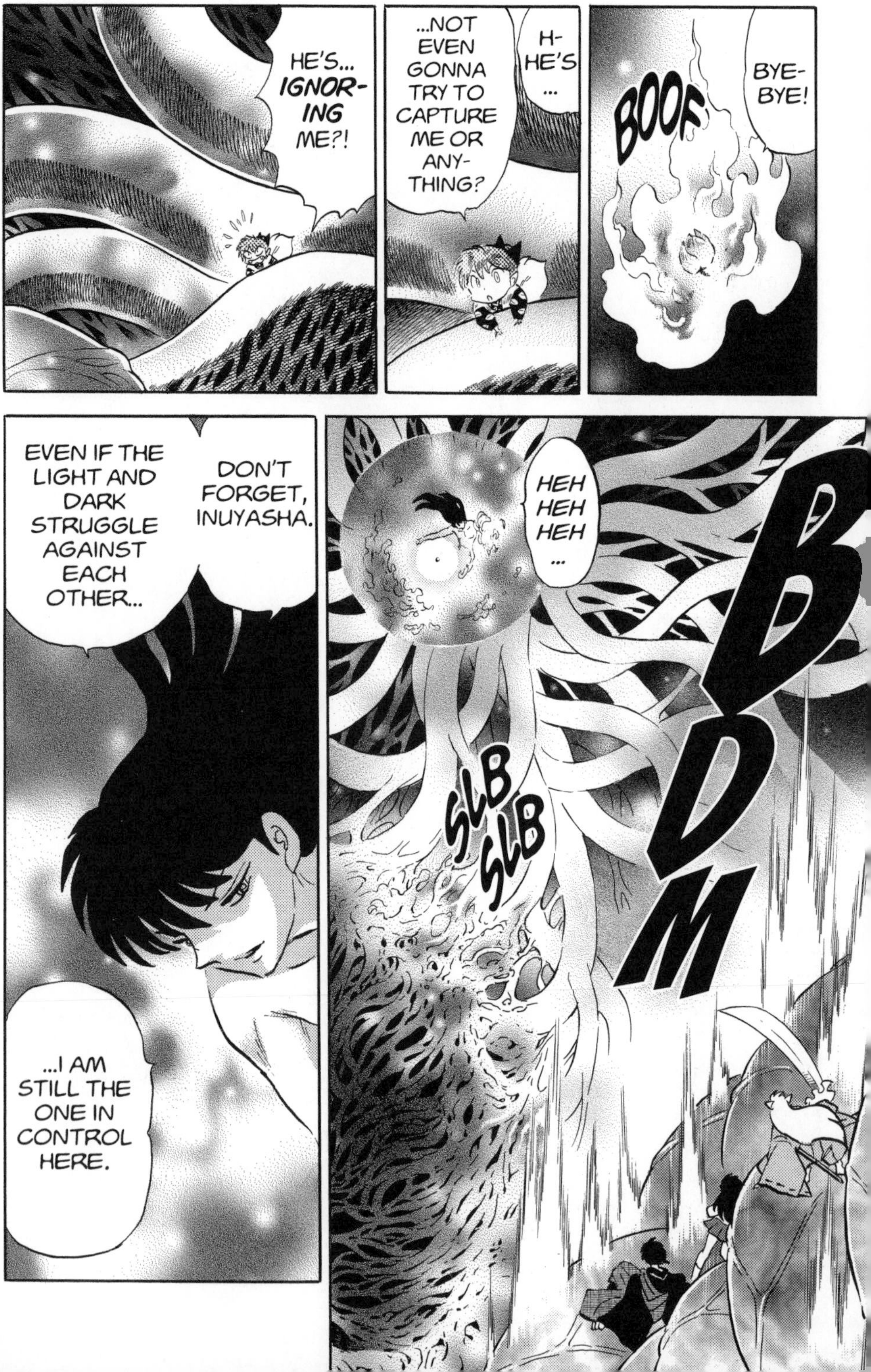
BYE-BYE!
BOOF
H-HE'S...
...NOT EVEN GONNA TRY TO CAPTURE ME OR ANYTHING?
HE'S... IGNORING ME?!
HEH HEH HEH...
BDM
SLB SLB
DON'T FORGET, INUYASHA.
EVEN IF THE LIGHT AND DARK STRUGGLE AGAINST EACH OTHER...
...I AM STILL THE ONE IN CONTROL HERE.

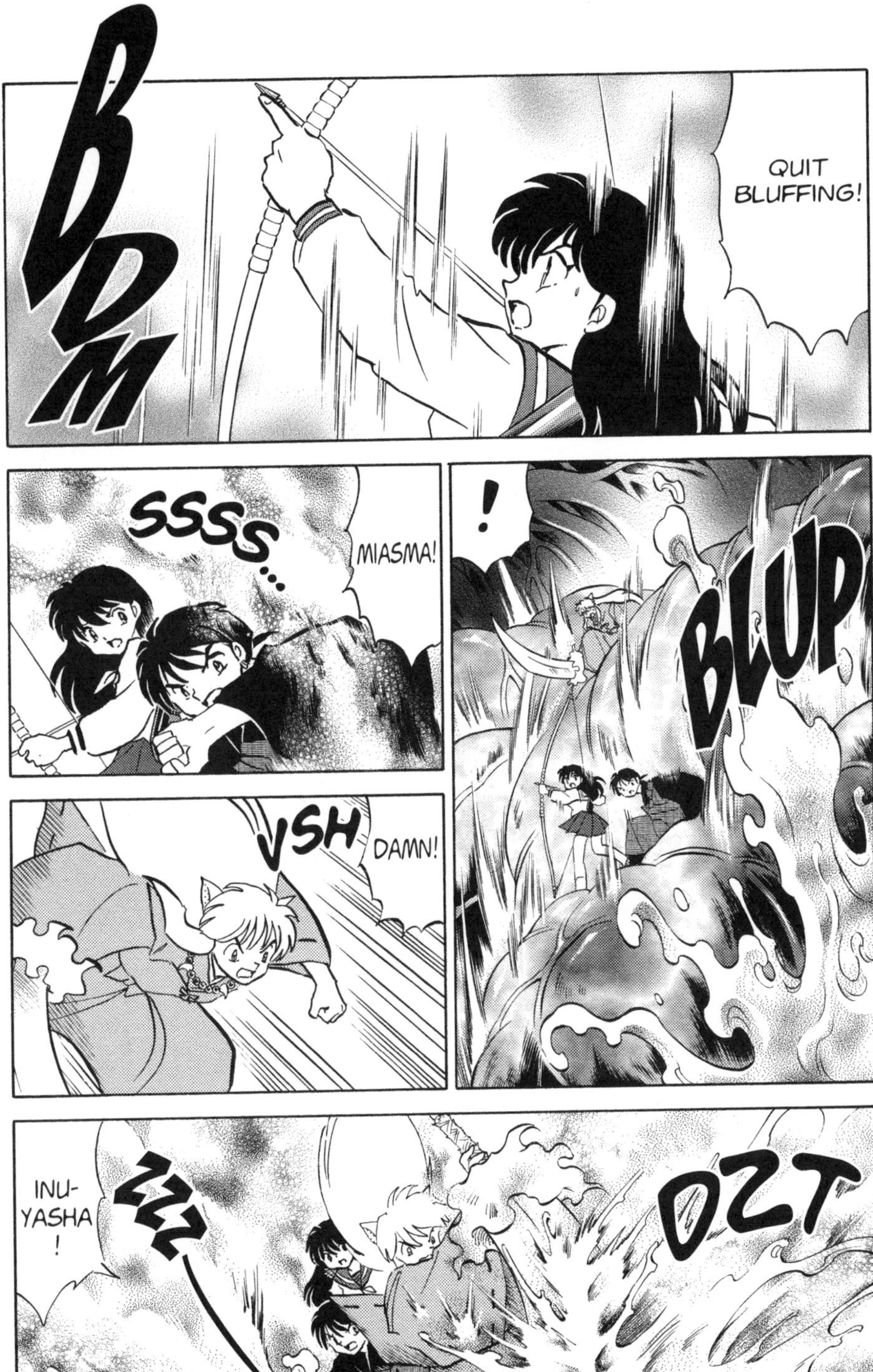
QUIT BLUFFING!
BDM
!
BLUP
MIASMA!
SSSS...
DAMN!
VSH
DZT
ZZZ
INU-YASHA!

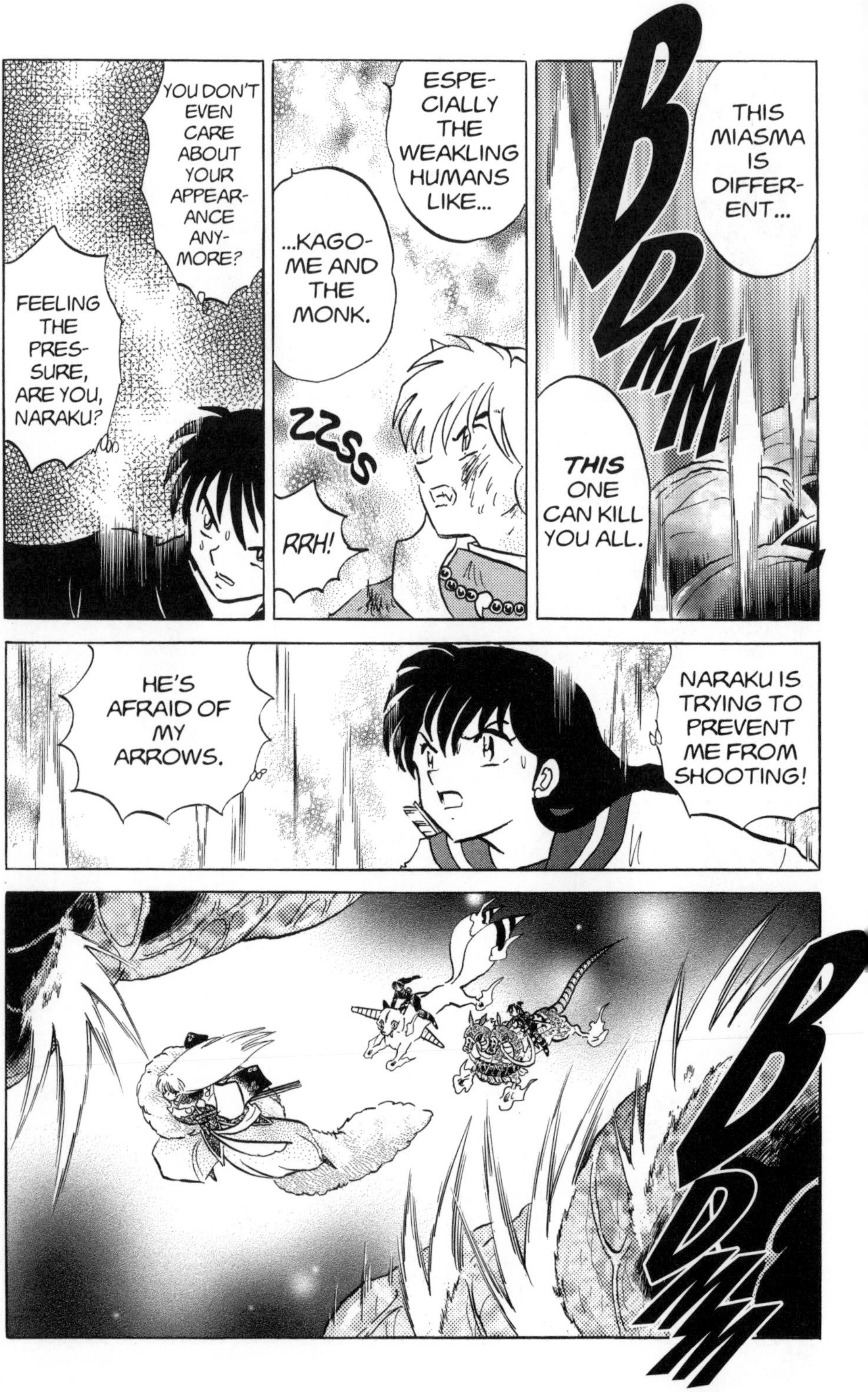
BDMM
THIS MIASMA IS DIFFERENT...
THIS ONE CAN KILL YOU ALL.
ESPECIALLY THE WEAKLING HUMANS LIKE...
...KAGOME AND THE MONK.
ZZSS
RRH!
YOU DON'T EVEN CARE ABOUT YOUR APPEARANCE ANYMORE?
FEELING THE PRESSURE, ARE YOU, NARAKU?
NARAKU IS TRYING TO PREVENT ME FROM SHOOTING!
HE'S AFRAID OF MY ARROWS.
BDMM

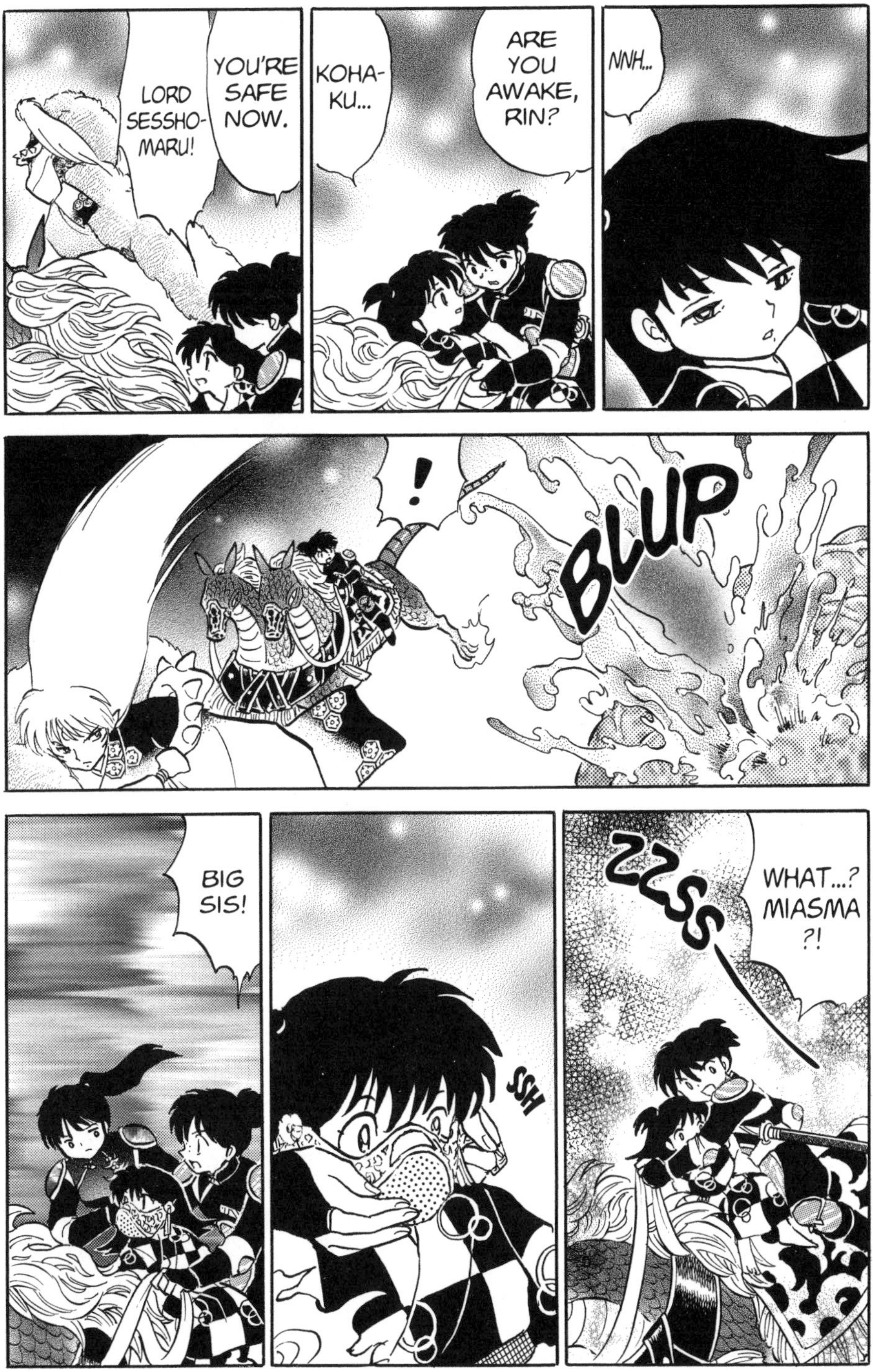
NNH...
ARE YOU AWAKE, RIN?
KOHA-KU...
YOU'RE SAFE NOW.
LORD SESSHO-MARU!
!
BLUP
WHAT...? MIASMA ?!
ZZSS
SSH
BIG SIS!

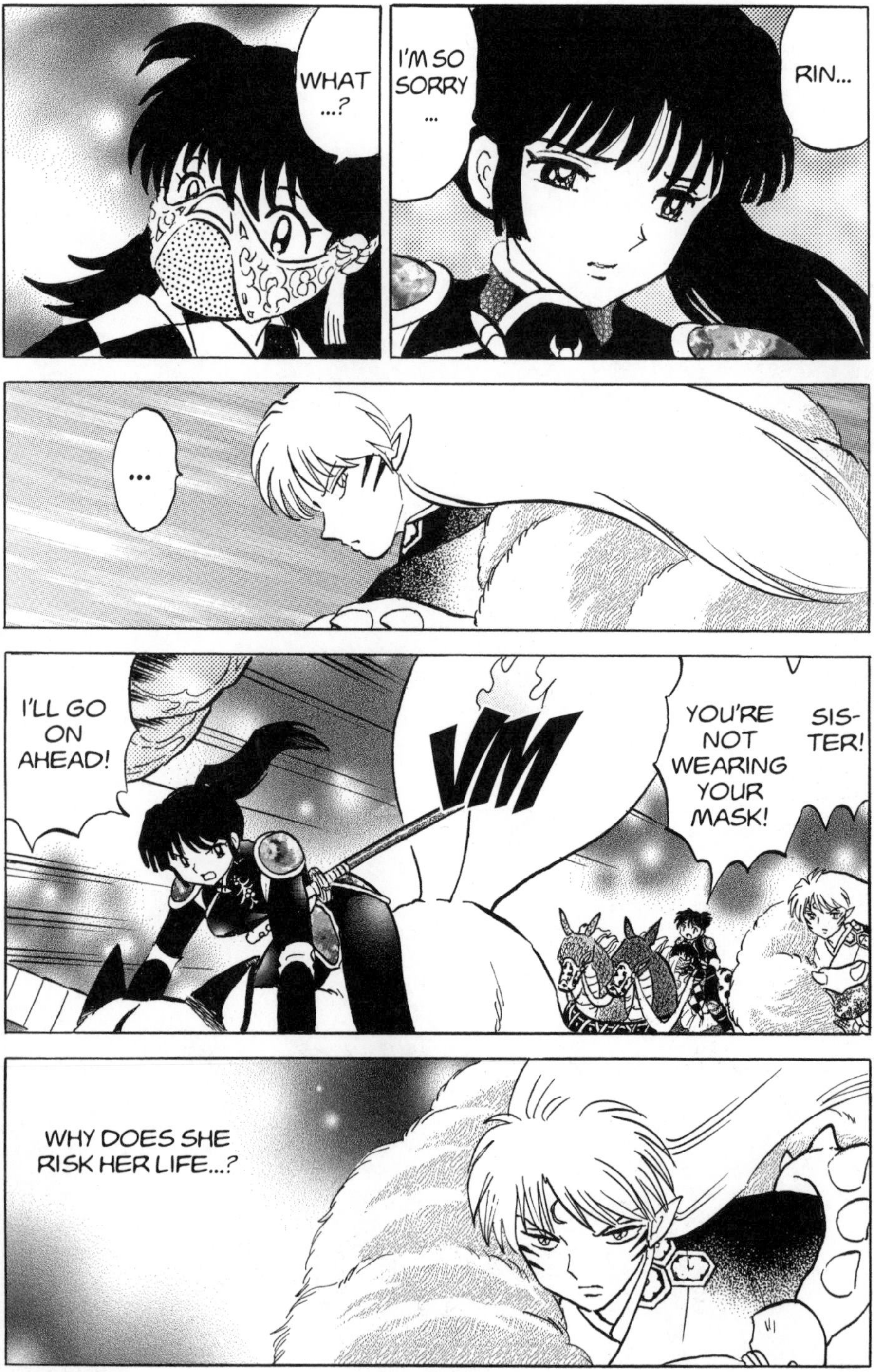
RIN...
I'M SO SORRY ...
WHAT ...?
...
SIS-TER!
YOU'RE NOT WEARING YOUR MASK!
VM
I'LL GO ON AHEAD!
WHY DOES SHE RISK HER LIFE...?

SCROLL SEVEN

DESPAIR

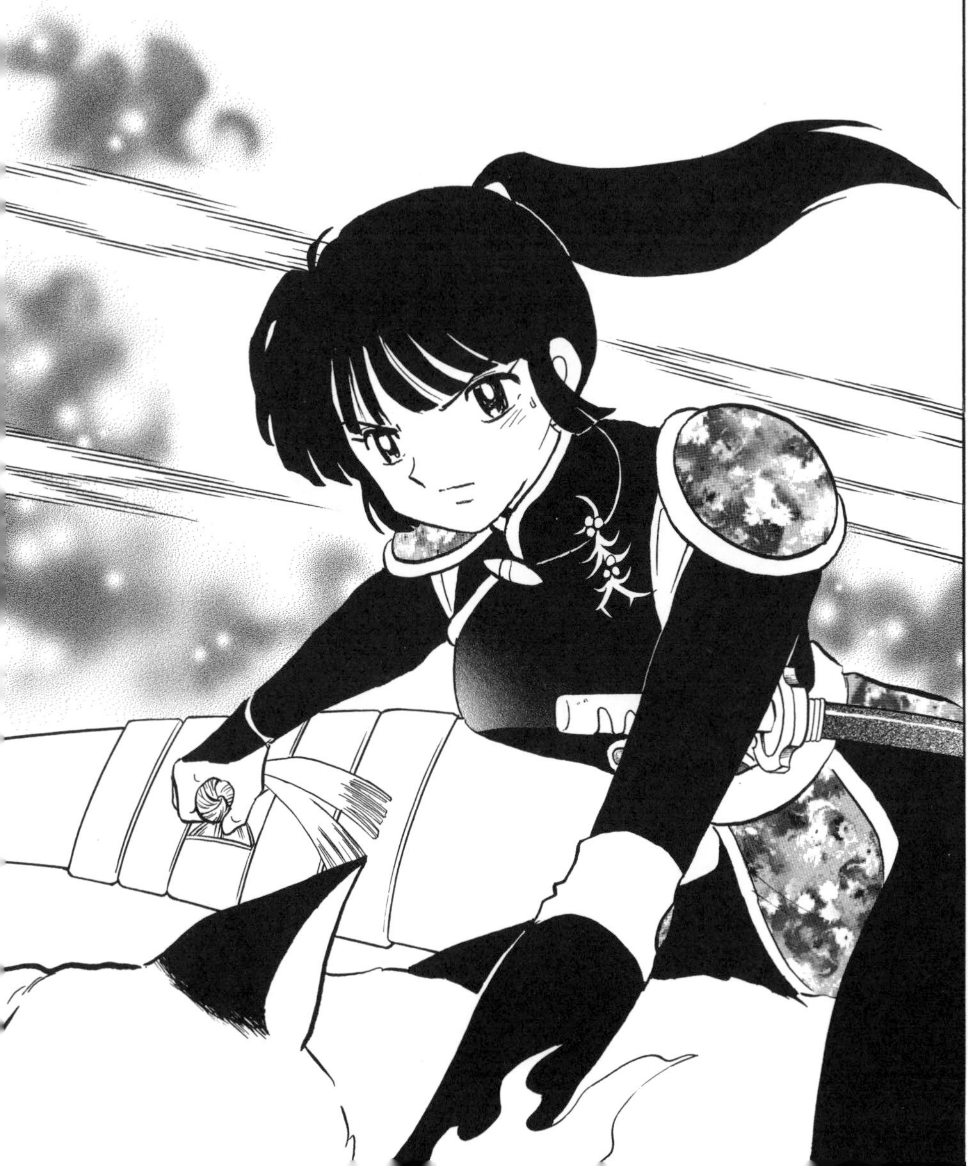

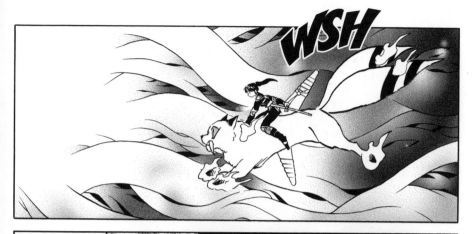

WSH
HURTS... TO BREATHE ...
SWOO...
FEELS LIKE THE MIASMA IS GETTING STRONGER...
LORD SESSHO-MARU! PLEASE GO AFTER LADY SANGO!
THE MIASMA WILL KILL HER!

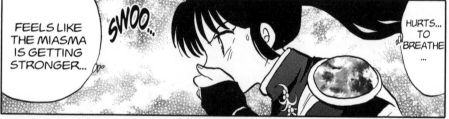

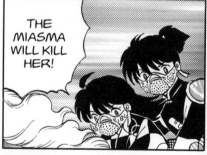

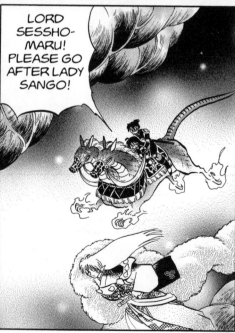

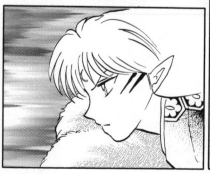

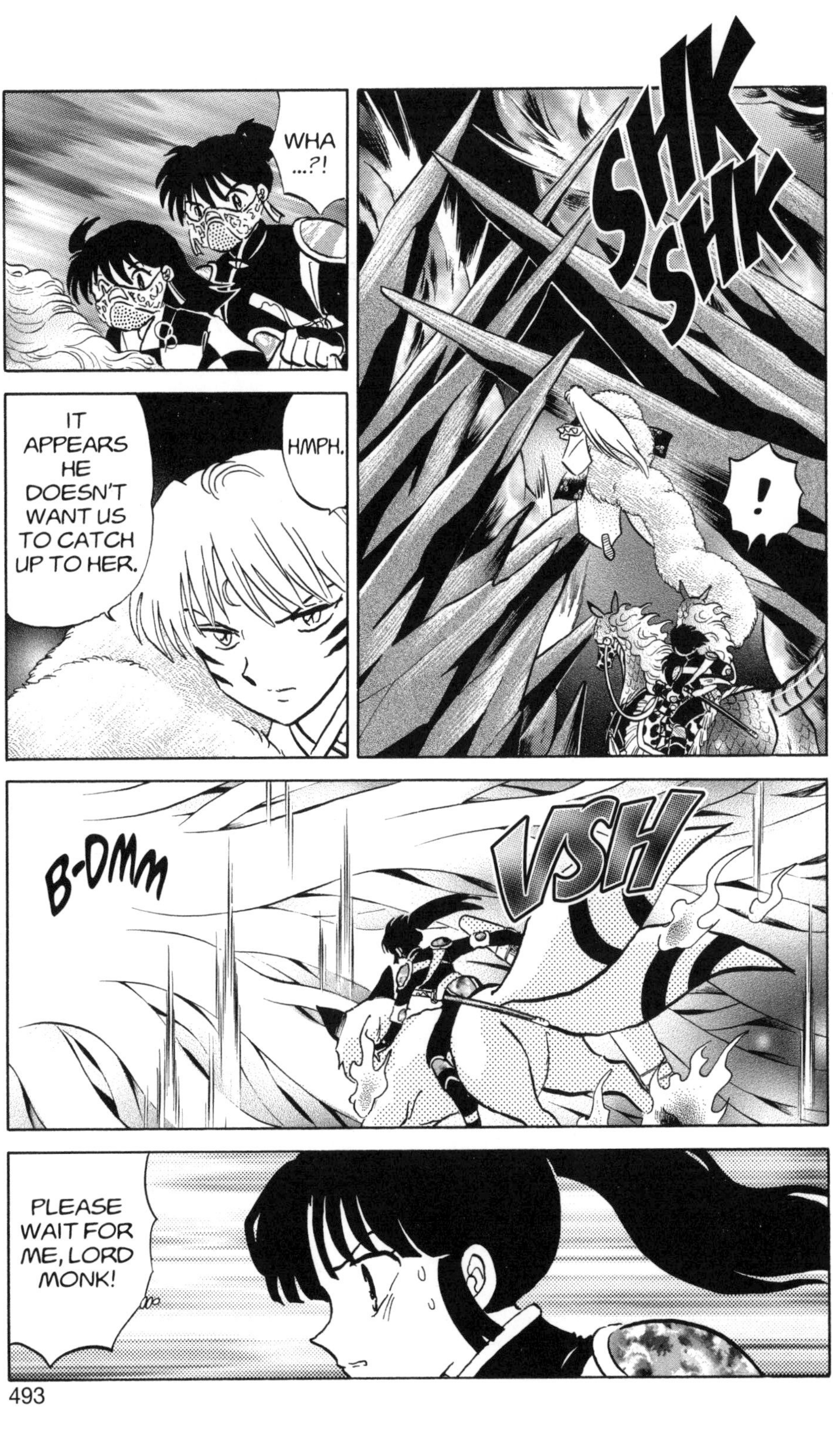
SHK SHK
!
WHA ...?!
HMPH.
IT APPEARS HE DOESN'T WANT US TO CATCH UP TO HER.
VSH
B-DMM
PLEASE WAIT FOR ME, LORD MONK!

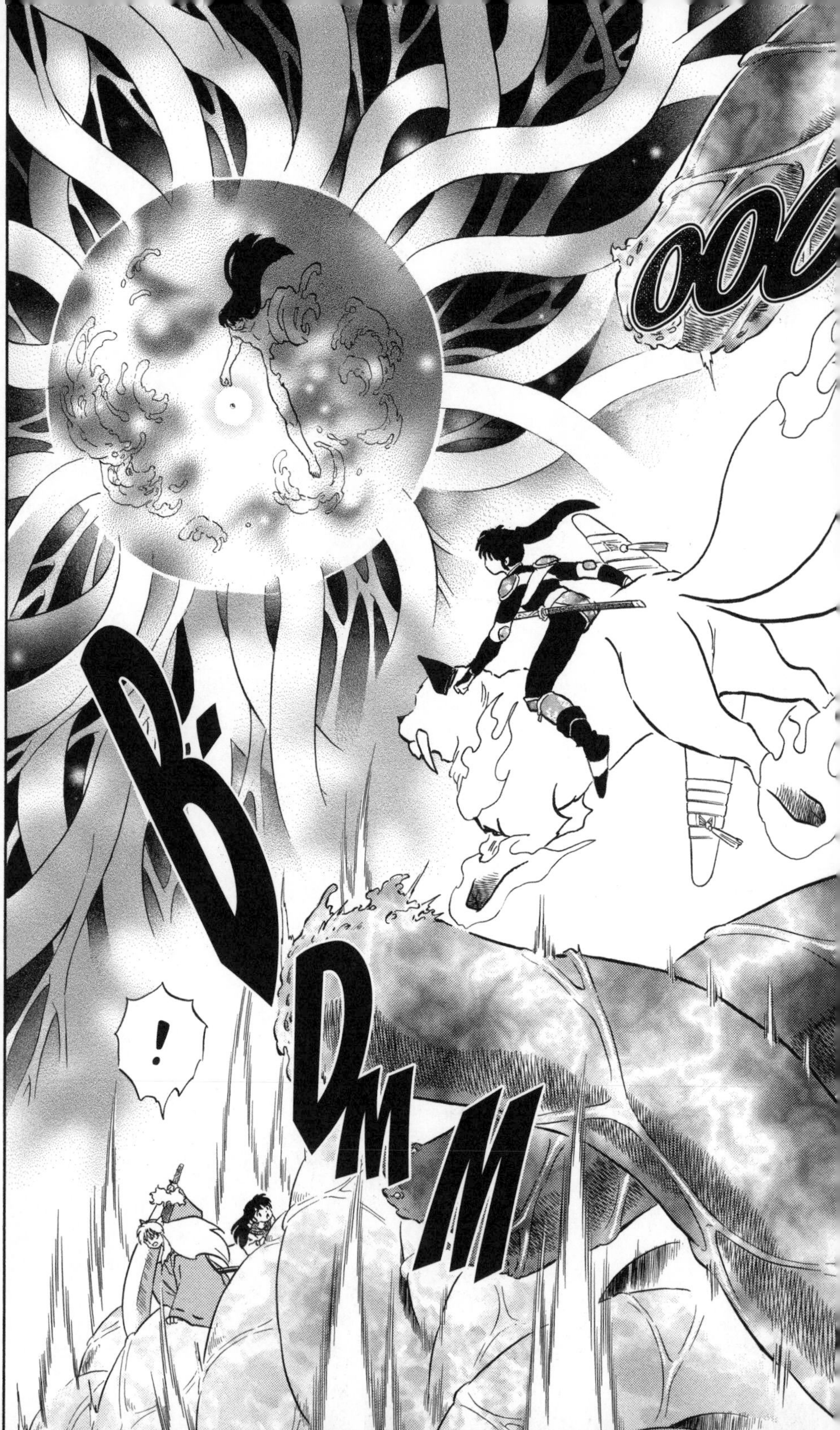

ooo
B
DMM
!

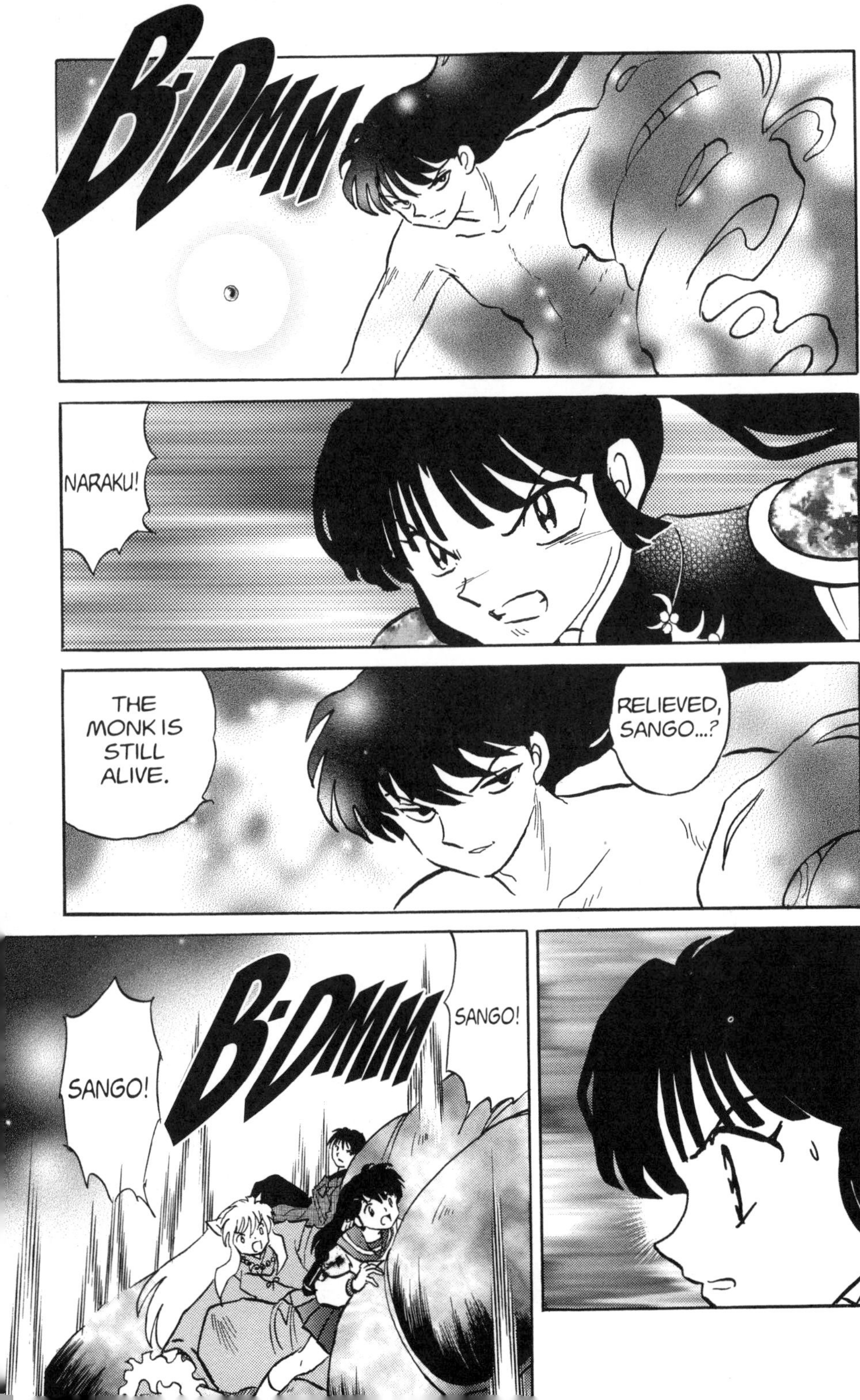
B-DMM
NARAKU!
RELIEVED, SANGO...?
THE MONK IS STILL ALIVE.
SANGO!
B-DMM
SANGO!

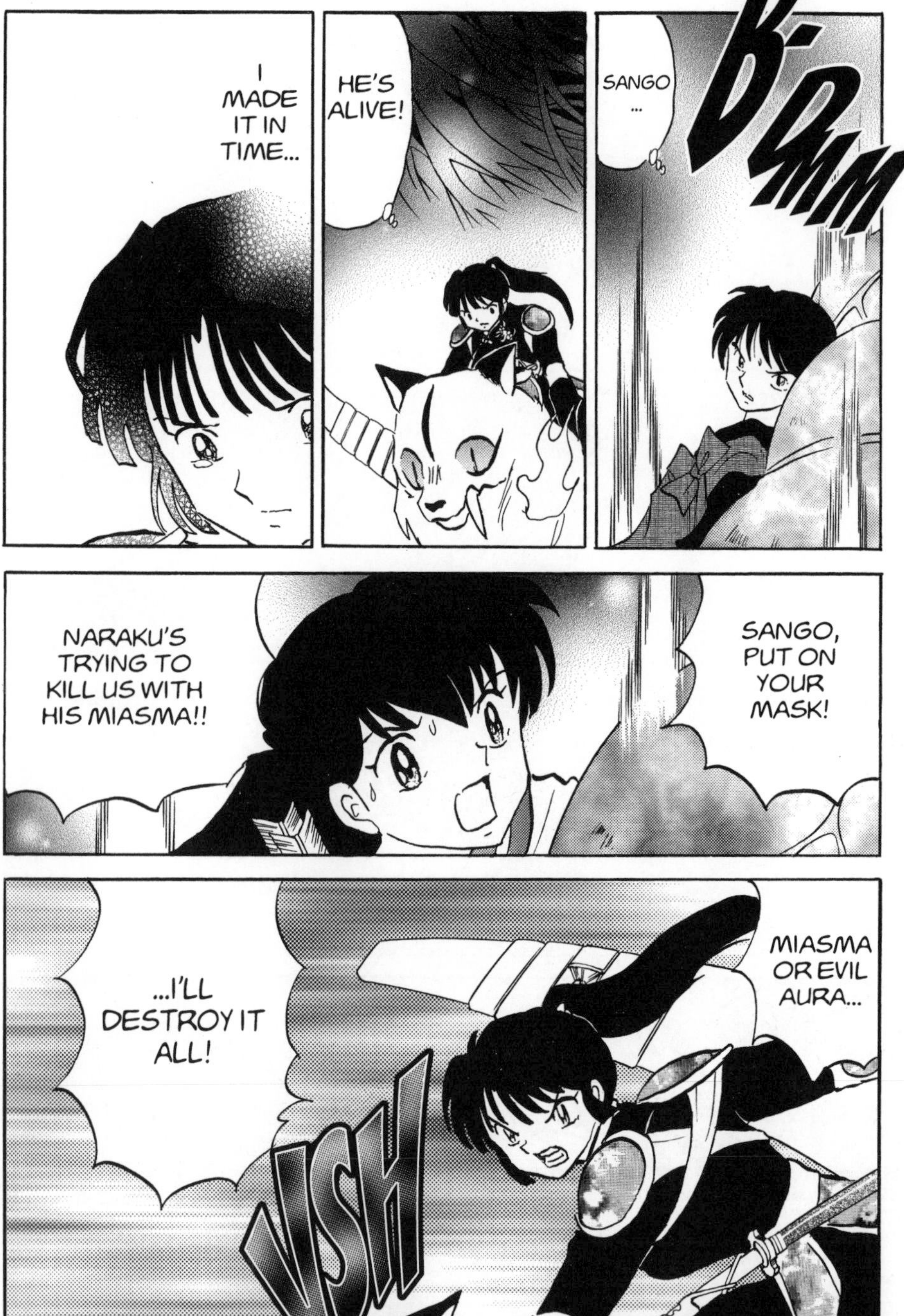
SANGO ...
BDMM
HE'S ALIVE!
I MADE IT IN TIME...
SANGO, PUT ON YOUR MASK!
NARAKU'S TRYING TO KILL US WITH HIS MIASMA!!
MIASMA OR EVIL AURA...
...I'LL DESTROY IT ALL!
VSH

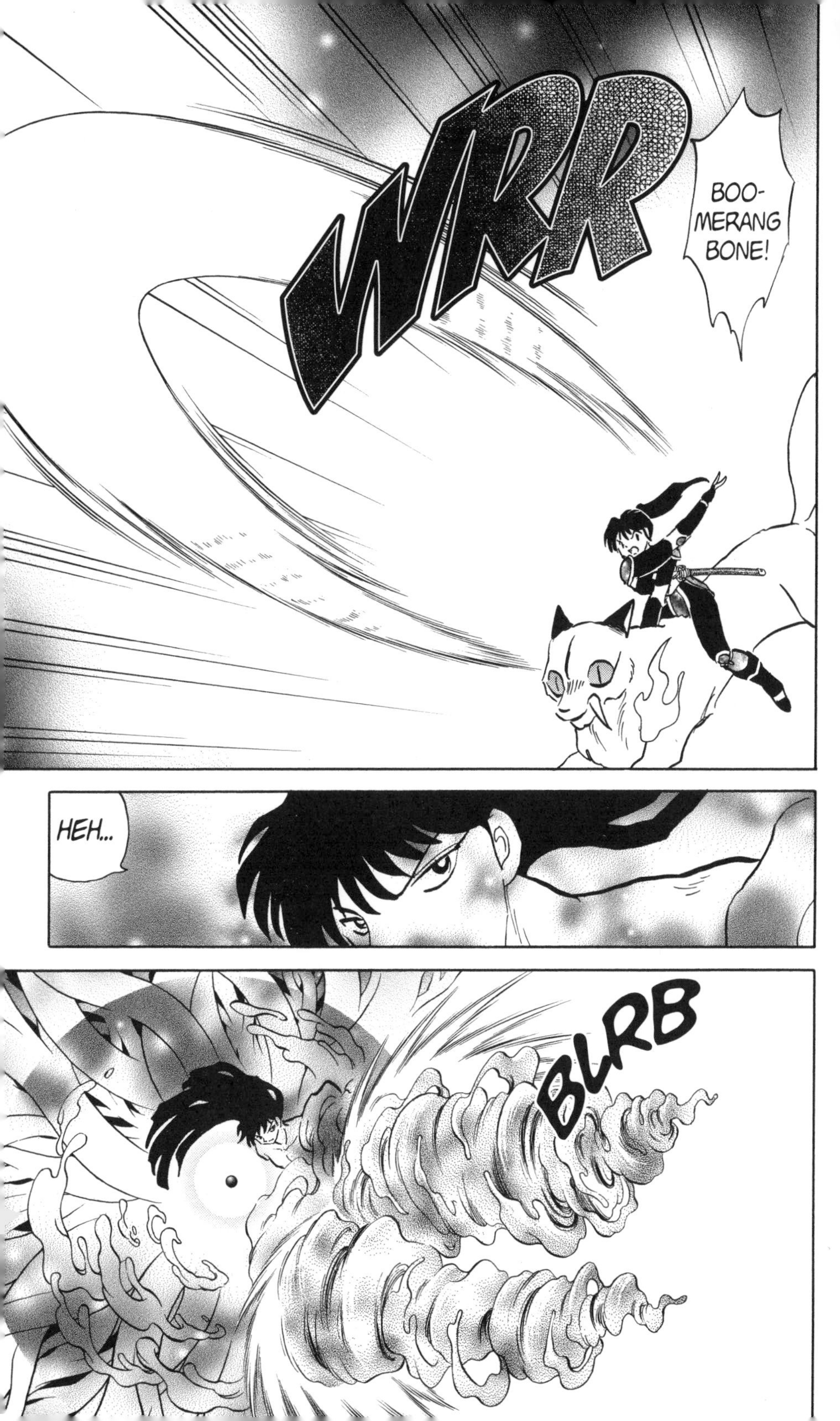
WRR
BOO-
MERANG
BONE!
HEH...
BLRB

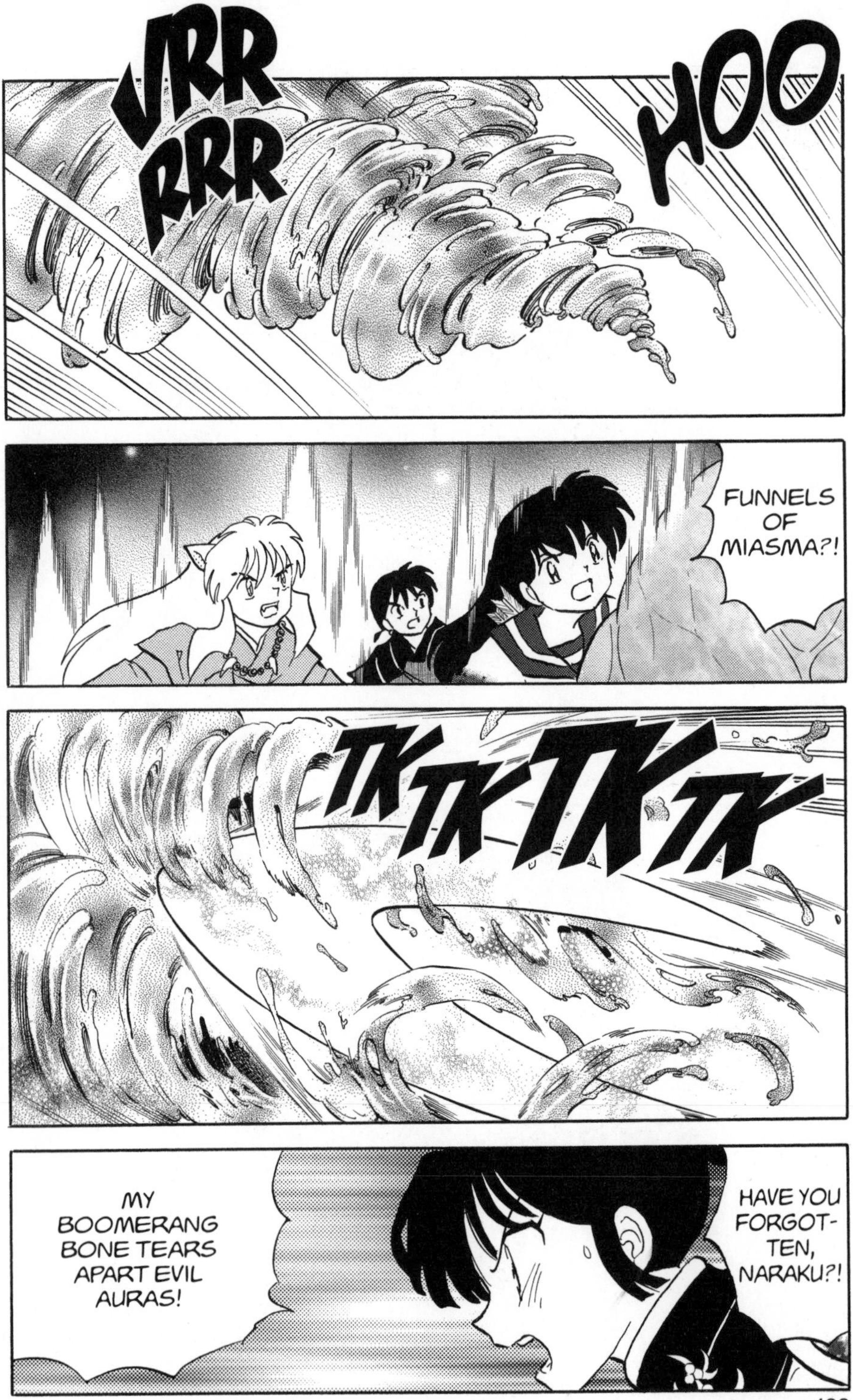
HOO
VRR RRR
FUNNELS OF MIASMA?!
TK TK TK TK
HAVE YOU FORGOT-TEN, NARAKU?!
MY BOOMERANG BONE TEARS APART EVIL AURAS!

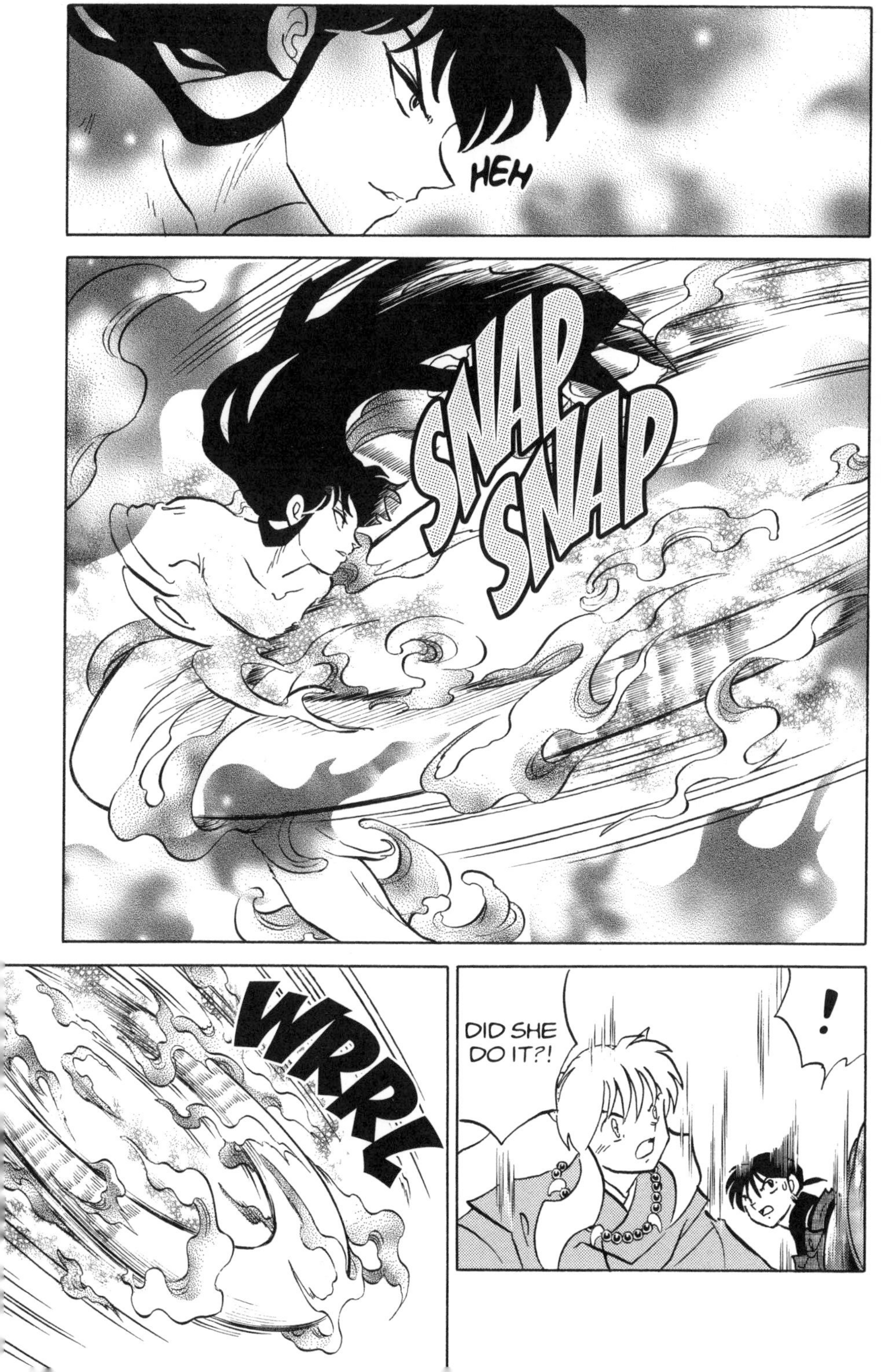
HEH
SNAP SNAP
!
DID SHE DO IT?!
WRRL

GRP

SSH...

WSH

TWNG

SAN-GO!

NO!

BOOM

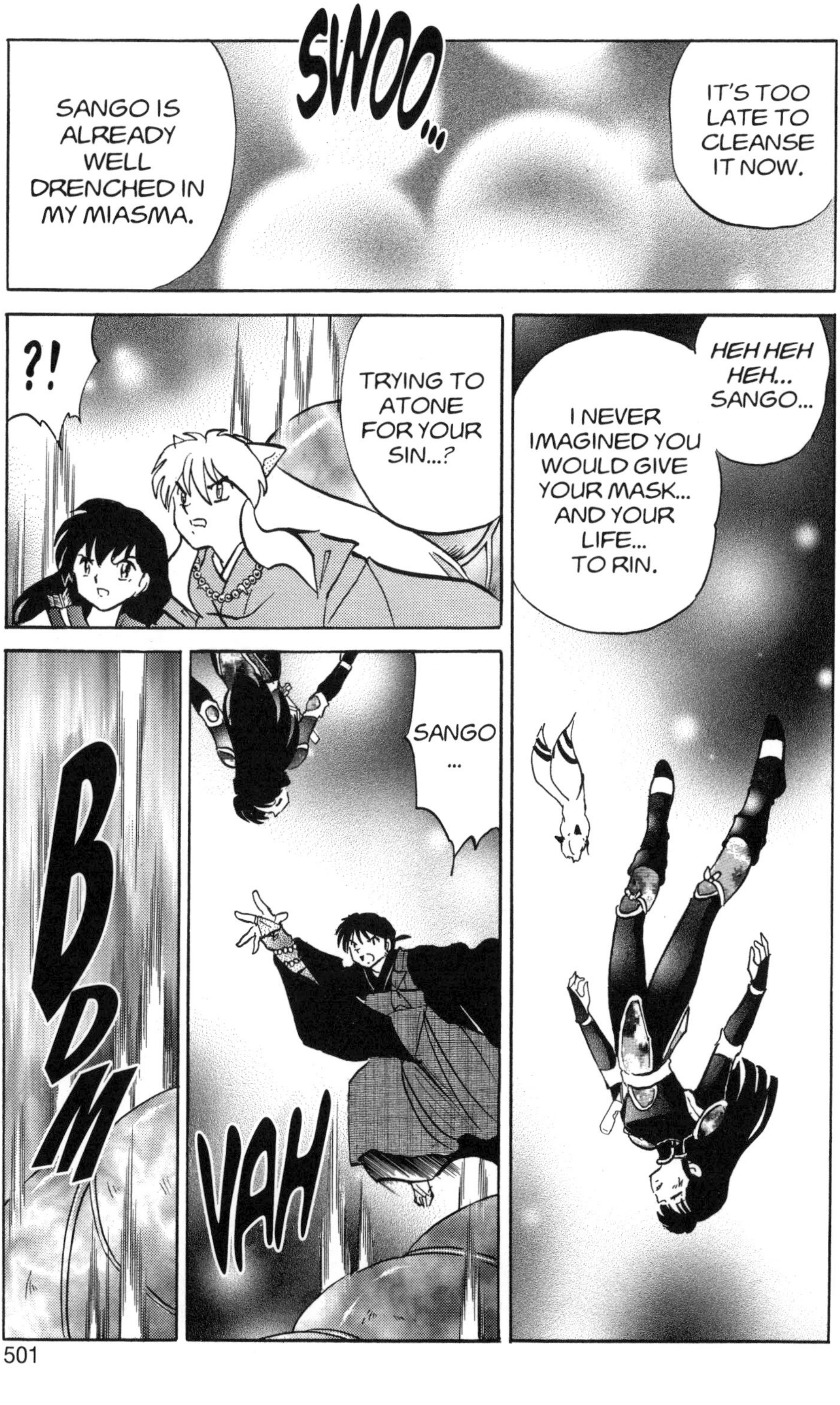
IT'S TOO LATE TO CLEANSE IT NOW.
SWOO...
SANGO IS ALREADY WELL DRENCHED IN MY MIASMA.
HEH HEH HEH... SANGO...
I NEVER IMAGINED YOU WOULD GIVE YOUR MASK... AND YOUR LIFE... TO RIN.
TRYING TO ATONE FOR YOUR SIN...?
?!
SANGO ...
VAH
BDM

LORD MIROKU! SANGO!

KAGO-ME!

WMP

YEEE!

CHAK
CHAK

SSH

RGH!

HSSSH

SHHM

RRRIP

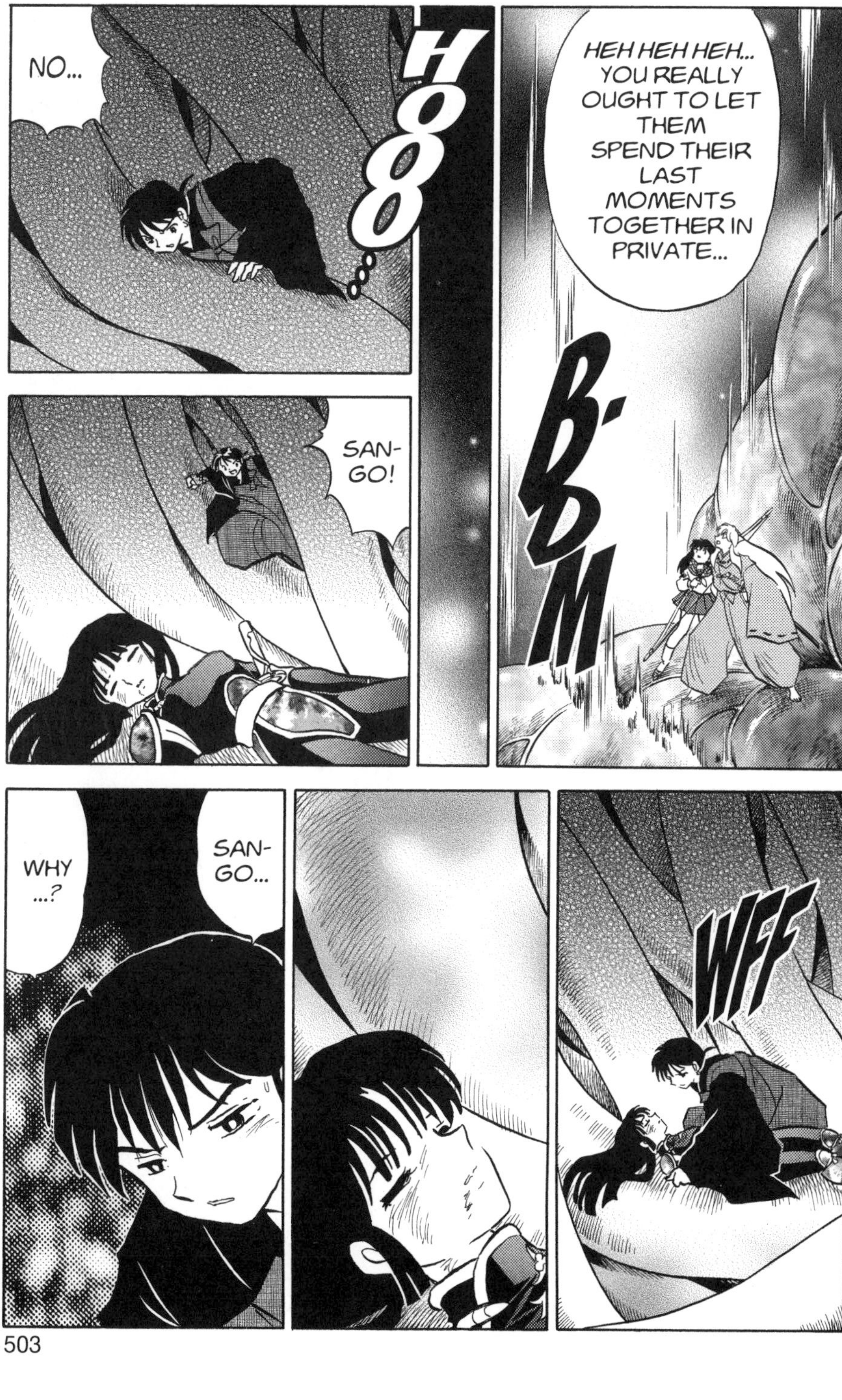
HEH HEH HEH... YOU REALLY OUGHT TO LET THEM SPEND THEIR LAST MOMENTS TOGETHER IN PRIVATE...
B-DM
NO...
SAN-GO!
WFF
SAN-GO...
WHY ...?

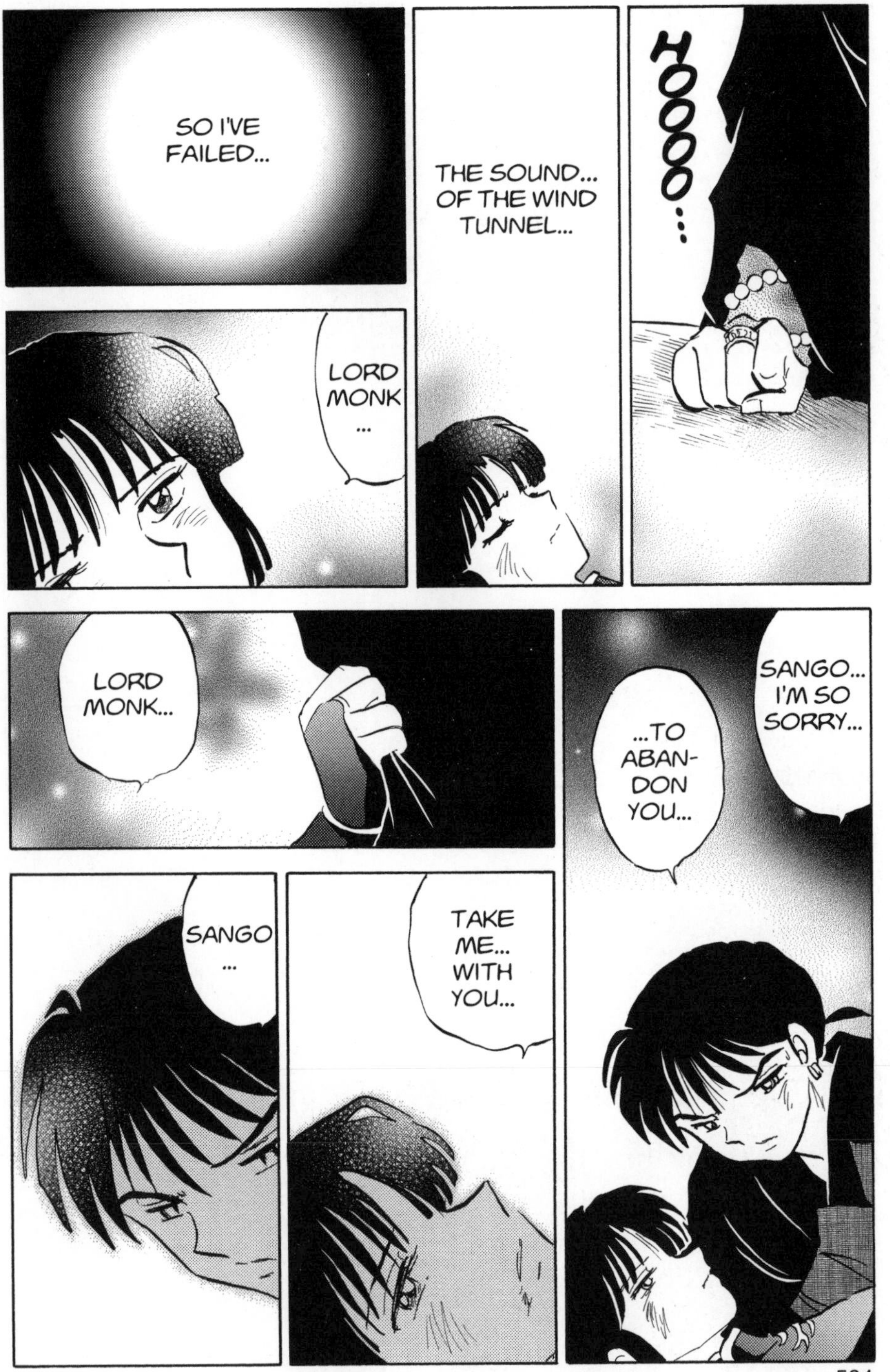
HOOOOO...
THE SOUND... OF THE WIND TUNNEL...
SO I'VE FAILED...
LORD MONK...
SANGO... I'M SO SORRY...
...TO ABANDON YOU...
LORD MONK...
TAKE ME... WITH YOU...
SANGO...

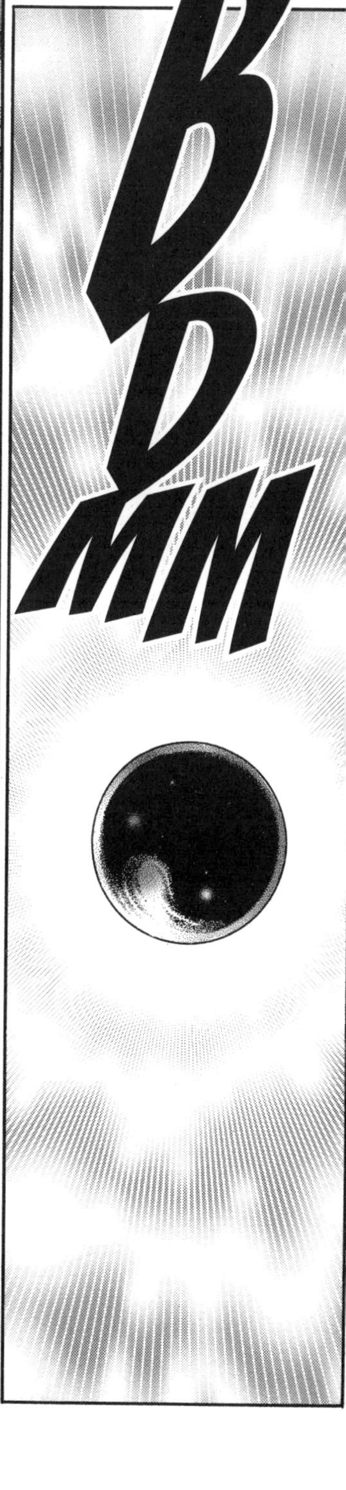
BDMM
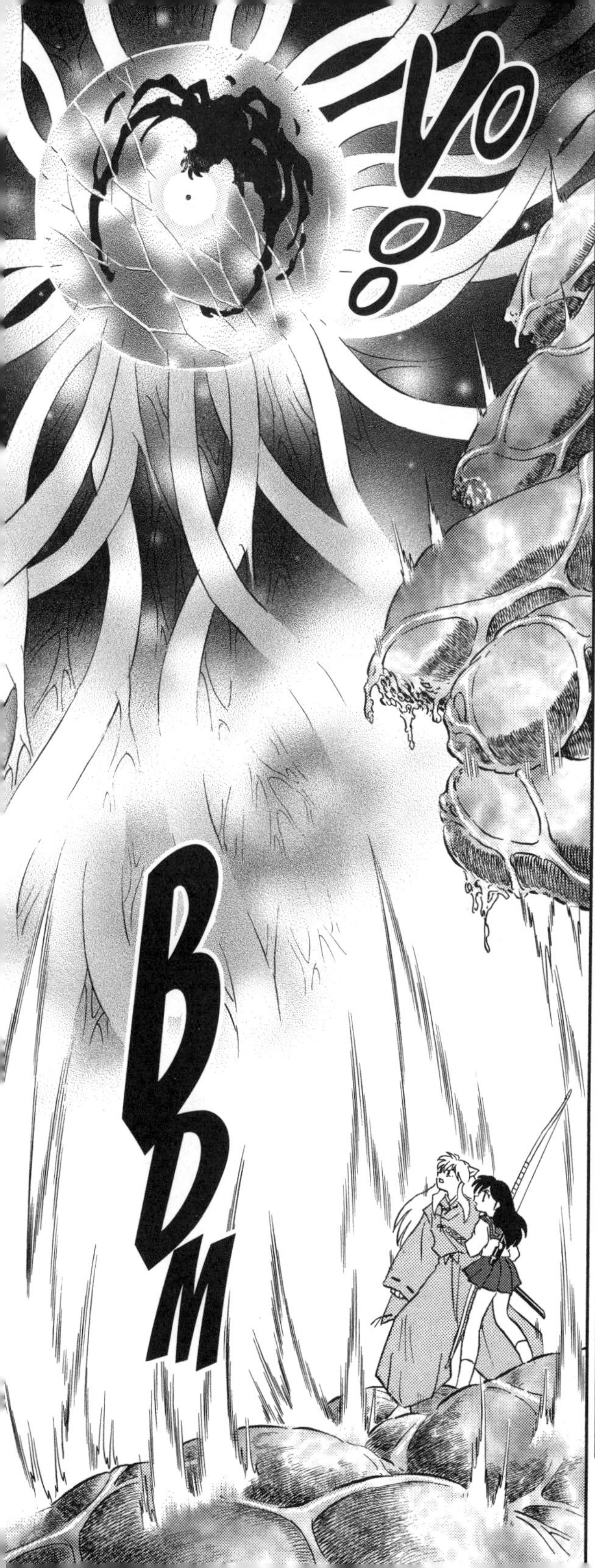
VOOO
BDM

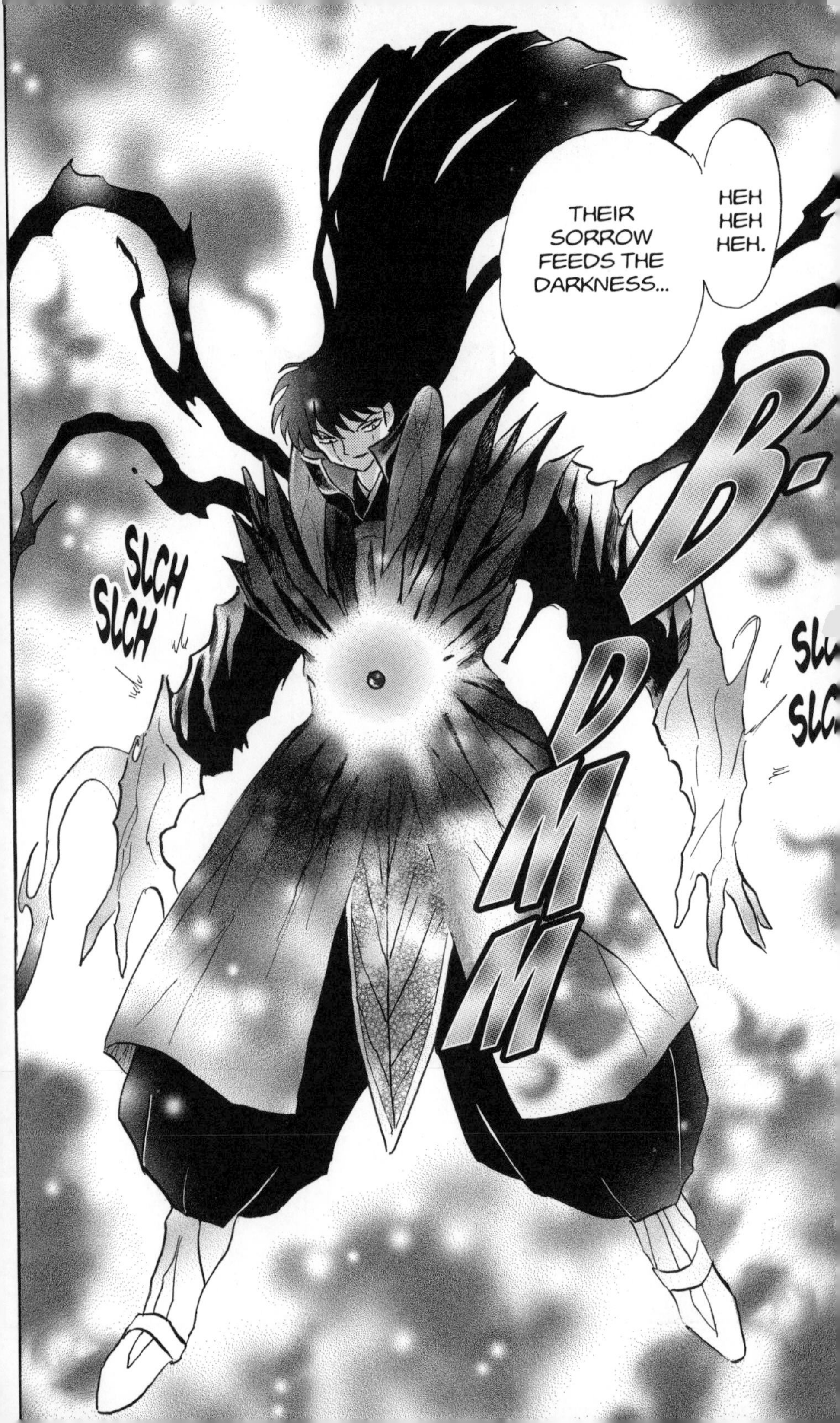
HEH HEH HEH.
THEIR SORROW FEEDS THE DARKNESS...
B-DMMM
SLCH SLCH

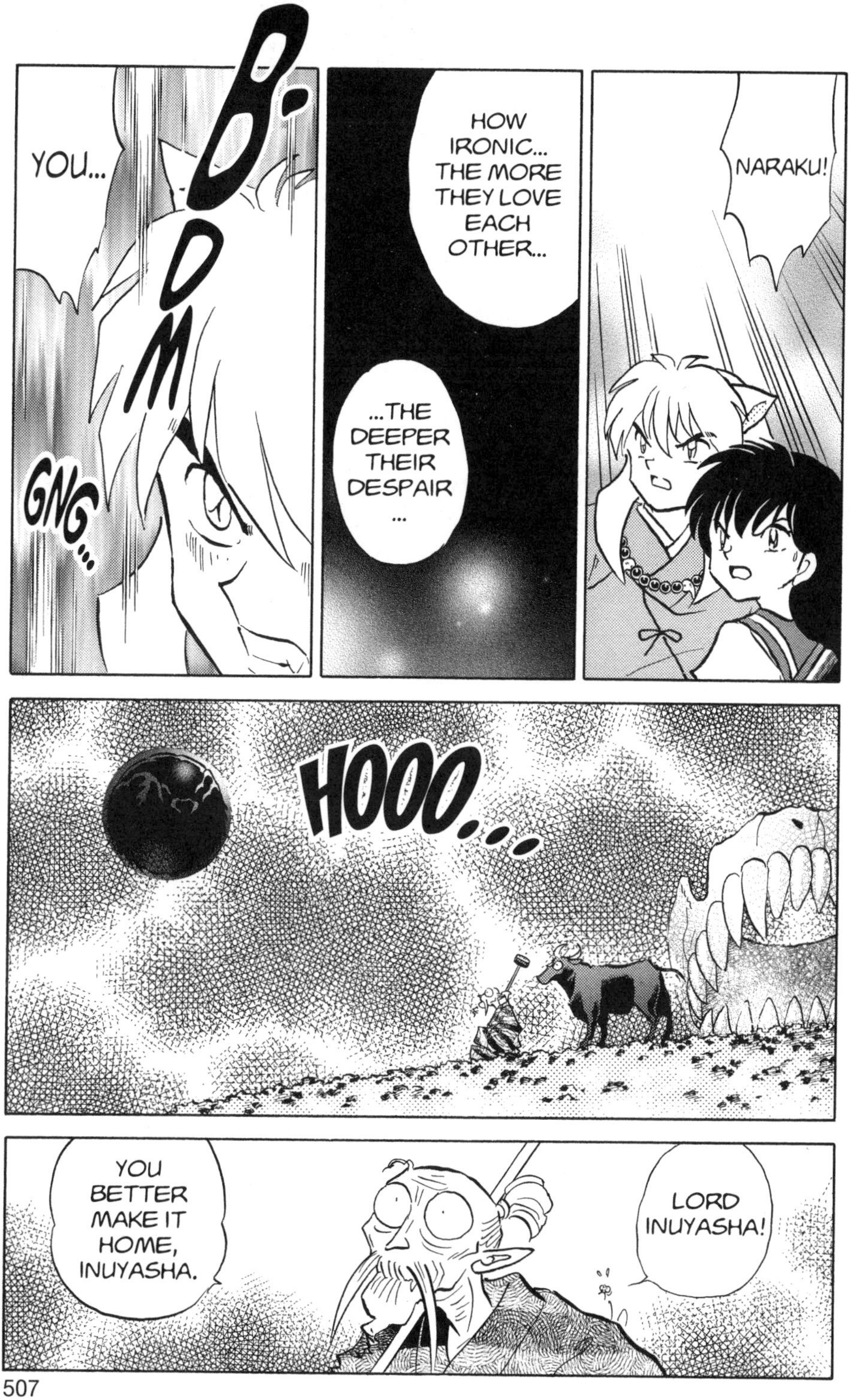
NARAKU!
HOW IRONIC... THE MORE THEY LOVE EACH OTHER...
...THE DEEPER THEIR DESPAIR ...
B-DOM
YOU...
GNG...
HOOO...
LORD INUYASHA!
YOU BETTER MAKE IT HOME, INUYASHA.

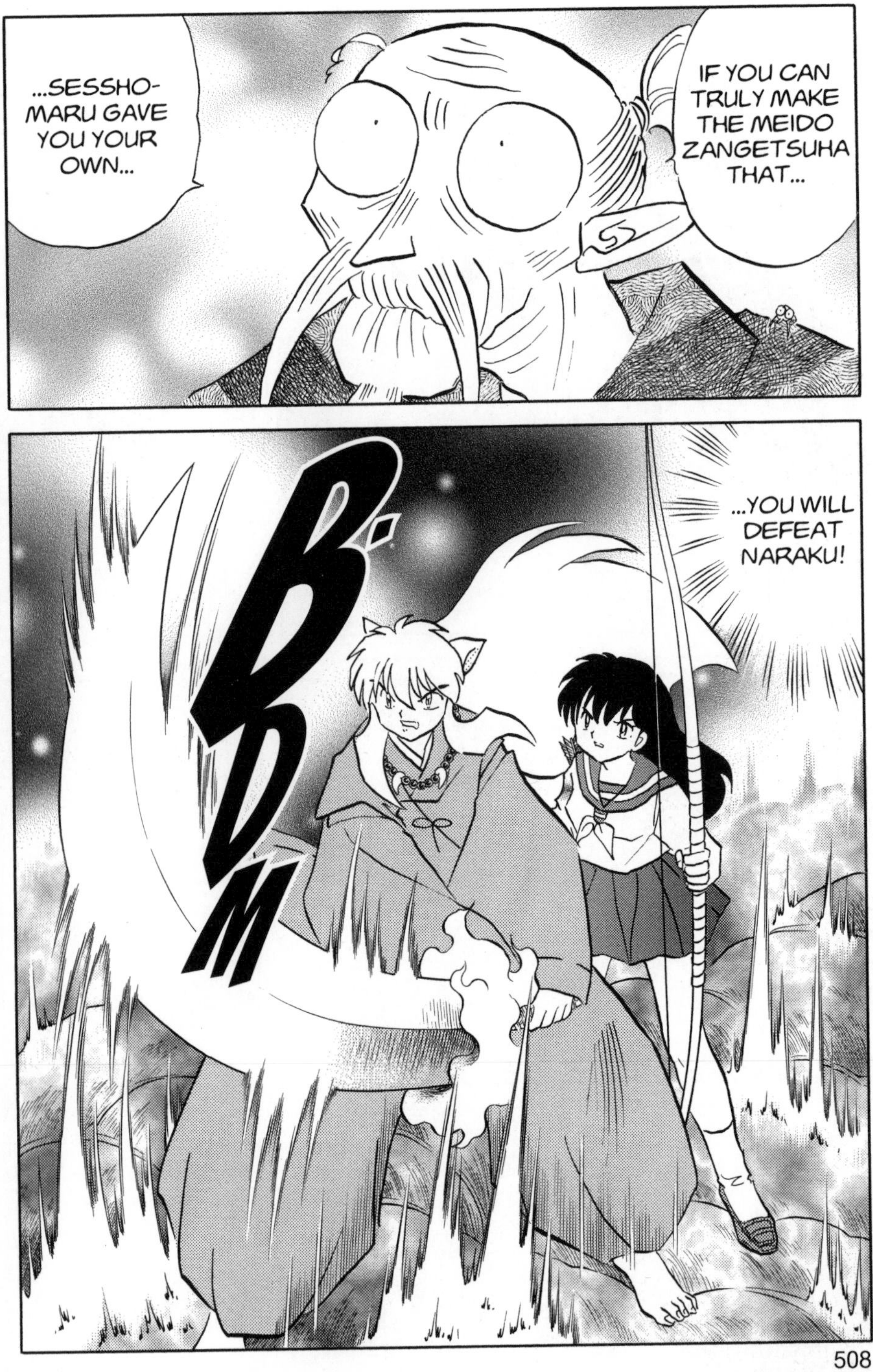
IF YOU CAN TRULY MAKE THE MEIDO ZANGETSUHA THAT...
...SESSHO-MARU GAVE YOU YOUR OWN...
...YOU WILL DEFEAT NARAKU!
BDM

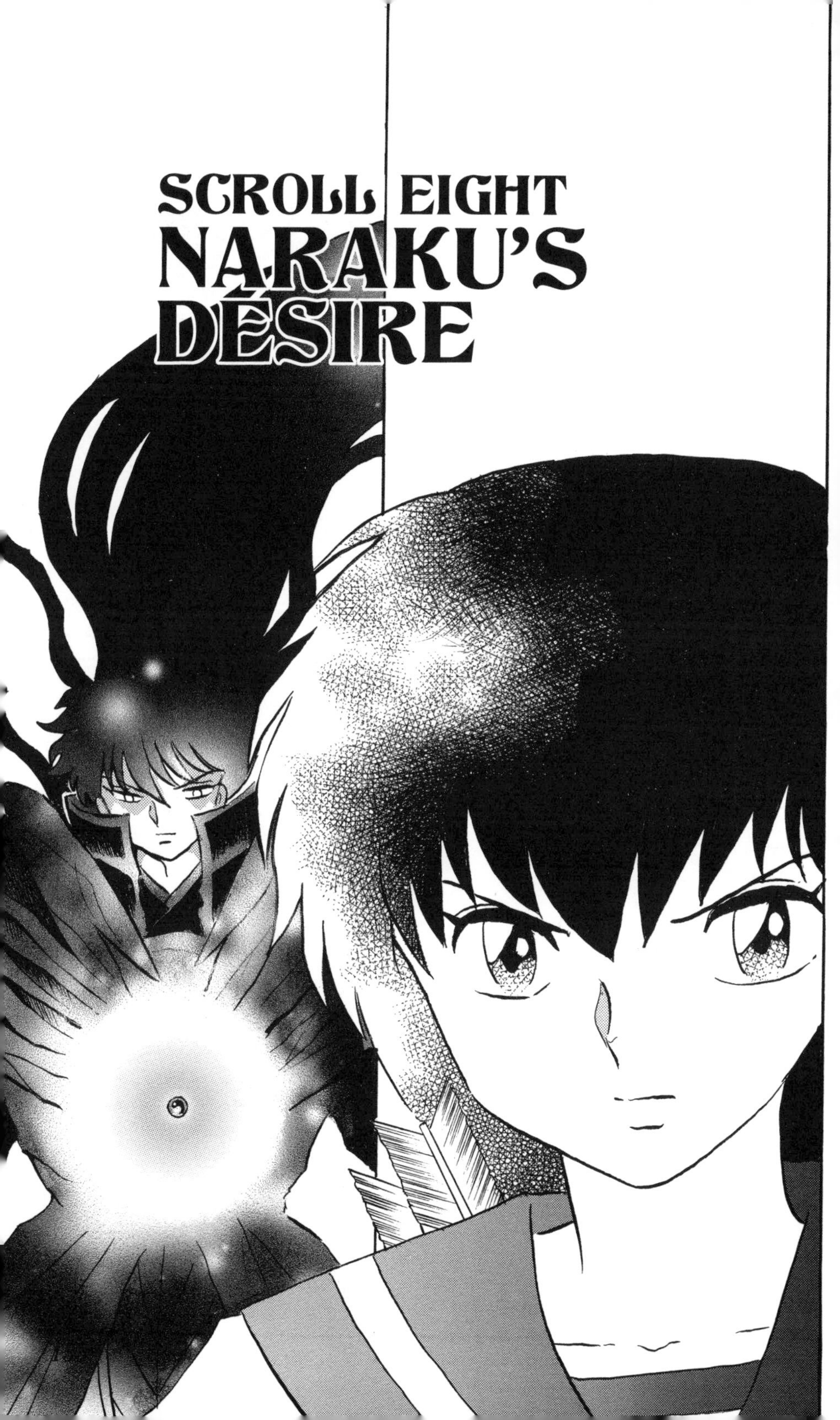
SCROLL EIGHT
NARAKU'S DÉSIRE

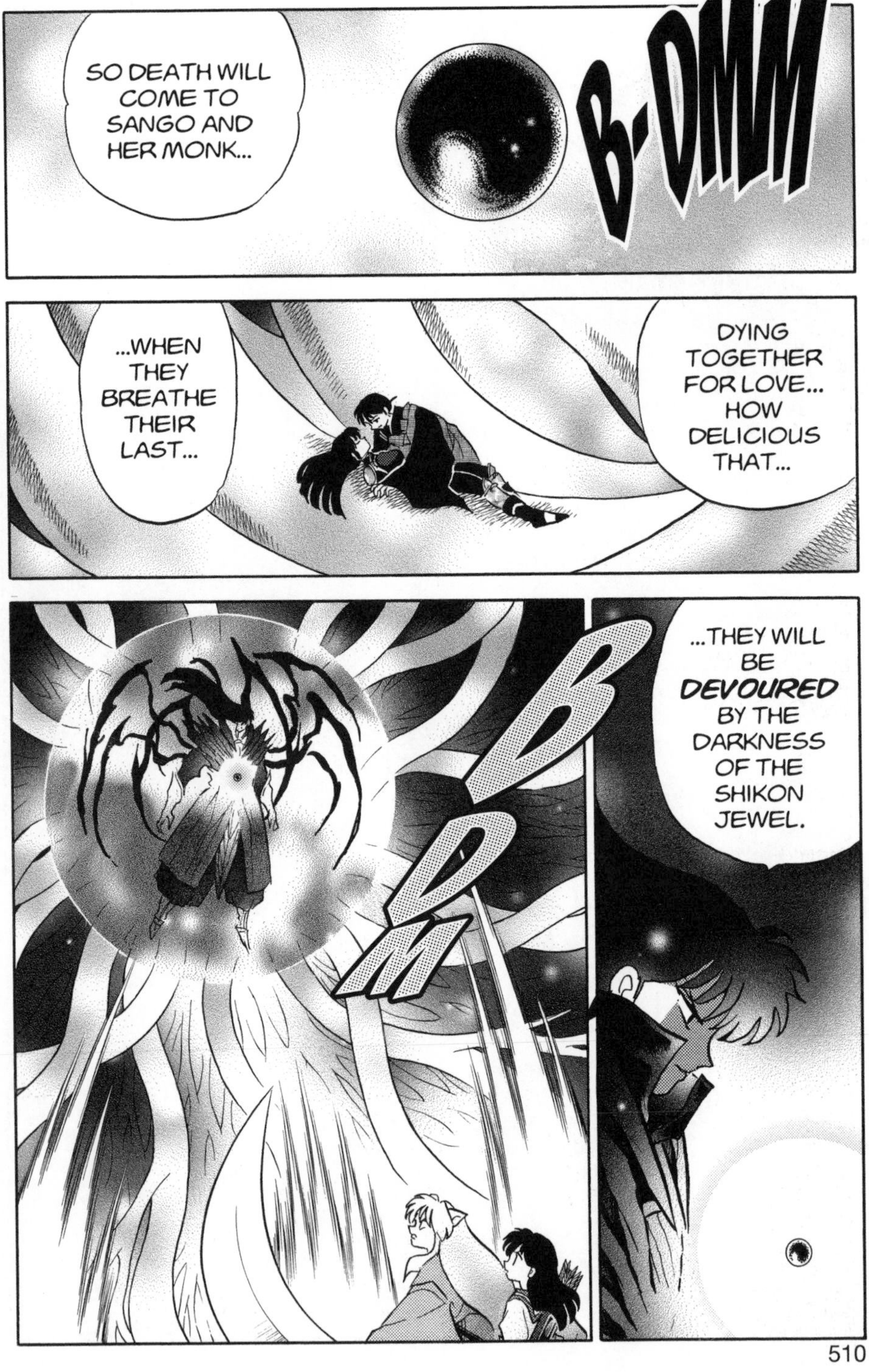
B-DMM
SO DEATH WILL COME TO SANGO AND HER MONK...
DYING TOGETHER FOR LOVE... HOW DELICIOUS THAT...
...WHEN THEY BREATHE THEIR LAST...
...THEY WILL BE **DEVOURED** BY THE DARKNESS OF THE SHIKON JEWEL.
BDM

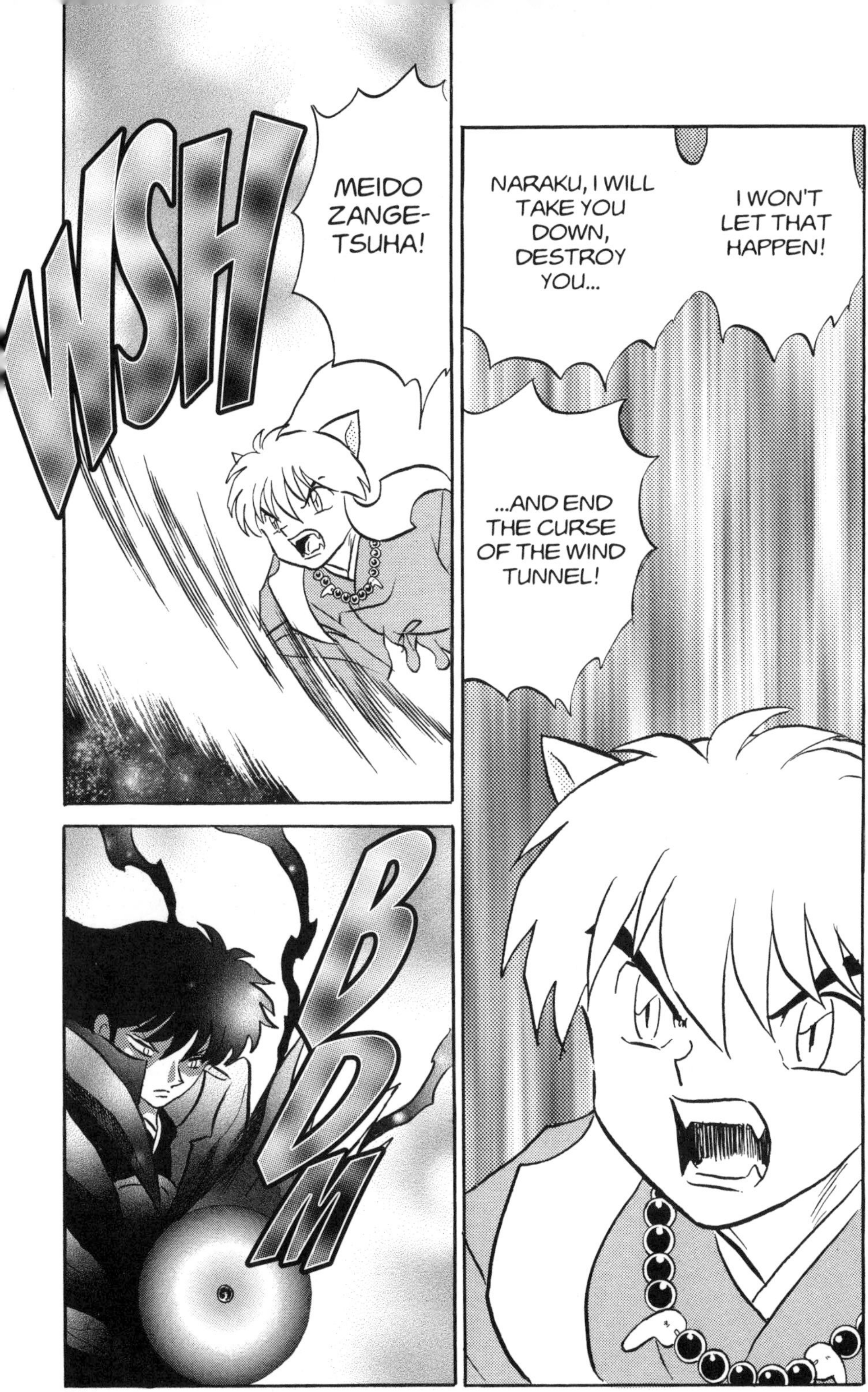
I WON'T LET THAT HAPPEN!
NARAKU, I WILL TAKE YOU DOWN, DESTROY YOU...
...AND END THE CURSE OF THE WIND TUNNEL!
MEIDO ZANGE-TSUHA!
WSH
BDM

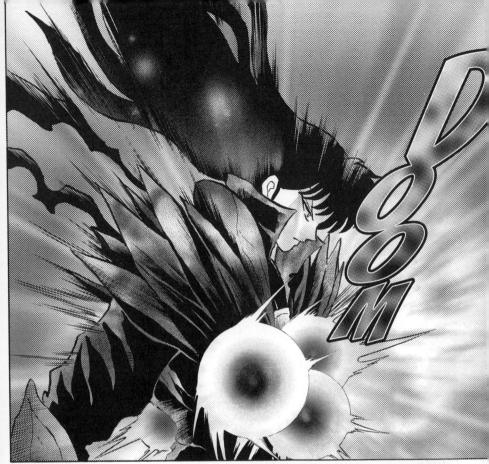

THE SHIKON JEWEL...

...HAS BECOME ONE WITH NARAKU!

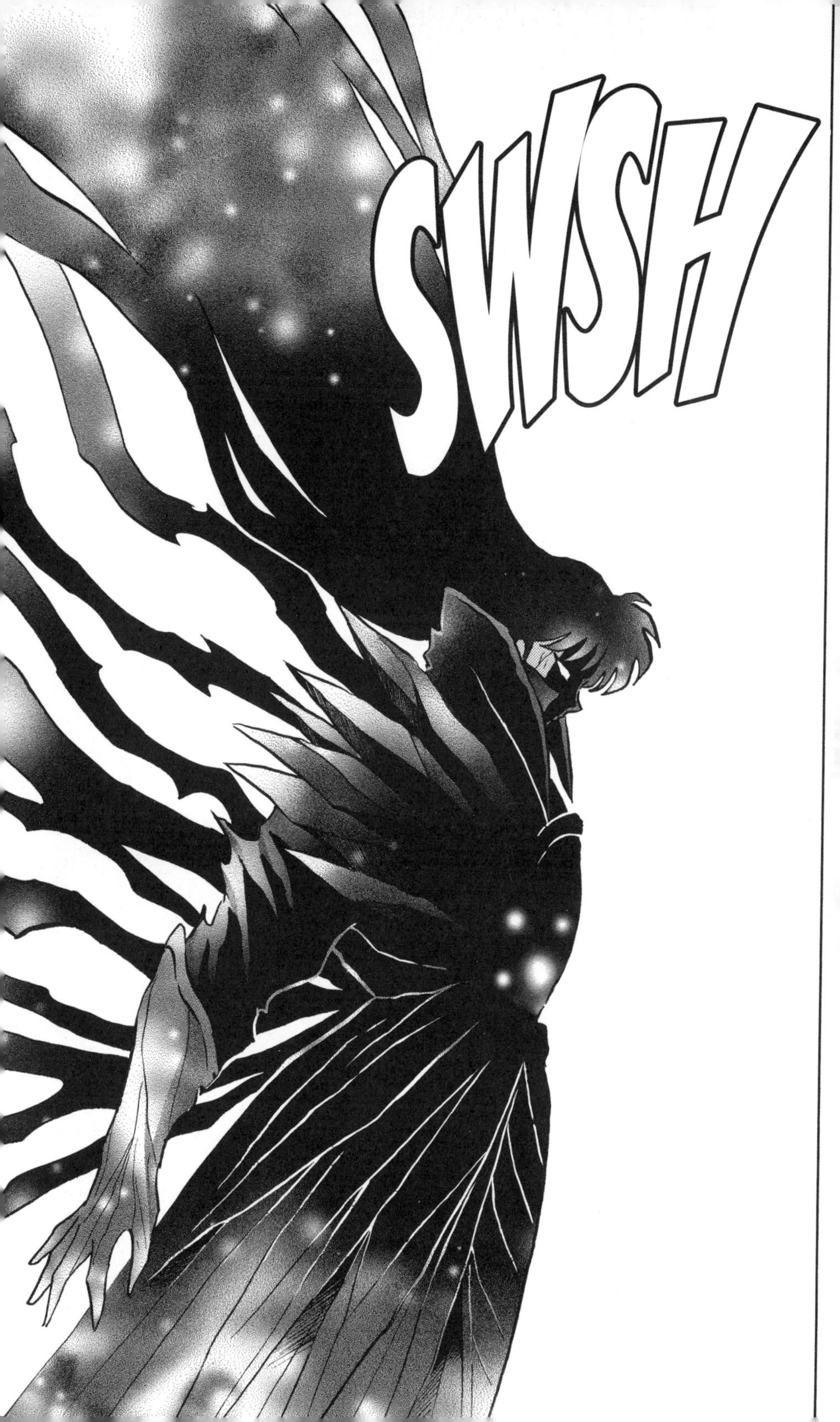
SWSH

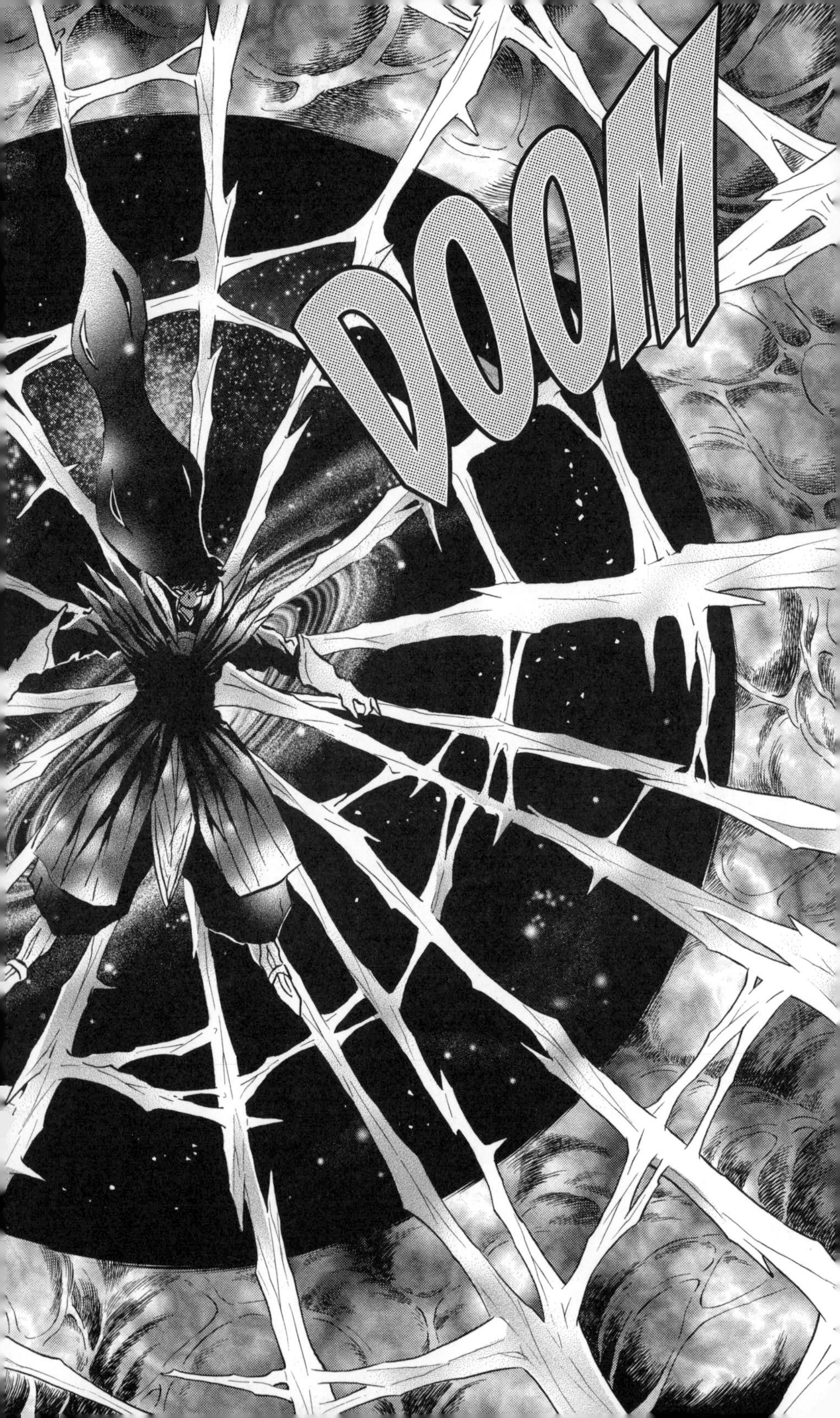
DOOM

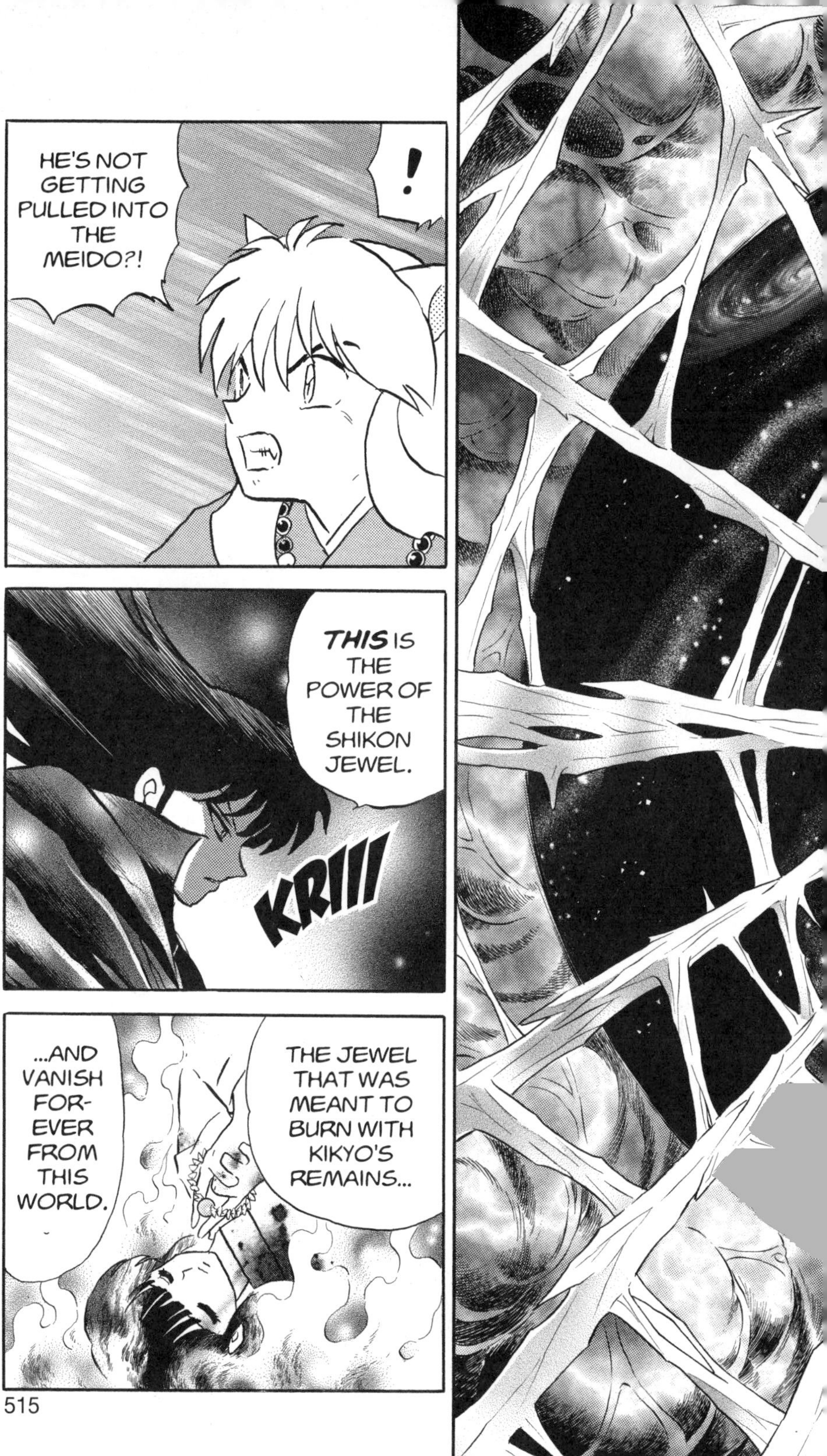
!
HE'S NOT GETTING PULLED INTO THE MEIDO?!
THIS IS THE POWER OF THE SHIKON JEWEL.
KRIII
THE JEWEL THAT WAS MEANT TO BURN WITH KIKYO'S REMAINS...
...AND VANISH FOR-EVER FROM THIS WORLD.

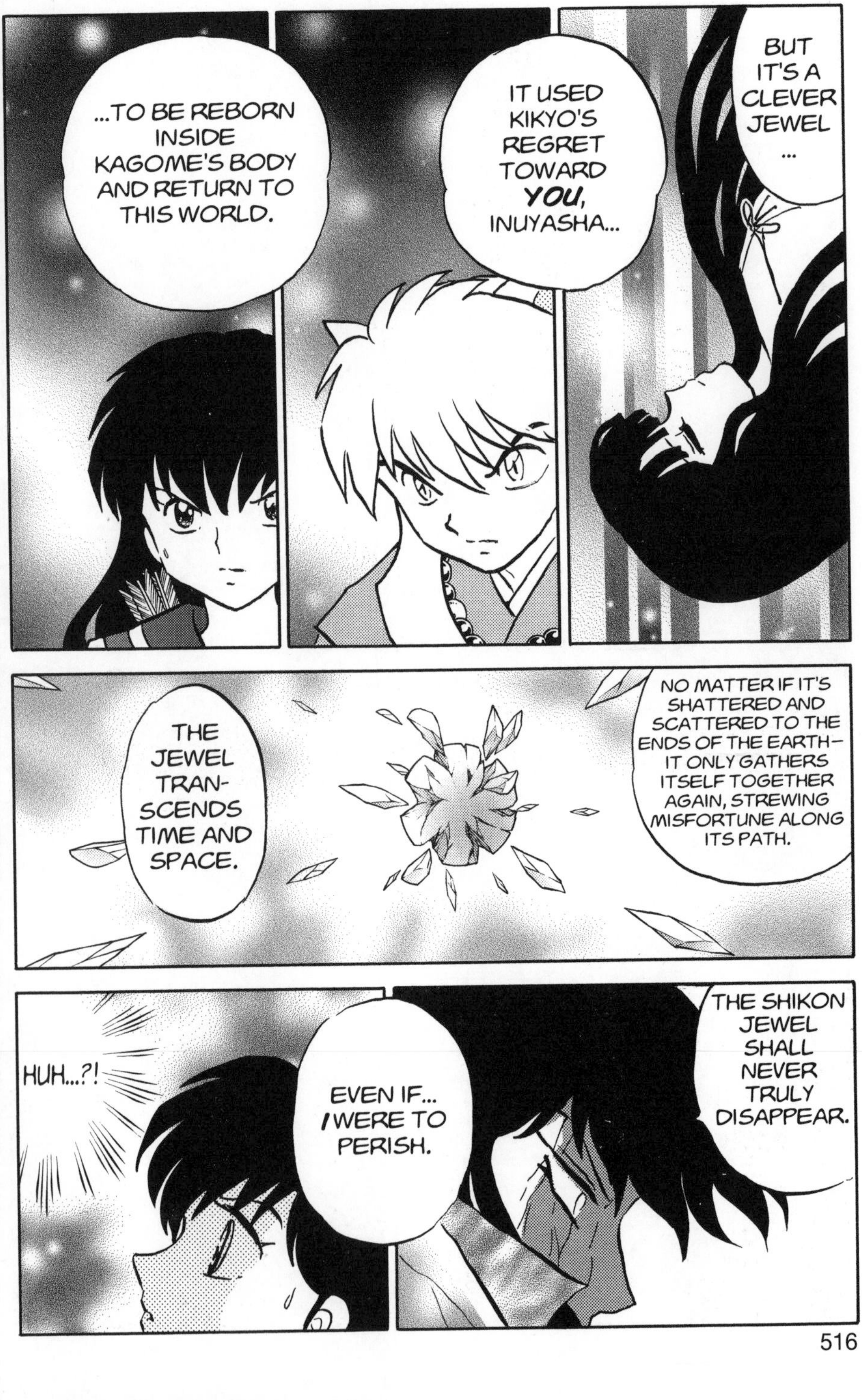
BUT IT'S A CLEVER JEWEL ...
IT USED KIKYO'S REGRET TOWARD *YOU*, INUYASHA...
...TO BE REBORN INSIDE KAGOME'S BODY AND RETURN TO THIS WORLD.
NO MATTER IF IT'S SHATTERED AND SCATTERED TO THE ENDS OF THE EARTH– IT ONLY GATHERS ITSELF TOGETHER AGAIN, STREWING MISFORTUNE ALONG ITS PATH.
THE JEWEL TRAN-SCENDS TIME AND SPACE.
THE SHIKON JEWEL SHALL NEVER TRULY DISAPPEAR.
EVEN IF... *I* WERE TO PERISH.
HUH...?!

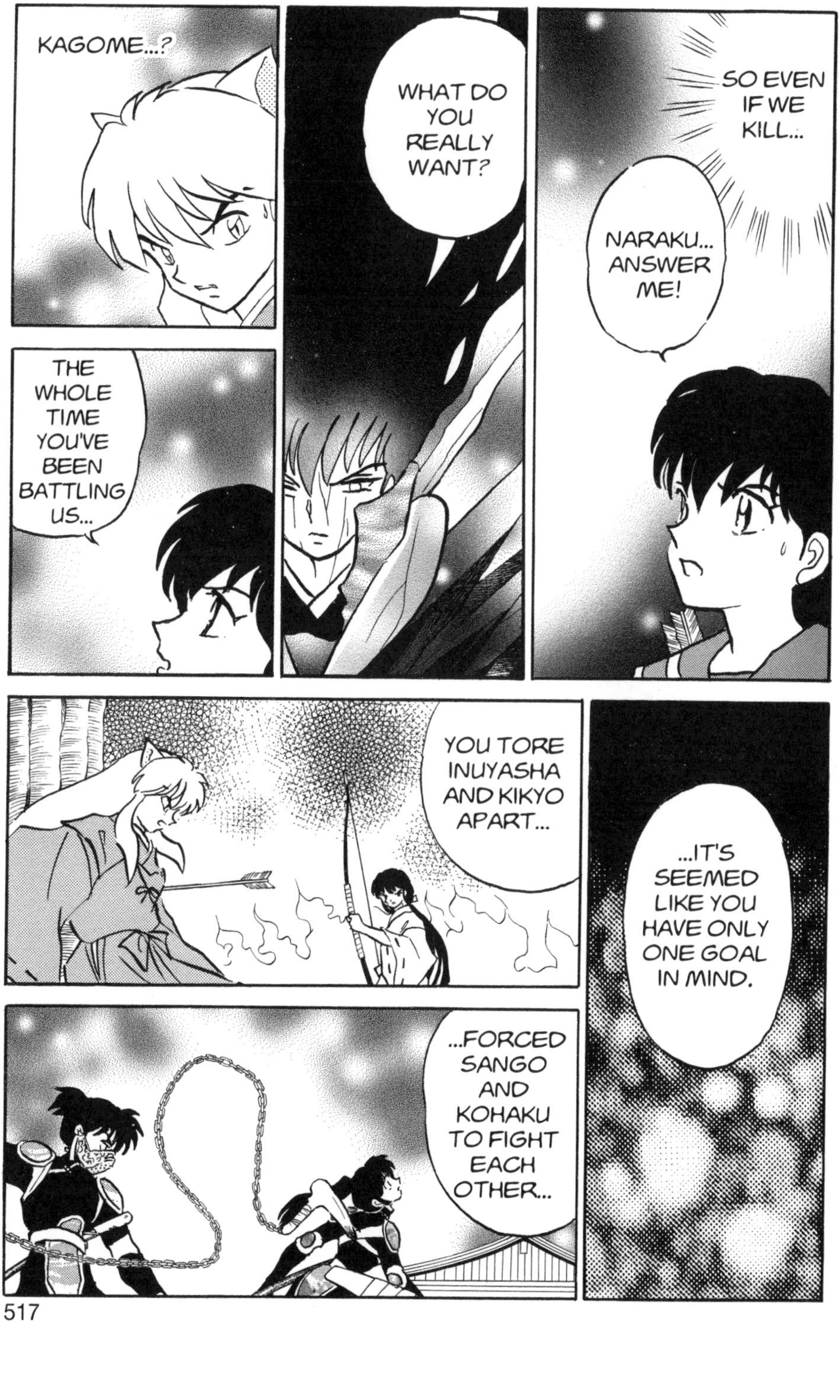
SO EVEN IF WE KILL...
NARAKU... ANSWER ME!
WHAT DO YOU REALLY WANT?
KAGOME...?
THE WHOLE TIME YOU'VE BEEN BATTLING US...
...IT'S SEEMED LIKE YOU HAVE ONLY ONE GOAL IN MIND.
YOU TORE INUYASHA AND KIKYO APART...
...FORCED SANGO AND KOHAKU TO FIGHT EACH OTHER...

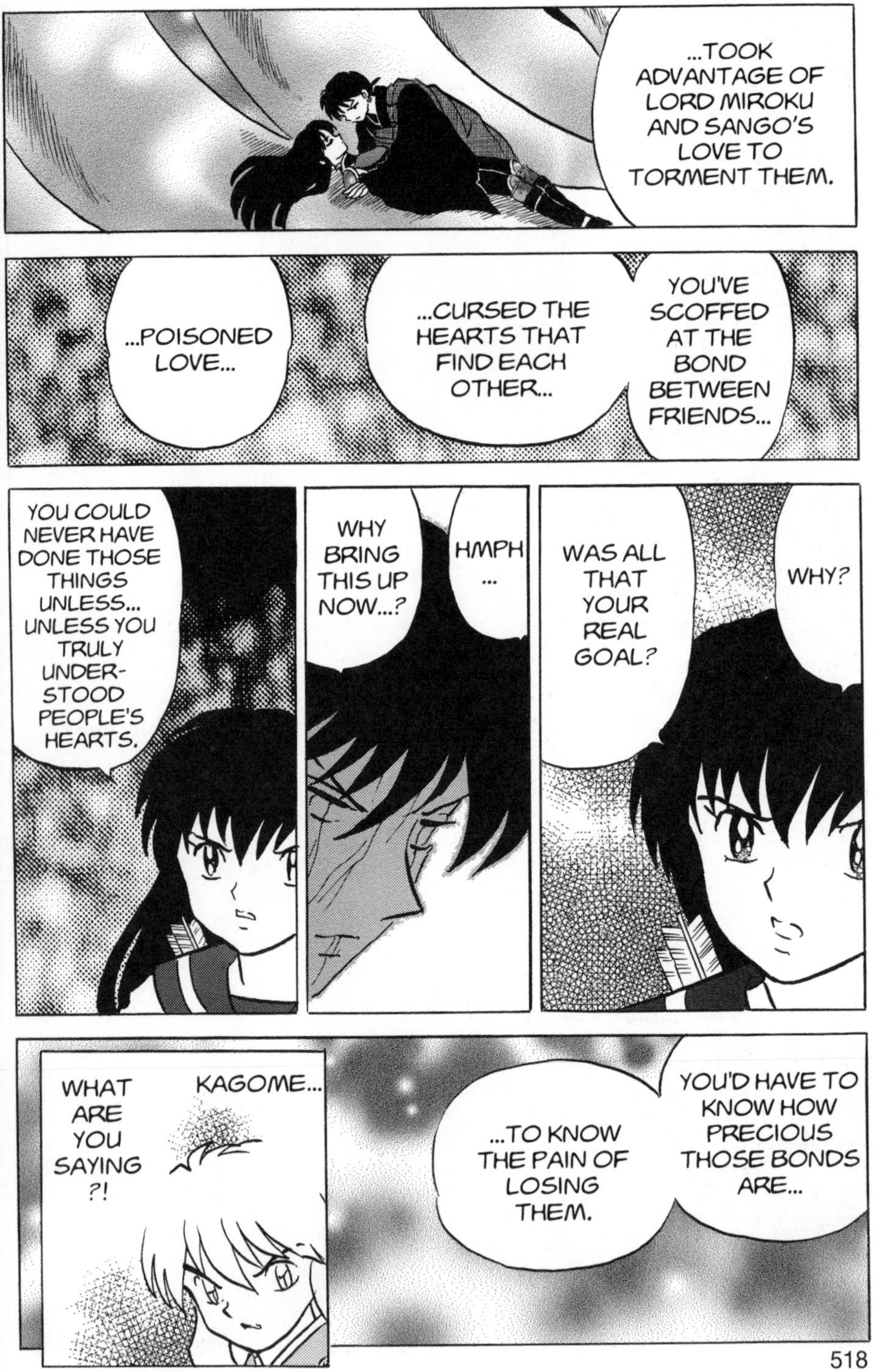
...TOOK ADVANTAGE OF LORD MIROKU AND SANGO'S LOVE TO TORMENT THEM.
YOU'VE SCOFFED AT THE BOND BETWEEN FRIENDS...
...CURSED THE HEARTS THAT FIND EACH OTHER...
...POISONED LOVE...
WHY?
WAS ALL THAT YOUR REAL GOAL?
HMPH ...
WHY BRING THIS UP NOW...?
YOU COULD NEVER HAVE DONE THOSE THINGS UNLESS... UNLESS YOU TRULY UNDER-STOOD PEOPLE'S HEARTS.
YOU'D HAVE TO KNOW HOW PRECIOUS THOSE BONDS ARE...
...TO KNOW THE PAIN OF LOSING THEM.
KAGOME...
WHAT ARE YOU SAYING ?!

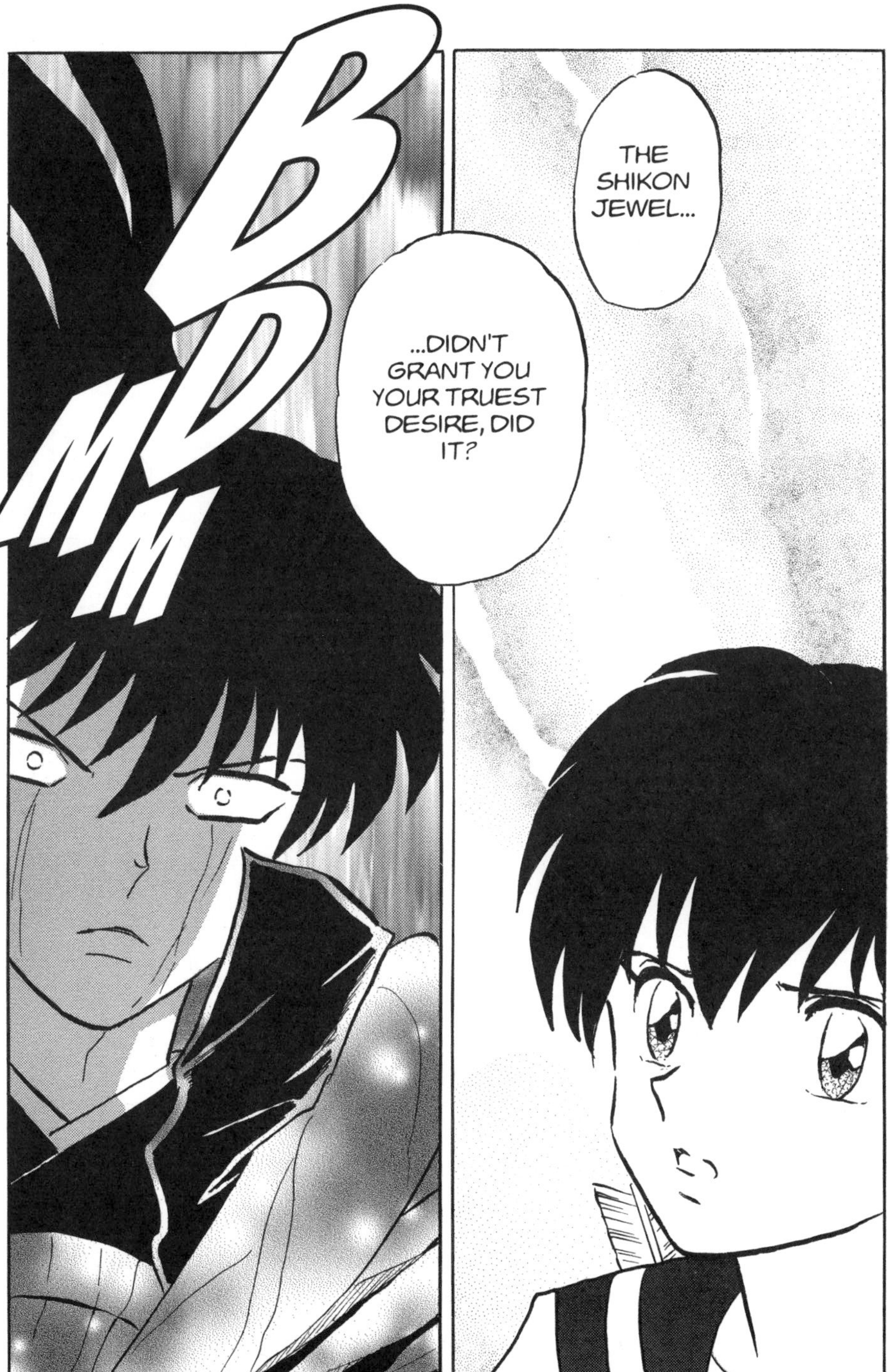
THE SHIKON JEWEL...
...DIDN'T GRANT YOU YOUR TRUEST DESIRE, DID IT?
BDMMM

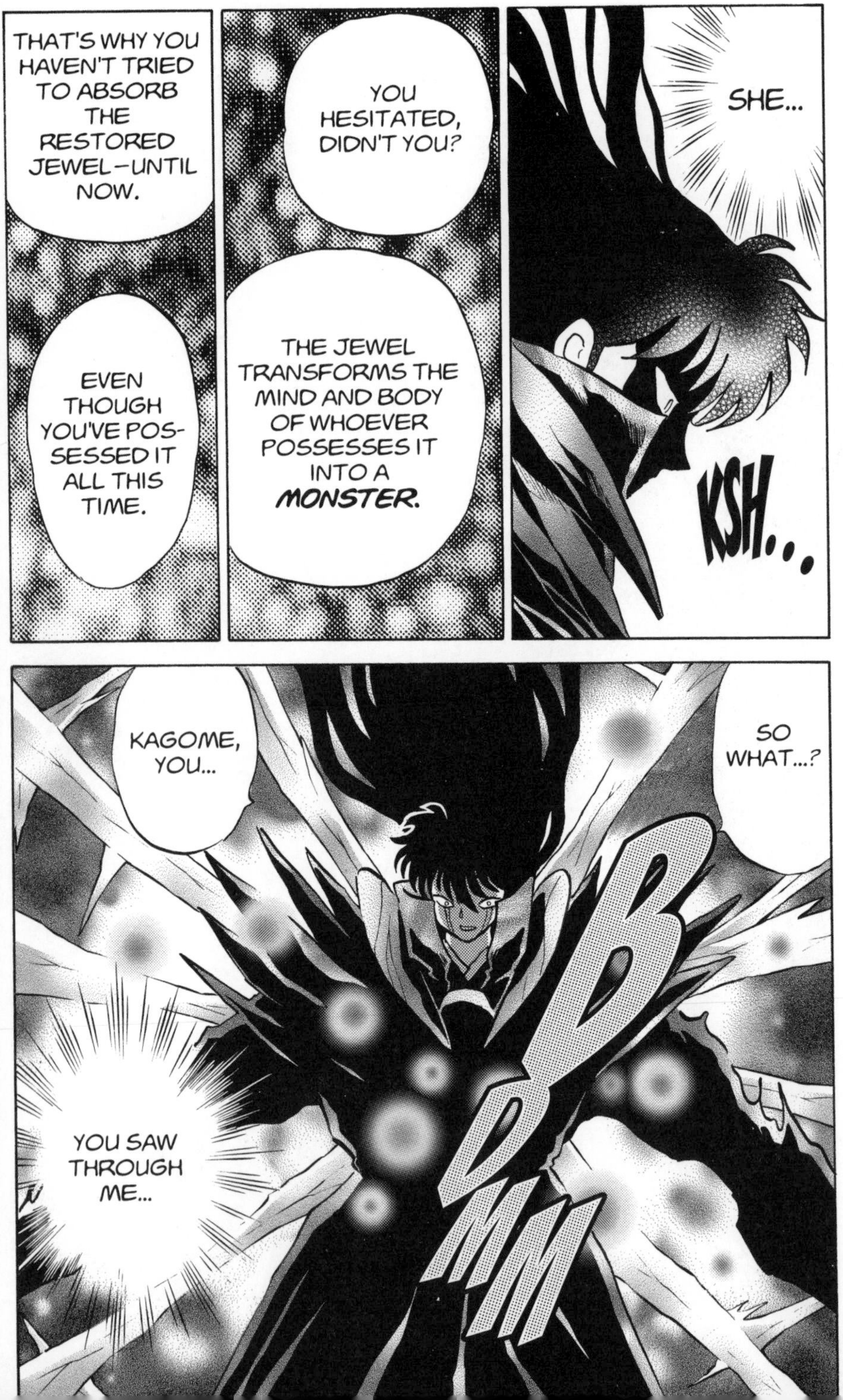
SHE...
KSH...
YOU HESITATED, DIDN'T YOU?
THE JEWEL TRANSFORMS THE MIND AND BODY OF WHOEVER POSSESSES IT INTO A **MONSTER**.
THAT'S WHY YOU HAVEN'T TRIED TO ABSORB THE RESTORED JEWEL—UNTIL NOW.
EVEN THOUGH YOU'VE POS-SESSED IT ALL THIS TIME.
SO WHAT...?
KAGOME, YOU...
YOU SAW THROUGH ME...

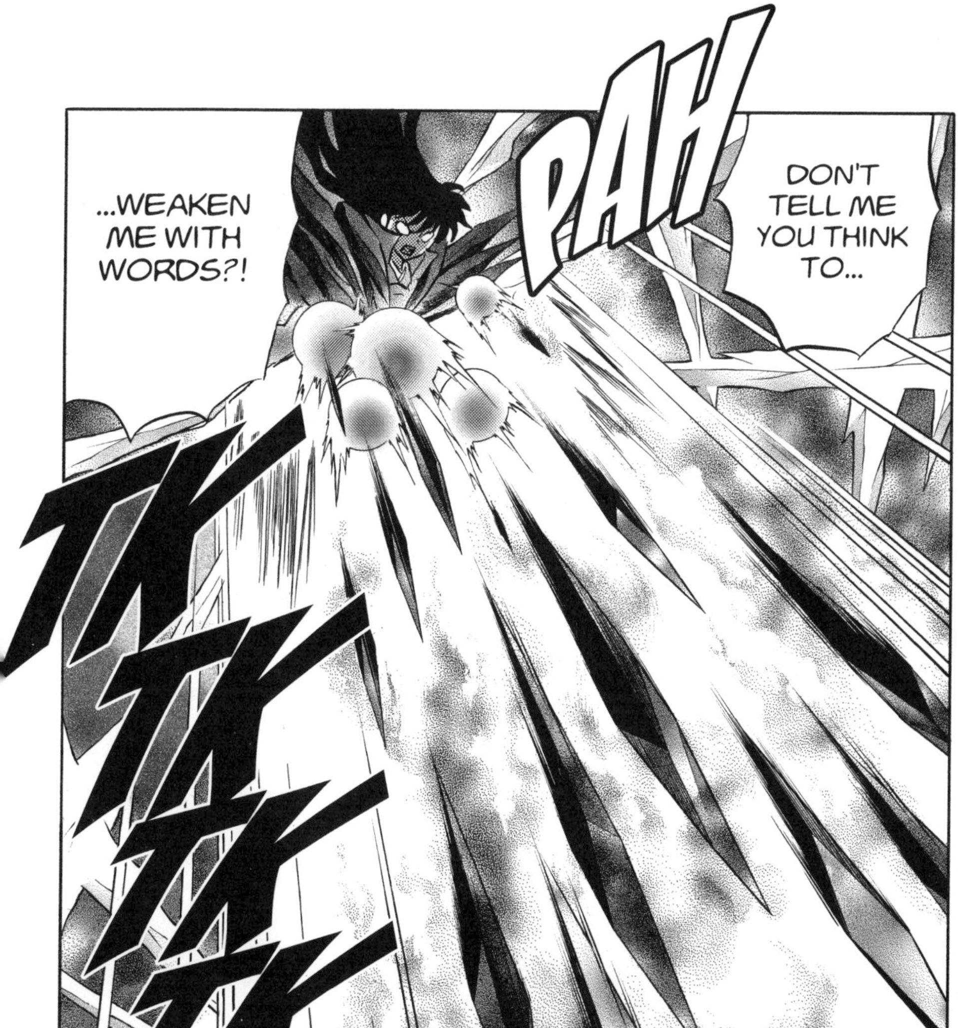
DON'T TELL ME YOU THINK TO...
PAH
...WEAKEN ME WITH WORDS?!

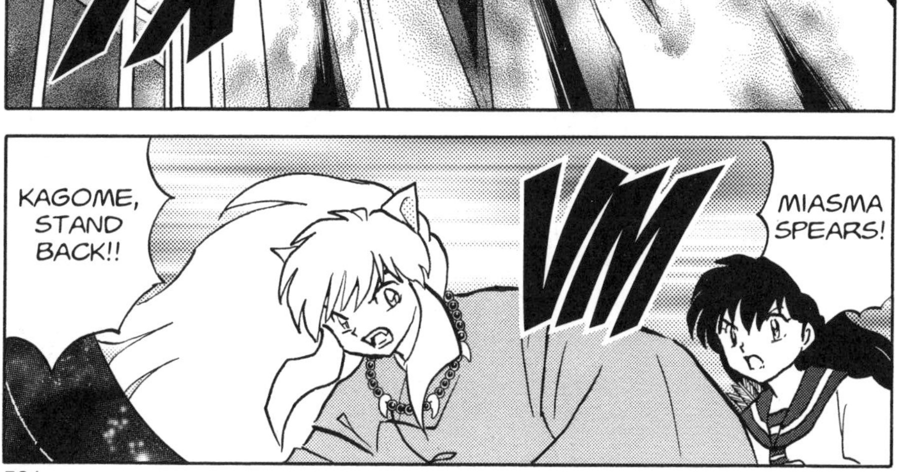
MIASMA SPEARS!
VM
KAGOME, STAND BACK!!

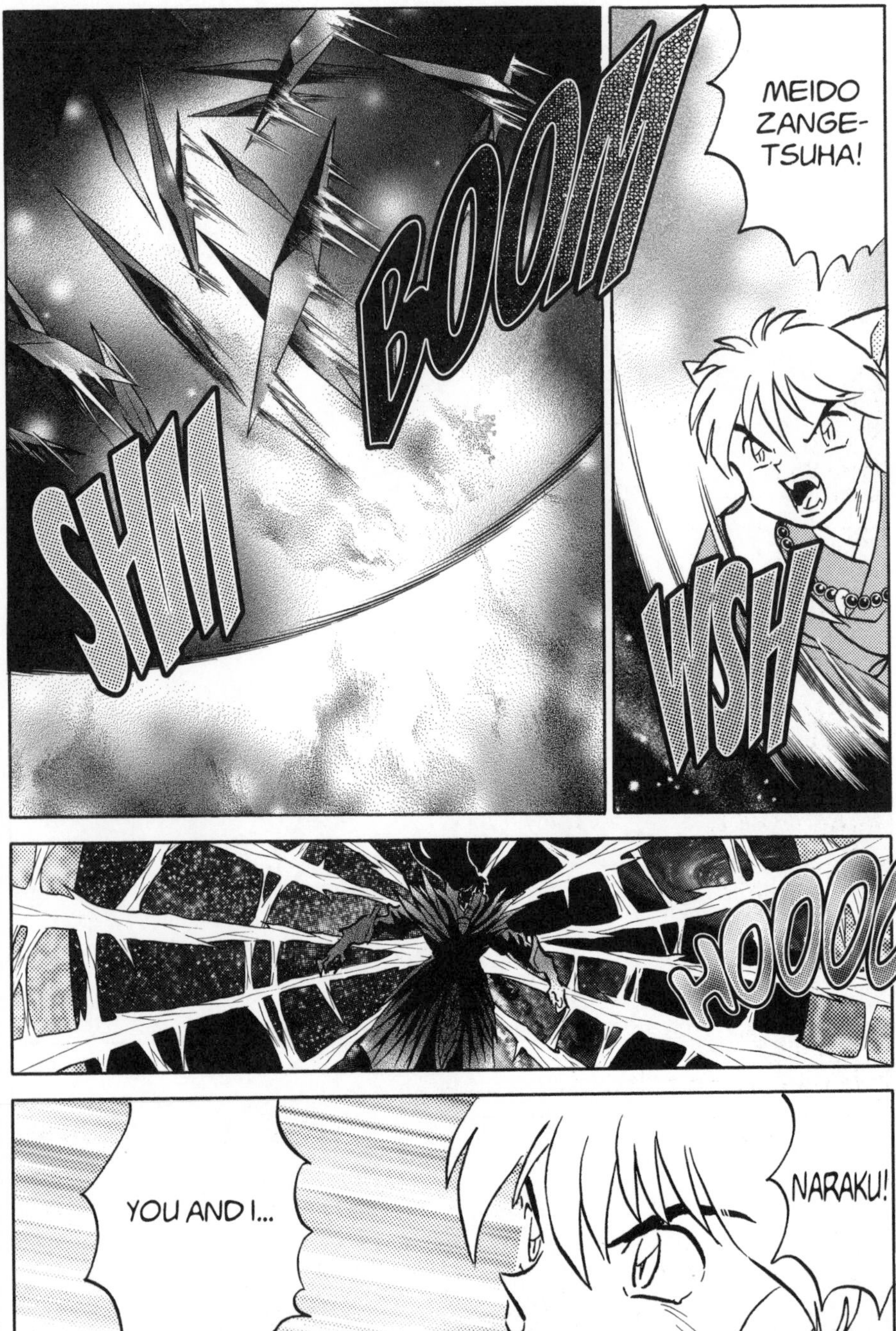
MEIDO ZANGE-TSUHA!
WSH
BOOM
SHM
WOOOO
NARAKU!
YOU AND I...

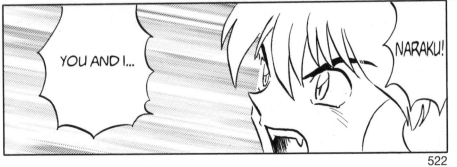

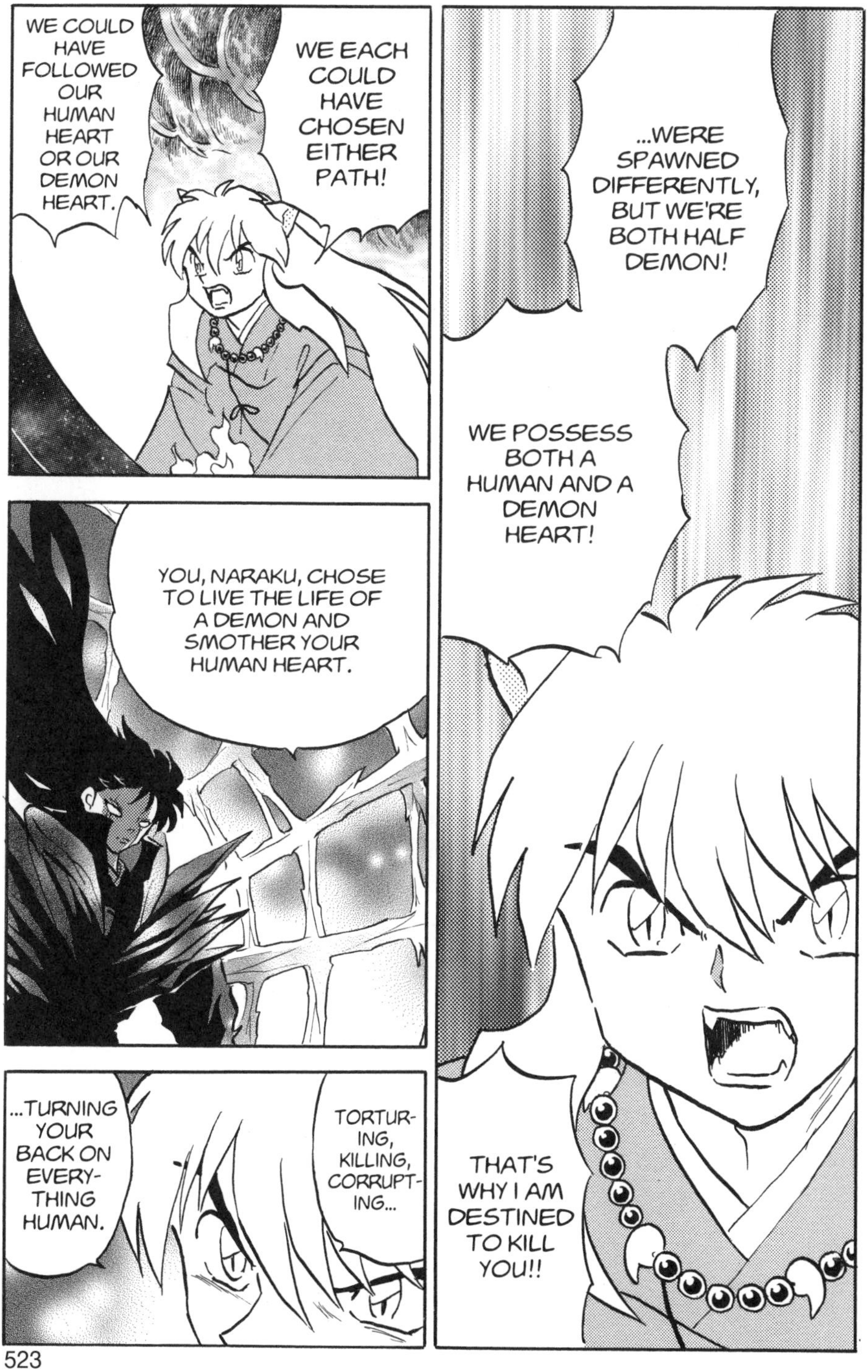
...WERE SPAWNED DIFFERENTLY, BUT WE'RE BOTH HALF DEMON!
WE POSSESS BOTH A HUMAN AND A DEMON HEART!
THAT'S WHY I AM DESTINED TO KILL YOU!!
WE EACH COULD HAVE CHOSEN EITHER PATH!
WE COULD HAVE FOLLOWED OUR HUMAN HEART OR OUR DEMON HEART.
YOU, NARAKU, CHOSE TO LIVE THE LIFE OF A DEMON AND SMOTHER YOUR HUMAN HEART.
TORTUR-ING, KILLING, CORRUPT-ING...
...TURNING YOUR BACK ON EVERY-THING HUMAN.

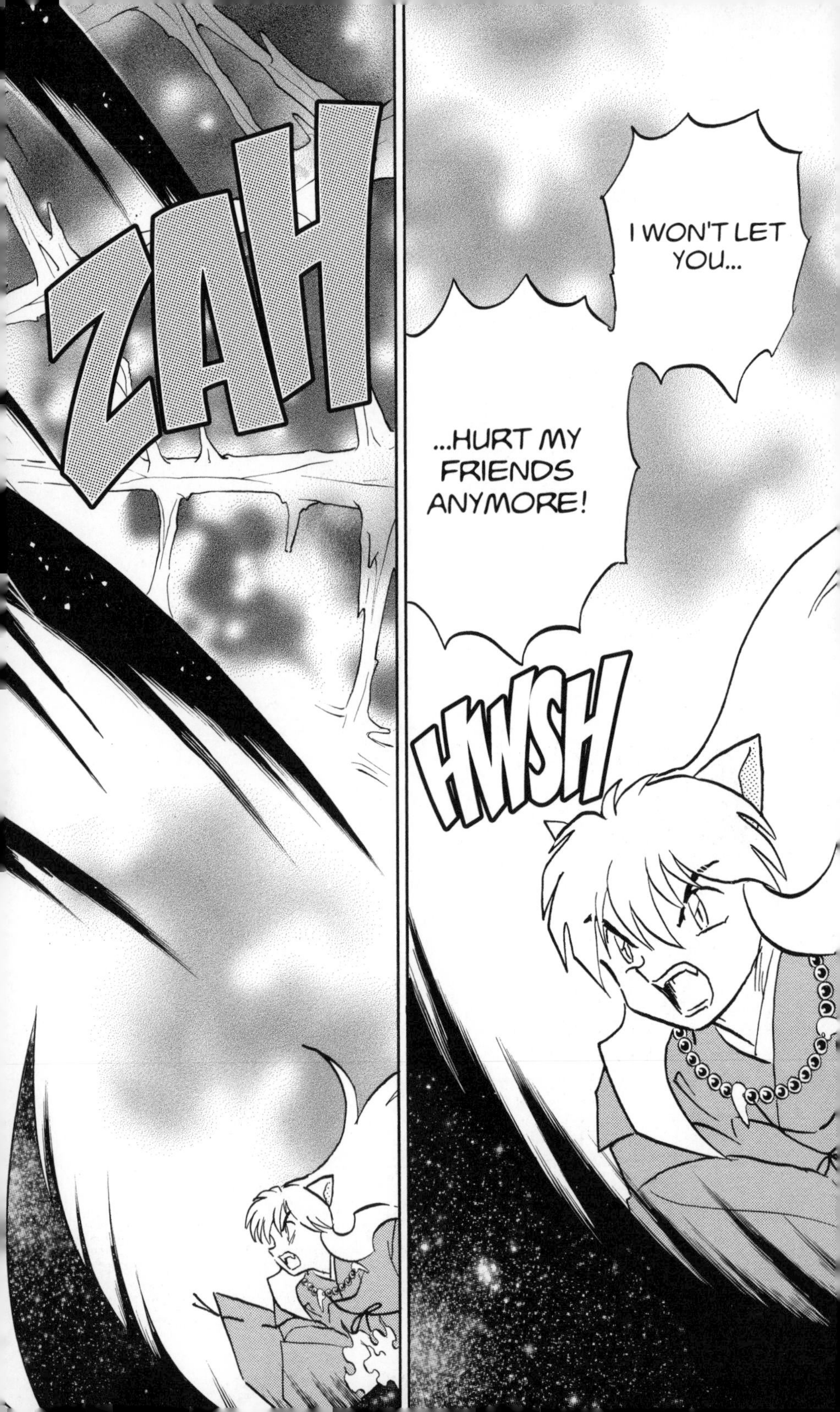
I WON'T LET YOU...
...HURT MY FRIENDS ANYMORE!
HWSH
ZAH

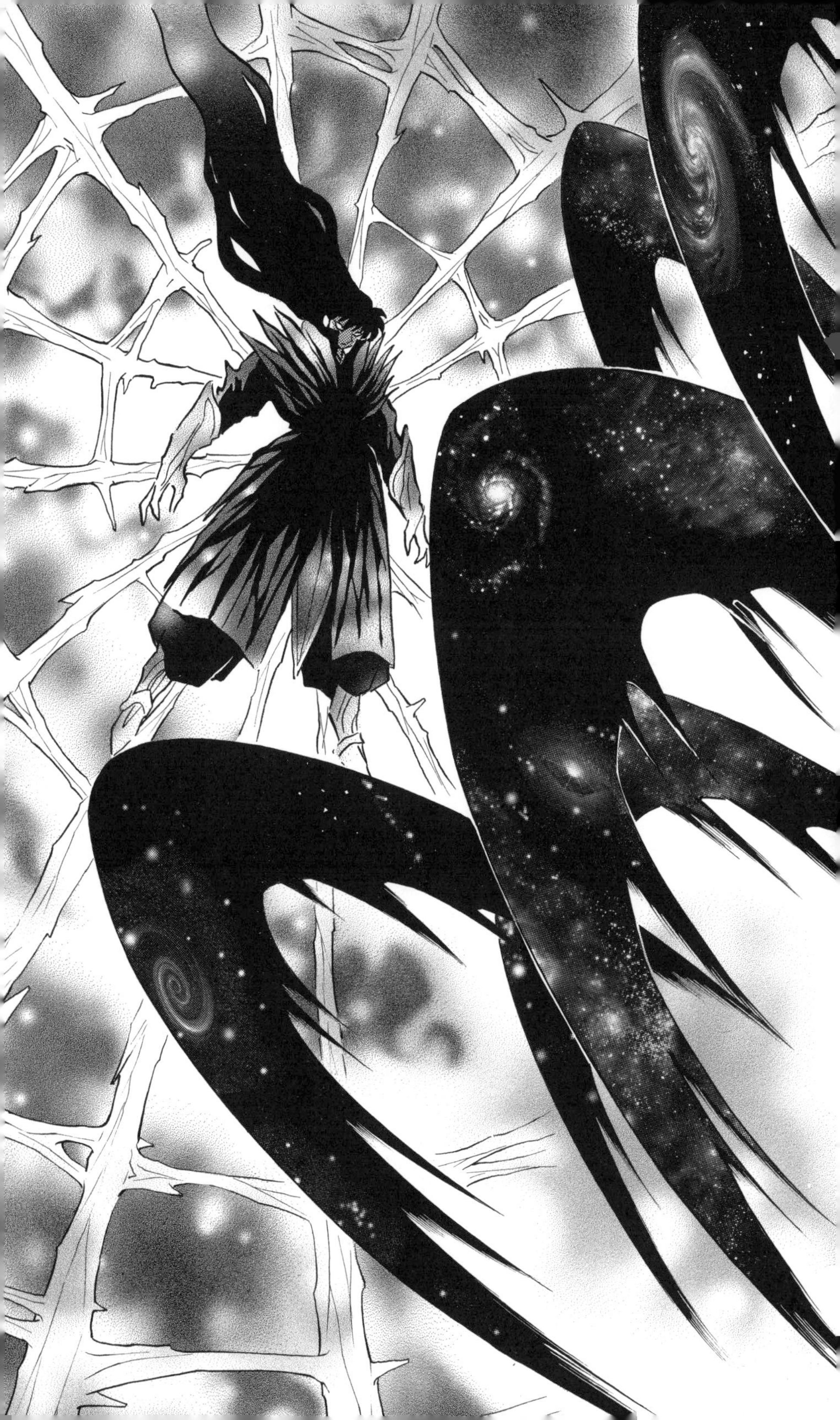

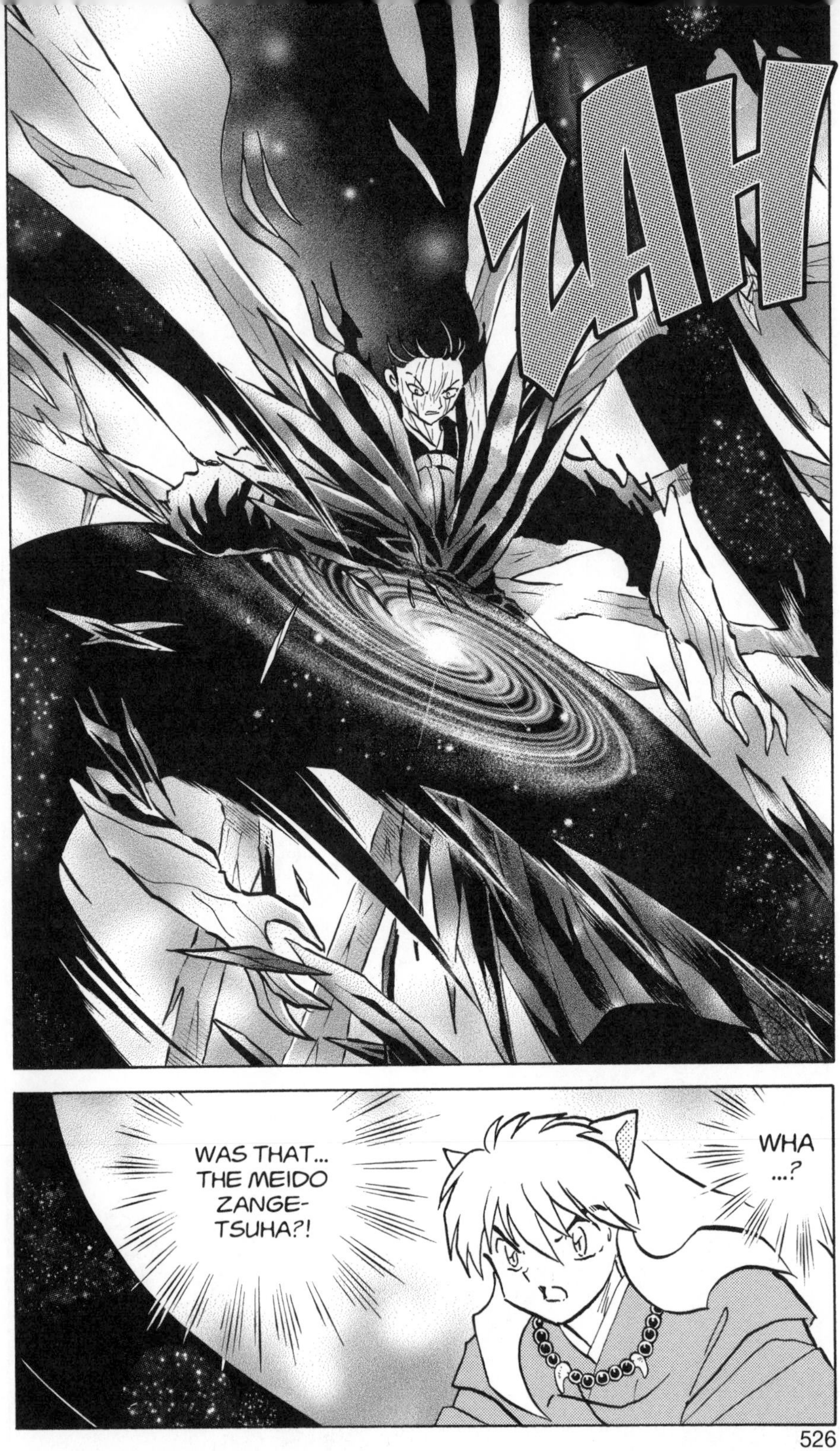
ZAH
WHA ...?
WAS THAT... THE MEIDO ZANGE-TSUHA?!

SCROLL NINE
A CUTTING MEIDO

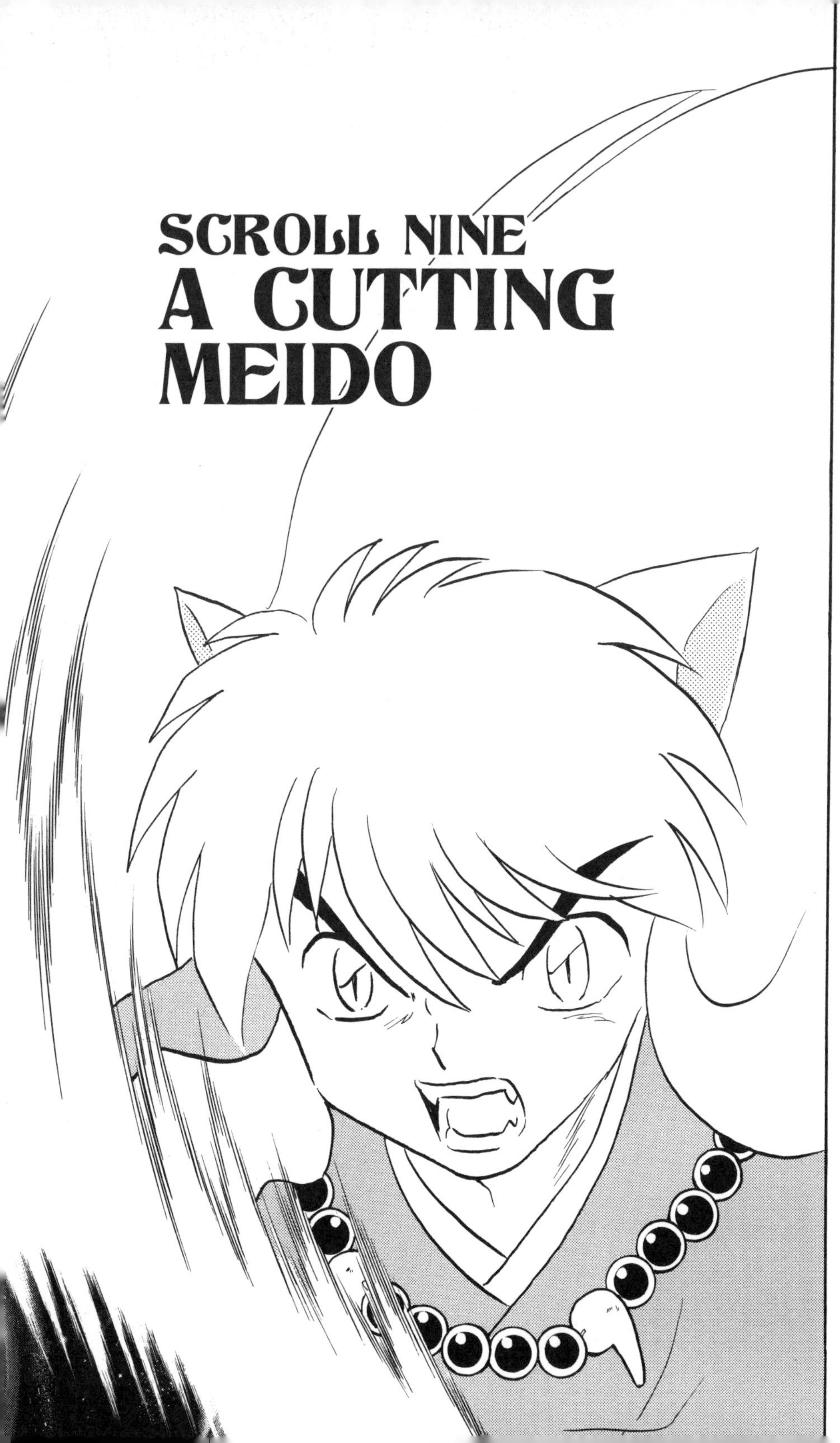

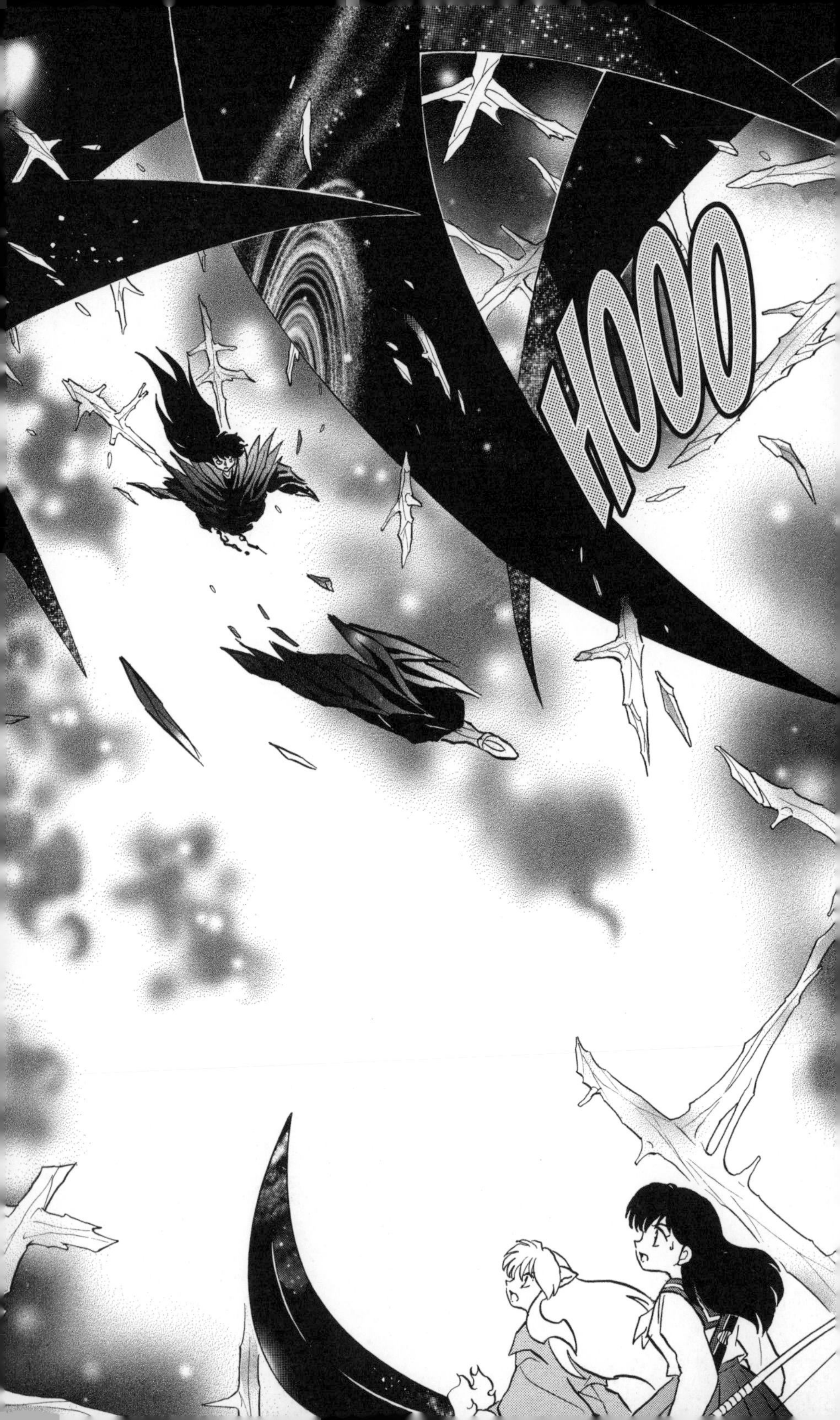
HOOO

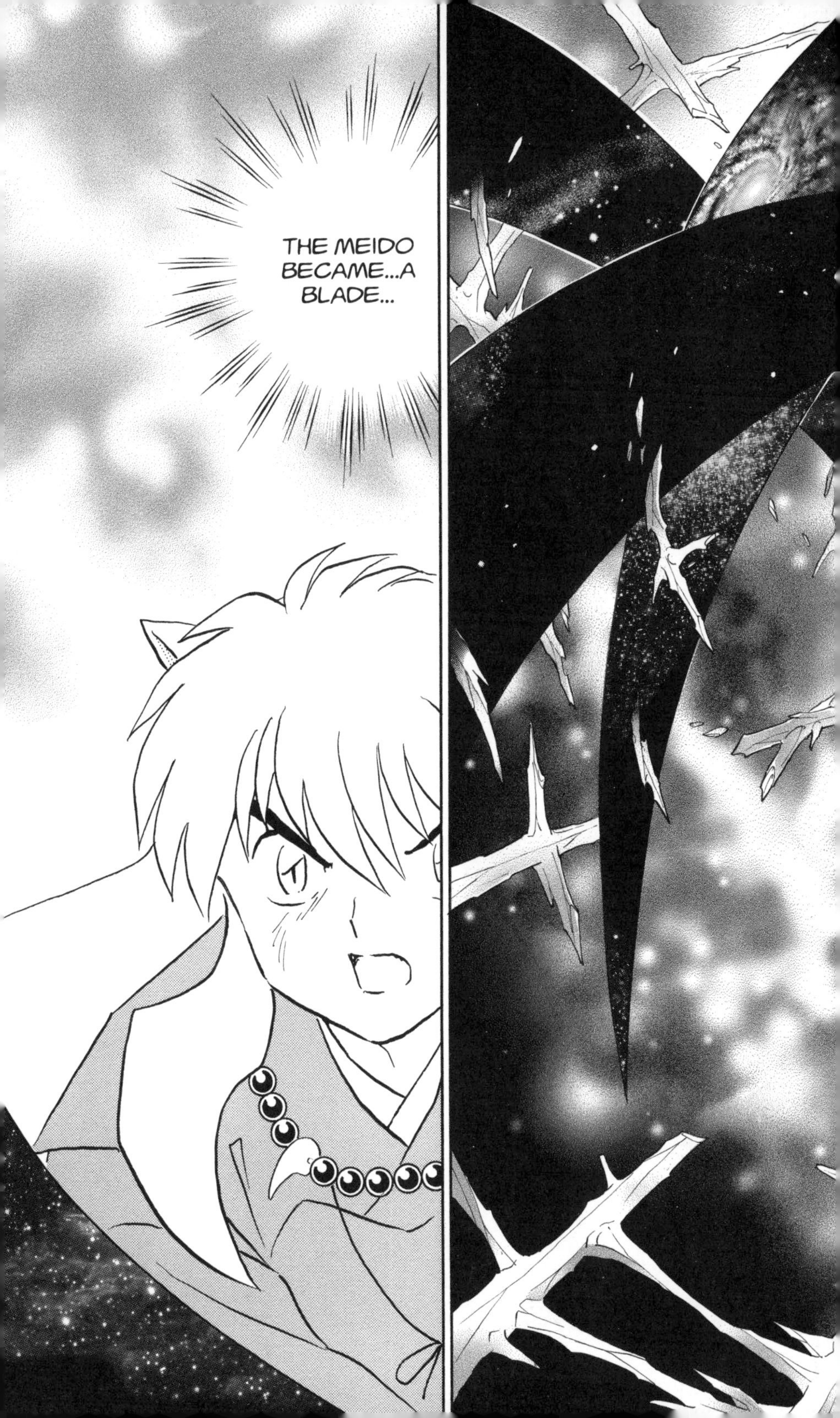
THE MEIDO BECAME...A BLADE...

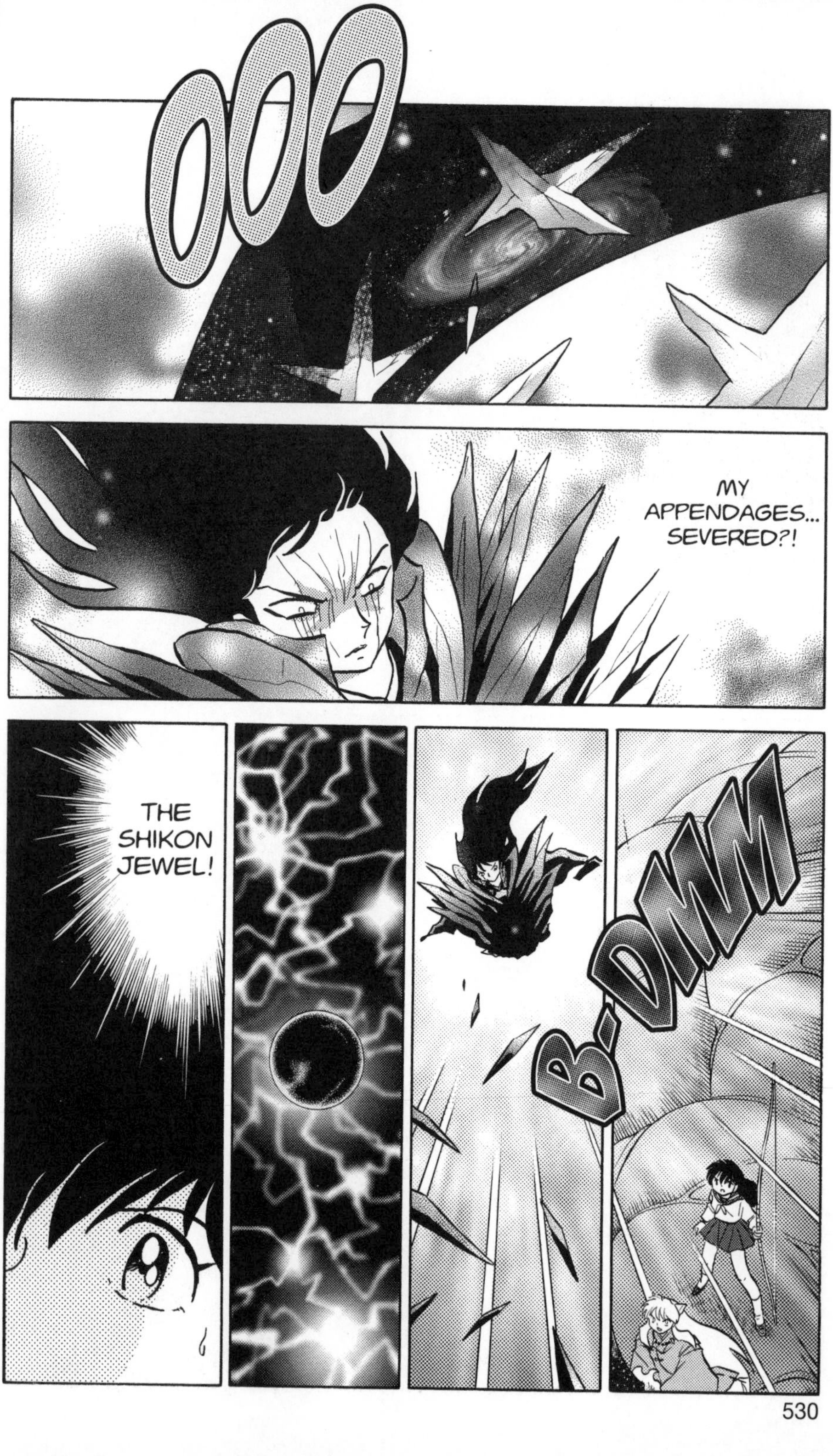
OOO
MY APPENDAGES... SEVERED?!
B-DMMM
THE SHIKON JEWEL!

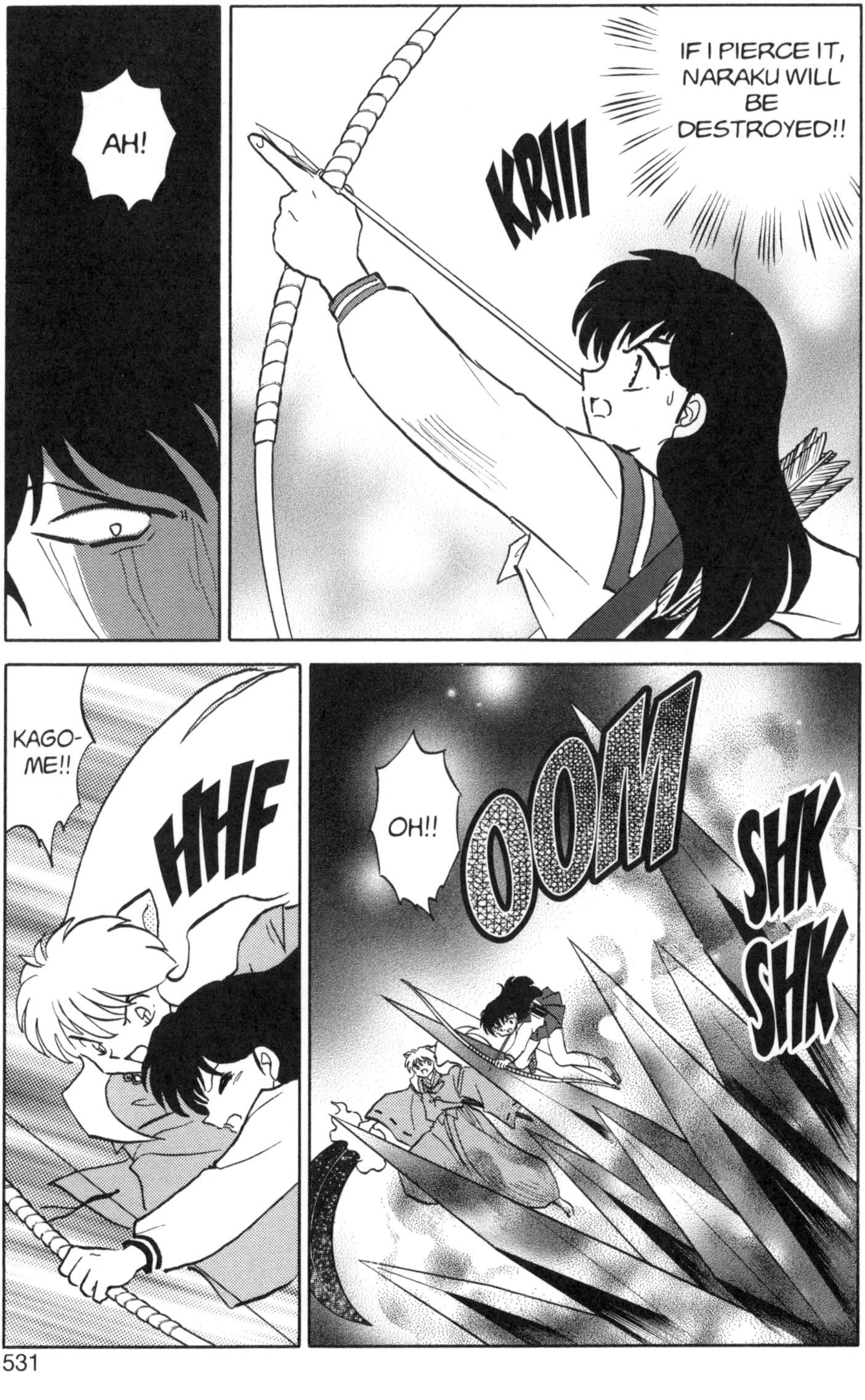
IF I PIERCE IT, NARAKU WILL BE DESTROYED!!
KRIII
AH!
OOM
SHK
SHK
OH!!
KAGO-ME!!
HHF

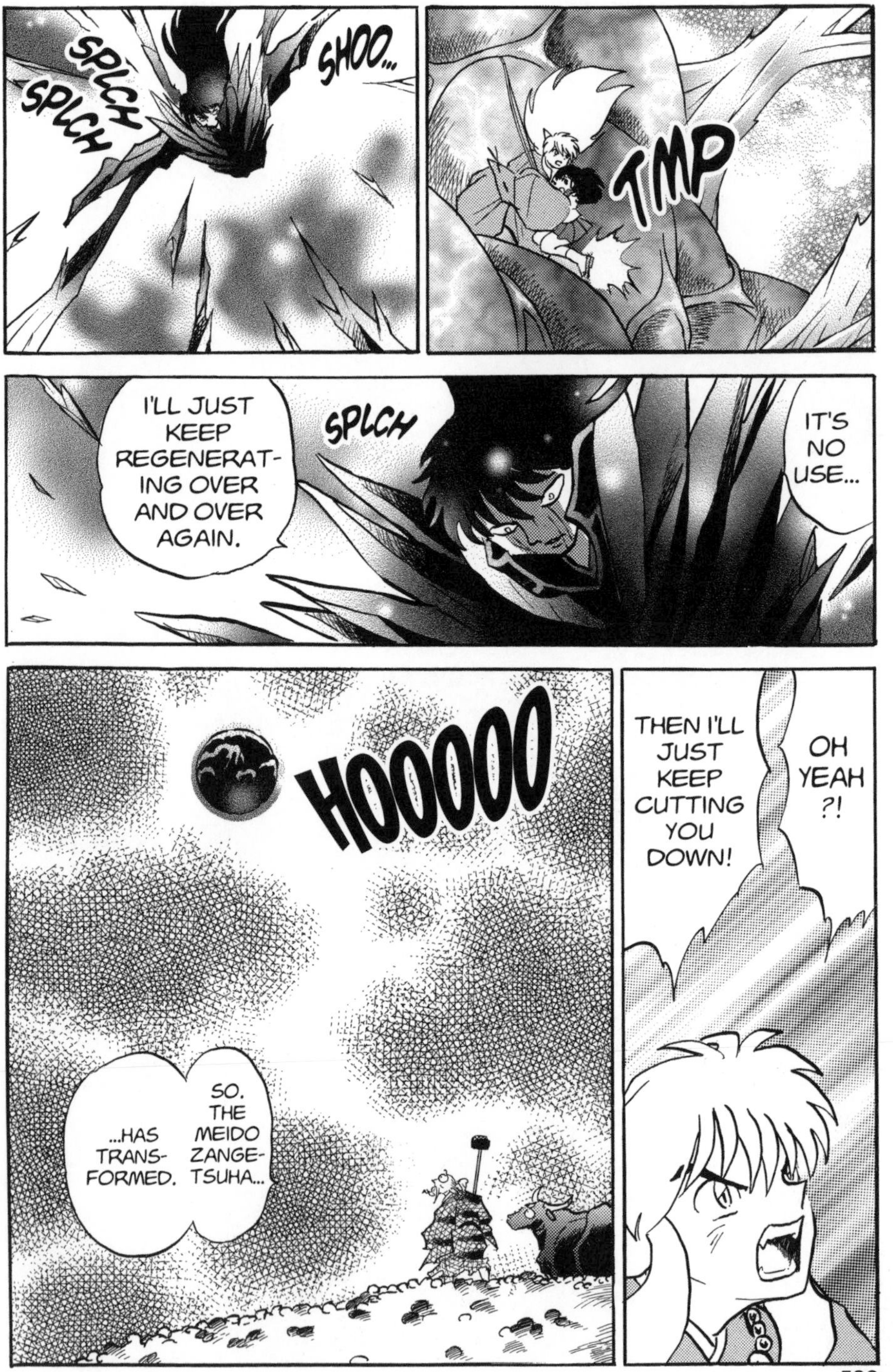
TMP
SHOO...
SPLCH SPLCH
IT'S NO USE...
SPLCH
I'LL JUST KEEP REGENERATING OVER AND OVER AGAIN.
OH YEAH?!
THEN I'LL JUST KEEP CUTTING YOU DOWN!
HOOOOO
SO. THE MEIDO ZANGETSUHA...
...HAS TRANSFORMED.

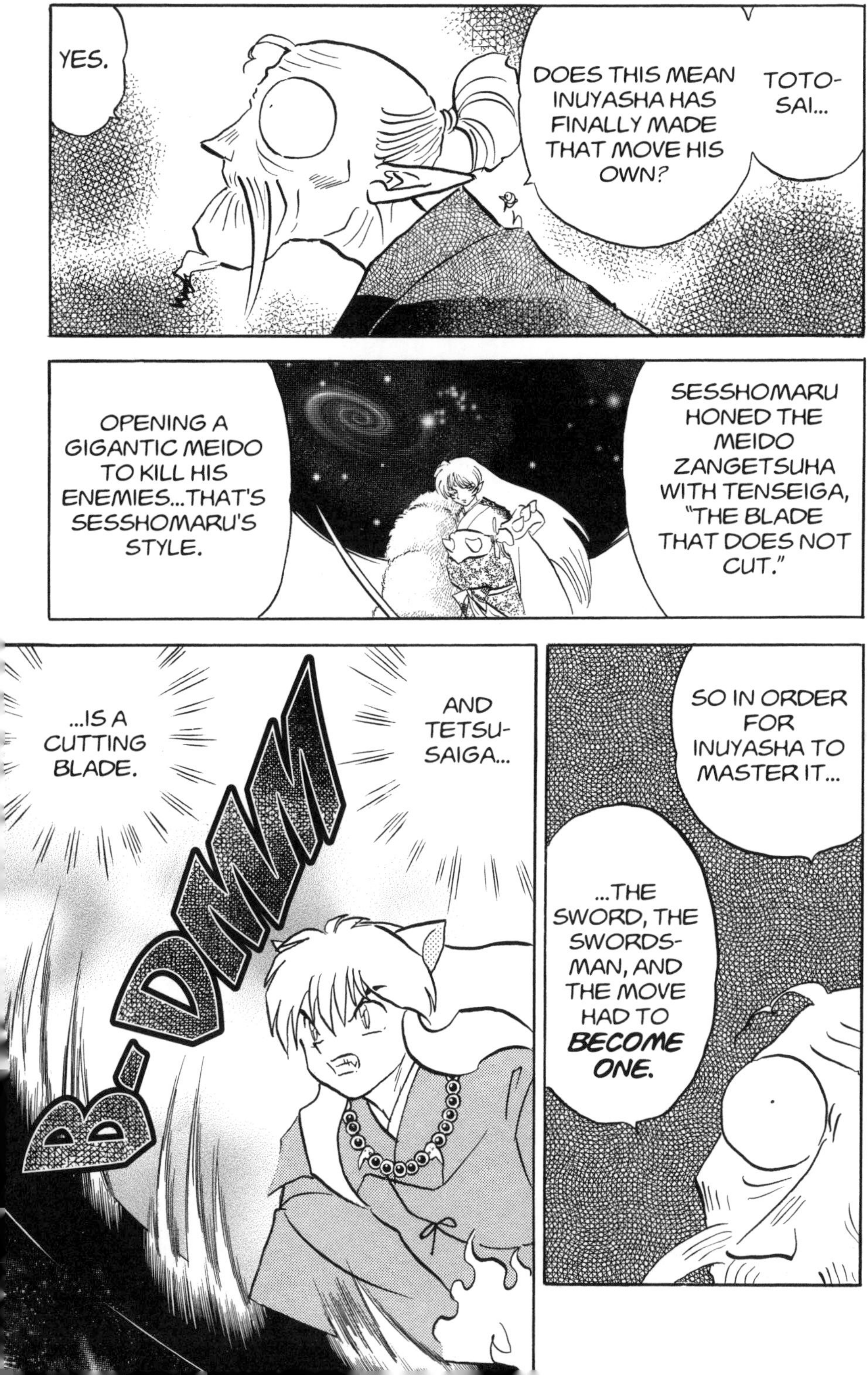
TOTO-SAI...
DOES THIS MEAN INUYASHA HAS FINALLY MADE THAT MOVE HIS OWN?
YES.
SESSHOMARU HONED THE MEIDO ZANGETSUHA WITH TENSEIGA, "THE BLADE THAT DOES NOT CUT."
OPENING A GIGANTIC MEIDO TO KILL HIS ENEMIES...THAT'S SESSHOMARU'S STYLE.
SO IN ORDER FOR INUYASHA TO MASTER IT...
...THE SWORD, THE SWORDS-MAN, AND THE MOVE HAD TO BECOME ONE.
AND TETSU-SAIGA...
...IS A CUTTING BLADE.
B-DMM

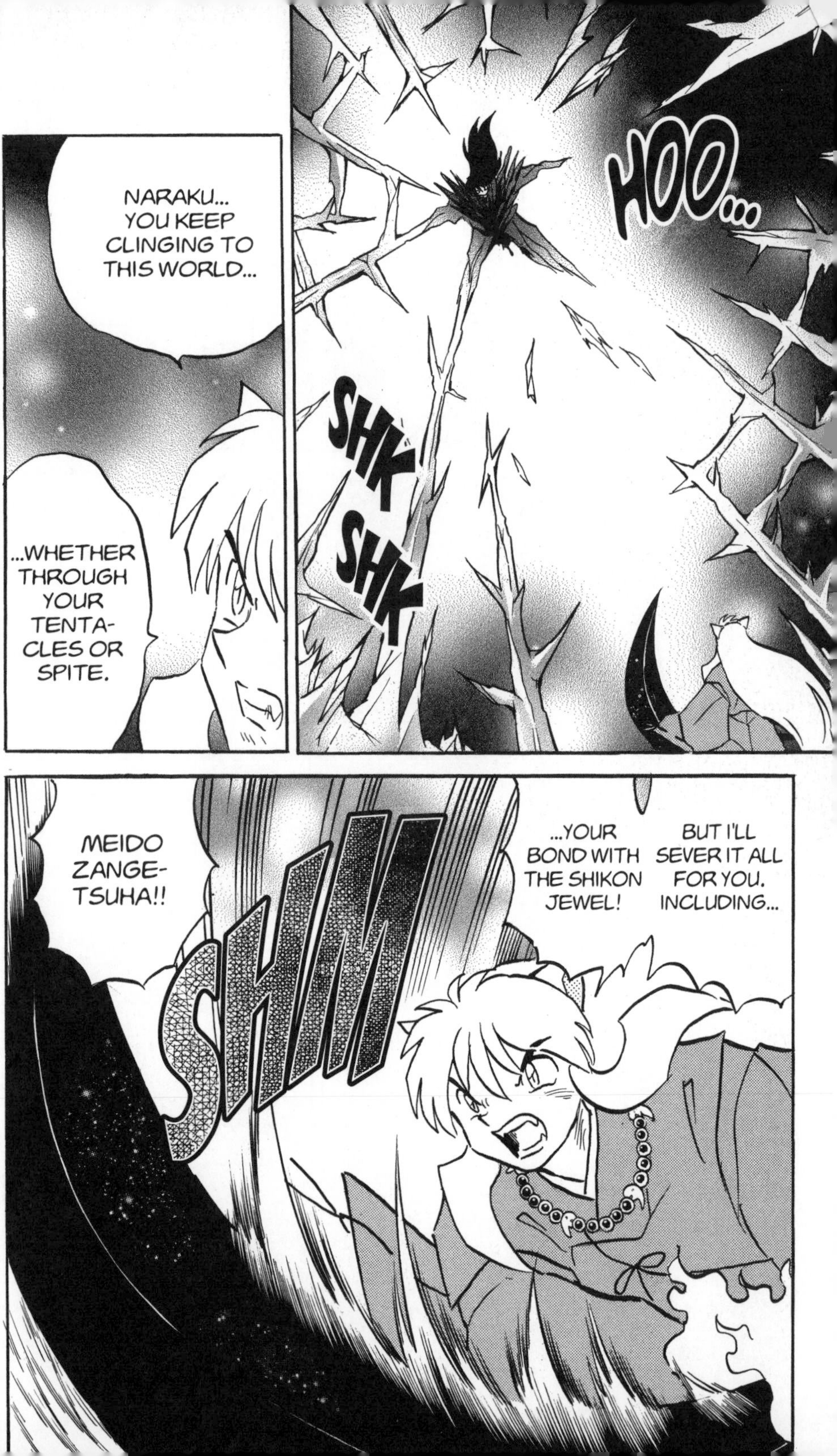
HOO...
SHK SHK
NARAKU... YOU KEEP CLINGING TO THIS WORLD...
...WHETHER THROUGH YOUR TENTA-CLES OR SPITE.
BUT I'LL SEVER IT ALL FOR YOU. INCLUDING...
...YOUR BOND WITH THE SHIKON JEWEL!
MEIDO ZANGE-TSUHA!!
SHIM

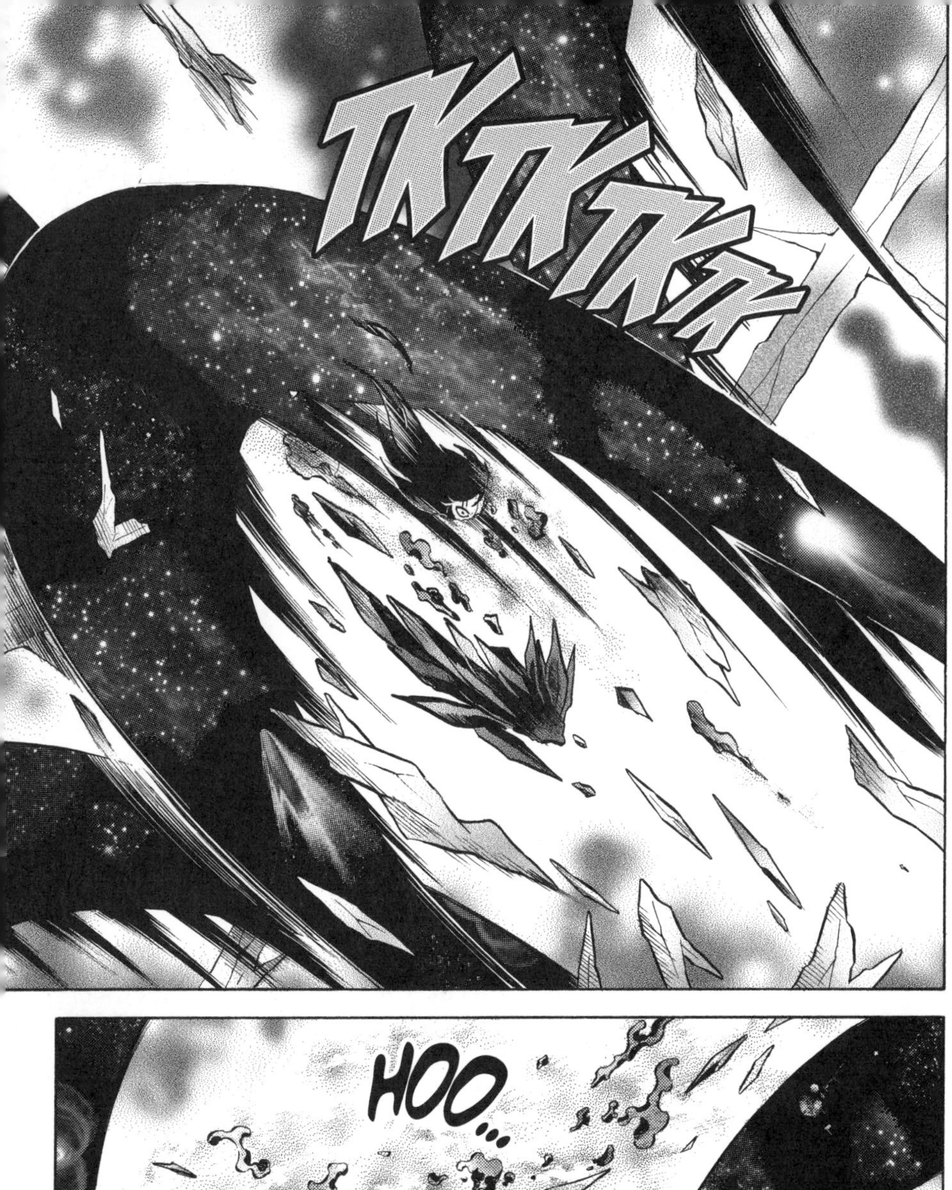
TKTKTKTKTK
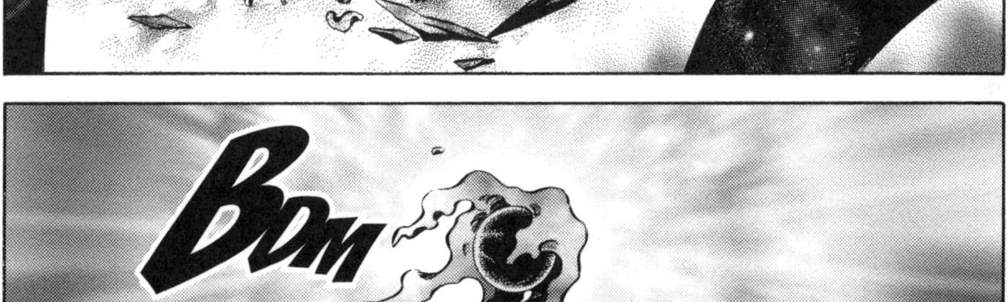
HOO...
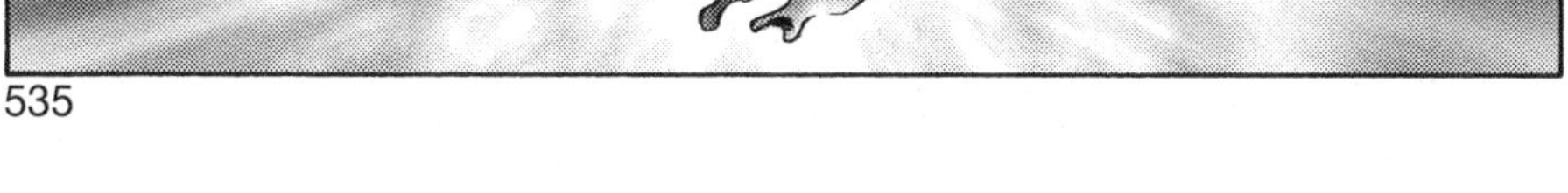
BOM

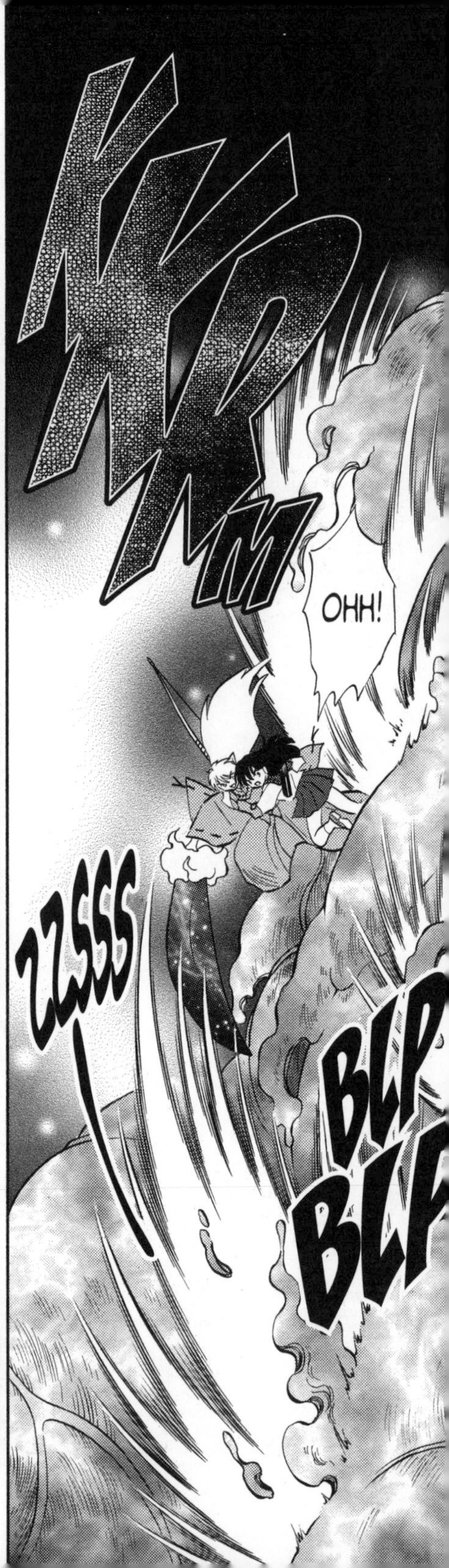
OHH!
ZZSSS
BLP
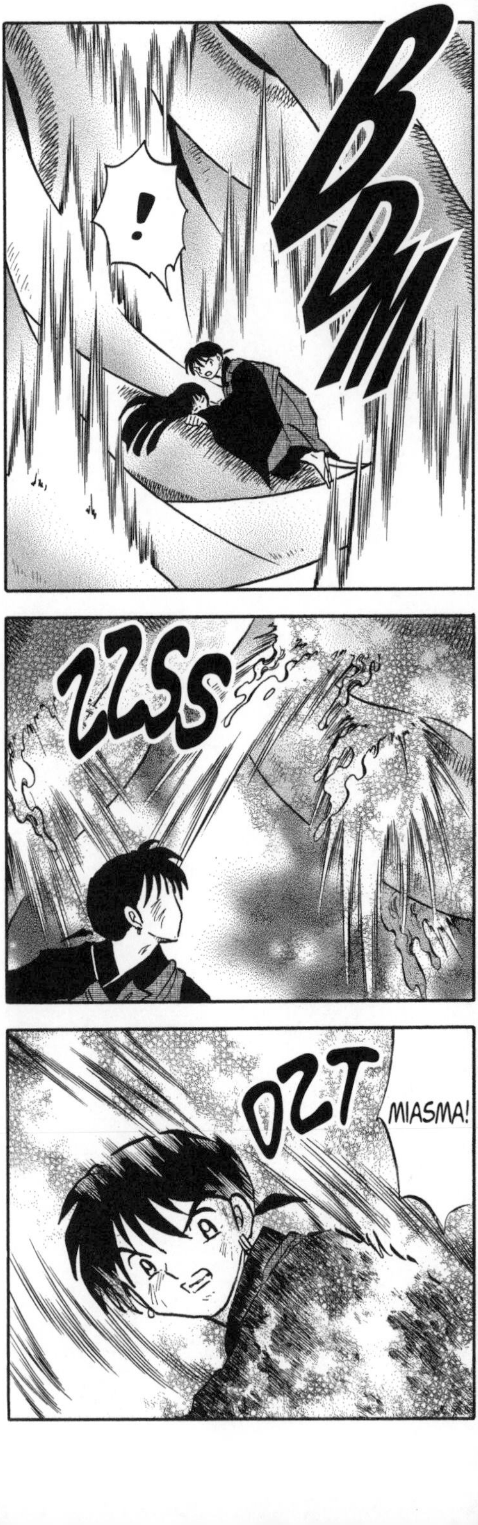
BOOM
!
ZZSS
DZT
MIASMA!

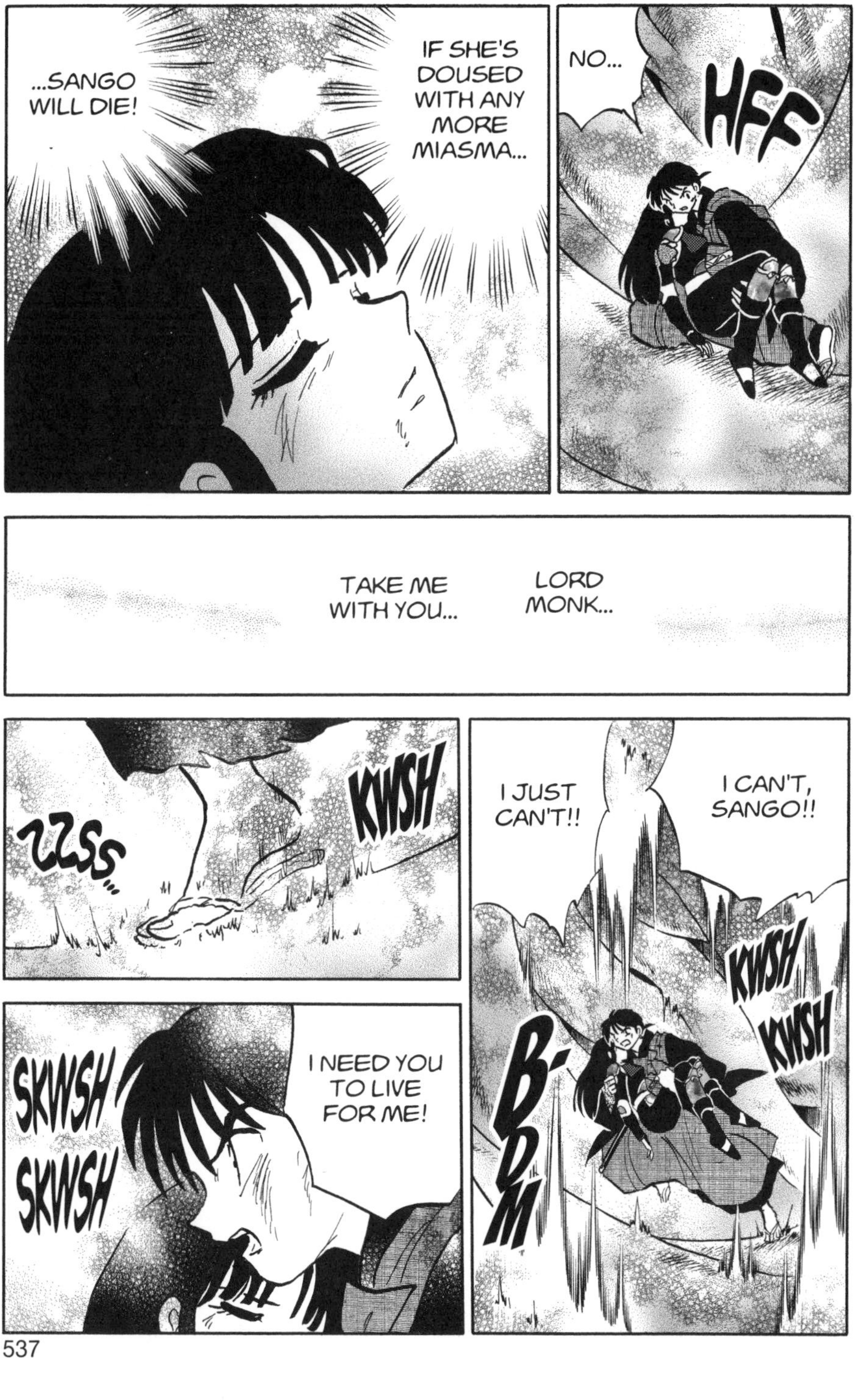
NO...
HFF
IF SHE'S DOUSED WITH ANY MORE MIASMA...
...SANGO WILL DIE!
LORD MONK...
TAKE ME WITH YOU...
I CAN'T, SANGO!!
I JUST CAN'T!!
KWSH
KWSH
B-DOM
KWSH
ZZSS...
I NEED YOU TO LIVE FOR ME!
SKWSH
SKWSH

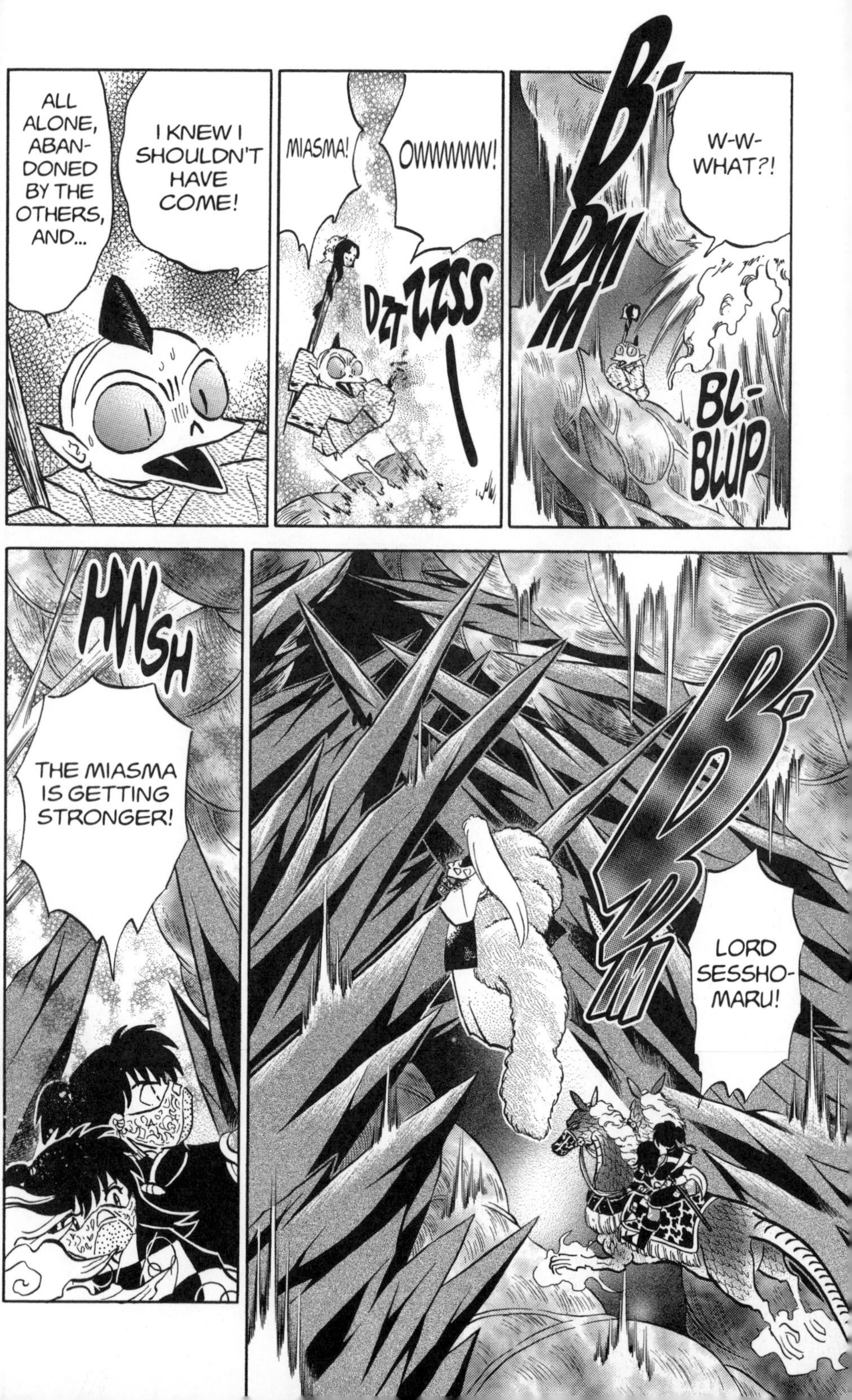
W-W-WHAT?!
B'DMM
BL-BLUP
OWWWWWW!
MIASMA!
DZT ZZSS
I KNEW I SHOULDN'T HAVE COME!
ALL ALONE, ABAN-DONED BY THE OTHERS, AND...
B'BMM
LORD SESSHO-MARU!
HWSH
THE MIASMA IS GETTING STRONGER!

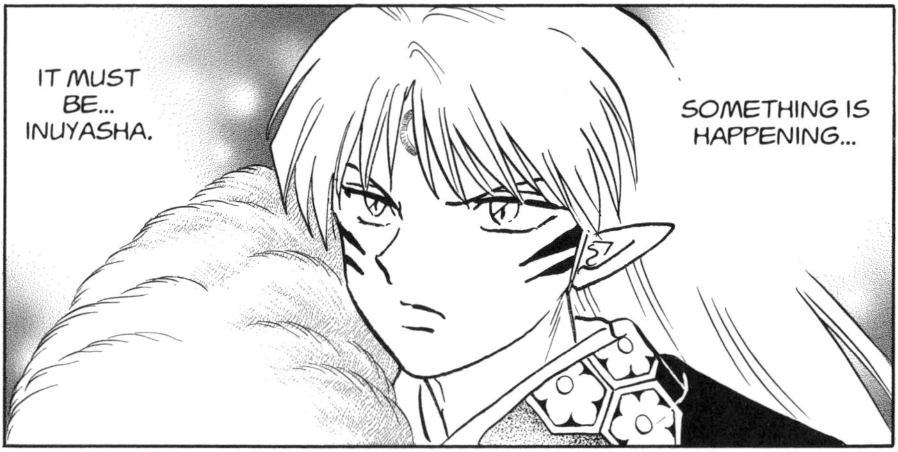
SOMETHING IS HAPPENING...
IT MUST BE... INUYASHA.
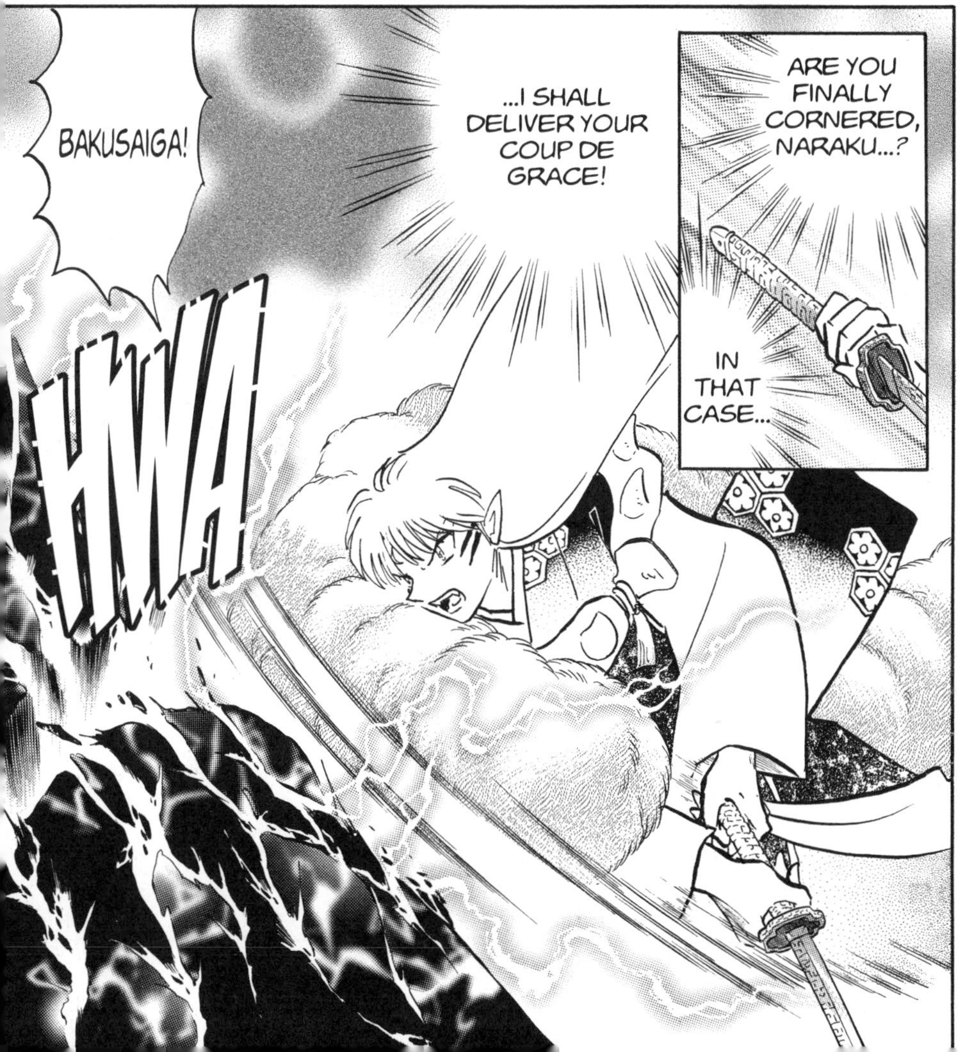
ARE YOU FINALLY CORNERED, NARAKU...?
IN THAT CASE...
...I SHALL DELIVER YOUR COUP DE GRACE!
BAKUSAIGA!
HWA

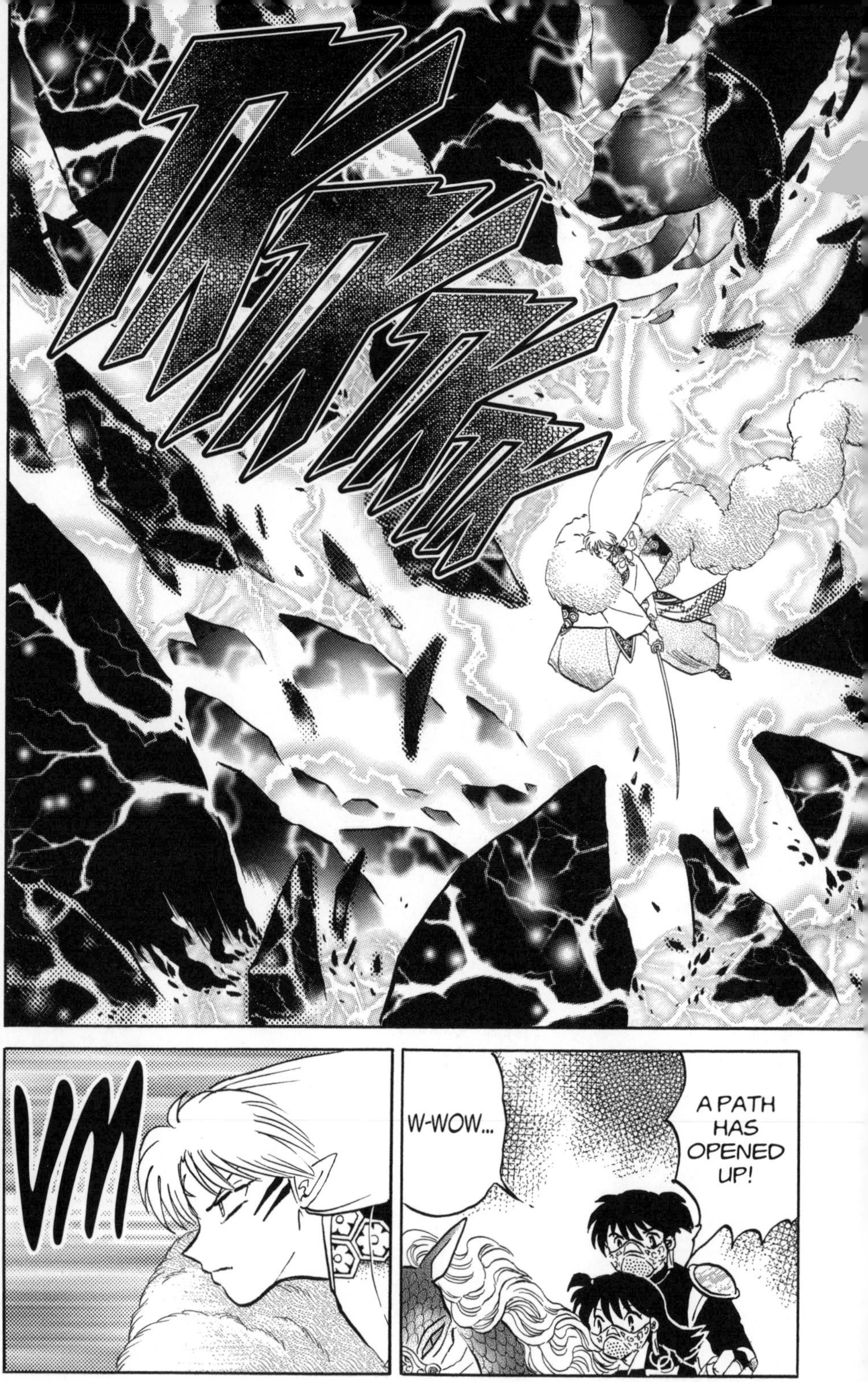
A PATH HAS OPENED UP!
W-WOW...
VM

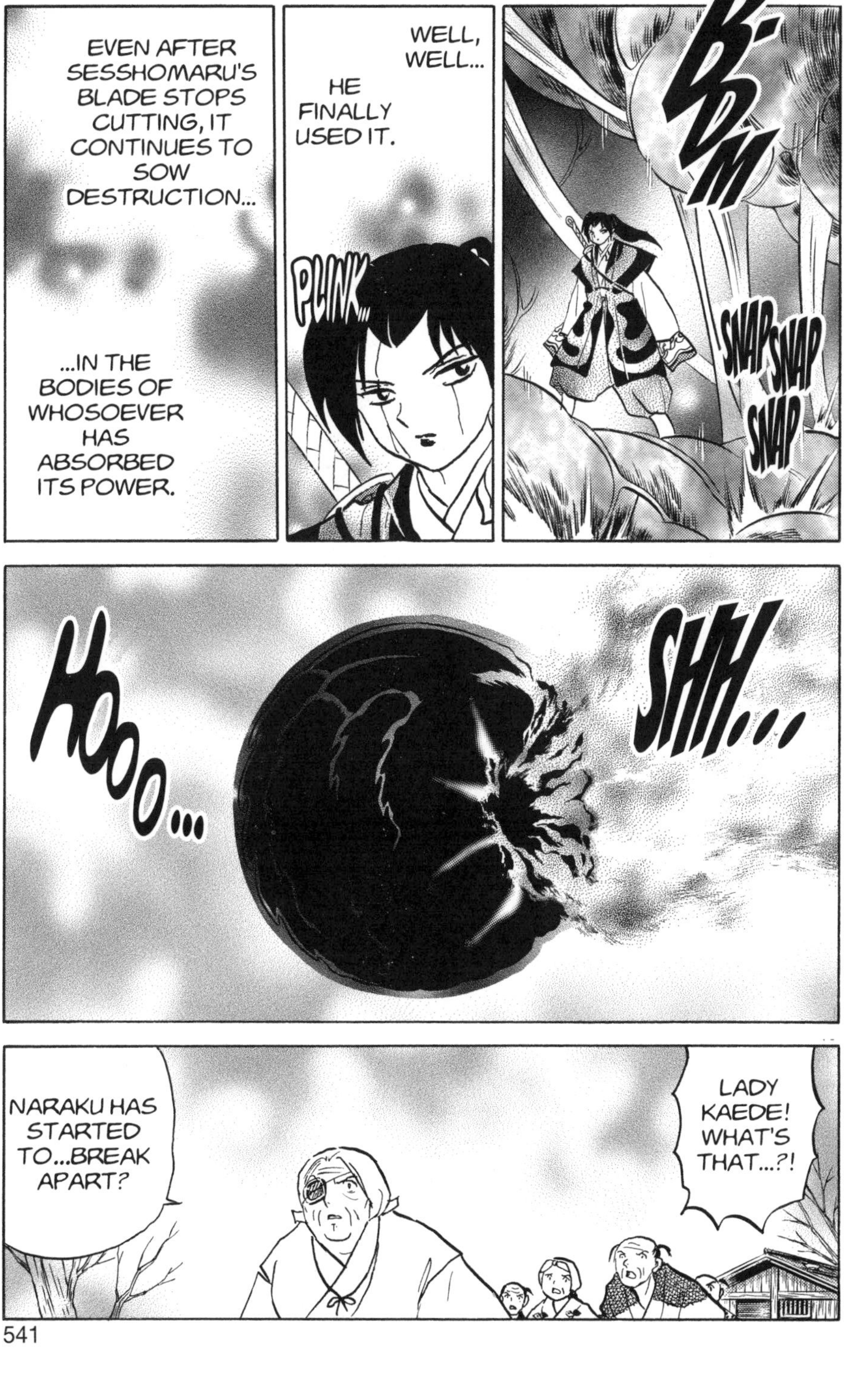
B-DOM
SNAP SNAP
SNAP
WELL, WELL...
HE FINALLY USED IT.
PLINK...
EVEN AFTER SESSHOMARU'S BLADE STOPS CUTTING, IT CONTINUES TO SOW DESTRUCTION...
...IN THE BODIES OF WHOSOEVER HAS ABSORBED ITS POWER.
SHH...
HOOO...
LADY KAEDE! WHAT'S THAT...?!
NARAKU HAS STARTED TO...BREAK APART?

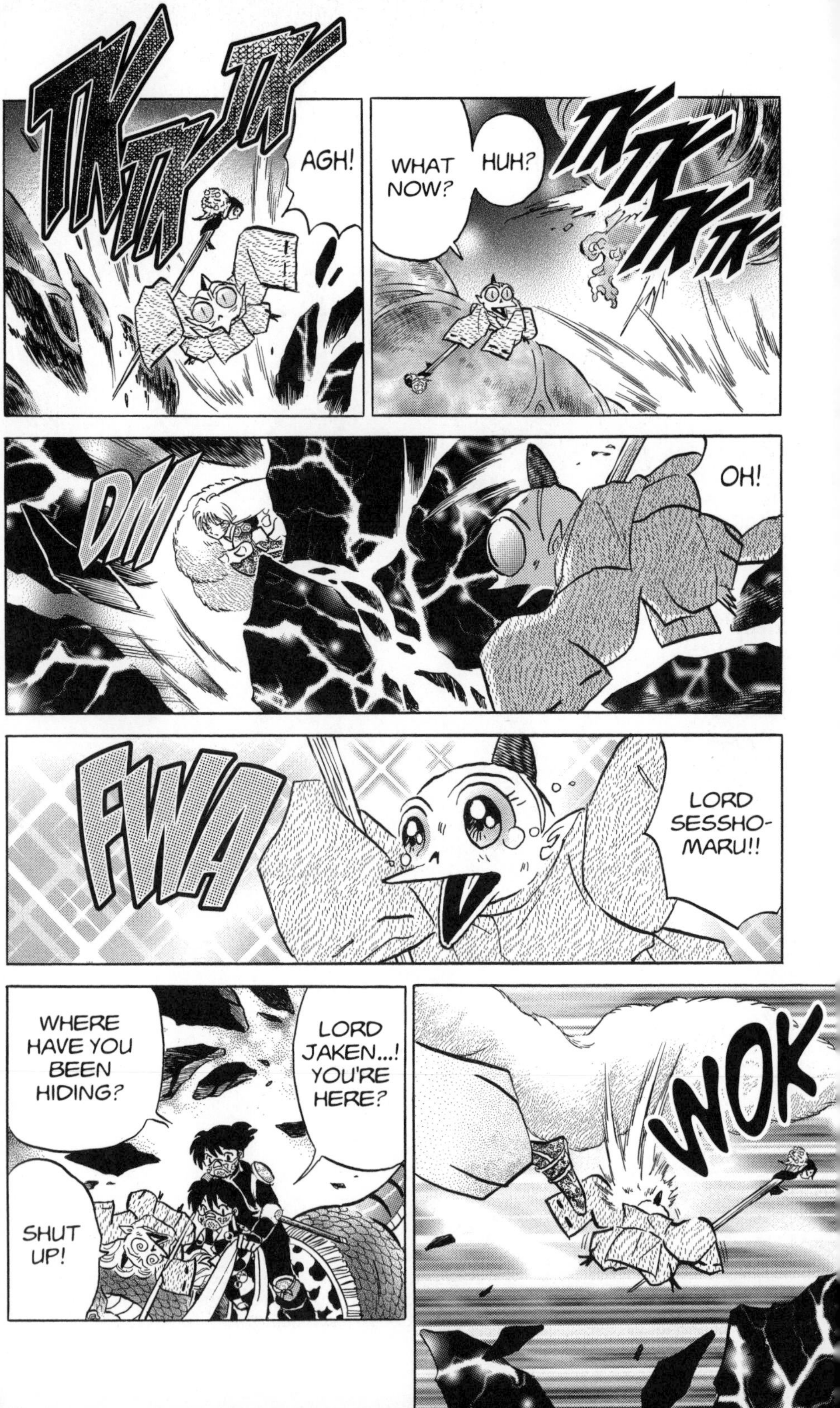
HUH?
WHAT NOW?
AGH!
OH!
DM
LORD SESSHO-MARU!!
FWA
WOK
LORD JAKEN...! YOU'RE HERE?
WHERE HAVE YOU BEEN HIDING?
SHUT UP!

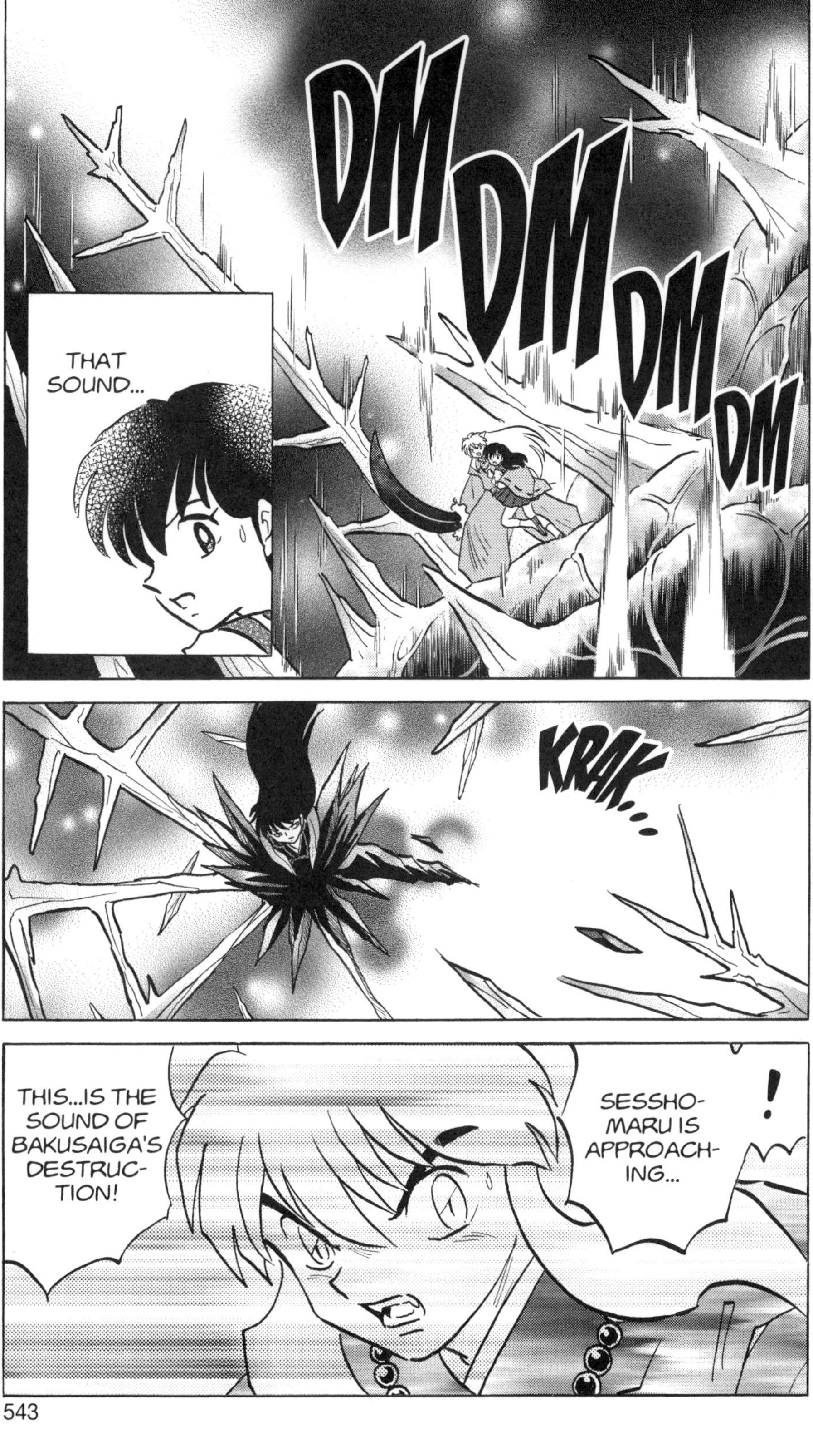
DM DM DM DM
THAT SOUND...
KRAK...
!
SESSHO-MARU IS APPROACH-ING...
THIS...IS THE SOUND OF BAKUSAIGA'S DESTRUC-TION!

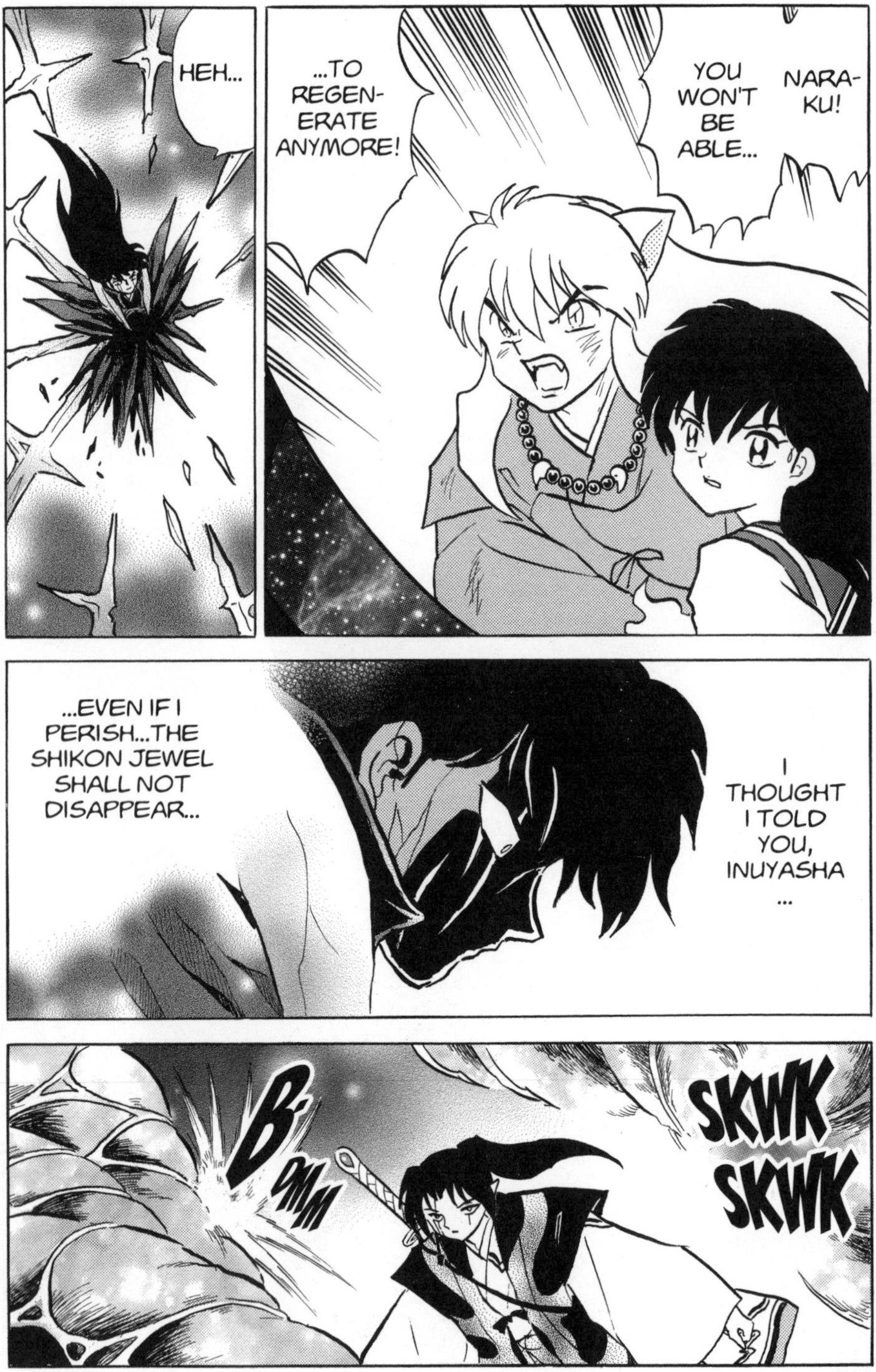
NARA-KU!
YOU WON'T BE ABLE...
...TO REGEN-ERATE ANYMORE!
HEH...
I THOUGHT I TOLD YOU, INUYASHA ...
...EVEN IF I PERISH...THE SHIKON JEWEL SHALL NOT DISAPPEAR...
SKWK SKWK
B-DMM

SCROLL TEN
BYAKUYA'S BLADE

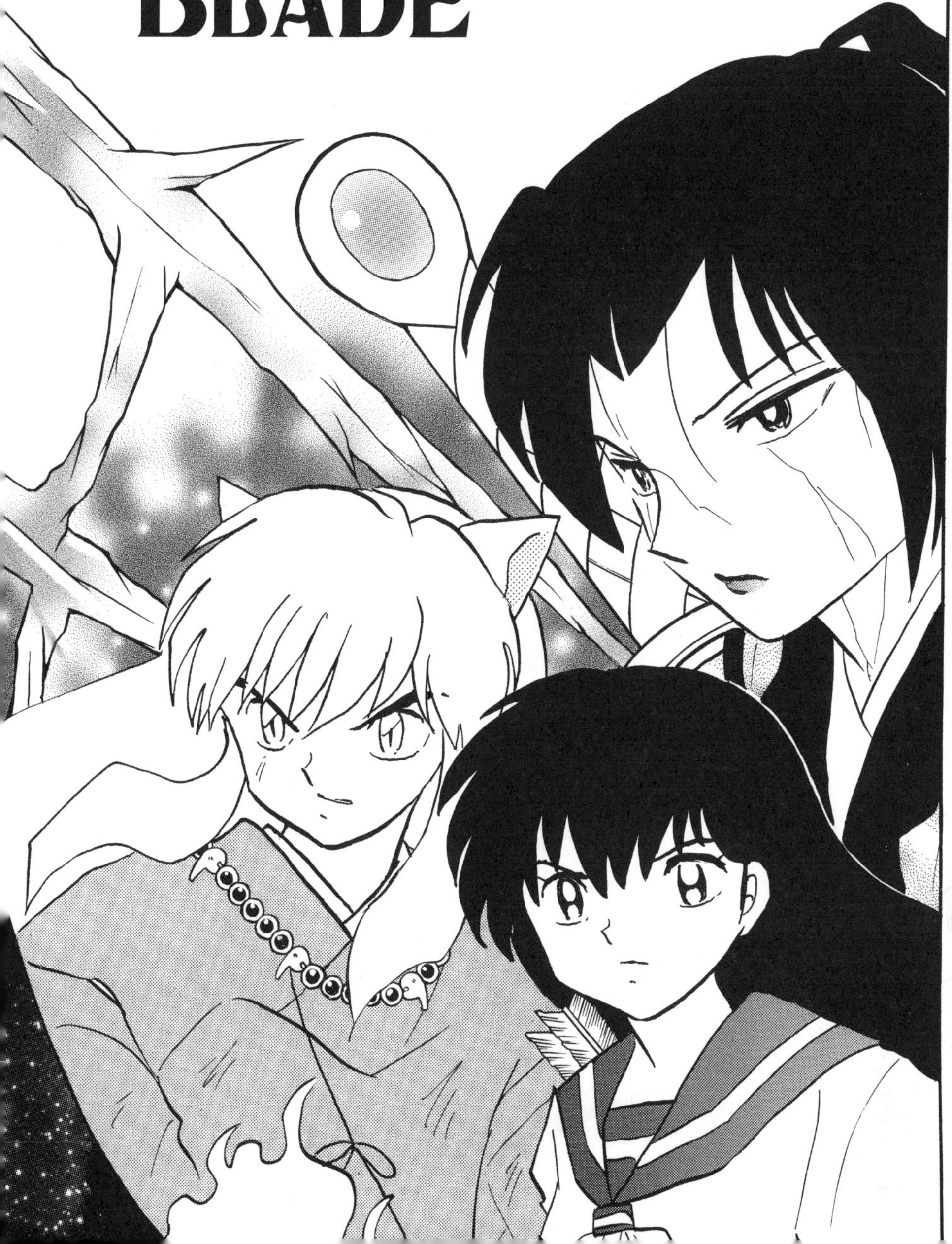

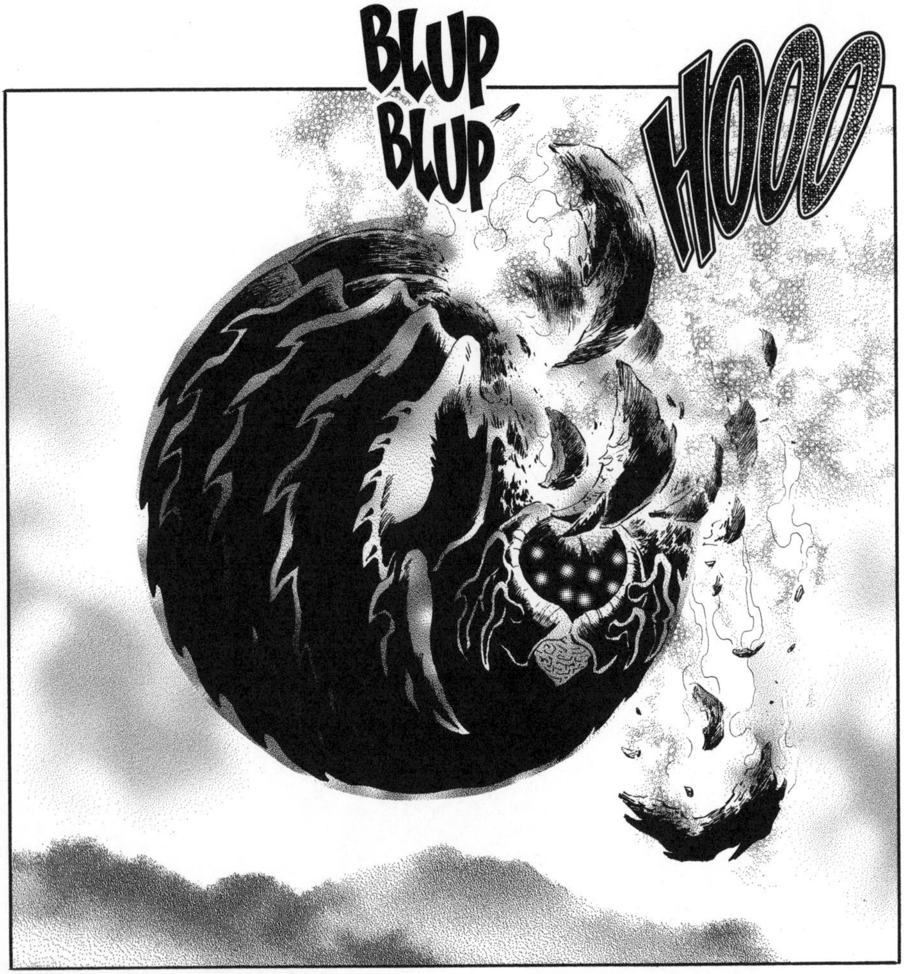
HOOO
BLUP
BLUP
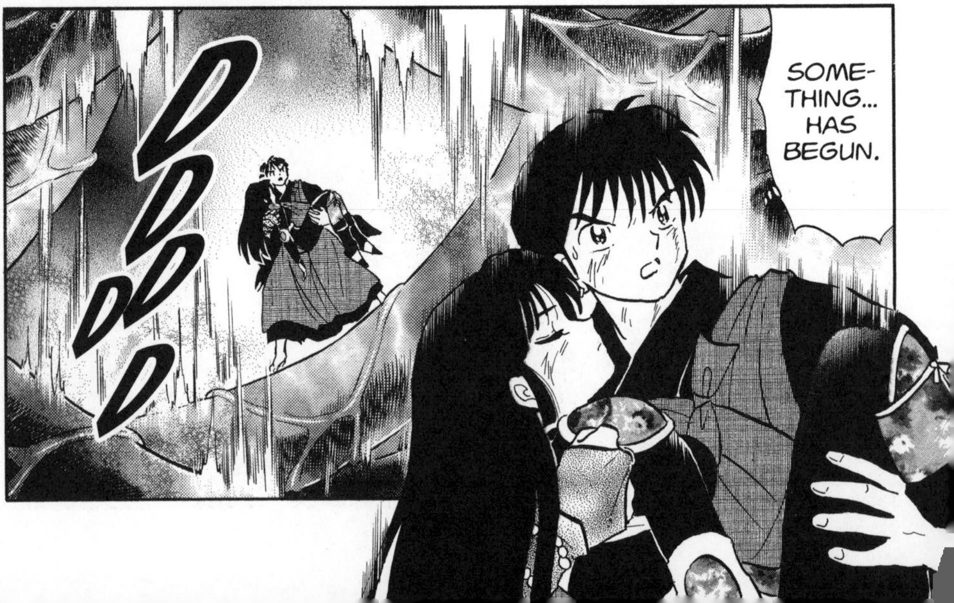
SOME-
THING...
HAS
BEGUN.
DDDDD

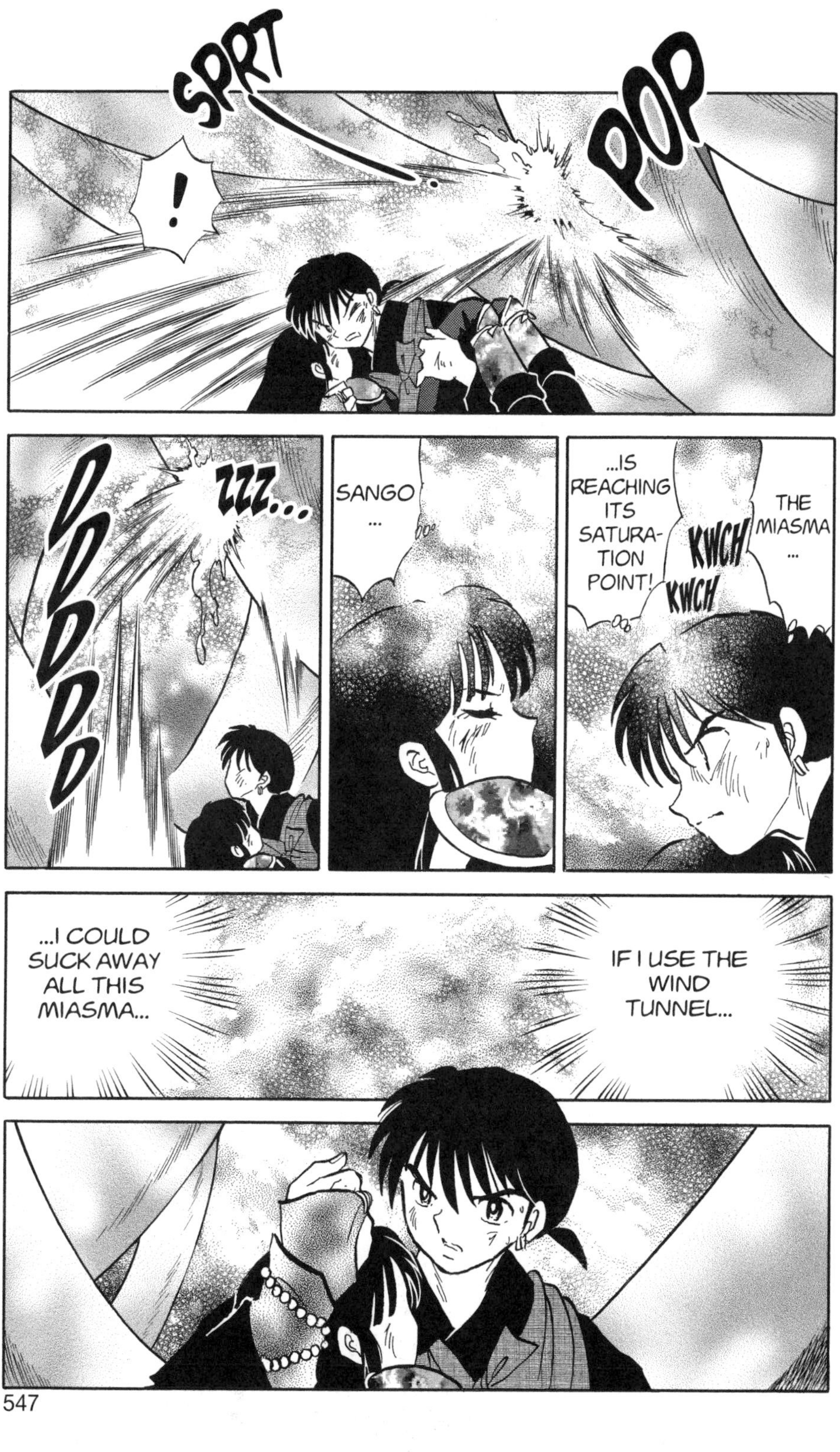
POP
SPRT
!
THE MIASMA...
KWCH
KWCH
...IS REACHING ITS SATURATION POINT!
SANGO...
ZZZ...
DDDDDD
IF I USE THE WIND TUNNEL...
...I COULD SUCK AWAY ALL THIS MIASMA...

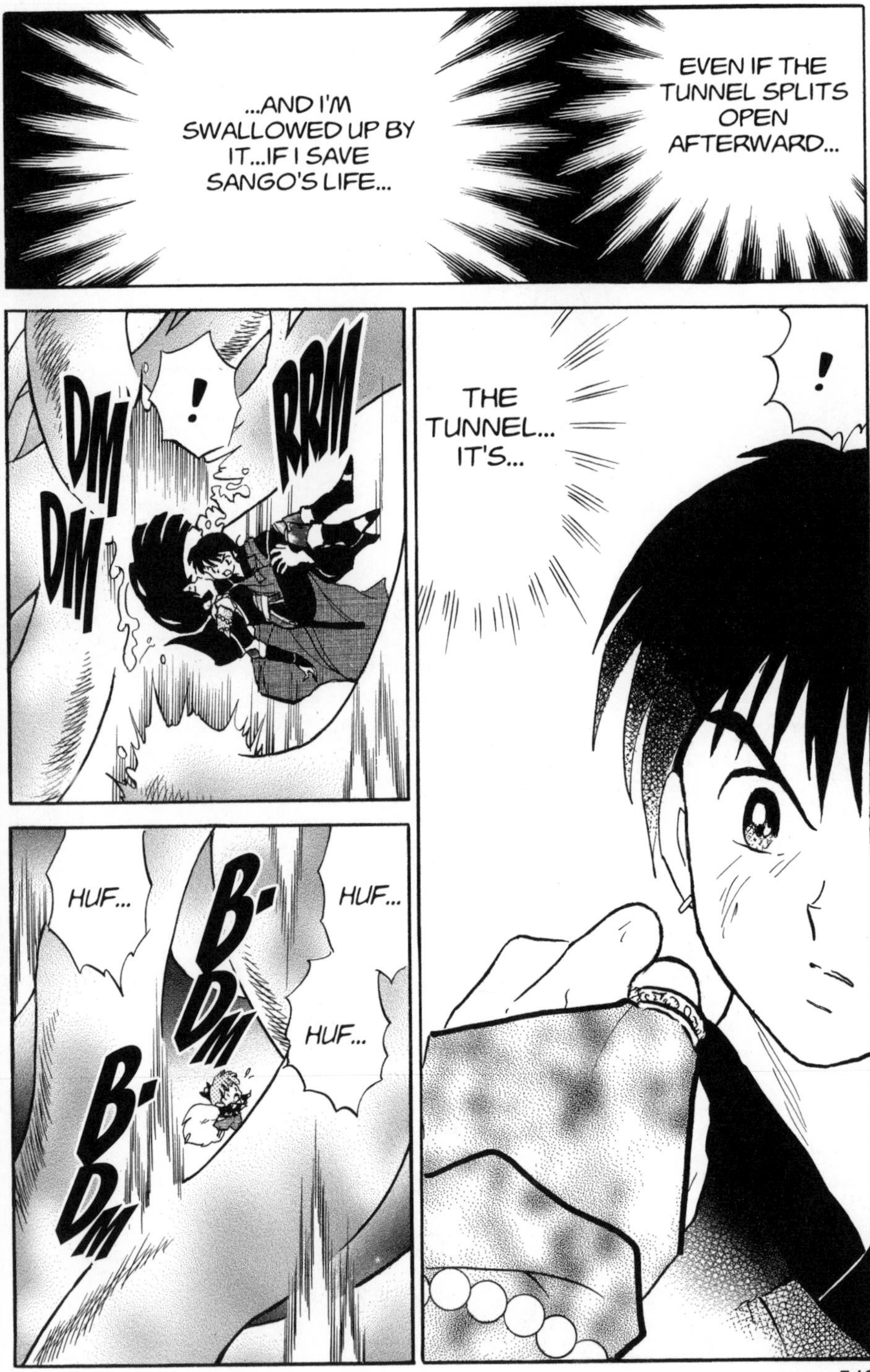
EVEN IF THE TUNNEL SPLITS OPEN AFTERWARD...
...AND I'M SWALLOWED UP BY IT...IF I SAVE SANGO'S LIFE...
!
THE TUNNEL... IT'S...
RRM
!
DM DM
HUF...
B-DM
HUF...
HUF...
B-DM

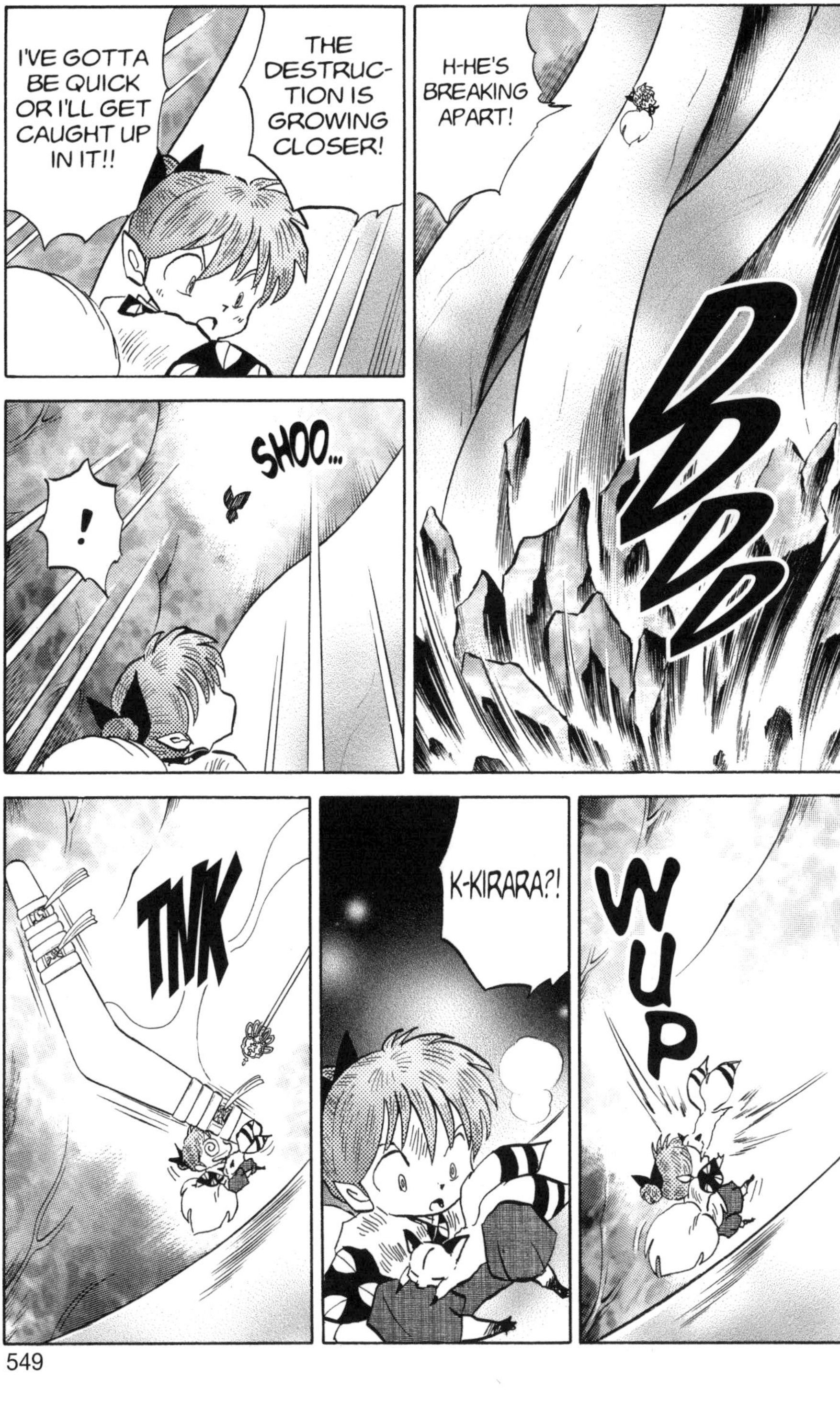
H-HE'S BREAKING APART!
THE DESTRUC-TION IS GROWING CLOSER!
I'VE GOTTA BE QUICK OR I'LL GET CAUGHT UP IN IT!!
SHOO...
!
WUP
K-KIRARA?!
TNK

ARGH!!

REEL

SWOO

GAH!

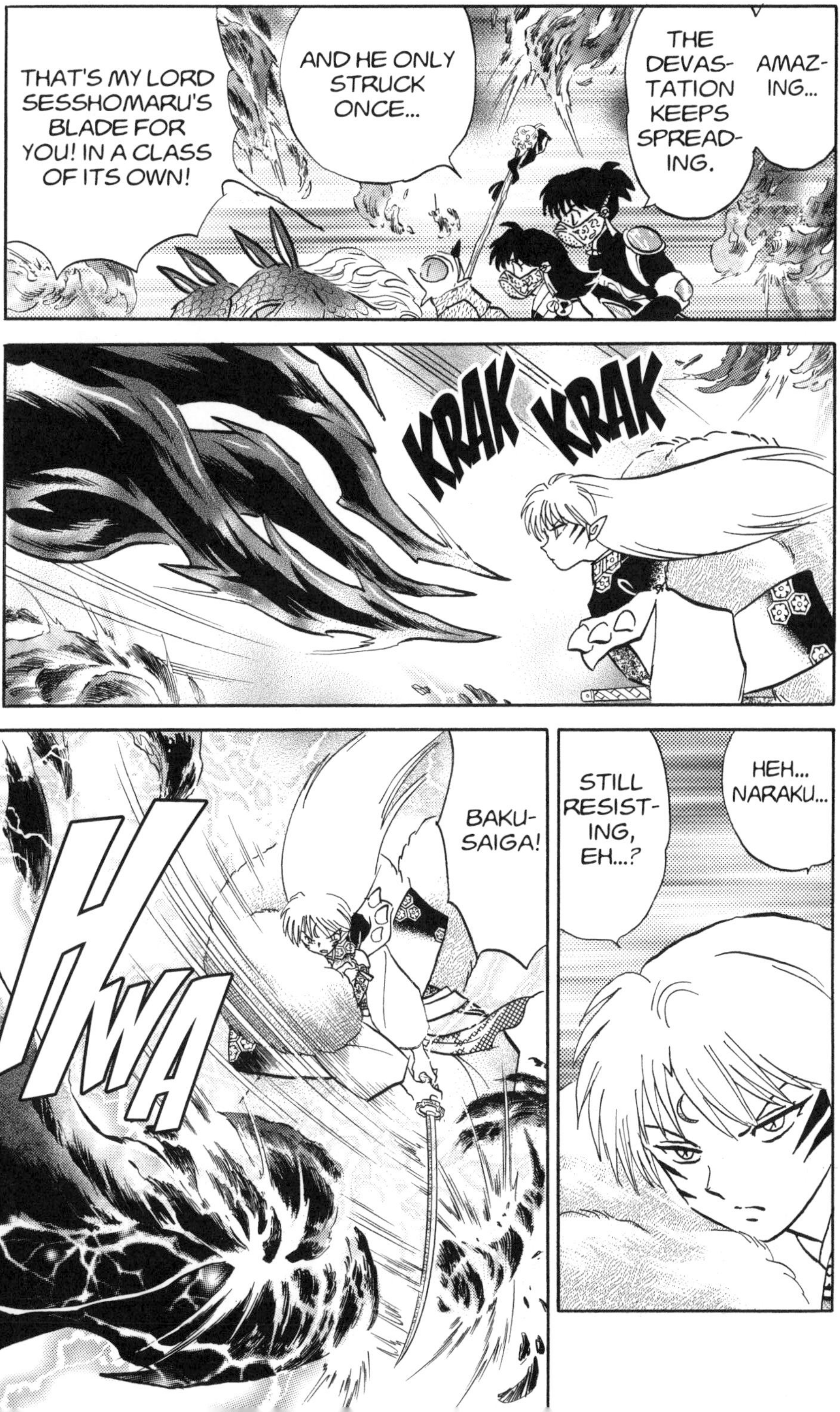
AMAZING...
THE DEVASTATION KEEPS SPREADING.
AND HE ONLY STRUCK ONCE...
THAT'S MY LORD SESSHOMARU'S BLADE FOR YOU! IN A CLASS OF ITS OWN!
KRAK KRAK
HEH... NARAKU...
STILL RESISTING, EH...?
BAKUSAIGA!
HWA

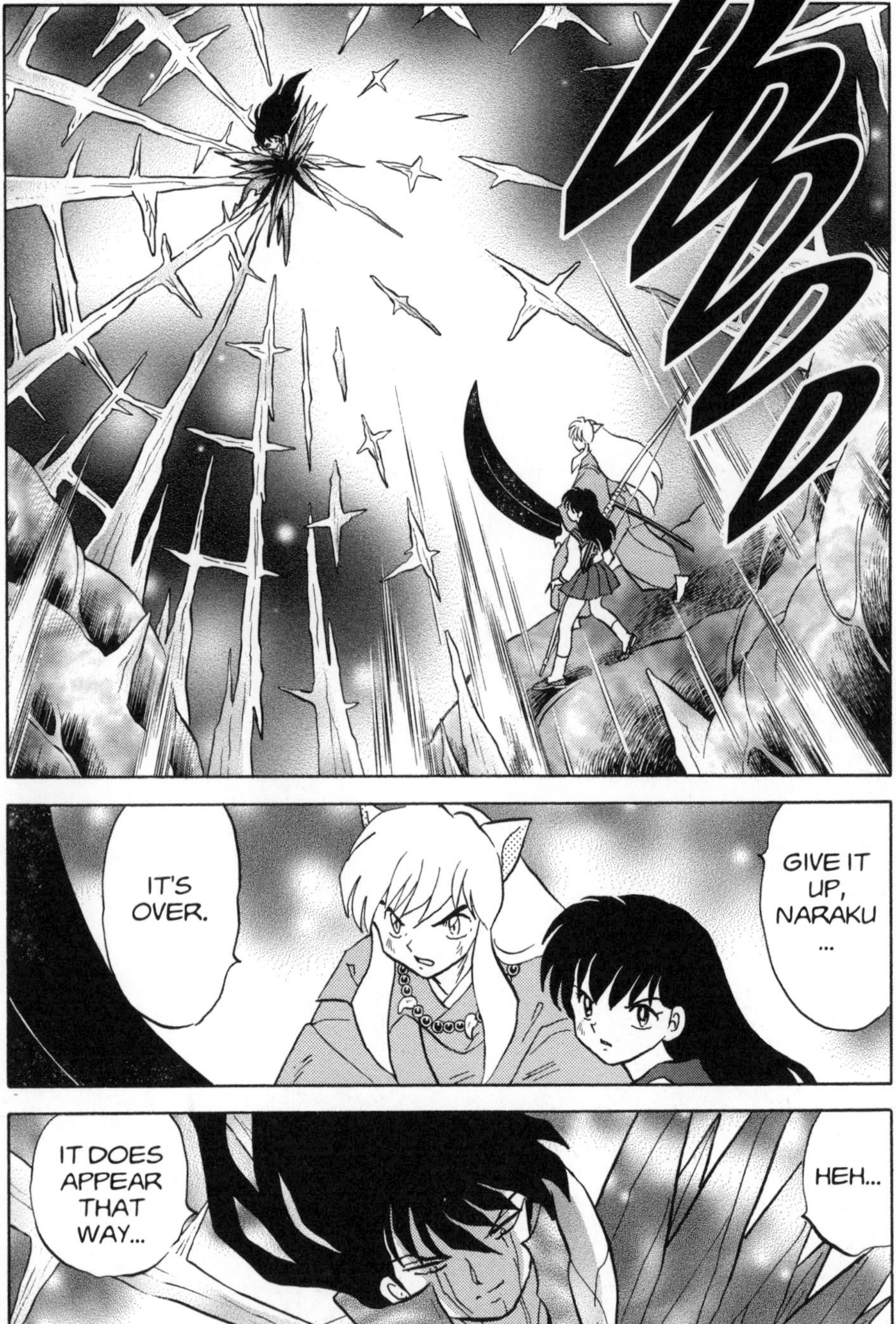
GIVE IT UP, NARAKU ...
IT'S OVER.
HEH...
IT DOES APPEAR THAT WAY...

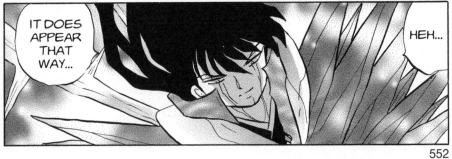

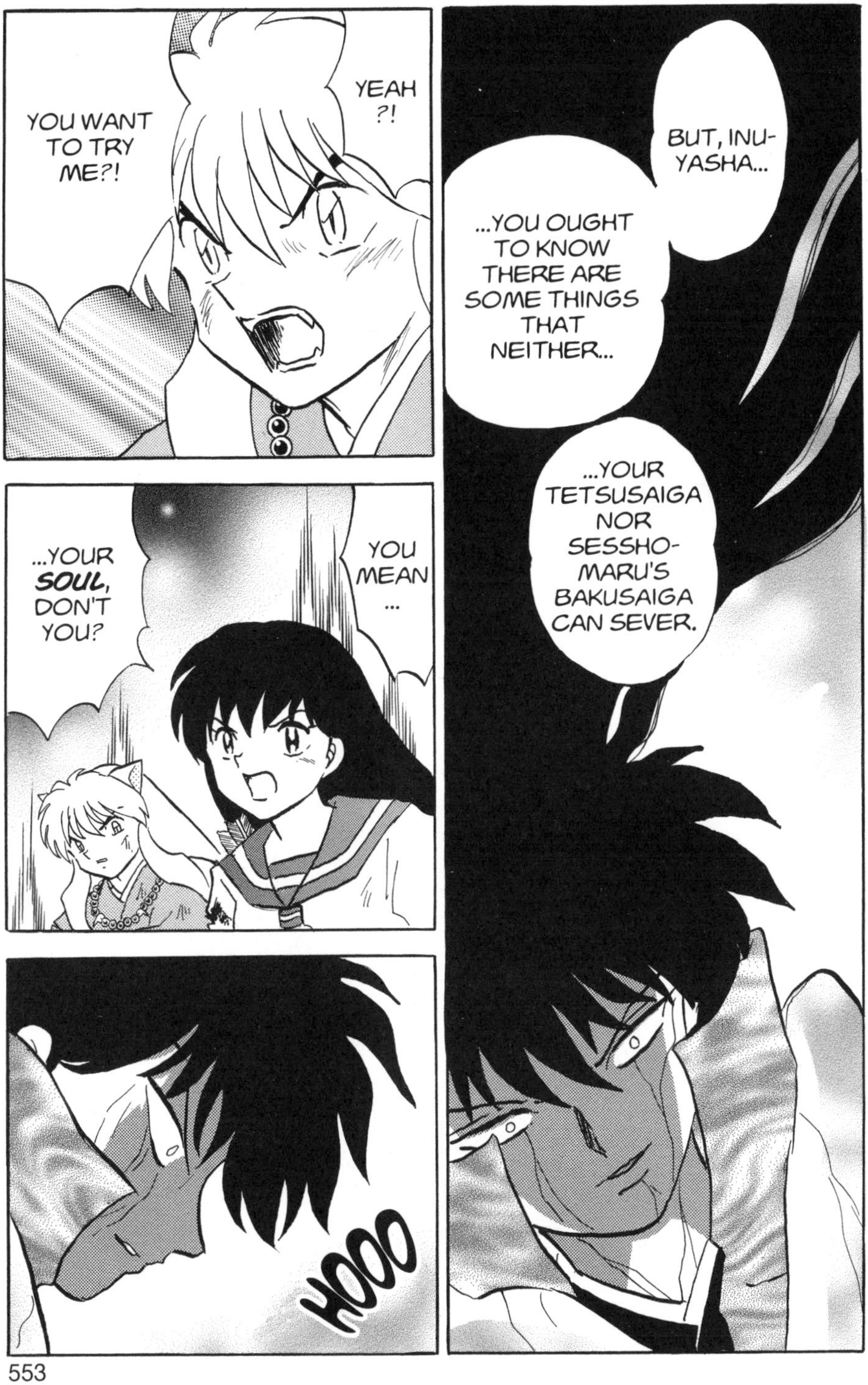
BUT, INU-YASHA...
...YOU OUGHT TO KNOW THERE ARE SOME THINGS THAT NEITHER...
...YOUR TETSUSAIGA NOR SESSHO-MARU'S BAKUSAIGA CAN SEVER.
YEAH ?!
YOU WANT TO TRY ME?!
YOU MEAN ...
...YOUR SOUL, DON'T YOU?
HOOO

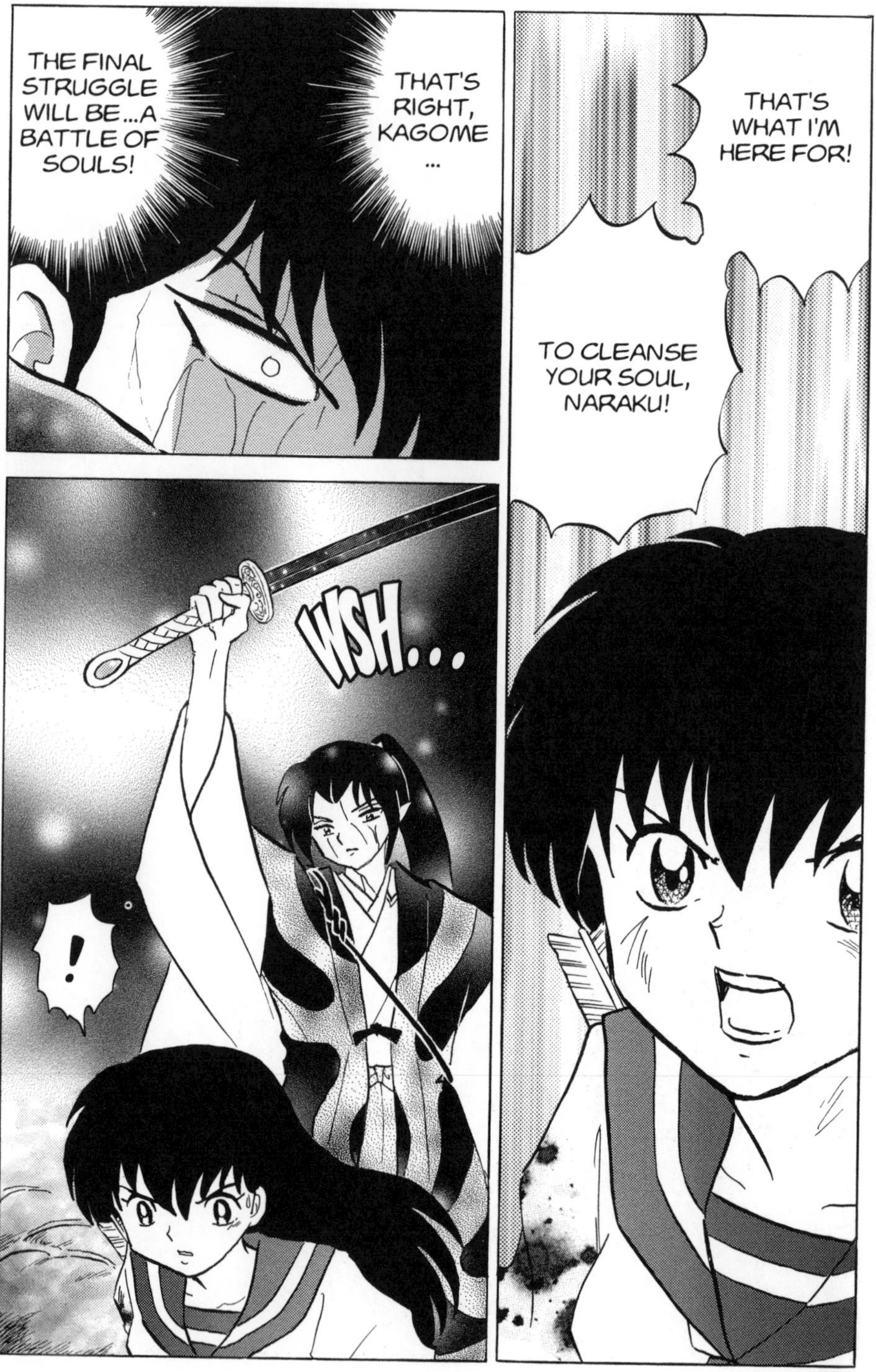
THAT'S WHAT I'M HERE FOR!
TO CLEANSE YOUR SOUL, NARAKU!
THAT'S RIGHT, KAGOME ...
THE FINAL STRUGGLE WILL BE...A BATTLE OF SOULS!
WSH...
!

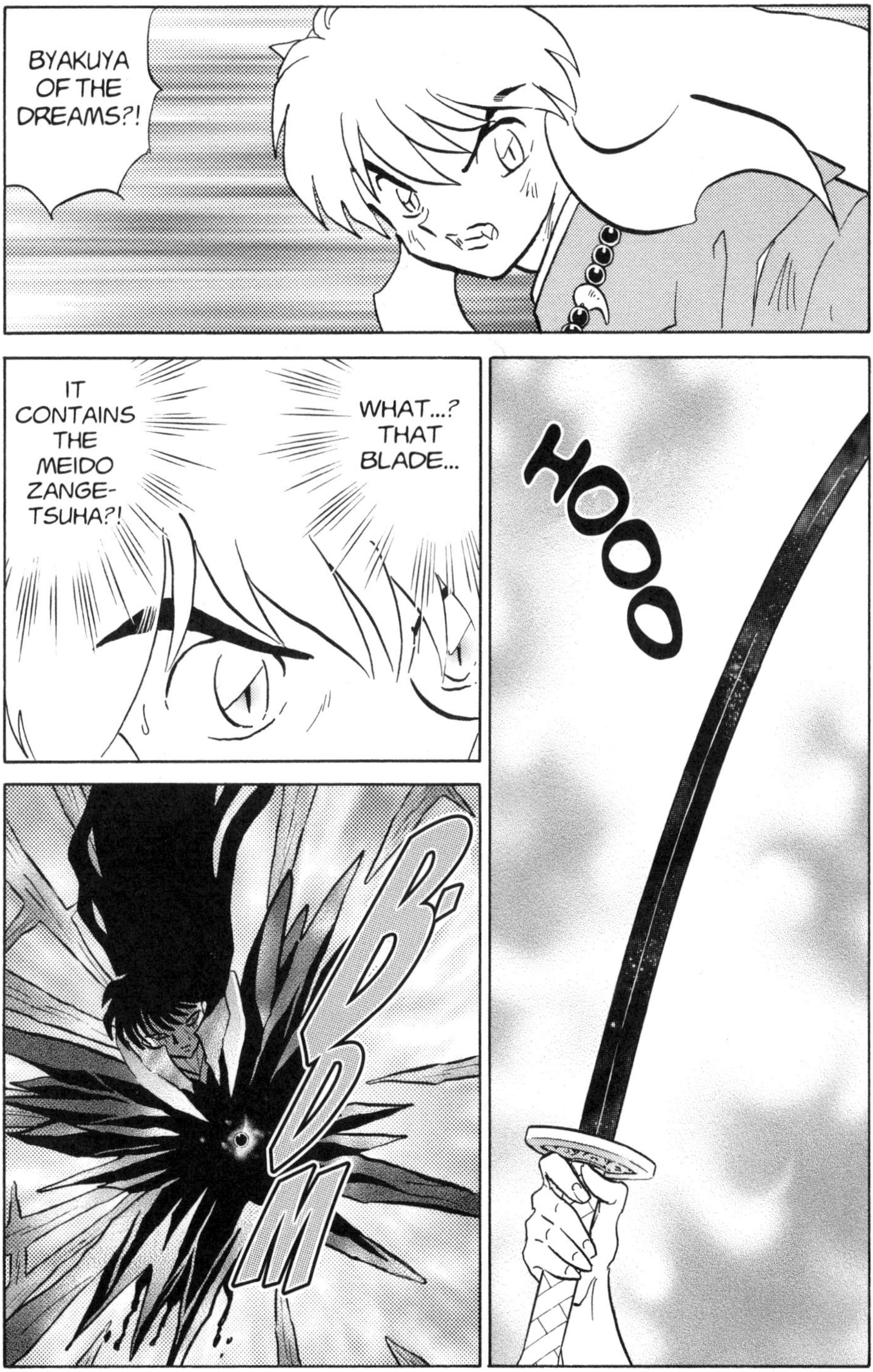
BYAKUYA OF THE DREAMS?!
HOOO
WHAT...? THAT BLADE...
IT CONTAINS THE MEIDO ZANGE-TSUHA?!
BOOM

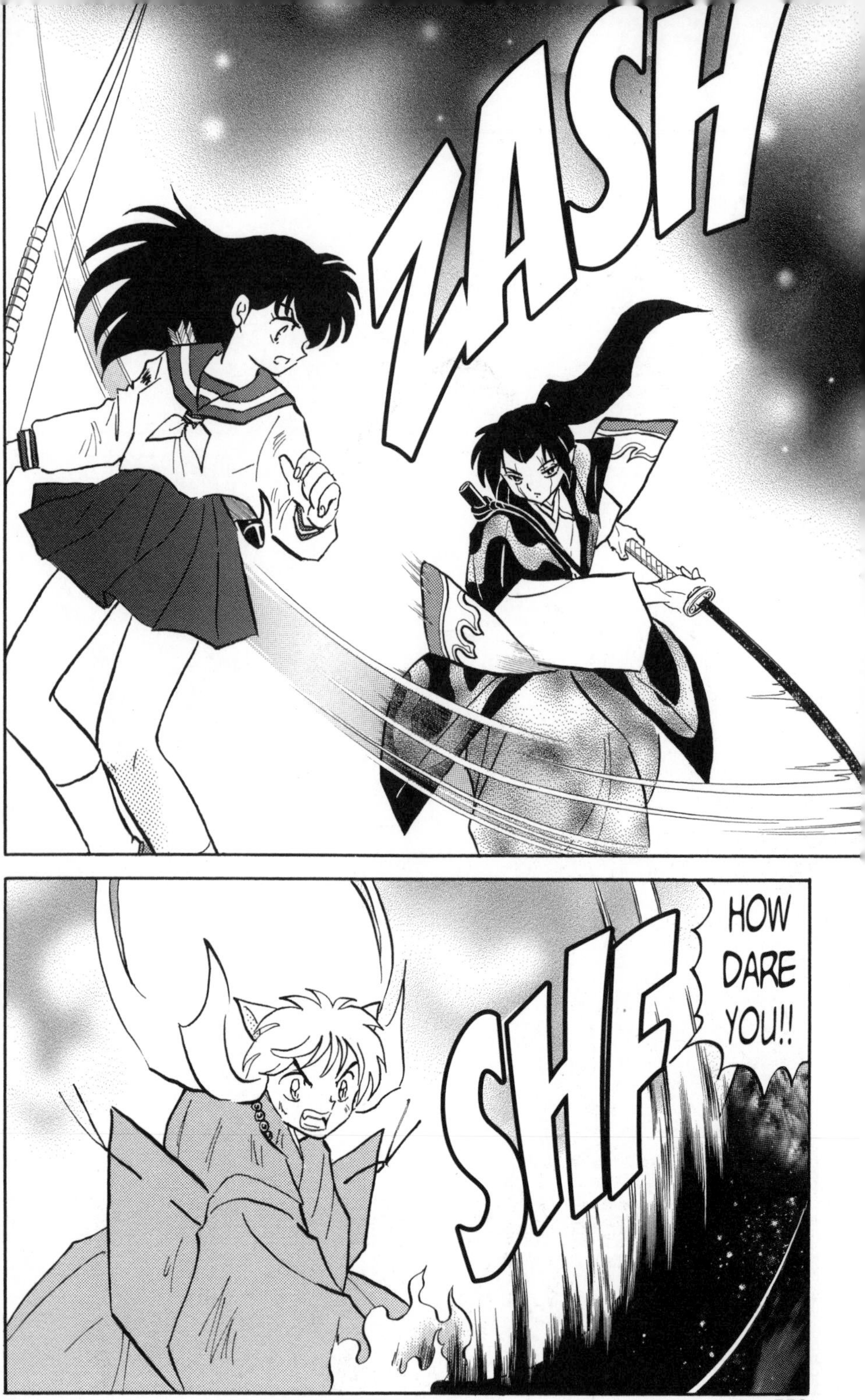
ZASH
HOW DARE YOU!!
SHF

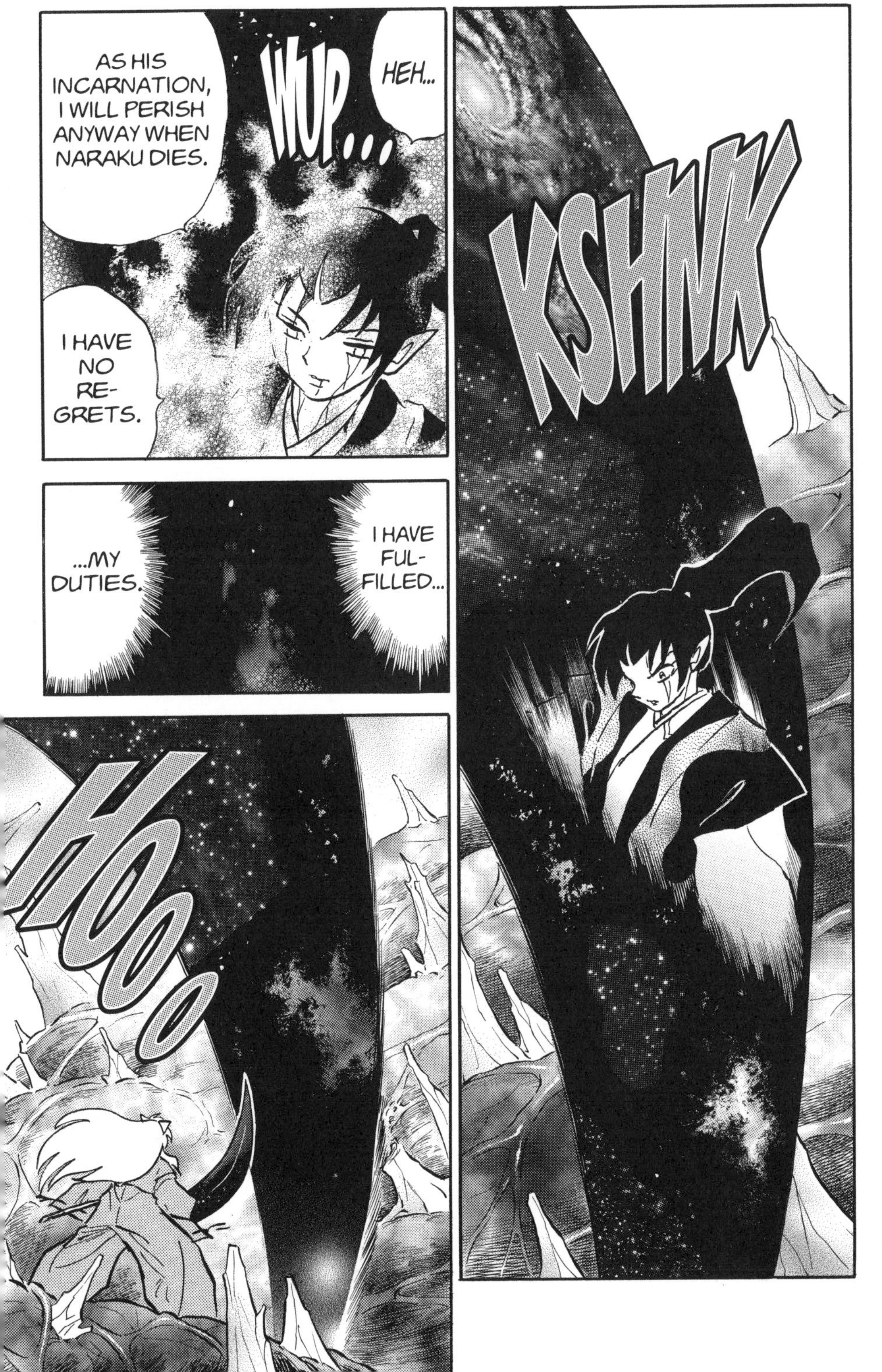
KSHNK
HEH...
WUP...
AS HIS INCARNATION, I WILL PERISH ANYWAY WHEN NARAKU DIES.
I HAVE NO RE-GRETS.
I HAVE FUL-FILLED...
...MY DUTIES.
HOOOO

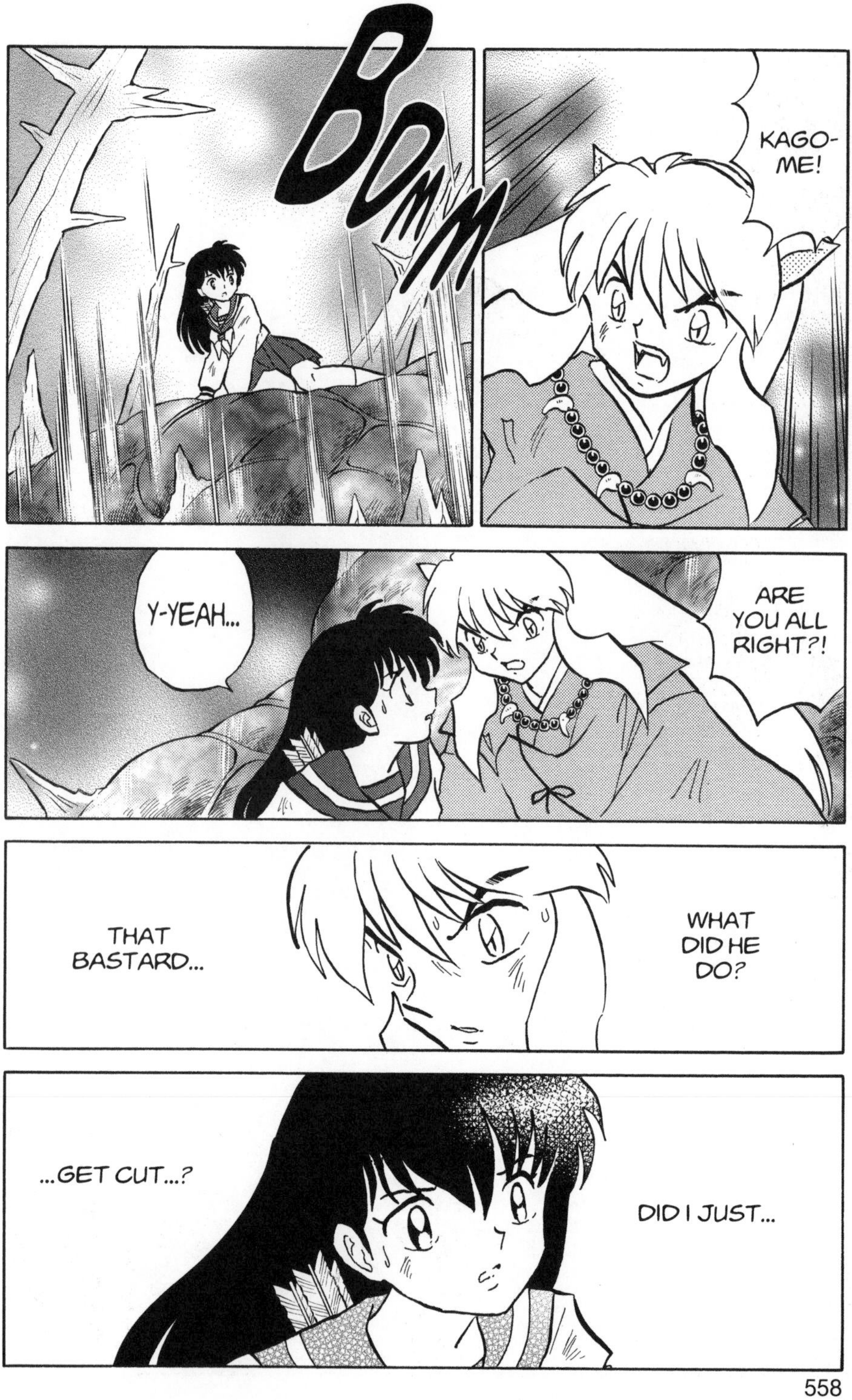
KAGO-ME!
BOMM
ARE YOU ALL RIGHT?!
Y-YEAH...
WHAT DID HE DO?
THAT BASTARD...
DID I JUST...
...GET CUT...?

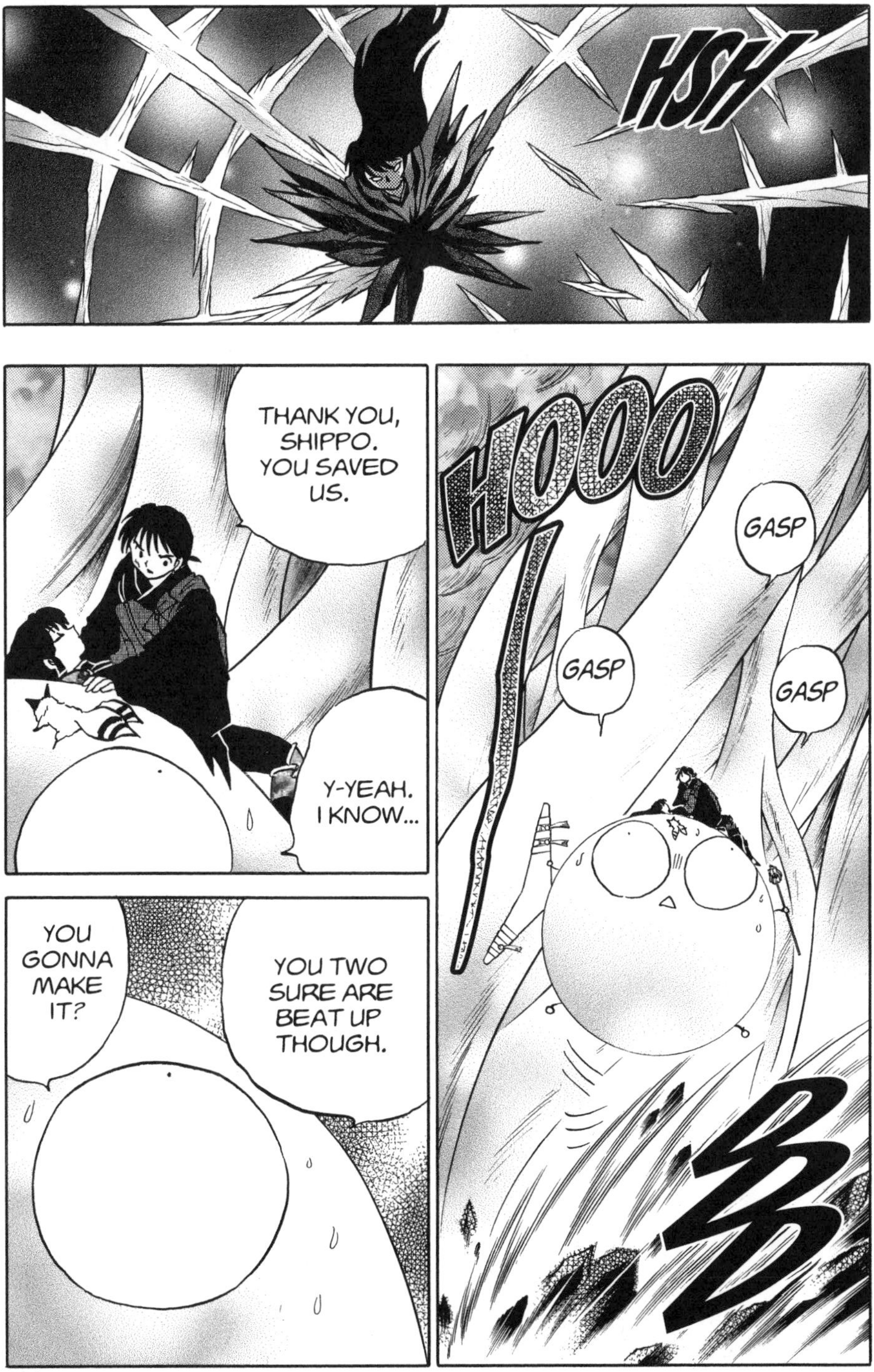
HSH
HOOO
GASP
GASP
GASP
THANK YOU, SHIPPO. YOU SAVED US.
Y-YEAH. I KNOW...
YOU TWO SURE ARE BEAT UP THOUGH.
YOU GONNA MAKE IT?

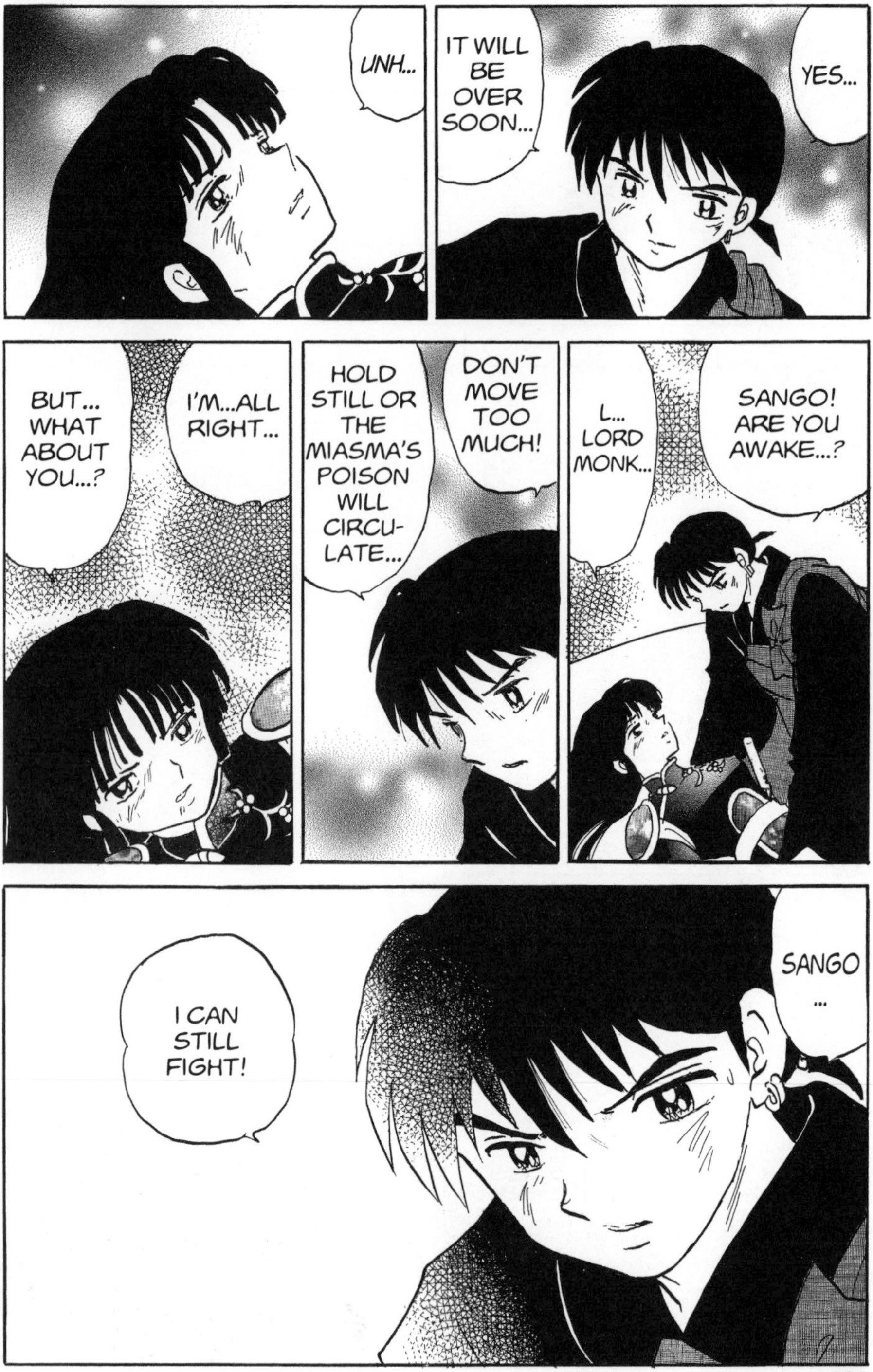

YES...
IT WILL BE OVER SOON...
UNH...
SANGO! ARE YOU AWAKE...?
L... LORD MONK...
DON'T MOVE TOO MUCH!
HOLD STILL OR THE MIASMA'S POISON WILL CIRCULATE...
I'M...ALL RIGHT...
BUT... WHAT ABOUT YOU...?
SANGO...
I CAN STILL FIGHT!

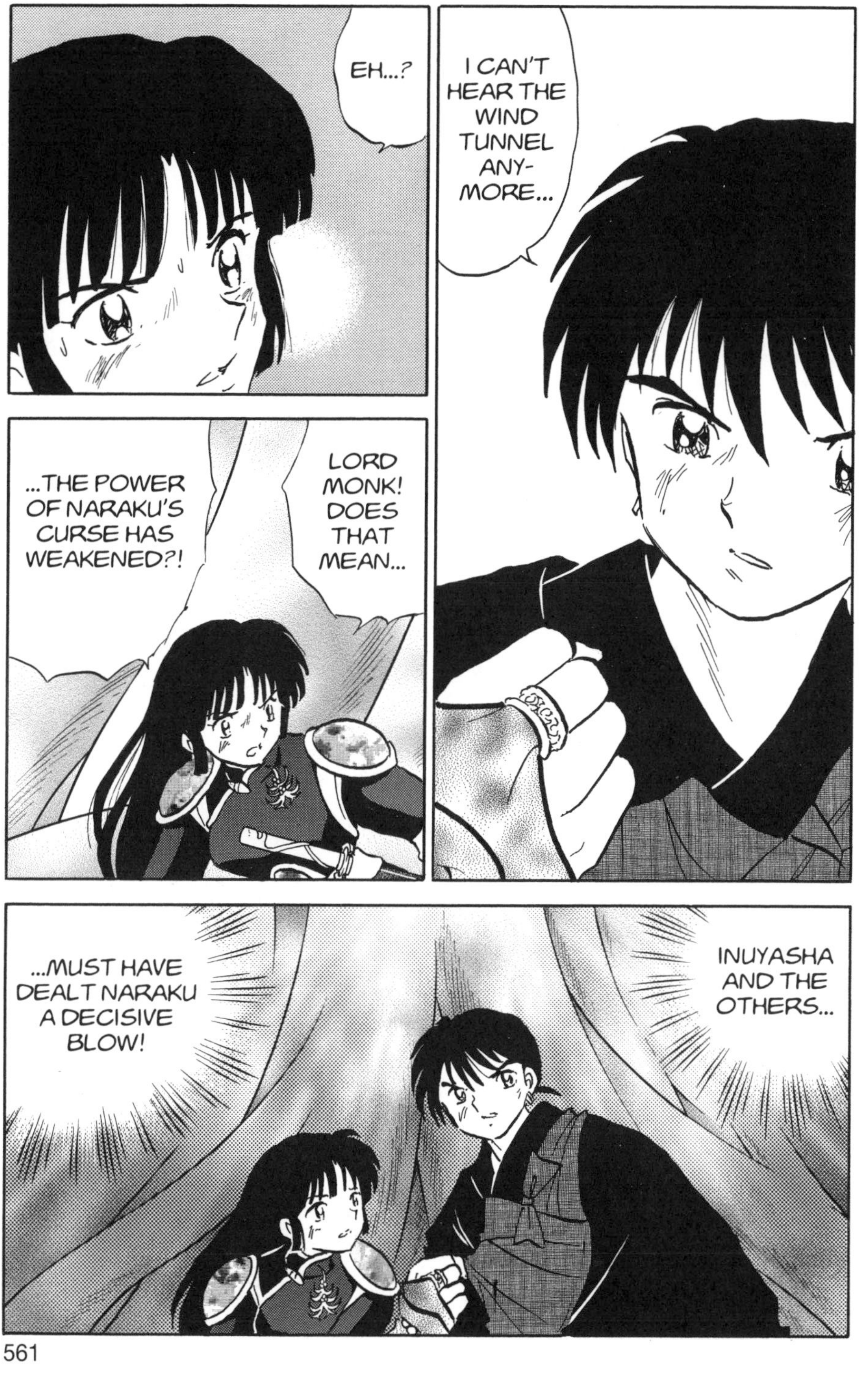
I CAN'T HEAR THE WIND TUNNEL ANY-MORE...
EH...?
LORD MONK! DOES THAT MEAN...
...THE POWER OF NARAKU'S CURSE HAS WEAKENED?!
INUYASHA AND THE OTHERS...
...MUST HAVE DEALT NARAKU A DECISIVE BLOW!

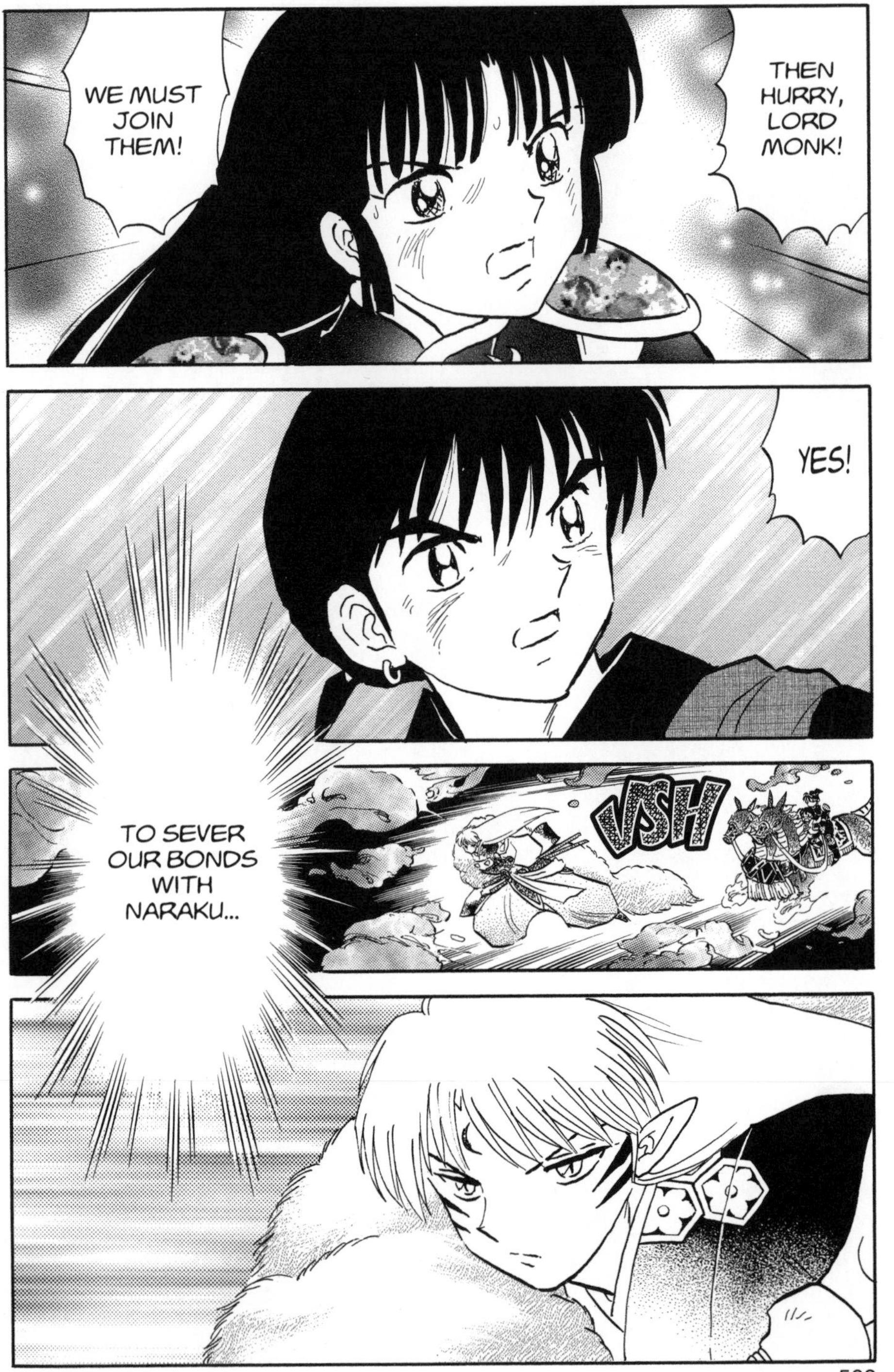
THEN HURRY, LORD MONK!
WE MUST JOIN THEM!
YES!
VSH
TO SEVER OUR BONDS WITH NARAKU...

InuYasha

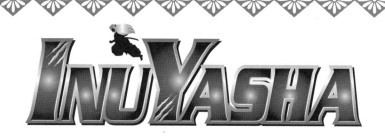

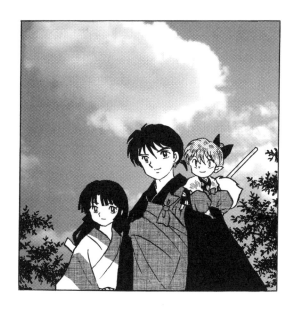

Volume 56

Tomorrow

SCROLL ONE
AMASSING FOR BATTLE

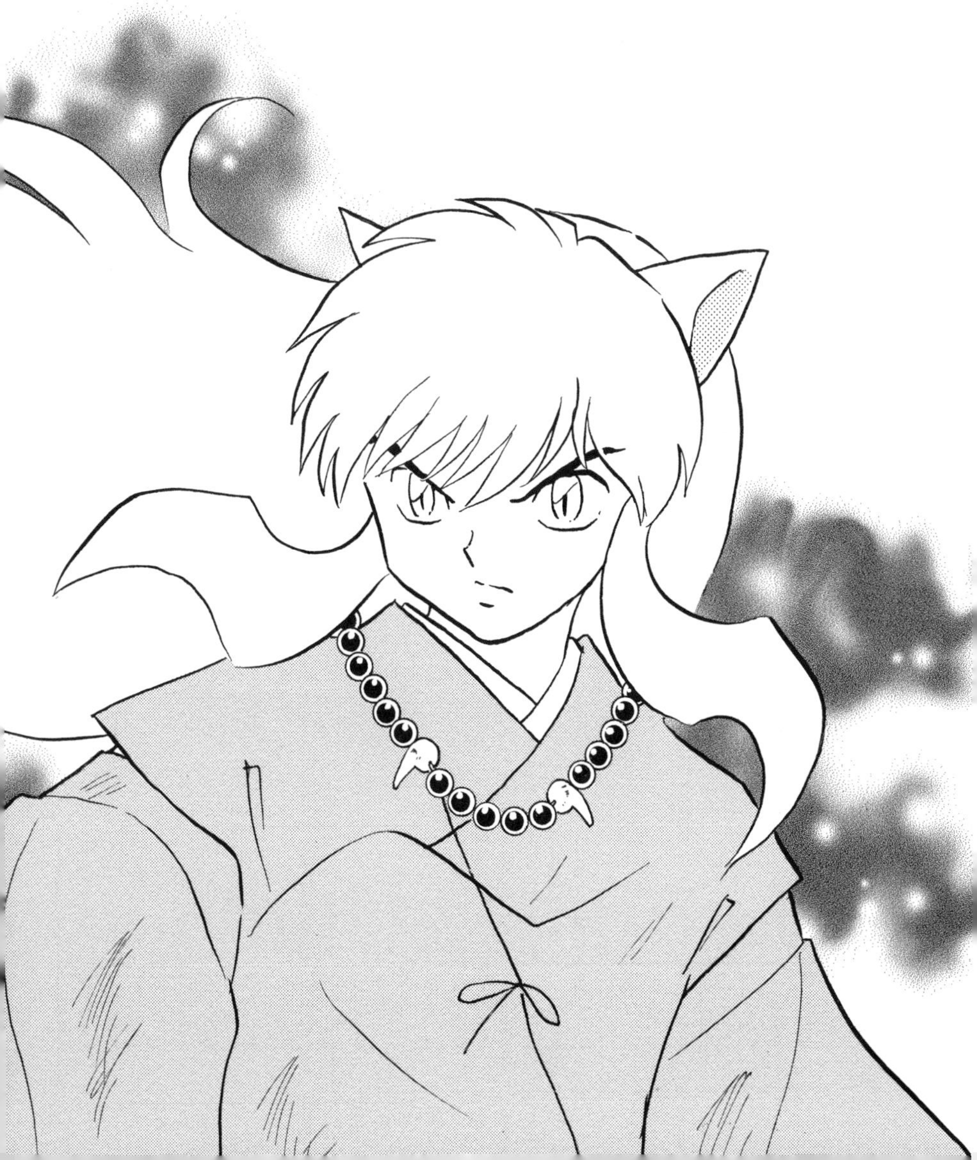

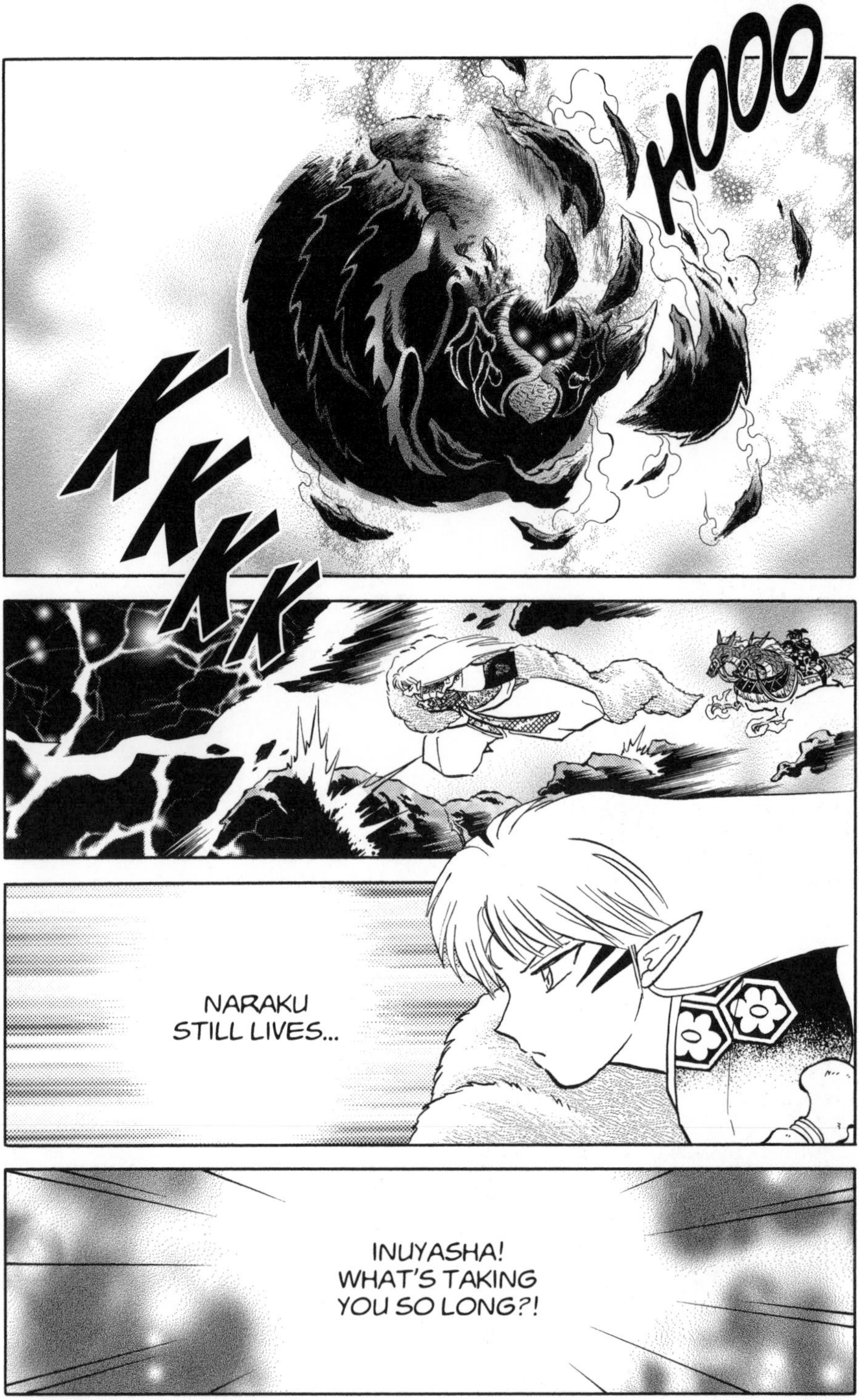
HOOO
KKKK
NARAKU STILL LIVES...
INUYASHA! WHAT'S TAKING YOU SO LONG?!

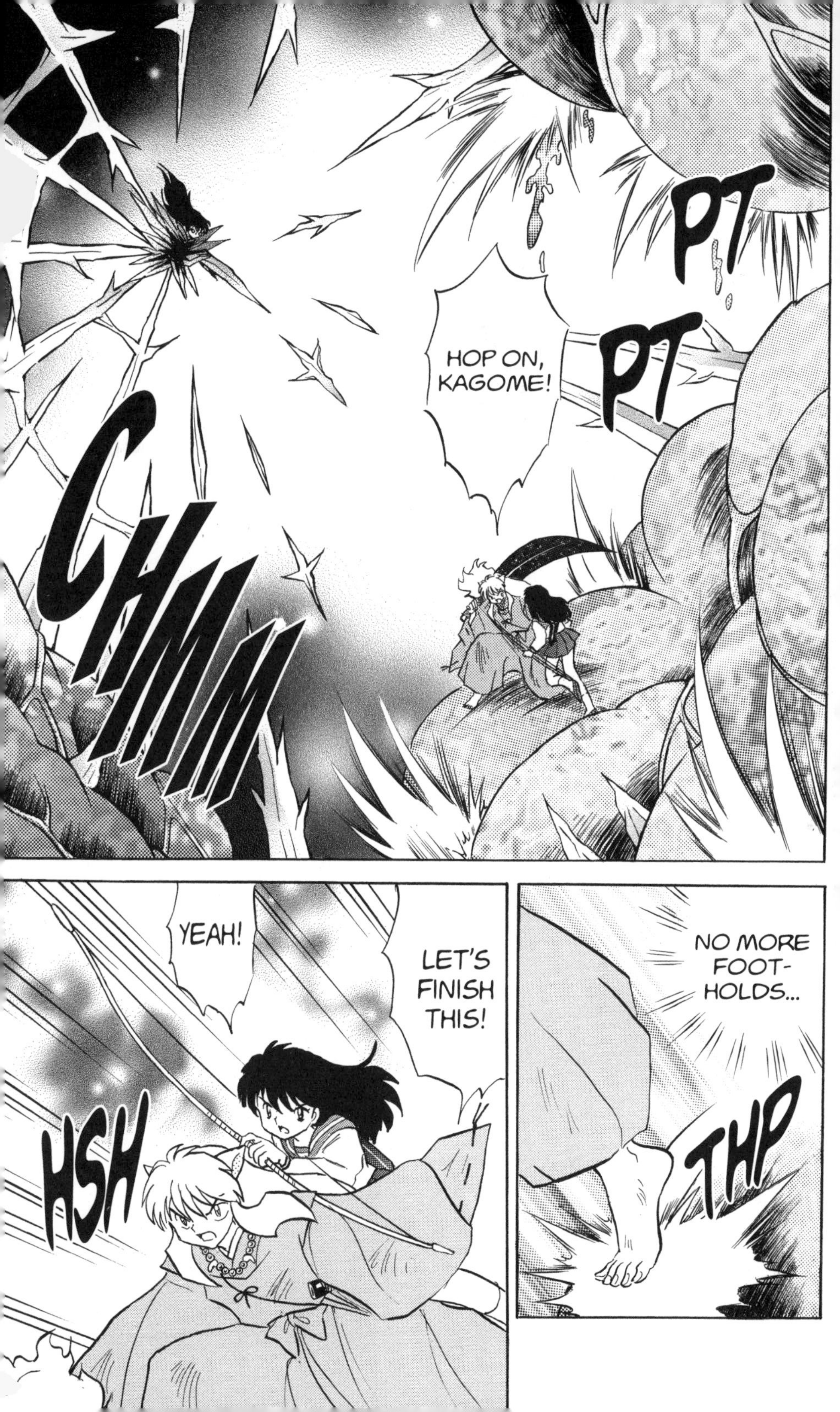
PT
PT
HOP ON, KAGOME!
CHMM
NO MORE FOOT-HOLDS...
THP
LET'S FINISH THIS!
YEAH!
HSH

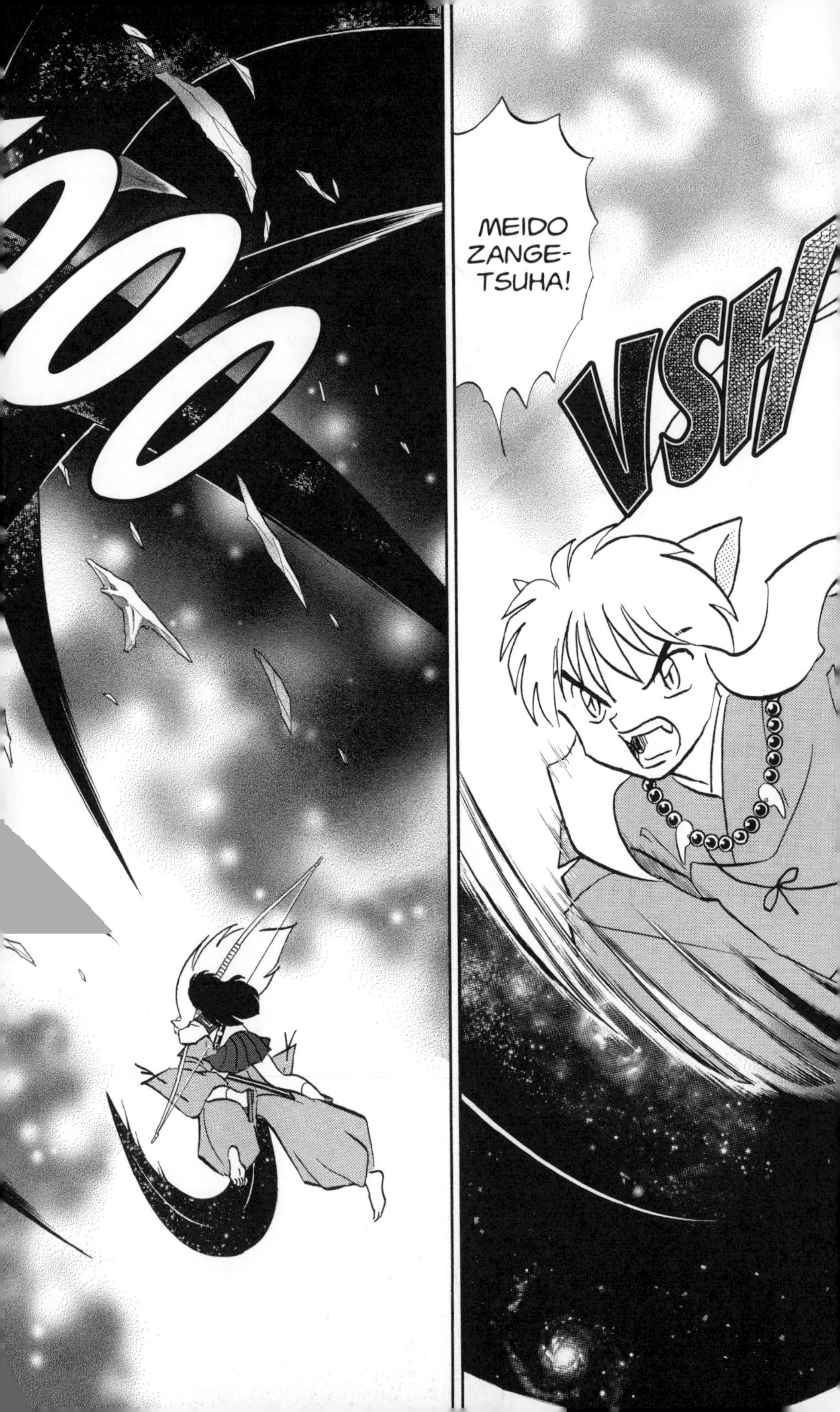
MEIDO ZANGE-TSUHA!
VSH

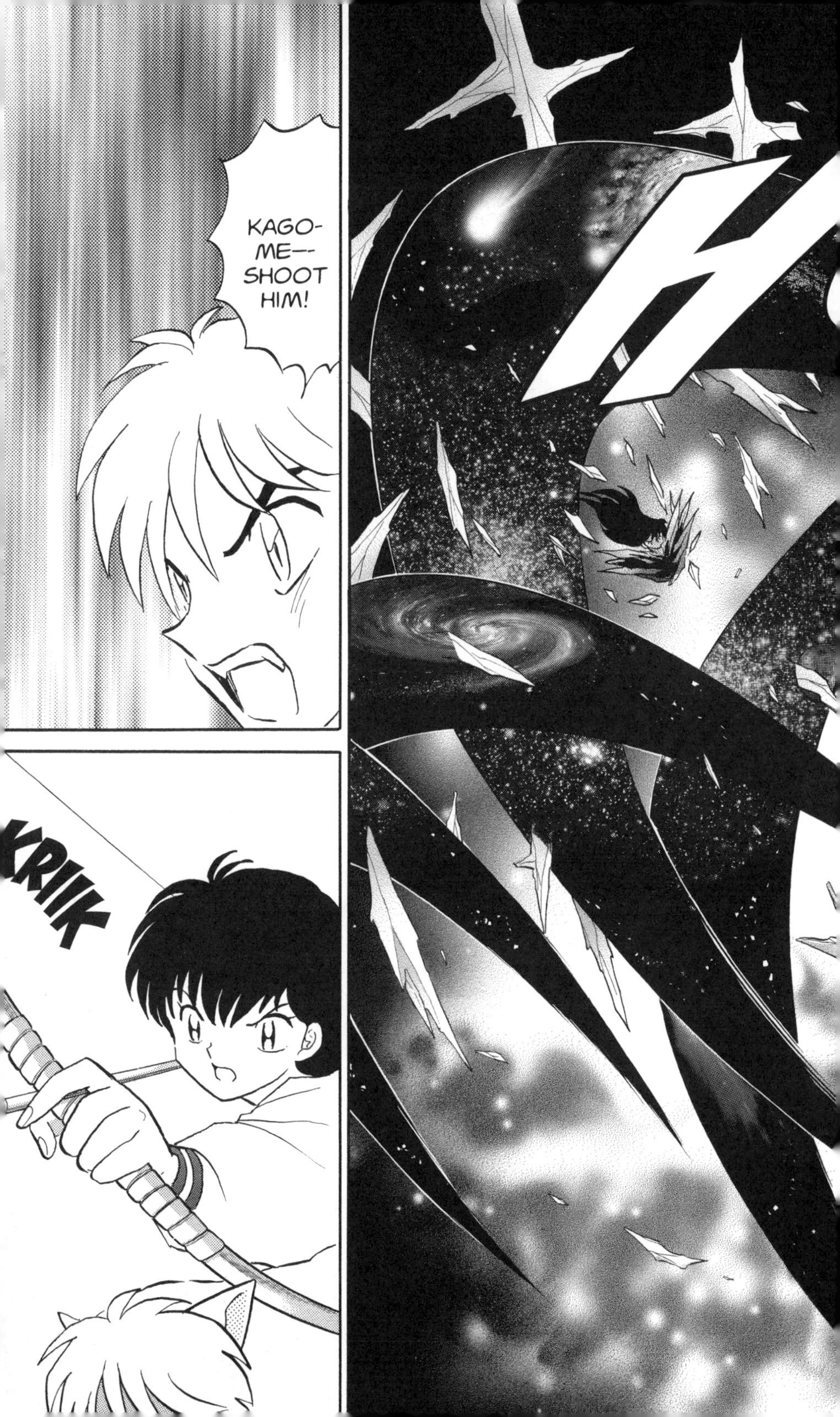
KAGO-
ME--
SHOOT
HIM!
KRIIK

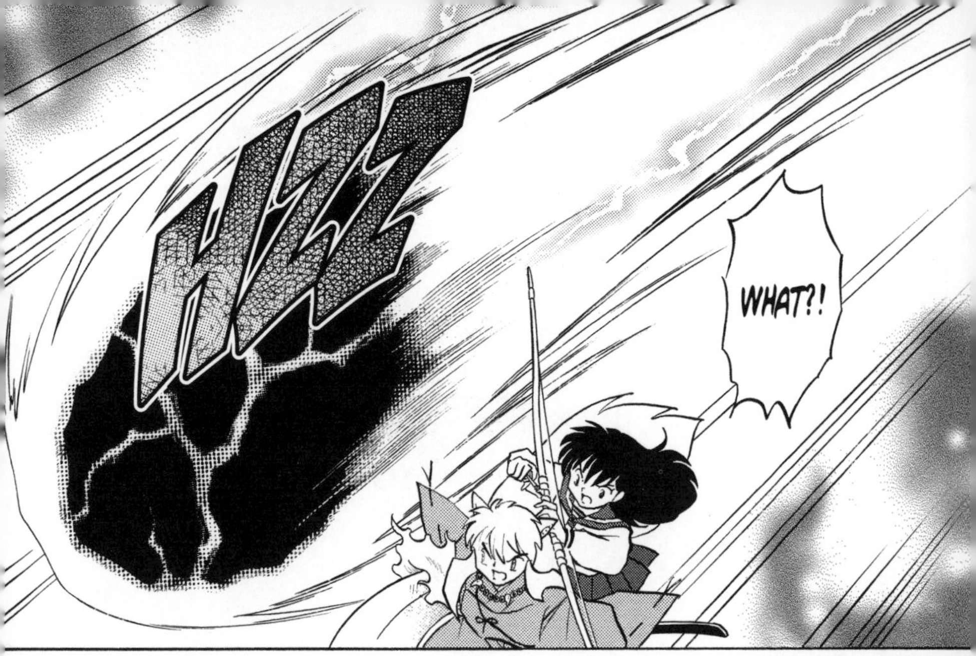
HZZ
WHAT?!
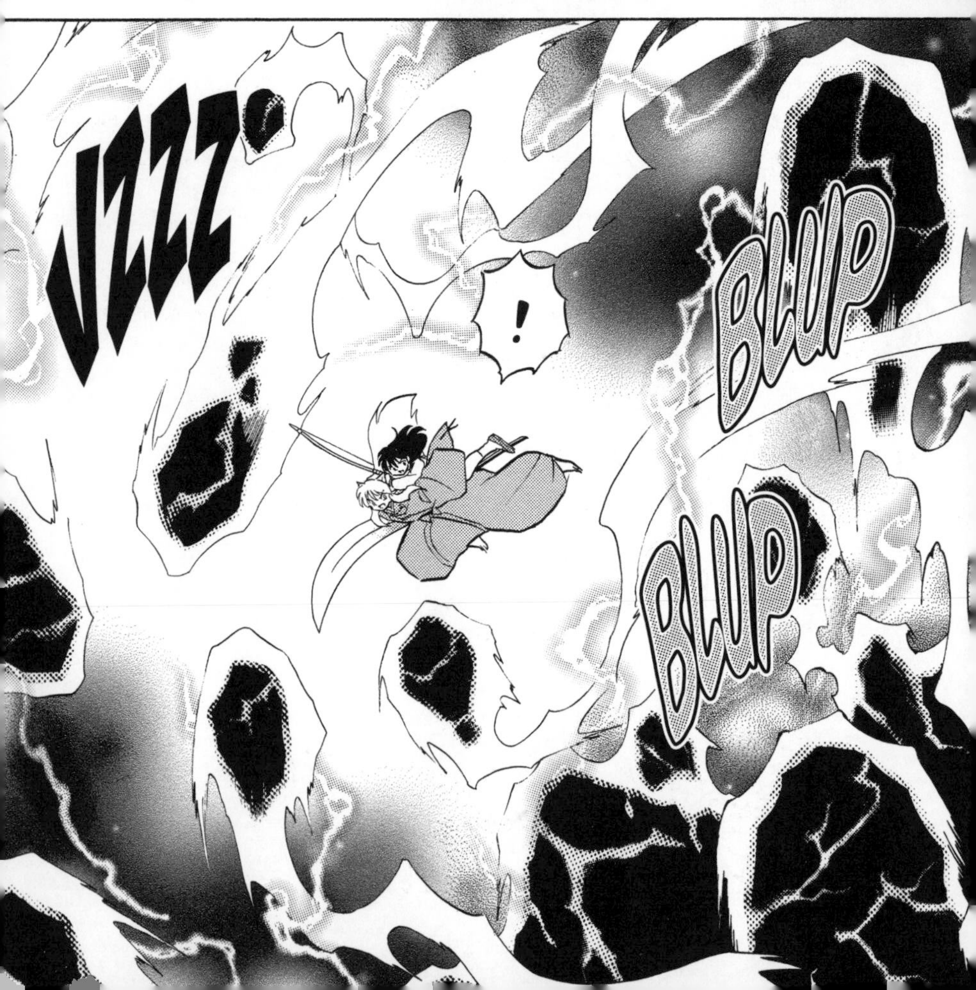
BLUP
BLUP
!
VZZZ

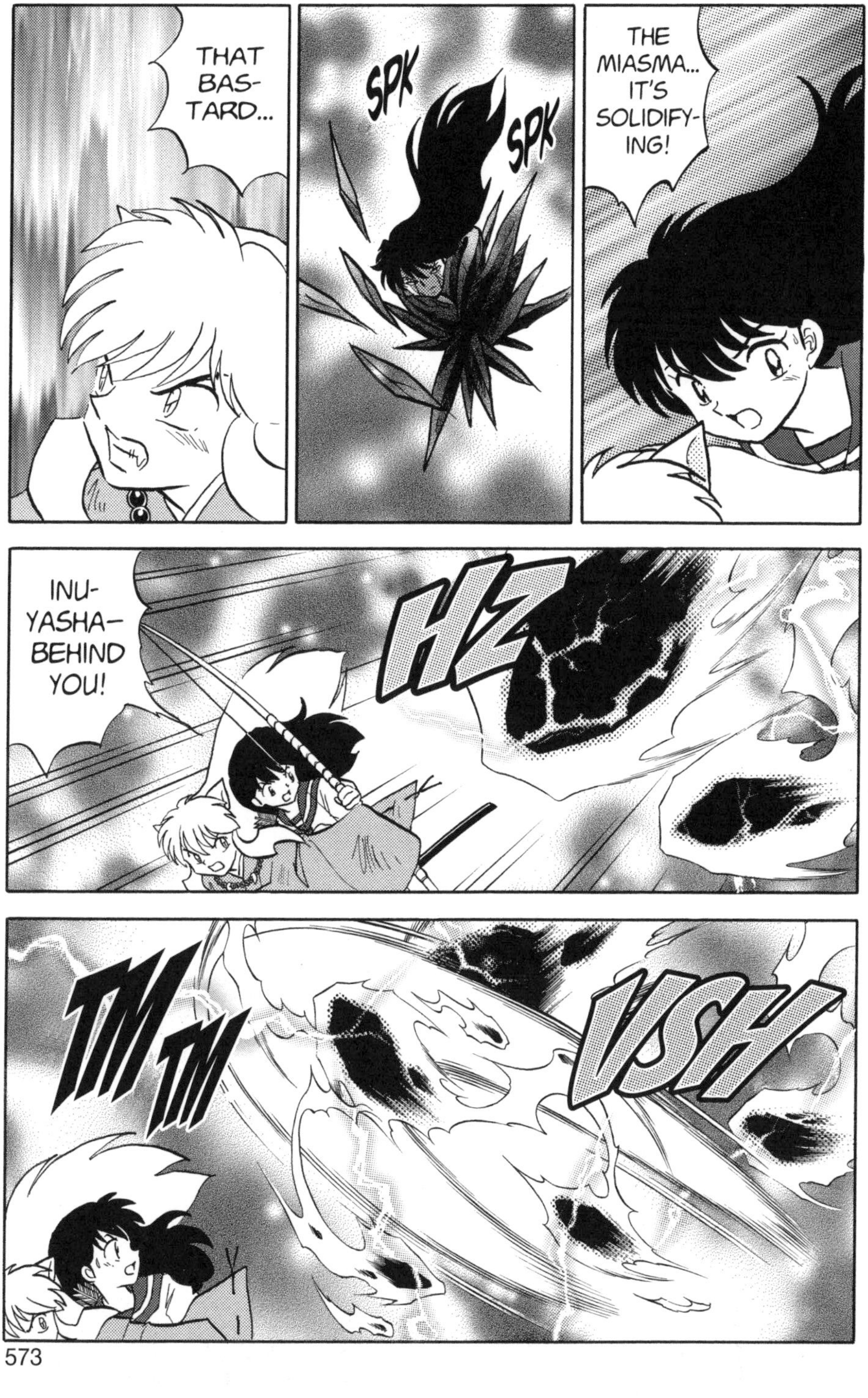
THE MIASMA... IT'S SOLIDIFYING!
SPK
SPK
THAT BASTARD...
HZ
INUYASHA—BEHIND YOU!
VSH
TM
TM

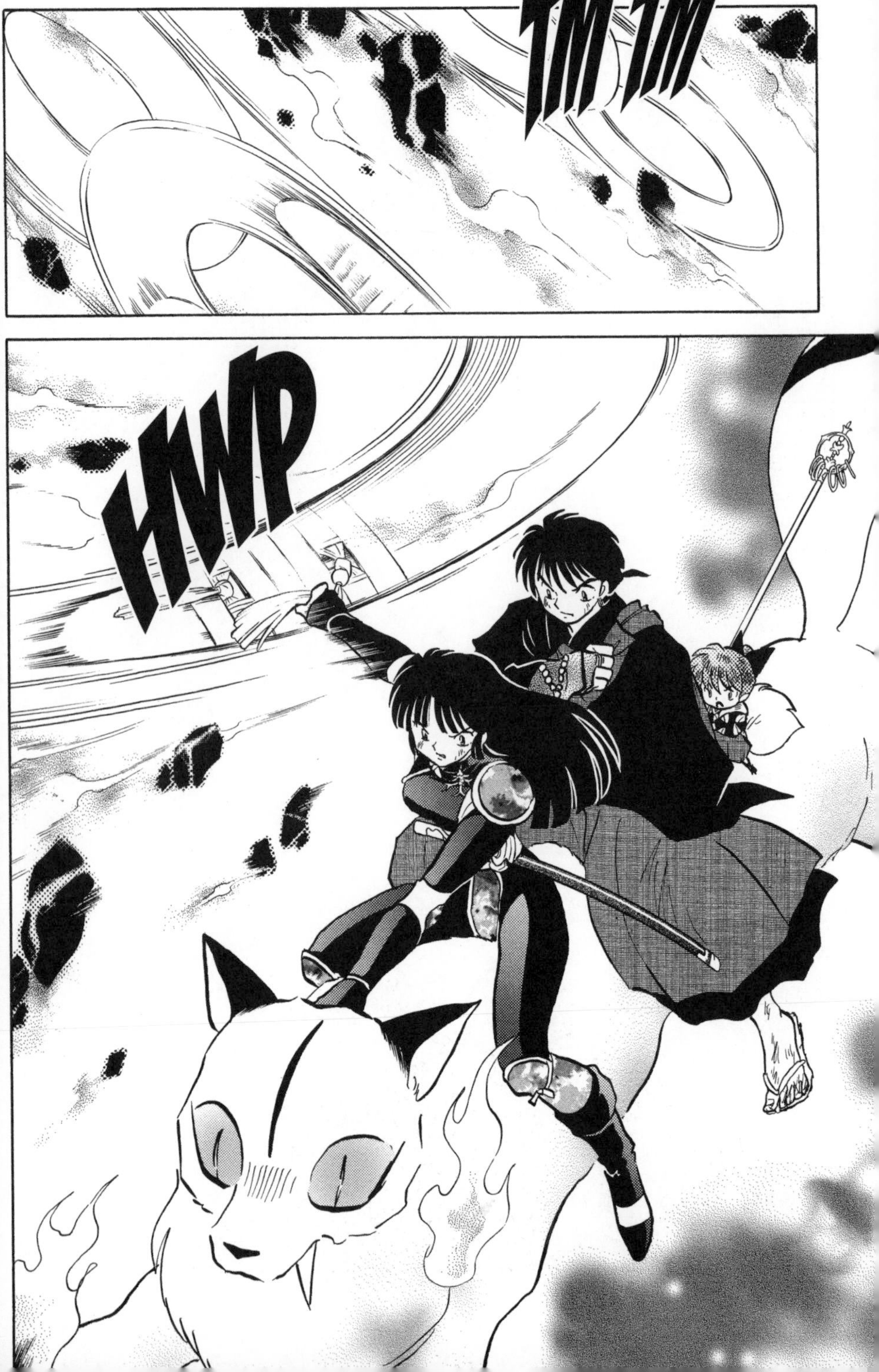
TM TM
HWP

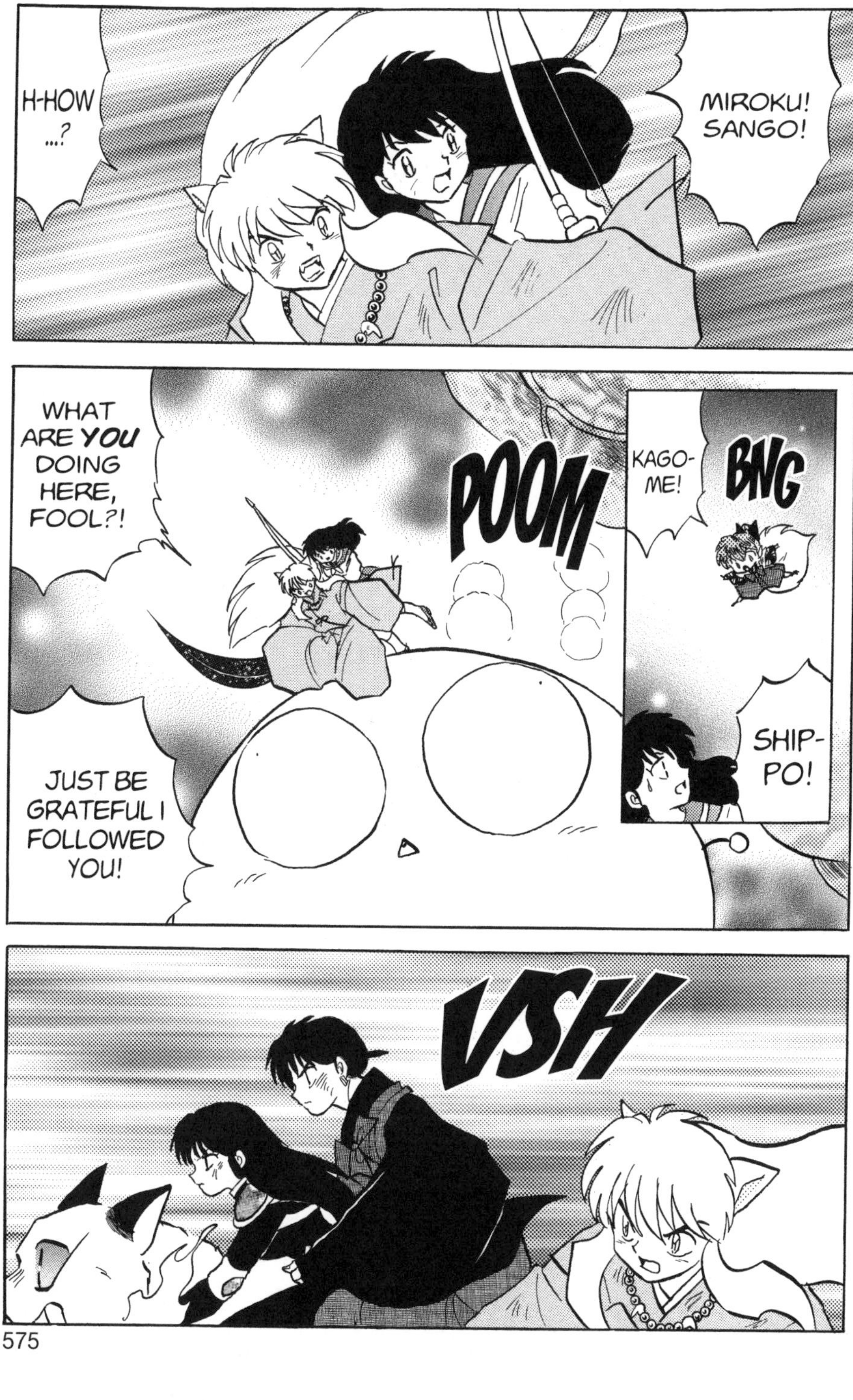
MIROKU! SANGO!
H-HOW ...?
KAGO-ME!
BNG
SHIP-PO!
POOM
WHAT ARE **YOU** DOING HERE, FOOL?!
JUST BE GRATEFUL I FOLLOWED YOU!
VSH

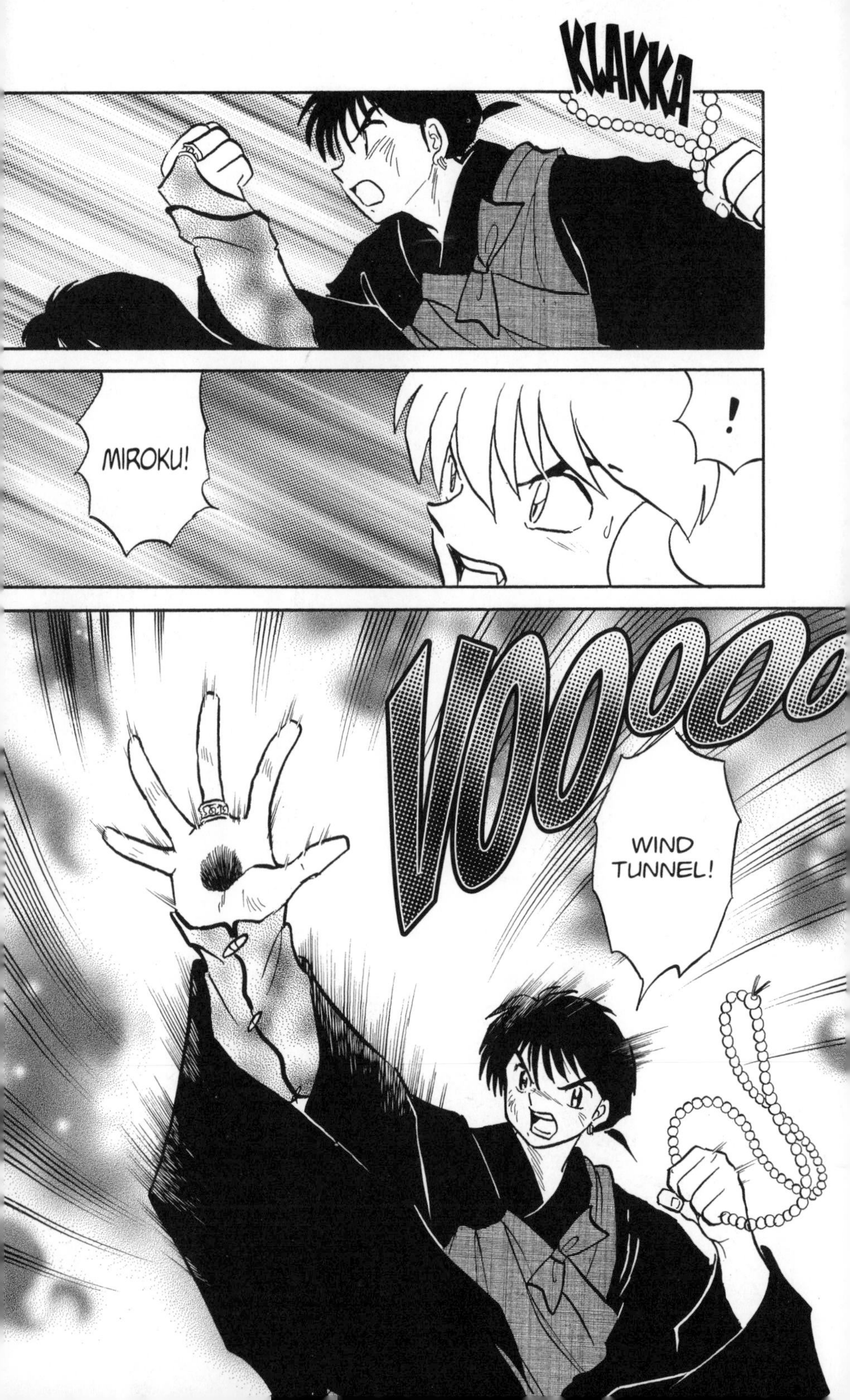
KLAKKA
!
MIROKU!
VOOOOO
WIND TUNNEL!

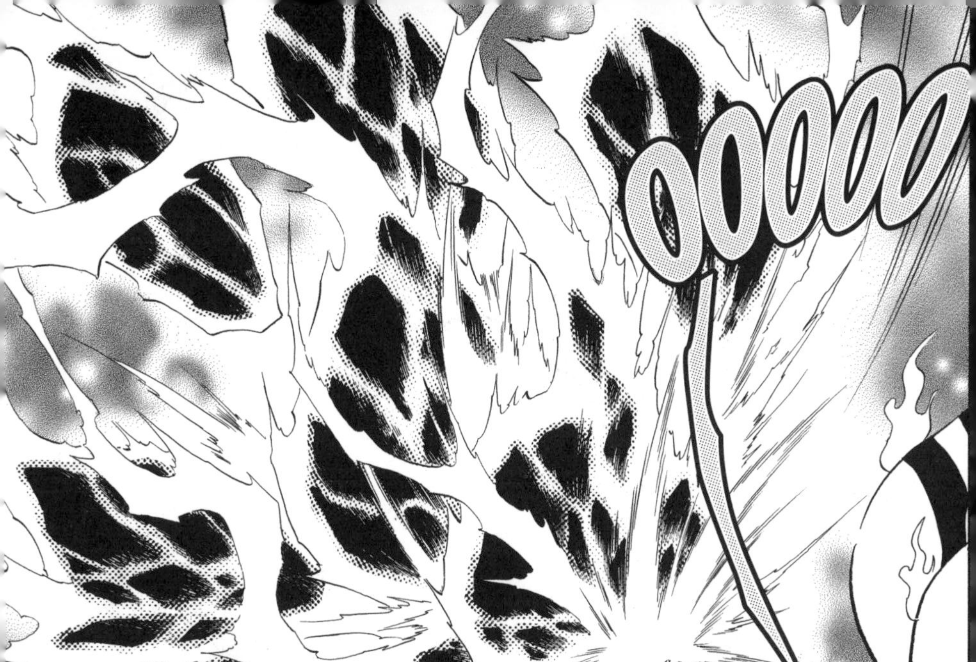
OOOOO
KKKKK

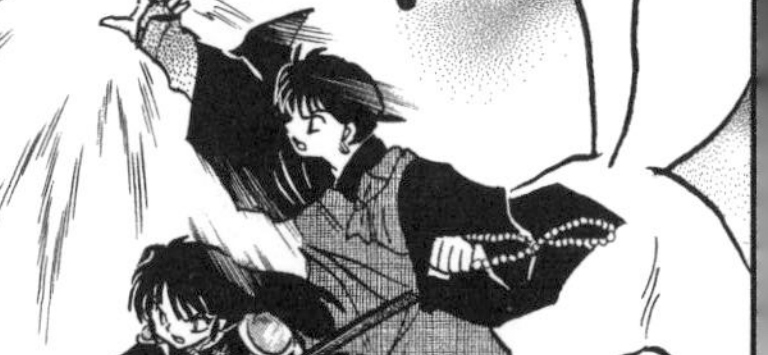
IT DIDN'T HURT ME!

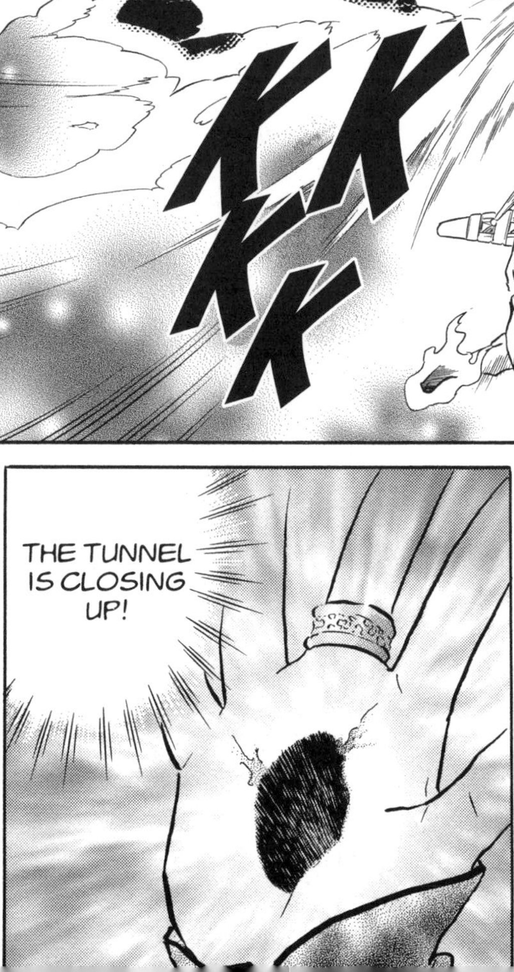
THE TUNNEL IS CLOSING UP!

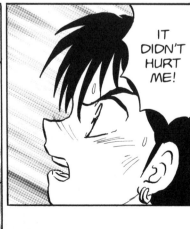

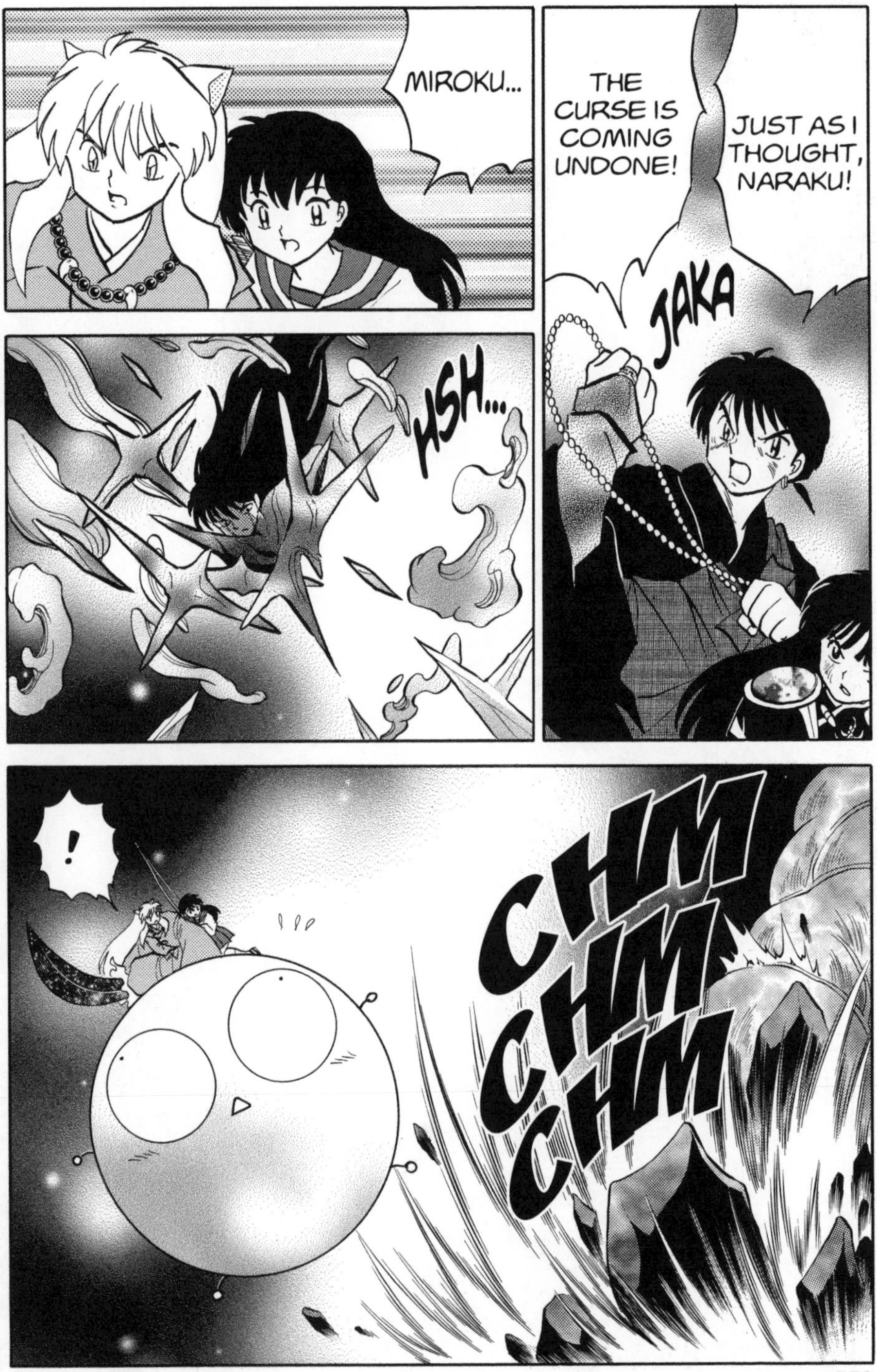
JUST AS I THOUGHT, NARAKU!
THE CURSE IS COMING UNDONE!
JAKA
MIROKU...
HSH...
!
CHM CHM CHM

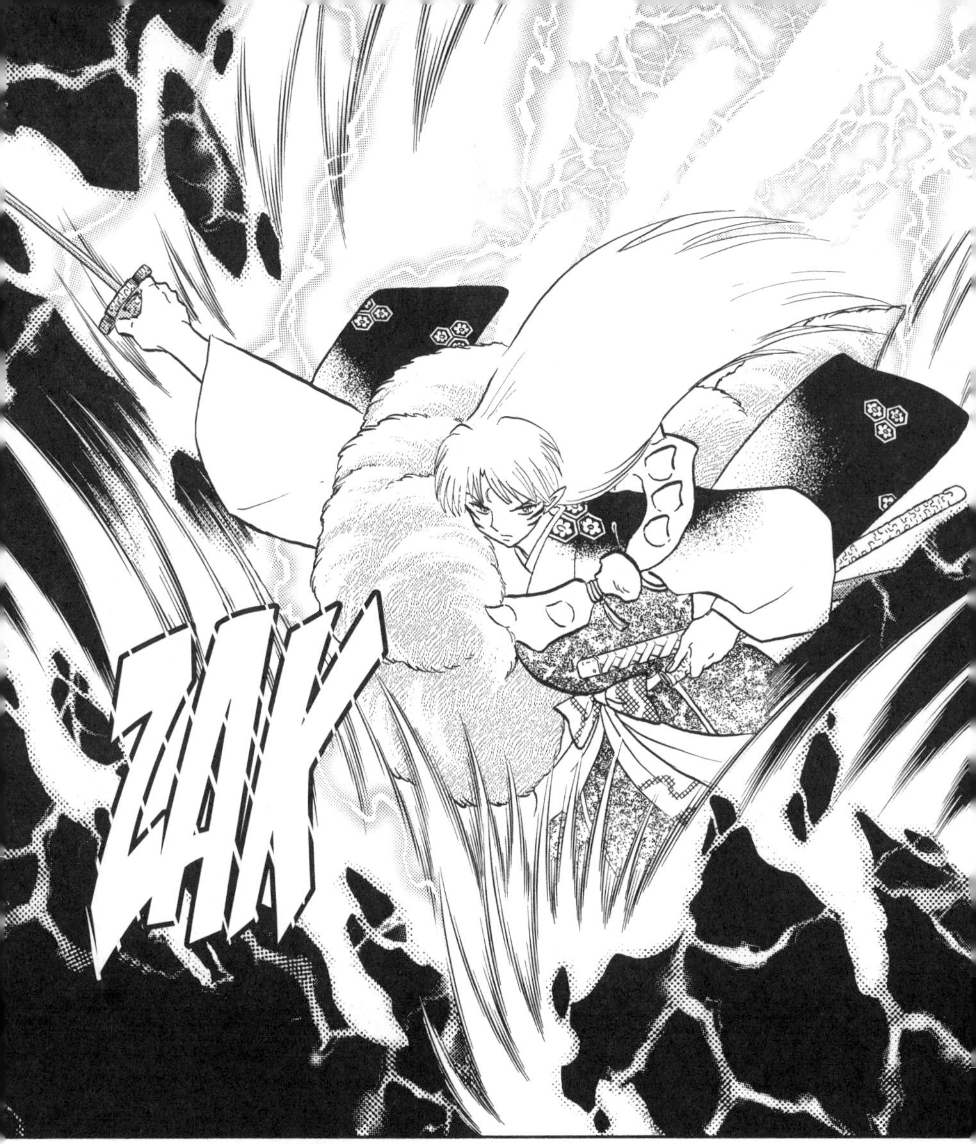
ZAK
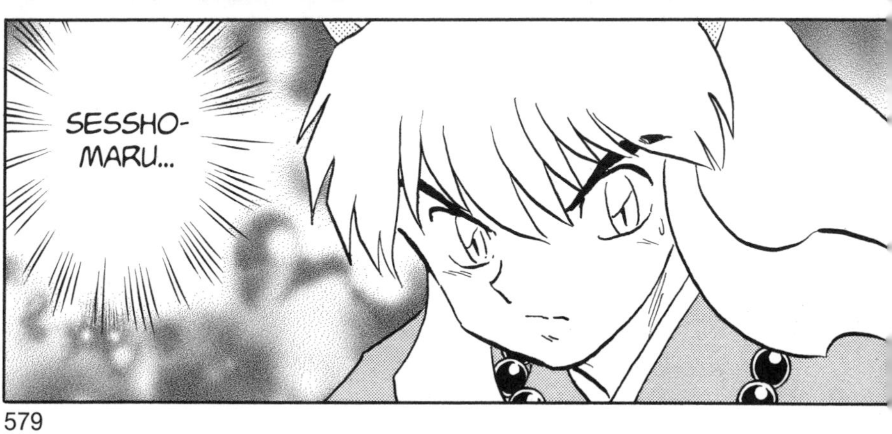
SESSHO-
MARU...

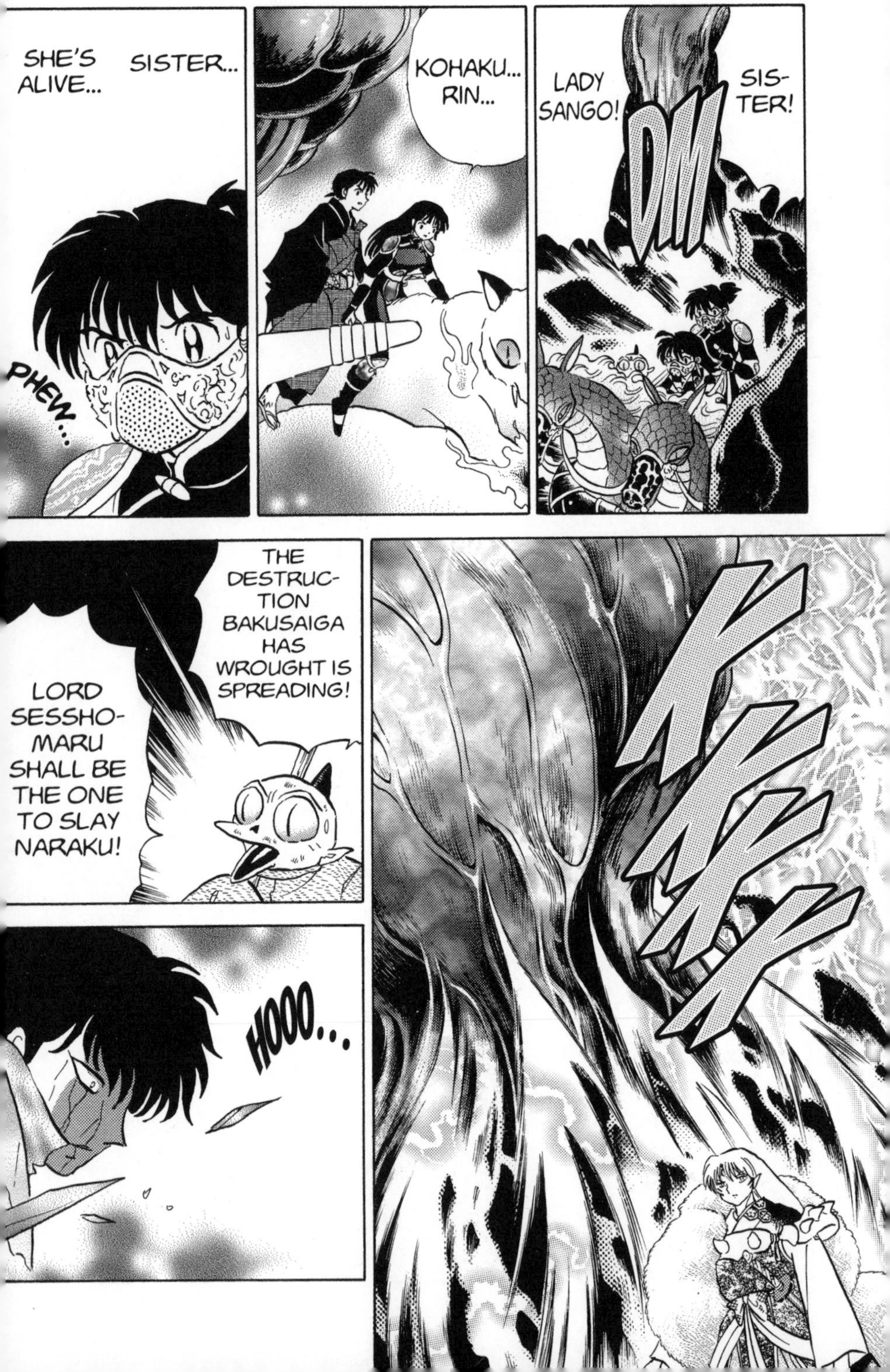
SIS-
TER!
LADY
SANGO!
DM
KOHAKU...
RIN...
SISTER...
SHE'S
ALIVE...
PHEW...
THE
DESTRUC-
TION
BAKUSAIGA
HAS
WROUGHT IS
SPREADING!
LORD
SESSHO-
MARU
SHALL BE
THE ONE
TO SLAY
NARAKU!
HOOO...

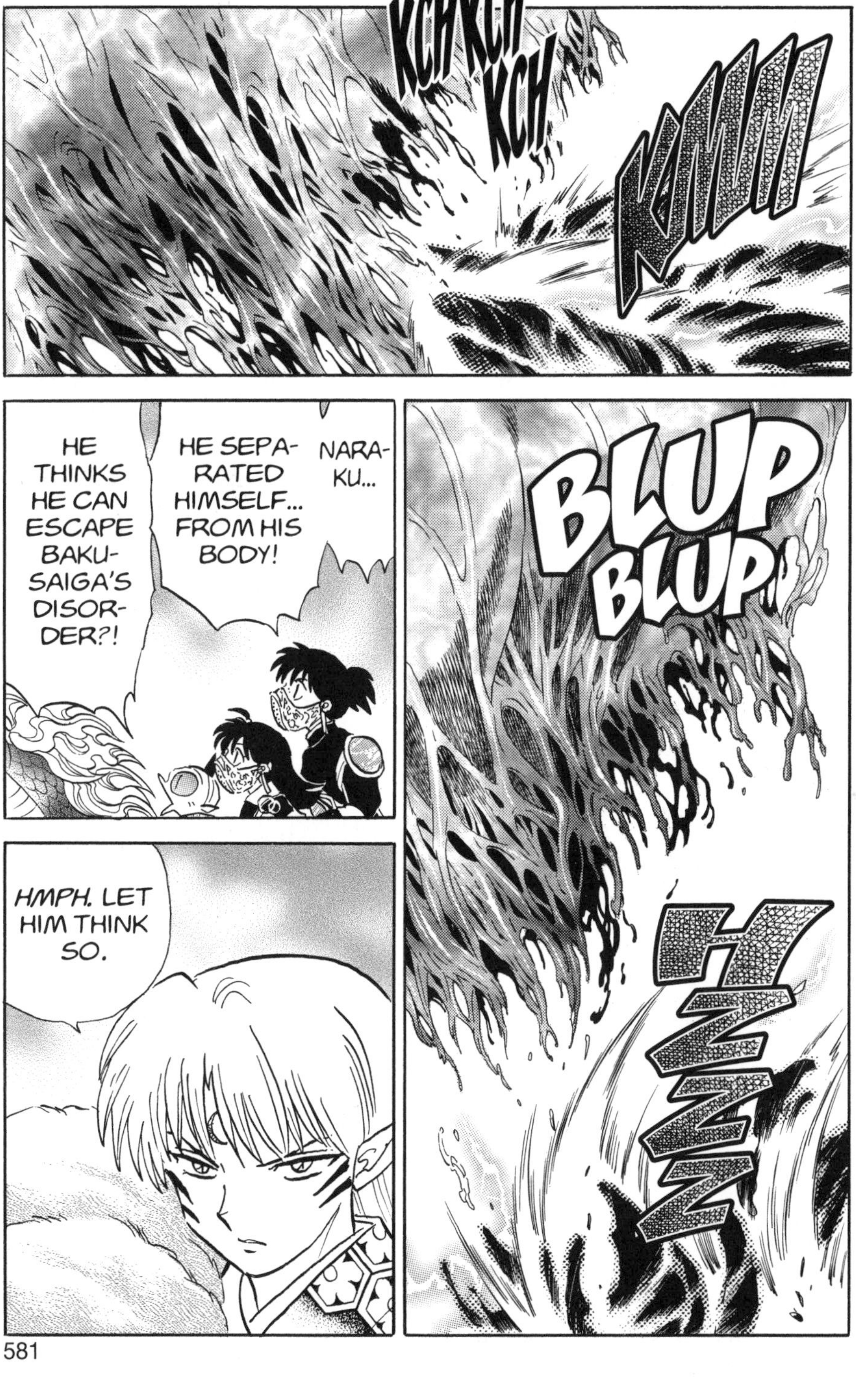
KCHKCH KCH
KMMM
BLUP BLUP
HMMMM
NARAKU...
HE SEPARATED HIMSELF... FROM HIS BODY!
HE THINKS HE CAN ESCAPE BAKUSAIGA'S DISORDER?!
HMPH. LET HIM THINK SO.

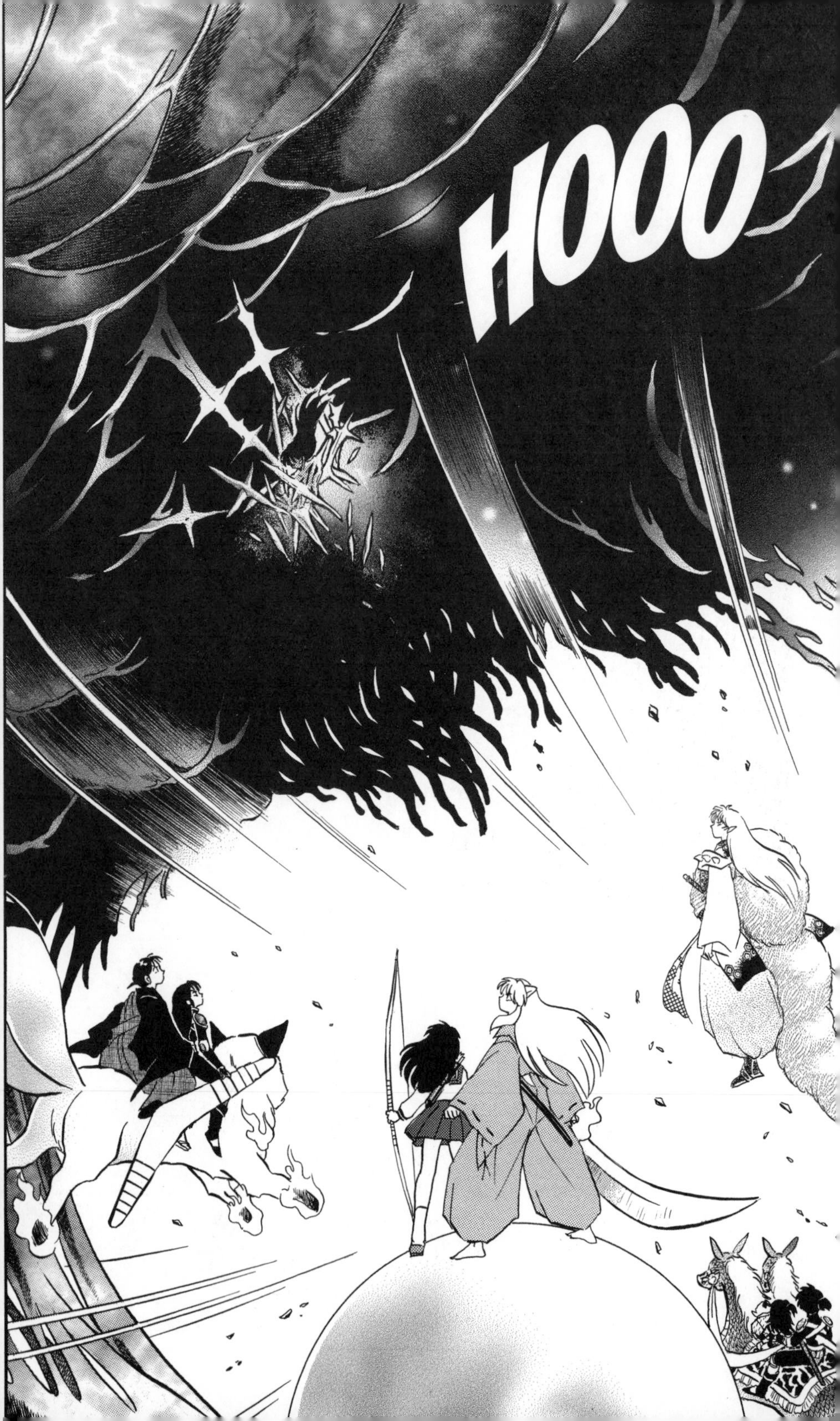
HOOO

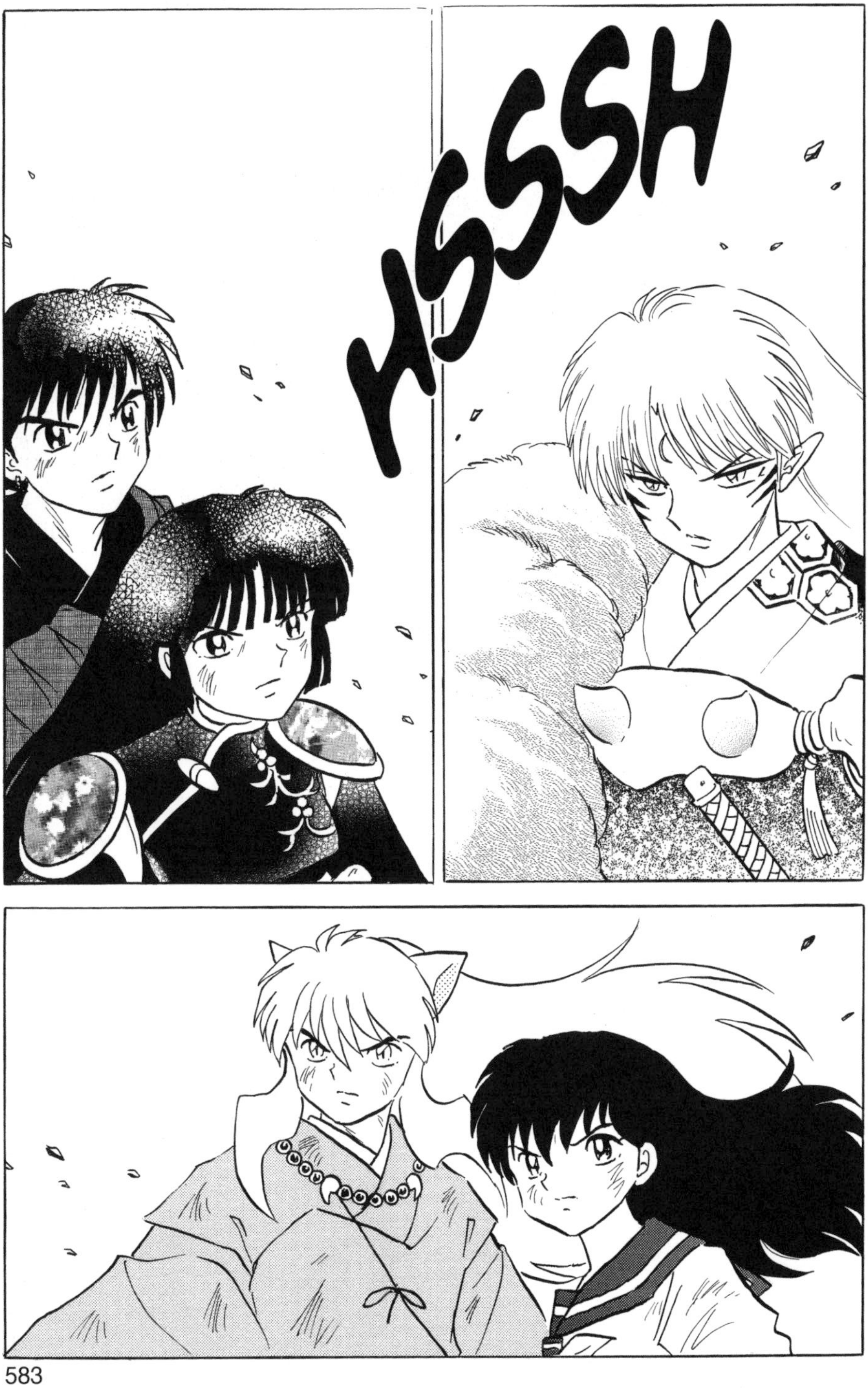
HSSSH

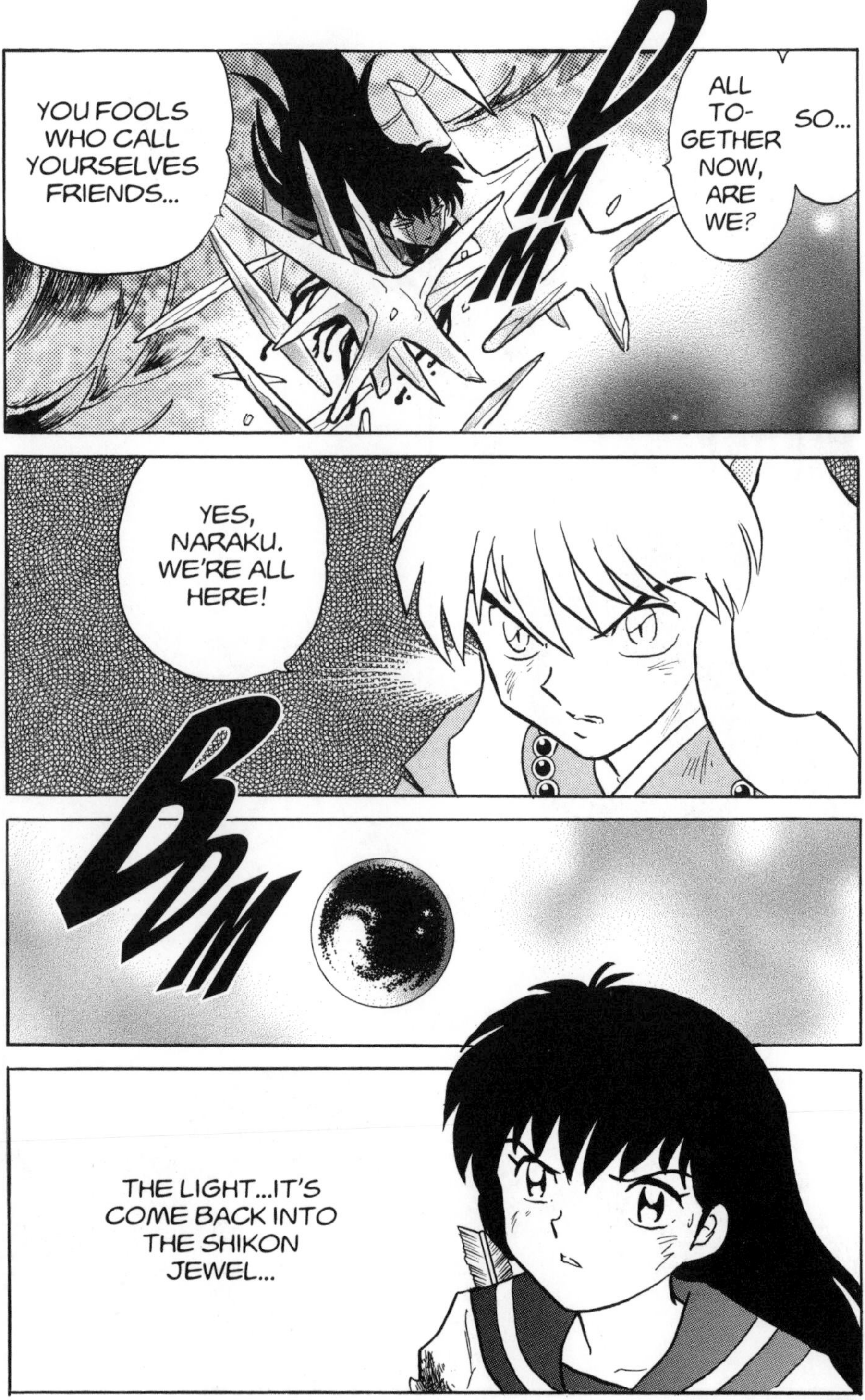
SO...
ALL TO-GETHER NOW, ARE WE?
YOU FOOLS WHO CALL YOURSELVES FRIENDS...
YES, NARAKU. WE'RE ALL HERE!
THE LIGHT...IT'S COME BACK INTO THE SHIKON JEWEL...

SCROLL TWO
COLLAPSE

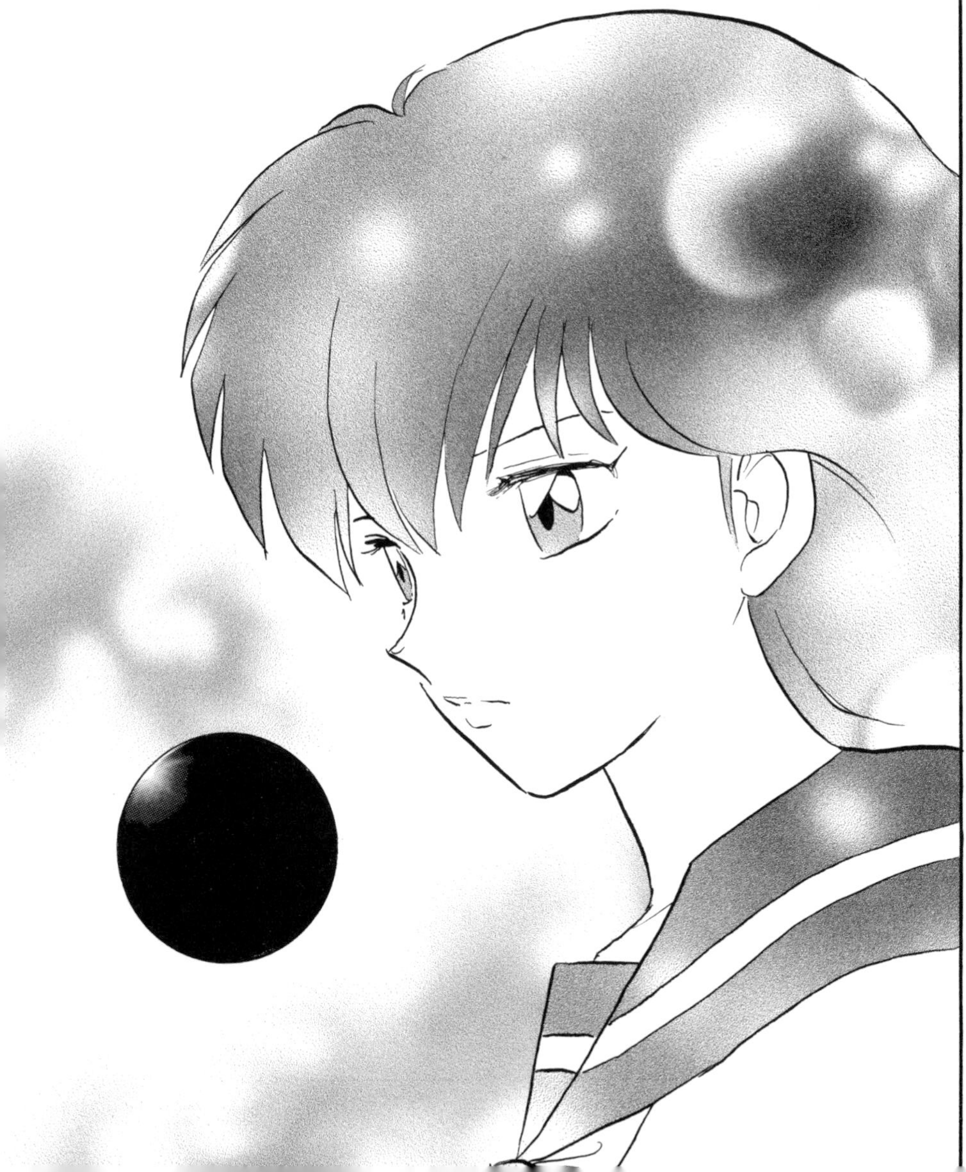

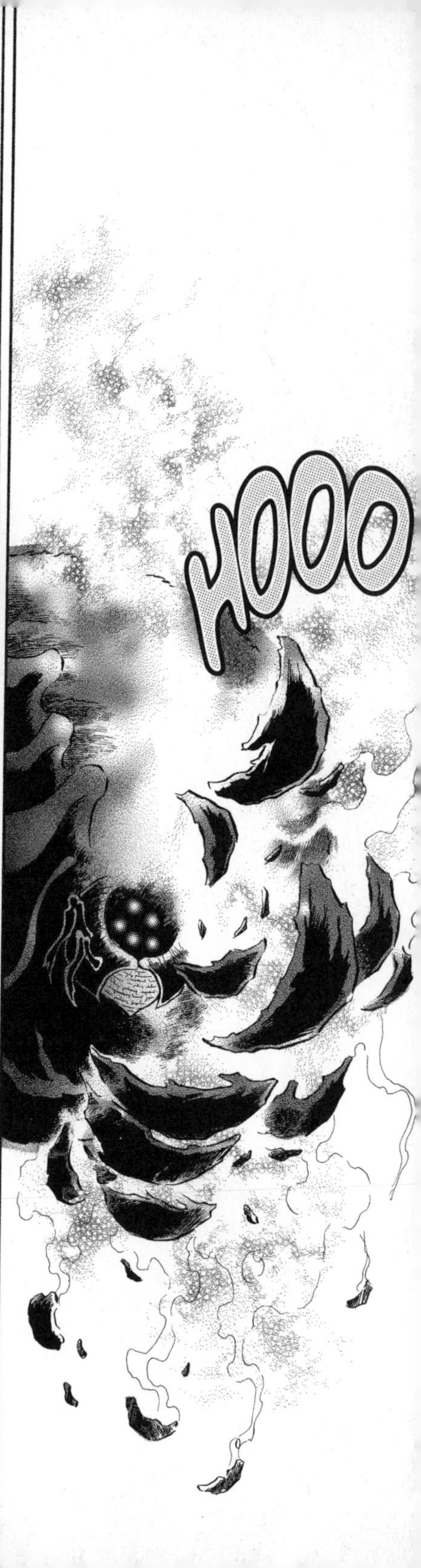
HOOO
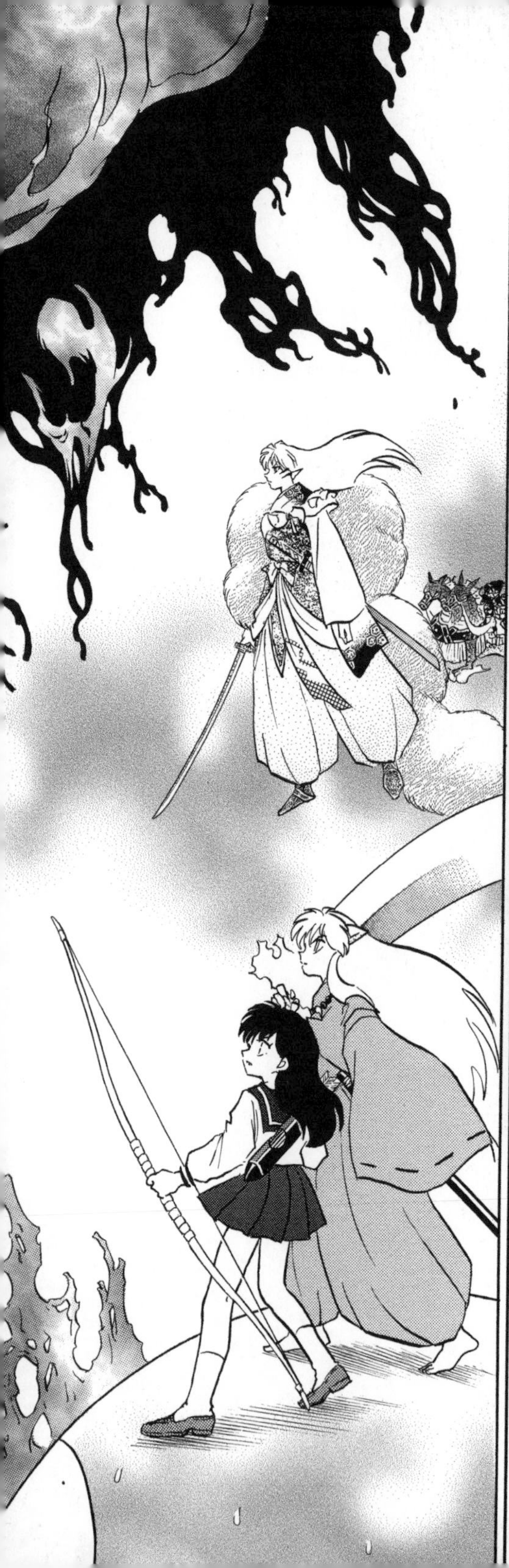

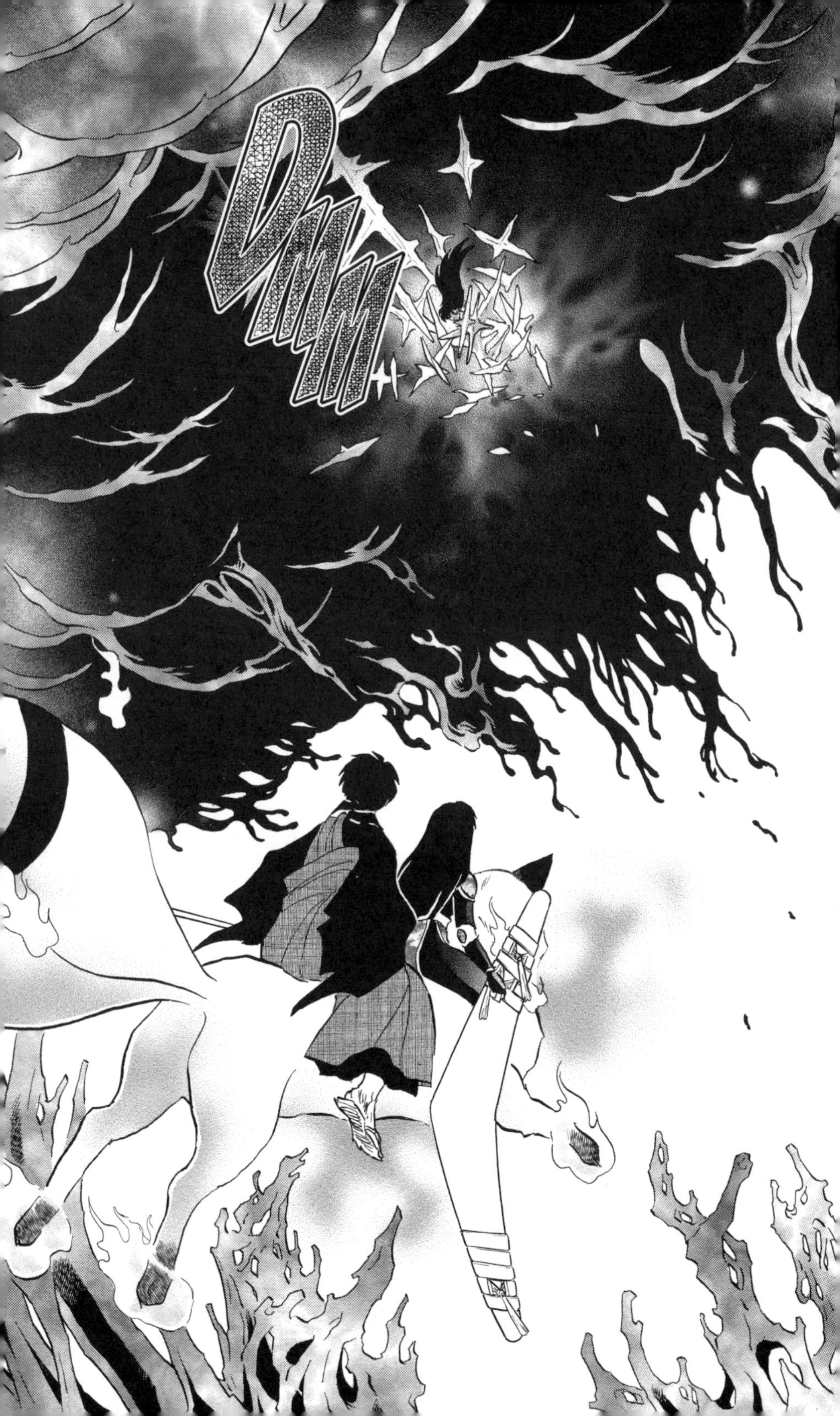
DMMM

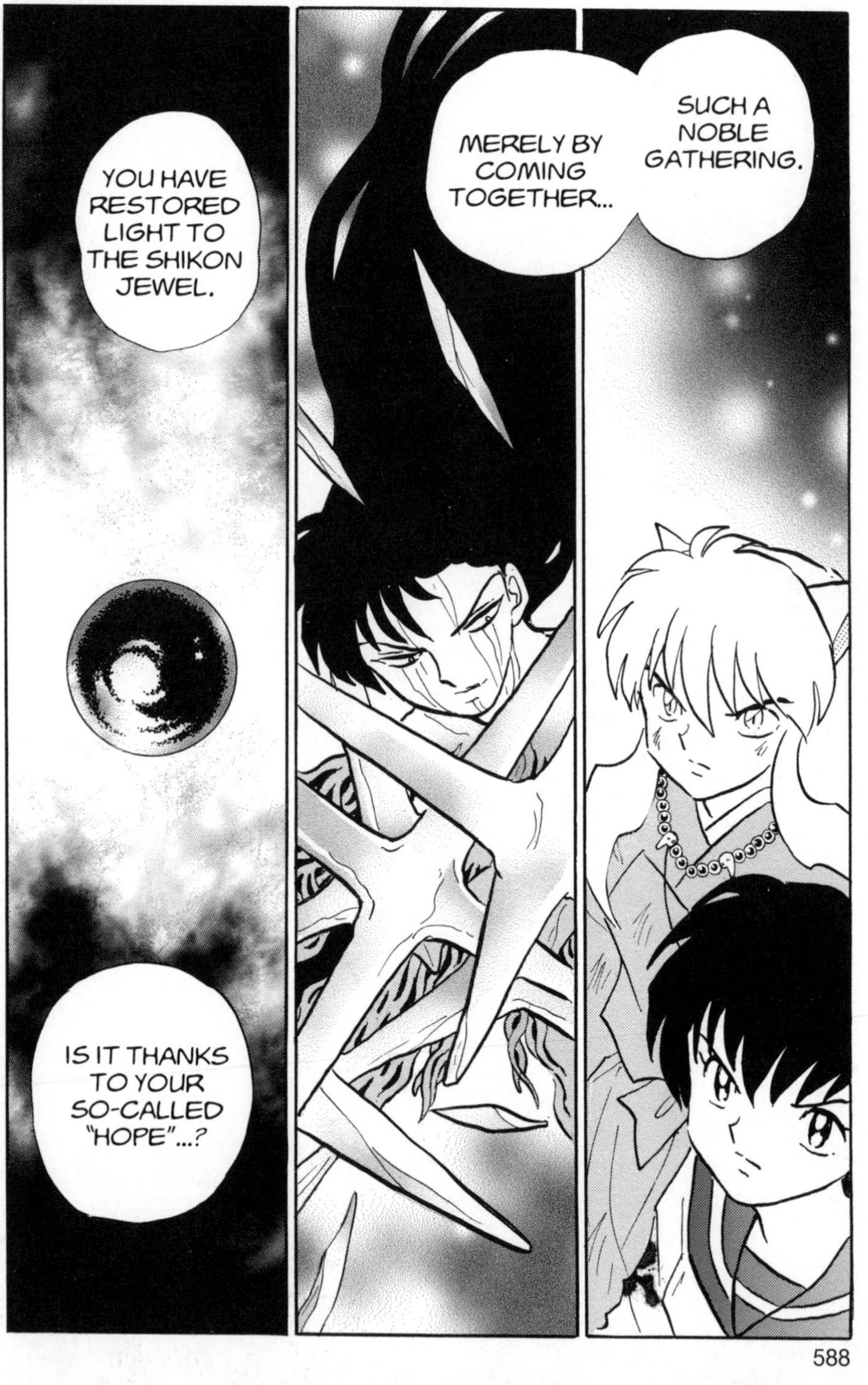
SUCH A NOBLE GATHERING.
MERELY BY COMING TOGETHER...
YOU HAVE RESTORED LIGHT TO THE SHIKON JEWEL.
IS IT THANKS TO YOUR SO-CALLED "HOPE"...?

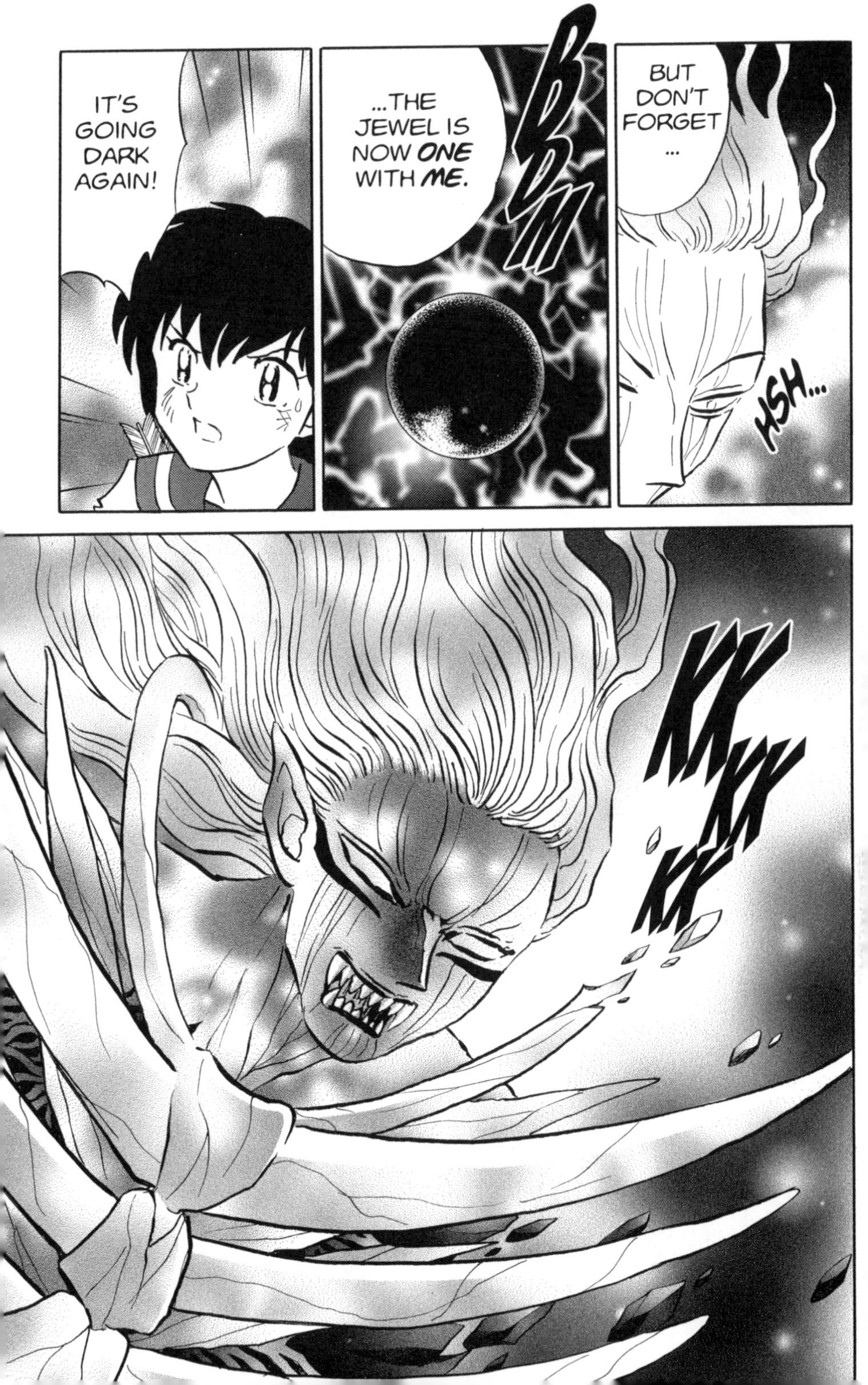
BUT DON'T FORGET ...
HSH...
...THE JEWEL IS NOW ONE WITH ME.
BDM
IT'S GOING DARK AGAIN!

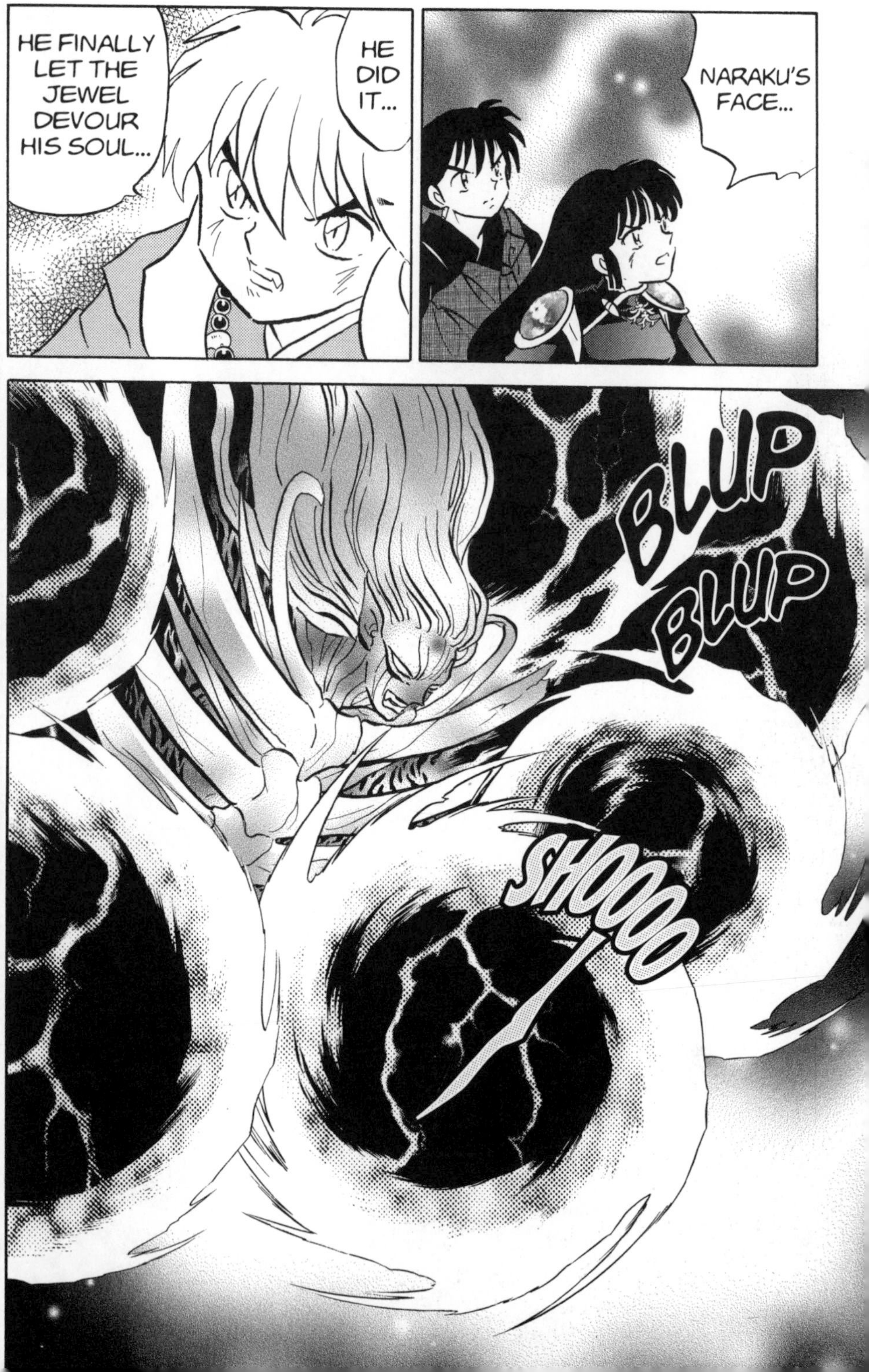
NARAKU'S FACE...
HE DID IT...
HE FINALLY LET THE JEWEL DEVOUR HIS SOUL...
BLUP BLUP
SHOOOO

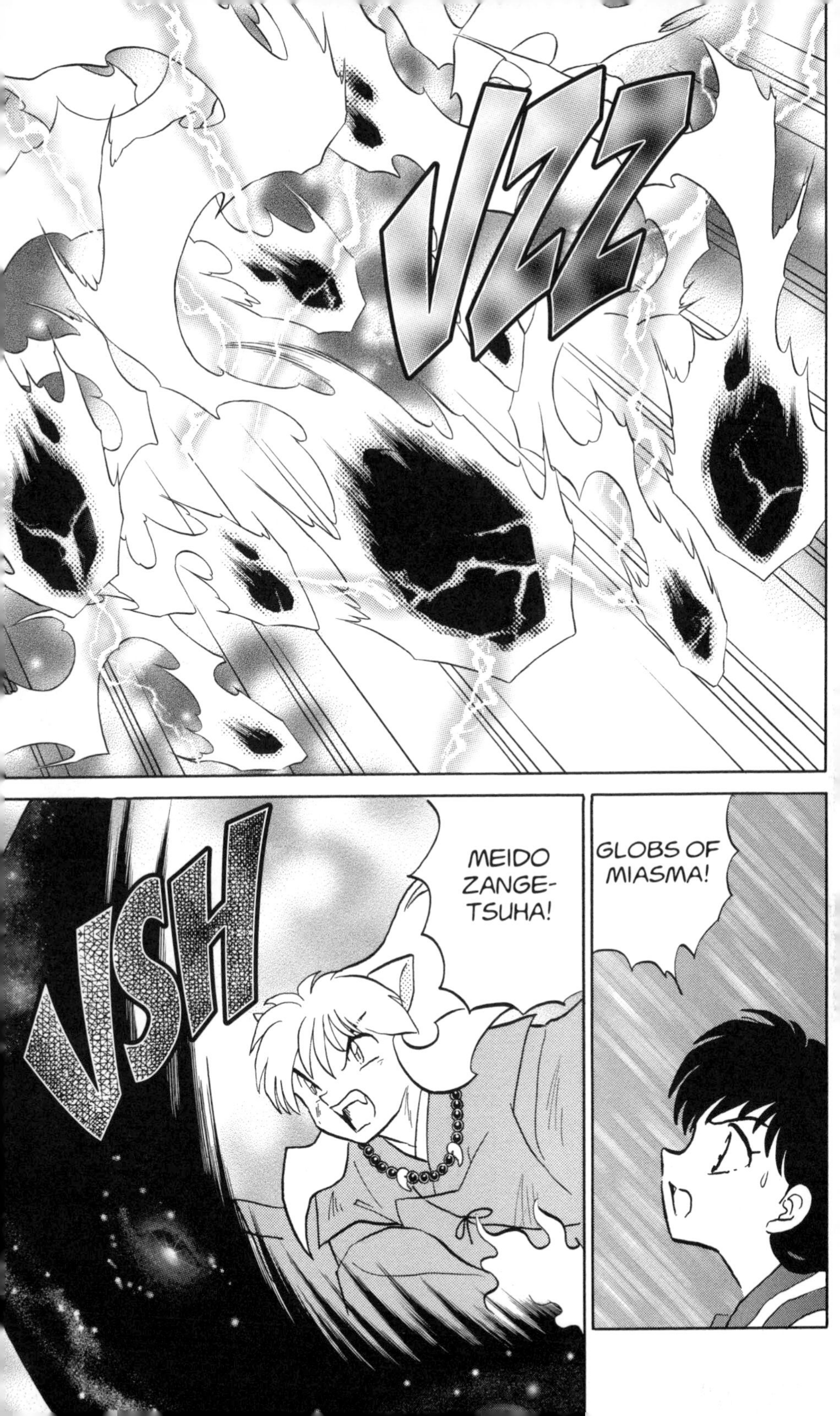
VIZZ
GLOBS OF MIASMA!
MEIDO ZANGE-TSUHA!
VSH

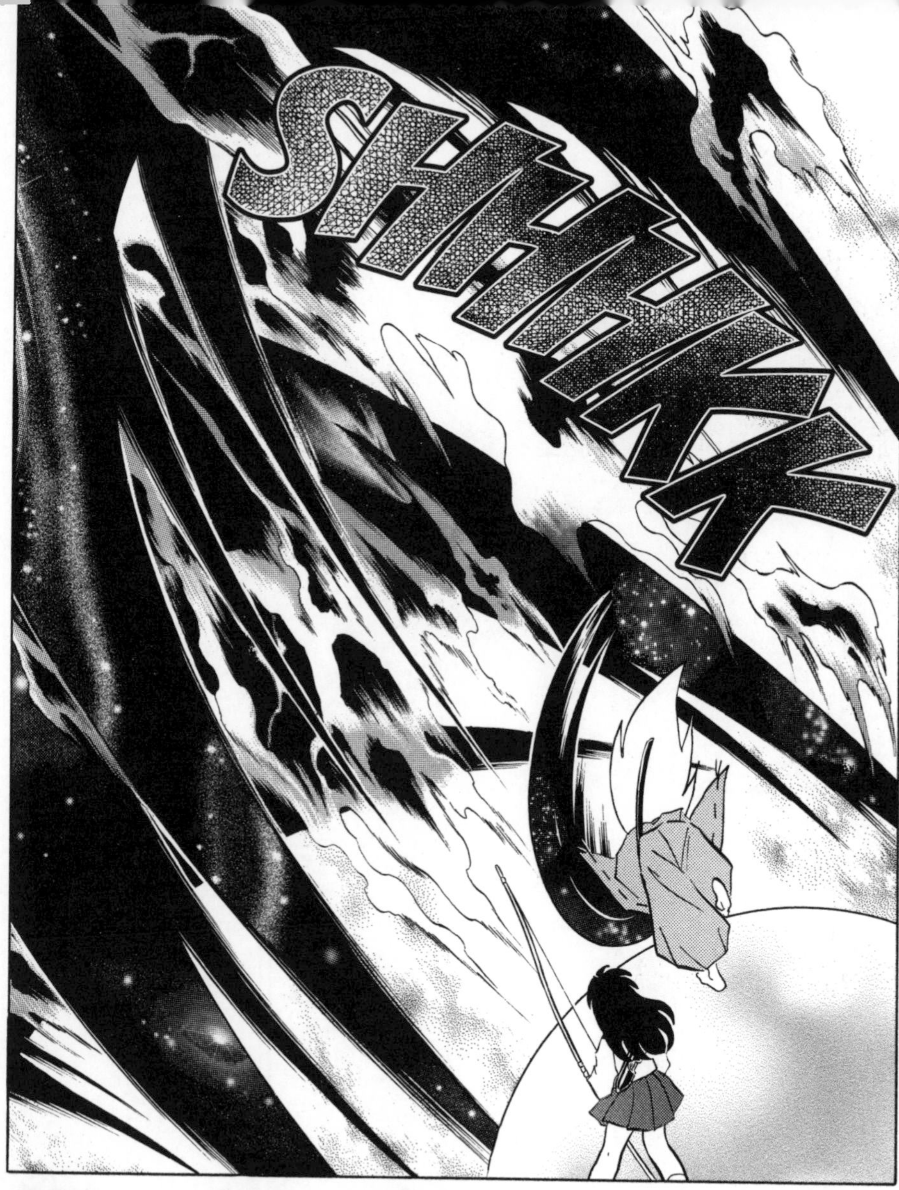
SHHHKK
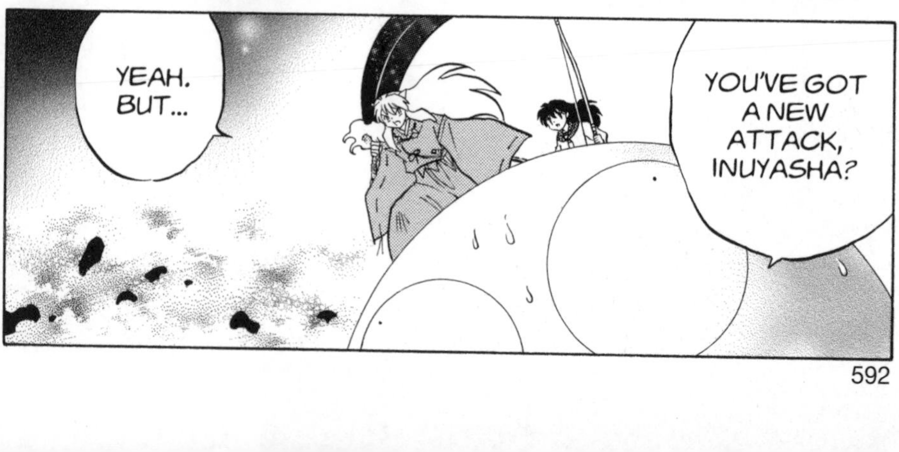
YOU'VE GOT A NEW ATTACK, INUYASHA?
YEAH. BUT...

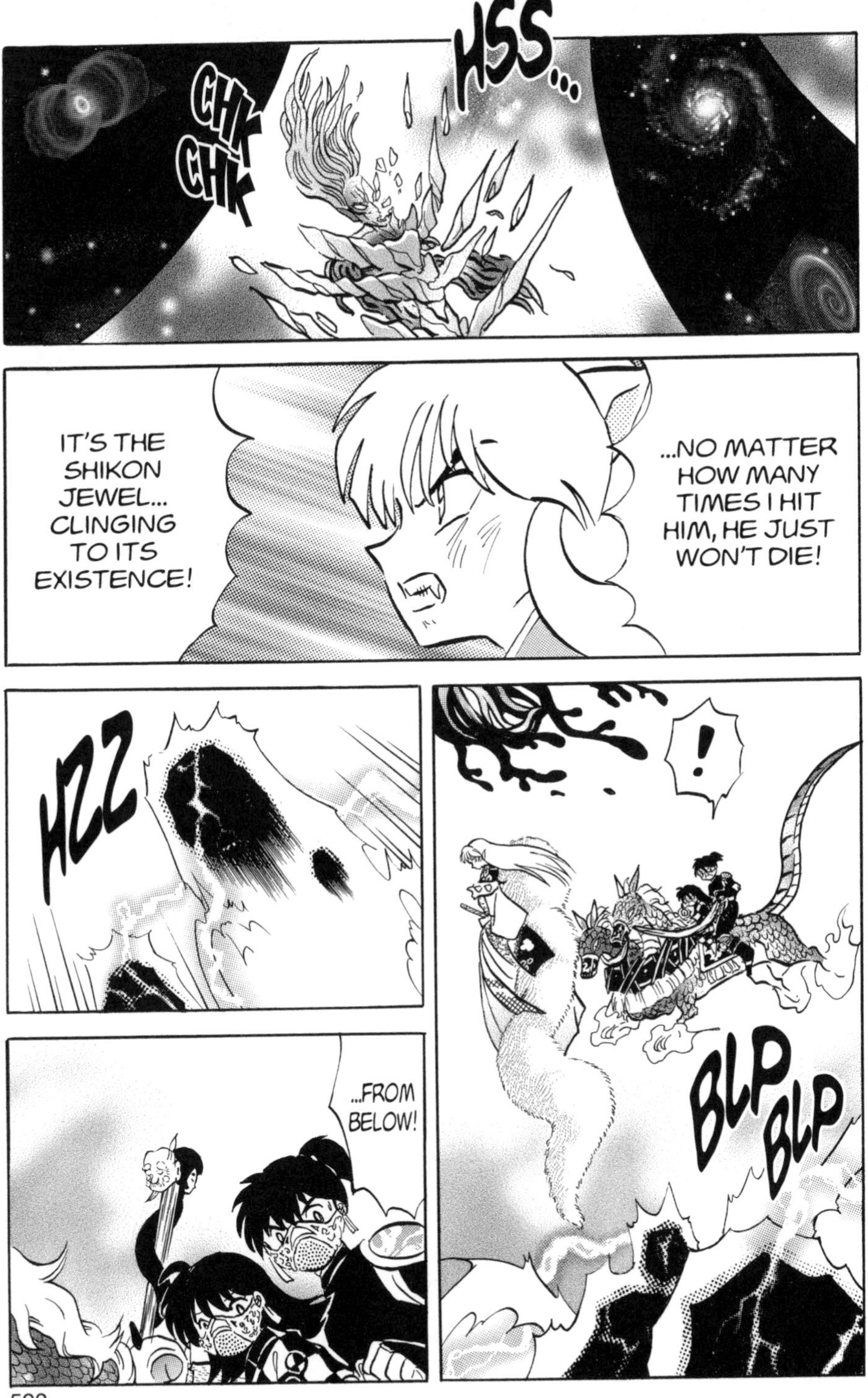
HSS...
CHK CHK
...NO MATTER HOW MANY TIMES I HIT HIM, HE JUST WON'T DIE!
IT'S THE SHIKON JEWEL... CLINGING TO ITS EXISTENCE!
!
BLP BLP
HZZ
...FROM BELOW!

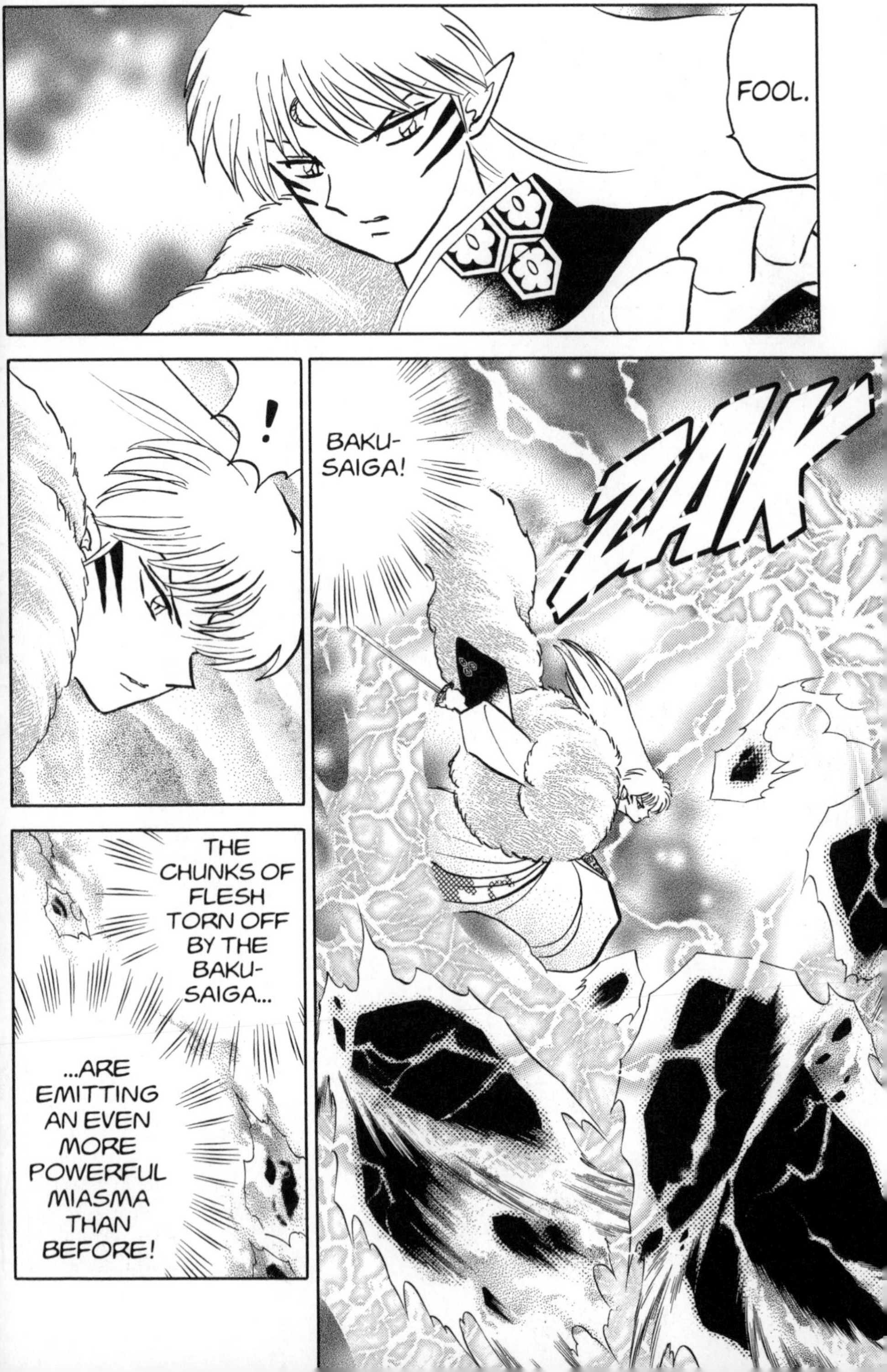
FOOL.
ZAK
BAKU-SAIGA!
!
THE CHUNKS OF FLESH TORN OFF BY THE BAKU-SAIGA...
...ARE EMITTING AN EVEN MORE POWERFUL MIASMA THAN BEFORE!

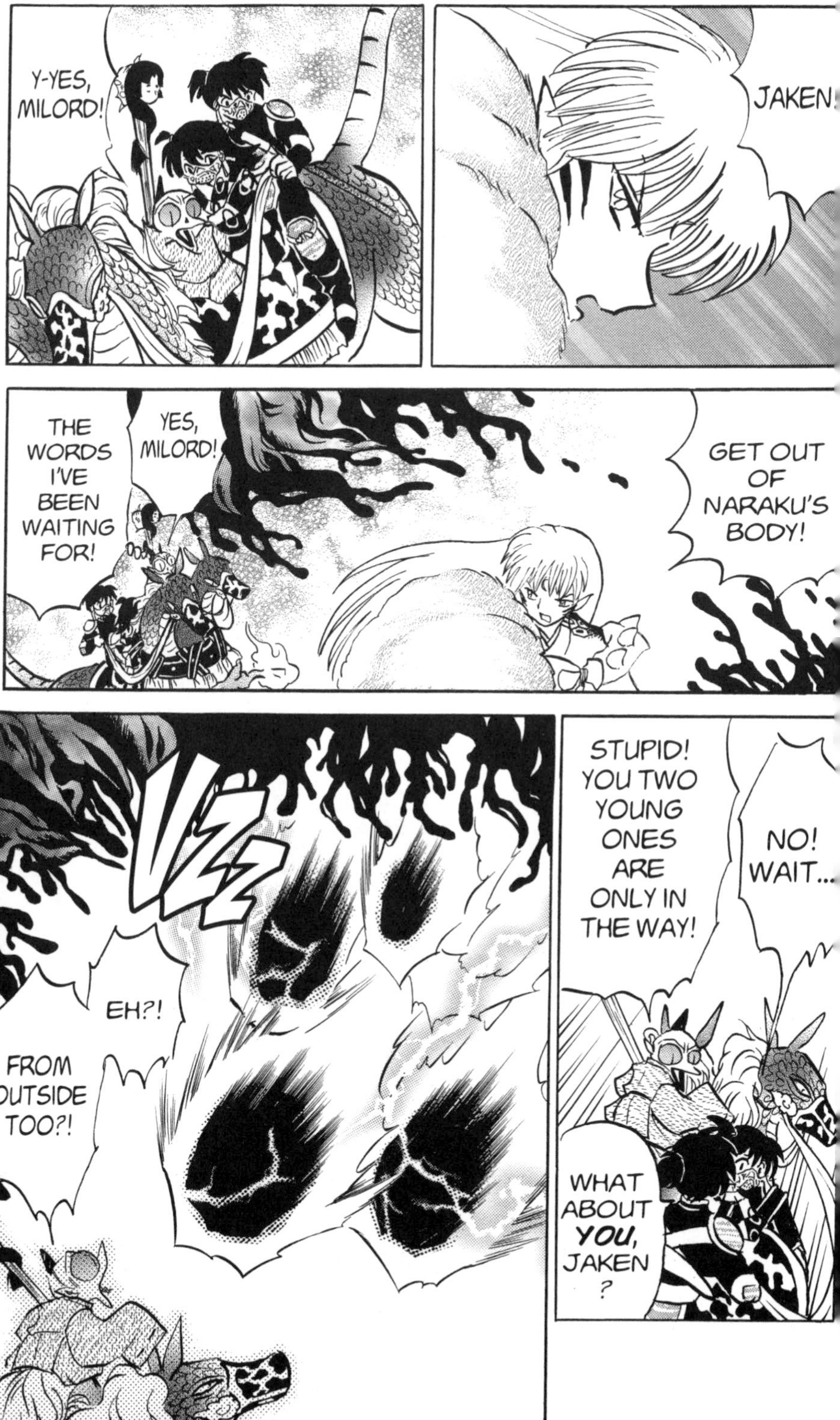
JAKEN!
Y-YES, MILORD!
GET OUT OF NARAKU'S BODY!
YES, MILORD!
THE WORDS I'VE BEEN WAITING FOR!
NO! WAIT...
STUPID! YOU TWO YOUNG ONES ARE ONLY IN THE WAY!
WHAT ABOUT *YOU*, JAKEN?
EH?!
FROM OUTSIDE TOO?!

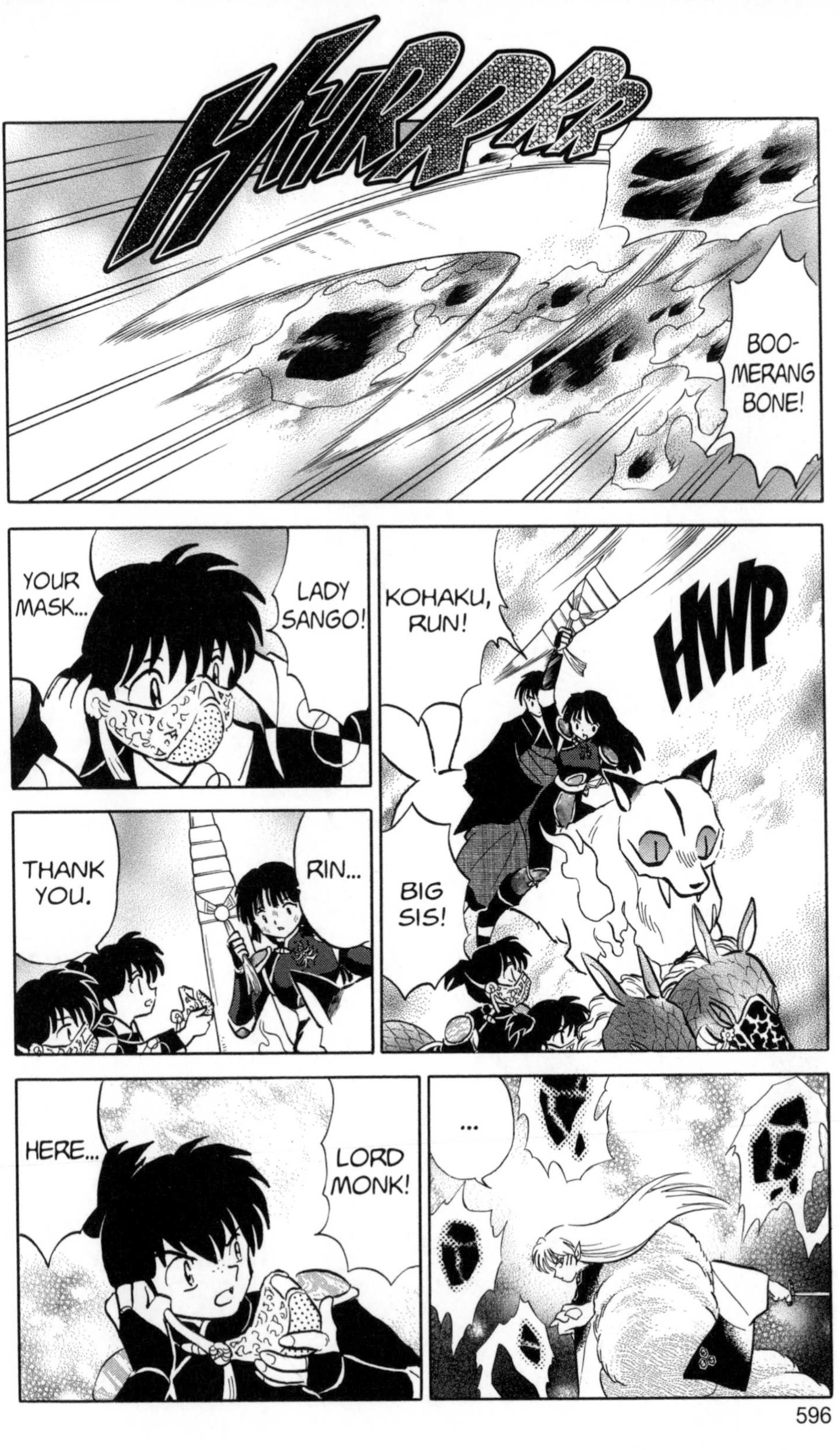
WHIRRRR
BOO-MERANG BONE!
HWP
KOHAKU, RUN!
BIG SIS!
LADY SANGO!
YOUR MASK...
RIN...
THANK YOU.
...
LORD MONK!
HERE...

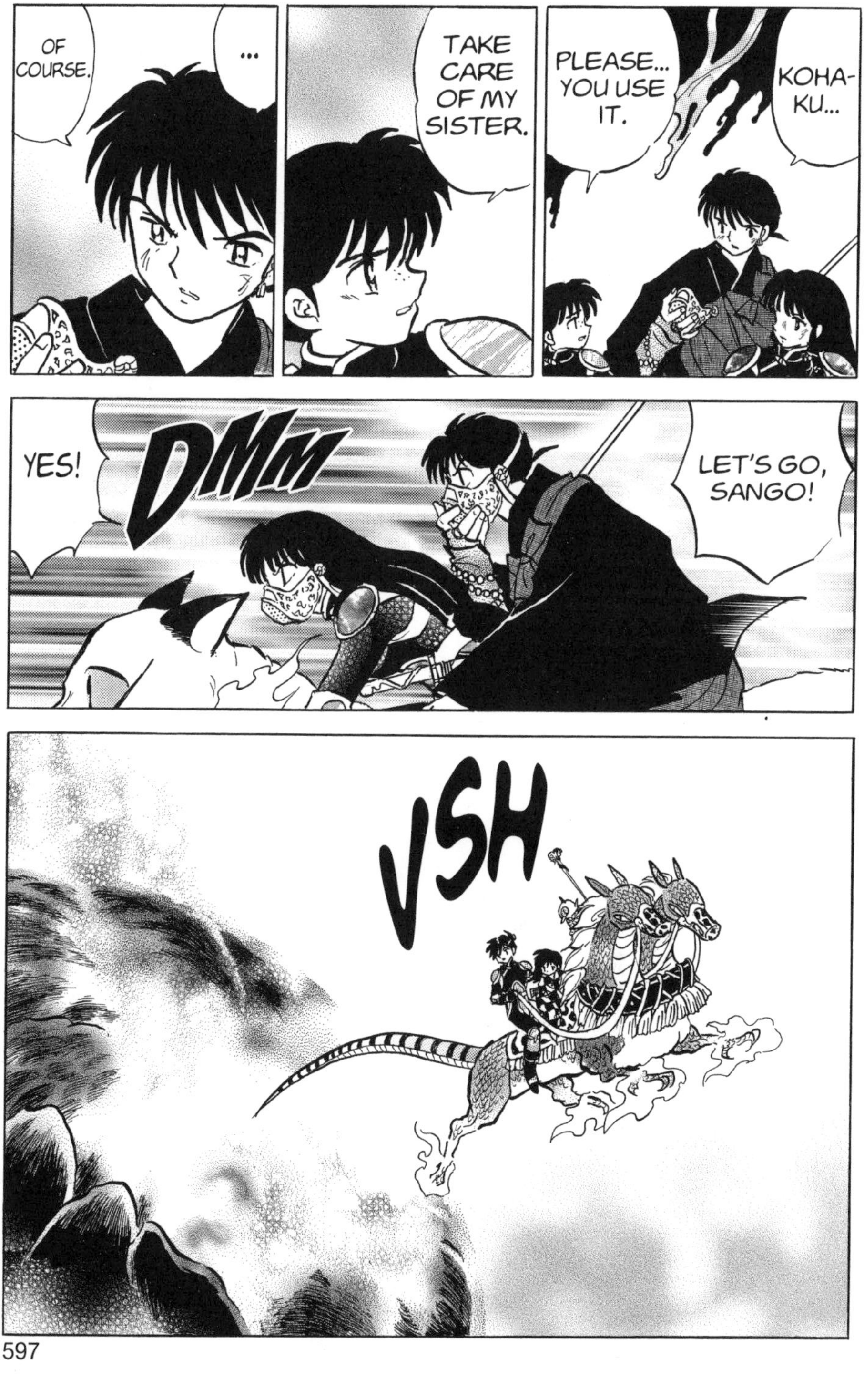
KOHAKU...
PLEASE... YOU USE IT.
TAKE CARE OF MY SISTER.
...
OF COURSE.
LET'S GO, SANGO!
DMM
YES!
VSH

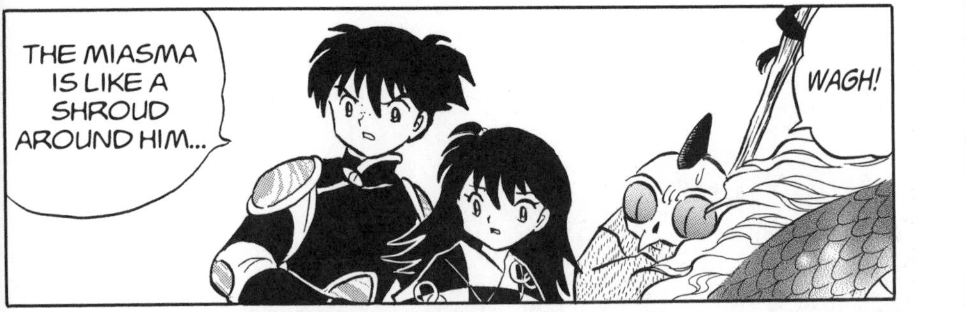
WAGH!
THE MIASMA IS LIKE A SHROUD AROUND HIM...

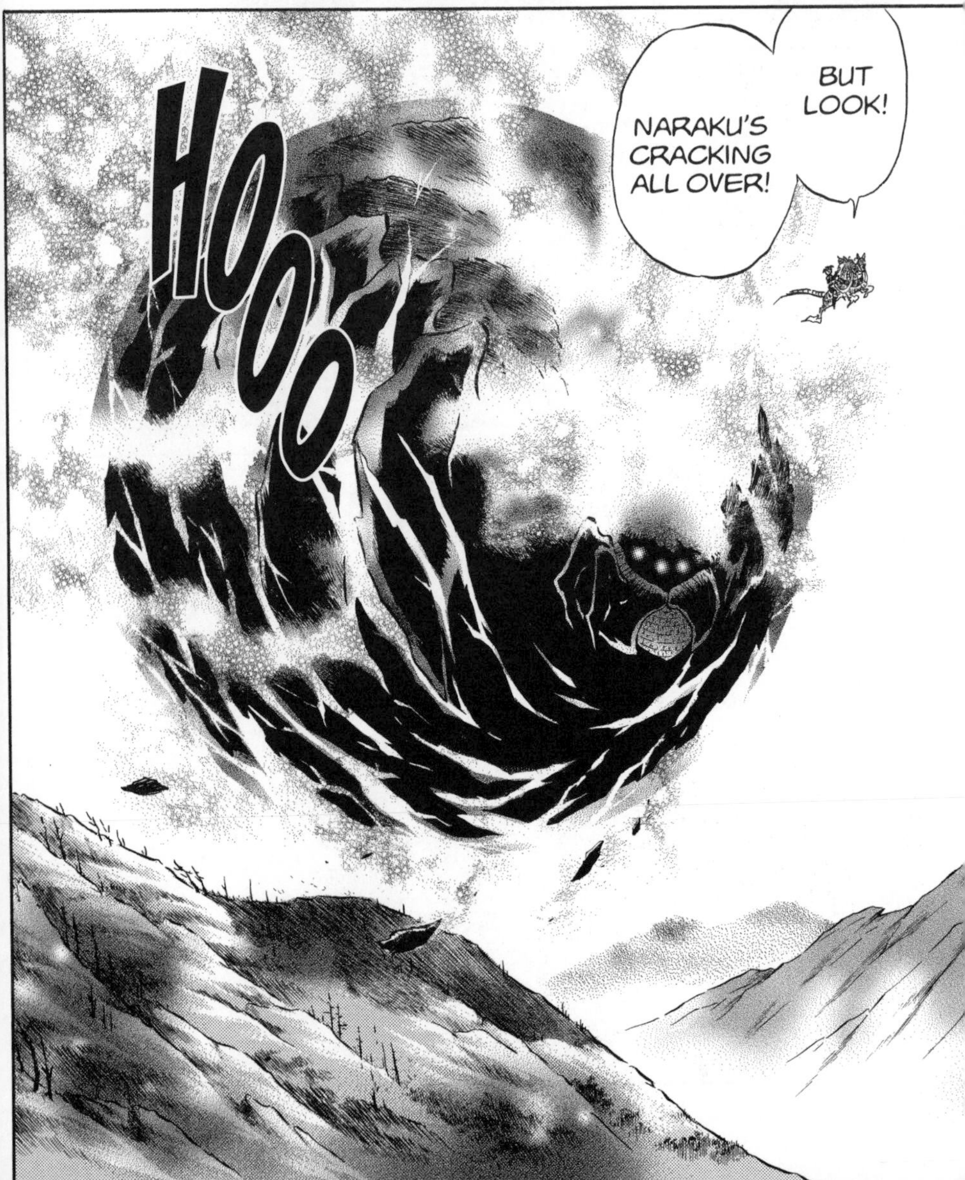
BUT LOOK! NARAKU'S CRACKING ALL OVER!
HOOOO

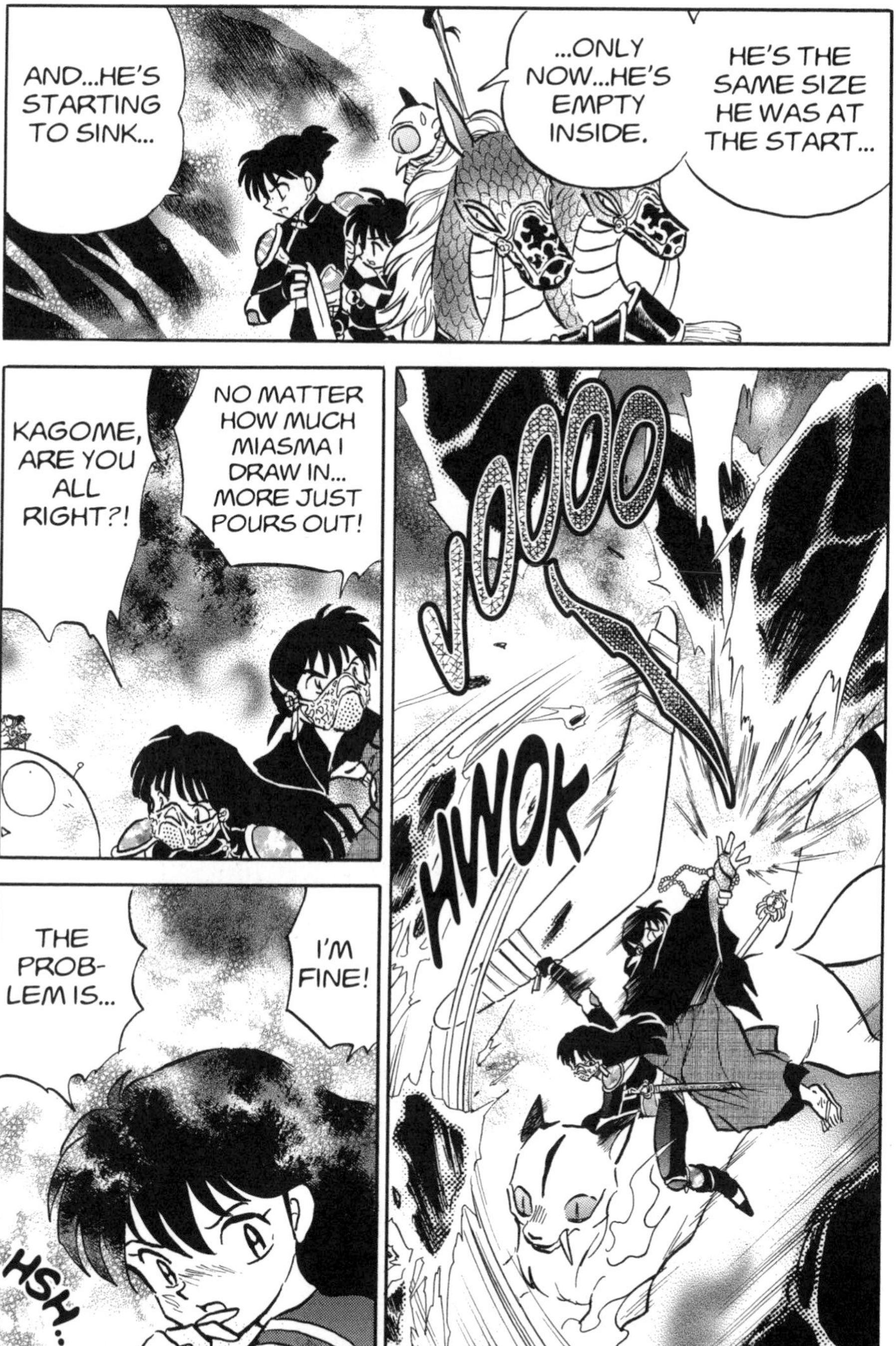
HE'S THE SAME SIZE HE WAS AT THE START...
...ONLY NOW...HE'S EMPTY INSIDE.
AND...HE'S STARTING TO SINK...
VOOOOO
HWOK
NO MATTER HOW MUCH MIASMA I DRAW IN... MORE JUST POURS OUT!
KAGOME, ARE YOU ALL RIGHT?!
I'M FINE!
THE PROB-LEM IS...
HSH...

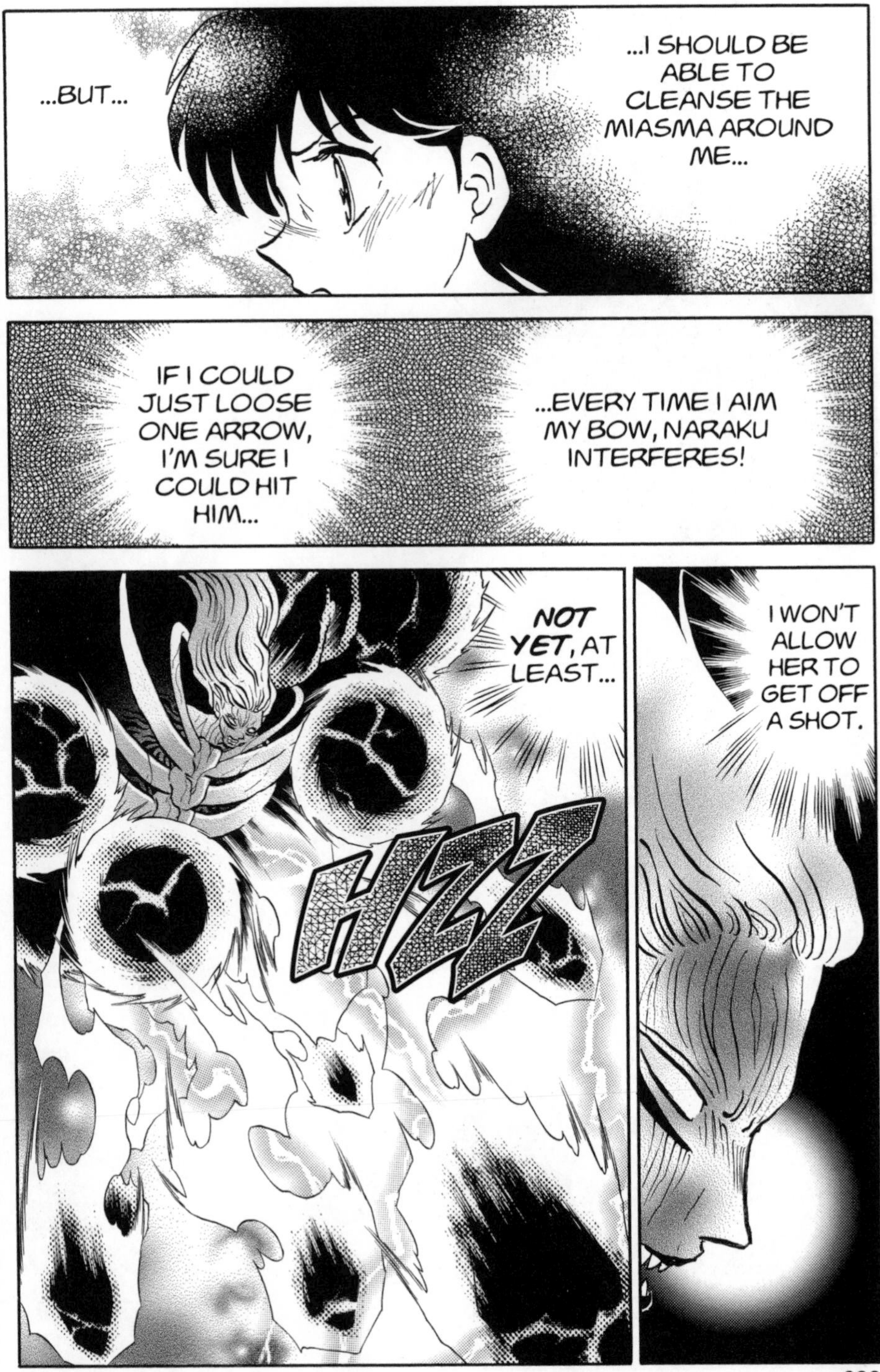

...I SHOULD BE ABLE TO CLEANSE THE MIASMA AROUND ME...
...BUT...
...EVERY TIME I AIM MY BOW, NARAKU INTERFERES!
IF I COULD JUST LOOSE ONE ARROW, I'M SURE I COULD HIT HIM...
I WON'T ALLOW HER TO GET OFF A SHOT.
NOT YET, AT LEAST...
HZZ

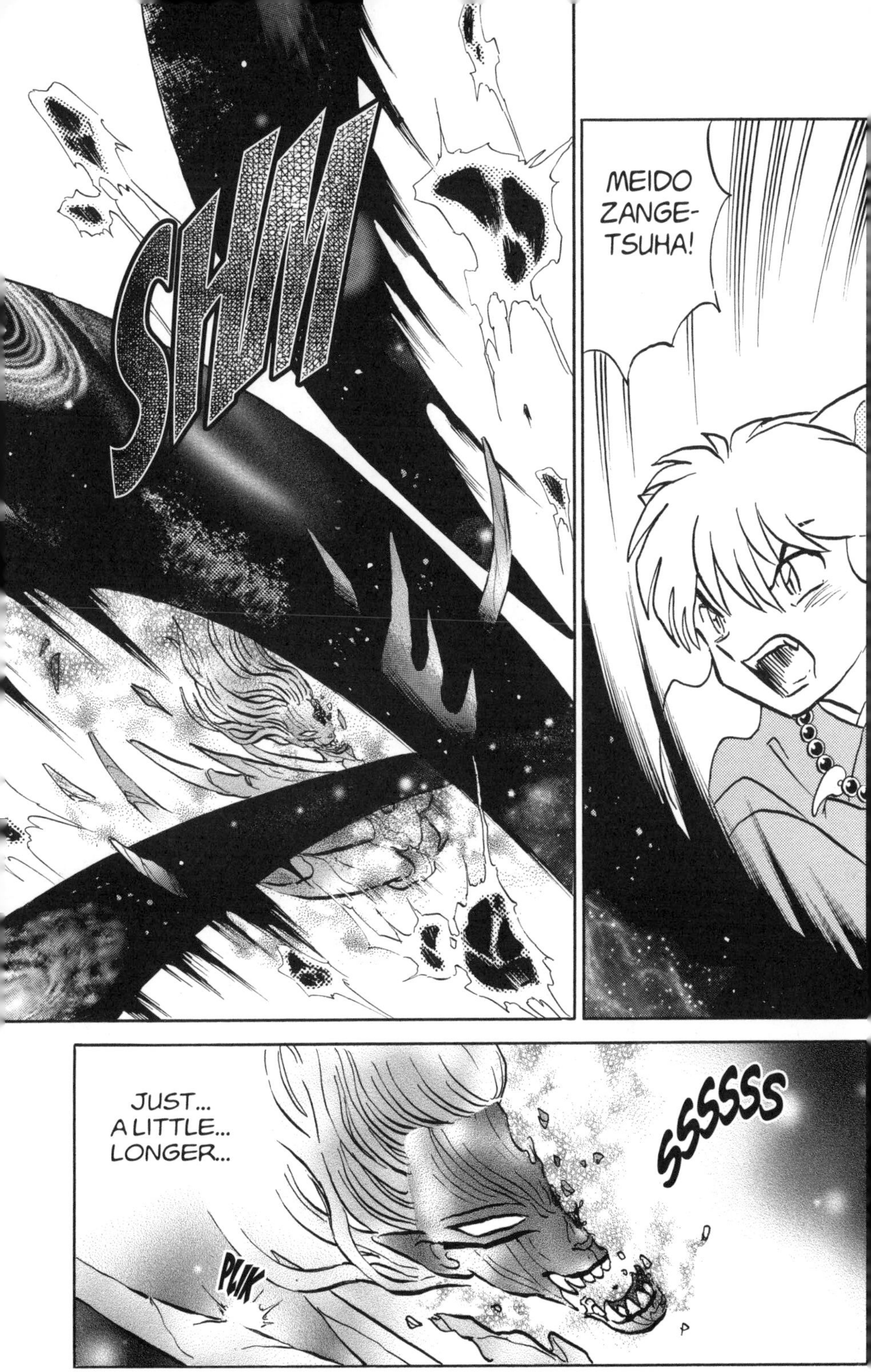
MEIDO ZANGE-TSUHA!
SHUM
SSSSSS
JUST... A LITTLE... LONGER...
PLIK

HSK...

HOO...

NARAKU
...

L-LADY
KAEDE?

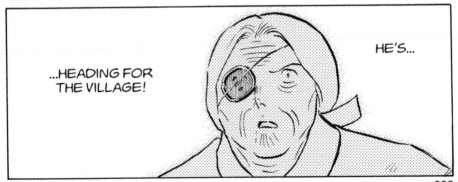

HE'S...

...HEADING FOR
THE VILLAGE!

SCROLL THREE
THE PLUNGE

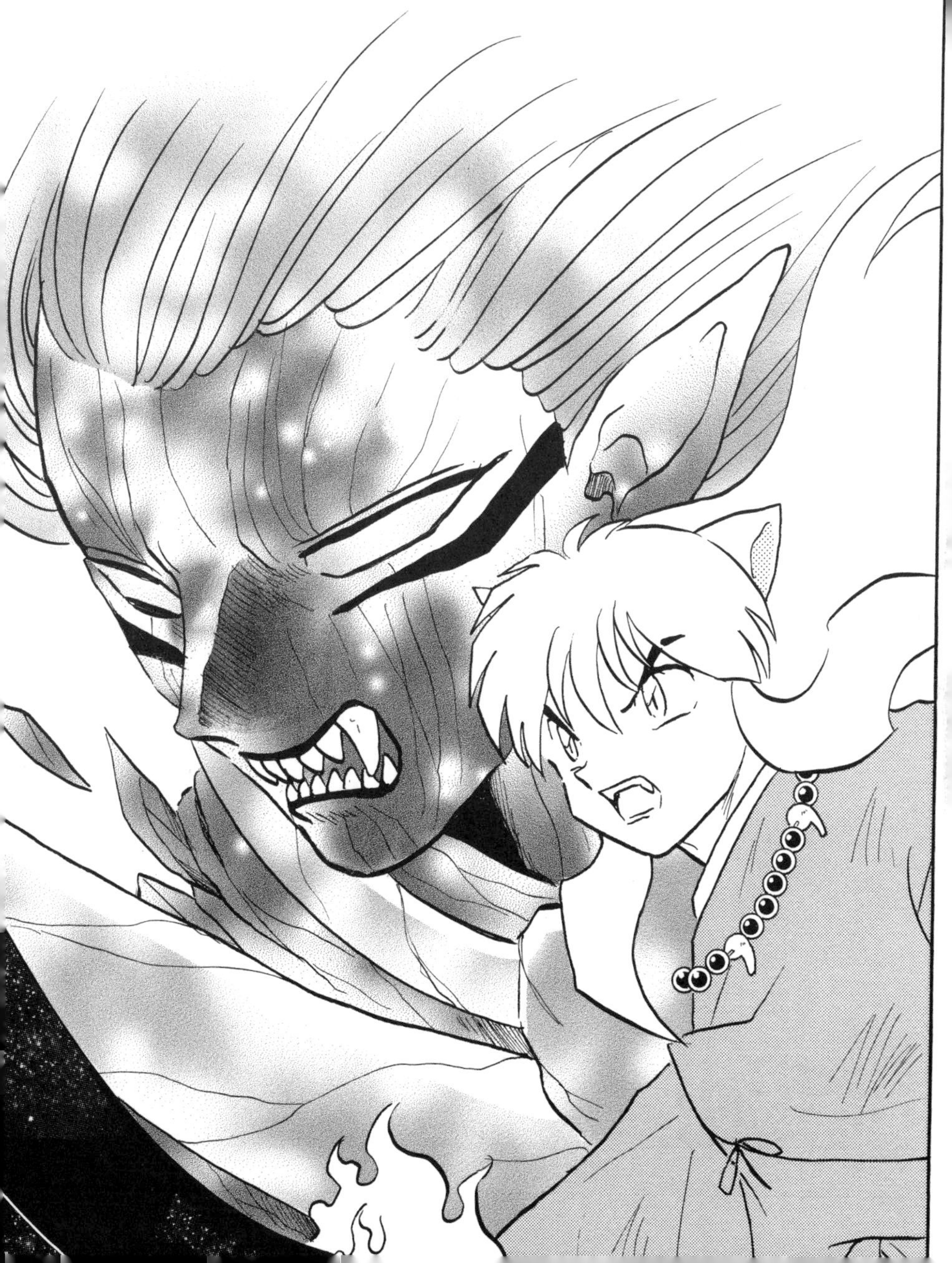

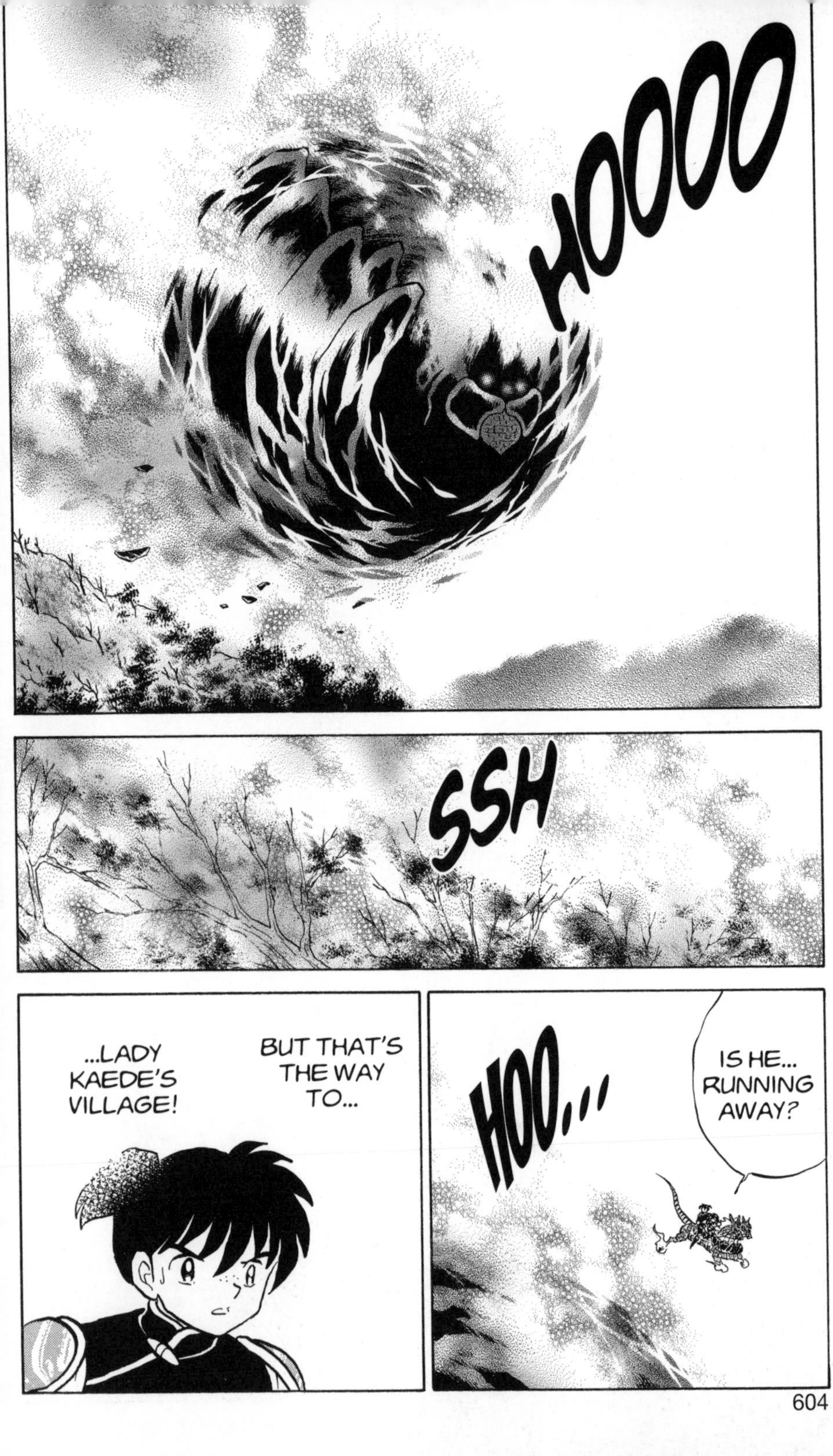
HOOOO
SSH
HOO...
IS HE... RUNNING AWAY?
BUT THAT'S THE WAY TO...
...LADY KAEDE'S VILLAGE!

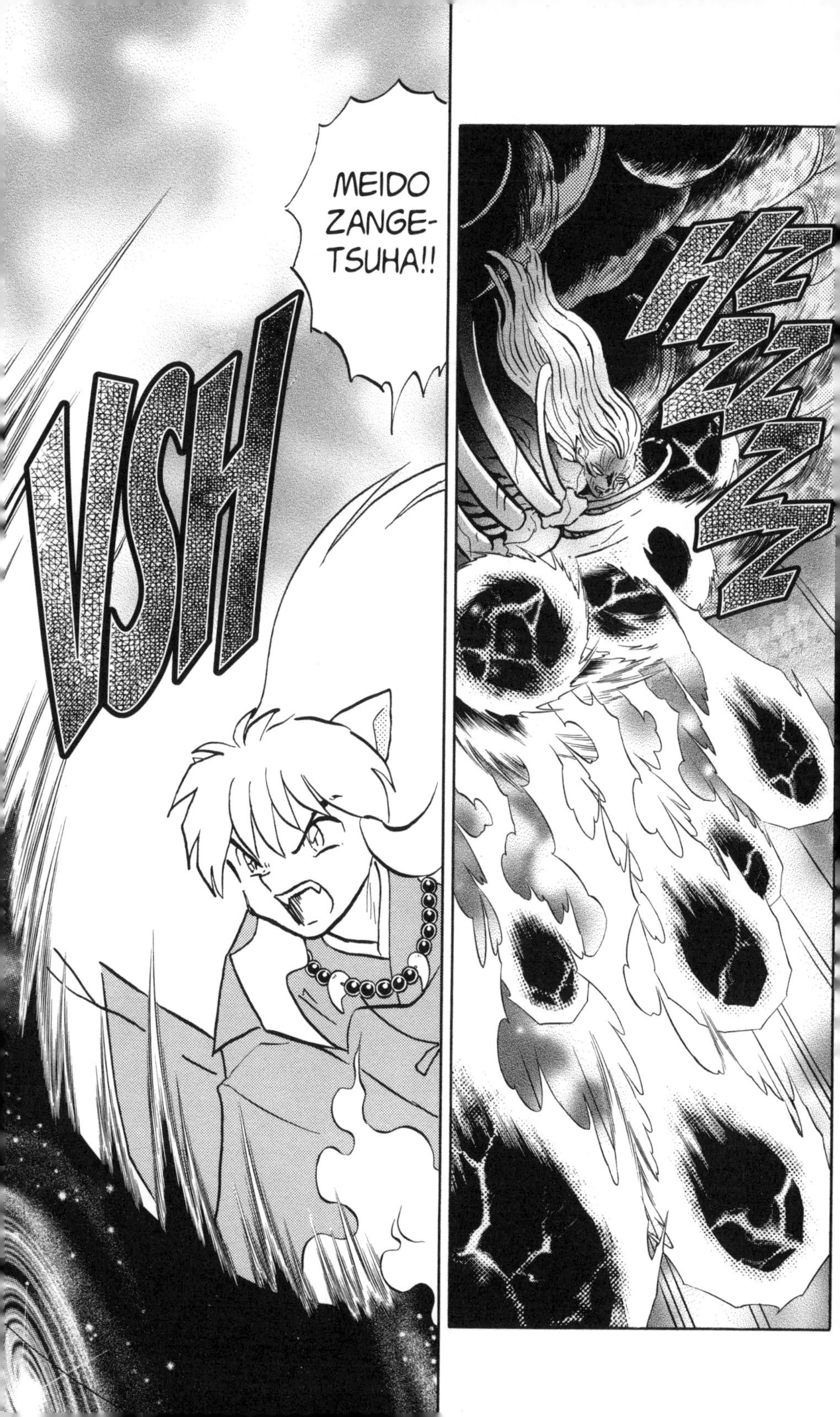
MEIDO ZANGE-TSUHA!!
VSH

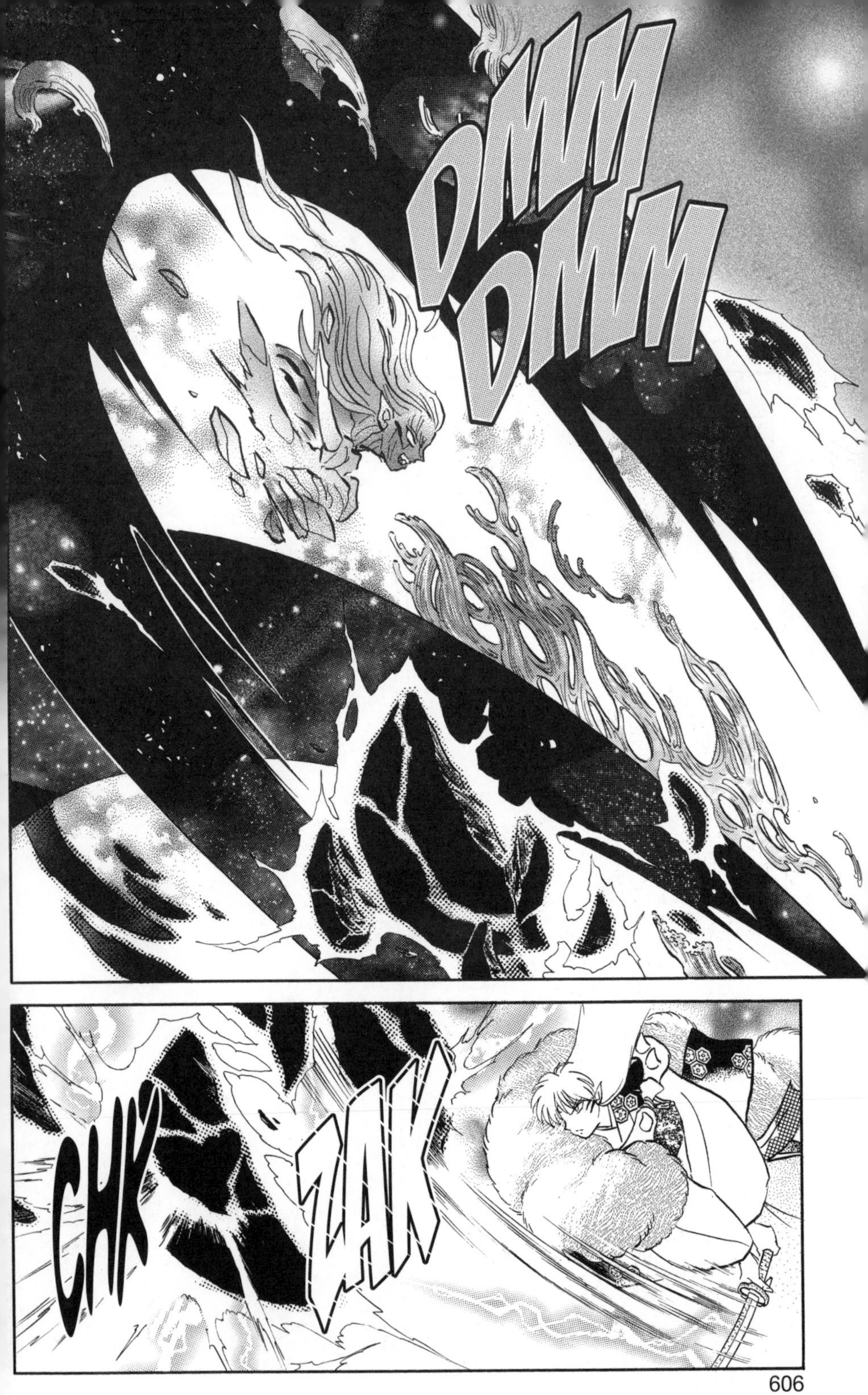
DMM DMM
ZAK
CHK

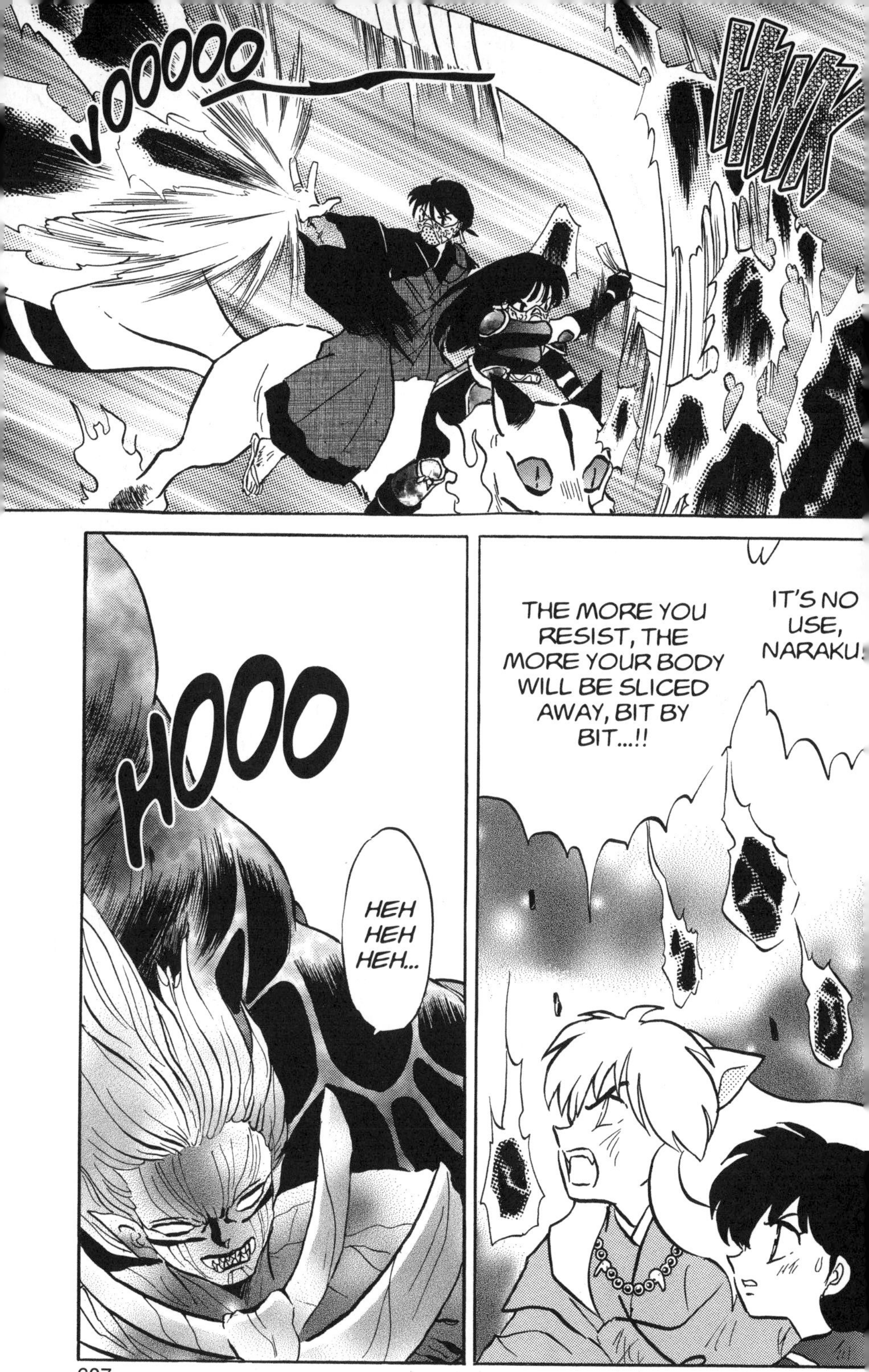
VOOOOO
HWWK
IT'S NO USE, NARAKU...!
THE MORE YOU RESIST, THE MORE YOUR BODY WILL BE SLICED AWAY, BIT BY BIT...!!
HOOO
HEH HEH HEH...

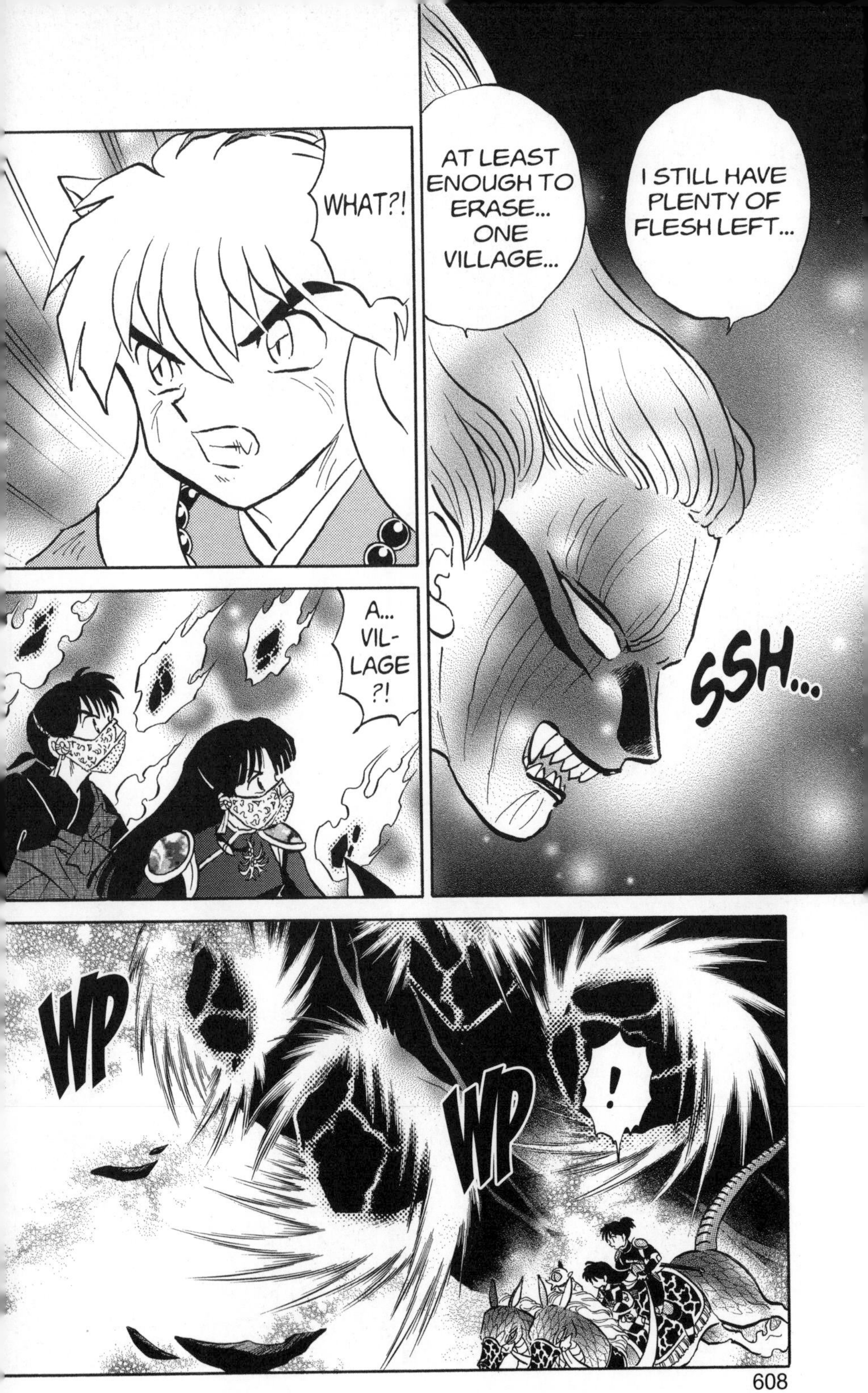
I STILL HAVE PLENTY OF FLESH LEFT...
AT LEAST ENOUGH TO ERASE... ONE VILLAGE...
SSH...
WHAT?!
A... VIL-LAGE?!
WP
WP
!

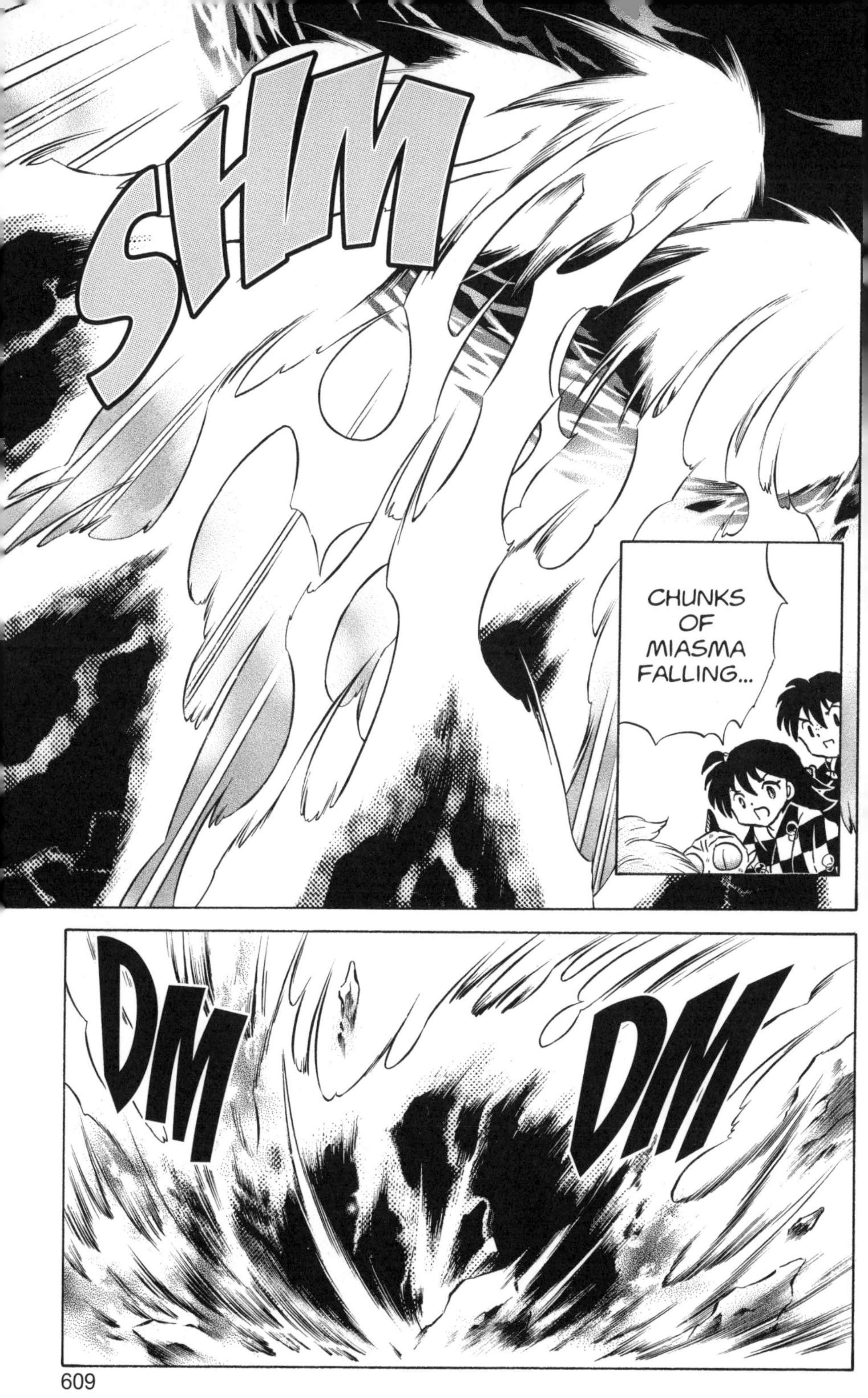
SHM
CHUNKS OF MIASMA FALLING...
DM
DM

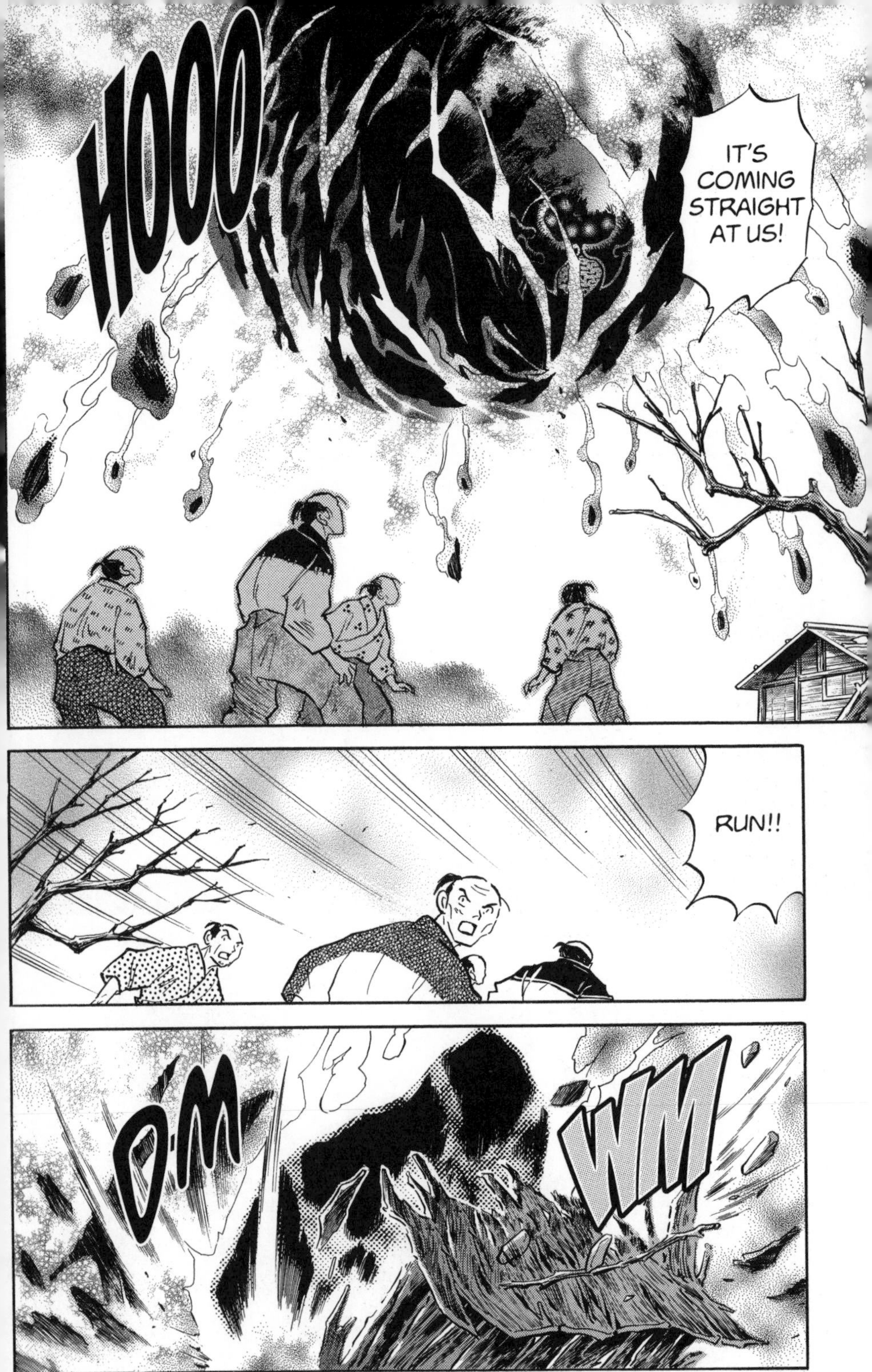
HOOO
IT'S COMING STRAIGHT AT US!
RUN!!
WM
DOM

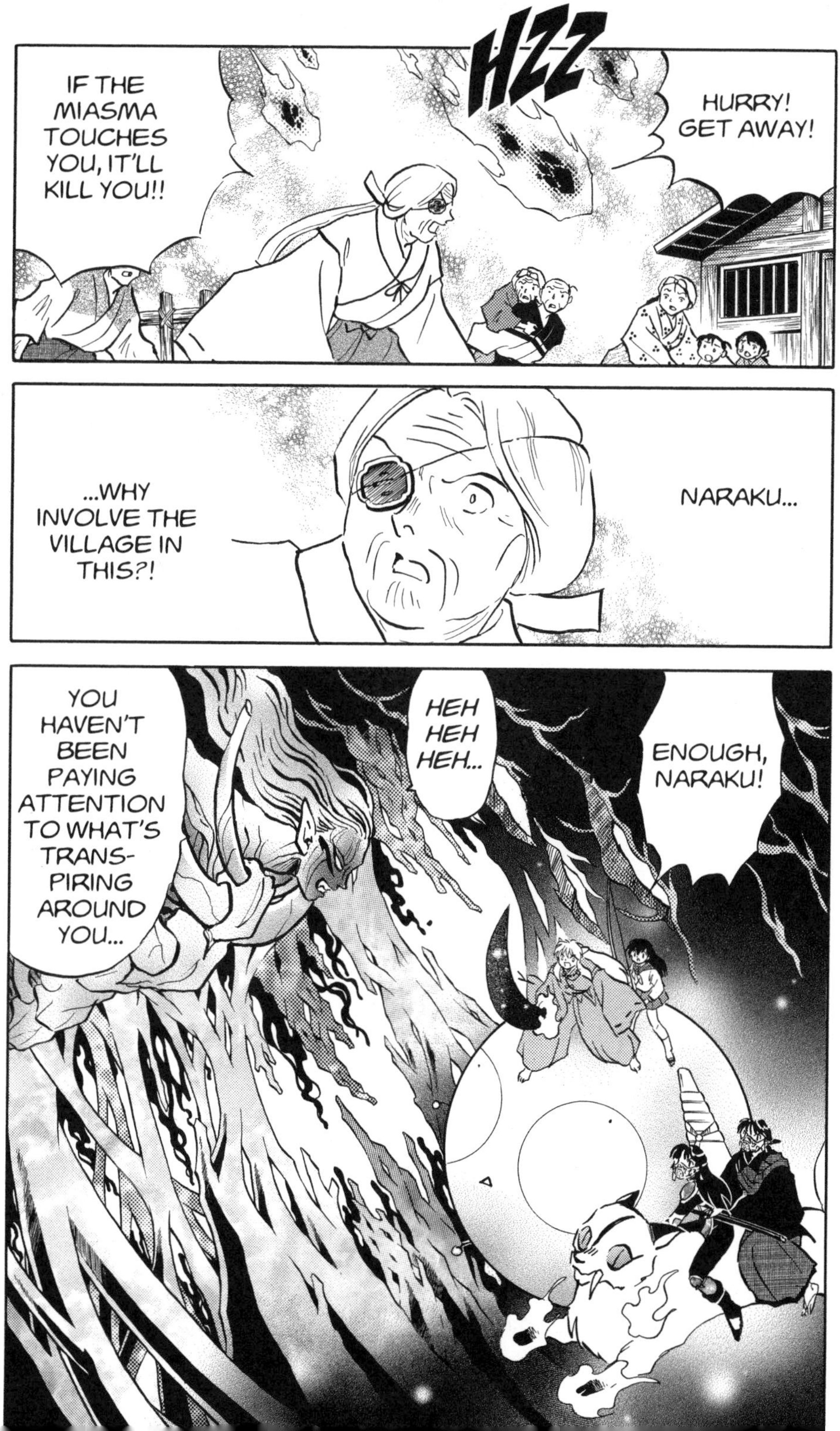
HURRY! GET AWAY!
HZZ
IF THE MIASMA TOUCHES YOU, IT'LL KILL YOU!!
NARAKU...
...WHY INVOLVE THE VILLAGE IN THIS?!
ENOUGH, NARAKU!
HEH HEH HEH...
YOU HAVEN'T BEEN PAYING ATTENTION TO WHAT'S TRANS-PIRING AROUND YOU...

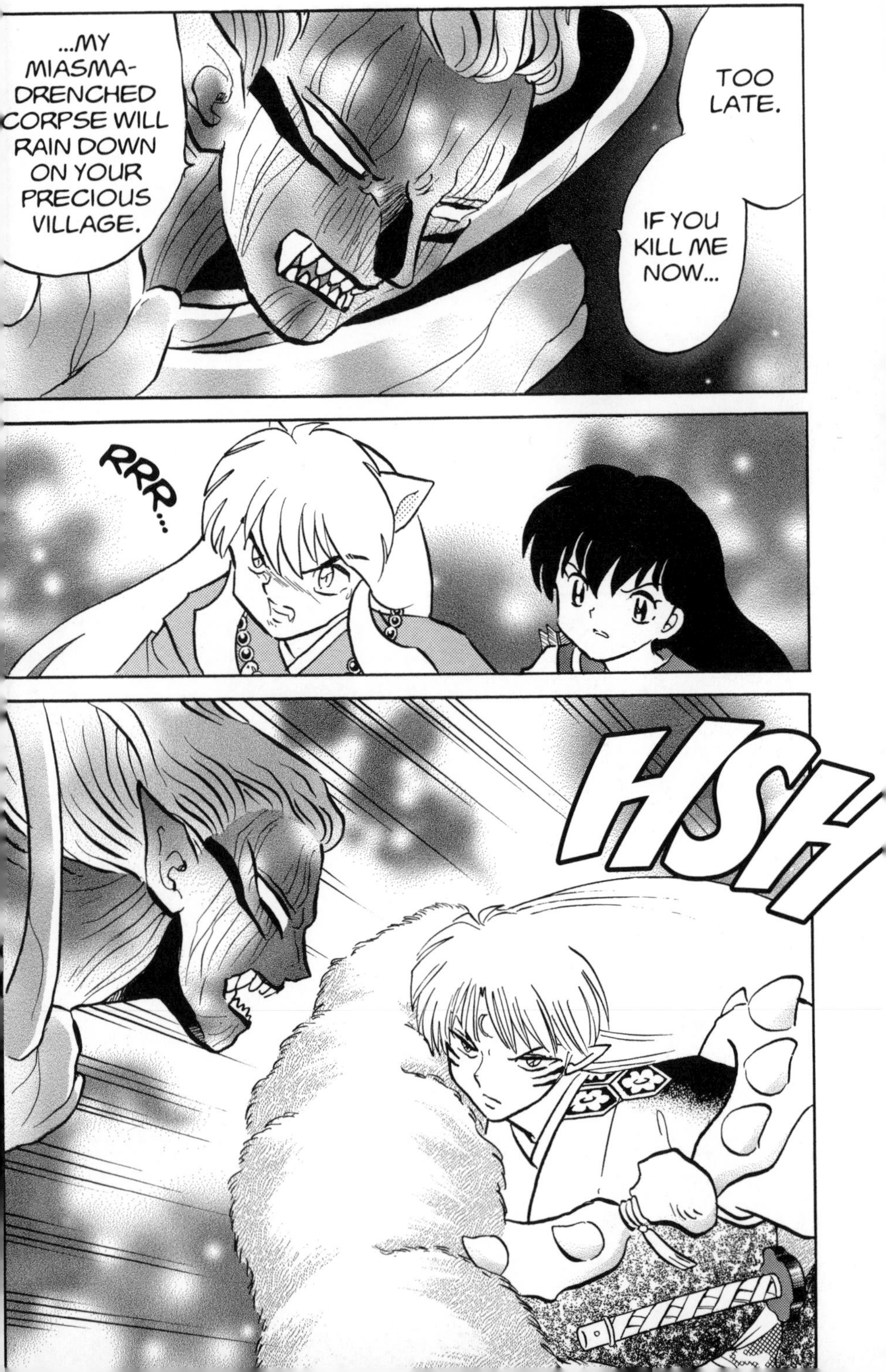
TOO LATE.
IF YOU KILL ME NOW...
...MY MIASMA-DRENCHED CORPSE WILL RAIN DOWN ON YOUR PRECIOUS VILLAGE.
RRR...
HSH

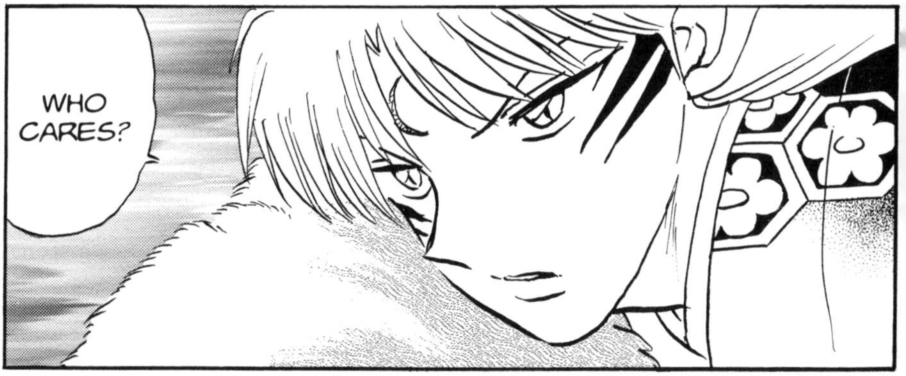
WHO CARES?

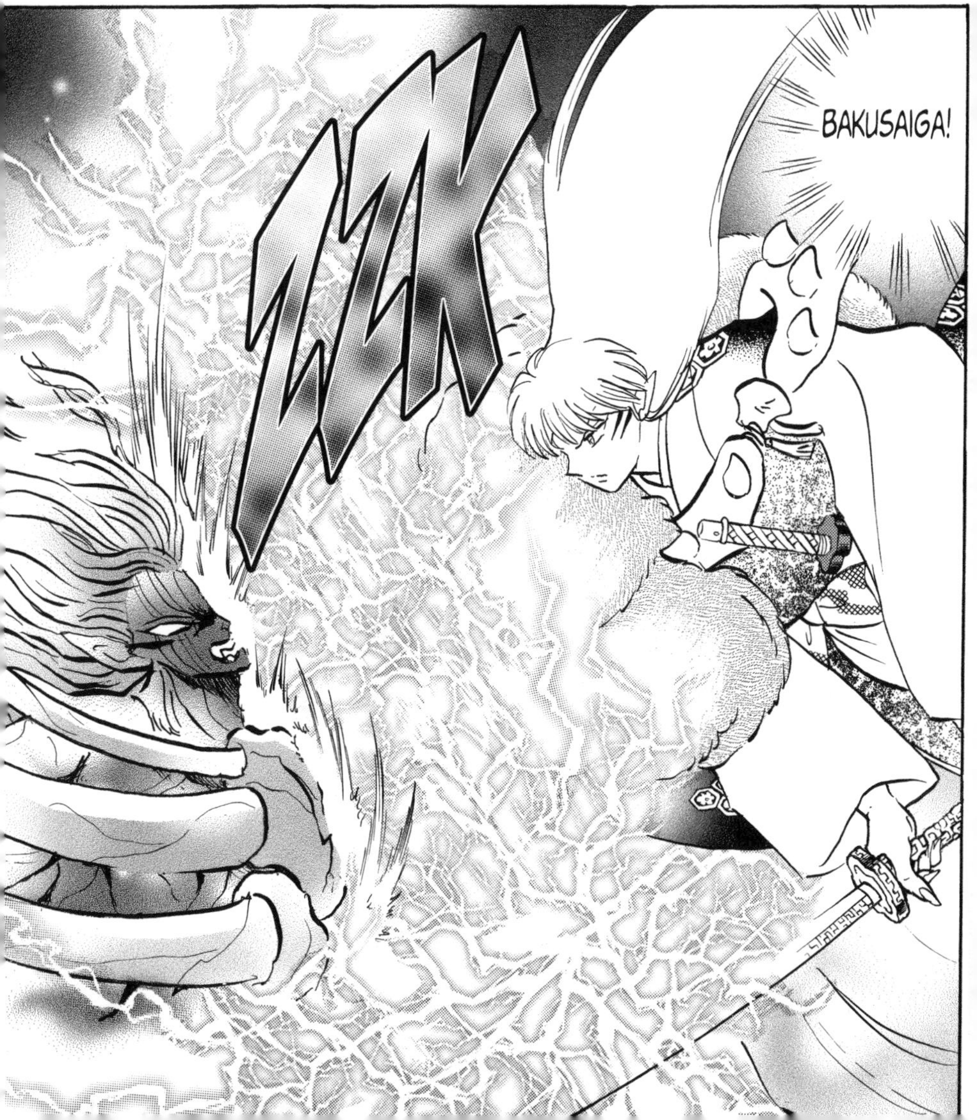
BAKUSAIGA!
ZZK

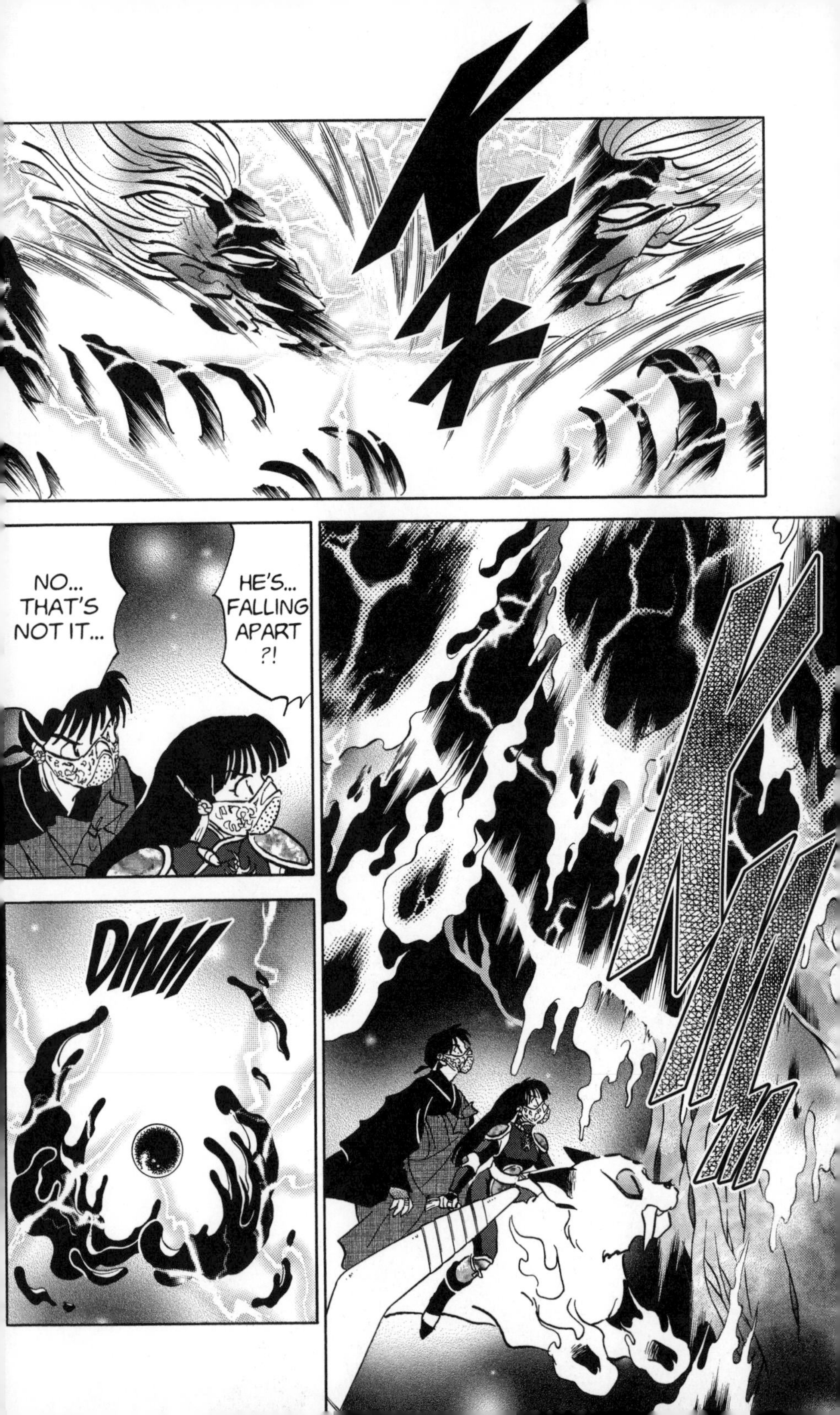
HE'S... FALLING APART ?!
NO... THAT'S NOT IT...
DMM

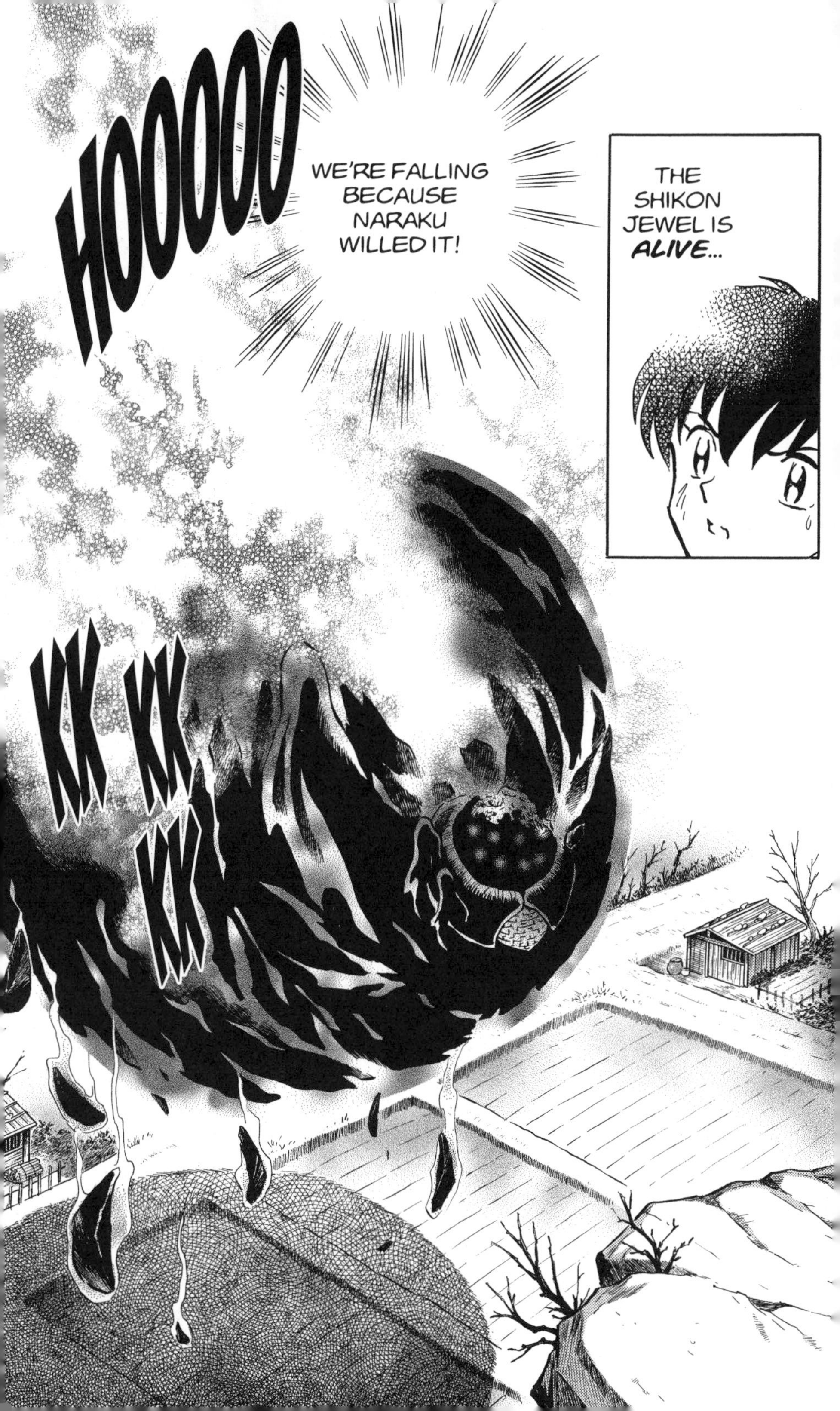
THE SHIKON JEWEL IS *ALIVE*...
WE'RE FALLING BECAUSE NARAKU WILLED IT!
HOOOOO
KK KK KK

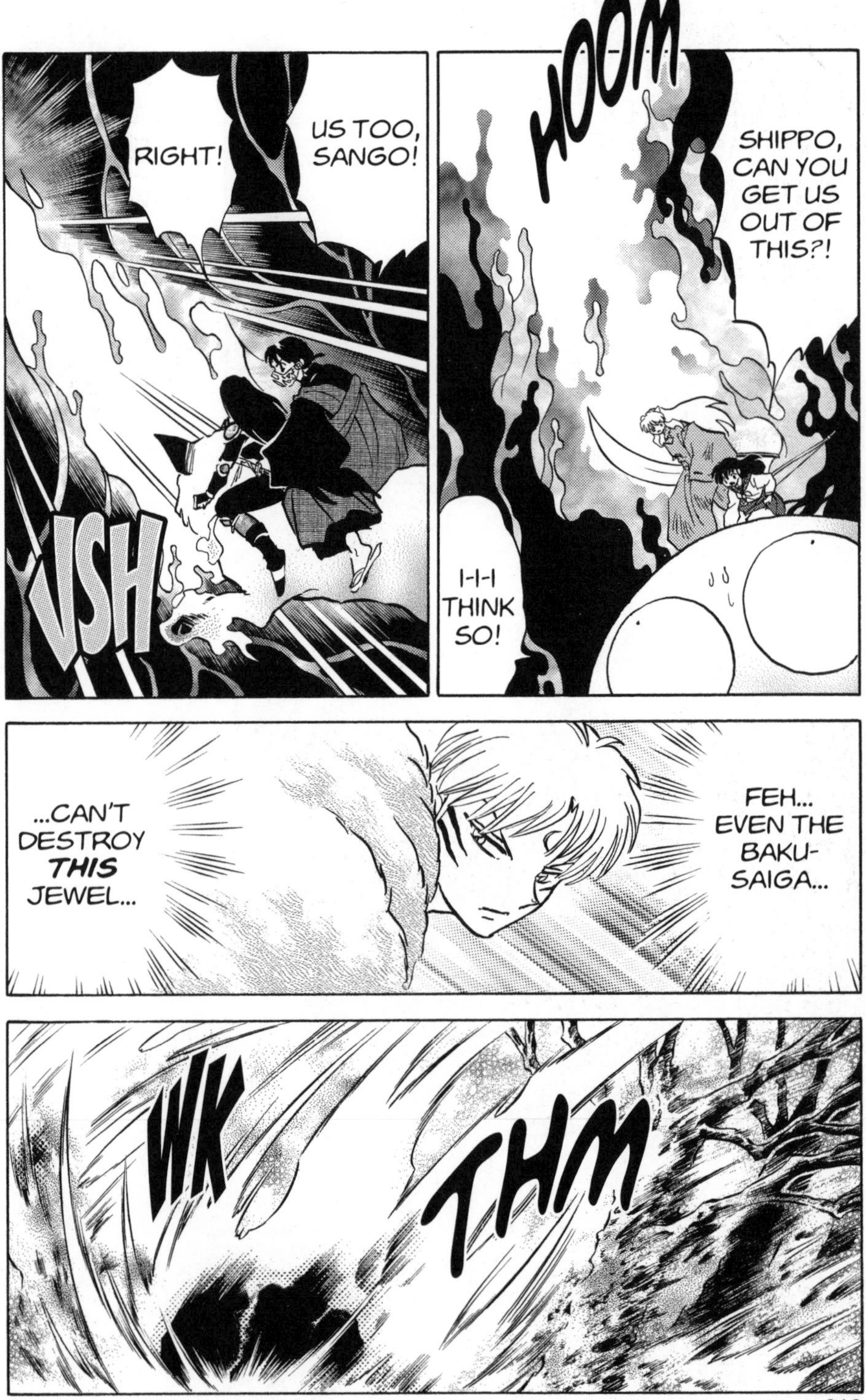
HOOM
SHIPPO, CAN YOU GET US OUT OF THIS?!
I-I-I THINK SO!
US TOO, SANGO!
RIGHT!
VSH
FEH... EVEN THE BAKU-SAIGA...
...CAN'T DESTROY **THIS** JEWEL...
WK
THM

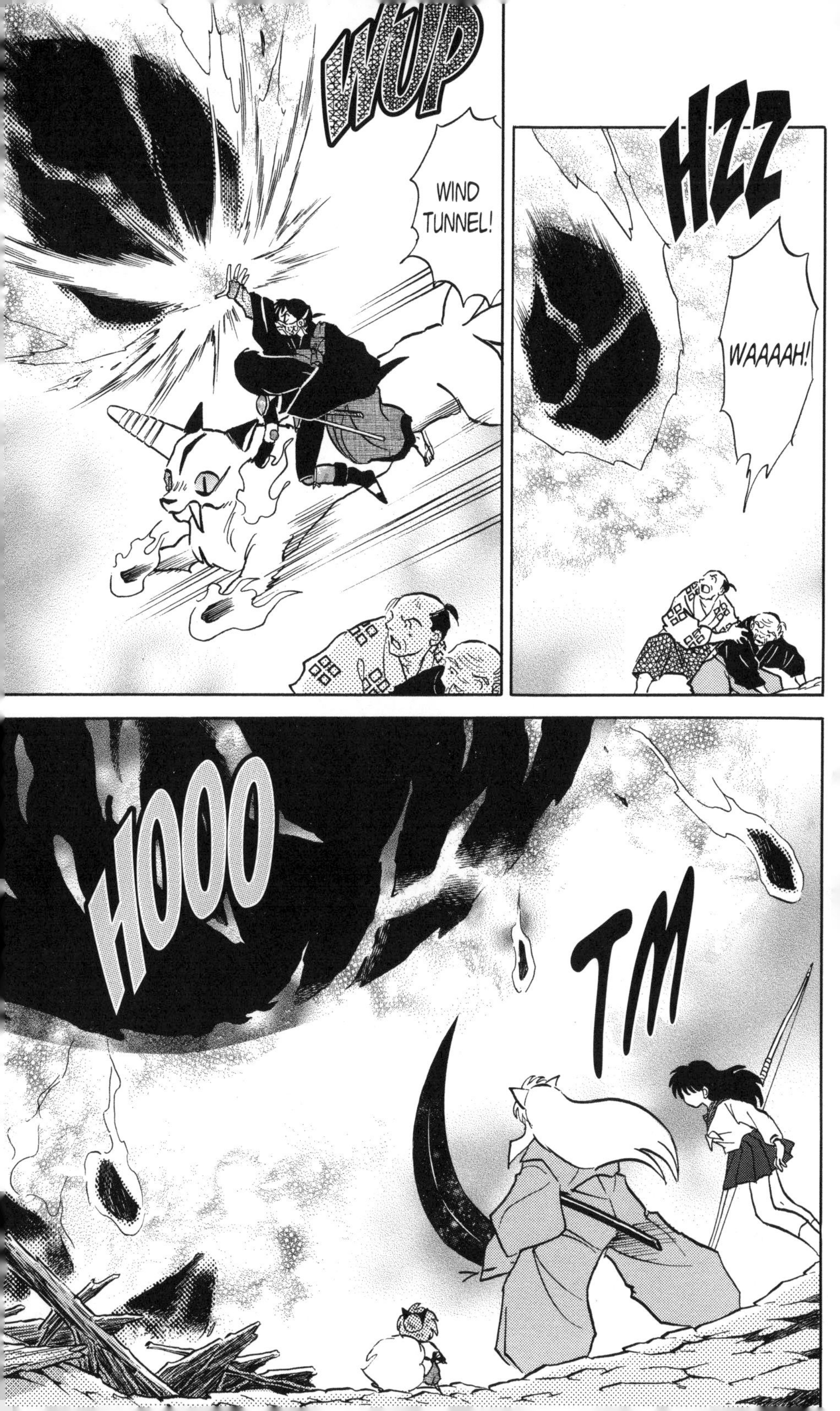
HZZ
WAAAAH!
WUP
WIND TUNNEL!
HOOO
TM

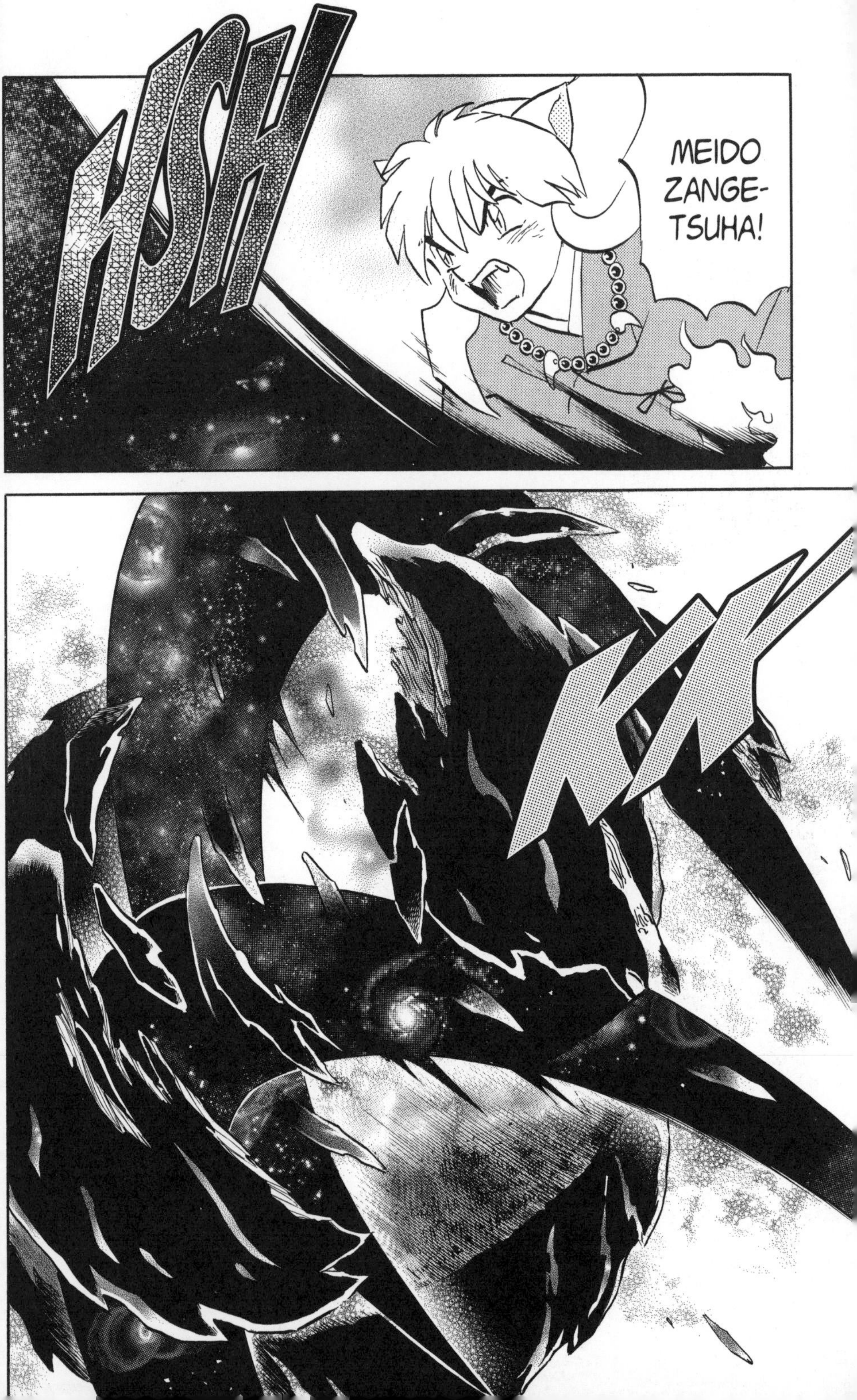
MEIDO ZANGE-TSUHA!
HSH
KK

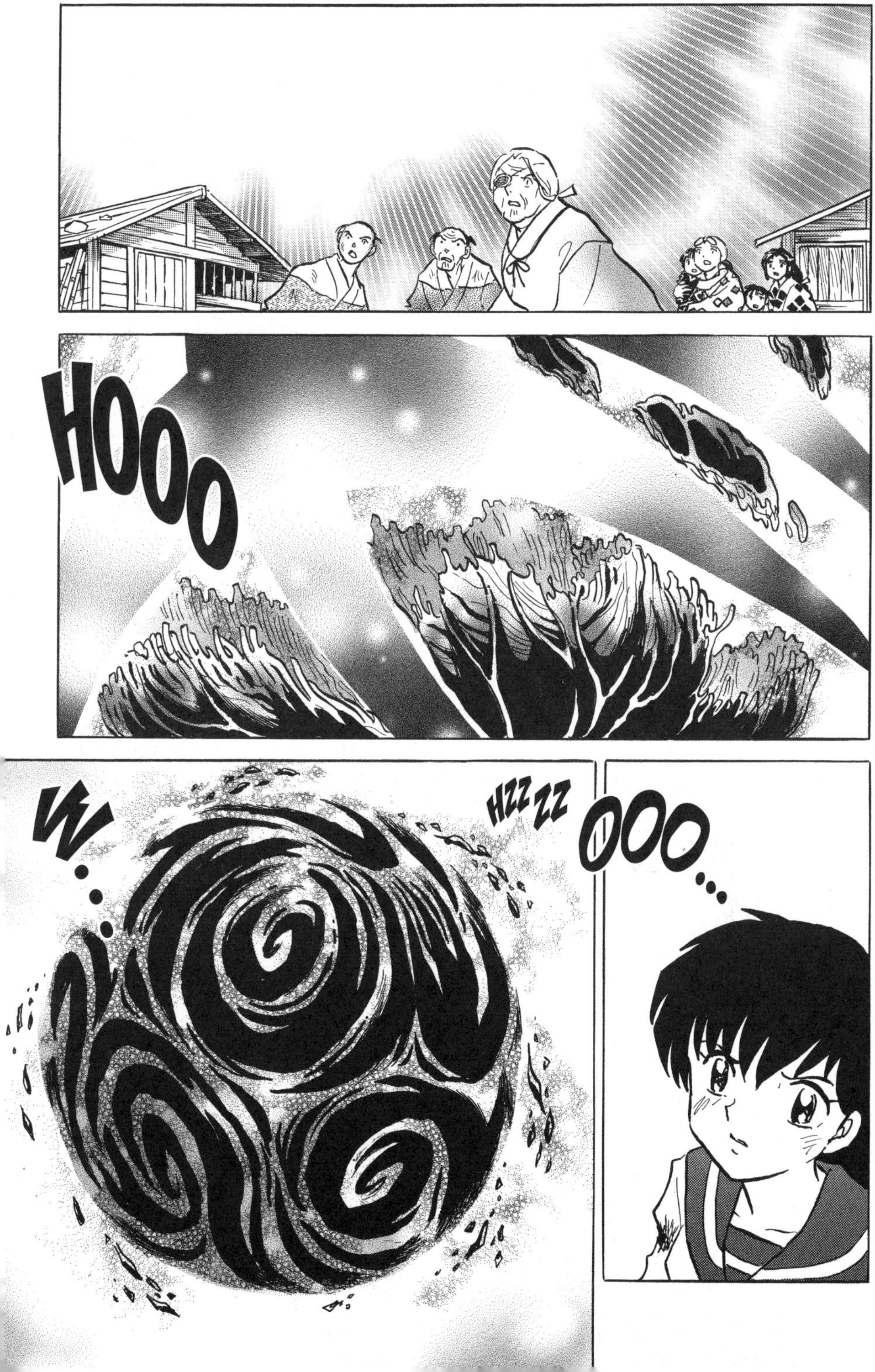
HOOO
OOO...
HZZZZ
W...

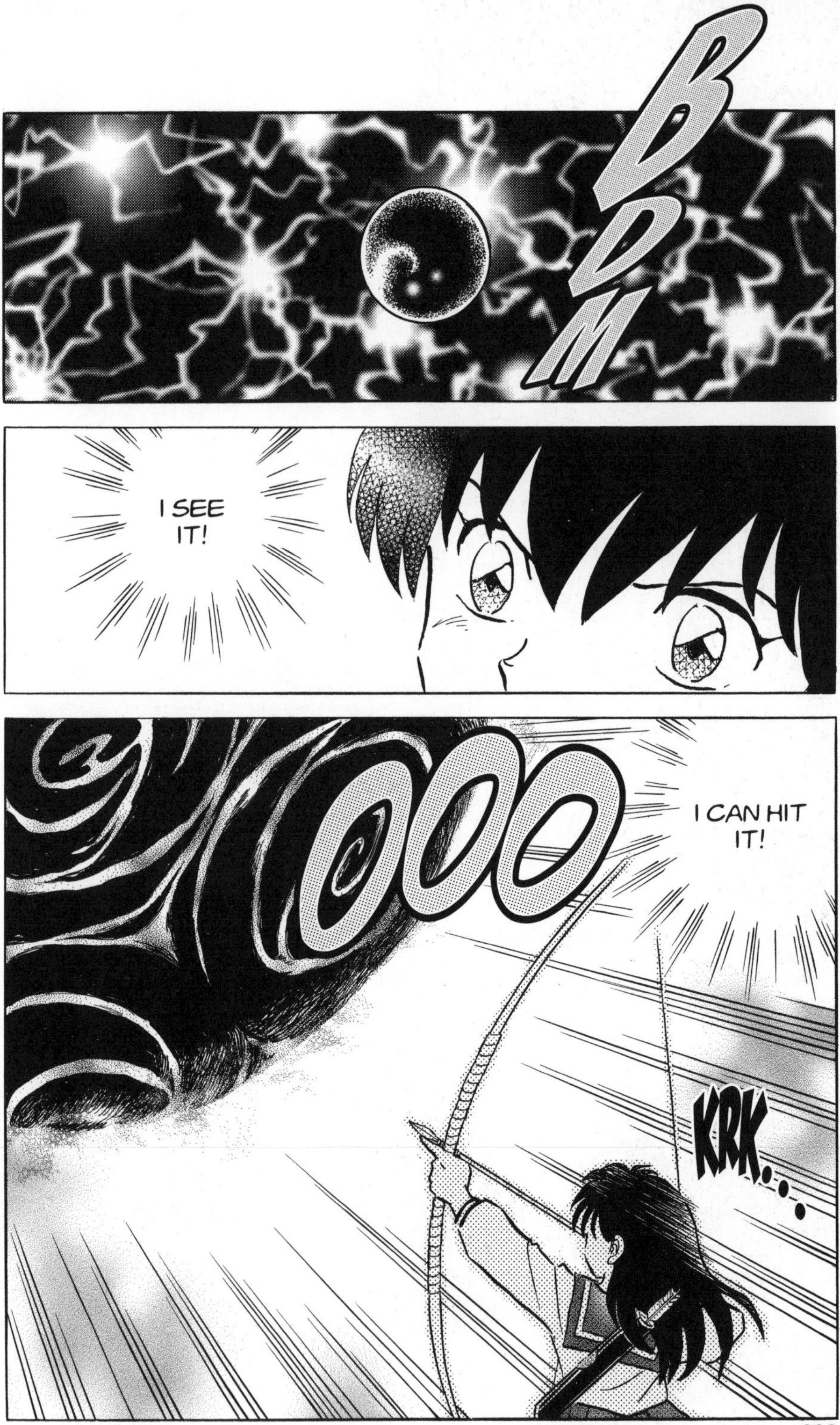
BDM
I SEE IT!
OOO
I CAN HIT IT!
KRK...

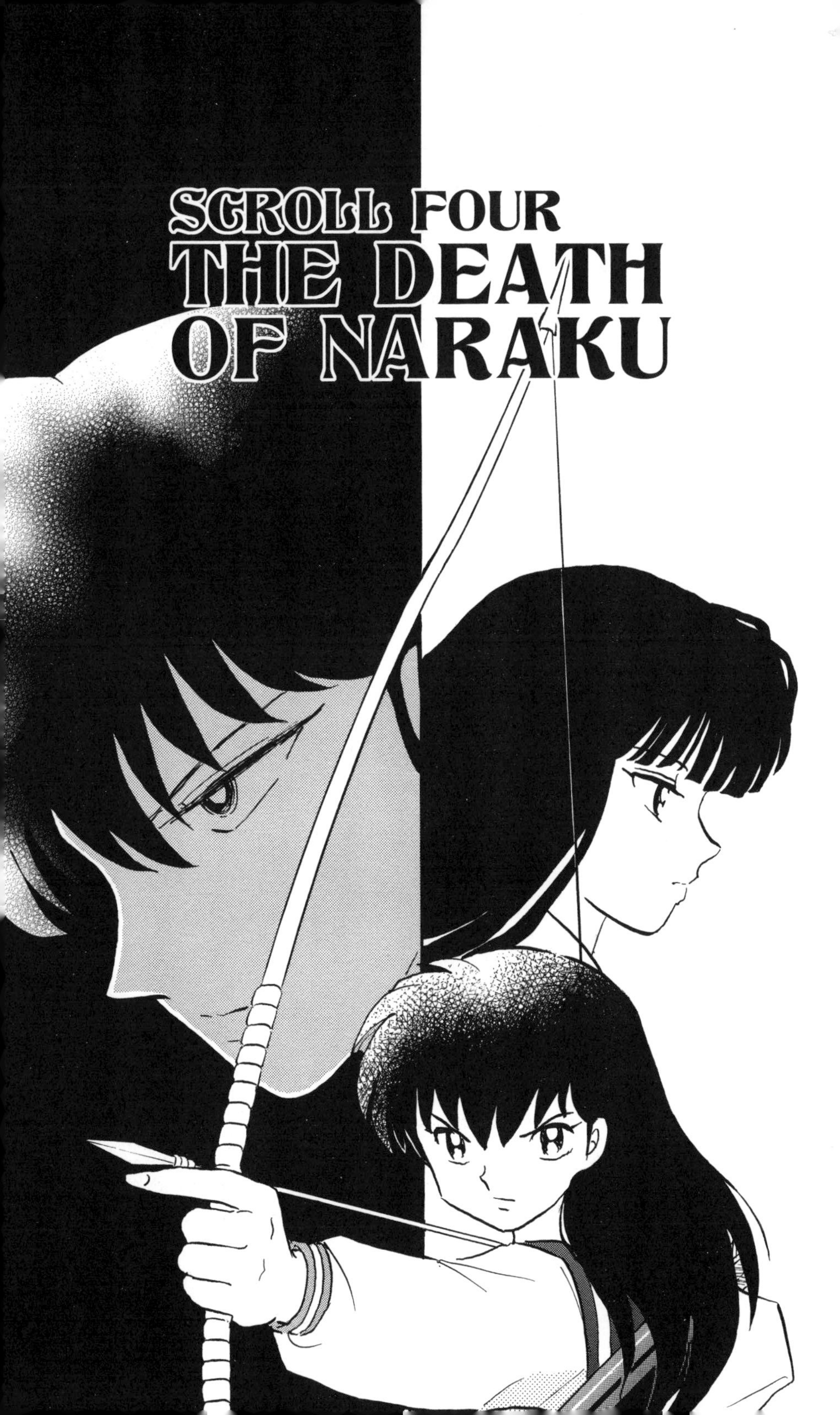
SCROLL FOUR
THE DEATH OF NARAKU

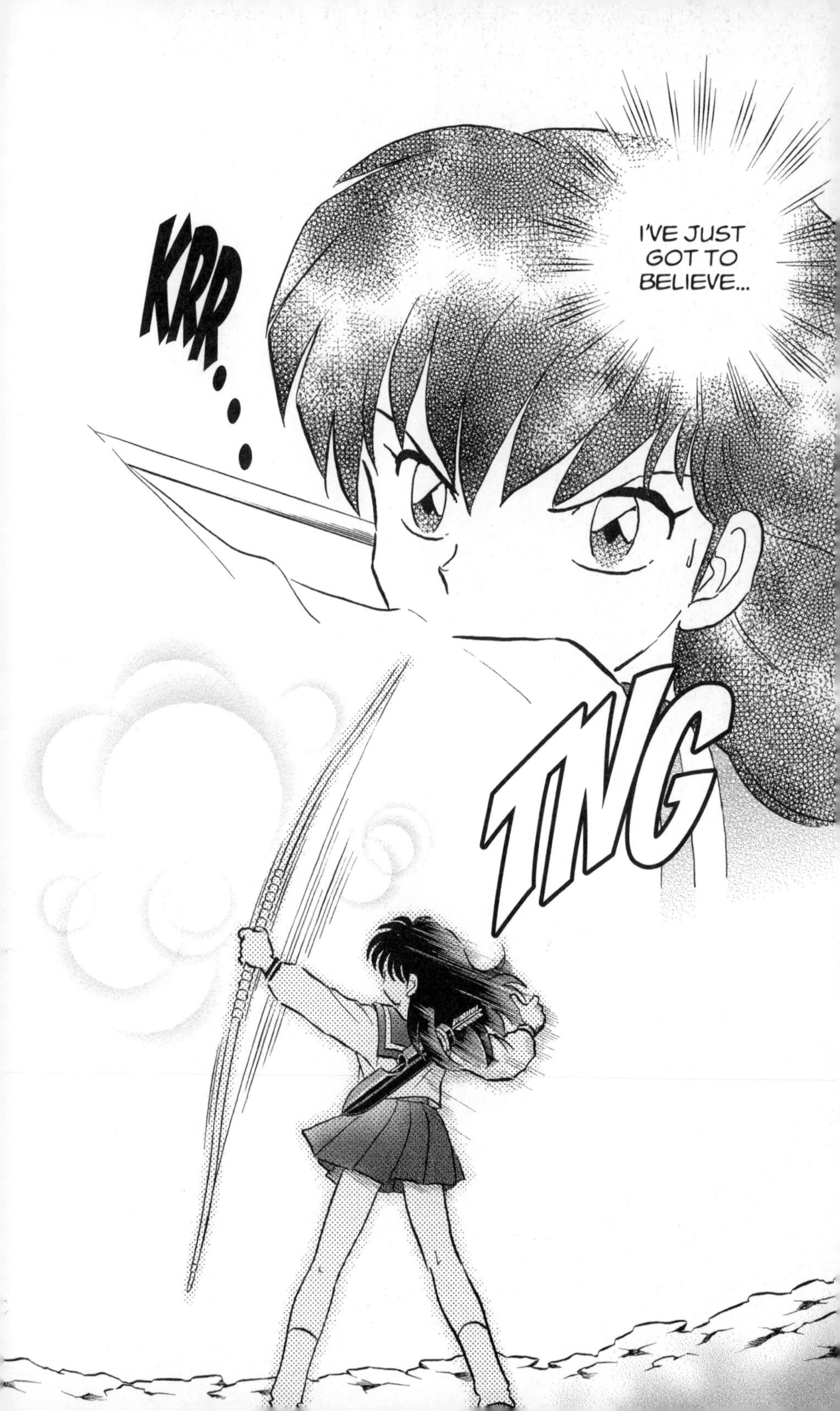
I'VE JUST GOT TO BELIEVE...
KRR...
TNG

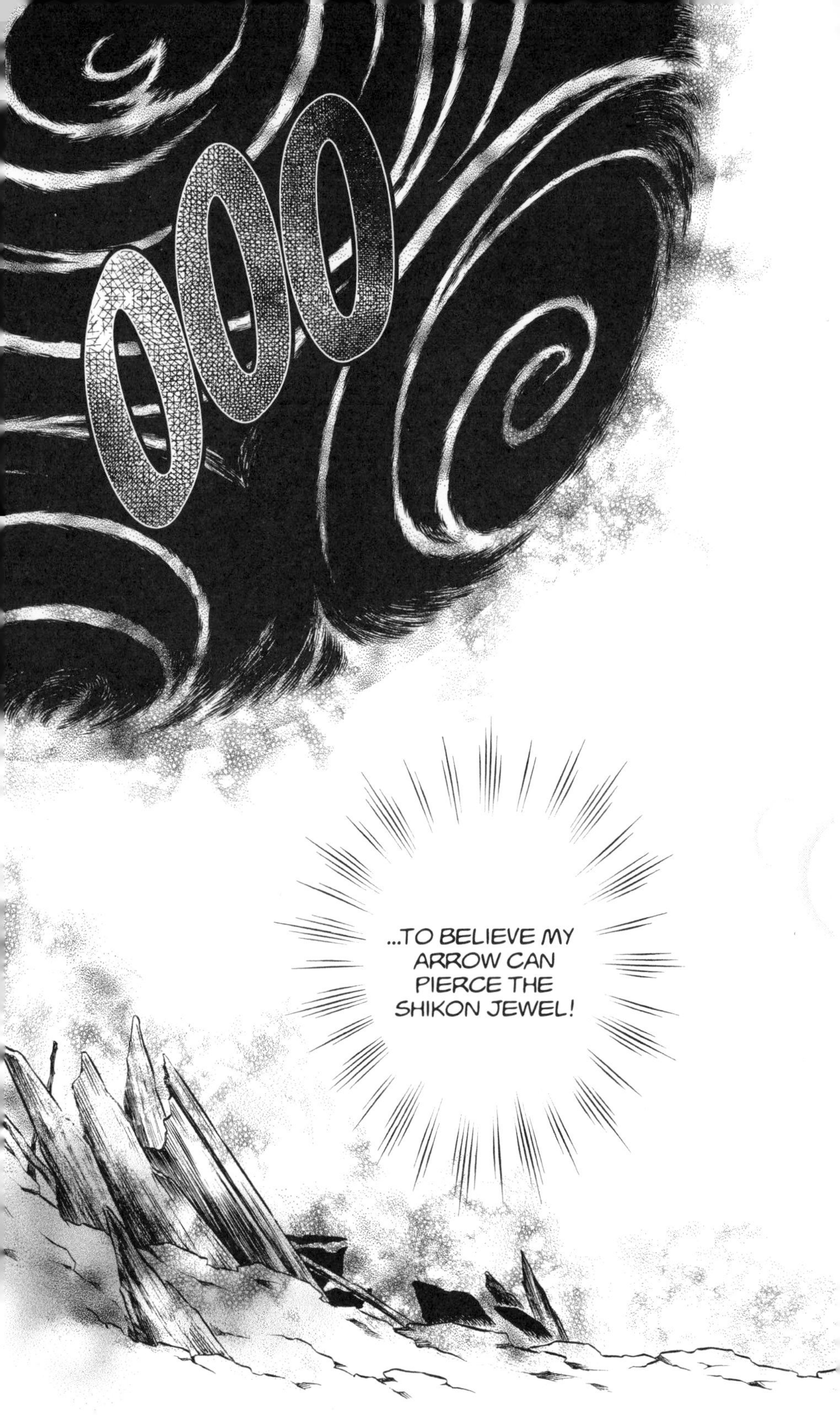
...TO BELIEVE MY ARROW CAN PIERCE THE SHIKON JEWEL!

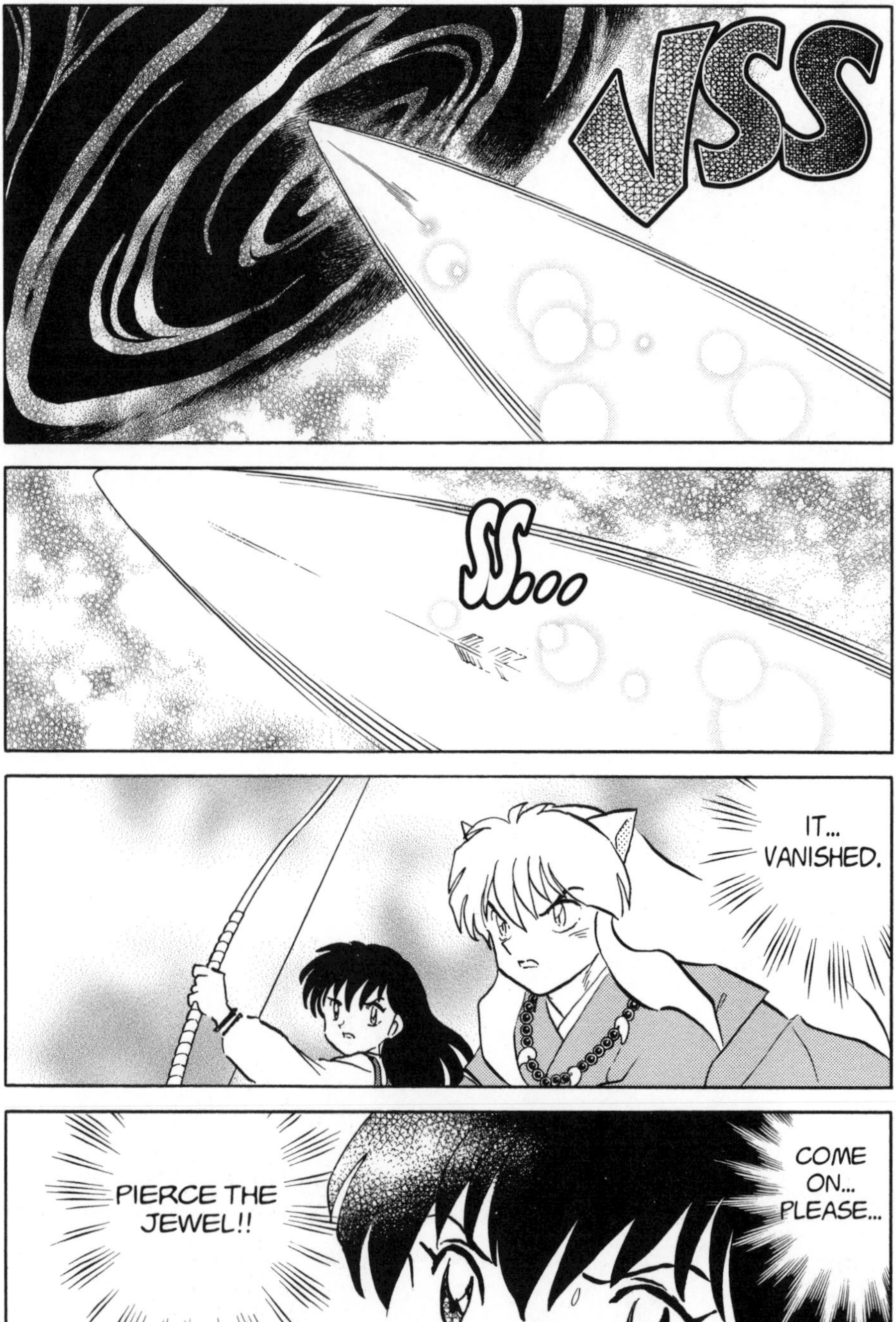
VSS
SSOOO
IT... VANISHED.
COME ON... PLEASE...
PIERCE THE JEWEL!!

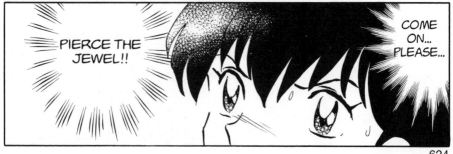

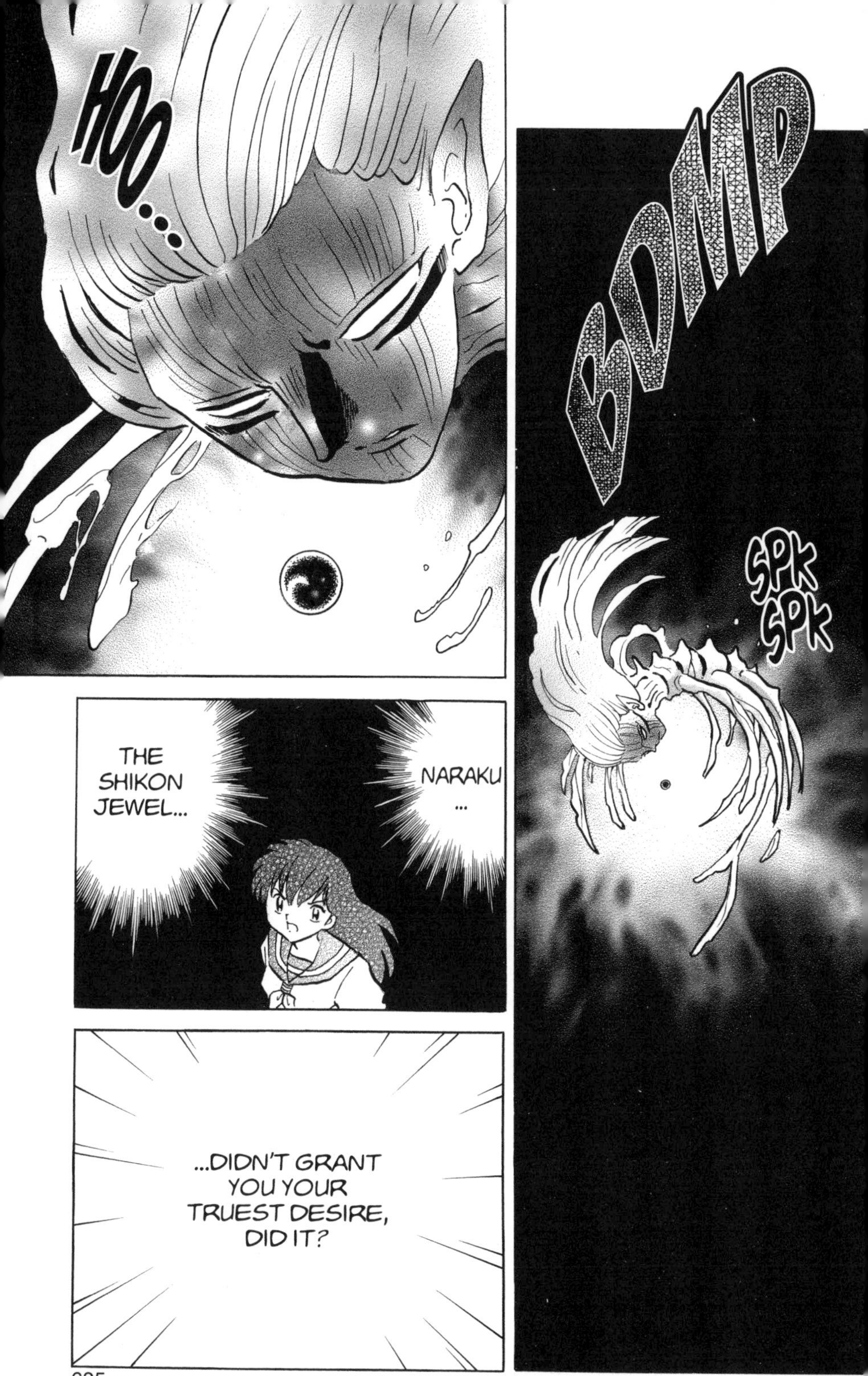
BOMP
SPK SPK
HOO...
NARAKU...
THE SHIKON JEWEL...
...DIDN'T GRANT YOU YOUR TRUEST DESIRE, DID IT?

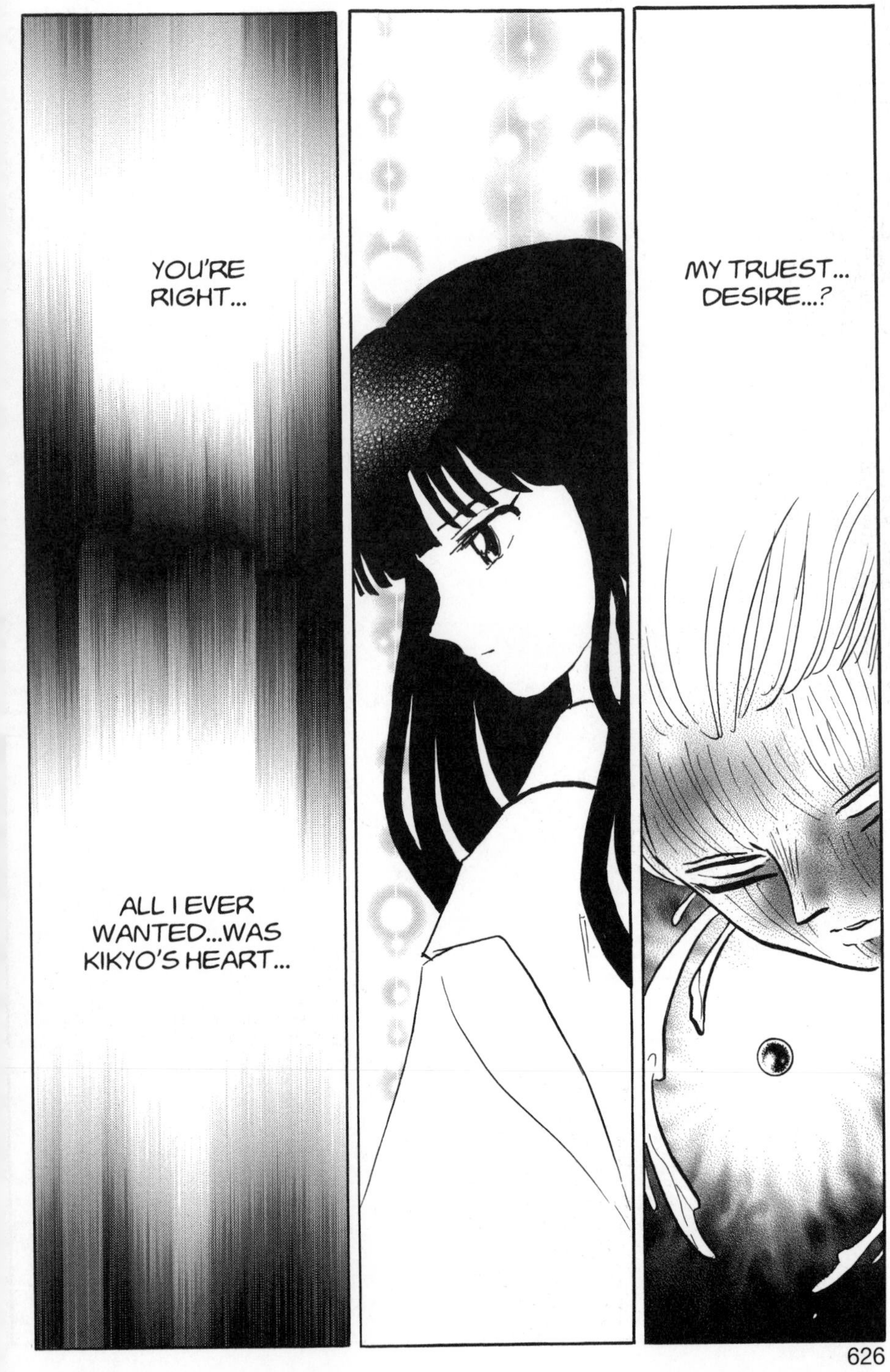
MY TRUEST...
DESIRE...?
YOU'RE
RIGHT...
ALL I EVER
WANTED...WAS
KIKYO'S HEART...

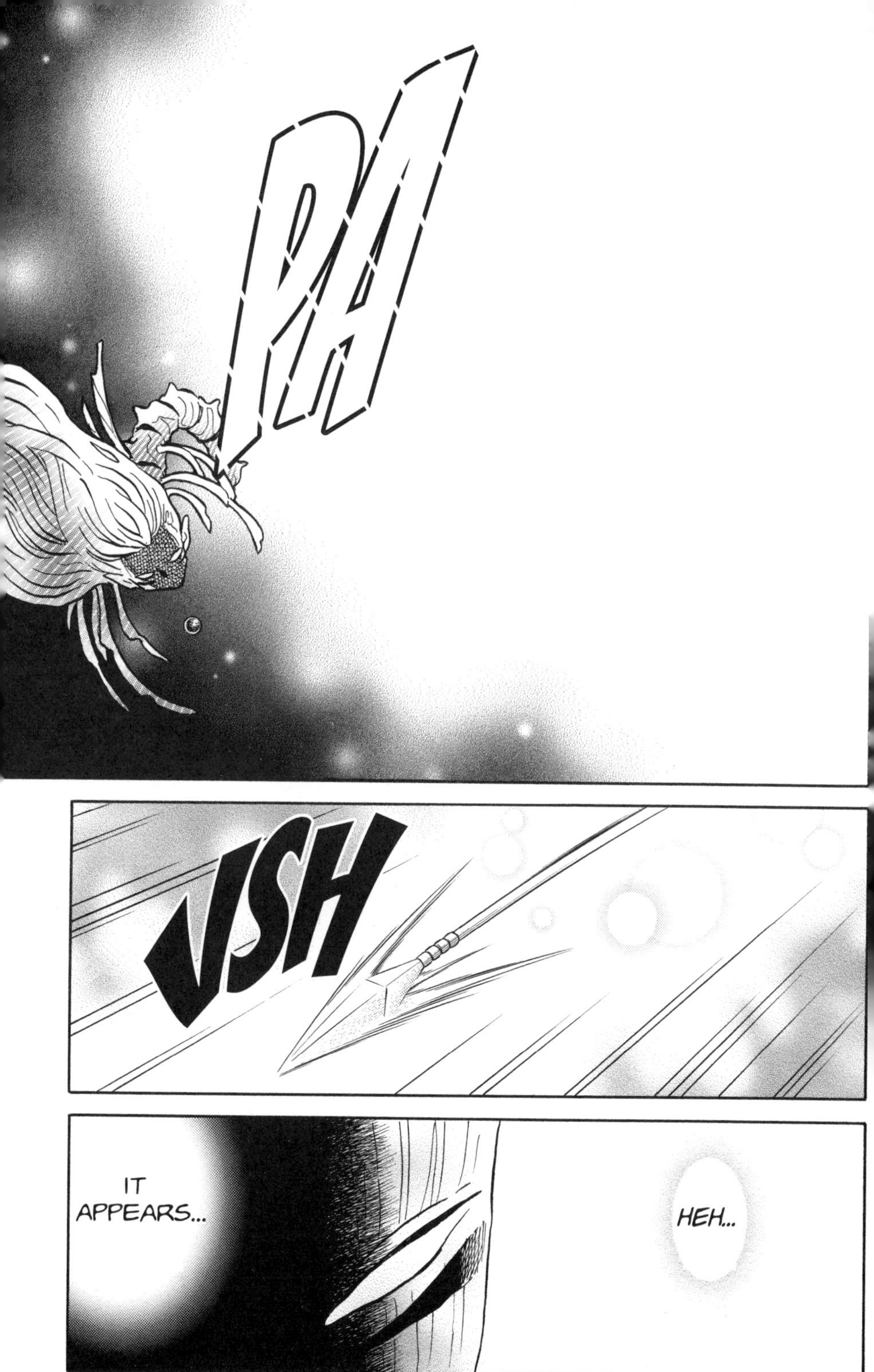
PA
VSH
HEH...
IT APPEARS...

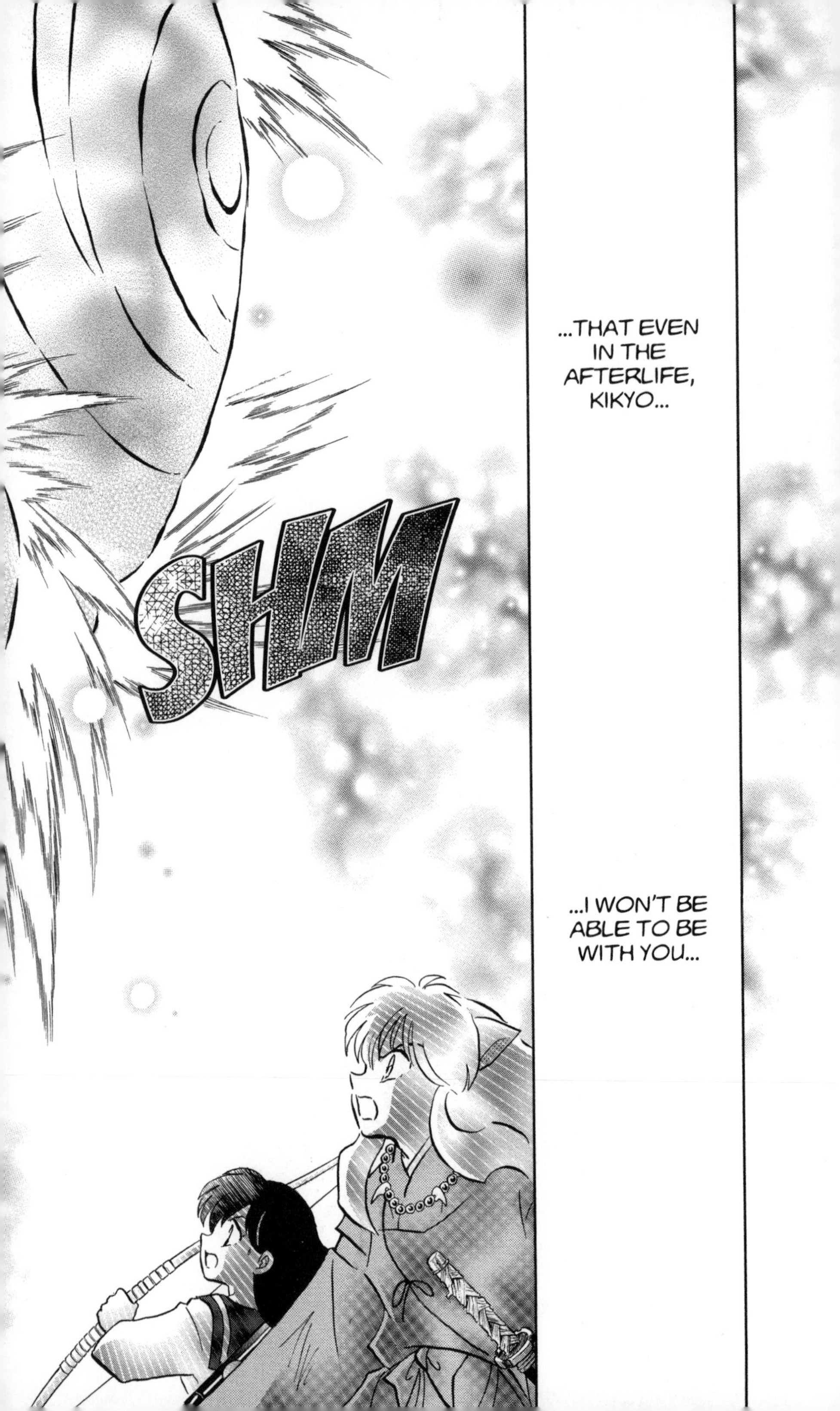
...THAT EVEN IN THE AFTERLIFE, KIKYO...
...I WON'T BE ABLE TO BE WITH YOU...
SHIM

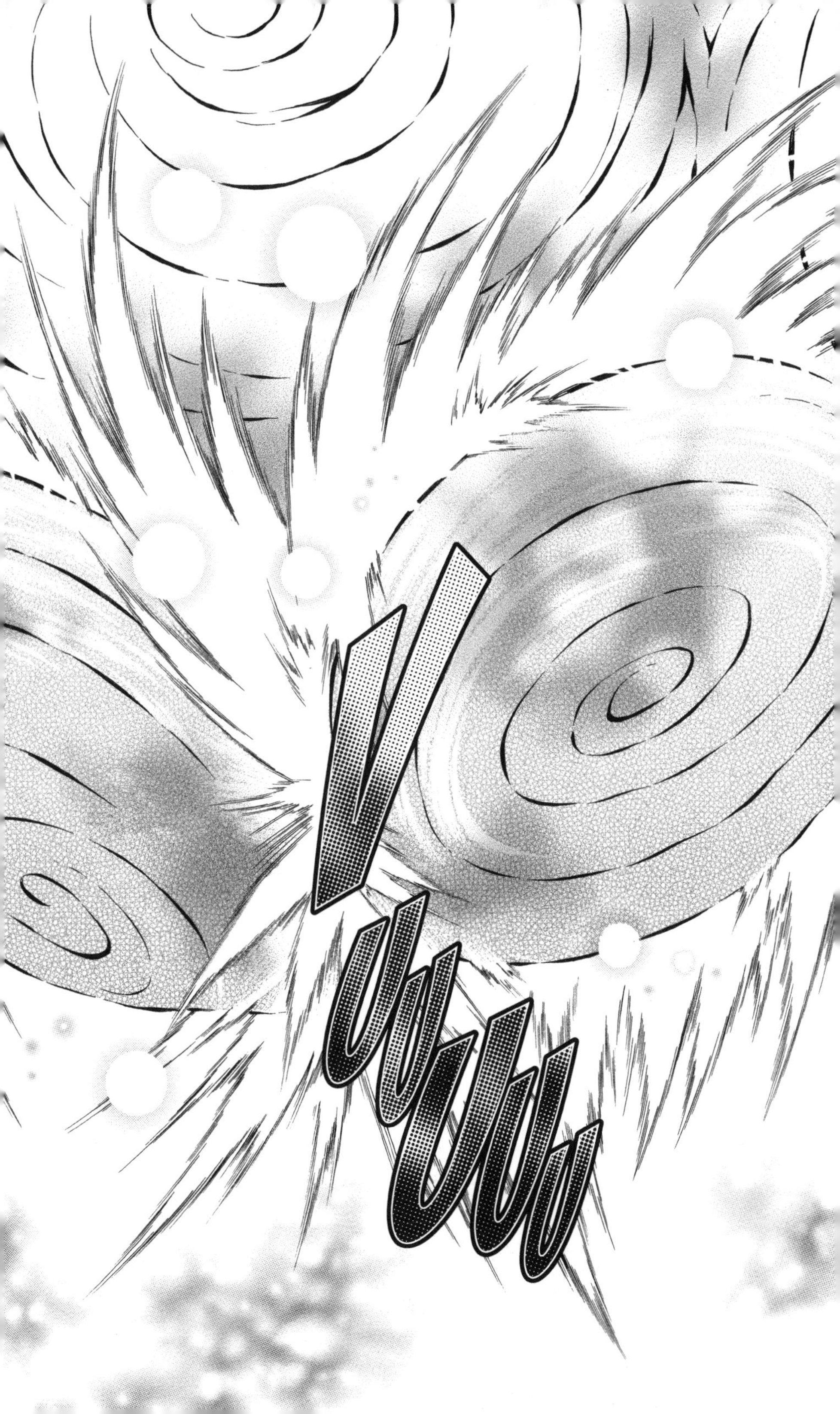

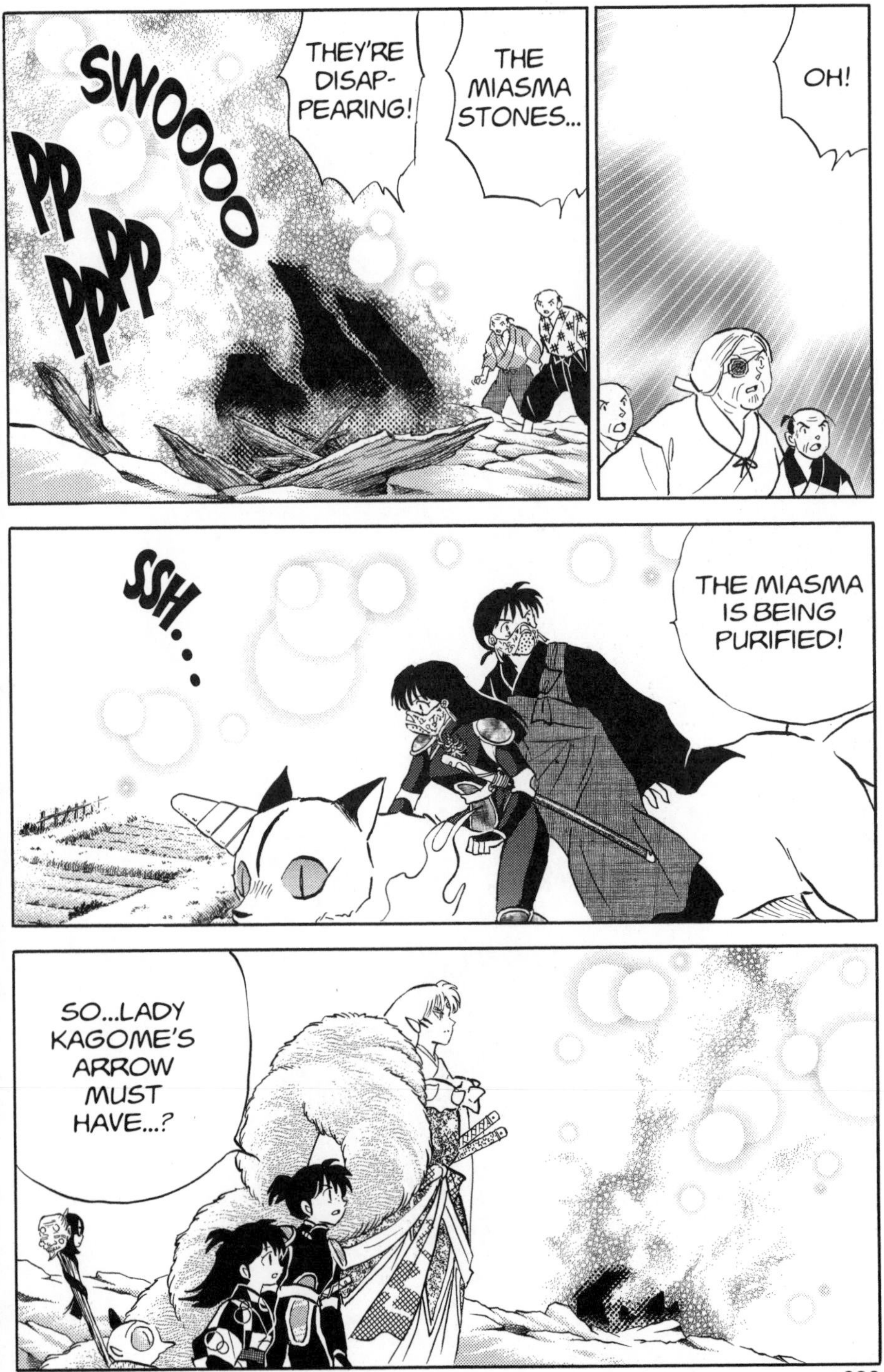
OH!
THE MIASMA STONES...
THEY'RE DISAP-PEARING!
SWOOOOPPPPPP
THE MIASMA IS BEING PURIFIED!
SSH...
SO...LADY KAGOME'S ARROW MUST HAVE...?

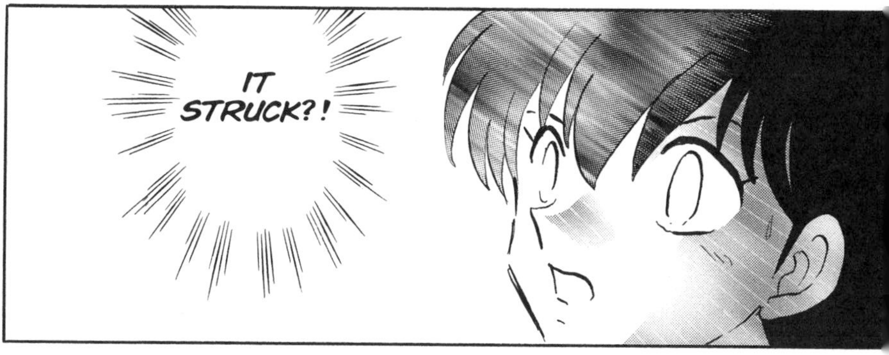
IT STRUCK?!

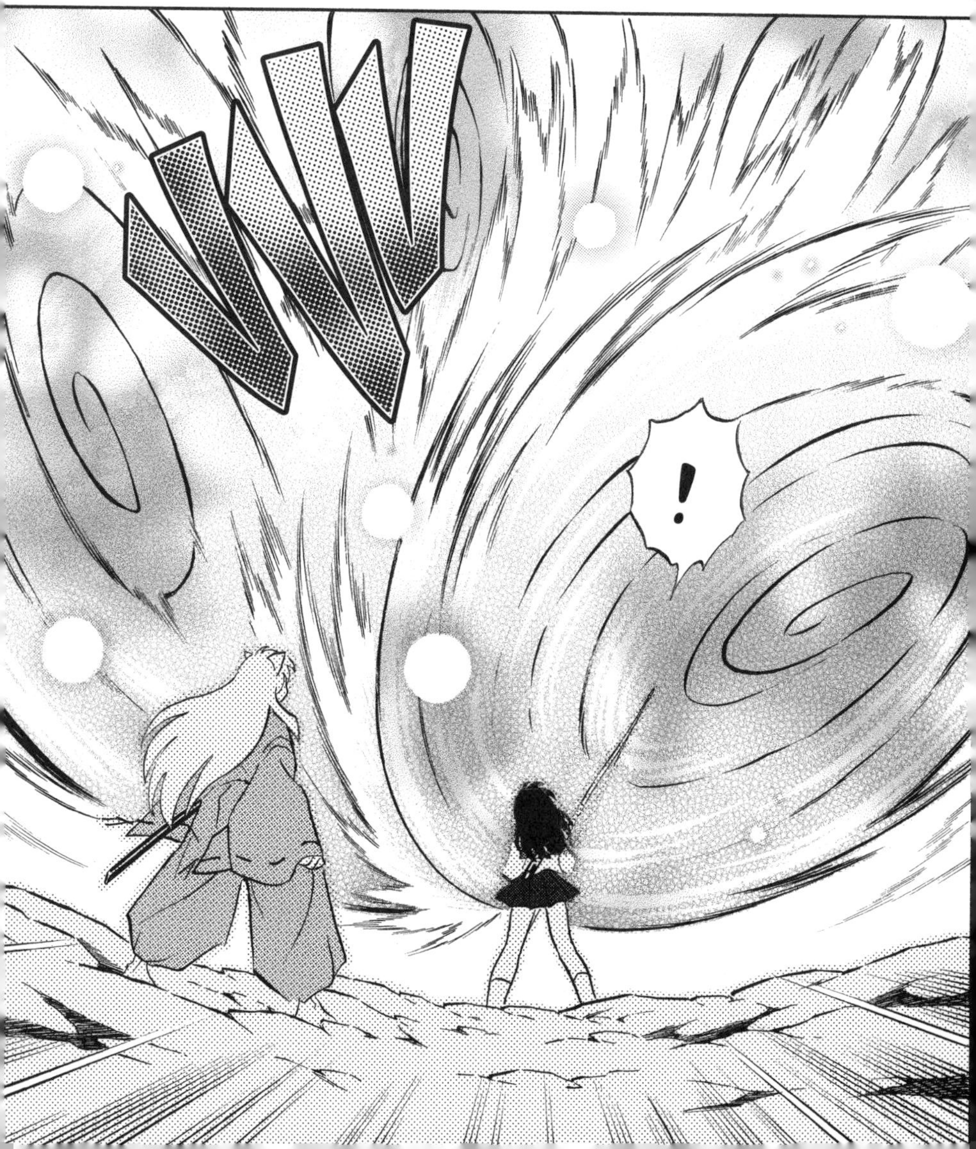
!

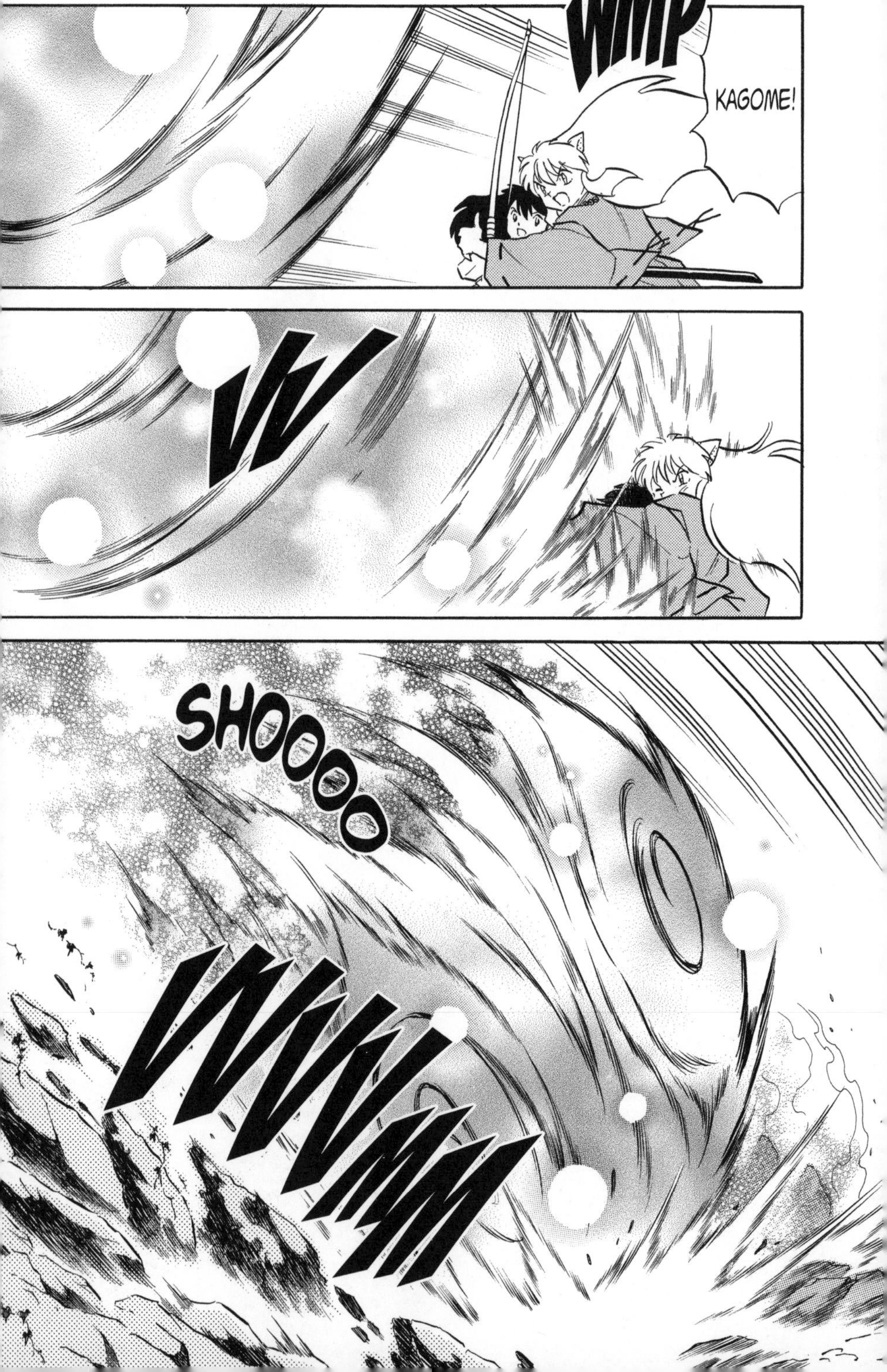
WMP
KAGOME!
SHOOOO

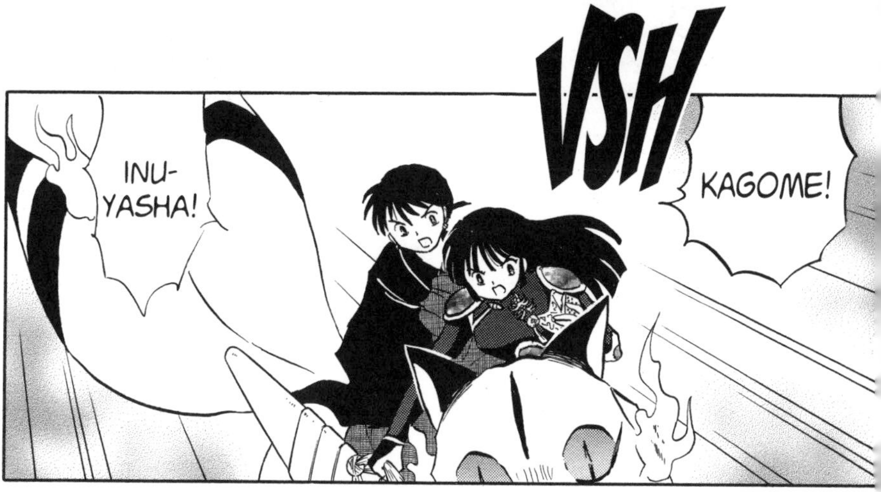
VSH
KAGOME!
INU-YASHA!

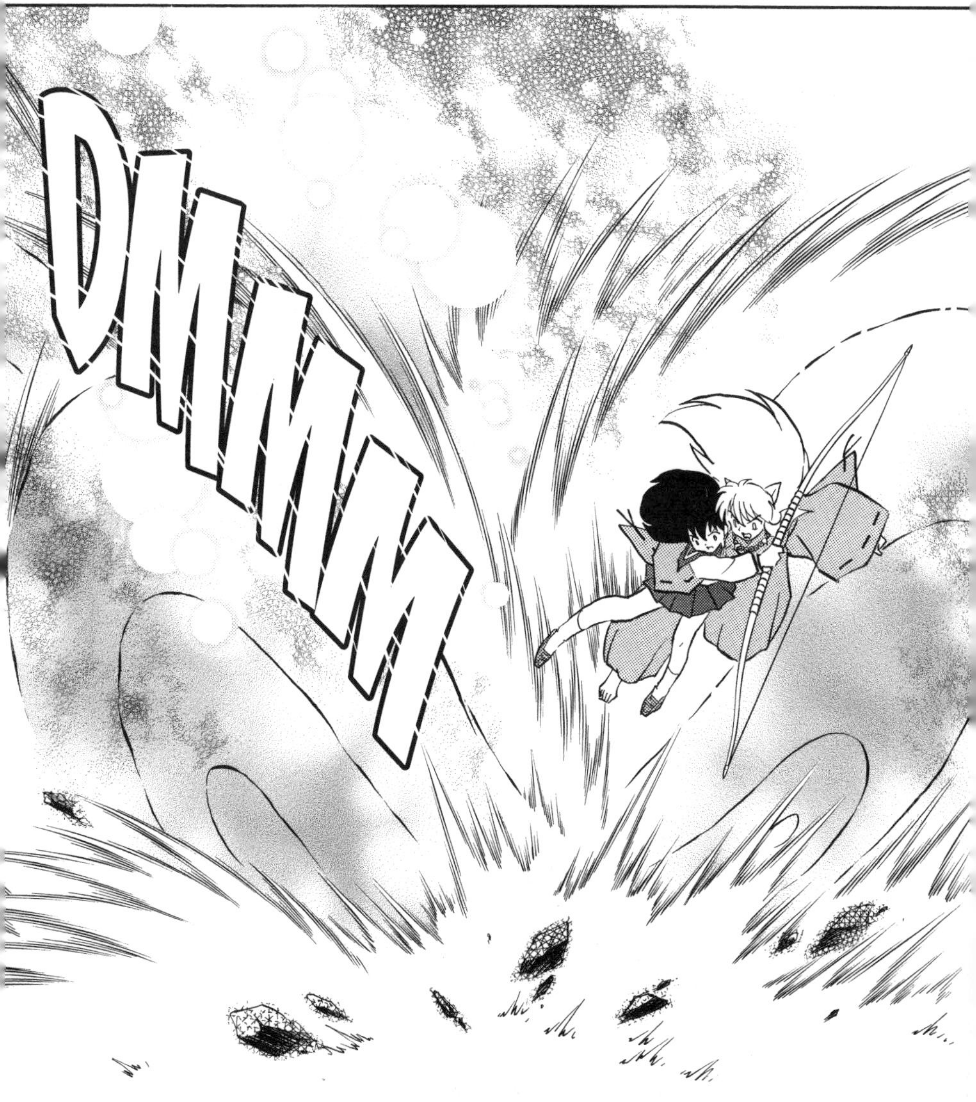
DMMMM

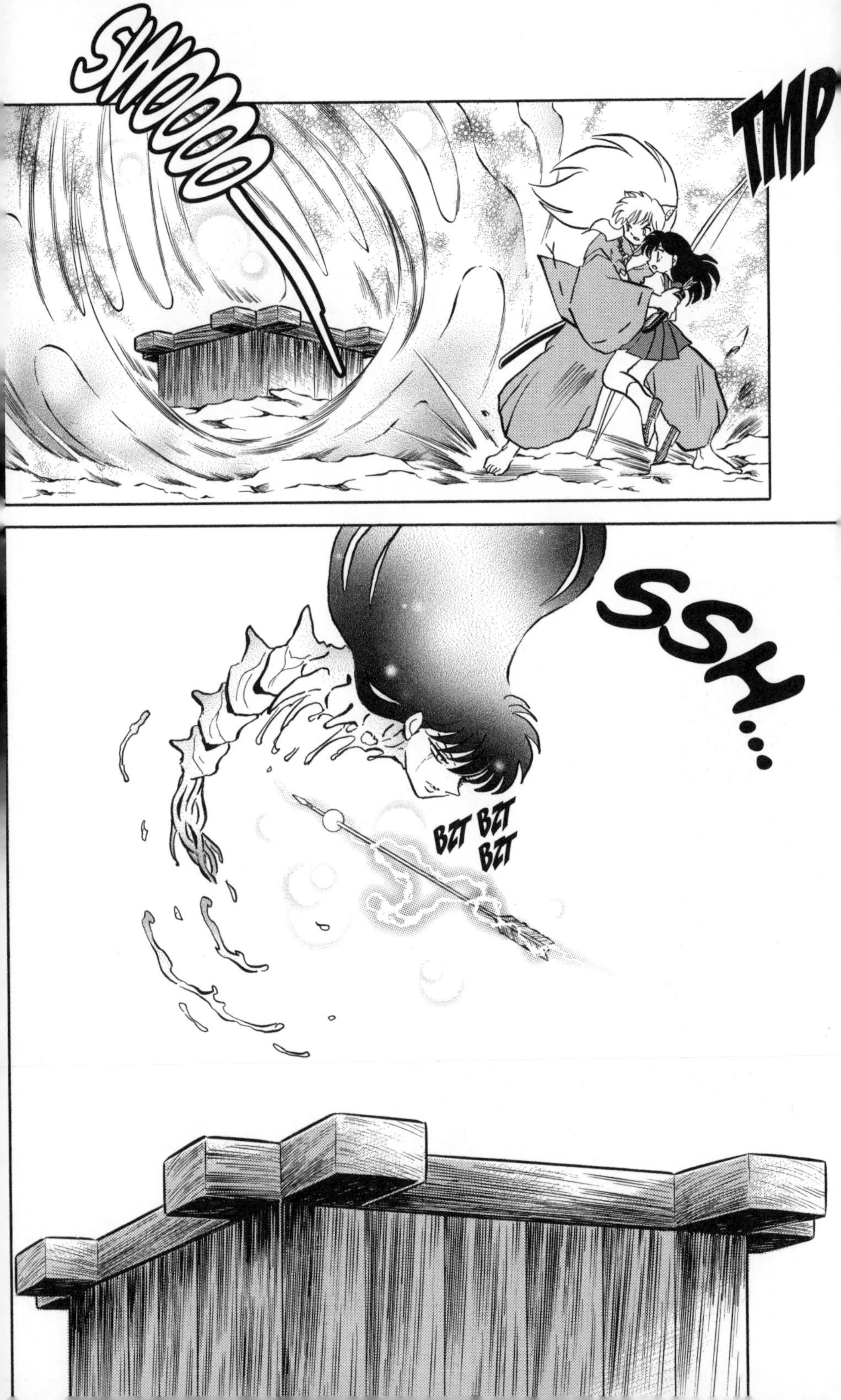
TMP
SHOOOO
SSH...
BZT BZT
BZT

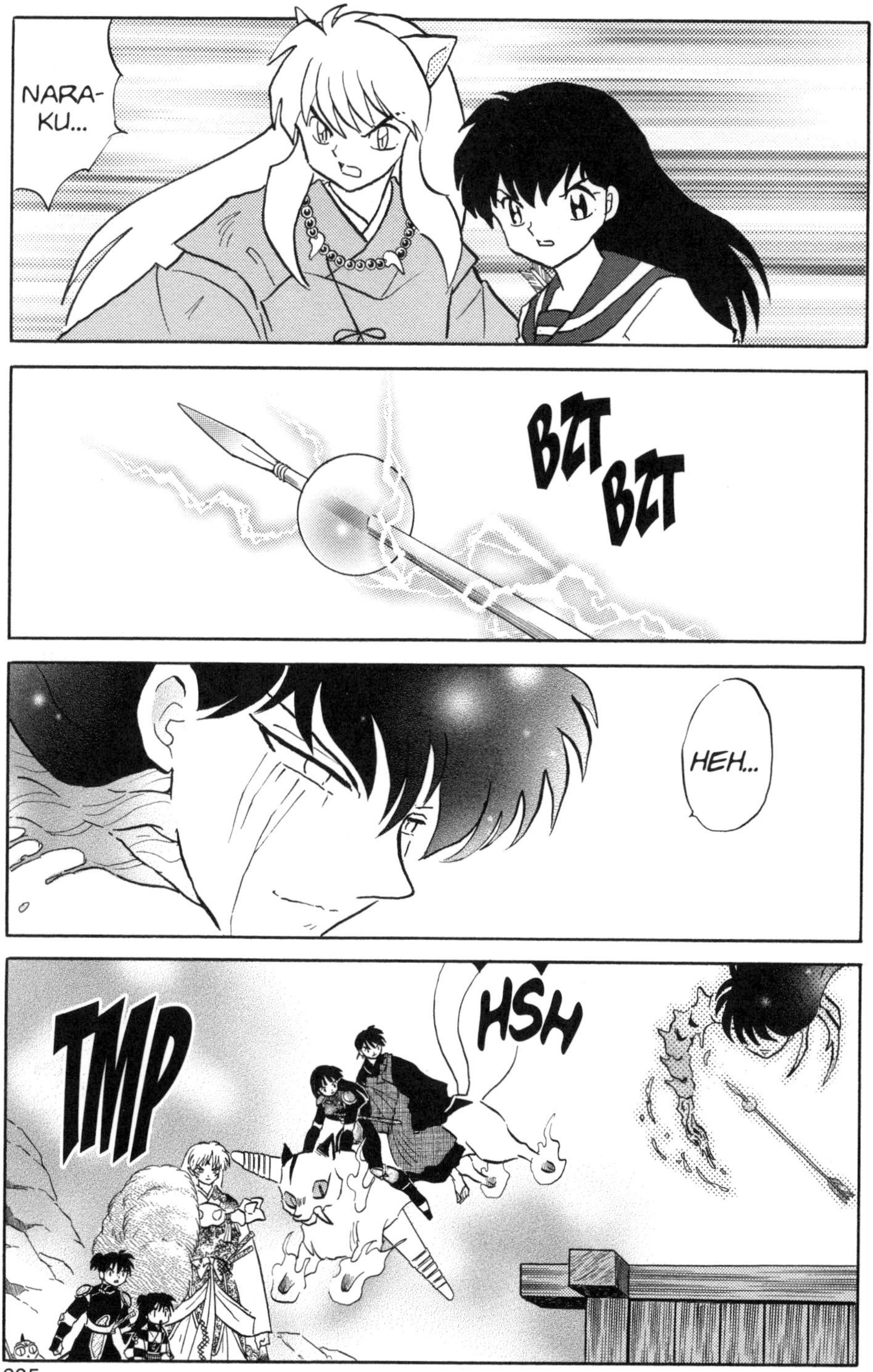
NARA-KU...
BZT BZT
HEH...
HSH
TMP

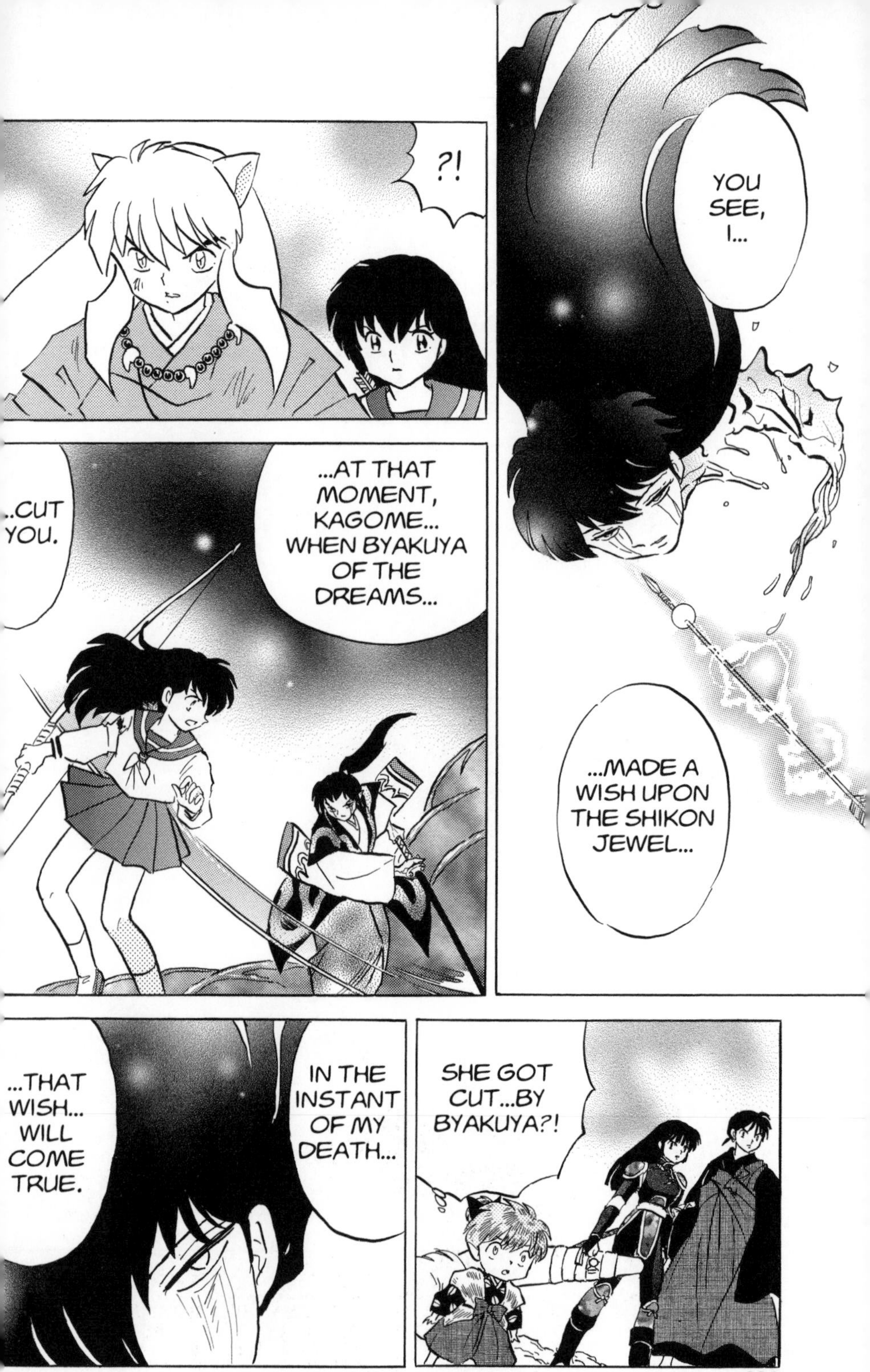
YOU SEE, I...
...MADE A WISH UPON THE SHIKON JEWEL...
?!
...AT THAT MOMENT, KAGOME... WHEN BYAKUYA OF THE DREAMS...
..CUT YOU.
SHE GOT CUT...BY BYAKUYA?!
IN THE INSTANT OF MY DEATH...
...THAT WISH... WILL COME TRUE.

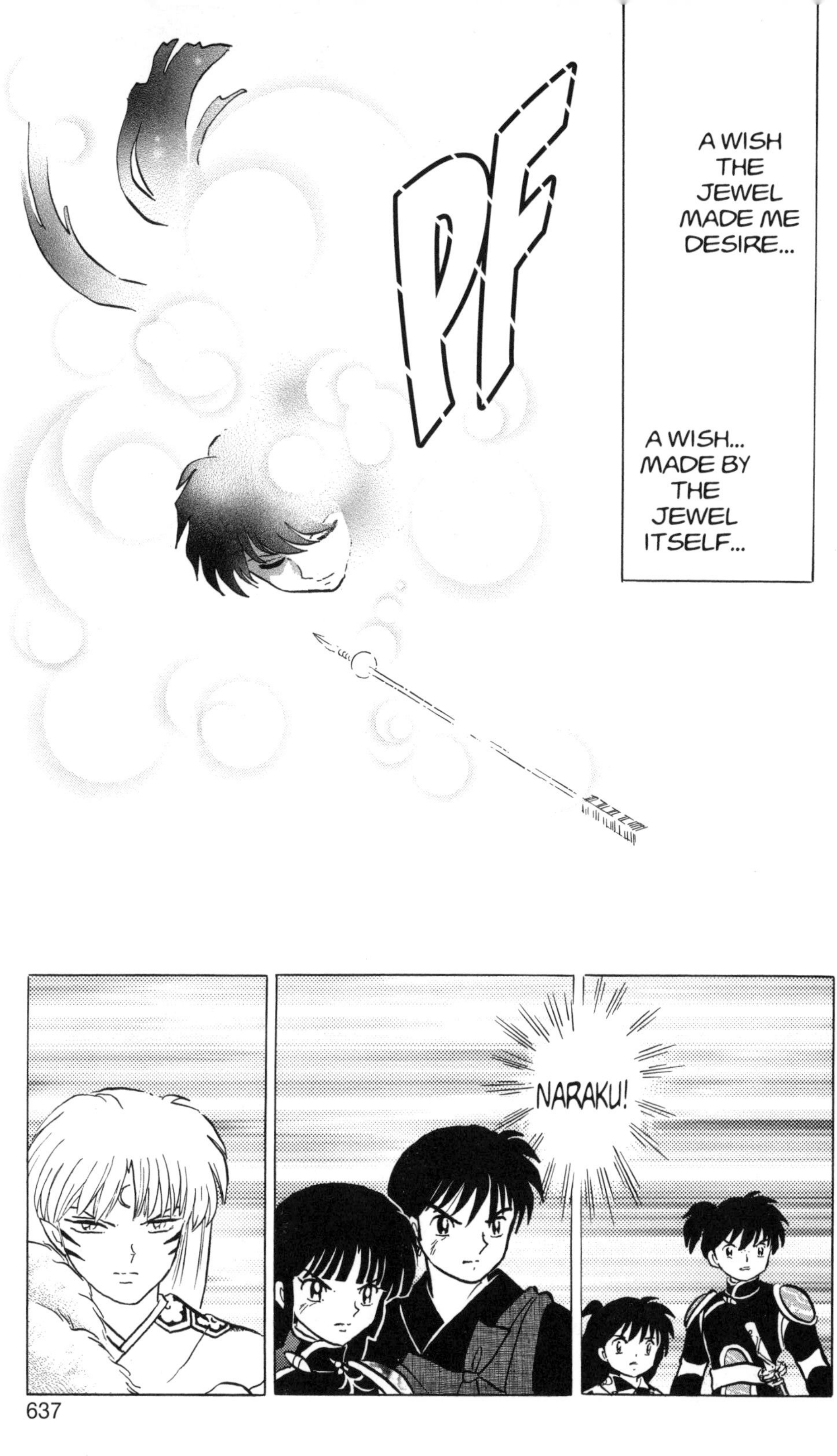
A WISH THE JEWEL MADE ME DESIRE...
A WISH... MADE BY THE JEWEL ITSELF...
PF
NARAKU!

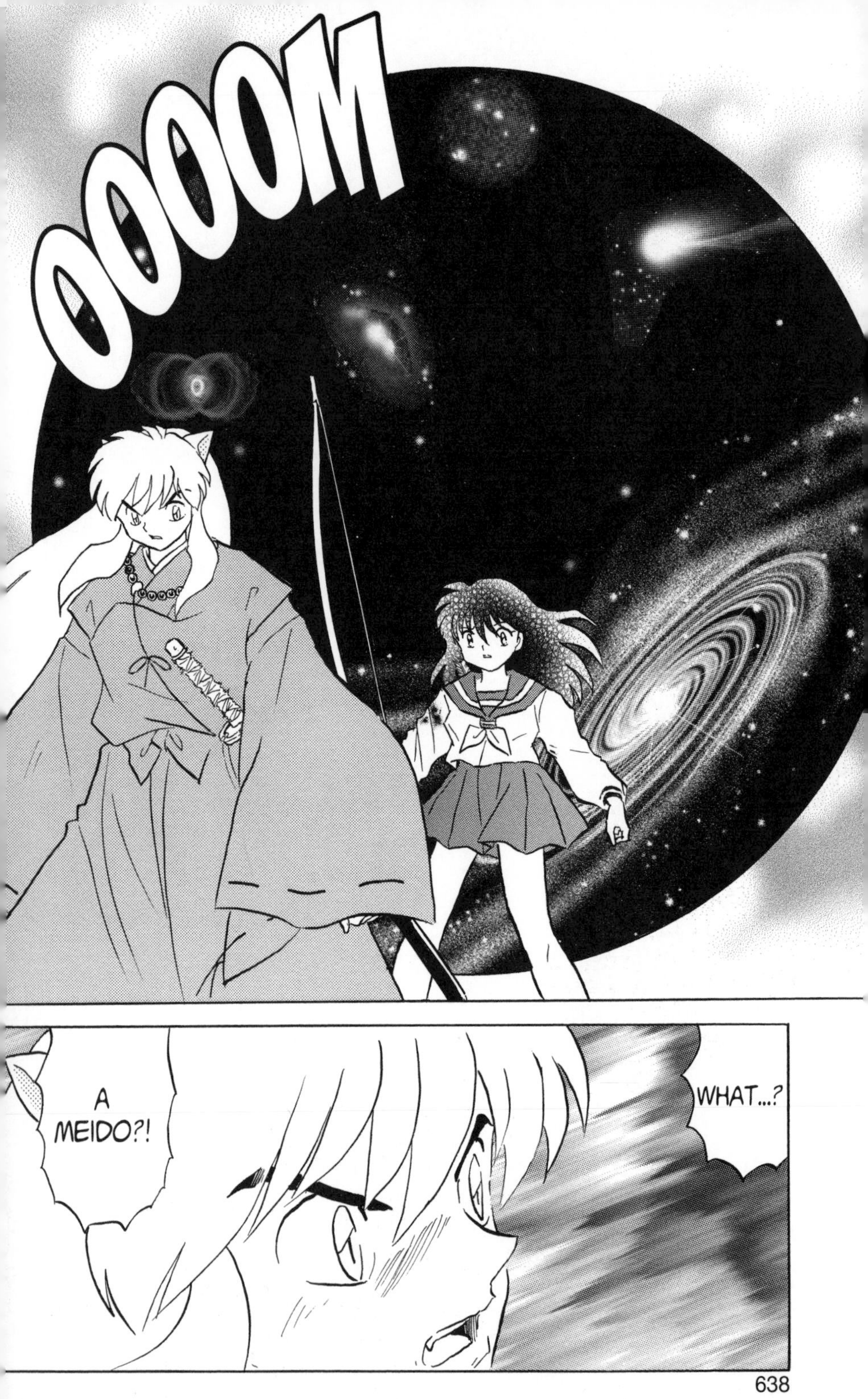
OOOOM
WHAT...?
A MEIDO?!

SCROLL FIVE
THE WELL TRANSFORMED

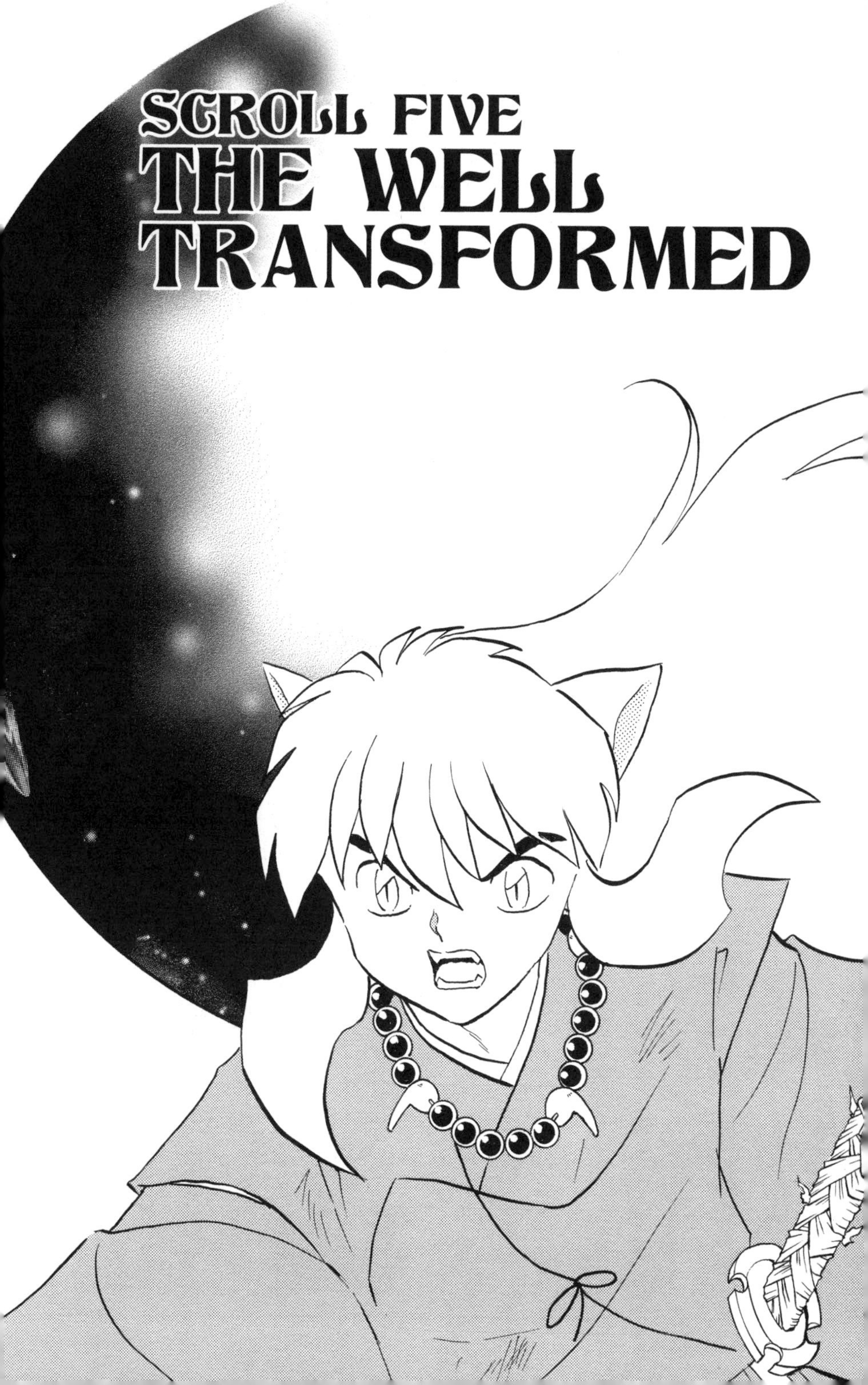

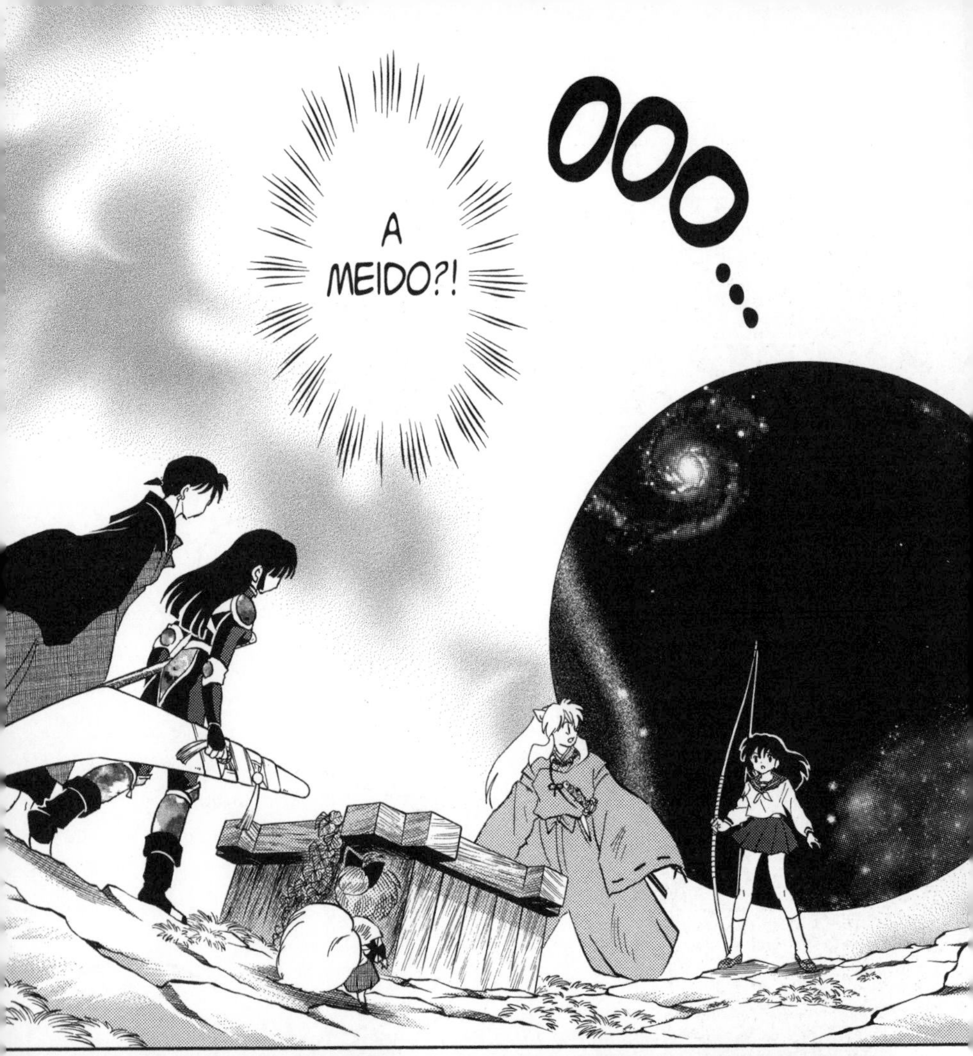
OOO...
A MEIDO?!

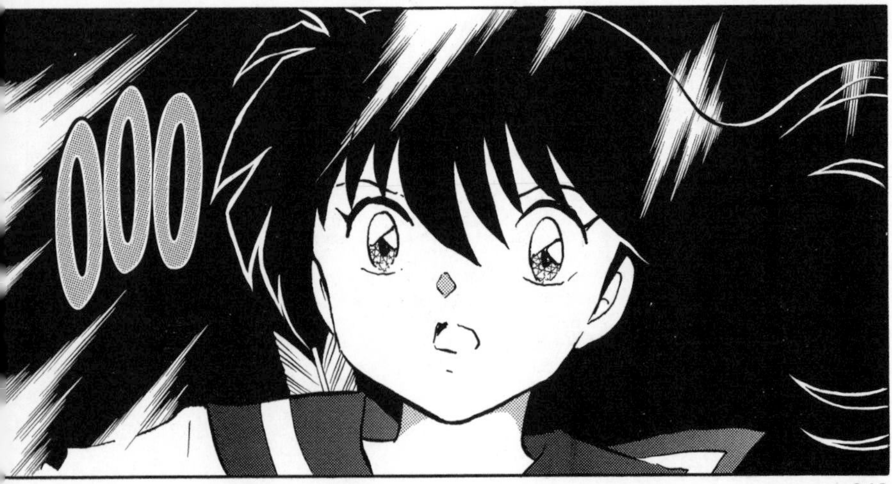
OOO

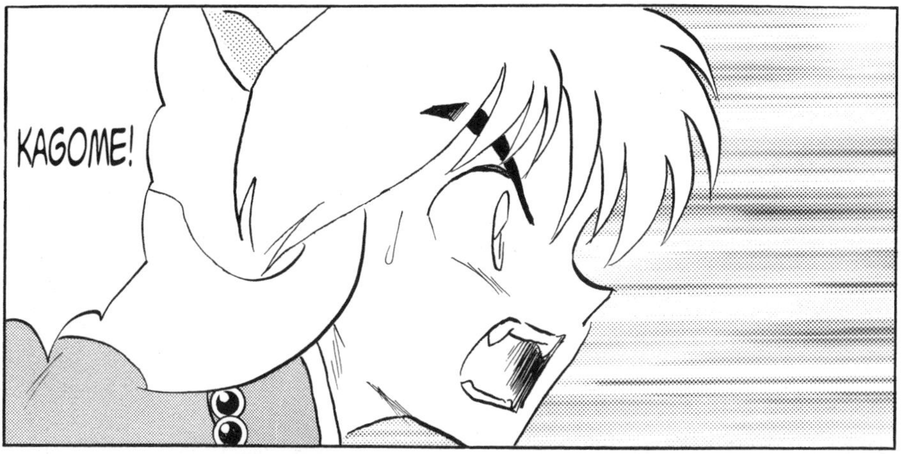
KAGOME!
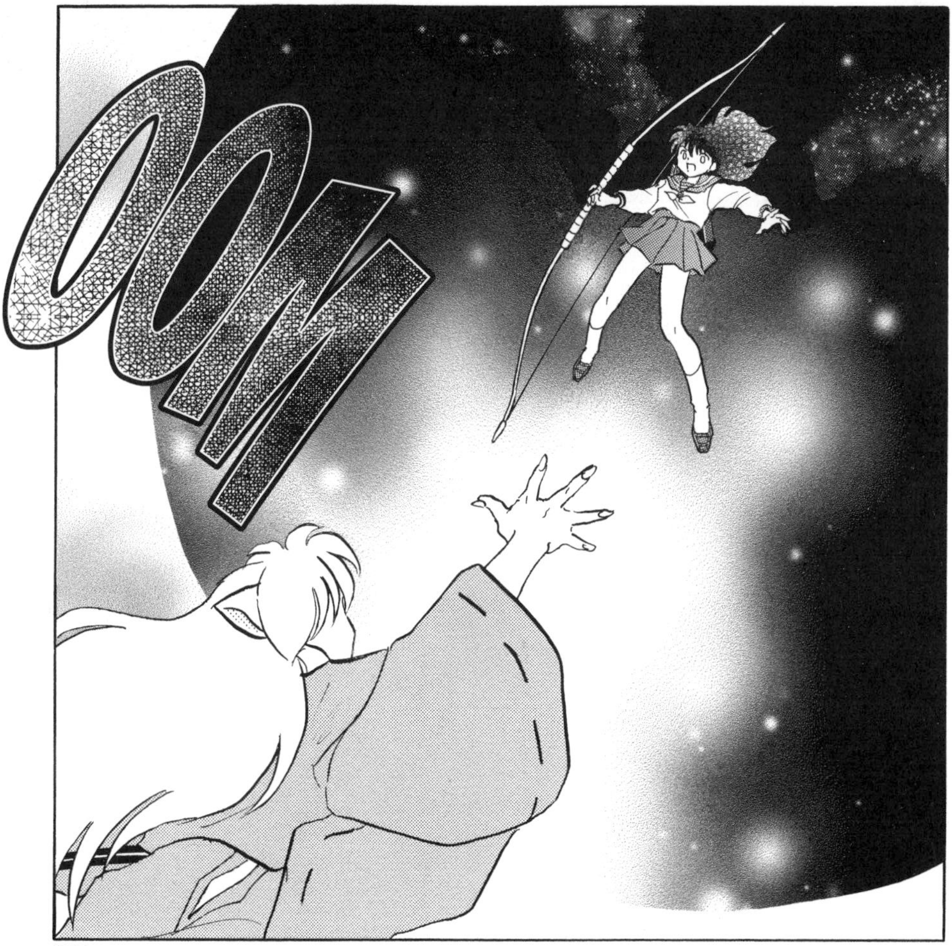
OOM

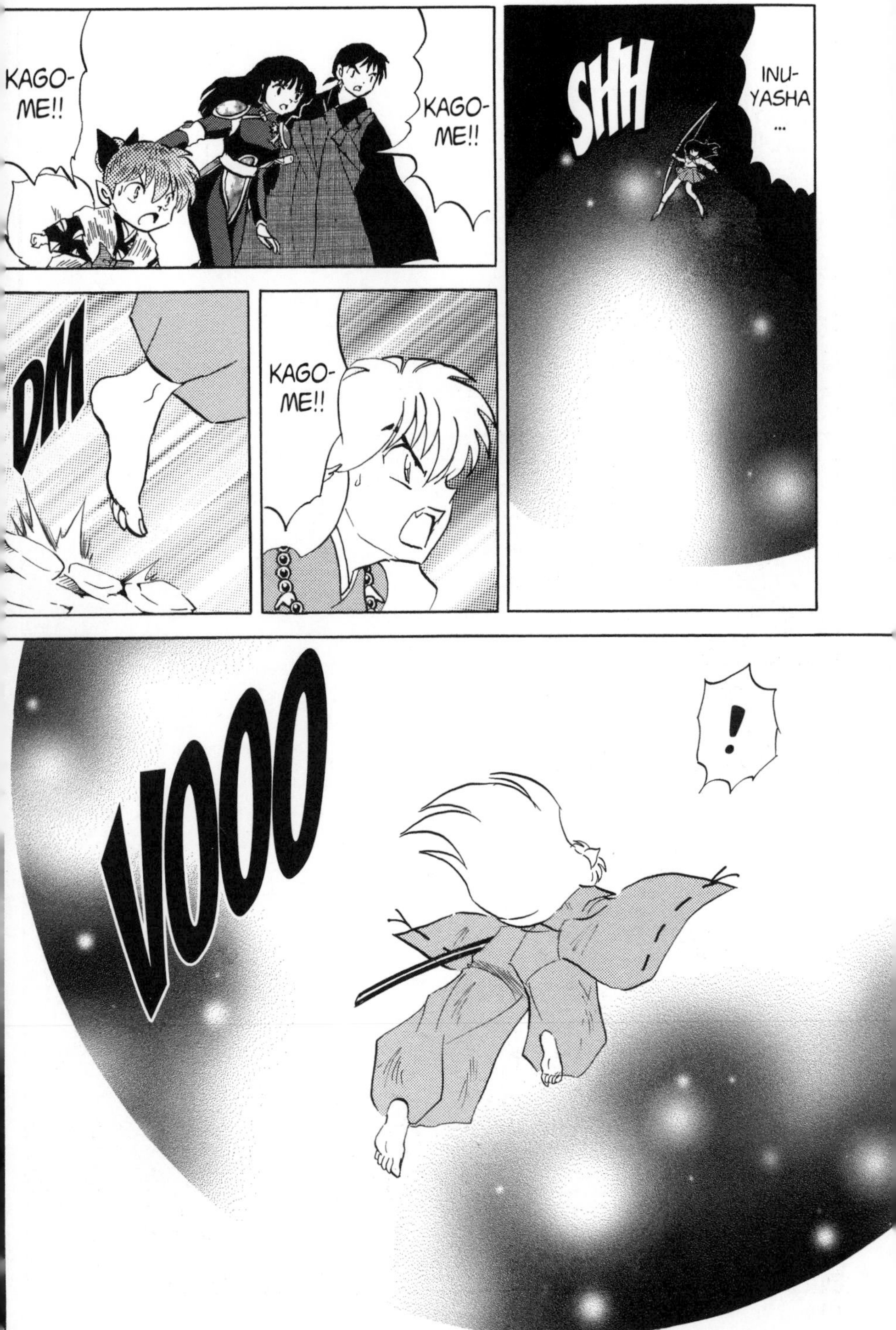
INU-YASHA ...
SHH
KAGO-ME!!
KAGO-ME!!
KAGO-ME!!
DM
!
VOOO

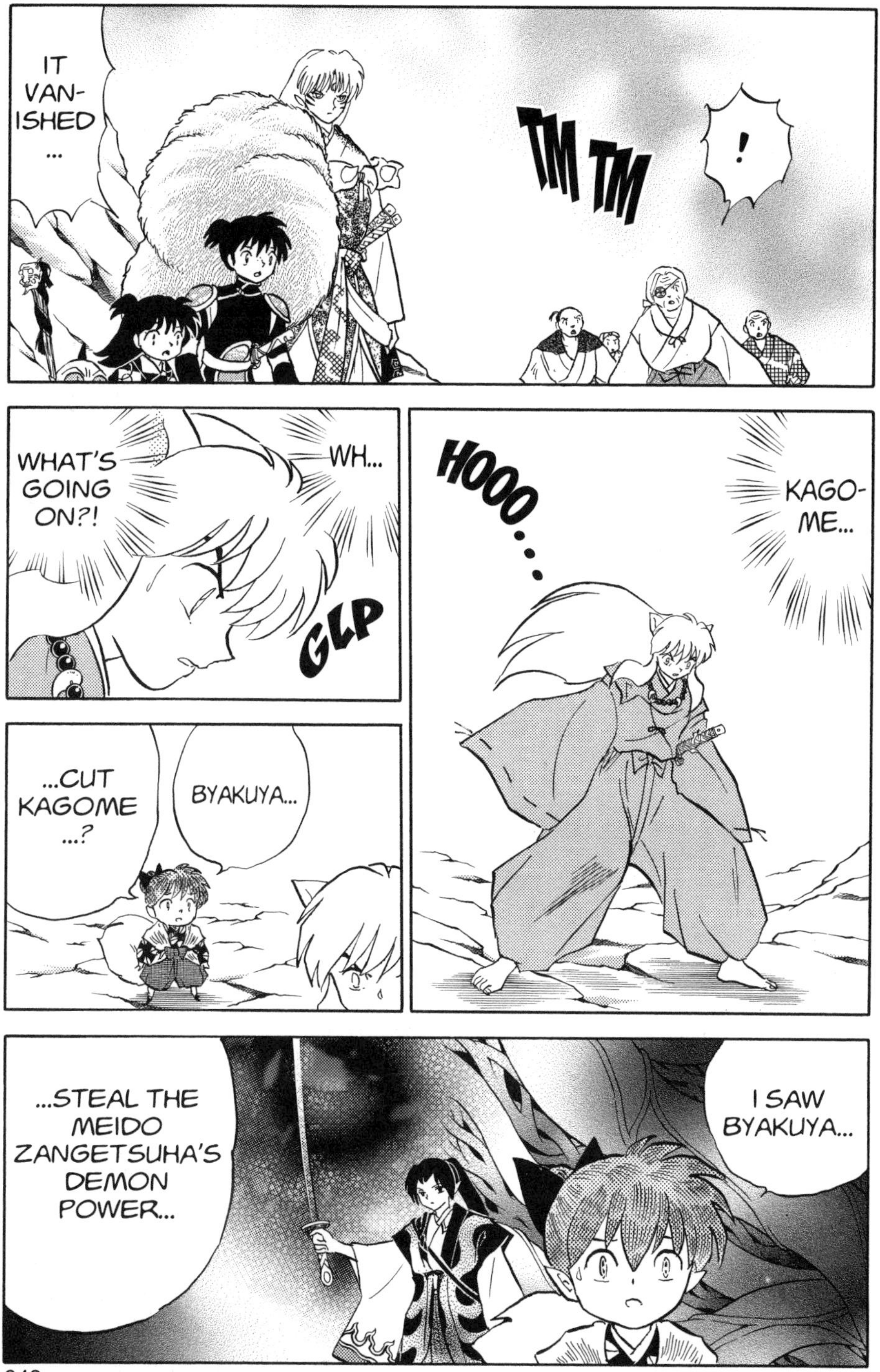
!
TM TM
IT VAN-ISHED ...
KAGO-ME...
HOOO...
WH...
WHAT'S GOING ON?!
GLP
BYAKUYA...
...CUT KAGOME ...?
I SAW BYAKUYA...
...STEAL THE MEIDO ZANGETSUHA'S DEMON POWER...

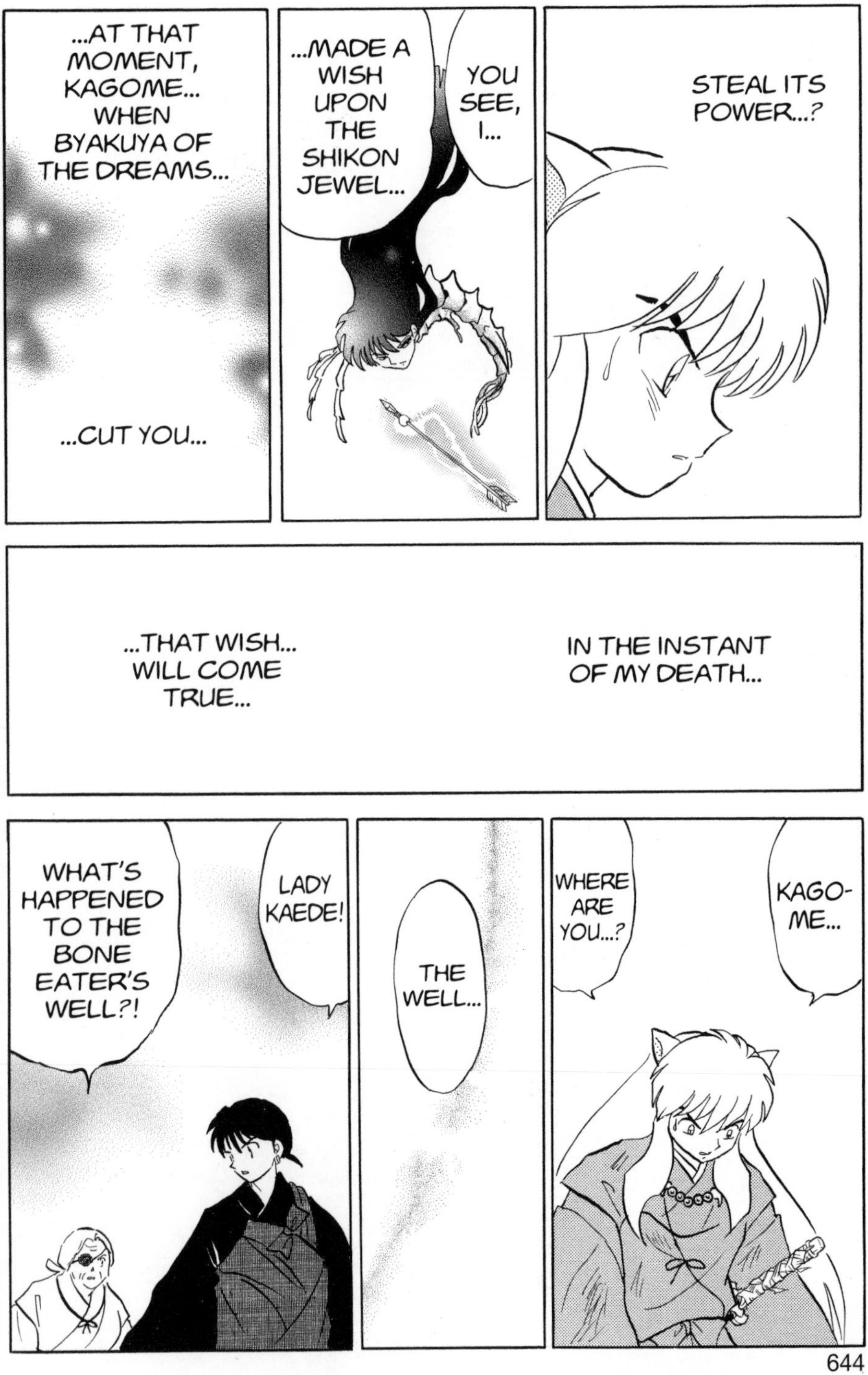

STEAL ITS POWER...?
YOU SEE, I...
...MADE A WISH UPON THE SHIKON JEWEL...
...AT THAT MOMENT, KAGOME... WHEN BYAKUYA OF THE DREAMS...
...CUT YOU...
IN THE INSTANT OF MY DEATH...
...THAT WISH... WILL COME TRUE...
KAGO-ME...
WHERE ARE YOU...?
THE WELL...
LADY KAEDE!
WHAT'S HAPPENED TO THE BONE EATER'S WELL?!

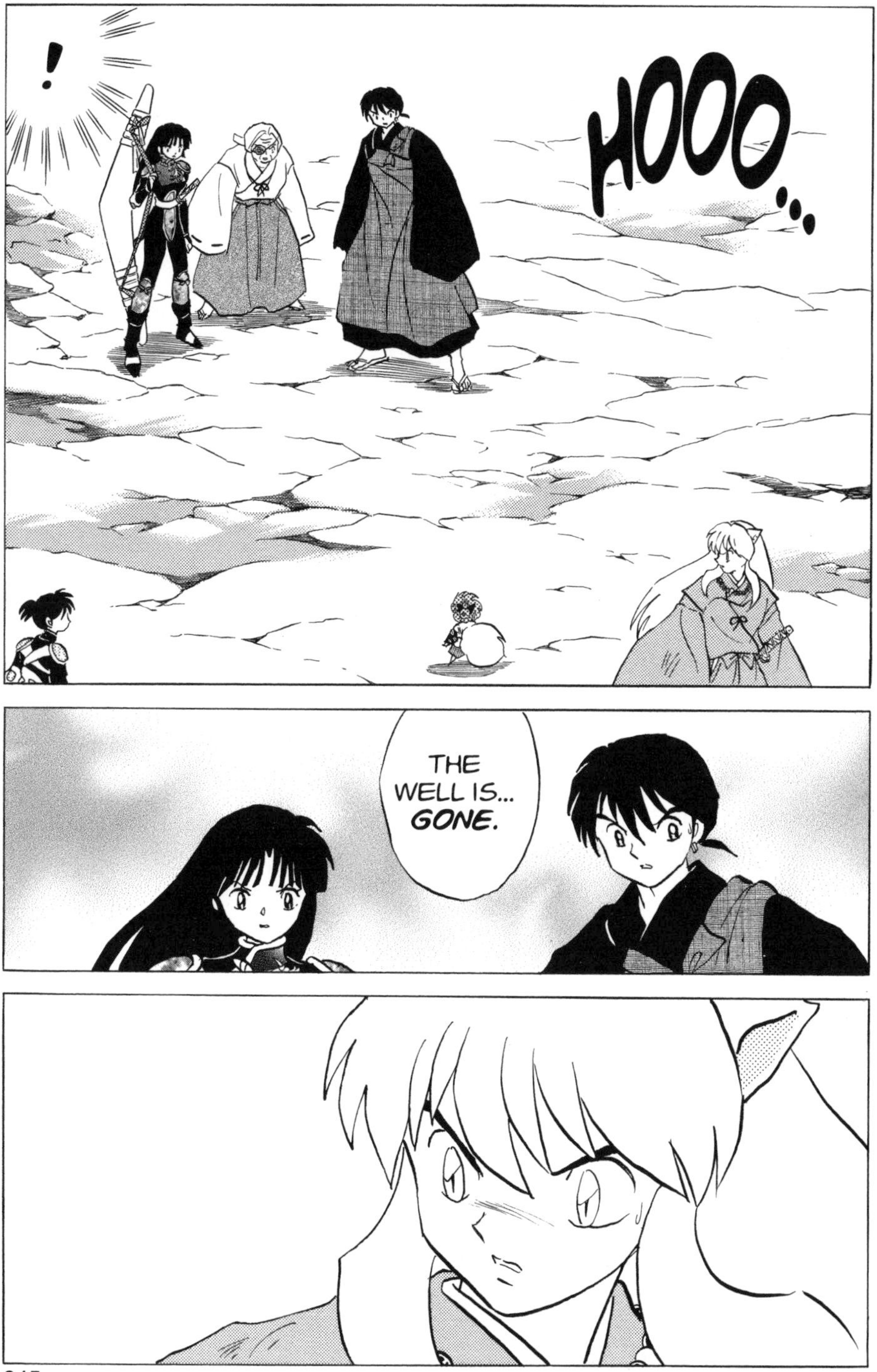
HOOO...
!
THE WELL IS... GONE.

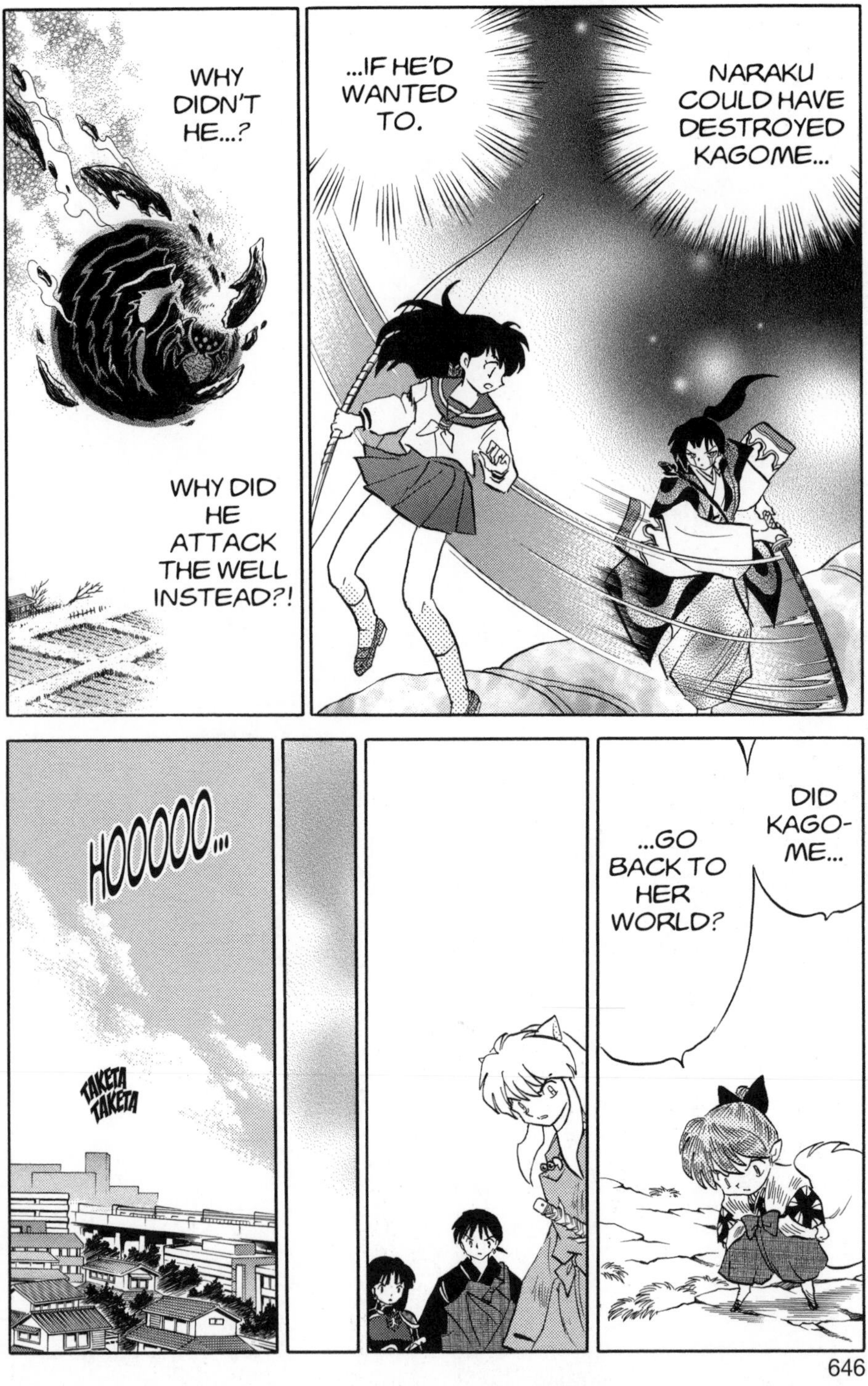
NARAKU COULD HAVE DESTROYED KAGOME...
...IF HE'D WANTED TO.
WHY DIDN'T HE...?
WHY DID HE ATTACK THE WELL INSTEAD?!
DID KAGOME...
...GO BACK TO HER WORLD?
HOOOOO...
TAKETA TAKETA

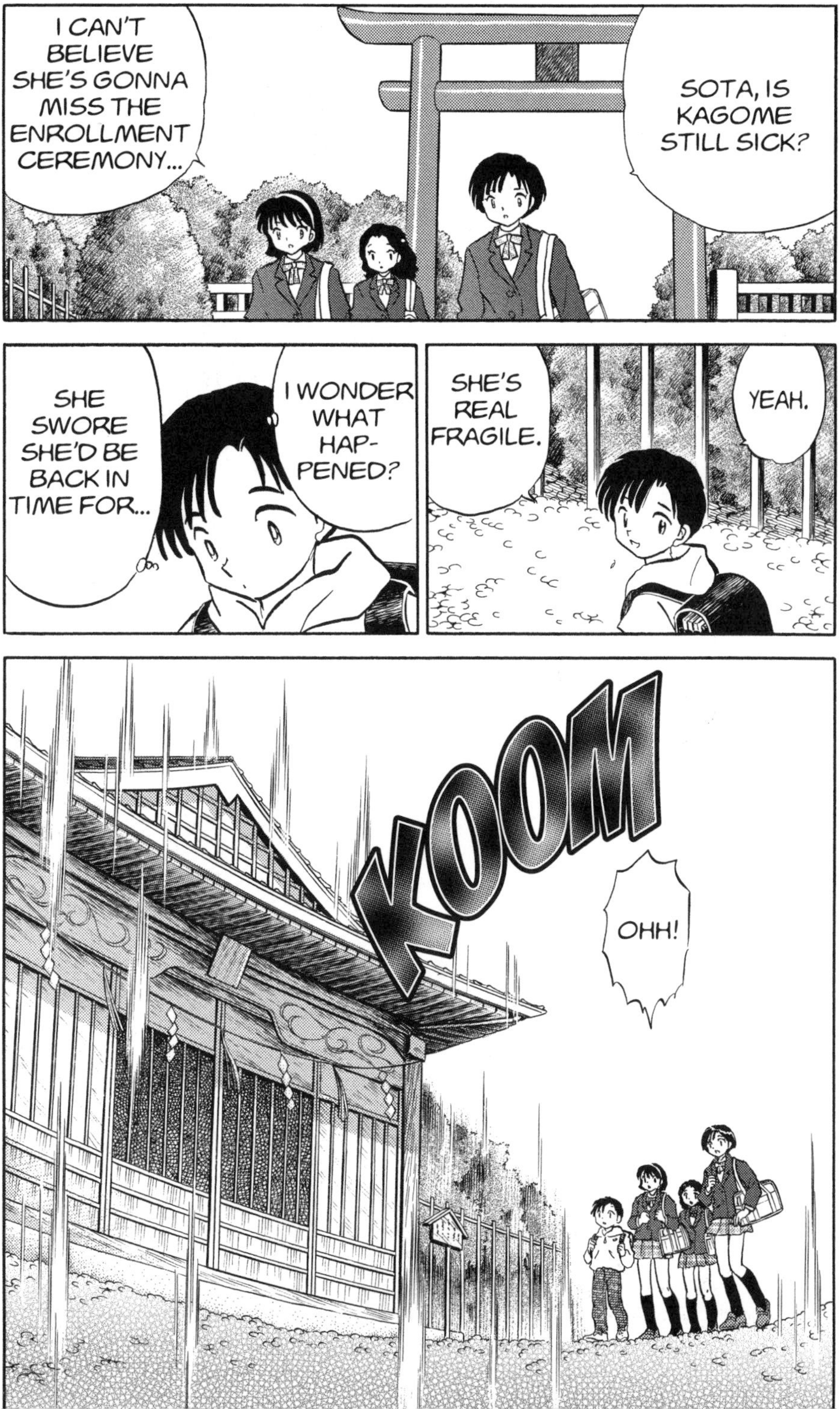
SOTA, IS KAGOME STILL SICK?
I CAN'T BELIEVE SHE'S GONNA MISS THE ENROLLMENT CEREMONY...
YEAH.
SHE'S REAL FRAGILE.
I WONDER WHAT HAP-PENED?
SHE SWORE SHE'D BE BACK IN TIME FOR...
KOOM
OHH!

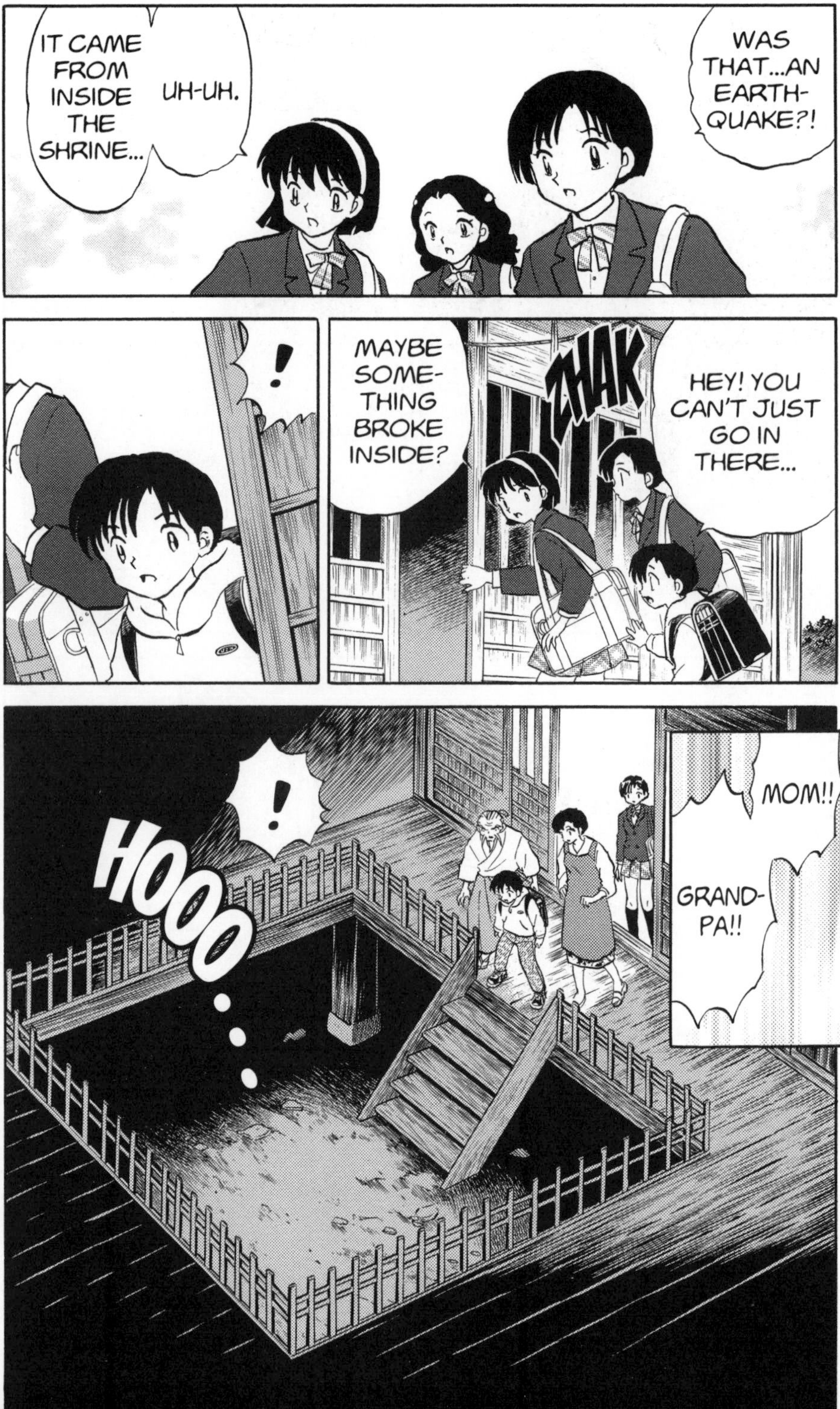
WAS THAT...AN EARTH-QUAKE?!
UH-UH.
IT CAME FROM INSIDE THE SHRINE...
HEY! YOU CAN'T JUST GO IN THERE...
ZHAK
MAYBE SOME-THING BROKE INSIDE?
!
MOM!!
GRAND-PA!!
!
HOOO...

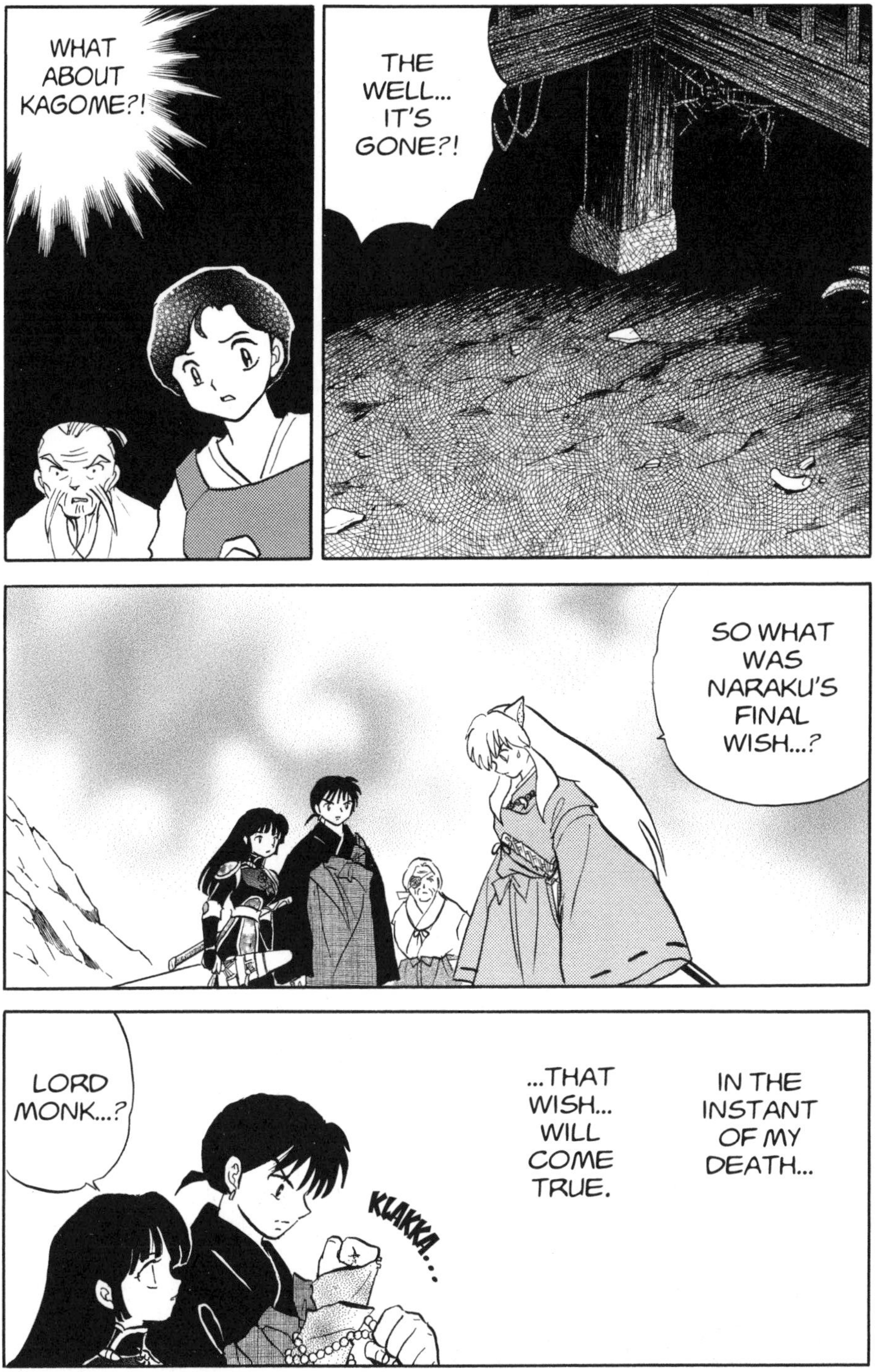
THE WELL... IT'S GONE?!
WHAT ABOUT KAGOME?!
SO WHAT WAS NARAKU'S FINAL WISH...?
IN THE INSTANT OF MY DEATH...
...THAT WISH... WILL COME TRUE.
LORD MONK...?
KLAKKA...

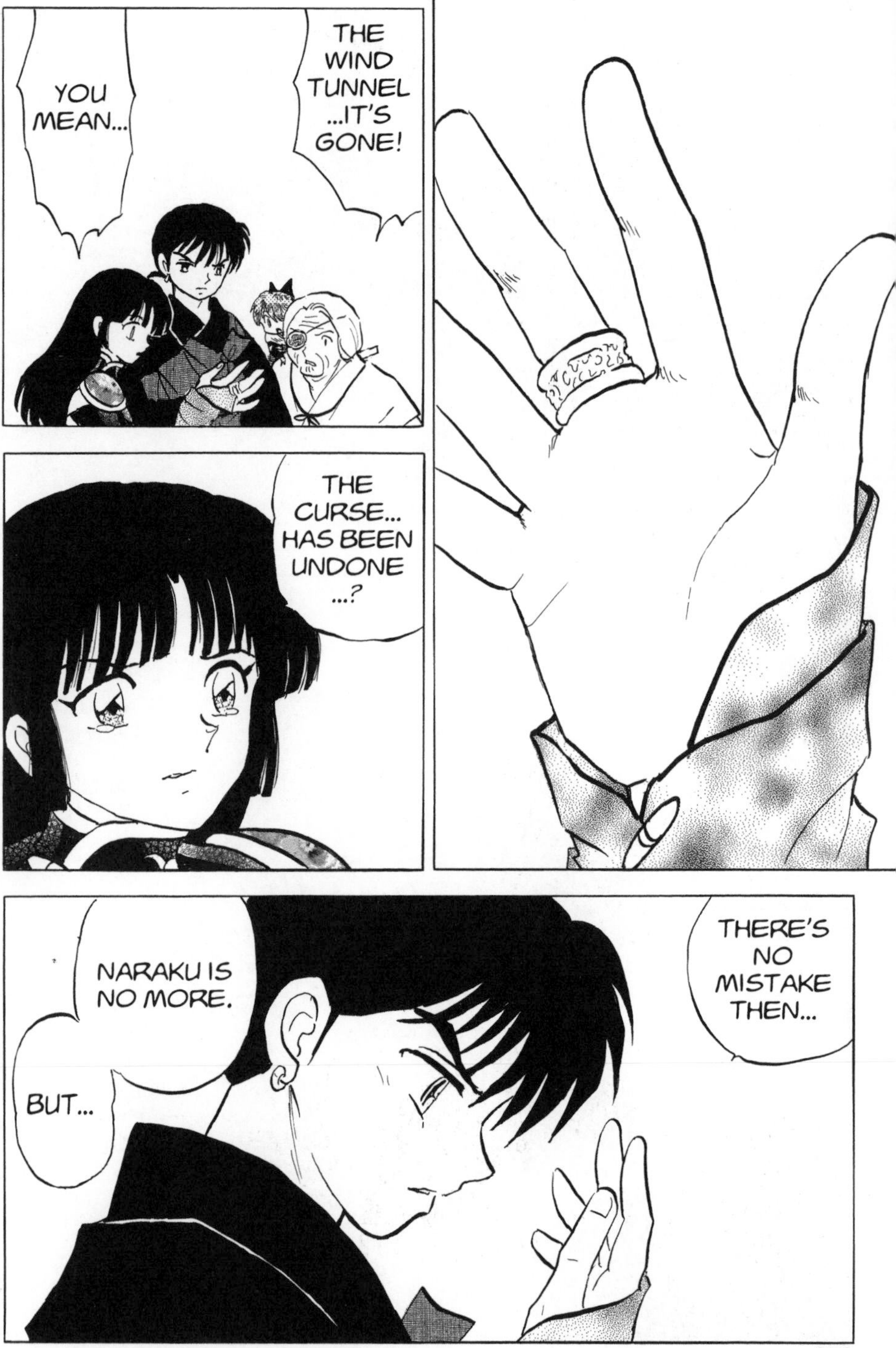
THE WIND TUNNEL ...IT'S GONE!
YOU MEAN...
THE CURSE... HAS BEEN UNDONE ...?
THERE'S NO MISTAKE THEN...
NARAKU IS NO MORE.
BUT...

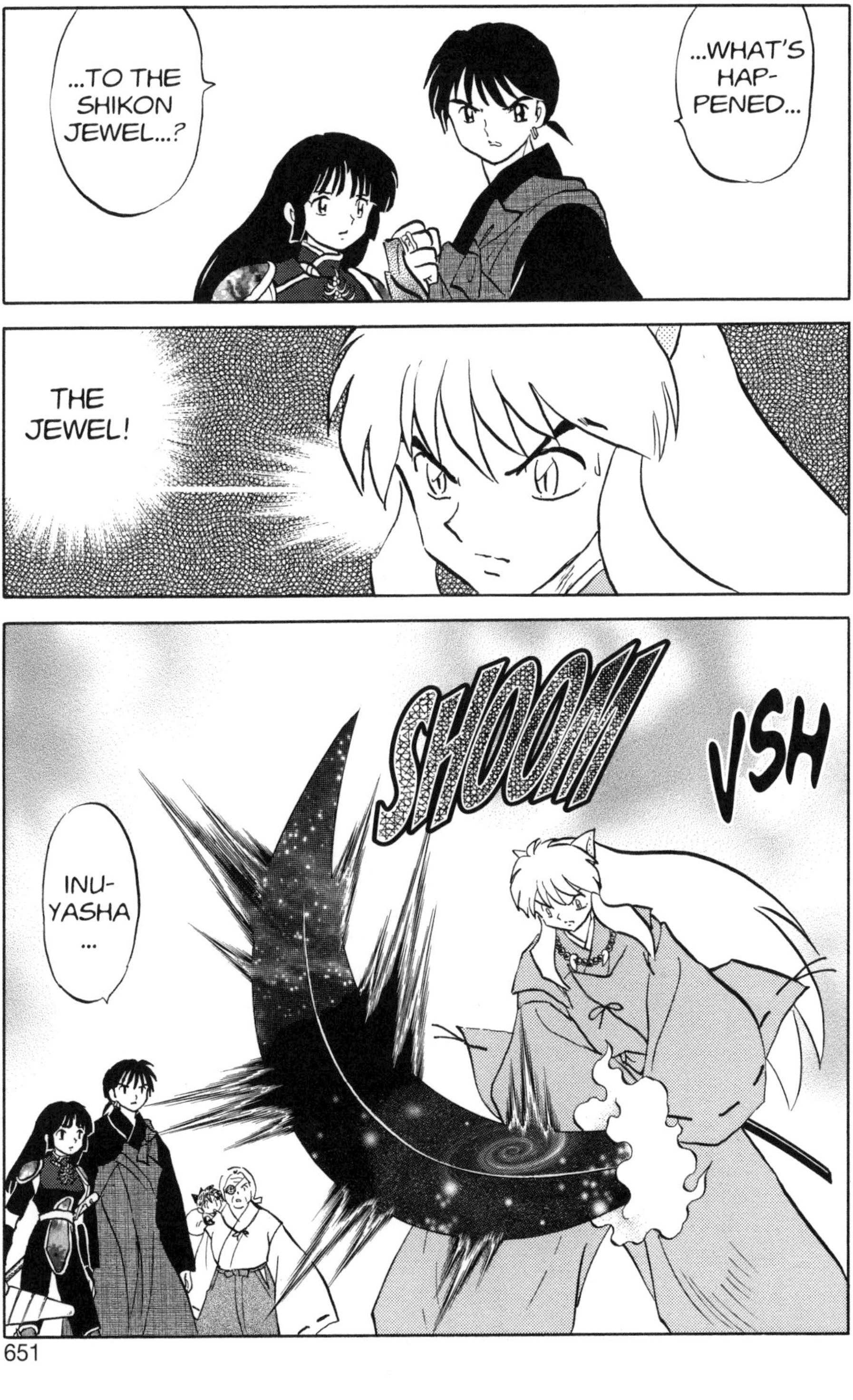
...WHAT'S HAP-PENED...
...TO THE SHIKON JEWEL...?
THE JEWEL!
VSH
SHOOM
INU-YASHA ...

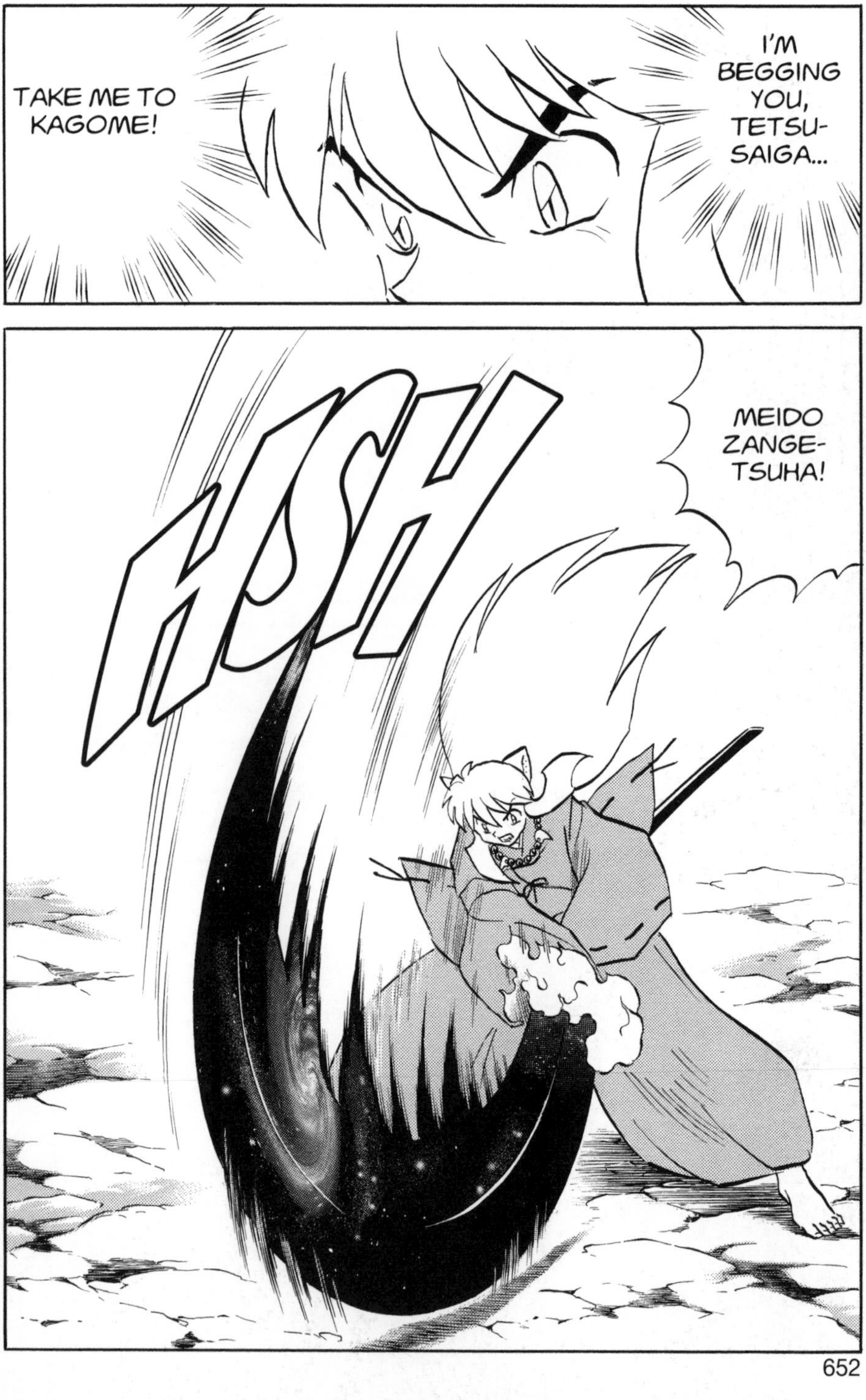
I'M BEGGING YOU, TETSU-SAIGA...
TAKE ME TO KAGOME!
MEIDO ZANGE-TSUHA!
HSH

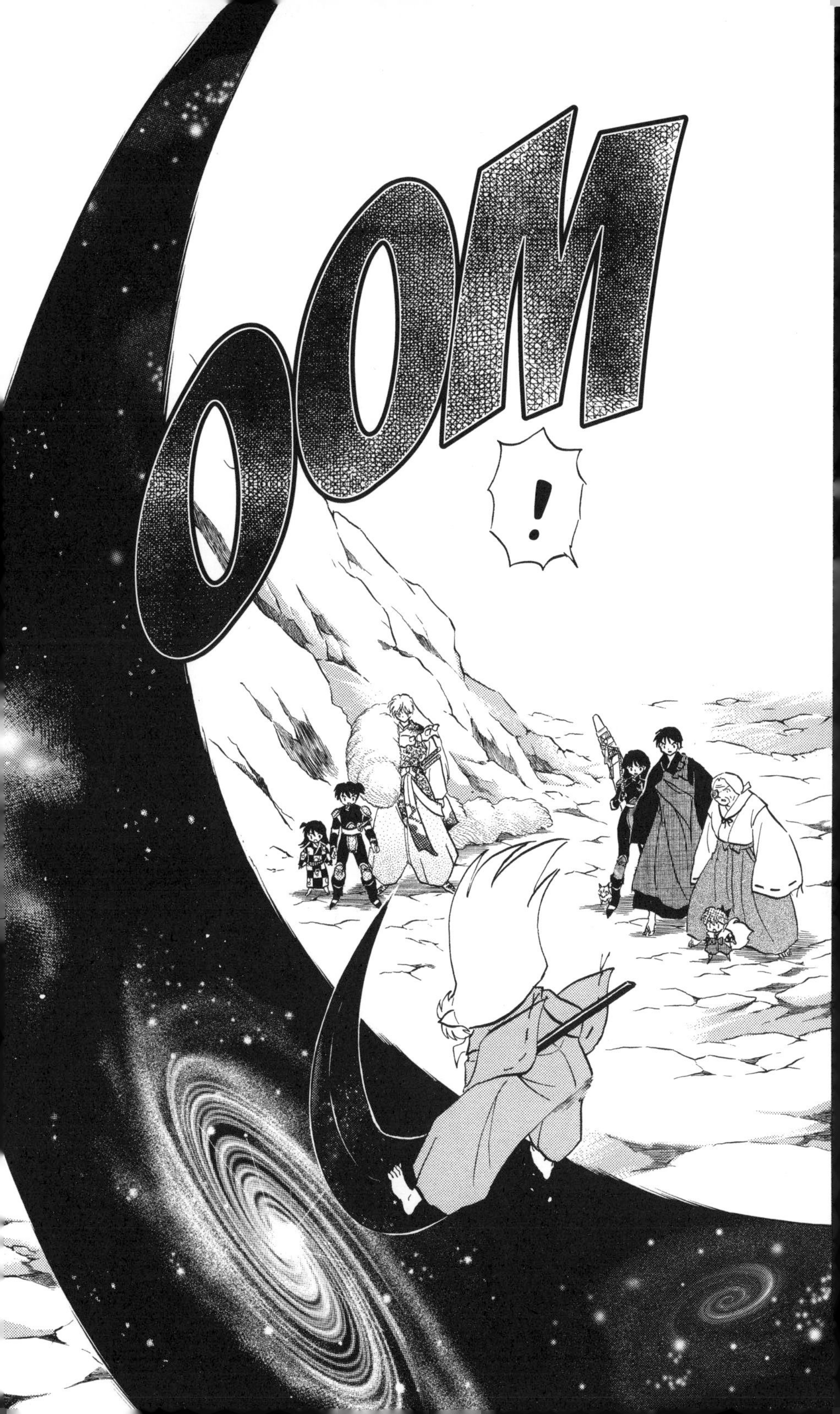
OOM
!

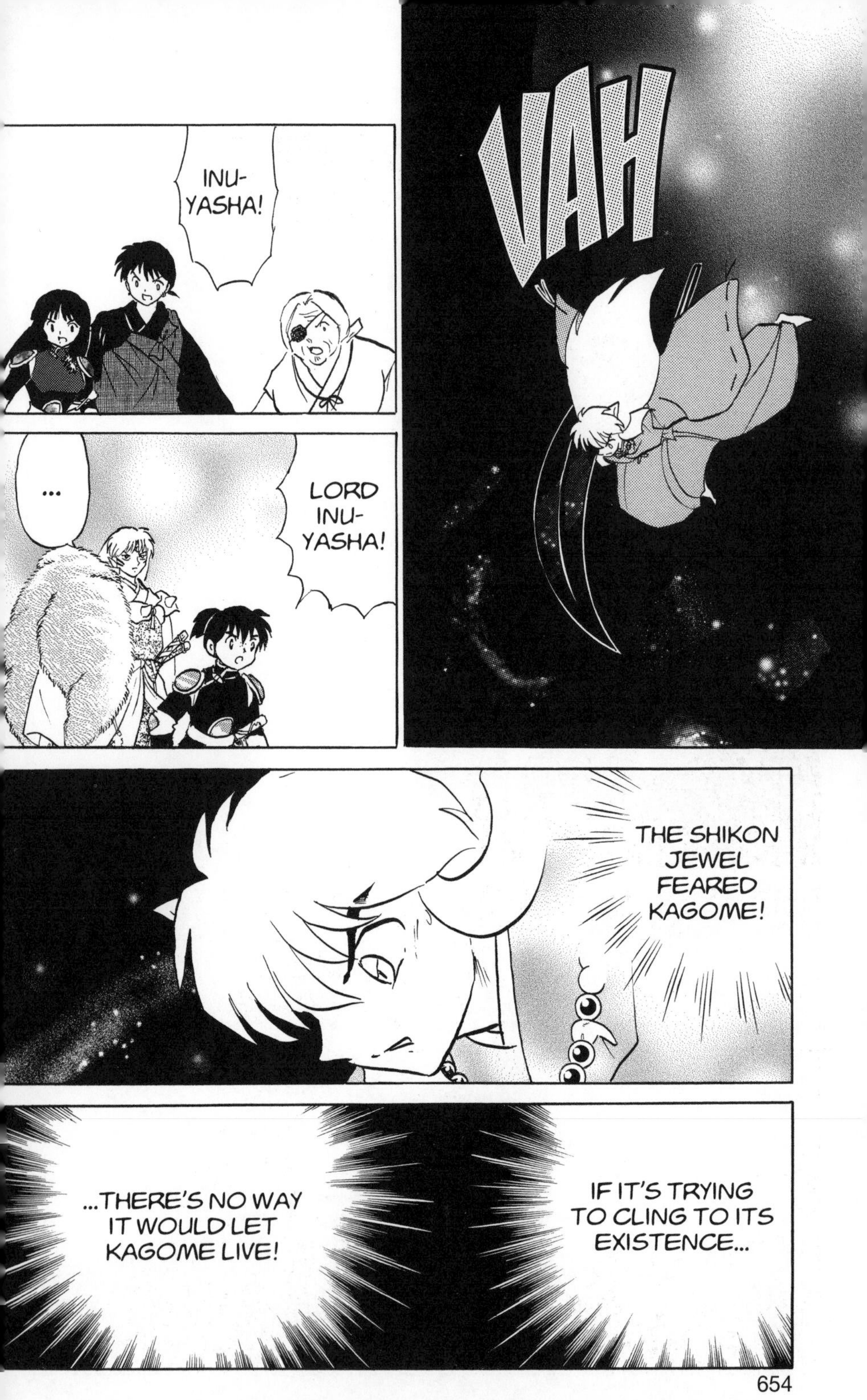
VAH
INU-YASHA!
LORD INU-YASHA!
...
THE SHIKON JEWEL FEARED KAGOME!
IF IT'S TRYING TO CLING TO ITS EXISTENCE...
...THERE'S NO WAY IT WOULD LET KAGOME LIVE!

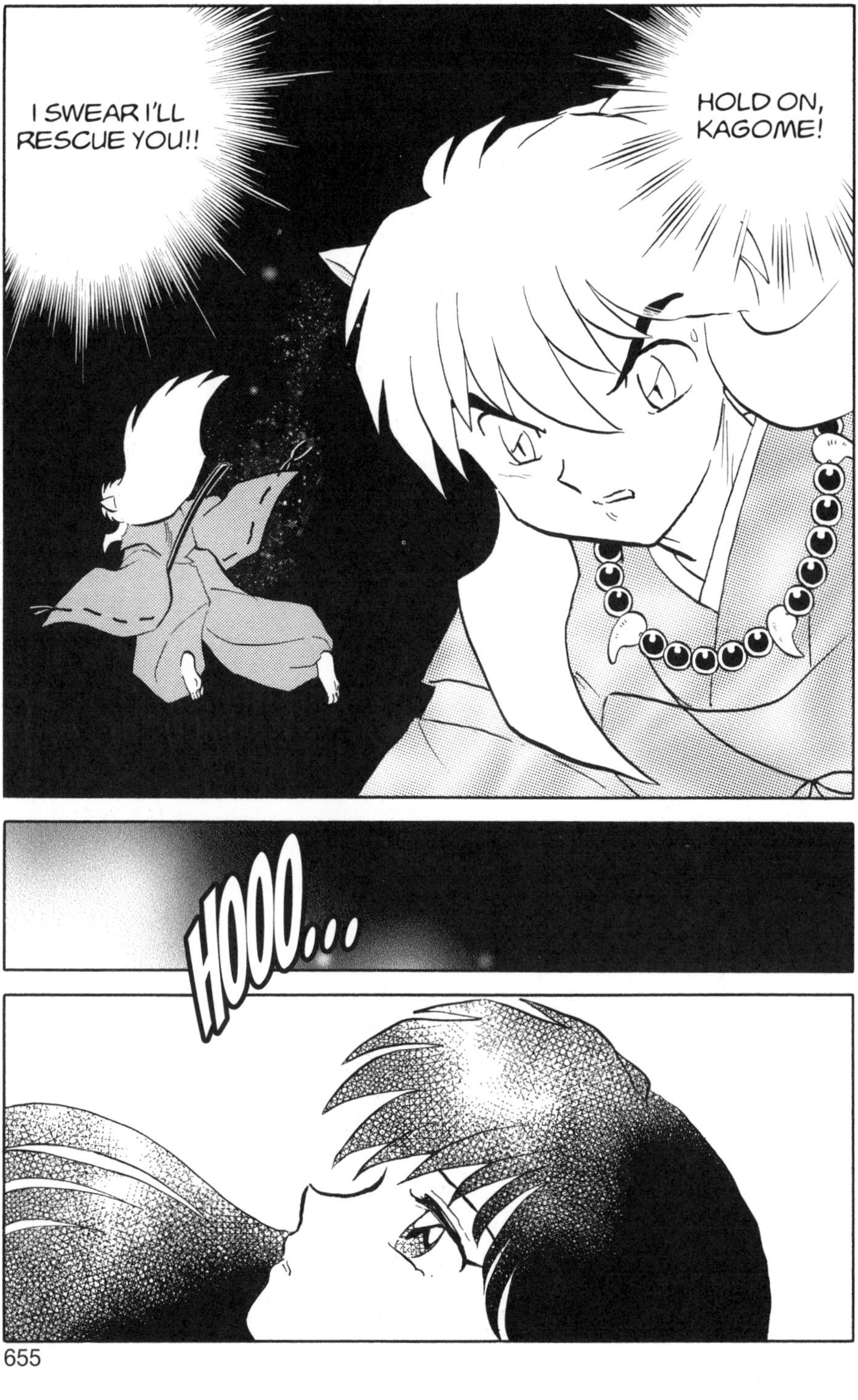
HOLD ON, KAGOME!
I SWEAR I'LL RESCUE YOU!!
HOOO...

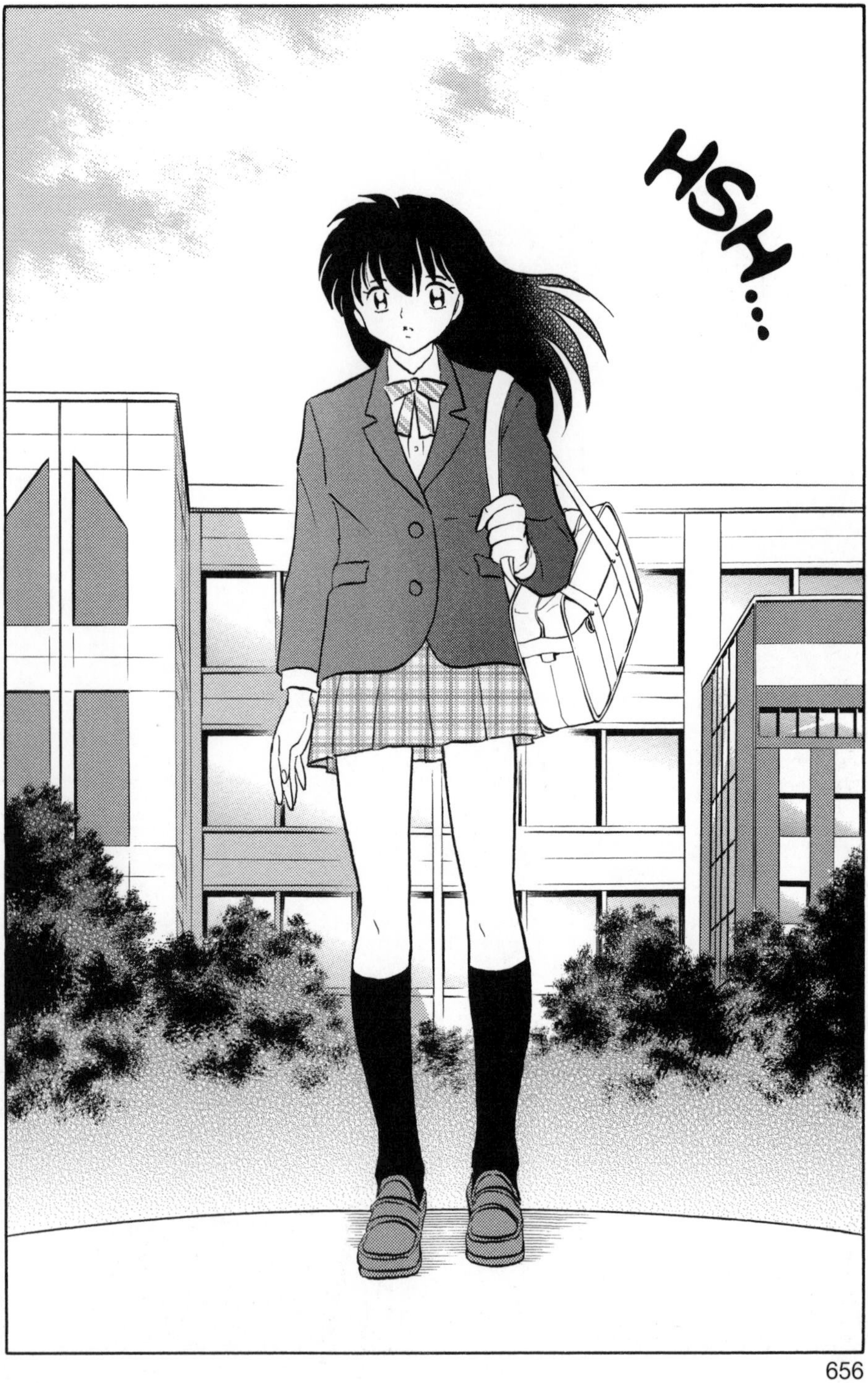
HSH...

SCROLL SIX
HIGH SCHOOL LIFE

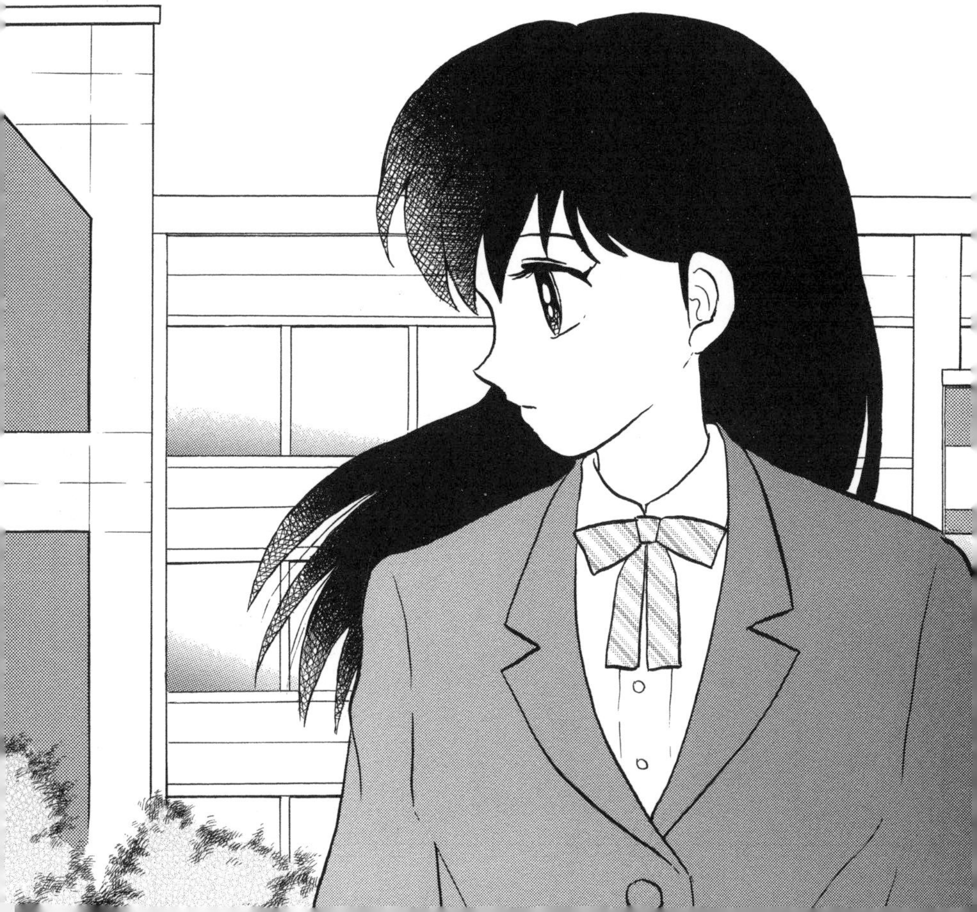

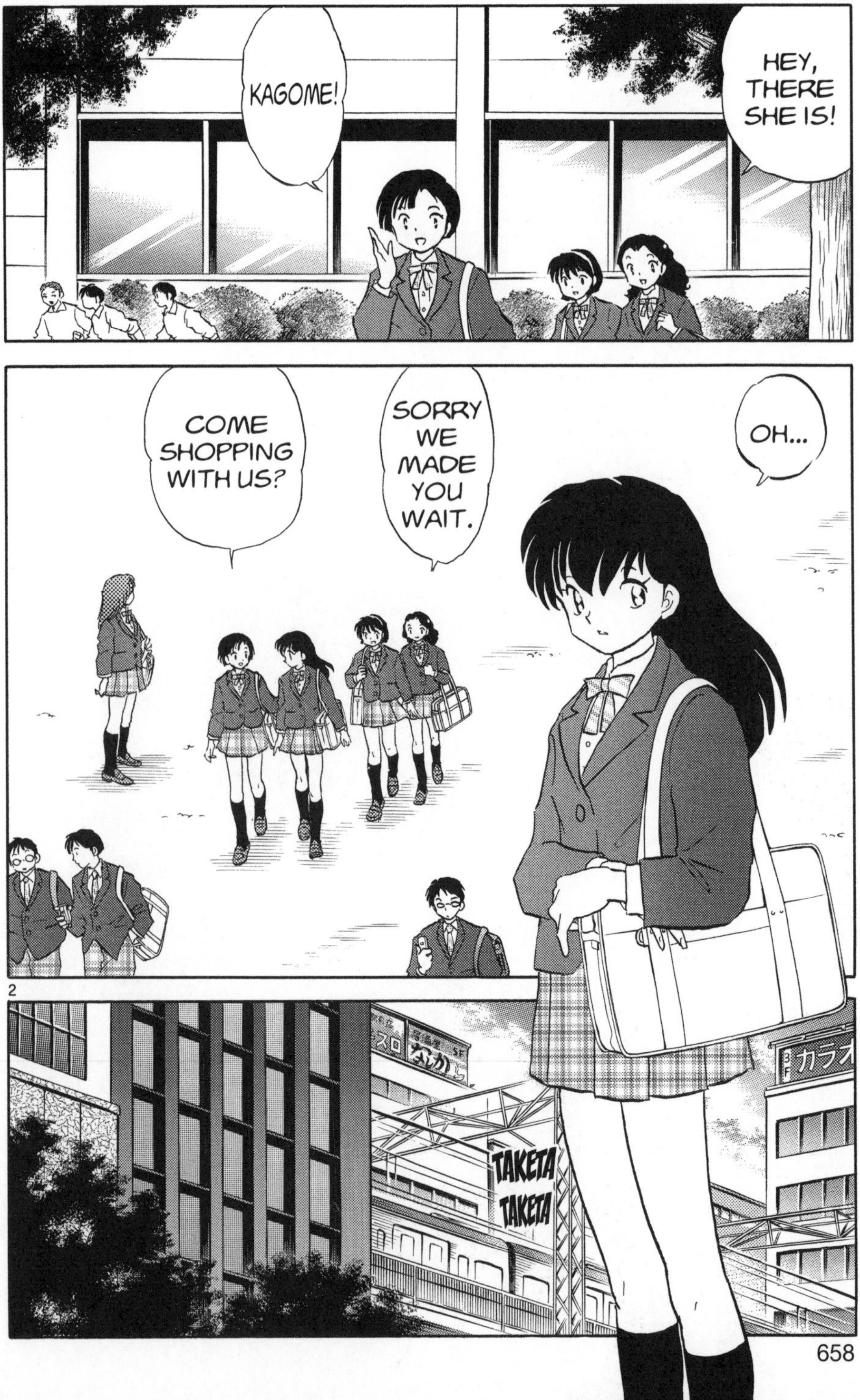
HEY, THERE SHE IS!
KAGOME!
OH...
SORRY WE MADE YOU WAIT.
COME SHOPPING WITH US?
TAKETA
TAKETA

2

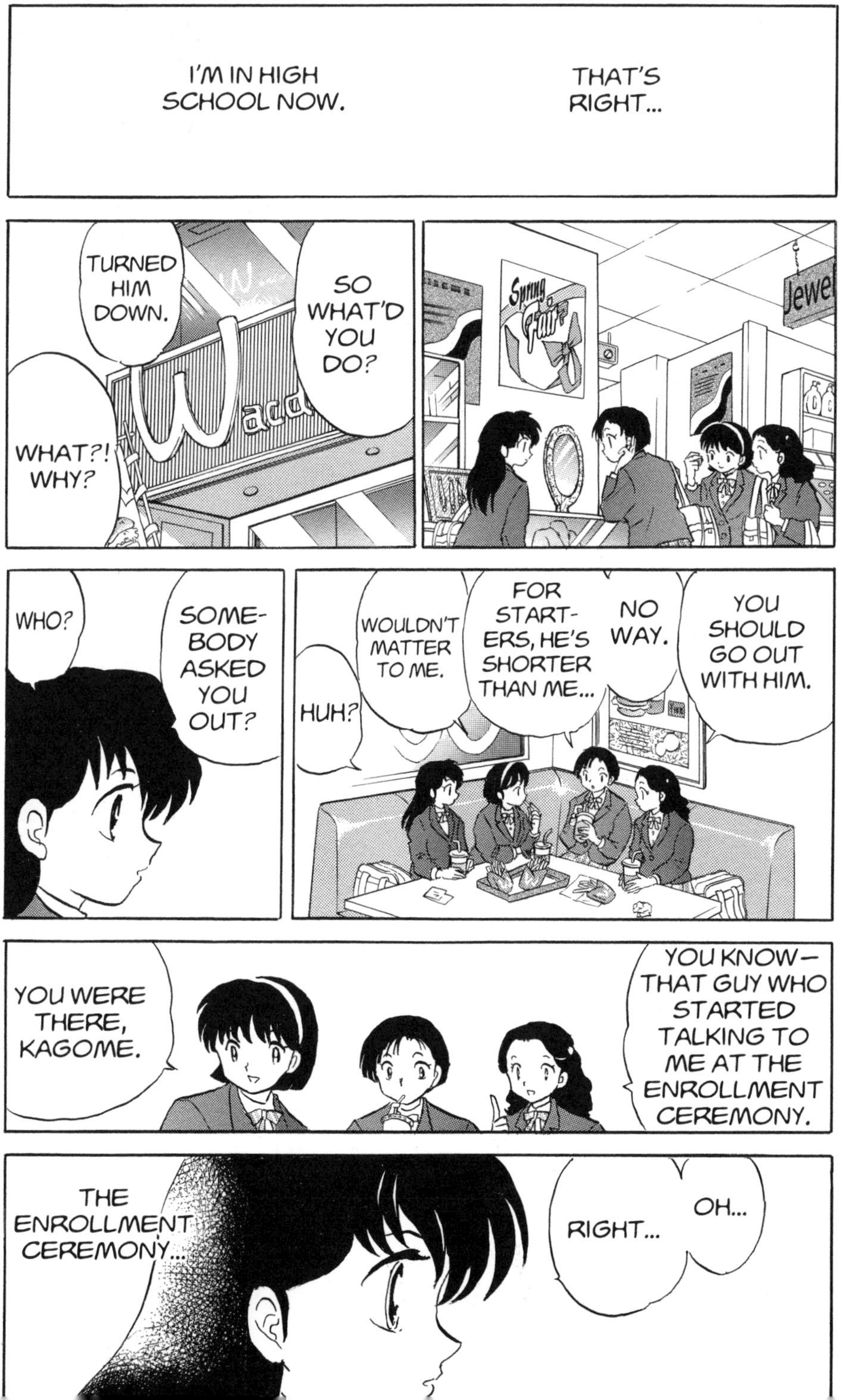
THAT'S RIGHT...
I'M IN HIGH SCHOOL NOW.
SO WHAT'D YOU DO?
TURNED HIM DOWN.
WHAT?! WHY?
YOU SHOULD GO OUT WITH HIM.
NO WAY.
FOR STARTERS, HE'S SHORTER THAN ME...
WOULDN'T MATTER TO ME.
HUH?
SOMEBODY ASKED YOU OUT?
WHO?
YOU KNOW— THAT GUY WHO STARTED TALKING TO ME AT THE ENROLLMENT CEREMONY.
YOU WERE THERE, KAGOME.
OH... RIGHT...
THE ENROLLMENT CEREMONY...

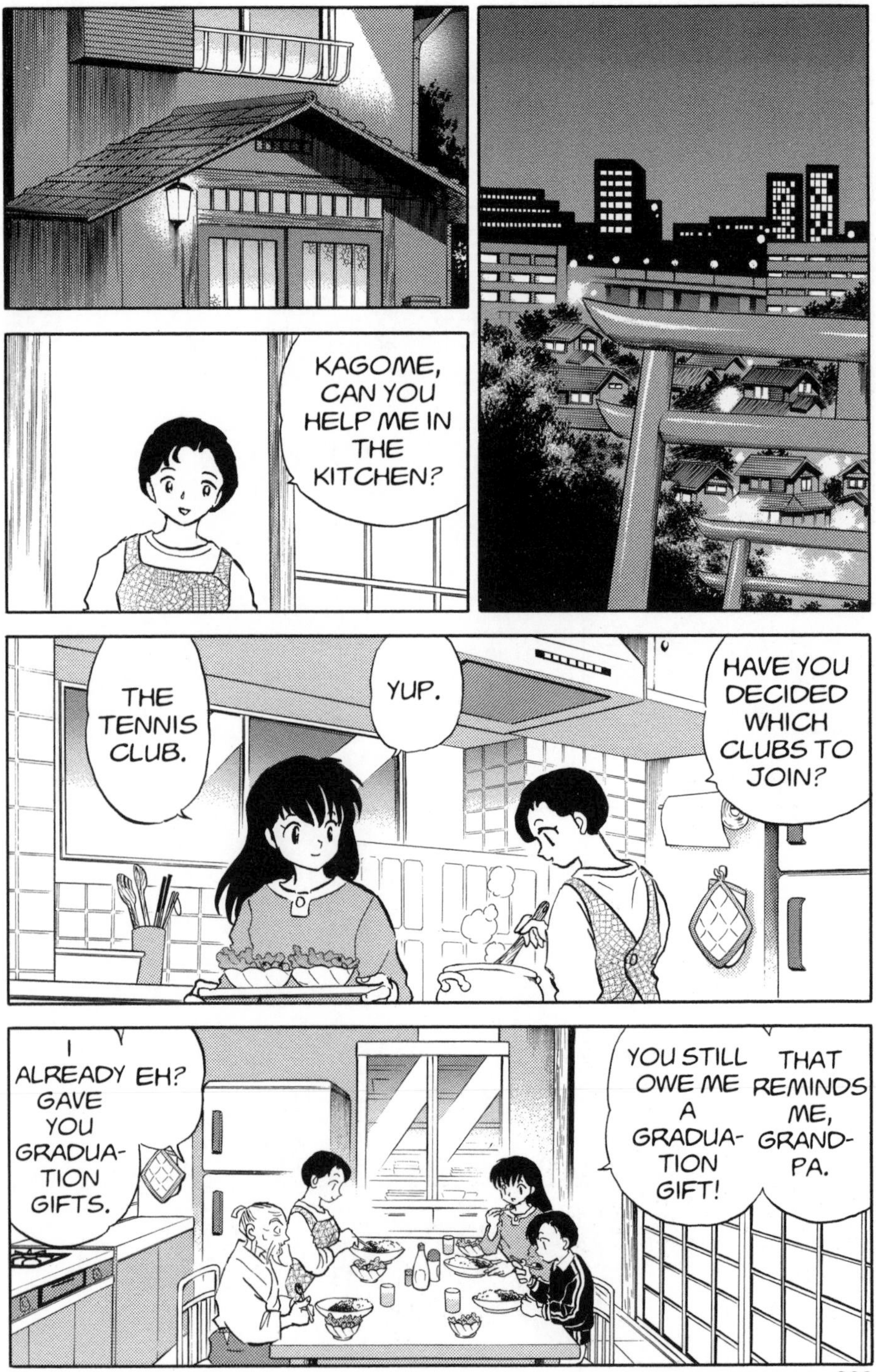
KAGOME, CAN YOU HELP ME IN THE KITCHEN?
HAVE YOU DECIDED WHICH CLUBS TO JOIN?
YUP.
THE TENNIS CLUB.
THAT REMINDS ME, GRAND-PA.
YOU STILL OWE ME A GRADUA-TION GIFT!
EH?
I ALREADY GAVE YOU GRADUA-TION GIFTS.

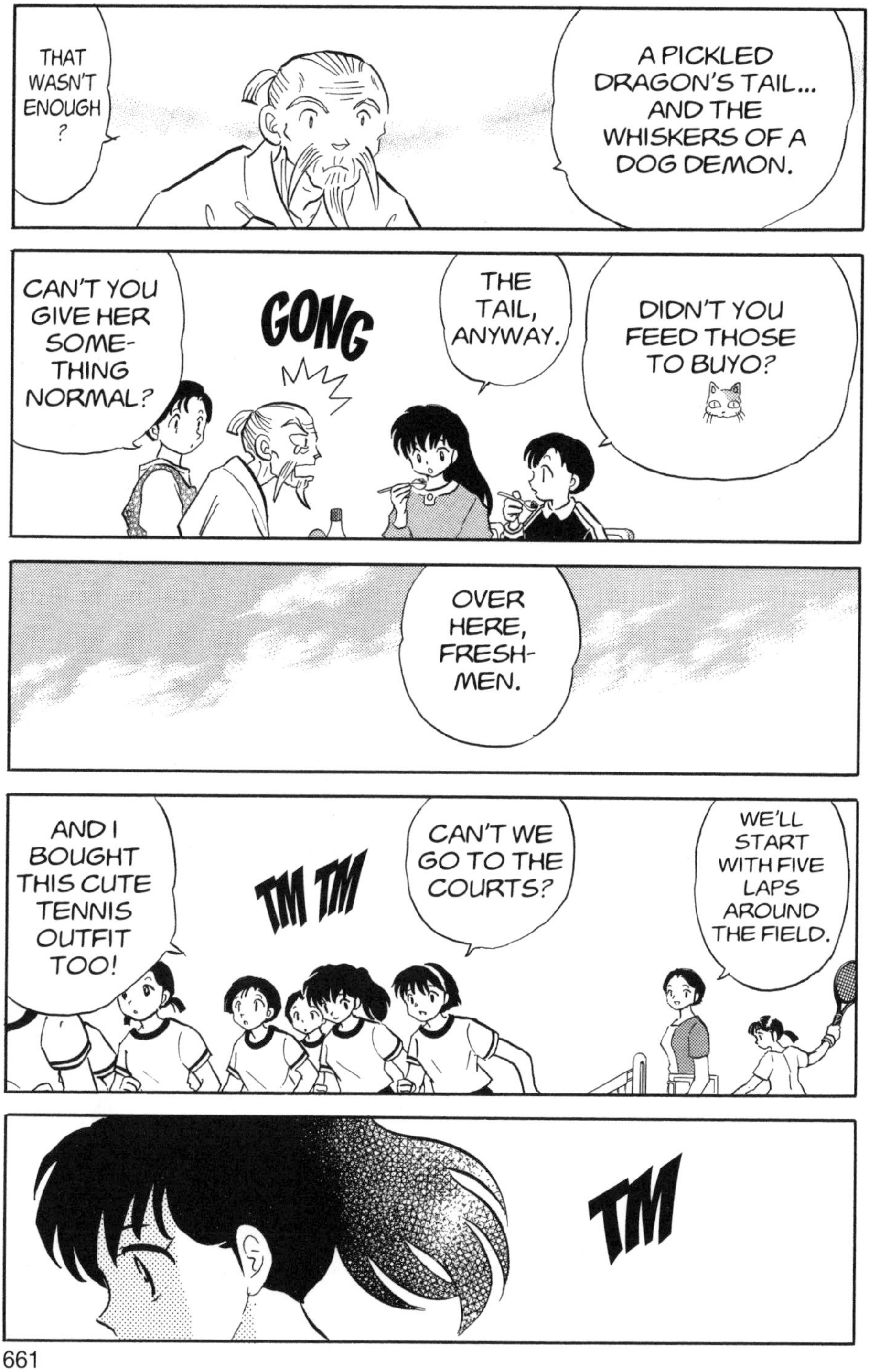
A PICKLED DRAGON'S TAIL... AND THE WHISKERS OF A DOG DEMON.
THAT WASN'T ENOUGH?
DIDN'T YOU FEED THOSE TO BUYO?
THE TAIL, ANYWAY.
GONG
CAN'T YOU GIVE HER SOME-THING NORMAL?
OVER HERE, FRESH-MEN.
WE'LL START WITH FIVE LAPS AROUND THE FIELD.
CAN'T WE GO TO THE COURTS?
TM TM
AND I BOUGHT THIS CUTE TENNIS OUTFIT TOO!
TM

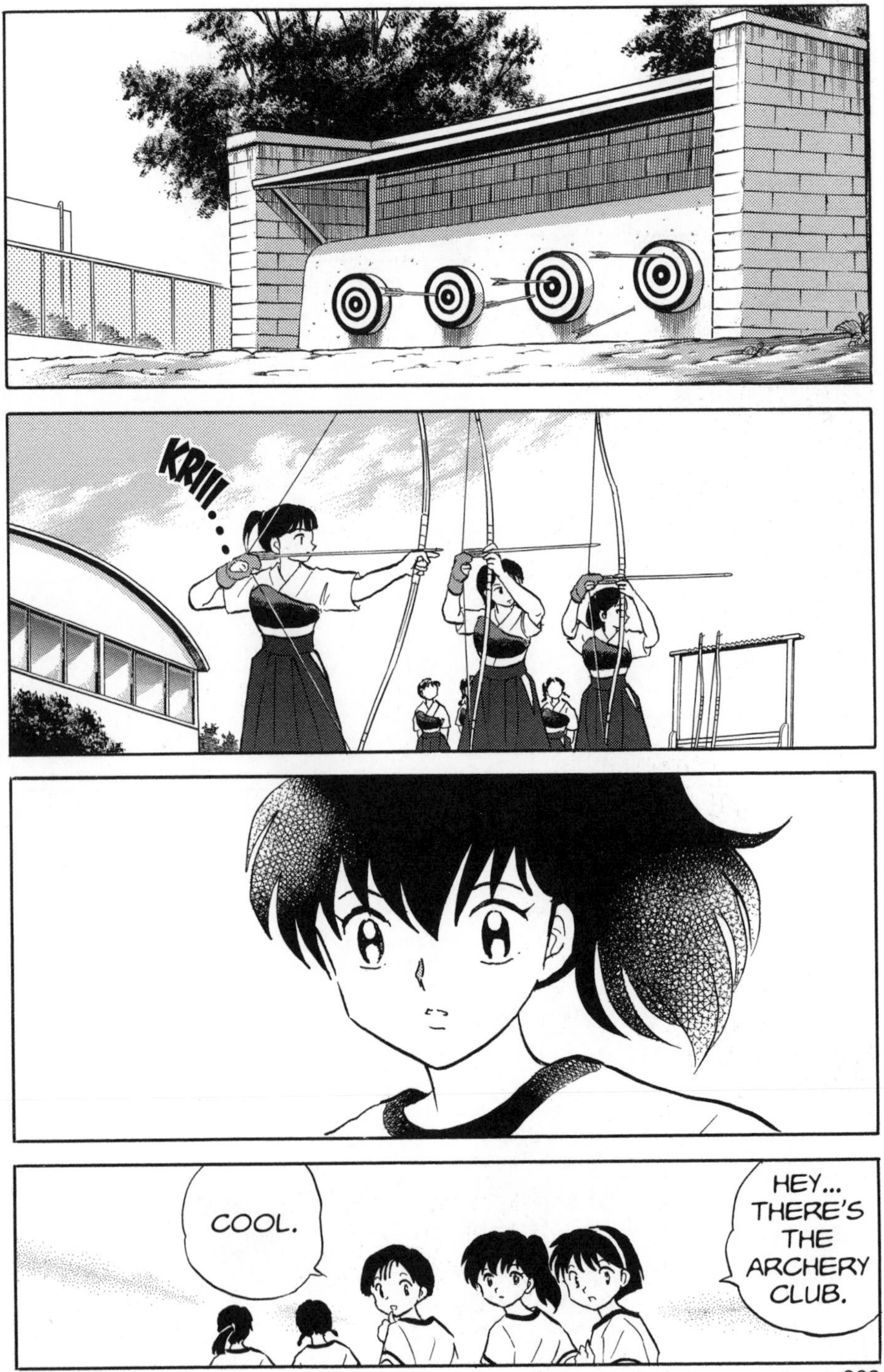
KRIII...
HEY... THERE'S THE ARCHERY CLUB.
COOL.

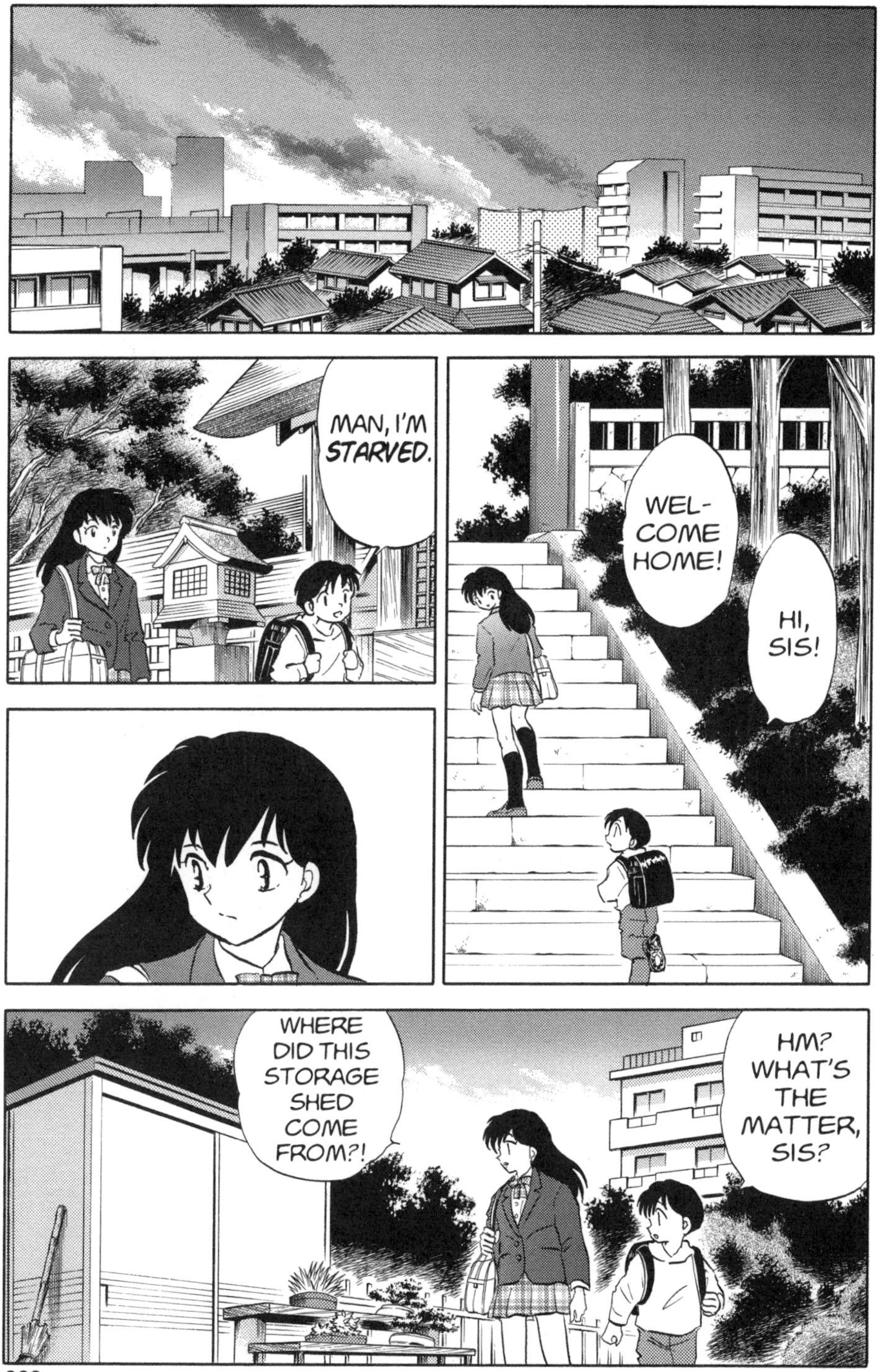
WEL-COME HOME!
HI, SIS!
MAN, I'M **STARVED**.
HM? WHAT'S THE MATTER, SIS?
WHERE DID THIS STORAGE SHED COME FROM?!

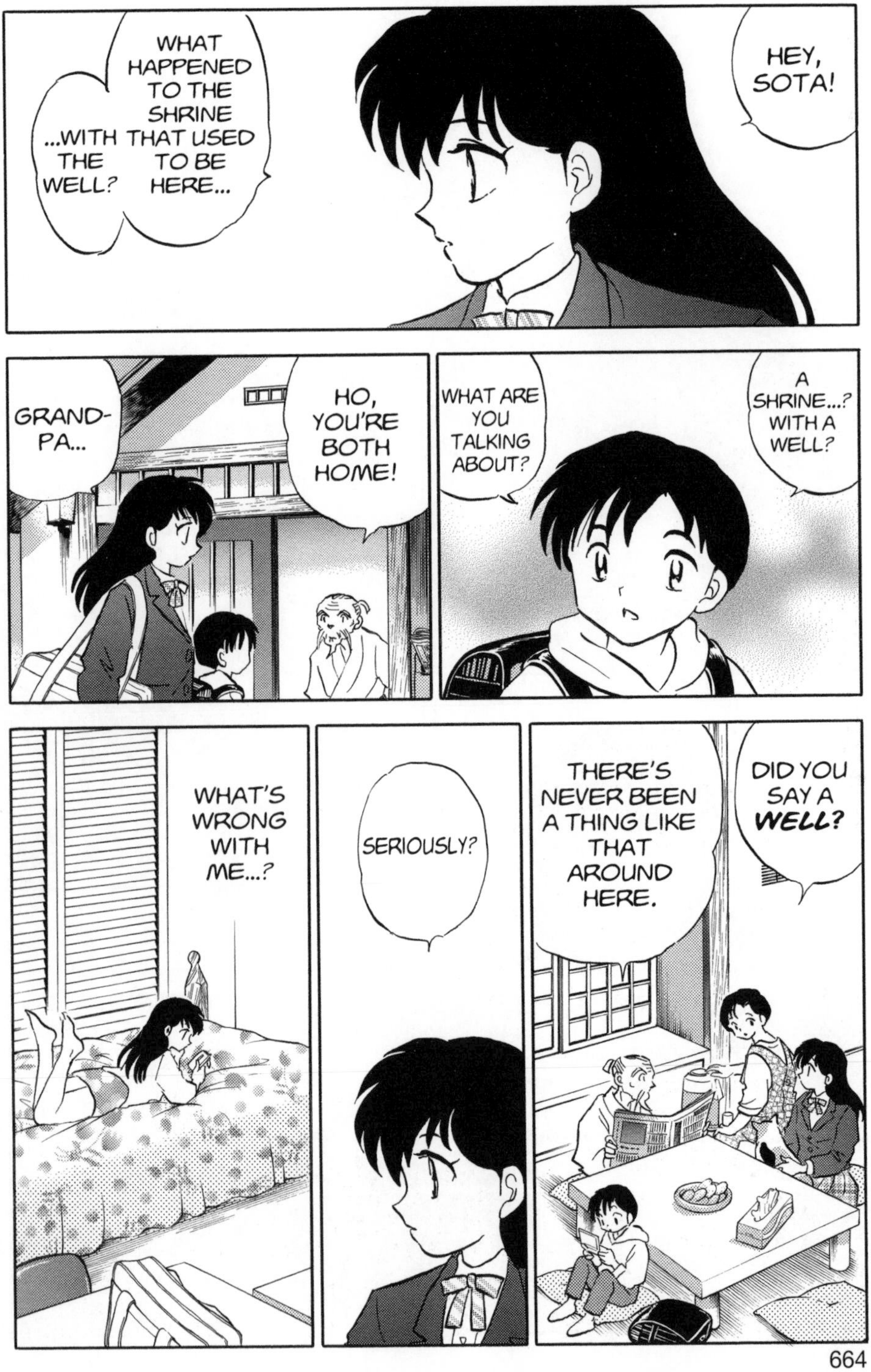
HEY, SOTA!
WHAT HAPPENED TO THE SHRINE THAT USED TO BE HERE...
...WITH THE WELL?
A SHRINE...? WITH A WELL?
WHAT ARE YOU TALKING ABOUT?
HO, YOU'RE BOTH HOME!
GRAND-PA...
DID YOU SAY A ***WELL?***
THERE'S NEVER BEEN A THING LIKE THAT AROUND HERE.
SERIOUSLY?
WHAT'S WRONG WITH ME...?

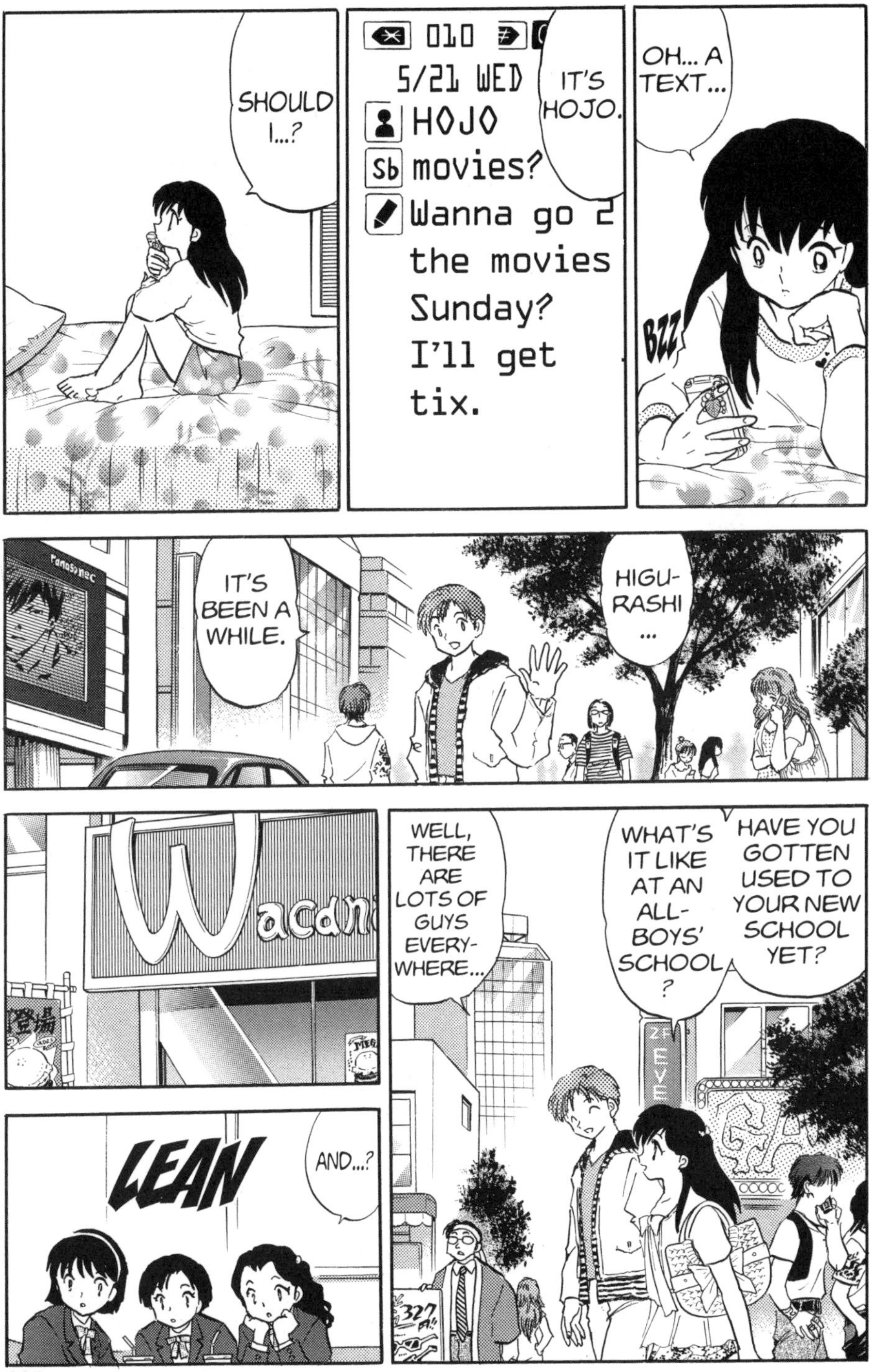
OH... A TEXT...
BZZ
IT'S HOJO.
010
5/21 WED
HOJO
Sb movies?
Wanna go 2 the movies Sunday? I'll get tix.
SHOULD I...?
HIGU-RASHI ...
IT'S BEEN A WHILE.
HAVE YOU GOTTEN USED TO YOUR NEW SCHOOL YET?
WHAT'S IT LIKE AT AN ALL-BOYS' SCHOOL?
WELL, THERE ARE LOTS OF GUYS EVERYWHERE...
LEAN
AND...?

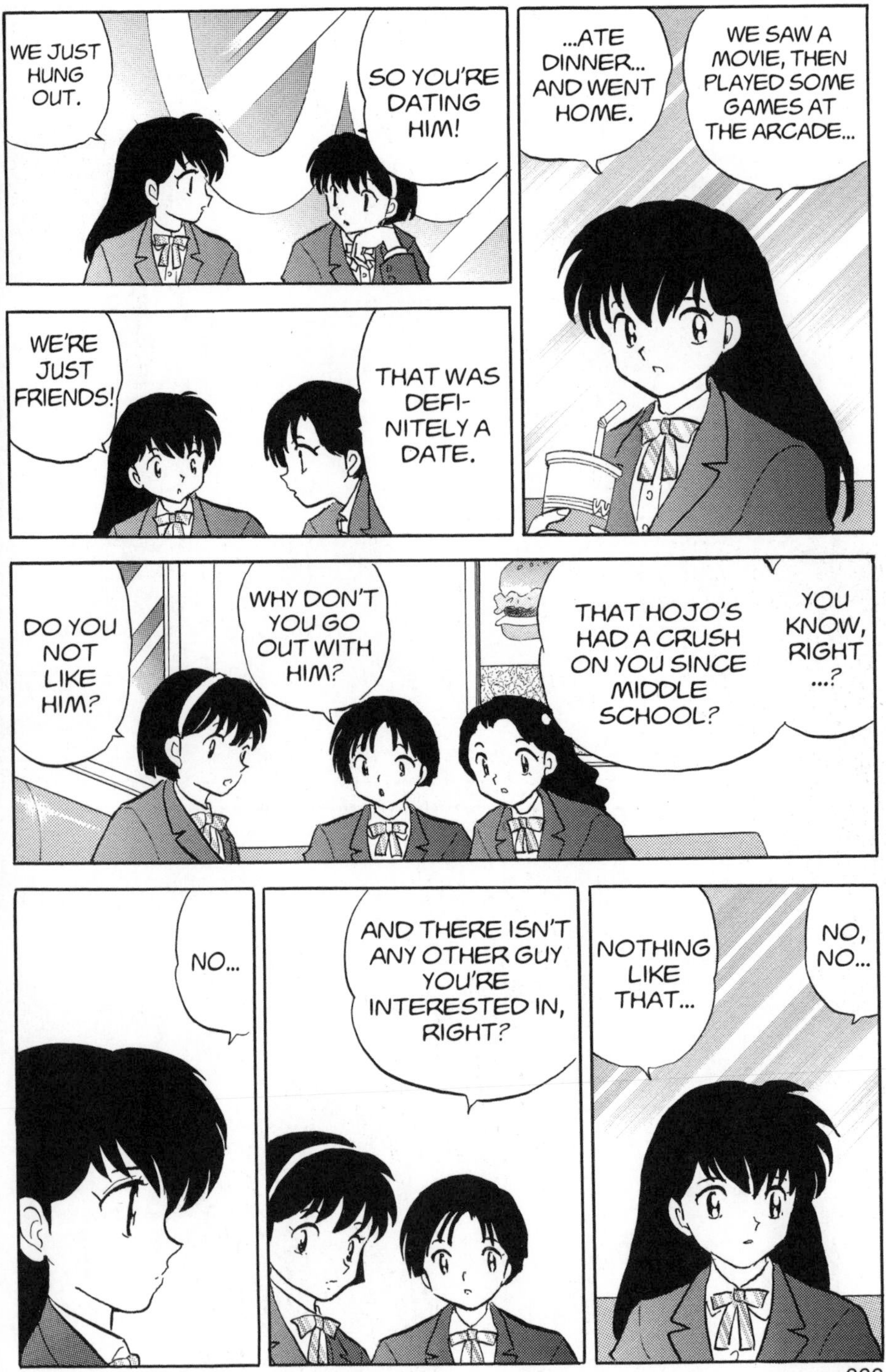
WE SAW A MOVIE, THEN PLAYED SOME GAMES AT THE ARCADE...
...ATE DINNER... AND WENT HOME.
SO YOU'RE DATING HIM!
WE JUST HUNG OUT.
THAT WAS DEFI-NITELY A DATE.
WE'RE JUST FRIENDS!
YOU KNOW, RIGHT ...?
THAT HOJO'S HAD A CRUSH ON YOU SINCE MIDDLE SCHOOL?
WHY DON'T YOU GO OUT WITH HIM?
DO YOU NOT LIKE HIM?
NO, NO...
NOTHING LIKE THAT...
AND THERE ISN'T ANY OTHER GUY YOU'RE INTERESTED IN, RIGHT?
NO...

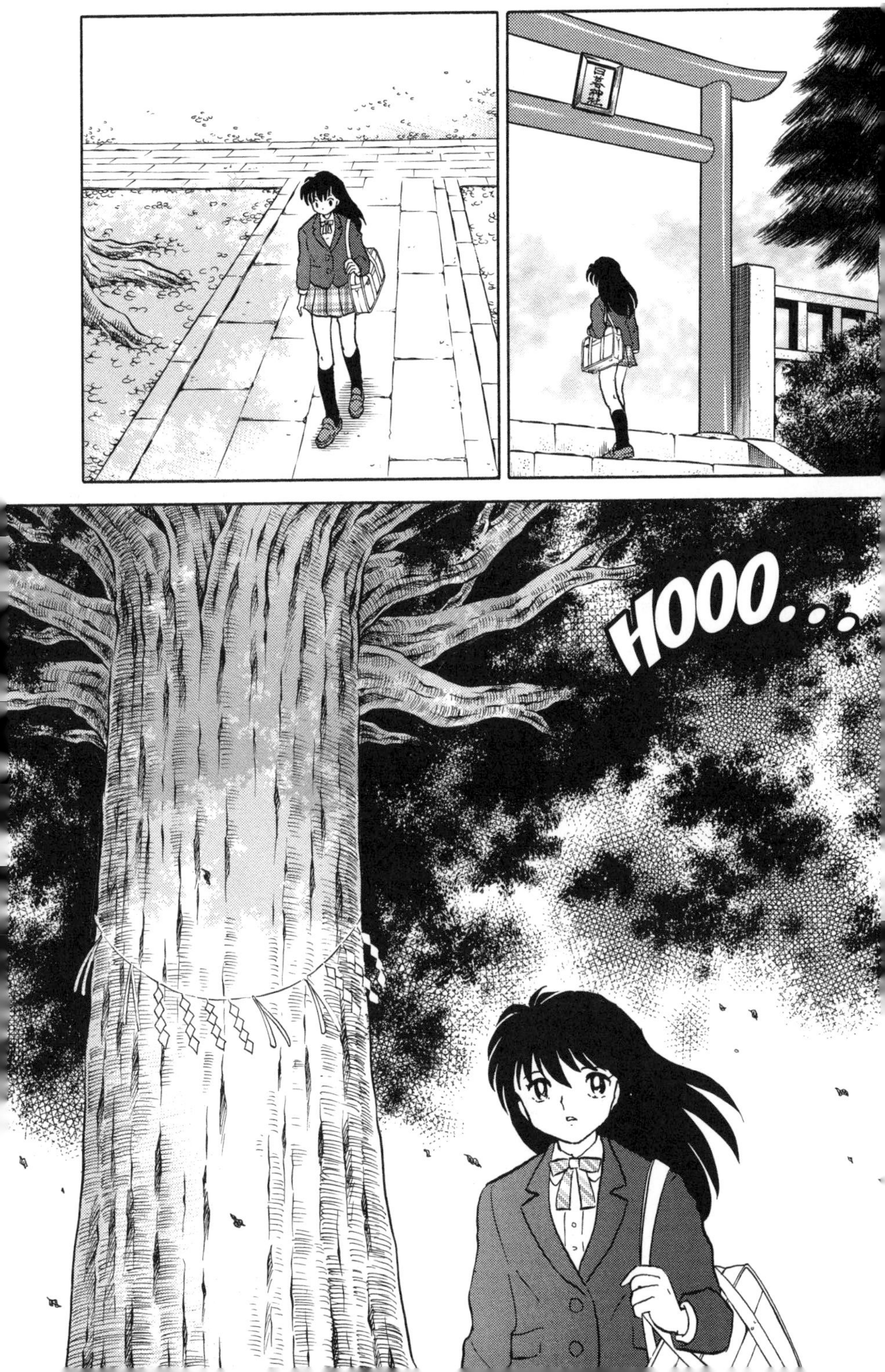
HOOO...

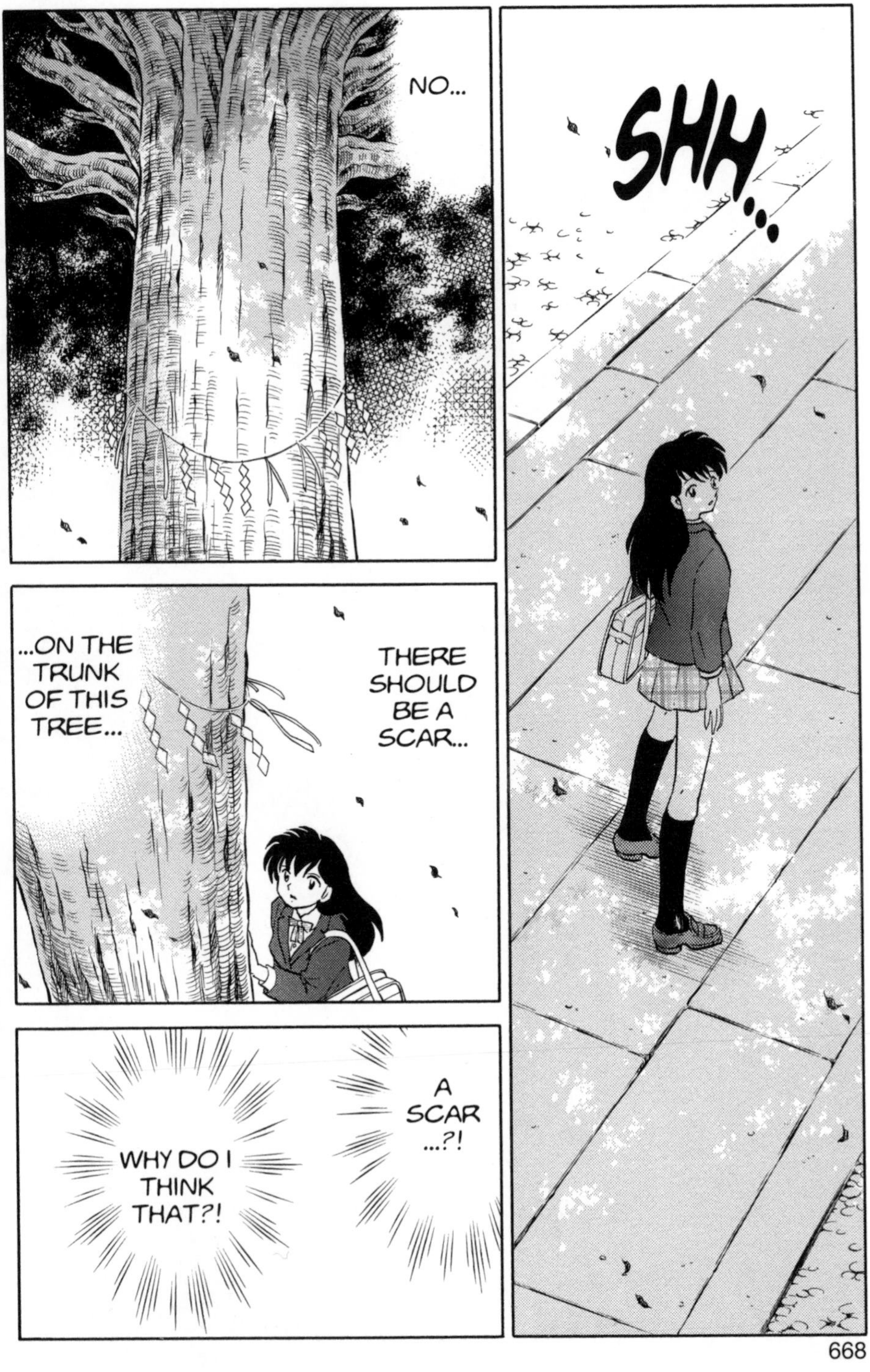
SHH...
NO...
THERE SHOULD BE A SCAR...
...ON THE TRUNK OF THIS TREE...
A SCAR ...?!
WHY DO I THINK THAT?!

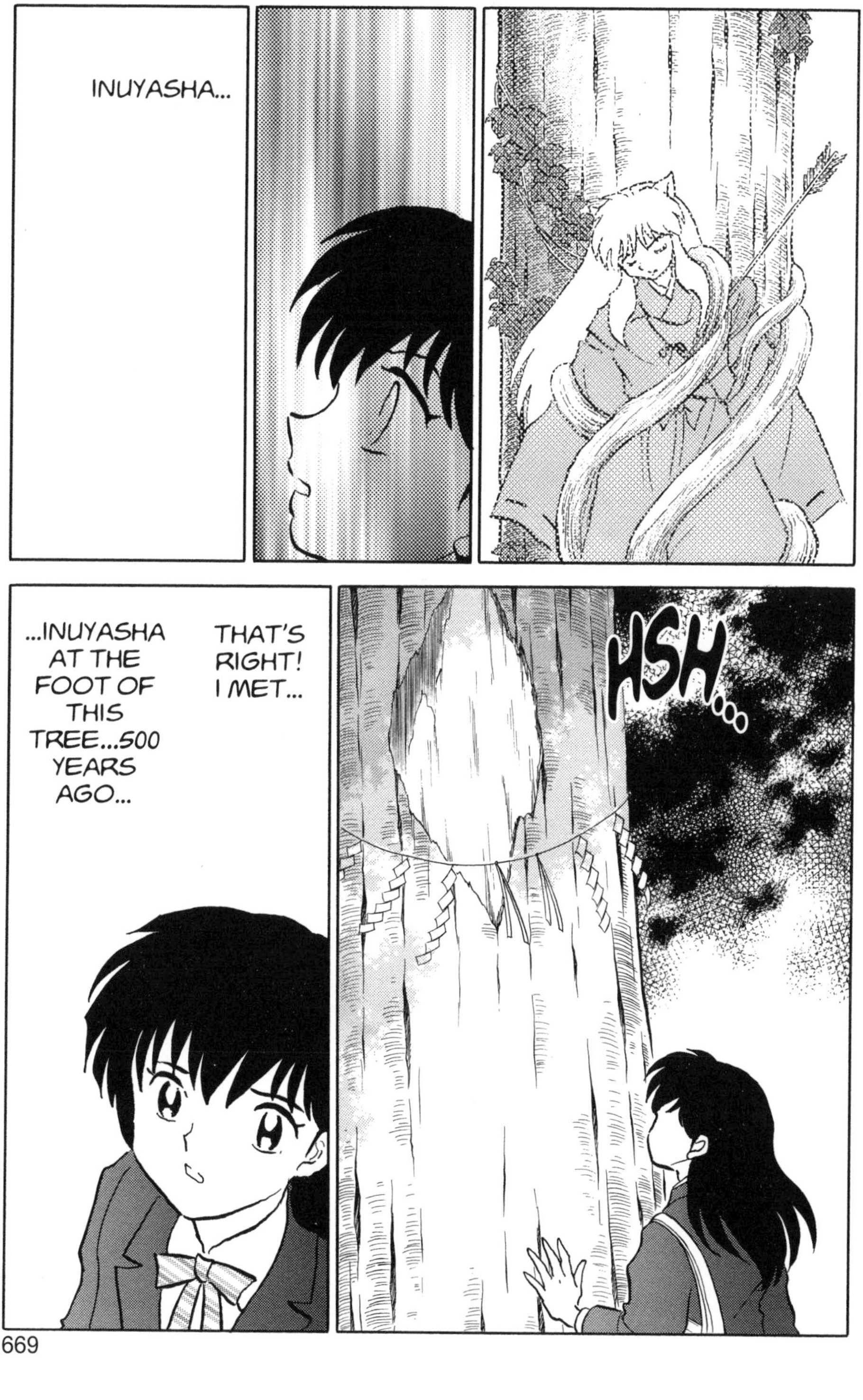
INUYASHA...
HSH...
THAT'S RIGHT! I MET...
...INUYASHA AT THE FOOT OF THIS TREE...500 YEARS AGO...

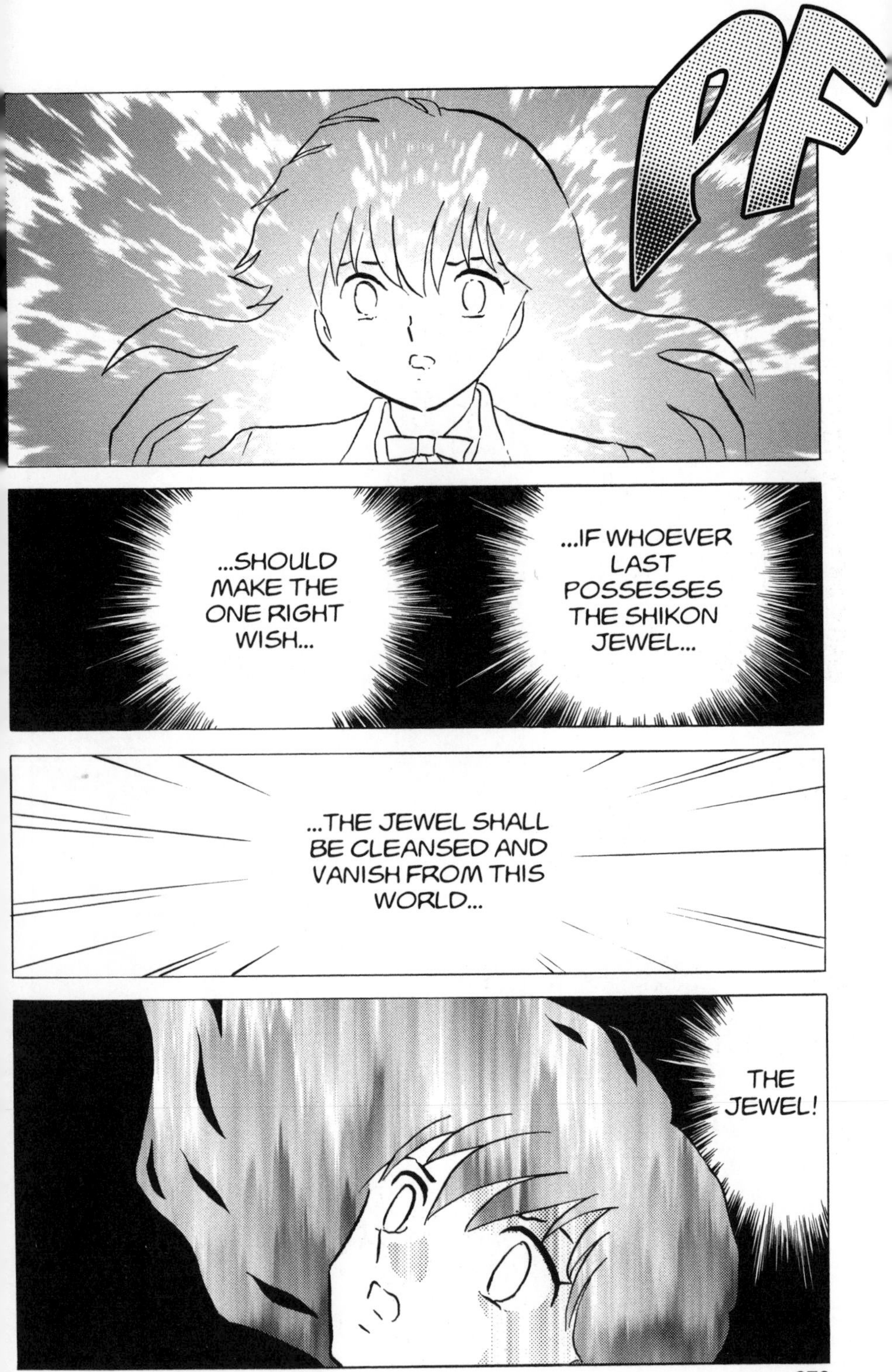
PF
...IF WHOEVER LAST POSSESSES THE SHIKON JEWEL...
...SHOULD MAKE THE ONE RIGHT WISH...
...THE JEWEL SHALL BE CLEANSED AND VANISH FROM THIS WORLD...
THE JEWEL!

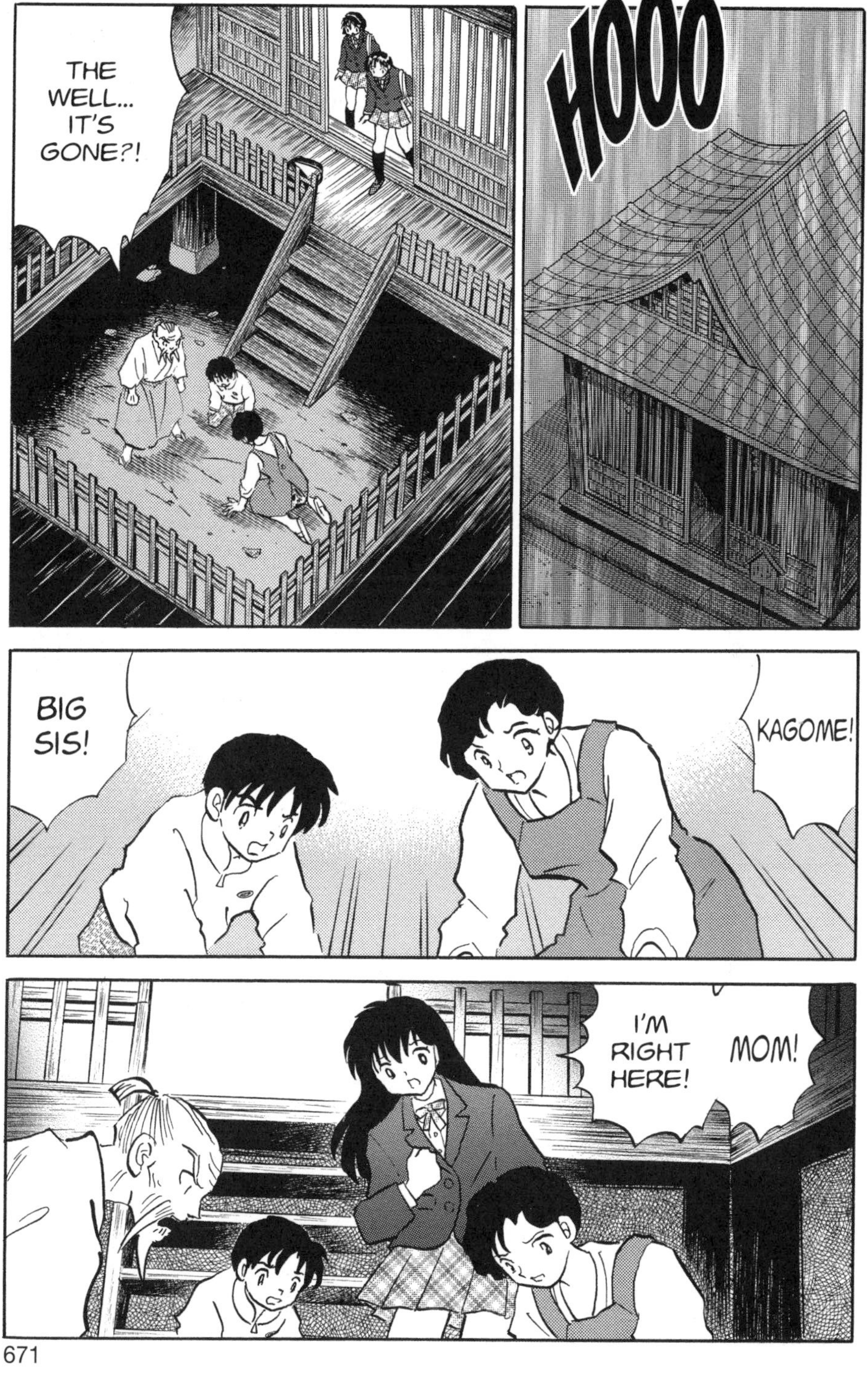
HOOO
THE WELL... IT'S GONE?!
KAGOME!
BIG SIS!
MOM!
I'M RIGHT HERE!

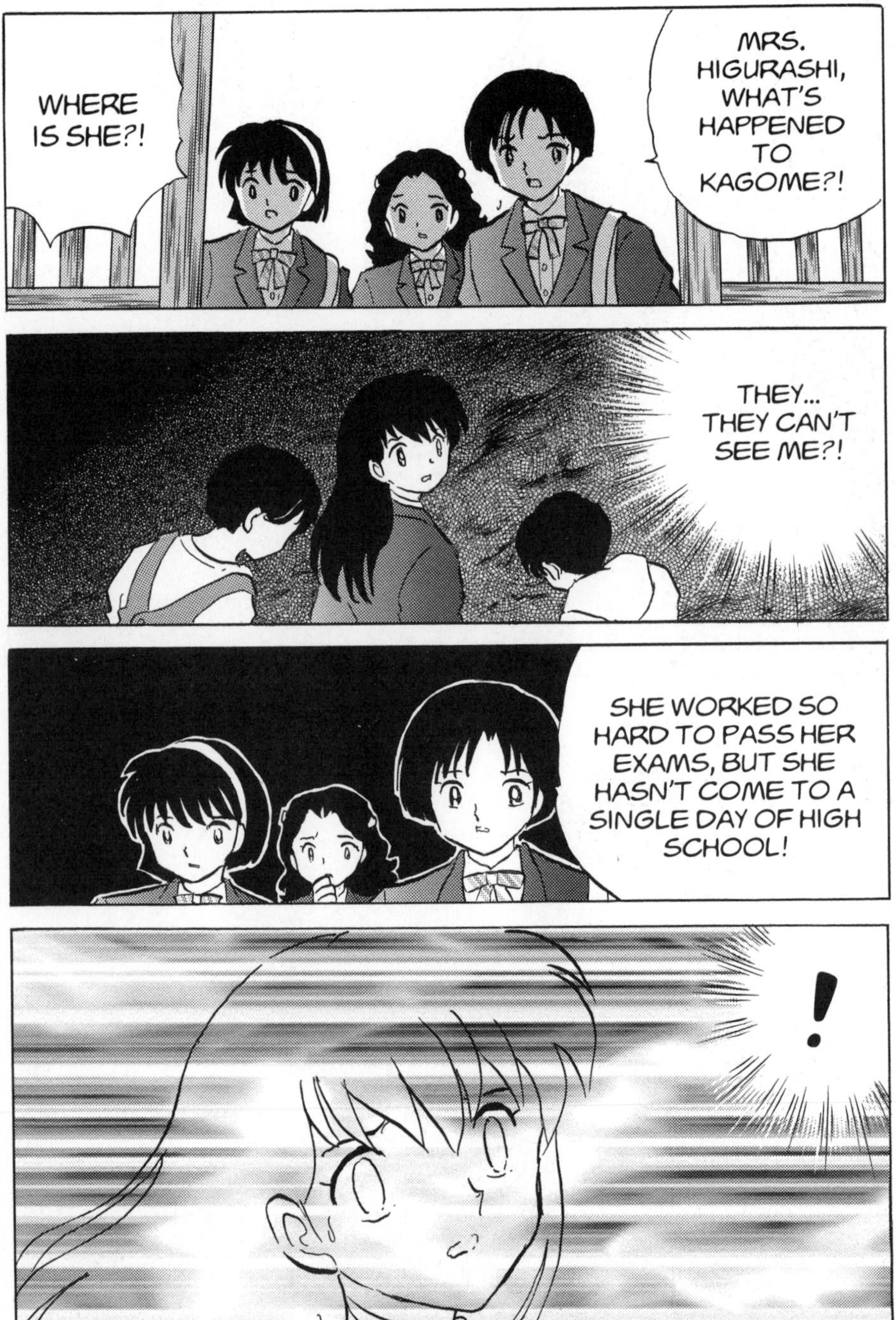
MRS. HIGURASHI, WHAT'S HAPPENED TO KAGOME?!
WHERE IS SHE?!
THEY... THEY CAN'T SEE ME?!
SHE WORKED SO HARD TO PASS HER EXAMS, BUT SHE HASN'T COME TO A SINGLE DAY OF HIGH SCHOOL!
!

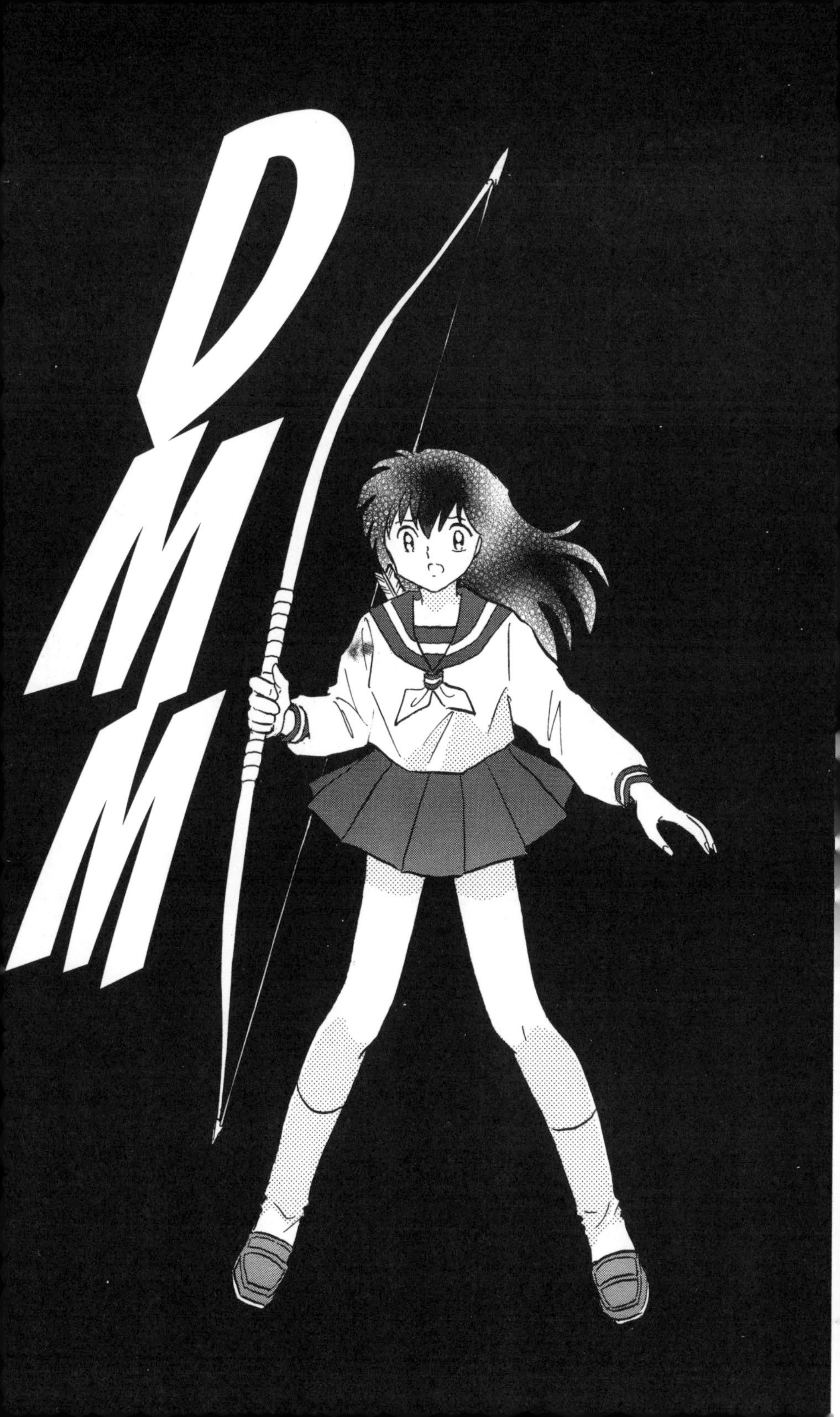
DMMM

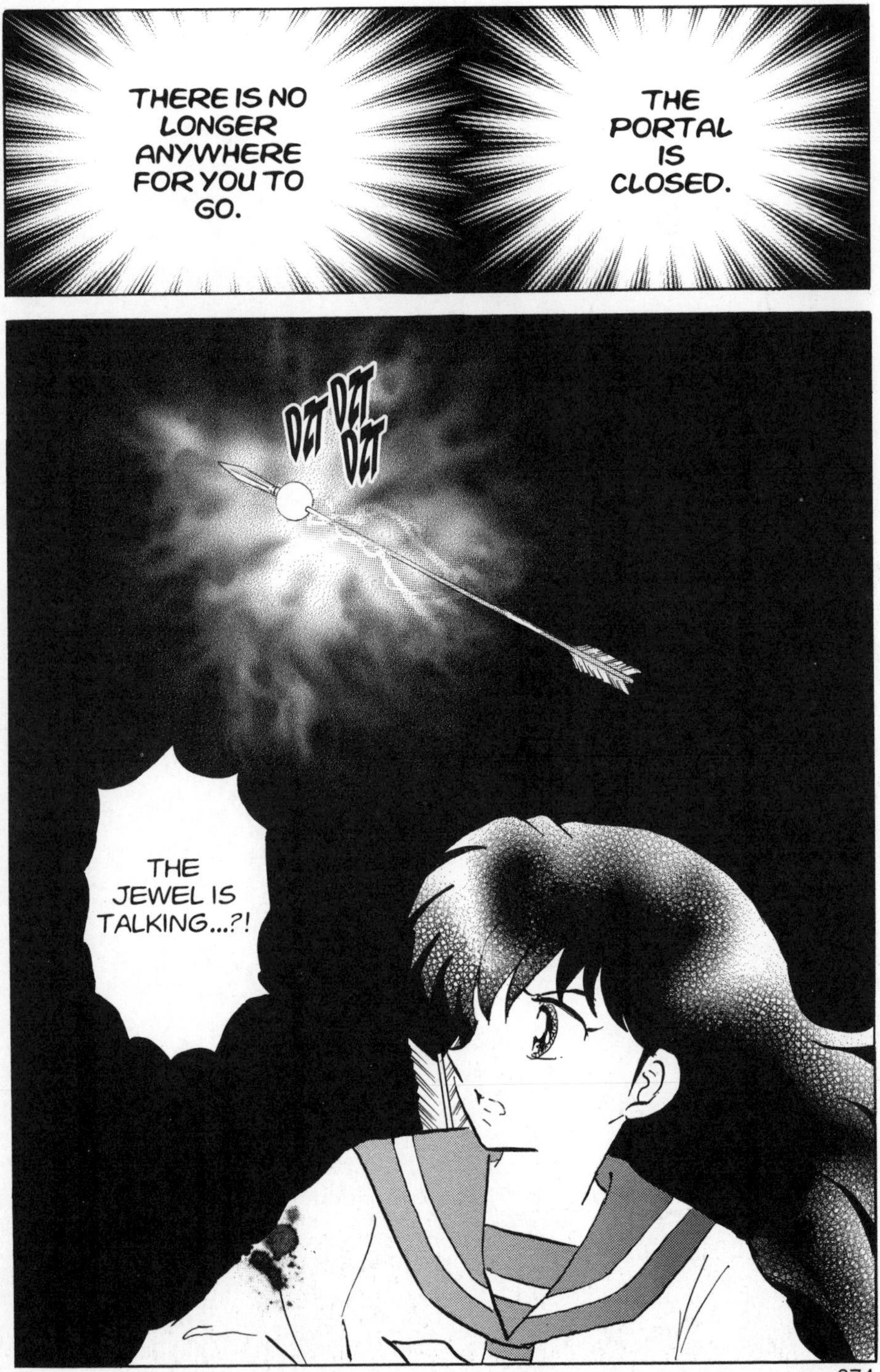
THE PORTAL IS CLOSED.
THERE IS NO LONGER ANYWHERE FOR YOU TO GO.
DZT DZT DZT
THE JEWEL IS TALKING...?!

SCROLL SEVEN
THE DARKNESS

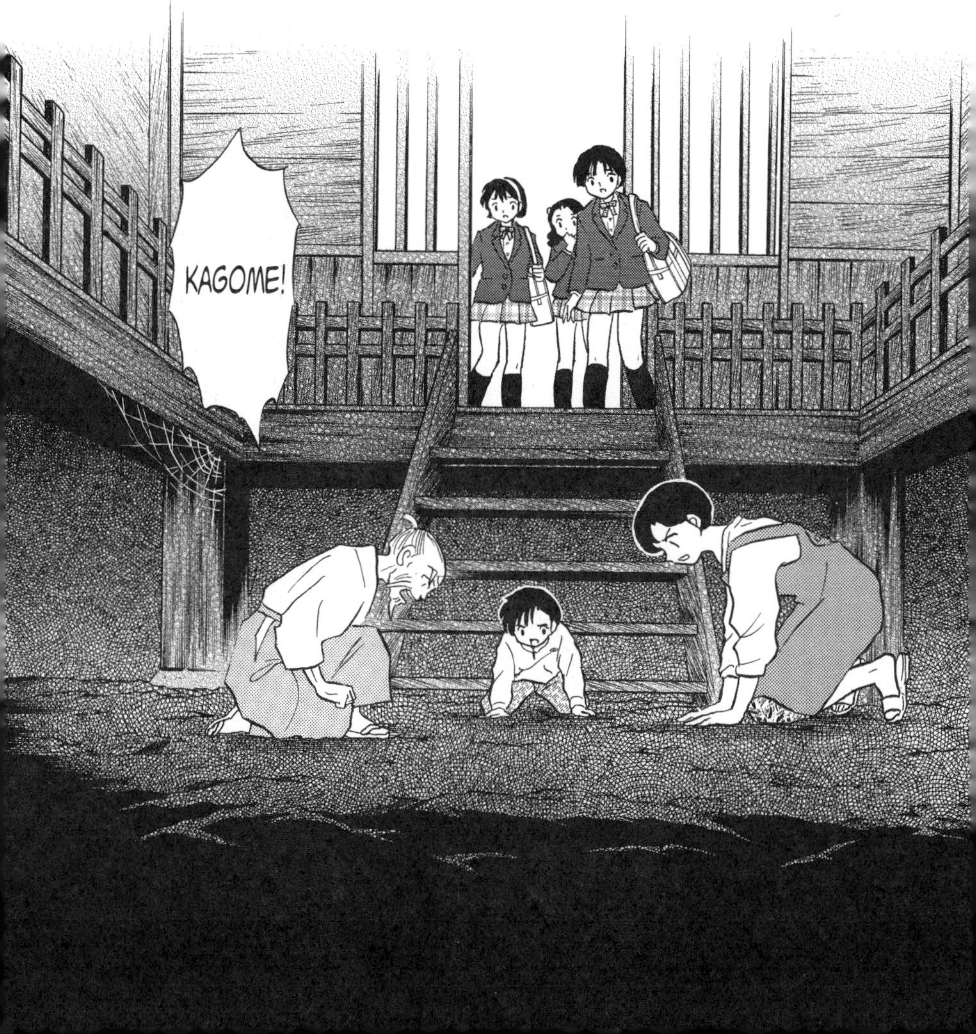
KAGOME!

KAGOME! WHERE ARE YOU?!

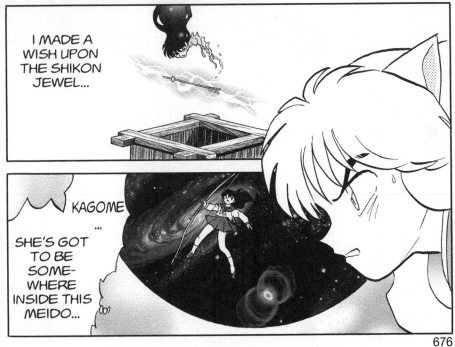

I MADE A WISH UPON THE SHIKON JEWEL...

KAGOME ...

SHE'S GOT TO BE SOME- WHERE INSIDE THIS MEIDO...

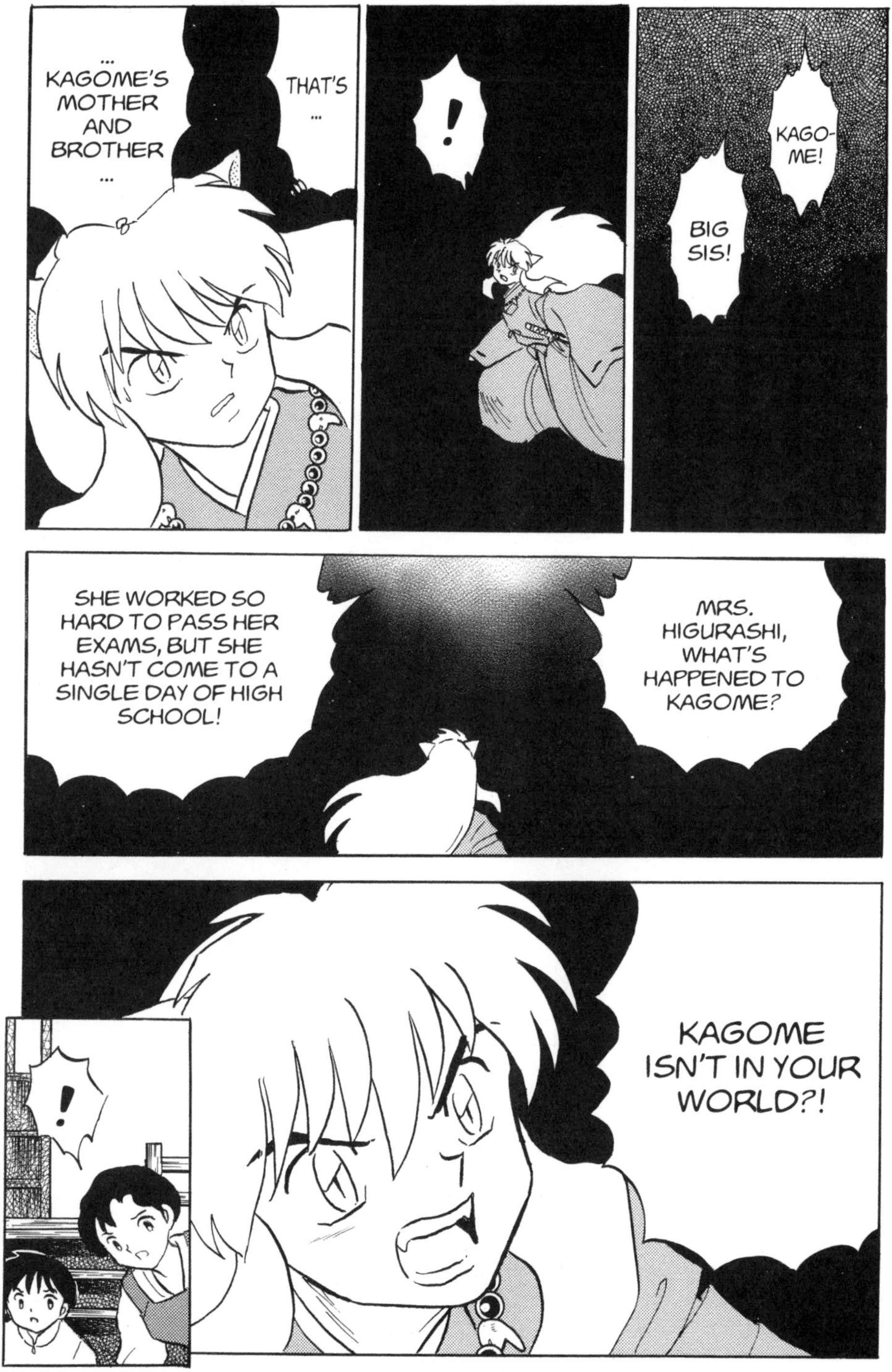
KAGO-ME!
BIG SIS!
!
THAT'S ...
... KAGOME'S MOTHER AND BROTHER ...
MRS. HIGURASHI, WHAT'S HAPPENED TO KAGOME?
SHE WORKED SO HARD TO PASS HER EXAMS, BUT SHE HASN'T COME TO A SINGLE DAY OF HIGH SCHOOL!
KAGOME ISN'T IN YOUR WORLD?!
!

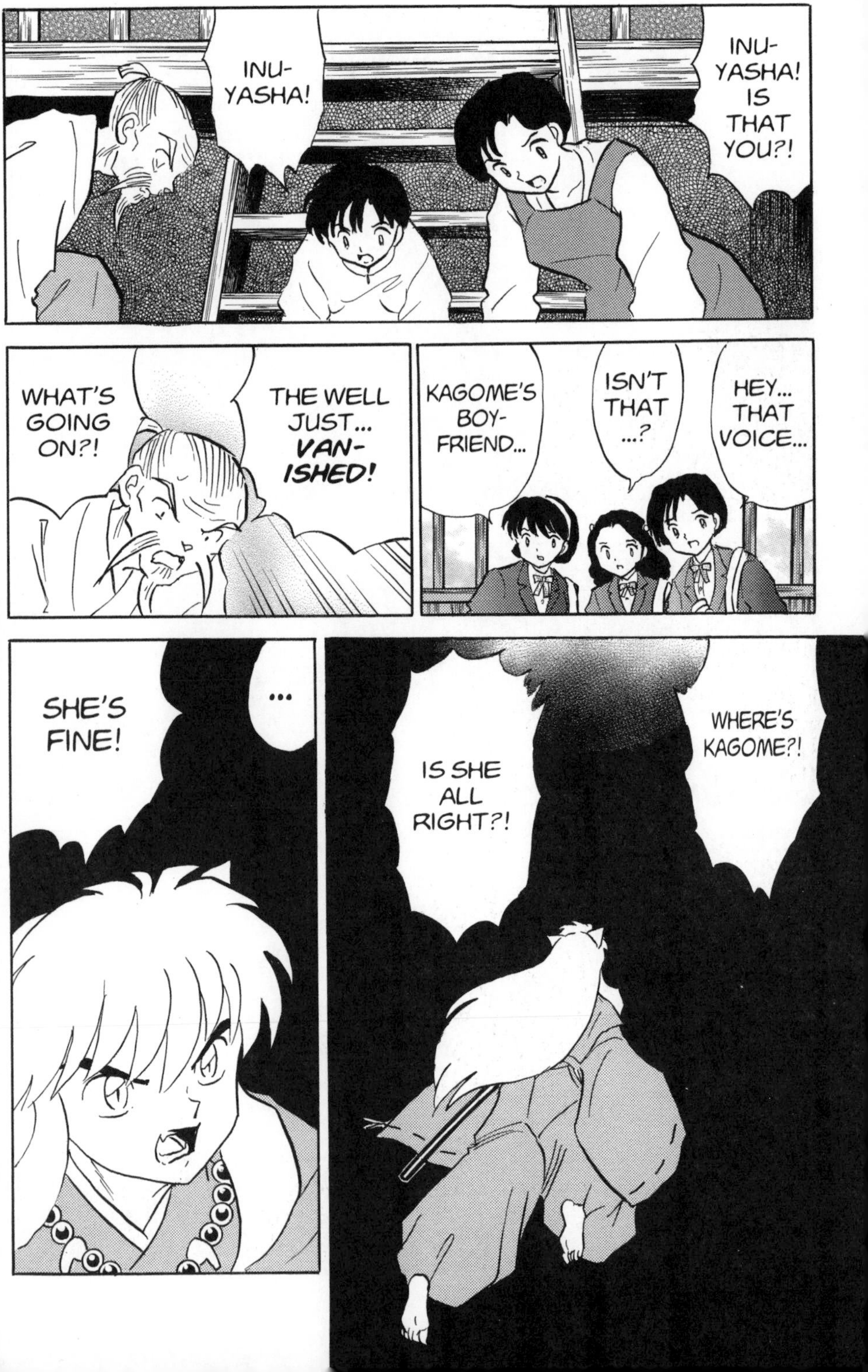
INU-YASHA! IS THAT YOU?!
INU-YASHA!
HEY... THAT VOICE...
ISN'T THAT ...?
KAGOME'S BOY-FRIEND...
THE WELL JUST... VAN-ISHED!
WHAT'S GOING ON?!
WHERE'S KAGOME?!
IS SHE ALL RIGHT?!
...
SHE'S FINE!

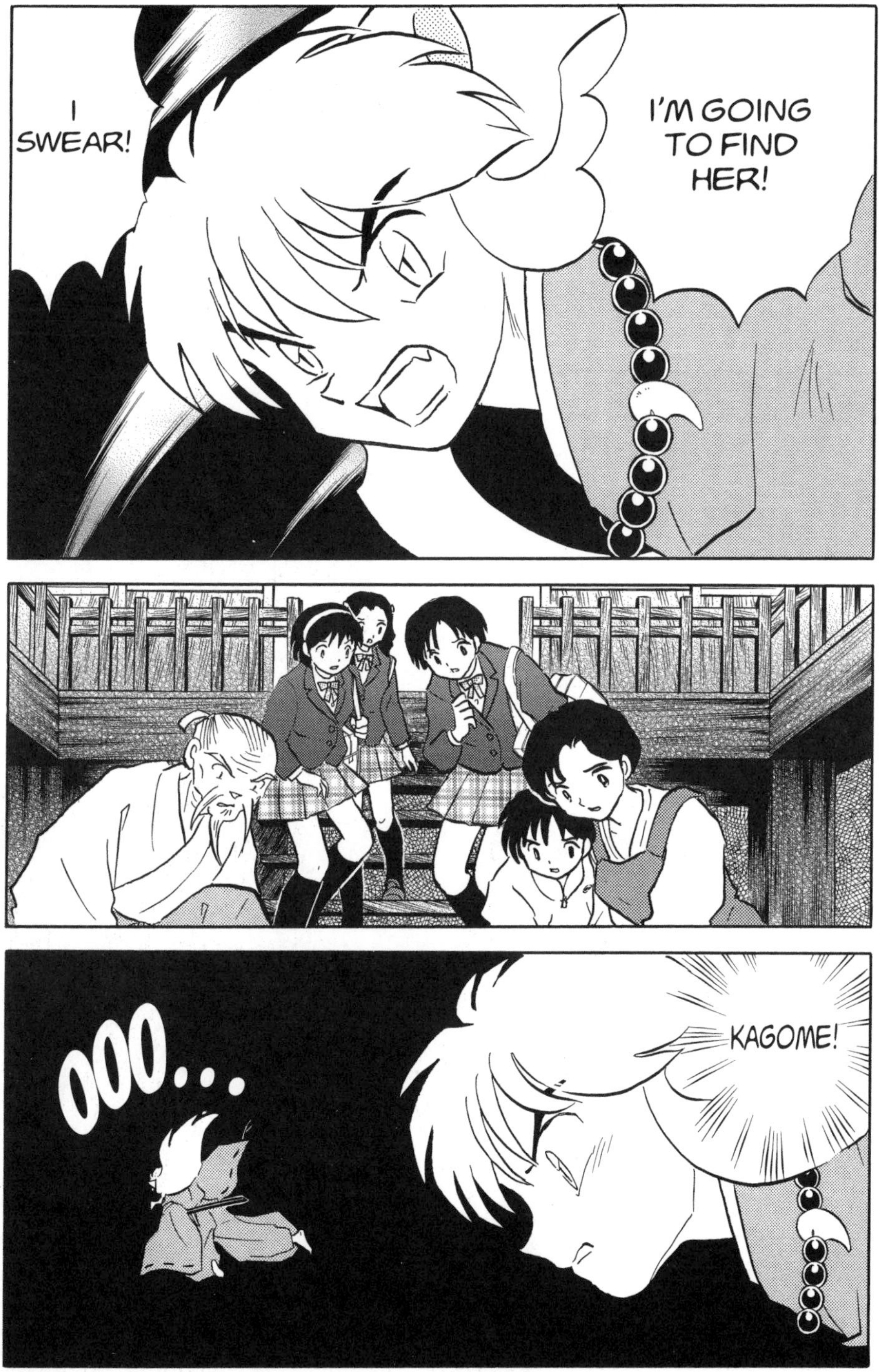
I'M GOING TO FIND HER!
I SWEAR!
KAGOME!
OOO...

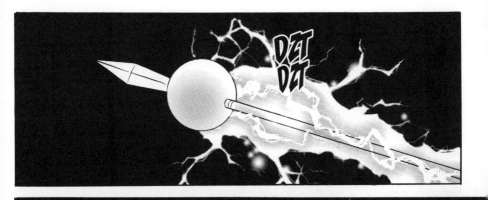

DZT
DZT

SHIKON
JEWEL...

WHERE
DID YOU
BRING
ME?!

WHERE
AM I?!

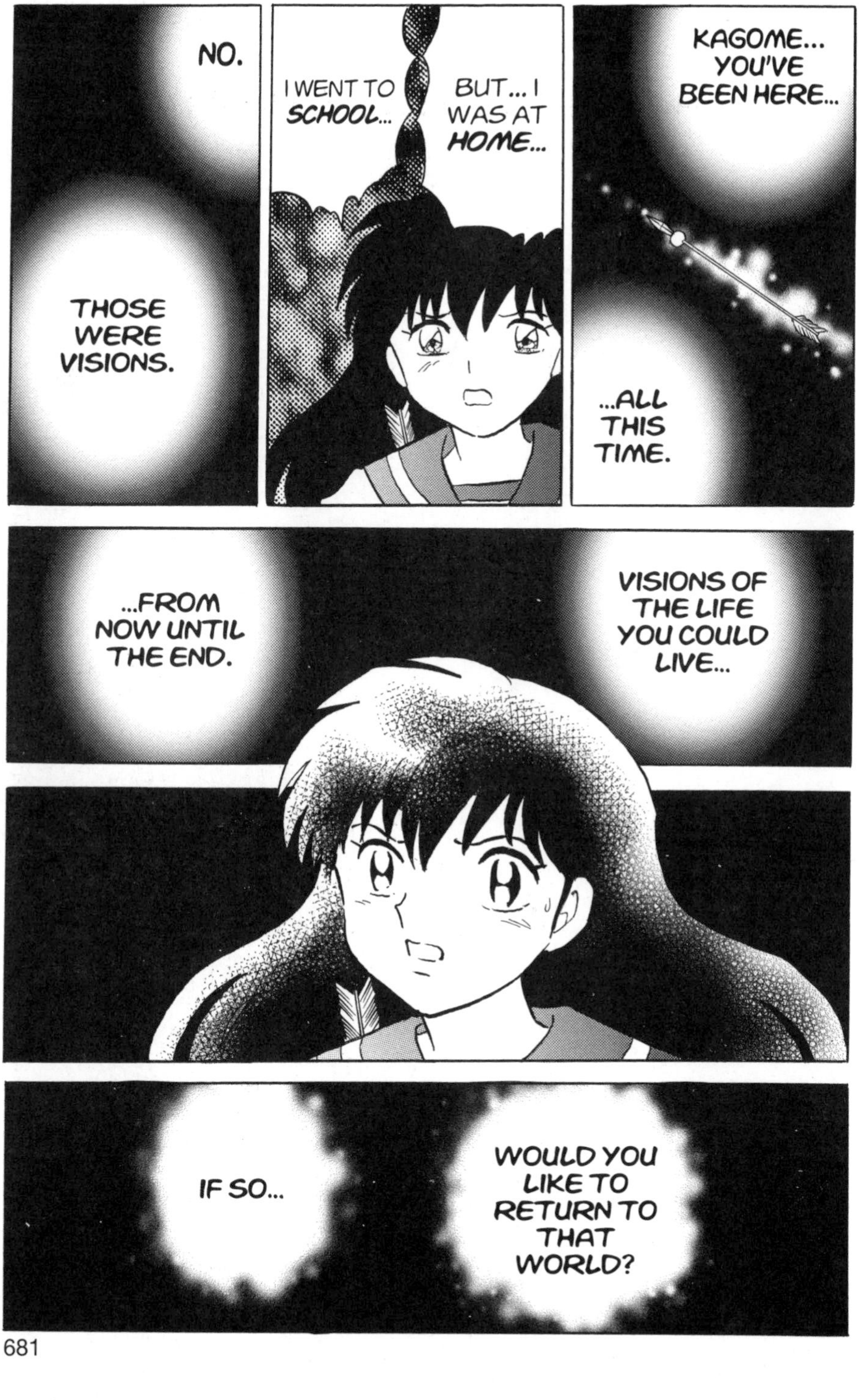
KAGOME... YOU'VE BEEN HERE...
...ALL THIS TIME.
BUT... I WAS AT HOME...
I WENT TO SCHOOL...
NO.
THOSE WERE VISIONS.
VISIONS OF THE LIFE YOU COULD LIVE...
...FROM NOW UNTIL THE END.
WOULD YOU LIKE TO RETURN TO THAT WORLD?
IF SO...

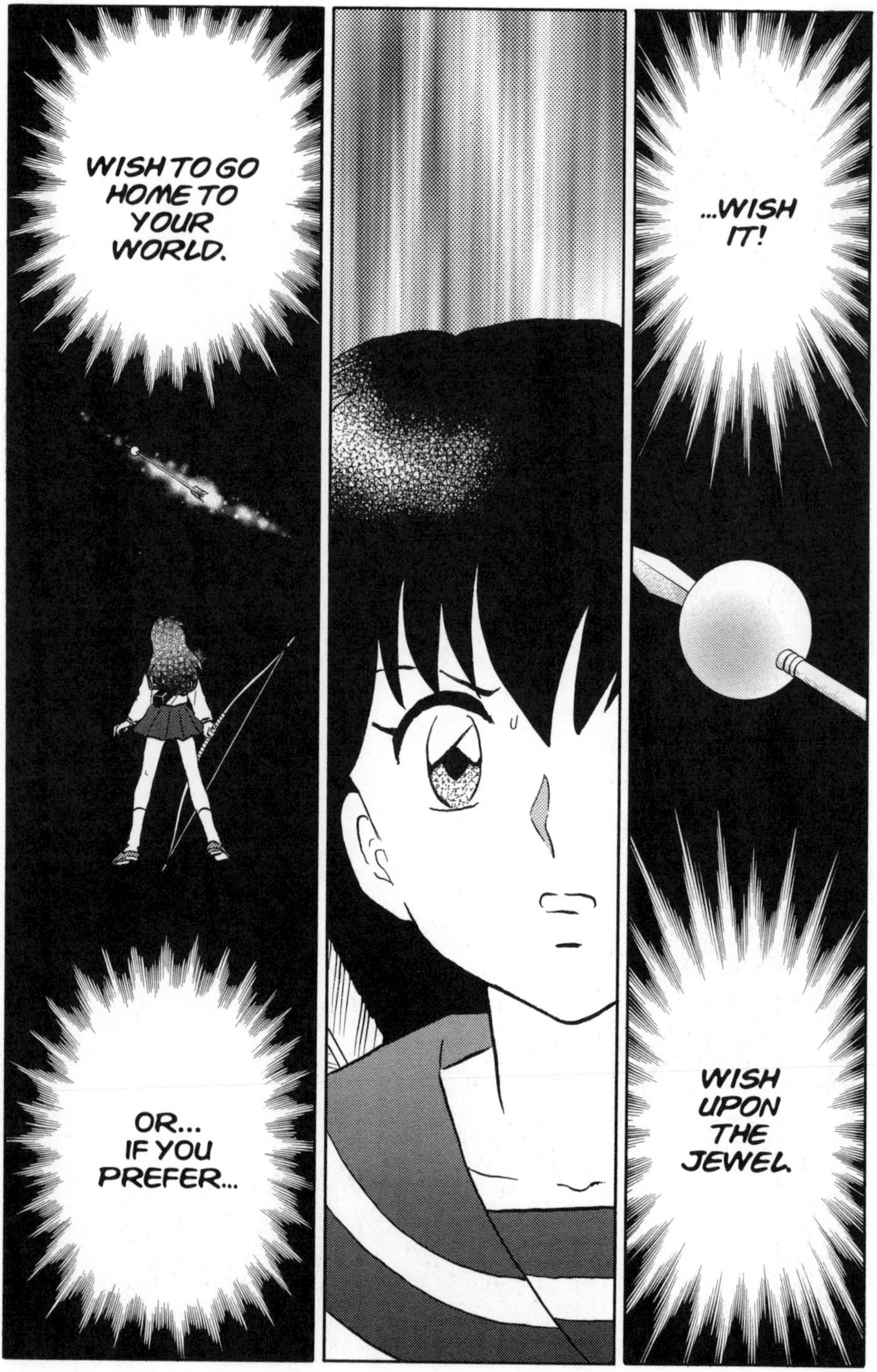
...WISH IT!
WISH UPON THE JEWEL.
WISH TO GO HOME TO YOUR WORLD.
OR... IF YOU PREFER...

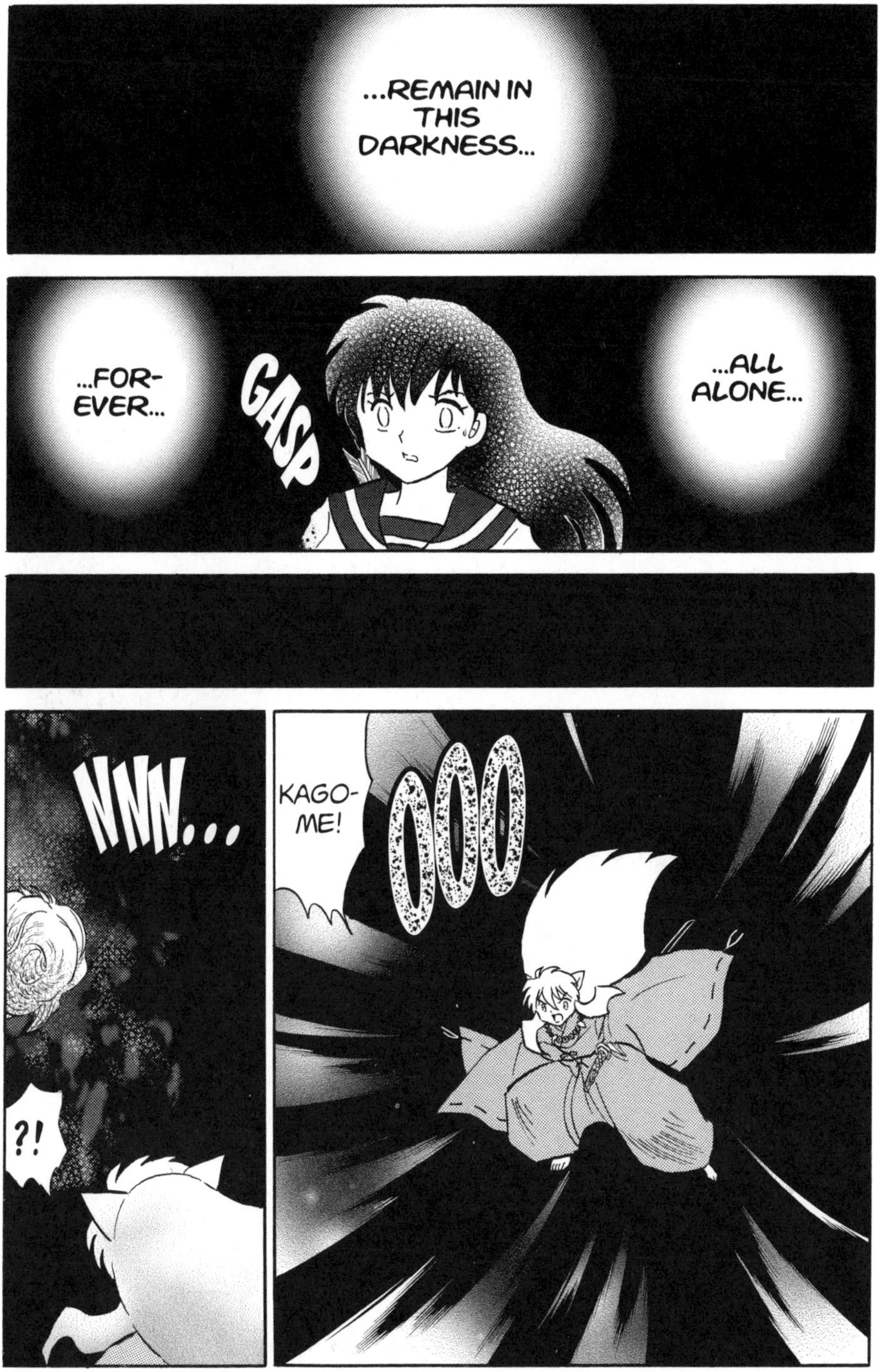
...REMAIN IN THIS DARKNESS...
...ALL ALONE...
GASP
...FOR-EVER...
KAGO-ME!
OOO
NNN...
?!

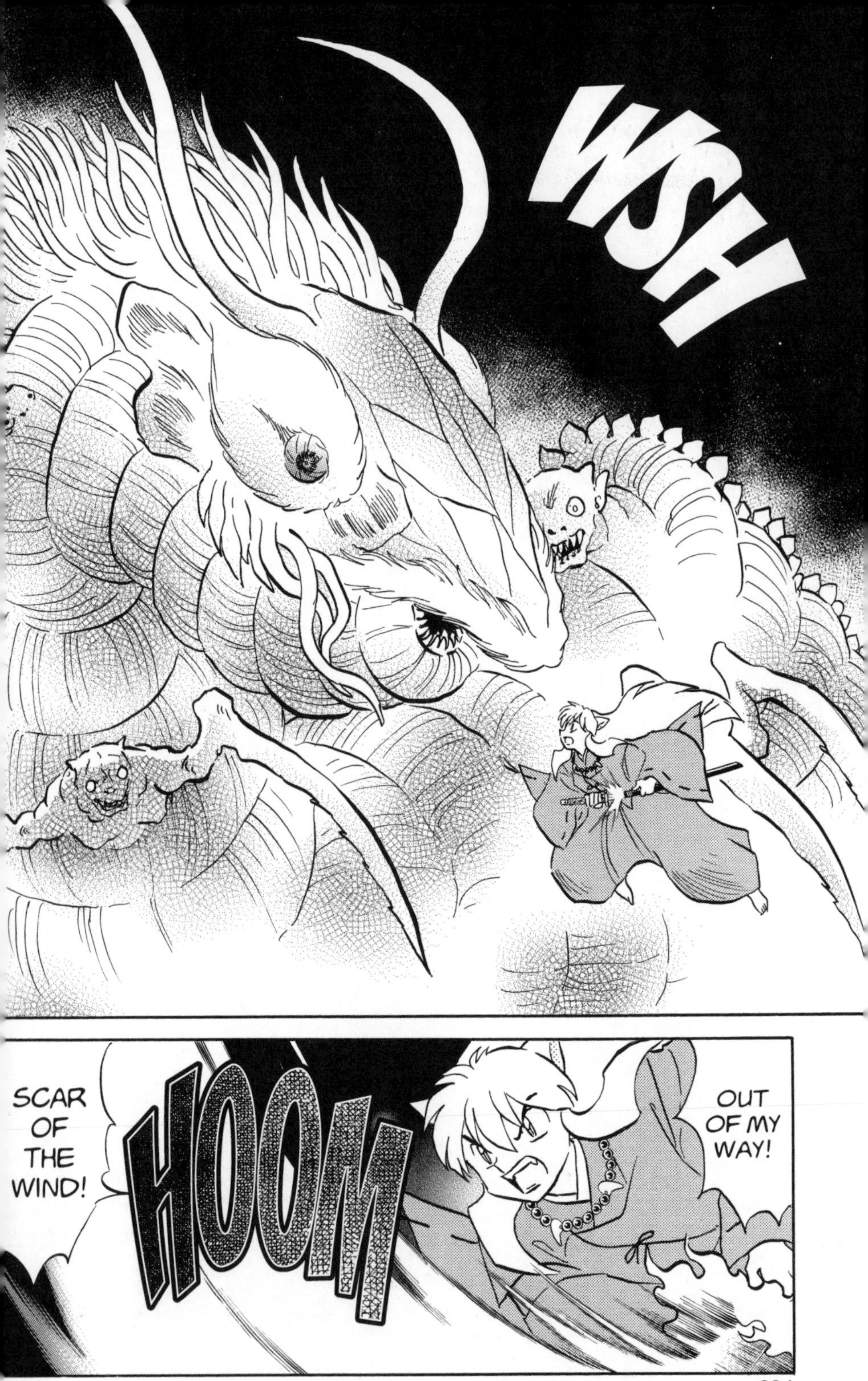
WSH
OUT OF MY WAY!
HOOM
SCAR OF THE WIND!

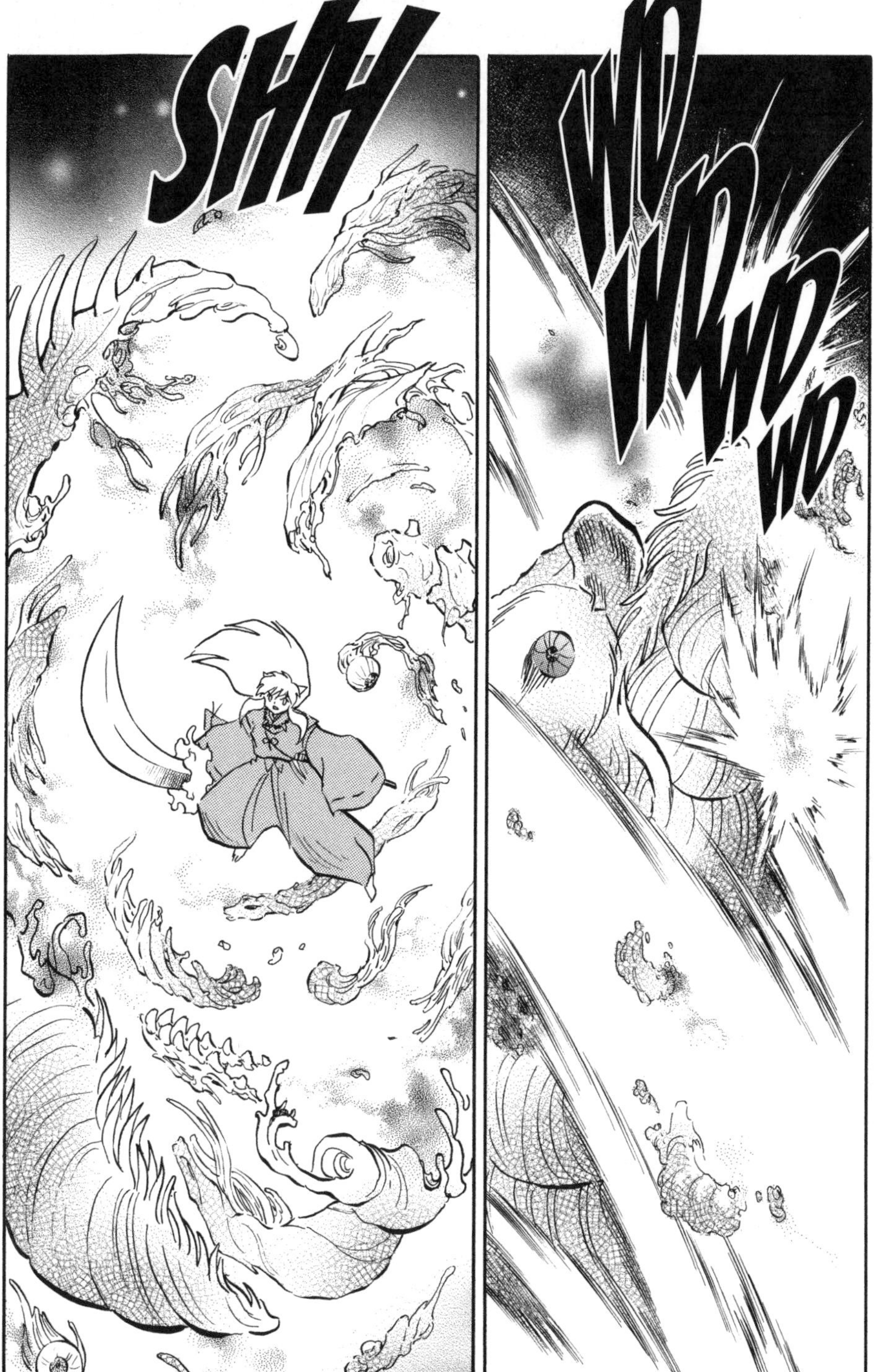
WD
WDWD
WD
SHH

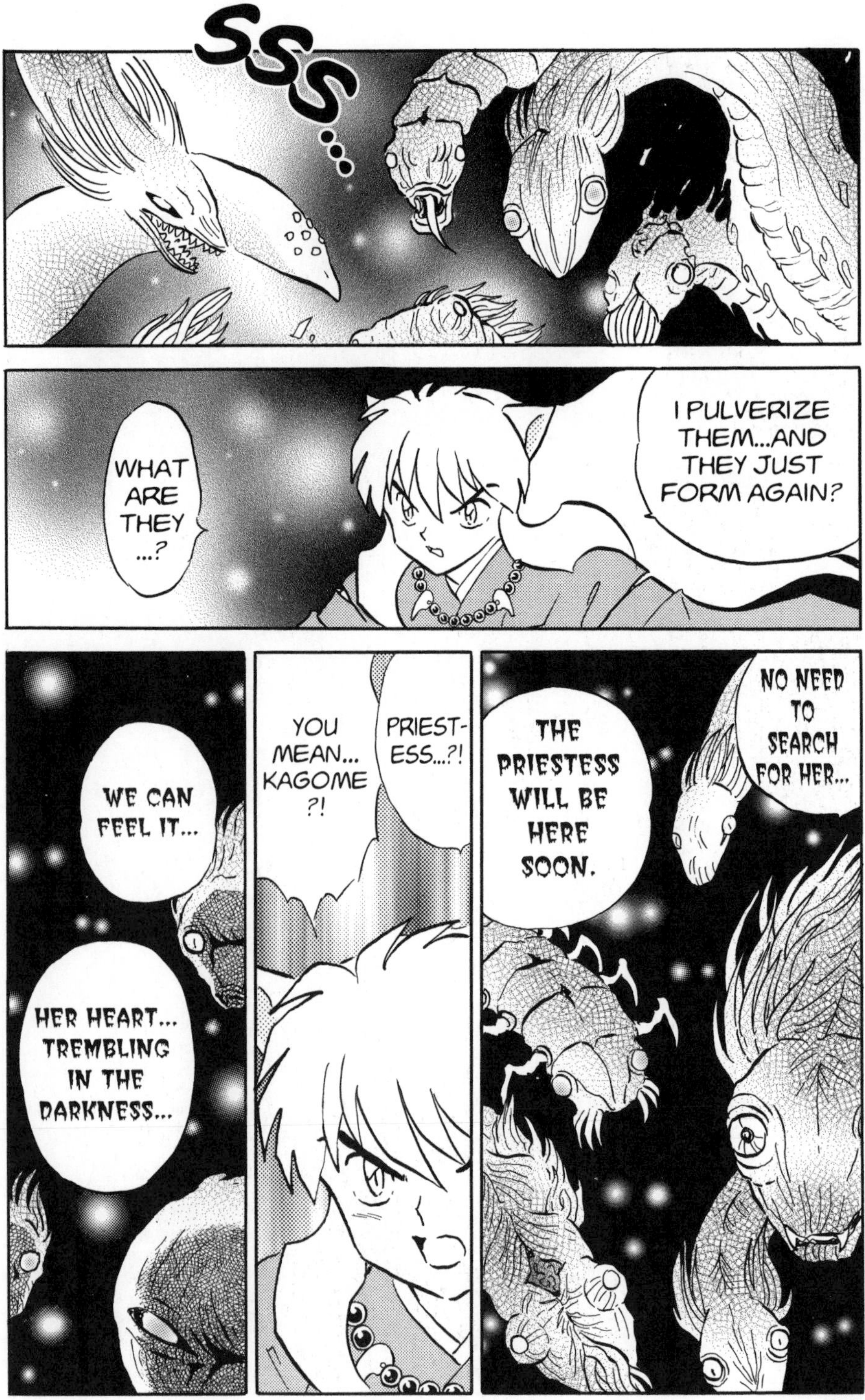
SSS...
I PULVERIZE THEM...AND THEY JUST FORM AGAIN?
WHAT ARE THEY ...?
NO NEED TO SEARCH FOR HER...
THE PRIESTESS WILL BE HERE SOON.
PRIEST-ESS...?!
YOU MEAN... KAGOME ?!
WE CAN FEEL IT...
HER HEART... TREMBLING IN THE DARKNESS...

...UN-LESS I WISH IT...?

I CAN'T GO BACK...

BDM

SOTA!

GRAND-PA!

MOM!

MIROKU! SANGO!

INU-YASHA!

SHIPPO!

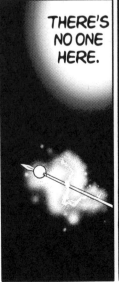

THERE'S NO ONE HERE.

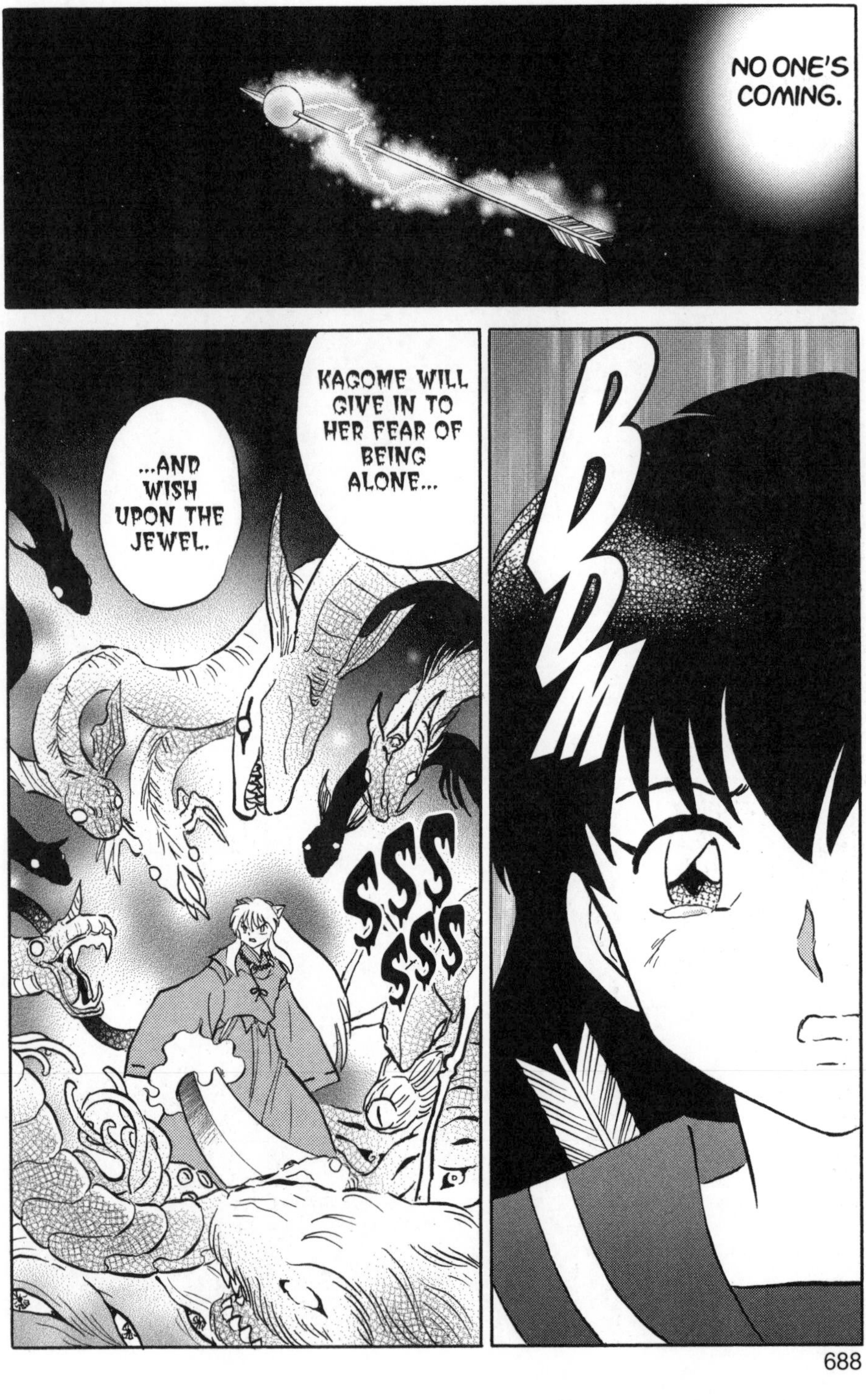
NO ONE'S COMING.
BDUM
KAGOME WILL GIVE IN TO HER FEAR OF BEING ALONE...
...AND WISH UPON THE JEWEL.
SSSSSS

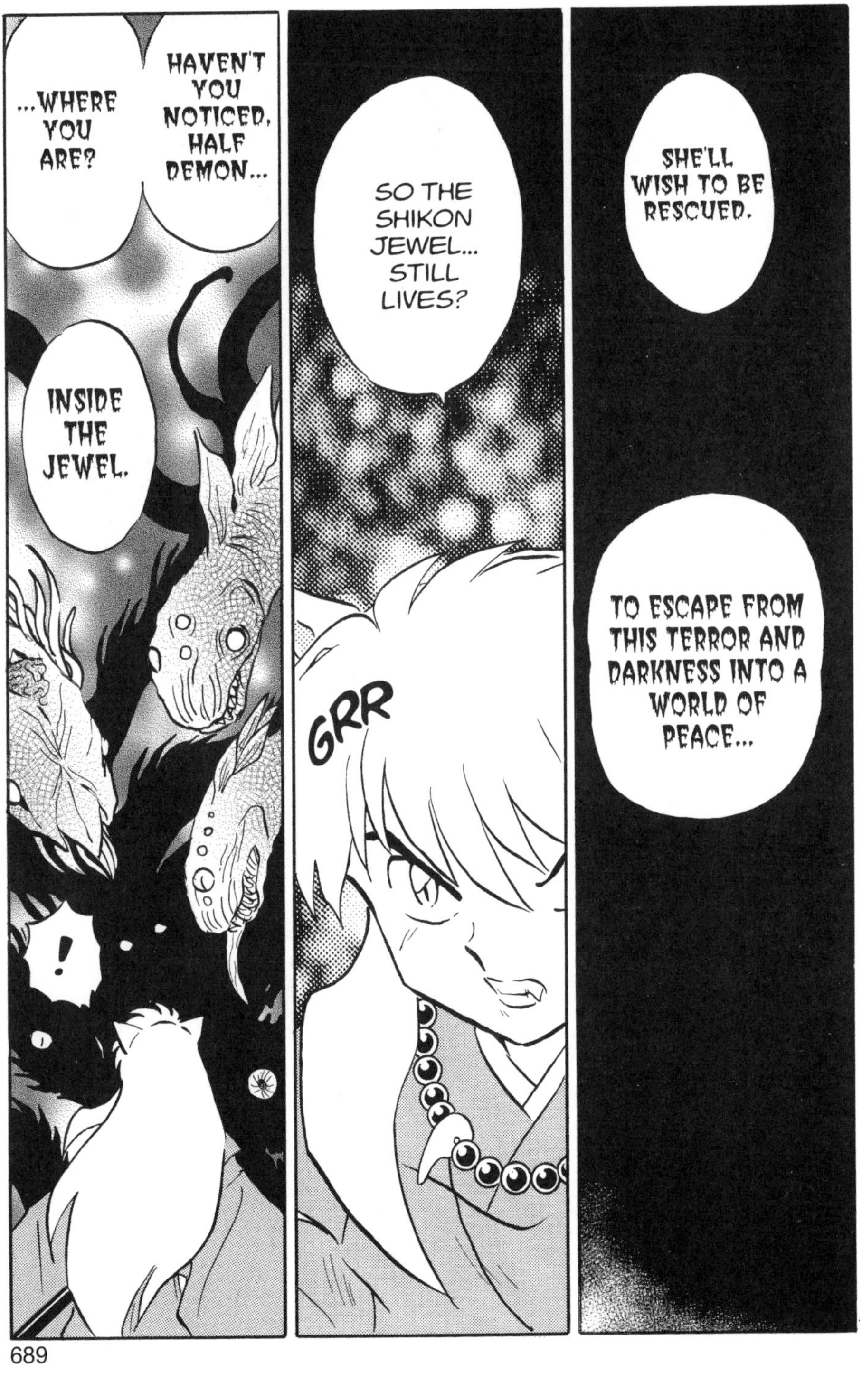
SHE'LL WISH TO BE RESCUED.
TO ESCAPE FROM THIS TERROR AND DARKNESS INTO A WORLD OF PEACE...
SO THE SHIKON JEWEL... STILL LIVES?
GRR
HAVEN'T YOU NOTICED, HALF DEMON...
...WHERE YOU ARE?
INSIDE THE JEWEL.
!

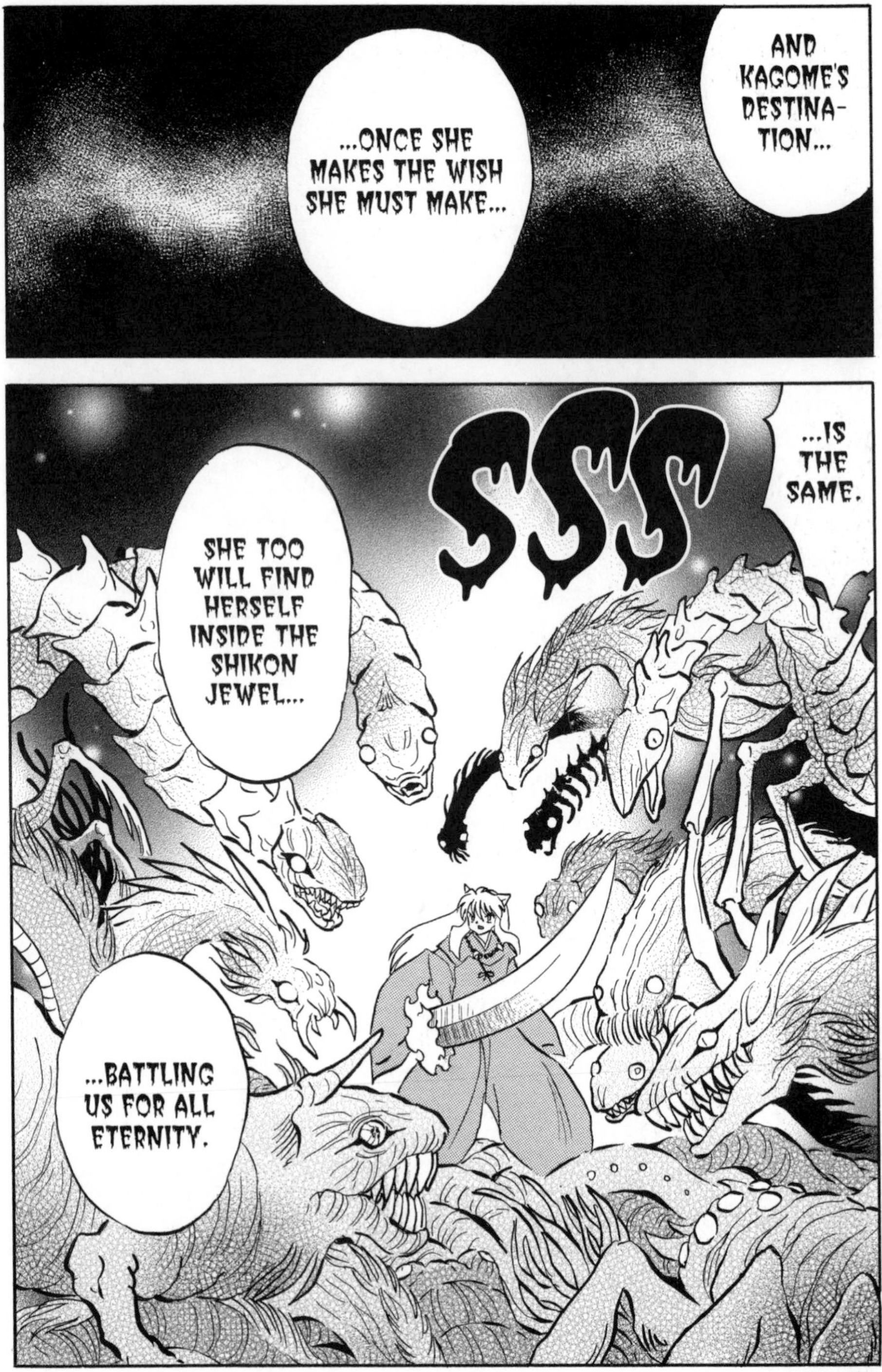
AND KAGOME'S DESTINATION...
...ONCE SHE MAKES THE WISH SHE MUST MAKE...
...IS THE SAME.
SSS
SHE TOO WILL FIND HERSELF INSIDE THE SHIKON JEWEL...
...BATTLING US FOR ALL ETERNITY.

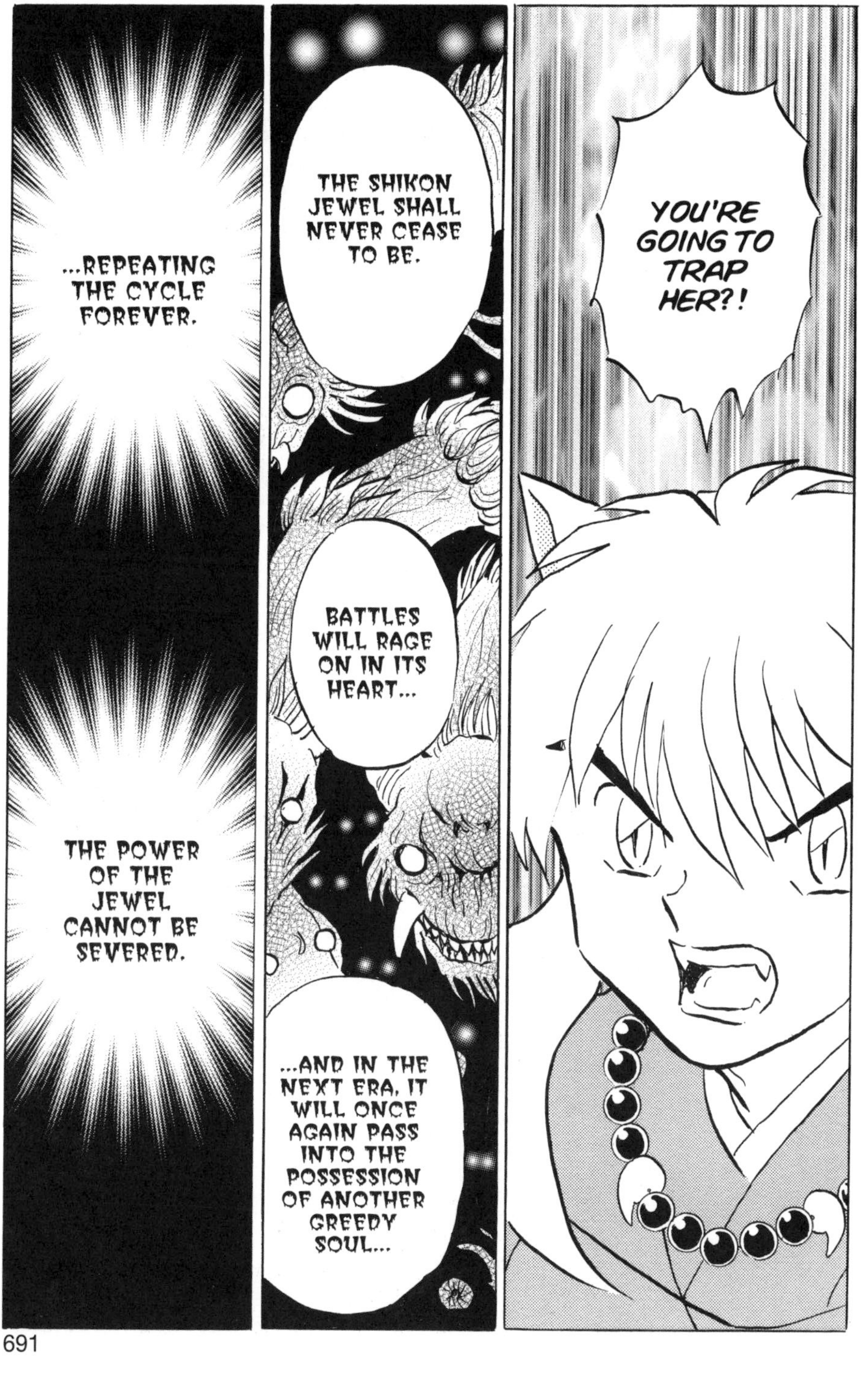
YOU'RE GOING TO TRAP HER?!
THE SHIKON JEWEL SHALL NEVER CEASE TO BE.
BATTLES WILL RAGE ON IN ITS HEART...
...AND IN THE NEXT ERA, IT WILL ONCE AGAIN PASS INTO THE POSSESSION OF ANOTHER GREEDY SOUL...
...REPEATING THE CYCLE FOREVER.
THE POWER OF THE JEWEL CANNOT BE SEVERED.

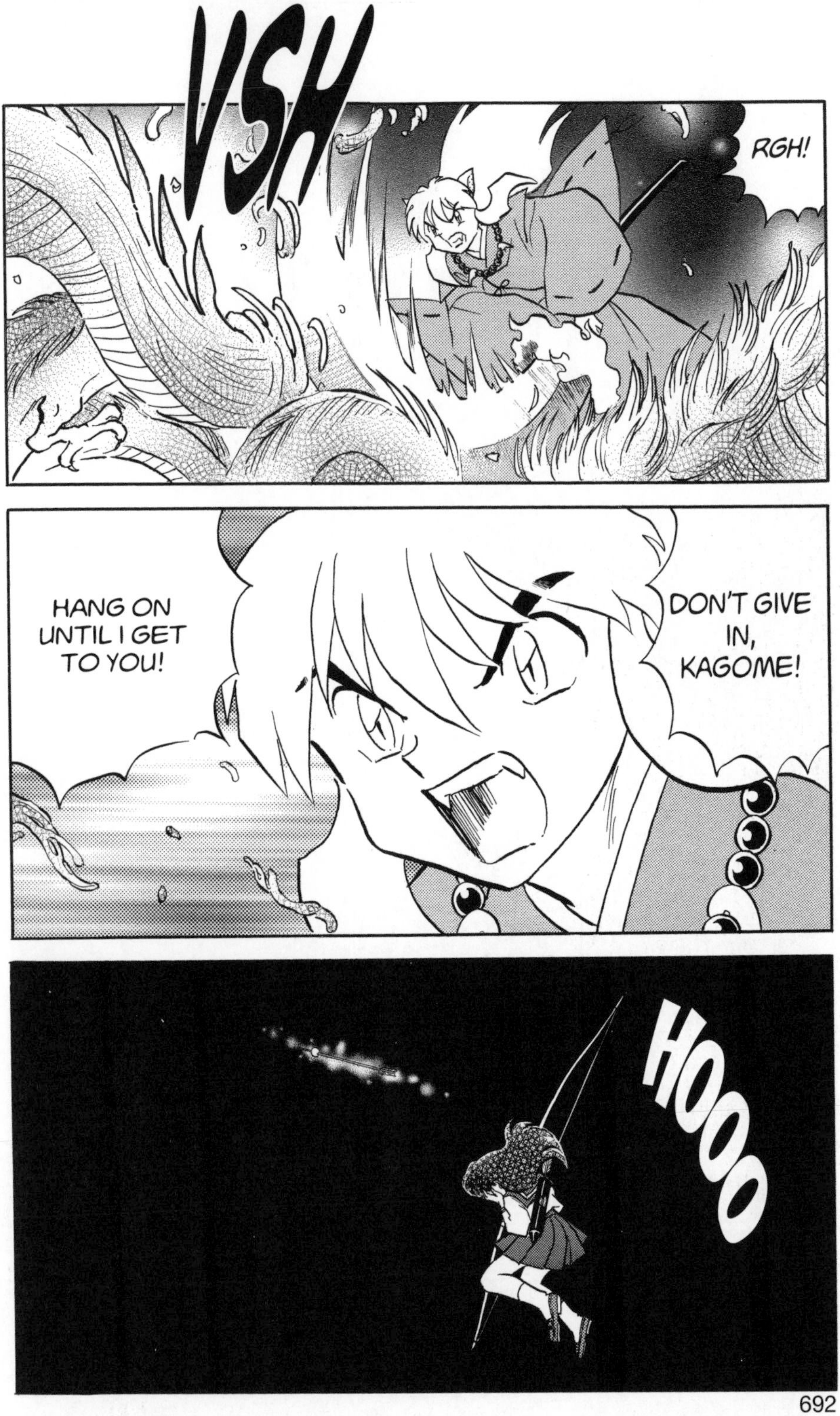
RGH!
VSH
DON'T GIVE IN, KAGOME!
HANG ON UNTIL I GET TO YOU!
HOOO

SCROLL EIGHT
DESTINY

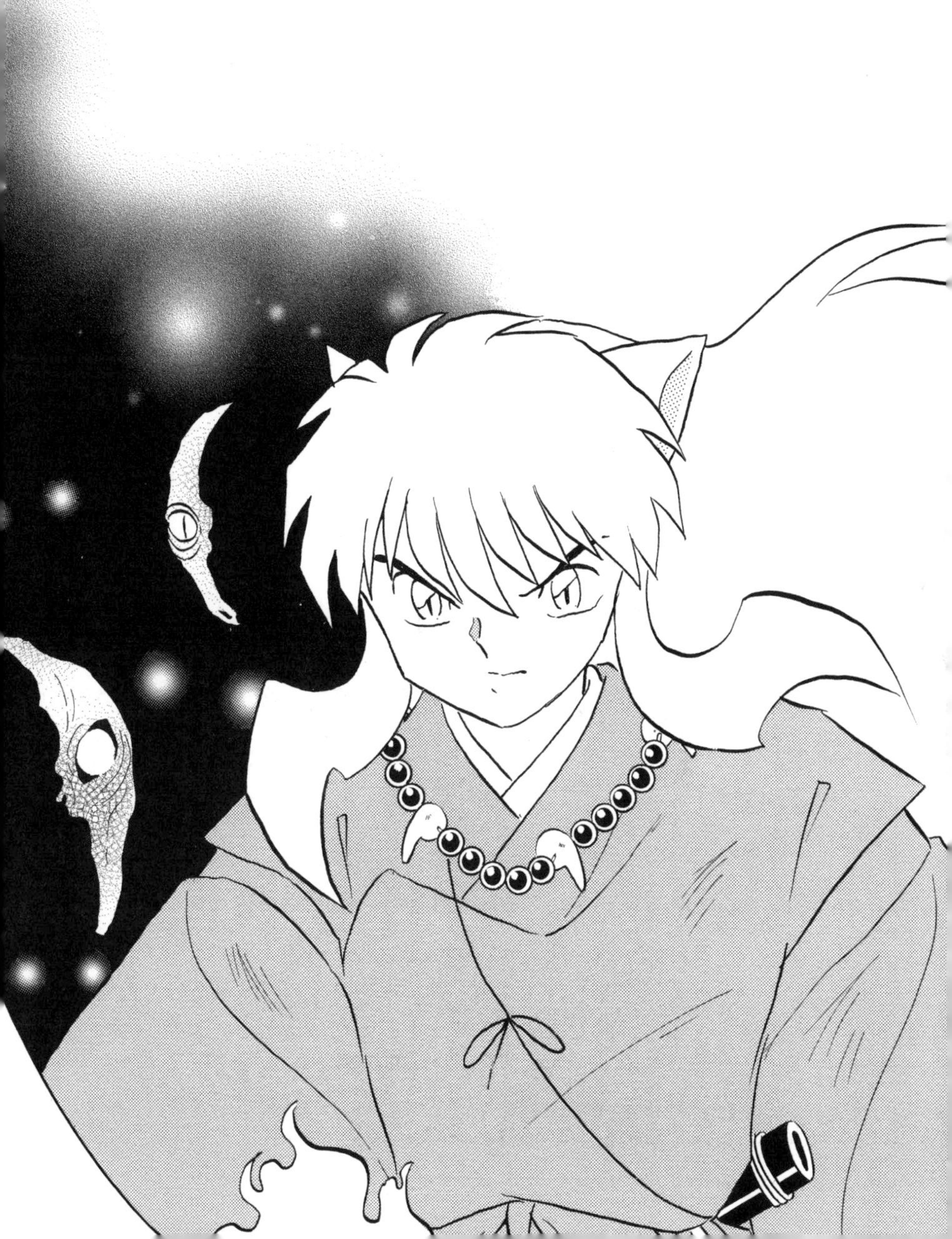

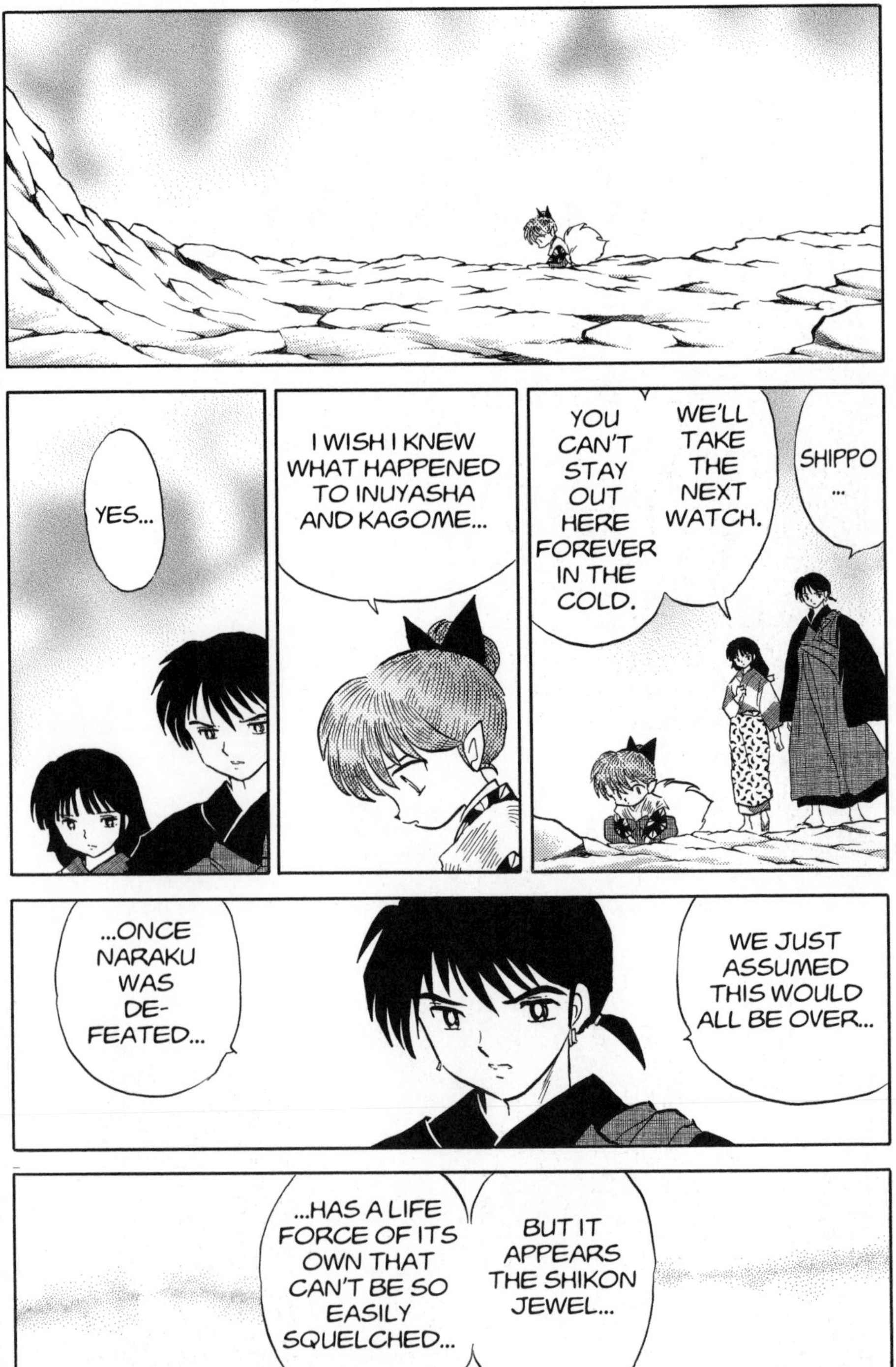
SHIPPO ...
WE'LL TAKE THE NEXT WATCH.
YOU CAN'T STAY OUT HERE FOREVER IN THE COLD.
I WISH I KNEW WHAT HAPPENED TO INUYASHA AND KAGOME...
YES...
WE JUST ASSUMED THIS WOULD ALL BE OVER...
...ONCE NARAKU WAS DE-FEATED...
BUT IT APPEARS THE SHIKON JEWEL...
...HAS A LIFE FORCE OF ITS OWN THAT CAN'T BE SO EASILY SQUELCHED...

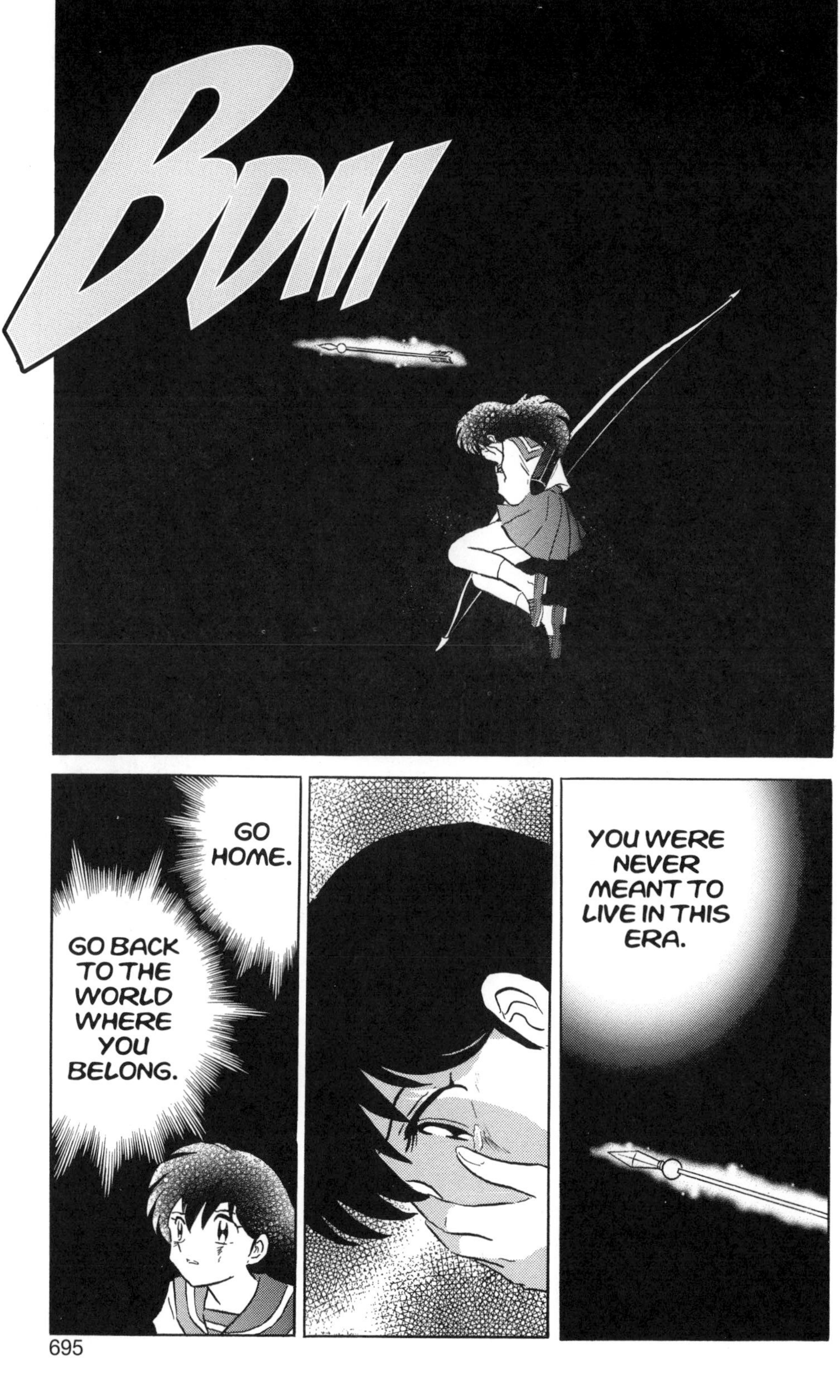
BDM
YOU WERE NEVER MEANT TO LIVE IN THIS ERA.
GO HOME.
GO BACK TO THE WORLD WHERE YOU BELONG.

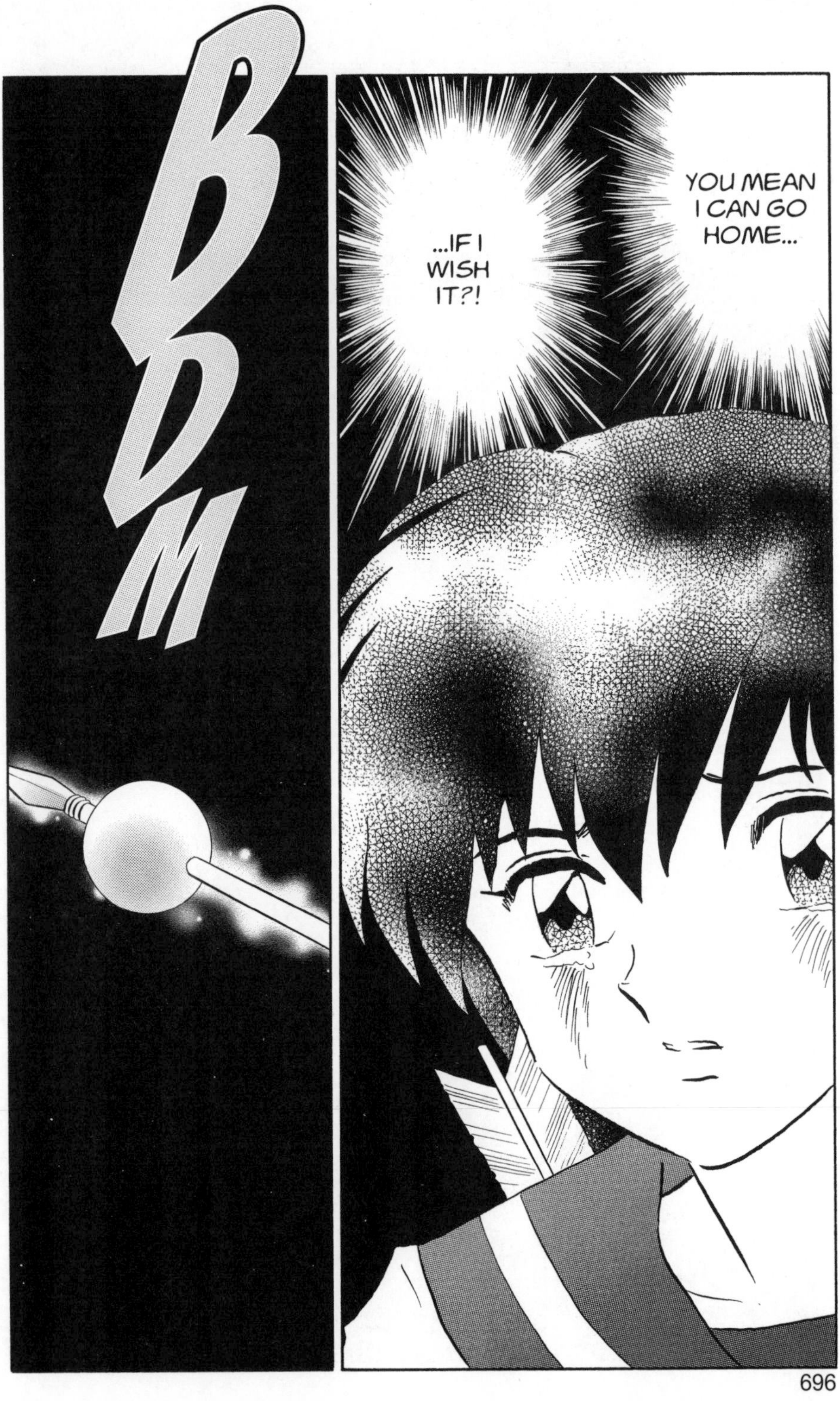
YOU MEAN I CAN GO HOME...
...IF I WISH IT?!
BDM

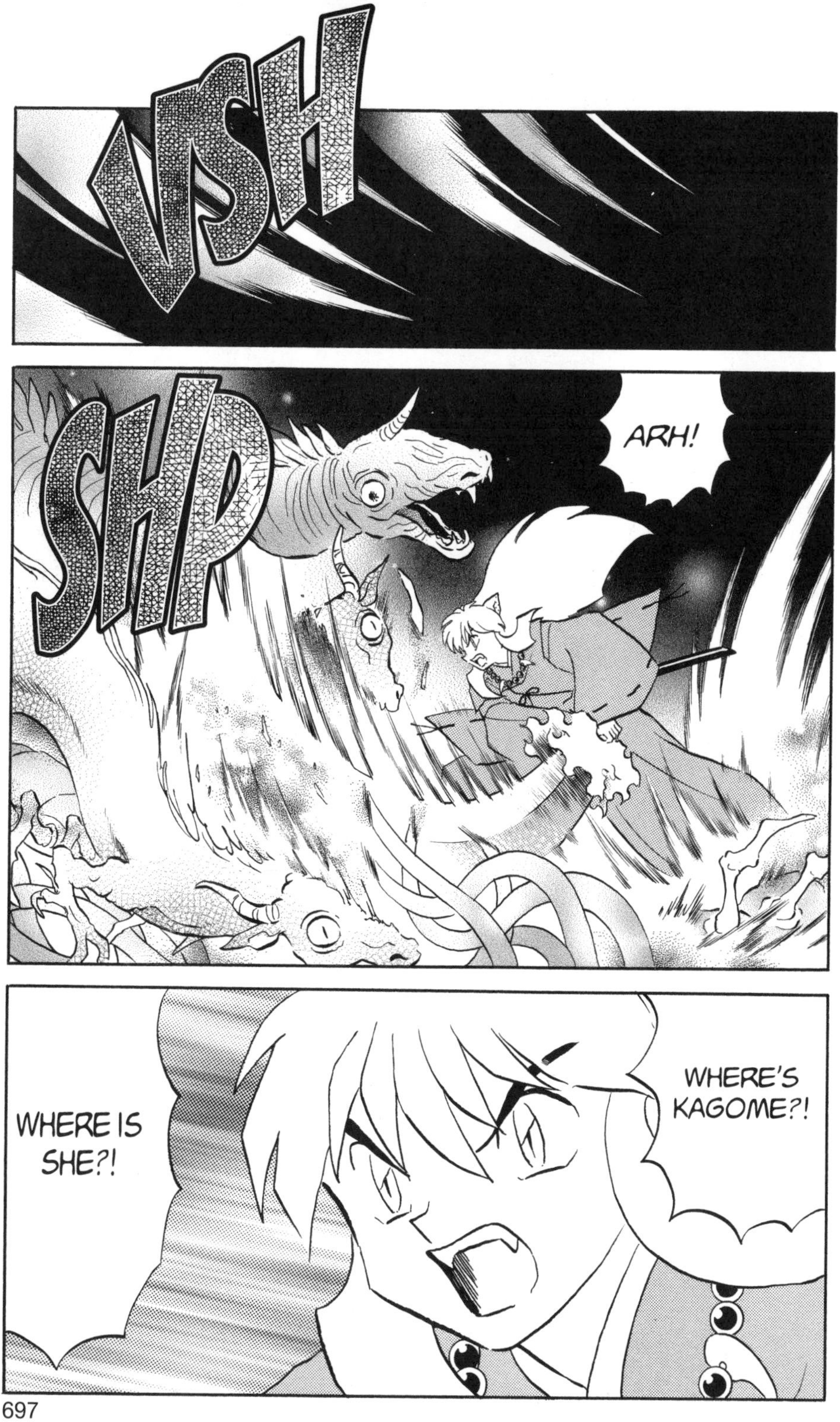
VSH
ARH!
SHP
WHERE'S KAGOME?!
WHERE IS SHE?!

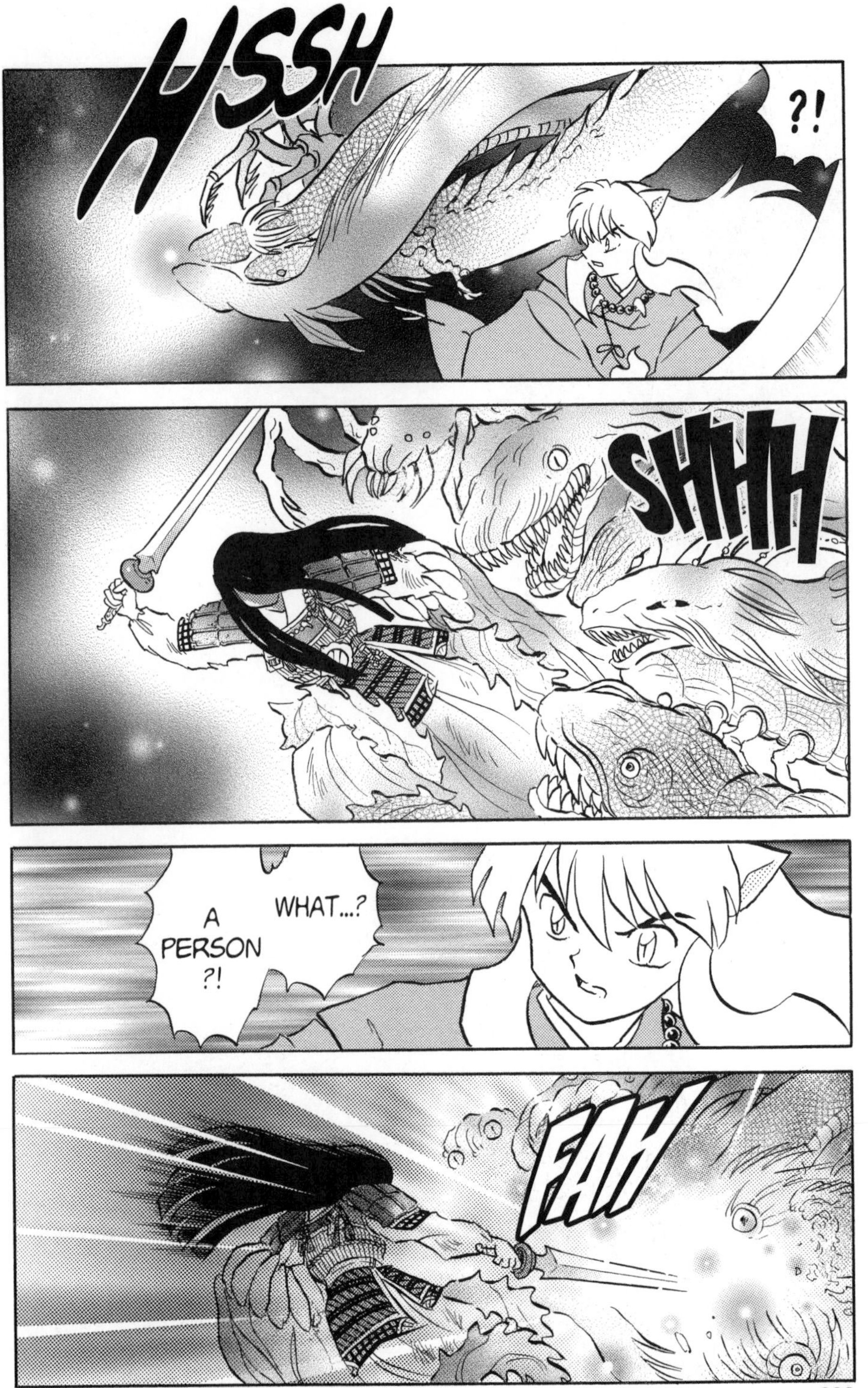
HSSH
?!
SHHH
WHAT...?
A PERSON ?!
FAH

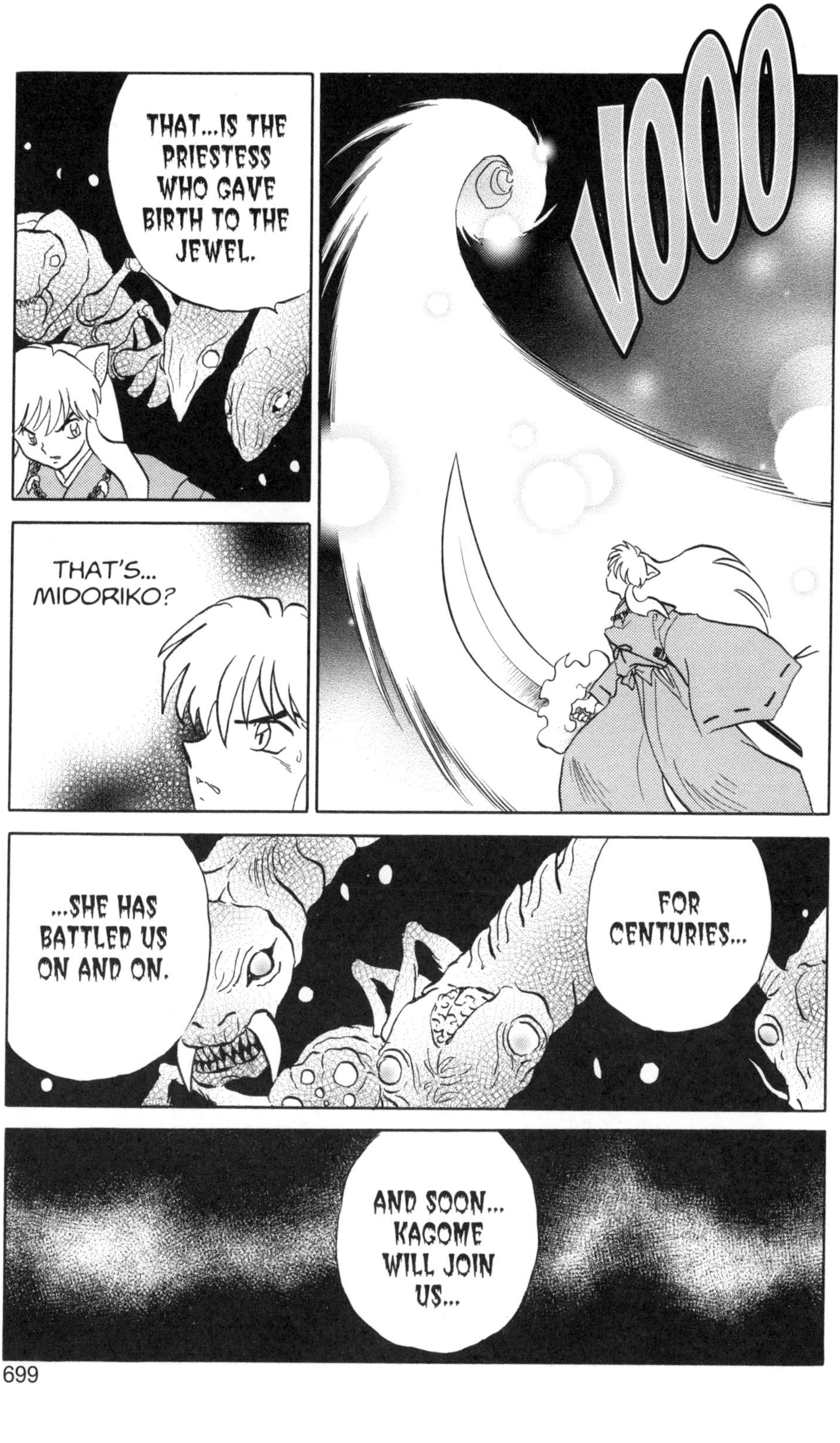
VOOO
THAT...IS THE PRIESTESS WHO GAVE BIRTH TO THE JEWEL.
THAT'S... MIDORIKO?
FOR CENTURIES...
...SHE HAS BATTLED US ON AND ON.
AND SOON... KAGOME WILL JOIN US...

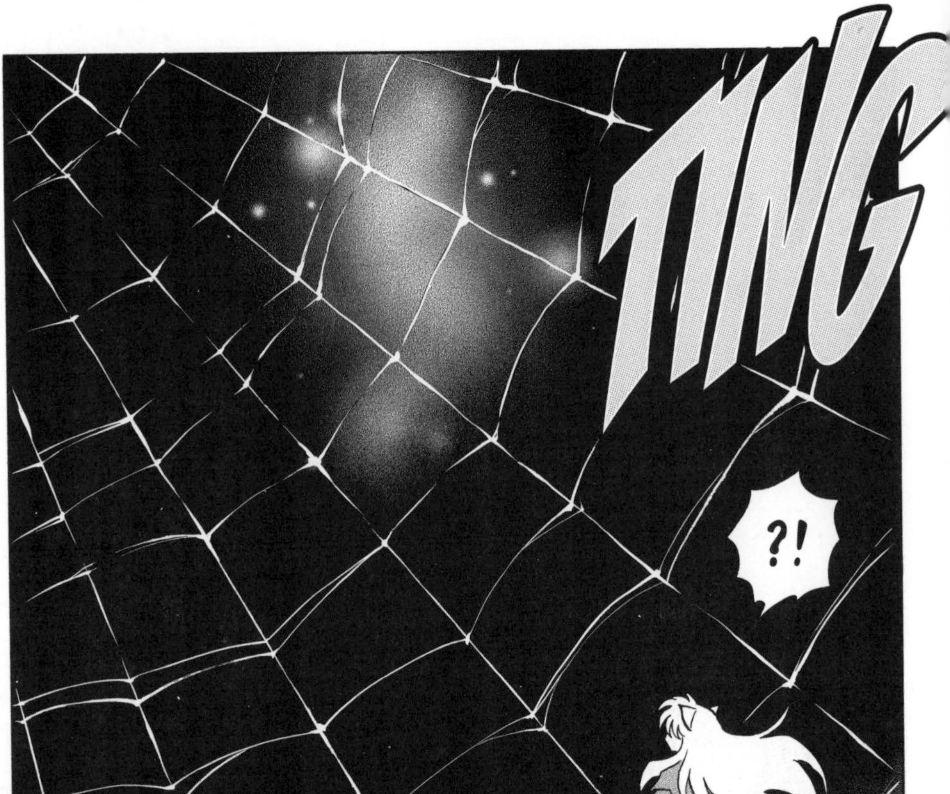
TING
?!
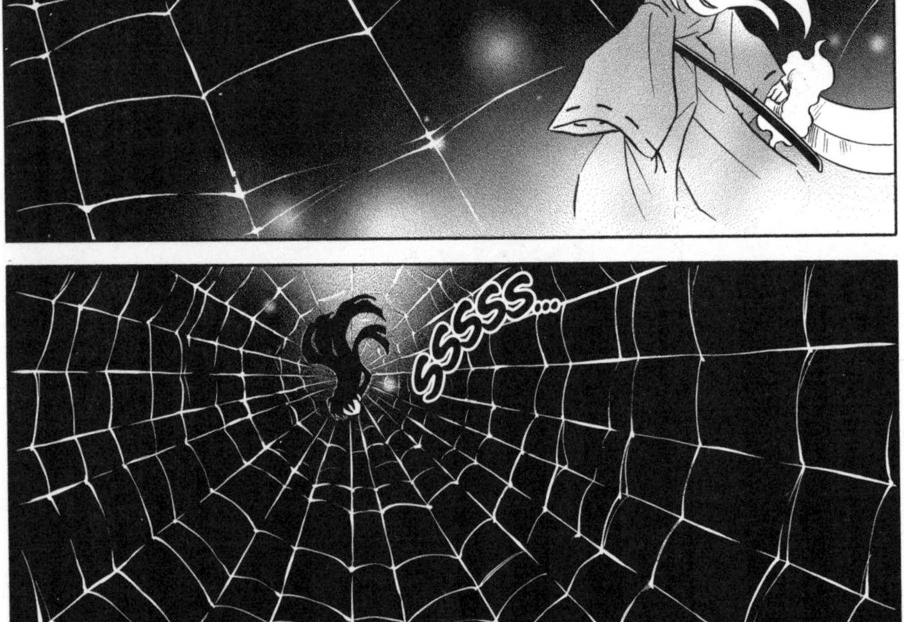
SSSSS...

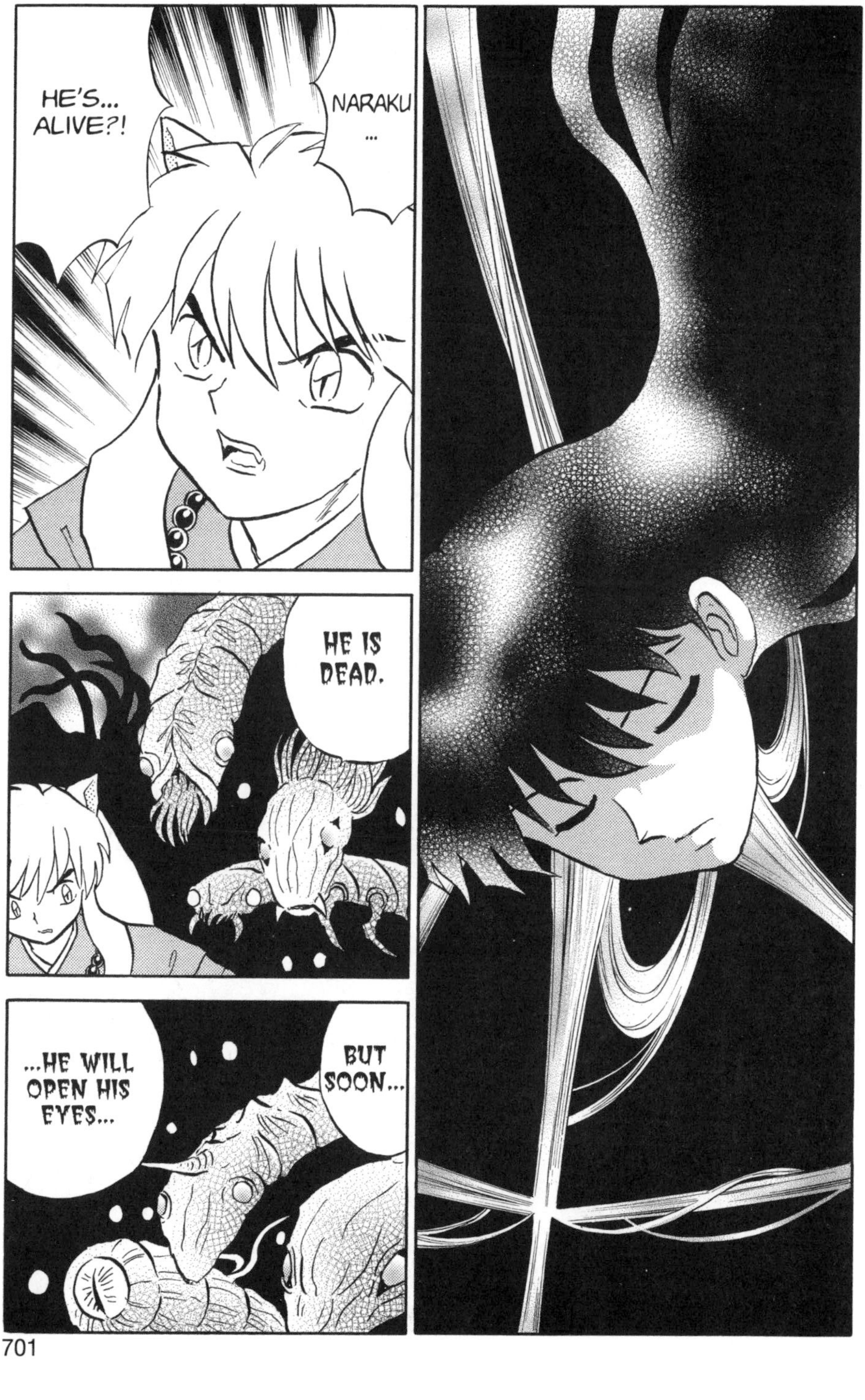
NARAKU ...
HE'S... ALIVE?!
HE IS DEAD.
BUT SOON...
...HE WILL OPEN HIS EYES...

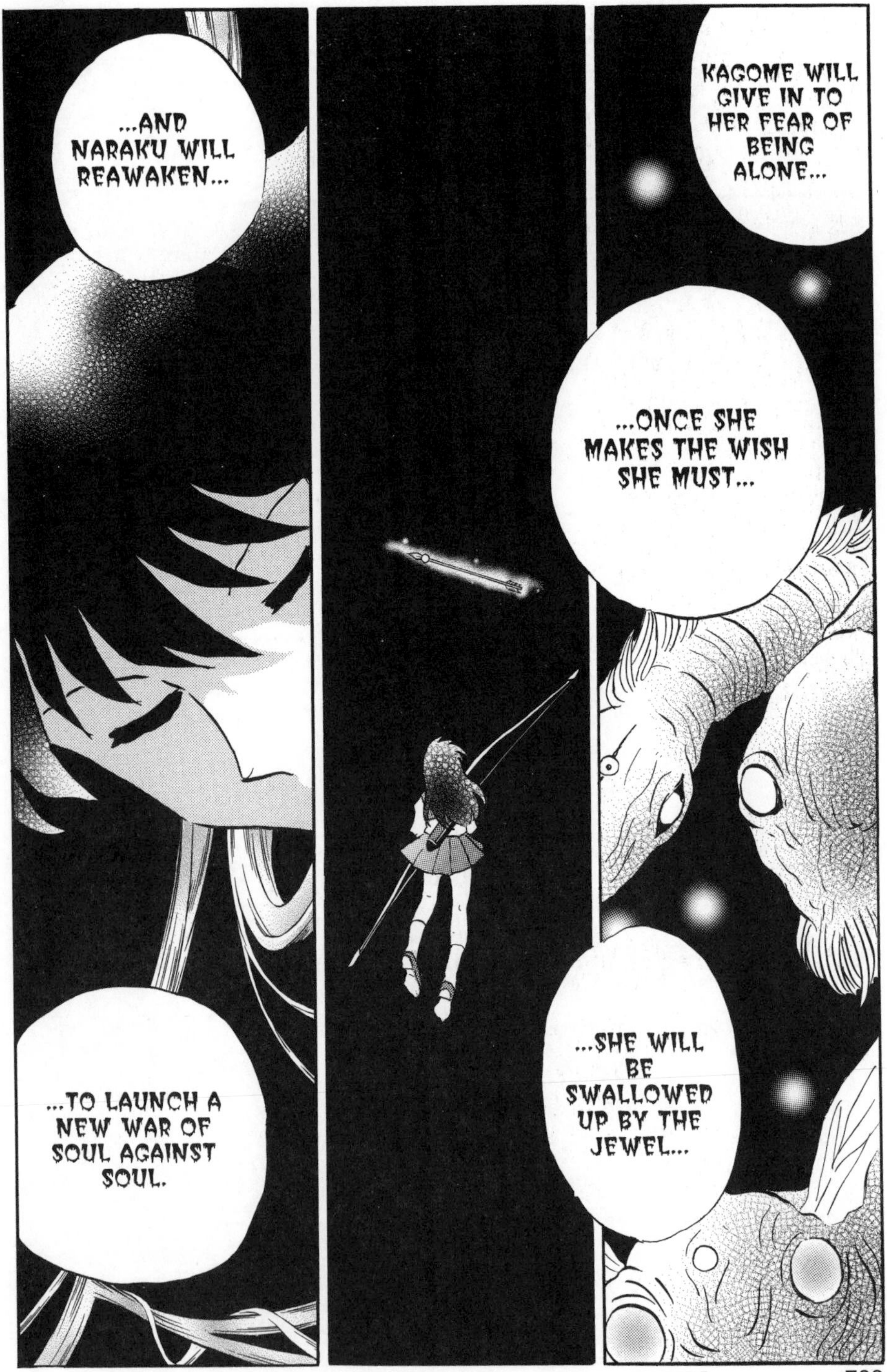
KAGOME WILL GIVE IN TO HER FEAR OF BEING ALONE...
...ONCE SHE MAKES THE WISH SHE MUST...
...SHE WILL BE SWALLOWED UP BY THE JEWEL...
...AND NARAKU WILL REAWAKEN...
...TO LAUNCH A NEW WAR OF SOUL AGAINST SOUL.

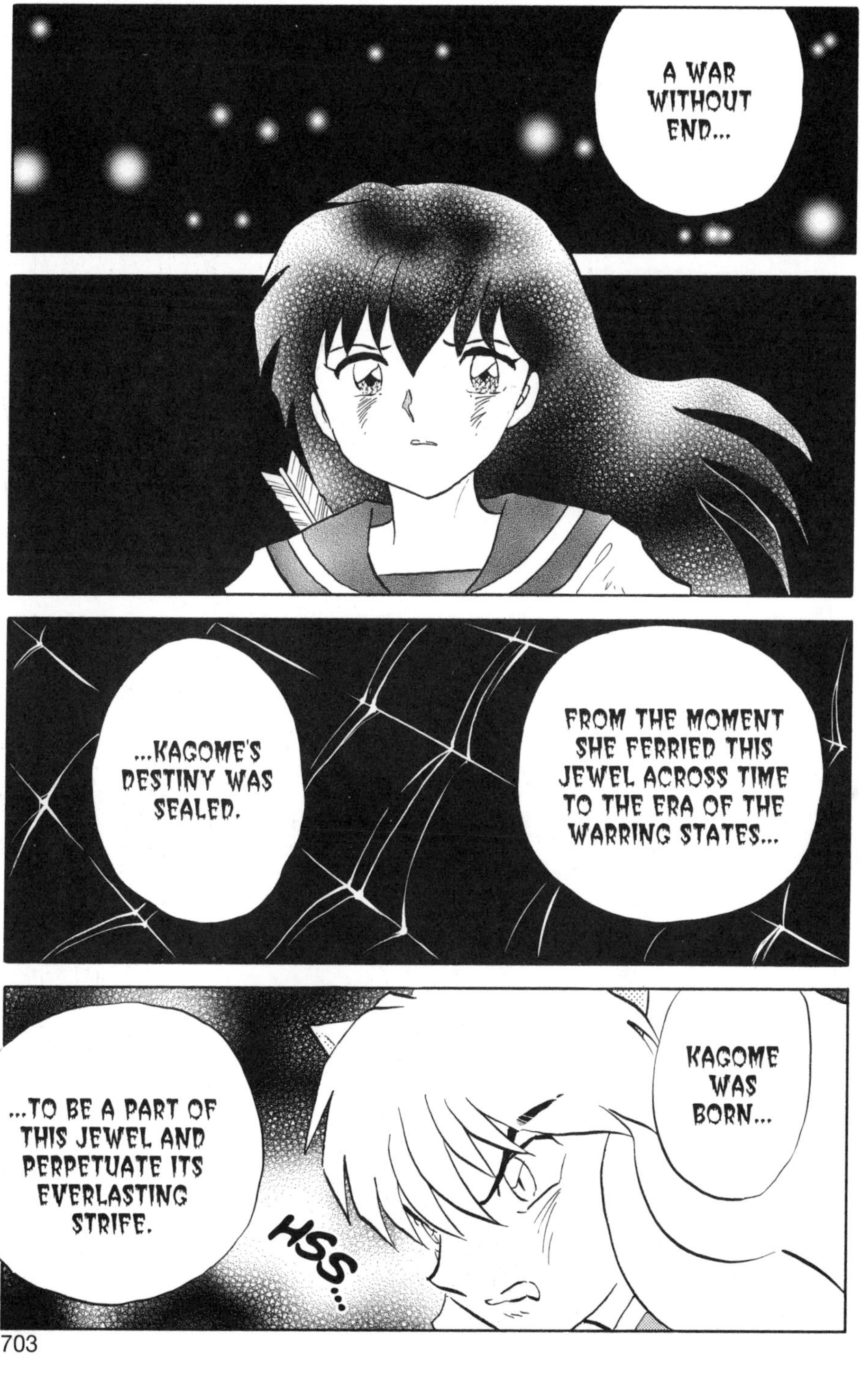
A WAR WITHOUT END...
FROM THE MOMENT SHE FERRIED THIS JEWEL ACROSS TIME TO THE ERA OF THE WARRING STATES...
...KAGOME'S DESTINY WAS SEALED.
KAGOME WAS BORN...
...TO BE A PART OF THIS JEWEL AND PERPETUATE ITS EVERLASTING STRIFE.
HSS...

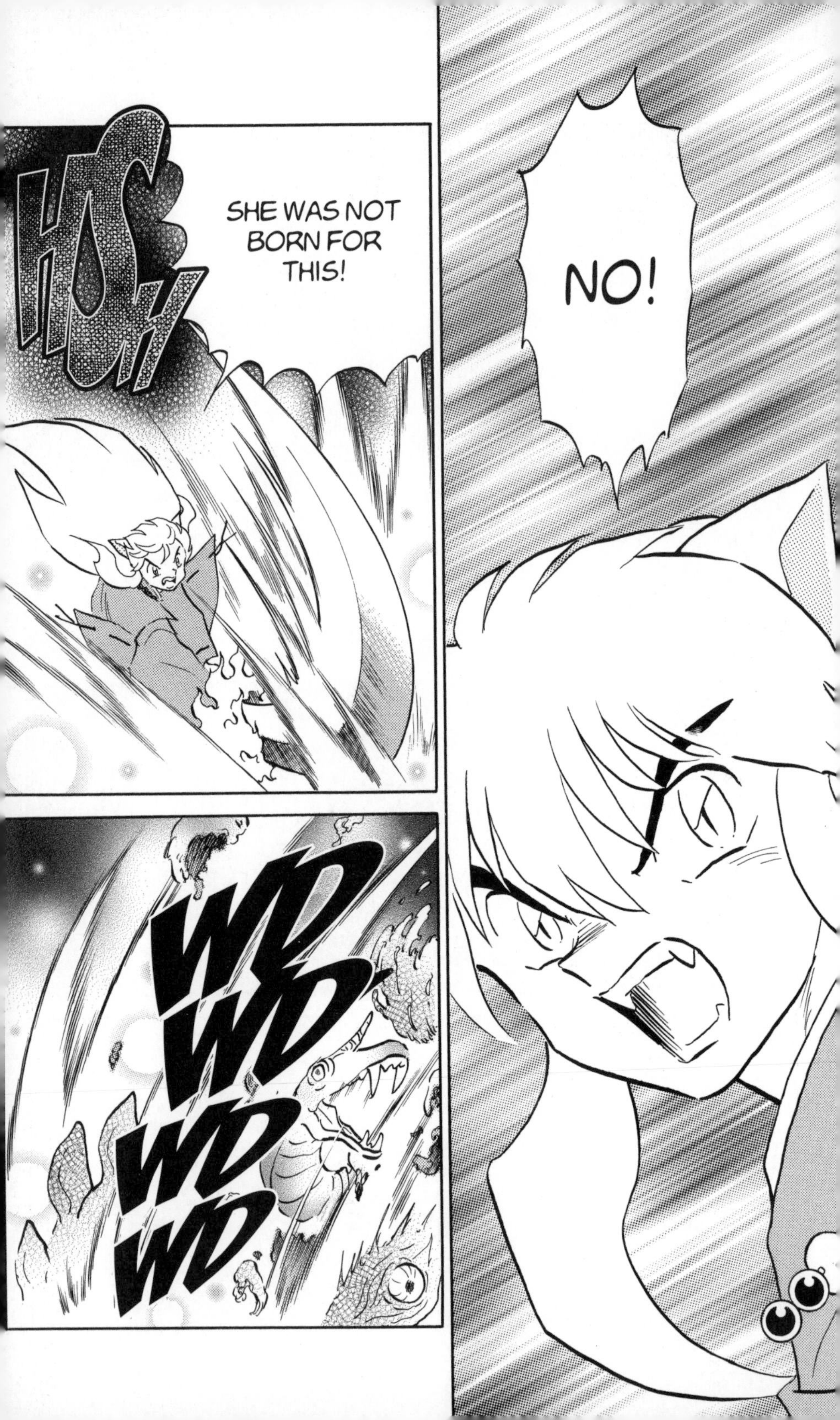
NO!
SHE WAS NOT BORN FOR THIS!

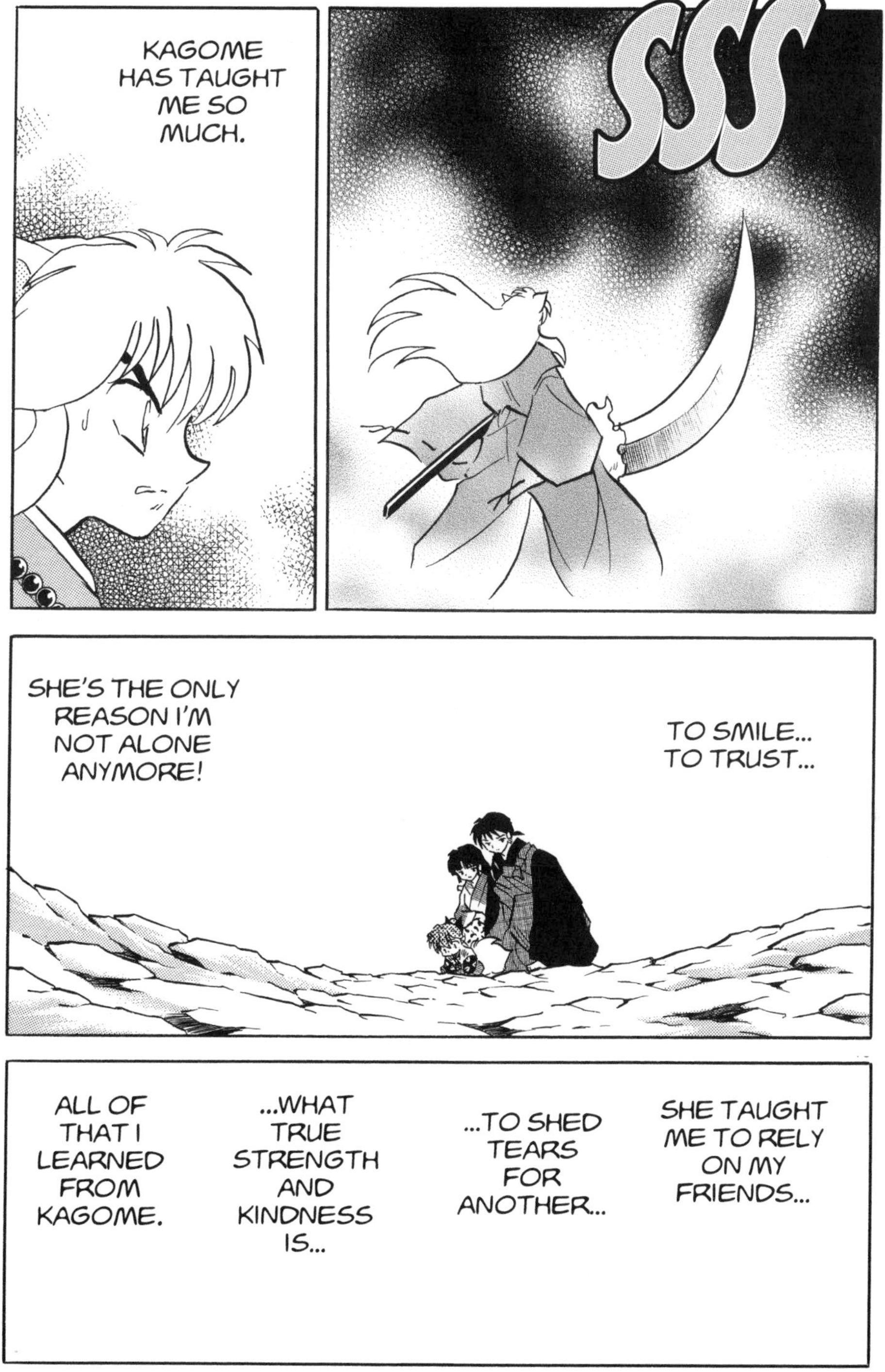
SSS
KAGOME HAS TAUGHT ME SO MUCH.
TO SMILE... TO TRUST...
SHE'S THE ONLY REASON I'M NOT ALONE ANYMORE!
SHE TAUGHT ME TO RELY ON MY FRIENDS...
...TO SHED TEARS FOR ANOTHER...
...WHAT TRUE STRENGTH AND KINDNESS IS...
ALL OF THAT I LEARNED FROM KAGOME.

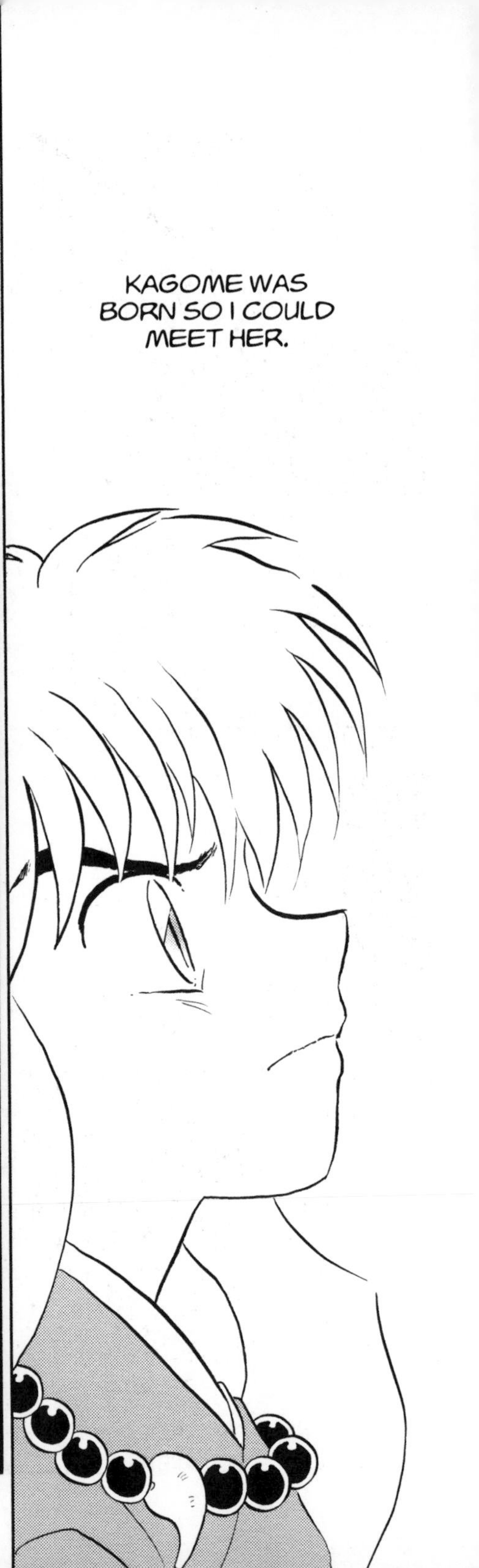
KAGOME WAS BORN SO I COULD MEET HER.

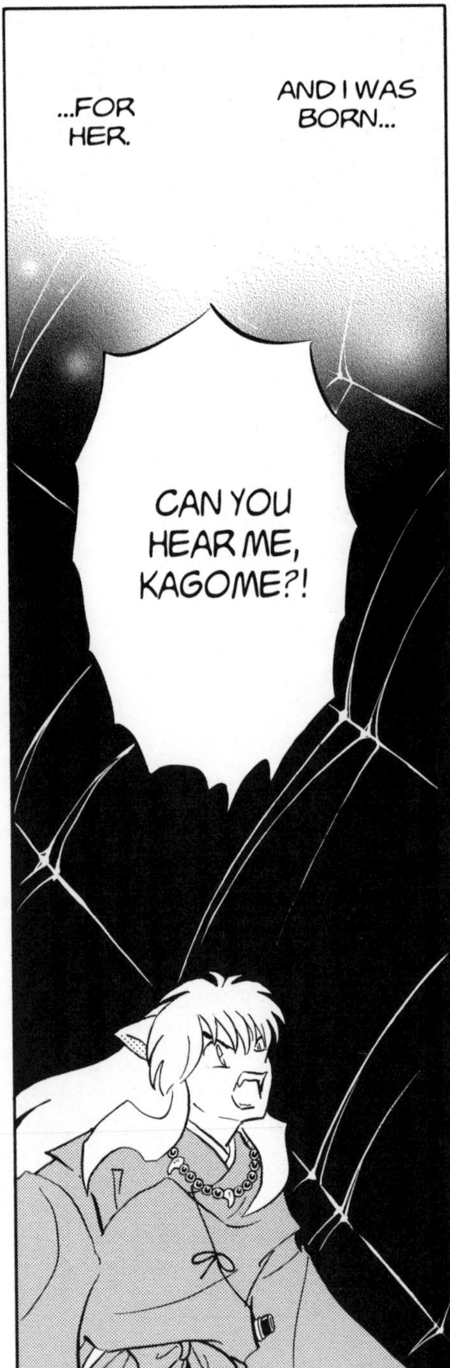
AND I WAS BORN...
...FOR HER.
CAN YOU HEAR ME, KAGOME?!

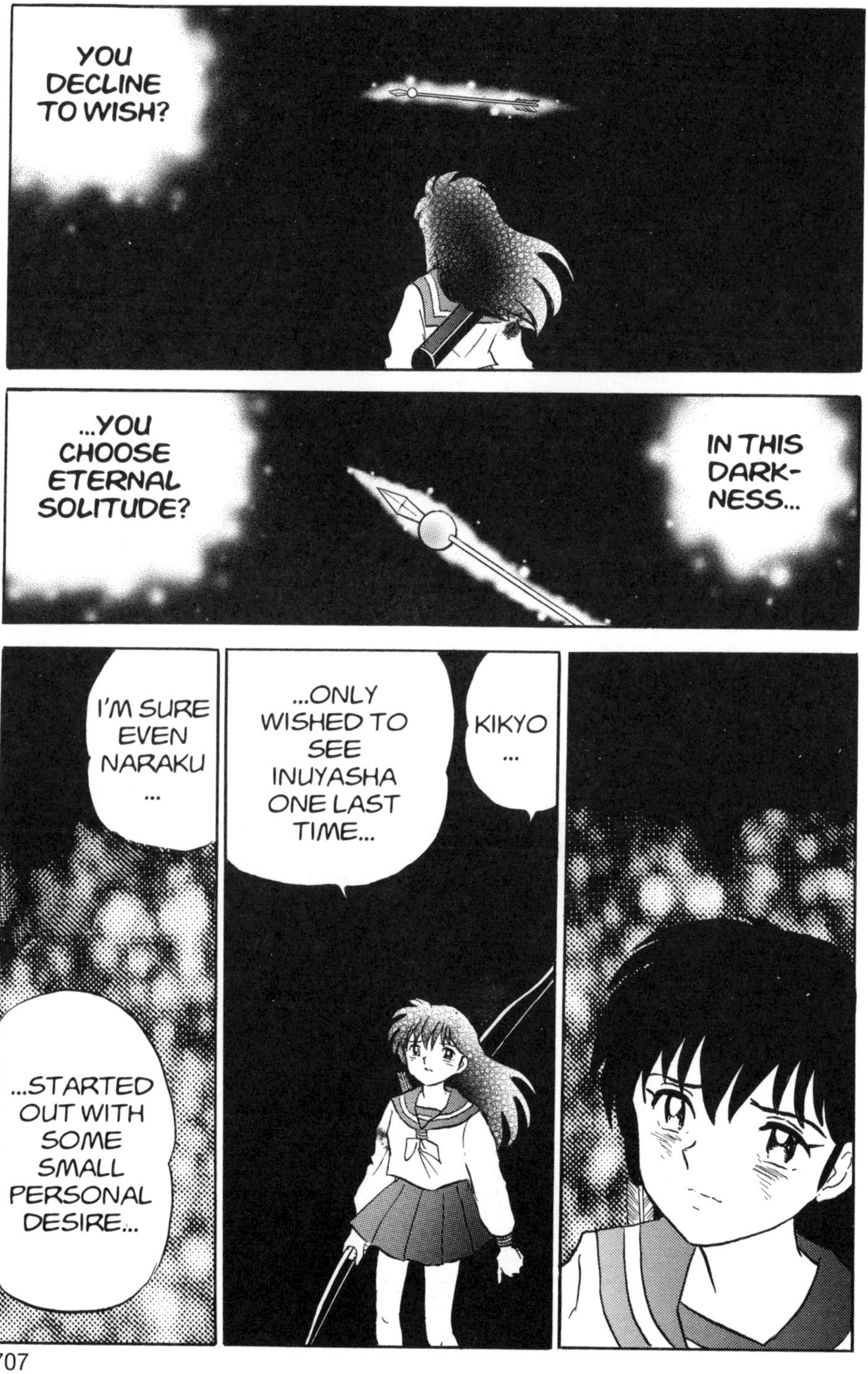
YOU DECLINE TO WISH?
IN THIS DARK-NESS...
...YOU CHOOSE ETERNAL SOLITUDE?
KIKYO...
...ONLY WISHED TO SEE INUYASHA ONE LAST TIME...
I'M SURE EVEN NARAKU...
...STARTED OUT WITH SOME SMALL PERSONAL DESIRE...

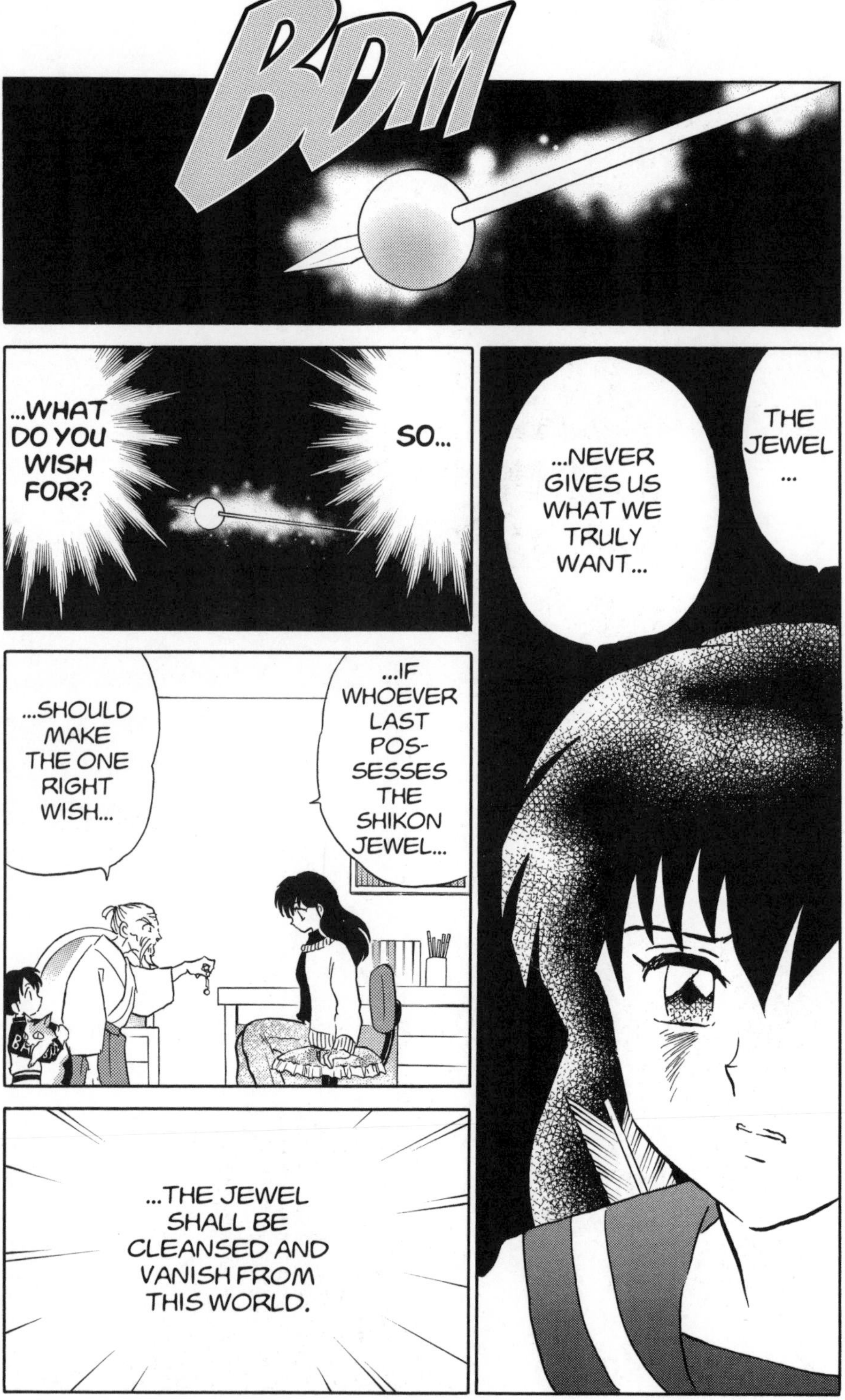
BDM
THE JEWEL...
...NEVER GIVES US WHAT WE TRULY WANT...
SO...
...WHAT DO YOU WISH FOR?
...IF WHOEVER LAST POS-SESSES THE SHIKON JEWEL...
...SHOULD MAKE THE ONE RIGHT WISH...
...THE JEWEL SHALL BE CLEANSED AND VANISH FROM THIS WORLD.

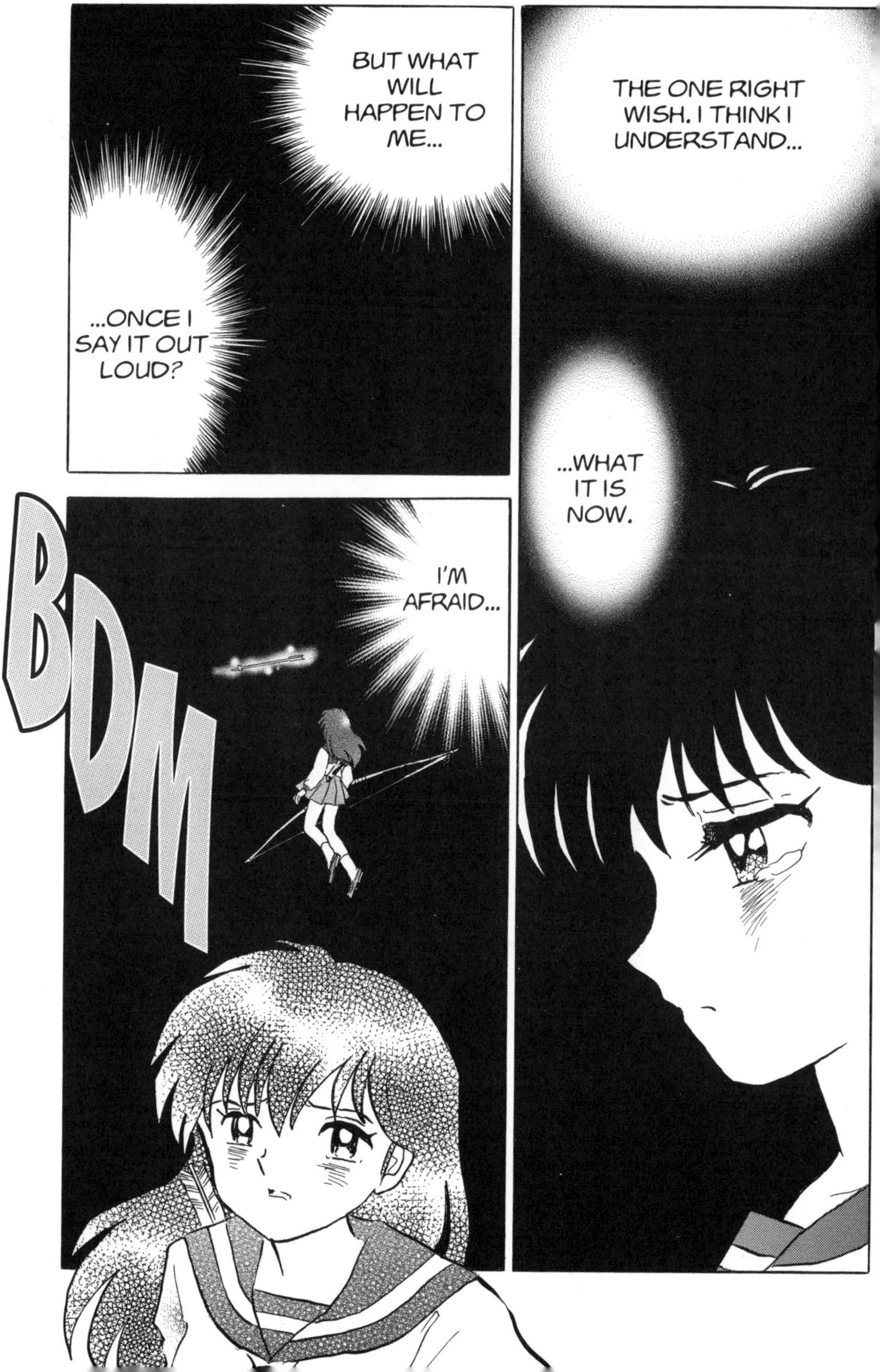

THE ONE RIGHT WISH. I THINK I UNDERSTAND...
...WHAT IT IS NOW.
BUT WHAT WILL HAPPEN TO ME...
...ONCE I SAY IT OUT LOUD?
I'M AFRAID...
BDM

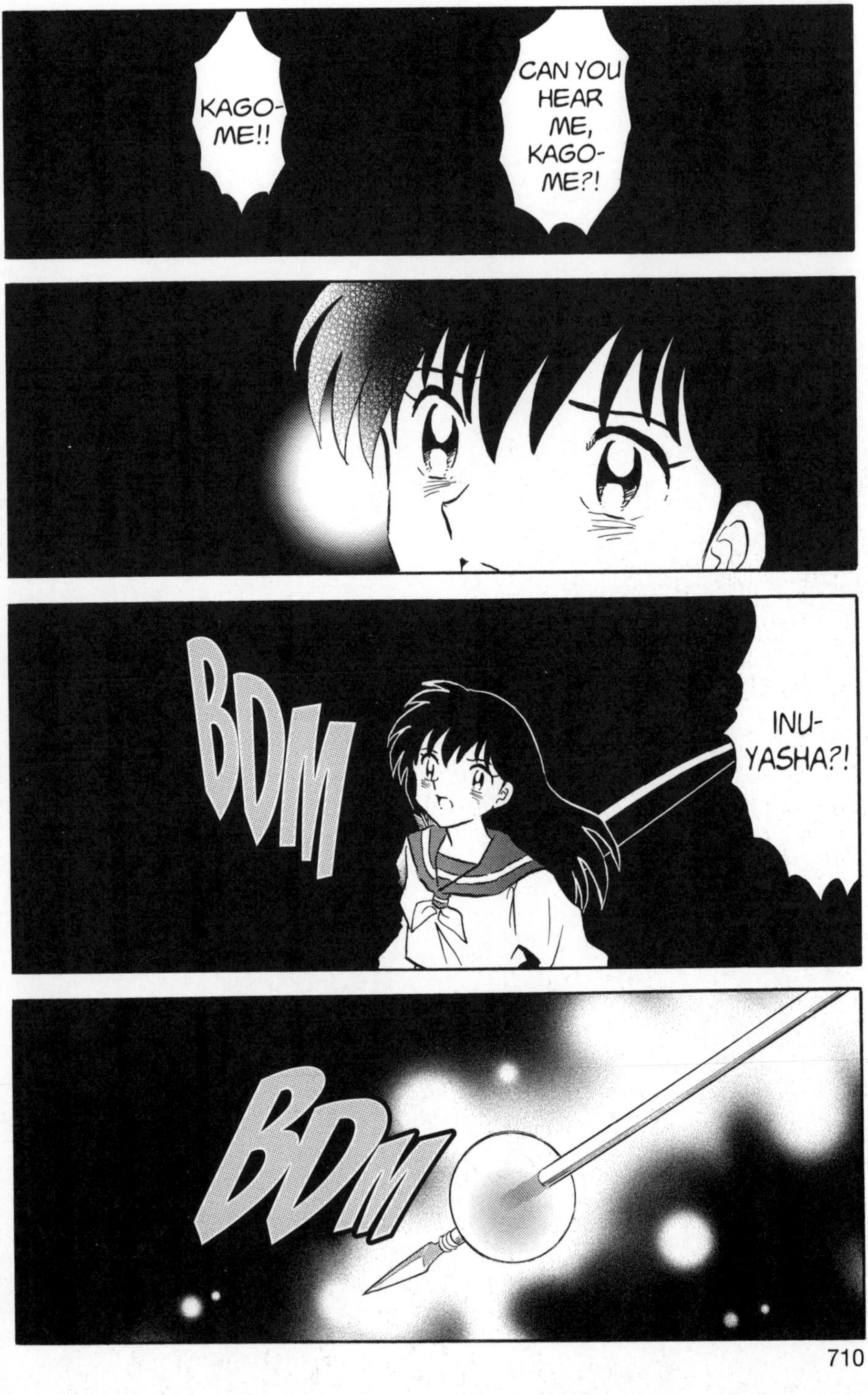
CAN YOU HEAR ME, KAGO-ME?!
KAGO-ME!!
INU-YASHA?!
BDM
BDM

SCROLL NINE
I WANT TO SEE YOU

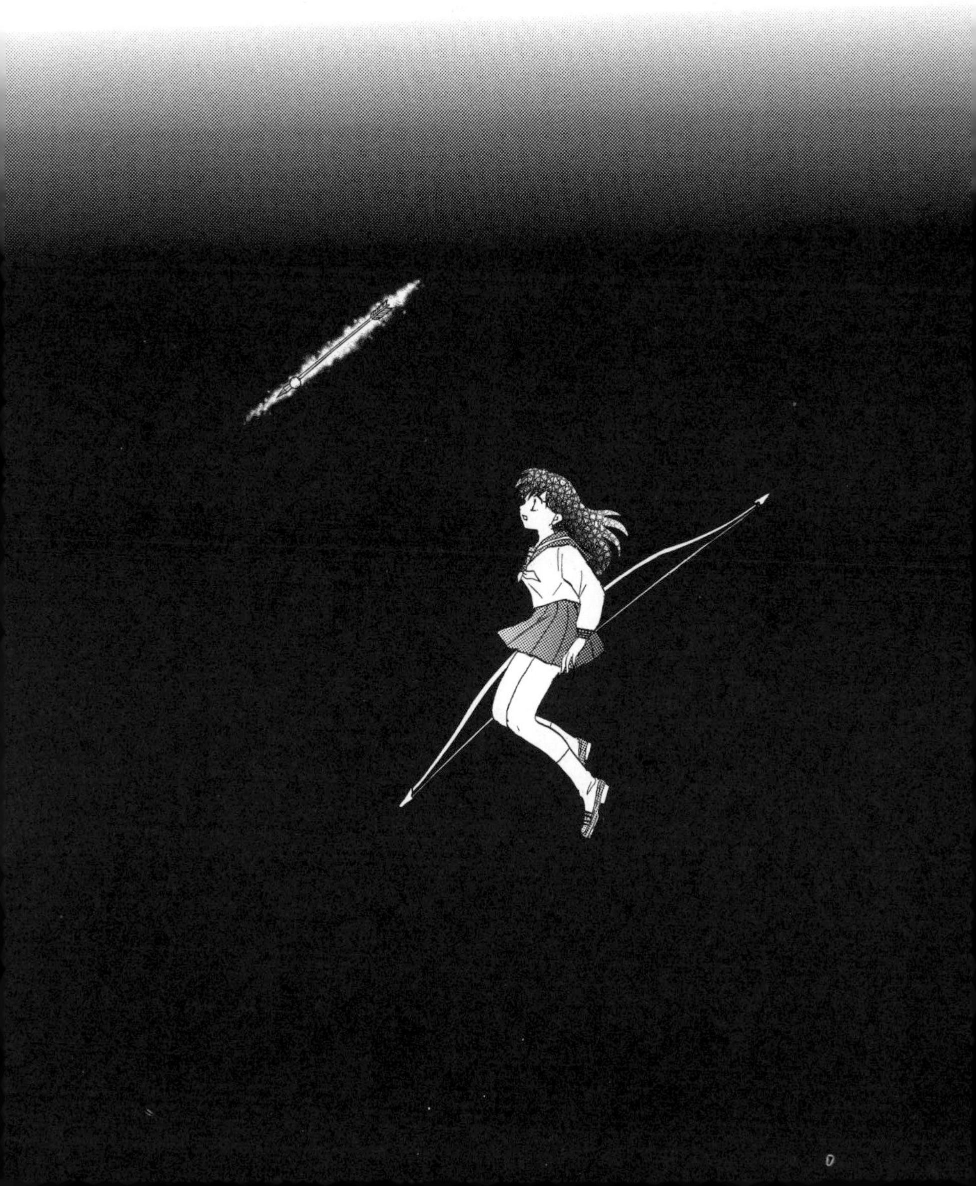

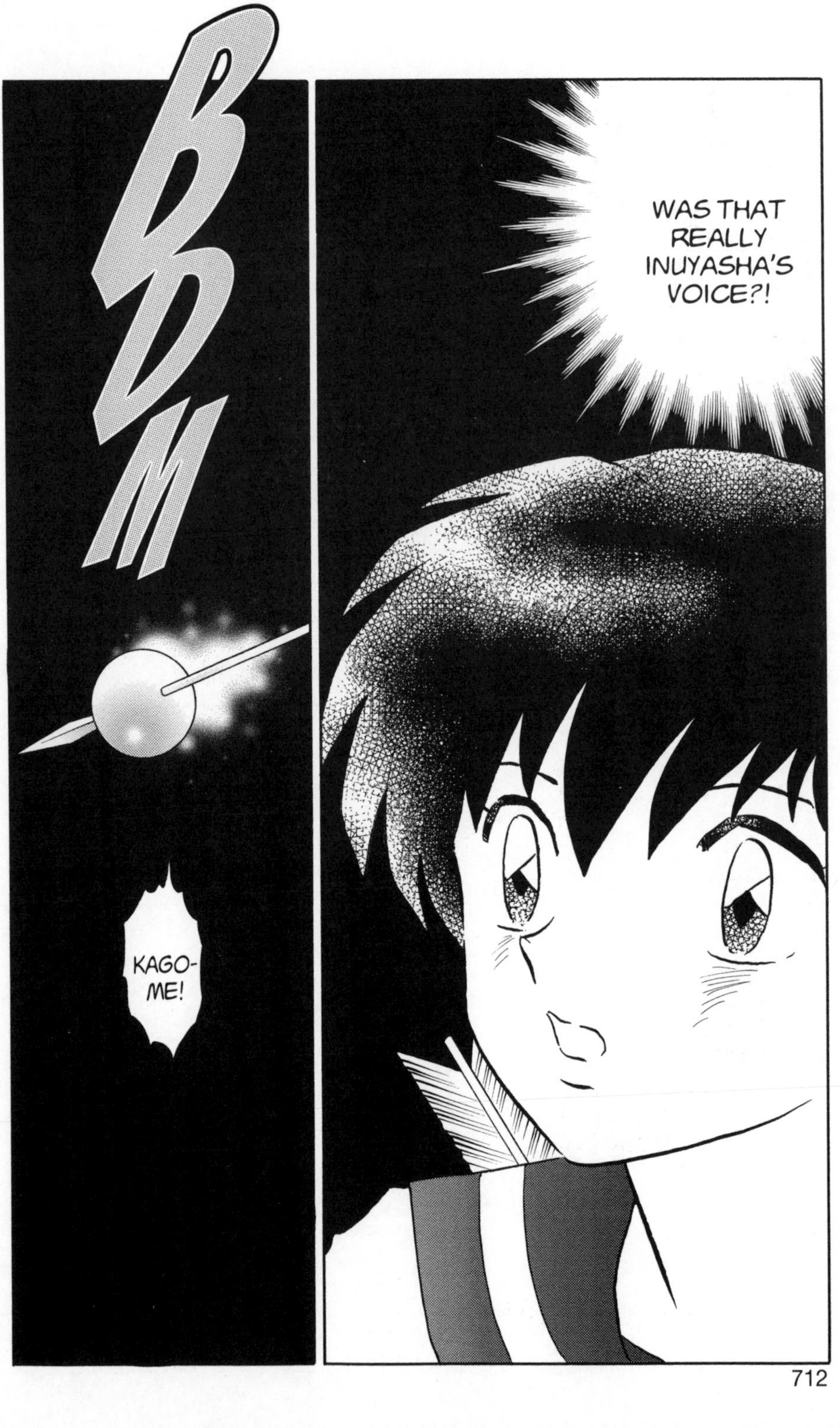
WAS THAT REALLY INUYASHA'S VOICE?!
BDM
KAGO-ME!

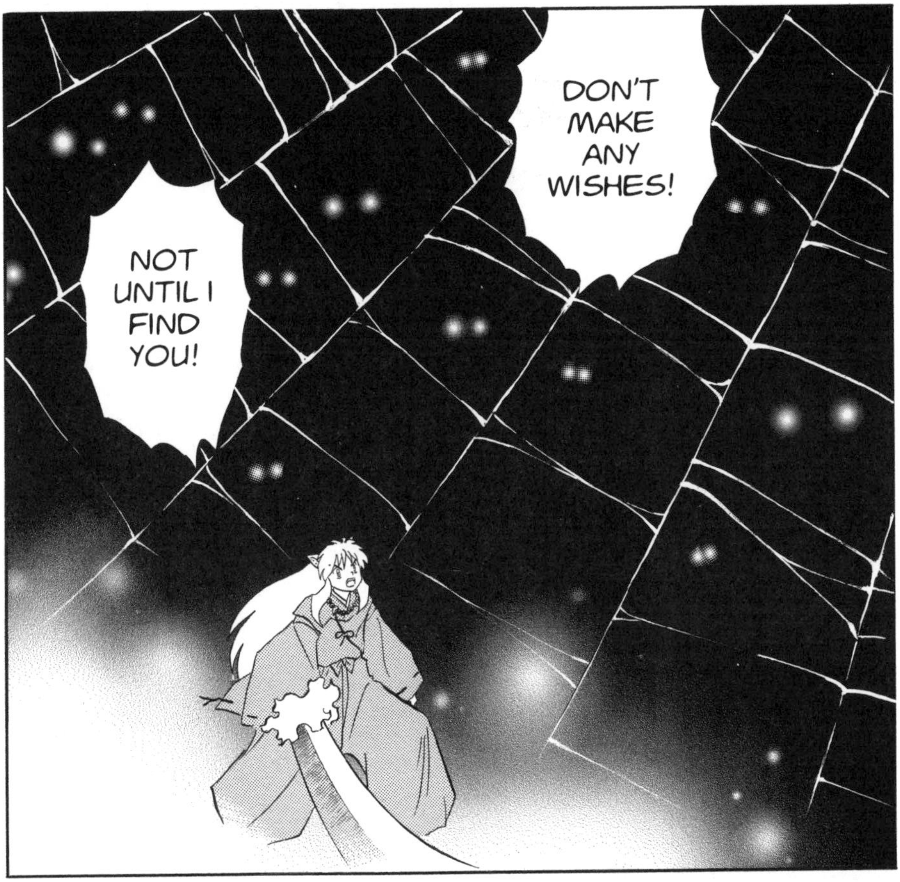
DON'T MAKE ANY WISHES!
NOT UNTIL I FIND YOU!

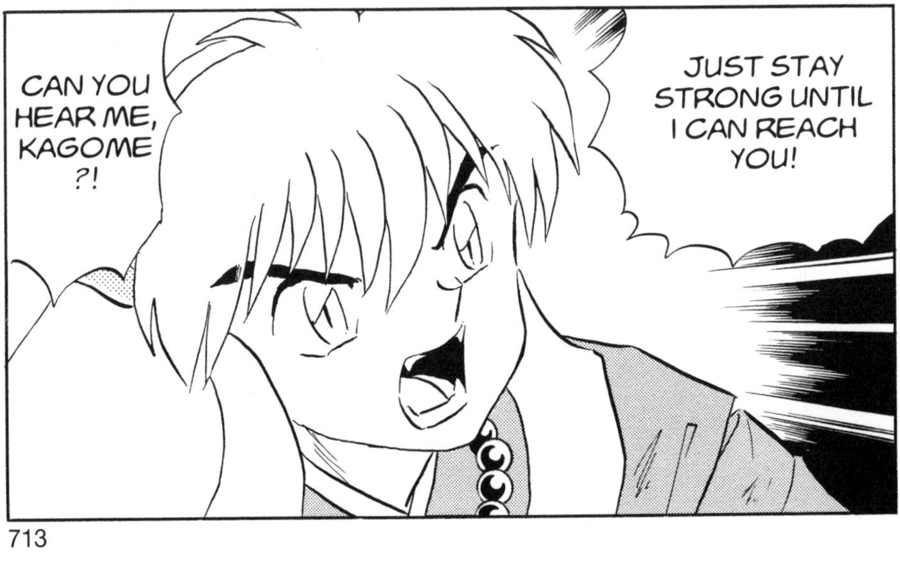
JUST STAY STRONG UNTIL I CAN REACH YOU!
CAN YOU HEAR ME, KAGOME ?!

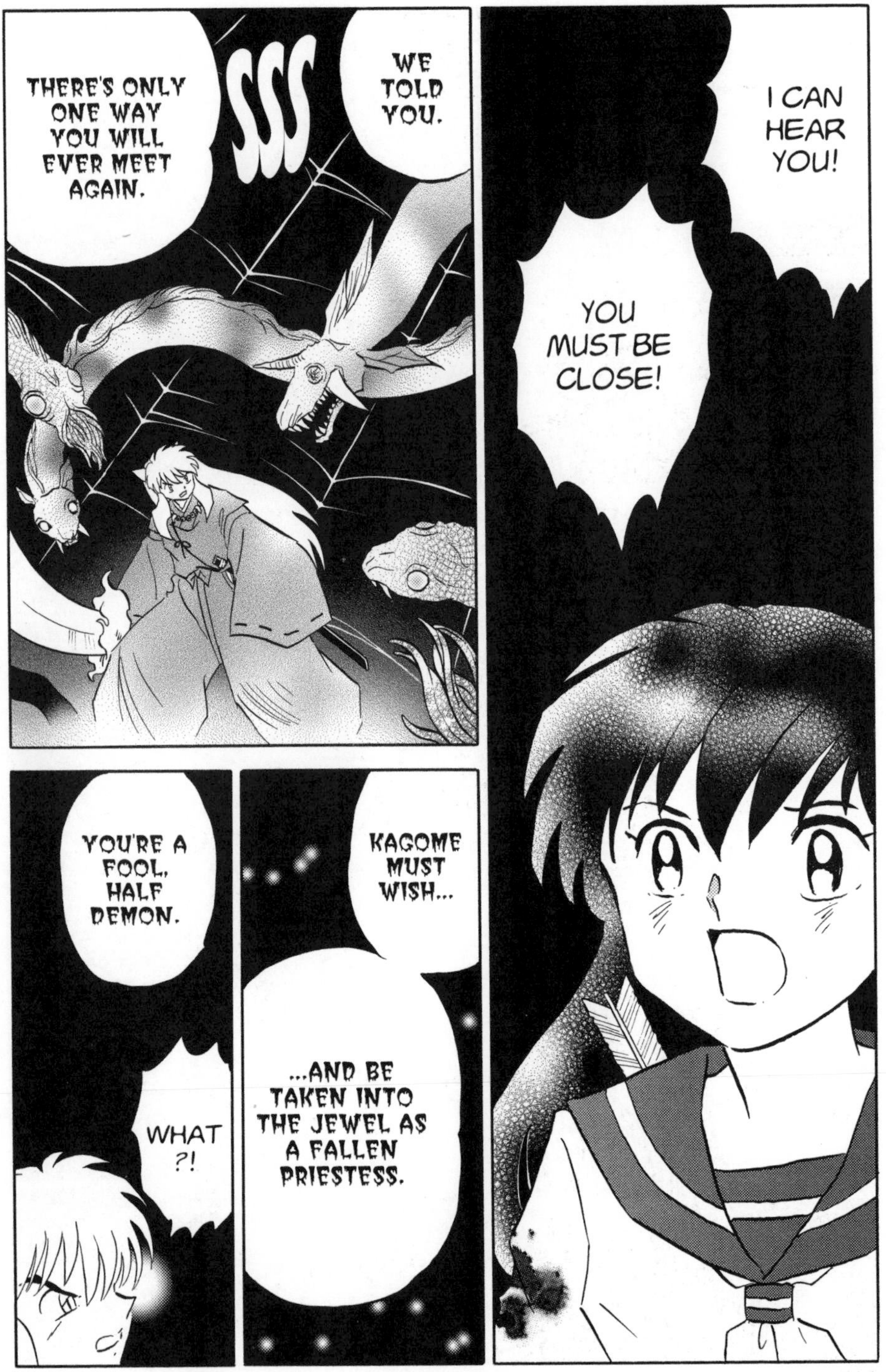
I CAN HEAR YOU!
YOU MUST BE CLOSE!
WE TOLD YOU.
SSS
THERE'S ONLY ONE WAY YOU WILL EVER MEET AGAIN.
KAGOME MUST WISH...
...AND BE TAKEN INTO THE JEWEL AS A FALLEN PRIESTESS.
YOU'RE A FOOL, HALF DEMON.
WHAT ?!

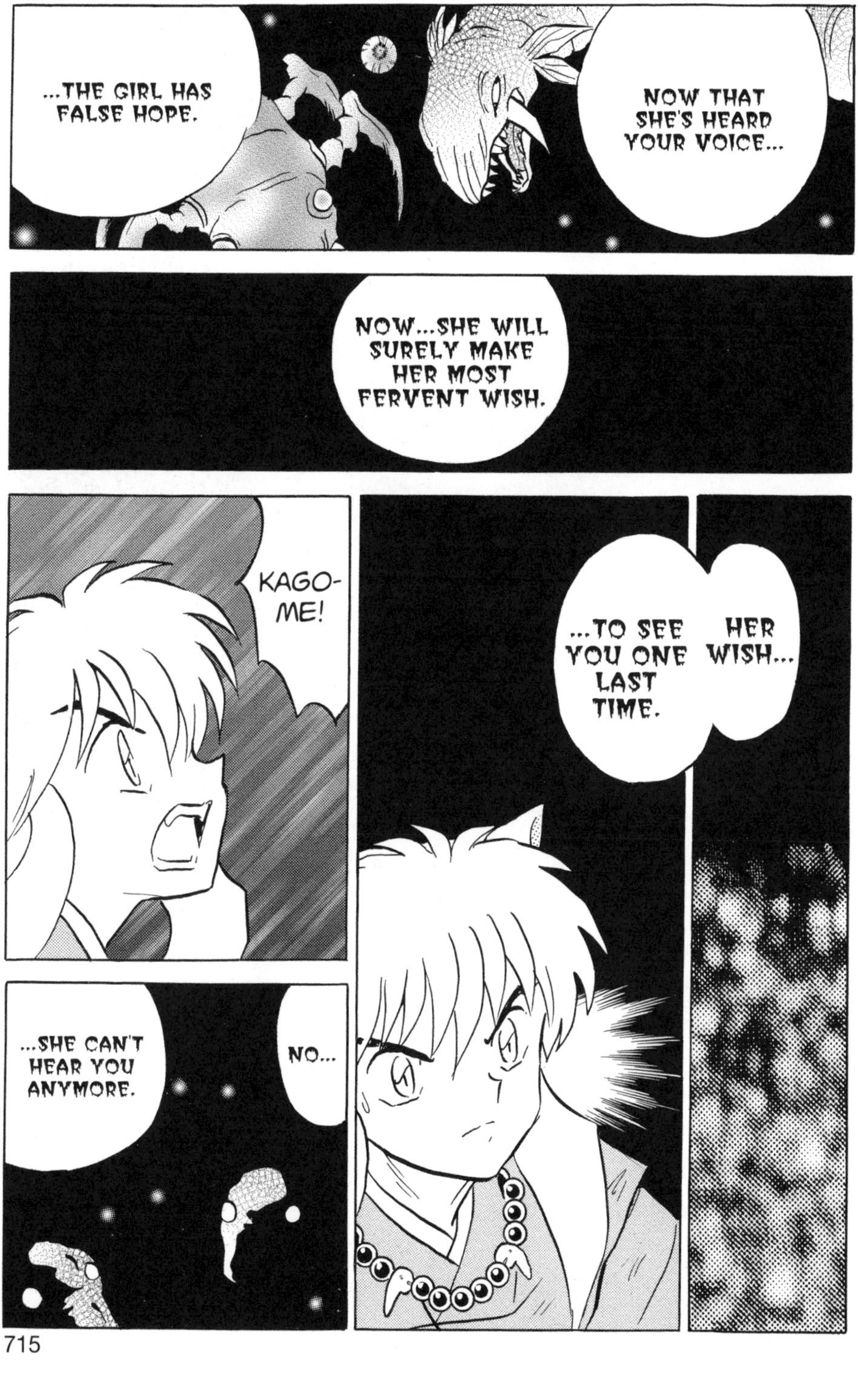
NOW THAT SHE'S HEARD YOUR VOICE...
...THE GIRL HAS FALSE HOPE.
NOW...SHE WILL SURELY MAKE HER MOST FERVENT WISH.
HER WISH...
...TO SEE YOU ONE LAST TIME.
KAGO-ME!
NO...
...SHE CAN'T HEAR YOU ANYMORE.

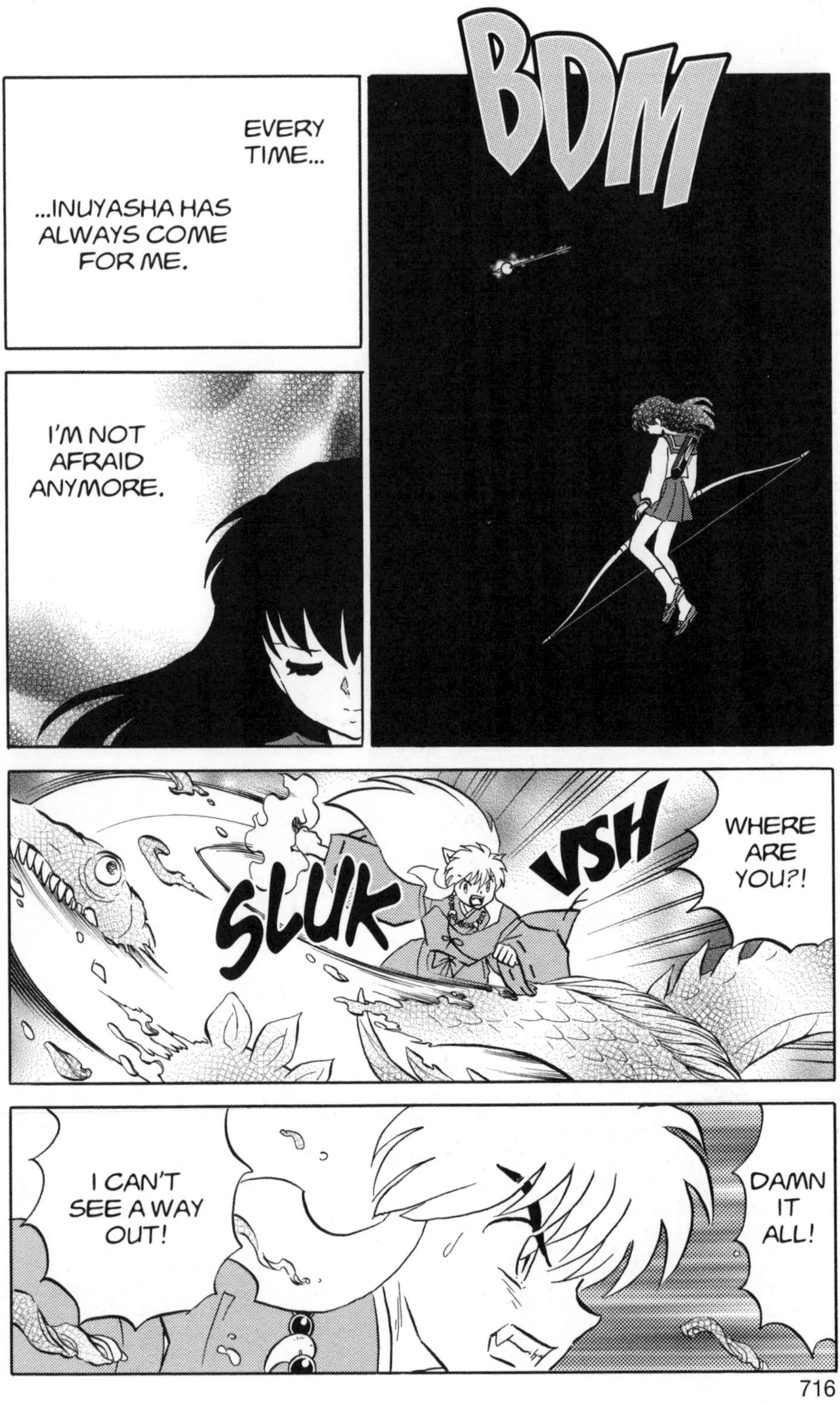
BDM
EVERY TIME...
...INUYASHA HAS ALWAYS COME FOR ME.
I'M NOT AFRAID ANYMORE.
WHERE ARE YOU?!
VSH
SLUK
DAMN IT ALL!
I CAN'T SEE A WAY OUT!

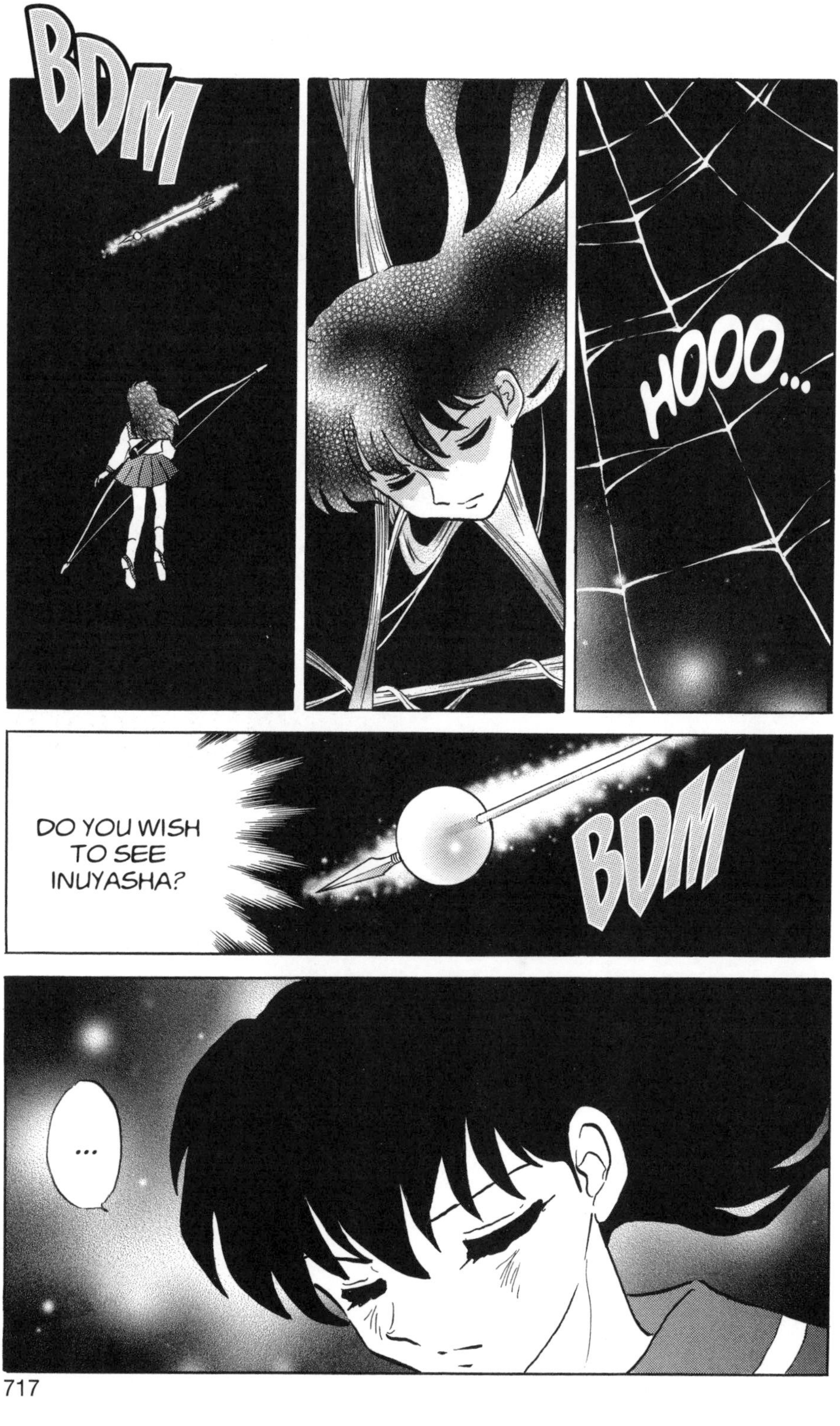
HOOO...
BDM
BDM
DO YOU WISH TO SEE INUYASHA?
...

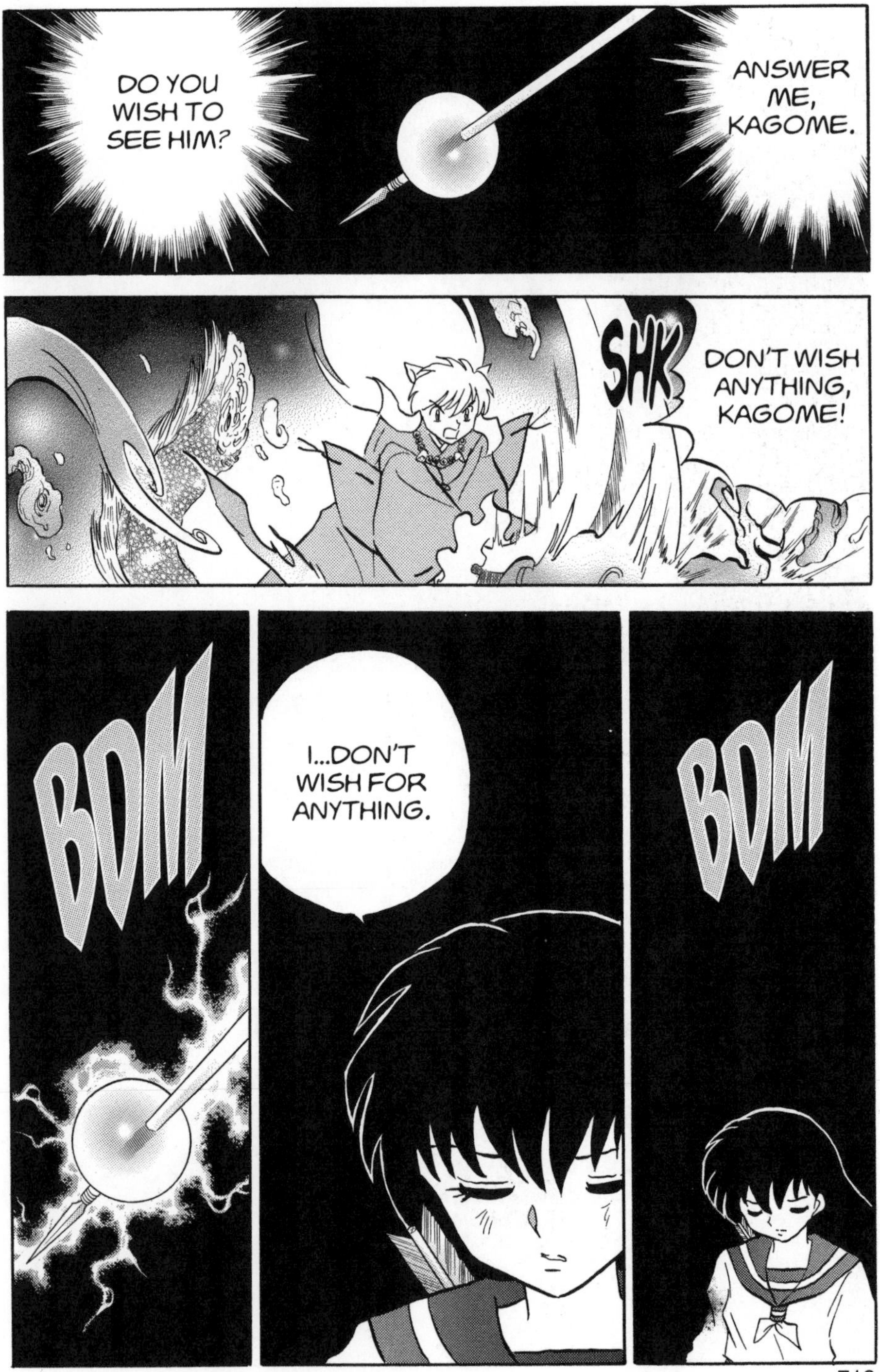
ANSWER ME, KAGOME.
DO YOU WISH TO SEE HIM?
SHK
DON'T WISH ANYTHING, KAGOME!
BOM
I...DON'T WISH FOR ANYTHING.
BOM

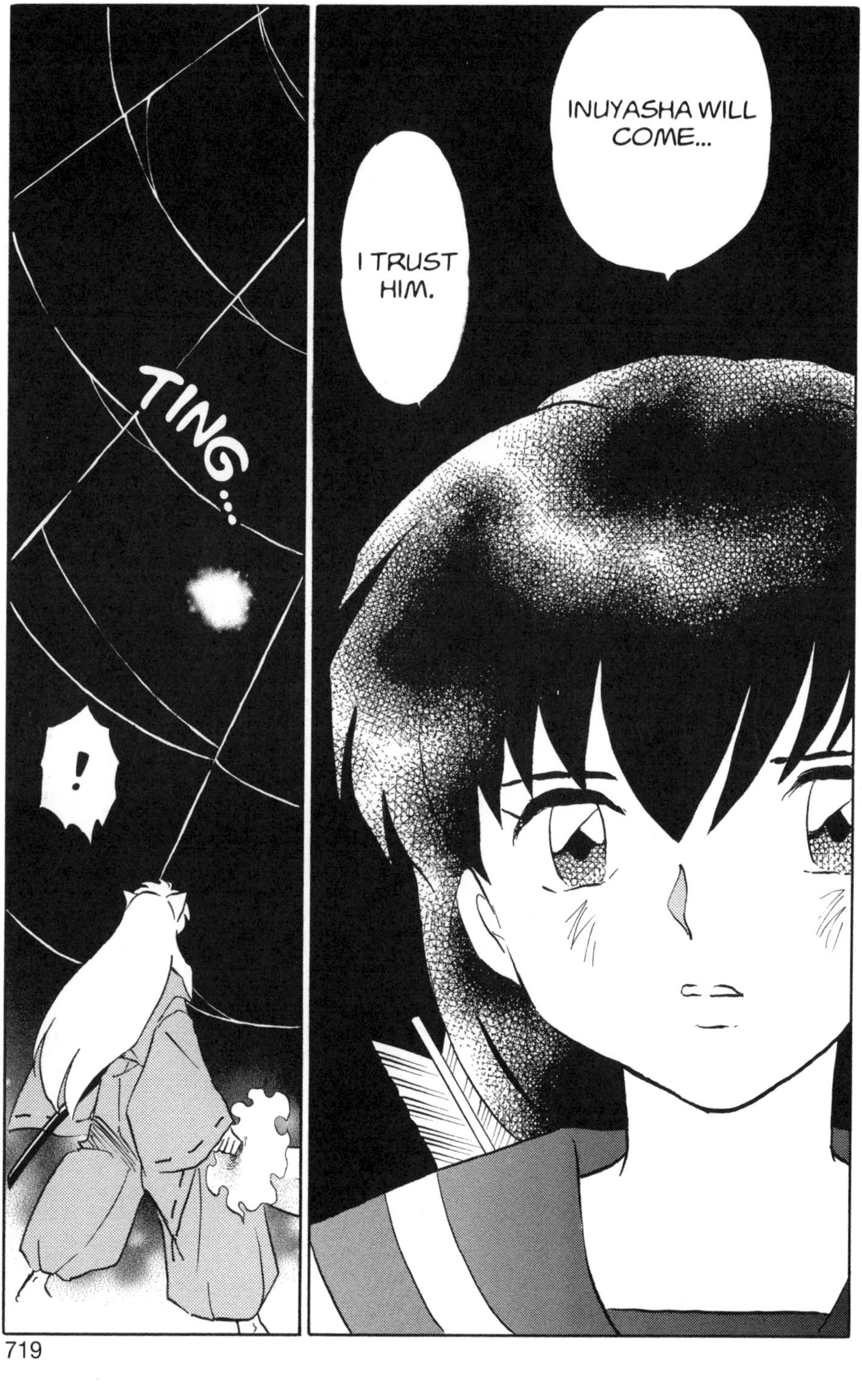
INUYASHA WILL COME...
I TRUST HIM.
TING...
!

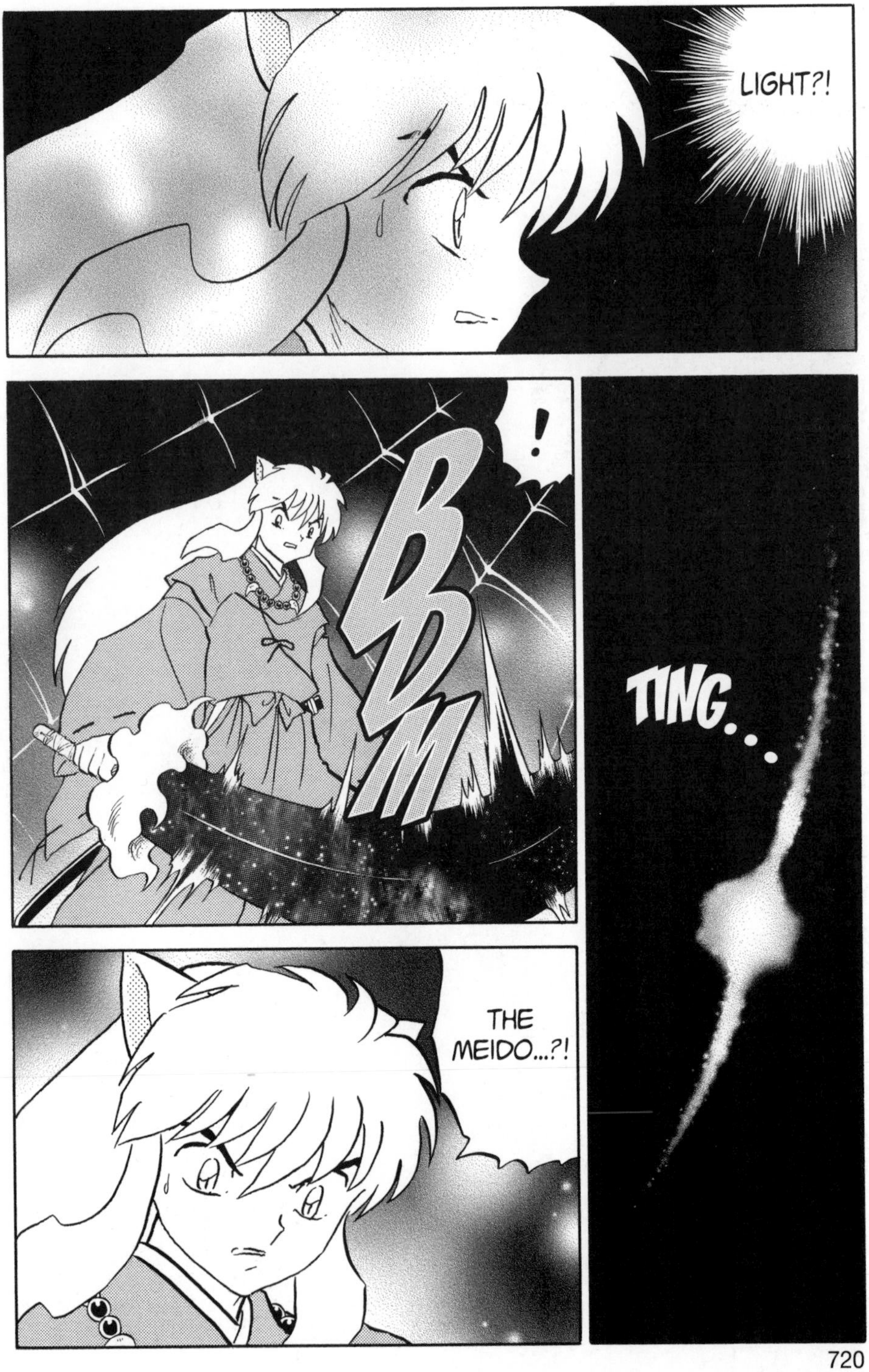
LIGHT?!
TING...
!
BVM
THE MEIDO...?!

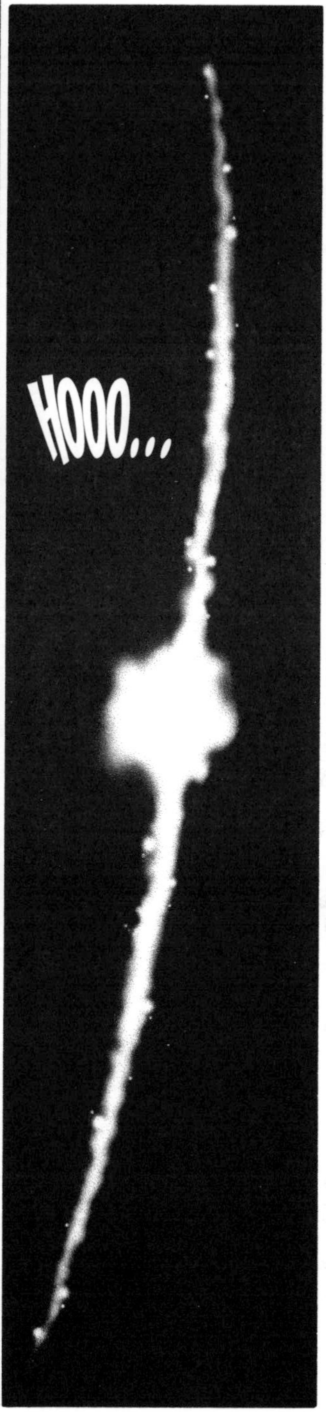
HOOO...

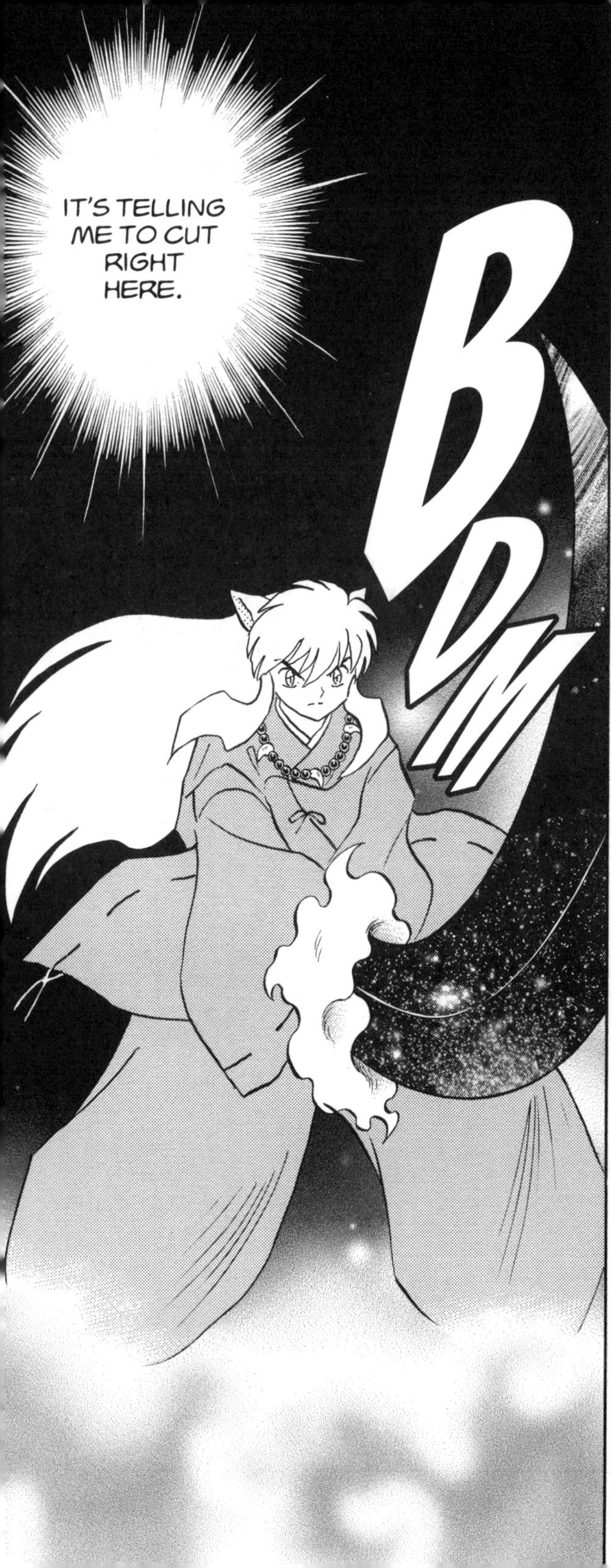
BDM
IT'S TELLING ME TO CUT RIGHT HERE.

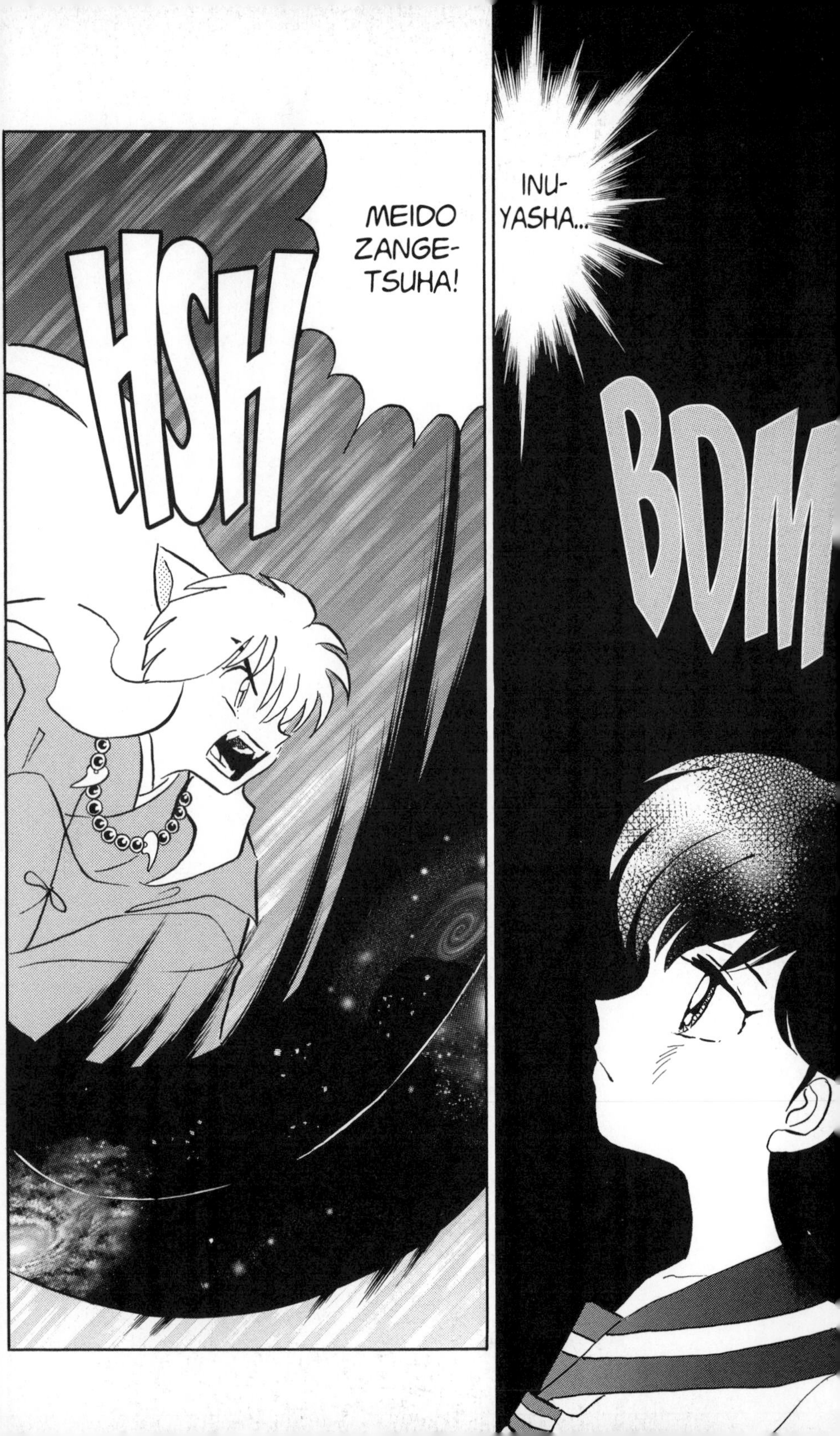
INU-YASHA...
BDM
MEIDO ZANGE-TSUHA!
HSH

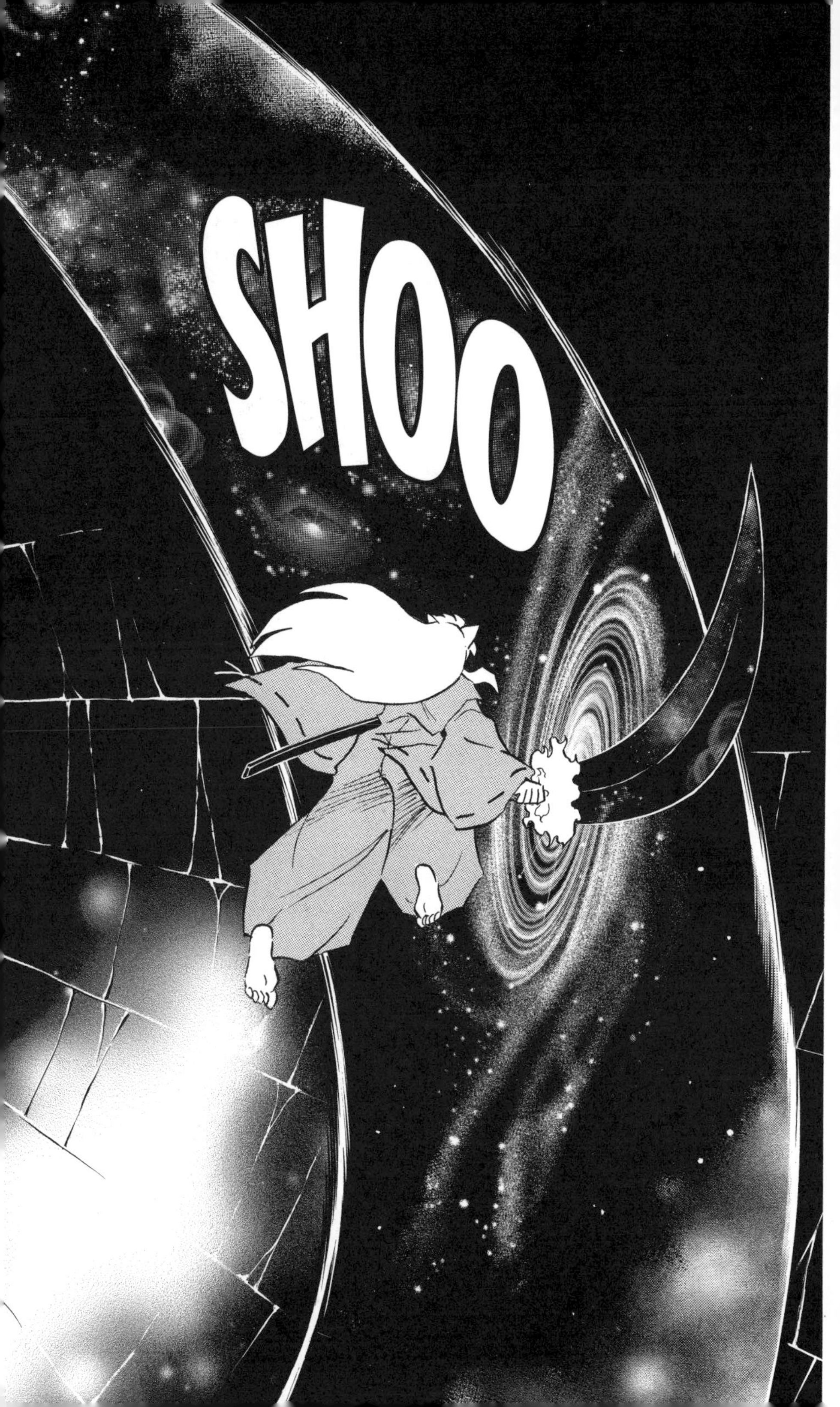
SHOO

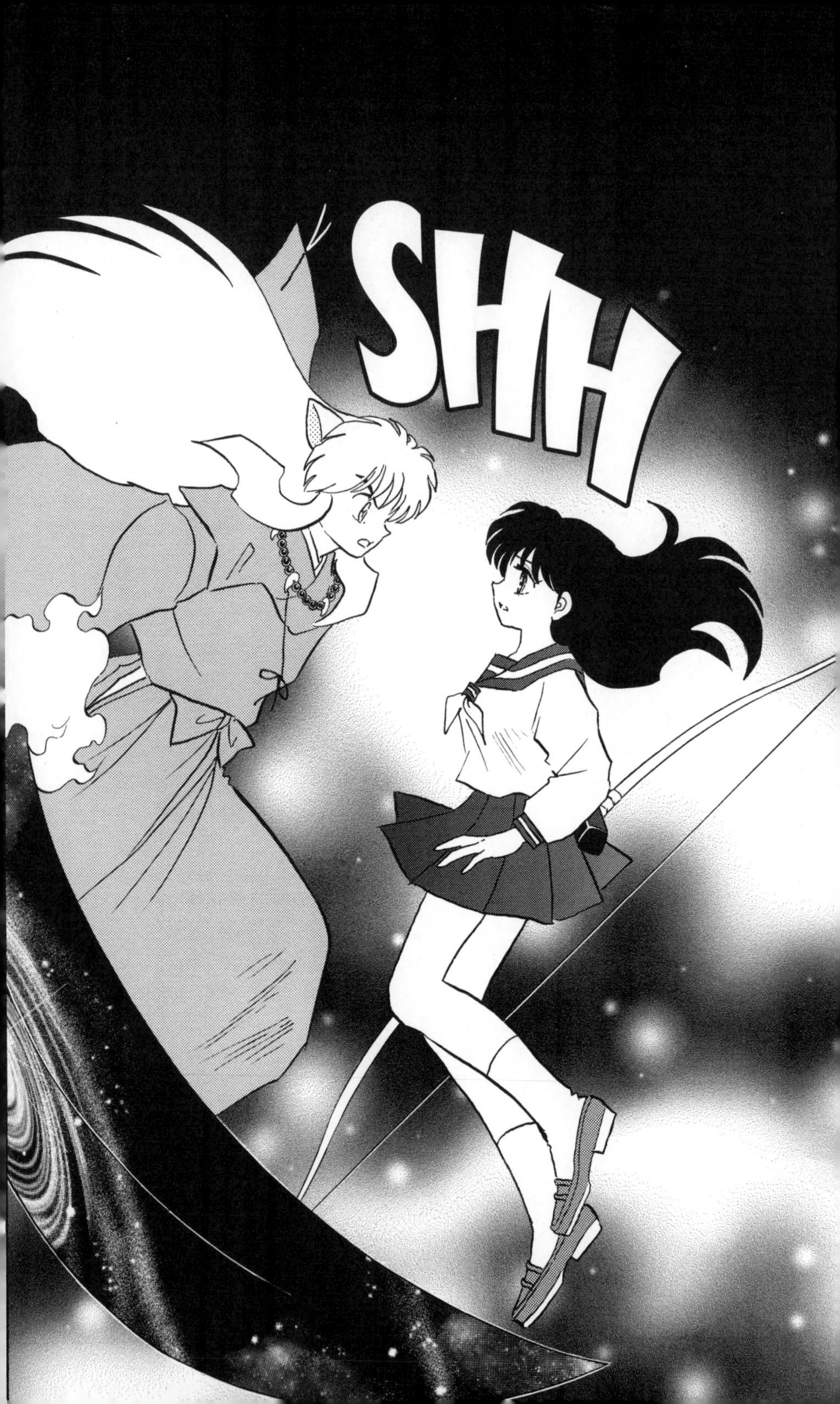
SHH

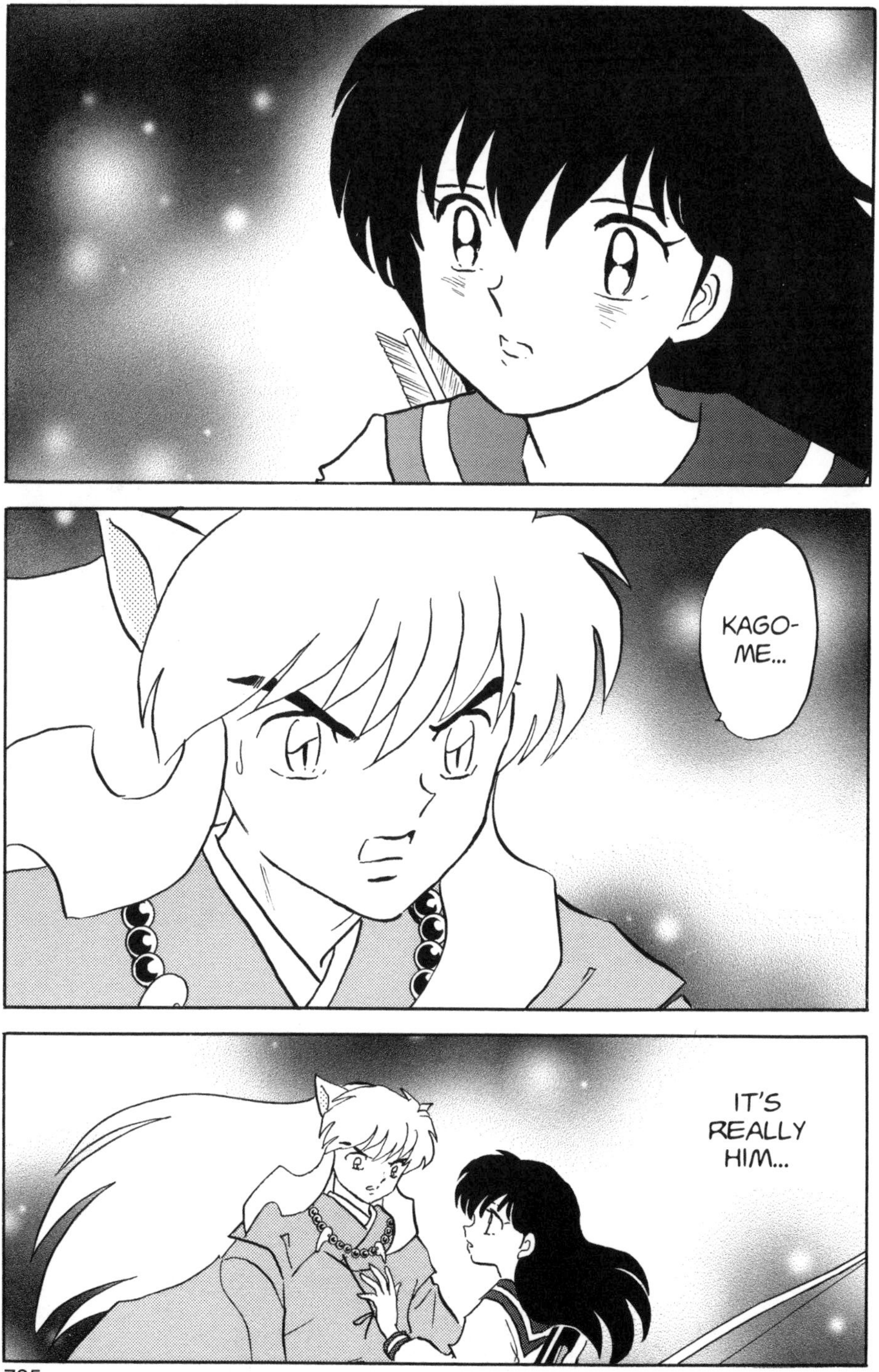
KAGO-
ME...
IT'S
REALLY
HIM...

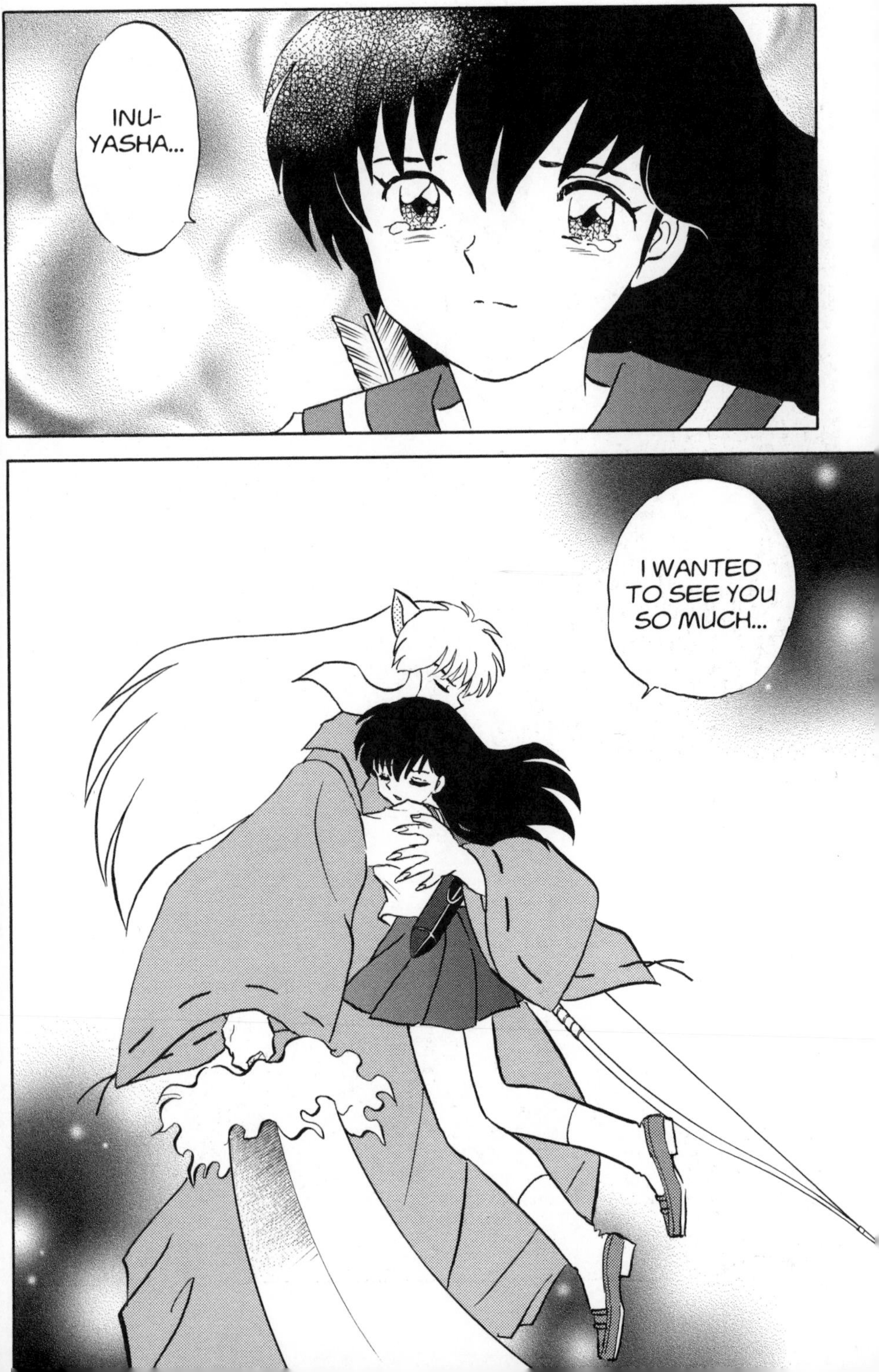
INU-
YASHA...
I WANTED TO SEE YOU SO MUCH...

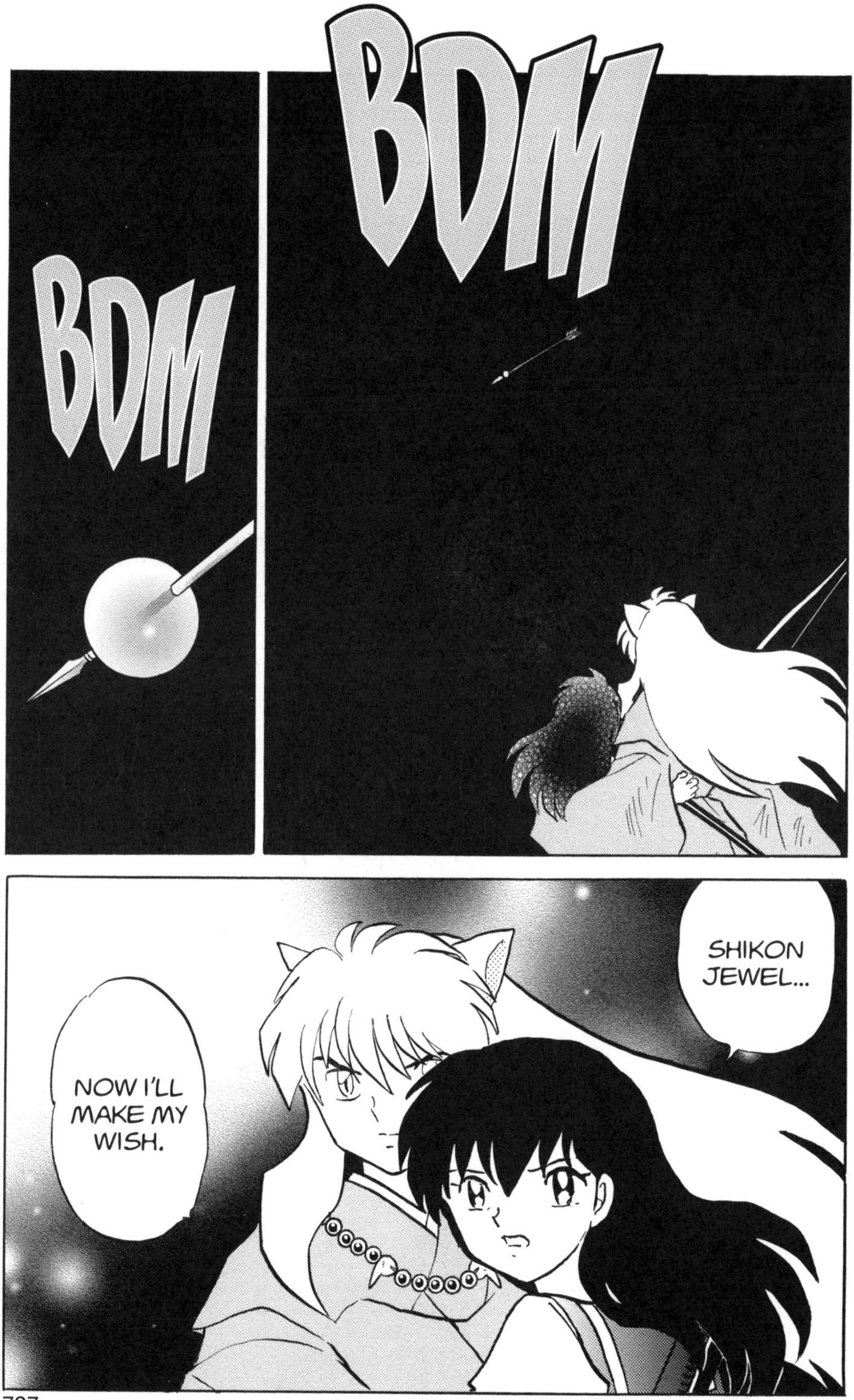
BDM
BDM
SHIKON JEWEL...
NOW I'LL MAKE MY WISH.

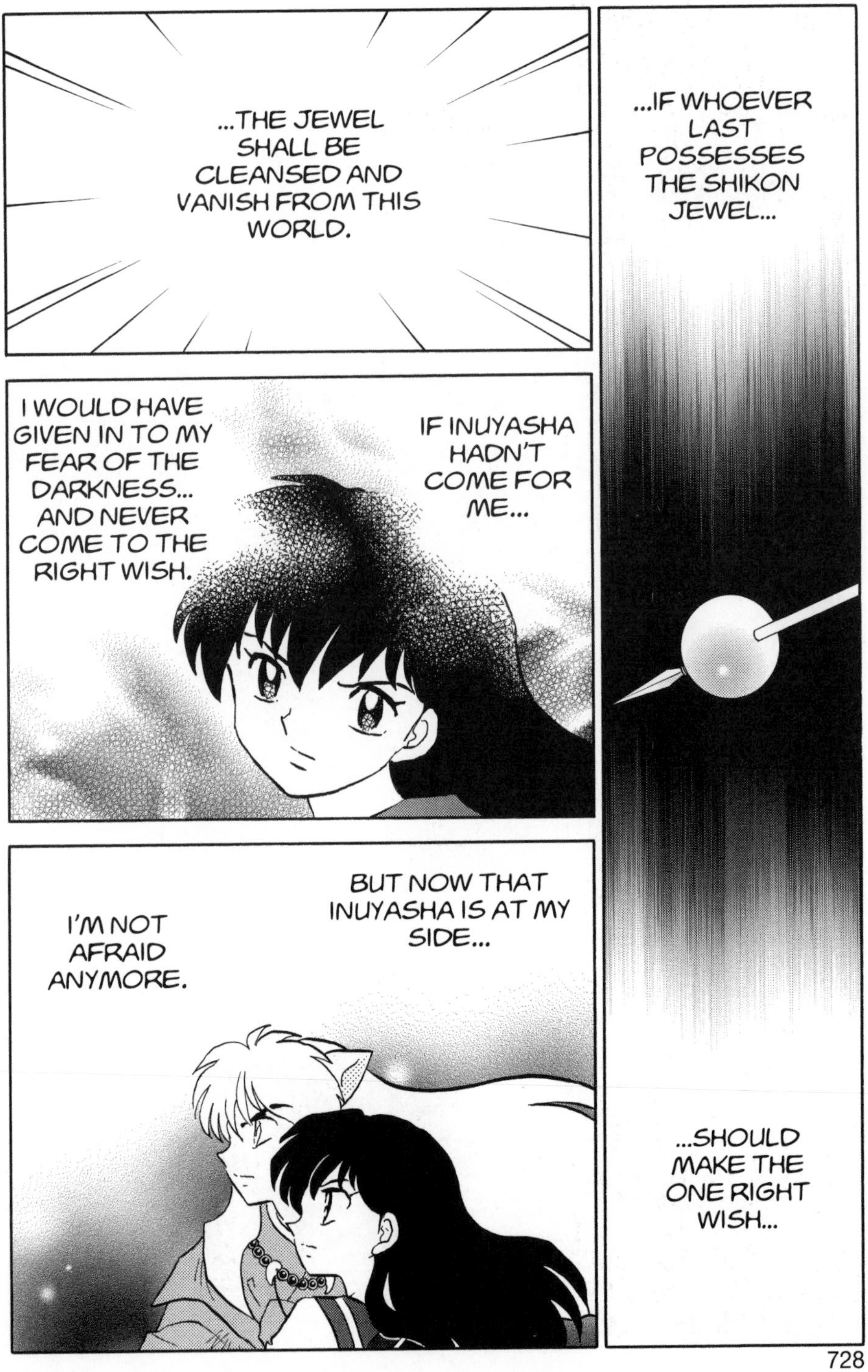
...IF WHOEVER LAST POSSESSES THE SHIKON JEWEL...
...SHOULD MAKE THE ONE RIGHT WISH...
...THE JEWEL SHALL BE CLEANSED AND VANISH FROM THIS WORLD.
IF INUYASHA HADN'T COME FOR ME...
I WOULD HAVE GIVEN IN TO MY FEAR OF THE DARKNESS... AND NEVER COME TO THE RIGHT WISH.
BUT NOW THAT INUYASHA IS AT MY SIDE...
I'M NOT AFRAID ANYMORE.

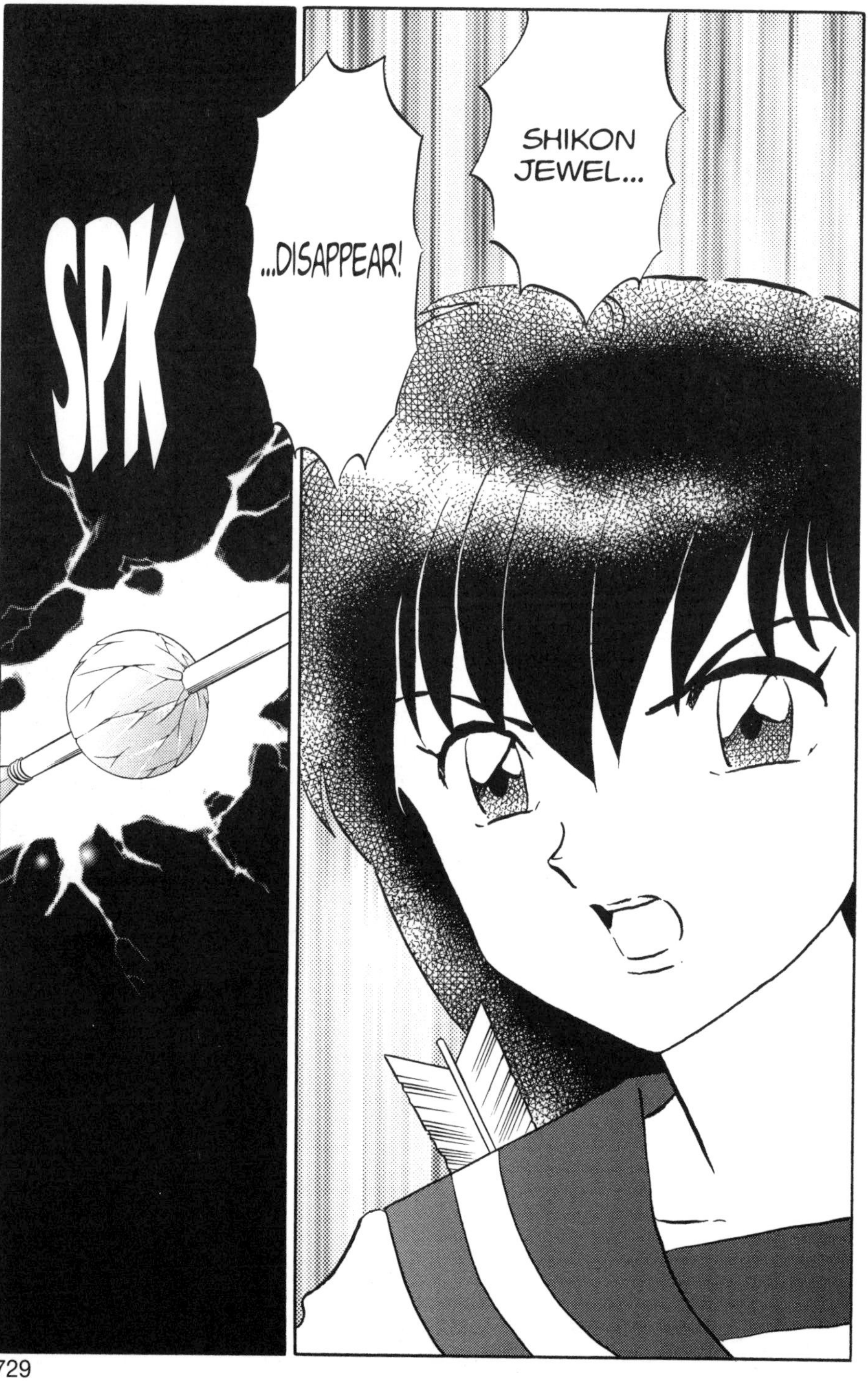
SHIKON JEWEL...
...DISAPPEAR!
SPK

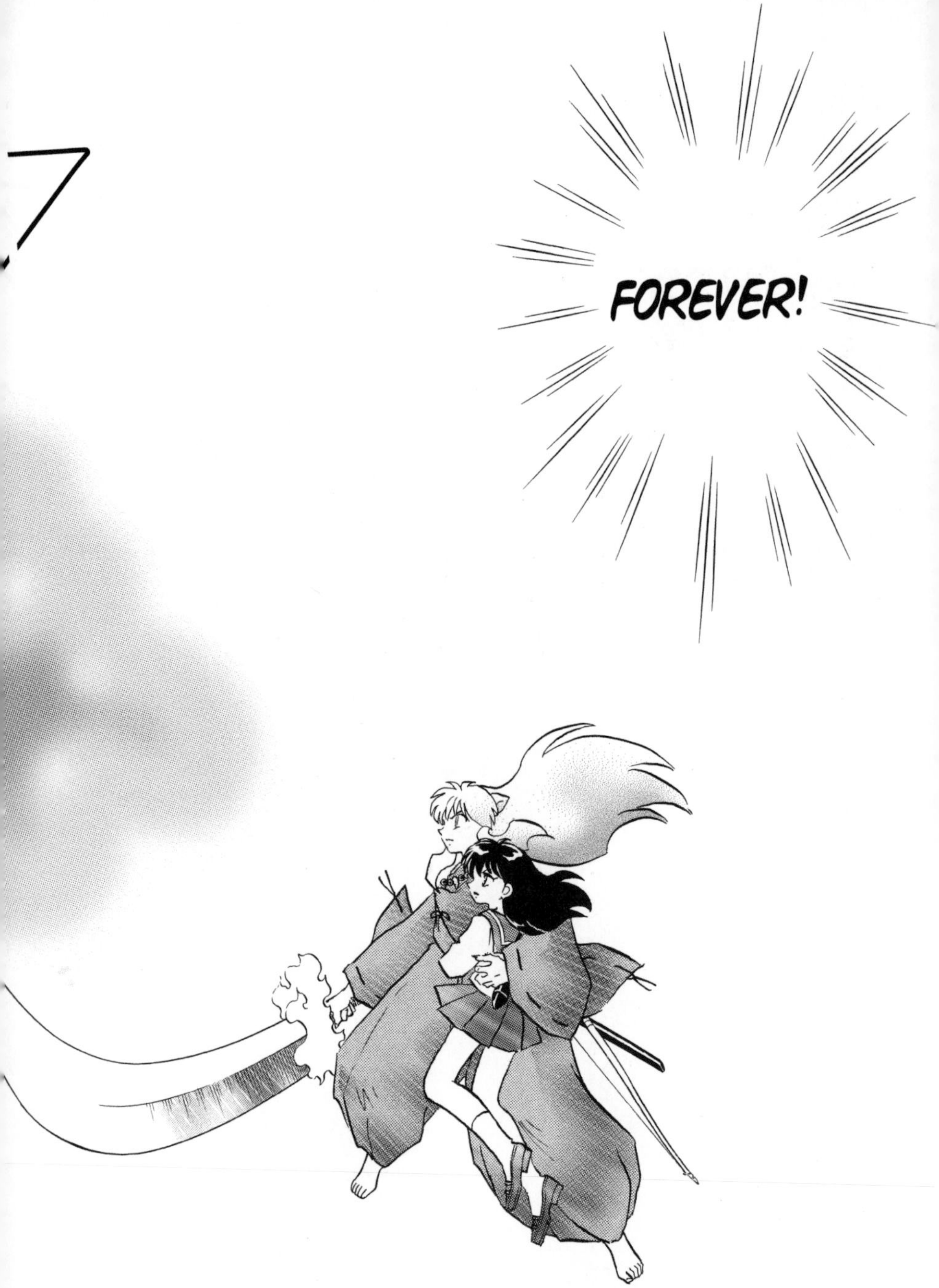
FOREVER!

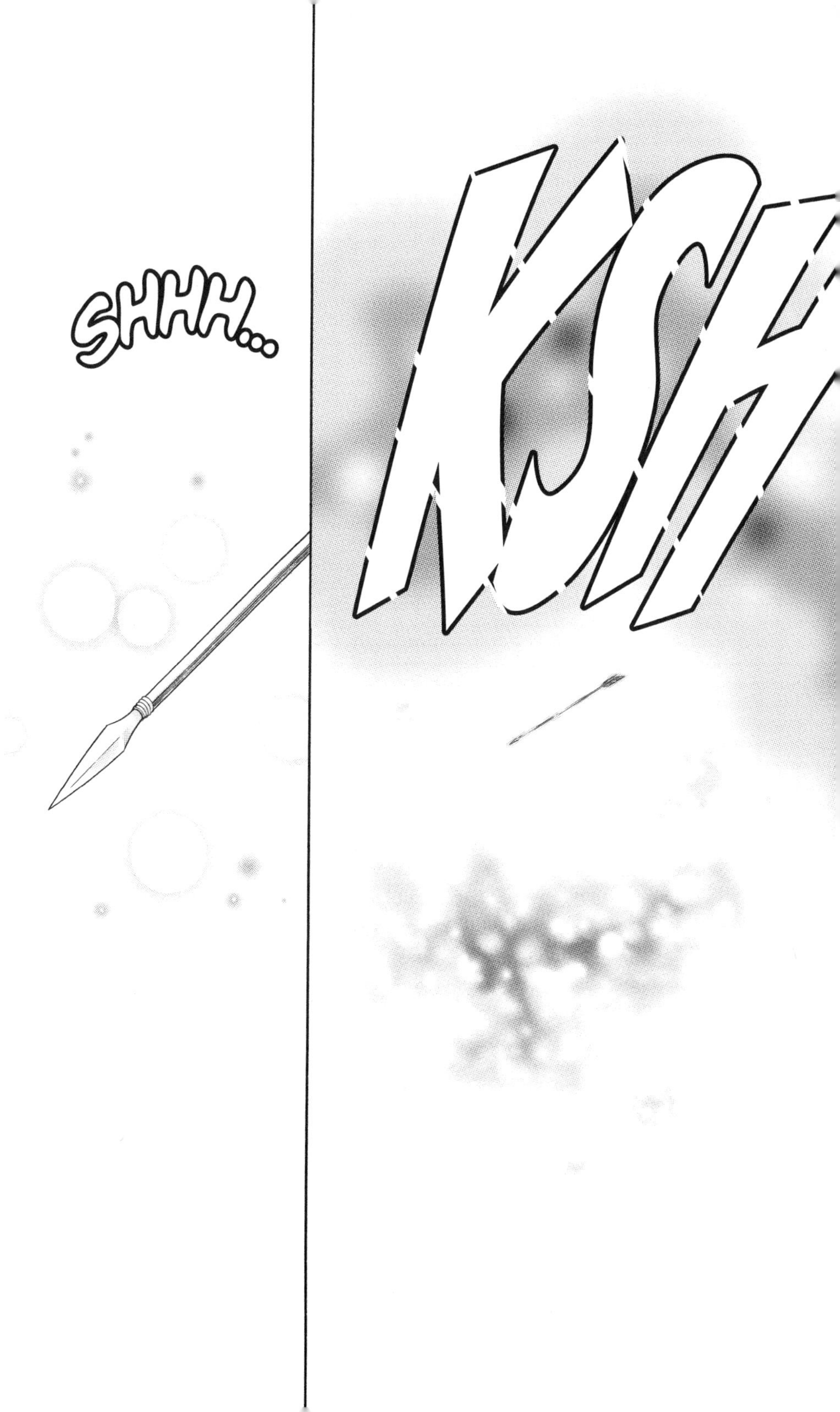
KSH
SHHH...

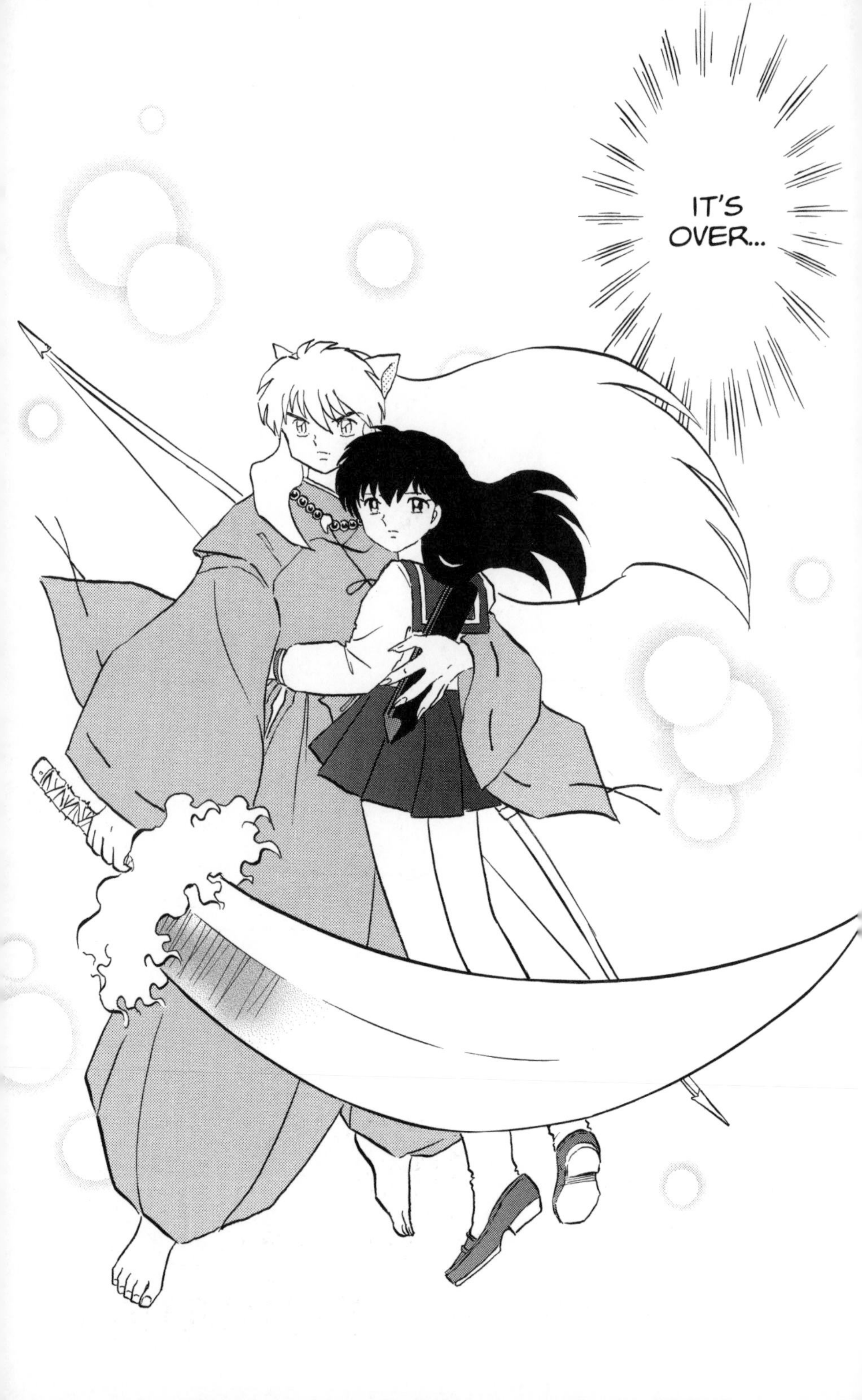
IT'S OVER...

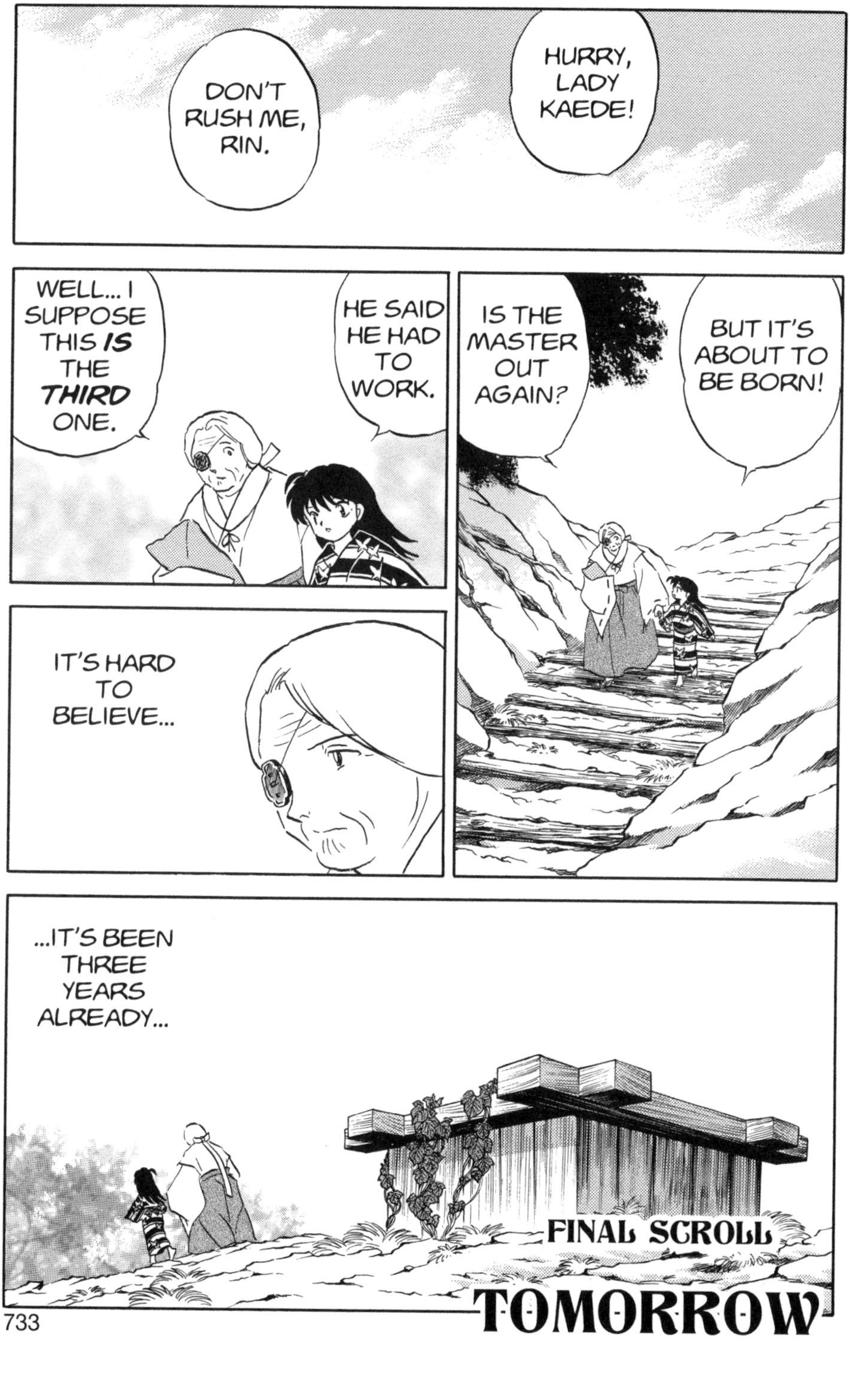
HURRY, LADY KAEDE!
DON'T RUSH ME, RIN.
BUT IT'S ABOUT TO BE BORN!
IS THE MASTER OUT AGAIN?
HE SAID HE HAD TO WORK.
WELL... I SUPPOSE THIS *IS* THE *THIRD* ONE.
IT'S HARD TO BELIEVE...
...IT'S BEEN THREE YEARS ALREADY...
FINAL SCROLL
TOMORROW

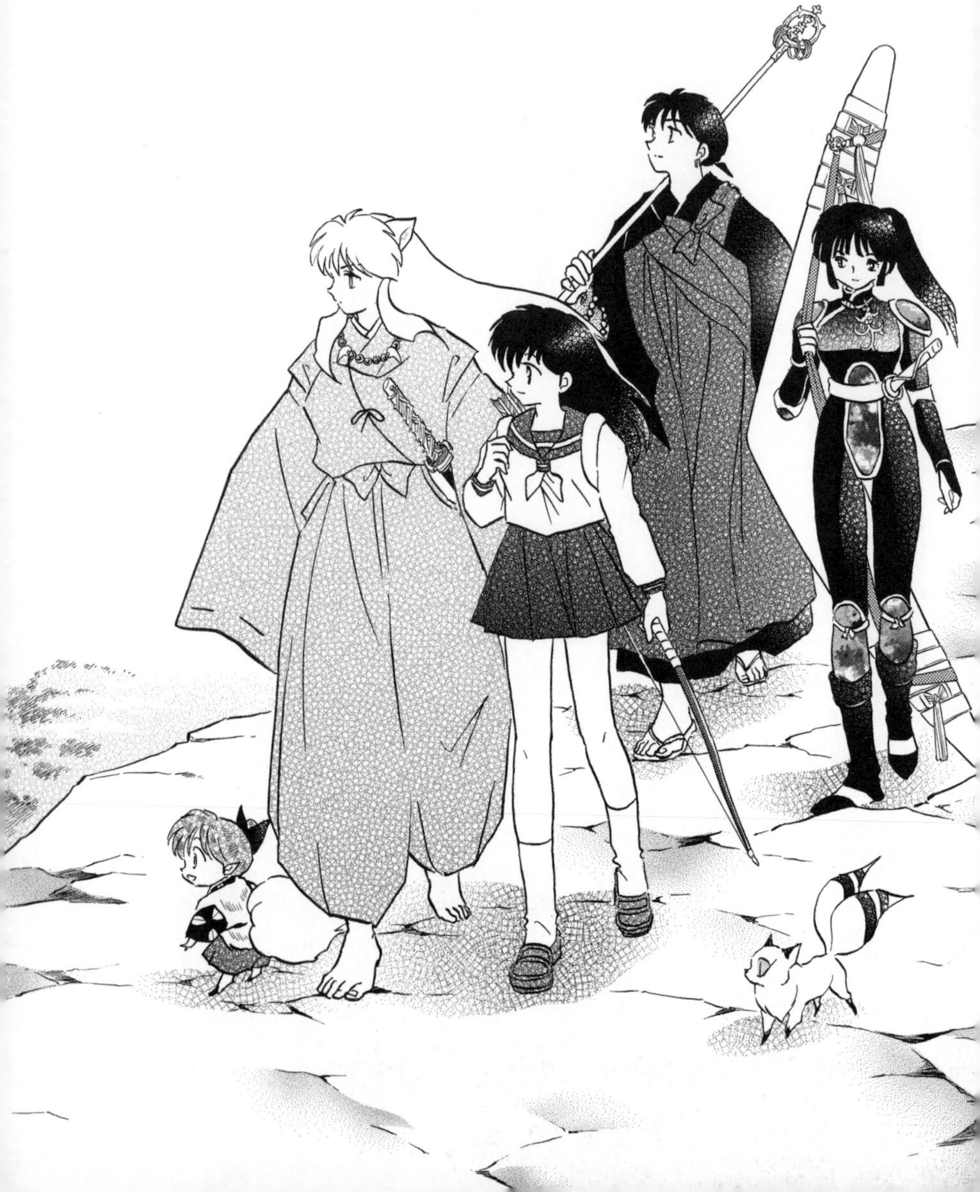

FINAL SCROLL
TOMORROW

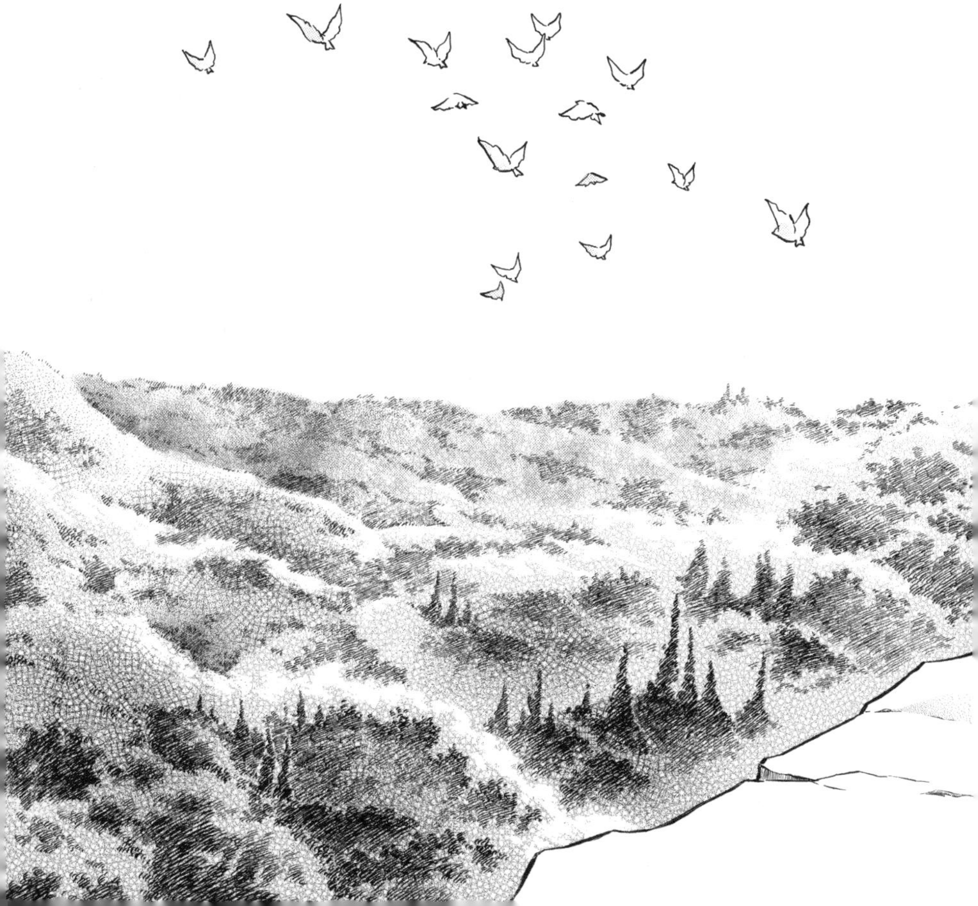

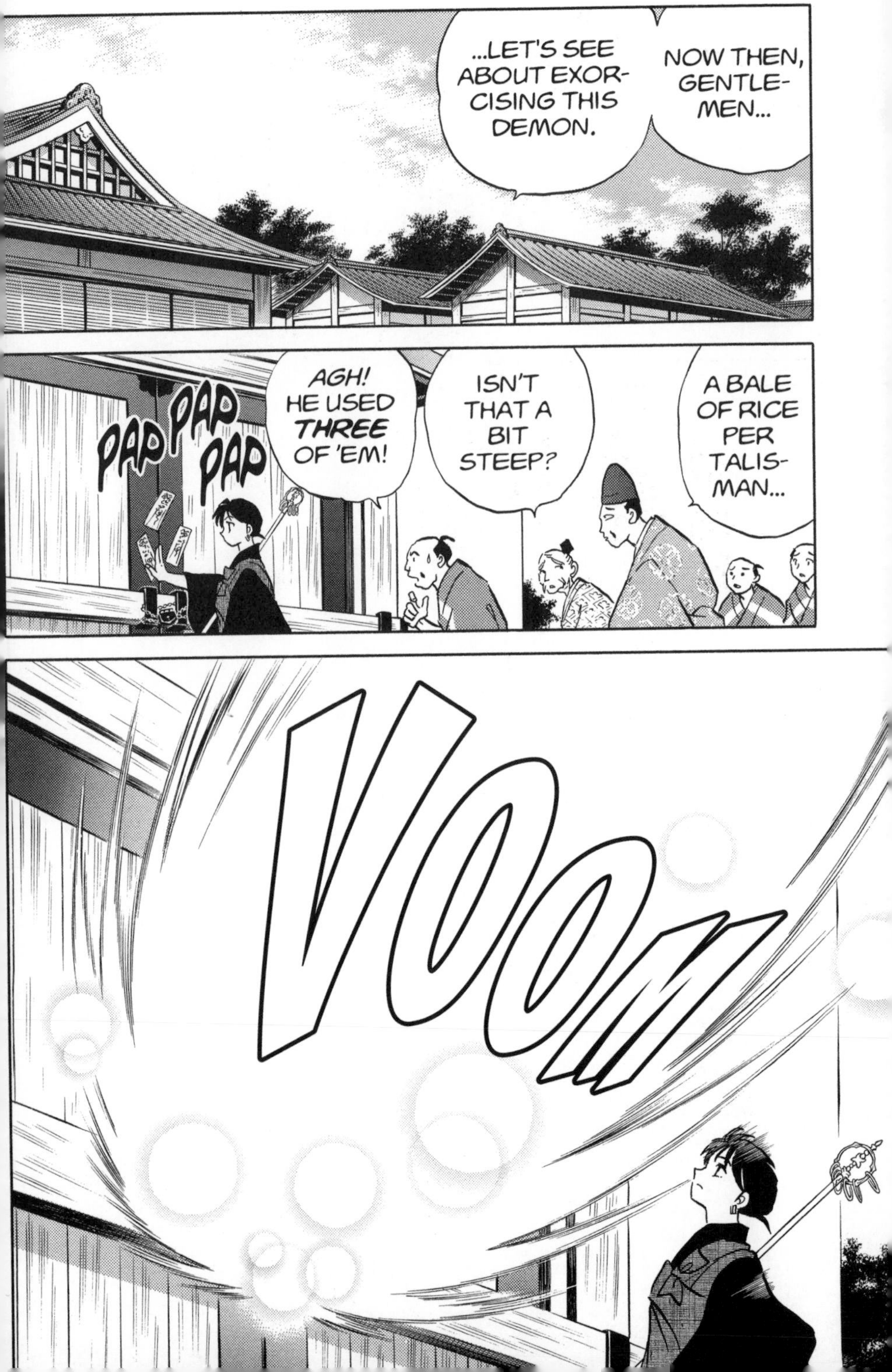
NOW THEN, GENTLE-MEN...
...LET'S SEE ABOUT EXORCISING THIS DEMON.
A BALE OF RICE PER TALIS-MAN...
ISN'T THAT A BIT STEEP?
AGH! HE USED THREE OF 'EM!
PAP PAP PAP PAP
VOOM

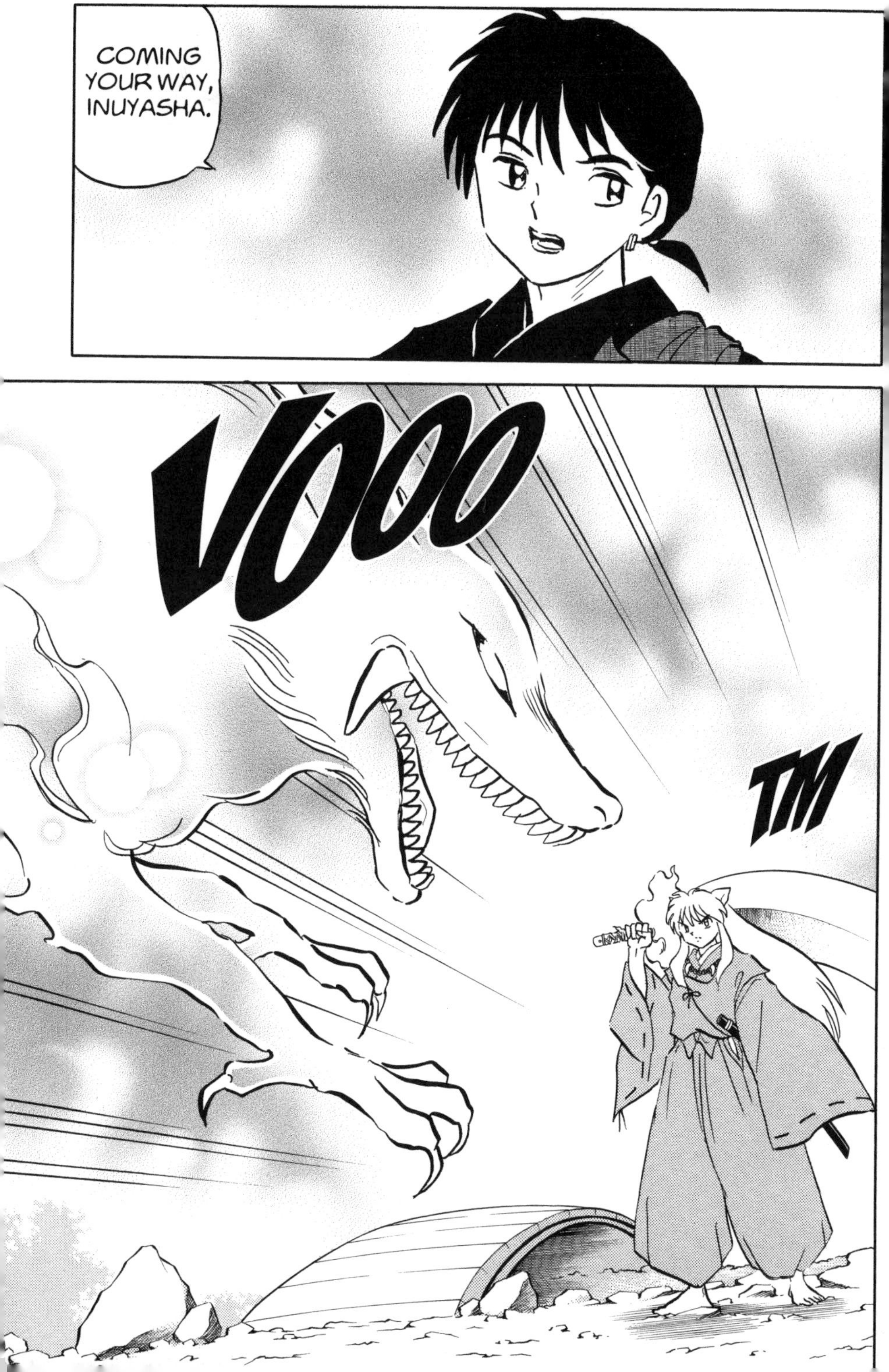
COMING YOUR WAY, INUYASHA.
VOOO
TM

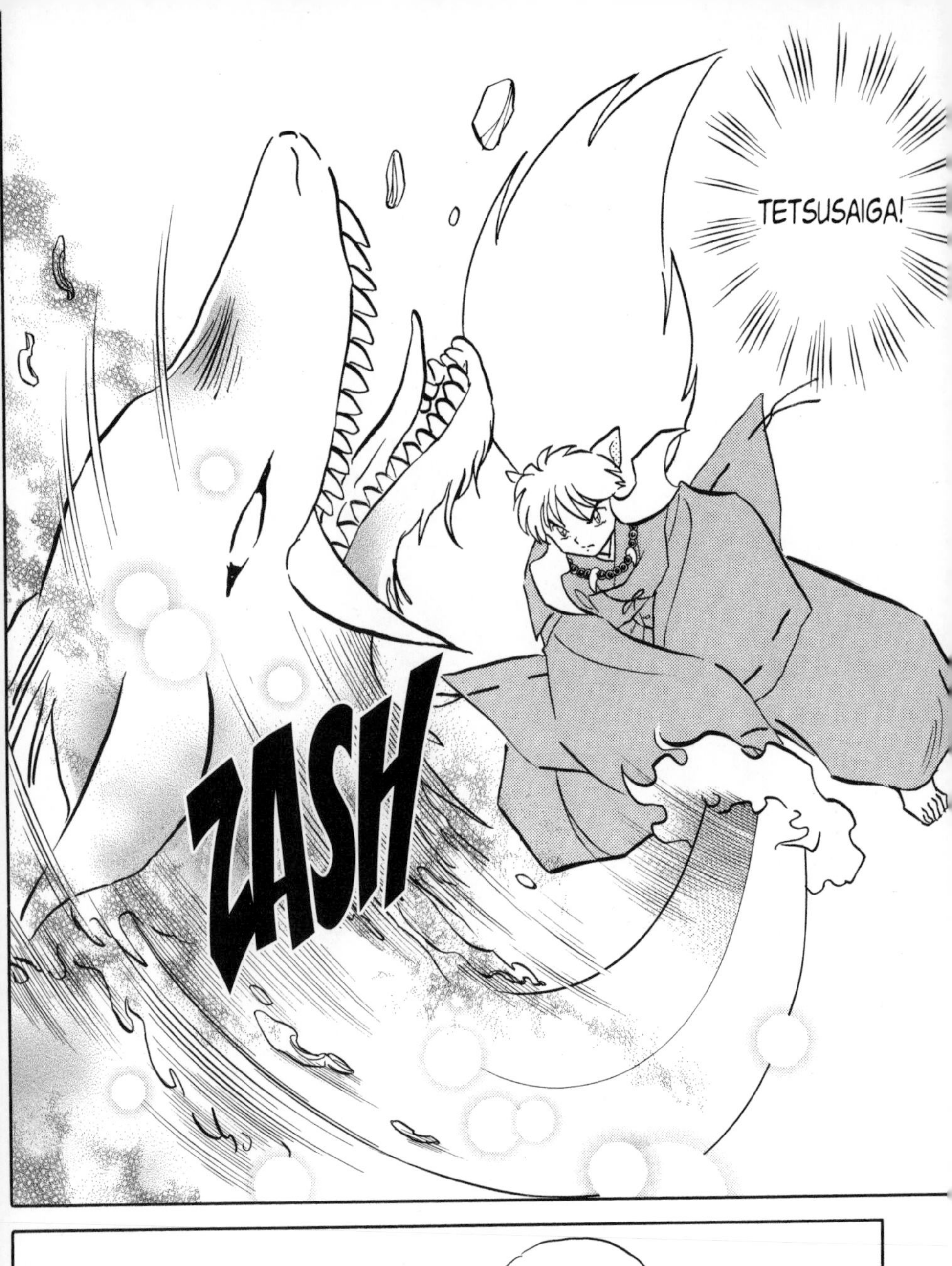
TETSUSAIGA!
ZASH

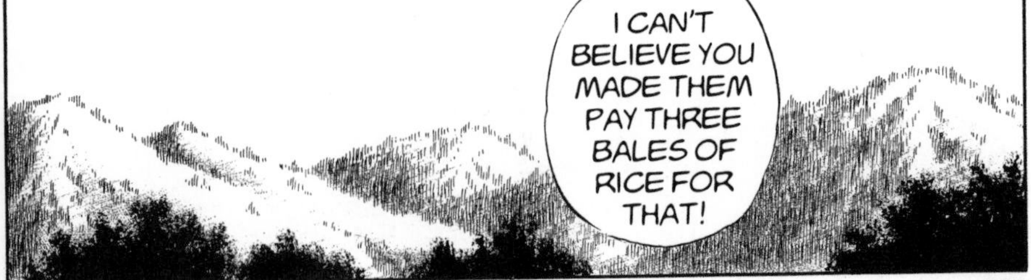
I CAN'T BELIEVE YOU MADE THEM PAY THREE BALES OF RICE FOR THAT!

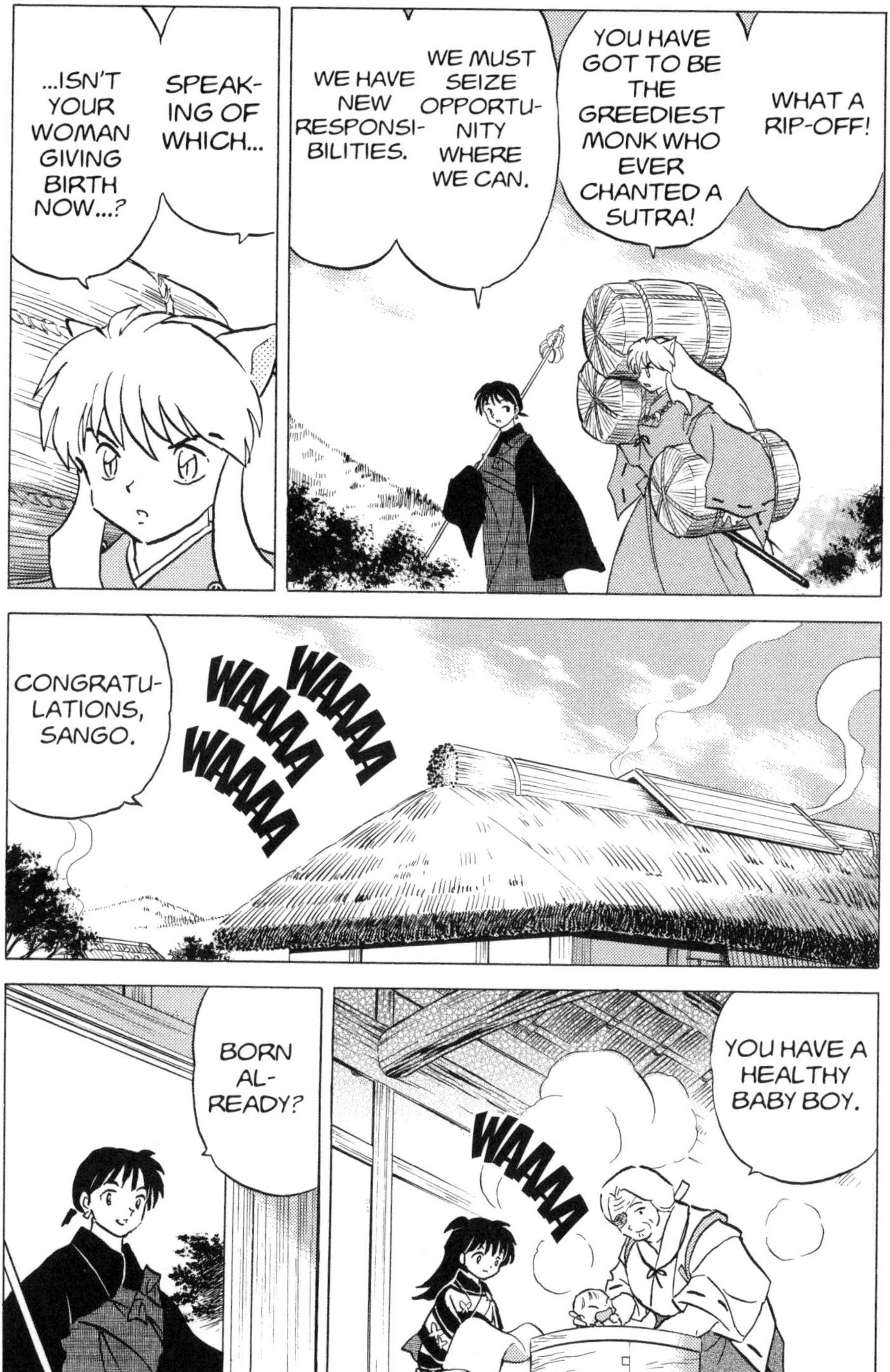
WHAT A RIP-OFF!
YOU HAVE GOT TO BE THE GREEDIEST MONK WHO EVER CHANTED A SUTRA!
WE MUST SEIZE OPPORTUNITY WHERE WE CAN.
WE HAVE NEW RESPONSIBILITIES.
SPEAKING OF WHICH...
...ISN'T YOUR WOMAN GIVING BIRTH NOW...?
WAAAAA
WAAAAA
WAAAAA
CONGRATULATIONS, SANGO.
YOU HAVE A HEALTHY BABY BOY.
WAAAAA
BORN ALREADY?

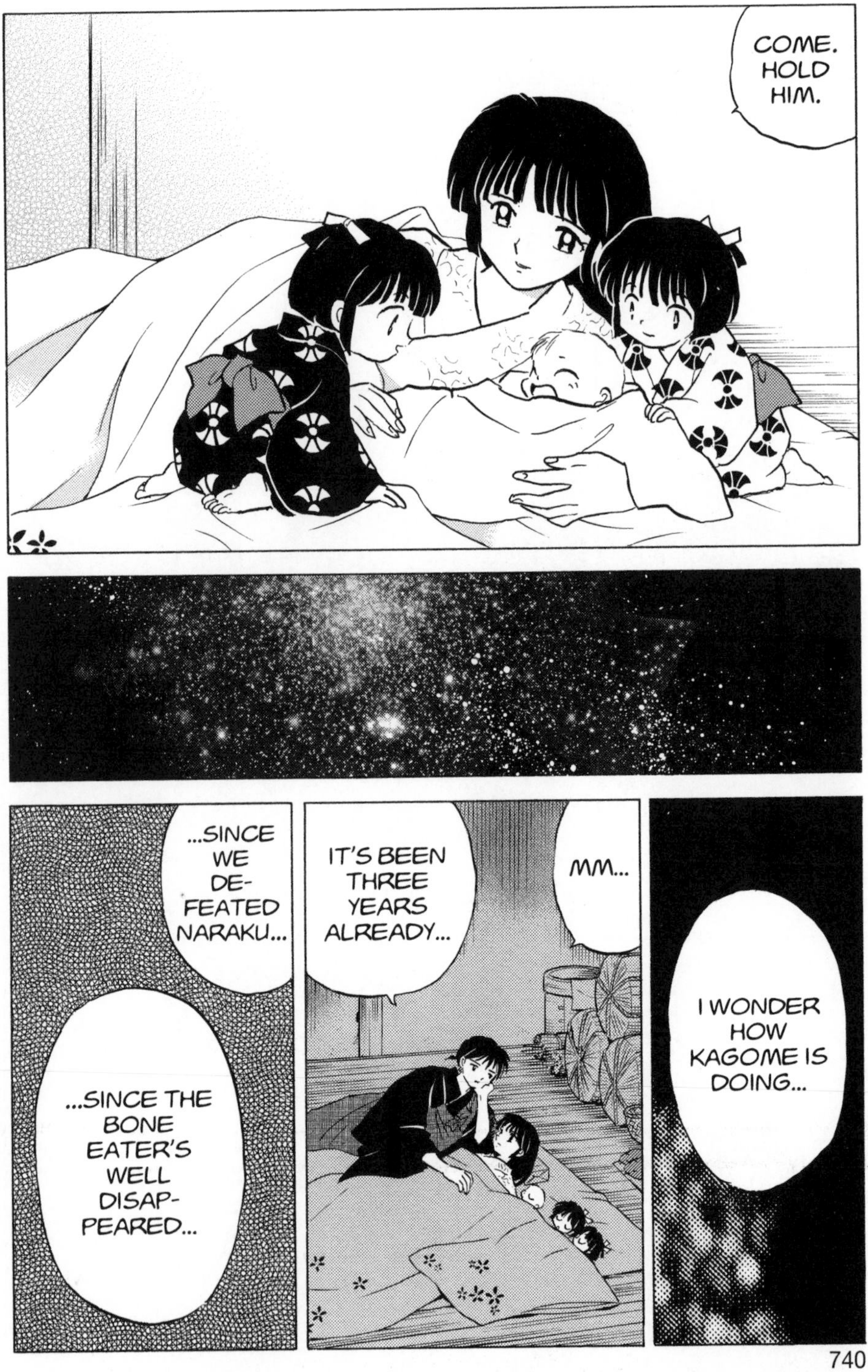
COME. HOLD HIM.
I WONDER HOW KAGOME IS DOING...
MM...
IT'S BEEN THREE YEARS ALREADY...
...SINCE WE DEFEATED NARAKU...
...SINCE THE BONE EATER'S WELL DISAPPEARED...

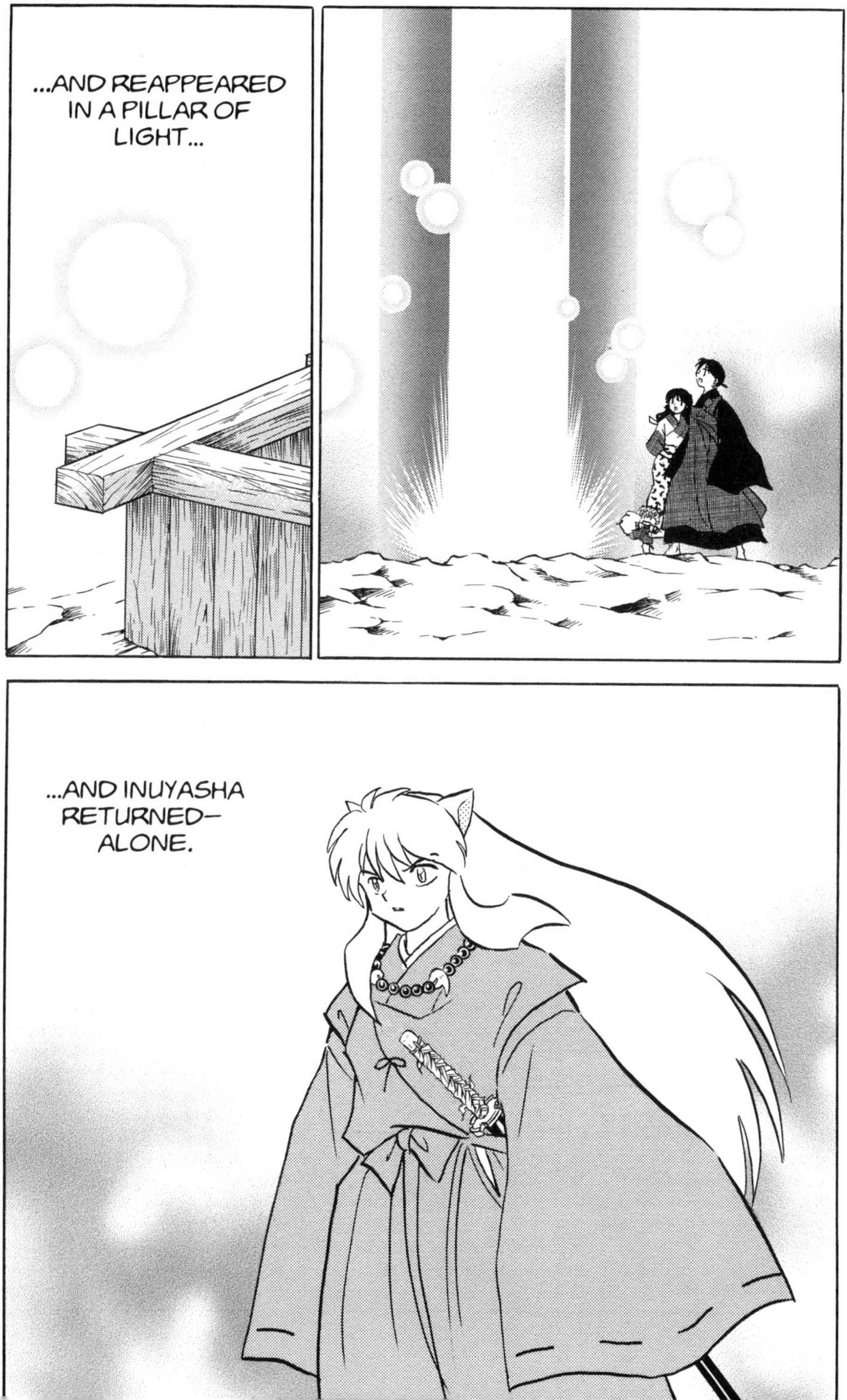
...AND REAPPEARED IN A PILLAR OF LIGHT...
...AND INUYASHA RETURNED— ALONE.

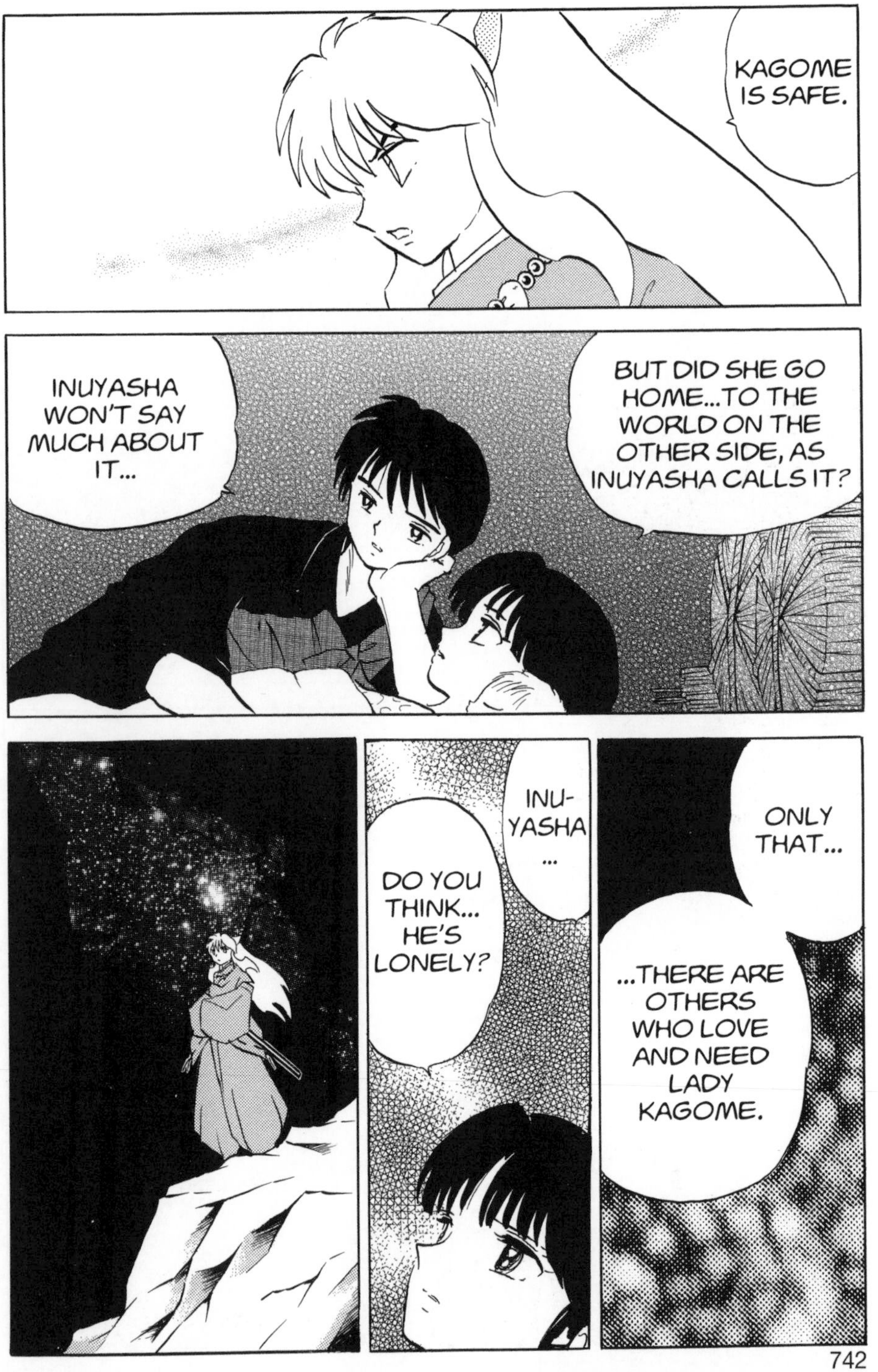
KAGOME IS SAFE.
BUT DID SHE GO HOME...TO THE WORLD ON THE OTHER SIDE, AS INUYASHA CALLS IT?
INUYASHA WON'T SAY MUCH ABOUT IT...
ONLY THAT...
...THERE ARE OTHERS WHO LOVE AND NEED LADY KAGOME.
INU-YASHA...
DO YOU THINK... HE'S LONELY?

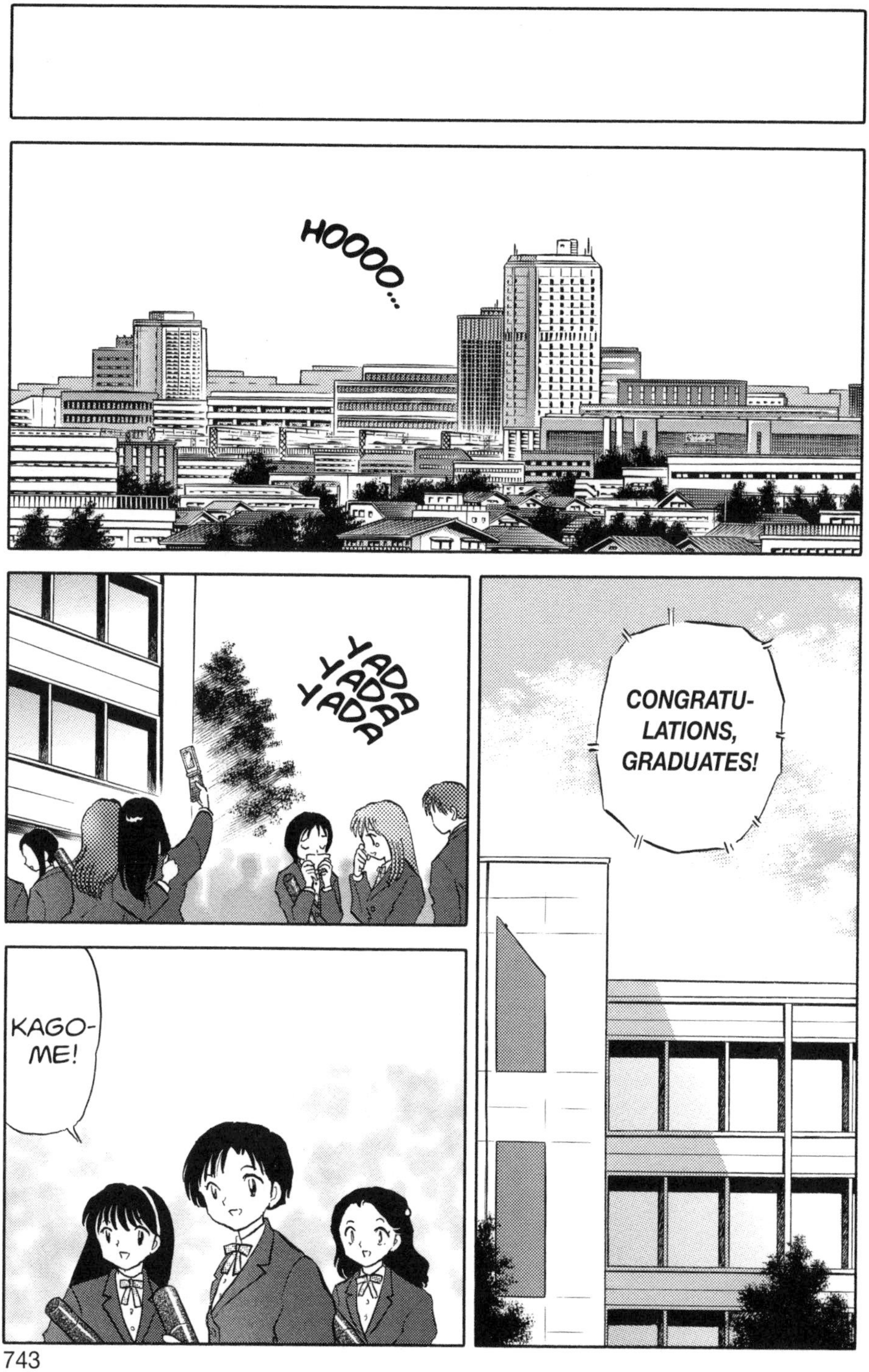
HOOOO...
CONGRATU-LATIONS, GRADUATES!
YADA YADA YADA
KAGO-ME!

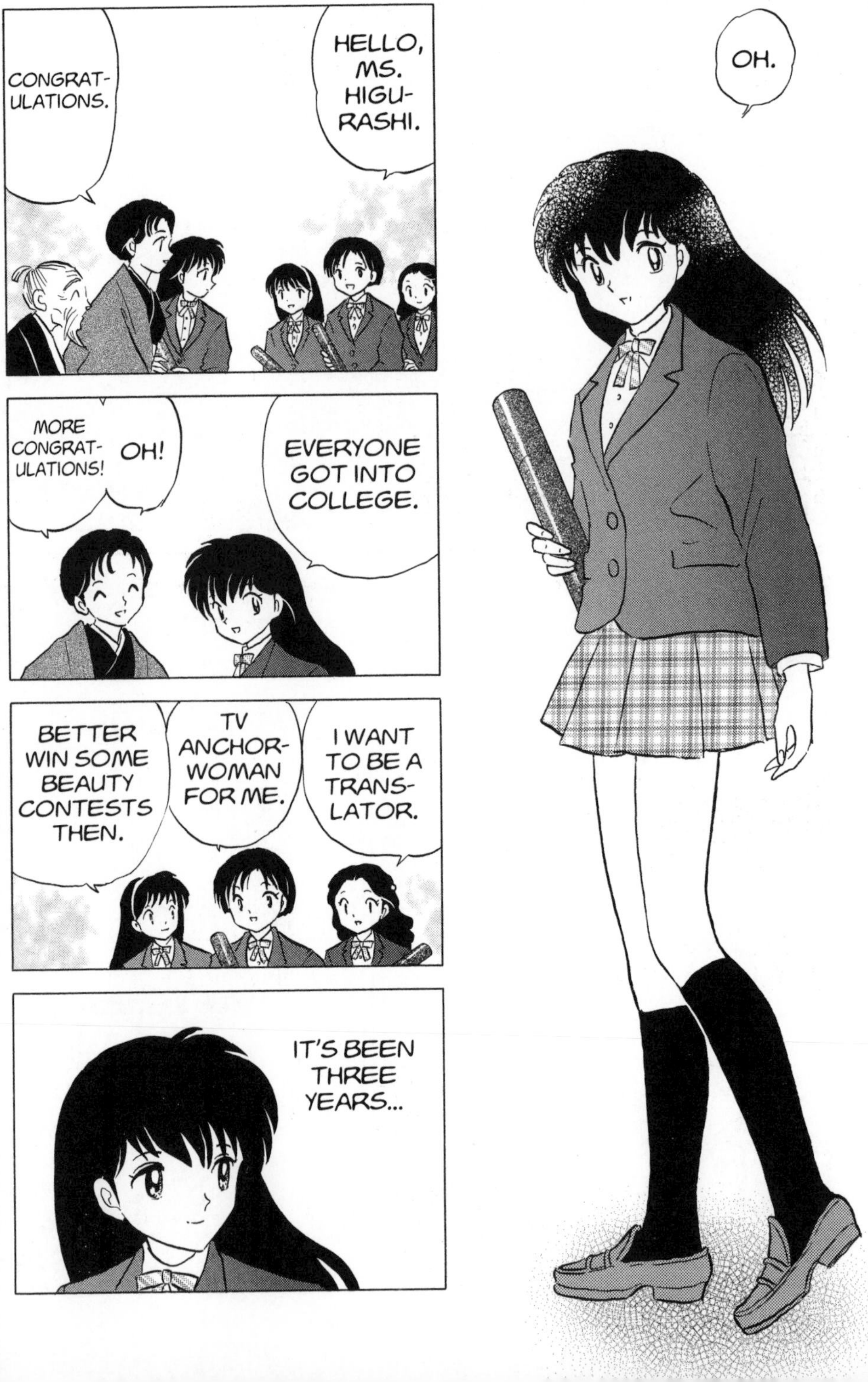
OH.
HELLO, MS. HIGU-RASHI.
CONGRAT-ULATIONS.
EVERYONE GOT INTO COLLEGE.
OH!
MORE CONGRAT-ULATIONS!
I WANT TO BE A TRANS-LATOR.
TV ANCHOR-WOMAN FOR ME.
BETTER WIN SOME BEAUTY CONTESTS THEN.
IT'S BEEN THREE YEARS...

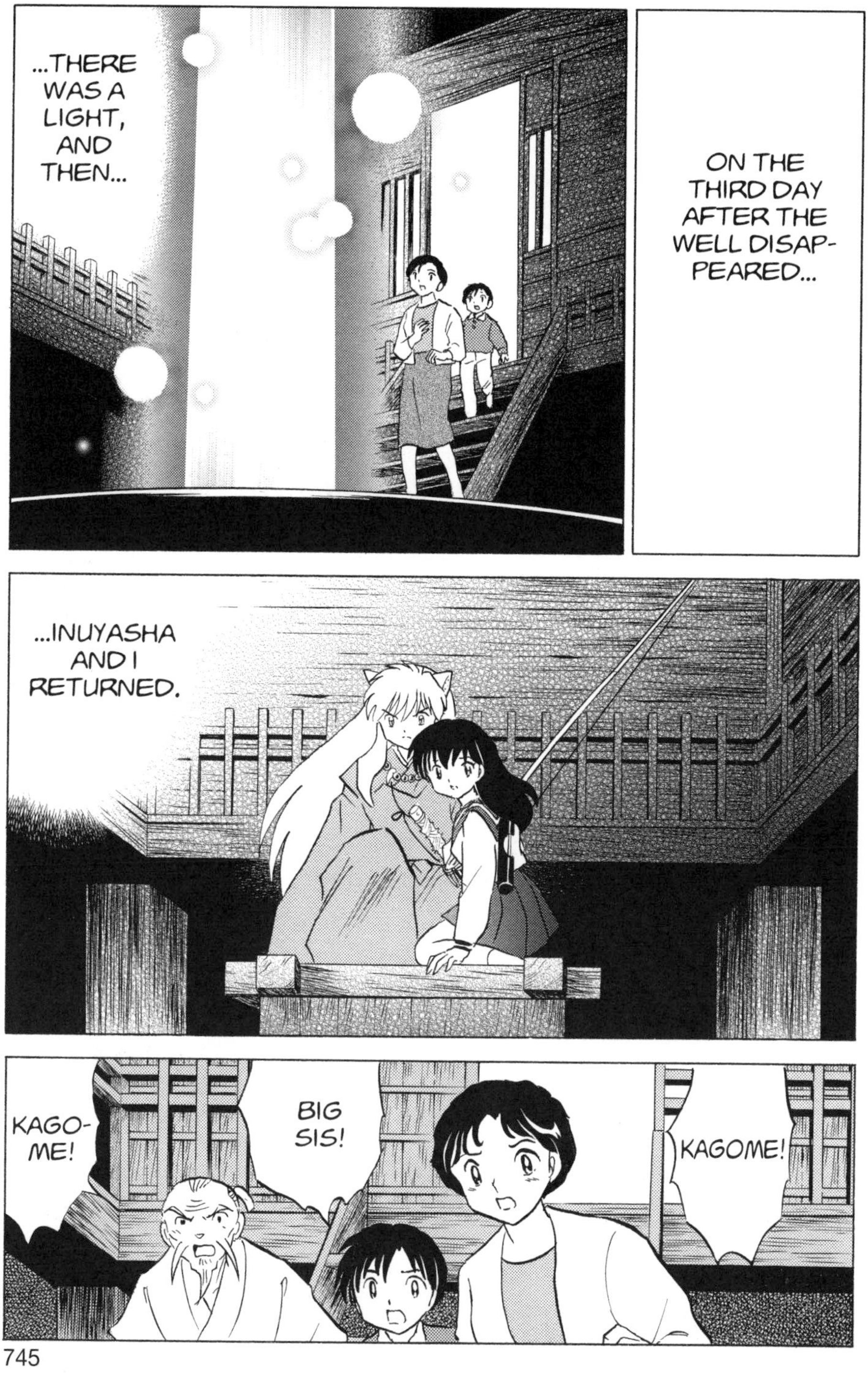
ON THE THIRD DAY AFTER THE WELL DISAP-PEARED...
...THERE WAS A LIGHT, AND THEN...
...INUYASHA AND I RETURNED.
KAGOME!
BIG SIS!
KAGO-ME!

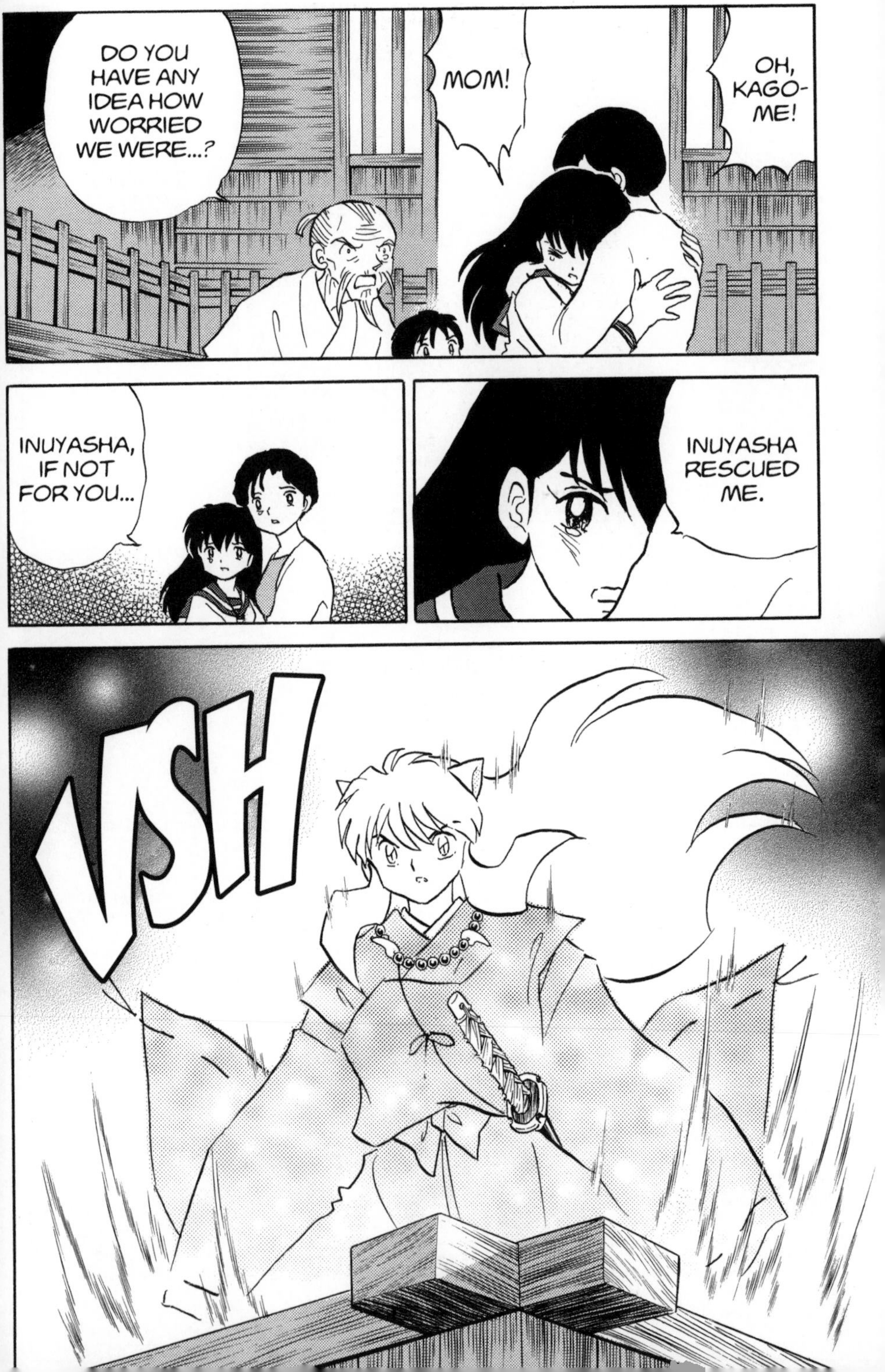
OH, KAGO-ME!
MOM!
DO YOU HAVE ANY IDEA HOW WORRIED WE WERE...?
INUYASHA RESCUED ME.
INUYASHA, IF NOT FOR YOU...
VSH

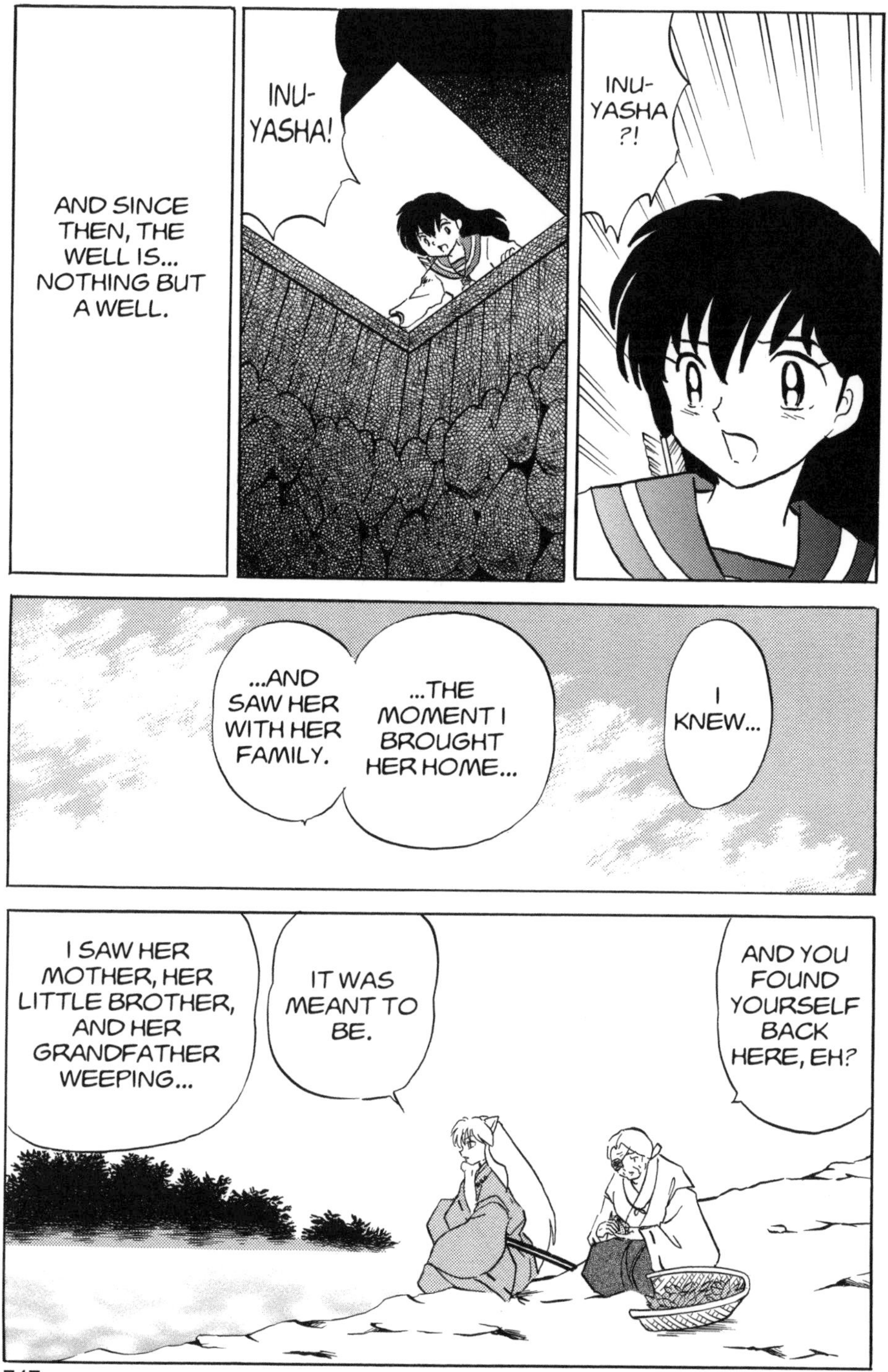
INU-YASHA?!
INU-YASHA!
AND SINCE THEN, THE WELL IS... NOTHING BUT A WELL.
I KNEW...
...THE MOMENT I BROUGHT HER HOME...
...AND SAW HER WITH HER FAMILY.
AND YOU FOUND YOURSELF BACK HERE, EH?
IT WAS MEANT TO BE.
I SAW HER MOTHER, HER LITTLE BROTHER, AND HER GRANDFATHER WEEPING...

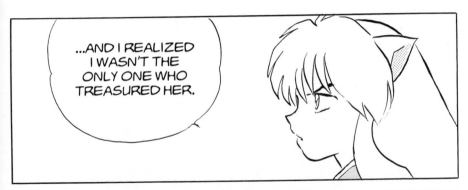

...AND I REALIZED I WASN'T THE ONLY ONE WHO TREASURED HER.
INU-YASHA...
I NEVER THOUGHT I'D HEAR SUCH WISDOM FALL FROM YOUR LIPS.
YEAH? WELL LISTEN TO THIS!
LALALA LALA LALA
SHIPPO!
HOW DID YOUR FOX DEMON EXAMS GO?
I AD-VANCED!
POP
UPPER JUNIOR 7TH
SO, MR. WISDOM ...
...HOW COME YOU KEEP JUMPING INSIDE THAT WELL EVERY THREE DAYS?

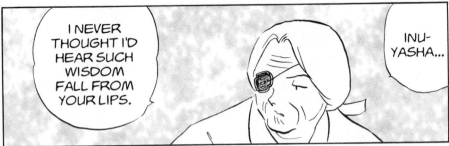

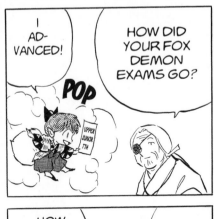

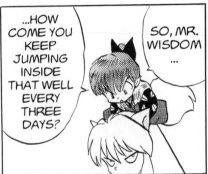

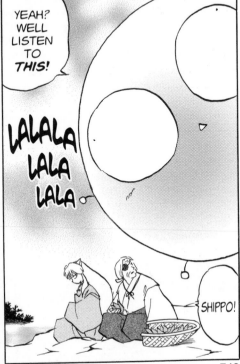

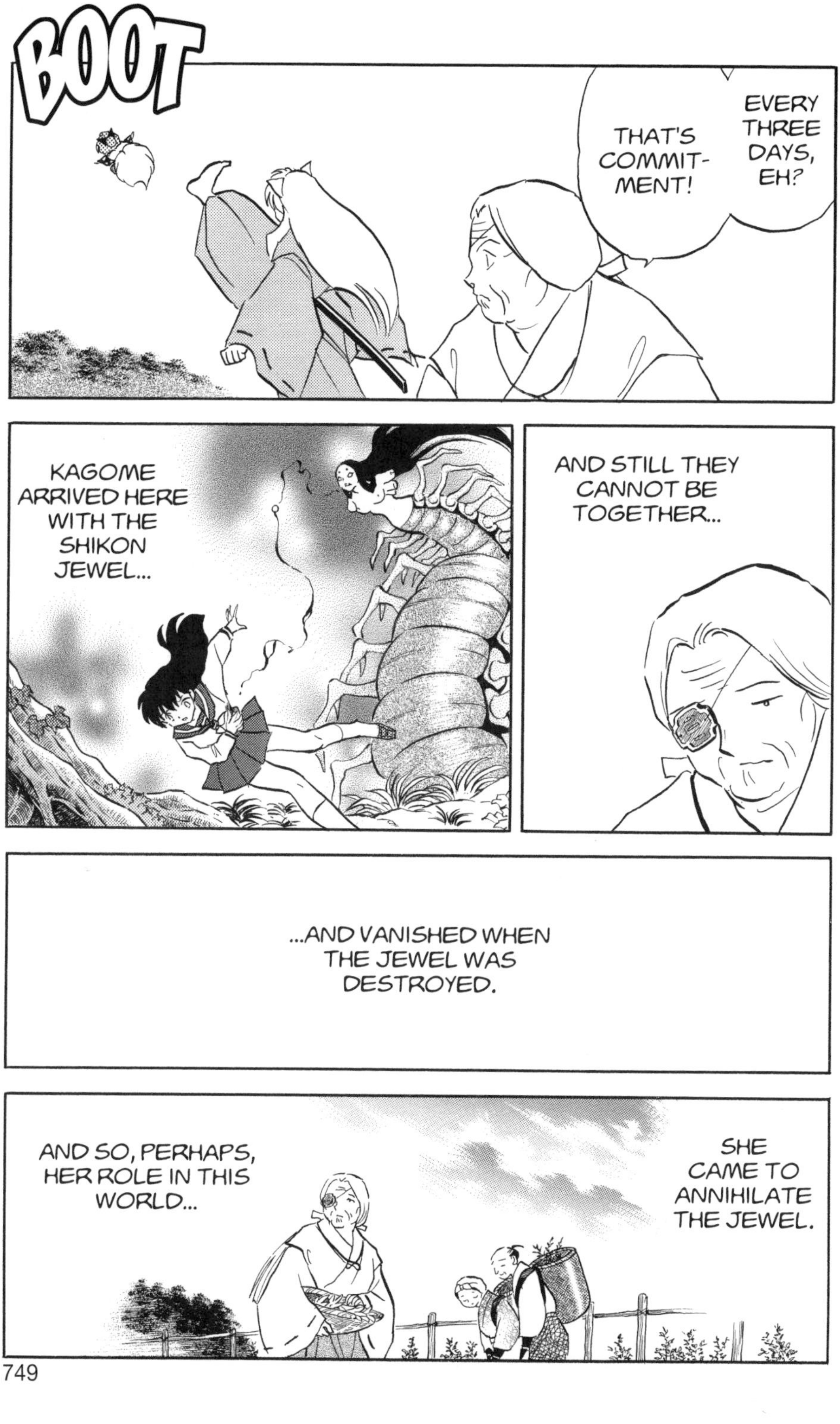
BOOT
EVERY THREE DAYS, EH?
THAT'S COMMIT-MENT!
AND STILL THEY CANNOT BE TOGETHER...
KAGOME ARRIVED HERE WITH THE SHIKON JEWEL...
...AND VANISHED WHEN THE JEWEL WAS DESTROYED.
SHE CAME TO ANNIHILATE THE JEWEL.
AND SO, PERHAPS, HER ROLE IN THIS WORLD...

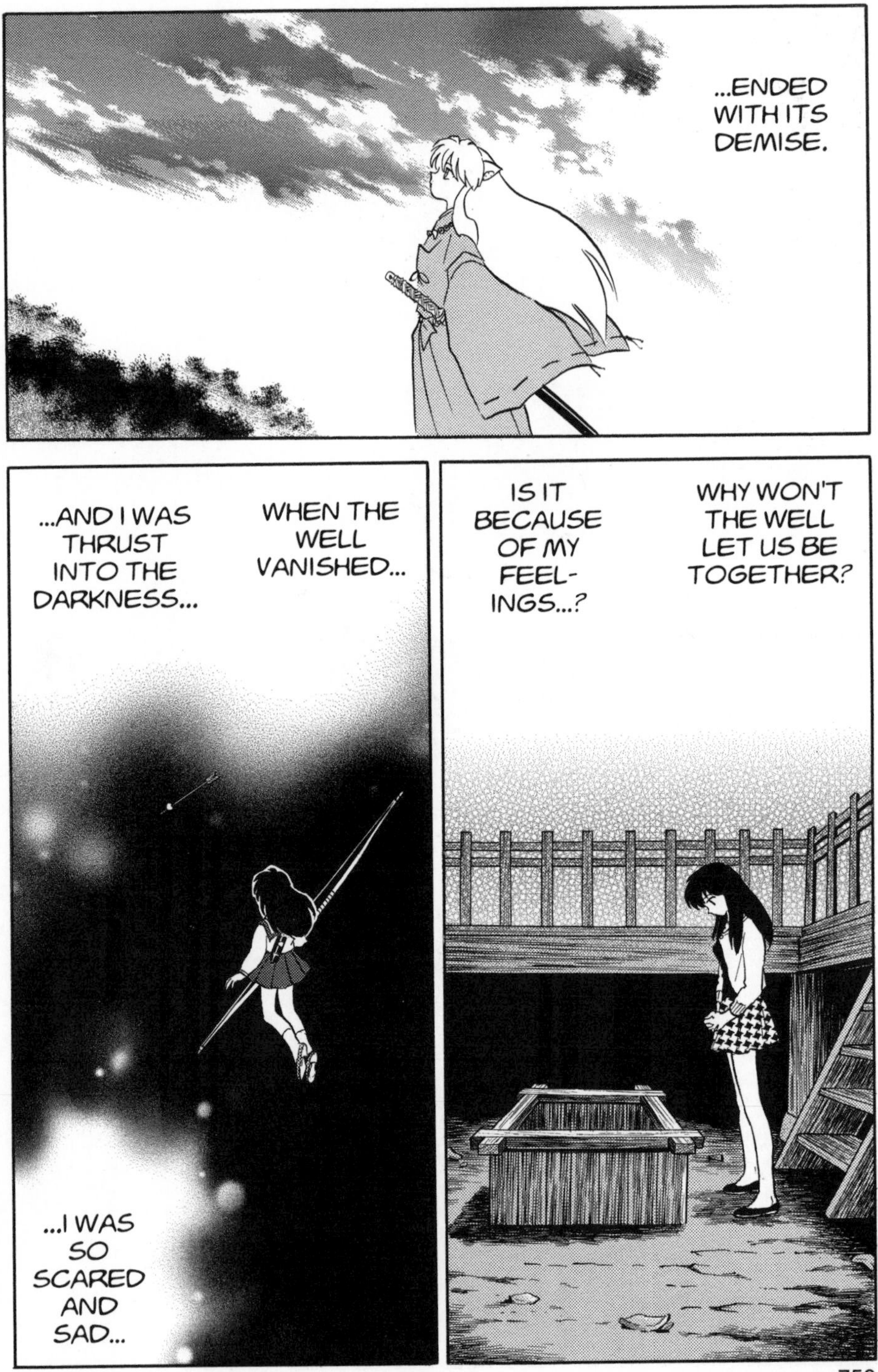
...ENDED WITH ITS DEMISE.
WHY WON'T THE WELL LET US BE TOGETHER?
IS IT BECAUSE OF MY FEEL-INGS...?
WHEN THE WELL VANISHED...
...AND I WAS THRUST INTO THE DARKNESS...
...I WAS SO SCARED AND SAD...

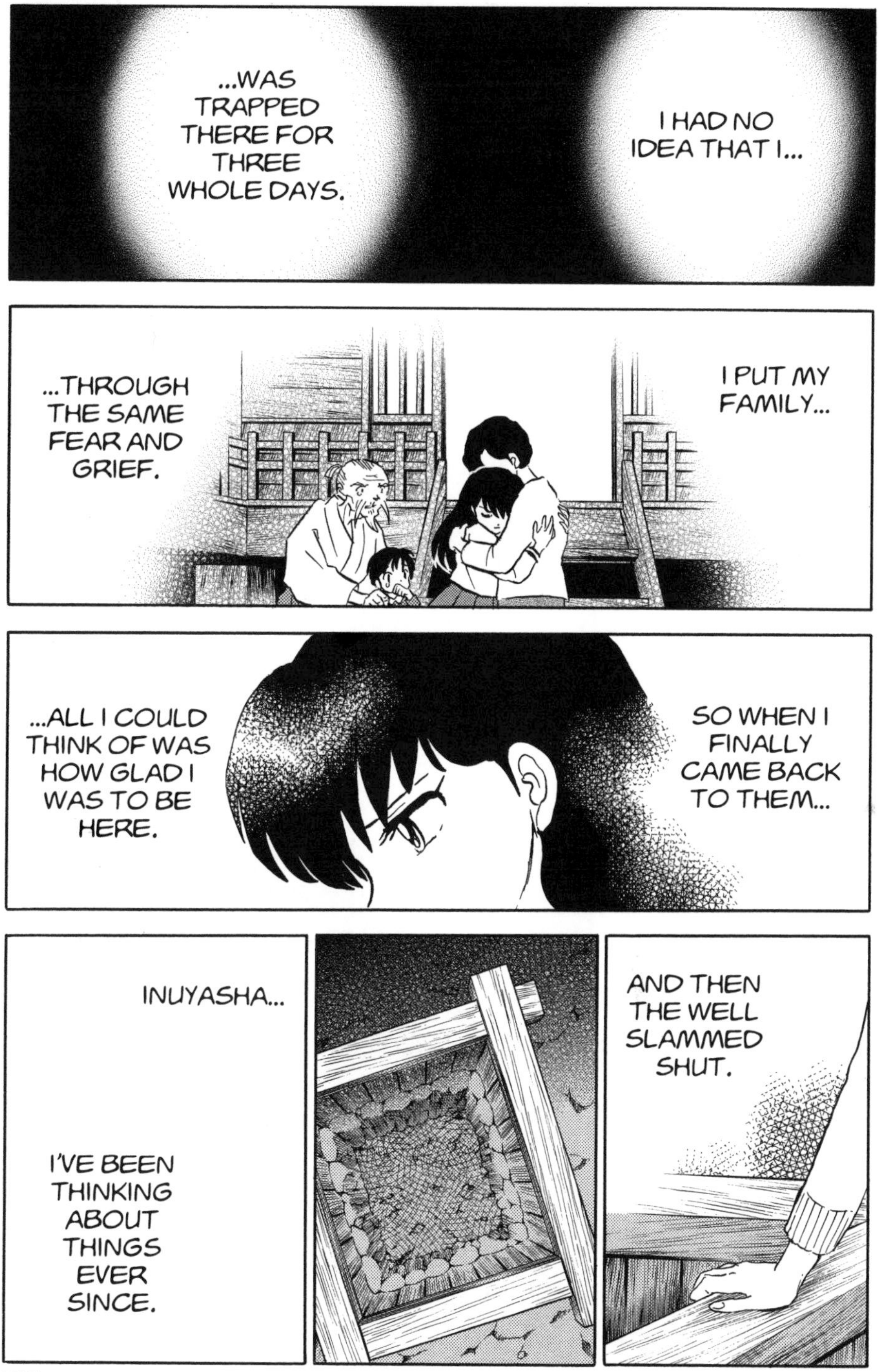
I HAD NO IDEA THAT I...
...WAS TRAPPED THERE FOR THREE WHOLE DAYS.
I PUT MY FAMILY...
...THROUGH THE SAME FEAR AND GRIEF.
SO WHEN I FINALLY CAME BACK TO THEM...
...ALL I COULD THINK OF WAS HOW GLAD I WAS TO BE HERE.
AND THEN THE WELL SLAMMED SHUT.
INUYASHA...
I'VE BEEN THINKING ABOUT THINGS EVER SINCE.

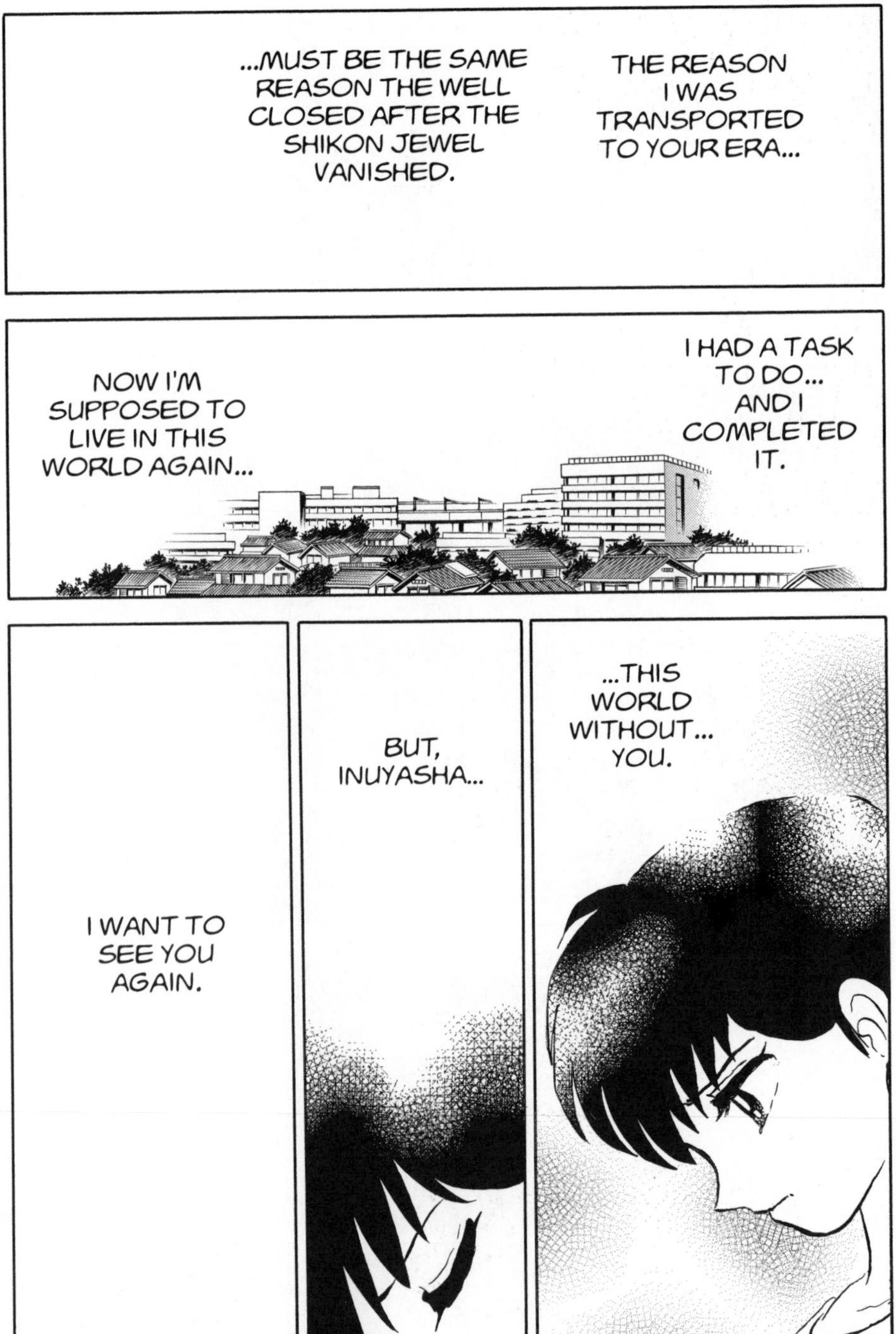
THE REASON I WAS TRANSPORTED TO YOUR ERA...
...MUST BE THE SAME REASON THE WELL CLOSED AFTER THE SHIKON JEWEL VANISHED.
I HAD A TASK TO DO... AND I COMPLETED IT.
NOW I'M SUPPOSED TO LIVE IN THIS WORLD AGAIN...
...THIS WORLD WITHOUT... YOU.
BUT, INUYASHA...
I WANT TO SEE YOU AGAIN.

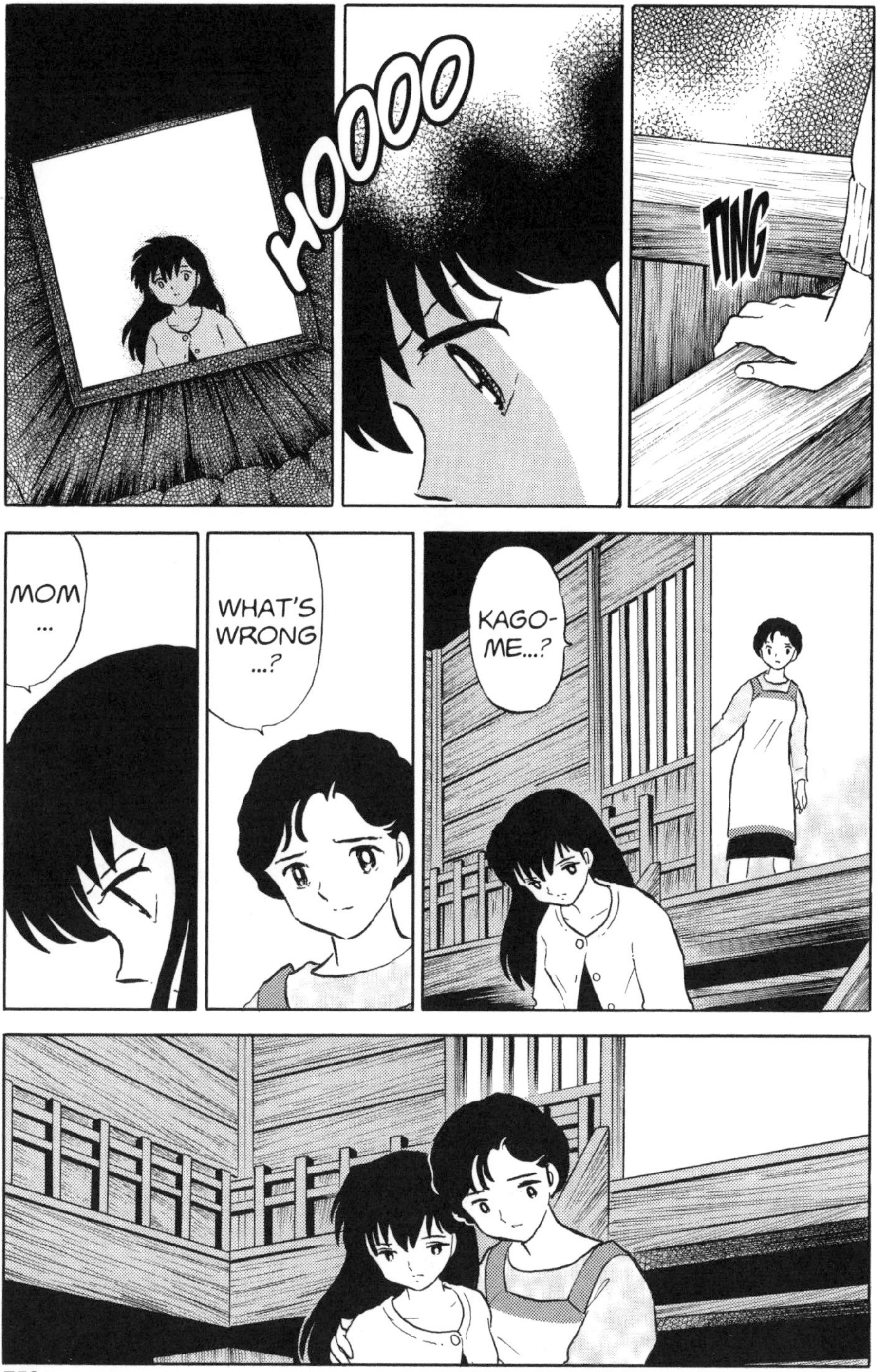
TING
HOOOO
KAGO-ME...?
WHAT'S WRONG ...?
MOM ...

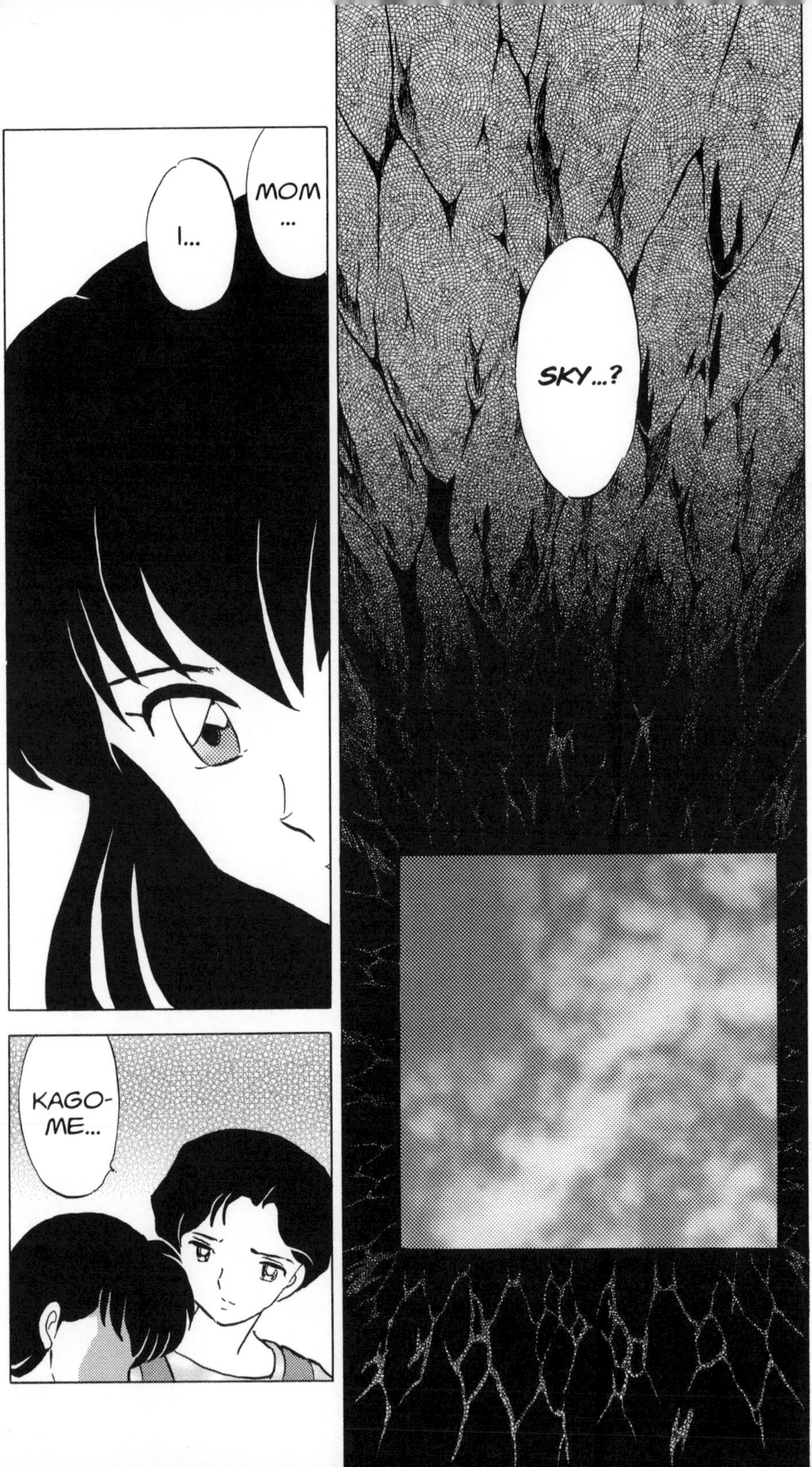
SKY...?
MOM ...
I...
KAGO-ME...

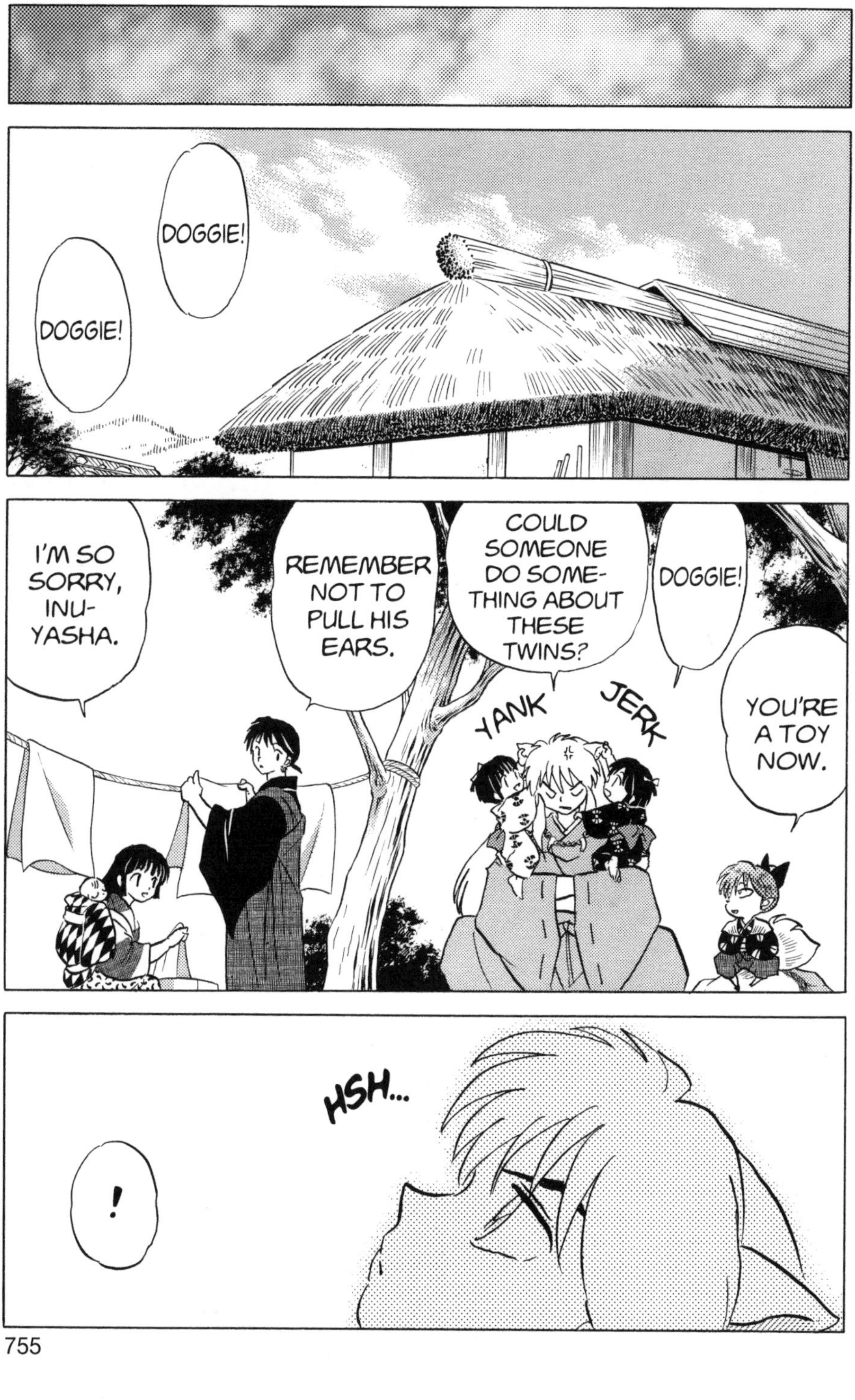
DOGGIE!
DOGGIE!
DOGGIE!
COULD SOMEONE DO SOMETHING ABOUT THESE TWINS?
JERK
YANK
YOU'RE A TOY NOW.
REMEMBER NOT TO PULL HIS EARS.
I'M SO SORRY, INUYASHA.
HSH...
!

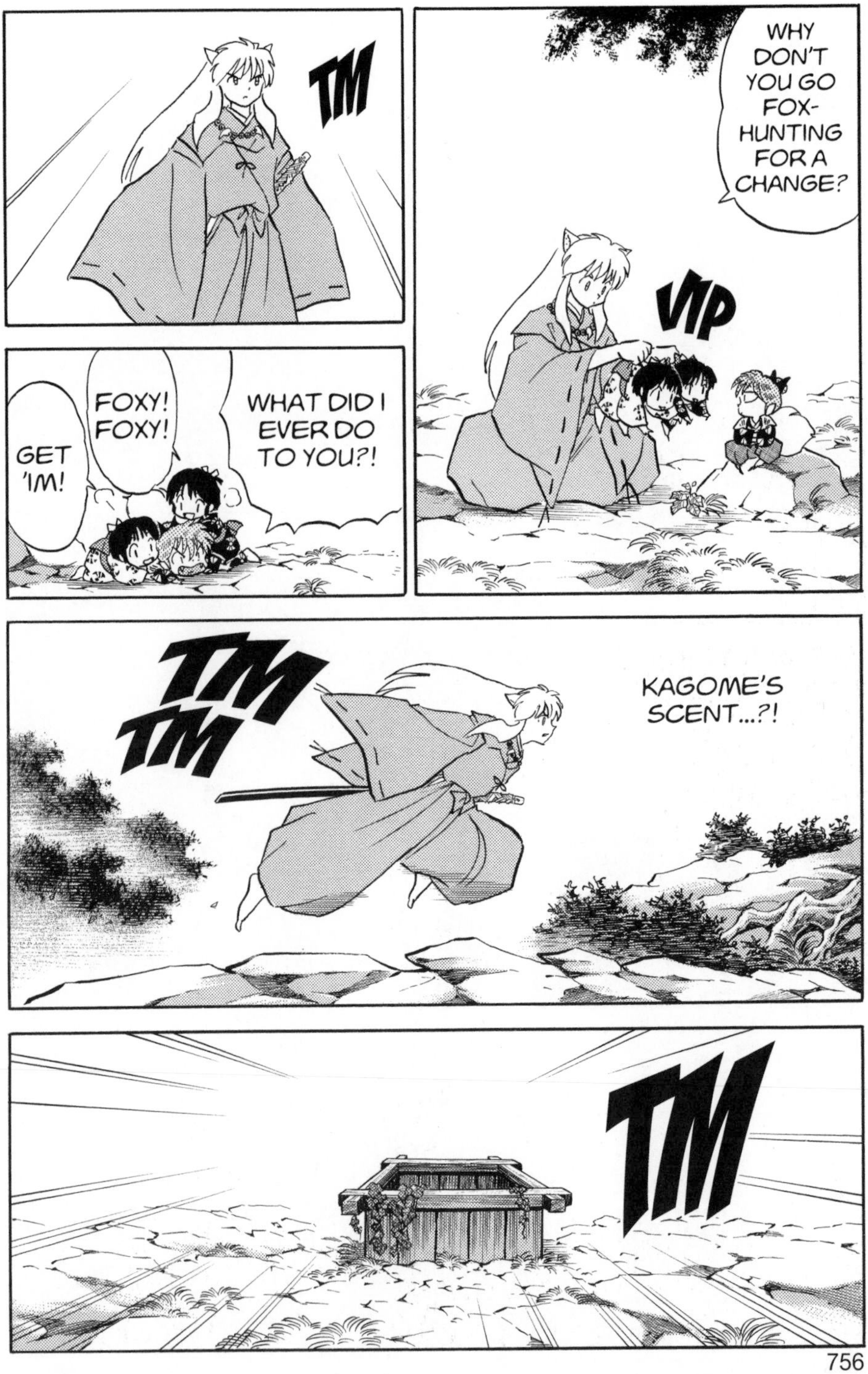
WHY DON'T YOU GO FOX-HUNTING FOR A CHANGE?
VIP
TM
WHAT DID I EVER DO TO YOU?!
FOXY! FOXY!
GET 'IM!
KAGOME'S SCENT...?!
TM TM
TM

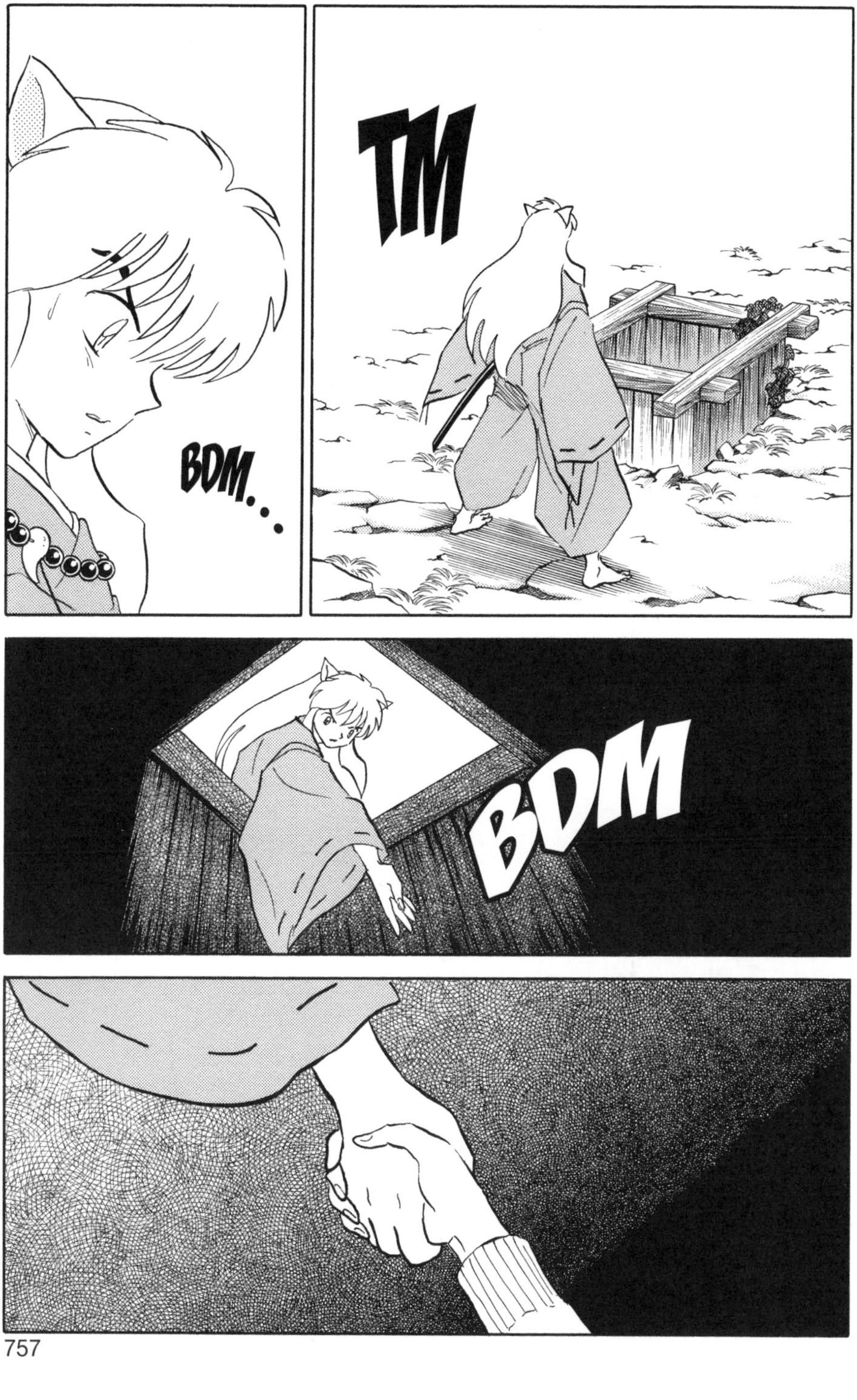
TM
BDM...
BDM

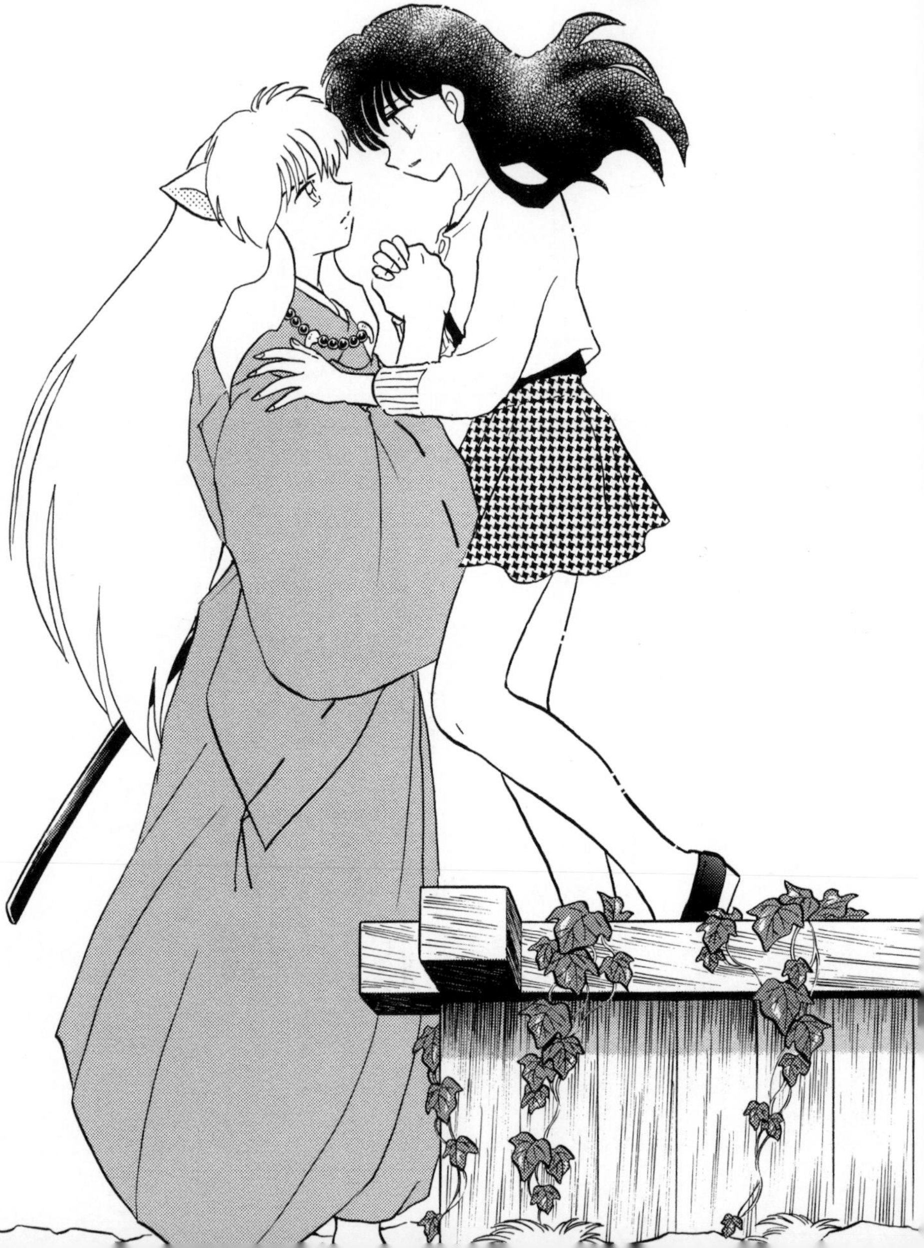
SHHH...

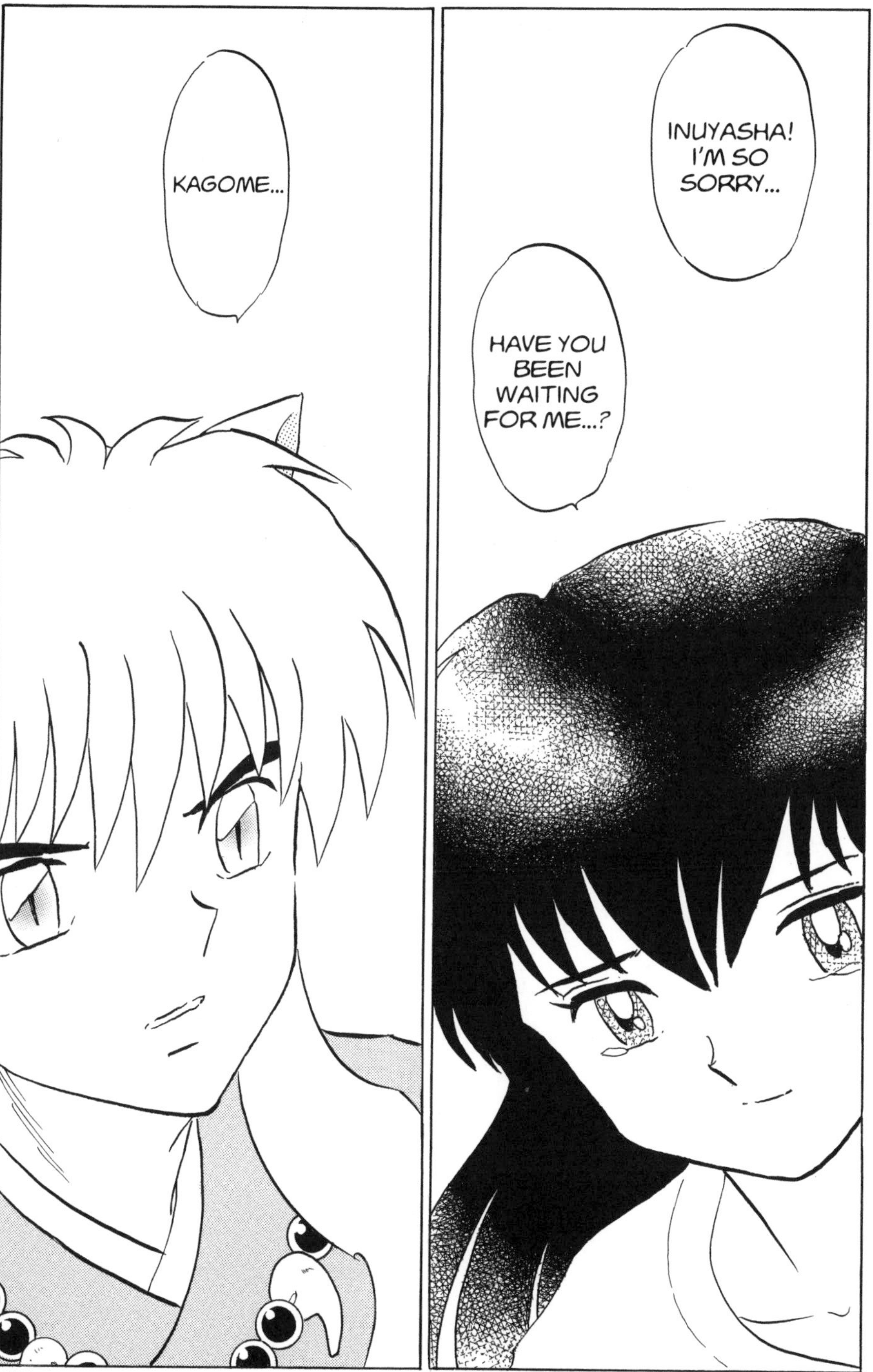
INUYASHA! I'M SO SORRY...
HAVE YOU BEEN WAITING FOR ME...?
KAGOME...

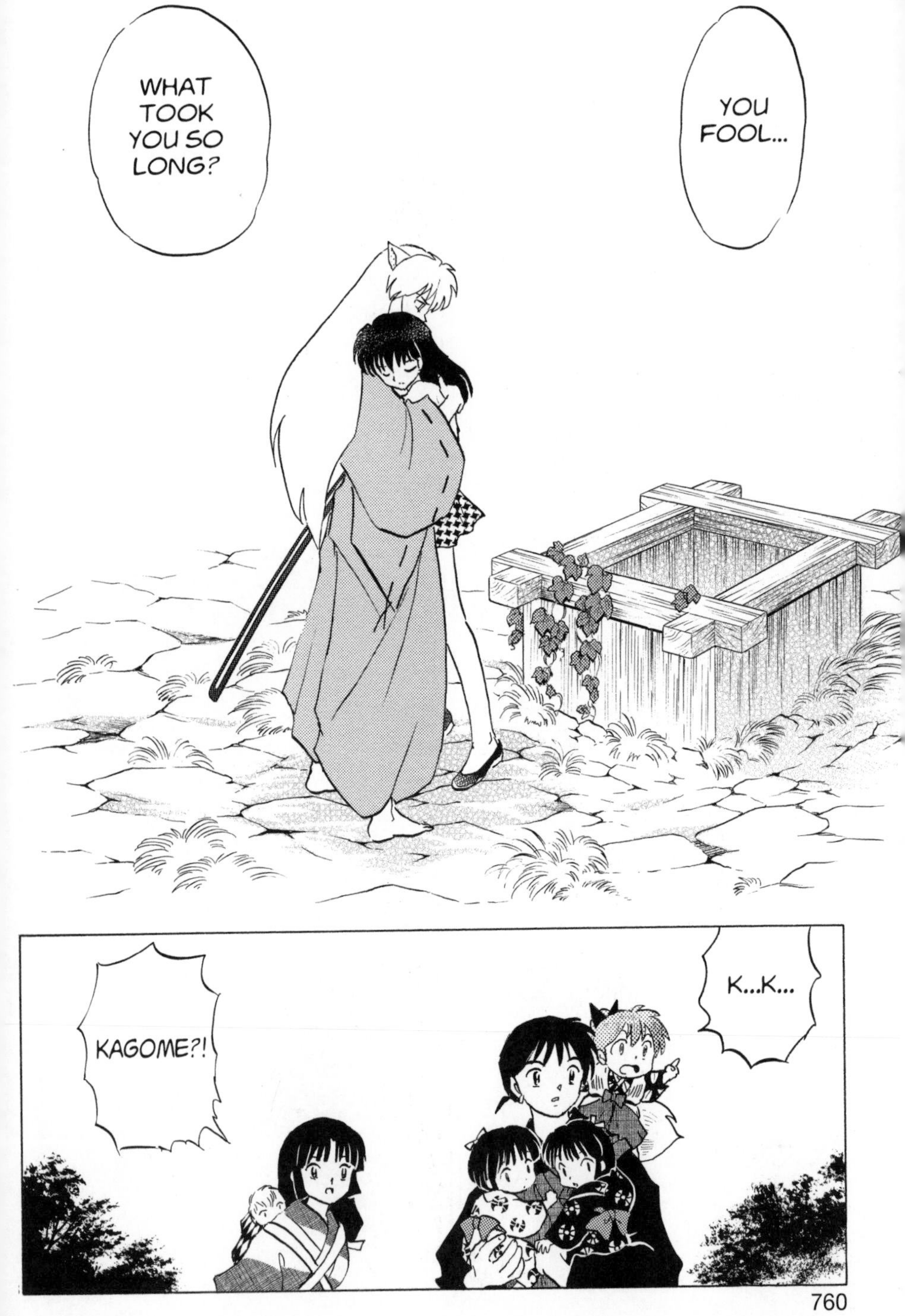
YOU FOOL...
WHAT TOOK YOU SO LONG?
K...K...
KAGOME?!

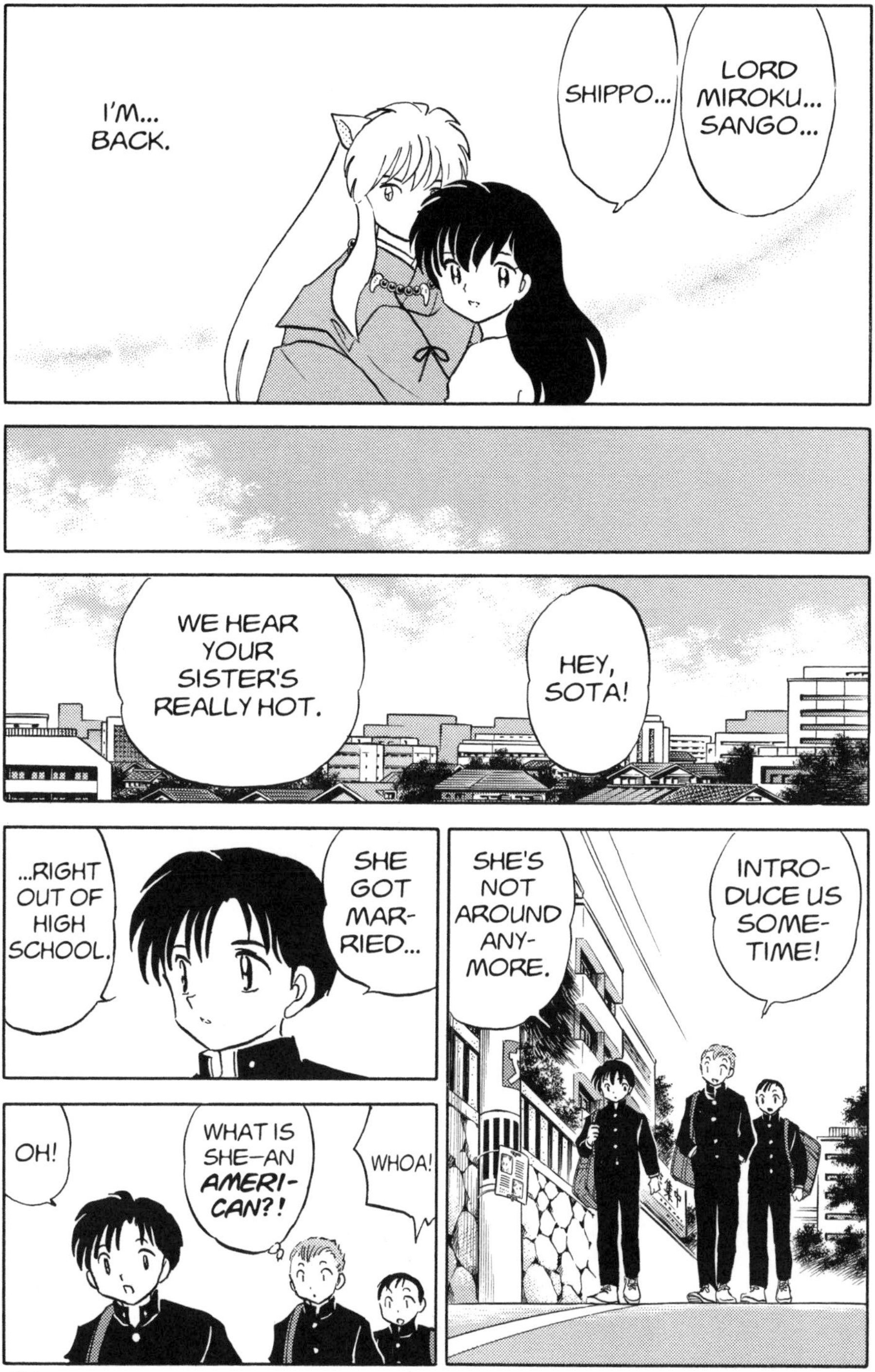
LORD MIROKU... SANGO...
SHIPPO...
I'M... BACK.
HEY, SOTA!
WE HEAR YOUR SISTER'S REALLY HOT.
INTRO-DUCE US SOME-TIME!
SHE'S NOT AROUND ANY-MORE.
SHE GOT MAR-RIED...
...RIGHT OUT OF HIGH SCHOOL.
WHOA!
WHAT IS SHE—AN ***AMERI-CAN***?!
OH!

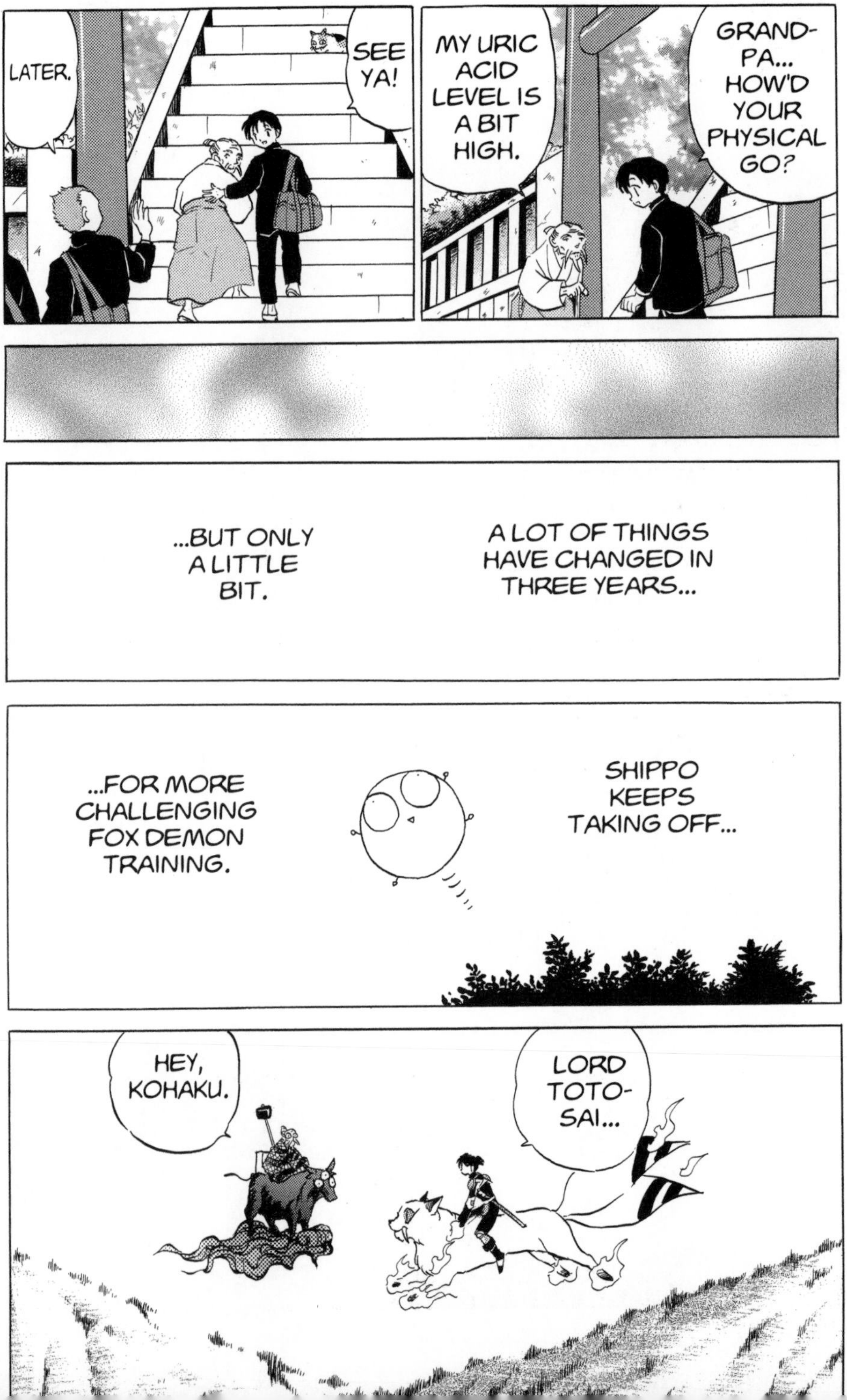
GRAND-PA... HOW'D YOUR PHYSICAL GO?
MY URIC ACID LEVEL IS A BIT HIGH.
SEE YA!
LATER.
A LOT OF THINGS HAVE CHANGED IN THREE YEARS...
...BUT ONLY A LITTLE BIT.
SHIPPO KEEPS TAKING OFF...
...FOR MORE CHALLENGING FOX DEMON TRAINING.
LORD TOTO-SAI...
HEY, KOHAKU.

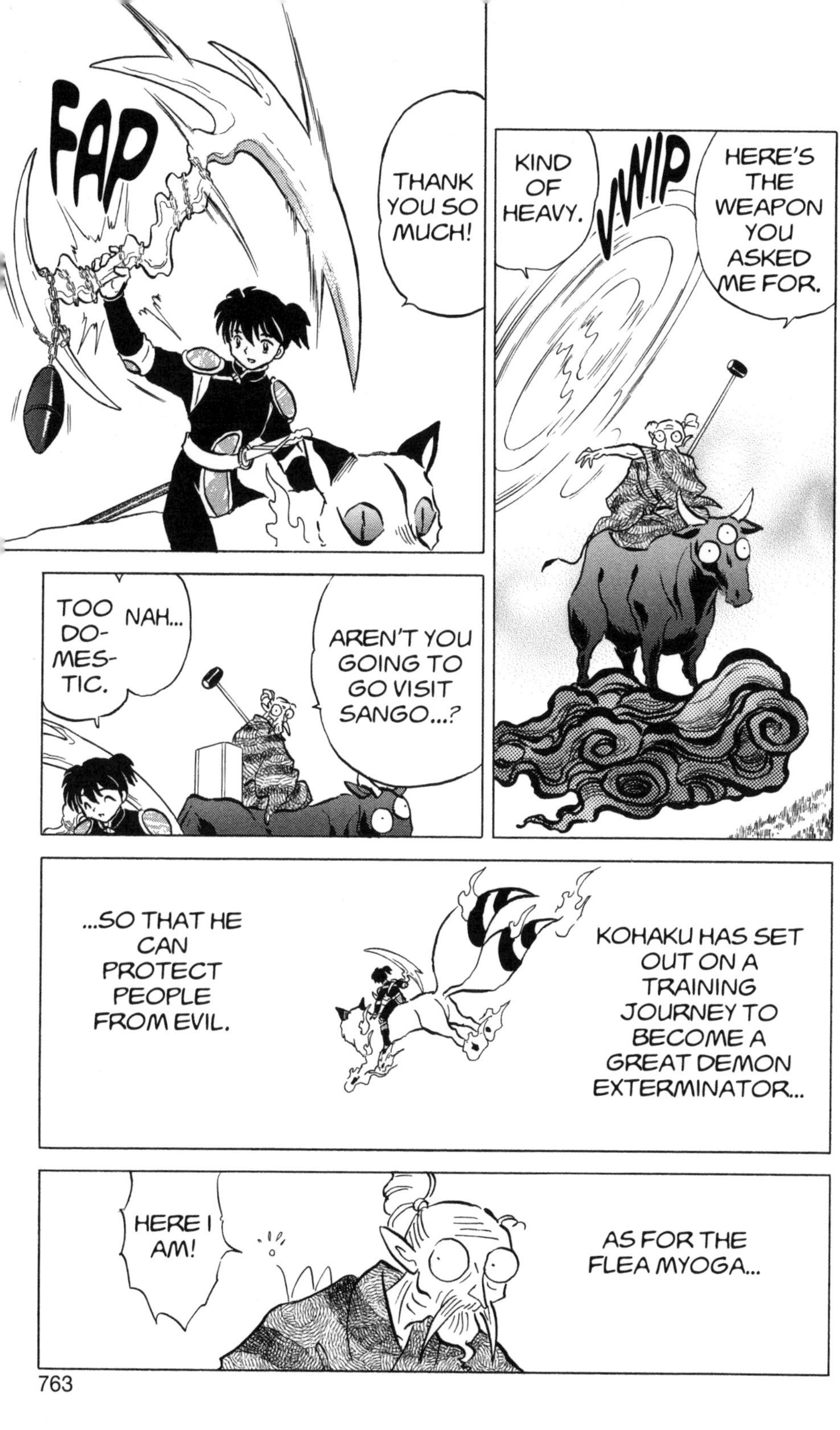
HERE'S THE WEAPON YOU ASKED ME FOR.
VWIP
KIND OF HEAVY.
FAP
THANK YOU SO MUCH!
AREN'T YOU GOING TO GO VISIT SANGO...?
NAH...
TOO DO-MES-TIC.
KOHAKU HAS SET OUT ON A TRAINING JOURNEY TO BECOME A GREAT DEMON EXTERMINATOR...
...SO THAT HE CAN PROTECT PEOPLE FROM EVIL.
AS FOR THE FLEA MYOGA...
HERE I AM!

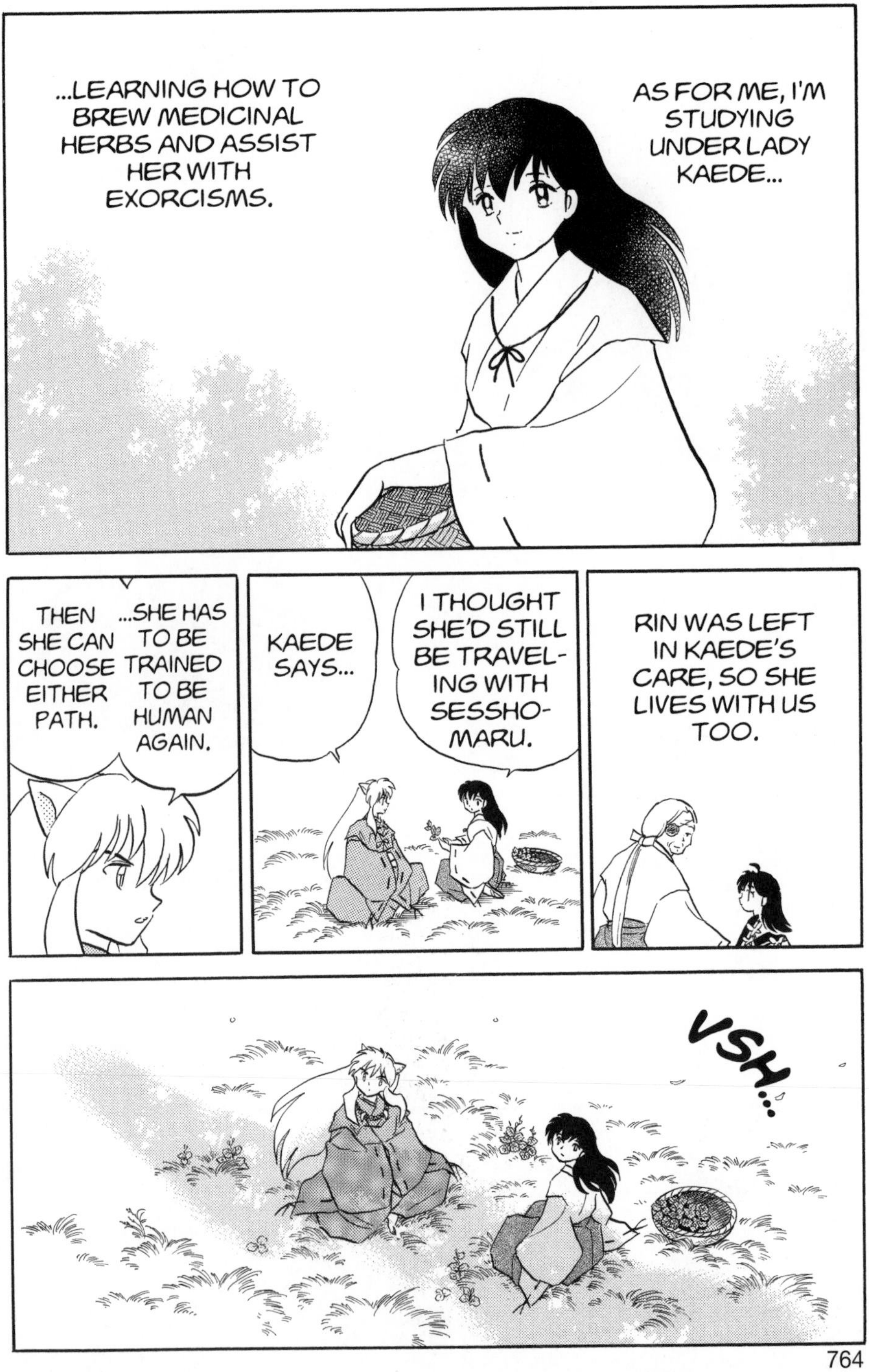
AS FOR ME, I'M STUDYING UNDER LADY KAEDE...
...LEARNING HOW TO BREW MEDICINAL HERBS AND ASSIST HER WITH EXORCISMS.
RIN WAS LEFT IN KAEDE'S CARE, SO SHE LIVES WITH US TOO.
I THOUGHT SHE'D STILL BE TRAVEL-ING WITH SESSHO-MARU.
KAEDE SAYS...
...SHE HAS TO BE TRAINED TO BE HUMAN AGAIN.
THEN SHE CAN CHOOSE EITHER PATH.
VSH...

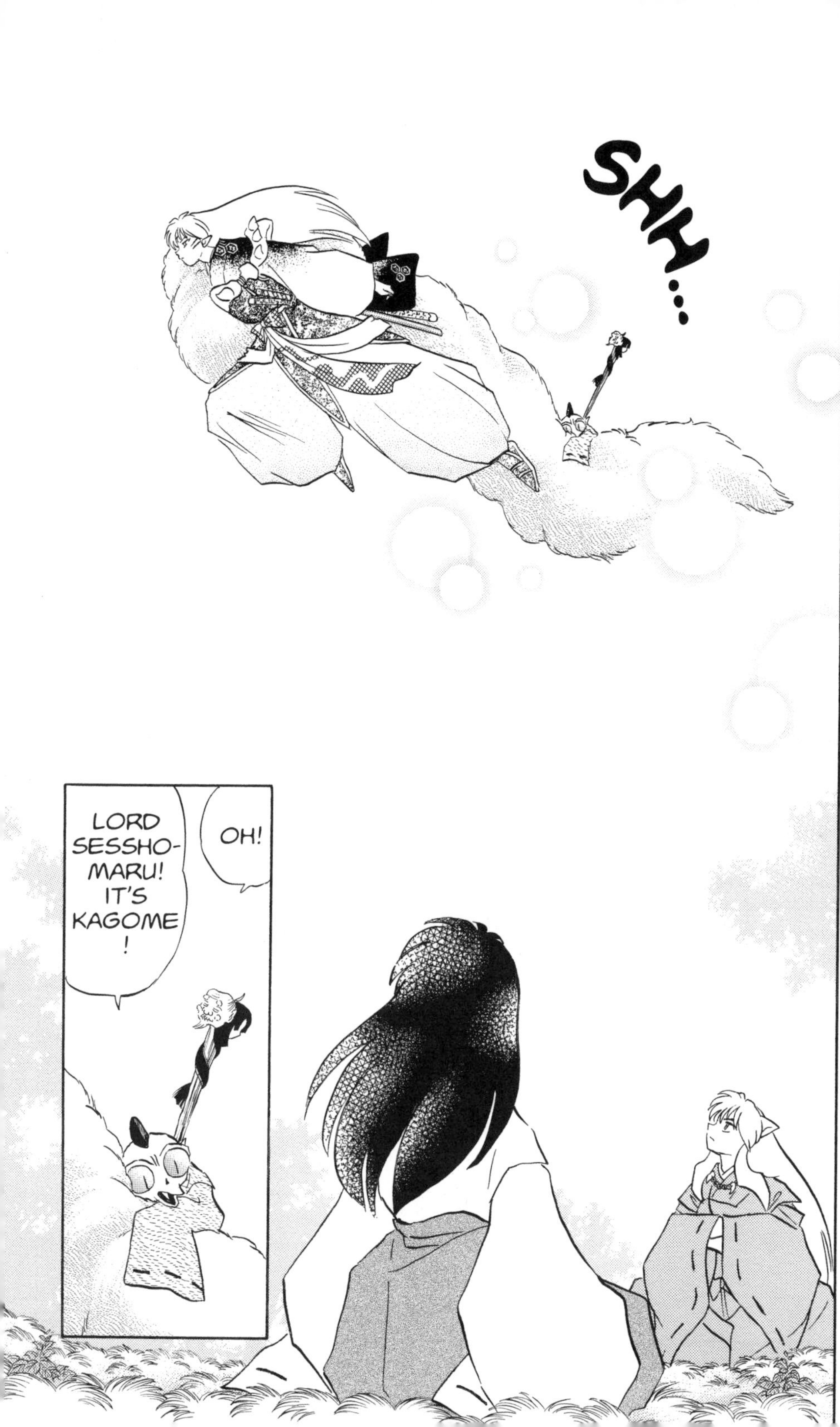
SHH...
OH!
LORD SESSHO-MARU! IT'S KAGOME!

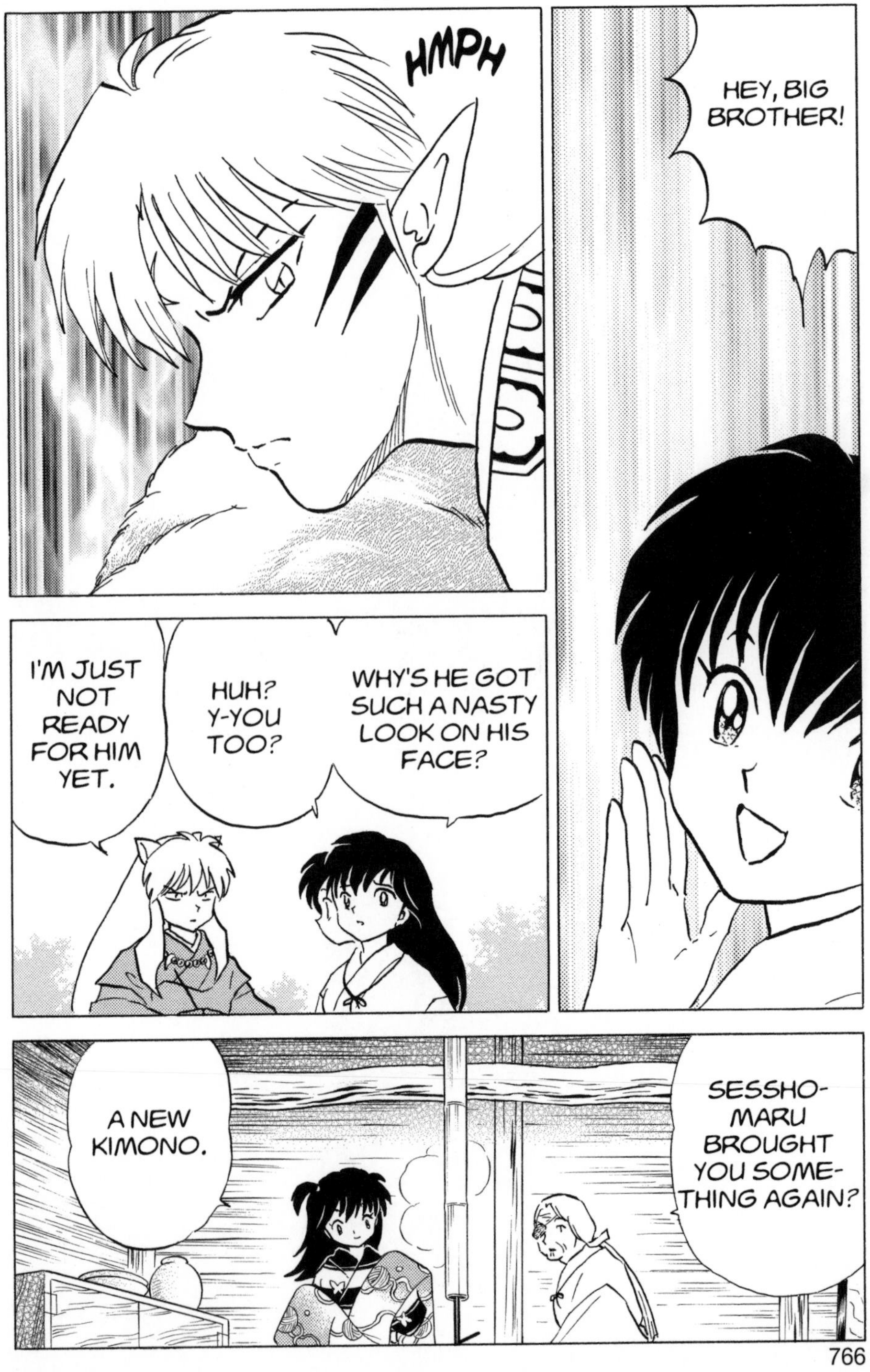

HEY, BIG BROTHER!
HMPH
WHY'S HE GOT SUCH A NASTY LOOK ON HIS FACE?
HUH? Y-YOU TOO?
I'M JUST NOT READY FOR HIM YET.
SESSHO-MARU BROUGHT YOU SOME-THING AGAIN?
A NEW KIMONO.

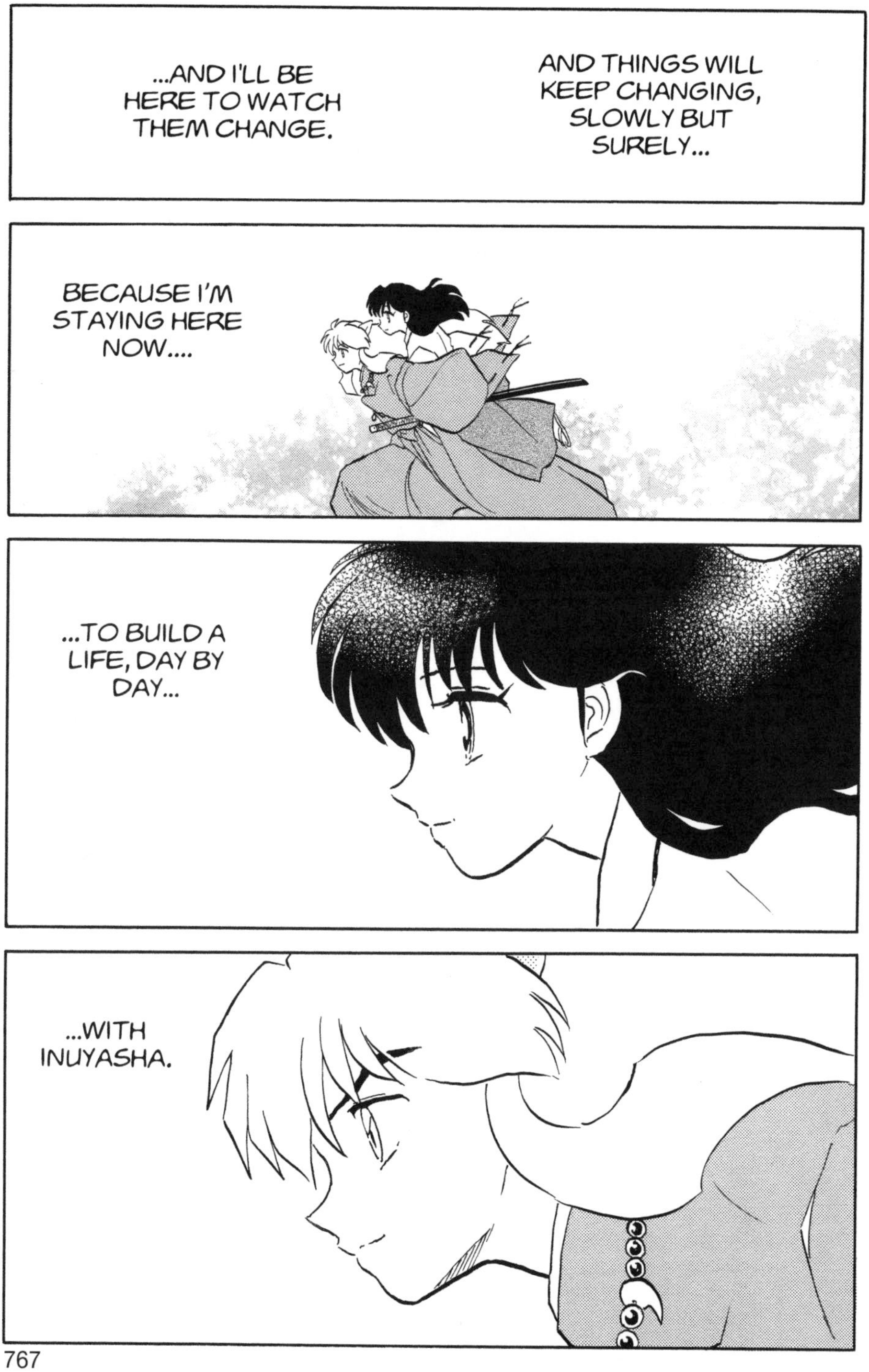

AND THINGS WILL KEEP CHANGING, SLOWLY BUT SURELY...
...AND I'LL BE HERE TO WATCH THEM CHANGE.
BECAUSE I'M STAYING HERE NOW....
...TO BUILD A LIFE, DAY BY DAY...
...WITH INUYASHA.

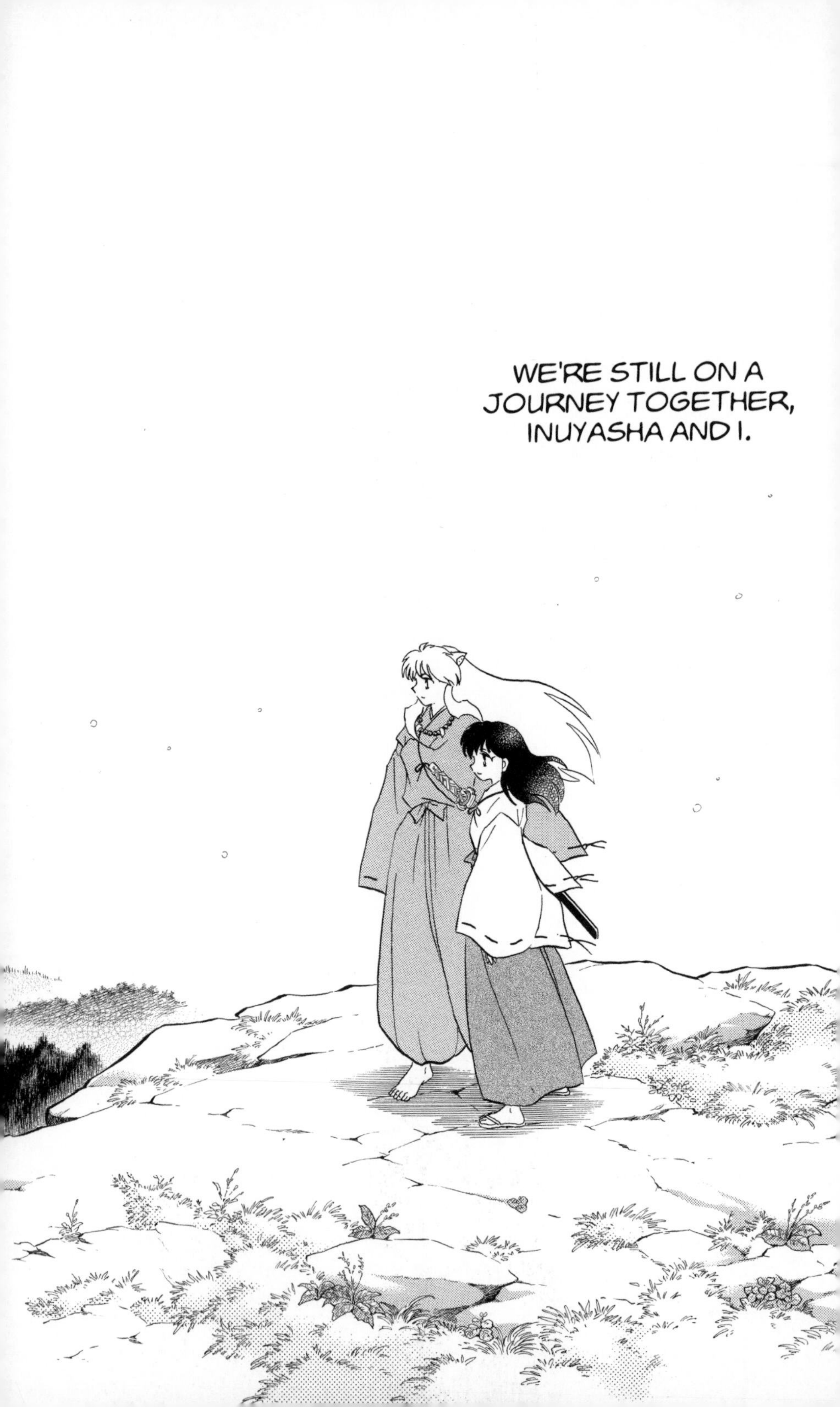
WE'RE STILL ON A JOURNEY TOGETHER, INUYASHA AND I.

BUT NOW WE'RE
JOURNEYING
TOWARD
TOMORROW.

ACKNOWLEDGEMENTS:

PRODUCTION
ASSISTANCE

KEIKO KOBAYASHI

TAKAKO GOTO

KIYOKO KAWANO

RIE KAWANO

TOMOMI ADACHI

HIROKO TANAKA

MOEKO FUJII

NAOKO OSAKA

EDITORIAL STAFF

TOSHIYUKI SENOU

MASAKI NAWATA

KAZUTO YOSHIDA

MASANAO MURAKAMI

TAKASHI KUMAGAI

SYUHOU KONDO

YOSUKE IZUKA

SHUNSUKE MOTEKI

INUYASHA
THE END

Original Cover Art Gallery

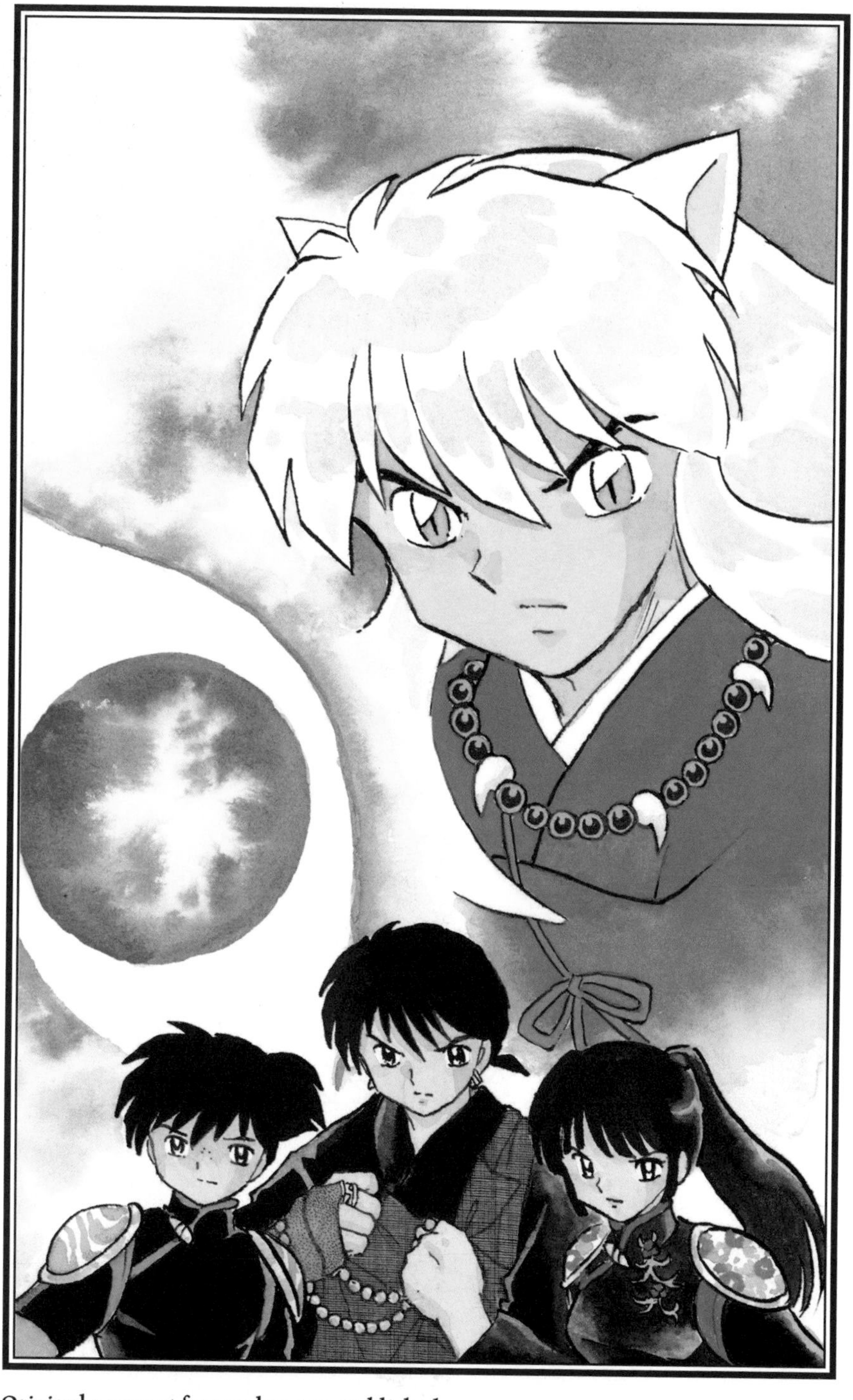

Original cover art from volume 53, published 2010

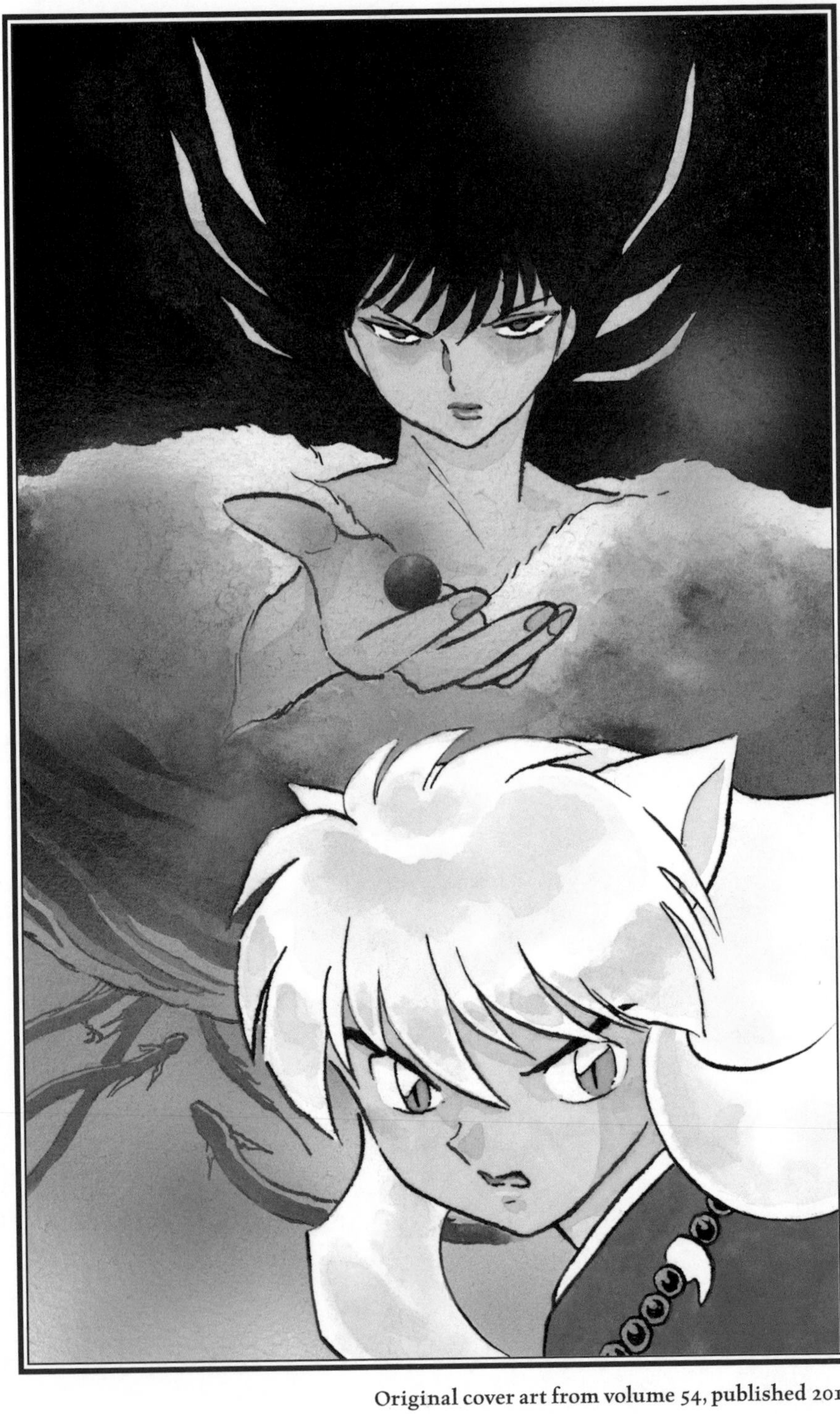

Original cover art from volume 54, published 2010

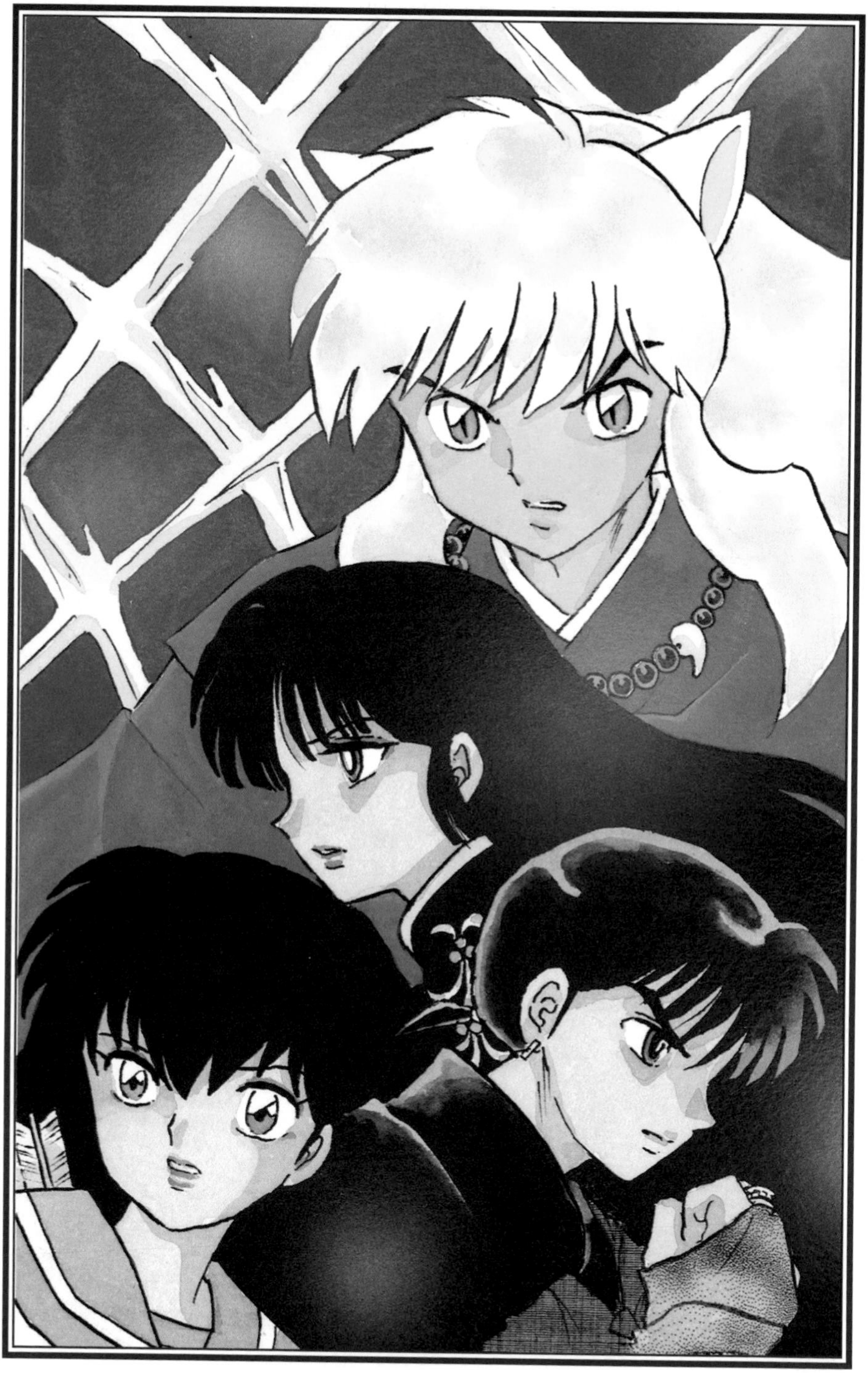

Original cover art from volume 55, published 2010

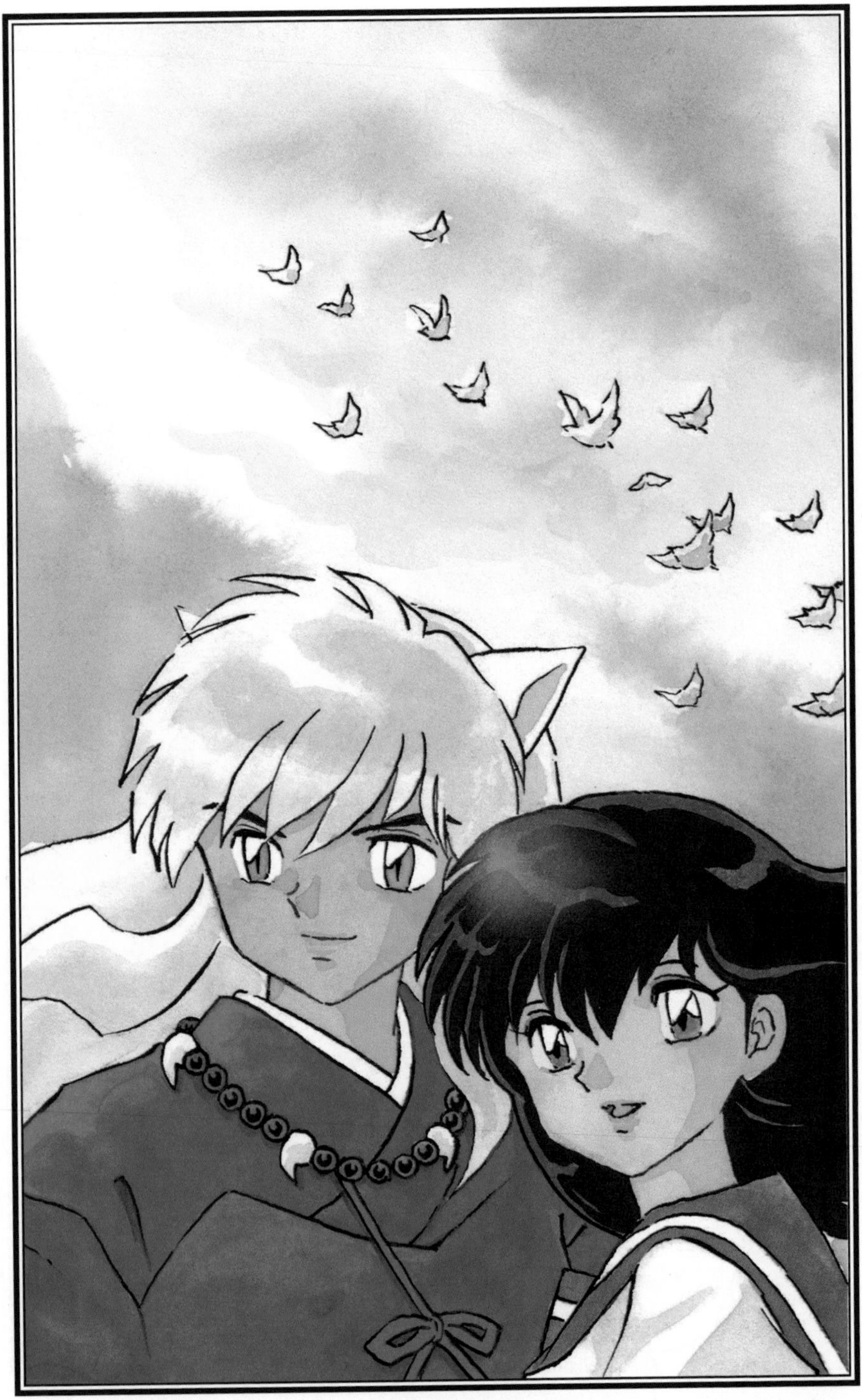

Original cover art from volume 56, published 2011